INTELLECTUAL PROPERTY LICENSING AND TRANSACTIONS

Intellectual property transactions underlie large segments of the global economy, from pharmaceuticals to computing, entertainment to digital content. This first-of-its-kind resource combines practical contract drafting and negotiation skills with substantive legal doctrine in the rapidly growing area of intellectual property transactions and licensing. Though primarily designed for classroom use, it is also a must-have legal reference work for every lawyer involved in the technology, biopharma, entertainment, media or financial services industries. It includes practical drafting models and explanations of key contractual provisions such as field of use, exclusivity, milestones, royalties, termination, indemnification and liability, and combines these with discussion of the latest cases interpreting these provisions. Numerous legal doctrines that affect the enforcement of IP agreements are also covered, including exhaustion, first sale, misuse, estoppel, antitrust and bankruptcy law, as well as chapters focusing on specialized fields such as trademark law, music licensing, technical standardization, and IP pooling. This book is also available as Open Access on Cambridge Core.

Jorge L. Contreras is Presidential Scholar and Professor of Law at the University of Utah S.J. Quinney College of Law. He has over thirty years of experience in intellectual property transactions and licensing, both as a practitioner at a large international law firm and as a leading legal academic.

Intellectual Property Licensing and Transactions
THEORY AND PRACTICE

JORGE L. CONTRERAS
University of Utah

CAMBRIDGE
UNIVERSITY PRESS

CAMBRIDGE
UNIVERSITY PRESS

University Printing House, Cambridge CB2 8BS, United Kingdom

One Liberty Plaza, 20th Floor, New York, NY 10006, USA

477 Williamstown Road, Port Melbourne, VIC 3207, Australia

314–321, 3rd Floor, Plot 3, Splendor Forum, Jasola District Centre, New Delhi – 110025, India

103 Penang Road, #05–06/07, Visioncrest Commercial, Singapore 238467

Cambridge University Press is part of the University of Cambridge.

It furthers the University's mission by disseminating knowledge in the pursuit of
education, learning, and research at the highest international levels of excellence.

www.cambridge.org
Information on this title: www.cambridge.org/9781316518038
DOI: 10.1017/9781009049436

First published 2022

A catalogue record for this publication is available from the British Library.

Library of Congress Cataloging-in-Publication Data
NAMES: Contreras, Jorge L., author.
TITLE: Intellectual property licensing and transactions : theory and
practice / Jorge L Contreras, University of Utah.
DESCRIPTION: Cambridge, United Kingdom ; New York, NY : Cambridge
University Press, 2022. | Includes index.
IDENTIFIERS: LCCN 2021052130 (print) | LCCN 2021052131 (ebook) | ISBN
9781316518038 (hardback) | ISBN 9781009048804 (paperback) | ISBN
9781009049436 (ebook)
SUBJECTS: LCSH: Intellectual property. | License agreements. | Patent
licenses.
CLASSIFICATION: LCC K1405 .C66 2022 (print) | LCC K1405 (ebook) | DDC
346.04/8–dc23/eng/20211223
LC record available at https://lccn.loc.gov/2021052130
LC ebook record available at https://lccn.loc.gov/2021052131

ISBN 978-1-316-51803-8 Hardback
ISBN 978-1-009-04880-4 Paperback

Contents

Figures

Tables

Acknowledgments

This book represents the culmination of many years of counseling, drafting, negotiating and teaching in the area of IP transactions and licensing. I am indebted to those who took the time to train, educate and mentor me when I embarked on this little-known but rewarding practice more than thirty years ago. Professors Lloyd Weinreb, Michael Boudin, Stephen Breyer and William Alford at Harvard Law School inspired in me an early appreciation for the intricacies of intellectual property, international law and technology regulation. Ron Laurie, my first law firm mentor in this area, remains a leader in the field. I owe a significant debt of gratitude to those partners at Hale and Dorr in Boston (now WilmerHale) who spent countless hours teaching me the ropes of the corporate and transactional world, including the things that never appear in case books and law review articles: Mike Bevilacqua, John Burgess, Bill Benjamin, David Westenberg, and many others. I am also grateful to the many law firm colleagues, clients, co-counsel and academics with whom I have collaborated over the years, each of whom has added to my store of knowledge of the field, and especially Laura Blood, my colleague in post-firm law practice, whose skill and attention to detail are unmatched. My first experience teaching IP transactions and licensing was at Washington University in St. Louis, where I co-taught the course with Blythe Burkhardt, who, with great experience and good humor, helped me to translate years of esoteric knowledge into a format suitable for students.

Several people contributed to the planning and development of this book. The late Professor Ray Nimmer at University of Houston Law Center was the initial inspiration for this project, and I used his excellent 2007 case book for years as I developed my own approach to teaching the subject. Greg Vetter at University of Houston and Jennifer Carter-Johnson and Jeff Carter-Johnson at Michigan State University provided invaluable input and support in the planning of this book. Matt Gallaway at Cambridge University Press was strongly committed to the open access nature of this book and made its publication possible. Patti Beekhuizen and Matthew Whitehead at the University of Utah provided invaluable help in preparing the manuscript, and many of my students over the years suffered through half-written chapters and notes as the book coalesced into its final form.

The "beta" version of this book was used by several brave instructors during 2021 and 2022 and I am grateful for their feedback and suggestions regarding its usability and improvement. I am particularly grateful to Jacques de Werra, Louis Brucculeri and, most especially, Jim Farrington at University of Notre Dame for reviewing and commenting on the manuscript.

Finally, I must thank my wife, Kimberly Kaphingst, whose endless patience allowed me to miss far too many birthdays, anniversaries and holidays while I was negotiating IP transactions around the world and grappling with the issues that are now presented in this book.

Introduction

Intellectual property (IP) law – broadly consisting of patent, copyright, trademark, trade secret and a handful of other doctrinal areas – is a key topic in today's legal and business curriculum. IP issues motivate some of the largest transactions, lawsuits and governmental policies of our day, and an increasing number of lawyers around the world practice in this area. The U.S. Patent and Trademark Office has reported that in 2019, IP accounted for 41% of all domestic economic activity and that IP-intensive industries supplied 63 million jobs.

IP transactions cover a broad range of business arrangements among IP holders and users, including IP licensing, R&D, development, joint venture, distribution, publishing, agency, manufacturing, service and other agreements. Much of the IP work performed by in-house attorneys falls into the transactional category, and IP transactional knowledge is highly relevant to attorneys working at law firms, government agencies, academic institutions, nonprofit organizations and international bodies.

There are two traditional modes in which IP law is taught today: *prosecution* – the practice of obtaining patents and trademarks from the US Patent and Trademark Office and corresponding international offices – and *litigation* – legal disputes over the ownership, infringement and misappropriation of IP assets. This book covers the third major leg of the IP triangle: *transactions*. In today's legal education marketplace, an increasing number of schools are offering courses, seminars and clinics that address transactional IP issues. This book caters to those educational settings.

FORMAT OF THIS BOOK

In many ways, this book resembles a traditional case book of the variety used in law schools for more than a century to teach subjects ranging from property to evidence to civil procedure. Admittedly, it contains edited judicial opinions (more on this below), but it also differs from traditional case books in a few important ways. Each chapter contains several distinct types of pedagogical material, the purpose and intent of which are summarized below:

1. *Edited cases* – when Christopher Columbus Langdell, the Dean of Harvard Law School from 1870 to 1895, developed the case method of legal education, he did so in an effort to link legal education to the actual mechanism by which the common law develops – judicial decisions. Reading and interpreting cases, Langdell and law professors over the subsequent 150 years have asserted, inures students to the methods of judicial reasoning, prepares them to present their own cases to courts, and elucidates the rules and doctrines that constitute the warp and weft of the common law. Today, the case method is under attack from various

quarters. Much of modern American law is statutory and administrative, not grounded in the common law, and in many fields, the number of cases that result in a published judicial opinion is vanishingly small. What's more, the growing corps of attorneys who deal primarily in contracts and transactions may never see the inside of a courtroom nor a person dressed in black robes during the course of a full and distinguished legal career. So why does a book that aspires to educate new transactional attorneys include so many cases?

The answer is simple. While the daily bread of the transactional attorney is the contract, a document rich in its own breed of linguistic legerdemain, contractual clauses do not exist in a vacuum. That is, with apologies to Donne, no contract is an island. Rather, the words of a contract represent merely the tip of an interpretive iceberg. Especially in the world of IP, every clause of a contractual arrangement is shaped by the scope and nature of the underlying rights, whether statutory or common law, as well as a host of limiting doctrines and a bevy of commercial and business practices. The attorney who seeks to draft and negotiate anything but the simplest IP agreement without a deep understanding of the underlying law and business context risks nothing short of legal malpractice. And, regrettably, examples of such missteps abound – patent licenses that violate the rule against post-expiration royalties, trademark licenses that fail to include adequate quality control provisions, copyright transfers that do not account for profits owed to co-owners, contractual provisions that are impermissibly conditioned on the filing of a bankruptcy action, agreements that illegally divide markets or fix prices, employee policies that assume that a works-made-for-hire doctrine exists under patent law, or that it applies to copyrighted software. These and hundreds of other pitfalls and traps for the unwary await the attorney who assumes that a contract is a contract is a contract, and that the so-called "four corners rule" ensures that the words printed on the page are all that one needs to understand the subject of an IP agreement.

It is for this reason that a large number of judicial decisions, as well as agency opinions and review letters, are included and discussed in this book. Ignore them at your peril!

2. *Statutory and regulatory text* – in addition to cases, IP law is, in many cases, a creature of statute. The Patent Act, Copyright Act and Lanham Act establish the basic contours of three of the major forms of IP in the United States, and other major statutes – the Bankruptcy Code, the Sherman Act, the Uniform Commercial Code – are routinely invoked. Thus, relevant statutory text is included throughout the book.

3. *Contractual language examples* – despite my strong plug for cases and statutes above, the crux of any course in IP licensing and transactions is the contractual language that instantiates the parties' agreement. Students should become familiar with recognized forms of most common contractual provisions, which will build up their own contractual vocabularies to a degree that will eventually enable them to draft language for unfamiliar and bespoke situations. This book includes examples of contractual language throughout each chapter, along with drafting notes intended to elucidate subtleties and inflection points where negotiation can occur. In addition to these excerpted selections, an online supplement includes several full-length sample contracts of different types, which can be used for further study or exercises.

4. *Notes and questions* – the primary reading material in each chapter is followed by a set of notes and questions. These are intended to draw out the main points of the reading material and to prompt students to consider their implications and to extend them to other situations. Responses may be assigned to students as homework and/or discussed in class.

5. *Problems* – each chapter also contains one or more hypothetical "Problems" that require students to apply the concepts learned in the chapter to a simulated client scenario, usually by drafting appropriate contractual language based on the examples contained in the chapter.

ORGANIZATION AND TOPICS

As indicated by the table of contents, this book consists of four principal parts. Part I covers materials preliminary to the negotiation of an IP transaction. Chapter 1 covers the business assumptions and goals behind IP transactions; Chapter 2 covers issues surrounding the assignment and ownership of IP, including the issues surrounding joint ownership; Chapter 3 covers some of the theoretical issues surrounding the nature of an IP "license" and how it compares to similar rights of usage in the context of real and personal property; Chapter 4 deals with implied licenses that are recognized by the law absent a written agreement; and Chapter 5 address precursors to the drafting and negotiation of an IP agreement, including term sheets, letters of intent and confidentially agreements.

Part II covers the "building block" components of IP licensing and similar agreements. The principal components of these agreements are divided among eight chapters that progress in logical order from the "front" to the "back" of a typical agreement, starting with the scope of the license grant itself (Chapters 6 and 7), then moving to the financial clauses defining up-front payments, royalties, milestones, cost recovery and related issues such as most-favored clauses and royalty audits (Chapter 8), then addressing clauses allocating IP ownership, management and control (Chapter 9), and finally addressing more general, but critical, agreement terms such as representations, warranties and indemnification (Chapter 10), litigation-related clauses such as IP enforcement, settlement, choice of law and alternative dispute resolution (Chapter 11), term, breach and termination, including statutory termination provisions (Chapter 12) and a number of "boilerplate" clauses that can have significant ramifications for licensing transactions (force majeure, assignment, waiver, merger, etc.) (Chapter 13). It is intended that these chapters form the core of any course utilizing the book, and it is recommended that instructors cover each of these chapters.

Part III then turns to a number of industry-specific licensing topics that are intended for use by instructors with an interest in the topics, but are not required for every course in IP licensing. Chapter 14 covers academic technology transfer – the licensing of inventions and works developed by academic institutions, often with federal funding and concomitant restrictions and limitations. Significant attention is given to the Bayh–Dole Act of 1980, which modernized university technology transfer and has given rise to debates over government march-in rights and other issues. Chapter 15 addresses special topics relevant to the licensing of trademarks and brands, including franchise agreements, quality control requirements and trademark marking and usage requirements. Chapter 16 covers the complex world of music licensing, including the bifurcated copyright status of musical compositions and performances, the US compulsory licenses for mechanical reproduction, the ASCAP and BMI performing rights organizations, issues arising from music streaming and sampling, and more. Chapter 17 addresses the evolution of consumer software and other licenses, from shrinkwrap packaging to electronic click-through agreements to online browsewrap agreements, discussing their enforceability, use and development. Chapter 18 turns to commercial software and database licensing with attention to issues surrounding reverse engineering, database protection, software-as-a-service and the cloud. Chapter 19 addresses open source code software and other public licenses, such as the Creative Commons suite of online content licenses, as well as more recent pledges made by IP holders to support platform evangelization, standardization and social causes. Finally, Chapter 20 discusses the fraught issue of standards-essential patent licensing, focusing on IP disclosure obligations and commitments to license on fair, reasonable and nondiscriminatory (FRAND) terms.

Part IV turns from industry-specific topics to more advanced, but generally applicable, licensing topics. Again, instructors may choose to cover only a subset of these issues in a given course, depending on their focus and interest. Chapter 21 addresses bankruptcy law issues that affect IP licensing, including the automatic stay of actions, the bar on *ipso facto* clauses and the rejection of executory contracts and Section 365(n) of the Bankruptcy Act. Chapter 22 covers the doctrines of licensee and assignee estoppel, as well as the evolving enforceability of no-challenge clauses in licensing agreements. Chapter 23 addresses the first sale and exhaustion doctrines in copyright, trademark and patent law, including issues surrounding gray market imports. Chapter 24 covers IP misuse doctrines including the impermissible expansion of temporal and geographic scope, the 1988 Patent Misuse Reform Act, issues surrounding package licensing and noncompetition restrictions. Chapter 25 presents a broad overview of antitrust issues germane to IP licensing transactions, including the DOJ–FTC Guidelines and Supreme Court precedent relating to market allocation, tying, market power and monopolization, with specific attention to so-called reverse payment settlements in the pharmaceutical industry and antitrust issues arising in technical standards development. Chapter 26 concludes with an overview of IP pooling arrangements, with a focus on the commercial and antitrust issues that they present.

As noted above, an online supplement (https://iptransactions.org) contains sample agreements that illustrate the concepts discussed throughout the text.

LIMITATIONS: WHAT YOU WILL NOT FIND IN THIS BOOK

This book is intended to provide students with an overview of the issues and considerations relevant to IP licensing today. It is not a comprehensive treatise, and it does not cover every issue or contractual clause in this broad and rapidly evolving field. Readers who want a more in-depth treatment of any particular issue are referred to several excellent treatises on IP licensing that are available online and in most academic libraries. These resources are cited throughout this book.

The focus of this book is US law. While it does address a few non-US issues, they are mentioned inasmuch as they may be useful to US practitioners negotiating international licensing agreements. This book should not be viewed as an authoritative source for non-US law.

This book assumes that the reader is familiar with the basic modes of IP protection in the US – patents, copyrights, trademarks and trade secrets. It does not offer a primer on these subjects, and readers wishing to learn more about the basic forms of IP protection are referred to a wealth of online and published materials on these topics.

The primary materials contained in this book (cases, articles, statutes) are edited for readability and to accommodate space constraints. Most internal citations, footnotes and references have been omitted. Thus, the text of these materials should not be viewed as definitive and should not be quoted without reference to the original source material.

CAREFUL DRAFTING PAYS

Every transactional lawyer dreads the day that one of his or her agreements is litigated, when he or she is abruptly transformed from a learned advisor to a fact witness. Unfortunately, this scenario recurs all too often in today's litigious environment. Believe me, when you are deposed by litigation counsel about the intended meaning of some obscure contractual clause that you drafted at 2 a.m. and then negotiated while on a cell phone in the back seat of a taxi cab, you will thank yourself for having drafted an agreement that is clear, unambiguous and reflective of your client's intent.

Likewise, there are few professional achievements as gratifying to the transactional lawyer as reading praise for one's work from the bench. In short, this is the standard that you should strive for in any agreement that you draft:

> There is simply nothing ambiguous about the Settlement Agreement. It is a well written, fully-integrated contract carefully molded on the contours of the 1993 License Agreement, which explicitly defined all essential terms while laying out the exact scope of the license and the parties' respective rights and obligations.[1]

It is a goal of this book to give you the tools – theoretical, doctrinal and practical – that are necessary to meet this standard in every agreement that you draft and negotiate. Happy drafting!

---

[1] *Cozza v. Network Assocs.*, 2005 U.S. Dist. LEXIS 11263 at *11 (D. Mass. 2005).

PART I

Introduction to Intellectual Property Licensing

1

The Business of Licensing

1.1 THE LICENSING INDUSTRY

Students of intellectual property (IP) law are often steeped in the theory and practice of IP litigation. Record labels sue parodists and illegal downloaders, patent owners sue infringers, luxury brands sue counterfeiters, employers sue employees who leak their valuable secrets. All of these cases and the doctrines that they create could lead to a view of the world of IP as a battlefield. Like armaments, firms acquire IP rights solely to attack others, to bludgeon competitors or extract rent from consumers.

But this view is wrong. It arises from the unfortunate fact that legal education emphasizes reported judicial decisions over all else, and judicial decisions arise from litigation. The reality, however, is that the vast majority of economic activity involving IP arises from transactions – business arrangements among firms and with consumers and, sometimes, the government.

According to one industry group, global revenues for product licensing – the licensing of brands, images and logos for products of various kinds – were nearly $300 billion in 2019.[1] In 2019, recorded music sales, including digital streaming, were approximately $20 billion,[2] sales of enterprise software were $439 billion,[3] and global sales of smartphones exceeded $400 billion. All told, trillions of dollars every year change hands on the basis of IP licenses and transactions – far more than the total sum of all the IP litigation that has ever been brought.

Whichever of these figures most resonates with you, it is undeniable that IP licensing is a major economic activity with far-reaching implications both in the United States and worldwide. Virtually every product, every financial transaction and every communication on Earth depends, in some way, on an IP license.

This chapter lays the groundwork for the detailed study of IP licensing that follows in this book. It describes the business and economic motivations behind IP transactions, and seeks to give the reader an appreciation for the scope and range of IP licensing in the marketplace.

---

[1] Licensing Int'l, 6th Annual Global Licensing Survey (discussed in Chapter 15).
[2] IFPI, IFPI issues annual Global Music Report, May 4, 2020, www.ifpi.org/ifpi-issues-annual-global-music-report (visited August. 22, 2020).
[3] Brookings Inst., Trends in the information technology sector, March 29, 2019, www.brookings.edu/research/trends-in-the-information-technology-sector (visited August 22, 2020).

1.2 WHY LICENSE?

The government grants the owner of an IP right the exclusive authority to exploit that right in its jurisdiction. At first blush, this seems like a golden opportunity for the IP owner to go into business. It can make, use, sell, display and perform the IP-protected thing with no competition from others for the entire duration of the relevant right. Build the better mousetrap, show the new masterpiece, storm the market with the new brand.

A moment's thought, however, dispels these aspirations to grandeur. In reality, many owners of IP cannot, or are not willing to, exploit their IP to the fullest degree, if at all.[4] The author of the next Great American Novel would be foolish to self-publish her work using nothing but a laser printer or a personal website. She needs a publisher that can exploit the full range of print and electronic distribution channels that exist today. The university researcher who develops an improved method of satellite navigation can't afford the hundreds of millions of dollars necessary to launch a satellite into orbit – her invention is best utilized by a company or government that is already in the satellite business. The producer of an independent animated film can't be expected to open a factory to produce the myriad lunchboxes, backpacks, T-shirts and action figures demanded by the fans of the film. Those tasks are best left to others already in the manufacturing trade. The list goes on.

The fact is that IP owners are often not in the best position to exploit their own IP. They need help. And the way to get that help is through licensing. Through a license, an IP owner legally grants somebody else – a "licensee" – the right to exploit some or all aspects of a particular IP right. In return, the IP owner – the "licensor" – usually receives some form of compensation, often money, but sometimes services, equity in a company, or a license to IP held by the licensee. All of these arrangements have as their goal a more efficient allocation of rights among the owner and others who may be in a better position to exploit those rights. The result of that allocation is the most efficient use of the IP rights, maximizing the profit that can collectively be achieved by the licensor and its licensees. As such, we can say that the goal of nearly all IP licensing transactions is to optimize allocative efficiency among IP owner and users. When this is accomplished properly, the greatest overall value will result, thus maximizing the social value of a given IP right.

> "the goal of nearly all IP licensing transactions is to optimize allocative efficiency among the IP owner and users."

With the principle of allocative efficiency in mind, consider the following economic rationales that motivate IP licensing from the perspectives of the IP owner (the licensor) and the potential user of that IP (the licensee).[5]

1.2.1 *Market Expansion (Divide and Conquer)*

The owner of an IP right – whether a patent, a copyright, a trademark or something else – may not have the internal capacity to exploit that right to its fullest extent, or at all. By licensing that IP right to someone with different capabilities and resources, segments of the market that are otherwise

---

[4]   Sometimes, of course, an IP owner may wish to use its IP to exclude others from the market and to dominate the market with its own products or services. Cynthia Cannady refers to this as the "fortress" IP strategy. See Cynthia Cannady, Technology Licensing and Development Agreements 46–48 (Oxford Univ. Press, 2013).

[5]   For a more detailed analysis of the economic factors motivating IP licensing see, e.g., Jonathan Barnett, *Why Is Everyone Afraid of IP Licensing?* 30 Harv. J.L. & Tech. 123 (2017) and Cannady, *supra* note 4, at 45–72.

unaddressed may be addressed. For example, a small biotech company discovers a new process for detecting DNA variants. The process will be valuable to the company's own research on diabetes therapies, but could be used in many other applications as well. When different licensees use the process in their own research, its use is expanded far beyond that of the original IP owner. Likewise, the creator of a popular comic book character may not manufacture consumer goods. But if it licenses the copyright in the character to consumer product companies, the character will appear on lunchboxes, backpacks and self-adhesive stickers that otherwise would not exist. Nor does a famous auto maker like Ferrari or Porsche produce T-shirts, key chains or sunglasses, but by licensing its marks to manufacturers of those products, it can satisfy consumer demand that would otherwise go unfulfilled. Some IP owners, such as universities and government laboratories, are unable to go into business at all, making licensing one of the only routes to commercialization of their IP.[6] Each of these examples illustrates the creation of new product and service markets for IP rights that might not exist without the IP owner's ability to license its rights to others.[7]

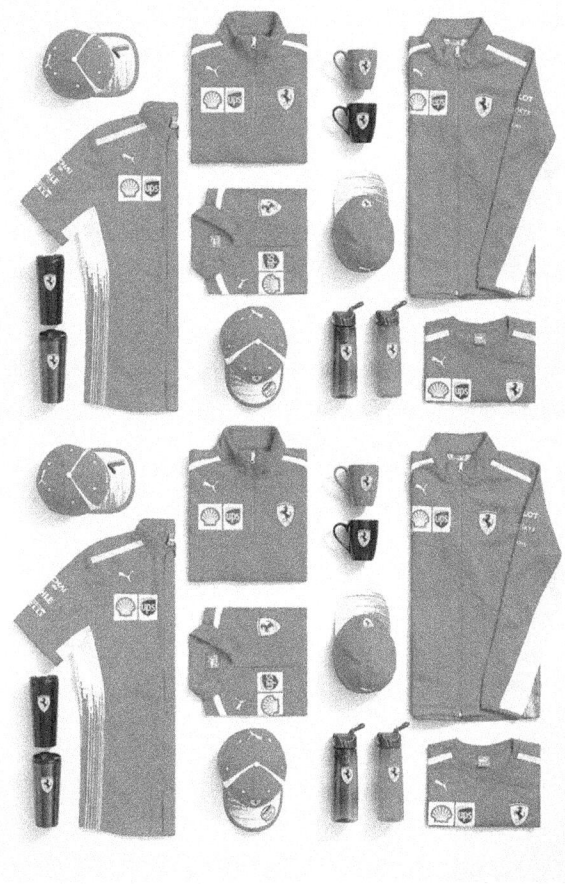

FIGURE 1.1 Auto makers like Ferrari do not manufacture the merchandise that bears their famous logos. This merchandise exists thanks to licensing.

[6]   University and government licensing are discussed in Chapter 14.

[7]   And even if the IP owner has the theoretical capability to address all of the different markets that can be addressed by an IP right, it is likely that licensing rights to others in some of those markets will result in the more *rapid* deployment of new products and services (i.e., retaining all rights in the original IP owner could create bottlenecks in the development of new products and services). See Jorge L. Contreras & Jacob S. Sherkow, *CRISPR, Surrogate Licensing, and Scientific Discovery*, 355 Science 698 (2017).

1.2.2 *Geographic Expansion*

Like market expansion, IP licensing enables IP owners to expand the territorial reach of their IP rights.[8] Many products and services have international appeal, but local markets are often difficult to enter without assistance. Depending on the product and the market, significant regulatory approvals and clearances may be required, advertising and packaging materials must be localized, and adequate distribution channels must be identified and secured. Large multinationals sometimes do all of this by themselves, but most IP owners, even those of considerable size, cannot. Thus, in order to distribute products and services worldwide, local manufacturing, distribution, sales, support and agency partners are often needed. And to the extent that these local partners will be manufacturing, reproducing, modifying or displaying anything covered by IP rights, licenses will be required.

THE RISK OF CANNIBALIZATION[9]

"Licensing for market expansion raises the issue of cannibalization. The licensor company will analyze at what point its licensees' product sales may eat into (cannibalize) its own profits. Apple Computer faced this difficult challenge in the 1990s when it considered licensing its proprietary operating system to PC system manufacturers such as Dell, Vobis, Olivetti, and Acer. If Apple licensed to these companies for cloning, they would reduce the cost of manufacture, eliminate extras like design features, and drag the Apple technology and pricing – and possibly its brand – into commodity status. No one at Apple was able to assess systematically the cannibalization risk, or suggest ways to limit it, other than to exclude Apple's most profitable geographic markets from the licenses. But those markets were precisely the markets that attracted the potential licensees. At the time they were not interested in making Apple clones only for the "rest of world" or "ROW" market (not Asia, Europe, or the United States). The potential licensees also wanted freedom to innovate based on Apple's operating system, a competition that was potentially frightening to Apple. Apple ultimately decided not to pursue licensing its operating system."

Cynthia Cannady, Technology Licensing and Development Agreements 51–52 (Oxford Univ. Press, 2013).

1.2.3 *Capacity Expansion*

In many cases, an IP owner may not possess the internal resources needed to exploit its rights fully, and can only do so with the financial or other assistance of others. A small biotech company does not have hundreds of millions of dollars required to conduct the clinical trials necessary to obtain regulatory approval for a new drug, nor do most screenwriters have the means to produce a television series based on a new script. In other words, an IP right may have value, but it is incomplete or not ready for market without further inputs – money, expertise, resources or additional innovation. In order to put these IP rights to productive use, assistance from others is often required. To do so, the biotech company can license its IP to a large pharmaceutical firm, and the screenwriter can license her script to a film studio or production company. In both cases, a product will be produced where none might exist otherwise, and the licensee and licensor will share the profits of the result.

---

[8] Many IP rights – particularly patents and trademarks – are strictly national in scope, and some IP rights such as the right of publicity exist in some countries but not in others. The issue of obtaining international IP protection is a complex one and the subject of many other books. We will assume, for our purposes, that such rights are available to IP owners in jurisdictions of interest.

[9] Cannady, *supra* note 4, at 51–52. Despite its unpleasant connotations, the term "cannibalization" is used widely in the industry.

1.2.4 *Modularization*

Even for large firms that theoretically have the capacity to take all the steps necessary to commercialize their IP, it may not be efficient for them to do so. First, there is substantial evidence that firms can increase efficiency and save costs by allocating specific tasks along the production chain to specialized (and lowest cost) suppliers, rather than performing these tasks internally.[10] This approach is sometimes referred to as "modularization" – the division of a multi-step process into discrete modules that can be performed by independent actors. For example, suppose that FryCo has developed an innovative, environmentally friendly coating for nonstick cookware. FryCo could, conceivably, purchase a fleet of delivery trucks to ensure that every consumer and retailer in the country had access to its wares. But unless FryCo's sales volume is huge, it would be far more efficient to allocate delivery to a specialized service such as FedEx or UPS, allowing FryCo to focus on its core competencies. Likewise, if FryCo's principal contribution is its secret nonstick coating, then it could focus its manufacturing efforts on production of that coating, while allocating the production of iron skillets to an established manufacturer of such products and granting it a license to apply FryCo's proprietary coating to their surfaces. As Professor Jonathan Barnett observes, "licensing enables firms to select the sequence of 'make/buy' transactions that deliver innovations (or products and services embodying innovations) at the lowest possible cost."[11]

A related benefit of supply chain modularization is risk mitigation. Put simply, if FryCo manufactured its own iron skillets and its skillet factory burned down, it would suffer a significant business interruption. However, if FryCo sourced skillets to its specifications from, say, three different vendors in different locations, then the loss of any one of them would not be catastrophic. Modularization enables the producer to reduce its reliance on any single source of necessary components, thereby reducing risk in the production process.[12]

Finally, modularization can enable firms to invest in multiple projects concurrently, rather than focusing all of their resources on one project at a time. As a result, a firm can spread its risk among a portfolio of projects, some of which may succeed and some of which may fail.[13]

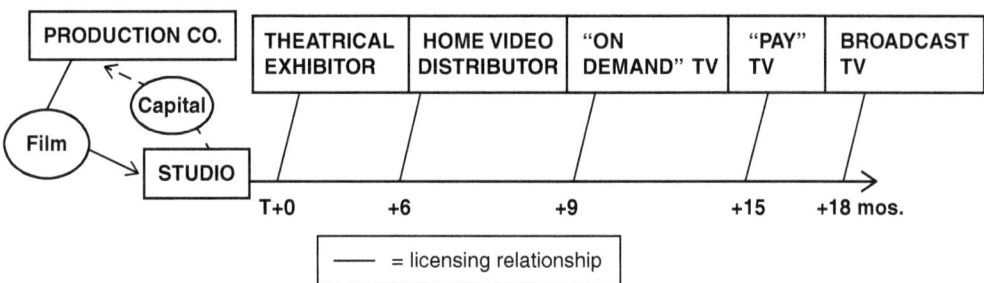

FIGURE 1.2 Jonathan Barnett illustrates how licensing enables motion picture firms to divide distribution rights among multiple entities, each with a specific role in the supply chain.[14]

---

[10] See Barnett, *supra* note 5, at 133–34 (discussing efficient disaggregation of production functions in the semiconductor chip industry).

[11] Barnett, *supra* note 5, at 130.

[12] There are, of course, many examples of components that are only available from a single source, particularly those that are covered by IP of their own.

[13] Professor Barnett offers examples from the motion picture and biopharmaceutical industries to illustrate this point (Figure 1.2). Barnett, *supra* note 5, at 136–37.

[14] Barnett, *supra* note 5, at 140, Fig. 5 [reprinted with permission].

1.2.5 *Monetization: Direct*

In some cases an entity acquires IP rights primarily to earn revenue from licensing them. This is the case with research universities, which spend large sums on research, but which never intend to bring products or services to the commercial market. Their primary goal in obtaining IP rights – usually patents – is to license them to the private sector so that others can exploit them in exchange for payments. This business model is discussed in greater detail in Chapter 14.

Commercial entities can also find themselves in possession of IP rights that they do not have the capacity or desire to exploit themselves, but which they can profitably license to others. Sometimes, this occurs when business priorities shift, or when product lines that were covered by patents are no longer successful in the marketplace, leaving behind few product sales, but a rich portfolio of patent rights to license. Prominent product manufacturers like Palm, Blackberry, Nokia, Motorola and Ericsson saw the virtual evaporation of their product markets (mostly phones and other handheld communications devices), but were left with sizeable portfolios of patents representing substantial opportunities for licensing income.

Licensing for income generation is also practiced by companies that remain active in product markets, but which find themselves with portfolios of valuable patents that can be licensed. IBM, for example, earned more than $723 million in annual IP licensing revenue in 2018, and chip maker Qualcomm earns between $1 billion and $1.5 billion from its licensing business *per quarter*. This type of licensing revenue need not be related to products sold by the IP owner. For example, from about 2011 to 2015, Microsoft aggressively asserted and licensed patents covering Google's Android operating system against smartphone makers such as Samsung, LG, HTC and Foxconn, earning Microsoft billions of dollars in revenue in a market segment in which it was a marginal player, at best.[15]

ROYALTIES FOR SALE

Many IP licenses involve the payment of ongoing royalties to the licensor. In some cases these royalties can be quite high. But sometimes a licensor needs cash quickly, and cannot afford, or does not want, to wait for years to collect the total value of its IP. Licensors may thus resort to well-known financial instruments used in industries such as equipment leasing and mortgage financing to "sell" future royalty streams for an immediate, up-front sum.

Who buys IP royalty streams? One publicly traded firm, Royalty Pharma (RPRX – NASDAQ), specializes in pharmaceutical royalties. According to one source, Royalty Pharma spent $3.3 billion to acquire a share of the Cystic Fibrosis Foundation's royalties from Vertex Pharmaceuticals' cystic fibrosis treatments, and $1.24 billion for the University of California's royalties from the prostate cancer drug Xtandi, among many others.[16] Likewise, the Canadian Pensions Plan Investment Board agreed to pay LifeArc $1.3 billion for its royalty interest in Merck's Keytruda cancer immunotherapy drug.

In some cases, royalty streams can be auctioned to the public. A share of the famous "perpetual" Listerine royalty (see Section 12.2.3) earning $32,000 per year was sold to an anonymous bidder for $560,000 at an auction in 2020.[17]

---

[15] Interestingly, in 2018 Microsoft joined the Open Innovation Network and thereby agreed not to assert its patents against users of Linux and Android operating systems. See Chapter 19 for a discussion of the business motivations behind this and similar pledges.

[16] Adam Houldsworth, *Five Key Insights into 2020's Drug Royalty Transactions*, Intell. Asset Mgt., December 16, 2020.

[17] Ryan Davis, Rare Listerine Royalty Auction Tied to 1881 Contract Flub, Law360, July 21, 2020.

But perhaps the most creative IP royalty sale was the 1997 securitization and public offering of 7.9 percent coupon bonds backed by the income from twenty-five pre-1990 recordings by singer David Bowie. The so-called "Bowie Bonds," all of which were purchased by The Prudential Insurance Co., earned Bowie $55 million in a single transaction, and by 2016 had reportedly served as the model for more than 100 similar transactions in the music industry.[18]

More recently, with the onset of the COVID-19 pandemic and the indefinite suspension of live musical performances, an increasing number of artists, including legendary performers like Neil Young and Bob Dylan, have sold off the rights in their song catalogs to make ends meet.[19]

1.2.6 *Monetization: Indirect*

Sometimes, the owner of an IP right may lack the ability and the resources to commercialize that IP right. For example, an individual inventor may make a breakthrough discovery in a field dominated by large players with which he or she cannot effectively compete, a start-up company may fail to raise sufficient funding to stay afloat, a company with a rich IP portfolio may be liquidated in bankruptcy, a company may be acquired by another firm that offers a competing product and a large firm may decide to discontinue a business line to which it holds IP rights. In all of these cases, the IP owner holds an asset that it spent valuable resources to create, but which it can no longer utilize productively. As a result, the IP owner's best (or only) option may be to license or sell the underutilized IP right to an entity that can make productive use of it. But finding such an entity may be difficult, and the small inventor, the failed start-up, the bankruptcy trustee and the disinterested acquirer may lack the ability to do so.

Enter the middlemen, known variously as patent licensing firms, nonpracticing entities (NPEs), patent assertion entities (PAEs) and patent "trolls."[20] These entities acquire IP rights from any of the sources described above and then seek to license them to others purely for economic gain, without creating or selling products or developing IP of their own. Despite the heated rhetoric that pervades this discussion, there is nothing inherently illegal or immoral about seeking to monetize IP assets, just as there is nothing wrong with financial institutions transacting in portfolios of consumer loans, mortgages or credit card debt.

THE DEBATE OVER PATENT TROLLS

"Patent troll" is a pejorative moniker commonly assigned to [non-practicing entities] (NPEs) because they allegedly wait for an industry to develop, then appear to exact a toll on companies who commercialize the technology. According to the detractors' narrative, trolls are recent fly-by-night shops that assert business-method and internet patents. Trolls assert low-quality patents in low-quality litigation. They obtain patents from failed companies in fire sales. Worse, because trolls do not make anything, their patents do not provide anything

---

[18]   See Emma Channing, *Bowie: Rock God or Tax Genius?*, February 7, 2016, https://papers.ssrn.com/sol3/papers .cfm?abstract_id=2729014.

[19]   Thomas Seal, Neil Young Sells 50% Stake in 1,180-Song Catalog to Hipgnosis, Bloomberg Law, January 6, 2021.

[20]   While these entities have attracted the most attention in relation to patents, assertion entities exist in the copyright world as well. See Matthew Sag, *Copyright Trolling, An Empirical Study*, 100 Iowa L. Rev. 1105 (2014) and Shyamkrishna Balganesh & Jonah B. Gelbach, *Debunking the Myth of the Copyright Troll Apocalypse*, 101 Iowa L. Rev. Online 43 (2016).

of value to society. In short, according to their critics, patent trolls represent a significant break from past practices and foreshadow the downfall of innovative society.

NPEs are not, however, without their defenders. According to their proponents, NPEs create patent markets, and those markets enhance investment in start-up companies by providing additional liquidity options. NPEs help businesses crushed by larger competitors – competitors who infringe valid patents with impunity. NPEs allow individual inventors to monetize their inventions. These functions, the proponents argue, justify the existence of NPEs.

Michael Risch, *Patent Troll Myths*, 42 Seton Hall L. Rev. 457, 459 (2012)

We need not delve into the debate over NPEs, PAEs and patent trolls, which has been ongoing for years. It involves questions well beyond the scope of this book, including the appropriateness of certain litigation tactics and the underlying quality of many patents that are asserted in litigation. While some PAEs shoot first and negotiate later, others would seemingly prefer to license their IP assets without resorting to expensive and risky litigation. The common motivating factor for licensing among these entities is the generation of financial returns.

1.2.7 *Rights Aggregation*

In some cases an entity's IP protects only a portion of an overall product, or constitutes an improvement on somebody else's IP. In these cases an entity's IP cannot practically be exploited without the cooperation of others. Sometimes, no one entity can act in a field without obtaining permissions from others – such fields are said to be characterized by "blocking" positions. For example, in *Standard Oil Co. (Indiana) v. United States*, 283 U.S. 163 (1931), four large oil companies each held patents necessary to perform the process of "cracking" crude oil to make gasoline. Each company's patents were blocking – none could perform the process without the cooperation of the others.[21] Likewise, in *Nadel v. Play-By-Play Toys & Novelties, Inc.*, 208 F.3d

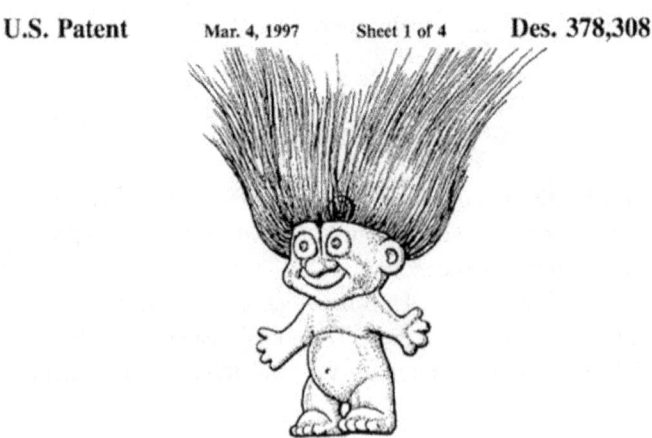

U.S. Patent   Mar. 4, 1997   Sheet 1 of 4   **Des. 378,308**

FIGURE 1.3 The debate over "patent trolls" has been raging for over a decade.

---

[21]   This important case is discussed and excerpted in Section 26.2.

368 (2d Cir. 1999),[22] an independent toy designer created a spinning plush toy based on Warner Bros. "Tazmanian Devil" character. He could not market his toy without the permission of Warner Bros., nor could Warner Bros. market the toy without his permission.

One important function of IP licensing is enabling entities to overcome these blocking positions, so that they may operate productively in the field. That is, without licensing an entity would have to acquire ownership of all blocking rights or create an entirely new product or service that does not infringe the IP of others. Both of these alternatives are often impossible, making licensing the best and only option for the productive use of one's own IP. Licensing of this nature can occur through individual licensing negotiations, cross-licenses (in which each party grants parallel licenses to the other), or pursuant to IP pools in which the rights of multiple IP owners are licensed on an aggregated basis (discussed in Chapter 26). While these transactions are often quite different in nature, they share the common feature of eliminating barriers to the efficient utilization of IP within a market sector.

1.2.8 *Platform Leadership*

In some instances the developer of a technology or creative platform may wish to license rights to others to encourage the broad use of its platform. This approach was adopted early by the makers of video game consoles (Sony, Nintendo, Microsoft), which sought to encourage game developers to write games optimized for their platforms. Today, the Apple App Store and Google Play exemplify a similar approach.[23] Similar motivations are at work in the area of open source software (Section 19.2), technical interoperability standards (Chapter 20) and many patent "pledges" (Section 19.4).

In each case, the owner of a platform technology makes it available, often without charge, to encourage the independent development of products and services compatible with the platform. With a platform's growth and adoption, the IP owner can sell ancillary products and services, effectively using the broadly licensed rights as "loss leaders" to promote other revenue-generating activities. For example, IBM's open source licensing of its Linux-based operating system led to substantial revenue from the sale of Linux servers and professional services, and Google's release of its Android operating system on an open source basis led to its widespread adoption and substantial ad revenue for Google.[24] Likewise, the developers of important interoperability standards such as Bluetooth and USB license patents covering these standards on a royalty-free basis, as the broad adoption of these standards enables them to sell more products and services (e.g., laptops, routers, chips, network services) that rely on those standards.

Notes and Questions

1. *Cannibalization.* What is cannibalization of a market? Why did cannibalization concerns deter Apple from licensing its operating system to other manufacturers, as Microsoft had done?
2. *Unplugging bottlenecks.* As noted in note 7, Professors Contreras and Sherkow claim that "even if the IP owner has the theoretical capability to address all of the different markets that can be addressed by an IP right, it is likely that licensing rights to others in some of those markets will result in the more *rapid* deployment of new products and services (i.e.,

---

[22] Discussed in Section 4.2.
[23] For additional examples from the computer and biotechnology industries, see Cannady, *supra* note 4, at 52–54.
[24] See Yochai Benkler, The Wealth of Networks: How Social Production Transforms Markets and Freedom 46 (Yale Univ. Press, 2006); Jorge L. Contreras, *Patent Pledges*, 47 Ariz. St. L.J. 543, 586 (2015).

FIGURE 1.4 Large information technology companies like IBM and Google embraced the open source Linux operating system to support the sale of associated hardware, services and advertising.

retaining all rights in the original IP owner could create bottlenecks in the development of new products and services).” Why would an IP owner's retention of rights create developmental bottlenecks? How can these bottlenecks be avoided?

3. *The troll debate.* What objections can be raised to the monetization of IP rights? Is there anything inherently wrong with using IP as a money-making investment? What types of litigation behavior might have made PAEs unpopular in many circles?

4. *Platforms.* How do the Apple App Store and Google Play exemplify a platform leadership strategy? What goals do you think Apple and Google have with respect to these platforms? What other online platforms have a similar strategy?

5. *Giving it away.* What would motivate the holder of a valuable IP right to give it away for free? Is this behavior irrational? How would you decide when a "give away" strategy is worth pursuing? Consider these issues when you read about open source software and patent pledges in Chapter 19.

Problem 1.1

Which IP licensing model would you recommend for each of the following companies? State any assumptions about the company's business that support your recommendation.

a. FryCo, a small chemical company that has developed an environmentally friendly nonstick cooking surface.
b. Twenty-First Century Films, an independent documentary film producer.
c. DeLuxe, a luxury brand known for its high-end leather accessories such as handbags, wallets and belts.
d. Droplet Labs, a start-up company that has patented a process for testing a single drop of a patient's blood for twenty different pathogens.

Problem 1.2

Your client Fizzy Cola is a producer of craft soft drinks based in Milwaukee, Wisconsin. Fizzy tells you that it would like to expand internationally to South America, the European Union, China, Japan and South Korea. What licensing and internationalization strategy would you recommend for Fizzy?

2

Ownership and Assignment of Intellectual Property

SUMMARY CONTENTS

The owner of an intellectual property (IP) right, whether a patent, copyright, trademark, trade secret or other right, has the exclusive right to exploit that right. Ownership of an IP right is thus the most effective and potent means for utilizing that right. But what does it mean to "own" an IP right and how does a person – an individual or a firm – acquire ownership of it? This chapter explores transfers and assignments of IP ownership, first in general, and then with respect to special considerations pertinent to patents, copyrights and trademarks. Assignments and transfers of IP *licenses*, another important topic, are covered in Section 13.3, and attempts to prohibit an assignor of IP from later challenging the validity of transferred IP (through a contractual no-challenge clause or the common law doctrine of "assignor estoppel") are covered in Chapter 22.

2.1 ASSIGNMENTS OF INTELLECTUAL PROPERTY, GENERALLY

Once it is in existence, an item of IP may be bought, sold, transferred and assigned much as any other form of property. Like real and personal property, IP can be conveyed through contract, bankruptcy sale, will or intestate succession, and can change hands through any number of corporate transactions such as mergers, asset sales, spinoffs and stock sales.

The following case illustrates how IP rights will be treated by the courts much as any other assets transferred among parties. In this case, the court must interpret a "bill of sale," the document listing assets conveyed in a particular transaction. Just as with bushels of grain or tons of steel, particular IP rights can be listed in a bill of sale and the manner in which they are listed will determine what the buyer receives.

Systems Unlimited v. Cisco Systems

228 Fed. Appx. 854 (11th Cir. 2007) (cert. denied)

Per Curiam

Following the settlement of a dispute between Systems Unlimited, Inc. and Cisco Systems, Inc. over the ownership of certain intellectual property, Cisco agreed to covey the property to Systems. In the resulting bill of sale, Cisco:

> granted, bargained, sold, transferred and delivered, and by these presents does grant, bargain, sell, transfer and deliver unto [Systems], its successor and assigns, the following:
> Any and all of [Cisco]'s right, title and interest in any copyrights, patents, trademarks, trade secrets and other intellectual property of any kind associated with any software, code or data, including without limitation host controller software and billing software, whether embedded or in any other form (including without limitations, disks, CDs and magnetic tapes), and including any and all available copies thereof and any and all books and records related thereto by [Cisco]

Cisco never delivered [copies of] any of the software to Systems. Alleging that it had been damaged by the non-delivery, Systems sued Cisco for breaching the bill of sale contract and for violating the attendant obligations to deliver the software under the Uniform Commercial Code.

Systems contends that the district court erred in granting summary judgment in favor of Cisco because: (1) the plain language of the bill of sale required Cisco to deliver the software; (2) the bill of sale, when read in conjunction with other contemporaneous agreements, required delivery; and (3) the UCC, which governs the bill of sale, requires that all goods be delivered at a reasonable time. Systems is wrong on each point.

The bill of sale is interpreted in accord with its plain language absent some ambiguity. Here, the parties agree that the bill of sale is clear and unambiguous.

The bill of sale provides that Cisco will "grant, bargain, sell, transfer and deliver unto [Systems] … [a]ny and all of [Cisco]'s right, title and interest in any copyrights, patents, trademarks, trade secrets and other intellectual property of a kind associated with any software, code or data." As the district court explained, this language unambiguously means that Cisco was required by the bill of sale to transfer to Systems all of its rights in intellectual property associated with certain software and data. There is no mention in the plain language of the contract itself of Cisco being obligated to transfer the actual software, and we will not imply any such obligation absent some good reason under law.

Systems says there are two good reasons to imply an obligation by Cisco to transfer the software. First, Systems argues that the bill of sale must be interpreted in conjunction with the settlement agreement between Systems and Cisco and other documents relating to the intellectual property. These other agreements, Systems claims, include an obligation by Cisco to deliver the software with any conveyance of intellectual property.

Assuming without deciding that the other agreements include language requiring Cisco to deliver the software, they are not relevant here because Systems has never alleged Cisco violated these other agreements. Systems' complaint alleges only a violation of the bill of sale contract, and there is no obligation in that contract to deliver the software. The bill of sale does not reference or incorporate any other agreement.

To get around this point, Systems argues that "when instruments relate to the same matters, are between the same parties, and made part of substantially one transaction, they are
to be taken together." It is true that this is one of the canons for construing a contract under
California law. But it is also true that this canon, as with most others, is inapplicable where
the contract that is alleged to have been breached is unambiguous. Here, the language of
the bill of sale is unambiguous. Thus, there is no need to apply any canons of construction.

Systems also argues that the UCC imposes a duty on Cisco to deliver the software. We
will assume without deciding that Systems' reading of the UCC is correct. Even so, the
provisions of the UCC only apply to contracts that deal predominately with "transactions
in goods." The sale of intellectual property, which is what is involved here, is not a transaction in goods. Thus, the UCC does not apply. Accordingly, the plain language of the
bill of sale governs and, as the district court held, it does not include a provision requiring
Cisco to deliver any software.

AFFIRMED.

Notes and Questions

1. *IP and the UCC.* The court in *Systems v. Cisco* holds that IP licenses and other transactions
   are not governed by Article 2 of the UCC, which pertains to sales of goods. In Section 3.4 we
   will discuss whether and to what degree Article 2 applies to IP *licenses*. But this case relates
   not to a license, but to a "sale" of software. Why doesn't UCC Article 2 apply? Should it?
2. *Delivery of what?* What does this language from the bill of sale refer to, if not delivery of
   software: "including any and all available copies thereof"? Does this language represent a
   drafting mistake by Systems' attorney? Or an intentional omission by Cisco?
3. *The need for software.* Why is Systems so upset that Cisco has allegedly refused to deliver the
   software in question? How useful is an assignment of copyright and other IP to someone who
   is not in possession of the software code that is copyrighted? Has Cisco "pulled a fast one" on
   Systems and the court, or is there a valid business reason that could justify Cisco's failure to
   deliver the software?
4. *Statute of frauds.* Assignments of copyrights, patents and trademarks must all be in writing
   (17 U.S.C. § 204(a), 35 U.S.C. § 261, 15 U.S.C. § 1060(3)). Why? This requirement does
   not apply to most licenses, which may be oral. Can you think of a good reason for this
   distinction?
5. *State law and mutual mistake.* Despite the federal statutory nature of patents, courts have
   long held that the question of who holds title to a patent is a matter of state contract law.[1]
   This issue arose in an interesting way in *Schwendimann v. Arkwright Advanced Coating, Inc.*,
   959 F.3d 1065 (Fed. Cir. 2020). In *Schwendimann*, the plaintiff's former company purported
   to assign her a patent application in 2003. Due to a clerical error by the law firm handling
   the matter, the assignment document filed with the patent office listed the wrong patent
   name and number. In 2011, the plaintiff filed an action asserting the patent against an alleged
   infringer. The defendant, discovering the incorrect assignment document from 2003, moved
   to dismiss on the ground that the plaintiff did not hold any enforceable rights at the time she
   filed suit and thus lacked standing. The district court, interpreting applicable state law, held
   that the 2003 assignment was the result of a "mutual mistake of fact" that did not accurately
   reflect the intent of the parties. Accordingly, the erroneous document could be reformed

---

[1] See *Enovsys LLC v. Nextel Commc'ns Inc.*, 614 F.3d 1333, 1342 (Fed. Cir. 2010).

and was sufficient to support standing to bring suit. The Federal Circuit affirmed. Judge Reyna dissented, reasoning that, irrespective of the district court's later reformation of the erroneous assignment, the plaintiff's failure to own the patent at the time her suit was filed necessarily barred her suit under Article III of the Constitution. Which of these positions do you find more persuasive? Notwithstanding the holding in favor of the plaintiff, is there a claim for legal malpractice against the law firm in question?

2.2 ASSIGNMENT OF COPYRIGHTS AND THE WORK MADE FOR HIRE DOCTRINE

Under § 201(a) of the Copyright Act, copyright ownership "vests initially in the author or authors of the work." A copyright owner may assign any of its exclusive rights, in full or in part, to a third party. The assignment generally must be in writing and signed by the owner of the copyright or his or her authorized agent (17 U.S.C. § 204(a)).

If a work of authorship is prepared by an employee within the scope of his or her employment, then the work is a "work made for hire" and the employer is considered the author and owner of the copyright (17 U.S.C. § 201(b)). In addition, if a work is not made by an employee but is "specially ordered or commissioned," it will be considered a work made for hire if it falls into one of nine categories enumerated in § 101(2) of the Act: a contribution to a collective work, a part of a motion picture or other audiovisual work, a translation, a supplementary work, a compilation, an instructional text, a test, answer material for a test, or an atlas. Commissioned works that do not fall into one of these nine categories (for example, software) are not automatically considered to be works made for hire, and copyright must be assigned explicitly through a separate assignment or sale agreement.

Warren v. Fox Family Worldwide, Inc.

328 F.3d 1136 (9th Cir. 2003)

HAWKINS, Circuit Judge.

In this dispute between plaintiff-appellant Richard Warren ("Warren") and defendants-appellees Fox Family Worldwide ("Fox"), MTM Productions ("MTM"), Princess Cruise Lines ("Princess"), and the Christian Broadcasting Network ("CBN"), Warren claims that defendants infringed the copyrights in musical compositions he created for use in the television series "Remington Steele." Concluding that Warren has no standing to sue for infringement because he is neither the legal nor beneficial owner of the copyrights in question, we affirm the district court's Rule 12 dismissal of Warren's complaint.

Warren and Triplet Music Enterprises, Inc. ("Triplet") entered into the first of a series of detailed written contracts with MTM concerning the composition of music for "Remington Steele." This agreement stated that Warren, as sole shareholder and employee of Triplet, would provide services by creating music in return for compensation from MTM. Under the agreement, MTM was to make a written accounting of all sales of broadcast rights to the series and was required to pay Warren a percentage of all sales of broadcast rights to the series made to third parties not affiliated with ASCAP or BMI. These agreements were renewed and re-executed with slight modifications in 1984, 1985 and 1986.

Warren brought suit in propria persona against Fox, MTM, CBN, and Princess, alleging copyright infringement, breach of contract, accounting, conversion, breach of fiduciary duty, breach of covenants of good faith and fair dealing, and fraud.

Warren claims he created approximately 1,914 musical works used in the series pursuant to the agreements with MTM; that MTM and Fox have materially breached their obligations under the contracts by failing to account for or pay the full amount of royalties due Warren from sales to parties not affiliated with ASCAP or BMI; and that MTM and Fox infringed Warren's copyrights in the music by continuing to broadcast and license the series after materially breaching the contracts. As to the other defendants, Warren claims that CBN and Princess infringed his copyrights by broadcasting "Remington Steele" without his authorization. Warren seeks damages, an injunction, and an order declaring him the owner of the copyrights at issue.

Defendants argu[ed] that Warren's infringement claims should be dismissed for lack of standing because he is neither the legal nor beneficial owner of the copyrights. The district court dismissed Warren's copyright claims without leave to amend and dismissed his state law claims without prejudice to their refiling in state court, holding that Warren lacked standing because the works were made for hire, and because a creator of works for hire cannot be a beneficial owner of a copyright in the work. Warren appeals.

The first agreement [between the parties], signed on February 25, 1982, states that MTM contracted to employ Warren "to render services to [MTM] for the television pilot photoplay now entitled 'Remington Steele.'" It also is clear that the parties agreed that MTM would "own all right, title and interest in and to [Warren's] services and the results and proceeds thereof, and all other rights granted to [MTM] in [the Music Employment Agreement] to the same extent as if … [MTM were] the employer of [Warren]." The Music Employment Agreement provided:

> As [Warren's] employer for hire, [MTM] shall own in perpetuity, throughout the universe, solely and exclusively, all rights of every kind and character, in the musical material and all other results and proceeds of the services rendered by [Warren] hereunder and [MTM] shall be deemed the author thereof for all purposes.

FIGURE 2.1 Warren claimed that he created 1,914 musical works for the popular 1980s TV series *Remington Steele*.

The parties later executed contracts almost identical to these first agreements in June 1984, July 1985, and November 1986. As the district court noted, these subsequent contracts are even more explicit in defining the compositions as "works for hire." Letters that Warren signed accompanying the later Music Employment Agreements provided: "It is understood and agreed that you are supplying [your] services to us as our employee for hire … [and] [w]e shall own all right, title and interest in and to [your] services and the results and proceeds thereof, as works made for hire."

That the agreements did not use the talismanic words "specially ordered or commissioned" matters not, for there is no requirement, either in the Act or the caselaw, that work-for-hire contracts include any specific wording. In fact, in *Playboy Enterprises v. Dumas*, 53 F.3d 549 (2d Cir. 1995), the Second Circuit held that legends stamped on checks were writings sufficient to evidence a work-for-hire relationship where the legend read: "By endorsement, payee: acknowledges payment in full for services rendered on a work-made-for-hire basis in connection with the Work named on the face of this check, and confirms ownership by Playboy Enterprises, Inc. of all right, title and interest (except physical possession), including all rights of copyright, in and to the Work." Id. at 560. The agreements at issue in the instant case are more explicit than the brief statement that was before the Second Circuit.

In this case, not only did the contracts internally designate the compositions as "works made for hire," they provided that MTM "shall be deemed the author thereof for all purposes." This is consistent with a work-for-hire relationship under the Act, which provides that "the employer or other person for whom the work was prepared is considered the author." 17 U.S.C. § 201(b).

Warren argues that the use of royalties as a form of compensation demonstrates that this was not a work-for-hire arrangement. While we have not addressed this specific question, the Second Circuit held in *Playboy* that "where the creator of a work receives royalties as payment, that method of payment generally weighs against finding a work-for-hire relationship." 53 F.3d at 555. However, *Playboy* clearly held that this factor was not conclusive. In addition to noting that the presence of royalties only "generally" weighs against a work-for-hire relationship, Playboy cites *Picture Music, Inc. v. Bourne, Inc.*, 457 F.2d 1213, 1216 (2d Cir. 1972), for the proposition that "[t]he absence of a fixed salary … is never conclusive." 53 F.3d at 555. Further, the payment of royalties was only one form of compensation given to Warren under the contracts. Warren was also given a fixed sum "payable upon completion." That some royalties were agreed upon in addition to this sum is not sufficient to overcome the great weight of the contractual evidence indicating a work-for-hire relationship.

Warren also argues that because he created nearly 2,000 musical works for MTM, the works were not specially ordered or commissioned. However, the number of works at issue has no bearing on the existence of a work-for-hire relationship. As the district court noted, a weekly television show would naturally require "substantial quantities of verbal, visual and musical content."

The agreements between Warren and MTM conclusively show that the musical compositions created by Warren were created as works for hire, and Warren is therefore not the legal owner of the copyrights therein.

AFFIRMED.

Notes and Questions

1. *Employee v. Contractor.* In *Warren v. Fox* the musical compositions created by Warren fell into one of the nine categories of "specially commissioned works" that qualify as works made for hire under § 101(2) of the Copyright Act (audiovisual works), even if they were not made by employees of the commissioning party. They will thus be classified as works made for hire so long as they can be shown to have been "specially commissioned" – the focus of the debate in *Warren*. A slightly different question arose in *Community for Creative Non-Violence v. Reid*, 490 U.S. 730 (1989). In that case Reid, a sculptor, was engaged by a non-profit organization, CCNV, to create a memorial "to dramatize the plight of the homeless." Sculpture is not one of the nine enumerated categories of commissioned works. Thus, even if Reid's sculpture were "specially commissioned" (as it probably was), it would not be classified as a work made for hire under § 101 unless Reid were considered to be an *employee* of CCNV. CCNV argued that it exercised a certain degree of control over the subject matter of the sculpture, making it appropriate to classify Reid as its employee. The Court disagreed:

   Reid is a sculptor, a skilled occupation. Reid supplied his own tools. He worked in his own studio in Baltimore, making daily supervision of his activities from Washington practicably impossible. Reid was retained for less than two months, a relatively short period of time. During and after this time, CCNV had no right to assign additional projects to Reid. Apart from the deadline for completing the sculpture, Reid had absolute freedom to decide when and how long to work. CCNV paid Reid $15,000, a sum dependent on completion of a specific job, a method by which independent contractors are often compensated. Reid had total discretion in hiring and paying assistants. Creating sculptures was hardly regular business for CCNV. Indeed, CCNV is not a business at all. Finally, CCNV did not pay payroll or Social Security taxes, provide any employee benefits, or contribute to unemployment insurance or workers' compensation funds.

   Does the structure of the works made for hire doctrine under § 101(2) of the Copyright Act make sense? Why should specially commissioned works be considered works for hire only if they fall into one of the nine enumerated categories? Why is a musical composition treated so differently than a sculpture?

2. *Manner of compensation.* The form of compensation received by the author is mentioned in both *Warren v. Fox* and *CCNV v. Reid*. Why is this detail significant to the question of works made for hire? Are the courts' conclusions with respect to compensation consistent between these two cases?

3. *Software contractors and assignment.* For a variety of professional, financial and tax-planning reasons, software developers often work as independent contractors and are not hired as employees of the companies for which they create software. And, like the sculpture in *CCNV v. Reid*, software is not one of the nine enumerated categories of works under § 101(2) of the Copyright Act. Thus, even if it is specially commissioned, software will not be considered a work made for hire. As a result, companies that use independent contractors to develop software must be careful to put in place copyright assignment agreements with those contractors. And because contractors often sit and work beside company employees with very little to distinguish them, neglecting to take these contractual precautions is one of the most common IP missteps made by fledgling and mature software companies alike. If you were the general counsel of a new software company, how would you deal with this issue?

4. *Recordation.* Section 205 of the Copyright Act provides for recordation of copyright transfers with the Copyright Office. Recordation of transfers is not required, but provides priority if the owner attempts to transfer the same copyrighted work multiple times:

> § 205(d) Priority between Conflicting Transfers. — As between two conflicting transfers, the one executed first prevails if it is recorded, in the manner required to give constructive notice … Otherwise the later transfer prevails if recorded first in such manner, and if taken in good faith, for valuable consideration or on the basis of a binding promise to pay royalties, and without notice of the earlier transfer.

   As students of real property will surely observe, this provision resembles a "race-notice" recording statute under state law. As such, the second transferee of a copyright may prevail over a prior, unrecorded transferee if the second transferee records first without notice of the earlier transfer. Note also that this provision is applicable only to copyrights that are registered with the Copyright Office.

5. *Statutory termination of assignments.* Sections 203 and 304 of the Copyright Act provide that any transfer of a copyright can be revoked by the transferor between 35 and 40 years after the original transfer was made.[2] This remarkable and powerful right is irrevocable and cannot be contractually waived or circumvented. It was intended to enable authors who were young and unrecognized when they first granted rights to more powerful publishers to profit from the later success of their works. For example, in 1938 Jerry Siegel and Joseph Shuster, the creators of the Superman character, sold their rights to the predecessor of DC Comics for $130. Siegel and Shuster both died penniless in the 1990s, while Superman earned billions for his corporate owners.

   Though Sections 203 and 304 were originally directed to artists, writers and composers, these provisions apply across the board to all copyrighted works including software and technical standards documents. The possibility that an original developer of Microsoft Windows could suddenly pull the plug on millions of existing licenses is somewhat ameliorated because the reversion does not apply to works made for hire or derivative works. Nevertheless, one must ask why these reversionary rights apply to software and technical documents at all. If such works of authorship are excluded as works made for hire under Section 101(2), why shouldn't they also be excluded from Sections 203/304?[3] Is there any justification for allowing developers of copyrighted "technology" products to terminate assignments made decades ago?

6. *Divisibility of copyright.* Prior to the Copyright Act of 1976, copyright ownership was not divisible. That is, the owner of a copyright, say in a book, could not assign the exclusive right to produce a film based on that book to a third party. The right to produce a film could be licensed to a third party, but an attempted assignment of the right would potentially be invalid or treated as a license.[4] But today, under 17 U.S.C. § 201(d)(2), "Any of the exclusive rights comprised in a copyright, including any subdivision of any of the rights specified by section 106, may be transferred … and owned separately." What do you think was the rationale for this change in the law? Why would, say, a film studio prefer to "own" the right to produce a film based on a book rather than have a license to do so?

---

[2]   See also Section 12.4, Note 4, discussing these statutory provisions as mechanisms for terminating copyright *licenses*.

[3]   *See* Timothy K. Armstrong, *Shrinking the Commons: Termination of Copyright Licenses and Transfers for the Benefit of the Public*, 47 Harv. J. Legis. 359, 405–09 (2010) (discussing implications for software) and Jorge L. Contreras & Andrew Hernacki, *Copyright Termination and Technical Standards*, 43 U. Baltimore L. Rev. 221 (2014) (discussing implications for technical standards).

[4]   See Jonathan M. Barnett, *Why Is Everyone Afraid of IP Licensing?* 30 Harv. J.L. & Tech. 123, 126 (2017).

FIGURE 2.2 The creators of the Superman character died in near poverty while the Man of Steel went on to form a multi-billion-dollar franchise. Sections 203 and 304 of the US Copyright Act were enacted to enable authors and their heirs to terminate any copyright assignment or license between 35 and 40 years after originally made in order to permit them to share in the value of their creations.

2.3 ASSIGNMENT OF PATENT RIGHTS

As with other IP rights, patents, patent applications and inventions may be assigned. Patent rights initially vest in inventors who are, by definition, individuals. Unlike copyright, there is no work made for hire doctrine under US patent law. However, if an employee is "hired to invent" – that is, to perform tasks intended to result in an invention – then the employee may have a legal duty to assign the resulting invention to his or her employer.[5]

Unfortunately, the "hired to invent" doctrine is murky and inconsistently applied.[6] Thus, most employers today contractually obligate their employees to assign rights in inventions and patents to them when made within the scope of their employment and/or using the employer's resources or facilities. This requirement exists in the private sector, at nonprofit universities and research institutions, as well as government agencies. The initial assignment from an inventor to his or her employer is often filed during prosecution of a patent on a form provided by the Patent and Trademark Office. If such an assignment is not filed, the inventor's employer obtains

---

[5] See *Standard Parts Co. v. Peck*, 264 U.S. 52 (1924) (employee hired to invent a specific improvement owed a duty to assign patent rights to the employer even though the employment contract did not specifically mention patent rights).

[6] See 8 Chisum on Patents § 22.03[2] ("The line between these 'hired-to-invent' and 'general employment' categories is a fine one, and it often must be drawn on the basis of sharply conflicting testimony … [*Standard Parts Co. v. Peck*] has served as a precedent for a multitude of decisions by lower federal courts, both finding (1) an employment to invent and (2) the absence of such employment.")

no rights in an issued patent other than so-called "shop rights" that allow the employer to use the patented invention on a limited basis.[7]

Beyond the initial assignment from the inventor(s), the owner of a patent may assign it to a third party as any other property right. The following case turns on whether an inventor assigned his rights to his employer at the time the invention was conceived, or when the patent was issued.

Filmtec Corporation v. Allied-Signal Inc.
939 F.2d 1568 (Fed. Cir. 1991)

PLAGER, CIRCUIT JUDGE

Allied-Signal Inc. and UOP Inc. (Allied), defendants-appellants, appeal from the preliminary injunction issued by the district court. The trial court enjoined Allied from "making, using or selling, and actively inducing others to make use or sell TFCL membrane in the United States, and from otherwise infringing claim 7 of United States Patent No. 4,277,344 ['344]." Because of serious doubts on the record before us as to who has title to the invention and the ensuing patent, we vacate the grant of the injunction and remand for further proceedings.

The application which ultimately issued as the '344 patent was filed by John E. Cadotte on February 22, 1979. The patent claims a reverse osmosis membrane and a method for using the membrane to reduce the concentration of solute molecules and ions in solution. Cadotte assigned his rights in the application and any subsequently issuing patent to plaintiff-appellee FilmTec. This assignment was duly recorded in the United States Patent and Trademark Office. Defendant-appellant Allied manufactured a reverse osmosis membrane and FilmTec sued Allied for infringing certain claims of the '344 patent.

John Cadotte was one of the four founders of FilmTec. Prior to founding FilmTec, Cadotte and the other founders were employed in various responsible positions at the North Star Division of Midwest Research Institute (MRI), a not-for-profit research organization. MRI was principally engaged in contract research, much of it for the United States (Government), and much of it involving work in the field of reverse osmosis membranes.

The evidence indicates that the work at MRI in which Cadotte and the other founders were engaged was being carried out under contract (the contract) to the Government. The contract provided that MRI

> agrees to grant and does hereby grant to the Government the full and entire domestic right, title and interest in [any invention, discovery, improvement or development (whether or not patentable) made in the course of or under this contract or any subcontract ... thereunder].

It appears that sometime between the time FilmTec came into being in 1977 and the time Cadotte submitted his patent application in February of 1979, he made the invention that led to the '344 patent. As we will explain, just when in that period the invention was made is critical.

---

7   As explained by Professor Chisum, "The classic 'shop right' doctrine provides that an employee who uses his employer's resources to conceive an invention or to reduce it to practice must afford to his employer a nonexclusive, royalty-free, nontransferable license to make use of the invention, even though the employee subsequently obtains a patent thereon. The shop right is not an ownership interest in the patent. Rather it constitutes a defense to a charge of patent infringement by the employee or his/her assignee." 8 Chisum on Patents § 22.03[3].

Cadotte left MRI in January of 1978. Cadotte testified that he conceived his invention the month after he left MRI. Allied disputes this, and alleges that Cadotte conceived his invention and formed the reverse osmosis membrane of the '344 patent earlier—in July of 1977 or at least by November of 1977 when he allegedly produced an improved membrane.

Allied alleges that the evidence establishes that the contract between MRI and the Government grants to the Government "all discoveries and inventions made within the scope of their [i.e., MRI's employees] employment," and that the invention claimed in the '344 patent was made by Cadotte while employed by MRI. From this Allied reasons that rights in the invention must be with the Government and therefore Cadotte had no rights to assign to FilmTec. If FilmTec lacks title to the patent, FilmTec has no standing to bring an infringement action under the '344 patent. FilmTec counters by arguing that the trial court was correct in concluding that the most the Government would have acquired was an equitable title to the '344 patent, which title would have been made void under 35 U.S.C. § 261 by the subsequent assignment to FilmTec from Cadotte.

The parties agree that Cadotte was employed by MRI and that the contract between MRI and the Government contains a grant of rights to inventions made pursuant to the contract. However, the record does not reflect whether the employment agreement between Cadotte and MRI either granted or required Cadotte to grant to MRI the rights to inventions made by Cadotte. Allied argues that Cadotte's inventions were assigned nevertheless to MRI. Allied points to the provision in the contract between MRI and the Government in which MRI warrants that it will obligate inventors to assign their rights to MRI.

While this is not conclusive evidence of a grant of or a requirement to grant rights by Cadotte, it raises a serious question about the nature of the title, if any, in FilmTec. FilmTec apparently did not address this issue at the trial, and there is no indication in the opinion of the district court that this gap in the chain of ownership rights was considered by the court.

Between the time of an invention and the issuance of a patent, rights in an invention may be assigned and legal title to the ensuing patent will pass to the assignee upon grant of the patent. If an assignment of rights in an invention is made prior to the existence of the invention, this may be viewed as an assignment of an expectant interest. An assignment of an expectant interest can be a valid assignment.

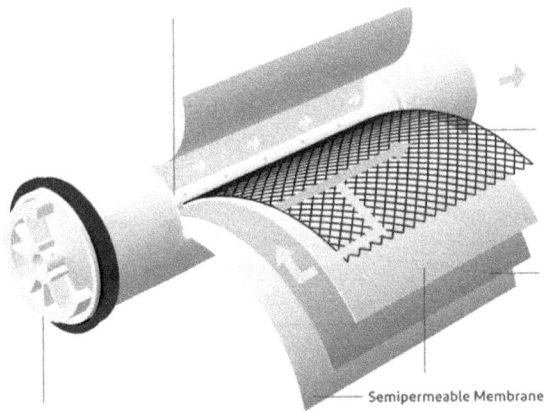

Semipermeable Membrane

FIGURE 2.3 FilmTec reverse osmosis membrane filter.

Once the invention is made and an application for patent is filed, however, legal title to the rights accruing thereunder would be in the assignee, and the assignor-inventor would have nothing remaining to assign. In this case, if Cadotte granted MRI rights in inventions made during his employ, and if the subject matter of the '344 patent was invented by Cadotte during his employ with MRI, then Cadotte had nothing to give to FilmTec and his purported assignment to FilmTec is a nullity. Thus, FilmTec would lack both title to the '344 patent and standing to bring the present action.

The district court was of the view that if the Government was the assignee from Cadotte through MRI, the Government would have acquired at most an equitable title, and that legal title would remain in Cadotte. The legal title would then have passed to FilmTec by virtue of the later assignment, pursuant to Sec. 261 of the [Patent Act]. *Sigma Eng'g v. Halm Instrument*, 33 F.R.D. 129 (E.D.N.Y. 1963).

But *Sigma*, even if it were binding precedent on this court, does not stretch so far. The issue in *Sigma* was whether the plaintiff, assignee of the patent rights of the inventors, was the real party in interest such as to be able to maintain the instant action for patent infringement. Defendant claimed that the inventors' employer had title to the invention by virtue of the employment contract which obligated the inventors to transfer all patent rights to inventions made while in its employ. As the court expressly noted, no such transfers were made, however, and the court considered any possible interest held by the employer in the invention to be in the nature of an equitable claim.

In our case, the contract between MRI and the Government did not merely obligate MRI to grant future rights, but expressly granted to the Government MRI's rights in any future invention. Ordinarily, no further act would be required once an invention came into being; the transfer of title would occur by operation of law. If a similar contract provision existed between Cadotte and MRI, as MRI's contract with the Government required, and if the invention was made before Cadotte left MRI's employ, as the trial judge seems to suggest, Cadotte would have no rights in the invention or any ensuing patent to assign to FilmTec.

Because of the district court's view of the title issue, no specific findings were made on either of these questions. As a result, we do not know who held legal title to the invention and to the patent application and therefore we do not know if FilmTec could make a sufficient legal showing to establish the likelihood of success necessary to support a preliminary injunction.

It is well established that when a legal title holder of a patent transfers his or her title to a third party purchaser for value without notice of an outstanding equitable claim or title, the purchaser takes the entire ownership of the patent, free of any prior equitable encumbrance. This is an application of the common law bona fide purchaser for value rule.

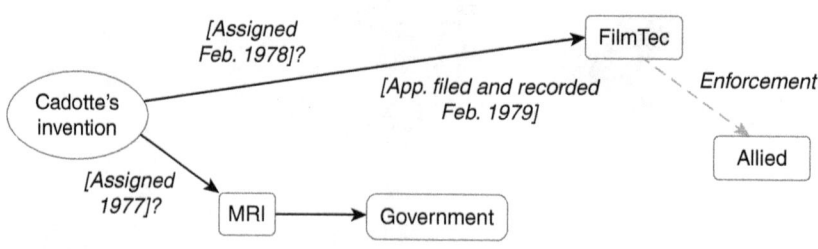

FIGURE 2.4 Schematic showing possible assignment pathways for Cadotte's invention.

Section 261 of Title 35 goes a step further. It adopts the principle of the real property recording acts, and provides that the bona fide purchaser for value cuts off the rights of a prior assignee who has failed to record the prior assignment in the Patent and Trademark Office by the dates specified in the statute. Although the statute does not expressly so say, it is clear that the statute is intended to cut off prior legal interests, which the common law rule did not.

Both the common law rule and the statute contemplate that the subsequent purchaser be exactly that—a transferee who pays valuable consideration, and is without notice of the prior transfer. The trial judge, with reference to FilmTec's rights as a subsequent purchaser, stated simply that "FilmTec is a subsequent purchaser from Cadotte for independent consideration. There is no evidence presented to imply that FilmTec was on notice of any previous assignment." The court concluded that, even if the MRI contract automatically transferred title to the Government, such assignment is not enforceable at law as it was never recorded.

> "the bona fide purchaser for value cuts off the rights of a prior assignee who has failed to record the prior assignment in the Patent and Trademark Office by the dates specified in the statute."

Since this matter will be before the trial court on remand, it may be useful for us to clarify what is required before FilmTec can properly be considered a subsequent purchaser entitled to the protections of Sec. 261. In the first place, FilmTec must be in fact a purchaser for a valuable consideration. This requirement is different from the classic notion of a purchaser under a deed of grant, where the requirement of consideration was a formality, and the proverbial peppercorn would suffice to have the deed operate under the statute of uses. Here the requirement is that the subsequent purchaser, in order to cut off the rights of the prior purchaser, must be more than a donee or other gratuitous transferee. There must be in fact valuable consideration paid so that the subsequent purchaser can, as a matter of law, claim record reliance as a premise upon which the purchase was made. That, of course, is a matter of proof.

In addition, the subsequent transferee/assignee—FilmTec in our case—must be without notice of any such prior assignment. If Cadotte's contract with MRI contained a provision assigning any inventions made during the course of employment either to MRI or directly to the Government, Cadotte would clearly be on notice of the provisions of his own contract. Since Cadotte was one of the four founders of FilmTec, and the other founders and officers were also involved at MRI, FilmTec may well be deemed to have had actual notice of an assignment. Given the key roles that Cadotte and the others played both at MRI and later at FilmTec, at a minimum FilmTec might be said to be on inquiry notice of any possible rights in MRI or the Government as a result of Cadotte's work at MRI. Thus once again, the key to FilmTec's ability to show a likelihood of success on the merits lies in the relationship between Cadotte and MRI.

In our view of the title issue, it cannot be said on this record that FilmTec has established a reasonable likelihood of success on the merits. It is thus unnecessary for us to consider the other issues raised on appeal concerning the propriety of the injunction. The grant of the preliminary injunction is vacated and the case remanded to the district court to reconsider the propriety of the preliminary injunction and for further proceedings consistent with this opinion.

VACATED AND REMANDED.

Notes and Questions

1. *Recording of title*. As noted in Section 2.1, Note 4, assignments of patents may be recorded at the Patent and Trademark Office. As provided in 35 U.S.C. § 261,

   An interest that constitutes an assignment, grant or conveyance shall be void as against any subsequent purchaser or mortgagee for a valuable consideration, without notice, unless it is recorded in the Patent and Trademark Office within three months from its date or prior to the date of such subsequent purchase or mortgage.

   This provision is a modified form of the familiar "race-notice" recording statute that applies to real estate transactions.[8] Unlike the comparable provision of the Copyright Act (17 U.S.C. § 205(d), discussed in Section 2.2), the second assignee of a patent may prevail over a prior, unrecorded assignee if the second assignee records first without notice of the earlier assignment *unless* the first assignee records within three months of the first assignment. An assignee of a patent thus has a three-month grace period in which to record its transfer without fear of being superseded by a second assignment. What is the reason for this three-month grace period, which exists neither in copyright nor real property law?

2. *Inquiry notice*. The court in *FilmTec* borrows the notion of "inquiry notice" from the law of real property recording. What is inquiry notice?[9] How does it differ from actual notice and constructive notice?

3. *Present v. Future Grants of Patent Rights*. The court in *FilmTec* explains that "the contract between MRI and the Government did not merely obligate MRI to grant future rights, but expressly granted to the Government MRI's rights in any future invention. Ordinarily, no further act would be required once an invention came into being; the transfer of title would occur by operation of law." That is, disregarding MRI's failure to record the transfer, MRI's *present* grant of rights in a future patent to the government (assuming that MRI had previously obtained the requisite rights from Cadotte) would *automatically* convey those rights to the government as soon as an invention was made.

   A similar fact pattern arose in *Stanford v. Roche*, 563 U.S. 776 (2011) (reproduced, in part, in Section 14.1). In that case, a Stanford researcher who was obligated under Stanford's policies to assign inventions to Stanford also signed an agreement assigning his future invention rights to Cetus Corp. while visiting the company to use its equipment. The Federal Circuit ruled for Cetus, reasoning that, under *FilmTec*, the researcher's *present* assignment of future patent rights to Cetus automatically became effective when a patent application was filed, leaving nothing for him to assign to the holder of a future *promise* of assignment (i.e., Stanford). Stanford successfully sought *certiorari* on different grounds (whether the Bayh–Dole Act overrode these contractual provisions), and the Supreme Court affirmed the judgment for Cetus without reaching the assignment issue.

   However, Justices Breyer and Ginsburg dissented (joined by Justice Sotomayor, who concurred in the judgment) on the ground that the Federal Circuit's 1991 rule in *FilmTec* seemingly contradicted earlier precedent. Citing one 1867 treatise and a 1958 law review note, Justice Breyer proposed that before *FilmTec*, "a present assignment of future inventions (as in both contracts here) conveyed equitable, but not legal, title" and that this equitable interest "grants equitable enforcement to an assignment of an expectancy but demands a further act, either reduction to possession or further assignment of the right when it comes into existence." In other words, the researcher's present "assignment" of his future patent rights

---

[8]   See, e.g., Jesse Dukeminier et al., Property 716 (8th ed., Wolters Kluwer Law & Business, 2014).

[9]   For a discussion and lively critique of this doctrine, see Carol M. Rose, *Crystals and Mud in Property Law*, 40 Stan. L. Rev. 577 (1988).

to Cetus would give Cetus an equitable claim to seek "legal title" once an invention existed or a patent application was filed. On this basis, Justice Breyer concludes,

> Under this rule, both the initial Stanford and later Cetus agreements would have given rise only to equitable interests in Dr. Holodniy's invention. And as between these two claims in equity, the facts that Stanford's contract came first and that Stanford subsequently obtained a postinvention assignment as well should have meant that Stanford, not Cetus, would receive the rights its contract conveyed.

Despite Justice Breyer's dissatisfaction with the holdings of *FilmTec* and *Stanford v. Roche*, their approach to future assignments still appears to be the law.[10] Which approach do you think most accurately reflects the intentions of the parties? What policy ramifications might each rule have?

4. *Shall versus does.* The result in *Stanford v. Roche* turns on the wording of two competing legal instruments – Dr. Holodniy's assignments to Cetus and Stanford. As noted by the Federal Circuit in the decision below, Holodniy's initial agreement with Stanford constituted a mere *promise* to assign his future patent rights to Stanford, whereas his agreement with Cetus acted as a *present* assignment of his future patent rights to Cetus, thus giving the patent rights to Cetus (583 F.3d 832, 841–842 (2009)). As explained by Justice Breyer in his dissent:[11]

> In the earlier agreement—that between Dr. Holodniy and Stanford University—Dr. Holodniy said, "I agree to assign … to Stanford … that right, title and interest in and to … such inventions as required by Contracts and Grants." In the later agreement—that between Dr. Holodniy and the private research firm Cetus—Dr. Holodniy said, "I will assign and do hereby assign to Cetus, my right, title, and interest in" here relevant "ideas" and "inventions." The Federal Circuit held that the earlier Stanford agreement's use of the words "agree to assign," when compared with the later Cetus agreement's use of the words "do hereby assign," made all the difference. It concluded that, once the invention came into existence, the latter words meant that the Cetus agreement trumped the earlier, Stanford agreement. That, in the Circuit's view, is because the latter words operated upon the invention automatically, while the former did not.

What could Stanford have done to avoid this problem? How do you think the result of *Stanford v. Roche* affected the wording of university patent policies and assignment documents in general?[12] Given this holding, should an assignment agreement ever be phrased in

---

[10] Professor Sean O'Connor analyzes the *FilmTec* rule and Justice Breyer's critique in Sean O'Connor, *The Aftermath of Stanford v. Roche: Which Law of Assignments Governs?*, 24 Intell. Prop. J. 29 (2011). Professor Dennis Crouch considers these issues in the context of patent prior art in Dennis Crouch, Not-Yet Filed Invention Rights, Patently-O, December 2, 2020, https://patentlyo.com/patent/2020/12/filed-invention-rights.html.

[11] For a discussion of the substance of Justice Breyer's dissent in *Stanford v. Roche*, see Section 2.3, Note 3.

[12] *See* Parker Tresemer, *Best Practices for Drafting University Technology Assignment Agreements after FilmTec, Stanford v. Roche, and Patent Reform*, 2012 U. Ill. J.L. Tech. & Pol'y 347 (2012) (offering concrete proposals for the improvement of university assignment documents), Sean M. O'Connor, *The Real Issue Behind Stanford v. Roche: Faulty Conceptions of University Assignment Policies Stemming from the 1947 Biddle Report*, 19 Mich. Telecomm. & Tech. L. Rev. 379, 421 (2013) (noting that "it is not clear that universities will be able or willing to impose new present assignment agreements upon their faculty without some form of consideration or shared governance consultation"). Notwithstanding the notoriety of *Stanford v. Roche*, not all universities appear to have gotten the message. For example, in *Omni Medsci, Inc. v. Apple Inc.*, 7 F.4th 1148 (Fed. Cir. 2021), the Federal Circuit held that a University of Michigan bylaw providing that intellectual property in a faculty member's inventions "shall be the property of the University" did not automatically assign the inventor's rights in the invention to the university. It explains that "On its face, [the clause] does not unambiguously constitute either a present automatic assignment or a promise to assign in the future. It does not say, for example, that the inventor 'will assign' the patent rights—language that this court has previously held to constitute an agreement to assign rather than a present assignment. Nor does it say that the inventor 'agrees to grant and does hereby grant' title to the patent—language that this court has previously held to constitute a present automatic assignment of a future interest. We conclude that [the clause] is most naturally read as a statement of intended disposition and a promise of a potential future assignment, not as a present automatic transfer."

any way other than "Assignor *hereby grants* to Assignee … "? Was Dr. Holodniy himself at fault in this situation? What, if anything, should he have done differently?

5. *Breadth of employee invention assignments.* As noted in the introduction to this section, employers who wish to obtain assignments of the inventions created by their employees must do so pursuant to written assignment agreements. But how broad can these assignments be? In *Whitewater West Indus. v. Alleshouse,* 2020 U.S. App. LEXIS 36394 (Fed. Cir. 2020), the Federal Circuit reviewed an employee assignment agreement that contained the following provision:

a. Assignment: In consideration of compensation paid by Company, Employee agrees that all right, title and interest in all inventions, improvements, developments, trade-secret, copyrightable or patentable material that Employee conceives *or hereafter may make or conceive,* whether solely or jointly with others:

(a) with the use of Company's time, materials, or facilities; or (b) resulting from or suggested by Employee's work for Company; or (c) in any way connected to any subject matter within the existing or contemplated business of Company

shall automatically be deemed to become the property of Company as soon as made or conceived, and Employee agrees to assign to Company, its successors, assigns, or nominees, all of Employee's rights and interests in said inventions, improvements, and developments in all countries worldwide. Employee's obligation to assign the rights to such inventions shall survive the discontinuance or termination of this Agreement for any reason.

This provision, on its face, appears to require not only that current employees assign their inventions to the company (a typical provision in employment agreements), but also that former employees continue to make such assignments indefinitely in the future, so long as such inventions are "in any way connected to any subject matter within the existing or contemplated business of Company." Needless to say, this provision is quite aggressive.

Richard Alleshouse, a designer of water park attractions, was hired by Wave Loch, Inc., a company operating in California, in October 2007. In September 2008, Alleshouse signed a Covenant Against Disclosure and Covenant Not to Compete containing the above assignment clause. In 2012, Alleshouse left Wave Loch to cofound a new company in the same line of business. There, he continued to develop and patent features of surfing-based water park attractions. In 2017, Wave Loch (through its successor Whitewater West) sued Alleshouse for breach of contract and correction of inventorship, seeking to acquire title to three patents on which Alleshouse was listed as a co-inventor following his departure from Wave Loch.

In evaluating Wave Loch's claim, the Federal Circuit considered California Business and Professions Code § 16600, which states: "Except as provided in this chapter, every contract by which anyone is restrained from engaging in a lawful profession, trade, or business of any kind is to that extent void." This statutory provision has traditionally been interpreted to prohibit companies from imposing noncompetition restrictions on former employees. In this case, however, the Federal Circuit extended its reach to prohibit assignments of future IP rights not based on the company's own IP. In assessing the over-breadth of the provision, the court noted that:

No trade-secret or other confidential information need have been used to conceive the invention or reduce it to practice for the assignment provision to apply. The obligation is unlimited in time and geography. It applies when Mr. Alleshouse's post-employment invention is merely "suggested by" his work for Wave Loch. It applies, too, when his post-employment invention is "in any way connected to any subject matter" that was within Wave Loch's "existing or contemplated" business when Mr. Alleshouse worked for Wave Loch.

Under these circumstances, the court invalidated the assignment provision, reasoning that it "imposes [too harsh a] penalty on post-employment professional, trade, or business prospects—a penalty that has undoubted restraining effect on those prospects and that a number of courts have long held to invalidate certain broad agreements with those effects."

Interestingly, Wave Loch cited *Stanford v. Roche* in its defense, arguing that the court there interpreted § 16600 to uphold the invention assignment provision used by Cetus. The Federal Circuit rejected this argument, however, stating that in *Stanford*, unlike *Whitewater*, "there was simply no evidence of a restraining effect on [the researcher's] ability to engage in his profession." But as pointed out by Professor Dennis Crouch, "The weak point of the Federal Circuit's decision [in *Whitewater*] is that it is seemingly contrary to its own prior express statement [in *Stanford*] that 'section 16600 [applies] to employment restrictions on departing employees, not to patent assignments.'"[13]

Which view do you find more persuasive? Should Alleshouse have been required to assign his post-departure patents to Wave Loch? What would the result be in a state that did not have an analog to California's § 16600? Should this question be resolved under Federal patent law?

6. *When does an assignable invention exist?* Another twist relating to employee invention assignments involves the point in time when an "invention" actually comes into existence and can thus be assigned. In *Bio-Rad Labs, Inc. v. ITC and 10X Genomics* (Fed. Cir. 2021), two employees each agreed to assign to Bio-Rad, their employer, any IP, including ideas, discoveries and inventions, that he "conceives, develops or creates" during his employment. Both employees left Bio-Rad to form 10X Genomics, which competed with Bio-Rad. Four months later, 10X began to file patent applications on technology that the employees had worked on while at Bio-Rad. The employees claimed that, while their work at 10X was related to their work at Bio-Rad, they did not actually "conceive" the inventions leading to their patents until after they had joined 10X. The Federal Circuit, applying California

FIGURE 2.5 Richard Alleshouse was the product manager for Wave Loch's FlowRider attraction, shown here as installed on the upper deck of a Royal Caribbean cruise ship.

13   Dennis Crouch, Overbroad Assignment Agreement: Invalid under California Law, Patently-O, November 19, 2020, https://patentlyo.com/patent/2020/11/overbroad-assignment-california.html.

employment and contract law, agreed, holding that the assignment clause in the Bio-Rad agreements related to "intellectual property" and that an unprotectable "idea," even if later leading to a patentable invention, was not IP and could thus not be assigned. That is, the court found that the assignment duty under the agreement was "limited to subject matter that itself could be protected as intellectual property." If this is the case, then why did the Bio-Rad agreement expressly call for the assignment of "ideas" in addition to inventions and other forms of IP?

  Professor Dennis Crouch contrasts *Bio-Rad* with *Dana-Farber Cancer Inst., Inc. v. Ono Pharm. Co., Ltd.*, 964 F.3d 1365 (Fed. Cir. 2020), in which unpatentable, pre-conception ideas did give rise to a claim for ownership of patentable inventions conceived later.[14] Which approach do you think most accurately reflects the intentions of the parties? How would you draft an assignment agreement to unambiguously cover pre-conception ideas, or to avoid such assignments?

7. *Indivisibility of patent rights.* Unlike copyrights (see Section 2.2, Note 5), the rights "within" a patent are indivisible. That is, the owner of a patent may not assign one claim of the patent to another, nor may it assign the exclusive right to make or sell one particular type of product. As set out by the Supreme Court in *Waterman v. MacKenzie*, 138 U.S. 252 (1891), a patent owner's only options are to assign (1) the whole patent, (2) an undivided part or share of the whole patent, or (3) the patent rights "within and throughout a specified part of the United States" (a rarity these days). Thus, when a patent owner, under option (2), assigns "an undivided part" of a patent, the assignee receives an undivided interest in the whole, becoming a tenant in common with the original owner and any other co-owners (the rights and duties of such joint patent owners are discussed in greater detail in Section 2.5). Why do patents and copyrights differ in this regard? Should patents be "divisible" like copyrights? What advantages or disadvantages might arise from such divisibility?

8. *Past infringement.* The general rule in the United States is that "one seeking to recover money damages for infringement of [a] patent … must have held the legal title to the patent during the time of the infringement." *Arachnid, Inc. v. Merit Indus., Inc.* 939 F.2d 1574, 1579 (Fed. Cir. 1991). Thus, the assignee of a patent only obtains the right to sue for infringement that occurred while it owned the patent. As the Supreme Court held a century and a half ago, "It is a great mistake to suppose that the assignment of a patent carries with it a transfer of the right to damages for an infringement committed before such assignment." *Moore v. Marsh*, 74 U.S. (7 Wall.) 515 (1868). This rule often acts as a trap for the unwary (see, e.g., *Nano-Second Technology Co., Ltd. v. Dynaflex International*, 2013 U.S. Dist. LEXIS 62611 (N.D. Cal.) (language purporting to assign "the entire right, title and interest" to a patent failed to convey the right to sue for past infringement)). As a result, if the assignee wishes to sue for infringement occurring prior to the date of the assignment, the assignment must contain an express conveyance of this right. Does this rule still make sense today? Why might an assignor of a patent not wish to assign the right to sue for past infringement to a purchaser of the patent? What language would you use in an assignment clause to convey this important right to the assignee?

[14] See Dennis Crouch, Pre-Invention Innovations Not Captured by Employment Agreement Duty to Assign, Patently-O, April 29, 2021, https://patentlyo.com/patent/2021/04/invention-innovations-employment.html.

Problem 2.1

The Brokeback Institute (BI) is a leading medical research center. The IP assignment clause in its standard consulting agreement reads as follows:

Consultant hereby assigns to BI all of its ownership, right, title, and interest in and to all Work Product. An Invention will be considered "Work Product" if it fits any of the following three criteria: (1) it is developed using equipment, supplies, facilities, or trade secrets of BI; (2) it results from Consultant's work for BI; or (3) it relates to BI's business or its current or anticipated research and development.

How would you react to and/or revise this clause if you represented a consultant who was one of the following:

a. A software developer being engaged by BI for a six-month, full-time engagement to update BI's medical records software database.
b. A Nobel laureate biochemist with a faculty appointment at Harvard who will be visiting BI to teach a three-week summer class to freshman pre-med students.
c. A brain researcher from Oxford who has been invited to serve on the scientific advisory board of a BI grant-funded neurosurgery project, which will involve participation in one telephonic board meeting per calendar quarter.
d. A pathologist who will advise BI on the design of its new pathology lab, which is expected to require fifty hours of work over the next year.

Problem 2.2

Help out Stanford University by drafting an IP assignment clause applicable to its faculty members, including those who occasionally visit other institutions and companies to use their equipment and facilities.

2.4 TRADEMARK ASSIGNMENTS AND GOODWILL

Like copyrights and patents, trademarks may be assigned by their owners. But as IP rights, trademarks differ in important respects from copyrights and patents. Most fundamentally, as discussed in the following case, an assignment of a registered trademark is invalid unless it is accompanied by an assignment of the associated business goodwill.

Sugar Busters LLC v. Brennan

177 F.3d 258 (5th Cir. 1999)

KING, Chief Judge

Plaintiff-appellee Sugar Busters, L.L.C. (plaintiff) is a limited liability company organized by three doctors and H. Leighton Steward, who co-authored and published a book entitled "*SUGAR BUSTERS! Cut Sugar to Trim Fat*" in 1995. In "*SUGAR BUSTERS! Cut Sugar to Trim Fat*," the authors recommend a diet plan based on the role of insulin in obesity and cardiovascular disease. The authors' premise is that reduced consumption of insulin-producing food, such as carbohydrates and other sugars, leads to weight loss and a more healthy lifestyle. The 1995 publication of "*SUGAR BUSTERS! Cut Sugar to Trim*

Fat" sold over 210,000 copies, and in May 1998 a second edition was released. The second edition has sold over 800,000 copies and remains a bestseller.

Brennan then co-authored "*SUGAR BUST For Life!*," which was published in May 1998. "*SUGAR BUST for Life*" states on its cover that it is a "cookbook and companion guide by the famous family of good food," and that Brennan was "Consultant, Editor, Publisher, [and] Sales and Marketing Director for the original, best-selling '*Sugar Busters!*™ *Cut Sugar to Trim Fat.*'" Approximately 110,000 copies of "*SUGAR BUST for Life!*" were sold between its release and September 1998.

Plaintiff filed this suit in the United States District Court for the Eastern District of Louisiana on May 26, 1998. Plaintiff sought to enjoin [Brennan] from selling, displaying, advertising or distributing "*SUGAR BUST for Life!*," to destroy all copies of the cookbook, and to recover damages and any profits derived from the cookbook.

The mark that is the subject of plaintiff's infringement claim is a service mark that was registered in 1992 by Sugarbusters, Inc., an Indiana corporation operating a retail store named "Sugarbusters" in Indianapolis that provides products and information for diabetics. The "SUGARBUSTERS" service mark, registration number 1,684,769, is for "retail store services featuring products and supplies for diabetic people; namely, medical supplies, medical equipment, food products, informational literature and wearing apparel featuring a message regarding diabetes." Sugarbusters, Inc. sold "any and all rights to the mark" to Thornton-Sahoo, Inc. on December 19, 1997, and Thornton-Sahoo, Inc. sold these rights to Elliott Company, Inc. (Elliott) on January 9, 1998. Plaintiff obtained the service mark from Elliott pursuant to a "servicemark purchase agreement" dated January 26, 1998. Under the terms of that agreement, plaintiff purchased "all the interests [Elliott] owns" in the mark and "the goodwill of all business connected with the use of and symbolized by" the mark.

The district court found that the mark is valid and that the transfer of the mark to plaintiff was not "in gross" because

> [t]he plaintiff has used the trademark to disseminate information through its books, seminars, the Internet, and the cover of plaintiff's recent book, which reads "*Help Treat Diabetes and Other Diseases.*" Moreover, the plaintiff is moving forward to market and sell its own products and services, which comport with the products and services sold by the Indiana corporation. There has been a full and complete transfer of the good will related to the mark ...

A trademark is merely a symbol of goodwill and has no independent significance apart from the goodwill that it symbolizes. Therefore, a trademark cannot be sold or assigned apart from the goodwill it symbolizes. The sale or assignment of a trademark without the goodwill that the mark represents is characterized as in gross and is invalid.

The purpose of the rule prohibiting the sale or assignment of a trademark in gross is to prevent a consumer from being misled or confused as to the source and nature of the goods or services that he or she acquires. Use of the mark by the assignee in connection with a different goodwill and different product would result in a fraud on the purchasing public who reasonably assume that the mark signifies the same thing, whether used by one person or another. Therefore, if consumers are not to be misled from established associations with the mark, [it must] continue to be associated with the same or similar products after the assignment.

Plaintiff's purported service mark in "SUGARBUSTERS" is valid only if plaintiff also acquired the goodwill that accompanies the mark; that is, "the portion of the business or service with which the mark is associated." [Brennan] claim[s] that the transfer of the "SUGARBUSTERS" mark to plaintiff was in gross because "[n]one of the assignor's underlying business, including its inventory, customer lists, or other assets, were transferred to [plaintiff]." [Brennan's] view of goodwill, however, is too narrow. Plaintiff may obtain a valid trademark without purchasing any physical or tangible assets of the retail store in Indiana – the transfer of goodwill requires only that the services be sufficiently similar to prevent consumers of the service offered under the mark from being misled from established associations with the mark.

In concluding that goodwill was transferred, the district court relied ... on its finding that "plaintiff is moving forward to market and sell its own products and services, which comport with the products and services sold by the Indiana corporation." Steward testified, however, that plaintiff does not have any plans to operate a retail store, and plaintiff offered no evidence suggesting that it intends to market directly to consumers any goods it licenses to carry the "SUGAR BUSTERS!" name. Finally, we are unconvinced by plaintiff's argument that, by stating on the cover of its diet book that it may "[h]elp treat diabetes and other diseases" and then selling some of those books on the Internet, plaintiff provides a service substantially similar to a retail store that provides diabetic supplies. We therefore must conclude that plaintiff's purported service mark is invalid.

Notes and Questions

1. *Acquiring goodwill.* The Servicemark Purchase Agreement between Elliott and Sugar Busters, LLC clearly purported to transfer "the goodwill of all business connected with the use of and symbolized by" the SUGARBUSTERS mark. Given this language, why did the Fifth Circuit find that the goodwill of the business was not transferred? In view of the court's holding, how would you advise a client if it desires to acquire a trademark but not to conduct the same business as the prior owner of the mark?

2. *Consumer confusion.* Generally, trademark infringement cases hinge on whether an alleged infringer is causing consumer confusion as to the source of goods or services. A similar theory applies to the Fifth Circuit's rule on in gross trademark assignments: If the new goods sold under the mark are significantly different than the old goods sold under the mark, then consumers might be confused as to the source and nature of the goods being sold. Why is this the case? What is the harm in this confusion?

3. *Effect of an in gross transfer.* Professor Barton Beebe notes, in discussing the *Sugar Busters* case, that "In most situations ... the assignee may claim exclusive rights in the mark, but the basis of and the priority date for those rights stems only from the assignee's new use of the mark, not from any previous use by the assignor."[15] This conclusion is sensible – without the accompanying goodwill, the acquirer gets nothing from the original mark owner, but may begin to use the mark afresh and may build up goodwill based on its own use. But does this reasoning correspond with the holding of *Sugar Busters*? Note the date on which the plaintiff purported to acquire the trademark from Elliott (January 26, 1998), when Brennan's allegedly infringing book was released (May 26, 1998) and when the plaintiff brought suit

15 Barton Beebe, Trademark Law: An Open Source Casebook, version 4.0 at Part III, 127 (2017).

against Brennan (May 26, 1998). Even if the plaintiff acquired no trademark rights at all from Elliott, wouldn't it have acquired some enforceable rights between January and May, 1998? And what about any common law trademark rights that the plaintiff accrued from the 1995 publication of its first *Sugar Busters* book?

4. *Toward free transfer?* Professor Irene Calboli argues that the rule requiring transfer of goodwill with trademarks is an outdated trap for the unwary that should be abolished. She hypothesizes a transaction in which a new company acquires the Coca-Cola Company, observing all the proper formalities, and then decides to apply the famous Coca-Cola mark not to carbonated colas, but to salty snacks. Will consumers be confused? Possibly, but the new owner is perfectly within its rights to apply the mark to its snack products rather than colas. Would consumers be worse off if the transaction documentation had neglected to reflect a transfer of goodwill? Calboli reasons that

   the rule of assignment "with goodwill" is failing to meet its purpose and ... rather than focusing on a sterile and confusing requirement, the courts should focus directly on the assignee's use of the mark. If this use is likely to deceive the public, the courts should declare the assignments at issue void. Yet, if no likelihood of confusion or deception results from the transaction, the courts should allow the assignments to stand.[16]

   Do you agree? Does the prohibition on *in gross* transfers of trademarks serve any useful purpose today?[17]

5. *Recordation.* The recordation requirements for trademarks are similar to those for patents. As provided under 15 U.S.C. § 1060(3):

   An assignment shall be void against any subsequent purchaser for valuable consideration without notice, unless the prescribed information reporting the assignment is recorded in the United States Patent and Trademark Office within 3 months after the date of the assignment or prior to the subsequent purchase.

   As with patents, this provision is a modified form of "race-notice" recording statute. The second assignee of a trademark may prevail over a prior, unrecorded assignee if the second assignee records first without notice of the earlier assignment *unless* the first assignee records within three months of the first assignment.

6. *Security interests and mortgages.* The recording statute for patents 35 U.S.C. § 261 refers to "a subsequent purchaser or mortgagee" of a patent, whereas the statute for trademarks refers only to "a subsequent purchaser." Why does the trademark statute omit mention of mortgagees? Can a trademark be mortgaged? What might prevent this from happening effectively?

7. *Short-form assignments.* Intellectual property rights are often conveyed as part of a larger corporate merger or acquisition transaction. In order to avoid filing the entire transaction agreement with the Patent and Trademark Office for recording purposes, the parties often execute a short-form assignment document that pertains only to the assigned patents or trademarks. This short-form document is then recorded at the Patent and Trademark Office. A sample of such a short-form assignment follows.

---

[16] Irene Calboli, *Trademark Assignment "With Goodwill": A Concept Whose Time Has Gone*, 57 Fla. L. Rev. 771, 776 (2005).

[17] Note that the requirement that a trademark *license* be accompanied by a transfer of goodwill was rejected in *Dawn Donut Co. v. Hart's Food Stores, Inc.*, 267 F.2d 358 (2d Cir. 1959), discussed in Section 13.1.

This assignment is made as of the _____ day of _____ by ASSIGNOR INC., a _____ corporation having a principal place of business at _____, hereinafter referred to as the ASSIGNOR, to ASSIGNEE CORP., a _____ corporation, having a • principal place of business at _____, hereinafter referred to as ASSIGNEE.

WHEREAS, ASSIGNOR is the owner of the registered trademarks and trademark applications, hereinafter collectively referred to as the TRADEMARKS, identified on Schedules "A" and "B" attached hereto, together with the good will and all rights which may have accrued in connection therewith.

WHEREAS, ASSIGNEE is desirous of acquiring the entire right, title and interest of ASSIGNOR in and to said TRADEMARKS together with said rights and the good will of the business symbolized thereby.

NOW, THEREFORE, for good and valuable consideration paid by the ASSIGNEE, receipt of which is hereby acknowledged, ASSIGNOR does hereby sell, assign, transfer and set over to ASSIGNEE, its successors and assigns, ASSIGNOR's entire right, title and interest in and to the TRADEMARKS, together with said good will of the business symbolized thereby, said TRADEMARKS to be held and enjoyed by the ASSIGNEE, its successors and assigns as fully and entirely as the same would have been held and enjoyed by the ASSIGNOR had this assignment not been made.

ASSIGNOR covenants and agrees to execute such further and confirmatory assignments in recordable form as the ASSIGNEE may reasonably require to vest record title of said respective registrations in ASSIGNEE.

IN WITNESS WHEREOF, ASSIGNOR has caused this Assignment to be executed by a duly authorized officer.

ASSIGNOR

By: _____ Date: _____

2.5 ASSIGNMENT OF TRADE SECRETS

Like other IP rights, trade secrets may be assigned by their owners. As the leading treatise on trade secret law announces in the heading of one of its chapters, "Trade Secrets Are Assignable Property."[18] Yet the assignment of trade secrets is perhaps the least developed and understood among IP types.

Part of the complexity arises from the fact that the term "trade secret" refers to two distinct concepts: A trade secret is, on one hand, a piece of information that derives value from being kept secret. Yet the term also refers to the set of enforceable legal rights that give the "owner" of that information legal redress for its improper acquisition or usage. In some ways, this dichotomy is similar to that seen with patents and copyrights. On one hand, there is an invention, and on the other hand, a patent right that gives its owner enforceable legal rights with respect to that invention. Likewise, a work of authorship and the copyright in that work of authorship. Unfortunately, trade secrecy law is hobbled by the existence of only a single term to describe both the *res* that is protected, and the legal mode of its protection.

[18] Milgrim on Trade Secrets, § 2.02.

It is for this reason that the few courts that have considered issues surrounding trade secret assignment have distinguished between "ownership" of a trade secret and its "possession." In *DTM Research, L.L.C. v. AT&T Corp.*, 245 F.3d 327, 332 (4th Cir. 2001), the court held that "While the information forming the basis of a trade secret can be transferred, as with personal property, its continuing secrecy provides the value, and any general disclosure destroys the value. As a consequence, one 'owns' a trade secret when one knows of it, as long as it remains a secret." Accordingly, the court held that a party possessing secret information is entitled to seek redress against another party that misappropriated it, even if the first party lacks "fee simple" title to that information (i.e., if the first party itself allegedly misappropriated the information from another).

Possession of a trade secret also figures prominently in cases that discuss the assignment of trade secrets. When the owner of a copyrighted work of art transfers the copyright to a buyer, the transferor loses its right to reproduce the work further. Likewise, when the owner of a trade secret transfers that secret to a buyer, the transferor loses its right to exploit that secret further. As the court explained in *Memry Corp. v. Ky. Oil Tech., N.V.*, 2006 U.S. Dist. LEXIS 94393 at *16 (N.D. Cal. 2006), "in giving up all rights to use of the secrets through assignment, the assignor is implicitly and legally bound to maintain the secrecy of the information contained in the trade secrets."

2.6 JOINT OWNERSHIP

Just like real and personal property, IP may be co-owned by multiple parties. But the laws regarding joint ownership of IP are different than those affecting real and personal property. To make matters worse, they also differ based on the kind of IP involved, and they vary from country to country. As a result, planning for joint ownership of IP can become fraught with risks and traps for the unwary. As one waggish practitioner has written, "'Joint ownership of IP' – no words strike more terror into the heart of an IP practitioner than the task of having to provide appropriate contractual provisions in such a situation."[19]

Joint ownership of IP rights impacts prosecution of patents and trademarks, exploitation of those rights, and licensing and enforcement of rights. These principles are discussed below in the context of patents, copyrights, trade secrets and trademarks under US law.

2.6.1 *Patents*

When more than one individual makes an inventive contribution to an invention, the resulting patent will be jointly owned. As explained by the Federal Circuit in *Ethicon v. United States Surgical Corp.*, 135 F.3d 1456, 1465 (Fed. Cir. 1998), "in the context of joint inventorship, each co-inventor presumptively owns a pro rata undivided interest in the entire patent, no matter what their respective contributions."

The rights of joint owners of patents are described in 35 U.S. Code § 262:

> In the absence of any agreement to the contrary, each of the joint owners of a patent may make, use, offer to sell, or sell the patented invention within the United States, or import the patented invention into the United States, without the consent of and without accounting to the other owners.

Thus, each co-owner of a patent may independently exploit the patent without the consent of its co-owners. But unlike copyrights, joint owners of patents do not owe one another a duty of

---

[19] Neil Wilkof, *Joint Ownership of a Trade Mark: The Tribulations of Termination*, IPKat, November 26, 2010, https://ipkitten.blogspot.com/2010/11/joint-ownership-of-trade-mark.html.

accounting or sharing of profits. Thus, the co-owner of a patented process that uses it to embark on a profitable new manufacturing venture has no obligation to share any of its earnings with the co-owners of the patent.

Any co-owner of a patent may also license it to others, again with no obligation to share royalties or other amounts received with its co-owners.[20] While a co-owner may grant an exclusive license to a third party, and that exclusivity may operate to prevent the granting co-owner from granting further licenses to others, it has no effect on the other co-owners of the patent, who may continue to exploit or grant other licenses under the patent.

Likewise, any co-owner of a patent may bring suit to enforce it against an infringer, but in order for the suit to proceed, it must join all other co-owners in the suit (see Section 11.1.5). Moreover, as illustrated in *Ethicon*, a retroactive license from any co-owner will serve to authorize the infringer's conduct, thus defeating a suit brought by fewer than all co-owners.

2.6.2 *Copyrights*

There are some similarities between the treatment of joint owners under US copyright and patent law. Under US copyright law, each co-owner of a copyright may independently exploit the copyright without permission of the other co-owners. This exploitation includes performance, reproduction, creation of derivative works and all other exclusive rights afforded by the Copyright Act. However, unlike patents, a copyright co-owner who earns profits from the exploitation of a jointly owned work must render an accounting to his or her co-owners and share the profits with them on a pro rata basis. Thus, if three members of a band compose a song, and one of them quits to pursue a solo career, the soloist must account to the other two for any profits that he or she earns from performing the song (or a derivative of it) for the duration of the copyright.

Likewise, any co-owner of a copyright may license the copyright to others. As with patents, an exclusive license granted by a single co-owner will not be particularly valuable to the licensee, as the other co-owners are free to license the same rights to others. Such an exclusive license will thus be considered nonexclusive for purposes of standing to sue.[21] As with other exploitation, the copyright licensor must account to the other co-owners for any profits earned based on the license.

Finally, any co-owner of a copyright may sue to enforce the copyright against an infringer without the consent of the other co-owners. As with patents, a license from any co-owner will serve to authorize the infringer's conduct. But unlike patent infringement litigation, notice to the co-owners of a copyright, and their joinder in an infringement suit, is not mandatory, but discretionary in the court (see 17 U.S.C. § 501(b), discussed in greater detail in Section 11.1.5, Note 5).

2.6.3 *Trade Secrets*

There is scant case law, and little reliable commentary, discussing the rights and obligations of joint owners of trade secrets to one another. Yet from the authority that exists, it appears that joint owners of trade secrets, unlike joint owners of patents and copyrights, are *not* free to exploit jointly owned trade secrets without the consent of their co-owners.

---

[20] See *Schering Corp. v. Roussel-UCLAF SA*, 104 F.3d 341, 344 (Fed. Cir. 1997) ("Each co-owner's ownership rights carry with them the right to license others, a right that also does not require the consent of any other co-owner").
[21] See *Sybersound Records, Inc. v. UAV Corp.*, 517 F.3d 1137 (9th Cir. 2008).

Thus, in *Morton v. Rank Am., Inc.*, 812 F. Supp. 1062, 1074 (C.D. Cal. 1993), one co-owner of trade secrets relating to the operations of the Hard Rock Café chain sued another co-owner who used the information in violation of a noncompetition agreement. The court held that, under California law, being the co-owner of a trade secret does not necessarily insulate one from a claim of trade secret misappropriation. In *Jardin v. DATAllegro, Inc.*, 2011 U.S. Dist. LEXIS 84509 *15 (S.D. Cal. 2011), another California court, citing *Morton*, held that a joint owner of a trade secret could be liable for disclosing the trade secret in a patent application without the permission of his co-owner.

It also appears, in at least one case, that a co-owner of a trade secret may sue a third party for misappropriation of that trade secret without the consent of the other co-owner(s). In *MGP Ingredients, Inc. v. Mars, Inc.*, 465 F. Supp. 2d 1109 (D. Kan. 2006), MGPI and SNM jointly owned trade secrets relating to the formulation of the popular Greenies® dog chews. MGPI alleged that SNM impermissibly disclosed these trade secrets to Mars, Inc., which then began to manufacture its own dog chews using the secret formula. The court rejected Mars' motion to dismiss MGPI's suit for trade secret misappropriation against both SNM and Mars on the basis that SNM was a co-owner of the trade secrets.

2.6.4 *Trademarks*

Unlike patents, copyrights and trade secrets, the primary purpose of a trademark is to act as an indication of the source of goods or services. The ownership of a single mark by two or more entities contradicts this fundamental principle and is thus "disfavored" by the law. As the Sixth Circuit cautions in *Yellowbook Inc. v. Brandeberry*, 708 F.3d 837, 845 (6th Cir. 2013),

> Joint ownership is disfavored in the trademark context. By their nature, trademarks derive their value from exclusively identifying a particular business. If customers are confused about which business the mark refers to, one of the users may unfairly benefit from the goodwill of the other, or the goodwill of the mark may be dissipated entirely. Beneficial joint ownership or licensing schemes may be devised, but courts are not well placed to fill in these details, and parties (and customers) are typically best served by exclusive ownership.

Nevertheless, the PTO permits joint ownership of registered marks. One scenario in which this is permitted is when the joint owners are related companies that exhibit a "unity of control" that eliminates consumer confusion because the joint owners are, for practical purposes, operating as a single unit.[22] In another scenario, two parties may be granted "concurrent" registrations for the same mark in connection with a similar product in different geographic markets.[23] In addition, the owner of a trademark registration may assign a partial interest in that registration to a third party, after which both parties will be co-owners of the registration.[24] This situation occurs, *inter alia*, as a result of the break-up of joint ventures and the inheritance of businesses by multiple heirs or testamentary beneficiaries.[25]

---

[22]   See Trademark Manual of Examining Procedure (TMEP), 1201.07(b)(ii).
[23]   15 U.S.C. § 1052(d) ("Concurrent registrations may also be issued by the Director when a court of competent jurisdiction has finally determined that more than one person is entitled to use the same or similar marks in commerce. In issuing concurrent registrations, the Director shall prescribe conditions and limitations as to the mode or place of use of the mark or the goods on or in connection with which such mark is registered to the respective persons").
[24]   Trademark Manual of Examining Procedure (TMEP), 501.06.
[25]   See, e.g., *Iskenderian v. Iskenderian*, 144 Cal. App. 4th 1162 (Cal. App. 2006) (trademark in family restaurant was validly transferred by late parent to three children).

When a jointly owned trademark serves as an indication of source, no individual co-owner has the right to exploit that mark separately from the collective use made by the joint owners. For example, the four original members of the musical group "The Commodores" held common law trademark rights in the group's name. When Thomas McClary, one of the group's members, left the group and began to perform under the names "The 2014 Commodores" and "The Commodores Featuring Thomas McClary" the other group members sued him for trademark infringement and a number of other causes. The Eleventh Circuit held in *Commodores Entm't Corp. v. McClary*, 879 F.3d 1114 (11th Cir. 2018) that "The rights to use the name 'The Commodores' remained with the group after McClary departed, and the corollary is also true: McClary did not retain rights to use the marks individually."

Notes and Questions

1. *Vive la difference?* Why is there such discord among four areas of US IP law regarding the rights of joint owners? Would there be value in harmonizing these different systems? How would you recommend that such harmonization be pursued?

2. *Economic justifications.* Judge Richard Posner offers a potential economic justification for the discrepancies in the treatment of jointly owned copyrights and patents.

   > In both domains, a joint owner is allowed to use or license the jointly owned work without the permission of the other owner or owners; this rule reduces transaction costs by eliminating bilateral monopoly. But the joint owner of a copyright who uses or licenses a copyright must account to the other owners for the profits of the use and share them with those others, while the joint owner of a patent need not. The latter rule provides greater encouragement to inventors to keep working to improve their inventions, consistent with the continuously improving quality of technology, but not of the arts.[26]

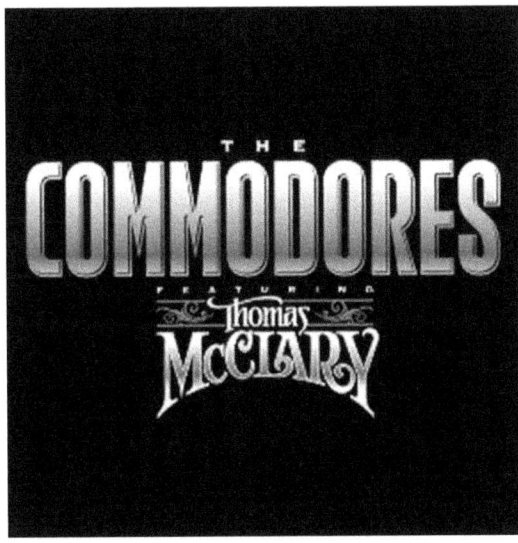

FIGURE 2.6 Though he was an original member of the musical group The Commodores, Thomas McClary did not retain rights to utilize the group's name after he left the band in 1984.

---

[26] Richard A. Posner, *Intellectual Property: The Law and Economics Approach*, 19 J. Econ. Persp. 57, 70 (2005).

What do you think of this explanation? Would requiring the co-owner of a patent to share its profits from the exploitation of the patent with its co-owners decrease innovation? Why doesn't the accounting requirement similarly dampen creative activity?

3. *International inconsistency.* Commentators have long observed that US law is out of step with the laws of many other countries in how it handles jointly owned IP. For example, in many countries in Europe and Asia, IP rights may not be exploited, licensed or asserted without the consent of all joint owners. Is this approach preferable? What does it mean for joint owners of IP?

In 1990, Professor Robert Merges and Lawrence Locke analyzed the laws of the United States and various other countries regarding their handling of joint patent owners. They concluded, among other things, that:

> The American rule permitting co-owners to work their patent without compensating the other co-owners is preferable to the French rule requiring compensation … [T]he French rule can lead to a situation where both co-owners elect not to work the patent, in hopes of forcing the other co-owner to work it and split the profits. Since society has an obvious interest in seeing patented technology developed, the American rule is better.
>
> The right of co-owners to license and assign their full interest, or any portion of it, should be restricted according to the rule in effect on the continent, in Great Britain and in Japan: consent of all co-owners should be required. This will prevent one co-owner from taking advantage of the others …[27]

Do you concur with these recommendations? Why or why not? Should any of Merges and Locke's recommendations be applied to forms of IP other than patents?

---

[27] Robert P. Merges & Lawrence A. Locke, *Co-ownership of Patents: A Comparative and Economic View*, 72 J. Pat. & Trademark Off. Soc'y 586 (1990).

3

The Nature of an Intellectual Property License

What is an intellectual property (IP) license? The answer to this seemingly straightforward question is far from obvious, and it has engendered no small amount of judicial hand-wringing and scholarly debate over the years. We are all familiar, of course, with the licensing *agreement*. A licensing agreement is a contract, whether oral or written, whether signed with a pen, affirmed by a handshake or assented with a click. And, as such, the rules of contract law apply – rules that have been developed over centuries of common law.

But a licensing agreement, according to some, is more than an ordinary contract, just as a rental agreement for an apartment is more than a mere contract. It conveys an interest in a property right. Thus, while a rental agreement is a contract, interpreted in accordance with the laws of contract, it also conveys a leasehold interest, a property interest that has an existence that is both dependent on, but also independent of, the contract that created it. That is, there are aspects of a leasehold that need not be written into a rental agreement, but which exist nonetheless – the result of even more centuries of common law development.

Similarly, we can talk about *licenses* separately from *licensing agreements*. While these two legal creations are often inextricably linked, they have separate qualities as well. In contrast to a licensing agreement, a license is an authorization to exploit some exclusive right that the law confers on the owner of IP. For example, under the U.S. Patent Act, "whoever *without authority* makes, uses, offers to sell, or sells any patented invention, within the United States or imports into the United States any patented invention during the term of the patent therefor, infringes the patent" (35 U.S.C. § 271(a) (emphasis added)). The "authority" referenced in the Act is typically referred to as a "license" to practice the patent. A license "[i]n its simplest form … means only leave to do a thing which the licensor otherwise would have a right to prevent."[1]

---

[1] *Western Elec. Co., Inc. v. Pacent Reproducer Corp.*, 42 F.2d 116, 118 (2d Cir. 1930).

The importance of treating a licensing agreement as distinct from a license is illustrated by the following example: Under a particular licensing agreement the licensor may grant a license under a copyright and under a patent. If the copyright license terminates for some reason (e.g., nonpayment of the royalty), the overall licensing agreement may continue, as may the patent license. Likewise, an agreement may terminate, yet a license granted under the agreement may be specified to continue in perpetuity after that termination.[2] The duration of a license and the licensing agreement under which it is granted need not be concurrent or identical.

But is an IP license a "property" interest, like a leasehold? The answer to that question depends on an even deeper question, which is the degree to which intellectual property itself constitutes "property." That, too, is the subject of significant debate, and the answer may vary depending on the type of IP involved.[3]

In this chapter we will explore some of the metaphysical issues surrounding the nature of an IP license – issues that sometimes have a very real effect on parties and transactions.

3.1 LICENSE VERSUS OWNERSHIP OF IP

Perhaps the easiest way to begin to think about the nature of an IP license is to compare it to its counterpart – IP ownership (discussed in Chapter 2). Just as every lease requires a lessor, every license requires a licensor. The licensor of an IP right may be its owner, or it may simply be another licensee who is sublicensing certain of its rights (just as a lessee of real property may sublease the leased premises). But for our purposes, it is useful to compare the rights that an IP licensee has with those possessed by an IP owner – one who has come into possession of legal title to IP through creation or assignment.

Professor Ray Nimmer explained this distinction as follows:

> Licenses are often contrasted with assignments of rights in information. The novice can think of an "assignment" as the equivalent of a sale of all rights in the intangible subject matter and not be far wrong. Commercial practice, however, frequently blurs the line between a license and an assignment. The fundamental difference is that, while licenses and assignments both focus on rights in, or use of, information, in an assignment the original rights owner tends to divest itself of rights in the subject matter, while in a license the transferor ("licensor") retains more rights in the subject matter of the license. It can do this not only because the parties have agreed to a transaction that enables a split of ownership and use rights in the information, but because unlike hard goods, information can be both transferred and retained.[4]

Table 3.1 offers a quick summary of the differences between the rights held by IP owners and licensees (both exclusive and nonexclusive).

Thus, as shown in Table 3.1, after A assigns IP right X to B, it is owned by B, and B has all rights to exploit, enforce, license and maintain X. Moving to the next column, if A grants B an exclusive license with respect to X, its ownership remains with A, but the right to exploit belongs to B (see Chapter 6 for a discussion of the rights and obligations of exclusive licensees). The right to enforce, further license and maintain X, however, may vary based on the terms of the exclusive licensing agreement between A and B. In some cases, B may obtain the right to

---

[2] Issues concerning the term and duration of licenses and licensing agreements are discussed in detail in Chapter 12.

[3] For a window into the extensive academic debate on this topic, see Molly Shaffer Van Houweling, *Intellectual Property as Property*, in Research Handbook on the Economics of Intellectual Property, Vol. I (Peter S. Menell and Ben Depoorter, eds., Edward Elgar, 2019).

[4] Raymond T. Nimmer, Licensing of Intellectual Property and Other Information Assets 3–4 (Carolina Academic Press, 2nd ed., 2007).

TABLE 3.1 *Rights in an item of IP (X) after a transaction between A and B*

After the transaction, which party (A or B):	Assignment	License (exclusive)	License (nonexclusive)
Owns X?	B	A	A
Has the right to exploit/use X	B	B	B/A
Has the right to prevent others from using X (i.e., enforcement)?	B	B/A	A
Has the right to grant further licenses to X?	B	B/A	A
May maintain rights in X?	B	B/A	A

enforce X (see Section 11.2), to grant sublicenses of X (see Section 6.5) and to maintain X (see Section 9.5). In contrast, under a nonexclusive license both A and B have the right to exploit X, while only A has the right to enforce, further license and maintain X.

3.2 COVENANT NOT TO SUE

Various courts and commentators have weighed in on the legal nature of an IP license. One view, exemplified by the Federal Circuit in *Spindelfabrik Suessen-Schurr Stahlecker & Grill v. Schubert & Salzer Maschinenfabrik AG*, 829 F.2d 1075 (Fed. Cir. 1987), is that a license is simply a covenant by the licensor not to sue the licensee for IP infringement under certain conditions:

> [A] patent license agreement is in essence nothing more than a promise by the licensor not to sue the licensee. Even if couched in terms of "[l]icensee is given the right to make, use, or sell X," the agreement cannot convey that absolute right because not even the patentee of X is given that right. His right is merely one to exclude others from making, using or selling X. Indeed, the patentee of X and his licensee, when making, using, or selling X, can be subject to suit under other patents. In any event, patent license agreements can be written to convey different scopes of promises not to sue, *e.g.*, a promise not to sue under a specific patent or, more broadly, a promise not to sue under any patent the licensor now has or may acquire in the future.

Professor Chris Newman, however, has challenged the characterization of a license as a "covenant not to sue." In the below excerpt, he compares licenses in the real property context to copyright licenses:

> If I sell you an admission ticket to my theater, I take on a contractual duty to allow you to enter the premises at the appointed time and place (as well as possibly to provide specified entertainment of some sort). If, when you arrive, I bar your entry, I violate my contractual duty, and you have a claim for breach of contract. But suppose I do allow (i.e., take no steps to obstruct or forbid) your entry as agreed. May I nevertheless charge you with trespass on the ground that while our contract imposed a duty on me to let you come in, it could not and did not grant you any privilege to do so? The answer is no … Selling you an admission ticket would be understood by all as manifesting the intent to grant you permission to enter, and so it would effectively exercise my power as a titleholder to grant you that privilege. The privilege would thus result from the same acts that give rise to a binding contract, but it would not flow from or depend upon contract formation as a legal matter. The privilege would be valid even if some technicality of contract law (say, failure to comply with a statute of frauds) prevented the creation of binding contractual duties. Even in the face of such a failure, if you were to show up at the time designated on the ticket and enter the premises, you would not be trespassing unless and until I revoked the privilege by asking you to leave.

If, on the other hand, we were to take seriously the notion that a license consists of nothing but a contractual obligation not to sue, then my hypothetical would have real bite. Under this reasoning, even though I am bound by contract to let you enter the theater, you are still technically a trespasser when you do so – it's just that I have a contractual duty not to bring a claim charging you as one. If this sounds absurd, the absurdity resides in the contract theory of license. After all, if you were not still a trespasser, it would be superfluous to speak of my having a contractual "duty not to sue" you – sue you for what? The notion that a license is a "contract not to sue" thus assumes the implicit (and correct) premise that contracts do not create privileges. Once a privilege has been granted on the other hand, there is no need for a contract "not to sue," though there may be for a contract not to revoke the privilege.

Is there any practical difference between having a privilege to use my property and having a right not to be sued for doing so? Indeed there is. Suppose my contractual duty not to sue you for trespass is part of a larger agreement in which you undertake other duties to me, some of which are due to be performed soon after your bargained-for use of my property is complete. If you then refuse or fail to perform in such a way as to constitute a material breach of the agreement, the contract may be terminated, thus relieving me prospectively of my duties under it, including the duty to refrain from suing you. This means that even though your prior uses of my property took place while the license (i.e., the contract) was still in force, if they are still within the statute of limitations for trespass I am now free to sue you over them. The contract theory of license cannot explain or justify the rule that licensed actions taken while the license remains in force are forever immune from claims of infringement.

Nor is the contract theory of license reconcilable with the phenomenon, common in copyright law, of multiple co-owners, each of whom is empowered to grant nonexclusive licenses without the others' consent.[5] Were such a license a contract, it would bind only the grantor and not other co-owners, who would remain free to sue for infringement. One might seek to explain this by theorizing that co-owners of the same work exist in some sort of privity such that a license agreement by one contractually binds the others, but clearly copyright law does not hold this to be the case. If it were, a single co-owner should be equally capable of granting an exclusive license binding on all other co-owners and rendering void any subsequent attempts of theirs to grant conflicting licenses. Instead, the law prevents the creation of conflicting exclusive licenses by holding that where there are co-owners, the power to create exclusive rights can only be wielded by all of them acting jointly.[6]

Notes and Questions

1. *Covenant or not?* Why does the Federal Circuit in *Spindelfabrik* refer to a patent license as a "covenant not to sue"? Why does Newman disagree with this characterization? How does he conceptualize an IP license? Does it matter that *Spindelfabrik* dealt with a patent license, whereas Newman is largely discussing copyright licenses?

2. *Nonproperty rights.* One of the difficulties with a property-based characterization of the IP license is that it does not fully account for permissions that are granted with respect to intangibles that are not generally considered to be property – data, know-how, unpatented inventions and the like.[7] How would you reconcile Newman's description with such licenses? Are they property interests? Or is a "covenant not to sue" a better description?

---

[5]   For a discussion of the rights and duties of co-owners of intellectual property, see Section 2.5.

[6]   Christopher M. Newman, *A License Is Not a "Contract Not To Sue": Disentangling Property and Contract in the Law of Copyright Licenses*, 98 Iowa L. Rev. 1101, 1130–31 (2013).

[7]   Professor Ray Nimmer made much of this point in advocating for the adoption of specific state legislation to govern IP licensing transactions. See Section 3.3.4 and Raymond T. Nimmer, *Licensing in the Contemporary Information Economy*, 8 Wash. U. J. L. & Pol'y 99 (2002).

3. *Future rights.* Another area in which conceptualizations of IP licenses are challenged is future IP rights. Licensing agreements often purport to grant rights with respect to IP that is created in the future (see, e.g., *Stanford v. Roche*, discussed in Section 2.3, Note 3, and *Aronson v. Quick Point Pencil*, discussed in Section 24.3). Are these future grants merely contractual commitments to grant licenses in the future, or are they present grants of future interests, analogous to future interests in estates that exist with respect to real property? For example, can an easement exist across a road that has not yet been built? Or is a contract relating to such an easement merely a contractual commitment to grant an easement once, and if, the road is built?

3.3 THE GOVERNING LAW OF IP LICENSES

Closely related to the legal nature of IP licenses is the question of which law governs such licenses. There are several possible choices:

- the state common law of contracts
- the state common law of property
- the Uniform Commercial Code enacted in various states
- federal statutory law governing certain licensed IP rights (e.g., patents, copyrights, registered trademarks and federal trade secrets)
- state statutory law governing certain licensed IP rights (e.g., state trade secrets)
- state common law governing certain licensed IP rights (e.g., common law trademarks and rights of publicity)
- federal common law relating to IP licenses.

Though there is no single, clear answer to this question, a significant amount of ink has been spilled wrangling over it. It is complicated, of course, by the diversity of IP types, which have their origins in federal statutes, state statutes and state common law. Below are various perspectives on this difficult question.

3.3.1 *State Common Law of Contracts*

The District Court in *Sun Microsystems, Inc. v. Microsoft Corp.*, 81 F. Supp. 2d 1026 (N.D. Cal. 2000) held that "[t]he rules of contract construction embodied in California law control the interpretation of the [License Agreement] to the extent that such rules are consistent with federal copyright law and policy." This position is a common one: because a licensing agreement is a contract, and because contracts are governed by state law, then the relevant state's common law of contracts governs the interpretation and enforcement of the licensing agreement.

Of course, any interpretation supplied by state contract law cannot be inconsistent with federal law that defines the licensed IP rights. Thus, for example, a state court could not hold that a copyright licensing agreement with a duration of fifty years is too long, given that the duration of copyright protection often exceeds that period. Likewise, a state court could not create a new standard for evaluating the scope of patent claims to determine which products are subject to a royalty obligation. But the interpretation of contractual terms, whether or not they deal with federally created IP rights, is generally performed under state contract law.

3.3.2 *State Common Law of Property*

A slightly different approach is taken by Judge Pauline Newman of the Federal Circuit, who suggests that it is not the state common law of contracts, but that of property that should be understood as governing IP licenses:

> The jurisprudence governing property interests is generally a matter of state law. Even when the property is the creation of federal statute, private rights are usually defined by state laws of property. This has long been recognized with respect to patent ownership and transfers.[8]

Professor Christina Mulligan, writing about software end user license agreements (EULAs, discussed in greater detail in Chapter 17), offers efficiency-based rationales to distinguish between a contractual and a property-based understanding of licensing agreements:

> One large difference between contract and property is that the number of people involved in contractual and property relationships changes how much negotiation over rights and duties is possible. Where two individuals sit down to hammer out a unique agreement for services from scratch, the costs each of them must shoulder, in terms of time and resources, to understand their agreement will be about the same. Moreover, to the extent that their contract covers unique circumstances, both parties may have similar interests in negotiating highly specific or idiosyncratic terms that advance their preferences for how the contract will be performed. And because the contract terms primarily affect those who are party to the contract, their idiosyncrasies won't impose information-cost burdens on others.
>
> On the other hand, the transfer and form of property rights affects many people besides the owner of the property. As a result, property rights tend to be more standardized, because the existence of idiosyncratic property rights raises the costs of understanding their scope for third parties who must respect others' rights.[9]

3.3.3 *The Uniform Commercial Code*

Article 2 of the Uniform Commercial Code relates to sales of goods. In general, IP licenses are not sales of goods, but the extension of rights in intangibles. Thus, as a formal matter, Article 2 does not apply to IP licenses. As Professor Ray Nimmer has observed, "In most licensing agreements and court decisions on licensing law issues, Article 2 is irrelevant and never even considered."[10]

Nevertheless, the familiarity that many attorneys have with Article 2 leads almost irresistibly to comparisons and analogies between contractual terms relating to sale of goods and transactions in IP. For example, UCC definitions of "good faith," "bona fide purchaser" and different forms of warranty routinely inform discussions of licensing agreements, both among attorneys and in judicial decisions.[11] Similar comparisons were made between sale and lease transactions, which led to the adoption in 1987 of Article 2A of the UCC pertaining to leases of personal property.

A similar effort – proposed UCC Article 2B – was initiated in 1995 with respect to license agreements. Yet, due to disagreements between consumer and software industry groups and

---

[8] *Ethicon, Inc. v. United States Surgical Corp.*, 135 F.3d 1456, 1471 (Fed. Cir. 1998) (Newman, dissenting) (citations omitted).

[9] Christina M. Mulligan, *Licenses and the Property/Contract Interface*, 93 Indiana L.J. 1073, 1083 (2018).

[10] Raymond T. Nimmer and Jeff C. Dodd, Modern Licensing Law, Vol. 1, 96 (Thomson Reuters, 2016–17).

[11] See, e.g., *Rhone-Poulenc Agro, S.A. v. Dekalb Genetics Corporation*, 284 F.3d 1323 (Fed. Cir. 2002), discussed in Section 6.4.

within IP academic circles, Article 2B was never adopted.[12] Instead, it was released in 1999 as a free-standing uniform law called the Uniform Computer Information Transactions Act (UCITA), which was adopted in only two states, Maryland and Virginia.[13]

3.3.4 *Federal Common Law*

First-year law students are taught that the concept of federal common law was abolished when the Supreme Court held in *Erie Railroad v. Tompkins*, 304 U.S. 64 (1938) that there is no "federal general common law." Yet pockets of federal common law survive to this day in a range of areas including admiralty, antitrust and bankruptcy law, as well as some areas of IP licensing. One area in which federal common law directly affects IP licensing agreements is the assignment of licensing agreements, which is discussed in Section 13.3.2.

Professor Shyamkrishna Balganesh points to the work of Professor Richard Epstein in describing the federal common law tradition in intellectual property:

> Intellectual property law, or the law relating to the delineation and enforcement of rights and privileges in informational resources, remains a prominent example here. Patent, copyright and trademark law in the U.S. are today seen as statutory areas that Congress alone is authorized to modify. Together with the complex rules of federal preemption, they purport to dominate the landscape of American intellectual property law.
>
> Yet, hidden away in the interstices of these statutory areas is a rather robust body of law that applies common law ideas, methods and principles to various informational resources without running afoul of preemption concerns. "Common law intellectual property," as it is often referred to, represents a set of legal causes of action that create various rights, duties, and enforceable liabilities for otherwise non-rival and non-excludable assets. Its hallmark lies in its common law origins, having been developed and adapted by judges in individual cases through the deployment of the common law's core concepts and principles.[14]

The following case illustrates how courts wrestle with these seemingly esoteric issues in a real-world dispute.

Bassett v. Mashantucket Pequot Tribe

204 F.3d 343 (2d Cir. 2000)

LEVAL, CIRCUIT JUDGE

Background

According to the allegations of the complaint: Plaintiff Debra Bassett operates a business, Bassett Productions, that produces films and television programs. Defendant Mashantucket Pequot Tribe is a federally recognized Indian tribe with a reservation located within the geographical boundaries of the State of Connecticut. Defendant Mashantucket Pequot Museum is a Connecticut corporation located on the Pequot Reservation.

---

[12] For the flavor of this debate, compare Mark A. Lemley, *The Law and Policy of Intellectual Property Licensing*, 87 Cal. L. Rev. 111 (1999) with Nimmer, supra note 6.

[13] The checkered history of UCC Article 2B and UCITA is summarized in Pratik A. Shah, *The Uniform Computer Information Transactions Act*, 15 Berkeley Tech. L.J. 85 (2000).

[14] Shyamkrishna Balganesh, *The Genius of Common Law Intellectual Property*, 48 J.L. Stud. (2019).

In October 1994, Bassett met with representatives of the Tribe to discuss the possibility of producing a film for the Museum about the Pequot War of 1636–38. In November, Defendant Theresa Bell, acting individually and as a representative of the Tribe, signed a "confidential disclosure agreement" in which she agreed that all information received from Bassett Productions was proprietary, and was to be returned to Bassett Productions at its request. In May 1995, Defendant Jack Campisi, communicating with Bassett on behalf of the Tribe, advised her that the Tribe intended to hire her to produce the film, contingent on the negotiation of a satisfactory contract and the Tribe's acceptance of a script for the film.

In August 1995, Bassett Productions entered into a letter agreement with the Tribe (the "Letter Agreement") for the development and production of a film about the 1636–38 Pequot War. The Letter Agreement identified Bassett Productions as the "Producer" and the Tribe as the "Owner," but did not define these terms. It stipulated that Bassett Productions would "hire and supervise the development and writing of a screenplay by Keith Merrill and George Burdeau," and that the Tribe would "compensate" Bassett Productions for development costs according to an agreed schedule. It also stipulated that "at such time" that the Tribe approved the final draft of the screenplay, Bassett Productions would have exclusive rights to produce the film for exhibition at the Pequot Museum.

Some time before October 30, 1995, Bassett had delivered to the Tribe a script that she herself had written based on a "script scenario" she had developed with assistance from her associate Allan Eckert. The script was prominently marked on its first page, "Copr. 1995 Bassett Entertainment Corporation."

On October 30, 1995, Bassett received a notice from the Tribe terminating the Letter Agreement. The notice asserted that Bassett had not "perform[ed] the contract as the parties anticipated." Following the termination of the Letter Agreement, the Tribe continued to pursue the development and production of a film on the 1636–38 Pequot War for exhibition at the Museum. In October 1996, filming was completed on a motion picture entitled, "The Witness." Bassett asserts the Tribe intends to screen the film at the Museum "in the near future" as part of "an interstate-driven tourist attraction."

In September 1996, Bassett commenced this lawsuit in the United States District Court for the District of Connecticut. The complaint sought an injunction as well as other copyright remedies on the ground that the Tribe and the Museum used Bassett's copyrighted script without her consent or license in order to produce their own film; it further alleged that they breached the Letter Agreement, and that they committed various state-law torts resulting in injury to Bassett … The district court granted Defendants' motion to dismiss the complaint, and Bassett appealed.

Discussion

28 U.S.C. § 1338(a) states that federal district courts "shall" have exclusive, original jurisdiction "of any civil action arising under any Act of Congress relating to … copyrights." It is well-established that not every complaint that refers to the Copyright Act "arises under" that law for purposes of Section 1338(a). See, e.g., *T.B. Harms Co. v. Eliscu*, 339 F.2d 823, 824 (2d Cir.1964) (Friendly, J.) (noting that this principle traces to "precedents going back for more than a century"). In particular, "the federal grant of a … copyright has not been thought to infuse with any national interest a dispute as to ownership or contractual enforcement turning on the facts or on ordinary principles of contract law." Here, the district court, relying on our discussion in dictum in *Schoenberg v. Shapolsky Publishers, Inc.*, 971 F.2d 926, 932–33 (2d Cir.1992), dismissed the claims based on the conclusion that

FIGURE 3.1 The Mashantucket Pequot Museum & Research Center in Ledyard, Connecticut, commissioned a film about the Pequot War of 1636–38.

Bassett's "copyright infringement claims ... do not 'arise under' federal copyright laws for purposes of 28 U.S.C. § 1338(a), but are merely incidental to [her] state law [contract] claims." Bassett contends that the court erred in dismissing her claims on the basis of *Schoenberg*. She argues that her copyright claims neither depend on nor result from claims for breach of contract. She further maintains that, because she sought a remedy expressly granted by the Copyright Act, her copyright claims do "arise under" the Act pursuant to the rule of *T.B. Harms*.

Whether a complaint asserting factually related copyright and contract claims "arises under" the federal copyright laws for the purposes of Section 1338(a) "poses among the knottiest procedural problems in copyright jurisprudence." 3 Melville B. Nimmer & David Nimmer, Nimmer On Copyright § 12.01[A], at 12–4 (1999). Such claims characteristically arise where the defendant held a license to exploit the plaintiff's copyright, but is alleged to have forfeited the license by breaching the terms of the licensing contract and thus to infringe in any further exploitation.

Prior to our landmark decision in *T.B. Harms*, several district courts in the Second Circuit resolved the issue of jurisdiction under Section 1338 for "hybrid" claims raising both copyright and contract issues by attempting to discern whether the copyright issues constituted the "essence" of the dispute, or whether instead the copyright issues were "incidental to" the contract dispute. That approach, however, left a class of plaintiffs who suffered copyright infringement bereft of copyright remedies. Plaintiffs whose federal lawsuits were dismissed for lack of subject matter jurisdiction on the ground that their copyright claims were "incidental to" their contract claims had no way either to obtain an adjudication of infringement or to obtain relief provided by the Copyright Act, because the Act confers exclusive jurisdiction over copyright claims on federal courts.

In *T.B. Harms*, Judge Friendly recognized the complexity of the problem of defining when a case "arises under" the Copyright Act. In synthesizing Supreme Court cases that had considered the issue of federal jurisdiction in a variety of contexts, Judge Friendly established a test for this circuit that focused on whether and how a complaint implicates the Copyright Act.

Judge Friendly began his analysis by examining Supreme Court precedent addressing the question when a federal court properly exercises jurisdiction under Section 1338, which creates jurisdiction in the federal courts in "any civil action arising under any Act of Congress relating to patents … [and] copyrights," among others. He identified two lines of authority as particularly important. First, in *American Well Works Co. v. Layne & Bowler Co.*, 241 U.S. 257, 260 (1916), Justice Holmes explained that a "suit arises under the law that creates the cause of action." According to Judge Friendly, Justice Holmes' interpretation of Section 1338 explained the exercise of federal jurisdiction "in a great many cases, notably copyright and patent infringement actions, both clearly authorized by the respective federal acts, and thus unquestionably within the scope of 28 U.S.C. § 1338." Judge Friendly observed that "in the many infringement suits that depend only on some point of fact and require no construction of federal law, no other explanation may exist." Second, Judge Friendly discussed *Smith v. Kansas City Title & Trust Co.*, 255 U.S. 180 (1921), in which the Supreme Court held that a claim created by state law might still "arise under" federal law "if the complaint discloses a need for determining the meaning or application of such a law."

Synthesizing the Supreme Court authorities, Judge Friendly concluded that a suit "arises under" the Copyright Act if:

(1) the complaint is for a remedy expressly granted by the Act, e.g., a suit for infringement or for the statutory royalties for record reproduction; or,

(2) the complaint … asserts a claim requiring construction of the Act

FIGURE 3.2   Chief Judge Henry T. Friendly, the author of the opinion in *T.B. Harms*, served on the US Court of Appeals for the Second Circuit from 1959–1986.

As the suit in *T.B. Harms* did not fall within any of these enumerated categories, the court found that it did not "arise under" the copyright laws for purposes of Section 1338 and that jurisdiction was therefore lacking.

The *T.B. Harms* test differed significantly from the essence-of-the-dispute or merely-incidental test. The analysis under *T.B. Harms* turns on what is alleged on the face of the complaint, while the essence-of-the-dispute or merely-incidental test looks rather at what defense will be proffered. For example, if the complaint alleges copyright infringement or seeks an injunction under the Copyright Act, under *T.B. Harms* the federal court has jurisdiction; under the other test, in contrast, the court must ascertain whether the defendant will defend only by reference to state law matters, such as a claim of contractual entitlement, or will raise defenses based on the Copyright Act.

The *T.B. Harms* test avoids problems that result from the essence-of-the-dispute test. By rejecting reliance on whether the copyright claim could be characterized as "incidental" and instead focusing the inquiry under Section 1338 on whether a plaintiff's complaint "[was] for a remedy expressly granted by the Act," *T.B. Harms* ensured that plaintiffs who sought copyright remedies that depended on a prior showing of contractual entitlement would not be left without the remedies promised by the Copyright Act. *T.B. Harms* also obviated the need for courts to determine at the outset of litigation whether copyright claims were incidental to contract claims – a difficult determination to make even after discovery and trial, and one that cannot be made reliably on the basis of the complaint alone.

Judge Friendly's solution to the problem posed by Section 1338 has been widely admired by the leading copyright scholars. The *T.B. Harms* test has been adopted by all the circuits that have considered the question whether a suit arises under the Copyright Act for purposes of Section 1338, if the disputed issues include non-copyright matters.

Nearly thirty years after the *T.B. Harms* decision, a panel of this court in *Schoenberg* undertook in dictum to state the test for determining the existence of Section 1338 jurisdiction in cases alleging violations of the Copyright Act resulting from breach of contract. The plaintiff, an author, alleged that he had licensed the defendant, a publisher, to publish plaintiff's work. The license obligated the defendant to publish within six months of plaintiff's delivery of the manuscript, to promote and market the work, and to license foreign language editions. According to plaintiff's allegations, the publisher breached numerous obligations of the license. As a result of these failures, plaintiff claimed that the license was terminated and that defendant's further publication of the work constituted an infringement. Although the appeal related to a different issue, the opinion undertook to state "the appropriate test under the *T.B. Harms* paradigm, for determining whether a suit 'arises under' the Copyright Act when it alleges infringement stemming from a breach of contract."

The opinion acknowledged that [i]n *T.B. Harms*, Judge Friendly wrote that, "an action 'arises under' the Copyright Act if and only if the complaint is for a remedy expressly granted by the Act," and that "[b]ecause Schoenberg is seeking damages for the alleged infringement as well as an injunction against future infringements, his complaint on its face asserts a claim 'arising under' the Copyright Act." It observed, however, that notwithstanding the *T.B. Harms* formulation, some district courts had "looked beyond the complaint in order to determine whether the plaintiff was really concerned with the infringement of his copyright, or, alternatively, was, in fact, more interested in" free enjoyment of his property or other non-copyright issues. Other courts, it noted, had adopted the even "broader proposition that no claim arises under the Copyright Act whenever an infringement would necessarily result from the breach of a contract that licensed or assigned a copyright."

In undertaking to reconcile the varying approaches of those district court opinions (and perhaps concluding that the authority of *T.B. Harms* extended only to disputes over copyright ownership and not to hybrid copyright/contract claims), *Schoenberg* created a new, complex three-step test; the first step of the test was precisely that which *T.B. Harms* had rejected – whether the claim for copyright remedies is "merely incidental" to a determination of contract rights. The opinion declared that in hybrid copyright and contract cases Section 1338 jurisdiction should be analyzed in the following manner:

> A district court must first ascertain whether the plaintiff's infringement claim is only "incidental" to the plaintiff's claim seeking a determination of ownership or contractual rights under the copyright ... If it is determined that the claim is not merely incidental, then a district court must next determine whether the complaint alleges a breach of a condition to, or a covenant of, the contract licensing or assigning the copyright ... [I]f a breach of a condition is alleged, then the district court has subject matter jurisdiction ... But if the complaint merely alleges a breach of a contractual covenant in the agreement that licenses or assigns the copyright, then the court must undertake a third step and analyze whether the breach is so material as to create a right of rescission in the grantor. If the breach would create a right of rescission, then the asserted claim arises under the Copyright Act.

We believe for a number of reasons that the *Schoenberg* test is unworkable. At the outset, it overlooks that, because the Copyright Act gives federal courts exclusive jurisdiction to enforce its provisions, a plaintiff who is denied access to a federal forum on the theory that his copyright claims are incidental to a contract dispute is thereby absolutely denied the benefit of copyright remedies. Such a denial of copyright remedies undermines the Act's capacity to protect copyright interests. A plaintiff with meritorious copyright claims and entitlement to the special remedies provided by the Act is deprived of these remedies merely because the first hurdle of proving entitlement is a showing of a contractual right.

A second problem with the *Schoenberg* test is that it is vague. *Schoenberg* characterizes the first part of its test in two ways: whether "the 'essence' of the plaintiff's claim" is in contract or copyright, or whether the "infringement claim is only 'incidental' to the plaintiff's claim seeking determination of ownership or contractual rights under the copyright." The meaning of either of these phrases is difficult to discern. At one juncture, *Schoenberg* suggests that the focus of inquiry should be on the plaintiff's motivations ("whether the plaintiff was really concerned with the infringement of his copyright or, alternatively, was, in fact, more interested in whether he would be allowed to enjoy his property free from the contract claims of the defendant"). District courts applying the "only incidental" test, in turn, have construed it in various other ways.

Furthermore ... the *Schoenberg* test requires the court to make complex factual determinations relating to the merits at the outset of the litigation – before the court has any familiarity with the case. Ascertaining what are a plaintiff's principal motives in bringing suit, and what issues will loom largest in the case, may well require extensive hearings and fact finding. The need for such fact finding recurs at each stage of *Schoenberg's* three-step formula. Thus, if a court finds that a copyright claim is not "merely incidental to" a contract claim (step one), it must still determine whether the contractual term alleged to have been breached was in the nature of a covenant or a condition (step two). And if it finds that the alleged breach was of a covenant, the court must next determine "whether the breach is so material as to create a right of rescission," failing which the case must be dismissed (step three). This third inquiry in particular, which entails an assessment of the importance of the particular covenant, as well as the seriousness of the breach, raises questions that are not appropriately, easily or reliably answered at the start of litigation.

"When a complaint alleges a claim or seeks a remedy provided by the Copyright Act, federal jurisdiction is properly invoked."

For the reasons discussed above, we conclude that, for claims of infringement arising from, or in the context of, an alleged contractual breach, this circuit's standard for determining jurisdiction under Section 1338 is furnished by *T.B. Harms*, and not by *Schoenberg*. When a complaint alleges a claim or seeks a remedy provided by the Copyright Act, federal jurisdiction is properly invoked.

Applying the *T.B. Harms* standard to this case leads us to conclude that Bassett's copyright claims "arise under" the Copyright Act for purposes of Section 1338. Unlike the complaint in *T.B. Harms*, the complaint in this case alleges that the defendants, without authority, used plaintiff's copyrighted script to produce a new film intended and advertised for imminent exhibition. The amended complaint alleged copyright infringement and sought "a remedy expressly granted by the Act," specifically, an injunction against further infringement of Bassett's copyrighted script. Because the complaint alleges the defendants violated the Copyright Act and seeks the injunctive remedy provided by the Act, under the rule of *T.B. Harms*, the action falls within the jurisdictional grant of Section 1338. The district court's contrary holding was in error.

Notes and Questions

1. *Contract versus property.* The question of whether state contract or property law governs IP licensing agreements reflects the debate discussed in Section 3.2 over the nature of IP licenses themselves. How would conceptualizing a license as a "covenant not to sue" impact governing law?

2. *The legacy of UCITA.* After the early 2000s, little was said about UCITA or the effort to develop a consistent national body of law for IP licenses and licensing agreements. Should legislative efforts in this area be restarted? How has the law of licensing developed without such a uniform code?

3. *Arising under.* How do the tests under *T.B. Harms* and *Schoenberg* fundamentally differ? How often do you think these different tests would result in different outcomes? Could the court in *Bassett* have reached the same result using the *Schoenberg* test? The effect of applying the *T.B. Harms* test may be to authorize federal jurisdiction in many more cases and thus remove those cases from state courts. What is the impact of such a shift?

4. *Contractual override?* Section 11.3 discusses contractual provisions by which parties specify the law that they wish to govern their licensing agreements. If an agreement contains such a clause, are the issues discussed in this section relevant? How do you think these legal principles interact with contractual preferences of parties? How often do you think parties select "Federal common law" to govern their licensing agreements?

3.4 OBLIGATION AS CONDITION VERSUS COVENANT

When a license is granted, the licensee obtains the right to perform particular acts under specified rights held by the licensor in designated fields of use. These define the "scope" of the license (which is discussed in greater detail in Chapter 6). If the licensee performs some activity outside the scope of the license, but which still infringes the licensor's intellectual property rights, then the licensee is an infringer. The license does not grant the licensee any rights outside the scope of the license, and the licensor is within its rights to sue the licensee for infringement of those out-of-scope IP rights.

Likewise, if the grant or continuation of a license is *conditioned* on the licensee's taking certain actions, then the licensee's failure to comply with those obligations can render the license void. For example, language such as the following could be considered a condition: "Licensor grants Licensee a non-exclusive license *so long as* Licensee complies with the following conditions." Because the license is conditioned on licensee's compliance with the stated conditions, the licensee's failure to comply with those conditions will void the license and the licensor can proceed against it in an infringement action.

If, on the other hand, the licensee violates an ordinary covenant or obligation in a license agreement (e.g., the obligation to pay royalties), then the licensor can sue the licensee for breach of contract and seek contractual damages and other remedies. It can also seek to terminate the license agreement if the provisions of the agreement permit termination for the alleged breach (see Section 12.2, discussing breach and termination of licenses). But so long as the license remains in effect, the licensee is operating under a license and is not infringing the licensor's IP rights. Thus, a breach of a license covenant, unlike operating outside the scope of the license grant, only gives rise to contractual remedies, but not infringement claims, so long as the license remains in effect.

One of the most important remedies available for claims of IP infringement is the injunction – a court order prohibiting conduct that constitutes infringement. Injunctive relief is relatively rare in contractual actions, in which monetary damages are the normal remedy. Thus, it is often advantageous to the licensor to argue that a particular contractual provision that the licensee has violated is a condition of the license rather than a mere contractual covenant. The following case illustrates this point.[15]

MDY Industries, LLC v. Blizzard

629 F.3d 928 (9th Cir. 2011)

CALLAHAN, CIRCUIT JUDGE

Blizzard Entertainment, Inc. ("Blizzard") is the creator of World of Warcraft ("WoW"), a popular multiplayer online role-playing game in which players interact in a virtual world while advancing through the game's 70 levels. MDY Industries, LLC and its sole member Michael Donnelly ("Donnelly") (sometimes referred to collectively as "MDY") developed and sold Glider, a software program that automatically plays the early levels of WoW for players.

---

[15] The important distinction between conditions and covenants in licensing agreements also figures prominently in *Jacobson v. Katzer*, reproduced in Section 19.2.5 (discussing whether requirements in an open source software licensing agreement are covenants or conditions).

MDY brought this action for a declaratory judgment to establish that its Glider sales do not infringe Blizzard's copyright or other rights ...

In November 2004, Blizzard created WoW, a "massively multiplayer online role-playing game" in which players interact in a virtual world. WoW has ten million subscribers, of which two and a half million are in North America.

WoW players roleplay different characters, such as humans, elves, and dwarves. A player's central objective is to advance the character through the game's 70 levels by participating in quests and engaging in battles with monsters. As a player advances, the character collects rewards such as in-game currency, weapons, and armor. WoW's virtual world has its own economy, in which characters use their virtual currency to buy and sell items directly from each other, through vendors, or using auction houses.

Each WoW player must read and accept Blizzard's End User License Agreement ("EULA") and Terms of Use ("ToU") on multiple occasions. Players who do not accept both the EULA and the ToU may return the game client for a refund.

Donnelly is a WoW player and software programmer. In March 2005, he developed Glider, a software "bot" (short for robot) that automates play of WoW's early levels, for his personal use. A user need not be at the computer while Glider is running. Glider ... moves the mouse around and pushes keys on the keyboard. You tell it about your character, where you want to kill things, and when you want to kill. Then it kills for you, automatically. You can do something else, like eat dinner or go to a movie, and when you return, you'll have a lot more experience and loot.

Glider does not alter or copy WoW's game client software, does not allow a player to avoid paying monthly subscription dues to Blizzard, and has no commercial use independent of WoW.

The parties dispute Glider's impact on the WoW experience. Blizzard contends that Glider disrupts WoW's environment for non-Glider players by enabling Glider users to advance quickly and unfairly through the game and to amass additional game assets. MDY contends that Glider has a minimal effect on non-Glider players, enhances the WoW experience for Glider users, and facilitates disabled players' access to WoW by auto-playing the game for them.

In summer 2005, Donnelly began selling Glider through MDY's website for fifteen to twenty-five dollars per license. As of September 2008, MDY had gross revenues of $3.5 million based on 120,000 Glider license sales.

Blizzard claims that from December 2004 to March 2008, it received 465,000 complaints about WoW bots, several thousand of which named Glider. Blizzard spends $940,000 annually to respond to these complaints.

As to the scope of the license [to use WoW], ToU § 4(B), "Limitations on Your Use of the Service," provides:

> You agree that you will not ... (ii) create or use cheats, bots, "mods," and/or hacks, or any other third-party software designed to modify the World of Warcraft experience; or (iii) use any third-party software that intercepts, "mines," or otherwise collects information from or through the Program or Service.

A copyright owner who grants a nonexclusive, limited license ordinarily waives the right to sue licensees for copyright infringement, and it may sue only for breach of contract. However, if the licensee acts outside the scope of the license, the licensor may sue for copyright infringement. Enforcing a copyright license raises issues that lie at the intersection of copyright and contract law.

We refer to contractual terms that limit a license's scope as "conditions," the breach of which constitute copyright infringement. We refer to all other license terms as "covenants," the breach of which is actionable only under contract law. We distinguish between conditions and covenants according to state contract law, to the extent consistent with federal copyright law and policy.

A Glider user commits copyright infringement by playing WoW while violating a ToU term that is a license condition. To establish copyright infringement, then, Blizzard must demonstrate that the violated term—ToU § 4(B)—is a condition rather than a covenant. Blizzard's EULAs and ToUs provide that they are to be interpreted according to Delaware law. Accordingly, we first construe them under Delaware law, and then evaluate whether that construction is consistent with federal copyright law and policy.

A covenant is a contractual promise, i.e., a manifestation of intention to act or refrain from acting in a particular way, such that the promisee is justified in understanding that the promisor has made a commitment. A condition precedent is an act or event that must occur before a duty to perform a promise arises. Conditions precedent are disfavored because they tend to work forfeitures. Wherever possible, equity construes ambiguous contract provisions as covenants rather than conditions. However, if the contract is unambiguous, the court construes it according to its terms.

Applying these principles, ToU § 4(B)(ii) and (iii)'s prohibitions against bots and unauthorized third-party software are covenants rather than copyright-enforceable conditions. Although ToU § 4 is titled, "Limitations on Your Use of the Service," nothing in that section conditions Blizzard's grant of a limited license on players' compliance with ToU § 4's restrictions.

To recover for copyright infringement based on breach of a license agreement, (1) the copying must exceed the scope of the defendant's license and (2) the copyright owner's complaint must be grounded in an exclusive right of copyright (e.g., unlawful reproduction or distribution). Contractual rights, however, can be much broader.

> "To recover for copyright infringement based on breach of a license agreement ... the copyright owner's complaint must be grounded in an exclusive right of copyright"

[C]onsider a license in which the copyright owner grants a person the right to make one and only one copy of a book with the caveat that the licensee may not read the last ten pages. Obviously, a licensee who made a hundred copies of the book would be liable for copyright infringement because the copying would violate the Copyright Act's prohibition on reproduction and would exceed the scope of the license. Alternatively, if the licensee made a single copy of the book, but read the last ten pages, the only cause of action would be for breach of contract, because reading a book does not violate any right protected by copyright law.

Here, ToU § 4 contains certain restrictions that are grounded in Blizzard's exclusive rights of copyright and other restrictions that are not. For instance, ToU § 4(D) forbids creation of derivative works based on WoW without Blizzard's consent. A player who violates this prohibition would exceed the scope of her license and violate one of Blizzard's exclusive rights under the Copyright Act. In contrast, ToU § 4(C)(ii) prohibits a player's disruption of another player's game experience. A player might violate this prohibition while playing the game by harassing another player with unsolicited instant messages. Although this conduct may violate the contractual covenants with Blizzard, it would not violate any of Blizzard's exclusive rights of copyright. The antibot provisions at issue in this case, ToU § 4(B)(ii) and (iii), are similarly covenants rather than conditions. A Glider user violates the covenants with Blizzard, but does not thereby commit copyright infringement because Glider does not infringe any of Blizzard's exclusive rights. For instance, the use does not alter or copy WoW software.

Were we to hold otherwise, Blizzard—or any software copyright holder—could designate any disfavored conduct during software use as copyright infringement, by purporting to condition the license on the player's abstention from the disfavored conduct. The rationale would be that because the conduct occurs while the player's computer is copying the software code into RAM in order for it to run, the violation is copyright infringement. This would allow software copyright owners far greater rights than Congress has generally conferred on copyright owners.

We conclude that for a licensee's violation of a contract to constitute copyright infringement, there must be a nexus between the condition and the licensor's exclusive rights of copyright. Here, WoW players do not commit copyright infringement by using Glider in violation of the ToU. MDY is thus not liable for secondary copyright infringement, which requires the existence of direct copyright infringement.

Notes and questions

1. *Grounded in exclusive rights of copyright.* The Ninth Circuit in MDY holds that a license condition is created when a contractual restriction is grounded in the licensor's exclusive rights of copyright. Other types of restrictions are simply contractual covenants. What kinds of contractual restrictions are "grounded in the exclusive rights of copyright"?

2. *Beyond copyright.* Should the Ninth Circuit's reasoning in MDY apply when distinguishing between license conditions and contractual covenants in licensing agreements that related to IP other than copyright? What about licenses of information not covered by any statutory form of IP, such as data and know-how? What might be an "exclusive right of patents" giving rise to a condition?

3. *Drafting conditions rather than covenants.* In *Sun Microsystems, Inc. v. Microsoft Corp.*, 188 F.3d 1115 (9th Cir. 1999) (decided prior to MDY), the Ninth Circuit found that a provision to ensure compatibility between the licensor's (Sun's) and licensee's (Microsoft's) software was a covenant rather than a condition of the license grant. As a result, Microsoft's failure to ensure compatibility was a breach of contract rather than infringement of Sun's intellectual property rights. The relevant sections of the licensing agreement between Sun and Microsoft are set forth below:

   § 2.1(a) Sun grants to Licensee a perpetual non-exclusive development license under the Intellectual Property Rights of Sun to make, access, use, copy, distribute, view, display, modify, adapt, and create Derivative Works of the Technology and resulting Products.

   § 2.6(a)(vi) Licensee agrees that any new version of a Product that Licensee makes commercially available to the public after the most recent Compatibility Date shall only include the corresponding Compatible Implementation.

   Do you think it would have been possible for Sun to draft §2.6(a)(vi) as a condition of the license grant? Could the two provisions have been combined so as to ensure that continued compatibility was a clear condition of the license grant? Why might Microsoft object to this provision as a condition, but consent to it as a covenant?

4. *Breach over infringement?* If a licensee uses licensed IP beyond the scope of the license, can the licensor bring a breach of contract claim in addition to, or in lieu of, an IP infringement claim? The answer may depend on the language of the license grant clause. If the grant simply allows the licensee to use the licensed IP for Purpose A, and the licensee in addition uses the IP for Purpose B, it is not clear that the licensee has breached the contractual provisions authorizing it to use the IP for Purpose A. On the other hand, if the license grant states that the licensee may use the licensed IP for the sole and exclusive purpose of pursuing Purpose A, then its use of the IP in pursuit of Purpose B might violate the terms of the agreement. Consider *Eli Lilly & Co. v. Emisphere Techs., Inc.*, 408 F. Supp. 2d 668, 685 (S.D. Ind. 2006), in which the court reasoned as follows:

> Emisphere granted Lilly an exclusive license to use Emisphere information for the "Field," which was defined as oral delivery of PTH. Section 2.1 concludes: "Lilly shall not have any rights to use the Emisphere Technology … other than insofar as they relate directly to the Field and are expressly granted herein." By its plain terms, this provision bars Lilly from using Emisphere Technology … outside the agreed field of PTH research.

> Do you agree with the court? Does the language "Lilly shall not have any right to use the [Technology] other than insofar as they relate directly to the Field" create a contractual prohibition that Lilly breached by using the Technology outside the Field? Or does "shall not have any right" define the scope of the license, meaning that Lilly's operation outside of the Field constitutes an infringement of Emisphere's IP? And if, as the court holds, Lilly breached the licensing agreement, could Emisphere *both* terminate the contract and sue for contractual damages, as well as bring suit for IP infringement?

3.5 EFFECT OF IP TRANSFER ON LICENSES

If an IP license is akin to a property interest, like a lease or a servitude upon land, then what happens to that license when the original licensor assigns the licensed IP to someone else? Does the license "run with the IP," as a real property servitude often (but not always) "runs with the land"? Or is the licensee out of luck (i.e., an infringer) when its licensor divests itself of the IP rights underlying the license?

The Copyright Act expressly addresses this issue in 17 U.S.C. § 205(e), which provides that:

> A nonexclusive license, whether recorded or not, prevails over a conflicting transfer of copyright ownership if the license is evidenced by a written instrument signed by the owner of the rights licensed or such owner's duly authorized agent, and if
> (1) the license was taken before execution of the transfer; or
> (2) the license was taken in good faith before recordation of the transfer and without notice of it.

Thus, a nonexclusive copyright license will survive a transfer of the underlying copyright if the license was granted before the transfer. It will also survive if the license was granted *after* the licensor transferred the copyright but before the transfer was recorded with the Copyright Office, so long as the licensee acted in good faith and did not have notice of the transfer.[16] Interestingly, § 205(e) does not apply to exclusive copyright licenses, presumably on the theory

---

[16] This "good faith" requirement is analogous to the standard of "inquiry notice" in real property transactions. See *Vapac Music Publ'g, Inc. v. Tuff 'N' Rumble Mgmt.*, 2000 U.S. Dist. LEXIS 10027 (S.D.N.Y. 2000).

that exclusive licenses should be recorded if the licensee wishes to guard against the loss of its rights as a result of future transfers.[17]

Unlike the Copyright Act, the Patent Act does not explicitly address the issue of a transfer of underlying rights. Nevertheless, it has been long-established in the case law that "the purchaser of a patent takes subject to outstanding licenses"[18] and "a [patent] license is good against the world, whether it is recorded or not. A purchaser of a patent takes it subject to all outstanding licenses."[19]

But what about the multitude of other contractual obligations contained in a licensing agreement? Licensor obligations relating to service, maintenance, technical assistance, indemnification and confidentiality are not likely to constitute part of the core licensed property interest that travels with the patent, so what happens to them when the licensor transfers the underlying IP to a new owner without assigning the entire agreement? In *Datatreasury Corp. v. Wells Fargo & Co.*, 522 F.3d 1368, 1372 (Fed. Cir. 2008), the Federal Circuit considered whether a contractual requirement to arbitrate disputes followed patents to their new owner. The court held that it did not, reasoning that

> the legal encumbrances deemed to "run with the patent" in these cases involved the right to use the patented product, not a duty to arbitrate. The cases do not support a conclusion that procedural terms of a licensing agreement unrelated to the actual use of the patent (e.g. an arbitration clause) are binding on a subsequent owner of the patent.

So what becomes of these non-transferred contractual obligations? One theory is that the original licensor and patent owner remains obligated to perform these contractual obligations so long as they have not been assigned to (and assumed by) someone else. Thus, if the original licensor does not assign a licensing agreement to the acquirer of the underlying IP, the original licensor is still required to perform these obligations. But this requirement may offer only cold comfort to the licensee, as the original licensor may have few remaining resources with which to perform those obligations, and without the underlying IP may be unable to perform some of those obligations. Section 13.3.5 discusses contractual provisions that help to ensure that these contractual licensor obligations are transferred to the new owner of the underlying IP.[20]

Notes and Questions

1. *Other forms of IP.* The principles discussed in this section are seldom raised in the context of trademark or trade secret licenses. Why? If a suitable case arose, do you think that a trademark or trade secret license should "run with the right"? What would be the practical effect of such a rule?

---

[17] See Sections 2.2–2.4 for a discussion of the recording requirements for assignments of patent, copyright and trademark rights.

[18] *Sanofi, S.A. v. Med-Tech Veterinarian Prods.*, 565 F. Supp. 931, 939 (D.N.J. 1983) (citing *Chambers v. Smith*, 5 F. Cas. 426, 427 (C.C. Pa. 1844)).

[19] *Sanofi*, 565 F. Supp. at 940 (quoting 4 Walker on Patents § 401 (2d ed.)).

[20] This issue is somewhat different than that of post-sale restraints (such as single-use requirements) that patent licensors seek to impose on purchasers of patented goods. These restraints, which some commentators have also analogized to real property covenants running with the land (see Herbert Hovenkamp, *Post-Sale Restraints and Competitive Harm: The First Sale Doctrine in Perspective*, 66 N.Y.U. Ann. Surv. Am. L. 487, 542 (2011)), are of questionable enforceability following the Supreme Court's 2017 decision in *Impression Products v. Lexmark*, discussed in Section 23.5.

2. *Running of the FRAND commitment.* Chapter 20.6 discusses the effect of a transfer of a patent on the original owner's obligation to license that patent to others on "fair, reasonable and nondiscriminatory" (FRAND) terms. As mentioned in Note 3 of that section, courts have generally not been amenable to treating such FRAND commitments as property-like encumbrances on patents. How does this reluctance square with the reasoning of courts in this section? Do FRAND commitments more resemble licenses, which do run with the rights, or arbitration commitments, which do not?

3. What contractual provisions might parties wish to add to their agreements to ensure that obligations follow a transfer of IP? (Hint: It's impossible to bind an unknown future buyer of an IP right, but not the future seller of that right.)

4

Implied Licenses and Unwritten Transactions

We generally think of license agreements as written documents signed (or clicked) by the parties. However, there are numerous situations in which a license or other rights may be implied through the conduct of the parties, a course of dealing or industry custom. Yet the law of implied licenses, and implied contracts more generally, is somewhat incoherent. As one leading treatise observes:

> [In] many modern implied license cases, courts attempt to describe the doctrine in terms of categories or types of implied licenses. In our view, most of these efforts are incomplete or worse; they create overlapping categories to the point that the categories confuse, rather than aid in analysis ... The fact that the doctrine involves overlapping, difficult to describe concepts, however, does not mean that implied license cases are random; it means, rather, that so many different concepts are brought into this concept that understanding it as a single theme is difficult.[1]

Implied license theories crop up in other chapters of this book, including those relating to scope of the license (Section 6.1), first sale and exhaustion (Chapter 23), and the licensing of technical standards (Chapter 20). The common theme among the cases dealing with implied licenses, if any exists, is that implied licenses may be recognized by a court in order to achieve some just end when express contractual terms are not up to the job. In this chapter we will consider a few special scenarios in which implied licenses and other rights may arise, bearing in mind that the potential to argue for the existence of an implied license is limited only by the ingenuity of the lawyers involved.

4.1 STATUTES OF FRAUDS

Implied licenses are, by their very nature, unwritten. Statutes of frauds are legal requirements that, to be enforceable, particular types of transactions must be in writing, typically accompanied by authorized signatures and, sometimes, other formalities. On one hand, a rule requiring written documentation serves important functions of preventing fraud, giving effective notice,

---

[1] Raymond T. Nimmer & Jeff Dodd, Modern Licensing Law § 10.02 (Thomson Reuters, 2016–17).

signaling the legal significance of a promise, and providing a record of the terms of the agreement. On the other hand, a writing requirement enables bad actors to avoid unwritten promises, increases transaction costs and introduces the likelihood that otherwise legitimate agreements will be invalidated on purely technical (and increasingly archaic) grounds.

As discussed in Chapter 2, federal copyright, patent and trademark law all contain rules that relate to the transfer and assignment of these rights. But is a license an "assignment" for the purposes of the statute of frauds? There is little statutory guidance regarding this question, but the answer is likely no. The Copyright Act, however, expressly includes "exclusive licenses" among the types of transactions requiring a written instrument. Does this mean that nonexclusive licenses need not be written? In many cases this is probably the rule (see *I.A.E. v. Shaver*, *infra*, Section 4.3).

State law statutes of frauds vary, but none specifically refers to licenses or transfers of intellectual property. This being said, the Restatement (Second) of Contracts § 110(e) notes that "a contract that is not to be performed within one year from the making thereof" is subject to the statute of frauds. The one-year requirement, to the extent recognized by a court, could seriously impact many licensing transactions. For example, in *Commonwealth Film Processing, Inc. v. Courtaulds United States, Inc.*, 717 F. Supp. 1157 (W.D. Va. 1989), the executives of two companies engaged in patent litigation met at an airport to discuss the settlement of their claims through a licensing arrangement. At that meeting, "certain basic understandings were reached on issues relevant to a possible license agreement" between the parties.

In holding that the oral settlement and license agreement were unenforceable under the one-year rule, the court reasoned that

> It is clear from the allegations in Commonwealth's complaint that the license agreement they contend was reached cannot be fully performed within one year. In paragraph 11a of the complaint, Commonwealth alleges that the license agreement would be "continuous." Paragraph 11b states that the alleged agreement contained a provision for royalty payments which were to continue for five years. Consequently, the license agreement which is alleged by Commonwealth falls squarely within the statute of frauds and is unenforceable unless saved by a recognized exception to the statute.

At least one state supreme court has criticized the one-year rule. In *C.R. Klewin, Inc. v. Flagship Properties, Inc.*, 600 A.2d 772 (Conn. 1991), the court reasons that the rule no longer supports the policies that gave rise to the statute of frauds and observes that the "only remaining effect" of the one-year rule "is arbitrarily to forestall adjudication of possible meritorious claims." The *Klewin* court thus adopts what is now the majority rule: an unwritten contract is not void under the one-year rule unless it cannot be performed within the one-year period under any circumstances. The fact that a contract is not *likely* to be performed within one year is not enough to void such an unwritten contract.

4.2 PITCHES AND IDEA SUBMISSIONS

In many industries, the owner of an IP right may approach a potential licensee to "pitch" a new idea, whether a business plan, a screenplay, a concept for a new reality TV show or, as in the *Nadel* case below, the idea for a new toy. In most cases, no documents have changed hands, let alone been executed. Yet in some cases, the submitter of an idea may be able to claim that use of that idea by a recipient gives rise to an implicit obligation to be compensated. The implied license doctrine in the context of idea submissions is discussed in the cases that follow.

Nadel v. Play-By-Play Toys & Novelties, Inc.
208 F.3d 368 (2d Cir. 1999)

SOTOMAYOR, CIRCUIT JUDGE

Craig P. Nadel (Nadel) brought this action against Play-By-Play Toys & Novelties, Inc. (Play-By-Play) for breach of contract, quasi contract, and unfair competition …

Background

Nadel is a toy idea man. Toy companies regularly do business with independent inventors such as Nadel in order to develop and market new toy concepts as quickly as possible. To facilitate the exchange of ideas, the standard custom and practice in the toy industry calls for companies to treat the submission of an idea as confidential. If the company subsequently uses the disclosed idea, industry custom provides that the company shall compensate the inventor, unless, of course, the disclosed idea was already known to the company.

In 1996, Nadel developed the toy concept at issue in this case. He transplanted the "eccentric mechanism" found in several hanging Halloween toys then on the market [and] placed the mechanism inside of a plush toy monkey skin to develop the prototype for a new table-top monkey toy. This plush toy figure sat upright, emitted sound, and spun when placed on a flat surface.

In October 1996, Nadel met with Neil Wasserman, an executive at Play-By-Play who was responsible for the development of its plush toy line. According to Nadel, he showed his prototype monkey toy to Wasserman, who expressed interest in adapting the concept to a non-moving, plush Tazmanian Devil toy that Play-By-Play was already producing under license from Warner Bros. Nadel contends that, consistent with industry custom, any ideas that he disclosed to Wasserman during their October 1996 meeting were subject to an agreement by Play-By-Play to keep such ideas confidential and to compensate Nadel in the event of their use.

Nadel claims that he sent his prototype monkey toy to Wasserman as a sample and awaited the "Taz skin" and voice tape, which Wasserman allegedly said he would send, so that Nadel could make a sample spinning/laughing Tazmanian Devil toy for Play-By-Play. Wasserman never provided Nadel with the Taz skin and voice tape, however, and denies ever having received the prototype monkey toy from Nadel.

Notwithstanding Wasserman's denial, his secretary, Melissa Rodriguez, testified that Nadel's prototype monkey toy remained in Wasserman's office for several months. According to Ms. Rodriguez, the monkey toy was usually kept in a glass cabinet behind Wasserman's desk, but she remembered that on one occasion she had seen it on a table in Wasserman's office. Despite Nadel's multiple requests, Wasserman did not return Nadel's prototype monkey toy until February 1997, after Play-by-Play introduced its "Tornado Taz" product at the New York Toy Fair.

The parties do not dispute that "Tornado Taz" has the same general characteristics as Nadel's prototype monkey [toy]. Nadel claims that, in violation of their alleged agreement, Play-By-Play used his idea without paying him compensation. Play-By-Play contends, however, that it independently developed the Tornado Taz product concept and that Nadel is therefore not entitled to any compensation. Specifically, Play-By-Play maintains that, as early as June or July of 1996, two of its officers – Wasserman and Slattery – met in Hong Kong and began discussing ways to create a spinning or vibrating Tazmanian Devil, including the possible use of an eccentric mechanism. Furthermore, Play-By-Play claims that in late September or early October 1996, it commissioned an outside manufacturing agent – Barter Trading of Hong Kong – to begin developing Tornado Taz.

Play-By-Play also argues that, even if it did use Nadel's idea to develop Tornado Taz, Nadel is not entitled to compensation because Nadel's concept was unoriginal and non-novel to the toy industry in October 1996.

Discussion

I. Nadel's Claims

On January 21, 1999, the district court granted Play-By-Play's motion for summary judgment dismissing Nadel's claims for breach of contract, quasi contract, and unfair competition. Interpreting New York law, the district court stated that "a party is not entitled to recover for theft of an idea unless the idea is novel or original." Applying that principle to Nadel's claims, the district court concluded that, even if the spinning toy concept were novel to Play-By-Play at the time Nadel made the disclosure to Wasserman in October 1996, Nadel's claims must nonetheless fail for lack of novelty or originality because "numerous toys containing the characteristics of [Nadel's] monkey were in existence prior to October 1996."

A. Submission-of-Idea Cases under New York Law

Our analysis begins with the New York Court of Appeals' most recent discussion of the law governing idea submission cases, *Apfel v. Prudential-Bache Securities, Inc.*, 616 N.E.2d 1095 (1993). In *Apfel*, the Court of Appeals discussed the type of novelty an idea must have in order to sustain a contract-based or property-based claim for its uncompensated use. Specifically, *Apfel* clarified an important distinction between the requirement of "novelty to the buyer" for contract claims, on the one hand, and "originality" (or novelty generally) for misappropriation claims, on the other hand.

Under the facts of *Apfel*, the plaintiff disclosed his idea to the defendant pursuant to a confidentiality agreement and, subsequent to disclosure, entered into another agreement wherein the defendant agreed to pay a stipulated price for the idea's use. The defendant used the idea but refused to pay plaintiff pursuant to the post-disclosure agreement on the asserted ground that "no contract existed between the parties because the sale agreement lacked consideration." The defendant argued that an idea could not constitute legally sufficient consideration unless it was original or novel generally and that, because plaintiff's

FIGURE 4.1 Tornado Taz.

idea was not original or novel generally (it had been in the public domain at the time of the post-disclosure agreement), the idea provided insufficient consideration to support the parties' post-disclosure contract.

In rejecting defendant's argument, the Court of Appeals held that there was sufficient consideration to support plaintiff's contract claim because the idea at issue had value to the defendant at the time the parties concluded their post-disclosure agreement. The *Apfel* court noted that "traditional principles of contract law" provide that parties "are free to make their bargain, even if the consideration exchanged is grossly unequal or of dubious value," and that, so long as the "defendant received something of value" under the contract, the contract would not be void for lack of consideration.

The *Apfel* court explicitly rejected defendant's contention that the court should carve out "an exception to traditional principles of contract law" for submission-of-idea cases by requiring that an idea must also be original or novel generally in order to constitute valid consideration. In essence, the defendant sought to impose a requirement that an idea be novel in absolute terms, as opposed to only the defendant buyer, in order to constitute valid consideration for the bargain. In rejecting this argument, the *Apfel* court clarified the standards for both contract-based and property-based claims in submission-of-idea cases. That analysis guides our decision here.

The *Apfel* court first noted that "novelty as an element of an idea seller's claim" is a distinct element of proof with respect to both (1) "a claim based on a property theory" and (2) "a claim based on a contract theory." The court then proceeded to discuss how the leading submission-of-idea case – *Downey v. General Foods Corp.*, 286 N.E.2d 257 (1972) – treated novelty with respect to property-based and contract-based claims. First, the *Apfel* court explained that the plaintiff's property-based claims for misappropriation were dismissed in Downey because "the elements of novelty and originality [were] absent," i.e., the ideas were so common as to be unoriginal and known generally. Second, the *Apfel* court explained that the plaintiff's contract claims in Downey had been dismissed on the separate ground that the "defendant possessed plaintiff's ideas prior to plaintiff's disclosure [and thus], the ideas could have no value to defendant and could not supply consideration for any agreement between the parties."

By distinguishing between the two types of claims addressed in Downey and the different bases for rejecting each claim, the New York Court of Appeals clarified that the novelty requirement in submission-of-idea cases is different for misappropriation of property and breach of contract claims ...

Thus, the *Apfel* court refused to read Downey and "similar decisions" as requiring originality or novelty generally in all cases involving disclosure of ideas. Rather, the *Apfel* court clarified that the longstanding requirement that an idea have originality or general novelty in order to support a misappropriation claim does not apply to contract claims. For contract-based claims in submission-of-idea cases, a showing of novelty to the buyer will supply sufficient consideration to support a contract.

Moreover, *Apfel* made clear that the "novelty to the buyer" standard is not limited to cases involving an express post-disclosure contract for payment based on an idea's use. The *Apfel* court explicitly discussed the pre-disclosure contract scenario present in the instant case, where "the buyer and seller contract for disclosure of the idea with payment based on use, but no separate postdisclosure contract for the use of the idea has been made." In such a scenario, a seller might, as Nadel did here, bring an action against a buyer who allegedly used his ideas without payment, claiming both misappropriation of property and breach of an express or implied-in-fact contract. The *Apfel* court recognized that these cases present courts with the difficult problem of determining "whether the idea the buyer was using was, in fact, the seller's." Specifically, the court noted that, with respect to a misappropriation of property claim, it is difficult to "prove that the buyer obtained the idea from [the seller] and nowhere else." With respect to a breach of contract claim, the court noted that it would be inequitable to enforce a contract if "it turns out upon disclosure that the buyer already possessed the idea." The court then concluded that, with respect to these cases, "[a] showing of novelty, at least novelty as to the buyer" should address these problems.

We note, moreover, that the "novelty to the buyer" standard comports with traditional principles of contract law. While an idea may be unoriginal or non-novel in a general sense, it may have substantial value to a particular buyer who is unaware of it and therefore willing to enter into contract to acquire and exploit it. In fact, the notion that an unoriginal idea may still be novel (and valuable) to a particular buyer is not itself a novel proposition ... In contrast to contract-based claims, a misappropriation claim can only arise from the taking of an idea that is original or novel in absolute terms, because the law of property does not protect against the misappropriation or theft of that which is free and available to all ...

Finally, although the legal requirements for contract-based claims and property-based claims are well-defined, we note that the determination of novelty in a given case is not always clear. The determination of whether an idea is original or novel depends upon several factors, including, inter alia, the idea's specificity or generality (is it a generic concept or one of specific application?), its commonality (how many people know of this idea?), its uniqueness (how different is this idea from generally known ideas?), and its commercial availability (how widespread is the idea's use in the industry?).

Moreover, in assessing the interrelationship between originality and novelty to the buyer, we note that in some cases an idea may be so unoriginal or lacking in novelty that its obviousness bespeaks widespread and public knowledge of the idea, and such knowledge is therefore imputed to the buyer. In such cases, a court may conclude, as a matter of law, that the idea lacks both the originality necessary to support a misappropriation claim and the novelty to the buyer necessary to support a contract claim.

In sum, we find that New York law in submission-of-idea cases is governed by the following principles: Contract-based claims require only a showing that the disclosed idea was novel to the buyer in order to find consideration. Such claims involve a fact-specific inquiry that focuses on the perspective of the particular buyer. By contrast, misappropriation claims require that the idea at issue be original and novel in absolute terms. This is so because unoriginal, known ideas have no value as property and the law does not protect against the use of that which is free and available to all. Finally, an idea may be so unoriginal or lacking in novelty generally that, as a matter of law, the buyer is deemed to have knowledge of the idea. In such cases, neither a property-based nor a contract-based claim for uncompensated use of the idea may lie.

In light of New York's law governing submission-of-idea cases, we next consider whether Nadel's toy idea was original or novel in absolute terms so as to support his misappropriation claim and whether his idea was novel as to Play-By-Play so as to support his contract claims.

B. Nadel's Misappropriation Claim

[In] this case, the district court did not decide whether Nadel's idea – a plush toy that sits upright, emits sounds, and spins on a flat surface by means of an internal eccentric motor – was inherently lacking in originality. We therefore remand this issue to the district court to determine whether Nadel's idea exhibited "genuine novelty or invention" or whether it was "a merely clever or useful adaptation of existing knowledge."

Moreover, insofar as the district court found that Nadel's idea lacked originality and novelty generally because similar toys were commercially available prior to October 1996, we believe that there remains a genuine issue of material fact on this point. While the record contains testimony of Play-By-Play's toy expert – Bert Reiner – in support of the finding that Nadel's product concept was already used in more than a dozen different plush toys prior to October 1996, the district court cited the "Giggle Bunny" toy as the only such example. Nadel disputes Reiner's contention and claims, furthermore, that the district court erroneously relied on an undated video depiction of the Giggle Bunny toy to conclude that upright, sound-emitting, spinning plush toys were commercially available prior to October 1996.

With respect to the Giggle Bunny evidence, we agree with Nadel that the Giggle Bunny model depicted in the undated video exhibit is physically different from the earlier Giggle Bunny model known to be commercially available in 1994. Drawing all factual inferences in Nadel's favor, we cannot conclude as a matter of law that the upright, sound-emitting, spinning plush Giggle Bunny shown in the video exhibit was commercially available prior to October 1996, and we certainly cannot conclude based on this one exhibit that similar toys were in the public domain at that time.

Moreover, although we find highly probative Mr. Reiner's testimony that numerous toys with the same general characteristics of Nadel's toy idea were commercially available prior to October 1996, his testimony and related evidence are too ambiguous and incomplete to support a finding of unoriginality as a matter of law. Mr. Reiner's testimony fails to specify precisely which (if any) of the enumerated plush toys were designed to (1) sit upright, (2) on a flat surface, (3) emit sounds, and (4) spin or rotate (rather than simply vibrate like "Tickle Me Elmo," for example). Without this information, a reasonable finder of fact could discount Mr. Reiner's testimony as vague and inconclusive.

On remand, the district court is free to consider whether further discovery is warranted to determine whether Nadel's product concept was inherently original or whether it was novel to the industry prior to October 1996. A finding of unoriginality or lack of general novelty would, of course, preclude Nadel from bringing a misappropriation claim against Play-By-Play. Moreover, in evaluating the originality or general novelty of Nadel's idea in connection with his misappropriation claim, the district may consider whether the idea is so unoriginal that Play-By-Play should, as a matter of law, be deemed to have already possessed the idea, and dismiss Nadel's contract claims on that ground.

C. Nadel's Contract Claims

Mindful that, under New York law, a finding of novelty as to Play-By-Play will provide sufficient consideration to support Nadel's contract claims. [Reading the] record in a light most favorable to Nadel, we conclude that there exists a genuine issue of material fact as to whether Nadel's idea was, at the time he disclosed it to Wasserman in early October 1996, novel to Play-By-Play. Notably, the timing of Play-By-Play's development and release of Tornado Taz in relation to Nadel's October 1996 disclosure is, taken alone, highly probative. Moreover, although custom in the toy industry provides that a company shall promptly return all samples if it already possesses (or does not want to use) a disclosed idea, Play-By-Play in this case failed to return Nadel's prototype monkey toy for several months, despite Nadel's multiple requests for its return. According to Wasserman's secretary, Melissa Rodriguez, Nadel's sample was not returned until after the unveiling of "Tornado Taz" at the New York Toy Fair in February 1997. Ms. Rodriguez testified that from October 1996 through February 1997, Nadel's sample was usually kept in a glass cabinet behind Wasserman's desk, and on one occasion, she remembered seeing it on a table in Wasserman's office. These facts give rise to the reasonable inference that Play-By-Play may have used Nadel's prototype as a model for the development of Tornado Taz.

None of the evidence adduced by Play-By-Play compels a finding to the contrary on summary judgment. With regard to the discussions that Play-By-Play purportedly had in June or July of 1996 about possible ways to create a vibrating or spinning Tazmanian Devil toy, those conversations only lasted, according to Mr. Slattery, "a matter of five minutes." Play-By-Play may have "discussed the concept," as Mr. Slattery testified, but the record provides no evidence suggesting that, in June or July of 1996, Play-By-Play understood exactly how it could apply eccentric motor technology to make its Tazmanian Devil toy spin rather than, say, vibrate like Tickle Me Elmo. Similarly, although Play-By-Play asserts that it commissioned an outside manufacturing agent – Barter Trading of Hong Kong – to begin developing Tornado Taz in late September or early October of 1996, Play-By-Play admits that it can only "guess" the exact date. Play-By-Play cannot confirm that its commission of Barter Trading pre-dated Nadel's alleged disclosure to Wasserman on or about October 9, 1996. Nor has Play-By-Play produced any documents, technical or otherwise, relating to its purported business venture with Barter Trading or its independent development of a spinning Tornado Taz prior to October 1996. Based on this evidence, a jury could reasonably infer that Play-By-Play actually contacted Barter Trading, if at all, after learning of Nadel's product concept, and that Play-By-Play's development of Tornado Taz is attributable to Nadel's disclosure.

We therefore conclude that there exists a genuine issue of material fact as to whether Nadel's idea was, at the time he disclosed it to Wasserman in early October 1996, novel to Play-By-Play. As to whether the other elements necessary to find a valid express or implied-in-fact contract are present here, e.g., mutual assent, legal capacity, legal subject matter, we leave that determination to the district court to address, if necessary, on remand.

Conclusion

For the foregoing reasons, we affirm that part of the district court's judgment dismissing Play-By-Play's counterclaims. We vacate that part of the district court's judgment granting Play-By-Play's motion for summary judgment and dismissing Nadel's complaint and remand for further proceedings consistent with this opinion.

Wrench LLC v. Taco Bell Corp.

256 F.3d 446 (6th Cir. 2001)

GRAHAM, DISTRICT JUDGE

This case raises a question of first impression in this circuit regarding the extent to which the Copyright Act preempts state law claims based on breach of an implied-in-fact contract. Plaintiffs-Appellants Wrench LLC, Joseph Shields, and Thomas Rinks brought this diversity action against Defendant-Appellee Taco Bell Corporation ("Taco Bell"), claiming breach of implied contract and various torts related to Taco Bell's alleged use of appellants' ideas.

I. Background

Appellants Thomas Rinks and Joseph Shields are creators of the "Psycho Chihuahua" cartoon character which they promote, market, and license through their wholly-owned Michigan limited liability company, Wrench LLC. The parties have described Psycho Chihuahua as a clever, feisty dog with an attitude; a self-confident, edgy, cool dog who knows what he wants and will not back down.

In June 1996, Shields and Rinks attended a licensing trade show in New York City, where they were approached by two Taco Bell employees, Rudy Pollak, a vice president, and Ed Alfaro, a creative services manager. Pollak and Alfaro expressed interest in the Psycho Chihuahua character, which they thought would appeal to Taco Bell's core consumers, males aged eighteen to twenty-four. Pollak and Alfaro obtained some Psycho Chihuahua materials to take with them back to Taco Bell's headquarters in California.

Upon returning to California, Alfaro began promoting the Psycho Chihuahua idea within Taco Bell. [After] several meetings with non-marketing executives, Alfaro showed the Psycho Chihuahua materials to Vada Hill, Taco Bell's vice president of brand management, as well as to Taco Bell's then-outside advertising agency, Bozell Worldwide. Alfaro also tested the Psycho Chihuahua marketing concept with focus groups to gauge consumer reaction to the designs submitted by Rinks and Shields.

During this time period, Rinks told Alfaro that instead of using the cartoon version of Psycho Chihuahua in its television advertisements, Taco Bell should use a live dog, manipulated by computer graphic imaging, with the personality of Psycho Chihuahua and a love for Taco Bell food. Rinks and Alfaro also discussed what it was going to cost for Taco Bell to use appellants' character, and although no specific numbers were mentioned, Alfaro understood that if Taco Bell used the Psycho Chihuahua concept, it would have to pay appellants.

In September 1996, Rinks and Shields hired Strategy Licensing ("Strategy"), a licensing agent, to represent Wrench in its dealings with Taco Bell. [On] November 18, 1996, Strategy representatives forwarded a licensing proposal to Alfaro. [Taco Bell] did not accept this proposal, although it did not explicitly reject it or indicate that it was ceasing further discussions with Wrench.

On December 5, 1996, Alfaro met with Hill, who had been promoted to the position of chief marketing officer, and others, to present various licensing ideas, including Psycho Chihuahua. On February 6, 1997, Alfaro again met with appellants and representatives of Strategy to review and finalize a formal presentation featuring Psycho Chihuahua that was to be given to Taco Bell's marketing department in early March 1997. At this meeting, appellants exhibited examples of possible Psycho Chihuahua promotional materials and also orally presented specific ideas for television commercials featuring a live dog manipulated by computer graphics imaging. These ideas included a commercial in which a male dog passed up a female dog in order to get to Taco Bell food.

Alfaro was unable to arrange a meeting with the marketing department during March 1997 to present the Psycho Chihuahua materials. On April 4, 1997, however, Strategy made a formal presentation to Alfaro and his group using samples of uniform designs, T-shirts, food wrappers, posters, and cup designs based on the ideas discussed during the February 6, 1997, meeting. Alfaro and his group were impressed with Strategy's presentation.

On March 18, 1997, Taco Bell hired a new advertising agency, TBWA Chiat/Day ("Chiat/Day"). Taco Bell advised Chiat/Day that it wanted a campaign ready to launch by July 1997 that would reconnect Taco Bell with its core group of consumers. Chuck Bennett and Clay Williams were designated as the creative directors of Taco Bell's account.

On June 2, 1997, Bennett and Williams proposed a commercial to Taco Bell in which a male Chihuahua would pass up a female Chihuahua to get to a person seated on a bench eating Taco Bell food. Bennett and Williams say that they conceived of the idea for this commercial one day as they were eating Mexican food at a sidewalk cafe and saw a Chihuahua trotting down the street, with no master or human intervention, "on a mission." Bennett and Williams contend that this image caused them jointly to conceive of the idea of using a Chihuahua as a way of personifying the intense desire for Taco Bell food. Williams subsequently wrote an advertisement script using a Chihuahua, which Taco Bell decided to produce as a television commercial.

When, in June 1997, Alfaro learned that Chiat/Day was planning to use a Chihuahua in a commercial, he contacted Hill again about the possibility of using Psycho Chihuahua. Hill passed Alfaro on to Chris Miller, a Taco Bell advertising manager and the liaison between Taco Bell's marketing department and Chiat/Day. On June 27, 1997, Alfaro gave Psycho Chihuahua materials to Miller along with a note suggesting that Taco Bell consider using Psycho Chihuahua as an icon and as a character in its advertising. Miller sent these materials to Chiat/Day, which received them sometime between June 28 and July 26.

Taco Bell aired its first Chihuahua commercial in the northeastern United States in July 1997, and received a very positive consumer reaction [and] launched a nationwide advertising campaign featuring Chihuahua commercials in late December 1997.

Appellants brought suit in January 1998, alleging breach of implied-in-fact contract as well as various tort and statutory claims under Michigan and California law. Appellee filed a motion to dismiss, which the district court granted in part and denied in part ...

II. Discussion

Appellants assert that the district court erred in determining that novelty was required to sustain their contract claim. The district court found that Michigan law required appellants to prove the originality or novelty of their ideas in order to maintain their claims, concluding that appellants' ideas were not novel because they "merely combined themes and executions that had been used many times in a variety of commercials for different products." The district court thus granted summary judgment in favor of appellee on this alternative basis. We conclude that the district court erred in finding that Michigan law requires novelty in a contract-based claim.

FIGURE 4.2 "Psycho Chihuahua" and the Taco Bell chihuahua

The district court seems to have assumed, without further discussion, that if the novelty requirement applied to appellants' conversion and misappropriation claims, it would also apply to appellants' implied-in-fact contract claim.

Conversion is based on property law principles. Courts have usually refused to protect ideas on a property theory, but when they have, it has generally been subject to the requirements of novelty and concreteness ... Most courts apply a different rule to contract claims, modifying the requirement of novelty in some circumstances and dispensing with it altogether in others. The reason for the distinction is this: property rights are rights against the world and courts are generally unwilling to accord that kind of protection to ideas; contract rights on the other hand are limited to the contracting parties and it should be for them to decide if an idea is sufficiently valuable to be purchased.

Nevertheless, many courts do require novelty in an action based upon an implied contract theory on the ground that there can be no consideration for an implied promise to pay if the idea does not constitute "property."

Sarver v. Detroit Edison Co., 51 N.W.2d 759 (Mich. App. 1997) tells us where Michigan likely stands on this issue. In *Sarver*, plaintiff brought an action against her employer seeking damages for conversion and breach of contract based on the allegation that defendant appropriated an idea which she submitted through an employee suggestion program. The court rejected plaintiff's conversion cause of action finding that plaintiff's idea "was neither novel nor unique" and "did not constitute property subject to a conversion cause of action." The *Sarver* court went on to hold, however, that plaintiff had stated a breach of contract claim, stating "to the extent that plaintiff seeks compensation for formulating, drafting, and submitting her idea pursuant to defendant's employee suggestion program, rather than for the idea itself, she has stated a breach of contract claim." The *Sarver* court did not impose a requirement of novelty on plaintiff's contract claim.

[The] *Sarver* court quoted with approval the decision of the Supreme Court of Alaska in *Reeves v. Alyeska Pipeline Service Co.* In *Reeves*, plaintiff had proposed the idea of creating a visitor center at a location where visitors could view the Alaska oil pipeline. He brought an action alleging tort and contract claims against the pipeline servicing company, which subsequently established such a visitor center. The Supreme Court of Alaska held that the element of novelty was not required for plaintiff's implied contract claim:

> Relying largely on cases from New York, Alyeska argues that novelty and originality should be required in an implied-in-fact claim. Reeves responds that we should follow California's example and not require novelty as an essential element of this sort of claim. Idea-based claims arise most frequently in the entertainment centers of New York and California, but New York requires novelty, whereas California does not. We prefer the California approach. An idea may be valuable to the recipient merely because of its timing or the manner in which it is presented ... Implied in fact contracts are closely related to express contracts. Each requires the parties to form an intent to enter into a contract. It is ordinarily not the court's role to evaluate the adequacy of the consideration agreed upon by the parties. The bargain should be left in the hands of the parties. If parties voluntarily choose to bargain for an individual's services in disclosing or developing a non-novel or unoriginal idea, they have the power to do so.

Reeves, 926 P.2d at 1130, 1141–1142. Since the Michigan court in *Sarver* quoted *Reeves* on the requirement of novelty in an action based on conversion and went on to hold that the plaintiff's contract claim survived notwithstanding lack of novelty, we conclude that

Michigan follows *Reeves* and the California cases which dispense with the requirement of novelty in actions based on implied-in-fact contracts …

While we conclude that Michigan would not impose a requirement of novelty in an action based upon a contract implied in fact, it does not appear that the result of this case would change even if Michigan were to follow the New York view, which requires only novelty to the defendant. Here, Taco Bell does not claim that it was aware of appellants' ideas prior to disclosure. Accordingly, we find that the district court erred in granting summary judgment to the appellee on the ground that appellants failed to show that their ideas were novel or original.

The judgment of the district court is REVERSED.

Notes and Questions

1. *Ideas versus trade secrets.* What is the difference between an "idea," such as the ideas shared in *Nadel* and *Wrench*, and a trade secret? Would you consider the ideas in these cases to constitute trade secrets? Would it have made a difference if the purveyor of the idea asked the recipient to sign a nondisclosure agreement? What if the recipient refused to sign? Should an idea's status as a trade secret affect a court's recognition of an implied license?

2. *Industry practice.* The *Nadel* court refers to trade practices in the toy industry. Why are those practices relevant? Would a court reach the same result in a different industry, say motion pictures or aerospace engineering?

3. *Idea disclaimers.* Some companies want to ensure that they are *not* obliged to individuals who pitch ideas to them. Consider the following disclaimer posted on the IBM website:

> IBM does not want to receive confidential or proprietary information from you through our Web site. Please note that any information or material sent to IBM will be deemed NOT to be confidential. By sending IBM any information or material, you grant IBM an unrestricted, irrevocable license to use, reproduce, display, perform, modify, transmit and distribute those materials or information, and you also agree that IBM is free to use any ideas, concepts, know-how or techniques that you send us for any purpose.[2]

Why doesn't IBM want your ideas? Would a disclaimer like IBM's be appropriate in the motion picture industry? Would it be enforceable? Would the enforceability of such a disclaimer work differently depending on whether an idea submitter argued in contract versus property?

Another company, satellite provider EchoStar, explains the following in its idea submission policy:

> EchoStar views patent protection as important for our own inventions and ideas as well as those you are offering to us. As a matter of policy, we normally receive unsolicited ideas from the general public only after the idea submitters have first taken steps to obtain patent protection for such ideas. We expect idea submitters to seek and rely wholly upon their patent rights, as defined by the claims of an issued patent, just as our company is required to do in order to protect its own rights.[3]

How does EchoStar's policy differ from IBM's? Why do you think EchoStar adopted this approach? Which of these two policies, if either, would you advise a client to adopt?

---

[2] IBM, Terms of Use, August 15, 2015, www.ibm.com/legal (visited August 17, 2020).
[3] Echostar, Unsolicited Ideas Policy Statement and Agreement.

4. *Novelty*. The court in *Wrench* holds that under Michigan law, following the California rule, novelty is not required to prevail on a breach of contract claim. For a property-based misappropriation claim, however, novelty would still be required. Is the idea of a clever, feisty chihuahua pitching Tex-Mex food novel enough to prevail on a misappropriation claim?

5. *Rights against the world*. The *Wrench* court notes that "property rights are rights against the world" (so-called *erga omnes* rights) whereas contract rights only affect the parties bound by the contract. Why does this distinction matter in deciding whether a novelty standard should apply?

6. *State versus federal law*. Does state or federal law govern the creation and interpretation of implied licenses pertaining to IP rights created under federal statute? In *Foad Consulting Group, Inc. v. Musil Govan Azzalino*, 270 F.3d 821 (9th Cir. 2001), a copyright case, the Ninth Circuit noted that:

> while federal law answers the threshold question of whether an implied, nonexclusive copyright license can be granted (it can), state law determines the contract question: whether a copyright holder has, in fact, granted such a license. As a general matter, we rely on state law to fill in the gaps Congress leaves in federal statutes. Thus, where the Copyright Act does not address an issue, we turn to state law ... so long as state law does not otherwise conflict with the Copyright Act. There is no reason we should treat implied copyright licenses any differently.

Not every circuit has addressed this issue. Do you think the Ninth Circuit's reasoning in *Foad* should be followed elsewhere?

7. *Parol evidence and implied licenses*. *Foad* dealt with the application of California's parol evidence rule to an implied copyright license. The parol evidence rule permits a court to consider evidence extrinsic to the four corners of a contract when the contract is ambiguous. But what is parol evidence when an implied (unwritten) contract is under consideration? Or, put another way, what is *not* parol when the contract itself is unwritten? The Ninth Circuit in *Foad* stated that "application of California's parol evidence rule in interpreting a contract that a party purports to have granted an implied copyright license does not conflict with the Act or its underlying policies." What does the court mean?

8. *Idea registration*. In Hollywood, aspiring screenwriters, directors and idea brokers regularly pitch ideas to movie studios and television networks. Generally, no contract is signed before or during a pitch, which can just as easily be made in a taxicab, a restaurant or even the proverbial elevator in a studio executive's office.[4] So how do pitchers prevent their ideas from being stolen by their (sometimes less than ethical) recipients? One solution is idea registration. The Writers Guild of America, West (WGAW) Registry allows individuals, for a small fee, to upload and register their scripts, treatments,[5] lyrics, short stories, poems, commercials, drawings and written ideas. Such registration offers no explicit legal protection, as might a copyright registration, but it does provide some benefits to the registrant. As explained by WGAW:

---

[4] Take the example of Robert Kosberg, known as Hollywood's "Mr. Pitch." Each year, Kosberg pitches twenty to fifty ideas for new films to major motion picture studios, of which he sells about eight. He sold New Line Cinema an idea for a horror film about a rampaging dog that he described as "Jaws on Paws." The film became *Man's Best Friend*. In one case, a grandmother from Ozark, Arizona, sent Kosberg a 3" × 5" card suggesting a story about a man who lives in the Statue of Liberty. He fleshed out the story and sold it to Polygram as "Keeper of the Flame." Kosberg paid the originator of the idea about $100,000. See Anna Muoio, *Meet Hollywood's Mr. Pitch*, Fast Company, October 1999, p.124.

[5] A "treatment" is a short (usually 1–3 pages) summary of the major characters and plot elements of a story intended for film or television.

The registration process places preventative measures against plagiarism or unauthorized use of an author's material. While someone else may have the same storyline or idea in his or her material, your evidence lies in your presentation of your work. Registering your work does not disallow others from having a similar storyline or theme. Rather, registering your work would potentially discourage others from using your work without your permission.

Though the Registry cannot prevent plagiarism, it can produce the registered material as well as confirm the date of registration. Registering your work creates legal evidence for the material that establishes a date for the material's existence. The WGAW Registry, as a neutral third party, can testify for that evidence.[6]

Of course, the Library of Congress also permits the registration of most of these materials for a similarly low fee, and a copyright registration does afford the registrant some legal rights. Why might someone choose WGAW registration over copyright registration?

10. *"Handshake culture" under threat?* California law requires lawyers' contingency fee agreements to be in writing. In 2018, actor Johnny Depp sued his longtime attorney to recover an estimated $30 million in fees that Depp had paid the attorney since 1999. The reason? The agreement – which entitled the attorney to the customary 5 percent share of Depp's earnings – was never put in writing. A Los Angeles trial judge agreed with Depp and ruled that the agreement between Depp and his attorney was not valid. The ruling was met with alarm by many in Hollywood, who bemoaned the death of the industry's "handshake culture."[7] Do you agree with the result of Depp's action? Is "handshake culture" at risk? Is it worth saving? Why or why not?

Problem 4.1

Julia, who recently received her PhD in satellite engineering, has an idea for a method of increasing the bandwidth of satellite transmissions. Julia is currently looking for a job, and has not filed a patent application for her invention (nor has she developed it enough to satisfy the formal requirements to obtain a patent). In a job interview with Conic Dynamics Corp. (CDC), Julia describes her idea to Paul, one of CDC's senior engineers. She tells him that she would be happy to work with him on improving her method if she is hired. Four weeks later, CDC informs Julia that she was not selected for the job. What legal recourse, if any, does Julia have in each of the following cases:

a. Julia hears nothing further from CDC, but a year after her interview an article describing her method is published in a technical journal. Paul is one of the article's co-authors.

b. Two years after Julia's interview, a friend informs her that he came across a patent application filed by CDC that claimed an invention remarkably similar to Julia's method.

c. Given the facts in (a) and (b), assume that a week after Julia's interview she received a letter from CDC stating that "CDC's official policy, as described on its website, is that all ideas submitted to it automatically become CDC's property and CDC will accept no obligations with respect to any submissions made to it unless the submission was requested in writing by a CDC representative."

d. Would the result in (a) or (b) change if CDC began a research project based on the same idea one year before Julia's interview?

e. Would the result in (a) or (b) change if Julia had given Paul a detailed set of diagrams and a written description of her method during the interview?

[6] www.wgawregistry.org/regfaqs.html#quest2 (accessed August 21, 2018).

[7] See, e.g., Sara Randazzo, *Ruling in Johnny Depp Lawsuit Threatens Hollywood Lawyers' Handshake Culture*, Wall St. J., August 29, 2018.

4.3 IMPLIED LICENSES AND COMMISSIONED WORKS

The cases in Section 4.2 address a situation in which an idea was submitted to a recipient and was used by the recipient in its business (the spinning toy idea in *Nadel* and the chihuahua restaurant promotion idea in *Wrench*). In both cases, the principal question was whether the *originator* of the idea had either a claim (property or contractual) to compensation for the use of the disclosed idea. In this section we turn to the question of what implied right the *recipient* of an intellectual asset (in these cases, copyrighted material, but also potentially ideas, patented inventions, etc.) may have to use the asset after it is delivered, even if the recipient has not fully complied with its obligation to pay the originator.

I.A.E., Inc. v. Shaver

74 F.3d 768 (7th Cir. 1996)

RIPPLE, CIRCUIT JUDGE

Architect Paul D. Shaver appeals the district court's summary judgment ruling that there was no infringement of Mr. Shaver's copyrighted schematic design drawings. The court concluded that Mr. Shaver had granted an implied nonexclusive license to utilize his drawings in the completion of Gary Regional Airport's air cargo building. For the reasons that follow, we [affirm].

I Background

In July 1992, two construction companies formed a joint venture. I.A.E., Inc. and its president Ramamurty Talluri joined with BEMI Construction and its president William Brewer to become the I.A.E./BEMI Joint Venture ("Joint Venture"). On December 21, 1992, the Joint Venture entered into a contract with the Gary Regional Airport Authority ("Airport") to design and to construct an air cargo/hangar building. Under the contract, Joint Venture was to provide all of the civil, structural, mechanical and electrical engineering services and architectural design services needed to construct the air cargo building.

In furtherance of that goal, Joint Venture subcontracted with Paul D. Shaver, an architect with extensive experience in designing airport facilities, to prepare the schematic design drawings for the airport building. The parties agree that there are four phases to the architectural design of a building: schematic design, preliminary design, final design and construction supervision. The schematic design documents are the product of the first phase of designing a building. They outline the scope of the project and are the basis of the owner's approval for the building design. Schematic design documents are often used as a reference base for further design development.

Mr. Shaver's letter of January 14, 1993, to Mr. Talluri, which constitutes the written contract between the architect and Joint Venture, contained Mr. Shaver's agreement to prepare the schematic design drawings for the Airport building: "With the assistance of your office and the [Airport] staff, agreed design parameters can be established initially to permit the Project to proceed in a normal development manner." The contract price for his services was $10,000 plus reimbursable expenses, less deductions for the participation of I.A.E.'s staff. The contract specifically set forth the services Mr. Shaver intended to perform:

To prepare, with the assistance of your office and BEMI, Inc., staff, standard Design Documents ... which would describe the agreed scope of the Project, we estimate a 4–5 week period of time including two or three scheduled approval meetings with your office and [Airport] Authority personnel. These documents would consist of the following which are customarily prepared to describe the scope of the Project and also for general reference: Drawings, 5, Title Sheet, Site Plan, Floor Plans, Elevations and Building Sections Preliminary Construction Cost Estimate.

[W]e are prepared to complete the required Schematic Design Document preparation for $10,000 subject to adjustment with deductions resulting from participation of staff from your office and your Architectural associate ...

Please advise us if you need any additional data concerning our understanding of the scope of work.

Mr. Shaver believed that, once a design had been approved, he would execute further written contracts for the remaining phases of the architectural work.

After Mr. Shaver attended several meetings with the Airport, he prepared his schematic design drawings of the proposed Airport building. He then delivered copies of his schematic drawings to the Airport, Joint Venture, and other parties involved in the Project. These drawings were submitted with a notice of copyright. The copyrights of those drawings, both as technical drawings and as architectural works, were effective June 2, 1993. Their validity has not been challenged. Mr. Shaver and Mr. Talluri later presented to the Airport the completed schematic designs. On February 22, 1993, the Airport approved one of them. Mr. Shaver was paid $5,000 of his fee on that date.

On March 1, 1993, Joint Venture retained H. Seay Cantrell & Associates ("Cantrell") to perform the remaining architectural work for the air cargo building. When Mr. Shaver realized that he and his firm were no longer involved in the Project, he took two actions. On March 3, 1993, Mr. Shaver wrote to the Airport's Executive Director, Levelle Gatewood, acknowledging that he and his staff were, "under the circumstances, no longer in a position to participate or contribute to the development of the east Air Cargo Building Project." The letter, with enclosed copies of Mr. Shaver's schematic design drawings, also stated:

We trust that our ideas and knowledge exhibited in our work will assist the Airport in realizing a credible and flexible use Cargo/Hangar facility.

Mr. Shaver's second act, one week later, was to seek collection of the amount that Joint Venture still owed him for the services he had rendered and to notify Joint Venture that he intended to enforce his copyrights if necessary. Mr. Shaver, by his attorney, claimed that he was owed an additional $5,000 fee, plus his out-of-pocket expenses ($887.29), plus (a new claim) a $7,000 payment for the purported "assignment" of his copyright on the schematic design documents. The attorney's letter of March 10, 1993 offered Mr. Talluri a settlement of Mr. Shaver's claim against Joint Venture for $12,887.29. Mr. Talluri agreed to pay the contract costs, $5,887.29, as final payment. According to Mr. Talluri, Mr. Shaver "had never previously raised the issue of copyright, copyright infringement or his alleged entitlement to moneys, in addition to the contract amount, for 'assignment' of his copyright on the schematic design drawings."

Once it was clear that Mr. Shaver and Joint Venture would not reach an accord concerning any amount still owing to Mr. Shaver under the contract, on August 5, 1993, I.A.E. and Mr. Talluri filed this action. They sought a declaratory judgment that they did not infringe any copyrights owned by Mr. Shaver and that they had a right to use Mr. Shaver's drawings;

they also sought damages. Mr. Shaver counterclaimed against I.A.E. and Mr. Talluri, seeking damages for copyright infringement and breach of contract. He also filed third-party complaints against Cantrell, BEMI and its president Mr. Brewer, and the Airport, alleging that all the named defendants had infringed his copyrights in the schematic design documents or that they had conspired to do so by copying and using elements of his design in the final bid documents for the Airport Project. Joint Venture and the Airport responded that they had used Mr. Shaver's drawings only as Mr. Shaver had intended their use, to build the Airport's air cargo building. All parties then filed cross-motions for summary judgment.

The district court granted summary judgment on the ground that there was no copyright infringement.

A.

Proof of copyright infringement requires two showings: first, that the claimant has a validly owned copyright, and second, that the "constituent elements of the work that are original" were copied. The first element is not in contention; there is no challenge to the validity of Mr. Shaver's copyrights. It is the second prong of infringement that is at issue; Mr. Shaver asserted that his work was copied. The district court determined, however, that the use of his works was permissible because Mr. Shaver had granted an implied nonexclusive license.

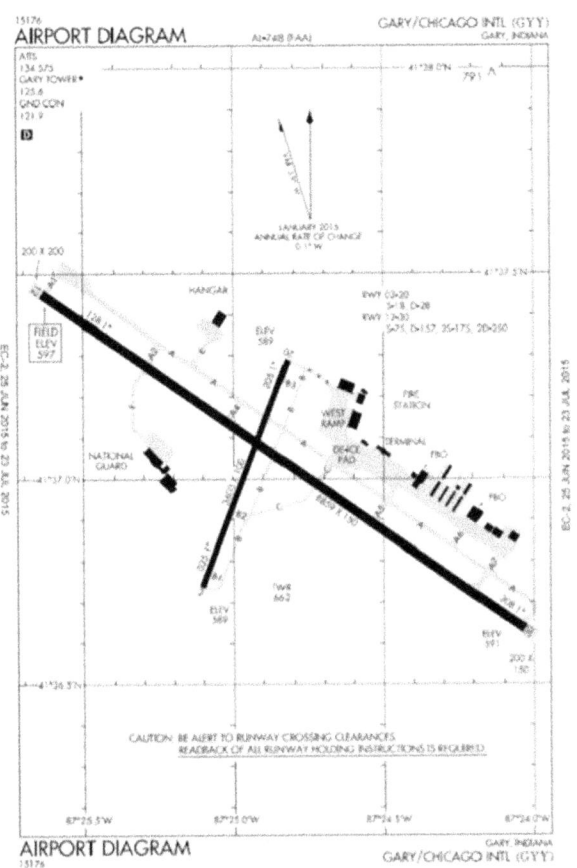

FIGURE 4.3 *I.A.E. v. Shaver* involved an architect's plans for an air cargo building at Gary Regional Airport (now Gary/Chicago International Airport (GYY)).

A copyright owner may transfer to another person any of the exclusive rights the owner has in the copyright; however, such a transfer must be made in writing. 17 U.S.C. § 204(a). [The] "transfer of copyright ownership" is defined, in the Copyright Act, as an exclusive license or some other instrument of conveyance. The definition expressly excludes a non-exclusive license. Therefore, even though section 204(a) of the Copyright Act invalidates any transfer of copyright ownership that is not in writing, section 101 explicitly removes a nonexclusive license from the section 204(a) writing requirement. We turn, therefore, to the differences between exclusive and nonexclusive licenses.

In an exclusive license, the copyright holder permits the licensee to use the protected material for a specific use and further promises that the same permission will not be given to others. The licensee violates the copyright by exceeding the scope of this license. The writing requirement serves the goal of predictability and certainty of copyright ownership.

By contrast, in the case of an implied nonexclusive license, the licensor-creator of the work, by granting an implied nonexclusive license, does not transfer ownership of the copyright to the licensee. The copyright owner simply permits the use of a copyrighted work in a particular manner. In contrast to an exclusive license, a "nonexclusive license may be granted orally, or may even be implied from conduct." … In fact, consent given in the form of mere permission or lack of objection is also equivalent to a nonexclusive license and is not required to be in writing. Although a person holding a nonexclusive license has no standing to sue for copyright infringement, the existence of a license, exclusive or nonexclusive, creates an affirmative defense to a claim of copyright infringement. The concept of an implied nonexclusive license has been recognized [by] the courts, including this one, which universally have recognized that a nonexclusive license may be implied from conduct. Indeed, implied licenses are like implied contracts, which are well recognized in the field of architecture. As the district court noted, the Ninth Circuit, in [*Effects Associates, Inc. v. Cohen*, 908 F.2d 555 (9th Cir. 1990)], held that an implied nonexclusive license has been granted when (1) a person (the licensee) requests the creation of a work, (2) the creator (the licensor) makes that particular work and delivers it to the licensee who requested it, and (3) the licensor intends that the licensee-requestor copy and distribute his work.

B.

In light of these principles, we now turn to the record before us. In our analysis, we find helpful, as did the district court, the opinion of our colleagues in the Ninth Circuit in *Effects*. In the case before us, [Shaver] maintains that his expectation was that he would be the architect who would be preparing the final drawings, presumably from his own preliminary drawings, to be used for the construction. We therefore must determine whether the record will support a determination that such an interpretation had any objective foundation.

Effects suggests several objective factors to guide the judicial inquiry as to whether an implied license exists: the language of the copyright registration certificate, the letter agreement, and deposition testimony; and the delivery of the copyrighted material without warning that its further use would constitute copyright infringement. When we apply these factors to the circumstances before us, we must conclude that there is no genuine issue of triable fact and that the district court concluded correctly as a matter of law that Mr. Shaver granted an implied nonexclusive license to Joint Venture.

FIGURE 4.4 *Effects Associates* involved the development of a gruesome special effect for the horror film *The Stuff*.

We note first that Mr. Shaver's certificates of registration, entitling the drawings "East Air Cargo Building, Gary Regional Airport, Indiana: Not Yet Constructed," state that copyrighted designs are to be used for the "Airport Facility." We now turn to the language of the contract itself. The contract in this case was a letter written by Mr. Shaver. This letter, apparently in confirmation of an earlier telephone conversation, demonstrates that the relationship of independent contractor for the purpose of creating the preliminary drawings for the Airport Project existed between Mr. Shaver and Joint Venture. It defines his role in the Airport Project and, specifically, his "understanding of the scope of work": preparation of the preliminary schematic design drawings … Mr. Shaver stated that his drawings are the type "customarily prepared to describe the scope of the project and also for general reference." Mr. Shaver also quoted the consideration for his work, $10,000. Mr. Shaver's statement that "agreed design parameters can be established initially to permit the Project to proceed in a normal development manner," certainly suggests that he considered his contribution to be in furtherance of the entire Project. In short, his letter was clear, to-the-point, and unambiguous. No other work is listed; no expectation of a further role in the Project is mentioned in the contract. Therefore, although Mr. Shaver tells us that he anticipated he would be the architect to take the Project to completion, nothing in his contract gives the slightest indication of that belief. Although Indiana law allows contractual terms to be implied from the intent and action of the parties, the "intent relevant in contract matters is not the parties' subjective intent but their outward manifestation of it." Here the contract is clear.

The plain language of the contract is supported by common sense. As we have already pointed out, Mr. Shaver created a work – preliminary architectural drawings – and handed them over to the Joint Venture for use on the Airport Project. For that work the architect received $10,000 compensation. As the Ninth Circuit concluded in *Effects*:

> To hold that *Effects* did not at the same time convey a license to use the footage in "The Stuff" would mean that plaintiff's contribution to the film was "of minimal value," a conclusion that can't be squared with the fact that Cohen paid Effects almost $56,000 for this footage. Accordingly, we conclude that *Effects* impliedly granted nonexclusive licenses.

908 F.2d 555, 558. This understanding is reflected throughout the parties' depositions and affidavits. Joint Venture clearly expected to use Mr. Shaver's drawings for the Project. Mr. Talluri expected that Mr. Shaver's schematic design drawings were to be used in the Airport Project for which they were intended and stated that the drawings were used only in that manner, despite the fact that Mr. Shaver was not the continuing architect.

Not only the language of the copyright registration certificates, the letter contract, and the depositions and common sense support the conclusion of the district court that the defendants had an implied nonexclusive license to use Mr. Shaver's drawings in the Airport Project; Mr. Shaver's actions and subsequent writing also unequivocally support that conclusion. Mr. Shaver delivered his copyrighted designs without any warning that their further use would constitute copyright infringement. In his March 3, 1993 letter, Mr. Shaver acknowledged that he was no longer a contributor to the Project's development, but that he expected "that our ideas and knowledge exhibited in our work will assist the Airport in realizing a credible and flexible use Cargo/Hangar facility." This statement, accompanied by the delivery of copies of his drawings, certainly constitutes a release of those documents to the Airport for its Project and clearly validates a determination that all the objective factors support the existence of an implied license to use Mr. Shaver's drawings in the construction of the air cargo building.

On this record, we cannot conclude that Mr. Shaver has raised a genuine issue of material fact on the issue of the parties' intent. His contention that he never intended to grant a license for the use of his drawings past the drafting stage unless he was the continuing architect is simply not supported by the record.

C.

Mr. Shaver also makes several alternative arguments that accept the existence of a nonexclusive implied license, but suggest that, under the circumstances established by the record, it cannot be enforced. We believe that these arguments cannot be maintained in light of our analysis, but we shall address them briefly for the sake of completeness.

Mr. Shaver submits that, even if there was an implied license for the use of his drawings, the Airport, Cantrell and Joint Venture exceeded the scope of that license by allowing another architect, Cantrell, to use the designs. He relies on *Oddo v. Ries*, 743 F.2d 630 (9th Cir.1984). *Oddo* held that Ries, a publisher, had an implied nonexclusive license to use Oddo's articles to create a particular book. However, Ries exceeded the scope of that implied license when it hired another writer and created a different work, one which included much new material written by the second writer as well as large portions of

Oddo's manuscript. By publishing the other writer's book, which was distinct from the plaintiff's manuscript originally licensed for use, the defendant exceeded the scope of the partnership's implied license. In our case, however, the record contains written authorization for the use of Mr. Shaver's copyrighted drawings to "describe the agreed scope of the Project" for Joint Venture and the Airport. The use of his drawings was therefore within the scope of that agreement. Mr. Shaver's assertion that he did not grant the right to further use of his drawings unless he was the architect continuing the Project is simply not supported by the contract. Mr. Shaver's reliance on *Oddo* is therefore of no benefit to him.

Mr. Shaver also asserts that, because only half of the contract sum was paid, the implied license "did not spring into existence." In *Effects*, the Ninth Circuit rejected a virtually identical argument that there could be no implied license until the full payment of the contract price was made. That court recognized that the appellant was treating the complete payment of the contractual consideration as a condition precedent to the use of the copyrighted material. After noting that "conditions precedent are disfavored and will not be read into a contract unless required by plain, unambiguous language," it found nothing in the agreement between the parties indicating such an agreement. Similarly, in the case before us, nothing in the contract or in Mr. Shaver's later letter indicates that full payment was a condition precedent to the use of his drawings. In fact, he first distributed his drawings before any payment was made, and next handed them over to the Airport, with no mention of payment, after half the dollar amount of the contract had been tendered. Clearly at that point a license to use the drawings had impliedly been granted. Mr. Shaver did not state that failure to pay would be viewed as copyright infringement until the March 10, 1993 letter from his attorney.

Conclusion

Mr. Shaver created an implied nonexclusive license to use his schematic design drawings in the Airport Project. Accordingly, there was no infringement of Mr. Shaver's copyrighted works. We conclude that, because there are no genuine issues of material fact before us, we must affirm the judgment of the district court.

Notes and questions

1. *Contract versus property.* In both *Shaver* and *Effects*, the customer of a commissioned work failed to pay the full amount due for the work, yet was found to have an implied license to use the work in the manner intended by the creator. Why wouldn't the customer's license be conditioned on making the full payment? Should it be? The court in *Shaver* wrote that "conditions precedent are disfavored and will not be read into a contract unless required by plain, unambiguous language." Can an implied license have "plain, unambiguous language"? For a further discussion of license conditions versus contractual covenants, see Section 3.4.

2. *Scope of implied license.* In *Johnson v. Jones*, 46 USPQ2d 1482 (6th Cir. 1998), the Sixth Circuit held that Johnson, an architect, did not grant an implied license for his client to alter and use his drawings. Johnson had submitted a draft contract containing the following language to his prospective client, Jones:

   The drawings, specifications and other documents furnished by the Design/Builder are instruments of service and shall not become the property of the Owner whether or not the project for which they are made is commenced. Drawings, specifications and other documents shall not be used by the Owner on other projects, additions to this project, or ... for completion of this Project by others, except by written agreement relating to use, liability and compensation.

Although Johnson began work, Jones did not sign the contract. Later, Johnson was terminated and Jones retained a different architect to complete the project. The new architect (Tosch) claimed that he had an implied license to use the drawings produced by Johnson, citing the *Effects* case. The court explained that:

> In *Effects*, defendant, a movie-maker, asked plaintiff, a special effects company, to create footage to enhance action sequences in a film defendant was making. Unhappy with the footage provided by plaintiff, defendant paid only half of the expected amount. Subsequently, defendant incorporated plaintiff's footage into the film and released the film to another company for distribution. The Effects court held that plaintiff had granted defendant an implied non-exclusive license to incorporate the footage into the film and then distribute the film.
>
> The circumstances in *Effects* differ materially from those in the present case. Almost every objective fact in the present case points away from the existence of an implied license. Johnson submitted two AIA contracts, both of which contained express provisions that he would retain ownership of his drawings, and that those drawings would not be used for completion of the Jones house by others, except by written agreement with appropriate compensation. These contractual provisions, although never signed by Jones, speak to Johnson's intent; they demonstrate that Johnson created the drawings with the understanding that he would be the architect in charge of the project. They further demonstrate that Johnson would not have allowed Tosch to finish the project using his drawings without a written agreement, and additional compensation.

How would you distinguish *Johnson* and *Shaver*, if at all? Which case do you feel better reflects the intentions of the parties?

3. *Implied rights to sublicense*. An interesting twist on the implied license doctrine has arisen in the context of tattoos. Tattoos are generally understood to comprise artistic works in which the tattoo artist obtains copyright. However, courts have also held that the individual on whom the tattoo is placed has an implied license to reproduce the tattoo, for example, in photographic images of himself or herself. The issue has become commercially significant when tattoos are visible on the bodies of celebrities such as sports figures. In *Solid Oak Sketches, LLC v. 2K Games, Inc.*, 449 F. Supp. 3d 333 (S.D.N.Y. 2020), the court found that NBA players LeBron James, Eric Bledsoe and Kenyon Martin had implied licenses to display and reproduce their tattoos (all created by the same artist) "as part of their likenesses," and that they were authorized to grant the NBA the right to license their likenesses, including the tattoos, to the producer of NBA-based video games.

Problem 4.2

Arti, a freelance graphic designer, is hired by a publisher to create the artwork for an undergraduate economics textbook. Arti produces the artwork and is paid $2,500, per their agreement, which is silent regarding copyright. Two years later, the publisher releases a second edition of the book. Because Arti is now working as a full-time employee of a rival publishing house, the publisher hires Bob to make slight revisions to the original artwork for the second edition. Two years after that, the book is ready for its third edition, and the publisher decides to modify the artwork further using its own in-house designer. Arti comes across a copy of the third edition online and realizes that the artwork has been altered without her consent. What legal remedies, if any, does Arti have against the publisher (assuming that she owns the copyright in the original artwork)?

FIGURE 4.5 NBA star LeBron James is reported to have twenty-four tat-toos, many of which were created by LA-based artist gangatattoo.

4.4 IMPLIED LICENSES IN LAW

McCoy v. Mitsuboshi Cutlery, Inc.

67 F.3d 917 (Fed. Cir. 1995)

RADER, CIRCUIT JUDGE

Duncan McCoy, Alex Dorsett, and Alex-Duncan Shrimp Chef, Inc. (McCoy) sued Mitsuboshi Cutlery, Inc. (Mitsuboshi) and Admiral Craft Equipment Corp. (Admiral Craft) for infringing McCoy's intellectual property rights and committing business torts. McCoy's sales organization had hired Mitsuboshi to make and supply shrimp knives covered by McCoy's patent and trademarks. When Mitsuboshi produced the knives, McCoy refused to pay for them. Mitsuboshi resold the knives to Admiral Craft. McCoy sought damages from Mitsuboshi and Admiral Craft for selling the knives to third parties. Admiral Craft settled with McCoy before trial.

Background

McCoy owns U.S. Patent No. 4,759,126 on a shrimp knife that peels, deveins, and butterflies in one motion. McCoy arranged for Mitsuboshi, a Japanese knife manufacturer, to produce shrimp knives embodying the patented invention. At McCoy's request, Mitsuboshi stamped the knives with McCoy's registered U.S. Trademarks Nos. 1,687,589 and 1,702,878. From 1988 to 1990, Mitsuboshi manufactured and sold large quantities of these knives to McCoy.

In 1991, McCoy's separate marketing organization, A.T.D. Marketing, Inc. (ATD), ordered 150,000 of the knives from Mitsuboshi. Mitsuboshi produced the knives. When Mitsuboshi timely offered the knives, ATD refused to accept or pay for them. ATD's refusal left Mitsuboshi holding the 150,000 knives in its warehouse in Japan. The record contains no suggestion that the knives were defective.

McCoy acknowledged its responsibility for ATD's refusal to pay. McCoy, however, accepted and paid for only about 20,000 of the 150,000 knives ordered. McCoy refused to pay for the other 130,000 knives. On the basis of these facts, the jury found that McCoy breached its contract with Mitsuboshi. McCoy did not appeal this jury verdict.

Following McCoy's partial payment, Mitsuboshi continued to negotiate for payment and delivery of the remaining 130,000 knives. McCoy, however, remained silent, unable to pay for them. In the face of this silence, Mitsuboshi repeatedly notified McCoy of its intent to resell the knives to mitigate damages. At length, Mitsuboshi sold 6,456 of the knives to Admiral Craft, a mail-order wholesaler of restaurant supplies. Admiral Craft sold 958 of the knives in the United States to restaurants and supply houses in 1993 through its mail catalog.

McCoy sued Mitsuboshi and Admiral Craft for patent and trademark infringement, unfair competition in violation of both federal and Texas law, and several Texas state law torts. Admiral Craft settled, but Mitsuboshi persevered, counterclaiming for breach of contract. At the close of evidence, Mitsuboshi moved for judgment as a matter of law that it was entitled to resell the knives. The trial court denied Mitsuboshi's motion. The jury found against Mitsuboshi on the infringement, unfair competition, and tortious interference counts, and for Mitsuboshi on the breach of contract count. Mitsuboshi then renewed its motion for judgment as a matter of law. The trial court again denied the motion. Mitsuboshi appeals.

Discussion

I.

The jury found, and McCoy does not contest, that McCoy breached its contract with Mitsuboshi. This appeal thus raises the purely legal question of the effect of McCoy's breach on his intellectual property rights in the knives. This court confronts this question for the first time.

A patent confers on its holder the right to exclude others from making, using, or selling what is described in its claims. This court has recognized that these intellectual property rights, like any other property rights, are subject to the contractual obligations of their owner and the applicable law:

> Th[e] right to exclude may be waived in whole or in part. The conditions of such waiver are subject to patent, contract, antitrust, and any other applicable law, as well as equitable considerations such as are reflected in the law of patent misuse. As in other areas of commerce, private parties may contract as they choose, provided that no law is violated thereby.

Mallinckrodt, Inc. v. Medipart, Inc., 976 F.2d 700, 703 (Fed.Cir.1992). Thus, a patent or trademark owner may contract to confer a license on another party. In most instances under contract law, a patent or trademark owner intentionally creates an express license. A licensee, of course, has an affirmative defense to a claim of patent infringement.

In some circumstances, however, the entire course of conduct between a patent or trademark owner and an accused infringer may create an implied license. The Supreme Court stated:

> Any language used by the owner of the patent or any conduct on his part exhibited to another from which that other may properly infer that the owner consents to his use of the patent in making or using it, or selling it, upon which the other acts, constitutes a license and a defense to an action ...

U.S. Pat. 4,759,126

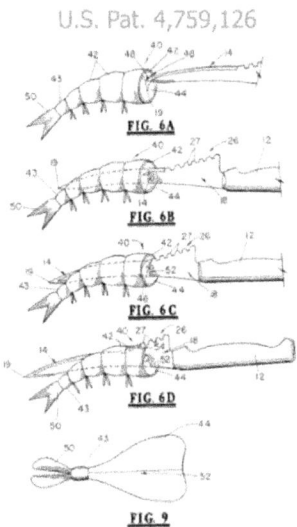

"Alex Duncan" Shrimp Chef knife

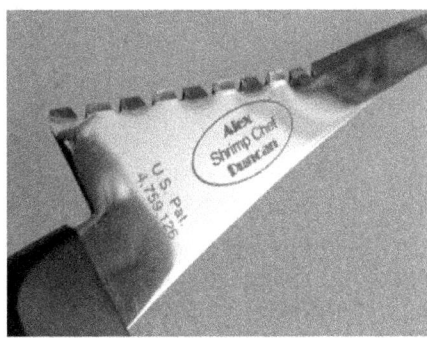

FIGURE 4.6 The patented shrimp knife and deveiner at issue in *McCoy*.

De Forest Radio Tel. Co. v. United States, 273 U.S. 236, 241 (1927). When warranted by such a course of conduct, the law implies a license.

Whether express or implied, a license is a contract "governed by ordinary principles of state contract law." Moreover the law may imply licenses "to make effective the contracts of the patentee." An implied license, however, must not exceed the limits necessary to make the contract effective.

To enforce the contracts of the patentee, the law may imply a license where a patent holder sells or authorizes the sale of a patented product – a voluntary sale. Thus, "an authorized sale of a patented product places that product beyond the reach of the patent." Under this implied license, a patent holder receives a reward for inventive work in the first sale of the patented product. As the Supreme Court stated:

> Patentees ... are entitled to but one royalty for the patented machine, and consequently when a patentee has himself constructed the machine and sold it, or authorized another to construct and sell it, or to construct and use and operate it, and the consideration has been paid to him for the right, he has then to that extent parted with his monopoly, and ceased to have any interest whatever in the machine so sold or so authorized to be constructed and operated.

Bloomer v. Millinger, 68 U.S. (1 Wall.) 340, 350 (1863).

In some cases, the law implies a license where a patent holder does not authorize the sale of a patented product – an involuntary sale. *See, e.g., Wilder v. Kent*, 15 F. 217, 219 (C.C.W.D.Pa.1883). For example, in *Wilder*, the patent holder sued an individual for infringement who purchased a machine at a sheriff's sale. The court dismissed the complaint finding the purchaser had acquired the right to use the patented machine through the purchase at the sheriff's sale. The court reasoned: "To deny to the sheriff's vendee the right to use such machine would in effect prevent its sale upon an execution at law ... and practically withdraw it from the reach of the owner's execution creditors." While appreciating the unique nature of patent rights, the court noted that "a patented machine is susceptible of manual seizure, and the unrestricted sale thereof does not involve the transfer of any interest in the patent."

Justice Story [in *Sawin v. Guild*, 21 F.Cas. 554, 554–55 (C.C.D.Mass.1813)] reasoned that statutes must be construed where possible to avoid introducing "public mischiefs, or manifest incongruities." Justice Story felt a great public mischief would result if courts construed the patent laws to permit an action against a sheriff for selling a patented product at a sheriff's sale.

More recently, in an opinion authored by Judge Friendly, the United States Court of Appeals for the Second Circuit expressly recognized and extended this implied license doctrine to the sale of products by an aggrieved seller to remedy a buyer's breach. *Platt & Munk Co. v. Republic Graphics, Inc.*, 315 F.2d 847 (2d Cir.1963). Platt & Munk owned copyrights on educational toys and contracted with Republic to supply them. After Republic began delivery, Platt & Munk alleged various defects and refused to pay for the balance of the toys. Republic then informed Platt & Munk of its intent to resell the toys to recover its production costs. Platt & Munk responded by seeking an injunction prohibiting Republic from reselling the toys without Platt & Munk's consent. The trial court granted a preliminary injunction without addressing whether the toys were actually defective or whether Platt & Munk had the right to refuse payment. Republic filed an interlocutory appeal.

The Second Circuit remanded to the trial court to determine whether Platt & Munk justifiably refused to pay for the toys. If not, it instructed the trial court to lift the injunction. In other words, if Platt & Munk breached the contract, Republic had a right to resell the toys notwithstanding any copyright protection. The Second Circuit based its holding on New York contract law, which provided a seller of goods the right to mitigate damages for contract breaches. Where Platt & Munk breached, the Second Circuit found that Platt & Munk's copyrights had no effect on Republic's state law right to resell:

> We see no reason why the copyrighted character of the goods should preclude [resale] when – and the qualification is vital – the person for whom the goods were being made unjustifiably refuses to pay the price.

Platt, 315 F.2d at 855.

This ruling extended the implied license doctrine beyond sales under judicial decree to sales under self-help provisions in commercial law. Together, [these cases] demonstrate that the law may create an implied license to enforce the contract obligations of the patent holder and recognize legal rights of aggrieved parties … Absent an implied license in either case, patent holders could frustrate otherwise available commercial remedies.

Here, McCoy and Mitsuboshi had a long-standing business relationship whereby Mitsuboshi manufactured McCoy's patented knives. In 1991, McCoy placed a purchase order for 150,000 knives with Mitsuboshi. Mitsuboshi, in turn, accepted the order and performed its obligations under that agreement. When it tendered the knives to McCoy, McCoy breached the contract by failing to pay. At that point, rather than immediately act, Mitsuboshi continued to negotiate with McCoy in an effort to secure payment and deliver the knives. After repeated failed attempts, Mitsuboshi sold some of the knives to an American company.

The applicable state contract law in this case is Texas's version of the Uniform Commercial Code. Because this case involves the sale of goods, the Texas UCC entitles the seller to resell the goods upon the buyer's wrongful refusal to pay. Consequently, under Texas contract law, when McCoy breached the contract, Mitsuboshi had a right to resell the knives to recoup its losses without McCoy's consent.

As in *Platt*, an implied license properly enforces McCoy's contractual promise to pay for the knives, reflects Mitsuboshi's commercial efforts to resolve the matter, and recognizes Mitsuboshi's rights to mitigate under the Texas UCC. This court, like our sister circuit in *Platt*, sees no reason why the owner of intellectual property rights deserves to evade application of the ordinary contract remedy of resale for an unjustified refusal to pay.

This implied license does not offend the protection afforded patent and trademark rights by federal law. Instead, licenses, like other federal property and contract rights, conform to the applicable state laws. As this court observed in *Power Lift*, the Supreme Court has held that federal patent law does not preempt enforcement of contracts under state law. By the same reasoning, federal trademark law does not preempt contract enforcement either. Intellectual property owners "may contract as they choose," but their intellectual property rights do not entitle them to escape the consequences of dishonoring state contractual obligations.

Notes and Questions

1. *Public mischiefs and manifest incongruities.* Judge Rader's reasons for recognizing an implied license in *Mitsuboshi* are somewhat unclear. He first references *Bloomer v. Millinger* and *Wilder v. Kent*, two obscure nineteenth-century cases that relate to the creation of an implied license accompanying sale of patented products, a doctrine that today has largely been subsumed by the doctrine of patent exhaustion (see Chapter 23). He next cites the even older case of *Sawin v. Guild*, in which Justice Story justified the recognition of an implied license so as to avoid "public mischiefs" and "manifest incongruities," a sort of public interest analysis that never gained significant purchase in patent law.[8] Finally, Judge Rader leaps forward by more than a century to *Platt & Munk*, in which the Second Circuit held that New York contract law concerning the mitigation of damages preempted any right that the holder of a copyright might have to prevent the resale of copyrighted toys. Which of these prior cases is most relevant to the facts in *Mitsuboshi*? Why do you think that Judge Rader felt the need to ground his decision in nineteenth-century decisions such as *Bloomer*, *Wilder* and *Sawin*?

2. *Implied in fact or implied in law?* There are two general species of implied license: those that are implied in fact and those that are implied in law. As explained by Professor Annemarie Bridy,

   The existence of a license … implied in fact … is inferred from objective indicia that the work's creator assented to and intended the defendant's use of the work. In order to prove an implied-in-fact license, the defendant must make a showing of permissive intent on the rights holder's part.[9]

   A license implied in law, on the other hand, arises solely through operation of law, without reference to the contracting intentions of the parties:

   To prove the existence of an implied-in-law contract (or quasi-contract), there is no need for the proponent to prove that her counterparty had contractual intent. Rather, the court imposes a contractual duty on the counterparty in order to prevent injustice to the proponent. The theory is equitable and nonpromissory, resting on the principle that one party should not be unjustly enriched at the expense of another.[10]

---

[8] Justice Story is famous for introducing moralistic elements into his patent law decisions, most notably the "moral utility" doctrine. *See Bedford v. Hunt*, 3 F. Cas. 37, 37 (C.C.D. Mass. 1817) (Story, J.) (the utility requirement of patent law "simply requires, that [an invention] shall be capable of use, and that the use is such as sound morals and policy do not discountenance or prohibit").

[9] Annemarie Bridy, A Novel Theory of Implied Copyright License in Paparazzi Pics, Law360, August 6, 2010.

[10] Id.

Applying this classification scheme, how would you characterize the implied licenses in *Nadel, Wrench, Shaver* and *Mitsuboshi?*

3. *Later-issued patents.* In *TransCore, LP v. Elec. Transaction Consultants Corp.,* 563 F.3d 1271 (Fed. Cir. 2009), TransCore, the holder of patents covering the E-ZPass automatic toll-collection device, settled patent litigation with Mark IV Industries, a competing manufacturer. Under the settlement agreement, TransCore granted Mark IV a license under three issued patents. Several years later, Mark IV brought suit against ETC, an installer of toll-collection devices sold by Mark IV, under a number of patents, including a newly issued patent (the '946 patent, a "continuation" of one of the licensed patents) that covered the subject matter of the patents licensed to Mark IV. Because the '946 patent had not issued at the time of TransCore's settlement with Mark IV, it was not included in the settlement agreement. Mark IV argued, however, that it had an implied license under the '946 patent. The Federal Circuit agreed, noting that the '946 patent "was broader than, and necessary to practice, at least the '082 patent that was included in the TransCore–Mark IV settlement agreement."

[T]he district court properly concluded that in order for Mark IV to obtain the benefit of its bargain with TransCore, it must be permitted to practice the '946 patent to the same extent it may practice the '183, '275 and '082 patents. TransCore is, therefore, legally estopped from asserting the '946 patent against Mark IV in derogation of the authorizations granted to Mark IV under the '183, '275 and '082 patents. And Mark IV is, in turn, an implied licensee of the '946 patent.

Why does the court find such an implied license? What injustice would be done if no implied license were recognized?

4. *No implied rights clauses?* What if the parties to a licensing agreement, such as the ones in *Mitsuboshi* or *TransCore,* agreed to a contractual clause excluding any implied licenses? Can a court still recognize an implied license? The answer seems to be yes. In *TransCore,* the TransCore–Mark IV settlement agreement contained the following language: "No express or implied license or future release whatsoever is granted to MARK IV or to any third party," 563 F.3d at 1272. In addition, the parties made sure, they thought, that the license granted under the three specified patents would not be expanded to include future patents, agreeing, "This Covenant Not To Sue shall not apply to any other patents issued as of the effective date of this Agreement or to be issued in the future." So how did the court find an implied license that applied to a patent "issued in the future"? It reasoned that not recognizing an implied license to the '946 patent would "permit TransCore to derogate from the rights it has expressly granted" – in effect selling a right, then taking back part of what it has sold.

   The Federal Circuit cabined the reasoning of *TransCore* in *Endo Pharms., Inc. v. Actavis, Inc.,* 746 F.3d 1371 (Fed. Cir. 2014), another case involving a license and a later-issued patent. As in *TransCore,* the license agreement in *Actavis* contained a "No Implied Rights" clause. But this time the Federal Circuit gave more weight to the clause, as well as the fact that the newly issued patent in *Endo* was not a continuation of one of the licensed patents, as it was in *TransCore.* It held that "The lack of a continuation relationship between any of the asserted and licensed patents and explicit disclaimer of any other licenses not within the literal terms of the contract are dispositive," 746 F.3d at 1378. What do you make of this distinction? Does it matter that the court in *TransCore* made little of the fact that the '946 patent arose from a continuation application? Should this really be the dispositive factor in implied license cases?

FIGURE 4.7 The dispute in *TransCore v. Elec. Transaction Consultants* involved patents covering E-ZPass electronic tollbooth devices.

5. *Scope of implied license.* Once an implied license is recognized, what is its scope? The court in *TransCore* held that "Mark IV's rights under its implied license to the '946 patent are necessarily coextensive with the rights it received in the TransCore–Mark IV license agreement," 563 F.3d at 1279–80. Why is this scope appropriate? What happens to the implied license when the originally licensed patents expire?

   In the copyright cases discussed in Section 4.3, Note 2, the result is less clear. Which approach is the better one? Should the basis on which an implied license is found affect the scope of the implied license?

6. *An implied license in oneself?* In recent years, celebrities, including Gigi Hadid and Khloe Kardashian, have been sued for copyright infringement when they have publicly posted photographs of themselves taken by paparazzi. In these suits, the paparazzi claim that the celebrities are infringing their (the paparazzi) copyrights in the photographs, as the copyright in a photograph is held by the photographer, even if it was taken without the permission of the celebrity. Professor Annemarie Bridy has argued that celebrities like Hadid should have a license implied in law to post photographs of themselves on social media:

   Paparazzi photography is the product of a culture that worships and commoditizes glamour and celebrity. It is, at its base, a form of celebrity exploitation. The value of a paparazzi photo derives less from the photographer's creative choices, which copyright is designed to protect, than from the celebrity of its subject, which is not copyright's concern. In paparazzi photos, the photographer's creative rights and the subject's publicity rights are entangled. Equity suggests that the primary source of a paparazzi photo's value, its famous subject, should be entitled to share in that value to some extent.

Hadid's contributions to the photo's aesthetic and commercial value seem on par with – if they don't actually exceed – the photographer's own contributions in this particular case. Yet the photographer sought to extract damages from Hadid for her limited use of the photo on her own Instagram account. To deny Hadid a limited implied license to use the photo at issue in the suit would arguably be unjust, considering both the significance of her contribution to its value and the fundamentally exploitive nature of paparazzi photography.[11]

Do you agree with Professor Bridy's theory? How are unauthorized celebrity photographs similar to McCoy's shrimp peelers?

---

[11] Id.

5

Confidentiality and Pre-license Negotiations

Before a commercial agreement of any significance is entered, the parties generally engage in discussions and negotiations. Depending on the size and complexity of the transaction, negotiations can sometimes take weeks, months or even years to complete. Often, the parties will exchange one or more pre-transaction documents that set the stage for the negotiations and a framework for the final, or "definitive" agreement(s). This chapter considers several of the most common forms of such preliminary documents: (1) invitations to license, (2) confidentiality and nondisclosure agreements and (3) term sheets, letters of intent and memoranda of understanding.

5.1 INITIAL OVERTURES AND DECLARATORY JUDGMENTS

Often, licensing and other transactions are effected between parties that know one another through their respective employees or consultants or their reputations in the market. In these cases, the discussions leading to a transaction can be initiated through a simple phone call, email message or meeting. But in other cases, the parties may not have a pre-existing relationship and will need to query potential business partners "cold." For example, a neophyte author will generally send out dozens or hundreds of query letters to publishers and literary agents before finding one who is interested in her great American novel. This process for authors, journalists, toy designers, visual artists, film makers, freelance photographers and other holders of copyrights can be time consuming and frustrating, but generally not fraught with legal issues.

The situation is somewhat different, however, when patents are involved. As discussed in Chapter 1, an individual who invents a new type of widget may not have the resources, expertise or business network to embark on full-scale production and marketing of the device. Likewise, the widget may simply be one component of a more complex product such as a smartphone, automobile or geosynchronous satellite that is manufactured by other, much larger, companies. In all of these cases, the inventor may need to approach different market players about potential licensing arrangements.

But how will a large company react to a licensing overture by an inventor who holds a patent that is potentially relevant to some aspect of its business? In the best case, the company will invite the inventor to discuss the proposal, which may eventually lead to an agreement. Less good, but far more common, the large company may ignore the inventor's unsolicited proposal. But most risky for the inventor, the company, once it is alerted to the existence of his patent, might view it as a potential threat. If that is the case, the company could seek to challenge the patent preemptively by bringing a *declaratory judgment action* against the inventor seeking to invalidate the patent.[1]

In a case of actual controversy … any court of the United States … may declare the rights and other legal relations of any interested party seeking such a declaration.

Thus, when there is an "actual controversy," a party may avail itself of the Act by seeking a declaration of its rights in federal court. For example, if the holder of an intellectual property right threatens to sue a party for infringement of that right, the threatened party may seek a declaration either that it does not infringe or that the asserted right is invalid or unenforceable.

In *MedImmune, Inc. v. Genentech, Inc.*, 549 U.S. 118 (2007), the Supreme Court established the current standard for assessing the existence of an "actual controversy" in IP cases:

> Whether the facts alleged, under all circumstances, show that there is a substantial controversy between parties having adverse legal interests of sufficient immediacy and reality to warrant the issuance of a declaratory judgment.[2]

The Federal Circuit's most extensive analysis of declaratory judgment jurisdiction in patent licensing cases can be found in *SanDisk Corp. v. STMicroelectronics, Inc.*, decided two months after the Supreme Court's decision in *MedImmune*.

Sandisk Corp. v. STMicroelectronics, Inc.

480 F.3d 1372 (Fed. Cir. 2007)

LINN, CIRCUIT JUDGE

SanDisk Corporation ("SanDisk") appeals from a decision of the U.S. District Court for the Northern District of California granting STMicroelectronics' ("ST's") motion to dismiss SanDisk's … claims relating to declaratory judgment of noninfringement and invalidity for failure to present an actual controversy. Because the district court erred in dismissing the declaratory judgment claims for lack of subject matter jurisdiction, we vacate the judgment and remand the case to the district court.

I. Background

SanDisk is in the flash memory storage market and owns several patents related to flash memory storage products. ST, traditionally in the market of semiconductor integrated

---

[1] Patents may be invalidated on a variety of grounds, including anticipation, obviousness, non-enablement, unclean hands and others. A patent that has been invalidated can no longer be enforced by its owner.

[2] Discussed in greater detail in Section 22.3.

circuits, more recently entered the flash memory market and has a sizeable portfolio of patents related to flash memory storage products. On April 16, 2004, ST's vice president of intellectual property and licensing, Lisa Jorgenson ("Jorgenson"), sent a letter to SanDisk's chief executive officer requesting a meeting to discuss a cross-license agreement. The letter listed eight patents owned by ST that Jorgenson believed "may be of interest" to SanDisk. On April 28, 2004, SanDisk responded that it would need time to review the listed patents and would be in touch in several weeks to discuss the possibility of meeting in June.

On July 12, 2004, having heard nothing further from SanDisk, Jorgenson sent a letter to SanDisk reiterating her request to meet in July to discuss a cross-license agreement and listing four additional ST patents that "may also be of interest" to SanDisk. On July 21, 2004, SanDisk's chief intellectual property counsel and senior director, E. Earle Thompson ("Thompson"), responded to ST's letter by informing Jorgenson of his "understanding that both sides wish to continue … friendly discussions" such as those between the business representatives in May and June. The discussions of May and June that Thompson referred to were discussions among managers and vice presidents of SanDisk and ST at business meetings held on May 18, 2004, and June 9, 2004, to explore the possibility of ST's selling flash memory products to SanDisk. The business meetings were unrelated to any patents.

On August 5, 2004, when the business representatives next met, SanDisk presented an analysis of three of its patents and orally offered ST a license. ST declined to present an analysis of any of its patents, stating instead that any patent and licensing issues should be discussed in a separate meeting with Jorgenson. Later that same day, Thompson wrote a letter to Jorgenson objecting to separating business and intellectual property issues and stating that "[i]t has been SanDisk's hope and desire to enter into a mutually beneficial discussion without the rattling of sabers." On August 11, 2004, Jorgenson replied, stating that it was her understanding that the parties were going to have a licensing/intellectual property meeting later that month "to discuss the possibility for a patent cross-license." She said that SanDisk should come to that meeting prepared to present an analysis of the three SanDisk patents it identified during the August 5th business meeting, as well as "any infringement analyses of an ST device or need for ST to have a license to these patents." She also said that ST would be prepared at that meeting to discuss the twelve patents identified in her prior letters. In closing, Jorgenson said that ST was "look[ing] forward to open and frank discussions with SanDisk concerning fair and reasonable terms for a broad cross-license agreement."

On August 27, 2004, the licensing meeting was held. Jorgenson, two ST licensing attorneys, and three technical experts retained by ST to perform the infringement analyses of SanDisk's products, attended on behalf of ST. Thompson and an engineer attended on behalf of SanDisk. At the meeting, Jorgenson requested that the parties' discussions be treated as "settlement discussions" under Federal Rule of Evidence 408. ST then presented a slide show which compared statistics regarding SanDisk's and ST's patent portfolios, revenue, and research and development expenses, and listed SanDisk's various "unlicensed activities." This slide show was followed by a four- to five-hour presentation by ST's technical experts, during which they identified and discussed the specific claims of each patent and alleged that they were infringed by SanDisk. According to Thompson, the presentation by ST's technical experts included "mapp[ing] the elements of each of the allegedly infringed claims to the aspects of the accused SanDisk products alleged to practice the elements." Thompson declares that "the experts liberally referred to SanDisk's (alleged) infringement of [ST's] products." SanDisk's engineer then made a presentation, describing several of SanDisk's patents and analyzing how a semiconductor chip product sold by ST infringes.

At the end of the meeting, Jorgenson handed Thompson a packet of materials containing, for each of ST's fourteen patents under discussion, a copy of the patent, reverse engineering reports for certain of SanDisk's products, and diagrams showing how elements of ST's patent claims cover SanDisk's products. According to SanDisk, Jorgenson indicated (in words to this effect):

> I know that this is material that would allow SanDisk to DJ [ST] on. We have had some internal discussions on whether I should be giving you a copy of these materials in light of that fact. But I have decided that I will go ahead and give you these materials.

Jorgenson further told Thompson that "ST has absolutely no plan whatsoever to sue SanDisk." Thompson responded to Jorgenson that "SanDisk is not going to sue you on Monday" and that another meeting might be appropriate.

On September 1, 2004, Jorgenson wrote to Thompson, enclosing copies of ST's general slide presentation from the August meeting and also enclosing a hard copy booklet containing each of the engineering reports "for each claim on all products where ST demonstrated coverage by the 14 ST patents to-date [sic]." Jorgenson requested that SanDisk provide ST with a copy of SanDisk's presentation and information about the three SanDisk patents presented. On September 8, 2004, Thompson replied by e-mail, confirming receipt of the package from ST, attaching a copy of SanDisk's presentation, indicating it was his "personal feeling … that we have got to trust one another during these negotiations," and seeking a non-disclosure agreement. Thompson also wrote "I still owe you the rates quoted."

On October 15, 2004, after several further e-mails and phone calls between the business representatives trying to establish another meeting, SanDisk filed the instant lawsuit. SanDisk alleged infringement of one of its patents and sought a declaratory judgment of noninfringement and invalidity of the fourteen ST patents that had been discussed during the cross-licensing negotiations. On December 3, 2004, ST filed a motion to dismiss

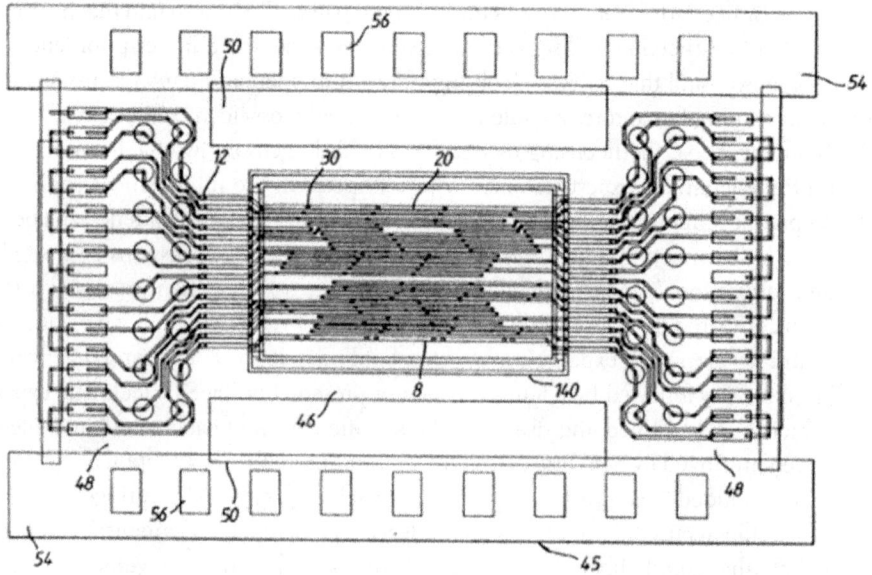

FIGURE 5.1 Figure from US Patent No. 5,073,816, "Packaging semiconductor chips," which ST claimed that SanDisk infringed.

SanDisk's declaratory judgment claims for lack of subject matter jurisdiction, maintaining that there was no actual controversy at the time SanDisk filed its complaint.

The district court granted ST's motion to dismiss, holding that no actual controversy existed for purposes of the Declaratory Judgment Act because SanDisk did not have an objectively reasonable apprehension of suit, even though it may have subjectively believed that ST would bring an infringement suit. The district court reasoned that "SanDisk has presented no evidence that ST threatened it with litigation at any time during the parties' negotiations, nor has SanDisk shown other conduct by ST rising to a level sufficient to indicate an intent on the part of ST to initiate an infringement action." The district court found that the studied and determined infringement analyses that ST presented to SanDisk did not constitute the requisite "express charges [of infringement] carrying with them the threat of enforcement." The district court also found that the totality of the circumstances did not evince an actual controversy because ST told SanDisk that it did not intend to sue SanDisk for infringement. In a footnote, the court indicated that, as an alternative basis for its ruling, even if it did have jurisdiction, it would exercise its discretion and decline to hear the case.

SanDisk appealed the dismissal to this court.

II. Discussion

SanDisk argues that the district court erred as a matter of law by requiring an express accusation of patent infringement coupled with an explicit threat of judicial enforcement to support declaratory judgment jurisdiction, and that, under the correct legal standard articulated by this court in *Arrowhead*, the facts of this case illustrate that SanDisk's apprehension of an infringement suit was objectively reasonable. SanDisk asserts that the infringement analysis presented by ST and its experts at the August 27, 2004 licensing meeting constituted an allegation of infringement and that the totality of the circumstances shows that ST's conduct gave rise to an actual case or controversy. SanDisk further points out that negotiations regarding licensing had ceased by the time SanDisk filed its claims for declaratory judgment.

ST counters that the district court applied the correct legal standard and argues that SanDisk ignores the line of cases that have followed and interpreted [*Arrowhead Indus. Water, Inc. v. Ecolochem, Inc.*, 846 F.2d 731 (Fed. Cir. 1988)]. ST asserts that the cases following *Arrowhead* reveal that the bare mention of infringement, particularly during license negotiations, is not sufficient to meet the standard set forth in *Arrowhead*. ST asserts that its conduct at the August 27, 2004 licensing meeting was to strengthen its position during licensing negotiations and that, under the totality of the circumstances, SanDisk has not shown that ST's conduct gave rise to declaratory judgment jurisdiction ...

1. Case or Controversy

The first question we address is whether the facts alleged in this case show that there is a case or controversy within the meaning of the Declaratory Judgment Act, 28 U.S.C. § 2201(a).

The Declaratory Judgment Act provides, in relevant part, that

[i]n a case of actual controversy within its jurisdiction ... any court of the United States, upon the filing of an appropriate pleading, may declare the rights and other legal relations of any interested party seeking such declaration, whether or not further relief is or could be sought.

The "actual controversy" requirement of the Declaratory Judgment Act is rooted in Article III of the Constitution, which provides for federal jurisdiction over only "cases and controversies." Thus, our jurisdiction extends only to matters that are Article III cases or controversies.

The Supreme Court, in the context of a patent license dispute, recently examined Article III's case or controversy requirement as it relates to the Declaratory Judgment Act. See *MedImmune, Inc. v. Genentech, Inc.*, 549 U.S. 118 (2007). In *MedImmune*, the Supreme Court considered "whether Article III's limitation of federal courts' jurisdiction to 'Cases' and 'Controversies,' reflected in the 'actual controversy' requirement of the Declaratory Judgment Act requires a patent licensee to terminate or be in breach of its license agreement before it can seek a declaratory judgment that the underlying patent is invalid, unenforceable, or not infringed."

The Supreme Court began its analysis

with the recognition that, where threatened action by government is concerned, [the Court] do[es] not require a plaintiff to expose himself to liability before bringing suit to challenge the basis for the threat—for example, the constitutionality of a law threatened to be enforced. The plaintiff's own action (or inaction) in failing to violate the law eliminates the imminent threat of prosecution, but nonetheless does not eliminate Article III jurisdiction.

The Supreme Court quoted its earlier decision in *Maryland Casualty Co. v. Pacific Coal & Oil Co.*, 312 U.S. 270, 273 (1941), where the Court stated that "the question in each case is whether the facts alleged, under all the circumstances, show that there is a substantial controversy, between parties having adverse legal interests, of sufficient immediacy and reality to warrant the issuance of a declaratory judgment." The Supreme Court emphasized that Article III requires that the dispute at issue be "'definite and concrete, touching the legal relations of parties having adverse legal interests'; and that it be 'real and substantial' and 'admi[t]' of specific relief through a decree of a conclusive character, as distinguished from an opinion advising what the law would be upon a hypothetical state of facts.'" *Id.* The Supreme Court stated that, when faced with a genuine threat of enforcement that the government will penalize a certain private action, Article III "d[oes] not require, as a prerequisite to testing the validity of the law in a suit for injunction, that the plaintiff bet the farm, so to speak, by taking the violative action." As the Supreme Court noted, "the declaratory judgment procedure is an alternative to pursuit of the arguably illegal activity." The Supreme Court clarified that, although a declaratory judgment plaintiff may eliminate an "imminent threat of harm by simply not doing what he claimed the right to do[,] ... [t]hat did not preclude subject-matter jurisdiction [where] the threat-eliminating behavior was effectively coerced." *Id.* "The dilemma posed by that coercion—putting the challenger to the choice between abandoning his rights or risking prosecution—is a dilemma that it was the very purpose of the Declaratory Judgment Act to ameliorate."

The Supreme Court then applied these principles to the facts of the case and remarked that "the requirements of [a] case or controversy are met where payment of a claim is demanded as of right and where payment is made, but where the involuntary or coercive nature of the exaction preserves the right to recover the sums paid or to challenge the legality of the claim." *Id.* The Supreme Court held that "[t]he rule that a plaintiff must destroy a large building, bet the farm, or (as here) risk treble damages and the loss of 80 percent of its business, before seeking a declaration of its actively contested legal rights finds no support in Article III."

With regard to patent disputes, prior to *MedImmune*, this court articulated a two-part test that first considers whether conduct by the patentee creates a reasonable apprehension on the part of the declaratory judgment plaintiff that it will face an infringement suit, and second examines whether conduct by the declaratory judgment plaintiff amounts to infringing activity or demonstrates concrete steps taken with the intent to conduct such activity. See *Arrowhead*, 846 F.2d at 736.

The Supreme Court's opinion in *MedImmune* represents a rejection of our reasonable apprehension of suit test. The Court first noted that "the continuation of royalty payments makes what would otherwise be an imminent threat at least remote, if not nonexistent … Petitioner's own acts, in other words, eliminate the imminent threat of harm." The Court nonetheless concluded that declaratory judgment jurisdiction existed relying in particular on its earlier decision in *Altvater v. Freeman*, 319 U.S. 359 (1943). There, the patentee brought suit to enjoin patent infringement, and the accused infringer filed declaratory judgment counterclaims of invalidity. The district court found that there was no infringement and that the patent was invalid. The appellate court affirmed the finding of noninfringement but vacated the finding of invalidity as moot. The Supreme Court held that the declaratory judgment counterclaims were not mooted by the finding of noninfringement. In finding declaratory judgment jurisdiction in *MedImmune*, the Court specifically addressed and rejected our reasonable apprehension test:

> [e]ven if *Altvater* could be distinguished as an "injunction" case, it would still contradict the Federal Circuit's "reasonable apprehension of suit" test. A licensee who pays royalties under compulsion of an injunction has no more apprehension of imminent harm than a licensee who pays royalties for fear of treble damages and an injunction fatal to his business. The reasonable-apprehension-of-suit test also conflicts with our decisions in *Maryland Casualty*, where jurisdiction obtained even though the collision-victim defendant could not have sued the declaratory-judgment plaintiff-insurer without first obtaining a judgment against the insured; and *Aetna Life Ins. Co. v. Haworth*, 300 U.S. 227, 239 (1937), where jurisdiction obtained even though the very reason the insurer sought declaratory relief was that the insured had given no indication that he would file suit. It is also in tension with *Cardinal Chemical Co. v. Morton Int'l, Inc.*, 508 U.S. 83, 98 (1993), which held that appellate affirmance of a judgment of noninfringement, eliminating any apprehension of suit, does not moot a declaratory judgment counterclaim of patent invalidity.
>
> *MedImmune*, 127 S. Ct. at 774 n.11.

The Supreme Court in *MedImmune* addressed declaratory judgment jurisdiction in the context of a signed license. In the context of conduct prior to the existence of a license, declaratory judgment jurisdiction generally will not arise merely on the basis that a party learns of the existence of a patent owned by another or even perceives such a patent to pose a risk of infringement, without some affirmative act by the patentee. But Article III jurisdiction may be met where the patentee takes a position that puts the declaratory judgment plaintiff in the position of either pursuing arguably illegal behavior or abandoning that which he claims a right to do. We need not define the outer boundaries of declaratory judgment jurisdiction, which will depend on the application of the principles of declaratory judgment jurisdiction to the facts and circumstances of each case. We hold only that where a patentee asserts rights under a patent based on certain identified ongoing or planned activity of another party, and where that party contends that it has the right to engage in the accused activity without license, an Article III case or controversy will arise and the party need not risk a suit for infringement by engaging in the identified activity before seeking a declaration of its legal rights.

...

Under the facts alleged in this case, SanDisk has established an Article III case or controversy that gives rise to declaratory judgment jurisdiction. ST sought a right to a royalty under its patents based on specific, identified activity by SanDisk. For example, at the August 27, 2004 licensing meeting, ST presented, as part of the "license negotiations," a thorough infringement analysis presented by seasoned litigation experts, detailing that one or more claims of its patents read on one or more of SanDisk's identified products. At that meeting, ST presented SanDisk with a detailed presentation which identified, on an element-by-element basis, the manner in which ST believed each of SanDisk's products infringed the specific claims of each of ST's patents. During discussions, the experts liberally referred to SanDisk's present, ongoing infringement of ST's patents and the need for SanDisk to license those patents. ST also gave SanDisk a packet of materials, over 300 pages in length, containing, for each of ST's fourteen patents under discussion, a copy of the patent, reverse engineering reports for certain of SanDisk's products, and diagrams showing a detailed infringement analysis of SanDisk's products. ST communicated to SanDisk that it had made a studied and determined infringement determination and asserted the right to a royalty based on this determination. SanDisk, on the other hand, maintained that it could proceed in its conduct without the payment of royalties to ST. These facts evince that the conditions of creating a substantial controversy, between parties having adverse legal interest, of sufficient immediacy and reality to warrant the issuance of a declaratory judgment were fulfilled. SanDisk need not "bet the farm," so to speak, and risk a suit for infringement by cutting off licensing discussions and continuing in the identified activity before seeking a declaration of its legal rights.

2. Promise Not to Sue

We next address whether Jorgenson's direct and unequivocal statement that "ST has absolutely no plan whatsoever to sue SanDisk" eliminates any actual controversy and renders SanDisk's declaratory judgment claims moot.

We decline to hold that Jorgenson's statement that ST would not sue SanDisk eliminates the justiciable controversy created by ST's actions, because ST has engaged in a course of conduct that shows a preparedness and willingness to enforce its patent rights despite Jorgenson's statement. Having approached SanDisk, having made a studied and considered determination of infringement by SanDisk, having communicated that determination to SanDisk, and then saying that it does not intend to sue, ST is engaging in the kinds of "extra-judicial patent enforcement with scare-the-customer-and-run tactics" that the Declaratory Judgment Act was intended to obviate. ST's statement that it does not intend to sue does not moot the actual controversy created by its acts.

Conclusion

For the above reasons, we conclude that the dismissal was improperly granted. The dismissal is vacated, and the case is remanded for further proceedings consistent with this opinion.

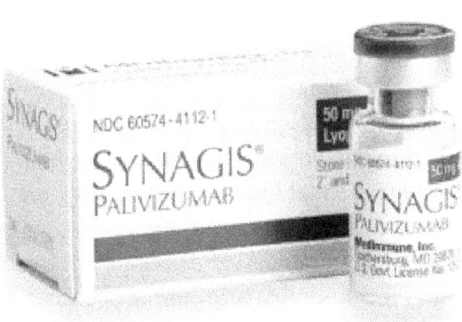

FIGURE 5.2 The dispute in *MedImmune v. Genentech* involved a Genentech patent claiming antibody technology. Because MedImmune's allegedly infringing drug Synagis generated 80 percent of its revenue, MedImmune accepted a license from Genentech and paid royalties "under protest," then sought to invalidate the patent.

Notes and Questions

1. *Declaratory judgment actions.* Why would a potential licensee bring a declaratory judgment action seeking to invalidate a patent offered to it for license? If the potential licensee does not wish to enter into a license, why not simply wait until the patent holder sues for infringement, and then raise any available defenses of invalidity?

2. *FRE 408 settlement negotiations.* Federal Rule of Evidence 408 states that:

   Evidence of the following is not admissible – on behalf of any party – either to prove or disprove the validity or amount of a disputed claim or to impeach by a prior inconsistent statement or a contradiction:
   (1) furnishing, promising, or offering – or accepting, promising to accept, or offering to accept – a valuable consideration in compromising or attempting to compromise the claim; and
   (2) conduct or a statement made during compromise negotiations about the claim – except when offered in a criminal case and when the negotiations related to a claim by a public office in the exercise of its regulatory, investigative, or enforcement authority.

   In *SanDisk*, the parties seemingly agreed to conduct their August 27 meeting under FRE 408. What is the significance of this decision? Why should it be relevant to declaratory judgment jurisdiction?

3. *No reasonable apprehension of suit.* In *MedImmune*, the Supreme Court explicitly rejected the Federal Circuit's "reasonable apprehension of suit" test for declaratory judgment jurisdiction. How do you think SanDisk's action would have fared under that test? Is ST's representation that it had no intention to sue still relevant under *MedImmune*?

4. *MedImmune's impact.* In his concurring opinion in *SanDisk*, Judge Bryson predicted that the Supreme Court's decision in *MedImmune*, which the Federal Circuit was bound to follow, would cause "a sweeping change in our law regarding declaratory judgment jurisdiction." Why? Do you think that such a sweeping change was justified? Would Judge Bryson, as the majority suggests, require SanDisk to "bet the farm" before bringing a declaratory judgment action? What impact is *MedImmune* likely to have on licensing negotiations?

5. *Patent applications.* In addition to issued patents, licenses are often granted with respect to patent applications (see Section 6.1). How might the presence of patent applications in a portfolio offered for license affect the declaratory judgment analysis under *MedImmune* and *SanDisk*? What other risks might exist for a potential licensor in offering patent applications for license?

6. *Invitations to license.* Following the decisions in *MedImmune* and *SanDisk*, patent holders must thread a particularly thin needle when approaching potential licensees. If they are too aggressive in arguing that the potential licensee is infringing, they may trigger a declaratory judgment action by the potential licensee in the court of its choice. If, on the other hand, they are too vague regarding the scope of their patents and the potential infringement, they may not persuade potential licensees that a license is necessary. Compare the two models of licensing "inquiry letters" below and consider what approach you might advise a client to use in crafting a licensing invitation that is not likely to lead the potential licensee to bring a declaratory judgment action.

Letter A is a traditional pre-*MedImmune* licensing invitation. But is the patentee better off with the informal and nonspecific approach in Letter B?

LICENSE INQUIRY LETTER A: DIRECT APPROACH

To: Company CEO
From: General Counsel, Patentee
  You are hereby notified that Company's XYZ product infringes U.S. Patent No. x,xxx,xxx owned by Patentee. Unless you return a signed copy of the attached license agreement to Patentee within 10 days of this letter, Patentee will initiate litigation against Company in the Eastern District of Texas.

LICENSE INQUIRY LETTER B: INDIRECT APPROACH

Hey Joe [CEO of Company Y] –
  I heard the XYZ product got great press at ComDex! ☺
  Let's grab sushi next time you're in Cupertino. My treat – we can catch up and maybe do some biz. I have a great idea for how our companies might be able to cooperate on a terrific new idea.
  Ciao!
  Jim

---

7. *Demand letter statutes.* More than thirty states have enacted statutes intended to curb abusive litigation by patent "trolls" by imposing fines for sending misleading or abusive letters that allege infringement and demand payment from recipients. In May 2021, the attorney general of Washington enforced such a law against a company that allegedly sent identical demand letters to 1,200 small businesses in forty-eight states over an eighteen-month period, all demanding $65,000 to license a patent covering financial transaction processing.[3] Do

---

[3] *State of Wash. v. Landmark Technology A LLC*, No. 21-2-06348-5 (King Co. Sup. Ct., filed May 13, 2021).

such laws make legitimate licensing overtures even more risky? How can patent owners address these risks?

8. *Demand letters and personal jurisdiction.* Does sending a patent demand letter to a potential licensee give the federal or state courts in the recipient's state personal jurisdiction over the sender? This controversial issue is addressed in Section 22.3, Note 4.

Problem 5.1

You represent I.C.E., the holder of a portfolio of US patents covering machines used in the packaging of ice cream for consumer resale. Draft a proposed licensing inquiry letter to the CEO of MechanIce, a long-time competitor in the manufacture of ice cream packaging machines.

Now assume that MechanIce refuses to respond, and you wish to bring it to the negotiating table by making its customers aware of your patents. Draft a licensing inquiry letter that can be sent to more than 3,000 supermarkets and grocery store chains in the United States that sell ice cream packaged using MechanIce machines (assume that the packaging itself is covered by the claims of one of your patents). How advisable is it to send this letter? What risks are involved?

5.2 CONFIDENTIALITY AND NONDISCLOSURE AGREEMENTS

During the proposal and negotiation of a licensing or other business transaction, it is often the case that one or both parties will be required to disclose information to the other that is not generally known to the public. Depending on the type of transaction that is contemplated, this information could include technical product details, input costs, names of existing and potential customers, details of unpublished patent applications, and much more.

In the United States, trade secrets are protected under both federal and state law. The Uniform Trade Secrets Act (UTSA), which has been adopted in most states, defines a trade secret as:

> information, including a formula, pattern, compilation, program, device, method, technique or process, that:
> 1. Derives independent economic value, actual or potential, from not being generally known to, and not being readily ascertainable by proper means by other persons who can obtain economic value from its disclosure, and
> 2. Is the subject of efforts that are reasonable under the circumstance to maintain its secrecy.[4]

Thus, much of the information that the parties are likely to disclose to one another would fall under this definition. But part 2 of the definition requires the party claiming a piece of information as a trade secret to take reasonable efforts to "maintain its secrecy." An unrestricted disclosure of even the most valuable information will result in the loss of its status as a trade secret, and the receiving party will be under no obligation to limit its use or disclosure of that information.

For this reason, it is often critical that parties enter into a written nondisclosure agreement (NDA) (also known as a confidentiality agreement) before any confidential information is disclosed. One of the most common agreements that a junior attorney will be given to draft and negotiate is an NDA. Below is a relatively customary form of NDA that is used in transactions like these.

---

[4]   UTSA § 1(3). In 2016, Congress enacted the Defend Trade Secrets Act (DTSA) (18 U.S.C. § 1836), which provides a federal cause of action for trade secret misappropriation. The DTSA definition of trade secrets does not differ significantly from that of the UTSA.

EXAMPLE: MUTUAL NONDISCLOSURE AGREEMENT

Agreement dated _____ (the "Effective Date"), between _____, and _____ (each a "Party" and together the "Parties").

1. *Background.* The Parties intend to engage in discussions and negotiations concerning a possible business relationship. In the course of such discussions and negotiations, [and in the course of any such business relationship], it is anticipated that each party will disclose or deliver to the other party and to the other party's directors, officers, employees, agents or advisors (including attorneys, accountants, consultants, bankers, financial advisors and members of advisory boards) (collectively, "Representatives") certain of its trade secrets or confidential or proprietary information for the purposes of enabling the other party to evaluate the feasibility of such business relationship [and to perform its obligations and exercise its rights under any such business relationship] (the "Purpose") [1]. As used in this Agreement, the party disclosing Confidential Information (as defined below) is referred to as the "Disclosing Party"; the party receiving such Confidential Information is referred to as the "Recipient."

2. *Confidential information.* [2] As used in this Agreement, the term "Confidential Information" means all information that is disclosed by the Disclosing Party or its Representatives to the Recipient [and which is designated as such in writing, whether by letter or by the use of an appropriate proprietary stamp or legend], [*or*] [which by its nature is of a type which is considered to be confidential and/or proprietary]. In addition, the term "Confidential Information" shall be deemed to include: (a) any notes, analyses, compilations, studies, interpretations, memoranda or other documents prepared by the Recipient or its Representatives which contain, reflect or are based upon, in whole or in part, any Confidential Information; and (b) the existence or status of, and any information concerning, the discussions between the parties concerning the Purpose.

3. *Duration.* This Agreement shall apply to all Confidential Information disclosed between the parties hereto from the Effective Date until [the first anniversary of the Effective Date] [3]. The obligations imposed by this Agreement shall continue with respect to a particular item of Confidential Information until the [fifth anniversary] of the disclosure of such Confidential Information to Recipient pursuant to this Agreement; provided, however, that the confidentiality obligations imposed by this Agreement with respect to [_____] included in the Confidential Information shall continue [in perpetuity/for a period of [__] years/for the duration of applicable trade secret protection under the law].

4. *Use and disclosure.* [4] The Recipient shall use the Confidential Information of the Disclosing Party only for the Purposes. The Recipient shall hold the Confidential Information in confidence with at least the same degree of care as it uses to keep its own proprietary information confidential, which shall in no event be less than reasonable care, and shall not intentionally disclose or publicly release any Confidential Information of the Disclosing Party.

5. *Limitations.* The obligations of the Recipient specified in section 4 shall not apply, and the Recipient shall have no further obligations, with respect to any Confidential Information to the extent that the Recipient can prove that such Confidential Information: (a) is

generally known to the public at the time of disclosure or becomes generally known without the Recipient violating this Agreement; (b) is in the Recipient's possession at the time of disclosure; (c) becomes known to the Recipient through disclosure by sources other than the Disclosing Party without such sources violating any confidentiality obligations to the Disclosing Party; or (d) is independently developed by the Recipient without access or reference to the Disclosing Party's Confidential Information [5]. Moreover, this Agreement shall not prohibit the Recipient from disclosing Confidential Information of the Disclosing Party to the extent required in order for the Recipient to comply with applicable laws, regulations, court orders and stock exchange rules, provided that the Recipient provides prior written notice of such required disclosure to the Disclosing Party, takes reasonable and lawful precautions to avoid and/or minimize the extent of such disclosure and cooperates with the Disclosing Party to obtain confidential treatment for such Confidential Information from the relevant authority.

6. *Ownership*. The Recipient agrees that it shall not receive any right, title or interest in, or any license or right to use, the Disclosing Party's Confidential Information or any patent, copyright, trade secret, trademark or other intellectual property rights therein, by implication or otherwise. Each of the parties hereto represents, warrants and covenants that the trade secrets which it discloses to the other party pursuant to this Agreement have not been stolen, appropriated, obtained or converted without authorization. [A prohibition on reverse engineering is sometimes included here, as well. [8]]

7. *Return of Confidential Information*. The Recipient shall, upon the written request of the Disclosing Party, return to the Disclosing Party, or destroy, all Confidential Information received by the Recipient from the Disclosing Party and all copies and reproductions thereof, including any notes, reports or other documents prepared by the Recipient which contain Confidential Information of the Disclosing Party [provided, however, that the Recipient shall not be required to locate or delete copies of Confidential Information that are stored on its internal or external computer backup media as part of its standard system backup and disaster recovery processes, so long as such Confidential Information is accessible only to the relevant computer operations personnel]. Notwithstanding the return or destruction of the Confidential Information, the Recipient will continue to be bound by its obligations of confidentiality and other obligations hereunder.

[8. OPTIONAL: *Residuals*. Notwithstanding anything to the contrary contained in this Agreement, either party shall be free to use any information disclosed hereunder to the extent that it is retained in the unaided memory of its employees.] [9]

9. *Representatives*. Recipient shall be permitted to disclose Confidential Information received from the Disclosing Party to those of its Representatives who have a need to know such Confidential Information for the Purposes, provided that such Representatives are legally bound to maintain the confidentiality of such Proprietary Information at least to the degree that Recipient is so bound hereunder. Any breach of any obligation of confidentiality by a Representative shall constitute a breach by Recipient hereunder, and Recipient shall be jointly and severally liable with all such Representatives for such breaches. Recipient shall maintain a written log of Representatives to whom the Confidential Information is disclosed and shall share such log with the Disclosing Party upon its request. [6]

10. *Injunctive relief.* The provisions of this Agreement are necessary for the protection of the business and goodwill of the parties and are considered by the parties to be reasonable for such purpose. The Recipient agrees that any breach of this Agreement [will/may] [7] cause the Disclosing Party substantial and irreparable injury which cannot be remedied by monetary damages alone, and, therefore, in addition to other remedies which may be available, the Disclosing Party shall have the right to [seek] [7] specific performance and other injunctive and equitable relief to prevent any such breach or its continuation without the necessity of posting a bond.

DRAFTING NOTES

[1] *Purpose* – Each NDA should define the purpose for which information is exchanged. Sometimes the purpose is narrowly limited to a specific potential transaction (often an acquisition), and sometimes it broadly covers any business transaction between the parties.

[2] *Confidential Information* – some NDAs use the term "Proprietary Information" instead of "Confidential Information." The intent is largely the same, though "Proprietary" connotes ownership as opposed to simple confidentiality (e.g., a party may hold third-party information that it does not "own," but which it is obligated to keep confidential).

[3] *Time of disclosure* – in some cases, the parties may have exchanged information before the NDA is signed, in which case retroactive effect should be considered.

[4] *Use and nondisclosure* – section 4 contains the two principal obligations that should be included in every NDA: the recipient's obligation not to use the disclosing party's confidential information for any purpose other than the purpose, and not to disclose or release that confidential information to others. Many NDAs inadvertently omit one of these key obligations – don't let this happen to you!

[5] *Independent development* – this exception generally becomes relevant in two contexts: (1) When the recipient is a large enterprise with multiple independent groups conducting research and development on potentially related topics, often in different geographical locations; if confidential information is disclosed to a group in the Austin, Texas office, but similar information is created by the recipient's Moscow office, the information should not be protected. (2) If the recipient knows that its developers are "contaminated" with confidential information, it can form a new development group with individuals who are assured to have no access to the confidential information and ask them to develop similar information independently. This is called a "clean room" approach, and has been upheld by the courts if conducted carefully. See *NEC Corp. v. Intel Corp.*, 1989 WL 67434 (N.D. Cal.).[5]

[6] *Recipient personnel* – in some cases, the disclosing party may wish to limit the recipient's personnel that are authorized to access and use its confidential information. Such

---

[5]   Note that independent development is not a defense to patent infringement, which is a strict liability tort that requires neither intent nor knowledge, though it may rebut a claim for enhanced damages for "willful" infringement under 35 U.S.C. § 284.

limitations can be structured to list the names and/or titles of such personnel, or the groups or departments in which they are based (e.g., "Confidential Information shall be made accessible only to attorneys who are members of Recipient's Office of General Counsel"). Alternately, certain groups can be expressly excluded from access to confidential information (e.g., "No Confidential Information shall be provided or made accessible to the members of Recipient's Mark V development team").

[7] *Injunctive relief* – this clause is intended to enable the disclosing party to obtain an injunction to prevent disclosure (or further disclosure) of its confidential information without proving every element typically required to obtain injunctive relief. As such, the recipient sacrifices significant legal protections by agreeing to this language in its "strong" form. The [alternative] language represents a recipient's standard push-back against this clause.

[8] No *reverse engineering* – if confidential information includes proprietary materials, chemical compounds, circuitry, software or other items from which other trade secrets may be derived, the disclosing party should consider the inclusion of a "no reverse engineering" clause, discussed in detail in Section 18.2.5.

[9] *Residuals* – section 8 is a "residuals" clause, which permits the recipient to continue to use any confidential information retained in the "unaided memory" of its personnel. Such a clause is almost always controversial, and its use and acceptance are generally industry-dependent. IBM is reputed to have "invented" this clause to enable its engineers to think freely, even after they had been exposed to competitors' confidential information. While a residuals clause does not permit the recipient to use any written, electronic or other artificial means to preserve confidential information that it is no longer permitted to use, it is certainly possible that some individuals may have exceptional (or even photographic) memories, which could enable them to use the disclosing party's confidential information long after a proposed transaction has failed to materialize.

Notes and Questions

1. *Purpose.* One of the most heavily litigated issues arising under an NDA is whether the recipient used confidential information for some purpose beyond the stated "purpose" of the disclosure. For example, in *Le Tote Inc. v. Urban Outfitters Inc.*, (E.D. Pa. 2021), Le Tote described its mail-order fashion rental business model to Urban Outfitters under an NDA for the purpose of enabling Urban Outfitters to evaluate a potential acquisition of Le Tote. Urban Outfitters did not acquire Le Tote, but did start its own mail-order fashion rental business. Le Tote alleged that it did so using Le Tote's confidential information. If you had represented Urban Outfitters, what language might you have drafted to protect your client from such allegations? For a sense of just how large the stakes can be in such matters, see *Martin Marietta Materials, Inc. v. Vulcan Materials Co.*, 56 A.3d 1072 (Del. Ch. 2012), aff 'd, 68 A.3d 1208 (Del. 2012) (injunction of a $5.5 billion hostile takeover on the basis of the interpretation of the word "between" in a confidentiality agreement).

2. *NDA versus definitive agreement.* In section 1 of the sample NDA, what is the purpose of the language in the definition of "Purposes" that reads "and to perform its obligations and exercise its rights under any such business relationship that is formalized between the parties"?

Is it advisable to allow a pre-agreement NDA to continue to cover information disclosed after a definitive license or other agreement is signed? Another approach is to limit the NDA to pre-agreement discussions, and then to include a comprehensive confidentiality clause in the "definitive" agreement between the parties. Or the parties may draft the confidentiality clause in the definitive agreement broadly enough to encompass information disclosed under the NDA and then supersede and cancel the NDA in the definitive agreement. What are the advantages and drawbacks of each of these approaches?

3. *Marking.* In section 2, the [bracketed] language shows that the central definition of "Confidential Information" can be cast in two ways: either as all information that the disclosing party marks as confidential (e.g., with a "CONFIDENTIAL" legend) or as *all* information that the disclosing party discloses to the recipient. What is the significance of including a marking obligation on the disclosing party? Which form of this definition would you choose if you were representing the disclosing party? The recipient?

4. *Confidential information versus trade secrets.* Why do NDAs go to such lengths to define confidential information, rather than simply relying on existing statutory and common law definitions of trade secrets? Are there significant differences between proprietary/confidential information and trade secrets? Why require any terms in an NDA beyond a simple acknowledgment that certain information is a trade secret?

5. *Timing and duration.* Section 3 of the NDA addresses timing and duration issues. The first sentence limits the obligations under the NDA to information disclosed prior to a particular cutoff date. Why would such a cutoff be advisable? If a cutoff is used, the parties must be careful to remember that the NDA is no longer in place after that date, as information disclosed afterwards will not be covered. An alternative is to eliminate the cutoff entirely. Under what circumstances would this approach be advisable?

   The next sentence describes how long the obligations under the NDA last with respect to information disclosed under it. Sometimes this duration has two tiers, a shorter term for most information (e.g., a five-year term) and a perpetual or longer term for highly sensitive or valuable information (e.g., the formula for Coca-Cola, key computer source code, etc.). Why should obligations of confidentiality ever expire? What other kinds of information might merit perpetual protection?

   Note the final drafting "option" in this sentence. It provides that all confidential information that constitutes a "trade secret" will remain protected for the duration of its trade secret status. Does this provision introduce some circularity to the duration of protection for this information?

6. *Residuals.* As noted in Drafting Note [9], residuals clauses are almost always controversial. If you represented the disclosing party in a transaction, how would you respond to the recipient's request for a residuals clause in an NDA? When might such a clause be reasonable? Could a residuals clause be interpreted as granting the recipient an implied license under the disclosing party's patents? How might this implication be avoided? How would a residuals clause have helped Urban Outfitters in the case discussed in Note 1?

7. *Exceptions.* Section 5 of the NDA provides several exceptions to the recipient's obligations of confidentiality. Which of these, if any, would you wish to eliminate or modify if you represented the disclosing party? How? The *Celeritas* case discussed below addresses one of the most common of these exceptions, that concerning information that is in the public domain. What is the purpose of the exception at the end of this section pertaining to the disclosing party's compliance with law and regulations? Why isn't this exception included with the other exceptions listed in Section 5?

FIGURE 5.3 The formula for Coca-Cola, which is allegedly stored in this imposing vault in Atlanta, has been a trade secret since 1886.

Celeritas Technologies, Ltd. v. Rockwell International Corp.

150 F.3d 1354 (Fed. Cir. 1998)

LOURIE, CIRCUIT JUDGE

Rockwell International Corporation appeals from the decision of the United States District Court for the Central District of California denying Rockwell's motions for judgment as a matter of law and for a new trial following a jury verdict that Rockwell willfully infringed Celeritas Technologies, Ltd.'s patent, misappropriated its trade secrets, and breached a non-disclosure agreement relating to the protected subject matter. [We affirm.]

On July 28, 1993, Michael Dolan filed a patent application for an apparatus for increasing the rate of data transmission over analog cellular telephone networks [using "de-emphasis" technology]. The resulting patent, U.S. Patent 5,386,590, assigned to Celeritas, was issued on January 31, 1995.

[In] September 1993, Dolan and other officials of Celeritas met with representatives from Rockwell to demonstrate their proprietary de-emphasis technology. Rockwell is the leading manufacturer of modem "chip sets" which contain the core functions of commercial modems, including the modulation function where de-emphasis is performed. The parties entered into a non-disclosure agreement (NDA), which covered the subject matter of the meeting and provided in pertinent part that Rockwell "shall not disclose or use any Proprietary Information (or any derivative thereof) except for the purpose of evaluating the prospective business arrangements between Celeritas and Rockwell."

The agreement provided that proprietary information "shall not include information which ... was in the public domain on the date hereof or comes into the public domain other than through the fault or negligence of [Rockwell]." [In] March 1994, AT&T Paradyne began to sell a modem that incorporated de-emphasis technology. In that same month, Rockwell informed Celeritas that it would not license the use of Celeritas's proprietary technology, and concurrently began a development project to incorporate de-emphasis technology into its modem chip sets. Significantly, Rockwell did not independently develop its own de-emphasis technology, but instead assigned the same engineers who had learned of Celeritas's technology under the NDA to work on the de-emphasis development project. In January 1995, Rockwell began shipping its first prototype chip sets that contained de-emphasis technology. By the time of trial in 1997, Rockwell's sales were surpassing its projections.

On September 22, 1995, Celeritas sued Rockwell, alleging breach of contract, misappropriation of trade secrets, and patent infringement. The jury returned a verdict for Celeritas on each of the three theories, awarding Celeritas $57,658,000 each on the patent infringement and breach of contract claims, and $26,850,000 each in compensatory and exemplary damages on the trade secret misappropriation claim. [Rockwell] moved for JMOL on liability and for a new trial on damages.

Rockwell first argues that the district court erred by denying its motion for JMOL on the breach of contract claim. Citing the prior art submitted to the United States Patent and Trademark Office (PTO) by Celeritas, Rockwell argues that the evidence at trial clearly demonstrates that the de-emphasis technology disclosed to Rockwell was already in the public domain. Even if the technology were proprietary at the time of disclosure, Rockwell argues, the technology had entered the public domain before Rockwell used it, concededly no later than March 1994. Specifically, Rockwell asserts that AT&T Paradyne had already placed the technology in the public domain through the sale of a modem incorporating de-emphasis technology ("the modem"). Rockwell asserts that the technology was "readily ascertainable" because any competent engineer could have reverse engineered the modem. Rockwell further argues that any confidentiality obligation under the NDA regarding de-emphasis technology was extinguished once the '590 patent issued in January 1995.

FIGURE 5.4 A Rockwell 33.6 K analog modem, *c.*1990s.

Celeritas responds that substantial evidence supports the jury's verdict that Rockwell used its proprietary information. Celeritas argues that in order for a trade secret to enter the public domain in California, it must actually have been ascertained by proper means, and not merely have been ascertainable. Celeritas maintains that, in any event, the only evidence at trial supports the jury's implicit finding that the information was not readily ascertainable from inspection of the modem. Celeritas also argues that the issuance of its patent in 1995 is immaterial because Rockwell had already breached the agreement by using its proprietary information in 1994.

We agree with Celeritas that substantial evidence supports the jury's conclusion that Rockwell breached the NDA. The jury implicitly found that the information given to Rockwell by Celeritas was proprietary. Unrebutted testimony established that Celeritas disclosed to Rockwell implementation details and techniques that went beyond the information disclosed in the patent. Thus, even if every detail disclosed in the patent were in the prior art, a fact never alleged by Rockwell, that fact would not undermine the jury's conclusion that Celeritas revealed proprietary information to Rockwell which it then used in developing its modem chip sets. Accordingly, Rockwell's reliance on the prosecution history of the '590 patent and the prior art submitted to the PTO is misplaced.

The jury also implicitly found that the technology had not been placed in the public domain by the sale of the modem. California law appears somewhat unsettled regarding whether a trade secret enters the public domain when it is "readily ascertainable" or whether it must also be "actually ascertained" by the public. Because the judgment is supportable under either standard, we need not attempt to resolve this issue of state law. Suffice it to say that substantial evidence supports a finding that the technology implementing the de-emphasis function in the modem was not "readily ascertainable." In fact, Dolan's testimony, the only evidence cited by Rockwell, belies its contentions. [Dolan] stated that (1) a spectrum analyzer would be needed to discover the de-emphasis technology, (2) most engineers that he talked to did not have spectrum analyzers, and (3) only if an engineer had a spectrum analyzer and knew what to look for could the engineer discover that the modem had de-emphasis technology. His express caveat that the use of de-emphasis could have been discovered if it was being affirmatively pursued is not an admission that the technology would be "readily ascertainable." Because substantial evidence supports the conclusion that the information disclosed to Rockwell had not entered the public domain before its unauthorized use by Rockwell, the court did not err in denying Rockwell's motion for JMOL regarding its breach of the NDA.

Notes and Questions

1. *Public domain information.* In *Celeritas*, the NDA did not apply to "information which [was] in the public domain on the date hereof or comes into the public domain other than through the fault or negligence of [Rockwell]." Why is such information excluded? Given the result in *Celeritas*, how might you adjust this language for future transactions?

2. *Patent applications.* Beginning in 2000, US patent applications have been published by the Patent and Trademark Office eighteen months after filing, unless the applicant chooses to waive foreign filing rights (35 U.S.C. § 122). The patent application in the *Celeritas* case, which was filed prior to 2000, was not subject to this requirement. What effect is the publication of patent applications likely to have on the information that they contain? How might this affect the recipient's obligations under a typical NDA?

3. *Issued patent.* Rockwell also argued that the issuance of Celeritas' patent in 1995 eliminated any obligation of confidentiality that Rockwell may have had. Is this correct? Why doesn't the court discuss this argument? What would the result have been if Rockwell had waited to begin development of its de-emphasis modem technology until Celeritas' patent had issued (disregarding the potential need for a patent license)?

4. *Contract versus trade secret.* Are there any advantages in bringing an action for contractual breach of an NDA as opposed to an action for misappropriation of trade secrets under either state law and/or the federal DTSA? When might you bring *both* a contractual and a trade secret misappropriation action?

Problem 5.2

Referring to the sample mutual NDA above, what are the top ten terms that you would seek to negotiate if you represented the party most likely to be the disclosing party? The recipient? What if you are not sure, at the outset, which party will be likely to disclose more proprietary information during discussions? Draft a mutual NDA that would be both reasonable but favorable to each of these negotiation positions.

5.3 PRELIMINARY DOCUMENTS

In addition to confidentiality agreements, parties negotiating licensing and other transactions often exchange, and sometimes sign, preliminary documents that summarize the terms of an anticipated transaction, as well as the premises under which negotiations are anticipated to occur. These preliminary documents are variously called term sheets, letters of intent, heads of agreement, memoranda of understanding, and a host of similar designations. In almost all cases, with a few notable exceptions, they are intended to be nonbinding.

In a recent article, Professor Cathy Hwang points out the high stakes that can ride on such preliminary documents and explores why they are used:

> In 2015, the Delaware Supreme Court awarded $113 million in expectation damages when a sophisticated party did not honor the terms of an unsigned, two-page preliminary agreement marked "non-binding." Over a ten-year battle, the Delaware courts' four decisions in *SIGA Technologies Inc. v. PharmAthene Inc.* stirred up a storm of interest from deal lawyers. They also brought to light a long-standing and puzzling practice in dealmaking: the use of non-binding agreements. Why do parties use non-binding agreements to memorialize high-stakes deals, especially when they have the option to use formal, binding contracts?
>
> This inquiry reveals that parties primarily use non-binding agreements to add formality to an otherwise murky pre-contractual deal process. Preliminary agreements mark the moment when deal parties have resolved most deal uncertainty and are likely to do a deal together, whether or not they sign a preliminary agreement. Instead of causing parties to behave well, preliminary agreements merely mark the moment when parties were already primed to behave well, with or without an agreement.[6]

Cynthia Cannady discourages the use of such preliminary documents whenever possible:

> Letters of intent and Memoranda of Understanding (MOUs) are quasi-agreements and are a risky practice with few benefits. Unlike interim agreements, they are often phrased in such a

---

[6] Cathy Hwang, *Deal Momentum*, 65 UCLA L. Rev. 376, 378–79 (2018). The term sheet in *PharmAthene* was not a standalone document, but set forth terms over which other (binding) agreement required the parties to negotiate in good faith.

way that it is unclear if they record a binding agreement. The parties may create a similarly confusing document by signing term sheets or other documents that do not express agreements on material terms. These types of documents are often entered into because the parties have not reached agreement on material terms that have proven intractable in negotiation, however, the parties still wish to proceed with a development project or a public announcement.

For example, the parties may enter into a letter of intent to avoid the risks of negotiation failure on the question of which party will own foreground IP in a development agreement, and the additional time pressure that delay places on the engineering teams when they begin work. Expressions like "good faith" and "best efforts" are often used in such agreements to describe the efforts of the parties to agree and/or produce a deliverable. However, after six months of joint engineering work, with no agreement on IP ownership, the parties are still likely to find it hard to agree. They may also rest on the comfort of a signed MOU and devote themselves to the engineering tasks at hand.[7]

Notes and Questions

1. *Value of preliminary documents.* As the above excerpts from Hwang and Cannady demonstrate, there is some disagreement regarding the value, or even advisability, of preliminary documents. Which of these viewpoints do you find more persuasive? How would you advise a client who came to you with a request to prepare a nonbinding letter of intent for a transaction?

2. *Texaco v. Pennzoil.* One of the most notorious pre-transaction documents in history involved three oil industry giants. In early January 1984, Pennzoil negotiated and signed a "Memorandum of Agreement" with certain large shareholders of Getty Oil whereby Pennzoil would acquire the outstanding shares of Getty at a price of $110 per share. The Memorandum of Agreement was subject to approval of Getty's Board of Directors, which rejected the offer as too low. Following further negotiations, the Board counter-proposed a price $5 above Pennzoil's original offer. Pennzoil accepted the counteroffer and both parties issued press releases announcing the deal. The next day, however, Texaco offered $125 per share to acquire all outstanding shares of Getty. Getty's Board voted to withdraw its previous counterproposal to Pennzoil and to accept Texaco's higher offer instead. Getty and Texaco signed a definitive merger agreement two days later. Pennzoil then sued Texaco for tortious interference and was awarded $7.53 billion in compensatory and $3 billion in punitive damages by a jury in Houston, Texas – the largest civil verdict in history. *Texaco, Inc. v. Pennzoil Co.*, 729 S.W.2d 768 (Tex. App. 1987).

3. *Nonbinding language.* In the wake of *Texaco v. Pennzoil*, lawyers became keenly aware of the need to be very clear when they did not intend preliminary documents to be binding. Robert Lloyd, reflecting on the judgment in that case, recommends language along the following lines:

Although the parties may exchange proposals (written or oral), term sheets, draft agreements or other materials, neither party will have any obligations or liability to the other party unless and until both parties' authorized representatives sign definitive written agreements. Exchanged terms are non-binding to the extent they are not included in such definitive written agreements. Either party can end these discussions at any time, for any reason (or for no

---

7   Cynthia Cannady, The Three No's: Letters of Intent, Memoranda of Understanding, and Standstill Agreements, in Technology Licensing and Development Agreements 469–70 (Oxford Univ. Press, 2013).

FIGURE 5.5 The record-breaking verdict in *Texaco v. Pennzoil* reinvigorated the popular notion that a handshake is a binding commitment.

reason at all), and without liability to the other party. Each party remains free to negotiate and to enter into contracts with others.[8]

Do you think this language is necessary to demonstrate that no contract is being formed by preliminary documents? What about merely including the word "nonbinding" in the document header?

4. *Binding terms – confidentiality, exclusivity, break-up fees.* Though most provisions of preliminary documents are nonbinding, a few provisions sometimes do bind the parties. First, and most commonly, confidentiality terms are often included in preliminary documents and are generally drafted to be binding on the parties. Beyond these are two less conventional forms of binding terms: exclusivity and so-called break-up fees. Exclusivity provisions require that the parties negotiate exclusively with each other for a specified period, which could be days, weeks or months. Break-up fee (also referred to as "bust-up" or "walk-away") provisions require that one party pay the other a specified amount if the parties fail to reach a binding agreement within a certain period of time. Why would parties agree to exclusivity and break-up fees before they have executed a definitive agreement?

5. *The term sheet.* Some forms of preliminary documentation look very much like contracts and are signed by the parties (as they were in *Texaco v. Pennzoil*). However, in many cases these documents are not signed, further bolstering arguments as to their nonbinding nature. The simplest form of preliminary documentation is probably the term sheet: a list of key terms that the parties anticipate including in a definitive agreement, assuming that they can get the details ironed out. Well-drafted term sheets may also include pointers to important but unresolved issues that need to be ironed out in the definitive agreement. Do you see value in such a nonbinding document?

[8] Robert M. Lloyd, *Pennzoil v. Texaco, Twenty Years After: Lessons for Business Lawyers*, 6 Transactions: Tenn. J. Bus. L. 321, 352 (2005).

NONBINDING TERM SHEET: SUBJECT TO NEGOTIATION AND DEFINITIVE AGREEMENT

Licensor	ElectroBev Co., a Delaware corporation
Licensee	Sunbelt, SA de CV, a Mexican corporation
Licensed Rights	Proprietary formula for ElectroBev soft drinks
	ElectroBev word and design marks in the Territory (Licensed Marks)
Licensed Products	Canned and bottled ElectroBev soft drinks for sale in consumer retail stores, convenience stores, restaurants, kiosks and vending machines. Excludes fountain drinks.
Territory	South and Central America (including Caribbean)
Rights Granted	Manufacture, promote and sell Licensed Products in the Territory under the Licensed Marks
Exclusivity	Exclusive (other than Electro's Brazilian subsidiary – which will retain rights in a manner to be agreed)
Up-Front Fee	$100,000
Royalty	5% of Net Sales up to $10,000,000
	3% above $10,000,000
Term	5 years, with 1-year automatic renewals
Target execution date	Jan. 30, 2020

6. *Term sheet terms.* How do you decide which terms to reflect in a term sheet? How might such terms differ from those in the above sample trademark license term sheet if the transaction involved (a) a feature-length film to be based on a popular foreign-language book; (b) a new lightweight silicone-based coating with high heat resistance; (c) a chemical compound with medicinal properties that has recently been extracted from a rare tropical insect; and (d) the lyrics to twenty Broadway musicals composed by a recently deceased songwriter?

7. *Interim agreements.* Lying somewhere between nonbinding preliminary documents and definitive transaction agreements are short-term "interim" agreements that parties some-times enter while they are considering whether a longer-term arrangement is advisable. Cannady explains the rationale for such agreements in the technology sector:

> Evaluation is part of the negotiation process. An evaluation agreement permits the parties to work together for a period of time and exchange information, and develop new information and ideas for the purpose of testing collaboration opportunities. It is like an NDA but per-mits a closer cooperation between the parties and may also specify which information will be exchanged.
>
> A prototype agreement goes further than evaluation and commits the parties to make one or more prototypes by a certain date. The agreement's material terms relate to the allocation of costs and duties, payment of expenses, and IP ownership and rights. Prototype agreements are mini-development agreements, but with a reduced [statement of work] and a shortened time frame.
>
> Interim agreements are used to permit the parties to work together for a period of time pending negotiation of the agreement. These agreements clarify which party will bear what costs, IP ownership and rights, and other critical issues. They provide that the agreement

will terminate by a certain date, usually a matter of a month or two. These agreements are risky because they tend to "let the horse out of the barn"; the parties rely on them as if they had successfully negotiated the full agreement. Just like development agreements, interim agreements require resolution of IP ownership and other difficult issues, but within a short time frame. In some cases, they are useful in helping parties find an interim solution pending negotiation.[9]

Do you agree with Cannady's assessment of the risks and benefits of interim agreements? How would you protect your client's interests if they wished to enter into such an agreement?

8. *Beta testing agreements.* One type of interim agreement that is sometimes used in the software industry is called a "beta testing" or "early release" agreement. This is essentially a license agreement that permits the use of a pre-release version of a software program. Because the software is not ready for commercial release, it is usually provided "as is" without warranties of any kind and at no or low cost to the user. In addition, the vendor often requires the user to report all bugs and errors in the software and to provide feedback on its features and functionality, which the vendor is then permitted to build into subsequent versions of the software (i.e., through a form of "grantback" license – see Section 9.1.2). What do you think happens under a typical beta agreement if a user conceives a patentable improvement to the software that she has been licensed to use? What risks might the assignment of improvements to the vendor pose for a beta user?

Problem 5.3

Your client, Cook E. Mawnster, has developed an innovative and delicious new recipe for chocolate-chip cookies. Until now she has been baking cookies and selling them at local bake sales and farmers' markets with resounding success. Now, she would like to enter into an agreement with a commercial baked goods company to produce and sell her cookies on a national basis. Draft the pre-transaction documents that you would recommend she use when approaching these companies.

---

[9] Cynthia Cannady, Technology Licensing and Development Agreements 470 (Oxford Univ. Press, 2013).

License Building Blocks

This part focuses on the principal terms of an intellectual property (IP) licensing agreement. Contrary to popular belief, save for online and "shrinkwrap" agreements (see Chapter 17), no two licensing agreements are exactly the same. Nevertheless, many licensing agreements share the same general layout and structure. Below is a rough summary of the different parts of a licensing agreement, with a few pointers regarding provisions that don't merit a full discussion in the chapters that follow. In the Online Appendix to this book are samples of several different types of licensing and other transaction agreements, which you may wish to refer to as you use this book.

INTRODUCTORY MATERIAL

The first few paragraphs of the agreement typically include the title of the agreement, the names of the parties, the effective date, and recitals framing the purpose of the agreement (see Section 13.1).

DEFINITIONS

Though they may seem routine, the defined terms in an agreement (those Capitalized or ALL CAPS terms that appear throughout the document) are among its most important terms. Many agreements include a section listing defined terms at the beginning (or, less frequently, at the end) of the agreement. The alternative to including a section devoted to defined terms is to define terms throughout the agreement "in line" (e.g., "the Parties shall conduct the research and development activities at 123 South Infinite Loop, Cupertino, California (the 'Facility')"). We will discuss important defined terms throughout the following chapters as they arise.

ACTIVITIES AND DELIVERABLES

Many agreements require one or both parties to perform some activity or service – the development of a new technology, the manufacture of a product, the provision of an online service, or any of a thousand other things. The general framework for the performance of these activities is usually laid out in the agreement, along with references to any products, prototypes, plans or designs that are required to be delivered (usually referred to as "Deliverables"). If the services or deliverables are complex, then they may be described in more detail in any number of schedules or exhibits to the main agreement. Services relating to the development of IP are discussed in Section 9.2.

LICENSE GRANTS AND EXCLUSIONS

The core of any license agreement is the license grant. Chapters 6 and 7 focus on the drafting and issues surrounding this key set of provisions.

IP OWNERSHIP AND MANAGEMENT

Sometimes each party brings IP to a collaboration; sometimes new IP is developed during the course of a collaboration. These provisions describe which party or parties owns particular categories of IP, and how the parties allocate responsibility for managing that IP (e.g., prosecuting patents). These issues are discussed in Chapter 9.

PAYMENTS

Most license agreements involve the payment of funds by one party to the other. Chapter 8 addresses the many different variants by which parties are paid.

REPRESENTATIONS, WARRANTIES AND INDEMNIFICATION

By this point in a license agreement, most businesspeople have stopped reading. We are now entering lawyers' territory, with a set of provisions that is both important and underappreciated. Representations, warranties and indemnification, discussed in Chapter 10, allocate liability among the parties for a host of potential issues.

TERM AND TERMINATION

It is the rare agreement that lasts forever, so every agreement contains clauses relating to its duration and eventual end. These provisions are discussed in Chapter 12.

THE BOILERPLATE

At the end of every agreement comes a set of terms – often running to several pages – that are seldom negotiated, but can become critically important under the right circumstances. These are covered in Chapter 13.

SIGNATURES

Every agreement must evidence the mutual assent of the parties. Today, assent can be manifested in many ways – through email, text, spoken word or handshake. But by far the most common method used in license agreements, other than consumer clickwrap agreements, is the personal signature of an authorized representative of the signing party. If the identity of the signatory needs to be verified, signatures can be notarized.

SCHEDULES

After the body of the agreement often come a variety of attachments. Schedules often contain lists or descriptions responsive to a particular section of the agreement. For example, if section 2.4 of the agreement requires the licensor to list all employees who are responsible for developing a particular technology, that list could be provided on schedule 2.4. The schedule is part of the agreement, but placed at the end for convenience.

EXHIBITS

Like schedules, exhibits come after the main body of the agreement. Though these two terms are often used interchangeably, traditionally an "exhibit" is a pre-existing document or item that is appended to the agreement, as opposed to a schedule, which is created specifically for the purposes of the agreement. Thus, exhibits to a license agreement might include a registration document for the licensed IP, a copy of an existing sublicense or a form of document that the parties will sign in conjunction with the license agreement, such as a promissory note, an assignment, a guaranty or a security interest form.

A FEW NOTES ON CONTRACT DRAFTING

Part II of this book concerns itself with the drafting of contractual clauses, what they mean, how they vary, and how they have been interpreted by the courts over the years. As such, it is worth spending a few words on the process of contract drafting itself.

Forms and Templates

Today, it is seldom the case that one sits before a blank computer screen to begin drafting a new agreement. Almost all agreements are based, at least in part, on forms, templates and precedents, of which there are vast troves to be found in online databases, law firm files and even the publicly searchable EDGAR database maintained by the Securities and Exchange Commission. One would be foolhardy to attempt to reinvent the wheel with each new agreement. Thus, it is both natural and efficient to rely on prior examples when beginning to draft a new agreement.

Yet, it is also important not to rely too heavily on precedent documents. Every IP licensing transaction other than the most routine consumer-facing nonexclusive licenses is different. The parties have different needs, desires and sensitivities. It is a mistake to assume that the current deal will be exactly like the last deal. Thus, the diligent attorney must approach every agreement clause with care and attention to the specific transaction and client at hand.

Rules versus Standards

In terms of specific drafting advice, it is important always to keep in mind the delicate balance between detail and generality. As one set of commentators aptly explains:

> In legislation, treaties, private contracts, and many other dealmaking areas, drafters must make a decision between using a rule or a standard to express meaning. Rules—"deliver the goods on October 1, at 7 p.m. Eastern, unless it is already dark, in which case, deliver the next day"—are more time-consuming to negotiate and draft, but easier to enforce. Standards—"deliver the goods at a reasonable time"—are the opposite: they are easier to draft, but harder to enforce.[1]

No matter how detailed a contract may be, it cannot take into account every eventuality that can arise in the complex hurly-burly of modern business and technology. Thus, do not strain to

---

[1]   Cathy Hwang & Matthew Jennejohn, *Deal Structure*, 113 Nw. L. Rev. 279, 285 (2018).

address every possible eventuality, but become comfortable with broader standards of conduct except where specificity is needed to protect the known interests of your client.

Constructive Ambiguity

Some lawyers feel the urge to specify every detail of a commercial transaction to the *n*th degree. Detail is, of course, critical in complex commercial arrangements. Delivery schedules, payment amounts, acceptance criteria and myriad other details must be negotiated and recorded in an agreement before it is signed. Failing to do so can, and often does, lead to disagreements down the road.

But not every detail needs to be specified in a contract, particularly when the parties already have a good working relationship. The common law provides a number of flexibilities that enable parties to rely on concepts like reasonable efforts, promptness and good faith as default regimes that can fill gaps in detail that the parties did not reduce to writing at the time of execution. Michal Shur-Ofry and Ofer Tur-Sinai refer to this approach as "constructive ambiguity," and find that in certain contractual areas and transactions a limited degree of flexibility and ambiguity can be more efficient than the often futile and imperfect attempt to predict every detail that will arise in a complex commercial arrangement.[2] This said, intentional flexibility is not the same as lazy drafting – some obligations *do* need to be spelled out in detail, and failing to do so is inadvisable.

Balance

When you, as an attorney, draft an agreement, you are usually doing so on behalf of a client. It is thus natural to draft in a manner that is favorable to your client and a bad idea to draft an agreement that disadvantages your client unnecessarily. That being said, the first draft of an agreement should not be viewed as a declaration of total war. Every clause need not favor your client and disfavor the other party. For example, limitations of liability that only benefit one party, confidentiality provisions that only protect information disclosed by your client, indemnification clauses that only run one way. Any competent lawyer representing the other party will markup these clauses to be more balanced, and may even go further than he or she ordinarily would because of your initial aggressive approach. More importantly, such one-sided agreements seldom serve their purpose or facilitate reaching a mutually acceptable deal. Worse still, I have seen instances in which such a one-sided agreement has triggered a phone call by a business executive on the receiving end to the executives of the well-intentioned attorney's client. Comments like "your lawyer obviously doesn't understand this business relationship or the way this industry works" do little to further one's legal career. In sum, drafting a totally one-sided agreement wastes time, money and goodwill on both sides. A much better approach is to draft a balanced agreement that puts your client's best foot forward, but does not seek to destroy the other party. Doing so will earn you the respect of both your client and the opposing party and its counsel.

---

[2] Michal Shur-Ofry & Ofer Tur-Sinai, *Constructive Ambiguity: IP Licenses as a Case Study*, 48 U. Mich. J. L. Reform 391 (2015).

Comprehension

There is no excuse for not understanding the agreement that you have drafted. When a law firm partner or an opposing counsel in a negotiation asks, "what does this clause mean?", there is no situation in which "I don't know" is an acceptable response. Nor is it acceptable to respond, "because that clause was in the form that I copied from." One of the goals of this book is to illuminate many of the types of contractual provisions found in IP licensing agreements. But there are many, many more, and it is up to you, as the drafter of an agreement, to take responsibility for understanding everything that is in it and being capable of explaining it to your co-counsel, your client and the opposing parties.[3]

Precision, Simplicity and Clarity

Words matter. An agreement serves many different purposes and has many different audiences. An agreement memorializes the terms pursuant to which a business transaction is carried out. It will often be read by managers and corporate representatives to guide their conduct. An agreement, particularly an IP licensing agreement, also serves as a legal instrument by which particular rights are granted – an adjunct to the formal grant of rights by the Patent and Trademark Office or which otherwise exists under the law. As such, an agreement is like a promissory note or a debenture – it is a document with independent legal effect that defines valuable asset classes held by different entities. Agreements also define the boundaries of permitted conduct by the parties and, too often, become the subject of disputes. When this happens, the words of agreements are parsed carefully by courts and, sometimes, juries to determine the obligations and liability of the parties.

Each of these scenarios argues for the careful drafting of agreements. But more importantly, they suggest that agreements should be written for a broad audience. The best agreement is one that can easily be comprehended by a lay juror who sees its words displayed on a projection screen in a courtroom. Obscurity generally benefits no one (or at least the party who will benefit cannot easily be predicted).

As a result, clarity in drafting is of paramount importance. Below are a few drafting tips that experienced practitioners abide by:

- *The fewer words, the better.* Don't use five words when you can use two. Instead of saying "any obligation of any type, nature or kind arising under or pursuant to this Agreement," you can usually just say "any obligation hereunder." Don't say "shall mean" when you can just say "means."
- *Be consistent.* All agreements have defined terms (see above and Section 13.2). Use them, and use them consistently. If you define "Term" to mean the term of the agreement, use "Term" every time you refer to the term of the agreement, and don't say "the term of this Agreement" when you just mean "Term."
- *Be modular.* A good agreement, like a good computer program, is modular in nature. This means that concepts, particularly definitions, should be contained in chunks that refer to one another, rather than spun out in huge paragraphs that are difficult for anyone but the

---

[3] One exception to this rule arises in the context of large M&A agreements, in which highly specialized representations and warranties are included on subjects such as environmental compliance, data privacy, retirement plans, taxes and the like. Generally, these provisions are drafted and negotiated by specialists, and the general agreement "quarterback" is not expected to understand or negotiate their details.

drafter to follow. This is not just a stylistic preference. Modular agreements are much easier to change, both during negotiation and later, if they need to be amended.

- *Avoid legalese.* Always remember that the ultimate audience for your agreement may be a jury of non-lawyers. Most jurors don't speak Latin. There is simply no need to show off your erudition by using terms like *"inter alia"* when you can just say "among others."

IP law is not quantum physics. There are few legal concepts or contractual commitments that a lay person cannot understand, so long as they are expressed clearly and concisely. As you draft agreement clauses, imagine that they will be read by your favorite elderly relative. Will he or she understand what you have drafted, given sufficient interest and patience? If not, consider revising your language.

Trust No One, Proofread, and Don't be Lazy

Lawyers are busy people, and it is often tempting to cut corners. This is human nature. But there are some circumstances under which you, as a lawyer, should never take shortcuts, and these include ensuring that an agreement that you drafted, negotiated or reviewed accurately reflects the deal that was made, and the intentions of your client. Ultimately, your client is paying you to vouch for the agreement. He or she won't read it in detail – that is your job, and neglecting to do this can be a career-ending mistake. Take, for example, the unfortunate facts in *D.E. Shaw Composite Holdings, L.L.C. v. Terraform Power, LLC* (N.Y. Sup. Ct., Dec. 22, 2020), in which one extraneous letter "s" among hundreds of pages of complex M&A documents resulted in a $300 million liability for one party, and a malpractice suit against the law firms that made the mistake.[4] Or consider *PBTM LLC v. Football Northwest, LLC* (W.D. Wash. 2021), a case involving the proposed sale of PBTM's VOLUME 12 and LEGION OF BOOM trademarks to the Seattle Seahawks football franchise. Though negotiations stalled over PBTM's price for the VOLUME 12 mark, the parties reached a deal on the LEGION OF BOOM mark. The court explains what happened next:

> General counsel for the Seahawks drafted a purchase agreement for the trademark, which [the] parties signed on August 24, 2014.
>
> PBTM claims that parties did not discuss the VOLUME 12 mark during negotiations and was therefore "surprised to see later drafts" of the LEGION OF BOOM Agreement that included clauses about VOLUME 12. PBTM claims that it specifically objected to paragraphs 21 and 22 and "wanted them deleted," since they contained language requiring PBTM to obtain the Seahawks' consent prior to marketing a BOOM or VOLUME 12 product. However, Seahawks management allegedly insisted that paragraphs 21 and 22 remain but promised to modify the language so that PBTM would not be required to obtain the Seahawks' consent prior to marketing a BOOM or VOLUME 12 product.
>
> PBTM claims that notwithstanding [the] parties' discussions about paragraphs 21 and 22, the Seahawks did not revise paragraph 22 to remove the mandatory consent provision. PBTM alleges that as a result of pressure from Seahawks management to immediately sign the agreement, and because [the] parties previously had a cordial working relationship, PBTM only gave the execution version a "cursory review." Consequently, it failed to notice that paragraph 22 was not revised as PBTM requested …

---

[4] *Terraform Power, LLC v. Orrick, Herrington & Sutcliffe LLP* and *Cleary Gottlieb Steen & Hamilton LLP* (N.Y. Supreme Ct., filed October 13, 2021).

Shortly after signing, PBTM discovered that the Seahawks had omitted the language PBTM requested in paragraph 22 to make the Seahawks' consent non-mandatory, and PBTM "promptly protested this omission several times." Although the Seahawks reassured PBTM that its general counsel would add the "not mandatory" language to paragraph 22 to make the consent provision non-obligatory, the language was never added and the Seahawks have since refused to do so.

When PBTM finally brought an action for contract reformation on the basis of unilateral mistake, the statute of limitations had run. And even if it had not, it is not clear that such an action would have been successful.

The moral of this story? Don't trust opposing counsel to make "agreed" changes to a draft agreement without checking that they were actually made. Better still, don't trust anyone to do your work without checking that it was done. Ultimately, you, as an attorney, will be held responsible for mistakes such as these, and the facts recited above would not play well in a legal malpractice action or a bar disciplinary proceeding.

6

License Grant and Scope

The license grant is the heart of any intellectual property (IP) license. This chapter explores many of the issues that arise in defining what rights are granted under a license agreement.

6.1 LICENSED RIGHTS

One of the most fundamental things that every license agreement must define is the set of rights that are being licensed. This definition must answer two related questions: what *type* of rights are being licensed (e.g., patents, copyrights, trademarks, etc.), and *which* of those rights are being licensed (e.g., which of the licensor's patents, copyrights, trademarks, etc.)? Though this exercise may sound straightforward, there are many ways that licensed rights can be identified, with significant ramifications for both the licensor and licensee. (Note that the definition of licensed rights is often tailored to the type of IP being licensed, so that a patent license agreement might refer to "Licensed Patents" instead of "Licensed Rights" and a trademark license may refer to "Licensed Trademarks," "Licensed Marks," "Licensed Brands" or some other variant.)

6.1.1 *Enumerated Rights*

One way to identify licensed rights is by enumerating those rights specifically and individually. Such an enumeration can refer to the governmental registrations for those rights, such as patent, trademark and copyright registrations. If there are too many rights to list conveniently in the text of a definition, a separate list can be attached as an exhibit to the agreement. Here is a simple example involving registered trademarks.

Single Registered Mark

"Licensed Mark" means U.S. Trademark Reg. No. 999,999 "SUPER-BEV".

Multiple Registered Marks

"**Licensed Marks**" means those U.S. and foreign trademark registrations listed in Exhibit A to this Agreement.

Unregistered IP can also be enumerated, so long as it can be described in a manner that clearly identifies and distinguishes it. Thus, unregistered (common law) trademarks can be included as part of a license grant, as can unregistered copyrights and even inventions and trade secrets that are not (yet) subject to any patent application. Some examples include the following.

Enumerated Rights Including Unregistered IP

"**Licensed Marks**" means those Marks that are listed in Exhibit A to this Agreement.
  "**Marks**" means trademarks, service marks and designs, whether or not registered.
"**Licensed Rights**" means all Authorship Rights throughout the world subsisting in the
  work THE GREAT AMERICAN NOVEL by Author.
  "**Authorship Rights**" means copyrights and related rights of authors, including
  moral rights.
"**Licensed Rights**" means all Know-How in Licensor's proprietary method for curing rubber utilizing heat modulation calibrated using the Arrhenius equation, as described in
  the confidential specification delivered by Licensor to Licensee on October 31, 2020.
    "**Know-How**" means all know-how, trade secrets, discoveries, inventions, data, spec-
  ifications and other information [, including biological, chemical, pharmacological, toxi-
  cological, pharmaceutical, analytical, safety, manufacturing and quality control data and
  information, study designs, protocols, assays and clinical data], whether or not confidential, proprietary or patentable and whether in written, electronic or any other form.[5]

DRAFTING NOTE

The above definitions include both a generic definition of the category of IP, as well as a definition of the licensed IP that incorporates the generic category. Using this modular structure in all but the simplest licensing agreements is advisable, as the generic IP category may be referred to elsewhere in the agreement (e.g., in the indemnification section) and it is best to use consistent terminology throughout.

Patents pose some additional issues. Like trademarks, patents are registered (and there are no common law patent rights analogous to common law trademarks). Yet many different patents may relate to the same basic invention. That is, during the patent prosecution process, patent applications may be subdivided, amended, continued and extended through a variety of differ-ent procedural mechanisms. Thus, one invention can end up being claimed by a dozen differ-ent patents that are issued for years following the issuance of the initial patent. Foreign patent applications can also be filed in multiple countries under the Patent Cooperation Treaty (PCT)

---

[5] Know-how is discussed in greater detail in Section 6.1.3.

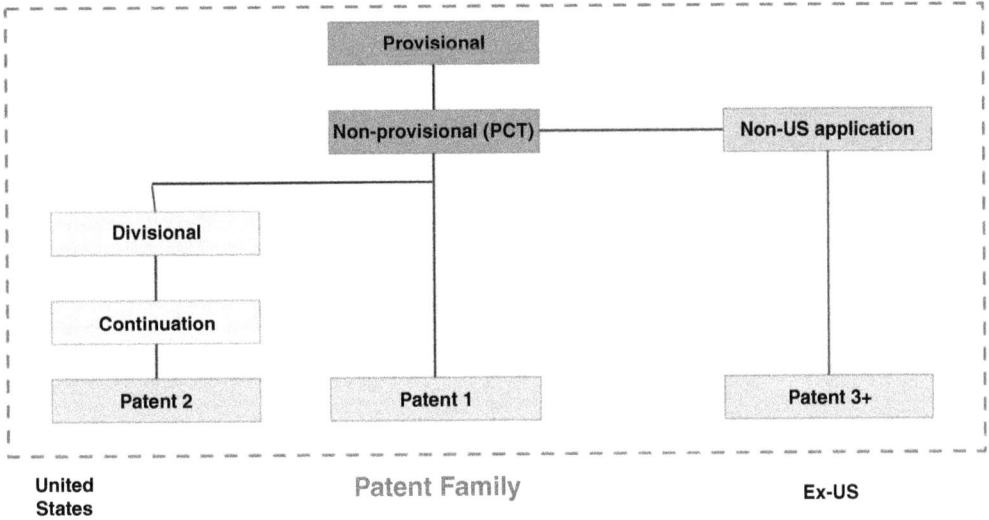

FIGURE 6.1 Graphical representation of a patent "family."

based on an original application in one country. These groups of related patents are often called a "patent family," and licensing is often conducted at the family level rather than the level of individual patents. The unifying trait of a patent family is often the ability to trace the origin of a patent to a single "ancestor" application filed on a date that is known as the "priority date" for the family and its other members. Figure 6.1 illustrates the different members of such a patent family. An example of a patent family definition follows.

LICENSED PATENTS AS SINGLE PATENT FAMILY

"**Licensed Patents**" means U.S. Patent No. x,xxx,xxx entitled "Improved Method for Slicing Bread and Apparatus Therefor" (September 9, 1999), together with all Patents claiming the same priority as such patent. [1]

    "**Patents**" means (a) patents and patent applications [4], and all divisional, continuation, and continuation-in-part applications of any such patent applications; (b) all patents issuing from any of the foregoing applications; and (c) all reissues, reexaminations, extensions, foreign counterparts [2] and supplementary protection certificates [3] of any of the patents described in clauses (a) or (b).

DRAFTING NOTES

[1] *Priority* – the "priority date" of a patent is the date on which the earliest utility patent application in the "family" of related applications was filed.
[2] *Foreign counterparts* – this term refers to foreign patents and patent applications, often filed under the Patent Cooperation Treaty, that derive from the same parent application.
[3] *Supplementary protection certificates* – these are European rights that protect certain pharmaceutical and other regulated compositions after their patent protection has expired.

[4] *Applications* – even though patent applications convey no enforceable rights, they can, and often are, licensed. Doing so is a convenient way to ensure that any patent rights that eventually emerge from such applications are licensed. The alternative would be to require the licensor to be extremely diligent in adding patents to the license grant as they are issued, a responsibility that benefits neither party.

The following case illustrates the importance of including the "right" rights in a license agreement.

Spindelfabrik Suessen-Schurr Stahlecker & Grill v. Schubert & Salzer Maschinenfabrik Aktiengesellschaft

829 F.2d 1075 (Fed. Cir. 1987)

BALDWIN, SENIOR CIRCUIT JUDGE

In 1983, Suessen, brought an action in the district court for infringement of two patents relating to improvements in the technology of open-end spinning devices, U.S. Patent No. 4,059,946 (the '946 patent) and U.S. Patent No. 4,175,370 (the '370 patent).

Schubert argues that it has an implied license under the '946 patent. Its argument involves two agreements.

The first was a license agreement entered in 1982 between Schubert and Murata Machinery, Ltd. (Murata). That agreement, entered into before the filing of this suit in 1983, in pertinent part reads:

> Murata hereby grants to Licensee [Schubert] a non-exclusive worldwide license under the Patents to make, use and sell the patented device only as part of the open end spinning machines of the License. The License hereby granted is a limited license, and Murata reserves all rights not expressly granted.

The "Patents" were defined [to] include U.S. Patent No. 4,022,011 ('011 patent) and other patents belonging to Murata in the name of Hironorai Hirai. Schubert asserts that, notwithstanding any infringement of '946, its accused infringement is merely a practicing of the '011 invention, which it is licensed to do under the 1982 agreement.

The second agreement, entered in 1984 after this lawsuit began, involved Suessen's purchase of the '011 and [other] patents from Murata. The agreement reads, in pertinent part:

> Suessen has been advised by Murata that a non-exclusive license of the patents and patent applications mentioned under 1. above had been granted by Murata to [Schubert] (hereinafter called the Licensee). Suessen hereby agrees to purchase the patents and patent applications mentioned under 1. above together with the License Agreement as of 23rd/28th July, 1982, with the said Licensee and agrees that you and your business/license concerns will maintain the licensed rights of the Licensee under the License Agreement as stipulated during the life of the patents and patent applications mentioned under 1. above.

Schubert asserts that, per the 1984 agreement, Suessen "stepped in the shoes of Murata" [and] cannot – just as Murata cannot – sue under the '946 or any other patent for infringement based on practicing the '011 invention. To allow such a suit, Schubert argues, would unfairly take away what it paid for in 1982. Schubert labels its argument one of "legal estoppel."

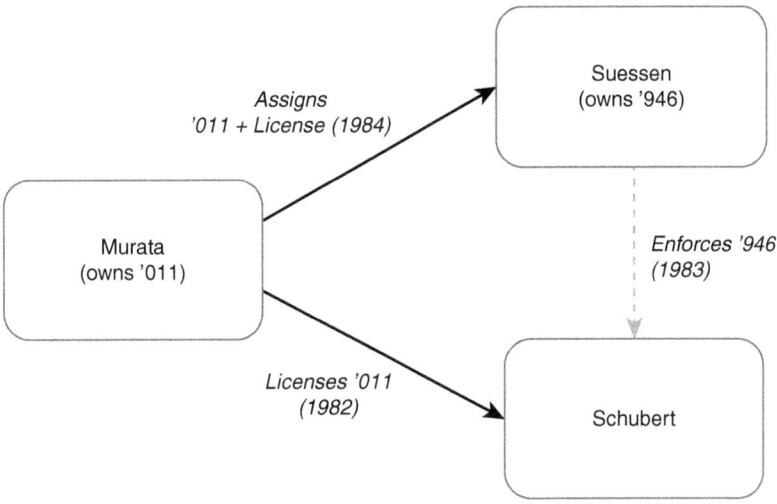

FIGURE 6.2 Ownership and license of '011 and '946 patents in *Spindelfabrik*.

[Schubert] asserts an implied license based on its theory of legal estoppel. Though we recognize that theory in appropriate circumstances, it does not work for Schubert here. Legal estoppel is merely shorthand for saying that a grantor of a property right or interest cannot derogate from the right granted by his own subsequent acts. The rationale for that is to estop the grantor from taking back that for which he received consideration. Here, however, we have a suit by a third party, Suessen, under a patent owned by Suessen. The license by the grantor, Murata, did not purport to, and indeed could not, protect Schubert from a suit by Suessen under '946. Hence, Suessen, by filing in 1983 and now maintaining its suit under '946, does not derogate from the right given by Murata in the 1982 license agreement.

Schubert nevertheless urges this three prong argument: (1) "legal estoppel" would prevent Murata from suing under the '946 patent if it were to acquire it; (2) Suessen "stepped into" Murata's shoes in 1984 when Suessen acquired the Hirai patents and committed to maintain Schubert's licensed rights; and hence, (3) just as Murata could not, Suessen cannot sue under the '946 patent. We reject that argument.

As a threshold matter, a patent license agreement is in essence nothing more than a promise by the licensor not to sue the licensee. Even if couched in terms of "[l]icensee is given the right to make, use, or sell X," the agreement cannot convey that absolute right because not even the patentee of X is given that right. His right is merely one to exclude others from making, using or selling X. Indeed, the patentee of X and his licensee, when making, using, or selling X, can be subject to suit under other patents. In any event, patent license agreements can be written to convey different scopes of promises not to sue, e.g., a promise not to sue under a specific patent or, more broadly, a promise not to sue under any patent the licensor now has or may acquire in the future.

As stated previously, the first prong of Schubert's three part "stepping in the shoes" argument is that legal estoppel would prevent Murata from suing Schubert under the '946 patent if Murata were to acquire that patent. However, even assuming, arguendo, that such estoppel against Murata exists, the final two prongs of Schubert's "stepping in the shoes" argument would fail. Given the assumption of estoppel against Murata, the 1982 license agreement would necessarily be a promise by Murata not to sue under any patent, including those acquired by Murata in the future. In the 1984 agreement, Suessen incurred what

Murata promised in 1982. Thus, Suessen would be committed to forebear from suit under (1) the transferred patents and (2) any of Murata's nontransferred patents (future and present). That commitment does not include a promise not to sue under Suessen's own '946 patent.

Schubert's "standing in the shoes" argument, however, would add to Suessen's commitment a promise not to sue under Suessen's separate patents that Murata never owned. On the facts of this case, we cannot interpret the 1984 agreement so broadly, at least not with respect to the '946 patent.

The district court correctly determined that there is nothing in the 1984 agreement about the '946 or other Suessen patent rights. Schubert points to no extraneous evidence tending to show any understanding on the part of either contracting party that Suessen was to forego rights under the '946 or any other patent then owned by Suessen. To the contrary, that a lawsuit under '946 was ongoing but not mentioned in the 1984 agreement indicates strongly that there was no intent by the parties to have Suessen forfeit its rights under '946. Furthermore, an implied promise by Suessen to forego its '946 suit is inconsistent not only with Suessen maintaining its lawsuit after the 1984 agreement but, also, with the course of events leading up to the 1984 contract. In sum, we agree with the district court's conclusion that the 1984 agreement did not impose on Suessen any obligation to stop its ongoing suit under the '946 patent.

Schubert argues that not implying a license in this case is unfair because Schubert paid valuable consideration for the right to practice the '011 invention but is in danger of losing that right as a result of doing no more than that for which it paid. We disagree. The right Schubert paid for in the 1982 agreement was freedom from suit by Murata, not Suessen. Indeed, when Schubert signed the 1982 agreement, it was aware of possible suit by Suessen, who had previously denied Schubert a license under the '946 patent. Moreover, Schubert has not shown us that it has lost any obligation Murata may still owe it under the 1982 license agreement, e.g., not to sue under any patents Murata still has or may acquire. To rule that the Suessen acquisition of the '011 patent somehow bestows on Schubert an absolute defense to a suit already filed by Suessen under '946, would result in an unintended windfall to Schubert that makes no sense under the facts of this case.

AFFIRMED

Notes and Questions

1. *Implied licenses.* In Chapter 4 we saw several examples in which courts implied licenses based on the conduct of the parties. How is *Spindelfabrik* different than these cases? If you were the judge, would you have recognized an implied license from Suessen to Schubert?
2. *Patent families.* How might the patent family definition suggested above have helped the parties in the *TransCore* and *Endo* cases discussed in Section 4.3, Notes 3–4?
3. *The importance of timing?* In *Spindelfabrik*, under the 1982 agreement, Murata licensed the '011 patent to Schubert. In 1984, Murata assigned the '011 patent and Schubert's license to Suessen. Prior to that, Suessen asserted the '946 patent against Schubert. The court held that nothing about Suessen's purchase of the '011 patent and license committed it to license the '946 patent to Schubert. But what if Suessen had purchased the '011 patent and license *before* it asserted the '946 patent against Schubert? Would this have changed the outcome? What if the '946 patent had originally been owned by Murata, but not included in the 1982 agreement, and then assigned to Suessen at the same time as the '011 patent? Would Schubert's estoppel argument be stronger?

4. *Products versus patents.* The *Spindelfabrik* case is really about product versus rights licenses (see the box "Rights Licenses versus Product Licenses"). Schubert argues that because it licensed the '011 patent, it had an absolute right to manufacture the product covered by the '011 patent. But it did not. The licensee of a patent only has the right to operate under the licensed patent and no more. How might the license agreement have been written to achieve what Schubert hoped, or assumed, it had achieved?

6.1.2 *Portfolio Rights*

Defining licensed rights by reference to a specific registered (or unregistered) IP right and its associated family members is relatively precise and avoids ambiguities regarding what is and is not licensed. Yet enumerating individual licensed rights can be both an administrative burden and a trap for the unwary. Suppose that a licensee wishes to obtain a license not to one, but a thousand different patents covering a complex product such as a smartphone or a computer. If the licensor were required to list every one of the licensed patents, it is possible that one or more patents might be overlooked. And, given cases like *Spindelfabrik*, it is difficult to argue that a right that is not enumerated in a list of licensed IP should be included in a license.

To get around this problem, parties have developed language under which groups of IP rights can be licensed without enumerating every one of them. Below is an example of such a "portfolio."

PATENT PORTFOLIO

"**Licensed Patents**" means all Patents throughout the Territory that are Controlled by Licensor or any of its Affiliates at any time during the Term [1] and that (a) claim all or any part of Licensor's Super-Slicer bread slicing device, or the use thereof [2], and (b) have a priority date earlier than January 1, 2021 [3].

"**Control**" means with respect to any intellectual property right, possession of the power and right to grant a license, sublicense, or other right to or under such intellectual property right as provided for in this Agreement without violating the terms of any agreement or other arrangement with any third party [4].

DRAFTING NOTES

[1] *Temporal portfolio constraint* – this clause applies to every patent that is in the licensor's portfolio during the term, including patents that the licensor acquires after the effective date of the agreement. If the parties wish to limit the portfolio to patents held as of the effective date, "during the Term" can be changed to "prior to the Effective Date."

[2] *Portfolio scope* – the above definition is said to cover the licensor's portfolio of patents pertaining to a particular device. If the licensor wishes instead to grant a license of its *entire* patent portfolio, then clause (a) would be eliminated.

[3] *Cutoff date* – clause (b) serves to exclude new inventions from a portfolio license. This approach can be useful if, for example, the license fee is paid in a lump sum (as it may be in a settlement agreement – see Section 11.6) based on the value of the licensor's existing patent portfolio. Note that the cutoff date in clause (b) may be prior to or after

the effective date of the agreement itself and would not exclude newly acquired patents so long as they meet the cutoff date.

[4] *Third-party licenses* – the definition of control is intended to encompass rights that the licensor owns or otherwise has the power to license. If it has already granted an exclusive license with respect to a right, then it cannot license it again (see Section 7.2.1), so such rights are not included in the license. Of course, a licensee that is concerned about such exclusions (e.g., the Swiss cheese effect) should insist that the licensor make representations and warranties (see Chapter 10.1) regarding the scope of the portfolio that is licensed and any exclusive licenses that could potentially remove necessary IP from the rights granted.

Notes and Questions

1. *Which portfolio?* In the patent portfolio definition set forth above, the licensed portfolio is defined by reference to a specific product sold by the licensor. Are there other ways that you could define a licensed portfolio? When might a licensor wish to grant a licensee a license with respect to its entire portfolio of patents?

2. *Cutoff date.* In the patent portfolio definition, there is a cutoff date beyond which patents controlled by the licensor are not included in the license. Would such a cutoff date ever be useful in a license in which the licensed rights are specifically enumerated? The cutoff date in clause (b) may be prior to or after the date of the agreement itself – when would it be useful to have a cutoff date that is after the date of the license agreement?

3. *Control.* In order to be licensed, patents (and other IP rights) must be owned or controlled by the licensor. This is the principal reason that Schubert's claim failed in *Spindelfabrik* – Murata could not license the '946 patent to Schubert because Murata did not own that patent. Accordingly, the patent portfolio definition set forth above defines licensed patents as those that are owned or controlled by the licensor or its corporate affiliates (see Note 4). Why is this language not needed when the licensed rights are enumerated specifically?

4. *Affiliates.* The term "Affiliates" is often used in licensing agreements to signify the other members of a party's corporate "family" – parent, subsidiary and sibling entities. Including IP held by affiliates in definitions such as the licensed rights is important, as large multinational organizations often hold or exploit IP rights in various entities for tax and accounting purposes. It is common to define "Affiliates" using the definition provided under the Securities Exchange Act of 1934:

   An "affiliate" of, or a person "affiliated" with, a specified person, is a person that directly, or indirectly through one or more intermediaries, controls, or is controlled by, or is under common control with, the person specified.
   The term "control" (including the terms "controlling," "controlled by" and "under common control with") means the possession, direct or indirect, of the power to direct or cause the direction of the management and policies of a person, whether through the ownership of voting securities, by contract, or otherwise.

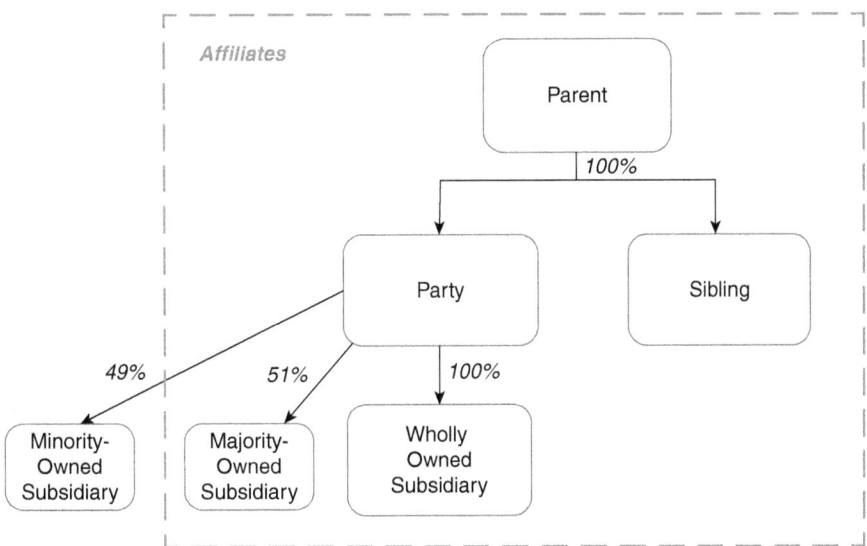

FIGURE 6.3 Affiliate relationships in a corporate "family."

Under this definition, "control" typically means ownership of at least 50 percent of the voting securities or interests of an entity.[6] As such, majority-owned subsidiaries of an entity are included within the definition of "Affiliates." Can you think of any reasons that the parties might prefer to define "control" as the ownership of 100 percent of the voting securities or interests of an entity (e.g., limited to wholly owned subsidiaries only)?

There are several contexts in which it is particularly important to pay careful attention to rights and IP held by affiliates:

• Alpha grants Beta an exclusive license under "all of Alpha's and its Affiliates' IP covering technology x"; Alpha is then acquired by Gamma, a larger company that also works in technology x. Does the license now cover Gamma's IP as well? What if the license was paid-up at the time of grant?

• Instead, assume that Alpha's subsidiary Delta also holds IP relating to technology x, and Alpha then sells Delta to Epsilon. Is Delta's IP still licensed to Beta? Is Epsilon's?

• Now suppose that Beta has granted a license under its own IP to Alpha and its affiliates. Alpha sells Delta to Epsilon. Does Beta's license to Delta continue once it is owned by Epsilon? Does Epsilon now get a license under Beta's IP? Again, what if all of these licenses were paid-up at the time of grant?

Can you think of more scenarios in which the extent of corporate families can play an important role in IP transactions?

5. *IP divestitures.* As discussed in Chapter 3.5, licenses of IP rights generally continue even if the underlying IP right is sold by the licensor. Thus, when a licensor grants a portfolio license and then sells some of the IP rights in the portfolio, the licensee can generally

---

[6] Outside of the IP licensing context, at least one court has held that as little as 35 percent "ownership" of an entity may confer "control" over it if, for example, the owner has a voting agreement, the right to designate directors or an independent commercial relationship that, individually or collectively, confers the "power to direct." See *Voigt v. Metcalf*, 2020 WL 614999 ("It is impossible to identify or foresee all of the possible sources of influence that could contribute to a finding of actual control") (discussed in S. Michael Sirkin, Voigt v. Metcalf: Delaware Court of Chancery Adopts Innovative Approach to Assessing Allegations of Effective Control, M&A Lawyer, May 2020, at 11).

rely on the continuation of that license, and the buyer (or even a new exclusive licensee) takes subject to the earlier-granted license. If this is the case, then in *Spindelfabrik* why did Murata assign the 1982 license agreement with Schubert to Suessen when Murata sold the '011 patent to Suessen?

6. *Copyright (and trademark) portfolios.* Portfolio licenses are not limited to patents. In many cases, copyrights are licensed on a portfolio basis as well. For example, a television network may license all of its programming to a cable provider or online streaming service, and a performing rights organization such as ASCAP or BMI routinely licenses thousands of songs to its licensees for particular uses (see Chapter 16). Trademarks, however, are not typically licensed on a portfolio basis, but are usually enumerated, even if a large number of marks are being licensed. Why?

6.1.3 *The Puzzle of "Know-How" Licensing*

License agreements involving technology often include a grant of rights with respect to "know-how." What is "know-how"? It is not a recognized form of IP. Though it may encompass trade secrets, know-how is generally understood to be broader than trade secrets alone. Noted organizational theorist Eric von Hippel defines know-how as "the accumulated practical skill or expertise which allows one to do something smoothly and efficiently."[7] J. N. Behrman, who conducted some of the first empirical studies of IP licensing in the United States, defines it as:

> whatever unpatented or unpatentable information the licensor has developed and which the licensee cannot readily obtain on his own and is willing to pay for under the agreement; such as techniques and processes, the trade secrets necessary to make and sell a patented (or other) item in the most efficient manner, designs, blueprints, plant layouts, engineering specifications, product mixes, secret formulas, etc.[8]

KNOW-HOW VERSUS TRADE SECRETS

Unlike know-how, trade secrets are recognized IP rights protected in the United States by federal and state statutes as well as common law. As discussed in Chapter 5.2, in order to be considered a trade secret, information must derive independent value from being kept secret and must be the subject of reasonable efforts to maintain confidentiality. These requirements are not always easy to establish, and information that is conveyed during the course of technical training, product demonstrations and support calls may not always qualify as trade secrets, despite its value to the recipient.

The concept of "know-how" has thus evolved to include both trade secrets as well as other information that is conveyed by the licensor to the licensee. So long as information is conveyed – whether orally, visually or in writing – it can be "know-how." This lower bar is useful primarily to establish a basis for the payment of ongoing royalties with respect to the information conveyed. That is, if a license covered only trade secrets, and the information

[7]   Eric E. von Hippel, Cooperation between Rivals: Informal Know-How Trading in Industrial Dynamics: Studies in Industrial Organization, vol. 10, 157, 158 (B. Carlsson, ed., Springer, 1989).
[8]   J. N. Behrman, *Licensing Abroad under Patents, Trademarks, and Know-How by U.S. Companies*, 2 Pat. Trademark & Copyright J. Res. & Ed. 181, 182 (1958).

in question lost trade secret status for some reason, then it is unclear that the license would remain in effect or that the licensee would have a continuing obligation to pay royalties. But if the royalty were payable instead on know-how, then the loss of trade secret status with respect to some or all of that information would not affect the license or the obligation to pay royalties. Thus, know-how is a more flexible concept than trade secrets, supporting a stronger basis for the payment of royalties.

However it is defined, know-how is frequently featured in license agreements. As early as 1959, a study of more than 1,000 IP license agreements found that approximately 39 percent included grants of know-how rights.[9] More recently, Thomas Varner, in a study of over 1,400 publicly filed patent licenses and assignments, found that 56 percent included know-how.[10] So we know that know-how is being licensed, but what does this mean in practice?

There are two principal functions that know-how licensing plays in IP transactions. The first is straightforward. If the licensor provides training, support, consultation, expertise or some other technical services to the licensee, then the information and skills conveyed through those services are "licensed" as know-how. Even though most of this intangible knowledge is not protected (or even protectable) by formal IP rights, courts have long recognized that such information can be valuable and thus the subject of compensation.

In many cases, however, no such knowledge transfer is contemplated, yet the license agreement (usually a patent license agreement) still contains a license of know-how. In these cases, the know-how license is included simply as a clever way for the licensor to continue to collect royalties after the relevant patents expire. As we will see in Chapter 24, it is illegal under US law for a patent holder to continue to collect royalties for the use of a patented technology after the patent has expired. To get around this limitation, patent holders can license patents and know-how together, so that even after the patents expire, there is still a valuable asset to support the payment of royalties (albeit at a reduced level). The same logic applies to patents that are invalidated after being licensed, and to sales of products in countries where the patent holder does not seek patent protection. In all of these cases, royalties can be collected with respect to know-how, even though no enforceable patents are licensed.

COMBINED PATENT AND KNOW-HOW DEFINITION

"**Licensed Rights**" means the Licensed Patents and all associated Know-How conveyed by the Licensor to the Licensee hereunder.

 "**Know-How**" means trade secrets, knowledge, techniques, methods and other information, whether or not patentable.

---

[9] J. N. Behrman & W. E. Schmidt, *New Data on Foreign Licensing*, 3 Pat. Trademark & Copyright J. Res. & Ed. 357, 370, Table 6 (1959).

[10] Thomas R. Varner, *An Economic Perspective on Patent Licensing Structure and Provisions*, 47 Les Nouvelles 28, 31 (2012).

Notes and Questions

1. *The risks of know-how licensing?* In the 1950s and 1960s there was significant concern among scholars and policy makers that the licensing of vaguely defined know-how might run afoul of antitrust laws.[11] We will study antitrust issues arising in connection with licensing transactions in Chapter 25, but for now it is sufficient to understand that "licenses" of this amorphous set of rights were viewed as a potential cover-up for otherwise anticompetitive arrangements. What kind of anticompetitive behavior do you think a know-how license might conceal?

2. *Know-how licensing and patent trolling.* Professors Robin Feldman and Mark Lemley have observed that when a patent holder makes an unsolicited licensing proposal to a potential licensee (e.g., as a prelude to an express or tacit threat of litigation), the resulting licenses seldom include a transfer of know-how.[12] This result held whether the patent holder was a non-practicing entity, a university or a company. Professor Colleen Chien, in contrast, found in a study of publicly filed licenses of software patents that most patent licenses also included a license of know-how or software code.[13] She explains the difference between her results and those of Feldman and Lemley as follows:

   Patent licenses that include knowledge, know-how, personnel, or joint venture relationships are more likely to represent direct transfers of technology, whereas the transfer of "naked" patent rights is more likely to primarily represent a transfer of liability between the parties.[14]

   What does Chien mean by a "transfer of liability between the parties"? Why would know-how transfers be more frequent in a broad sampling of licensing transactions than patent-owner-initiated demands for a license?

3. *Taxing know-how.* In addition to antitrust, early concerns over know-how licensing arose from tax law. Was know-how a taxable asset, or was the transfer of know-how a service? In each case, how was it valued? Together with "goodwill" (see Chapter 2.4), know-how presents one of the more interesting tax issues in the field of IP licensing.[15]

6.1.4 Product Rights

So far, our consideration of licensed rights has focused on specific IP rights or groups of rights that the parties desire to license. This approach is natural when particular patents, copyrights, trademarks or trade secrets are known, or expected, to have value in themselves. However, it is often the case that a licensee is interested in exploiting a product that may be covered by a variety of IP rights held by the licensor, and neither the licensor nor the licensee knows, or particularly cares, which rights those may be.

Software programs often fall into this category. Software can be protected by large numbers of copyrights, patents, trade secrets, trade dress, trademarks and other forms of IP. But

---

[11] *See, e.g.,* Behrman, *supra* note 4, at 222–23 (listing 23 legal concerns raised by know-how licensing); David R. Macdonald, *Know-How Licensing and the Antitrust Laws,* 62 Mich. L. Rev. 351 (1964).

[12] Robin Feldman & Mark A. Lemley, *Do Patent Licensing Demands Mean Innovation?,* 101 Iowa L. Rev. 137, 156–75 (2015).

[13] Colleen V. Chien, *Software Patents as a Currency, Not Tax, on Innovation,* 31 Berkeley Tech. L. J. 1669, 1679 (2016).

[14] Id. at 1689.

[15] *See, e.g.,* John F. Creed & Robert B. Bangs, *Know-How Licensing and Capital Gains,* 4 Patent, Trademark & Copyright J. Res. & Education 93, 93 (1960).

if a distributor wishes to resell a software program via an online store, or a consumer wishes to use that software on her laptop computer, it is unlikely that they are aware of, or have any desire to know about, the specific IP rights covering that software. In fact, in many cases, even the owner of the software, particularly if it is a large company, may not be aware of the many different IP rights that protect it. Thus, in software and other industries, the common practice is to license all rights pertaining to a particular *product* without any attempt to list or even categorize them.

PRODUCT LICENSE RIGHTS

The term **"Licensed Software"** means the executable object code of the SOFTMICRO application (version 1.0) and all of Licensor's patent, copyright, trade secret, trade dress and other rights in and to such software application and its operation, but excluding trademarks.

In some cases, a licensor granting a license with respect to a full product, especially a software product, will not even recite the IP rights that are licensed at all, and will simply grant the license in the Grant clause of the agreement (see Section 6.3). Or, if it separately defines the licensed software, it will omit to mention any IP rights.

PRODUCT LICENSE RIGHTS: SIMPLIFIED

The term **"Licensed Software"** means the executable object code of the SOFTMICRO application (version 1.0).

RIGHTS LICENSES VERSUS PRODUCT LICENSES

There is a **critical** difference between licenses of *rights* and licenses of *products*. In a license of rights, for example a patent license, the licensee is permitted to create and exploit *any* product that it wishes within the bounds of the license grant (e.g., within the field of use and scope of license discussed in Section 6.2). Thus, if the licensed patent covers an amplifier, the licensee may make any amplifier that it wishes – large, small, low-power, portable, transistorized, heat-resistant, etc. In short, it may use the patented technology to create a product of its own. In contrast, a product license allows the licensee to make only the exact product that is licensed. Thus, if Microsoft licenses its Windows operating system to a PC manufacturer, the licensee is likely permitted to install Windows on its PCs, but not to create a new, improved version of Windows or any other operating system. This key difference is important to keep in mind when reviewing the many variants of license agreements that will be discussed in this book.

Notes and Questions

1. *Code.* The sample definition of "Licensed Software" relates to the "object code" version of the software. We will discuss the distinction between object code and source code in more detail in Section 18.2. For now, it is sufficient to understand that the object code version of software is the version that runs on a user's computer or device, but does not allow the user to understand the internal functions of the software or how it is "written." Why do you think most software distribution and use licenses are limited to object code?

2. *No trademarks.* Trademark rights are typically excluded from a product-based license or, if granted, are licensed separately. There are several reasons for this convention. First, a trademark license is not required to use a software program, even if the program displays the vendor's trademarks (we will discuss trademark licensing in greater detail in Chapter 15). A distributor or reseller may require a license to advertise a software program, but that license will contain numerous qualifications and requirements and is thus best granted separately from the right to distribute the program. Finally, doctrines in trademark law such as "nominative fair use" permit parties to refer to a trademarked term in a factual manner (e.g., "We service BMW vehicles"), without the need for a formal license. As a result, a well-drafted definition of product rights should generally exclude trademarks.

6.1.5 *Future Rights*

It is a somewhat metaphysical question whether an IP right can actually be "licensed" before it is created. Is the license of a future IP right – a patent claiming an invention not yet made, the copyright in a book not yet written – a *property interest* that exists independent of the right itself, like a contingent remainder or other future interest in real property, or is it merely a *promise* to license the IP right once it exists? This is a question that deserves to be debated in the law reviews, but is not one that we will answer here. For all practical purposes, as we saw in *Stanford v. Roche* (Chapter 2.3), interests in IP that is not yet created can clearly be bought, sold and licensed. Yet, as that case also suggests, there is an important difference between a present license of future inventions and a promise to grant a license in the future (with the former clearly preferable to the latter).

In fact, we have already seen licenses of future rights above, in our example of a patent portfolio license. If, during the term of the license, the licensor comes into possession of a new patent that meets the other criteria for a licensed right, then that new patent is licensed along with the rest. But future rights may be licensed more explicitly, and they often are.

FUTURE LICENSED RIGHTS

"**Licensed Work**" means the book that is written and delivered by Author hereunder, currently known under the working title THE GREAT AMERICAN NOVEL.

"**Licensed Rights**" means all patent, copyright, know-how, trade secret and other rights in all developments, inventions and discoveries in the Field made by Dr. Jekyll and the other members of the Jekyll Lab at Stevenson University during the Term.

Problem 6.1

For each of the following deals, draft a suitable definition of the "Licensed Rights":

a. Transatlantic Corp. has agreed to sell its fleet of Atlantic fishing vessels to United Fishfry. After the sale, Transatlantic will continue to operate its remaining fleet of seven passenger cruise ships. Several years ago, Transatlantic developed a patented method of radar enhancement that greatly improves navigation at sea. The enhancement is now used on all of Transatlantic's ships. The parties have agreed that, as part of the fleet sale, Transatlantic will grant an appropriate license to United.

b. Lobrow Corp. sells a popular line of children's toys in the United States based on the popular YouTube character "Bo Weevil." Assume that Lobrow owns all rights in and to this character and has protected it around the world. In an effort to go international, Lobrow has agreed to grant Downunder, Inc. the right to distribute Bo Weevil toys in Australia and New Zealand.

c. Don Juan has just published a bestselling memoir of his scandalous career in Hollywood. He was recently approached by RealTV, a producer, to develop the memoir into a Netflix television series.

d. Choco Corp. and PeaNot, Inc. are large snack food manufacturers. They have formed a joint venture (JV) to create and market a candy bar that combines the best features of each of their existing product lines (chocolate bars and synthetic peanuts). Each of them will receive 50 percent of the profits of the JV during its existence and has agreed to grant a license to the JV.

6.2 SCOPE OF THE LICENSE: FIELD OF USE, LICENSED PRODUCTS, AND TERRITORY

Once the licensed IP rights are defined, we must define the markets and applications in which the licensee will be permitted to exploit those rights. In some rare cases, a licensor may wish to cede all potential markets and applications of its IP to the licensee throughout the world. If this is the case, then these concepts can simply be incorporated into the grant clause, discussed in Section 6.3. However, if the licensor wishes to grant the licensee only a subset of the total rights available, then careful attention must be paid to defining the scope of the licensee's use. Three related definitions are often employed for this purpose: Field of Use, Licensed Products and Territory. While different agreements may combine some or all of these definitions, we will discuss each individually before considering how they can be combined.

6.2.1 *Field of Use*

The field of use (FOU) is the market segment or product category in which the licensee is authorized to exercise the licensed rights. There is a virtually unlimited range of fields that can be specified in an agreement, from extremely narrow to extremely broad. Following are examples of FOU for three different types of IP.

The limitation of a patent licensee's FOU was validated by the Supreme Court in *General Talking Pictures Corp. v. Western Electric*, 304 U.S. 175 (1938). In that case, Western Electric, the holder of a patent on electronic amplifiers, licensed the patent to two different licensees: Transformer Co., in the field of amateur radio, and General Talking Pictures, in the field of movie projectors. When Transformer Co. began to sell amplifiers to General Talking Pictures for use in its projectors, Western Electric sued, alleging that Transformer Co. was not licensed to sell amplifiers for use in the theatrical projection market, and was thus infringing Western Electric's patent. The Supreme Court agreed, holding that "patent owners may grant licenses extending to all uses or limited use in a defined field."

Fields of use come in two flavors: those that limit the technical application of a licensed right (e.g., "treating emphysema") and those that limit the customers to which products may be sold (e.g., manufacturers of amateur radio receivers versus movie projectors). In some respects, these two categories can appear to merge, as types of customers are easily defined by different technical applications (and the explicit allocation of customers is a violation of the antitrust laws – see Section 25.3). Nevertheless, analytically it is sometimes convenient to think of FOU as limiting either technical applications or customers.

Some agreements may define multiple fields of use: a licensee may have exclusive rights in some fields and nonexclusive rights in other fields; some fields may be prohibited to it; and it may have the option to acquire rights in still other fields, often upon the payment of a fee.

FIELD OF USE EXAMPLES

Biotech (e.g., a new molecule)

- Treatment of hereditary breast cancer using a therapeutic agent targeted to variants in the *BRCA1* or *BRCA2* genes;
- treatment of hereditary breast cancer using a therapeutic agent targeted to one or more genetic variants;
- treatment of hereditary breast cancer;
- treatment of breast cancer;
- treatment of cancer;
- human therapeutics;
- all therapeutic applications, human and veterinary;
- all applications, whether therapeutic, diagnostic, agricultural, industrial or military.

Electronics (e.g., part of a 5G telecommunications standard)

- Implementation of wideband wireless communication functionality conforming to the 5G standard in a consumer handheld smartphone device;
- implementation of wideband wireless communication functionality in a consumer handheld smartphone device;
- implementation of wideband wireless communication functionality in a consumer device;
- implementation of wideband wireless communication functionality in a communications device;
- implementation of wireless communication functionality;
- communications applications;
- all applications.

Literary (e.g., a popular novel)

- English-language print books for the US and Canadian market;
- Spanish-language editions;

- paperback editions;
- ebooks;
- magazine serializations;
- audiobooks;
- stage plays;
- television and film adaptations;
- action figures and other memorabilia;
- T-shirts and other apparel;
- theme park attractions.

Notes and Questions

1. *Going broad.* Generally, a licensee will desire an FOU that is as broad as possible, while the licensor will seek to limit the FOU so that it retains as many rights as possible to grant to others or exploit itself. Under what circumstances might a licensee be concerned about an FOU that is too broad?

2. *Biotech FOU.* In some industries, particularly biotechnology, there may be multiple potential uses for a licensed compound, such as a molecule, protein or gene. It is thus not uncommon in biotech licenses to see FOU that are limited to specific disease targets (e.g., cancer, cystic fibrosis, diabetes) or delivery mechanisms (e.g., intravenous, oral, topical, gene therapy). In many cases, license grants are exclusive with respect to these narrowly specified FOU. These licenses are typically granted at early stages of product research and development.

   However, once a relatively complete drug or therapy is licensed (e.g., from a biotech company to a pharmaceutical manufacturer that will seek regulatory approval and then manufacture and market the drug), it is not typical to limit use by disease indication. The reason is that physicians are generally free to prescribe a medication for any use (i.e., the indicated use as well as "off label" uses), and the distributing company has little means of policing whether those uses fall within the scope of its license.

3. *Anticompetitive fields?* In *General Talking Pictures*, discussed above, Justice Black dissented, expressing concern that the allocation of different "fields" to different patent licensees, especially if numerous patents held by different owners were pooled together, could have the effect of creating a series of submonopolies that limited competition. We will discuss antitrust issues in greater detail in Chapter 25, but based on what you now know about FOU, do you agree with Justice Black's concern?

4. *FOU and the lawyer's role.* The FOU definition is one of the few parts of a license agreement that does not depend on legal terminology so much as a deep and accurate understanding of the licensed rights, the market and the potential business relationship between the parties. Clients will often provide their attorneys with a definition of the FOU that they feel is adequate, and that definition may even be embedded in a term sheet or letter of intent before the license drafting begins (see Section 5.3). But the diligent attorney should consider whether there are unanticipated pitfalls in the client's FOU definition: Is it too broad or too narrow? Will it enable the licensee to carry out the business arrangement that is anticipated? How will it fare in the face of competition from others? Will the licensor have sufficient flexibility to license others in adjacent fields? Will the definition quickly become obsolete as technology advances? Asking questions like these, rather than cutting and pasting an FOU definition from a client's email or term sheet, will serve the interests of both parties to the transaction.

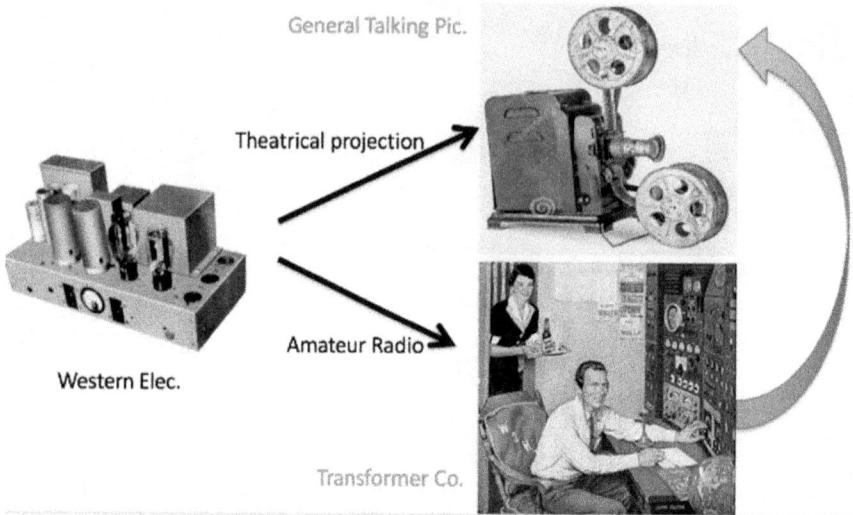

FIGURE 6.4 In *General Talking Pictures*, the Supreme Court validated the division of patent license rights according to technical fields of use.

Problem 6.2

For each of the following IP rights, describe the *broadest* FOU that you would realistically wish to obtain as the licensee, and the *narrowest* FOU that you would realistically wish to grant as the licensor:

a. a patented synthetic molecule that converts petroleum products into refined sugar;
b. the #1 R&B hit song "Bag of Fleas" by the megagroup Shag Shaggy Dog;
c. a little-known Bulgarian superhero comic character known as "Tarantula Man";
d. a patented software encryption methodology that would reduce the effectiveness of cyberattacks by 90 percent;
e. the world-famous "squish" brand/logo that Squish Corp. has popularized through a line of high-end sports footwear;
f. The persona of the recently deceased pop superstar formerly known as Princess.

6.2.2 *Licensed Product*

The term "Licensed Product" means, essentially, a product made or sold by the licensee that uses or is covered by some or all of the licensed IP rights. The term Licensed Product is important because it often (but not always) defines the licensee's payment obligation. That is, the licensee often must pay the licensor a royalty based on the licensee's revenue earned from sales of Licensed Products. So, every Licensed Product triggers a payment. For this reason, the definition of Licensed Product must specify that the product in question is covered by the licensed IP. The licensor is typically not legally entitled to collect royalties on a licensee's sale of products that are not covered by the licensor's IP, a practice that is referred to as "misuse" (see Chapter 24).

A basic example of a Licensed Product definition is set forth below. The *Cyrix* case discussed in Section 6.3 introduces additional complexities to this definition, particularly clause (a).

Licensed Product (Patent)

"**Licensed Product**" means a product that is (a) manufactured or sold by or for the Licensee or its Affiliates and (b) which is covered by any claim of the Licensed Patents.

Licensed Product (Patent + Know-How)

"**Licensed Product**" means a product that is (a) manufactured or sold by or for the Licensee or its Affiliates and (b) which is covered by any claim of the Licensed Patents or which embodies, or is manufactured using, any of the Licensed Know-How.

6.2.3 *Territory*

Every IP license has a territorial scope, whether implicitly through the inherent national character of intellectual property rights or, more typically, as defined in the agreement.

Some licenses are worldwide. That is, they allow the licensee to exercise the licensed rights everywhere in the world. Of course, no license is needed in countries and regions where the licensor does not possess IP protection for the licensed rights. A few countries lack patent laws entirely (e.g., Eritrea, Myanmar, Somalia), and it is only the most determined patentee that seeks and obtains patent protection in every country that does. In terms of copyright, 179 countries are parties to the international Berne Convention for the Protection of Literary and Artistic Works, but Iran, Iraq, Cambodia, Ethiopia and a handful of others are not. Moreover, national IP laws are not recognized in international waters, or in space. Thus, while truly "worldwide" licenses may be overkill, there is little downside in granting worldwide rights when the licensor does not wish to impose any territorial restriction on the licensee's activities.

Below the global level, parties may subdivide the world largely as they see fit. The territory of a license grant may be a city, state, country or larger region. Parties, however, often run into trouble when they try to define territories beyond national borders. Ill-defined regions such as "Asia Pacific"[16] the "Middle East" and the "US West Coast" (are Alaska and Hawaii included?) frequently appear in term sheets and letters of intent, but often lead to disagreements regarding the precise countries included within their scope. Even regions that may seem well-understood can harbor traps for the unwary. For example, when asked how many countries are in North America, many people will respond "three – Canada, the USA and Mexico." But this is incorrect. There are around forty countries that make up the North American continent, including Caribbean nations such as Cuba, Jamaica, Haiti and the Dominican Republic, the Central American countries of Panama, Costa Rica, Nicaragua, Honduras, El Salvador, Guatemala and Belize, as well as Bermuda, off the Atlantic coast of the United States, and the massive territory Greenland (currently held by Denmark).

The territory of "Europe" presents even more complexities. When speaking of Europe, one might mean the European Union (EU) (27 countries), the European Economic Area (the EU plus Iceland, Liechtenstein and Norway), the Eurozone (19 of the EU countries), the European Patent Convention (16 countries), or the traditional "continent" of Europe, which includes

---

[16] The author once served as his law firm's representative to a group called the Pacific Rim Advisory Council (PRAC), which included members not only from expected "Pacific Rim" countries such as Japan, South Korea, China and Singapore, but also countries including Venezuela, Argentina, Brazil and South Africa, with no known territory on the Pacific Ocean.

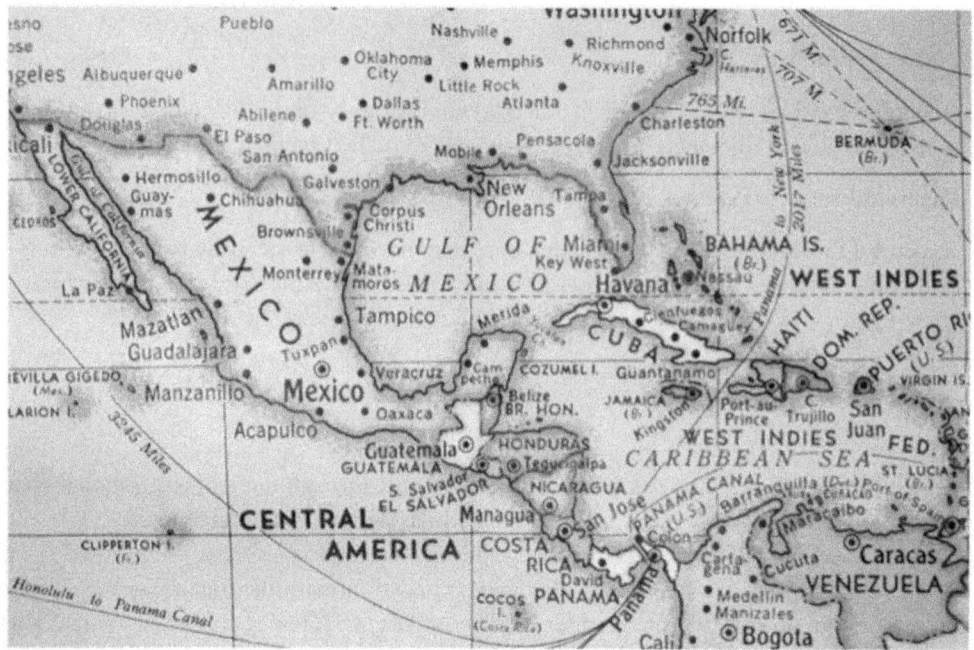

FIGURE 6.5 The territory of "North America" consists of about forty different countries.

Russia, Ukraine and other countries that are not a part of any of the major European trading coalitions. Moreover, even the EU is fluid, as the recent exit of the UK (via Brexit) demonstrates. License agreements that defined the licensee's territory as spanning the European Union suddenly contracted on January 31, 2020, when the UK exited the EU.

Perhaps the most precise manner of defining the territory of a license agreement is to list the specific countries included in the territory in a schedule or exhibit to the agreement, though this approach can have its hazards as well. Consider, for example, the patent and know-how licenses sponsored by the Medicines Patent Pool (MPP), an arm of the UN's World Health Organization. The MPP obtains licenses from multinational pharmaceutical companies for the manufacture and distribution of lifesaving drugs in the developing world. A company granting such a license could specifically list the "developing" countries to which the license applied. But countries change status occasionally. India and China are, by some measures, still developing countries, yet many companies would hesitate to lump them together with far poorer countries for essentially philanthropic purposes. Instead of listing countries, a licensor could refer to an external list or index, such as the Organisation for Economic Co-operation and Development (OECD) list of "least developed countries," a list that changes periodically.

A final note of caution with respect to territory definition is to ensure that the granting of licenses within defined territories is not a cover-up for the allocation of markets among competitors, a violation of the antitrust laws (see Section 25.3). Outside of the United States, competition laws and regional agreements may also limit the ability of parties to divide rights territorially. For example, the EU requires the free movement of goods, services, capital and persons among member states of the Union. Accordingly, agreements that prevent a party in one EU country from shipping goods to, or providing services in, another EU country may be invalid.

There is no foolproof method of correctly defining the territory of a license agreement, other than to draft carefully and thoughtfully with the intentions of the parties in mind and a good atlas at hand.

6.3 GRANT CLAUSE

With the nature of the licensed rights, and the markets in which the licensee may operate, established, the "grant" clause of a license agreement sets forth the precise legal rights that are granted to the licensee.

Grant Clause [Patent]

Licensor hereby grants [1] to Licensee a nonexclusive, [nonassignable] [2] license [3] under the Licensed Patent Rights, excluding the right to sublicense [4], to make, use, sell, offer for sale and import Licensed Products throughout the Territory.

Grant Clause [Copyright]

Licensor hereby grants [1] to Licensee a nonexclusive, [nonassignable] [2] license [3], excluding the right to sublicense [4], to reproduce, distribute, publicly perform and make derivative works of the Licensed Works throughout the Territory.

Grant Clause [Trademark]

Licensor hereby grants [1] to Licensee a nonexclusive, [nonassignable] [2] license [3], excluding the right to sublicense [4], to reproduce and display the Licensed Marks, without alteration, on Approved Products throughout the Territory and on advertising and promotional materials, tangible and electronic, promoting the Approved Products in the Territory.

DRAFTING NOTES

[1] *Present grant* – although *Stanford v. Roche* (discussed in Section 2.3, Note 3) involved an assignment of rights rather than a license, its lessons about clear present grants of rights hold equally true in the realm of licensing. Avoid variants in the grant clause such as "shall grant," "agrees to grant" and the like.

[2] *Assignability* – many license grants include the term "nonassignable." Doing so could, however, conflict with the express assignment clause usually contained toward the back of the agreement (see Section 13.3). Rather than attempt to sort out any contradictory language when a merger or other corporate transaction is on the horizon, it is preferable to omit "nonassignable" in the grant clause.

[3] *Right and license* – the grant is of a "license." Some agreements state that a "right and license" is granted, but this is unnecessary.

[4] *Sublicensing* – some licenses may be sublicensed (see Section 6.5), and if so, there will be a separate, often lengthy, section on sublicensing. However, if the intent is to prohibit sublicensing, it is efficient to do so in the grant clause.

Note that with respect to rights that are granted under statutory forms of IP (especially patents and copyrights), it is important to follow the statutory rights that are inherent in the licensed assets. Specifically:

- The Patent Act establishes that the owner of a patent has the exclusive right to **make, use, sell, offer for sale** and **import** a patented article (35 U.S.C. § 271(a)).

- The Copyright Act establishes that the owner of a copyright has the exclusive right to **reproduce, prepare derivative works, distribute, perform** and **display** various types of copyrighted works (17 U.S.C. § 106).
- The Lanham Act establishes that the registrant of a federal trademark or service mark has the exclusive right to **use in commerce, reproduce, copy**, and **imitate** the mark (15 U.S.C. § 1114).

Keeping these distinctions in mind is critical when drafting the grant clause. Thus, if a patent is being licensed, it is nonsensical to grant a licensee the right to "display" the patented article or to "produce derivative works" of it, as these are not rights granted under the Patent Act. Likewise, granting the licensee under a copyright the right to "use" the copyrighted work can cause no end of confusion, as demonstrated by the decision in *Kennedy v. NJDA*, discussed in Section 9.1 (interpreting the word "use" in a copyright license to encompass the making of derivative works).

It is also important to note that these rights can often be granted separately, and not all rights need be granted to every licensee. For example, some patent licenses permit *use* of a patented apparatus, but do not grant the licensee the right to *make* or *sell* that apparatus. By the same token, some exclusive patent licenses may grant the licensee an exclusive right to sell a licensed product, but do not extend exclusivity to the use of that product. Copyright licenses can be limited to the right to reproduce a work, but not to create *derivative* works of it.

For IP assets that are not statutorily defined, such as know-how, unregistered trademarks, rights of publicity, database rights and the like, the drafter can be more creative regarding the authority granted to the licensee. Yet this additional flexibility can also lead to disputes, so the drafter must pay particular attention to defining the rights granted as precisely as possible to achieve the client's objectives.

The *Cyrix* case excerpted below illustrates the importance of precisely defining the scope of the license granted.

Cyrix Corp. v. Intel Corp.

77 F.3d 1381 (Fed. Cir. 1996)

LOURIE, CIRCUIT JUDGE

Intel Corporation appeals from the decision of the United States District Court for the Eastern District of Texas entering judgment in favor of Cyrix Corporation, SGS-Thomson Microelectronics, Inc. (ST), and International Business Machines Corporation (IBM), and holding that IBM and ST acted within the scope of their respective patent license agreements with Intel when IBM made, and ST had made, products for Cyrix. [We] affirm.

Background

Cyrix designed and sold microprocessors. Since it did not have its own facility for manufacturing the microprocessors it designed, it contracted with other companies to act as its foundries. Under such an arrangement, Cyrix provided the foundries with its microprocessor designs, and the foundries manufactured integrated circuit chips containing those microprocessors and sold them to Cyrix. Cyrix then sold the microprocessors in the marketplace under its own brand name.

It was Cyrix's practice to use manufacturing facilities of companies that were licensed under Intel's patents. IBM was such a company; it had obtained a license to Intel's patents in a patent license agreement dated October 1, 1989. The granting clause of the IBM–Intel agreement provided as follows:

2.2 Subject to the provisions of Sections 2.7 and 3.3, INTEL, on behalf of itself and its Subsidiaries, hereby grants to IBM a worldwide, royalty-free, nonexclusive license under the INTEL Licensed Patents:

> 2.2.1 to make, use, lease, sell and otherwise transfer IBM Licensed Products and to practice any method or process involved in the manufacture or use thereof;
>
> …
>
> 2.2.3 to have made IBM Licensed Products … by another manufacturer for the use, lease, sale or other transfer by IBM.

The agreement defined "IBM Licensed Products" as follows:

> 1.23 "IBM Licensed Products" shall mean IHS Products, … Supplies and any combination of any, some or all of the foregoing …

Cyrix also used ST as a foundry. Initially, ST manufactured the chips, but when ST was unable to meet Cyrix's demands, ST requested its affiliate in Italy, SGS-Thomson Microelectronics S.r.L. (ST-Italy), to manufacture the needed chips, which ST then sold to Cyrix.

ST was operating under a license agreement between Mostek and Intel, which ST acquired by assignment. The agreement contains the following granting clause:

> INTEL grants and agrees to grant to MOSTEK non-exclusive, non-transferrable, worldwide licenses under INTEL PATENTS and INTEL PATENT APPLICATIONS to make, to have made, to use, to sell (either directly or indirectly), to lease and to otherwise dispose of LICENSED PRODUCTS.

The agreement defined "LICENSED PRODUCTS" as follows:

> "LICENSED PRODUCTS" shall mean any product manufactured, used or sold by either party covered by patents of the other party.

It is undisputed that ST-Italy is legally not a "subsidiary" of ST and is thus not licensed under the ST–Intel agreement. ST therefore relied upon its "have made" rights to obtain products from ST-Italy, which it then sold to Cyrix to fulfill its contractual obligation.

Cyrix filed a declaratory judgment action against Intel, alleging a "reasonable apprehension" that it would be sued for patent infringement.[17] Cyrix sought a declaration that it did not infringe the Intel patents, claiming immunity on the ground that IBM and ST were both licensed under the patents. Cyrix's view was that because IBM and ST acted within the scope of their respective licenses from Intel, its sales of microprocessors were shielded from any holding of infringement, the microprocessors having been obtained from authorized licensees.

---

[17] For a discussion of the standard for bringing a declaratory judgment action see Section 5.1. Note that this case also pre-dates the Supreme Court's decision in *MedImmune*, which rejected the Federal Circuit's "reasonable apprehension of suit" test.

IBM and ST intervened, seeking an adjudication of their rights under their respective agreements with Intel. On motions for summary judgment by Intel, IBM, and ST, the district court granted summary judgment for IBM and ST, and denied summary judgment for Intel. The district court also entered judgment for Cyrix.

The district court held that IBM had a right to act as a foundry in supplying microprocessors to Cyrix. It found that the definition of "IBM Licensed Products" in the IBM–Intel agreement did not limit the products it was licensed to sell to those designed by IBM. The district court distinguished *Intel Corp. v. U.S. Int'l Trade Comm'n*, 946 F.2d 821, 828 (Fed. Cir.1991) ("*Atmel*") (construing the term "Sanyo … products" in a license agreement as limiting the grant of rights to Sanyo-designed and Sanyo-manufactured products). The district court concluded that, unlike the situation in *Atmel*, an internal conflict in the IBM–Intel agreement was not created by construing the license grant to cover products other than IBM-designed products. The court considered the facts to be more analogous to those in *ULSI*, rather than to those in *Atmel*.

The district court also held that ST had the right to have microprocessors made for it by any third party, including ST-Italy, and the right to sell those microprocessors to Cyrix. The district court found that the microprocessors were made for ST, not Cyrix, and that the supply agreement between ST and ST-Italy was not a sublicense that exceeded ST's rights under the ST–Intel agreement. The district court thus distinguished the case that Intel cited in support of its position, *E.I. du Pont de Nemours and Co. v. Shell Oil Co.*, 498 A.2d 1108, 1114–15 (Del. 1985) (holding that a third-party's manufacturing of a product for itself under a licensee's "have made" rights was a prohibited sublicense). This appeal followed.

Discussion

A. IBM–Intel Agreement

Intel argues that the IBM–Intel agreement does not support a grant of foundry rights. Intel relies upon the word "IBM" as modifying the term "licensed products" in arguing that this modifier is a so-called "Sanyo limitation," limiting the scope of the products licensed and indicating that the parties did not intend to provide foundry rights. Intel also asserts that

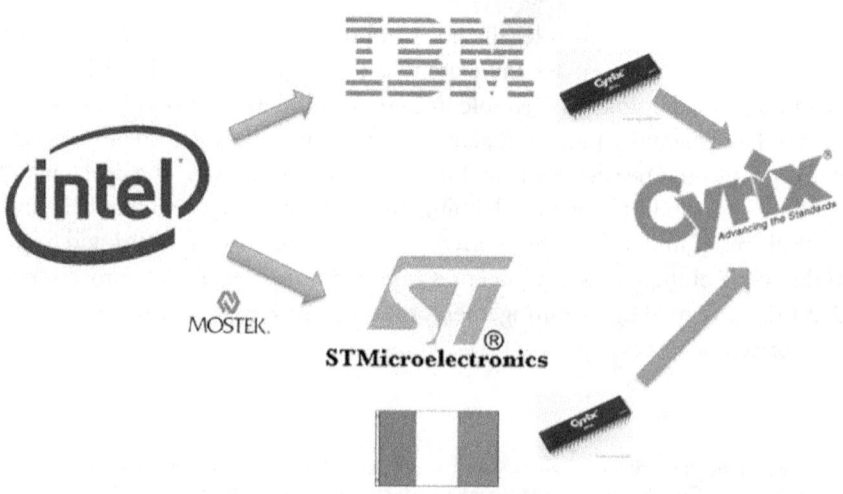

FIGURE 6.6 The complex flow of license rights in *Cyrix v. Intel*.

the "have designed" provision in the license does not provide IBM with the right to act as a foundry in manufacturing products designed by Cyrix.

Cyrix and IBM argue that the plain language of the IBM–Intel agreement grants to IBM the right to make and sell to Cyrix microprocessors that Cyrix designed. They argue that the "IBM" modifier in section 2.2.1 of the agreement was intended to distinguish "IBM Licensed Products" from "Intel Licensed Products," and that "IBM Licensed Products" as defined in the agreement are not limited to those products specifically designed by IBM and made for itself. They argue that the term "IBM" used in the term "IBM Licensed Products" is not a "Sanyo limitation."

We agree with the district court. The agreement granted IBM the right to make and sell "IBM Licensed Products," which are defined elsewhere in the agreement and are not limited to products designed by IBM. Sections 2.2.1, which grants a license to sell "IBM Licensed Products," and 1.23, which defines "IBM Licensed Products," must be read together. When this is done, the granting provision essentially reads as follows:

2.2.1 to make, use, lease, sell and otherwise transfer IHS Products, … Supplies and any combination of any, some or all of the foregoing … and to practice any method or process involved in the manufacture or use thereof;

The products so defined are not limited to IBM-designed products. They include categories of products defined without the IBM prefix. The agreement defined these items as follows:

1.1 "Information Handling System" shall mean any instrumentality or aggregate of instrumentalities primarily designed to compute, classify, process, transmit, receive, retrieve, originate, switch, store, display, manifest, measure, detect, record, reproduce, handle or utilize any form of information, intelligence or data for business, scientific, control or other purposes.

1.2 "IHS Product" shall mean an Information Handling System or any instrumentality or aggregate of instrumentalities (including, without limitation, any component or subassembly) designed for incorporation in an Information Handling System;

1.4 "Supply" shall mean, as to each party hereto, any article or matter designed for use in or by, and adapted to be effectively consumed in the course of operation of an IHS Product licensed herein to that party.

Accordingly, we conclude that the district court correctly held that "IBM Licensed Products" are not limited to products designed by IBM.

We also do not agree with Intel that the "IBM" modifier is analogous to the "Sanyo limitation" in *Atmel*. The agreement in *Atmel* contained the following provision:

Intel hereby grants and will grant to Sanyo an [sic] non-exclusive, world-wide royalty-free license without the right to sublicense except to its Subsidiaries, under Intel Patents which read on any Sanyo Semiconductor Material, Semiconductor Device, Magnetic Bubble Memory Device, Integrated Circuit and Electronic Circuit products, for the lives of such patents, to make, use and sell such products.

We construed the term "Sanyo" to limit the products listed after that term. Such a construction was required because it gave meaning to the term "Sanyo" which was consistent with other provisions of the contract. Otherwise, the term "Sanyo" would have lacked meaning, and a contract must be construed if possible to give meaning to all its provisions.

In contrast, the term "IBM Licensed Products" is thoroughly defined in the IBM–Intel agreement to provide no Sanyo-type limitation. Moreover, as argued by IBM, the "IBM" modifier is readily explained by its being distinguished from "Intel Licensed Products."

This case is more analogous to *ULSI* than *Atmel*. In *ULSI*, Hewlett-Packard Company (HP) acted as a foundry to make and sell math coprocessor chips to ULSI. HP obtained a license to Intel's patents under an agreement in which "each granted to the other an 'irrevocable, retroactive, nonexclusive, world-wide, royalty-free license.'" ULSI sought to be shielded from infringement of Intel's patents by purchasing the math coprocessor chips from HP, which was acting as an authorized seller. In concluding that HP's agreement with Intel provided HP with the right to act as a foundry for ULSI, we stated that, in contrast to the "Sanyo limitation" discussed in *Atmel*, "the licensing agreement between Intel and HP here contains no restriction on HP's right to sell or serve as a foundry." There was no "Sanyo limitation" in *ULSI*. The products that were licensed were defined broadly. Notwithstanding the presence of the modifier "IBM," the same is true here.

Intel also argues that section 2.2.3, providing a right to "have made" products only when the designs are furnished by IBM, limits IBM's right to have products designed by Cyrix. IBM did not have the products made for it, and thus this provision does not limit its rights to make and have designed the products it sold to Cyrix. In summary, IBM properly made and sold microprocessors under section 2.2.1; IBM properly had microprocessors designed under section 2.2.2; and IBM did not "have made" microprocessors under the more limited section 2.2.3. Thus, IBM did not act outside the terms of the Intel agreement.

Intel also makes a policy argument premised on a preamble clause in its agreement with IBM in which the parties stated that "each expects to continue a research and development effort which will produce further patents and each may require a nonexclusive license under such patents of the other." Intel argues that interpreting the agreement in favor of IBM would discourage the research the agreement was intended to foster. That argument totally misses the mark. The meaning of that clause is simply that the parties were entering into the agreement to facilitate their future research, i.e., to provide themselves with patent freedom for the future. Even if Intel never intended IBM to act as a foundry, this vague preamble cannot be interpreted to give effect to that intention if doing so would override clear operative language in the agreement. This agreement clearly gave IBM the right to make and sell to Cyrix microprocessors designed by Cyrix.

B. ST–Intel Agreement

Intel argues that the arrangement between ST and ST-Italy is in effect a sublicense, which it is clear is not permissible under the ST–Intel agreement. In particular, it argues that under ST's "have made" rights, ST is only permitted to have products made for itself. Intel posits that the arrangement among ST, ST-Italy, and Cyrix was a mere paper transaction, i.e., a "sham." *See E.I. du Pont*, 498 A.2d at 1116 (holding that a third party made a product for itself, not for a licensee, when it made a product and sold it to the licensee, who simultaneously sold it back to the third party).

ST and Cyrix argue that ST was acting within the scope of its "have made" rights. ST denies that its arrangement with ST-Italy was a "sham" and claims that it was using ST-Italy to manufacture products for it in order to meet its obligation to supply microprocessors to Cyrix. They distinguish *du Pont* on its facts, noting that in *du Pont* the party manufacturing under the "have made" right was also using the product itself, whereas here the product made under the "have made" right was sent to and eventually sold by the licensee.

We start with the clear proposition that, under its agreement, ST had the right to have the product made for it and to sell that product to third parties. It relied upon that right to have the product made by ST-Italy and to sell it to Cyrix. The district court found that the arrangement was distinguishable from that in *du Pont*. In *du Pont*, Carbide sought a license under du Pont's patent to manufacture a product known as methomyl, but du Pont refused to grant Carbide a license. Carbide then entered into an agreement with Shell, du Pont's licensee, whereby Carbide would manufacture methomyl for Shell under Shell's "have made" rights and Shell would sell it back to Carbide. Carbide would then use it (or sell it) as it wished. The Supreme Court of Delaware, whose law governed that agreement, concluded that the two agreements, one to enable Carbide to manufacture methomyl for Shell and the other whereby Shell sold it back to Carbide, were two halves of a single business transaction. The net result was that they enabled Carbide to make and use the patented product. The court held that that was in effect a sublicense, which was prohibited under the Shell–du Pont agreement.

The district court identified several important differences between the situation in *du Pont* and the arrangement among ST, ST-Italy, and Cyrix, and concluded in its Memorandum Opinion and Order as follows:

> The substance of the arrangement between Cyrix and ST and ST and ST-Italy is that when Cyrix needs wafers, it issues a purchase order to ST. ST then either manufactures the wafers itself at its Carrollton, Texas, facility or arranges for ST-Italy to manufacture the wafers at its Italian facility. ST is selling wafers. It is not selling or receiving payment for the use of its license from Intel. It has not authorized ST-Italy to make the wafers for or sell them to anyone other than ST. The production of the wafers is for the use of ST, the original licensee, and not for the use of ST-Italy. This is a valid exercise of the have-made rights granted under the License Agreement and does not constitute a sublicense.

We agree with the district court that the facts here are thoroughly distinguishable from those in *du Pont*. In *du Pont*, the arrangement was a sham. The third-party (Carbide)

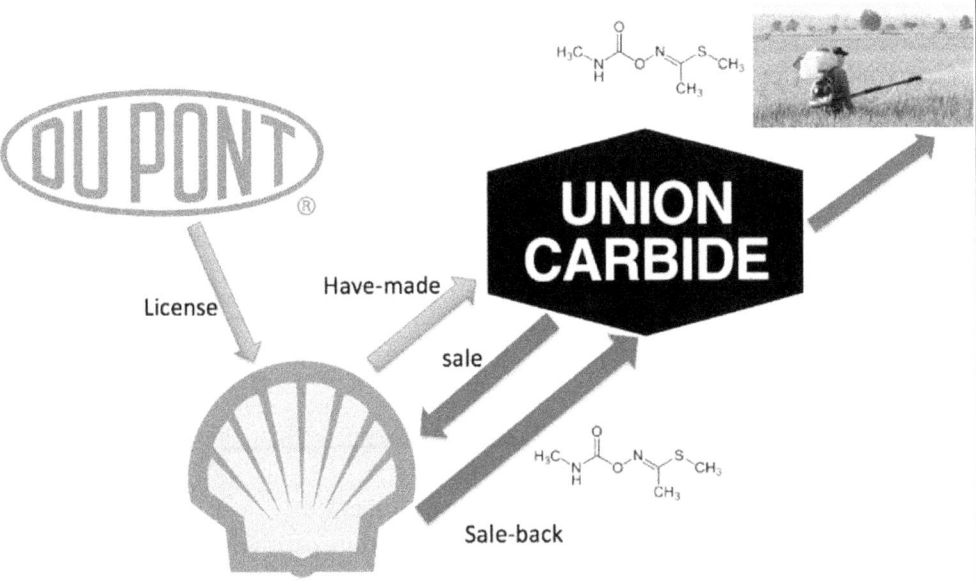

FIGURE 6.7 The "have-made" arrangements in *du Pont v. Shell*.

acting under Shell's "have made" rights was manufacturing and selling the product to Shell and then buying it back in what was only a set of paper transactions. Here, however, the third-party (ST-Italy) properly manufactured microprocessors under ST's "have made" rights, and ST then properly sold the products to a different entity, Cyrix. The two agreements, one permitting ST-Italy to manufacture microprocessors for ST and the other providing for ST's sale of microprocessors to Cyrix, were separate business transactions. As the district court found, ST was using both its own facility and ST-Italy's to satisfy its obligation to provide microprocessors to Cyrix. The products manufactured by ST-Italy were made for ST. If the facts in this case had been that Cyrix made the product for ST under ST's "have made" rights and then ST sold the product back to Cyrix, then they would have been analogous to those in *du Pont*, but those are not our facts. We accordingly conclude that the district court did not err in holding that the arrangements among ST, ST-Italy, and Cyrix were a valid exercise of ST's "have made" rights under its agreement with Intel. The district court thus did not err in granting a declaratory judgment of noninfringement in favor of Cyrix and ST.

AFFIRMED.

Notes and Questions

1. *Sublicensing.* Sublicenses, which are discussed in greater detail in Section 6.5, play a major role in the court's analysis in *Cyrix*. For now, suffice it to say that a sublicense is a grant by a licensee of a portion of the rights that it has received from the licensor. Sublicensing, like subleasing in the context of real property, may be prohibited by the "primary" license between the licensor and the licensee (i.e., the sublicensor). Did Intel's licensing arrangements with ST and IBM permit them to sublicense rights to Cyrix?

2. *Foundry use and the Sanyo limitation.* In the microelectronics industry, a "foundry" is a manufacturing facility where integrated circuits are manufactured to the order of a customer, usually using the customer's specifications. Because Cyrix lacked a license from Intel, Cyrix provided integrated circuit designs to ST and IBM, both Intel licensees, for manufacture. In effect, ST and IBM were acting as foundries for Cyrix. Why was Intel concerned about this arrangement? What is a "Sanyo limitation" and why did Intel argue that the license included one?

3. *Generality as permissiveness?* The *Cyrix* court interpreted Intel's license grant to IBM as including the right to make products designed by other entities. This determination was based in large part on the rather broad and general definitions given to the term "IBM Licensed Products." The license grant clause reads:

   [INTEL] hereby grants to IBM a worldwide, royalty-free, nonexclusive license under the INTEL Licensed Patents … to make, use, lease, sell and otherwise transfer IBM Licensed Products and to practice any method or process involved in the manufacture or use thereof …

   If you were to redraft the grant in a manner more favorable to Intel, how would you do so to prevent IBM from acting as a foundry for Cyrix?

4. *Have-made and foundry rights.* Unlike the right to "make," "use," "offer to sell" and "sell" a patented article, the right to have the article made by a third party is not one of the exclusive rights granted to a patent holder under 35 U.S.C. § 271(a). Courts thus have some flexibility in interpreting the have-made right, but have often interpreted it, at least in the electronics

industry, as specifically permitting a customer to have products manufactured by a foundry.[18] The have-made right then immunizes the foundry manufacturer from claims of infringement. Do you think that Intel granted IBM a "have-made right"? If not, would your interpretation change if Intel knew, at the time the license was negotiated, that IBM had all of its products fabricated by third parties? What is the difference between a "have-made" right and a sublicense?

5. *More on have-made and foundry rights.* If a have-made right has been granted, courts must often determine the limits of permitted foundry activity, and whether it includes the manufacture of products that are not made to the specifications of a particular customer, but are stock or off-the-shelf products. For example, in *Thorne EMI N. Am. v. Hyundai Elec. Indus.*, 1996 U.S. LEXIS 21170 (Dist. Del. 1996), the court held that "a foundry commissioned by IBM to manufacture [Hyundai] products would have the protection of the license agreement, [but] a manufacturer of 'off the shelf' products is not a foundry ... [and] therefore, whether or not it sold the products to IBM, would not be protected by the agreement." Assuming that Intel granted a have-made right to IBM, was IBM operating within its scope as a foundry for Cyrix?[19]

6. *Have-made under copyright.* Have-made rights are usually discussed in the context of patent licensing, but they can arise under copyright law as well. In *Great Minds v. Fedex Office & Print Servs., Inc.*, 886 F.3d 91, 94 (2d Cir. 2018), the court dismissed a copyright infringement action against a commercial printer that copied materials at request of an authorized licensee, noting the "mundane ubiquity of lawful agency relationships." Where the text of a license "provides no basis for distinguishing between" a licensee that directs its own employees to make copies versus one that "achieves an identical result by enlisting a temporary independent contractor—or a commercial duplication service," the contractor is not liable for infringement. How does this reasoning work in terms of the exclusive rights granted under the Copyright Act, which do not include a right to "make," but do include the right to "reproduce"? Does this decision effectively create a right to sublicense under copyright law, or should it be interpreted more narrowly, like the "have-made" right under patent law?

7. *Branding as a restriction.* Another way that licensors sometimes try to prevent their licensees from acting as third-party foundries is to limit the scope of their licenses to products bearing the licensee's brands. Thus, Intel could have limited IBM's license to the manufacture of products "marketed and sold under IBM's brands." This certainly would have prevented IBM from manufacturing Cyrix-branded chips. But how might such a restriction be circumvented by a determined licensee? Would such circumvention result in as effective a situation for the third-party customer?

8. *Granting what you have the right to grant: the legal authority limitation.* Recall the *Spindelfabrik* case from Section 6.1. Murata licensed the '011 patent to Schubert, then assigned the patent and the Murata–Schubert license to Suessen. Murata did not own the '946 patent. Schubert argued that Suessen, which did hold the '946 patent, should be deemed to have licensed it to Schubert when Suessen acquired the '011 patent and associated license. But the court disagreed, holding that the license could only convey to Schubert what the original licensor, Murata, could legally convey. Because Murata

---

[18] See, e.g., *CoreBrace LLC v. Star Seismic LLC*, 566 F.3d 1069, 1072–73 (Fed. Cir. 2009) ("The right to 'make, use, and sell' a product inherently includes the right to have it made by a third party, absent a clear indication of intent to the contrary").

[19] For an in-depth discussion of have-made rights in the context of electronics cases, see Michael P. Bregenzer, *"Have-Made" Rights: A Trap for the Unwary*, 10 Intell. Prop. Today 13 (July 2003).

never held the '946 patent, Murata could not license it to Schubert, and Suessen, which acquired the Murata–Schubert license, had no obligation to grant Schubert more than Murata did.

We discussed *Spindelfabrik* in the context of defining licensed rights (via the definition of "Control"). But the idea that a licensor cannot grant more than it holds also finds its way into license grant clauses. Consider the highlighted language in the following license grant.

> **GRANT CLAUSE WITH AUTHORITY LIMITATION**
>
> Licensor hereby grants to Licensee, during the Term of this Agreement, **and solely to the extent that Licensor has the authority to do so,** a nonexclusive, nonassignable worldwide right and license under the Licensed Rights, excluding the right to sublicense, to make, use, sell, offer for sale and import Licensed Products.

The above clause limits the license grant to rights that the licensor has the legal authority to grant. At first blush, this limitation might seem tautological: *of course* the licensor can't grant more rights than it has, as the court in *Spindelfabrik* emphasized. So is such a clause mere legal surplusage? Not exactly.

Suppose, for example, that "Licensed Rights" encompasses all of the licensor's worldwide patent rights with respect to a particular technology. Also suppose that the licensor previously granted to Company A an exclusive right to use such technology in France. When the licensor grants further rights to Company B, it cannot grant Company B the right to use the technology in France. So rather than modify the grant to exclude France (and every other country and subfield in which it has granted rights to others), the licensor can simply limit the license to the rights that the licensor has the authority to grant to Company B.

Should Company B, the licensee, be concerned about such a limitation? Absolutely. But it can protect itself by insisting that the licensor list any previous license grants with respect to the licensed rights in a schedule (see Section 10.2.2, Note 6). How might such a disclosure protect the licensee?

9. *Use not sell.* As noted in the introduction to this part, some nonexclusive patent licenses grant the right to use but not to sell a licensed product, and some exclusive licenses grant exclusivity with respect to the right to sell, but not the right to use. What is the reasoning behind splitting the use and sale rights in this manner? How might the right to make a licensed product be addressed in these scenarios?

6.4 CHANGES TO LICENSE SCOPE

Some IP rights – copyrights, trademarks, trade secrets – can last a very long time, sometimes in excess of a century and sometimes indefinitely. It is not surprising, therefore, that technologies and business practices that were contemplated when license agreements were drafted may change radically during the term of those agreements. How should unanticipated future uses be treated? The following cases explore this important issue.

Boosey & Hawkes Music Publishers, Ltd. v. The Walt Disney Co.

145 F.3d 481 (2d Cir. 1998)

LEVAL, CIRCUIT JUDGE

Boosey & Hawkes Music Publishers Ltd., an English corporation and the assignee of Igor Stravinsky's copyrights for "The Rite of Spring," brought this action alleging that the Walt Disney Company's foreign distribution in video cassette and laser disc format ("video format") of the film "Fantasia," featuring Stravinsky's work, infringed Boosey's rights. In 1939 Stravinsky licensed Disney's distribution of The Rite of Spring in the motion picture. Boosey, which acquired Stravinsky's copyright in 1947, contends that the license does not authorize distribution in video format ... We hold that summary judgment was properly granted to Disney with respect to Boosey's Lanham Act claims, but that material issues of fact barred the other grants of summary judgment. [We] remand all but the Lanham Act claim for trial.

I. Background

During 1938, Disney sought Stravinsky's authorization to use The Rite of Spring (sometimes referred to as the "work" or the "composition") throughout the world in a motion picture. Because under United States law the work was in the public domain, Disney needed no authorization to record or distribute it in this country, but permission was required for distribution in countries where Stravinsky enjoyed copyright protection. In January 1939 the parties executed an agreement (the "1939 Agreement") giving Disney rights to use the work in a motion picture in consideration of a fee to Stravinsky of $6000.

The 1939 Agreement provided that:

In consideration of the sum of Six Thousand ($6,000.) Dollars, receipt of which is hereby acknowledged, [Stravinsky] does hereby give and grant unto Walt Disney Enterprises, a California corporation ... the nonexclusive, irrevocable right, license, privilege and

FIGURE 6.8 Igor Stravinsky and Walt Disney.

authority to record in any manner, medium or form, and to license the performance of, the musical composition hereinbelow set out

Under "type of use" in ¶ 3, the Agreement specified that

The music of said musical composition may be used in one motion picture throughout the length thereof or through such portion or portions thereof as the Purchaser shall desire. The said music may be used in whole or in part and may be adapted, changed, added to or subtracted from, all as shall appear desirable to the Purchaser in its uncontrolled discretion.

The Agreement went on to specify in ¶ 4 that Disney's license to the work "is limited to the use of the musical composition in synchronism or timed-relation with the motion picture."

Finally, ¶ 7 of the Agreement provided that "the licensor reserves to himself all rights and uses in and to the said musical composition not herein specifically granted" (the "reservation clause").

Disney released Fantasia, starring Mickey Mouse, in 1940. The film contains no dialogue. It matches a pantomime of animated beasts and fantastic creatures to passages of great classical music, creating what critics celebrated as a "partnership between fine music and animated film." The soundtrack uses compositions of Bach, Beethoven, Dukas, Schubert, Tchaikovsky, and Stravinsky, all performed by the Philadelphia Orchestra under the direction of Leopold Stokowski. As it appears in the film soundtrack, The Rite of Spring was shortened from its original 34 minutes to about 22.5; sections of the score were cut, while other sections were reordered. For more than five decades Disney exhibited The Rite of Spring in Fantasia under the 1939 license. The film has been re-released for theatrical distribution at least seven times since 1940, and although Fantasia has never appeared on television in its entirety, excerpts including portions of The Rite of Spring have been televised occasionally over the years. Neither Stravinsky nor Boosey has ever previously objected to any of the distributions.

In 1991 Disney first released Fantasia in video format. The video has been sold in foreign countries, as well as in the United States. To date, the Fantasia video release has generated more than $360 million in gross revenue for Disney.

II. Discussion

Boosey's request for declaratory judgment raises … whether the general grant of permission under the 1939 Agreement licensed Disney to use The Rite of Spring in the video format version of Fantasia (on which the district court found in Disney's favor) …

Boosey contends that the license to use Stravinsky's work in a "motion picture" did not authorize distribution of the motion picture in video format, especially in view of the absence of an express provision for "future technologies" and Stravinsky's reservation of all rights not granted in the Agreement. Disputes about whether licensees may exploit licensed works through new marketing channels made possible by technologies developed after the licensing contract – often called "new-use" problems – have vexed courts since at least the advent of the motion picture.

In *Bartsch v. Metro-Goldwyn-Mayer, Inc.*, [391 F.2d 150 (2d Cir.1968)] we held that "licensees may properly pursue any uses which may reasonably be said to fall within the medium as described in the license." 391 F.2d at 155. We held in *Bartsch* that a license

FIGURE 6.9 The 1991 VHS videotape version of Disney's *Fantasia* sparked a dispute with Igor Stravinsky's estate.

of motion picture rights to a play included the right to telecast the motion picture. We observed that "if the words are broad enough to cover the new use, it seems fairer that the burden of framing and negotiating an exception should fall on the grantor," at least when the new medium is not completely unknown at the time of contracting.

The 1939 Agreement conveys the right "to record [the composition] in any manner, medium or form" for use "in [a] motion picture." We believe this language is broad enough to include distribution of the motion picture in video format. At a minimum, *Bartsch* holds that when a license includes a grant of rights that is reasonably read to cover a new use (at least where the new use was foreseeable at the time of contracting), the burden of excluding the right to the new use will rest on the grantor. The license "to record in any manner, medium or form" doubtless extends to videocassette recording and we can see no reason why the grant of "motion picture" reproduction rights should not include the video format, absent any indication in the Agreement to the contrary. If a new-use license hinges on the foreseeability of the new channels of distribution at the time of contracting – a question left open in *Bartsch* – Disney has proffered unrefuted evidence that a nascent market for home viewing of feature films existed by 1939. The *Bartsch* analysis thus compels the conclusion that the license for motion picture rights extends to video format distribution.

We recognize that courts and scholars are not in complete accord on the capacity of a broad license to cover future developed markets resulting from new technologies. The Nimmer treatise describes two principal approaches to the problem. According to the first view, advocated here by Boosey, "a license of rights in a given medium (e.g., 'motion picture rights') includes only such uses as fall within the unambiguous core meaning of the term (e.g., exhibition of motion picture film in motion picture theaters) and exclude any uses that lie within the ambiguous penumbra (e.g., exhibition of motion picture on television)." Under this approach, a license given in 1939 to "motion picture" rights would include only the core uses of "motion picture" as understood in 1939 – presumably

theatrical distribution – and would not include subsequently developed methods of distribution of a motion picture such as television videocassettes or laser discs.

The second position described by Nimmer is "that the licensee may properly pursue any
uses that may reasonably be said to fall within the medium as described in the license."
Nimmer expresses clear preferences for the latter approach on the ground that it is "less
likely to prove unjust." As Judge Friendly noted in *Bartsch*, "So do we."

We acknowledge that a result which deprives the author-licensor of participation in
the profits of new unforeseen channels of distribution is not an altogether happy solution.
Nonetheless, we think it more fair and sensible than a result that would deprive a contracting party of the rights reasonably found in the terms of the contract it negotiates.
This issue is too often, and improperly, framed as one of favoritism as between licensors
and licensees. Because licensors are often authors – whose creativity the copyright laws
intend to nurture – and are often impecunious, while licensees are often large business
organizations, there is sometimes a tendency in copyright scholarship and adjudication to
seek solutions that favor licensors over licensees. Thus in [*Cohen v. Paramount Pictures,
Inc.*, 845 F.2d 851 at 854 [(9th Cir. 1988)], the Ninth Circuit wrote that a "license must be
construed in accordance with the purpose underlying federal copyright law," which the
court construed as the granting of valuable, enforceable rights to authors and the encouragement of the production of literary works. Asserting that copyright law "is enacted for the
benefit of the composer," the court concluded that it would "frustrate the purposes of the
[copyright] Act" to construe the license as encompassing video technology, which did not
exist when the license was granted.

In our view, new-use analysis should rely on neutral principles of contract interpretation
rather than solicitude for either party. Although *Bartsch* speaks of placing the "burden of
framing and negotiating an exception … on the grantor," it should not be understood to
adopt a default rule in favor of copyright licensees or any default rule whatsoever. What
governs under Bartsch is the language of the contract. If the contract is more reasonably
read to convey one meaning, the party benefited by that reading should be able to rely
on it; the party seeking exception or deviation from the meaning reasonably conveyed by
the words of the contract should bear the burden of negotiating for language that would
express the limitation or deviation. This principle favors neither licensors nor licensees. It
follows simply from the words of the contract.

The words of Disney's license are more reasonably read to include than to exclude a
motion picture distributed in video format. Thus, we conclude that the burden fell on
Stravinsky, if he wished to exclude new markets arising from subsequently developed
motion picture technology, to insert such language of limitation in the license, rather than
on Disney to add language that reiterated what the license already stated.

Other significant jurisprudential and policy considerations confirm our approach to
new-use problems. We think that our view is more consistent with the law of contract
than the view that would exclude new technologies even when they reasonably fall within
the description of what is licensed. Although contract interpretation normally requires
inquiry into the intent of the contracting parties, intent is not likely to be helpful when
the subject of the inquiry is something the parties were not thinking about. Nor is extrinsic evidence such as past dealings or industry custom likely to illuminate the intent of the
parties, because the use in question was, by hypothesis, new, and could not have been the
subject of prior negotiations or established practice. Moreover, many years after formation
of the contract, it may well be impossible to consult the principals or retrieve documentary

evidence to ascertain the parties' intent, if any, with respect to new uses. On the other hand, the parties or assignees of the contract should be entitled to rely on the words of the contract. Especially where, as here, evidence probative of intent is likely to be both scant and unreliable, the burden of justifying a departure from the most reasonable reading of the contract should fall on the party advocating the departure.

Nor do we believe that our approach disadvantages licensors. By holding contracting parties accountable to the reasonable interpretation of their agreements, we encourage licensors and licensees to anticipate and bargain for the full value of potential future uses. Licensors reluctant to anticipate future developments remain free to negotiate language that clearly reserves the rights to future uses. But the creation of exceptional principles of contract construction that places doubt on the capacity of a license to transfer new technologies is likely to harm licensors together with licensees, by placing a significant percentage of the profits they might have shared in the hands of lawyers instead.

Neither the absence of a future technologies clause in the Agreement nor the presence of the reservation clause alters that analysis. The reservation clause stands for no more than the truism that Stravinsky retained whatever he had not granted. It contributes nothing to the definition of the boundaries of the license. And irrespective of the presence or absence of a clause expressly confirming a license over future technologies, the burden still falls on the party advancing a deviation from the most reasonable reading of the license to insure that the desired deviation is reflected in the final terms of the contract. As we have already stated, if the broad terms of the license are more reasonably read to include the particular future technology in question, then the licensee may rely on that language.

Bartsch therefore continues to articulate our "preferred" approach to new-use questions, and we hold that the district court properly applied it to find that the basic terms of Disney's license included the right to record and distribute *Fantasia* in video format.

Notes and Questions

1. *Other new uses.* In *Random House, Inc. v. Rosetta Books, LLC*, 150 F. Supp. 2d 613 (S.D.N.Y. 2002), aff'd, 283 F.3d 490 (2d Cir. 2002), the court held that an agreement granting Random House the exclusive right to "print, publish and sell" certain works by William Styron, Kurt Vonnegut and other prominent authors "in book form" did not convey a right to release the works in electronic form as "ebooks." The court explained,

   Manifestly, paragraph #1 of each contract – entitled either "grant of rights" or "exclusive publication right" – conveys certain rights from the author to the publisher. In that paragraph, separate grant language is used to convey the rights to publish book club editions, reprint editions, abridged forms, and editions in Braille. This language would not be necessary if the phrase "in book form" encompassed all types of books. That paragraph specifies exactly which rights were being granted by the author to the publisher. Indeed, many of the rights set forth in the publisher's form contracts were in fact not granted to the publisher, but rather were reserved by the authors to themselves. For example, each of the authors specifically reserved certain rights for themselves by striking out phrases, sentences, and paragraphs of the publisher's form contract. This evidences an intent by these authors not to grant the publisher the broadest rights in their works.

   The court distinguished *Boosey & Hawkes* and other early cases by characterizing them as encompassing within the licensed rights "new uses" within the "same medium as the

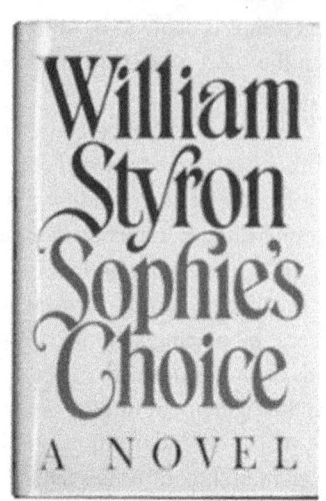

FIGURE 6.10 William Styron's *Sophie's Choice*, one of the titles at issue in *Random House v. Rosetta Books*.

original grant" (i.e., the display of a motion picture, whether on television or a videocassette). Ebooks, on the other hand, are "a separate medium from the original use – printed words on paper." Do you agree with this distinction? Is the difference between ebooks and printed books very different than the difference between videotapes and cinematic films? Or is it, as the court claims, merely "a determination, relying on neutral principles of contract interpretation"?

2. Tasini *and database rights*. The advent of digital formats such as databases and the Internet complicated the licensing of traditional print works such as newspaper articles. The Supreme Court in *New York Times Co., Inc. v. Tasini*, 533 U.S. 483 (2001) held that a newspaper that obtained the right to publish stories written by freelance journalists did not automatically obtain the right to place those stories in an online searchable database. After *Tasini*, a publisher specifically must obtain the right to publish the work both in the original newspaper or other compilation as well as on the Internet, in a database or in other digital formats. How do you think publishers reacted to the *Tasini* decision? Do you think that they made any changes to their standard agreements with freelance journalists?

Problem 6.3

Scent-o-Matic is a new technology for ebooks that gives users an olfactory overlay, such as providing the fragrance of baking bread in a recipe book or the aroma of a city back alley in a 1930s detective story. Scent-o-Matic is patented and works using software that causes certain scents to be produced when certain keywords are on the page. Scent-o-Matic is owned by Nile Books, a popular ebook publisher with existing licenses to deliver the numerous titles in its library to its ebook readers. The standard ebook publication license grants Nile Books the right to "reproduce and distribute the Work in English as an electronic book of the full-length verbatim text of the

Work, including any illustrations, in a digital format. Such digital format may include necessary modifications to allow an end user to access, read, and interact with the Work in digital format."

Analyze whether the Scent-o-Matic technology would be allowed under the license in the following circumstances.

a. The original ebooks are not altered – the Scent-o-Matic ebook reader contains a program that analyzes words on the screen and produces scents when it recognizes certain keywords.
b. Niles Books edits the original ebook by adding a non-visible notation to certain words such that when those words appear on the screen, Scent-o-Matic produces certain scents.
c. Your client is an established author with a new series of books soon to be published. She does not want Niles Books to deploy its Scent-o-Matic technology with her books. Redraft the language to make it clear that neither Scent-o-Matic nor any other technologies that add sensory inputs can be used with her books without her permission.

6.5 SUBLICENSING

A sublicense is a grant of rights by a licensee to a third party (the sublicensee) which encompasses some or all of the rights that have been granted to the licensee under a primary license agreement. Unlike an assignment of a license, the licensee that grants a sublicense generally remains bound by the terms of the original license. By the same token, the sublicense only exists so long as the underlying license remains in force.

Generally speaking, nonexclusive licensees may not grant sublicenses unless expressly permitted to do so in the primary license agreement. In some cases, however, exclusive licensees are permitted, under the law, to grant sublicenses without express permission from the licensor.[20] As a result, it is prudent, whether drafting an exclusive or a nonexclusive license, to specify whether, and to what degree, the licensee may grant sublicenses.[21]

If sublicensing will be permitted under a licensing agreement, the licensor will often seek to impose some degree of control over the nature and identity of sublicensees.

FIGURE 6.11 Graphical representation of license and sublicense rights.

EXAMPLE: SUBLICENSING

a. The licenses granted under this Agreement shall include the right to grant sublicenses without the consent of Licensor to any of Licensee's Affiliates for so long as it remains an Affiliate of Licensee. Except as provided above, Licensee has no right to sublicense any licenses granted under this Agreement without the prior written consent of Licensor [1], which shall not be unreasonably withheld or delayed [2].

---

[20] The rationale supporting this conclusion is similar to the rationale permitting exclusive licensees to assign their rights without the consent of the licensor. See Section 13.3.
[21] Professor Jim Farrington offers this rule of thumb: "If representing the Licensor: assume Licensee may sublicense without consent. If representing the Licensee: assume Licensee may not sublicense without consent."

b. [Any sublicense granted by Licensee for any in-kind or nonmonetary consideration (including, but not limited to, services, equipment, supplies, usage of facilities, advertising, barter, bandwidth, data, intellectual property of any kind, releases from liability, options, interests in litigation, security interests, loans, debt forgiveness, covenants not to sue or to assert rights, software, technology, know-how, marketing rights, improvements, capital stock, units, partnership interests or other ownership interests in entities of any kind, or rights to receive dividends, revenue, royalties or other monies in the future) may be granted only with Licensor's express prior written consent.] [3]

c. No sublicense shall relieve Licensee of its obligations under this Agreement, including the obligation to pay Licensor any and all fees, royalties and other amounts due. [4] Any breach of a sublicense agreement by the Sublicensee shall be deemed to constitute a breach of this Agreement by Licensee, and Licensee shall be liable for any action by a Sublicensee that would constitute a breach of this Agreement had it been committed by Licensee. [5]

d. Licensee shall provide a fully executed copy of each agreement pursuant to which it grants sublicense hereunder to Licensor immediately following its execution [6]. Without limiting the generality of the foregoing, each sublicense agreement shall provide that:

   (i)   Licensor shall have no responsibility, obligation or liability of any kind or manner to any Sublicensee;

   (ii)   Licensor shall be an express third party beneficiary of such sublicense, entitled to enforce it in accordance with its terms; [7]

   (iii) Sublicensees shall have no further right to grant sublicenses of the rights granted under this Agreement; [8]

   (iv)   in the event of any inconsistency between the terms of a sublicense agreement and this Agreement, this Agreement shall control; [9]

   (v)   in the event that any Sublicensee (or any entity or person acting on its behalf) initiates any proceeding or otherwise asserts any claim challenging the validity or enforceability of any Licensed Right in any court, administrative agency or other forum, Licensee shall, upon written request by Licensor, terminate forthwith the sublicense agreement with such Sublicensee, and the sublicense agreement shall provide for such right of termination by Licensee; [10]

   (vi)   such sublicense shall terminate automatically upon the termination of this Agreement. [11]

   (vii) the sublicensee shall be bound by provisions equivalent to those found in Sections xxx of this Agreement [e.g., audit, reporting, indemnification, non-competition, confidentiality, etc.]. [12]

DRAFTING NOTES

[1] *Approval rights* – the licensor often retains the right to approve sublicensees, though in some cases a licensee's Affiliates are automatically approved (this is especially the case when it is anticipated that the licensee will distribute a product through an international network of affiliated companies). In approving or rejecting sublicensees, the licensor must be careful to avoid potential antitrust issues that can arise from customer allocation and group boycotts (see Sections 25.3 and 25.7).

[2] *Reasonableness* – not all licensors will want to prove that their refusal to approve a sublicensee is "reasonable." Accordingly, "shall not be unreasonably withheld … " can be replaced by ", which approval licensor may extend or withhold in its sole discretion." As a compromise, the agreement can specify types of sublicensees that are either prohibited outright, or require approval of the licensor (e.g., competitors in the licensor's markets). Be careful, though. Naming specific companies to which sublicenses cannot be granted can run afoul of antitrust laws as concerted refusals to deal or group boycotts (see Section 25.7).

[3] *Nonmonetary compensation* – this clause is necessary to protect the licensor only if the licensee will pay the licensor a running royalty based on net sales or share sublicensing income with the licensor (see Section 8.4).

[4] *No release from obligations* – it is important that the licensee remain obligated to the licensor for all of its obligations under the prime licensing agreement. A sublicense is not intended to release the licensee from liability. If that were the case, the licensor could enter into a license agreement directly with the proposed sublicensee.

[5] *Cross-breach* – because the licensor lacks privity of contract with sublicensees, it is useful to attribute breaches by sublicensees to the prime licensee. Without such attribution, the licensor may have limited recourse against breaches by sublicensees (which may, in fact, be preferable to the licensee/sublicensor, who may argue that so long as it complies with its obligations under the prime license, the sublicensor–sublicensee relationship is not the concern of the prime licensor). See Section 12.3, Note 10, further discussing breach and termination by sublicensees.

[6] *Copies* – it is advisable for the licensor to obtain copies of all sublicenses granted when sublicensees will have substantial rights to exploit the licensed IP. It is unnecessary, for example, in the case of consumer end user sublicense agreements (see Section 17.1, Note 2). Licensees are sometimes reluctant to disclose sublicense agreements, but may agree to disclosure of redacted versions that contain at least the terms necessary to verify compliance with the sublicensing conditions, including financial terms when relevant to the licensor.

[7] *Third-party beneficiary* – under § 302(1) of the Restatement (Second) of Contracts, a third party's capacity to sue under a contract depends on whether that party is an intended beneficiary of the contract. If the contracting parties intended that a third party benefit from performance of the contract, then that third party is an intended beneficiary and is entitled to enforce the contract. As a result, a licensor may seek to declare itself a third-party beneficiary of each sublicense agreement.

[8] *No further sublicenses* – this restriction, like the limitation on the number of sublicensees, seeks to contain the dissemination of the licensed IP and the prime licensor's control over it.

[9] *Precedence* – see the discussion of order of precedence in Section 13.10.

[10] *No challenge* – see the discussion of no-challenge clauses in Section 22.4.

[11] *Termination* – it is often the case that sublicenses will terminate upon termination of the prime license, though there are exceptions – for example, in the case of software end user sublicenses. See Section 12.5.6 for a discussion.

[12] *Pass-down obligations* – if the licensor itself has licensed IP rights from a third party, then it may be required to pass down additional obligations to sublicensees.

The *Cyrix* case discussed in Section 6.1 turns to a great extent on whether or not ST was permitted to grant a sublicense to its affiliate in Italy. ST's primary license with Intel appears to have prohibited sublicensing. If sublicensing is permitted, however, the sublicensor (the primary licensee) can clearly not grant the sublicensee more rights than the sublicensor obtained from the primary licensor. The following case explores what happens when a sublicensee acquires a sublicense from a licensee/sublicensor that itself may not be in good standing with the primary licensor.

Rhone-Poulenc Agro, S.A. v. DeKalb Genetics Corporation

284 F.3d 1323 (Fed. Cir. 2002)

DYK, CIRCUIT JUDGE

Rhône-Poulenc Agro, S.A. ("RPA") appeals from the decision of the United States District Court for the Middle District of North Carolina granting summary judgment of non-infringement on the ground that Monsanto Co. ("Monsanto") has a valid license to U.S. Patent No. 5,510,471 ("the '471 patent"). The issue here is whether a sublicensee (Monsanto) that acquired the sublicense from a licensee (DeKalb Genetics Corp. ("DeKalb")), that acquired the original license by fraud, may retain the sublicense by establishing that the sublicensee was a bona fide purchaser for value …

We hold that the bona fide purchaser defense is governed by federal law and is not available to non-exclusive licensees in the circumstances of this case. Accordingly, we vacate the decision of the district court and remand for further proceedings consistent with this opinion.

Background

From 1991 through 1994, RPA and DeKalb collaborated on the development of biotechnology related to specific genetic materials. During this time, a scientist at RPA, Dr. DeRose, developed an optimized transit peptide ("OTP") with a particular maize gene, which proved useful in growing herbicide resistant corn plants. The OTP is covered by the claims of the '471 patent and is the subject of RPA's patent infringement claim against Monsanto.

In 1994, RPA, DeKalb, and non-party Calgene, Inc. ("Calgene") entered into an agreement (the "1994 Agreement") that provided:

> RPA and CALGENE hereby grant to DEKALB the world-wide, paid-up right to use the RPA/CALGENE Technology and RPA/CALGENE Genetic Material in the field of use of corn. DEKALB shall have the right to grant sublicenses to the aforementioned right to use without further payment being made to RPA or CALGENE.

The RPA/CALGENE Technology and RPA/CALGENE Genetic Material included the invention claimed in the '471 patent. In 1996, DeKalb sublicensed its rights to the RPA/Calgene Technology and Genetic Material to Monsanto. At the same time Monsanto granted to DeKalb licenses to use certain intellectual property related to genetically-engineered corn …

On October 30, 1997, RPA filed suit against DeKalb and Monsanto, seeking, inter alia, to rescind the 1994 Agreement on the ground that DeKalb had procured the license (the "right to use") by fraud. RPA also alleged that DeKalb and Monsanto were infringing the

'471 patent and had misappropriated RPA's trade secrets. Monsanto defended, inter alia, on the ground that it had a valid license to practice the invention of the patent and use the trade secrets, based on the rights owned under the 1994 Agreement that were transferred by DeKalb to Monsanto in 1996. At trial, a jury found, inter alia, that DeKalb had fraudulently induced RPA to enter into the 1994 Agreement. The district court ordered rescission of the 1994 Agreement. Nonetheless, Monsanto moved the district court for summary judgment that it had a valid license to the '471 patent and the right to use RPA's trade secrets because under the 1996 Agreement Monsanto was a bona fide purchaser for value of the sublicense to the patent and the trade secrets. The district court ... granted this motion and dismissed the infringement and misappropriation claims against Monsanto.

The district court found that, as a sublicensee of the '471 patent and the trade secrets, Monsanto was "entitled to be considered a bona fide purchaser, because it paid value for the right to use the technology without knowledge of any wrongdoing by DeKalb." Because "Monsanto [was] a bona fide purchaser of the ... technology, [it] therefore [could not] be liable as a patent infringer or a trade secret misappropriater." The district court explicitly did not reach the issues of whether Monsanto's bona fide purchaser defense would apply to any future licenses of RPA's technology or whether, in light of the 1994 RPA–DeKalb–Monsanto Agreement granting DeKalb the right to sublicense, the bona fide purchaser defense would benefit sublicensees of Monsanto.

RPA filed this timely appeal, which concerns only the validity of Monsanto's license to practice the '471 patent.

Discussion

In *Rhône-Poulenc I*, we affirmed the judgment of the district court, rescinding the 1994 licensing agreement based on a jury verdict finding that DeKalb acquired its patent license by fraud. RPA asserts that it necessarily follows that the Monsanto sublicense to the '471 patent is void, and that Monsanto can be sued for patent infringement. We agree ...

35 U.S.C. § 261 ... provides that a later bona fide purchaser for value without notice (a later assignee) prevails if the earlier assignment was not timely recorded in the patent office.[22] This case, however, involves a different situation – the circumstance in which the interest in the patent held by the grantor is voidable and the question is whether a grantee may retain its interest even if the grantor's interest is voided. Section 261 does not directly govern the resolution of this question.

Since section 261 does not apply directly, we must turn to other provisions of the Patent Act. Section 271 of the Act provides: "whoever without authority makes, uses, offers to sell, or sells any patented invention ... infringes the patent." 35 U.S.C. § 271(a). We are charged with the task of determining the meaning of the term "without authority." Under this provision, as under other provisions of the Patent Act, the courts have developed a federal rule, where appropriate, and have deferred to state law, where that is appropriate. This issue of whether to apply state or federal law has particular importance in this case because North Carolina state law, the law of the forum state, does not recognize a bona fide purchaser defense unless there has been a title transfer.

In general, the Supreme Court and this court have turned to state law to determine whether there is contractual "authority" to practice the invention of a patent. Thus, the

---

[22] See Chapter 2.

interpretation of contracts for rights under patents is generally governed by state law. *Aronson v. Quick Point Pencil Co.*, 440 U.S. 257, 262 (1979); *Lear, Inc. v. Adkins*, 395 U.S. 653, 661–62 (1969). Just as the interpretation of patent license contracts is generally governed by state law, so too the consequences of fraud in the negotiation of such contracts is a matter generally governed by state law. It may be argued that the impact of fraud upon the validity of a license as against a bona purchaser defense should also be governed by state law. However, we confront here a unique situation in which a federal patent statute explicitly governs the bona fide purchaser rule in some situations but not in all situations. It would be anomalous for federal law to govern that defense in part and for state law to govern in part. There is quite plainly a need for a uniform body of federal law on the bona fide purchaser defense.

On the related question of the transferability of patent licenses, many courts have concluded that federal law must be applied. In so holding, courts generally have acknowledged the need for a uniform national rule that patent licenses are personal and non-transferable in the absence of an agreement authorizing assignment, contrary to the state common law rule that contractual rights are assignable unless forbidden by an agreement.

In short, because of the importance of having a uniform national rule, we hold that the bona fide purchaser defense to patent infringement is a matter of federal law. Because such a federal rule implicates an issue of patent law, the law of this circuit governs the rule. Of course, the creation of a federal rule concerning the bona fide purchaser defense is informed by the various state common law bona fide purchaser rules as they are generally understood.

Congress has specifically provided that patents are to be treated as personal property. 35 U.S.C. § 261. At common law, a bona fide purchaser (also known as a "good faith buyer") who acquired title to personal property was entitled to retain the property against the real owner who had lost title to the property, for example, by fraud. Generally, a bona fide purchaser is one who purchases legal title to property in good faith for valuable consideration, without notice of any other claim of interest in the property. The bona fide purchaser rule exists to protect innocent purchasers of property from competing equitable interests in the property because "[s]trong as a plaintiff's equity may be, it can in no case be stronger than that of a purchaser, who has put himself in peril by purchasing a title, and paying a valuable consideration, without notice of any defect in it, or adverse claim to it .... " *Boone v. Chiles*, 35 U.S. 177, 210 (1836).

At common law, however, it was quite clear that one who did not acquire title to the property could not assert the protection of the bona fide purchaser rule. Many courts have held that a party to an executory contract to purchase title, the owner of a lease, or a purchaser from a vendor who did not have title cannot benefit from the bona fide purchaser rule. It is clear under the law of North Carolina (the state in which RPA filed suit) that "[i]n the absence of an estoppel, one is not entitled to protection as a bona fide purchaser unless he holds the legal title to the property in dispute."

Monsanto urges that the cases requiring that one obtain title to benefit from the bona fide purchaser defense are "antiquated," and the Uniform Commercial Code's ("U.C.C.") modern approach has rejected the requirement of title. In fact, the title rule is recognized in modern property law, and has been confirmed by the U.C.C. Under U.C.C. Article 2-403, even "[a] person with voidable title has power to transfer a good title to a good faith purchaser for value."

Monsanto also relies on statements from various treatises on patent licensing for the proposition that a sublicense continues, even when the principal license is terminated. But the statements address the situation where the original licensee is terminated as a matter of contract law, e.g., for breach of contract. These treatises do not address the operation of the bona fide purchaser rule with respect to sublicenses and do not state or suggest that a sublicense continues even when the principal license is rescinded because it has been obtained by fraud.

Even if the general common law extended the protection of the bona fide purchaser rule to holders of non-exclusive licenses, it would not be appropriate for us to extend such protection to non-exclusive licenses as a matter of federal common law. Section 261 of title 35 reflects a determination by Congress that only those who have obtained an "assignment, grant or conveyance" may benefit from the protection of the statute. This provision thus reflects a congressional judgment that the protections of the bona fide purchaser rule extend only to those who have received an "assignment, grant or conveyance." Under such circumstances, the Supreme Court has made clear that we must consider the purposes of federal statutes in framing a rule of federal common law, even if the statutes are not directly applicable.

Although our precedent has recognized that in some circumstances an exclusive patent license may be tantamount to an assignment of title to the patent, this is so only when "the licensee holds 'all substantial rights' under the patent." *Textile Prods., Inc. v. Mead Corp.*, 134 F.3d 1481, 1484 (Fed. Cir.), *cert. denied*, 525 U.S. 826 (1998). Here the license is non-exclusive, and there is no contention that the license agreement transferred "all substantial rights." Thus, an assignment did not occur, and in the absence of an "assignment, grant or conveyance," Congress contemplated that there would be no bona fide purchaser defense.

Conclusion

In sum, the bona fide purchaser defense does not apply to non-exclusive licensees. We accordingly vacate the decision of the district court and remand for further proceedings consistent with this opinion.

Notes and Questions

1. *Exclusive versus nonexclusive licensee*. The Federal Circuit in *Rhone-Poulenc v. DeKalb* holds that the bona fide purchaser defense does not apply to nonexclusive licensees. Why? Does the court imply that a different result might apply to exclusive licensees? Do you agree?

2. *Section 261 and bona fide purchasers*. Much like state recording statutes for real property, Section 261 of the Patent Act provides that a purchaser of a patent without notice of a prior sale will prevail over a previous purchaser of the same patent if the prior sale was not recorded at the Patent and Trademark Office within three months of the purchase. Why do you think that Congress enacted this rule? How does this rule differ from a traditional state "race-notice" or "notice" recording statutes for real property?

3. *Termination of sublicenses*. In arguing that its sublicense should continue notwithstanding DeKalb's original fraudulent license acquisition, Monsanto relies on treatise authors who suggest that a valid sublicense should continue notwithstanding the termination of the primary license. The Federal Circuit in *Rhone-Poulenc* sidestepped this issue, noting that the

question was not whether Rhône-Poulenc's sublicense was terminated, but whether it was ever valid in the first place, considering DeKalb's original fraudulent license. For some time after this decision, it was unclear whether a sublicense would survive the termination of its primary license. In 2018, however, the Federal Circuit clarified its position, holding in *Fraunhofer-Gesellschaft v. Sirius XM Radio*, 940 F.3d 1372, 1380 (Fed. Cir. 2018) that "our law does not provide for automatic survival of a sublicense" and expressly rejecting any implication to the contrary in *Rhone-Poulenc*. Which default rule do you find more persuasive: that sublicenses do or do not automatically survive the termination of the primary license?

Of course, the parties themselves provide for the survival of sublicenses by clearly stating in the primary license agreement that all sublicenses will, or will not, terminate upon termination of the primary license. See Section 12.3, Note 9, and Section 12.E.6, which discuss in greater detail issues surrounding the breach and termination of sublicenses.

4. *Licensor's approval of sublicenses.* If sublicensing is permitted under a primary license, the parties will sometimes agree to include the template for the sublicensing agreement that the licensee/sublicensor must use as an exhibit to the primary license. This gives the licensor comfort that the terms that its licensee will grant to sublicensees are understood and agreed up-front. In other cases, when a template sublicense agreement is not attached, the licensor may reserve the right to review and approve any sublicense agreements or individual sublicensees. If the primary licensor reserves the right to approve sublicensees, the reasons for rejection should usually be spelled out in the primary agreement so as to avoid allegations of anticompetitive behavior (see Chapter 25 relating to antitrust considerations in license agreements).

5. *Sublicensing in the biotech industry.* One of the industries in which sublicensing is standard practice is biotechnology. In many cases, a university will grant a license to a biotechnology company, which is sometimes a university spinout or start-up founded by university researchers (see Section 14.3). The scope of this license is often broad and exclusive, covering the entire output of a particular university laboratory. The biotech company will then continue the research begun by the university, often working alongside university researchers. The biotech company's goal is to develop or discover promising drug or diagnostic candidates that it can then sublicense on an individual basis to a larger pharmaceutical company, which will have the resources to conduct the large-scale clinical trials necessary to secure FDA approval for the product. Sometimes, the pharmaceutical company will license several compounds or drug candidates (each a different FOU) from the biotech company, often on an exclusive basis. The pharmaceutical company may also obtain an option to acquire licenses in additional FOUs, typically upon payment of an option fee. When a biotech company announces that it has signed a large deal with a pharmaceutical company, it is usually counting on the exercise of all such options, the payment of all milestone payments and an estimate of the royalty revenue that it will receive. As a licensee/sublicensor, the biotech company itself will be obligated to pay a portion of its earnings from the pharmaceutical company back to the university holding the patents and the primary license. This business pattern has been used for the last thirty years and has, to a large degree, defined the modern biotechnology industry. Nevertheless, as discussed in Section 14.3, Note 1, universities have been criticized for granting sublicenses of such breadth to for-profit companies that are not obliged to abide by the universities' public missions. What alternative licensing and sublicensing structures might exist to address these concerns?

7

Exclusive Licenses

One of the fundamental attributes of any intellectual property (IP) license is whether it is exclusive or nonexclusive. The principal distinction between an exclusive and a nonexclusive license is the extent to which the licensor may grant third parties licenses covering the same scope as the original license. An exclusive licensor relinquishes the right to license its IP again, while a nonexclusive licensor retains it.

Exclusivity need not be absolute. Often, the scope of a licensee's exclusivity is limited to a particular field of use, territory or time period, and may include any number of qualifications and restrictions. Figure 7.1 illustrates the complex network of exclusive rights that can be granted with respect to subfields within a broadly applicable technology such as CRISPR-Cas9 gene editing.

In addition, if specified in an agreement, a licensor can expressly authorize one or more additional parties to operate in a manner that overlaps with the rights granted to its exclusive licensee (in which case the licensee is termed a "co-exclusive" licensee). In some situations, the licensor itself may wish to continue to operate under the rights granted to an exclusive licensee, though it commits not to grant licenses to others. In these cases, the licensee is often referred to as a "sole" licensee.

Finally, exclusivity need not last forever. In some cases, a limited exclusive "head start" period of six months, one year or some other term can be offered to a licensee. In other cases, exclusivity may be offered initially, but may convert to nonexclusivity if the licensee fails to meet specified "milestone" targets, such as annual sales volume or progress toward regulatory approval. In still other cases, the licensee may be required to make periodic payments to maintain exclusivity.

The samples that follow illustrate some of the permutations that can exist with respect to exclusive, co-exclusive and sole licenses. As you review these samples, consider the business motivations that would drive each party to push for, or resist, such structures.

CRISPR-CAS9 licensing agreements

Exclusive licenses to surrogates for human therapeutics limit access to CRISPR as a platform technology.

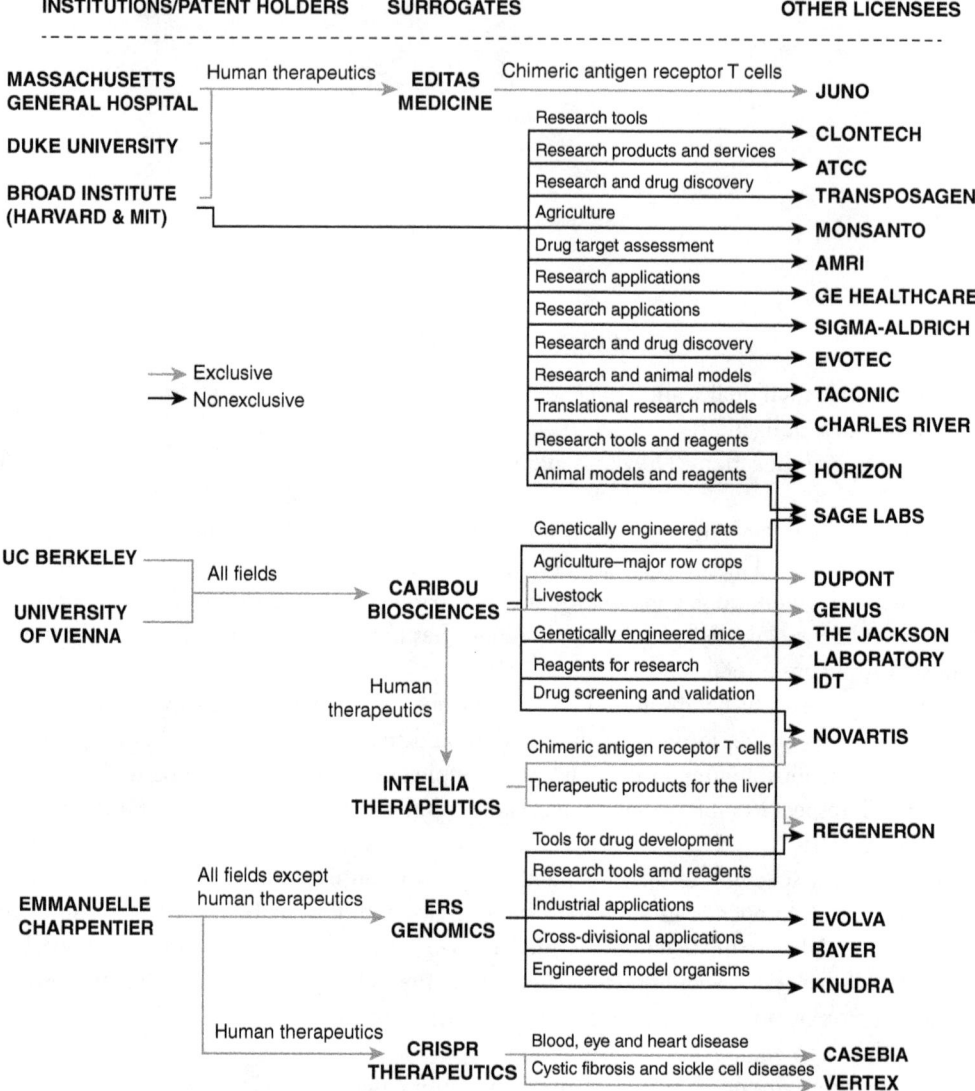

FIGURE 7.1 The complex, multi-tiered exclusive and nonexclusive licensing structure for CRISPR-Cas9 gene editing technology as it existed in early 2017.

SAMPLE EXCLUSIVE LICENSE GRANTS

Licensor hereby grants to Licensee the exclusive right and license:

a. to make, use, sell, have sold and import Licensed Products in the Territory;
b. to translate the Licensed Work into the Portuguese language and to reproduce and distribute such Portuguese translation in the Territory;

   c. to reproduce and display the Licensed Mark on Authorized Apparel Products for sale and distribution throughout the world, and in connection with their advertising and marketing;

   d. to conduct research, develop and make therapeutic products targeting the XYZ Gene which are covered by the Licensed Patents, expressly excluding the right to sell, have sold or distribute such products on a commercial basis;

   e. to operate one or more barbeque restaurants in Harris County, Texas under the Licensed Marks, which exclusivity shall be subject to Licensor's (or its assignee's) operation of its original barbeque restaurant on Kirby Drive under the Licensed Marks;

   f. to make, have made, use, sell, have sold and import semiconductor chips covered by the Licensed Patents on a worldwide basis for a period of one year, after which such license shall remain exclusive only in countries in which Licensee's Net Revenues from the sale of such semiconductor chips exceeds $10 million in the immediately preceding calendar year.

7.1 EXCLUSIVITY: RATIONALES AND POLICY

Why would an IP owner grant a particular licensee exclusive rights with respect to that IP? After all, the IP owner is giving up a lot when it grants an exclusive license. What commercial factors make up for the loss of control ceded by the IP owner granting an exclusive license?

One set of reasons that an IP owner may wish to grant an exclusive license relates to the relationship that the licensor wishes to build with its licensee. A single exclusive licensee can be viewed as a privileged business partner with respect to a particular geographic market or product category, and the existence of only one licensee in this territory/category may enable closer cooperation and knowledge sharing between the licensor and licensees. For example, it is not uncommon for regional distribution relationships to be exclusive, so that an Italian wine producer may appoint different exclusive distributors of its products in the United States, the EU, Australia and South America. In each jurisdiction, a distributor would be chosen based on its skill, experience, commercial network, reputation and relationship with the manufacturer. Granting all rights in a particular jurisdiction to a single exclusive licensee enables that licensee to obtain necessary import clearances, develop distribution channels, produce advertising and the like. Were multiple distributors permitted in each territory, no single distributor would have as great an incentive to produce marketing or advertising to promote the products (as the others would benefit as "free riders").

Another important consideration in determining whether to grant an exclusive license arises in connection with what the licensee will be expected to do in order to bring the licensed product or technology to market. If the licensee will simply be reselling a packaged commodity product, such as a nationally recognized snack food or software application, then it must make relatively few investments in order to successfully exploit its license rights, and a nonexclusive license may be appropriate. But if the licensee will be expected to make significant investments either in product or market development, then it may be unwilling to make those investments unless it is guaranteed that it will not have competitors in the relevant market, at least for some time period (and at least not authorized by the same licensor). For example, exclusive licensing is common in the biopharmaceutical industry, where universities and biotech companies routinely license early-stage discoveries and technologies to pharmaceutical developers on an exclusive basis, with the understanding that the licensee will be required to devote significant additional effort and resources to finalizing any product suitable for commercial use, and will then be required to conduct costly and time-consuming clinical trials necessary to obtain regulatory approval for the product. Without the promise of exclusive rights to sell the resulting product, and the profit to be earned from being the only firm selling a breakthrough new drug or other product, few firms would invest the hundreds of millions of dollars required to develop a final product in these markets.

Finally, a licensee may simply wish to obtain exclusive rights in a market in which it feels that it can maximize its profits through exclusivity. In such cases, the licensor may be indifferent whether an exclusive or nonexclusive license is granted, and may allow a prospective exclusive licensee to pay some premium in order to obtain exclusive rights, at least for a specified period. From the licensor's perspective, the additional compensation that it can charge for an exclusive license may make this option attractive.

The granting of exclusive rights is not always a private matter to be negotiated between an IP owner and its licensee. Public policy issues can come into play when a licensed technology has a significant public health or other social benefit. Thus, in 1999, the US National Institutes of Health adopted a policy urging its grant recipients to license patented research tools (technologies that enable the discovery or development of multiple other technologies) on a nonexclusive basis to promote their greatest utilization (Fed. Reg. 64(246): 72090 (1999)). Likewise, in 2007, eleven major US research universities, including the University of California, Berkeley, Harvard, and MIT, committed to a set of core licensing values, known as the "Nine Points," one of which states that universities should make patented research tools as broadly available as possible through nonexclusive licensing (see Section 14.3.2).

The remainder of this chapter will address the obligations that exclusivity imposes on both licensors and licensees. But before moving to these topics, you should be aware that one of the most important attributes of an exclusive license agreement is the exclusive licensee's right to bring an action for infringement of the licensed IP rights against third parties. This critical right will be discussed at length in Section 11.2.

7.2 LICENSOR'S OBLIGATIONS

While actual agreements vary widely, the defining feature of an exclusive license is a commitment by the licensor that it will not grant further licenses covering the same subject matter and scope or exploit the licensed IP itself. There are, however, potentially significant drafting and policy issues that arise when applying exclusivity to the licensor's conduct.

7.2.1. *Granting Other Licenses in the Exclusive Field*

One of the key benefits that a licensee obtains from an exclusive license is the ability to occupy a field to the exclusion of competitors. But exclusivity may not always work out that way, as illustrated by the following case.

Donald F. Duncan, Inc. v. Royal Tops Manufacturing Co., Inc.
343 F.2d 655 (7th Cir. 1965)

MAJOR, CIRCUIT JUDGE
This action was brought by plaintiff [Duncan] against defendants [Royal] for alleged trademark infringement of its registered trademarks, "Yo-Yo," "Genuine Duncan Yo-Yo"

and "Butterfly," unfair competition, false representation of goods and unauthorized use of plaintiff's trademarks. Defendants by answer denied all allegations of the complaint relevant to plaintiff's claim for relief.

Following a lengthy trial, the District Court entered its findings of fact, conclusions of law and a judgment order in favor of plaintiff, from which defendants appeal.

On July 23, 1948, [Duncan] entered into an agreement with Louis Marx & Company, Inc. and Charmore Company, whereby [Duncan] granted them a license to use the trademark "Yo-Yo." The agreement provided that "should Marx abandon the manufacture or/ and sale of the bandalore types of toy spinning tops, manufactured and sold by it, then Duncan shall have the right to cancel the license granted herein upon thirty (30) days' notice in writing given to Marx."

In 1951, Royal's predecessor brought an action for declaratory judgment in the District Court for the Northern District of Illinois, by which it sought a cancellation of plaintiff's registration, "Yo-Yo," on the ground that it was the generic or a descriptive name of the article upon which it was used.

On September 14, 1955, plaintiff entered into a license agreement with Royal by which it granted to Royal "an exclusive and non-transferable right to use Licensor's trade-mark, 'Yo-Yo,' on or upon or in association with bandalore tops." This agreement provided, "The parties hereto agree that they will enter into appropriate papers in the United States District Court in the aforesaid litigation (referring to the action for declaratory judgment) wherein said trade-marks shall be held to be valid and existing."

On November 21, 1955, a consent judgment was entered which found plaintiff to be the owner of the trademark registrations for "Yo-Yo" and for "Genuine Duncan Yo-Yo." The judgment recited, "Each of the above trademarks is applied and used in connection with a disc-shaped top manipulated up and down on a string, more commonly known as a bandalore top or quiz." The judgment determined that the trademarks "are valid."

On September 6, 1961, plaintiff's attorney directed a letter of cancellation to the Marx and Charmore Companies, the licensees named in the 1948 license agreement stating, "Please consider this letter as the thirty-days' written notice." This notice was given as required by a provision contained in that agreement.

Royal contends that ... plaintiff, as an inducement for the 1955 license agreement, fraudulently represented that there was no outstanding license agreement when as a matter of fact it knew or should have known the 1948 agreement with Louis Marx & Company, Inc. and Charmore Company was in force and effect. In any event, Royal argues that the [1955] license agreement was invalid because of a mutual mistake as to a material fact and that the consent decree was entered as a result of and as provided for in the license agreement and was, therefore, tainted with the same fraud or mutual mistake.

Plaintiff's response to these contentions is based upon a finding by the District Court. "This license (referring to the 1948 license to Marx and Charmore) was cancelled by mutual agreement in 1952," and "Correspondence between Marx and plaintiff indicates an acknowledgment of the cancellation of 1952." In our judgment, these findings as well as the argument predicated thereon are clearly erroneous and must be rejected.

Plaintiff in support of its cancellation theory relies upon the testimony of Donald Duncan, Sr., that the license was cancelled in 1952 by mutual agreement in a conversation with Marx. Admittedly he gave no thirty-day written notice of cancellation as required by the Duncan–Marx agreement. Nor was such a notice given until 1961, when it was given by plaintiff's attorney. Plaintiff attempts to bolster its contention on this score by inferences drawn from correspondence between Duncan and Marx following the alleged oral cancellation. An examination of this correspondence as a whole completely negates the inferences which plaintiff professes to discern. For instance, on July 14, 1961, the attorneys for Marx wrote plaintiff, stating, "Our client is licensed by you to use the name 'Yo-Yo' as provided in the 1948 agreement." On July 26, 1961, Marx wrote plaintiff, "We have an agreement to that effect (our right to use the name 'Yo-Yo') giving us full permission to use it." (This is the same Marx with whom Duncan claimed to have had the oral agreement of cancellation in 1952.)

Even after plaintiff's counsel gave written notice of cancellation in his letter of September 6, 1961, Marx was still contending that its 1948 agreement with plaintiff was in effect. In response to the written notice of cancellation, the attorneys for Marx wrote that they "... consider this attempted cancellation to be without validity or effect." It may be that when plaintiff's counsel gave written notice of cancellation in 1961, he was without knowledge of the alleged oral cancellation in 1952, or if he had such knowledge, recognized it as futile. In this connection it is pertinent to note that Donald F. Duncan, Jr., plaintiff's president, testified that to his knowledge the 1948 agreement with Marx and Charmore had not been cancelled and was still in full force and effect in 1955, when the license agreement was entered into between plaintiff and Royal.

Thus, the conclusion is inescapable that the 1948 license agreement between plaintiff and Marx and Charmore was in full force and effect at the time plaintiff entered into a license agreement with Royal and granted to it "an exclusive" right. Royal's president, Joseph T. Radovan, testified that he would not have settled Royal's suit against plaintiff for declaratory judgment if he had known there was an outstanding license agreement with some other company. The most charitable characterization which can be made of plaintiff's misrepresentation is that it was a mutual mistake, relied upon by Royal to its prejudice. The [1955] license agreement ... is, therefore, invalid.

Notes and Questions

1. *When an exclusive licensee wants more.* Royal had an exclusive license from Duncan. Even if there was an additional (and presumably nonpracticing) licensee from 1955 to 1961, by the time this case was decided in 1965, Royal was Duncan's only licensee. Why would Royal argue that its exclusive license should be invalidated?

2. *Prior licenses.* Can an IP holder grant an "exclusive" license if prior existing licensees already exist in a field? In *Mechanical Ice Tray Corp. v. Gen. Motors Corp.*, 144 F.2d 720 (2d Cir. 1944), the holder of patents covering ice trays granted a license to General Motors (GM) which provided "that the defendant was exclusively licensed under the patents within the United States ... with the sole exception of a non-exclusive license which had been granted to Westinghouse Electric & Manufacturing Company. It was agreed that if the Westinghouse license should be terminated the defendant should become the sole licensee." When the licensor claimed that GM breached the implied duty that an exclusive licensee has to exploit the licensed rights (see Section 7.3), GM argued that it was not an exclusive licensee due to the prior license that had been granted to Westinghouse. The court disagreed, reasoning as follows:

We think this license made the defendant an exclusive licensee though it is true that the non-exclusive license to Westinghouse remained in effect. The argument that the

Westinghouse license prevented the defendant from becoming an exclusive licensee does not take wholly into account the legal meaning of that term. [An exclusive license] is not the equivalent of "sole licensee." A license can have the attributes which make it exclusive in the legal sense though it is not the only license. There may be one or more previous licenses which are non-exclusive and by contrast with the exclusive license are called bare. When this is so the exclusive license does not, of course, cover the entire field but it binds the licensor not to enlarge thereafter the scope of other licenses already granted or increase the number of licenses.

Do you agree with the court's reasoning? Should the outcome have been different if GM had been unaware of the Westinghouse license? What if the licensor had intentionally withheld the existence of the Westinghouse license from GM?

3. *Yo-yo history*. The following excerpt from the online Museum of Yo-Yo History (www .yoyomuseum.com) offers additional background:

The modern story of the yo-yo starts with a young gentleman from the Philippines, named Pedro Flores. In the 1920s, he moved to the USA, and worked as a bellhop at a Santa Monica hotel. Carving and playing with wooden yo-yos was a traditional pastime in the Philippines, but Pedro found that his lunch break yo-yo playing drew a crowd at the hotel. He started a company to make the toys, calling it the Flores Yo-Yo Company. This was the first appearance of the name "yo-yo," which means "come-come" in the native Filipino language of Tagalog.

Donald F. Duncan, an entrepreneur who had already introduced Good Humor Ice Cream and would later popularize the parking meter, first encountered the yo-yo during a business trip to California. A year later, in 1929, he returned and bought the company from Flores, acquiring not only a unique toy, but also the magic name "yo-yo." About this time, Duncan introduced the looped slip-string, which allows the yo-yo to sleep – a necessity for advanced tricks.

Throughout the 1930s, 40s, and 50s, Duncan promoted yo-yos with innovative programs of demonstrations and contests. All of the classic tricks were developed during this period, as legendary players toured the country teaching kids and carving thousands of yo-yos with pictures of palm trees and birds. During the 1950s, Duncan introduced the first plastic yo-yos and the Butterfly® yo-yo, which is much easier to land on the string for complex tricks. Duncan also began marketing spin tops during this period.

The biggest yo-yo boom in history (until 1995) hit in 1962, following Duncan's innovative use of TV advertising. Financial losses at the end of the boom, and a costly lawsuit to protect the yo-yo trademark from competitors forced the Duncan family out of business in the late 60s. Flambeau Products, who made Duncan's plastic models, bought the company and still owns it today.

4. *Licensees versus infringers*. In *Duncan* and *Mechanical Ice Tray*, an exclusive licensee alleged that the licensor had breached its obligation to grant it an exclusive license due to the existence of one or more other licensees. What if the licensor has not granted other licenses, but has instead permitted a third party to infringe an exclusively licensed IP right? Should this constitute a breach of the licensor's obligation to grant its licensee exclusivity? What if both the licensor and the licensee were aware of the infringement at the time the exclusive license was granted?

Consider *Ryan Data Exchange v. Graco*, 913 F.3d 726 (8th Cir. 2019) (reproduced in Section 11.2). Rydex granted Graco an exclusive patent license in 2005. At that time, both Rydex and Graco were aware that a third party, Badger, was allegedly infringing the patent. Rydex sued Badger for infringement in 2011, but in 2012 settled with Badger in a manner

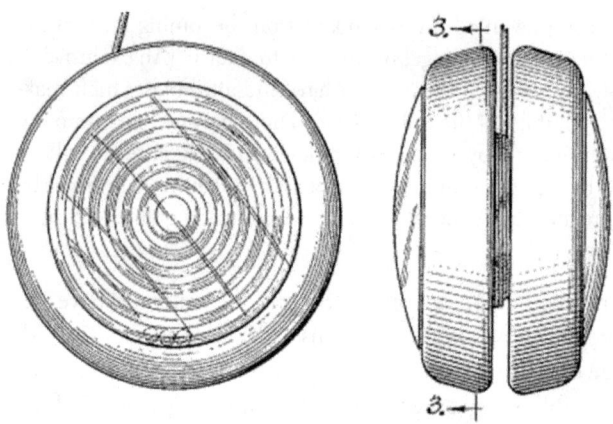

FIGURE 7.2 Illustration from one of Duncan's "Bandalore Toy"
patents, U.S. Pat. No. D175,022 (June 28, 1955).

that did not end its infringement. The patent expired in 2015. Graco sued Rydex for breaching its obligation to grant an exclusive license. The district court held, as a matter of law,
that Rydex breached its obligation to provide Graco with an exclusive license from 2012,
when Rydex settled its suit with Badger, until 2015, when the patent expired. Yet the court
allowed the jury to determine, as a question of fact, whether Rydex was in breach of that
obligation from 2005, when Rydex granted the exclusive license, until 2011, when it sued
Badger for infringement. The jury found that Rydex had not breached its obligation from
2005 to 2011. Why not?

5. *Semi-exclusive and sole licenses.* In some cases, a licensor will grant a license to more than
    one licensee, but will expressly limit the number of such licenses. These are called semi-
    exclusive licenses. Such arrangements sometimes occur when the owner of an IP right
    has granted a license that cannot be revoked, and a prospective new licensee wishes to be
    "exclusive" save for that prior license. In other cases, the licensor may wish to exploit the
    licensed IP itself, concurrently with a licensee, while at the same time committing that it
    will not grant further licenses to third parties. This is called a "sole license" (and is somewhat
    distinct from a licensor's "reserved rights" discussed in the next section, which are generally
    more limited). If you represented the licensee in these situations, what concerns might they
    raise?

Problem 7.1

Baker grants Mega an exclusive license to make, offer to sell, and sell patented bread-making
machines throughout the United States. The license bears a royalty of 10 percent of Mega's
net sales, with no up-front fee. Several months later, Mega discovers that Baker had previously granted a nonexclusive license to Texibake Corp. to make, offer to sell, and sell the same
machines in the state of Texas. Texibake sells approximately 100 machines per year.

a. What remedy, if any, does Mega have?
b. Now suppose that, three years after Baker granted the exclusive license to Mega, Texibake
    expands its sales force and starts to sell machines throughout the United States in violation
    of its license. Does Mega's remedy change?

7.2.2 *Licensor's Reserved Rights*

In some cases, a licensor may "reserve" certain rights to itself when granting exclusive rights to a licensee. The following case illustrates a fairly common set of licensor rights reservations for educational purposes.

Kepner-Tregoe, Inc. v. Vroom
186 F.3d 283 (2d Cir. 1999)

MOTLEY, DISTRICT JUDGE

This is an appeal of a civil judgment against Professor Victor H. Vroom for breach of contract and copyright infringement relating to an exclusive licensing agreement between Dr. Vroom and Kepner-Tregoe, Inc. (K-T). The licensing agreement provided K-T with the exclusive use of executive leadership training materials co-authored by Dr. Vroom in return for the payment of royalties to Dr. Vroom. The [issue] presented by this appeal [is] whether the district court's finding of liability against Dr. Vroom for intentional copyright infringement and breach of contract should be upheld. For the reasons discussed below, the decision of the district court is affirmed.

Background

In 1972, Dr. Vroom, a professor at Yale University's School of Organization and Management, entered into a licensing agreement with K-T, an international management training company. This agreement granted K-T the exclusive worldwide rights to specific copyrighted materials co-authored by Dr. Vroom. These materials, known as the Vroom–Yetton model, were used to teach managers how to make better decisions. In return, K-T agreed to pay Dr. Vroom and his co-author, Dr. Philip W. Yetton, royalties based on its exclusive use of the licensed materials. The licensing agreement also included a teaching clause that allowed Dr. Vroom to retain non-assignable rights to use the licensed materials for his "own teaching and private consultation work."

In the mid-1980s, Dr. Vroom created a more sophisticated software program, entitled "Managing Participation in Organizations" (MPO), which partially overlapped with the materials licensed to K-T. Dr. Vroom used the MPO program to conduct management training seminars for corporate executives at Yale University and other college campuses. Upon learning of Dr. Vroom's use of the copyrighted materials, K-T initiated this lawsuit in 1989.

K-T alleges that Dr. Vroom's use of the MPO program in his teaching of executives in the university setting infringes on its copyrights and constitutes a breach of the licensing agreement. It further alleges that Dr. Vroom breached the licensing agreement by assigning the rights to the MPO program, which infringed K-T's licensed materials, to Leadership Software Inc. (LSI), a Texas company founded by Dr. Vroom and his colleague, Dr. Arthur Jago. LSI was created to market the MPO program.

In 1990, K-T initiated a separate lawsuit against LSI and Dr. Jago in federal district court in Texas. Dr. Vroom was not a defendant in the suit because personal jurisdiction was unavailable. In that case, K-T alleged copyright infringement based on LSI's sales of the MPO program, which contained substantial similarities to the Vroom–Yetton model, the copyrighted materials exclusively licensed to K-T. The Texas district court found in favor of K-T and awarded it $46,000 in actual damages as well as injunctive relief.

After a five-day bench trial in April 1997, the district court in the present action held that Dr. Vroom's use of the licensed materials, including the infringing MPO program, in his teaching of executives in the university setting was not permitted under the teaching clause of the licensing agreement. The trial court found that the teaching clause was ambiguous as written and looked to other contemporaneous documentary evidence for clarification of the parties' intentions. The lower court interpreted the teaching clause to mean that Dr. Vroom was only allowed to use the copyrighted materials for his teaching of bona fide enrolled graduate and undergraduate students. Moreover, the district court found that Dr. Vroom willfully infringed the copyrighted material licensed to K-T and breached his contract with K-T when he taught the exclusively licensed materials to large groups of executives in the university setting.

Discussion

The central issue in this case involves the proper interpretation of the teaching clause of the licensing agreement, which allows Dr. Vroom to use the licensed materials in the course of his "own teaching and private consultation work." We find that the district court did not err in finding the teaching clause ambiguous. It properly looked to prior negotiations between the parties to determine the parties' intentions regarding the interpretation of the clause. Furthermore, credible evidence was presented at trial that supported the lower court's interpretation of the teaching clause so as to limit Dr. Vroom's teaching to only bona fide enrolled undergraduate and graduate students.

Dr. Vroom argues that the district court effectively rewrote the clear and unambiguous language of the licensing agreement by restricting his teaching of the licensed materials to only students. Dr. Vroom contends that the parties intended to allow him to retain broad and unlimited rights to use the licensed materials in his teaching, including his teaching of executives in the university setting. Dr. Vroom also claims that the trial court's decision will virtually deprive him of his right to earn a living because he is enjoined from using the MPO program in his courses for executives at Yale and other colleges.

We review the district court's construction of the text of the licensing contract *de novo*. To begin with, we agree with the district court that the teaching clause was ambiguous. K-T contends that this clause was only intended to allow the teaching of undergraduate and graduate students; Dr. Vroom argues that this clause, which also allowed "private consulting," also permitted him to teach classes to large groups of executives. We hold, as did the district court, that in the context of the agreement the word "teaching" was susceptible to the interpretation advanced by either Dr. Vroom or K-T. Accordingly, the district court was entitled to consider extrinsic evidence to interpret the contractual language.

We also affirm the district court's holding limiting the clause to the teaching of enrolled graduate and undergraduate students. The communications of the parties during the negotiation of the licensing agreement support this interpretation. K-T wrote a memorandum to Dr. Vroom in January of 1972, stating that it wanted to prevent "mass" teaching of the materials. Dr. Vroom produced no evidence at trial that he ever contradicted K-T's interpretation of the teaching clause in any communications with K-T throughout the remainder of the negotiations. The district court properly relied on this evidence to conclude that the teaching clause did not extend beyond the teaching of enrolled graduate and undergraduate students.

Notes and Questions

1. *Licensor's reserved rights.* The dispute in *Vroom* centers around the reserved uses that an exclusive licensor retains for itself. There was no question that Dr. Vroom reserved some rights to use the Vroom–Yetton model for his own purposes. The question was how much Dr. Vroom could do. How might Dr. Vroom have improved his case by drafting his reservation of rights more carefully? How would you have advised him in 1972?

2. *Drafting of reservations.* Another good illustration of an exclusive licensor's reservation of rights can be found in *Macy's Inc. v Martha Stewart Living Omnimedia, Inc.*, 127 A.D.3d 48 (N.Y. Sup. 2015), which involved an exclusive licensing agreement between Martha Stewart Living Omnimedia (MSLO) and the Macy's department store chain, as well as MSLO's subsequent agreement with J.C. Penney Corp. (JCP).

   In 2006, Macy's and MSLO entered into a licensing agreement granting Macy's certain exclusive rights with respect to products designed by MSLO. These products were defined in the agreement as "Exclusive Product Categories" and included bedding, bathware, housewares and cookware. In conjunction with Macy's, MSLO would design goods in those categories, which were branded with the MSLO mark. Macy's would manufacture the goods and sell them in Macy's stores. The agreement further provided that Macy's would be the exclusive outlet for sales of these items and that MSLO would not, without Macy's consent, enter into any new agreement or extend any existing agreement "with any department store or manufacturer or other retailer of department store merchandise that promotes the sale of any items" in Macy's Exclusive Product Categories that are branded with a Martha Stewart mark. The agreement further provided that if MSLO ultimately contracted, with Macy's approval, tacit or otherwise, to sell goods in the Exclusive Product Categories through other outlets, such goods were to be manufactured solely by Macy's and could not be sold through a downscale retailer. The agreement was subject to several limitations, the key one being MSLO's reservation of the right to open its own retail stores. These stores were defined as "retail store[s] branded with Martha Stewart Marks or Stewart Property that [are] owned or operated by MSLO or an Affiliate of MSLO or that otherwise prominently feature Martha Stewart Marks or Stewart Property." Even with respect to those MSLO stores, however, only Macy's could manufacture and sell products in its Exclusive Product Categories at Macy's cost plus 20%. This arrangement was designed to prevent MSLO stores from undercutting Macy's prices on those goods.

   In 2011, MSLO [negotiated a retail partnership with JCP]. The evidence in the record clearly shows that JCP executives knew that, in order to obtain this retail partnership, they would have to "break" the exclusivity provisions in the Macy's contract. In order to evade those provisions, JCP viewed the exemption for MSLO stores as a means to attain its goals of creating a retail partnership with MSLO. It proposed creating a "store-within-a-store." Under this concept, MSLO retail stores would be set up as a separate "store" within already established JCP stores. Entry to the store would be located wholly within the confines of JCP stores, i.e., it would not be a freestanding store with a separate outside entrance; the MSLO store would only be accessible by entering through the JCP store. MSLO would help design the branded goods and receive a royalty, just as with Macy's. However, JCP would manufacture the goods, own the inventory, own the retail space, employ the salespeople, book the sales, set the prices, set the promotions and bear all risk of loss.

   Macy's sued MSLO for breach of contract and JCP for tortious interference with contract. The lower court found that since JCP would manufacture the goods, own the inventory and, in short, control all aspects of the "store," this would run afoul of the clear language of the contract with MSLO and Macy's that requires Macy's to manufacture all MSLO goods in Exclusive Product Categories, even for MSLO stores. It also violated the prohibition on MSLO from entering into any agreement with any department store that promotes the design and sale of items within the Exclusive Product Categories, thus breaching, among other things, the exclusivity provisions of its contract with Macy's.

The court on appeal agreed, holding that "There are no exceptions to this exclusivity of manufacture, yet JCP's agreement with MSLO called for JCP to manufacture these products."

If you had represented MSLO in its negotiation with Macy's, how would you have drafted the exclusion from Macy's exclusive license to permit MSLO to enter into the desired arrangement with JCP?

7.2.3 *Licensor's Duties with Respect to the Licensed IP*

When a licensee obtains an exclusive license, it often pays a substantial sum to the licensor in advance and invests significant resources in creating complementary technology, building out physical manufacturing and distribution resources, developing a market for the licensed technology, training technical, sales and marketing personnel, and foregoing other business opportunities. As a result, licensees often expect that the licensor will "do its part" to maintain the value of the licensed IP, either by paying fees and taking routine steps at the Patent and Trademark Office to renew and otherwise maintain the licensed IP in force, or more assertively by enforcing the licensed IP against infringers in the licensee's exclusive field. Duties such as these can be imposed by contract, and often are (see Sections 9.5 and 11.2). But to what degree does the law impose such duties on an exclusive licensor?

The answer is: very little. Patent and trademark owners have significant latitude to protect, maintain and renew their registrations at their own discretion, and absent contractual requirements to the contrary, courts have been reluctant to recognize any duty that they do so. For example, in *Westowne Shoes, Inc. v. Brown Group, Inc.*, 104 F.3d 994, 997 (7th Cir. 1997), which involved an exclusive license of the Naturalizer trademark on footwear, Judge Richard Posner explained that

> The owner [of a trademark] can if he wants, unless contractually committed otherwise, abandon the trademark, dilute it, attach it to goods of inferior quality, attach it to completely different goods – can, in short, take whatever steps he wants to jeopardize or even completely destroy the trademark. When cases speak of the trademark owner's "duty to ensure the consistency of the trademarked good or service," they mean that it is a condition of the continued validity of the trademark, or a defense to a consumer's claim of having been fooled by the substitution of an inferior good, not that it is a ground for a licensee's being allowed to sue to force the trademark owner to take steps to assure the trademark's continued validity.
>
> We think that Westowne more or less understands all this, and is making solely a contract claim—that the trademark license obligated Brown to keep the Naturalizer mark up to snuff. A licensor might so promise, but this licensor did not. Westowne is asking us to make such a promise an implied term of every trademark licensing agreement, and that would be absurd. It would give licensees comprehensive power over the licensor's business … The office of implied contractual terms is to save contracting parties costs of negotiations by interpolating terms that they are pretty sure to have agreed to had they thought about the matter, not terms that they would

FIGURE 7.3 Martha Stewart display inside a J.C. Penney's store.

be almost sure to reject; for the interpolation of such terms would increase rather than decrease the costs of contracting as parties busied themselves contracting around the interpolated terms.

Similar reasoning has been applied to an IP owner's failure to enforce its IP against infringers. More than 100 years ago, the court held in *Martin v. New Trinidad Lake Asphalt Co.*, 255 F. 93, 96–97 (D.N.J. 1919) that an exclusive licensee had no action against a licensor who allegedly failed to prevent others from infringing the licensed patents. The court reasoned that "[t]he license agreement [contains] no provision that the licensor would protect the licensee from infringements by others. In the absence of such a provision, there was no obligation upon the part of the [licensor] to do so."

In the end, if an exclusive licensee wishes to ensure that its licensor maintains the licensed IP or enforces it against infringers, it is well advised to insist upon contractual commitments that the licensor do so.

Notes and Questions

1. *Why so few licensor obligations?* Why don't courts impose implied obligations on licensors to maintain the value of exclusively licensed IP rights? Compare the unwillingness of courts to extend these obligations to licensors with the implied obligations imposed on licensees in Section 7.3. How do you account for this difference? What language should a licensee seek to include in an agreement if it is concerned about the licensor's willingness to maintain its IP?

Problem 7.2

Proggo and Curio enter into an agreement whereby Proggo will develop a software program to help Curio forecast global demand for antique furniture. The program will be based on templates that Proggo has created for clients in other industries (e.g., jewelry, paintings, rare books), but Proggo expects to add about 100,000 new lines of customized code (of a total of one million) for Curio. Curio does not want any of its competitors to have access to the functionality that it will receive. How would you draft an exclusive license provision for the software program? How would your result differ if you represented Proggo versus Curio?

7.3 LICENSEE'S OBLIGATIONS: DUTY TO EXPLOIT

7.3.1 *Milestone and Diligence Requirements*

Because the licensor of an IP right often depends on its licensees for revenue, and because the licensor seldom exercises direct control over its licensees' activities, license agreements often contain provisions that measure the licensee's progress against certain commercial or technological goals (milestones). Milestones, sometimes referred to as "diligence requirements," serve several purposes. First, the achievement of a milestone is often coupled with a payment by the licensee (see Section 8.5). This permits the licensee to stagger payments, usually of increasing size, based on its progress toward full commercialization of the licensed rights. As such, milestone payments align the licensee's payment obligations with its likelihood of achieving commercial success. From the licensor's standpoint, milestone payments can provide needed cash before a commercial product is approved and launched – a process that can often take years.

A final reason that diligence requirements appear in license agreements is unrelated to milestone payments. Under the Bayh–Dole Act of 1980 (discussed in Section 14.1), academic institutions that obtain federal funding may patent their federally funded inventions, but are subject to a number of requirements. Among these is the obligation to report to the federal funding agency "on the utilization or efforts at obtaining utilization that are being made" by the institution and its licensees with respect to each federally funded invention (35 U.S.C. § 202(c)(5)). As a result, many licenses in fields that are heavily funded by the federal government (biotechnology, aerospace, agriculture, computer encryption) contain measurable indicia of utilization of the licensed technology.

Milestones are intended to reflect the achievement of defined goals along the road to the full commercial exploitation of a licensed IP right. As such, milestones can reflect steps along the regulatory, technological or commercial pathway to commercialization. In drafting milestones, it is critical that these be specified clearly and based on objective criteria (e.g., not "satisfactory completion of product testing" and other subjective measures).

Common examples of **regulatory** milestones include:

- the licensee files an investigational new drug (IND) application for a licensed product with the FDA;
- the licensee administers first dosing of the licensed product to a patient in phase I/II/III clinical trials;
- the licensee receives FDA approval to market a licensed product in the United States;
- the licensee receives regulatory approval to market a licensed product in a specific country.

Common examples of **technological** milestones include:

- a working licensed product prototype is demonstrated to the licensor;
- a specified technical/scientific threshold is met;
- the licensed product is certified by a recognized international certification body;
- the licensed technology is submitted to a recognized international standards body;
- the licensed technology is adopted by a recognized international standards body as an industry standard;

- a "beta" version of the licensed product is released.

Common examples of **commercial** milestones include:

- the licensed product is announced at a major trade show or event;
- the licensee enters into a manufacturing agreement for licensed products;
- the licensee completes construction of its manufacturing facility for the licensed products;
- the licensee appoints a distributor for the licensed product in a specific country or region;
- the licensee sells the first 100 units of the licensed product;
- the licensee's first sale of the licensed products in a specific country or region;
- the licensee earns $XXX from sales of the licensed products.

The licensee is often required to submit a periodic (often annual) report to the licensor indicating its progress toward achieving any as-yet-unmet milestones.

Milestones may be structured in a number of ways, and significant legal ramifications flow from the choices that are made:

- Milestones may be binding *commitments* – if the licensee does not achieve a milestone, it is in breach of the contract.
- Milestones may be *termination* triggers – if the licensee does not achieve a milestone, the licensor may have the right to terminate the agreement.
- Milestones may be *goals* – the licensee must expend some degree of effort to meet the milestones, but failing to meet them is not a breach.
- Milestones may be *payment* triggers – a payment is triggered when a milestone is achieved.
- Milestones may be requirements for maintaining *exclusivity* – if the licensee does not achieve a milestone, the licensor may convert some or all of the license (including specified fields of use) from exclusive to nonexclusive.

To make matters more complicated, the consequences of missed milestones are not mutually exclusive. For a discussion of the financial consequences of missed milestones, see *Law v. Bioheart, Inc.*, discussed in Section 8.5, and for a discussion of the licensor's right to terminate based on milestone failures, see Section 12.3, Note 1.

7.3.2 *Best Efforts*

Even without contractual milestones, courts often imply duties on exclusive licensees to use a degree of diligence in exploiting rights over which they have exclusive control. These implied obligations can range from duties to attempt to exploit the licensed rights in good faith, to more substantial obligations to employ "best efforts" in this pursuit. The case involving Lucy, Lady Duff Gordon, a classic of the contract law canon, introduces these issues, while *Permanence v. Kennametal* provides an overview of the recent case law addressing this topic.

Wood v. Lucy, Lady Duff Gordon
222 N.Y. 88 (N.Y. App. 1917)

CARDOZO, JUSTICE

The defendant styles herself "a creator of fashions." Her favor helps a sale. Manufacturers of dresses, millinery and like articles are glad to pay for a certificate of her approval. The things which she designs, fabrics, parasols and what not, have a new value in the public mind when issued in her name. She employed the plaintiff to help her to turn this vogue into money. He was to have the exclusive right, subject always to her approval, to place her indorsements on the designs of others. He was also to have the exclusive right to place her own designs on sale, or to license others to market them. In return, she was to have one-half of "all profits and revenues" derived from any contracts he might make. The exclusive right was to last at least one year from April 1, 1915, and thereafter from year to year unless terminated by notice of ninety days. The plaintiff says that he kept the contract on his part, and that the defendant broke it. She placed her indorsement on fabrics, dresses and mil-linery without his knowledge, and withheld the profits. He sues her for the damages, and the case comes here on demurrer.

The agreement of employment is signed by both parties. It has a wealth of recitals. The defendant insists, however, that it lacks the elements of a contract. She says that the plaintiff does not bind himself to anything. It is true that he does not promise in so many words that he will use reasonable efforts to place the defendant's indorsements and market her designs. We think, however, that such a promise is fairly to be implied. The law has out-grown its primitive stage of formalism when the precise word was the sovereign talisman, and every slip was fatal. It takes a broader view to-day. A promise may be lacking, and yet the whole writing may be "instinct with an obligation," imperfectly expressed. If that is so, there is a contract.

The implication of a promise here finds support in many circumstances. The defendant gave an exclusive privilege. She was to have no right for at least a year to place her own indorsements or market her own designs except through the agency of the plaintiff. The acceptance of the exclusive agency was an assumption of its duties. We are not to suppose that one party was to be placed at the mercy of the other. Many other terms of the agree-ment point the same way. We are told at the outset by way of recital that "the said Otis F. Wood possesses a business organization adapted to the placing of such indorsements as the said Lucy, Lady Duff-Gordon has approved." The implication is that the plaintiff's busi-ness organization will be used for the purpose for which it is adapted. But the terms of the defendant's compensation are even more significant. Her sole compensation for the grant of an exclusive agency is to be one-half of all the profits resulting from the plaintiff's efforts. Unless he gave his efforts, she could never get anything. Without an implied promise, the transaction cannot have such business "efficacy as both parties must have intended that at all events it should have". But the contract does not stop there. The plaintiff goes on to promise that he will account monthly for all moneys received by him, and that he will take out all such patents and copyrights and trademarks as may in his judgment be necessary to protect the rights and articles affected by the agreement. It is true, of course, as the Appellate Division has said, that if he was under no duty to try to market designs or to place certificates of indorsement, his promise to account for profits or take out copyrights would be valueless. But in determining the intention of the parties, the promise has a value. It helps to enforce the conclusion that the plaintiff had some duties. His promise to pay the defendant one-half of the profits and revenues resulting from the exclusive agency and to render accounts monthly, was a promise to use reasonable efforts to bring profits and reve-nues into existence. For this conclusion, the authorities are ample.

The judgment of the Appellate Division should be reversed, and the order of the Special Term affirmed, with costs in the Appellate Division and in this court.

FIGURE 7.4 Lucy Christiana Lady Duff Gordon (1863–1935).

Permanence Corp. v. Kennametal, Inc.

725 F. Supp. 907 (E.D. Mich. 1989)

FREEMAN, JUSTICE

In this diversity action, plaintiff seeks damages for the breach of an implied obligation of a licensing agreement. [Defendant, Kennametal, Inc.] obtained a non-exclusive license to manufacture and sell products "made from and pursuant to" certain listed patents. Two years later, Kennametal exercised a contractual option to convert the license to an exclusive license to manufacture and sell. Plaintiff alleges that Kennametal breached and continues to breach to date, its obligations under the aforementioned written agreement between the parties [to exercise its best efforts]. Defendant argues that "[a] best efforts clause will not be implied in a patent license agreement where (i) the agreement is adequately supported by consideration, (ii) the plaintiff was represented by counsel, and (iii) the agreement is expressly an integrated agreement."

In *Vacuum Concrete Corp v. American Machine & Foundry Co.*, 321 F. Supp. 771, 772–73 (S.D.N.Y. 1971), the court adequately summarized the competing interests in determining whether to infer an obligation of best efforts:

It is settled law that the court will imply a duty on the part of an exclusive licensee to exploit the subject matter of the license with due diligence, where such a covenant is essential as a matter of equity to give meaning and effect to the contract as a whole.

The reasoning [is that] it would be unfair to place the productiveness of the licensed property solely within the control of the licensee, thereby putting the licensor at his mercy, without imposing an obligation to exploit upon the licensee. In effect the court is merely enforcing an obligation which the parties overlooked expressing in their contract or which they considered unnecessary to be expressed. In such circumstances the implied obligation "must conform to what the court may assume would have been the agreement of the parties, if the situation had been anticipated and provided for. Thus whatever obligation is sought to be raised by legal implication, must be of such a character as the court will assume would have been made by the parties if their attention had been called to the subject, and their conduct inspired by principles of justice."

A typical example of an implied covenant to exploit is found in a leading case in New York on the subject, *Wood v. Lucy, Lady Duff-Gordon*. There the defendant, a fashion designer, gave the plaintiff the exclusive privilege of marketing defendant's design. Although the plaintiff did not expressly agree to exploit the design, the court implied such an obligation, since defendant's sole revenue was to be derived from plaintiff's sale of clothes designed by defendant and defendant was thus at the plaintiff's mercy. In this and in similar cases the circumstances revealed that such an obligation was essential to give effect to the contract between the parties and was in accord with their intent. On the other hand, where the parties have considered the matter and deliberately omitted any such obligation, or where it is unnecessary to imply such an obligation in order to give effect to the terms of their contract, it will not be implied.

[Our] starting point, of course, must be the terms of the written contract between the parties. Although the Agreement purported to grant an exclusive license to AMF, obligating it to pay royalties to Vacuum, it is readily apparent that Vacuum, unlike the licensors in those cases where an obligation to exploit has been implied, did not depend for its revenue solely upon sales of the licensed devices (Octopus Lifters) by AMF. In the first place according to the terms of the Agreement Vacuum retained the right itself to manufacture and sell up to $300,000 annually of Octopus Lifters within the licensed territory. The significance of this reservation as a factor negating an implied covenant to exploit is apparent from the undisputed fact that up to the date of the Agreement between the parties Vacuum's maximum gross annual income from sales or licensing of the lifting device in the licensed territory (U.S.) was $63,771 received in 1964, of which $47,939 represented income from the sale of a total of eight machines, parts, and services.

The decision in each case in which a party asserts an implied obligation of best efforts turns upon the circumstances of each case, although certain factors can be distilled from an evaluation of the reported cases. In the *Wood* case, for example, the most important factor in the decision was that the fashion designer would not receive any revenue unless the plaintiff sold the designer's clothes. As a matter of equity, Justice Cardozo held that the contract was "instinct with obligation" on the plaintiff to use reasonable efforts to sell the clothes.

In *Havel v. Kelsey-Hayes Co.*, 83 A.D.2d 380 (N.Y. App. Div. 1981), the agreement in issue provided as follows:

By agreement dated January 30, 1973, plaintiff granted to defendant an exclusive license for the use and dissemination of the patented process. Defendant agreed to pay plaintiff a percentage of the cost of super alloy powders used in the process and further agreed that plaintiff would receive 25% of all lump sum payments and 40% of all royalties paid to defendant by sublicensees. The agreement also provided for payment by defendant of minimum royalties of $20,000 per year. The minimum payment was not guaranteed, however, because plaintiff's sole right was to terminate the license on defendant's failure to make up the deficiency if plaintiff's share of the lump sum payments and royalties did not amount to $20,000 in any calendar year.

The court held that the contract, when read as a whole, was instinct with an obligation to use reasonable efforts to exploit the process. Of primary importance to the court was the provision for an exclusive license; of further importance was that the minimum royalty provision was not guaranteed and that public policy supports the use of patents, not their suppression.

In *Willis Bros., Inc. v. Ocean Scallops, Inc.*, 356 F. Supp. 1151 (E.D.N.C. 1972), the license agreement granted to the defendant,

> an exclusive, world wide right for the life of the patent to manufacture, use and sell a certain scallop shucking process on which plaintiffs had pending an application for letters patent. The plaintiffs agreed not to manufacture, use, or sell the equipment except as to commitments made prior to the agreement. In consideration for this exclusive licensing, the defendant agreed to pay plaintiffs an amount determined on a basis of three cents per net pound of product processed by use of the equipment and/or the processes. There is no minimum royalty provision in the contract. Although the Agency Agreement provides that Willis Brothers will serve as a nonexclusive agent for the defendant in the sale of scallop meat, there is no reservation of rights in the License Agreement permitting the plaintiffs to compete with the license. The Employment Contract provided that Willis was to receive consultant's fees. This agreement was cancelled by the defendant after one year. In order to enable the plaintiffs to pay the debts incurred by the development of the patent, the defendant loaned Willis Brothers seventy thousand dollars. Prepayment of the loan was to be made by application to the principal the royalties under the License Agreement and percentages of the amount payable to Willis Brothers under the Agency Agreement. The prepayment provision providing for payment of the loan from the royalties indicates that a "best efforts" provision is essential to give effect to the agreements between the parties.

Of importance to the court was that the agreement was for an exclusive license to work the patent and that the defendant must use due diligence in working the patent to allow plaintiff to repay the loan defendant made to it as part of the agreement.

In *Bellows v. E.R. Squibb & Sons, Inc.*, 184 U.S.P.Q. 473 (N.D. Ill. 1974), the agreement in issue provided in pertinent part:

> 4.01 Concurrently with the execution of this Agreement [Squibb] shall pay to [Bellows] the sum of … ($50,000.00), which shall represent a credit against future royalties, but shall not be refundable in whole or part in the event no royalties [accrue] to Bellows
>
> 8.02 [Squibb] may terminate this Agreement in its entirety … by giving [Bellows] written notice at least six (6) months prior to such termination.
>
> 8.03 In the event of any of the following, [Bellows] may, at his option, terminate this Agreement:
>
>   a) [Squibb] elects not to exploit the license granted hereunder, … and [Squibb] shall have so notified [Bellows]…
>
>   d) [Squibb] … has failed to market the Licensed Product … within eighteen (18) months of the date of this Agreement.
>
>   e) [Squibb] does not pay to [Bellows] a minimum royalty of ($50,000) for each year after 1974 and during the life of this Agreement.

The court held as a matter of law that there could be no implied duty of best efforts in the exploitation of the invention. The crucial factors in the case are that the agreement specifically recognized that Squibb might decide not to exploit the patent and provided for that contingency. The court also noted that the agreement was the result of arm's length bargaining with both parties assisted by counsel and that "no obligation should be implied to merely cure an unsatisfactory bargain."

Looking at the agreement in this case, the court notes several important factors. First, the defendant exercised its option to obtain the exclusive rights to exploit plaintiff's patents.

Second, plaintiff could only terminate the agreement upon a breach of the agreement by defendant; defendant, however, could terminate the agreement upon 90 days notice provided that it pay the royalties due up to the effective date of the cancellation. Unlike *Bellows*, this agreement does not contain any provision allowing plaintiff to terminate the agreement if best efforts were not used or if certain minimum royalties were not paid. This factor further supports plaintiff's position.

Third, the agreement contained an integration clause:

> This Agreement supersedes all other agreements, oral or written, heretofore made with respect to the subject matter hereof and the transactions contemplated hereby and contains the entire agreement of the parties.

Defendant relies upon this provision in arguing against any implied obligation of best efforts. In *Vacuum Concrete*, 321 F. Supp. at 773–74, the court stated:

> Other provisions of the Agreement which militate against implying a covenant to exploit with due diligence are … the stipulation that the Agreement constituted "the entire agreement between the parties." … For instance, the merger or integration clause …, by emphasizing that the formal contract, which contained no undertaking by AMF to exploit the device, constituted the "entire" Agreement between the parties, negates the thought that they intended to impose such a duty upon AMF.

Fourth, the parties have submitted contradictory affidavits regarding the drafting of the agreement and what was negotiated. *See* McKenna Affidavit para. 9 ("Kennametal responded in a letter dated March 11, 1985, pointing out that Permanence and Kennametal had discussed 'best efforts' during the negotiation and that the parties had agreed to pre-paid royalties instead …"); Krass Affidavit para. 4 ("Neither the completed agreement nor any of the draft agreements contained a 'best efforts' clause and, to the best of my knowledge, there were not negotiations with respect to the inclusion of such a clause").

Fifth, on February 8, 1979, defendant pursuant to the agreement paid to plaintiff $250,000, $100,000 of which was an advance payment of royalties. On February 5, 1981, defendant paid plaintiff a second up-front fee of $250,000, $100,000 of which was an advance payment of royalties. The agreement also contained royalty rates on the net sales price of products made by defendant using processes that fall under valid claims of the patents. This factor sways decidedly in defendant's favor.

Finally, there is no dispute that the agreement has no express reference to "best efforts" with regard to the use of the patent, although the court notes that in another portion of the agreement the parties agreed that "Kennametal shall use reasonable efforts to guard against the unauthorized use or disclosure of such technology and technical assistance." The inclusion of the phrase "reasonable efforts" in paragraph 6.4 and the absence of that phrase in any other section of the agreement militates against inferring an implied promise to use best efforts to exploit the patents. This agreement was negotiated at arm's length by competent counsel.

After considering these factors, the court holds that there is no implied obligation of best efforts. Of primary importance is that the defendant paid up-front over $500,000 in fees and advance royalties. Thus, unlike the seminal *Wood* case, plaintiff's sole revenue was not subject to the whim of defendant in exploiting the patents – plaintiff had money in hand and was to receive further royalties under the agreement. While the *Masco* case upon which defendant relies can be distinguished because it involved a nonexclusive license, the Michigan Court of Appeals in that case stated:

There is no showing by the parties that Masco Corporation ordinarily supplied best effort clauses to licensing agreements. The circumstances surrounding this agreement also do not support the contention that the best efforts clause was so clearly within the contemplation of the parties that they deemed it unnecessary to expressly stipulate it. The record discloses a dispute between the parties as to whether a best efforts clause was considered during negotiation of this agreement. This is not a dispute of fact which would preclude summary judgment. This dispute shows that the parties did not feel that a best efforts clause was so clearly implied that it was unnecessary to include it in the contract.

Similarly, in the instant case, the only disputed factual issue is what occurred during the negotiation of the agreement. The court has carefully read the agreement and holds that no best efforts clause can be implied to it.

Notes and Questions

1. *What standard?* Although the *Kennametal* court states that *Vacuum Concrete* "adequately summarized" the law regarding "best efforts," the quoted language refers to a duty of "due diligence" rather than best efforts. Do these standards differ? A review of the case law quickly reveals that a range of different standards are used to describe the implied obligations of exclusive licensees. For example, courts refer to "reasonable efforts," "best efforts for a reasonable time," "good faith efforts," "active exploitation in good faith," and many other formulations of this concept. Are these courts all attempting to describe the same nebulous standard of conduct, or are there dozens of different shades of effort that may be imposed on a licensee depending on the circumstances?

2. *How good are best efforts?* Many transactional lawyers will tell you that "best efforts" is a very high standard of performance, requiring a party to take extreme measures, even risking financial ruin, to achieve the desired end. There is even an oft-repeated hierarchy of efforts, running from best efforts, at the top, to reasonable best efforts to reasonable efforts to commercially reasonable efforts to good-faith efforts, at the bottom.

   But the case law belies this folk wisdom. Clearly, "best efforts" require more than "mere" good faith, but cases routinely hold that "best efforts" do not require a licensee to take measures that are unreasonable or destructive. For example, in *Perma Research & Dev. Co. v. Singer Co.*, 402 F. Supp. 881, 896, aff'd, 542 F.2d 111, 113 (2d Cir. 1976), a party agreed to "use its best efforts for a reasonable time" to perfect a particular product for commercial purposes. The court held only that the party was required to undertake research and development necessary to bring the product to market without unreasonable effort. Thus, even under a "best efforts" requirement, the case law generally allows a licensee to make a reasoned business decision to take, or omit to take, actions dictated by reasonable judgment in light of market realities and circumstances. In other words, "best efforts" are "reasonable efforts."

   Parties that do not wish to throw the dice in court sometimes try to define the level of efforts required under an agreement with a greater degree of specificity. For example, in *Elorac, Inc. v. Sanofi-Aventis Can., Inc.*, 343 F. Supp. 3d 789, 794 (N.D. Ill. 2018), the license agreement defined "Commercially Reasonable Efforts" as:

   efforts consistent with those generally utilized by companies of a similar size for their own internally developed pharmaceutical products of similar market potential, at a similar stage of their product life taking into account the existence of other competitive products in the marketplace or under development, the proprietary position of the product, the regulatory structure involved, the anticipated profitability of the product and other relevant factors. It is understood that such product potential may change from time to time based upon changing scientific, business and marketing and return on investment considerations.

Does this definition give the licensor more comfort than a simple obligation that the licensee use "reasonable efforts" to commercialize the product? Why? What specific aspects of this definition do you find the most helpful? To what degree is it still vulnerable to subjective interpretation?

3. *Good faith.* In general, an obligation of good faith is less stringent than a best efforts, negligence or reasonable care standard. Good faith is primarily concerned with whether conduct is fair and undertaken honestly, rather than the particular degree of care with which an act is performed. For example, UCC § 2-103(b) defines good faith as honesty in fact and conformance to commercial standards of fair dealing. In view of this distinction, what standard of conduct would you prefer to be held to as an exclusive licensee? What would you prefer as a licensor who has granted an exclusive license?

4. *Enumeration of obligations.* If a licensor wants to be sure that its exclusive licensee will take certain actions to promote a particular product or business, it can list those specific obligations in the agreement. For example, a licensee can be required to meet minimum annual sales or development milestones, achieve certain regulatory approvals, open a certain number of sales offices around the world, devote a certain number of full-time personnel to promotional activities, etc. Why don't all license agreement contain such specific lists of licensee actions? When might a general "best efforts" or "good faith" obligation be preferable? Absent a list of specific milestones or requirements, would you prefer that an exclusive licensing agreement state a general level of obligation such as "best efforts" or "good faith," or that it remain silent on this issue, allowing a court to determine the appropriate degree of effort depending on the facts and circumstances?

5. *Effect of advance payments.* Why does the court in *Permanence* emphasize the fact that the licensee made an advance payment to the licensor? What effect should advance payments have on an exclusive licensee's obligations?

6. *Merger clause.* The court in *Permanence* also gives weight to the presence of a "merger" or "integration" clause in the agreement between Permanence and Kennametal. This clause is typically considered part of the "boilerplate" that comes at the end of every agreement. Is it meaningful? Should the court give significant weight to standard clauses such as this, particularly if there is evidence that the parties had a different understanding? See Section 13.7 for a discussion of these standard clauses in licensing agreements.

7. *Remedies.* What is a licensor's remedy if its exclusive licensee fails to meet its standard of performance? If such a failure can be characterized as a breach of contract, then the licensor may have the right to terminate the agreement, either under the terms of the agreement or under the common law (see Chapter 12). But there are less severe remedies, as well. One of these is releasing the licensor from certain milestone or progress payments to the licensee (see Chapter 8.5). Another effective remedy is the licensor's ability to terminate the licensee's exclusivity, but otherwise to keep the license agreement in force. In effect, this remedy converts the exclusive license to a nonexclusive license. Depending on the agreement, such a conversion may also reduce the royalty rate payable by the licensee, eliminate further milestone payments by the licensor, and otherwise transform the financial profile of the agreement from an exclusive to a nonexclusive agreement. Both a release from payments and conversion to nonexclusivity are generally implemented through express contractual language rather than operation of law. Which remedy do you think is the most effective for

an exclusive licensee's failure to meet its commercialization obligations? Does your answer depend on whether you represent the licensor or the licensee?

Problem 7.3

Kitchen Corp. grants Garden Italiano, a national restaurant chain, a five-year exclusive license under Kitchen Corp.'s patented process for sharpening kitchen knives. Under the agreement, Garden Italiano is required to make an up-front payment of $75,000 and to pay running royalties of 15 percent on income that it obtains from sublicensing the process to others, and 0.25 percent of net sales from all Garden Italiano restaurants. A year after the agreement is executed, Garden Italiano determines that it would be more economical to subscribe to a national knife rental program that delivers newly sharpened knives to its outlets every week. Garden Italiano discontinues use of Kitchen Corp.'s sharpening process and makes no further effort to market the process to others. Three months later, Kitchen Corp, notices that Garden Italiano has stopped making payments under the licensing agreement. What legal actions, if any, would you advise Kitchen Corp. to take in response?

Problem 7.4

Big Film USA is a major motion picture producer and distributor. Its inventory includes thousands of motion picture scripts, many of which were created by independent screenwriters. In most cases, the screenwriter has granted Big Film USA all rights to exploit the script under a worldwide, perpetual, exclusive license agreement in exchange for an advance payment of a few thousand dollars plus a 5 percent running royalty on net profits from any motion picture based on the script. Five years ago, Hank Toms licensed Big Film USA the script for a film titled *Citizen Jane*, a darkly comedic look at the rise of a plucky young newspaper reporter. Upon signing the licensing agreement, Big Film USA's acquisitions manager told Hank that the script was a "masterpiece of modern cinema." Nevertheless, during the past five years, Big Film USA has made no progress toward producing a film based on the script, though it has produced at least ten other motion pictures in the same genre as *Citizen Jane*. One of these other films won two Academy Awards, but the other nine ranged from modest commercial successes to flops. None of the other films infringes Hank's copyright in *Citizen Jane*. Does Hank have a legal claim against Big Film USA? What arguments might you make on behalf of Big Film USA to contest Hank's claims? How might you draft future exclusive script licenses to avoid such claims from other screenwriters?

8

Financial Terms

While lawyers often obsess over the "legal" terms of an agreement, it is likely that the most important contractual language from the parties' perspective – at least the business representatives of the parties – is that describing their financial obligations to one another. Attorneys often give far too little time and attention to these financial clauses, assuming that the parties and their accountants, bankers and financial advisors will work out the "numbers" to their satisfaction. This assumption, however, is grossly inaccurate. The financial clauses of an agreement are rife with legal details that can have an inordinate impact on the deal. Thus, while attorneys need not opine as to the market value of a particular technology, they must be prepared to draft and negotiate language that gives effect to the business and financial assumptions of their clients.

This being said, there is a virtually unlimited array of financial clauses that can be deployed in a licensing agreement. Save for limited antitrust considerations (see Chapter 25) and voluntary restraints (e.g., the FRAND licensing commitments described in Chapter 20), there are few legal constraints on the form or amount of compensation that an intellectual property (IP) holder may charge for its IP. Accordingly, parties are relatively free to formulate whatever business arrangement they wish.

This chapter summarizes the most common forms of financial clauses that appear in IP and technology licensing agreements and illustrates how they are used in typical transactions.

8.1 FIXED PAYMENTS

Fixed payments are amounts that are predetermined and specified in a contract, usually without reference to the licensee's revenue or use of the licensed rights. Such payments can be due upon contract signing (or within a short period thereafter), in which case they are called **up-front** payments.

8.1.1 *Up-Front and Lump-Sum Payments*

Up-front payments are not uncommon in many types of licensing agreements. Often, privately held biotech companies require up-front payments from their licensees in order to fund their operations prior to the development, approval and marketing of a product. These up-front payments are often made in exchange for exclusive license rights in a particular field or fields of use and are often paid in addition to running royalties on products that are eventually created under the license.

EXAMPLE: UP-FRONT FEE

Licensee shall pay Licensor a nonrefundable, up-front fee of $1,000,000 within ten (10) business days from the Effective Date.

If an up-front payment represents the entire consideration for the license, and no further payments or royalties are due, then it is also referred to as a **lump-sum** payment. When you pay $1.99 for a new app at the Apple AppStore, you have paid a lump-sum fee for a nonexclusive license.

One of the best-known lump-sum license fees was that paid by Microsoft to Spyglass, Inc., the start-up that licensed the original "Mosaic" web browser from the University of Illinois. In the early 1990s, Microsoft realized that the WorldWide Web had significant commercial potential, yet Marc Andressen's Netscape Communications seemed to have a corner on the market for web browser technology with its then-ubiquitous Netscape Navigator program. To jump-start its own entry into the web browser market, Microsoft sought rights to distribute Mosaic from Spyglass. Microsoft's first offer was $100,000. As the CEO of Spyglass explained to the *New York Times*, "the first offer from Microsoft on licensing deals is always $100,000."[1] By December 1994, Spyglass negotiated Microsoft's lump-sum license fee up to $2 million, which entitled Microsoft to distribute Mosaic with its Windows 95 operating system. Microsoft renamed the browser "Internet Explorer" and began to give it away for free, a business model with which Netscape simply could not compete.

Depending on the industry, up-front fees in license agreements can be quite large. One recent study of more than 1,000 biopharmaceutical licenses entered into between 1998 and 2018 found that average up-front fees paid were $11.5 million, with a high of $240 million (for a tumor therapeutic licensed by Exelixis to Bristol-Myers Squibb).[2]

8.1.2 *Option Fees*

Option fees are also typically one-time payments of a fixed amount. Thus, if a company – often in the biotech or entertainment industries – grants another company an option to acquire exclusive license rights to IP at some time in the future, the option fee will be paid as a one-time fixed fee, and the purchase price or license fee payable upon exercise of the option will be a (usually larger) fixed fee.

---

[1]   Steve Lohr, *Spyglass, a Pioneer, Learns Hard Lessons About Microsoft*, NY Times, March 2, 1998, p. D1.
[2]   Mark Edwards, *Biopharma Milestone Payments: Negotiating and Equitable Value Allocation*, BioSciBD (January 6, 2019) (supporting data), https://bioscibd.com/biopharma-milestone-payments/#2.

FIGURE 8.1 Spyglass, Inc. licensed its Mosaic web browser code to Microsoft for $2 million. Mosaic became the basis for Internet Explorer.

EXAMPLE: OPTION FEE

Licensee shall pay Licensor a one-time, nonrefundable option fee of $1,000,000 within three (3) days of the Effective Date (the "Option Fee").

Licensee shall have the option ("Option") to elect to obtain an exclusive license to the Optioned Rights on the terms set forth in Section [x], which Option Licensee may exercise at any time prior to the fifth (5th) anniversary of the Effective Date by paying to Licensor the amount of $25,000,000 (the "Exercise Price").

Fixed payments need not be made in a single installment. In many cases, such payments can be due periodically – monthly, quarterly, annually or on some other schedule. Fixed annual license fees are not uncommon in some industries, such as enterprise software. Likewise, such arrangements often include charges for related services, such as software maintenance, support and updating, which is charged periodically (often annually) as a percentage of the annual license fee (often in the range of 15–25 percent of the annual license fee).

EXAMPLE: PERIODIC LICENSE FEE

Licensee shall pay Licensor a nonrefundable license fee of $1,000,000 no later than sixty (60) days prior to the beginning of each Contract Year hereunder.

8.1.3 *Nonrefundable Fees*

One question that is often raised in the context of fixed fees is the degree to which such fees are refundable if some future event, such as regulatory approval of a drug, does not occur. In general, up-front fees are **nonrefundable** (see the above drafting examples). They thus represent a risk to the licensee, which must pay whether or not the acquired rights turn out to be as valuable as promised. Yet, absent outright fraud by the licensor, there is little that a licensee can do to recover nonrefundable up-front fees once they have been paid.

In the summer of 2008, Myriad [Genetics, Inc.] announced the results of its eighteen-month clinical trial for Flurizan. It was a failure. The drug provided no significant benefit in treating Alzheimer's disease over the standard treatment regimen. Without further ado, the company discontinued its Flurizan development program.

Despite this blow to Myriad, Flurizan represented a personal victory for [CEO Pete] Meldrum. A little over a month before the clinical trial results were released, Meldrum had negotiated a deal with the CEO of Danish pharmaceutical manufacturer Lundbeck. Myriad granted Lundbeck the exclusive European marketing rights for Flurizan in exchange for an up-front, nonrefundable payment of $100 million. Lundbeck made the payment promptly. Forty days later, the clinical trial announcement was made and Flurizan was dead. Lundbeck's CEO balked, but the contract was airtight – the payment was nonrefundable. Meldrum walked away from the Flurizan fiasco with a cool $100 million and turned Lundbeck into an industry laughingstock. Biotech journalist Adam Feurstein called Meldrum's coup "one of the smartest drug licensing deals of all time." To recognize his achievement, TheStreet.com named Meldrum "Best Biotech CEO of the Year."

8.1.4 *Advances and Applicable Fees*

In some cases, up-front fees are characterized as advances against future payment obligations such as royalties. Such advances are common in the publishing, music and entertainment industries. In this model, authors and composers often receive an advance upon licensing their rights to a publisher. An advance can be paid before a work is delivered (common for nonfiction books) or upon the licensing of a manuscript (works of fiction) or sound recording.

The term "advance" indicates that such a payment is really a prepayment of applicable royalties that may be due during the life of an agreement. Yet, in many cases, authors and other rights licensors receive only their advance, as earned royalties never exceed the amount of the advance.

In some cases, an up-front payment will be referred to not as an advance, but as "applicable" to a future payment obligation. This is sometimes the case with option fees. For example, a $5,000 option fee may be described as "applicable to" the purchase price of the relevant right if the option is exercised. If the option fee is not applicable to the purchase price, then it is referred to as "nonapplicable."

8.2 RUNNING ROYALTIES: THE ROYALTY RATE

For many types of IP the most common form of payment is the royalty. A royalty is a periodic payment that is typically based on the licensee's manufacture, use or sale of a licensed product or service, whether a new drug, a book or an action figure. These payments are often referred to as "running" royalties because they are paid over the course of the agreement term. The term "earned" royalty is commonly used to refer to royalties based on the licensee's revenue, usually from sales of licensed products.

---

[3] From Jorge L. Contreras, *How the Gene Was Won* https://genomedefense.org.

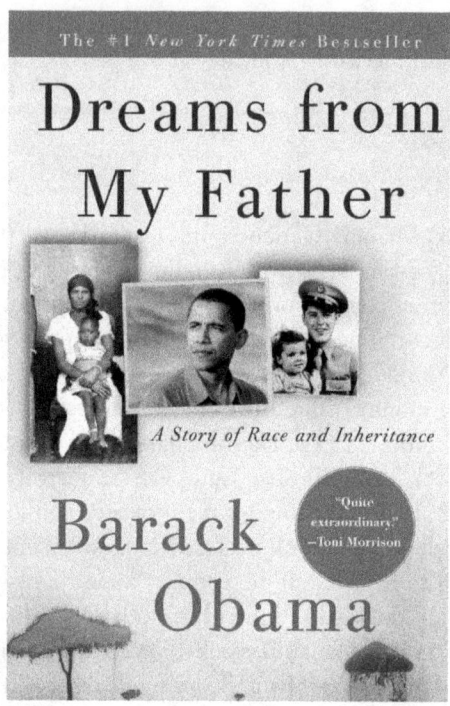

FIGURE 8.2 Former President Barack Obama received a $20 million advance in 2017 for his memoir *Dreams from My Father,* the largest single-book advance on record, though some argue that Bill Clinton's $15 million advance for his 2001 memoir *My Life* was larger in inflation-adjusted dollars.

Royalties are typically calculated and paid periodically over the course of an agreement – monthly, quarterly, annually or over some other fixed interval. Quarterly royalty payments are the norm in patent licensing agreements, though semi-annual payments are common in literary rights agreements. In general, royalties with respect to a particular period will be due and payable within some reasonable time after the end of the period (e.g., thirty days after the end of the relevant calendar quarter). A royalty report showing the basis for royalties paid is often required to accompany each royalty payment, and in Section 8.9 we will discuss audit and other mechanisms used by licensors to check the accuracy of these reports.

Royalties are popular forms of compensation because they tend to align the interests of the licensor and licensee. That is, they typically increase in proportion to increases in the licensee's own profits attributable to the licensed rights. Thus, if the licensee does well, so does the licensor. But while this general principle sounds straightforward, the calculation of royalties in licensing agreements can become devilishly complex, filled with room for interpretation and opportunistic behavior. This section addresses some of the basic concepts necessary to understand royalty calculations, and Section 8.3 addresses additional clauses used by parties when structuring their royalty arrangements.

8.2.1 *Per-Unit Royalties*

8.2.1.1 Flat-Rate Royalties

The simplest form of running royalty is one that sets a fixed charge for each unit of a licensed product sold or distributed by the licensee. An example of such a royalty provision follows.

EXAMPLE: PER-UNIT RUNNING ROYALTY

Licensee shall pay to Licensor earned royalties at the rate of $x.xx per unit of Licensed Product sold [*alternative*: manufactured].

Thus, if the royalty rate is $0.10 per unit, and the licensee sells 500,000 units during a particular calendar quarter, then the licensee will owe the licensor a royalty of $50,000 for that quarter. With a per-unit royalty, it does not matter how much the licensee earns from its sale of licensed products, whether it offers discounts or even whether it makes a profit (or loss) on those sales.

Examples of per-unit royalties abound. As discussed in Section 16.2.2, the US Copyright Royalty Board established a flat rate of 24¢ for every downloaded ringtone that includes a copyrighted musical work, whether composed by the Rolling Stones or your brother's weekend garage band. And, at its peak, the well-known DVDC6 patent pool charged disc manufacturers a flat rate of 7.5¢ per DVD disc. Because these per-unit rates are often denominated in cents on the dollar, they are sometimes referred to as "penny rates."

In some cases involving manufactured products, a licensor may not wish to wait to see whether a licensee sells the licensed products that it manufactures, and may require a per-unit royalty to be paid with respect to every licensed product that the licensee manufactures (or has manufactured on its behalf). This formulation tends to get the licensor paid earlier, and insulates the licensor from the vagaries of the licensee's sales efforts. Naturally, licensees will resist the manufacture of a product, rather than its sale, as the event triggering a royalty payment. After all, the licensee itself earns nothing when a product is manufactured but not sold, so the alignment of the parties' interests is weaker with such an arrangement. Nevertheless, licensors may find it easier to monitor or audit the output of a production line than dispersed sales across a wide geographic region, so there may be valid reasons that licensors insist on such provisions.

8.2.1.2 Tiered Royalty Schedules

Like percentage royalties (discussed in Section 8.2.2), per-unit royalties may be "flat" or "tiered." Flat royalties are the same no matter how many units of the licensed product are manufactured or sold, as illustrated in the example above. Tiered royalties, on the other hand, take volume into account, and usually decrease as the licensee's volume increases. For example, a tiered royalty schedule might look like that shown in Table 8.1.

Using this tiered royalty schedule, if, during the first quarter of the year, the licensee sold 60,000 units of the licensed product, it would owe the licensor $1.00 for each of the first 5,000 units (or $5,000), $0.85 for the next 45,000 units ($38,250) and $0.75 for the next 10,000 units ($7,500) for a total quarterly royalty payment of $50,750. In the second quarter, the count would

TABLE 8.1 *A tiered royalty schedule*

Units sold during quarter	Royalty per unit
0–5,000	$1.00
5,001–50,000	$0.85
50,001–100,000	$0.75
100,000+	$0.65

begin again from zero. Thus, if the licensee sold 100,000 units during the second quarter, it would owe $5,000 + $38,250 + $37,500, or a total of $80,750.

In some cases the parties may not wish to reset the volume counter at the beginning of each royalty period, and may instead wish the licensee's volume tiers to continue to accumulate over the full year or the entire term of the agreement. For example, suppose that the volume tiers continued to accumulate during the full term of the agreement above instead of resetting each quarter. During the first quarter the licensee would pay $50,750, as above. However, if the licensee sold 100,000 units during the second quarter, it would begin with the benefit of the third-tier royalty. Its second quarter royalty payment would be $0.75 for the first 40,000 units ($30,000) and $0.65 for the next 60,000 units ($39,000), for a total of $69,000, which is significantly less than what it would have paid had the tiers reset at the beginning of the second quarter.

8.2.2 *Percentage Royalties: The Royalty Rate*

For all of their advantages, per-unit royalties do not closely link the licensee's royalty obligation to its actual revenue from licensed product sales. As a result, many parties to licensing agreements choose to specify royalties in terms of a *percentage* rather than a fixed rate per product.

8.2.2.1 The Basics

A percentage royalty has two key components: the royalty rate and the royalty base. The royalty *base* is the amount of licensee revenue that is multiplied by the royalty *rate* to yield the royalty owed. In other words,

$$\text{Royalty } (\$) = \text{rate } (\%) \times \text{base } (\$).$$

The royalty base is often expressed in terms of the licensee's "net sales" of licensed products. The definition of net sales is often one of the most complex and most contentious in a licensing agreement, and is discussed in greater detail in the next subsection.

EXAMPLE: PERCENTAGE ROYALTY

Licensee shall pay to Licensor earned royalties at the rate of *x* percent on Net Sales of Licensed Products.

8.2.2.2 Tiered Royalties

Like per-unit royalties, percentage royalties may be flat or tiered. An example of a volume-based tiered percentage royalty schedule is given in Table 8.2:

TABLE 8.2 *A volume-based tiered percentage royalty schedule*

Units sold during quarter	Royalty rate (%)
0–5,000	2.5
5,001–50,000	2.0
50,001–100,000	1.5
100,000+	1.0

These royalty rates are *incremental* quarterly sales tiers. Thus, if the licensee sells 75,000 units in the quarter, and each unit results in net sales of $100, the licensee will pay:

Units 1–5,000:	$100 × 0.025 × 5,000 = $12,500
Units 5,001–50,000:	$100 × 0.02 × 45,000 = $90,000
Units 50,001–75,000:	$100 × 0.015 × 25,000 = $37,500
Total	**$140,000**

But tiered royalty schedules need not be based only on sales volume. For example, different royalty rates and rate schedules may be based on:

- the **geographic** market in which a licensed product is sold – for example, many pharmaceutical products are priced differently in different geographic markets, with rates in low-income countries only a fraction of what they are in high-income countries;
- the **type** of licensed product sold – for example, the DVD patent pools charged very different royalty rates depending on whether the licensee manufactured a DVD player or a DVD disc;
- the **date** on which the license is granted – for example, licensors sometimes seek to incentivize early adoption of their technology by offering rates that are determined based on when the license agreement was signed.

Finally, tiered royalty schedules may combine all of these, as well as percentage and per-unit royalty rates, in any number of variations.

8.2.2.3 Royalty Rate Levels

One thing that attorneys advising clients in licensing transactions are typically not called upon to do is determine the royalty rate at which the licensed rights will be licensed. The determination of royalty rates, just as the selling price of a product or service, is typically a decision left to business and financial experts. This being said, licensing attorneys should understand the general landscape of royalty rate determination, both to assist their clients during negotiations, and because the framework for negotiating royalty rates often becomes a key factor in IP infringement litigation.[4]

In truth, the establishment of a royalty rate in a licensing agreement depends to a large degree on custom and practice in the relevant industry, as well as the negotiation leverage of the parties.[5] For example, patent royalty rates in the semiconductor and electronics industries are often in the low single digits, while software licenses often carry a royalty of 40–50 percent. And even within these general categories there can be significant variation depending on the strength and desirability of the licensed IP, the size and reputation of the licensee, the type of licensed product being authorized, the exclusivity of the license and numerous other factors. For example,

---

[4] For example, 35 U.S.C. § 284 establishes that a patent holder is entitled to minimum damages for patent infringement equivalent to a "reasonable royalty" for use of the invention, and the federal courts in assessing such reasonable royalties typically look to the fifteen-factor test established in *Georgia-Pacific Corp. v. United States Plywood Corp.*, 318 F. Supp. 1116 (S.D.N.Y. 1970), which centers on the royalty rate that would have been agreed by the parties in a "hypothetical negotiation."

[5] This discussion assumes that there are no external constraints on the establishment of royalty rates, such as a patent holder's commitment to grant licenses at rates that are "fair, reasonable and nondiscriminatory" (FRAND) – see Chapter 20.

according to one industry source, the average royalty rate for licensing a brand or character for use in toys and games is approximately 8 percent.[6] Yet it has also been reported that Disney charges Hasbro between 20 and 25 percent for its exclusive toy/merchandise license of its *Star Wars* and *Marvel Comics* properties.[7]

SAMPLE ROYALTY RATES IN BOOK PUBLISHING

Book publishing agreements contain a range of royalty rates for different outlets and forms of publication. Below is a sample of the rates charged by a US publisher for a novel by a non-celebrity author:

US hardcover retail sales   10–15 percent of retail price
Export hardcover sales   6 percent of retail price
US paperback retail sales   7.5 percent of retail price
Export paperback sales   5 percent of retail price
Foreign-language editions   75 percent of publisher's royalty received
Electronic editions   25 percent of publisher's royalty received
Serialization   50 percent of publisher's royalty received

FIGURE 8.3 The Walt Disney Company owns some of the world's most valuable brands and is reported to earn 15.5 percent of all IP licensing revenue in the United States (IBISWorld, Intell. Prop. Licensing in the US p.35 (March 2020)).

---

6   www.thelicensingletter.com (May 1, 2020).
7   Leo Sun, *Disney's Pixar Could Become a New Growth Engine for Mattel*, The Motley Fool, May 2, 2019, www.fool .com/investing/2019/05/02/disneys-pixar-could-become-a-new-growth-engine-for.aspx.

- In an effort to analyze patent royalty rates more systematically, economists beginning in the 1970s postulated that a licensee should pay a royalty equivalent to 25 percent of its anticipated profit from sales of the licensed product. Thus, if the licensee's profit margin on sales of a licensed product were 16 percent, an appropriate royalty to the licensor would be 4 percent.

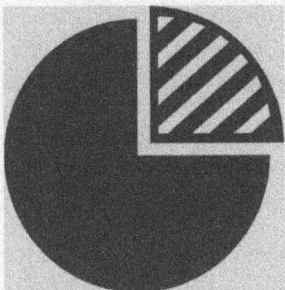

- As explained by the rule's leading proponent, Robert Goldscheider, the 25 percent rule is based on the "assumption [that] the licensee should retain a majority (i.e. 75 percent) of the profits, because it has undertaken substantial development, operational and commercialization risks, contributed other technology/IP and/or brought to bear its own development, operational and commercialization contributions."[8] Empirical work by Goldscheider and others seemed to corroborate the use of the 25 percent rule in a variety of licensing transactions.
- Yet the 25 percent rule has its detractors, who charge that it fails to account for both the importance of the licensed patents to the product sold and the relationship of the parties. In 2011, the Federal Circuit rejected use of the 25 percent rule in reasonable royalty patent damages calculations, calling it "fundamentally flawed" and holding that "there must be a basis in fact to associate the royalty rates used in prior licenses to the particular hypothetical negotiation at issue in the case. The 25 percent rule of thumb as an abstract and largely theoretical construct fails to satisfy this fundamental requirement."[9] The court also held that evidence of the reasonableness of a royalty rate based on the 25 percent rule failed to satisfy the minimum threshold for admissible "scientific, technical, or other specialized knowledge" under Federal Rule of Evidence 702, as interpreted under *Daubert v. Merrell Dow*, 509 U.S. 589 (1993). To illustrate the absurdity of the 25 percent rule in practice, the court hypothesized that it "would predict that the same 25%/75% royalty split would begin royalty discussions between, for example, (a) TinyCo and IBM over a strong patent portfolio of twelve patents covering various aspects of a pioneering hard drive, and (b) Kodak and Fuji over a single patent to a tiny improvement in a specialty film emulsion." From the court's standpoint, the 25 percent rule was dead.[10]

---

[8] Robert Goldscheider, John Jarosz & Carla Mulhern, *Use of the 25 Per Cent Rule in Valuing IP*, 37 Les Nouvelles 123, 124 (2002).

[9] *Uniloc USA v. Microsoft Corp.*, 632 F.3d 1292, 1315 (Fed. Cir. 2011).

[10] Goldscheider mounted a spirited defense of the "25 percent rule" following *Uniloc*: Robert Goldscheider, *The Classic 25% Rule and the Art of Intellectual Property Licensing*, 2011 Duke L. & Tech. Rev., No. 6 at 1 (2011): "it is inappropriate to condescendingly diminish [the rule] to a mere 'rule of thumb.' When properly understood and applied, the Classic 25% Rule is an effective discipline that achieves the high standards of reliability demanded by the U.S. Supreme Court in the *Daubert* and *Kumho Tire* cases."

8.2.2.4 Hybrid Royalty Rates

As we will discuss in greater detail in Section 24.3, US law does not permit a patent holder to charge a royalty with respect to a patent that is expired, or in a jurisdiction where the patent is not in force. Doing so is said to extend the temporal or geographic scope of the patent grant impermissibly, and is prohibited as patent "misuse."

As a result, patent licensors often combine licenses of patents with licenses of know-how or trade secrets.[11] Because trade secret rights have no natural expiration, a trade secret license may technically last in perpetuity.[12] Under such a structure, one royalty is charged when and where patent claims remain in effect, and a lower royalty is charged when/where no patent claims are in effect (i.e., the royalty is consideration only for the know-how). As the Ninth Circuit held in *Chromalloy Am. Corp. v. Fischmann*, 716 F.2d 683 (9th Cir. 1983), when a licensed patent is found to be invalid,

> while the licensor is not entitled to recover royalties as such under the patent license, compensation must be allowed to the extent that non-patent assets, such as know-how, are transferred to the licensee in the patent agreement.

But as the court went on to emphasize, it is important that the distinction between royalties for the patent rights and nonpatent rights be clearly delineated in the agreement and not blended in a single rate.

The key question, then, becomes how to allocate royalty payments between patents and know-how. One common approach is to set the know-how-only royalty at 50 percent of the patent + know-how royalty, but there is no precise formula for making this determination. One leading treatise notes that "[t]he prospect of long or perpetual royalties may create the temptation to skew the allocation in favor of the trade secret component" in such a hybrid license.[13] The author warns, however, that such gamesmanship (e.g., allocating 75 percent of the royalty to trade secrets when they represent only 25 percent of the value of the combined patent plus trade secret package) could backfire on the licensor:

> Suppose, for example, that a reasonable economic analysis of a bundle of patent and trade secret rights would require payment of 75% of the running royalty for the patents and only 25% for the trade secrets. Suppose further that a "clever" licensor, intent upon maximizing an entitlement to long term royalty and avoiding the risk of loss of royalty due to a finding of invalidity (or, for that matter, to expiration) of the patent, decides to shape the royalty allocation so that only 25% is allocated to the patents and 75% to the technology. The licensor may then, as a patentee, encounter a problem with other prospective licensees. Those licensees, interested in the patents, may not have any interest in the secret but unpatented technology, either because they have their own or believe they can develop it more cheaply than they can purchase it from the licensor ... And if the patent-only licensees insist upon most-favored licensee treatment, the prior license arrangement and its artificially low patent rate will haunt the licensor.
>
> Another risk is that the licensor, by deflating the contractual consideration for the patent license may be creating an evidentiary pitfall for the future. Suppose the licensor must establish the value of those patents in patent infringement litigation against third parties. Say that the total "package" rate for licensed patented and trade secret technology is 5%, of which 4% would have been fairly attributable to the patent component, but the licensor has adopted the practice of

---

[11] In addition to know-how, some biotechnology patent licenses seek to combine patent licenses with the provision of biomaterials such as cell lines, DNA samples or even modified organisms. See Patrick Gattari et al., *Beyond Hybrid Licenses: Strategies for Post Patent Expiration Payments in the United States*, 52 Les Nouvelles 31 (2017).

[12] See, e.g., *Warner-Lambert Pharm. Co. v. John J. Reynolds, Inc.*, 178 F. Supp. 655 (S.D.N.Y. 1959) (licensee's obligation to pay royalties on sale of Listerine indefinitely upheld).

[13] 3–18 Milgrim on Licensing § 18.12 (2012).

charging only 1% for the patents and 4% for the trade secret technology. A third party ... defendant in an infringement action, [could] argue that the licensor's licensing practices have established the true value of the licensed patents and hence supply the "reasonable royalty" measure of damages to which the licensor is entitled if it prevails in the patent infringement action.[14]

While courts have not analyzed the question of an appropriate split between patent and know-how royalties in a hybrid license, one data point of interest appears in Justice Kagan's opinion in *Kimble v. Marvel Entertainment, LLC*, 576 U.S. 446 (2015) (reproduced in Section 24.3):

> [P]ost-expiration royalties are allowable so long as tied to a non-patent right—even when closely related to a patent. That means, for example, that a license involving both a patent and a trade secret can set a 5% royalty during the patent period (as compensation for the two combined) and a 4% royalty afterward (as payment for the trade secret alone).

Another useful data point is the 50 percent royalty rate reduction seen in *Aronson v. Quick Point Pencil Co.*, 440 U.S. 257 (1979), which was triggered when Aronson failed to obtain a patent on her keyring design (see Section 24.3, Note 10).

Notes and Questions

1. *Fixed fees versus running royalties.* What are the comparative advantages and disadvantages of fixed fees versus running royalties? When would you advise a client to seek one over the other? Are there any circumstances under which you would advise your client to reject either of these options entirely?

2. *Royalty versus royalty share.* In the sample list of book publishing rates reproduced above, you will see that there are two ways in which a publisher calculates royalties due to an author: as a percentage of the retail price of the book, and as a percentage of the publisher's royalty received from a third party. What accounts for this difference in treatment? For additional thoughts on this approach, see Section 8.4 relating to sublicensing income.

3. *More rules of thumb.* In addition to the 25 percent rule, parties litigating the reasonableness of patent royalty rates have also drawn upon the work of Nobel laureate John Nash, whose work predicted that parties bargaining over a matter would reach agreement when they evenly split the profits attributable to the patented technology.[15] This 50–50 profit split became known as the Nash Bargaining Solution, and was frequently introduced in royalty rate cases. But in *VirnetX, Inc. v. Cisco Systems, Inc.*, 767 F. 3d 1308, 1333 (Fed. Cir. 2014), the Federal Circuit rejected the Nash 50–50 rule of thumb as well, on grounds similar to those that it cited in the earlier *Uniloc* case. Though the Federal Circuit rejected both of these rules of thumb on evidentiary grounds, economists and damages experts continue to employ them when advising clients regarding royalty rates. Is this continuing reliance on these rejected rules of thumb justified? Why or why not?

4. *Not too high.* Is it always in the licensor's interest to charge a royalty that is as high as possible? Consider the following assessment:

> Perhaps counterintuitively, maximizing the royalty rate may not always be in the best interests of the licensor. If the royalty rate is exceptionally high, it may serve as a disincentive to the licensee because the profit associated with the commercial product will be negatively affected by the royalty. An exceptionally high royalty rate may also incentivize a licensee to develop technology that works around the IP defined in the license agreement.[16]

---

[14] Id. (citations omitted).
[15] John Nash, *The Bargaining Problem*, 18 Econometrica 155 (1950).
[16] Michael A. Reslinski & Bernhard S. Wu, *The Value of Royalty*, 34 Nat. Biotechnol. 685, 689 (2016).

Do you agree? How might you advise your licensor client to approach the delicate issue of royalty rate determination?

Problem 8.1

Consider this clause from a license agreement between the University of Texas and IDEXX Laboratories for a veterinary (canine) diagnostic test reagent:

5.1.b [Upon University's receipt of a notice of allowance of the Patent, Licensee will pay University] a running royalty as follows:

i.   Four percent (4.0%) of Net Sales for all Licensed Products Sold to detect Lyme disease alone.
ii. One percent (1.0%) of Net Sales of all License Products Sold to detect Lyme disease in combination with one other veterinary diagnostic test or service (for example, but not limited to, a canine heartworm diagnostic test or service) …
iii. Two and one-half percent (2.5%) of Net Sales for all Licensed Products Sold as a product or service to detect Lyme disease in combination with one or more veterinary diagnostic products or services to detect tick-borne disease(s).

IDEXX sells a combined canine diagnostic test that detects Lyme disease, heartworm and at least one other tick-borne disease. What royalty rate should IDEXX pay with respect to this test? Is there an ambiguity in the agreement? How would you resolve it?[17]

Problem 8.2

Suppose that you represent Sy Scientific, an inventor who has just filed a patent covering a new polymer-rubber compound that has amazing tensile properties that it retains even at ultra-high temperatures. Sy anticipates applications of this substance, which he has named "slubber," in markets from space exploration to nuclear power to cooking utensils. Sy has also developed a novel technique for determining the length of time that a batch of slubber must be heated in order to give it optimal tensile properties. How would you go about advising Sy to develop a royalty program for slubber?

8.2.3 *Percentage Royalties: Royalty Base*

As noted above, the amount that the licensee must pay when a percentage royalty is charged depends both on the royalty rate, discussed above, and the royalty base.

8.2.3.1 Net Sales

In an agreement, the royalty base is often expressed in terms of the licensee's "net sales" of licensed products or services. Definitions of net sales are often highly contested and heavily negotiated. A simplified version might read as follows.

EXAMPLE: NET SALES (LICENSEE-FAVORABLE)

"Net Sales" means the actual amounts received by Licensee with respect to sales of Licensed Products.

[17] For the court's not very illuminating conclusion, see *Bd. of Regents of the University of Texas System v. IDEXX Laboratories, Inc.*, Cause No. 2018-08064 (Dist. Ct. Harris Co., Tex., Sep. 29, 2020).

As with many clauses involving payment, there are numerous variations on the themes set out above. For example, the licensee will generally favor defining Net Sales with reference to "actual amounts *received* by Licensee," as this is a reflection of the licensee's actual revenue from the licensed products. The licensor, on the other hand, may prefer a definition based on "amounts *invoiced* by Licensee," as this reflects the amounts that *should have been* paid for the licensed products, and is not dependent on the licensee's collection efforts or the compliance of the licensee's customers.

Likewise, it is not uncommon to define net sales with reference to amounts received or invoiced by "Licensee and its Affiliates," particularly if the licensee will be selling or distributing licensed products through its own foreign subsidiaries. Without this addition, net sales could be construed to mean the intercompany transfer prices that the licensee receives from its affiliates, which could be far below market rates.

EXAMPLE: NET SALES (LICENSOR-FAVORABLE)

"Net Sales" means the actual amounts invoiced by Licensee and its Affiliates with respect to sales of Licensed Products.

8.2.3.2 Licensed Products

Mathematically speaking, an infinite number of royalty rate and base combinations will yield the same per-unit royalty in any given situation. For example, a royalty rate of 1 percent charged on a $100 base yields a royalty payment of $1.00, as does a rate of 10 percent on a $10 base and a rate of 0.01 percent on a base of $10,000.

Yet, for many reasons, it is important to get the royalty base "right," particularly when royalty rates are based on general benchmarks in the industry. Thus, if an apparel manufacturer licenses a popular cartoon character for use on children's pajamas at a royalty rate of 5 percent, and then prints the character only on the pajama tops, must it also pay the 5 percent royalty on the matching pajama bottoms that do not display the character? What about a smartphone manufacturer that licenses a patented film that eliminates scratches on a smartphone screen – must the manufacturer pay the agreed royalty only on the price of the film, or on the entire smartphone? This detail is critical to define, either in the definition of net sales or, preferably, the definition of licensed products as to which net sales are calculated. Consider the following case in which this issue was raised.

Allen Archery, Inc. v. Precision Shooting Equipment, Inc.
865 F.2d 896 (7th Cir. 1989)

WOOD, JR., CIRCUIT JUDGE

This is a contract case arising out of a patent license granted by plaintiff-appellee Allen Archery, Inc. ("Allen") to defendant-appellant Precision Shooting Equipment ("Precision") and defendant Paul E. Shepley. The parties dispute the amount of royalties due Allen for the use by Precision of Allen's invention.

I. Factual Background

On December 30, 1969, United States patent No. 3,486,495 entitled "Archery Bow with Draw Force Multiplying Attachments" was issued to Holless W. Allen. The patent was assigned to plaintiff-appellant Allen Archery, Inc. in 1973 and it expired in 1986. The patent relates to an archery bow known commonly to archers and the archery industry as the "compound bow."

The longbow or straight bow has been in existence for centuries and consists of a single piece of material with a single bowstring attached to the ends of the limbs. Another traditional bow, the recurve bow, is similar to the longbow, but its limbs curve forward at the tips where the bowstring is attached. The crossbow is a weapon having a short bow known as a "prod." The prod is mounted crosswise at the end of a stock.

The compound bow system covered by Allen's patent employs rotatable pulleys or cams and multiple-line lacing of the bowstring or cable to create compound leverage. The important advantage of the compound bow, as opposed to more conventional bows, is that the compound bow casts an arrow at greater speed with increased striking power while reducing the amount of force needed to draw the bow … A compound bow comprises a handle section and a pair of limbs secured to the handle section. An eccentric wheel or cam is mounted on the end of each limb. A bowstring is trained around the wheels to present a central stretch and two end stretches. The central stretch includes a nocking point for receiving the nock or slotted tail of an arrow. The pulley wheels may be round or oval-shaped and are referred to as eccentrics since they are mounted off center in either case.

The compound bow quickly became popular in archery circles. Within eight years of obtaining a patent, Allen had licensed virtually the entire archery industry. When the compound bow first appeared, all of the compound bows built under the licenses were modifications of the longbow or straight bow. Not until 1982 was a crossbow developed that used a compound bow prod.

FIGURE 8.4 H.W. Allen (1909–1979) with a prototype of his compound bow invention.

Pursuant to an agreement dated July 1, 1973, Shepley became a licensee under the patent. Precision … is a sublicensee under the patent pursuant to a sublicensing agreement with Shepley dated November 1, 1975.

[The] disputes between Allen and Precision center on their differing interpretations of the licensing agreement. The agreement basically gives Precision a license to manufacture, use, and sell "bows embodying the inventions covered" by the compound bow patent held by Allen. Precision had to pay royalties to Allen during the life of the agreement on each bow sold and on replacement parts. The royalty schedule provided that Precision pay a royalty of 5 1/2 percent of the net selling price on the first 31,000 bows sold during a one-year period and a 5 percent royalty on any other bows sold during that same one-year period. The agreement stipulates that:

> Licensor agrees that royalties are not to be paid on accessories such as stabilizers and sights and their mountings, bow quivers and fish reels, which are invoiced, billed or sold as separate items from the complete basic operable bow.

Precision began manufacturing crossbows embodying the compound bow principle in 1982. Allen contends that the "complete basic operable bow" described in the licensing agreement includes both the stock and the prod of the crossbow. The Crossfire, Foxfire, and Spitfire crossbows, all manufactured and sold by Precision, utilize the compound principle. Precision argues that the "complete basic operable bow" is provided by the prod alone and that Allen is entitled to no royalties on the value of the stock. Precision notes that when a crossbow is shipped, the prod is not attached to the stock. Precision claims that the prod of the crossbow could be used as an operable bow. Precision values the prod alone at $75, an amount arrived at through a comparison with its regular bow line and also based on the manufacturing cost of the product.

The parties also dispute the definition of accessories that are exempted from the royalty obligation. Allen contends that the overdraw mechanism which is standard equipment on the Mach II model bow is not an accessory. An overdraw is a device that enables a bow to shoot a shorter-than-normal arrow. The overdraw uses a ledge mounted on the side of the bow handle to support the tip of the arrow. The tip of the arrow can then be supported behind the handle of the bow and does not need to project forward from the front of the bow as is usually the case. Precision claims that the overdraw is an accessory since the Mach II could be a "complete basic operable bow" without it. Allen also asserts that the special camouflage paint applied to some bows is part of the basic bow since it is invoiced and billed as part of the basic bow price. Precision states that the special paint is in reality sold separately and the royalty obligation does not apply.

II. Discussion

[The issues] revolve around the proper construction of the licensing agreement as it relates to crossbows and "accessories." *Richards v. Liquid Controls Corp.*, 26 Ill. App. 3d 111, 325 N.E.2d 775 (1975), sets out the method for construing contracts in Illinois:

> The primary objective is to give effect to the intention of the parties. This is to be determined solely from the language used in the executed agreement when there is not ambiguity, but a strict construction which reaches a different result from that intended by the parties should not be adopted. Previous agreements, negotiations and circumstances may be considered in finding the meaning of the words used and when there is an ambiguity,

or when the language used is susceptible of more than one meaning, extrinsic evidence is admissible to show the meaning of the words used.

Precision asserts that the language of the licensing agreement is ambiguous and it disputes the meaning of such terms as "complete basic operable bow," "bows embodying the inventions covered by said patent," and "accessories … invoiced, billed, or sold as separate items." The district court found that the language used in the agreement was not ambiguous. The court stated that there was no evidence before it concerning prior negotiations or agreements that could be considered in determining the meaning of the terms.

Examining the issue of how crossbows fit under the term "complete basic operable bow," the district court found that Precision was obligated to pay royalties on the full sale price of any crossbow embodying the Allen compound bow invention. The court rejected Precision's contention that the prod and the stock could be separated for the purposes of computing royalties. Finding that the agreement was meant to cover all bows embodying the inventions, the court stated that the stock of a crossbow was an integral part of the bow, not a mere accessory.

A review of the record indicates that the district court was correct in its determination that the entire sale price of a crossbow was subject to the royalty payment set forth in the licensing agreement. Precision, in paying royalties to Allen on its compound crossbow sales, had only paid royalties on the supposed value of the prod minus the stock. It unilaterally set this price at $75 per compound crossbow. Precision sold a large number of these compound crossbows, far more than its sales of conventional or noncompound crossbows. Each of these compound bows sold is marked with the Allen patent number.

It is strained logic to argue that because the prod can be separated from the stock, it can qualify as a "complete basic operable bow." In attempting to define those terms, we must find the "ordinary and usual connotation attributable to those words." While it may be possible for some people to fire an arrow from the prod minus the stock, it is clear that an ordinary user would not consider the prod on its own to be a complete bow. The owner's manual shipped with every crossbow clearly explains how the prod is to be mounted on the stock and drawn and shot only after it has been secured to the stock; nowhere is it suggested that the prod is operable as a separate unit. It is of no consequence that Precision did not manufacture crossbows at the time it obtained the license, since the agreement covers all bows embodying the patented principles, including those bows not yet designed or built. The district court's conclusion that royalties must be paid on the full sale price of the crossbows was correct.

Precision … argues that since the licensing agreement does not specifically detail how royalties should be apportioned for crossbows, overdraw mechanisms, and paint, the court should not include nonpatented elements in the determination of royalty obligations. Precision points to the case of *Velsicol Chemical Corp. v. Hooker Chemical Corp.*, 230 F. Supp. 998 (N.D. Ill. 1964), for the proposition that royalties should be computed in proportion to the use of the patented device. However, the *Velsicol* case involves a situation that in many ways is unique to the chemical industry. In *Velsicol*, the defendant's patented end product used the plaintiff's patented chlorendic as an ingredient. Unlike the present case, *Velsicol* concerns products where both the component and the end product are patented by the respective parties. The proportionate use argument does not apply here where there is no issue of relative contribution between the parties.

[We also] consider the question of whether the overdraw mechanism on the Mach II bow and the camouflage paint found on some bows qualify as accessories under the agreement. The district court found that they were not accessories within the meaning of the agreement and ordered that royalty payments be made on the full sale price of the bow including the overdraw and the camouflage paint. The district court emphasized the testimony of a Precision manager who stated that no accessories are attached to a bow when a bow is shipped. Working from that premise, the court determined that, since the overdraw mechanism and the camouflage paint were both attached to the bow when shipped, they could not be accessories.

While this proposition at first may seem to be an over-simplification, by looking closely at the licensing agreement, we conclude that the district court's finding that items attached to a bow cannot be accessories is correct. The licensing agreement provides that accessories will be excluded from royalty calculations if they are invoiced separately. Precision did not choose to invoice the paint jobs or the overdraw devices separately. It included them, as well as the crossbow stocks, in the invoice prices of the respective bows. This leads to the conclusion that they are part of the complete bow. Also, the agreement names items that it considers accessories, such as "stabilizers, sights, and their mountings, bow quivers, and fish reels." These items are all clearly separable from the "complete basic operable bow." Camouflage paint and overdraw mechanisms are not separable items and should not be considered as accessories.

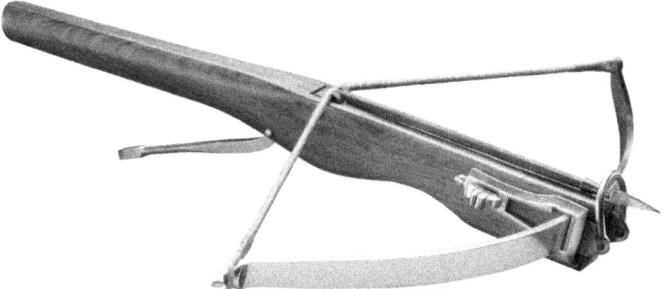

FIGURE 8.5 The court in *Allen Archery* held that a crossbow's stock, overdraw mechanism and camouflage paint were not "accessories" excluded from the royalty calculation, even if they were not covered by the patent claims and could be purchased separately.

Notes and Questions

1. *EMVR versus SSPPU*. The dispute in *Allen Archery* required the court to interpret the scope of the royalty base defined in the licensing agreement between Allen and Shepley. A similar analysis is often conducted in patent infringement cases in which no agreement exists between the patent holder and the infringer. In these cases, if infringement is proven, the court must determine both an appropriate royalty rate and a royalty base. When patents cover a single component of a multi-component product, such as the crossbow in *Allen Archery*, a smartphone or a computer, the court must decide whether the royalty base should be the price of the component covered by the patent or the larger product in which the component is used.

   The court considered this issue in *Cornell University v. Hewlett-Packard Co.*, 609 F. Supp. 2d 279 (N.D.N.Y. 2009). In that case, Cornell obtained a patent covering one component of an instruction buffer that could be embodied in a computer processor chip used in computer servers and workstations. Cornell sued Hewlett-Packard for infringement and was awarded damages at a royalty rate of 0.8 percent. The court then had to determine the base to which this royalty should be applied: H-P's sales of computer servers and workstations, CPU "bricks" including processors, coolant, external memory and power converters, or processors alone. Cornell argued that it was entitled to royalties on the $23 billion that H-P would have made if it had sold the infringing processors as bricks. The court disagreed, holding that Cornell was entitled to royalties only on a base that represented the "smallest salable patent practicing unit" or SSPPU. Though H-P primarily sold computer servers and workstations, it had in the past sold individual processors. Thus, the processor, and not the CPU brick, was the SSPPU that formed the base on which Cornell was entitled to royalties (still a substantial $8 billion sum).

The court in *Cornell* also held that in order for the holder of a patent covering a component of an end product to receive royalties on the basis of the sale price of an end product (the so-called "entire market value rule" or EMVR), three conditions must be met: (1) the infringing component must be the basis for customer demand for the entire product; (2) individual infringing and noninfringing components must be sold together to form a functional unit; and (3) individual infringing and noninfringing components must be analogous to a single functioning unit, not sold together for mere business advantage.

2. *Process royalties.* Not all patents relate to products that can be sold. Some patents cover processes or methods for performing services, for manufacturing goods, for improving efficiency, and for many other purposes. In these cases, the royalty base is often expressed in terms of the revenue that the licensee earns from using the patented process. For example, a license of patents covering an automated system for operating a customer service call center might bear royalties based on a percentage of the licensee's call center revenue, and a patented process for improving the efficiency of an assembly line might bear royalties based on the licensee's sales of products manufactured on that line. While such arrangements are not uncommon, they require significant analysis and negotiation in order to give the licensor a fair share of revenue derived from its licensed process without capturing value arising from the licensee's own know-how, techniques and other licensed technology.

3. *Reach-through royalties.* If a patent covers a research method or tool, it may not be practical for the patent holder to charge a royalty on the "sale" of products covered by that patent. Indeed, there may be no products sold at all. Rather, the research tool may be used to discover new compounds or drug targets, to locate subterranean oil reserves or to predict stock market movements. In each of these cases, use of the tool could result in the discovery or development of something hugely profitable – a new drug, an oil reservoir or a market windfall. On what basis should the patent holder charge a user for the use of the patented research tool? Traditionally, the developer of such a research tool – say, a microscope, chemical reagent or DNA sequencing technique – would charge a one-time fee for the use of the tool, either through the sale of a product such as a microscope or reagent, or as an up-front license fee for the use of a patented method. Some developers of research tools, however, have sought to collect royalties not only on the sale or use of their patented tool, but on the licensee's revenue derived from products discovered or developed *using* the research tool.[18] These royalties on downstream products are referred to as "reach-through" royalties.

---

[18] In some cases, a tool developer's patents claim not only the tool itself, but products resulting from the use of that tool. Yet it is not strictly necessary for the tool developer to have patent claims covering the products discovered using the research tool to charge a royalty on those products. We will consider this issue further in Chapter 24 relating to IP misuse.

Reach-through royalties have been highly controversial. The National Institutes of Health discourages the use of reach-through royalties with respect to federally funded discoveries, stating that:

[NIH grant] Recipients are expected to ensure that unique research resources arising from NIH-funded research are made available to the scientific research community … If the materials are patented or licensed to an exclusive provider, … royalty reach-through, or product reach-through rights back to the provider are inappropriate.[19]

In addition, many corporations disfavor the use of reach-through royalties by their potential licensors.[20] What justification can you see for charging reach-through royalties? Why might a licensee object to the payment of such royalties?[21]

4. *Including unlicensed products in the royalty base.* In *Automatic Radio Co. v. Hazeltine Research, Inc.*, 339 U.S. 827 (1950), Automatic Radio licensed a portfolio of more than 500 radio broadcasting patents from Hazeltine (an early patent assertion entity) in exchange for a royalty based on Automatic Radio's total sales of radio broadcasting receivers, whether or not they practiced the licensed patents. Four years into the agreement, Automatic Radio objected to paying the minimum royalty required under the license agreement, arguing that none of its products infringed the patents and that requiring it to pay a royalty amounted to patent misuse (discussed in greater detail in Section 24.4). The Court disagreed, holding that the royalty base established under the agreement was "a convenient mode of operation designed by the parties to avoid the necessity of determining whether each type of petitioner's product embodies any of the numerous Hazeltine patents."[22] How does the Court's reasoning in *Automatic Radio* compare to that of *Allen Archery*, in which the licensor was permitted to include the price of unpatented crossbow components in its royalty base?

5. *Allocation and copyright.* Royalty base issues also arise in copyright licenses. Consider a class action complaint filed by various textbook authors against McGraw Hill. The publication agreement between McGraw Hill and each author requires McGraw Hill to pay the author a percentage of the "selling price" of the book, whether in print or electronic form, less customary deductions. Beginning in 2009, McGraw Hill transitioned many of its textbooks to an electronic platform called Connect. At first, McGraw Hill paid the required royalty based on its sale price of each electronic book on Connect. But in 2020, McGraw Hill announced that it would pay royalties based only on "revenue attributed to the ebook component." In other words, it would allocate revenue from selling an ebook between the book and the Connect platform itself. The result was a reduction in author royalties of 25–35 percent. What result? See *Flynn v. McGraw Hill LLC*, Case 1:21-cv-00614-LGS (S.D.N.Y., filed Jan. 22, 2021).

---

[19] Natl. Inst. Health, Principles and Guidelines for Recipients of NIH Research Grants and Contracts on Obtaining and Disseminating Biomedical Research Resources: Final Notice, 64 Fed. Reg. 72,090, 72,094 (1999).

[20] See Gattari et al., *supra* note 11. For a discussion of allegations that reach-through royalties constitute patent misuse, see Section 24.2, Note 5.

[21] For a comprehensive discussion of reach-through royalties in the biopharmaceutical sector, see Alfred C. Server, Nader Mousavi & Jane M. Love, *Reach-Through Rights and the Patentability, Enforcement, and Licensing of Patents on Drug Discovery Tools*, 1 Hastings Sci. Tech. L.J. 21 (2009).

[22] Id. at 833

8.2.3.3 Exclusions from Net Sales

As most percentage-based running royalties are expressed in terms of the licensee's "net sales" of licensed products, the definition of net sales is often negotiated heavily. In addition to the scoping described above, there are a range of exclusions from net sales that often appear in licensing agreements. These generally permit the licensee to exclude from its royalty calculation "pass through" costs that, though billed to customers, do not contribute to the licensee's bottom line. An example of these follows.

EXAMPLE: NET SALES (WITH EXCLUSIONS)

"Net Sales" means the actual amounts [invoiced/received] by Licensee and its Affiliates with respect to sales of Licensed Products, less (a) shipping, packaging, delivery and freight insurance costs to the extent separately stated on the invoice; (b) standard quantity discounts, rebates and credits for returned goods; (c) applicable taxes and other duties assessed directly on sales of the Licensed Products; (d) bad debt; and (e) amounts received for training, technical assistance, maintenance, service and support.

Shipping and Packaging. Fees received by the licensee for shipping, packaging and delivery are often excluded from net sales because these fees are usually paid by the licensee to third-party fulfillment and shipping firms without markup and do not represent actual revenue to the licensee. If the licensee handles its own fulfillment, then this provision may be less appropriate.

Discounts. This exclusion is important if net sales are based on the amounts that the licensee invoices for licensed products. If the licensee invoices the customer $100 for a product but then extends a $10 discount to the customer, so that the licensee only receives $90, then it is fair for the licensee's royalty to be based on the invoiced price less the discount. Even so, the licensor may insist that net sales be reduced only for discounts that are "standard" and which relate to the quantity of products ordered, as the licensee should not be permitted to reduce its royalty base.

Rebates. In some cases the licensee will receive payment for a licensed product and then refund part of that payment to its customer in the form of a rebate. As the licensee does not retain those funds, it will often seek to exclude rebates paid from net sales. The licensor's response to this request could be that rebates should be considered promotional expenses paid by the licensee, similar to advertising, which are not appropriate reductions to the royalty due.

Returns. If the licensee sells 100 products but 5 are returned by customers for a refund, then the licensee may argue that its royalty obligation should only be with respect to the 95 products that were not returned. The licensor may respond that its royalties should not be reduced on account of the licensee's poor product quality. Depending on the industry, this exclusion can be heavily negotiated and may allow deductions from net sales up to an expected return rate (say 5 percent) or may simply adjust the royalty rate to take that return rate into account.

Taxes. If the licensee collects sales, use or value-added taxes from its customers in connection with the sale of licensed products or services (as it is often legally required to do), and then remits those amounts to the appropriate taxing authority, then it is customary to allow the licensee to deduct those amounts from the definition of net sales.

Bad Debt. Though the licensee may invoice a customer for a product, there is no assurance that the licensee will be paid. Thus, depending on the industry, the licensee may be allowed a credit for average bad debt (possibly in the 1–2 percent range) on invoiced amounts.

Licensee Services. If the licensee charges its customers for services (training, maintenance, etc.) as part of its sale of licensed products, then the licensee will often argue that such amounts (which are not paid with respect to the licensed products themselves) should not be used to calculate the royalty payable to the licensor. Licensors may disagree, arguing that such add-on services are enabled only because the licensed products are being sold, and may wish to prevent the licensee from shifting large amounts of revenue from the licensed product price to these services simply to reduce the royalty owed.

Notes and Questions

1. *In-kind compensation.* The typical percentage royalty arrangement is based on the licensee's net sales of licensed products or services. But what if some or all of the licensee's compensation is in the form of noncash consideration? Some noncash consideration – equity securities, marketed products, commodity services and even advertising space/time – is relatively easy to value and a net sales definition can be adjusted to reflect the cash-equivalent market value of such consideration on the date paid. Other noncash compensation – IP licenses, noncompetition covenants, technical assistance – may be more difficult to value, and the licensor will seek to ensure that the licensee is not circumventing its royalty obligations by accepting unreported noncash compensation in exchange for licensed products or services. By the same token, agreements normally contain a range of obligations in addition to payment (confidentiality, indemnification, etc.), and it would be unreasonable for a licensor to insist that each of these obligations be converted to a cash value for the purposes of royalty calculation. If you were a licensor, how might you seek to prevent your licensee from avoiding its royalty obligations through accepting noncash consideration?

8.3 RUNNING ROYALTIES: ADJUSTMENTS AND LIMITATIONS

Section 8.2 discusses the basic framework for defining and calculating running royalties. In this section we will discuss some additional provisions that are used in licensing agreements to modify and limit running royalties.

8.3.1 *Minimum Royalties*

It is sometimes the case that a licensor will require its licensee to pay a minimum level of royalties, whether or not those royalties are actually earned under the applicable royalty calculation formulas. Royalty minimums are often required if (a) the licensor has fixed cost commitments, such as facility and personnel costs, and few sources of income other than royalties, and (b) the licensee's income is seasonal, with significant variation among calendar quarters (e.g., toys, retail, vacation travel, etc.).

Minimum royalties may be structured in a variety of ways. The most straightforward method is to specify a minimum dollar amount that the licensee will pay during defined periods (e.g., every calendar quarter or year) during the term of the agreement.

If minimum royalties will be due on an annual basis instead of a quarterly basis, then the relevant provision must speak to the total earned royalties paid and payable over the course of the year, with the make-up payment being made with the fourth quarterly payment for the year.

EXAMPLE: QUARTERLY MINIMUM ROYALTIES (WITHOUT CREDITING)

In the event that the total earned royalties payable by Licensee to Licensor hereunder during any calendar quarter during the Term of this Agreement is less than $250,000 (the "Quarterly Minimum"), then concurrently with Licensee's payment of earned royalties to Licensor hereunder for such quarter, Licensee shall, in addition, pay to Licensor an amount (the "Make-Up Amount") equal to the difference between the Quarterly Minimum and the amount of earned royalties payable with respect to such quarter, such that the total amount payable by Licensee with respect to such quarter is the Quarterly Minimum.

But what happens if the licensee exceeds the quarterly (or annual) minimum during a particular calendar quarter (or year), but then falls short in a future quarter (or year)? May the licensee credit its overage against satisfaction of the minimum in a future period? This is often a topic of some negotiation. A licensor that is looking for an assured quarterly or annual payment is unlikely to wish to agree to crediting of prior overages against future minimum royalty commitments, even though it will, over the course of both periods in question, satisfy the minimum. If crediting of overages is allowed, another question to be answered is how long such credits can be applied: in the next quarter, the next x quarters or any time during the term of the agreement.

The following language addresses some of the issues arising from crediting overages against prior period minimums.

EXAMPLE: QUARTERLY MINIMUM ROYALTIES (WITH CREDITING)

In the event that the total earned royalties payable by Licensee to Licensor hereunder during any calendar quarter during the Term of this Agreement is less than $250,000 (the "Quarterly Minimum"), then concurrently with Licensee's payment of earned royalties to Licensor hereunder for such quarter, Licensee shall, in addition, pay to Licensor an amount (the "Make-Up Amount") equal to the difference between the Quarterly Minimum and the amount of earned royalties payable with respect to such quarter, such that the total amount payable by Licensee with respect to such quarter is the Quarterly Minimum. Licensee [**shall/shall not**] have the right to credit any overage of earned Royalties above the Quarterly Minimum in a given calendar quarter against any shortfall of earned Royalties below the calendar quarter Minimum during [any future/the next] calendar quarter.

8.3.2 *Royalty Caps*

The converse of a minimum royalty is a maximum royalty or royalty "cap." Royalty caps may be applied to any given period under the agreement (e.g., quarter or year), or may be aggregated over the entire term of the agreement.

EXAMPLE: ROYALTY CAP

Example 1

In no event shall Licensee be required to pay earned royalties hereunder during any calendar quarter in excess of $1,000,000.

Example 2

In no event shall Licensee be required to pay earned royalties hereunder in excess of a total of $10,000,000 during the Term of this Agreement.

In the case of a royalty cap that applies across the entire term of the agreement (example 2 above), once the licensee pays earned royalties equal to the cap, the license is typically considered to be paid-up.

Problem 8.3

LocCo has licensed FashO's famous "WOOSH" brand for use on apparel in the United States for a period of three years. The licensing agreement contains the following provision:

> LocCo will pay minimum earned royalties of $500,000 during each calendar quarter hereunder, with any overage carried forward one calendar quarter and no more, and provided that under no circumstances shall LocCo be required to pay earned royalties during the term of this Agreement in excess of $7,000,000.

Earned royalties under the Agreement are calculated at the following levels during each year.

Year	Q1	Q2	Q3	Q4
1	$350,000	$450,000	$500,000	$650,000
2	$400,000	$450,000	$550,000	$600,000
3	$650,000	$750,000	$850,000	$1,000,000

What payments is LocCo required to make with respect to each quarter during the term of the agreement?

8.3.3 *Royalty Buyouts*

Some license agreements permit the licensee to pay a lump sum in order to "buy out" its remaining running royalty obligation. This buyout option usually becomes available at some defined point during the term of the agreement, often when some milestone is achieved.

The buyout price should fairly compensate the licensor for its lost potential royalty revenue, though some licensors may accept a discount from the projected present value of the remaining royalty stream given the certainty of the lump-sum payment versus the inherent uncertainty of royalty income. The amount of the buyout can be specified in absolute terms (i.e., a fixed dollar figure) or, more often, as a multiple of prior quarterly royalty payments (assuming that royalty payments have commenced at the time of exercise).

From the licensee's standpoint, a one-time cash payment, even if greater than the expected royalty stream, may be more desirable from a revenue reporting and profitability perspective than a running royalty that must be paid every quarter.

8.3.4 *Royalty Escalation Clauses*

Generally, the payment provisions of licensing agreements are not subject to change unless changes are expressly provided for. Thus, even in the presence of changed circumstances or incorrect assumptions, unless there was fraud on the part of one of the parties or events rise to the level of force majeure (see Section 13.6), the parties must live with the deal that they have made.

Nevertheless, some agreements do permit changes to royalty rates and other financial terms under certain conditions. The following case illustrates these issues.

Arbitron, Inc. v. Tralyn Broadcasting, Inc.

400 F.3d 130 (2d Cir. 2005)

CALABRESI, Circuit Judge.

This breach of contract dispute raises the question of whether, under New York law, two parties entering into a licensing agreement for radio ratings and data may authorize one party to adjust the price of that data unilaterally at some point in the future. [W]e conclude that the contract before us delegated, with unmistakable clarity, price-setting authority to a single party, and that New York law does not invalidate such contracts. We therefore vacate the district court's order of summary judgment and remand for reconsideration.

I. Background

Plaintiff-appellant Arbitron, Inc. ("Arbitron"), a Delaware corporation, is a popular listener-demographics data provider for North American radio stations. Arbitron licenses its copyrighted listener data to regional AM and FM stations, which then use the demographic profiles of station listeners to attract advertisers. In 1997, Arbitron entered into one such license – a "Station License Agreement to Receive and Use Arbitron Radio Listening Estimates" (the "License Agreement") with defendant Tralyn Broadcasting, Inc. ("Tralyn"), a Mississippi corporation. The License Agreement permitted Tralyn's only radio station (WLUN-FM in the Gulfport, Mississippi area, later known as WLNF-FM) to use Arbitron listening data reports. Over its five-year term, the License Agreement charged Tralyn a monthly rate of $1,729.57 for the use of Arbitron's listening data reports by this single station.

Were this monthly license fee the only pricing portion of the License Agreement, this case would present an extremely simple contract dispute. But another clause of the agreement – which we shall call the "escalation clause" – provided that, were Tralyn or its successor to acquire additional radio stations in the same or adjacent regional markets, a new license fee would be charged. Upon acquiring such stations, Tralyn was required to notify Arbitron so that Arbitron could determine a new license fee, and, if necessary, approve the assignment of the licensing agreement to a new party in interest. Any new licensing fee would be set, according to the escalation clause, at Arbitron's discretion. The clause provided:

> In the event that Arbitron consents to the assignment of this Agreement, Arbitron reserves the right to redetermine the rate to be charged to the assignee … Station agrees that … if it is or was purchased or controlled by an entity owning or otherwise controlling other radio stations in this Market or an adjacent Market … Station … will report the change and the effective date thereof to Arbitron within 30 days of such change. In the event of such occurrence, Station further agrees that Arbitron may redetermine its Gross Annual Rate for the Data, Reports and Services licensed hereunder, as well as any Supplementary Services, effective the first month following the date of the occurrence. Notwithstanding Station's failure to notify Arbitron, pursuant to provisions of this paragraph, Arbitron may redetermine the Station's Gross Annual Rate for all Data, Reports and Services, as well as any Supplementary Services, based on the foregoing, effective the first month following the date of the occurrence.

Pursuant to this "escalation clause," Arbitron was given the right to increase the license fee as Tralyn purchased additional stations (or as entities owning additional stations purchased Tralyn). Thus, the escalation clause assumed that, as Tralyn acquired additional regional stations, it would share listener data among each of these stations, and, by allowing Arbitron to increase Tralyn's fees, the clause provided Arbitron with a mechanism to reflect this additional use.

On October 31, 1999, Tralyn was purchased by defendant-appellant JMD, Inc. ("JMD") a Mississippi corporation. At the time JMD acquired Tralyn and WLNF-FM, JMD also controlled at least four other stations in the Gulfport, Mississippi market (WROA-AM, WZKX-FM, WGCM-AM, and WGCM-FM). The purchase agreement between JMD and Tralyn assigned to JMD the License Agreement; JMD thereby assumed responsibility for paying Arbitron, and implicitly, for notifying Arbitron of the additional radio stations now operated by Tralyn's successor. But in violation of Paragraph 11 of the License Agreement, neither JMD nor Tralyn obtained Arbitron's prior written consent to the License Agreement's assignment. Nor did they provide Arbitron with notice of a change in ownership of WLNF-FM. Instead, from November 1999 until June 2002, JMD simply paid the original single-station monthly license fee ($1,729.57) directly to Arbitron. In return, Arbitron provided WLNF-FM with updated listening data (specifically, the Fall 1999 Ratings Book and Research Data – referred to by the parties as the "Fall Book" – which was published in February 2000).

In June 2000, Arbitron discovered, through its own diligence, that JMD had purchased Tralyn and that the terms of the License Agreement had been breached. Arbitron thereupon notified JMD by letter that it was exercising its right to increase the monthly licensing fee under the escalation clause of the License Agreement. Arbitron determined JMD's new annual license fee by multiplying the single-station license fee ($1,779.57) by five ($8,897.85) to reflect the five JMD stations that could now share Arbitron's listener data. It then reduced that figure by 35% to reflect the typical volume discount for licenses covering five or more stations. The result was a revised monthly charge of $5,784.93. Based on this new licensing fee, which Arbitron claimed should have been paid since the October 1999 purchase, Arbitron sent JMD an invoice for "incomplete" payments made between October 1999 and June 2000. It also sent an invoice indicating the additional payments that would be due for the next quarter's listening reports.

JMD never paid these invoices, and subsequently refused to pay anything – even the $1,779.57 due each month under the original one-station License Agreement. Arbitron therefore stopped sending JMD its listening data reports, as it was permitted to do under the License Agreement upon the licensee's nonpayment of the monthly licensing fee.

Arbitron filed the instant suit against Tralyn and JMD on November 1, 2001. Its complaint for breach of contract sought $172,394.22, representing all moneys due under the Licensing Agreement (plus interest) from June 1999 to the end of the contract's five-year term.

On June 5, 2003, the district court … granted summary judgment – but not monetary damages – to JMD. The district court concluded that because "[n]either the escalation clause in ¶ 11, nor any other section of the Agreement, contains any basis for determining the new rate to be paid Arbitron in the event changes in ownership occur," the License Agreement's escalation clause was unenforceably vague under New York law. Arbitron now challenges the district court's decision.

II. Discussion

The district court based its decision on three New York cases, each dealing with contracts for the sale or lease of real property. Upon review of these same cases, we conclude that the escalation clause is enforceable under the common law of New York. This is so because the clause before us is not an "agreement to agree," under which future negations between the parties must occur, but is instead an acknowledgment that, if certain conditions arise in the future, no new agreement is required before Arbitron may set new license terms. Such an agreement is not unenforceably vague under New York's common law.

The seminal New York precedent on unenforceably indefinite contracts is [*Joseph Martin, Jr., Delicatessen, Inc. v. Schumacher*, 52 N.Y.2d 105, 417 N.E.2d 541 (1981)]. There, the Court of Appeals was faced with an agreement between a landlord and a tenant to lease a commercial space for five years at a monthly rate beginning at $500 and escalating over five years to $650, with the option to renew the lease for another five-year term at a rent to be determined by the parties. At the close of the lease's five-year term, the landlord sought to increase the rent from $650 to $900 monthly. Surprised, the tenant employed an assessor, who appraised the market value of the premises at no more than $550 per month. The tenant sued for specific performance, seeking a new five-year lease at the fair market rate of $550. In resolving the case, the Delicatessen majority recognized that the U.C.C., as implemented by the New York legislature, counseled in favor of supplying missing price terms to save and enforce the agreement, and that the terms supplied by a court under the U.C.C. would correspond to a good's fair market value. Nevertheless, because the New York statute's terms made clear that leases or contracts for the sale of real property were not covered by the U.C.C., the Court of Appeals refused to enforce the agreement. It concluded that

> it is rightfully well settled in the common law of contracts in this State that a mere agreement to agree, in which a material term is left for future negotiations, is unenforceable. This is especially true of the amount to be paid for the sale or lease of real property. The rule applies all the more, and not the less, when, as here, the extraordinary remedy of specific performance is sought.

Upon review of *Delicatessen* [and other cases], we conclude that the License Agreement's escalation clause is indeed enforceable under the common law of New York. The escalation clause, unlike the promise to set a future rent rate collectively in *Delicatessen*, does not require the parties to reach an "agreement" on price at some point in the future. That is, the escalation clause is not an "agreement to agree." Instead ... it is a mechanism for objectively setting material terms in the future without further negotiations between both parties. It does so, moreover, with sufficient evidence that both parties intended that [pricing] arrangement. The escalation clause clearly and unambiguously states that, in the event that Tralyn or its successors acquired new radio stations in the same (or an adjacent) geographic market, "Arbitron may redetermine its Gross Annual Rate for the Data, Reports and Services licensed hereunder ... effective the first of the month following [the acquisition]." The escalation clause further provides, in unambiguous language, that Arbitron may exercise this power to "redetermine" the license fee "[n]otwithstanding Station's failure to notify Arbitron" that an acquisition had occurred.

The intent of the parties is manifest in the language of the agreement. Both Arbitron and Tralyn explicitly agreed that Arbitron was authorized to adjust the license fee in the event that Tralyn or its successors began to operate additional stations. This fact makes the instant case very different from those disputes in which courts are faced with "no objective evidence" of a shared intent to permit one party to set prices in the future. And it in no way leads a court enforcing the contract to "impos[e] its own conception of what the parties should or might have undertaken." Accordingly, we conclude that the district court erred in holding the License Agreement's escalation clause "impenetrably vague" under New York law.

Because we believe that the License Agreement's escalation clause is not inconsistent with New York law, we conclude that the district court erred in granting summary judgment to JMD. We therefore vacate the district court's order and remand the case for further proceedings.

Notes and Questions

1. *The sky's the limit?* The Second Circuit in *Arbitron* holds that ¶ 11 of the license agreement gives Arbitron the right to increase the royalty payable by JMD following an assignment of the agreement. As the court explains,

   Arbitron determined JMD's new annual license fee by multiplying the single-station license fee ($1,779.57) by five ($8,897.85) to reflect the five JMD stations that could now share Arbitron's listener data. It then reduced that figure by 35% to reflect the typical volume discount for licenses covering five or more stations. The result was a revised monthly charge of $5,784.93.

   Arbitron's recalculation seems reasonable, or at least grounded in the facts of the case. But the Court says that Arbitron has "complete discretion" to increase its rates. Does that mean that Arbitron, if it so chose, could have raised its rate to $10,000? $100,000? $1,000,000? Is there any cap on Arbitron's seemingly unfettered discretion?

2. *A drafting lapse?* As we will discuss in Chapter 17, an increasing number of online license agreements give the licensor the unilateral right to amend the agreement, subject only to contractual limitations on unconscionable behavior. Usually, consumers acceding to these terms have little knowledge or understanding of what they are agreeing to. But what about a commercial entity such as Tralyn? Why would it agree to give Arbitron seemingly unfettered discretion to raise its rates? Do you think that Tralyn and JMD made any mistakes in handling this transaction?

3. A *trade secret license*. Arbitron's license agreement covers "radio ratings and data" – factual information that is not covered by copyright, but which may qualify as a trade secret. Do trade secret licensors need to be particularly careful about the parties that are entitled to access licensed data – more so than licensors of other forms of IP? Why or why not?

4. *Royalty term*. Under some licensing agreements, the period during which royalties are payable (the "Royalty Term") is shorter than the full term of the agreement or the life of the licensed IP rights. Under what circumstances might such an arrangement be desired?

8.3.5 Royalty Stacking and Bundling

8.3.5.1 Royalty Stacking Clauses

Many products are covered by multiple IP rights. One industry group estimated in 2011 that a typical smartphone was covered by approximately 250,000 different patents.[23] A motion picture or video game often embodies rights from an adapted book, personal rights of publicity, fictional characters, original artwork and set designs, multiple musical works, the film's cinematography and choreography, as well as distinctive buildings, product designs and logos that are shown. Even biotechnology products can be subject to multiple patent claims – one analysis estimated that the vitamin A-rich genetically engineered product known as *golden rice* was covered by forty-five patents or patent families held by more than twenty different entities.[24] New vaccine products may be subject to patents covering research tools, recombinant techniques, cell lines, DNA sequences, transformation vectors, adjuvants and delivery means.

As a result of the proliferation of IP in many fields, a licensee seeking to commercialize such a product or work must obtain licenses from a number of separate rights holders. And if each, or some portion, of these rights holders demands a royalty, then the royalties will add up, possibly to a sizable sum. This phenomenon is known as royalty "stacking."

In most cases, royalty stacking is simply a cost of doing business in a rights-centric world. While there have been some attempts in particularly patent-heavy industries to coordinate and limit aggregate royalties charged by patent holders for a single product (see Chapter 20 relating to so-called FRAND licensing commitments for standardized products), and to aggregate both patents and copyrights in pools (see Chapter 26), such industry-wide efforts are uncommon.

As noted in Section 26.1, Note 6, patent pools are rare in the biopharmaceutical field. However, licensing practices have developed in the industry to account, at least partially, for royalty stacking concerns.

EXAMPLE: ROYALTY STACKING CLAUSE

In the event that Licensee, in connection with exercising the rights licensed to it under Section x, is required to pay license fees, royalties or similar amounts to a third party in addition to Licensor in respect of patents covering the manufacture, use or sale of the Licensed Products in any country solely by reason of the incorporation of Licensed Technology therein or the implementation of any of the claims of the Patent Rights ("Third Party Payments"), and such Third Party Payments exceed [25% of the Royalties payable to

---

[23] See RPX Corp., Registration Statement on Form S-1, p.55 (September 2, 2011).

[24] R. David Kryder, Stanley P. Kowalski & Anatole F. Krattiger, *The Intellectual and Technical Property-Components of proVitamin A Rice (Golden Rice): A Preliminary Freedom-to-Operate Review*. ISAAA Briefs No. 20 (2000), www.isaaa .org/resources/Publications/briefs/20/download/isaaa-brief-20-2000.pdf.

Licensor hereunder], then the Royalties payable hereunder with respect to the country as to which such Third Party Payments are made shall be reduced by [50% of] the amount of such Third Party Payments actually paid by Licensee with respect to Net Sales of Licensed Products during the same calendar quarter [, provided, however, that the amount of such reduction shall in no event exceed fifty percent (50%) of the Royalties otherwise due hereunder].

The above clause allows the licensee to reduce its royalty payments to the licensor if it is required to make patent-related payments to another party. In response, the licensor may seek various limitations, including (a) a threshold that must be met before any adjustment is made; (b) a discount on the amount of the third-party payment to be applied against royalties due to the licensor; and (c) a limit on the overall reduction of such royalties.

Royalty stacking clauses are most common in the biotechnology sector, though they do appear occasionally in licenses relating to semiconductors and other patented technologies. They are not widely used in connection with copyright licenses.

8.3.5.2 Royalties for Bundled Rights

A licensor will sometimes license a bundle of IP rights as a single package. In these cases, it usually charges a single royalty that does not differentiate among the multiple rights included in the bundle. In these arrangements, the royalty typically remains constant, whether or not individual rights (typically patents or copyrights) are added or subtracted from the bundle.

As discussed in Section 8.2.3, Note 4, bundled royalty arrangements were validated by the Supreme Court in *Automatic Radio Co. v. Hazeltine Research, Inc.*, 339 U.S. 827 (1950) (reproduced in Section 24.4), where a fixed royalty was charged for a portfolio of more than 500 patents, some of which would expire during the term of the agreement. The Court held that the bundled royalty was "a convenient mode of operation designed by the parties to avoid the necessity of determining whether each type of petitioner's product embodies any of the numerous Hazeltine patents."[25]

Since *Automatic Radio*, the pricing of bundled rights at a fixed rate has been further validated, including by a national review committee convened by the Attorney General in 1955:

Package licensing should be prohibited only where there is refusal, after a request, to license less than a complete package. Additionally, the licensor should not be required to justify on any proportional basis the royalty rate for less than the complete package, so long as the rate set is not so disproportionate as to amount to a refusal to license less than the complete package. For example, where a substantial group of patents are offered at a flat royalty rate, the deletion of one or several specified patents need not affect the rate.[26]

Nevertheless, the Supreme Court's 1964 decision in *Brulotte v. Thys*, 379 U.S. 29 (1964) (discussed in Section 24.3) established that post-expiration royalties are not permissible and constitute a form of patent misuse. However, *Brulotte* involved a portfolio of twelve patents,

[25] Id. at 833.
[26] Report of the Attorney General's National Committee to Study the Antitrust Laws 39-40 (March 31, 1955).

all of which had expired by the time of the royalty dispute. Cases following *Brulotte* indicate that so long as a single patent in a licensed portfolio remains in effect, the licensor need not decrease the portfolio royalty.[27]

This being said, some licensors have adopted the practice of adjusting bundled royalty rates downward as patents in the bundle begin to expire. One of the most notable of these was the DVD6C patent pool, which decreased its royalty for DVD players and discs every two years as patents in the portfolio began to expire.[28]

Notes and Questions

1. *The licensor's perspective.* It is clear why a licensee would wish to reduce the royalty payable to a licensor based on royalties payable to third parties, but why would a licensor accept a royalty stacking clause? In other words, why should a licensor of a valid IP right be penalized because the licensee's product will include IP owned by others?

2. *Bundling for convenience.* In *Automatic Radio*, the Supreme Court held that charging a single rate for a bundle of IP rights does not constitute patent misuse if agreed for the parties' mutual convenience. Conversely, in *Zenith Radio Corp. v. Hazeltine Research, Inc.*, 395 U.S. 100 (1969), the Court held that patent use may be found when "the patentee directly or indirectly 'conditions' his license upon the payment of royalties on unpatented products – that is, where the patentee refuses to license on any other basis and leaves the licensee with the choice between a license so providing and no license at all." How should a patentee thread the needle between these two cases? May it offer a "standard" licensing program for its portfolio which includes all patents for a single rate, or must it honor every licensee's request for a more limited license at a reduced rate?

8.4 SUBLICENSING INCOME

Running royalties are usually based on the licensee's (and its affiliates') revenue from the sale of licensed products. But what if the licensee does not itself sell licensed products, but instead sublicenses its rights to another party who distributes or sells those products? Such arrangements are common in a number of industries, including biotechnology, branded goods and literary works. If a sublicensee is in the picture, what should the licensee be required to pay the licensor? The answer to this question can have significant financial implications for the parties.

There are three general options that can be used to allocate sublicensing income between the licensor and the licensee:

1. *Include sublicensee's revenue in licensee's net sales:* "net sales" on which the licensee's royalty is based can include revenue received by the licensee, its affiliates and their sublicensees.

2. *Include licensee's sublicensing income in licensee's net sales:* "net sales" on which the licensee's royalty is based can include all amounts that the licensee receives from its sublicensees, including sublicensing fees, royalties and milestone payments.

---

[27] See, e.g., *McCullough Tool Co. v. Well Surveys, Inc.*, 43 F.2d 381, 410 (10th Cir. 1965), *cert. denied* 383 U.S. 933 (1966) (distinguishing *Brulotte*, in which the licensor "attempted to extend the period for paying royalties beyond the date of expiration of the last of the patents covered by the agreement"). But see *Rocform Corp. v. Acitelli-Standard Concrete Wall, Inc.*, 67 F.2d 678 (6th Cir. 1966) (licensor misused its patents by failing to reduce package royalty rate after the most important patent in the package had expired).

[28] DVD6C Licensing Group, Royalty Rates Under the DVD6C Licensing Program, www.dvd6cla.com/royaltyrate .html.

3. *Share licensee's sublicensing income:* the licensee can pay the licensor a specified percentage of all amounts that the licensee receives from its sublicensees, including sublicensing fees, royalties and milestone payments, which is at a different (and usually higher) rate than the running royalties that the licensee pays on its own net sales (e.g., 50 percent).[29]

The financial effects of these different payment structures can be illustrated by the below example.

a. The brand owner grants a US manufacturer (USM) the worldwide right to use a particular brand on apparel at a royalty rate of 25 percent.
b. The USM grants a Korean manufacturer (KM) the right to use the brand on apparel in South Korea.
c. The USM, knowing that profit margins on Korean branded apparel are very high, charges KM a royalty of 40 percent.
d. During a particular quarter, the USM earns $100,000 from sales of branded shirts, and KM earns $500,000.

The USM's royalty obligation to the brand owner for its US sales is 25 percent of $100,000 or $25,000.

The KM's royalty obligation to the USM is 40 percent of $500,000 or $200,000.

What, then, must the USM pay the brand owner with respect to KM's sales? This depends on the payment structure agreed by the owner and the USM.

If they chose Option 1, in which the USM's net sales are deemed to include the KM's sales revenue, then the KM's entire $500,000 revenue is counted in the USM's net sales, and the USM must pay 25 percent to the brand owner, a royalty of **$125,000**.

If they chose Option 2, in which the royalty income received by the USM from the KM is included in the USM's net sales, then the USM must pay the owner 25 percent of the $200,000 royalty paid by the KM to the USM, or a royalty of **$50,000**.

FIGURE 8.6 Sales illustrating the importance of carefully allocating sublicensing income.

29 Cf., *B.J. Thomas v. Gusto Records, Inc.*, 939 F.2d 395 (6th Cir. 1991) (according to industry custom, "the musician receives half of the fees received from licensing the masters to unaffiliated third parties").

If they chose Option 3, assuming that the USM and the owner have agreed to split the USM's sublicensing revenue 50–50, then the USM must pay the owner 50 percent of the $200,000 royalty paid by the KM to the USM, or **$100,000**.

This example demonstrates the significant financial effect that the treatment of sublicensing income can have. But the effect can be even more stark. Suppose that Korean margins on apparel are much lower than they are in the United States, and the KM can only pay the USM a royalty of 10 percent. In this case, the KM pays the USM a royalty of $50,000 on its revenue of $500,000, and the USM's payment to the owner is:

Option 1: 25 percent × $500,000 = $125,000
Option 2: 25 percent × $50,000 = $12,500
Option 3: 50 percent × $50,000 = $25,000

Note that under Option 1, the USM earns only $50,000 from the KM but pays $125,000 to the owner, resulting in a net loss to the USM of $75,000. Under this scenario, the individual who drafted the owner–USM license agreement would likely be out of a job.

In reality, Option 3 is the most common method for handling sublicensing income, with a split negotiated at, above or below the 50–50 level. However, attorneys should be vigilant to ensure that definitions of net sales do not inadvertently include sublicensing income in a manner that would distort the financial deal reached by the parties.

8.5 MILESTONE PAYMENTS

In Section 7.3.1 we discussed "milestone" or "diligence" obligations of exclusive licensees. In this section we will cover the financial obligations (i.e., payments by the licensor) that arise in connection with the licensee's achievement of successive milestones. Just as with up-front payments and royalties, there is no uniform methodology for determining the size of milestone payments. To some degree, these payments can be dictated by the licensee's anticipated cash needs as its commercialization program for the licensed IP progresses. For example, as a drug candidate advances along the development pathway, the scope and cost of human clinical trials increases dramatically.

Despite this variation, one thing that can generally be said about milestone payments is that the achievement of successive milestones usually triggers increasingly large payments. The following example illustrates this principle.

EXAMPLE: DUE DILIGENCE MILESTONES AND PAYMENTS

Licensee shall pay Licensor a nonrefundable, noncreditable milestone payment upon the satisfaction of the following diligence milestones within thirty (30) days following Licensee's written certification thereof:

Diligence milestone	Milestone payment	To be achieved by
First dosing of a patient in US Phase II clinical trial of Licensed Product	$15,000,000	March 1, 2022
First dosing of a patient in US Phase III clinical trial of Licensed Product	$25,000,000	January 1, 2024
US FDA grants marketing approval of Licensed Product	$50,000,000	January 1, 2026
First US sales of Licensed Product	$100,000,000	June 30, 2026

One study of more than 1,000 biopharma licensing deals signed between 1998 and 2018 found that average total milestone payments were approximately $31 million, with a high of $800 million (in a 2001 deal between Eli Lilly/ImClone and Bristol-Myers Squibb for the tumor drug Erbitux).[30]

"BIOBUCKS"

In the biopharmaceutical sector, licensing and development deals valued in excess of $1 billion are regularly announced in the press. But upon closer inspection, it turns out that few of these deals actually result in the advertised payments being made. For example, in 2016, Novartis and Xencor announced a $2.4 billion deal for two drugs targeted at acute myeloid leukemia and B-cell malignancies. But only $150 million was paid up-front, with the rest payable upon the achievement of regulatory and commercial milestones.[31] In an analysis of 700 biotech deals, STAT found that, on average, only 14 percent of the announced deal value was paid upon signing.[32] Another recent study of 100 biotech deals found that, on average, only about one-third of potential milestone payments were actually paid out over the term of the agreement.[33] So how can companies announce billion dollar deals when only a fraction of the stated amount is likely to be paid? Behold the magic of "BioBucks" – inflated dollar amounts that are useful for press releases, but little else.

Law v. Bioheart, Inc.

2009 U.S. Dist. LEXIS 21464 (W.D. Tenn. 2009)

DONALD, DISTRICT JUDGE

Findings of Fact

A. Plaintiffs

In 1991, Dr. [Peter K.] Law resigned his professorship at the University of Tennessee to launch the Cell Therapy Research Foundation (CTRF), a non-profit organization dedicated to developing cellular treatments for muscular dystrophy, particularly Duchenne muscular dystrophy. At the time Dr. Law separated from employment with the University of Tennessee, the University of Tennessee Research Foundation—the owner of patents developed by Dr. Law while in the university's employ—granted to Dr. Law … rights to the patent application that eventually, through Dr. Law's efforts, became U.S. Patent No. 5,130,141 ('141 patent). In addition to the '141 patent, Dr. Law has also developed other technologies that have been patented.

---

[30] Edwards, *supra* note 2.

[31] See Amy Reeves, *Novartis, Xencor Ink $2.4 Billion Licensing Deal in Blood Cancer*, Investor's Business Daily, June 28, 2016, www.investors.com/news/technology/novartis-xencor-ink-2-4-billion-licensing-deal-in-blood-cancer

[32] Damian Garde, *What's Behind Those Billion-Dollar Biotech Deals? Often, a Whole Lot of Hype*, STAT, November 18, 2016, www.statnews.com/2016/11/28/biobuck-deals

[33] Philip Gregg, *Biotechs Receive One-Third of the Milestone Payments Provided for in Licensing Agreements*, Born.to.Invest, January 2, 2020 (translated from French original), https://born2invest.com/articles/biotechs-receive-one-third-of-the-milestone-payments-provided-for-in-licensing-agreements

Beginning in 1991 with the founding of CTRF, Dr. Law concentrated his scientific work on treating sufferers of muscular dystrophy both in the United States and abroad by means of "Myoblast Transfer Therapy" (MTT). MTT involves the transfer of a normal human genome to a genetically abnormal patient through the injection of cultured myoblasts. A myoblast, sometimes called a satellite cell, is an immature skeletal muscle cell. In the treatment of muscular dystrophy by MTT, a small number of cells are taken from a genetically normal donor. Those cells are then cultivated into billions of additional cells over several weeks, and the cultivated cells are injected into the patient. The implanting of cells from one person into another, such as in MTT, is known as an allogenic process. By contrast, in an autologous process, the cells implanted are derived from cells extracted from the patient's own body.

[In 1997], Dr. Law formed Cell Transplants International, LLC (CTI), a Tennessee limited liability company, in order to commercialize his patents. In 2004, Dr. Law allowed the Tennessee Secretary of State to administratively dissolve CTI. CTI had become financially unsound and left numerous creditors at its dissolution.

In 1999, Dr. Law and CTRF became the subject of an investigation by the Food and Drug Administration ("FDA") after an inspection of CTRF's laboratory revealed a number of deficiencies. The FDA placed the MTT program, which at the time was in trials pursuant to an "investigational new drug" application (IND application), on clinical hold in October 1999, thereby precluding further trials and treatment. In the summer of 2000, the FDA seized Dr. Law's supply of myoblasts and notified Dr. Law that he had been disqualified as an FDA-approved clinical researcher. Dr. Law's myoblasts were destroyed by the FDA in February 2001. In November 2002, the FDA notified him that it intended to conduct a hearing on his qualifications. Dr. Law failed to appear at the FDA's hearing and did not otherwise contest the charges against him. Finally, in October 2006, the FDA officially disqualified Dr. Law from serving as an investigator in clinical trials.

B. Bioheart

Bioheart, a Florida corporation, maintains its principal place of business in Sunrise, Florida. In 1999, Howard Leonhardt, a businessman with many years of experience in the biotechnology sector, formed Bioheart with the goal of developing and commercializing cellular therapies designed to repair or regenerate damaged human heart muscle. After some initial research, Bioheart decided that it would utilize myoblasts, as opposed to other types of cells, in this process.

"MyoCell" is the trade name of the product Bioheart ultimately developed. MyoCell treatment involves first taking a skeletal muscle biopsy from the thigh of a patient who has suffered heart failure. Myoblasts are then removed from the biopsied muscle tissue. These myoblasts are isolated and cultured in a proprietary growth media, which causes the myoblasts to grow into millions or even billions of cells. Finally, the cultured myoblasts are implanted into the damaged heart muscle by means of a catheter. Bioheart's original plan did not call for Bioheart to culture myoblasts itself. Bioheart instead planned to contract this responsibility to outside manufacturers—namely Dr. Law and his facility.

As part of developing MyoCell, Bioheart sought out and acquired patents and other intellectual property that potentially possessed utility for its purposes ... Mr. Leonhardt concluded that Dr. Law's '141 patent might cover at least part of the process being developed by Bioheart. Bioheart, therefore, decided to contact Dr. Law in order to obtain rights to his '141 patent.

C. The License Agreement

In early 2000, Dr. Law and Bioheart exchanged draft proposals for an agreement by which Bioheart would acquire a license to practice the '141 patent. At this time, Bioheart and Mr. Leonhardt were operating under the impression that Dr. Law's procedures were FDA-compliant and that he was in the process of conducting human clinical trials; in reality, this was precisely when Dr. Law's problems with the FDA were escalating. Dr. Law represented that he could greatly assist Bioheart in the development of its product, including by becoming Bioheart's supplier of cultured myoblasts. Reliance upon Dr. Law would, Bioheart believed, enable it to progress quickly into clinical studies and then to commercialization of MyoCell. Ultimately, both sides reached an agreement, producing the first contract ("License Agreement") at issue in this case.

Mr. Leonhardt executed the License Agreement on behalf of Bioheart on February 7, 2000, and Dr. Law executed the License Agreement on February 9, 2000. Dr. Law repeatedly made representations to Mr. Leonhardt that he and CTI/CTAL could be Bioheart's supplier of cultured myoblasts, and Bioheart anticipated that they would act as its supplier.

D. The Addendum

Shortly after execution of the License Agreement, the parties recognized the need for revisions and modifications to its terms as well as the need to enter into additional agreements.

Consequently, the parties undertook discussions lasting from approximately February to July 2000 aimed at altering their original agreement. [O]n July 21, 2000, Dr. Law executed the Addendum ("Addendum") amending the License Agreement.

The Court summarizes the terms of the Addendum as follows:

Section 1. Dr. Law and CTI agree to sign four separate agreements along with the Addendum: (a) a Scientific Advisory Board Consultation Agreement ("Advisory Board Agreement"); (b) a Supply Agreement ("Supply Agreement") related to supplying cultured myoblasts; (c) an Inventions and Proprietary Rights Assignment and Confidentiality Agreement ("Inventions and Proprietary Rights Agreement"); and (d) a Warrant Certificate ("Warrant Certificate") related to obtaining stock in Bioheart ...

Section 2(a). ... Dr. Law and/or CTI shall provide Bioheart with "all pertinent and critical information" needed to obtain FDA approval of an IND application for the processes being developed by Bioheart.

Section 2(c). Bioheart agrees to make a $3 million milestone payment to CTI upon commencement of a "bona fide Phase II human clinical trial study that utilizes technology claimed under [the '141 patent] with [FDA] approval in the United States[.]" ...

E. Subsequent Relations Between Plaintiffs and Bioheart

In the period following execution of the Addendum, Bioheart was still preparing for the filing of its initial IND application with the FDA, but Dr. Law's operations in Memphis were already the subject of an ongoing FDA investigation into his practices. The parties had entered into the Supply Agreement on the premise that CTI would be Bioheart's primary, if not sole, supplier of cultured myoblast, but CTI was never able to perform the Supply Agreement in spite of Bioheart's repeated insistence that its performance was needed. Ultimately, Bioheart began seeking other suppliers, which had the effect of delaying its IND application.

As indicated above, Section 2(a) of the Addendum obligated Dr. Law and/or CTI to provide Bioheart with "all pertinent and critical information" needed "to file an IND with the FDA and to have [the IND application] approved by the FDA." Providing this information was a vital part of facilitating Bioheart's submission of an IND application. Dr. Law, however, never discharged this obligation as Bioheart had envisioned. Dr. Law failed to provide Bioheart with his complete standard operating procedures ("SOP's") for culturing myoblasts even though Bioheart needed them in order to file its IND application, and the SOP's Dr. Law did provide were either redacted or so vague as to be unhelpful. Declaring it to be proprietary information, Dr. Law also withheld information from Bioheart regarding the formulation of the culturing media employed in his processes, which was likewise required for the IND application. Similarly, Dr. Law never gave Bioheart all the information needed regarding the source of his media's ingredients, nor did he ever furnish the necessary certificates of analysis for these ingredients. Although Bioheart requested it, Dr. Law and CTI also refused Bioheart even limited access to their "drug master file" in relation to certifying the safety of Dr. Law's cell culturing media. Additionally, Dr. Law did not make available to Bioheart information on shipping and transporting cultured myoblasts.

Determining that Dr. Law's SOP's did not comply with the FDA's cGMP standards and facing a lack of necessary information about Dr. Law's processes and media, Bioheart elected to develop its own SOP's and culturing media rather than rely upon Dr. Law and CTI. Dr. Law insisted at trial that he only withheld the SOP's for yielding the billions of cells that he would produce in MTT because that number of cells would be too great for Bioheart's needs. The Court finds, however, that Dr. Law's failure to provide information was not as harmless as he contends.

After developing its own SOP's and culturing media, Bioheart filed an IND application in 2002. Bioheart also built a cGMP-compliant cell culturing facility. Subsequent attempts to consult with Dr. Law did not result in meaningful assistance, and Dr. Law continued to withhold information. At trial, Bioheart submitted that Dr. Law's failures severely hindered its IND application and forced it to develop SOP's and culturing media at a cost of $3,737,657.19.

MyoCell now depends upon processes and media that differ substantially in several significant ways from those developed by Dr. Law. Bioheart's first trial of MyoCell in the United States occurred in April 2003. The next significant step in the development process, FDA-approved Phase II/III human clinical trials, commenced in October 2007. No commercialization of MyoCell has yet occurred, although Bioheart has received partial reimbursement of certain expenses in relation to its clinical trials.

Conclusions of Law

Plaintiffs' Claim for the $3 Million Milestone Payment

Plaintiffs contend that they are entitled to the milestone payment under the Addendum because the conditions described in Section 2(c) of the Addendum have now occurred. Specifically, Plaintiffs argue that Bioheart has commenced a bona fide Phase II human clinical trial study in the United States utilizing technology claimed under the '141 patent with FDA approval. Bioheart makes several independent arguments in response. The Court concludes that Bioheart is entitled to judgment on Count Four of Plaintiffs' amended complaint.

Existence and Satisfaction of Condition Precedent

Bioheart [argues] that the milestone payment under Section 2(c) is subject to a condition precedent which neither Dr. Law nor CTI has satisfied. According to Bioheart's interpretation, Section 2 of the Addendum creates a condition precedent when it prefaces the terms of the new agreement with a recital stating that the contract is "[i]n consideration of Dr. Law's and CTI's execution, delivery and performance of the above-identified agreements … " In the provisions that followed, Bioheart agreed, among other things, to make the milestone payment upon "commencement of a bona fide Phase II human clinical trial study that utilizes technology claimed under [the '141 patent] with [FDA] approval in the United States." Bioheart now cites four ways in which, it says, the condition precedent has not been satisfied: (1) CTI never performed and never was able to perform the Supply Agreement under which CTI was to furnish Bioheart with FDA-quality myoblasts; (2) Dr. Law failed to comply with his obligation under the Inventions and Proprietary Rights Agreement to give Bioheart access to his information—including his formulae, processes, manufacturing techniques, and trade secrets—related to heart muscle regeneration and angiogenesis; (3) Dr. Law did not conduct research of "mutual interest" in exchange for receiving the $500,000 payment; and (4) Dr. Law did not provide Bioheart "with all pertinent and critical information in order to file an IND with the FDA and to have it approved by the FDA" as he was obligated to do by Section 2(a) of the Addendum. Plaintiffs' principal argument in response is that these are not part of a condition precedent to the milestone payment. Rather, they urge that the only condition to payment of the milestone is Bioheart's initiation of the Phase II human clinical study, an event that has occurred.

"A condition precedent generally is defined as 'an act or event, other than a lapse of time, which must exist or occur before a duty of immediate performance of a promise arises'" [citation omitted]. A condition precedent may be a prerequisite to the coming into existence of a binding contract, or it may be what causes a duty in an existing contract to arise. If it is subject to a condition precedent, a duty need not be performed until the condition occurs or the nonoccurrence of the condition is excused.

Plaintiffs correctly note that Tennessee law, like the law in other jurisdictions, does not favor contractual conditions precedent. Generally, where it is fairly debatable whether particular language in a contract creates a condition precedent, the language will be interpreted in favor of creating only a covenant or promise. Where, however, it is the parties' intention, as gleaned from the language of the contract and the surrounding circumstances, to create a condition precedent, it will be upheld. Although it does not require the use of any particular language, "[t]he presence of a condition is usually signaled by a conditional word or phrase such as 'if,' 'provided that,' 'when,' 'after,' 'as soon as,' and 'subject to.'"

Considering the Addendum as a whole, the Court concludes that the preface in Section 2 does not create a condition precedent to the $3 million milestone payment. First, Section 2 does not employ any of the terms or phrases usually associated with creation of a condition precedent. While the specific language of Section 2(c) does signal a condition by making Bioheart's payment due only "upon commencement" of a Phase II human clinical study "utilizing technology claimed" under the '141 patent, no reference is made within Section 2(c) to any other condition. And, as Plaintiffs note, in Section 1 of the Addendum, the parties indisputably set up a condition precedent to the Addendum's becoming an enforceable contract. There the Addendum reads, "It shall be an express condition precedent to the effectiveness of this Addendum that ... [the four described agreements] ... be executed and delivered by the parties hereto." Thus, Section 1 is compelling evidence to indicate that, when these parties unmistakably intended a condition precedent, they knew how to express their wish clearly. Presumably then, if the parties had intended Section 2 to also contain a condition precedent, they would have been just as explicit ... Taking all of these factors along with the legal presumption against finding conditions precedent, the Court finds that Bioheart's $3 million milestone payment is not subject to a condition precedent other than commencement of the clinical study described in Section 2(c). A party's failure to perform the duties Bioheart references could constitute a breach and be the basis of an independent claim for damages, but it would not amount to a failure of a condition precedent.

Notes and Questions

1. *Rationales for milestones.* What rationale do licensors typically have for including milestones in licensing agreements? What about licensees? What do you think are the typical points of contention in formulating milestones?
2. *Satisfaction of milestones.* In *Law v. Bioheart*, Dr. Law failed to fulfill several of his contractual obligations, yet the court was still willing to uphold his right to receive the $3 million milestone payment. On what ground did the court eventually reject his claim to the milestone?
3. *Conditions precedent.* What is the significance of determining whether or not certain obligations of Dr. Law constituted conditions precedent to Bioheart's payment of the $3 million milestone? What was the only condition that the court did recognize with respect to the milestone payment? Why does the court say that conditions precedent are disfavored under the law?
4. *Election of remedies.* The court notes that despite Dr. Law's breaches, "Bioheart chooses to embrace the Addendum rather than to have the Addendum rescinded." Why do you think Bioheart made this choice? What would have been the effect on the parties' obligations of rescinding the Addendum?
5. *The rest of the story.* Bioheart's business is commonly referred to as "stem cell therapy," a controversial and largely unregulated process that one Harvard stem cell biologist refers to as "the modern equivalent of snake oil."[34] Bioheart, whose investors included Dan Marino, former quarterback of the Miami Dolphins, changed its name to US Stem Cell in 2016. As noted by the court, beginning in 1999 the FDA investigated Dr. Law, seized and destroyed his stock of myoblasts and disqualified him as a clinical investigator in 2006. In 2017, Dr. Law, writing from his position at the Cell Therapy Institute in Wuhan, China, struck back. He published an article in which he accused the FDA of "character assassination," "non-scientific, unjust and possibly illegal practices" and "crime[s] against humanity," and insisted that his myoblast therapy for Duchenne muscular dystrophy is both safe and effective.[35]
6. *Licensor milestones versus options.* Throughout this section we have discussed milestone and diligence requirements imposed on licensees. But what about licensors? There are often obligations that licensors must fulfill, including the development and regulatory approval of products, before a product can be commercialized. Would it be possible to structure

---

[34] Sharon Begley, *Three Patients Blinded by Stem Cell Procedure, Physicians Say*, STAT, March 15, 2017 (quoting Dr. George Daley, dean of Harvard Medical School).
[35] Peter K. Law, *Crime against Humanity: Uncovering Two Decades of Corruption in the FDA Regarding DMD Treatment*, 6 Open J. Regenerative Med. 35 (2017).

milestone payments by the licensee based on the licensor's achievement of concrete progress toward commercialization? How would you draft such a clause?

As it turns out, industry practice does not typically characterize licensor steps toward commercialization as milestones. If a licensed right, such as a patent claiming a new drug candidate, requires significant development or regulatory approval that will be undertaken by the licensor, then the licensee is often granted an *option* to obtain a license once those steps have been successfully completed. That is, at the outset, when the technology still requires further licensor development/approval, the licensee will pay a modest "option fee," which gives it the exclusive right to obtain a full license once the development is completed or the approvals have been obtained. Upon exercise of the option, the licensee will pay a much larger "purchase price" to obtain an exclusive license.

Problem 8.4

You represent Western University, which has patented a promising new process for curing cheese. You are negotiating an exclusive license agreement with Cheesy Co., a small, local company that produces artisanal cheeses. The parties have agreed that Cheesy will pay up to $5 million in milestone payments to WU. Draft a "Milestones" section of the agreement that includes five reasonable milestones and accompanying payments, and that describes the schedule for milestone achievement and the consequences for nonachievement of milestones.

8.6 EQUITY COMPENSATION

When a licensee is a start-up company without substantial financial resources, a licensor may accept shares of the licensee's capital stock as full or partial compensation for a license. While this arrangement is most common in university spinout licenses (see Chapter 14), it occurs elsewhere as well.

FIGURE 8.7 Stanford University is reported to have earned $336 million by selling shares of Google stock in the company's 2004 IPO and subsequent offerings.

The issuance of stock involves corporate and securities laws that are beyond the scope of this book. However, even noncorporate attorneys should be familiar with the basic contractual terms surrounding the issuance of equity securities in licensing agreements.[36]

EXAMPLE: EQUITY COMPENSATION

Licensee will grant to Licensor _____ shares of the Licensee's common stock (the "Shares"), which represents ___ percent (____%) of the issued and outstanding equity securities of Licensee, calculated on a fully diluted, as converted basis, as of the Effective Date, after giving effect to the issuance of the Shares.

The Shares are fully paid as partial consideration for the license of certain intellectual property rights granted by Licensor to Licensee under this Agreement.

Such Shares shall be issued to Licensor and evidenced by a stock certificate, registered in the name of Licensor, that is delivered to Licensor within thirty (30) days following the Effective Date.

US universities generally seek equity compensation from start-up licensees in the range of 5–10 percent of the company shares. UK universities are known to seek higher equity shares, in the range of 50 percent.

But what does this percentage actually mean? Usually it refers to a percentage of the total outstanding company stock, including both common and preferred stock,[37] as of the effective date of the agreement. Unexercised options and warrants to acquire shares of the licensee's stock are usually not included in this calculation.

For example, suppose that the licensor wants equity compensation equal to 5 percent of the licensee's equity. Suppose that the licensee has a total of 50,000 shares of common stock issued to its founders, and 10,000 shares of preferred stock, which converts to common stock at a ratio of 1:5. The total outstanding shares, on an as-converted basis, at the effective date is thus 100,000. The licensor's share will be 5 percent of the total, taking into account the issuance of the licensor's shares. Thus, the licensor will receive 5,263 shares, as this equals 5 percent of 105,263.[38]

The term "fully diluted" in the above example refers to so-called "anti-dilution" provisions that are often contained in preferred stock terms. In short, these provisions result in the issuance of more shares of preferred stock if additional stock is issued to someone else. So the issuance of stock to the licensor itself could trigger an anti-dilution adjustment for the preferred stockholders, which would result in their having more stock, which would result in the licensor's share having to increase to reach the required level, and so on. The calculation can be done, but it is a bit complex.

---

[36] Further details can be found in Bryce Pilz, *Modern Intellectual Property Valuation in the Academic Technology Transfer Setting* in Research Handbook on Intellectual Property and Technology Transfer 166, 184–89 (Jacob Rooksby, ed., Edward Elgar, 2020).

[37] The term "as converted" means that shares of preferred stock are treated as though they have been converted to common stock, as most preferred stock can be, though sometimes on a basis greater than 1:1.

[38] A discussion of the mechanics of such transactions can be found in Mark Edwards, Fiona Murray & Robert Yu, *Gold in the Ivory Tower: Equity Rewards of Outlicensing*, 24 Nat. Biotechnol. 509 (2006).

These days, university licensors can ask for a range of additional equity-based protections and rights, including anti-dilution, the right to participate in future stock issuances, board observer rights and the like. The provisions are beyond the scope of most typical licensing agreements and generally require the involvement of attorneys familiar with capital markets and equity issuance laws.

Notes and Questions

1. *University equity.* Equity compensation is increasingly common in university licenses, but also appears in some business-to-business licenses. What features of university licenses might make equity compensation more popular in university licenses that others?
2. *Equity compensation trade-offs.* What risks might exist for licensors who accept equity as compensation in licensing transactions? Are there any risks for the licensee issuing the equity as compensation?

8.7 COST REIMBURSEMENT

When universities and small companies license patents, they often require that the licensee reimburse them for patent prosecution costs incurred prior to the execution of the agreement. If a license is exclusive, then the licensee often covers the entirety of these costs. If the license is co-exclusive, or if it is exclusive only in a particular field, then the cost is often split among licensees. Nonexclusive licensees typically do not reimburse the licensor for prosecution costs (or, if they do, that cost is built into their nonexclusive licensing fees).

The level of patent prosecution costs will vary depending on the complexity of the technology, the developmental stage of the technology, the stage of prosecution (e.g., provisional application, utility application, examination, issuance, post-grant opposition), how many applications and patents have been filed, whether foreign protection has been sought and whether competitors have, or are likely to, opposed the patent(s) at the Patent Trial and Appeals Board (PTAB). For "mature" patents, maintenance fees may also have been paid to the PTO. These costs, when aggregated across jurisdictions, can range from as little as $10,000 to several hundred thousand dollars or more per patent.

Of course, prosecution activity often continues after a license agreement is signed, and maintenance fees will continue to become due with respect to issued patents and trademarks.[39] In the United States, Europe and other countries, proceedings of various types (*inter partes review*, oppositions, etc.) can be initiated at patent offices to invalidate issued patents. Because these proceedings are semi-administrative in nature, and are not part of court-based litigation, they are sometimes treated as part of the patent prosecution process. This being said, the costs of these proceedings, while substantially lower than litigation, far surpass typical patent prosecution charges. As a result, parties should be careful about allocating the costs of these proceedings.

If the licensee has agreed to assume responsibility for prosecution matters (see Section 9.5), then the licensee will usually cover ongoing prosecution and maintenance costs. If the licensor retains this responsibility (e.g., if it has granted several exclusive licenses in different fields and has not granted prosecution responsibility to any one licensee), then the licensor may seek periodic reimbursement of at least a portion of its prosecution and maintenance costs. In some cases, these costs may be split evenly among all licensees.

---

[39] For patents, maintenance fees are $2,000 due 3.5 years after issuance, $3,760 due 7.5 years after issuance and $7,700 due 11.5 years after issuance. 37 CFR 1.20(e)-(g). Trademark renewal fees must be paid every ten years, accompanied by a fee of $425 per class of goods or services in the registration.

EXAMPLE: PROSECUTION COST REIMBURSEMENT

Licensor shall provide Licensee with a quarterly statement of its out-of-pocket costs and expenses [1] incurred in prosecuting and maintaining the Licensed IP, including filing, correction and issuance fees, maintenance payments, and the associated fees of external attorneys, experts, translators and illustrators ("Prosecution Costs") [2]. For the avoidance of doubt, Prosecution Costs shall include costs and expenses associated with defending the Licensed IP against invalidity and reexamination proceedings, oppositions, *inter partes review* and similar proceedings brought in any patent office or other administrative body, but excluding litigation proceedings brought in any court [3].

DRAFTING NOTES

[1] *Out-of-pocket costs* – it is typical to reimburse an IP holder for its costs and expenses paid to third parties and governmental agencies, but not for the time of its internal personnel. Some organizations that handle a large amount of prosecution internally may wish to charge a reasonable rate for the time of in-house personnel.
[2] *Illustrators* – patent drawings and figures are sometimes created by professional illustrators and drafters.
[3] *Validity proceedings* – as noted above, the cost of defending issued patents against invalidity proceedings can be high, so the parties should be careful to allocate these expenses.

8.8 MOST-FAVORED CLAUSES

"Most-favored" licensee clauses find their roots in the world of international statecraft, in which the most favorable trade status that can be afforded to another country is that of a "most-favored nation" or MFN. Most-favored clauses are not uncommon in licensing agreements, and often retain the label "MFN" even when used in this private law context.

Most-favored clauses protect the licensee against competitive disadvantage arising from the licensor's later grant of more favorable contractual terms to a competitor of the licensee. But with this type of clause, more than many others, the devil is in the details. Two examples of MFN clauses are provided here.

EXAMPLES: MOST-FAVORED LICENSEE

Example 1

If during the term of the Agreement the Licensor grants to any unaffiliated third party licensee ("Third Party") [that is of a similar size and geographic focus as Licensee] a license to the Licensed Patent in the Field of Use on financial terms that are [substantially] more favorable than those granted herein [for similar quantity and kind of Licensed Products], then Licensor shall promptly notify Licensee of such license, describing the Third Party's more favorable terms in reasonable detail, though the identity of the Third Party need not be revealed.

Licensee shall then have a period of [60 days] in which to consider whether to exercise its rights under this Section. If it so elects, it shall notify Licensor in writing, and thereupon this Agreement shall automatically be amended to provide for such more favorable terms. Such amendment shall be retroactively effective to the date on which the more favorable terms were granted to the Third Party. In the event that such amendment requires the parties to make any adjusting payments, these shall be made within sixty (60) days following Licensee's exercise of its rights hereunder.

Example 2

The aggregate Fees charged to Customer for [the Services/Software] during the term of this Agreement shall not exceed [ninety-five percent (95%) of] the aggregate fees contemporaneously charged by Licensor to any other [non-Affiliate customer/Competitor of Customer] for comparable services and software (taking into account product mix, term of use, number of seats/copies, and corresponding nonmonetary benefits received by Licensor). Licensor shall adjust the Fees charged to Customer on a going-forward basis so that such Fees do not exceed such threshold; provided that if Licensor reduces the Fees charged to Customer to comply with such requirement and then subsequently ceases to charge Licensor's [other customers/such Competitor] at or above the price that triggered such reduction, Licensor shall thereafter be entitled to increase the Fees charged to Customer to levels consistent with such pricing requirement, but in no case to levels above those originally charged under this Agreement. Notwithstanding the foregoing, under no circumstances shall Licensor be required to provide any refund, rebate or credit to Customer in respect of Fees paid prior to the charging of such lower fees to such other customer/Competitor.

The first question to ask when drafting (and negotiating) an MFN clause is how broad its scope should be in terms of *agreement coverage*. That is, what types of later agreements will need to be compared to the agreement with MFN treatment to determine whether their terms are more favorable? Should a patent license agreement be compared only to other patent license agreements? Or should other types of agreements, such as merger agreements, supply agreements and settlement agreements, also be subject to MFN comparison? This issue, which parties often fail to address in their drafting, is the subject of the *Kohle* case excerpted below.

The second issue of this nature concerns which future *licensees and fields of use* are subject to comparison under an MFN clause. That is, should the first licensee be entitled to terms as favorable as those granted by the licensor to entities of all descriptions or only entities that can reasonably be viewed as competing with the first licensee (it is generally accepted that MFN clauses do not apply to intercompany transactions between a licensor and its affiliated companies)? For example, suppose that a patent covers a method for rapidly recharging a lithium-ion battery, and it is licensed to an electric vehicle manufacturer at a flat rate of $7.50 per car. If the licensee has MFN protection, should that protection extend to licenses that the patent holder grants to manufacturers of smartphones at $1.00 per phone? Considering that the price of a smartphone is far less than that of a car, it might seem unreasonable to compare these two licenses. Likewise, a pharmaceutical manufacturer that is licensed to sell a patented drug in the United States should probably not be automatically entitled to the same rates as a manufacturer distributing the drug in the developing world. Finally, a trademark licensor might be reluctant to grant a small, specialty business – say, a producer of hand-crafted porcelain dolls – MFN protection against lower rates that it extends to a large multinational toy manufacturer that will produce far larger quantities of licensed goods at lower price points.

Once these initial scoping questions are decided, the parties must agree *which contractual terms* are subject to MFN treatment. Suppose that the first licensee pays a running royalty rate of 5 percent to manufacture and sell widgets covered by the licensor's patents. If the licensor grants a license to a second licensee at a royalty rate of 3 percent, the first licensee's MFN clause would be triggered. But what if the second licensee pays a large up-front fee in order to secure this lower royalty rate (like prepaying "points" on a mortgage in order to secure a lower monthly interest rate)? Should the first licensee be entitled to the benefit of the 3 percent rate if it made no up-front payment? Or should it be given the option to make a similar up-front payment in order to gain the advantage of the lower running royalty rate? Likewise, what if one licensee purchases equity of the licensor? Should the first licensee be required to make such a purchase in order to enjoy the lower royalty rates enjoyed by the second?

With respect to the comparison of financial terms, some MFN clauses contain a materiality or substantiality qualifier. Licensors will argue that an MFN adjustment should not be triggered based on trivial differences among licenses (e.g., slightly different interest rates for late payments, payment terms or foreign exchange rates). But once such a qualifier is introduced, there will always be an issue of what constitutes a "material" difference. When large amounts are at stake, the parties are well advised to be as specific as possible in this regard, perhaps specifying that any difference in royalty rates or total compensation of more than x percent will trigger an MFN adjustment.

Most MFN protection is limited to protection against more favorable *financial* terms, as there are hundreds of other contractual provisions – notice periods, warranties, indemnities, etc. – that will vary from agreement to agreement. If a later agreement gives a second licensee forty-five days to cure a breach rather than thirty days, should the first licensee's MFN clause give it the benefit of that longer cure period? What if the second license also has a less favorable confidentiality clause? Must the first licensee accept the bad terms of the second agreement in addition to the good? And what if some terms in the second license are entirely inapplicable to the first license – how would the electric vehicle manufacturer's license for battery charging technology be adjusted if a smartphone manufacturer received a large milestone payment upon approval by the Federal Communications Commission? The above example contains some possible limitations on the type, size and field of use of later licenses that are subject to MFN treatment, but additional language may be necessary, depending on the specifics of the parties' transaction.

Once these terms are decided, the process for implementing MFN treatment must be specified in some detail. This necessarily includes a notification by the licensor of the more favorable terms, a period during which the licensee may consider them, and some mechanism for the licensee to gain the benefit of the more favorable terms. In some cases, an agreement may specify that more favorable terms are automatically extended to the licensee. However, if the licensee would be required to make an up-front payment or the licensor would be required to refund amounts previously paid by the licensee, the parties should have a reasonable period of time in which to calculate and effect such reconciliation. This being said, some MFN clauses (such as example 2 above) specifically exclude any refund of prior amounts paid by the licensee.

Finally, the retroactive effect of an MFN adjustment must be considered. One approach is to make the more favorable terms apply retroactively to the date on which they were first granted to the second licensee. This eliminates any advantage that the licensor may gain by delaying its notification to the licensee. However, retroactive adjustments can have significant accounting and financial implications, which should encourage the licensor to notify the licensee as promptly as possible of the more favorable terms.

Studiengesellschaft Kohle m.b.H. v. Hercules Inc.

105 F.3d 629 (Fed. Cir. 1997)

MAYER, JUSTICE

In 1986, Studiengesellschaft Kohle m.b.H. (SGK) sued Hercules, Inc.; Himont U.S.A., Inc.; and Himont, Inc. (collectively "Hercules") for patent infringement. Hercules counterclaimed, alleging that SGK had breached the most favored licensee provision of their license agreement by failing to offer Hercules a license with the same terms it offered other licensees. But for the breach, Hercules argued, it would have been licensed under the patents at issue during the period in question, thereby insulating it from infringement. The district court agreed and entered judgment for Hercules. Because SGK has not established that the court made any clearly erroneous findings of fact or error of law, we affirm.

Background

SGK is the licensing arm of the Max Planck Institute for Coal Research in Germany. In the early 1950s, SGK invented a catalyst that could be used to make plastics, such as polyethylene and polypropylene. In 1954, SGK and Hercules entered a "polyolefin contract" (the "1954 contract") granting Hercules a nonexclusive license under SGK's "Patent Applications and Patents Issued Thereon." Although the United States had not issued SGK any patents at that time, the contract contemplated that Hercules would be licensed under any SGK patent issued in the future in the plastics field. The contract included a most favored licensee provision, set forth in pertinent part:

> If a license shall hereafter be granted by [SGK] to any other licensee in the United States or Canada to practice the Process or to use and sell the products of the Process under [SGK's] inventions, Patent Applications or Patents or any of them, then [SGK] shall notify Hercules promptly of the terms of such other license and if so requested by Hercules, shall make available to Hercules a copy of such other license and Hercules shall be entitled, upon demand if made three (3) months after receiving the aforementioned notice, to the benefit of any lower royalty rate or rates for its operations hereunder in the country or countries (US and Canada) in which such rates are effective, as of and after the date such more favorable rate or rates became effective under such other license but only for so long as and to the same extent and subject to the same conditions that such … lower royalty rate or rates shall be available to such other licensee; provided, however, that Hercules shall not be entitled to such more favorable rate or rates without accepting any less favorable terms that may have accompanied such more favorable rate or rates.

The contract also contained a termination clause, which granted SGK the right to terminate the agreement and the licenses upon sixty days written notice if Hercules failed to make royalty payments when due. However, Hercules had the right to cure its default by paying SGK "all sums then due under [the] Agreement," in which case the licenses would remain in full force and effect.

The parties amended the contract [in 1972] by granting Hercules "a fully paid-up" license through December 3, 1980, the date the '115 patent expired, under SGK's "U.S. Patent rights with respect to polypropylene … up to a limit of six hundred million pounds (600,000,000) per year sales." For sales exceeding that amount, Hercules was obligated to pay SGK royalties of one percent of its "Net Sales Price." As to SGK's patents expiring after December 3, 1980, Hercules possessed the right, upon request, to obtain "a license on terms no worse than the most favored other paying licensee of [SGK]." SGK concedes that this provision granted Hercules the "right to the most favored paying licensee's terms regardless of whether those terms had been granted before or after 1972." The amendment also provided that the terms and conditions of the 1954 contract remained in "full force and effect except as modified by, or inconsistent with, this amendment." SGK concedes that "the notice provision, indeed the whole [most-favored licensee] clause, 'survived the 1972 Agreement.'"

On November 14, 1978, SGK was issued U.S. Patent No. 4,125,698 ('698 patent) for the "Polymerization of Ethylenically Unsaturated Hydrocarbons." The parties agree that under the 1972 amendment Hercules was licensed under the '698 patent, without any additional payment, through December 3, 1980. It is also undisputed that this patent is covered by the 1954 agreement, as amended.

In March 1979, SGK sent Hercules a letter terminating the 1954 contract and the licenses granted under it "for failure to account and make royalty payments" when due. In accordance with the agreement, the letter stated that the termination would become effective in sixty days unless the "breach" had been corrected and the payments made. Hercules paid SGK $339,032 within the sixty-day period, which SGK accepted. Although SGK possessed the right to question any royalty statement made by Hercules, and to have a certified public accountant audit Hercules' books to verify or determine royalties paid or payable, it did not do so.

On May 1, 1980, more than seven months before the expiration of Hercules' "paid-up" license, SGK granted Amoco Chemicals Corporation (Amoco) a nonexclusive "paid-up" license to make, use, and sell products covered by SGK's polypropylene patents in the United States. In exchange, Amoco paid SGK $1.2 million. SGK does not dispute that the '698 patent is covered by this license or that it failed to apprise Hercules of the license at the time it was granted. Hercules first learned of Amoco's license in 1987, after SGK commenced this action. It demanded an equivalent license retroactive to December 3, 1980.

FIGURE 8.8 The SGK–Hercules agreement concerned patent rights in polypropylene, a plastic used to make a wide range of products from Tic-Tac containers to furniture.

SGK refused, contending that (1) Amoco was not a "paying licensee," as contemplated by the 1972 amendment; (2) Hercules' request was too late; and (3) Amoco's license was granted as part of a settlement agreement.

On December 3, 1986, SGK filed suit in the United States District Court for the District of Delaware, charging Hercules with infringement of the '698 patent. Hercules counterclaimed, alleging that the 1954 license, as amended, required SGK to notify it of the Amoco agreement in 1980, the terms of which it was entitled to obtain via the most favored licensee provision of the 1954 contract, as amended. Hercules argued that it would have exercised its right to obtain a license on Amoco's terms had SGK not breached that provision. It claimed, therefore, that it was entitled to such license, retroactive to December 3, 1980, upon paying SGK $1.2 million. The court agreed and entered judgment for Hercules. This appeal followed.

Discussion

SGK concedes that the notice provision was effective but argues that it was only obligated to provide Hercules with notice of any license with terms more favorable than Hercules' license. In 1972, Hercules obtained a "paid-up" license under SGK's patents through December 3, 1980. In 1978, the '698 patent issued. Hercules was licensed under that patent, without additional cost, by virtue of the 1972 license. Because Hercules obtained a "free" license under the '698 patent for the first 600 million pounds, no terms could be more favorable, according to SGK. So, it had no duty to apprise Hercules of the Amoco license.

SGK's interpretation does violence to the plain language of the 1954 contract. The notice clause did not condition SGK's obligation to inform Hercules of other licenses on whether such licenses were more favorable. It required SGK to notify Hercules promptly of the terms of a license granted "to any other licensee." Under SGK's construction, the power to determine whether another license was more favorable resided not with Hercules, but with SGK. That simply was not what the agreement provided. It is true that the 1954 contract granted Hercules the right, upon demand, to the benefit of any "more favorable rate or rates." However, that clause signified nothing more than the commercial reality that Hercules would opt only for a license whose terms it thought were more favorable than its own. It did not divest Hercules of the right to decide which terms were more favorable. Indeed, such a decision will not always be apparent when one considers the myriad combinations of royalty payments, lump-sum payments, and technology transfers a license can effect. Consequently, the court was correct that SGK's failure to provide notice constituted a breach of the license agreement.

SGK next says that it had no obligation to grant Hercules a license with terms equivalent to those in the Amoco license because Amoco was not a "paying licensee" within the meaning of the 1972 amendment. Again, we turn to the plain language of the license and interpret it anew. The 1972 amendment provided that for any of SGK's patents expiring after December 3, 1980, including the '698 patent, SGK would "grant Hercules, upon request, a license on terms no worse than the most favored other paying licensee of [SGK]." SGK contends that Amoco was not a "paying licensee" because it made just one lump-sum payment and no royalty payments; only licensees that make ongoing royalty payments are "paying licensee[s]."

In construing the term "paying licensee," we must give the words their ordinary meaning unless a contrary intent appears. The ordinary meaning of the term "paying licensee" is one who gives money for a license. See Webster's II New Riverside University Dictionary 863 (1984) (defining "pay" as "[t]o give money to in return for goods or services rendered").

SGK has not established that the parties intended that the term should mean something else. We see no distinction between one who makes an up-front, lump-sum payment and one who makes continuing royalty payments. Indeed, such a distinction would be doubly doubtful because a "paid-up" license presumably includes potential future royalty payments discounted to their net present value.

SGK also argues that the $1.2 million payment was in settlement of litigation; Amoco was not intended to be a "paying licensee." But the court found that Amoco paid SGK $1.2 million for a paid-up license for unlimited production under, inter alia, the '698 patent. SGK has not shown how this finding is clearly erroneous: Amoco was a "paying licensee."

Even were we to accept SGK's interpretation as reasonable, however, the provision would be ambiguous because Hercules' construction is also reasonable. Under such circumstances, and in the absence of any extrinsic evidence clearly establishing the parties' intent, we construe the term "paying licensee" against the drafter of the language – SGK – under the doctrine of contra proferentem. So, Hercules' interpretation would still prevail.

According to SGK, even if Hercules is entitled to terms equivalent to those in the Amoco license, it exercised its option too late to be effective. This argument fails because the only requirement in the 1954 contract or its amendments that limits the time in which Hercules must request a license is that it be within three months of receiving the required notice. Because SGK failed to notify Hercules of the Amoco license, that time limitation never began. The court found that Hercules first became aware of the Amoco license in 1987 through discovery in this case. Hercules demanded an equivalent license on or about March 16, 1987, so even if constructive notice could trigger the three-month limitation, Hercules met it.

SGK also contends that the court erred in concluding that Hercules was entitled to a license retroactive to December 3, 1980. It argues that for six years Hercules intentionally manufactured products covered by the '698 patent, which it thought was invalid, without a license. Only after this court ruled that the patent had not been proven invalid, did Hercules become interested in obtaining a license. It requested a license retroactive to the date its allegedly infringing activities began, thereby insulating itself from any infringement claim. SGK argues that "nothing in Hercules' option provides for such a right."

To be sure, neither we nor the parties can know with certainty whether Hercules would have exercised its right to a license on Amoco's terms in 1980, had it received the required notice. To that extent the prospect of absolving six years of alleged infringement via a retroactive license is troubling. But the uncertainty was caused by SGK's breach, the consequences of which it must bear. The 1954 contract expressly and unambiguously provides Hercules with the right to obtain the terms of another license "effective, as of and after the date such more favorable rate or rates became effective under such other license." The agreement must stand as written. Hercules is entitled to the terms of the Amoco license effective May 1980, when the Amoco license became effective.

Notes and Questions

1. *Different approaches to MFN.* Compare the example MFN clauses provided above. How do they differ? Which would you prefer if you were the licensee? The licensor?
2. *Dispute resolutions.* A surprising number of litigated cases in addition to *Kohle* involve disputes over the applicability of MFN clauses to settlement agreements, arbitral awards and other agreements arising from the resolution of disputes between the licensor and other

licensees.[40] How might you draft an MFN clause to avoid this potential issue? What factors might complicate any blanket exclusion of dispute resolution agreements from MFN comparisons?

3. *Exclusivity and MFN.* MFN clauses are typically granted in nonexclusive license agreements. Do you see why? What protection does an exclusive licensee have against future competitive licenses by the licensor?

4. *Favorable terms.* In *Kohle*, the MFN clause in the 1972 amendment required SGK to grant Hercules a license on terms no worse that the most favored other paying licensee. Amoco, which paid SGK $1.2 million, was found to be a paying licensee. But Hercules paid nothing for the right to operate under the patent through December 1980. Was Amoco's license truly "more favorable" than Hercules'?

5. *Timing.* What if a more favorable license is granted years after a license with an MFN clause, when the licensed patents are closer to expiration? The Fifth Circuit in *JP Morgan Chase Bank, N.A. v. DataTreasury Corp.*, 823 F.3d 1006 (5th Cir. 2016) held that the passage of time was not a factor in assessing the effect of an MFN clause. In that case, DataTreasury settled patent infringement litigation with JP Morgan Chase in 2005 pursuant to an agreement that required JP Morgan to pay $70 million over a seven-year period, and which contained an MFN clause. JP Morgan made the final payment in 2012, shortly before DataTreasury licensed the same patents to a third party for only $250,000. The licensed patents were scheduled to expire in 2016 and 2017. JP Morgan then sued DataTreasury for breach of the MFN clause. The court ruled in JP Morgan's favor, holding that it was entitled under the MFN clause to a refund of $69 million,[41] given that the scope of the license granted to the third party was essentially the same as that granted to JP Morgan.

Judge Higginson dissented in part, arguing that JP Morgan paid for the right to operate under DataTreasury's patents for a full seven years longer than the third party, making the grants dissimilar enough to avoid applying the MFN clause. Judge Higginson further argued that under the majority's reasoning, JP Morgan would be entitled to its $69 million refund even if DataTreasury had granted the third-party license "just a month before the licensed patents expired." Which view do you think is the sounder one? Should the amount of time before a patent expires factor into the application of the MFN clause? If so, how, and would an MFN clause be applicable to any license other than one granted on the very same day?

8.9 AUDIT CLAUSES

In many licensing agreements, the licensee's payments are based on information solely in the licensee's possession: its revenue and sales figures, its achievement of certain technical and commercial milestones and the like. As a result, the licensee is usually required to submit periodic reports to the licensor informing it of the facts underlying the payments due during the period. These are often referred to as royalty reports or statements.

---

[40] Compare *Kohle* with *Wang Laboratories v. OKI Electric Industry Co.*, 15 F. Supp. 2d 166 (D. Mass. 1998) ("Monies received as a settlement for past tortious use of patents are not the equivalent of royalties").

[41] Though the third party paid only $250,000, its licensing agreement also required payments of an additional $250,000 for each acquisition that it made. Because JP Morgan had made three acquisitions during the course of its own license, the court determined that it would have been required to pay $1 million under the terms of the more favorable agreement.

In most agreements, the licensor has the right to "audit" the licensee's records in order to verify the information stated in its royalty reports. Many of the cases involving royalty disputes originated with a royalty audit. Such audit provisions are complex to negotiate, however, as the information that they seek is often confidential to the licensee, and of significant commercial and competitive value. Below are two examples of financial audit clauses, illustrating provisions that are favorable to the licensor and the licensee, respectively.

EXAMPLE: AUDIT CLAUSES

Licensor-Favorable

Licensor may cause an audit to be made of the applicable Licensee records and facilities (including those of Licensee's Affiliates) in order to verify statements issued by Licensee and Licensee's compliance with the terms of this Agreement. Any such audit may be conducted by Licensor or its independent accountants or consultants during regular business hours at Licensee and/or Customer's facilities, with one (1) week's notice, unless Licensor has reason to believe that Section x or y has been breached, in which case Licensor may audit Licensee and/or Customer's activities upon 24 hours' notice. Licensee agrees to provide Licensor's designated audit team prompt access to the relevant records and facilities. Licensor will pay for any such audit, unless the amount of any underpayment is greater than [5 percent] of the amount due, or if the audit reveals a material breach of any provision of this Agreement. In this case, Licensee shall reimburse Licensor for such audit costs in addition to the underpaid amounts and applicable interest charges. Licensor reserves the right to disclose the results of any audit conducted under Section x to its own licensors that have a need to know.

Licensee-Favorable

Licensor will have the right, no more than once during any twelve-month period, to engage an independent certified public accounting firm reasonably acceptable to Licensee to audit the books and records of Licensee for the sole purpose of confirming the accuracy of Royalty Statements provided hereunder. The auditor shall be required to enter into a nondisclosure agreement with Licensee covering all information learned or derived during such audit, and shall not be permitted to disclose to Licensor any such information other than its determination that an underpayment may have occurred, and in what amount. All costs and expenses of such audit shall be borne by Licensor unless such audit reveals any previously undisclosed underpayment in excess of [10 percent] of the total amount due during any calendar year and such underpayment is confirmed in writing by Licensee or by a court of competent jurisdiction in a final judgment from which no appeal may be taken, in which case Licensee shall reimburse Licensor for the reasonable and customary fees of its external auditing firm.

As you can see, audit provisions can vary substantially based on which party drafts them. Below are some of the more contentious issues that are usually negotiated in such clauses:

Who Conducts the Audit? Perhaps the most controversial issue in an audit clause is who is authorized to conduct the audit. The licensor will prefer to inspect the licensee's book and records itself – this is cheaper than hiring an external firm and will also give the licensor insight into the licensee's internal accounting practices, sales figures and the like. The licensor's personnel may also be more attuned to the industry and be better able to recognize inconsistencies or suspicious entries. The licensee, on the other hand, will be concerned about the disclosure of its confidential business records to the licensor, which may compete with the licensee or deal with the licensee's competitors. As a result, the licensee usually prefers that the audit be conducted by an external auditing firm and that records disclosed to the auditor be subject to a confidentiality agreement. Using an external auditor increases the cost and hassle for the licensor, making an audit less likely, and also makes it easier for the licensee to conceal information that the auditors may not know to ask for. If the licensor agrees to hire an external audit firm, it may also insist that its own financial personnel be permitted to participate in the audit, or at least to view the records provided to the auditors.

What Records Are Subject to Audit? In an audit, the licensor will seek access to as many records of the licensee as possible – computer files, databases, sales receipts, invoices and the like. The licensee will seek to confine the subject of the audit to specific records supporting its royalty reports. A key question is whether the licensee will give the auditor the right to search records as it wishes, or whether records for review will be provided by the licensee.

Cost Shifting. Usually the licensor is responsible for the costs of conducting the audit, though there is a trigger for shifting that cost to the licensee. The trigger is usually an underpayment by the licensee, though the amount of the triggering underpayment can range from 0 to upwards of 10 percent. There is also a question of which costs are shifted – should the licensee cover only the licensor's out-of-pocket fees paid to an external audit firm, or should it also pay for the time and effort expended by licensor's internal personnel?

Disputing Audit Results. It is inevitable that in some cases the licensee will dispute the findings of the audit. If this happens, a path for resolution must be specified. If the agreement contains a general dispute resolution clause (see Section 11.4), then that mechanism may be used. If a dispute resolution clause is not included in the agreement, then the audit clause should include language specifying the mechanisms used to resolve disputes over the audit results (e.g., mediation and arbitration). If such mechanisms are not specified, then the licensee's only option may be to refuse to pay the underpayment detected by the auditor and allow the licensor to sue for breach (nonpayment), at which time a court will resolve the dispute.

9

Development, Allocation and Management of IP

In previous chapters we have largely focused on the licensing of existing intellectual property (IP) by a licensor to a licensee. But in many cases significant bodies of IP may be created by the parties during the term of the agreement. This IP may be created by a licensor who contracts to undertake technology development services for its licensee, or by a licensee that is given the right to make its own modifications and improvements to the licensed IP. Or, in some cases, IP may be developed jointly by the parties. In each of these cases, the parties must agree which of them will own the newly developed IP, and whether any licenses will be granted to the non-owning party, and how they will manage and prosecute that IP.

9.1 LICENSEE DEVELOPMENTS: DERIVATIVES, IMPROVEMENTS AND GRANTBACKS

When a licensor provides IP to a licensee, the licensee is sometimes permitted to develop its own IP based on the licensed IP. This section discusses some of the legal issues surrounding those licensee-developed works, and how they are handled in IP licensing agreements.

9.1.1 Derivative Works and Improvements

Section 101 of the Copyright Act defines a "derivative work" as

> a work based upon one or more preexisting works, such as a translation, musical arrangement, dramatization, fictionalization, motion picture version, sound recording, art reproduction, abridgment, condensation, or any other form in which a work may be recast, transformed, or adapted. A work consisting of editorial revisions, annotations, elaborations, or other modifications which, as a whole, represent an original work of authorship, is a "derivative work".

Under Section 106 of the Copyright Act, the owner of a copyright has the *exclusive* right to prepare derivative works based upon a copyrighted work. Derivative works that are made without the licensor's authorization have no copyright protection at all. Thus, if a licensee wishes to prepare derivatives of any kind based on a licensed copyrighted work, it must be very sure to obtain the right to make those derivatives under its license to the original work.

The following case considers the degree to which a licensee obtains the right to prepare derivative works absent clear permission to do so.

Kennedy v. National Juvenile Detention Association
187 F.3d 690 (7th Cir. 1999)

BAUER, CIRCUIT JUDGE

I. Background

On October 30, 1995, [Edwin] Kennedy and the [National Juvenile Detention Association ("NJDA")] entered into an agreement for Kennedy to provide consulting services, to conduct a study of the juvenile justice requirements of the Seventh Judicial Circuit of Illinois (the "circuit"), and to submit a written report of his findings. The study was funded by the [Illinois Juvenile Justice Commission ("IJJC")]. The goals of the study were to collect data regarding current juvenile detention practices, to recommend improvements in the juvenile detention process, and to estimate future juvenile detention requirements within the circuit. The contract was to run until September 30, 1996.

On September 20, 1996, Kennedy submitted a draft of his report to the NJDA. At the behest of the NJDA and IJJC, Kennedy made minor revisions to his report for no additional compensation. A few months later, the NJDA requested that Kennedy, in exchange for an additional $10,000, make more revisions to his report because the original changes were not as extensive as they had hoped. Kennedy refused to make the revisions because he was concerned about compromising the integrity of his work, and he subsequently applied to register a copyright in his work. The copyright was effectively registered on January 13, 1997. In the meantime, the NJDA requested that Kennedy provide a disk with his copy of the final report. Thinking this was a condition for payment according to the agreement, Kennedy supplied the NJDA with the disk. When the contract had expired and Kennedy had refused to make further revisions to his report, the NJDA hired Craig Boersema to supervise the completion of the report. Kennedy was fully compensated for his completed work.

On January 17, 1997, Anne Studzinski, administrator of the IJJC, hosted a meeting in Chicago, attended by the NJDA's Executive Director Earl Dunlap, and Boersema, for the purpose of altering Kennedy's report; Kennedy neither knew of nor assented to the revision. Studzinski defended her revision of the report based on a clause in the contract which states:

> Where activities supported by this contract produce original computer programs ... writing, sound recordings, pictorial reproductions, drawing or other graphical representations and works of any similar nature, the government has the right to use, duplicate and disclose, in whole or in part, such materials in any manner for any purpose whatsoever and have others do so. If the material is copyrightable, Edwin Kennedy may copyright such, but the government reserves a royalty-free non-exclusive and irreversible license to reproduce, publish, and use such materials in whole or in part and to authorize others to do so.

In March of 1997, Kennedy released his version of the report, and on April 1, 1997, Dunlap issued a press release discrediting Kennedy and his work in order to promote the revised version of the work. The NJDA published the official report in August of 1997.

Kennedy filed suit against the NJDA and IJJC for copyright infringement. The NJDA and IJJC filed motions to dismiss the claim based on lack of subject matter jurisdiction, lack of personal jurisdiction, improper venue, and failure to state a claim. The district court [granted] defendants' motions to dismiss for failure to state a claim, rejecting the other theories as well as the request for sanctions. [Kennedy appeals.] The NJDA re-asserts its contention that it had the right to produce derivative works from Kennedy's report or, in the alternative, that it had a right, as a joint author of the study, to publish its version of the report.

II. Analysis

Kennedy concedes that the contractual agreement conferred upon the NJDA the right to reproduce and publish his report, however he argues that it did not grant either the NJDA or IJJC the right to create derivative works from it.

[The] district court found, and we agree, that the consulting agreement granted the NJDA a nonexclusive license to reproduce, publish, and use Kennedy's copyrighted report. The court also found that the term "use" must give the defendants rights beyond those of reproduction and publication. Moreover, it found that, considering the broad, comprehensive grant of authority given to the NJDA and IJJC, it was irrelevant that the agreement did not specifically refer to the defendants' right to create derivative works from Kennedy's copyrighted materials. Therefore, the district court found that the agreement gave the defendants permission to alter Kennedy's report and create a derivative work from it.

The NJDA suggests in its brief that the word "use" in this case is synonymous with "prepare derivative works." While we will not go so far as to agree with this interpretation, in the context of the consulting agreement between Kennedy and the NJDA, the term "use" does encompass the act of creating derivative works. To read the agreement any other way would render the term "use" superfluous. [A]s the contract stands, it grants the defendants the right to use Kennedy's report for any purpose whatsoever.

[AFFIRMED.]

MANION, CIRCUIT JUDGE, concurring in part and dissenting in part.

[T]he issue is whether "use," the third verb in the clause, unambiguously grants to the defendants the right to prepare derivative works. The other two verbs in this clause are unambiguous because they are statutory terms of art. But the drafters of the contract (the defendants) chose not to use the third term of art – "prepare derivative works." Instead they used the vague term "use." This suggests that the parties intended "use" to mean something other than simply "prepare derivative works." They may have intended it to mean something more than prepare derivative works or perhaps something less. It is very possible that they intended it to mean only prepare derivative works. But their intention is not clear from the contract's text, and so this term is "ambiguous." Thus the parties should be given the opportunity to create a record to show what meaning was intended, and doubts should be construed against the drafters to the extent doing so does not otherwise frustrate the intentions of the parties. Thus I would reverse the district court's dismissal.

Notes and Questions

1. *"Use."* In the Patent Act, "use" is one of the statutory exclusive rights granted to a patentee, but the term is not defined in the Copyright Act. Should copyright law look to patent law when the word "use" is employed in a copyright license? Or should general dictionary definitions apply? For example, *Webster's New Collegiate Dictionary* defines the word "use" as "legal enjoyment of property that consists in its employment, occupation, exercise or practice." Should a dictionary definition be controlling? What about normal usage of the term within the trade? What might "use" mean if not "prepare derivative works"?

2. *Derivative works and trade usage.* Though the parties in *Kennedy* may not have been very precise about the right to make derivative works, parties in industries that depend on the making of derivatives as their life's blood (such as the literary and entertainment industries) are careful to delineate this right extremely carefully. How do you think that an agreement relating to the publication of a book, the translation of the book into another language, or the adaptation of a book for a film might address the issue of derivative works? Do you think that such agreements would simply grant a publisher or production company the right to "use" the licensed book?

3. *Improvements beyond copyright.* Questions regarding a licensee's right to produce modified versions of a licensed work are not exclusive to the copyright licenses. Though the term "derivative work" is unique to the Copyright Act, patent and know-how licenses often address similar issues using the terminology of "improvements." Thus, a licensee may be granted the right to make improvements to a licensed technology or may be expressly prohibited from doing so (though such a prohibition could run afoul of misuse and other rules, as we will see in Chapter 24). Trademark licensees are generally not permitted to create derivatives, modifications or improvements of the marks they are licensed. Why do you think this is the case?

4. *Ownership of improvements and derivatives.* Assuming that a licensee makes derivative works or improvements of a licensed work or technology, who owns such new works? Under US law there is a significant split between patent and copyright law in this regard. Under patent law, the inventor of an improvement to a patented invention will own that improvement, even though the improver may not be able to exploit that improvement without a license from the owner of the underlying (improved) invention. By the same token, the owner of the improved invention will have no right to use the patented improvement without a license from the improver. The patent on the improvement is thus called a "blocking patent." Copyright law is different. Under Section 106 of the Copyright Act, a derivative of a copyrighted work may not be made without the authorization of the copyright owner. There is no copyright at all in an unauthorized derivative work – the derivative is simply in the public domain. Does this divergence between patent and copyright law make sense?[1] Which approach do you prefer?

5. *Derivatives abroad.* European copyright law generally treats derivatives of copyrighted works similarly to improvements of patented inventions – the creator owns them. Which system to you think is preferable – that of the United States or Europe?

---

[1] Judge Richard Posner offers a possible economic justification for the different treatment of improvements under patent and copyright law: technological improvement is typically a continuous, collaborative process, and allowing unauthorized improvers to patent their improvements encourages maximum participation in efforts to improve the originally patented process or product. Progress is much less pronounced in the arts; we do not think that after Shakespeare wrote each of his plays, other playwrights would have been well employed trying to improve them. Richard A. Posner, *Intellectual Property: The Law and Economics Approach*, 19 J. Econ. Persp. 57, 70 (2005).

9.1.2 *Grantbacks*

If a licensee of an IP right creates an authorized derivative or improvement based on that IP right, it will generally be owned by the licensee – its creator. But an IP licensing agreement can attach requirements to the ownership or licensing of that derivative work. At one extreme, the licensor of the original IP right can require that the licensee assign back to it all derivatives and improvements based on the originally licensed IP. Short of an assignment of ownership, a licensor can require that the licensee grant it a license to use and otherwise exploit such derivative works. Such a license running from a licensee back to the licensor is often called a "grantback" license.

In some cases, grantbacks can be royalty-free – simply treated as part of the consideration paid by the licensee for the original license grant from the licensor. In other cases, the grantback license may be subject to royalties at a rate negotiated at the time of the original grant or which will be negotiated once the derivative or improvement is made.

The following discussion of grantback clauses dates to 1975, but is still relevant today.

> There are two principal reasons for the inclusion of grant-back clauses in patent licensing agreements. First, licensors who produce under their own patents or consider doing so may insist on a grantback clause to assure future access to improvement patents developed by their licensees. If the licensee develops a patentable improvement to the licensor's patent and becomes the sole patentee under that improvement patent, he alone will be able to exploit the improved technology while the licensor may be left with an obsolete and useless process. A grant-back provision in the licensing agreement protects the licensor from this result. A patentee may prefer not to sell rights to his patent without the assurance that he will not be forced to compete with his licensees at a disadvantage.
>
> Second, the parties may negotiate a grant-back arrangement to ensure unified control over an entire process. Just as a large undeveloped tract of urban land is more valuable than the sum of its constituent parts, an entire patented process is more valuable than the aggregate value of the component patents. The parties may, therefore, use grant-backs to maximize the overall efficiency of their relationship.[2]

EXAMPLE: GRANTBACK

Licensee hereby grants to Licensor a nonexclusive [1], worldwide, royalty-free, paid-up, irrevocable, fully sublicensable right and license to [exploit all *rights* [2]] in and to any derivative works, modifications and improvements made by or for the Licensee that include or are based upon the Licensed IP ("Improvements"). Licensee shall notify Licensor of each such Improvement and shall deliver all such Improvements to Licensor within [three (3) business days] after they are made [3].

DRAFTING NOTES

[1] *Exclusivity* – a grantback license may be exclusive or nonexclusive. An exclusive grantback requires the licensee to cede all rights in its improvements to the original licensor, a somewhat harsh requirement that would likely disincentivize the licensee from

[2] Richard Schmalbeck, *The Validity of Grant-Back Clauses in Patent Licensing Agreements*, 42 U. Chi. L. Rev. 733, 735 (1975).

making any improvements at all. If the licensor wishes to obtain exclusive rights to improvements, perhaps because it desires to incorporate all such improvements into later versions of its own products, the licensee could be permitted to retain a license to use its improvements internally, without the right to distribute them to others.

[2] *Rights granted* – like any license, a grantback license must specify what rights are being granted. When considering this question, ask what the purpose of the grantback license is. Is it intended to enable the original licensor to incorporate the licensee's work into its own products? If so, the grantback license should be quite broad. Is it to enable the licensor to use the licensee's work in its own enterprise? If so, then the grantback license can be limited to internal use, and exclude the right to distribute further.

[3] *Delivery* – a delivery obligation is often overlooked in grantback clauses, but it is important if the licensor has no way to know what developments the licensee is making with respect to the licensed IP. The timing of delivery may vary based on the type of technology or work being developed. A three-day delivery requirement is stringent, but could be important, for example, if the licensed IP relates to a vaccine technology that the licensee is testing for immediate use. If, on the other hand, the agreement relates to a film script or novel being translated into a foreign language, then delivery of the derivative work may be appropriate once completed, or a specified number of months after the license is granted.

Notes and Questions

1. *Why grantbacks?* Why do you think that a licensor might insist on a grantback clause in an IP licensing agreement? What concerns might a licensee have with respect to agreeing to such a term?

2. *Grantbacks and antitrust.* Grantback licenses can be used by licensors to extend the scope of their IP rights, thereby stifling competition, and have thus been subject to scrutiny by antitrust enforcement agencies (see Chapter 25). In their 2017 *Antitrust Guidelines for the Licensing of Intellectual Property*, the US Department of Justice and Federal Trade Commission make the following observations about grantbacks:

Grantbacks can have procompetitive effects, especially if they are nonexclusive. Such arrangements provide a means for the licensee and the licensor to share risks and reward the licensor for making possible further innovation based on or informed by the licensed technology, and both of these benefits promote innovation in the first place and promote the subsequent licensing of the results of the innovation. Grantbacks may adversely affect competition, however, if they substantially reduce the licensee's incentives to engage in research and development and thereby limit rivalry.

A non-exclusive grantback allows the licensee to practice its technology and license it to others. Such a grantback provision may be necessary to ensure that the licensor is not prevented from effectively competing because it is denied access to improvements developed with the aid of its own technology. Compared with an exclusive grantback, a non-exclusive grantback, which leaves the licensee free to license improvements technology to others, is less likely to harm competition.

Why do the antitrust agencies express concern with exclusive grantback licenses? How might the use of grantback licenses impact innovation?

3. *Share-alike and copyleft*. Grantback clauses typically require a licensee to grant a license to its licensor. In some cases, however, a license agreement will require the licensee to grant rights in its derivative works to a broad category of users or to the public at large. These provisions often occur in open source software licenses and Creative Commons online content licenses and are referred to as "share-alike" or "copyleft" licenses, and are discussed in greater detail in Section 19.2.

4. *Consumer grantbacks*. Below is a clause from an end user license agreement for a 3D printer:

> Customer hereby grants to Stratasys a fully paid-up, royalty-free, worldwide, non-exclusive, irrevocable, transferable right and license in, under, and to any patents and copyrights enforceable in any country, issued to, obtained by, developed by or acquired by Customer that are directed to 3D printing equipment, the use or functionality of 3D printing equipment, and/or compositions used or created during the functioning of 3D printing equipment … that is developed using the Products and that incorporates, is derived from and/or improves upon the Intellectual Property and/or trade secrets of Stratasys. Such license shall also extend to Stratasys' customers, licensors and other authorized users of Stratasys products in connection with their use of Stratasys products.[3]

> This license grants the printer manufacturer an irrevocable, royalty-free license to any IP pertaining to 3D printers that is created by a user while using the printer. Is this clause reasonable? How far can such grantback clauses go? Could the manufacturer also seek a royalty-free copyright or design patent license covering anything that the user prints on the printer? Keep these questions in mind when you read Chapter 24 covering IP misuse.

Problem 9.1

OverView Systems is the developer of the widely used "FloorMaster" software system for managing factory automation. Malden Robotics has developed a new humanoid robot, the "T-1000," that accurately mimics human motions. Malden Robotics would like to adapt the T-1000 for use in automotive plants and other factory settings. To do so, Malden Robotics needs to develop a software module that makes the T-1000 compatible with FloorMaster. Assume that you represent OverView, which is willing to grant Malden Robotics a license to "use" FloorMaster internally solely for the purposes of developing the T-1000 compatibility module. Should OverView insist on a grantback clause in this license? If so, draft the terms of the grantback and explain why you have requested them.

9.2 LICENSOR DEVELOPMENTS: COMMISSIONED WORKS

In Section 2.2 we discussed the work made for hire doctrine under copyright law, which establishes when the copyright in a commissioned work is owned by the commissioning party, as opposed to the creator. Yet there are many issues beyond the default rules for ownership that arise in the context of commissioned works and technology development.

9.2.1 *Allocation of IP for Commissioned Works*

When a work – whether it is a public sculpture, a screenplay or a software system – is commissioned, it is usually in the parties' interest to specify who will own the work that is produced and delivered, rather than relying on the default legal rules of ownership.

---

[3] www.stratasys.com/legal/terms-and-conditions-of-sale. Thanks to Professor Lucas Osborne for bringing this clause to my attention.

In the simplest cases this is merely a question of whether the developer or the customer will own the work, the answer to which is often dictated by industry norms and practices. For example, when a magazine or website commissions a freelance photographer to shoot a celebrity wedding, the copyright in the resulting photos is often retained by the photographer, while the magazine obtains a license to print one or more selected photos. But when a business hires a web designer to create a new corporate website, the copyright in the site is usually transferred to the business upon payment of the design fee. Complications arise, however, in more involved transactions.

9.2.1.1 Customizations

In some cases a customer may engage a developer not to create a new software system from scratch, but to modify an existing platform to work in the customer's environment. For example, a software vendor may have a system that manages logistics for the shipment of products around the world. A distributor in the wine and spirits business may wish to use the platform, but requires modifications to account for specific alcohol excise taxes and transport restrictions that are imposed by different US states and countries. In this case, the vendor is unlikely to assign the customer the copyright in the basic software system. However, the vendor *may* be willing to transfer copyright in the alcohol-specific customizations to the customer. On the other hand, the vendor may predict that the customizations that it develops relating to the wine and spirits trade may translate to other regulated industries, such as pharmaceuticals (not to mention other wine and spirits distributors). The vendor may thus be reluctant to assign copyright in those customizations to its customer. At this point, the parties must work out a mutually satisfactory business solution. Among the almost limitless possibilities are the following:

- The vendor retains copyright in the customizations, but agrees that it will not license them to any other wine or spirits distributor for a period of five years.
- The vendor retains copyright in the customizations, but agrees to pay the customer a royalty of 5 percent if it licenses them to any other wine or spirits distributor and a royalty of 2 percent if it licenses them to a customer in any other industry, which royalty obligation will expire ten years after delivery of the original customizations to the customer.
- The vendor transfers copyright to the customer, but retains a license authorizing it to create derivative works of the customizations for use in industries other than wine and spirits.

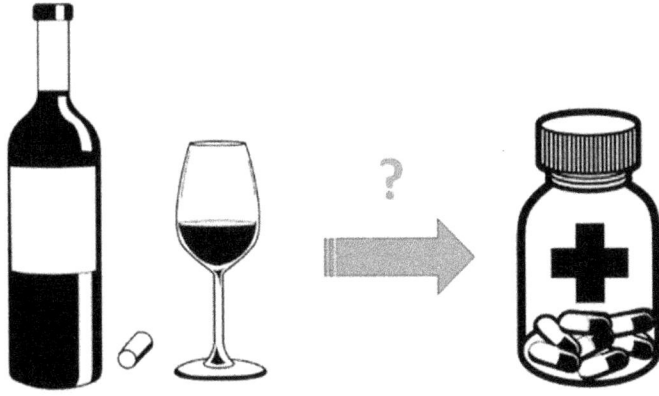

FIGURE 9.1 To what degree might a software logistics system customized for the wine and spirits market be useful in the pharmaceuticals market? The answer will dictate the degree to which the vendor wishes to retain rights to those customizations.

9.2.1.2 Third-Party Components

Many complex software systems, electronic devices and pieces of industrial equipment include technology and IP that are not originated by the vendor that makes delivery to a customer. As a result, a variety of third-party IP must be sublicensed by the vendor to its customer. In some cases the vendor's licensing terms may be sufficiently broad to encompass the rights extended by the third parties whose technology is included in its delivery. For example, the license agreement for Apple's Big Sur version of its MacOS operating system contains the following language:

A. The Apple software (including Boot ROM code), *any third party software*, documentation, interfaces, content, fonts and any data accompanying this License whether preinstalled on Apple-branded hardware, on internal storage, on removable media, on disk, in read only memory, on any other media or in any other form (collectively the "Apple Software") are licensed, not sold, to you by Apple Inc. ("Apple") for use only under the terms of this License. Apple *and/or Apple's licensors* retain ownership of the Apple Software itself and reserve all rights not expressly granted to you. You agree that the terms of this License will apply to any Apple-branded application software product that may be preinstalled on your Apple-branded hardware, unless such product is accompanied by a separate license, in which case you agree that the terms of that license will govern your use of that product (emphasis added).

> ...

P. Third Party Software. Apple has provided as part of the Apple Software package, and may provide as an upgrade, update or supplement to the Apple Software, access to certain third party software or services as a convenience. To the extent that the Apple Software contains or provides access to any third party software or services, Apple has no express or implied obligation to provide any technical or other support for such software or services. Please contact the appropriate software vendor, manufacturer or service provider directly for technical support and customer service related to its software, service and/or products.[4]

In some cases, however, third-party licensors may insist on including their own terms in the license granted by the vendor. For example, the Apple BigSur license also contains the following clause (and several more like it):

This product is licensed under the MPEG-4 Visual Patent Portfolio License for the personal and non-commercial use of a consumer for (i) encoding video in compliance with the MPEG-4 Visual Standard ("MPEG-4 Video") and/or (ii) decoding MPEG-4 video that was encoded by a consumer engaged in a personal and non-commercial activity and/or was obtained from a video provider licensed by MPEG LA to provide MPEG-4 video. No license is granted or shall be implied for any other use. Additional information including that relating to promotional, internal and commercial uses and licensing may be obtained from MPEG LA, LLC. See https://www.mpegla.com.

If a customer is concerned about the inclusion of third-party software or components in a deliverable that it is paying a vendor to develop for it, it may request that the vendor list all third-party components in a schedule and seek the customer's approval to include further third-party components in the system.

In addition to potential licensing issues, third-party components can present issues relating to performance, repair, maintenance, security and IP indemnification. As a result, customers are often justifiably wary of the inclusion of large numbers of third-party components in systems that are allegedly being developed to their specifications.

---

[4] www.apple.com/legal/sla/docs/macOSBigSur.pdf

9.2.1.3 Customer Materials

In many cases, such as the wine and spirits customization project described above, the vendor/developer will require information, data or even designs from its customer. The treatment of these "customer materials" is often a sensitive topic in licensing negotiations. On one hand, parties generally agree that the customer should retain ownership of such customer materials and that they should be treated as confidential information of the customer. However, disagreement can arise with respect to the ownership or use of customizations based on those customer materials.

9.2.2 *Technology Development Obligations*

Depending on the complexity and cost of a development project, the vendor's obligations may be spelled out in exceptional detail, including week-by-week tasks, deliverables, charges, required approvals and acceptance criteria.[5] The specifics of a development project are often listed in a "statement of work" or SOW – a document that is often created by technical and business personnel with minimal input from legal. It is a mistake, however, to assume that an SOW does not require careful legal review. Many SOWs, whether intentionally or not, contain significant legal obligations that can lead to disputes and eventual collapse of a relationship (see the case of *iXL*, below).

Depending on the generality of the services described in an SOW, many agreements also provide for individual projects to be authorized pursuant to work orders (also known as work releases and other variants). These documents, like SOWs, form part of the legally binding agreement between the developer and the customer, and are usually signed and appended to the agreement.

In addition to the documents detailing what work the developer must perform, many development agreements contain a document referred to as a specification ("spec"). The specification is generally a technical requirements document jointly developed by the parties which outlines the functionality, performance, reliability and other technical criteria for the system being developed.

In most complex development projects, issues are discovered during the course of development – either additional resources that are required by the developer, or additional requirements that the customer realizes that it has. When this happens, the parties may agree on one or more "change orders" to modify aspects of the then-current SOW or work orders. It is important to remember that change orders must be agreed by both parties – it is the rare agreement that allows one party alone to modify the performance obligations under an agreement.

EXAMPLE: CHANGE ORDERS

Neither this Agreement, nor any Work Order, may be modified or amended except via written Change Order signed by an authorized representative of both parties. If Client requests or Developer recommends changes during performance of a Work Order, Developer will provide Client with a written Change Order Proposal setting forth (a) a description of the

---

[5] A detailed analysis of each of these terms is beyond the scope of this book. For a discussion of technology development contracting practices, see Cynthia Cannady, Technology Licensing and Development Agreements (Oxford Univ. Press, 2013).

proposed change(s), (b) impact on price, (c) impact on the production schedule and (d) a revised Statement of Work. Client may, at its discretion, accept or reject any Change Order Proposal. A Change Order Proposal will be considered rejected if Client does not respond to the proposal within ten business days. If accepted, Change Orders will be effective upon execution by both parties. If rejected, Developer will be required to perform in accordance with any then-outstanding Work Orders according to their terms.

Notwithstanding the foregoing, Developer may make minor modifications to software design specifications if such modifications do not limit, diminish or affect the functional operation or use of the software or its output.

The following case illustrates some of the issues that can arise when a development agreement goes sour.

IXL, Inc. v. AdOutlet.Com, Inc.

2001 U.S. Dist. LEXIS 3784 (N.D. Ill. 2001)

SCHENKIER, MAGISTRATE JUDGE

I.

At its core, this case presents a basic contract dispute between iXL, Inc. ("iXL") and AdOutlet.Com, Inc. ("AdOutlet"). In its amended complaint, iXL claims that it entered into a contract with AdOutlet to provide consulting and web design services for a fee; that iXL provided the services; that iXL billed AdOutlet $2,913,708 for the work and expenses associated with those services; but that AdOutlet has paid only $1,195,505 of the billed amount, leaving a substantial shortfall that iXL now seeks to collect under theories of breach of contract, accounts stated, open book account, and quantum meruit. AdOutlet denies that it owes iXL anything beyond what AdOutlet already has paid; indeed, AdOutlet complains it has paid too much, and has asserted a breach of contract counterclaim seeking recovery of an unspecified amount for "significant costs and expenses" that AdOutlet allegedly has incurred because AdOutlet had to correct short-comings in iXL's performance.

iXL claims that AdOutlet is using computer source code property that iXL created, but for which AdOutlet has not paid, and that AdOutlet thus has committed misappropriation, conversion and unauthorized use of intellectual property in violation of common law, and copyright infringement … iXL has moved for a preliminary injunction, seeking to bar AdOutlet from using the computer code and intellectual property allegedly supplied by iXL on AdOutlet's web site.

On March 22, 2000, iXL and AdOutlet entered into a Master Service Agreement ("the Agreement"), pursuant to which iXL agreed to provide AdOutlet with consulting and web design services on an hourly fee and expense basis. As a substantial part of those services, iXL was to create computer "source code" to assist in the operation of AdOutlet's web site.

The Agreement contemplated that the specific tasks that iXL would perform, and the price for those tasks, would be set forth in separate Statements of Work ("S.O.W."), which would incorporate the terms of the Agreement.

Under the Agreement, iXL possessed the authority to "determine the method, details, and means of performing the services to be performed hereunder, subject to the standards set forth in the Statement of Work and the approval of Client, which shall not be unreasonably withheld." iXL warranted that it would perform services for AdOutlet "in material conformity to the specifications set forth in a Statement of Work contemplated hereunder in a professional and workmanlike manner." At the same time, the Agreement contained a disclaimer by iXL, stating that it did not warrant that its services would be "error free," or that AdOutlet would be able to obtain certain results due to the services provided by iXL, or that iXL was providing any warranty of merchantability, title, or fitness for a particular purpose.

The Agreement specified that for the services provided under the Agreement, AdOutlet "shall pay to iXL the fees in the amount and manner set forth in the Statement of Work," as well as expenses. The Agreement also set forth the remedies that iXL could pursue in the event of nonpayment by AdOutlet. If AdOutlet failed to pay for sixty days after the date of the invoice, the Agreement authorized iXL's "suspension of the performance of the services." The Agreement further provided that if iXL pursued legal action to recover on unpaid invoices, AdOutlet would be liable to pay "in addition to any amount past due, plus interest accrued thereon, all reasonable expenses incurred by iXL in enforcing this Agreement, including, but not limited to, all expenses of any legal proceeding related thereto and all reasonable attorneys' fees incurred in connection therewith."

The Agreement provided for various circumstances under which the Agreement could be terminated. For example, the Agreement provided that upon a default of payment by AdOutlet, which had not been cured within thirty days, iXL could terminate the Agreement upon written notice. The Agreement stated that upon termination of the Agreement for any of the specified reasons, AdOutlet "shall be obligated to pay iXL for all services rendered pursuant to any outstanding Statements of Work through the effective date of such termination."

Pursuant to the Agreement, the parties entered into six separate Statements of Work. The Statements of Work defined the "Services" that iXL would perform as those set forth in the Statement of Work, and "Works" as "all deliverables developed or prepared by iXL in the performance of Services hereunder." The Statements of Work contemplated that in performing Services and Works for AdOutlet, iXL would use certain "Pre-Existing Works" that already had been developed by iXL; that iXL also would use certain "Client Materials" obtained from AdOutlet, such as information and ideas; and that iXL would create certain new material for AdOutlet. Paragraph 3 of the consulting terms and conditions set forth the ownership rights in these three different categories of materials. Because it is central to the present motion, we set forth below that provision in its entirety:

> 3. "Work for Hire." Client shall retain all title to Client Materials, including all copies thereof and all rights to patents, copyrights, trademarks, trade secrets and other intellectual property rights inherent in such Client Materials. iXL shall not, by virtue of this Statement or otherwise, acquire any proprietary rights whatsoever in the Client Materials, which shall be the sole and exclusive property of Client. With the exception of Pre-Existing Works, the Services provided by iXL and the Works shall constitute "work made for hire" for Client … and Client shall be considered the author and shall be the copyright owner of the Works. If and to the extent that the foregoing provisions do not operate to vest fully and effectively in Client such rights, iXL hereby grants and assigns to Client all rights which may not have so vested, (except for rights in the Pre-Existing Works)

AdOutlet does not dispute that iXL actually worked the hours for which it billed AdOutlet.

During the summer of 2000, iXL sent portions of the source code to AdOutlet by e-mail. On or about October 1, 2000, iXL delivered to AdOutlet two compact discs containing the source code iXL created for the web site. As it was delivered to AdOutlet, the source code provided by iXL bore a legend stating that AdOutlet owns the copyright.

The payment disputes between the parties reflect the ongoing disagreements between the parties during iXL's performance of work ... AdOutlet claims that the source code prepared by iXL was fraught with defects, which over a period of several months iXL had difficulty in correcting and that, as a result, AdOutlet personnel had to fix. AdOutlet claims that the vast majority of the source code used for the AdOutlet web site thus was developed by AdOutlet, and not iXL.

While iXL does not directly dispute that it encountered some difficulties in supplying code and other information that met AdOutlet's requirements, iXL contends that iXL ultimately provided satisfactory code and other information – which iXL contends AdOutlet is using without paying for it.

Despite its criticisms about the quality of the code iXL supplied, AdOutlet admits that it has not exercised its option under paragraph 2.3 of the terms and conditions to the Statements of Work to reject the source code, to return it to iXL, and to terminate the Agreement. Rather, AdOutlet has installed the source code and continues to use it on its web site.

II.

The difficulty that iXL confronts is in establishing a likelihood of success on the proposition that iXL, rather than AdOutlet, is the owner of a copyright in the source code. On this point, iXL runs headlong into the language of the Agreement that iXL itself drafted. The Statements of Work specifically state that the Works and Services provided by iXL (which include the source code) are works made for hire for AdOutlet, and that AdOutlet "shall be considered the author and shall be the copyright owner of the works." This language plainly constitutes an express agreement that the source code is work made for hire, as required by 17 U.S.C. § 101. Under 17 U.S.C. § 201(b), the "person for whom the work was prepared [here, AdOutlet] is considered the author for purposes of this title, and, unless the parties have expressly agreed otherwise in a written instrument signed by them, owns all of the rights comprised in the copyright."

iXL contends that taken together, the Agreement and the Statements of Work show that the parties have "expressly agreed otherwise," by making full payment of the invoices a condition precedent to AdOutlet's ownership of the source code. In order for iXL to demonstrate likelihood of succeeding on this point, iXL must show both (1) that it is likely to succeed on its claim that AdOutlet breached the contract by nonpayment, and (2) that such a breach deprives iXL of ownership of the source code.

iXL has shown some likelihood of success on this first point. There is nothing here to suggest that the Agreement and the Statements of Work, signed by both parties, are not valid and enforceable. Nor is there any dispute that iXL has billed AdOutlet for some $2.9 million of time and expense that iXL actually incurred in providing services to AdOutlet, that AdOutlet has not paid nearly that full amount, and that as a result iXL has suffered injury – iXL admittedly has received some $1.7 million less than it billed AdOutlet. While AdOutlet asserts that iXL failed to perform adequately under the Agreement and that AdOutlet's failure to pay the full amount is thus not a breach, there is evidence that could establish AdOutlet has accepted iXL's work. The evidence shows that AdOutlet has not returned the source code submitted by iXL, and has not exercised the procedure set forth in the contract for termination upon iXL's failure to timely correct non-conforming works. To the contrary, the evidence shows that AdOutlet is using the source code developed by iXL on the web site, and that the source code developed by iXL is a critical component to the operation of AdOutlet's web site. Given these circumstances, the Court finds that iXL has established some likelihood of success on its claim of breach of contract.

However, iXL has not established a likelihood of success on the proposition that a breach of contract results in AdOutlet being deprived of ownership of the source code. The Statements of Work provide that the Services provided by iXL are "works made for hire" for AdOutlet. The Copyright Act provides that the person for whom the work was prepared is considered the author and owns the rights comprised in the copyright "unless the parties have expressly agreed otherwise in a written instrument signed by them." The Agreement and the Statements of Work contain no express agreement that AdOutlet will be considered the author of the source code and the owner of its copyright only after full payment of the invoices. Nor do these agreements state that AdOutlet is barred from using the source code in its web site if AdOutlet has failed to pay the full invoice amount. Indeed, when iXL delivered the CD ROMs containing the source code on or about October 1, 2000 – by which time AdOutlet already was nearly $900,000 in arrears in payment for more than 60 days – iXL nonetheless affixed to the code a legend identifying AdOutlet as the holder of the copyright.

In the absence of an express agreement, iXL attempts to cobble together an implied condition that AdOutlet cannot own (or use) the source code until it has made full payment of the invoice price to iXL. iXL points to two provisions in particular, neither of which bears the weight that iXL seeks to place on it.

First, iXL points to paragraph 2.2 of the terms and conditions of the Statements of Work, which state that AdOutlet "shall perform the tasks set forth in the Statement as a condition to iXL's obligations to perform hereunder." iXL claims that this language establishes that full payment by AdOutlet is a condition precedent to AdOutlet being deemed the author and copyright holder of the source code. iXL certainly could have made full payment by AdOutlet a condition precedent. But it is hard to read paragraph 2.2 as doing so. The word "tasks" is not defined in the Agreement or in the Statements of Work. The Court finds it plausible that paragraph 2.2 is to be read in conjunction with paragraph 2.4, which provides that iXL's obligation to meet contractual deadlines is contingent upon AdOutlet complying "in a timely manner, with all reasonable requests of iXL." But to construe "task" to mean "full payment" by AdOutlet, as iXL argues, would make no sense. Read that way, under paragraph 2.2 iXL would have absolutely no "obligations to perform" until AdOutlet first had paid the full contract price – which is clearly not what the parties intended, as measured both by the wording of the contract and the actual course of performance by the parties.

In this case, iXL drafted the Agreement and the Statements of Work, and negotiated it at arms length with AdOutlet. iXL had every opportunity, and presumably every incentive, to provide in the Agreement and the Statements of Work for adequate safeguards to insure payment – including a provision that conditioned AdOutlet's right of ownership in use of the copyrighted information upon payment of the full invoice price. Now that the contract has gone sour, iXL asks the Court to step in and provide it with a remedy (and with leverage) that iXL did not bargain for. The Court does not believe that iXL has shown some likelihood of succeeding in that effort.

Notes and Questions

1. *Third-party component anxiety.* Why might a customer be concerned about the inclusion of third-party components in a system that is being developed for it? What contractual provisions can the customer include in an agreement to mitigate the risk of these third-party components? To what degree would it be appropriate for the developer of a large enterprise software system to utilize the language about third-party components utilized by Apple in its Big Sur licensing agreement?

2. *Acceptance by use.* In *iXL*, the court makes note of the fact that AdOutlet did not reject the software delivered by iXL, but instead elected to use it to run its website. If AdOutlet were truly dissatisfied with the result of iXL's development project, what would you have advised AdOutlet to do?

3. *Conditions on use.* The court in *iXL* notes that "In the absence of an express agreement, iXL attempts to cobble together an implied condition that AdOutlet cannot own (or use) the source code until it has made full payment of the invoice price to iXL." Not surprisingly (given this lead-in), the court does not recognize the condition that iXL seeks to impose on AdOutlet's use of the software. If you had represented iXL, how would you have drafted the relevant contractual clauses to reflect your client's needs?

Problem 9.2

We-R-Toyz (WRT) is a national toy retailer that, in addition to selling products offered by Mattel, Hasbro and other leading manufacturers, has its own line of WRT toys. WRT's chief product designer, Max Headroom, has conceptualized a new baby doll that includes sophisticated software that can teach children up to five different languages (English, Spanish, Mandarin, Japanese and Swahili). He calls it "Baby Lingua." WRT's in-house design team has developed the plastic "shell" for the doll, as well as the software and hardware used to move its limbs and head. However, WRT lacks the in-house expertise to develop the language-teaching module.

As a result, Max wishes to contract with Dr. Beatrice Skinner, a world-renowned linguistic software expert and artificial intelligence designer, to develop the language-teaching module for Baby Lingua. Dr. Skinner is interested in the project, and has previously developed software that teaches English and Spanish that could easily be ported into Baby Lingua's computer processor. She will require help, however, to adapt her software to teach Mandarin, Japanese and Swahili. She thinks that she can identify experts in Beijing, Tokyo and Nairobi to perform the necessary work. Given that the holiday season is only eight months away, and sufficient quantities of Baby Lingua will require at least two months to produce, time is of the essence.

As the attorney for WRT, create a prioritized list of the seven most important contractual provisions that will need to be included in any contract with Dr. Skinner for the Baby Lingua project. What concessions do you think Dr. Skinner will request with respect to these provisions, and how would you respond?

9.3 JOINT DEVELOPMENTS: FOREGROUND AND BACKGROUND IP

It is often beneficial for independent parties to cooperate on the development of IP. Such cooperative projects exist in all fields of IP development, from film production to pharmaceutical research to software coding to product design. And while industry-specific norms and customs often dictate many of the aspects of these relationships, they share a number of common features and considerations regarding IP ownership and licensing.

9.3.1 *Foreground and Background IP*

Joint development projects often involve both pre-existing and newly developed IP. Intellectual property that one party controlled prior to the commencement of the joint development project is often referred to as that party's "background IP." Background IP can also include IP that is developed by a party after the commencement of the joint development project, but outside the context of the project (e.g., within a different company business unit). This newly developed, but unrelated, IP is sometimes referred to as "sideground IP," but is also commonly grouped together with background IP.

Background IP is often licensed by the party that owns it to the other party for use solely in connection with the joint development project. This license is typically nonexclusive and will last only as long as the project continues.

Intellectual property that is developed as part of the joint project is called "foreground IP." Foreground IP can be developed by one party or by both parties together. The legal rules regarding joint ownership of patents, copyrights and trade secrets, as well as works made for hire and employment agreements, will play a role in determining how foreground IP is owned (see Chapter 2). For the purposes of this analysis, assume that some IP developed during a joint development program will be solely owned by one party or the other, and some will be jointly owned by both parties.

As discussed in Section 2.5, joint ownership of IP is often inconvenient, as it requires coordination of the prosecution, maintenance, licensing and enforcement of such IP. As a result, parties in joint development arrangements often agree to divide ownership of jointly developed IP so that only one party owns any given item of jointly developed IP. This division is usually accomplished by a simple assignment of rights by the party that wishes to transfer its joint ownership interest to the other party. Following this transfer, ownership of the jointly developed IP resides in only one party, which can then grant a license to the other party in appropriate fields (see Section 9.3.2). In many cases this license will be irrevocable to ensure that a party is not divested of its right to ongoing use of IP that it helped to develop.

9.3.2 *Joint and Reserved Fields*

Most joint development agreements include a definition of the "joint field" in which the parties will conduct joint IP development. It is important to define this joint field carefully, as the parties often grant each other rights in their valuable background IP that they use or have licensed in other fields.

In addition to the joint field, each party often stakes out a "reserved field" of use that is core to its own business. A party's reserved field is often designated as a "no-fly zone" for the other party, at least with respect to jointly developed IP. That is, while the parties cooperate on the development of IP for use in the joint field, each may also agree not to tread on the other party's reserved field. For example, licenses of foreground IP often exclude the developing party's reserved field, and when joint IP is assigned to the other party, the developing party may retain a license in its own reserved field.

9.3.3 *Payments*

It is not typical for parties to pay royalties with respect to IP licenses granted in connection with joint development projects, with a few exceptions. First, when a party solely develops IP, or jointly developed IP is based on a party's solely owned IP, it may be appropriate for the other party to pay a royalty for the use of that IP outside of the joint field (i.e., in the nondeveloping party's reserved field).

Table 9.1 illustrates how parties may allocate IP ownership and licenses with respect to IP that they bring to a project and develop during the course of a project. For example, Party A would grant Party B a nonexclusive license to use Party A's background IP, and any foreground IP that is derivative of Party A's owned IP, solely in the joint field. But with respect to Party A's foreground IP that is derivative of Party B's owned IP, Party A would grant Party B an exclusive license (or assignment), retaining only a license to use that IP in the joint field and Party A's field. These allocations are merely examples; actual IP allocations will vary based on the nature of the collaboration and negotiation leverage of the parties.[6]

TABLE 9.1 *Sample allocation of joint development IP rights*

Type of IP	Developer of IP	
	Party A	Party B
Background	Nonexclusive license to B in joint field	Nonexclusive license to A in joint field
Sole foreground (developer derivative)	Nonexclusive license to B in joint field	Nonexclusive license to A in joint field
Sole foreground (new)	Nonexclusive license to B in joint field and B's field (royalty-bearing)	Nonexclusive license to A in joint field and A's field (royalty-bearing)
Sole foreground (partner derivative)	Exclusive license to B for all purposes (or assigned to B), with nonexclusive retained license for joint field and in A's field	Exclusive license to A for all purposes (or assigned to A), with nonexclusive retained license for joint field and in B's field
Joint foreground (developer derivative)	B assigns ownership to A; A grants B nonexclusive license in B's field	A assigns ownership to B; B grants A nonexclusive license in A's field
Joint foreground (partner derivative)	A assigns ownership to B; B grants A nonexclusive license in joint field and A's field	B assigns ownership to A; A grants B nonexclusive license in joint field and B's field
Joint foreground (new)	Jointly owned; A grants B exclusive license in B's field	Jointly owned; B grants A exclusive license in A's field

Notes and Questions

1. *Joint ownership.* As noted above, and as detailed in Section 2.5, the joint ownership of IP requires coordination of the prosecution, maintenance, licensing and enforcement of such IP, which can be costly and time-consuming. As a result, many attorneys shy away from joint ownership of IP and seek to achieve similar results using a combination of sole ownership and exclusive licenses. But a large number of joint development agreements nevertheless provide for joint ownership of jointly developed IP. Why?

2. *Reserved fields.* Why do you think that parties tend to seek exclusive rights to jointly developed IP in their reserved fields? What happens if IP has application both in the joint field and a party's reserved field?

[6] For a more comprehensive treatment of these issues, see Ronald S. Laurie, Managing Intellectual Property Allocation in Joint Ventures, in Licensing Best Practices: Strategic, Territorial, and Technology Issues (R. Goldscheider & A. H. Gordon, eds., Wiley, 2006).

Problem 9.3

American Livery Vehicle (ALV), a large but sagging Detroit manufacturer of light trucks and vans, wants to get into the electric vehicle market. DuraVac is a Japanese consumer battery manufacturer that wishes to enter the market for high-voltage electric vehicle batteries. ALV and DuraVac wish to collaborate to develop a new automotive battery that will meet both of their business needs. Develop a table modeled on Table 9.1 that outlines how the IP brought to the collaboration, and any IP developed during the collaboration, would be allocated between the parties.

9.4 IP IN JOINT VENTURES

A joint venture (JV) is a business arrangement in which two or more independent parties contribute resources (e.g., technology, capital, labor, expertise, manufacturing or distribution channels) to pursue a specific business goal. The joint venturers then share risks, rewards and control of the JV. There are many possible forms of JV, but the two most common are (1) a contractual arrangement that assigns each JV party specified rights and responsibilities in pursuing the JV's business goals ("contractual JV"); and (2) the formation of a new entity to pursue the JV's business goals ("entity JV"). A contractual JV is no more than a contractual arrangement specifying a set of rights and obligations of the parties; as such, it is no different than many of the contractual relationships that we have already studied.

In an entity JV, each of the forming parties typically holds an ownership or control interest in the new entity (which is often a limited liability company or limited partnership) and contributes some assets to the JV entity, whether cash, IP, equipment, facilities, services or some combination thereof. The JV operates semi-independently, often hiring its own employees, producing whatever product or service it is formed to pursue, and earning revenue from the sale of that product or service to customers. It may then retain its profits to further invest in the JV business, or distribute some of its earnings to the member parties. An entity JV often has independent management, though the members exercise oversight through their seats on a board of directors or direct voting on the JV's activities. Figure 9.2 illustrates the two principal JV structures.

9.4.1 *IP Contributions*

The contribution that each JV member makes to an entity determines the size of that member's ownership share in the JV. In the simplest case, each member would contribute an amount of cash to the JV and would receive a proportional share of the JV's ownership interests. However, it is often the case that JV members bring different assets to the JV: some have the necessary

FIGURE 9.2 The two principal JV structures.

financial resources to fund the JV's activities, some have know-how and expert personnel, some have technology and IP rights. All of these contributions may be necessary to ensure the success of the JV, though valuing them appropriately may be difficult.

Contributions of technology and associated IP to a JV can be conceptualized in terms of background IP and foreground IP, as discussed in Section 9.3. The presence of the entity JV itself, however, complicates the picture, as the JV, in addition to each of the members, may either own or license the foreground IP developed by the JV or its members.

Much of the discussion of IP allocation in JVs relates to patents, but significant copyright, trademark and trade secret IP are also contributed to JVs.

9.4.2 *IP Allocations*

Unlike joint development projects and contractual JVs (discussed in Section 9.3), the development of IP within an entity JV focuses most development activity within the entity JV itself. Thus, licenses to the parties' background IP are granted not to the JV member parties, but to the entity JV. Likewise, one of the advantages of creating a JV is to localize development work in the joint field within the JV. Thus, it is likely that the JV members themselves will not be engaged in the development of foreground IP within the JV field. As a result, the various assignments and licenses by the parties contemplated by joint development projects (per Table 9.1) are often absent in an entity JV arrangement.

When the JV itself develops new IP in the joint field, it usually retains such IP with no licenses to its members, on the theory that the entity JV was formed to commercialize IP in the joint field to the exclusion of its members. But when the JV develops IP that is outside the joint field, the members may wish to exploit that IP, at least in their respective reserved fields. As a result, the JV may be required to assign or exclusively license this IP to the members in their reserved fields. Depending on the negotiation leverage of the JV, it may also require that these licenses be royalty-bearing. A slightly different approach may be appropriate when the JV develops IP that is a derivative of background IP licensed to it by a member. In this case, the JV may assign that IP to the member that owns the underlying background IP, while retaining an exclusive license in the joint field.

TABLE 9.2 *Sample allocation of JV IP rights*

Type of IP	Developer of IP		
	Member A	Member B	Joint venture
Background	Exclusive license to JV in joint field	Exclusive license to JV in joint field	N/A
Sole foreground (developer derivative)	N/A	N/A	Exclusive (royalty-bearing) licenses to members in their respective reserved fields
Sole foreground (new)	N/A	N/A	Exclusive (royalty-bearing) licenses to members in their respective reserved fields
Sole foreground (member derivative)	N/A	N/A	Assigned to member that owns underlying IP, with exclusive reserved license in the joint field
Joint foreground	None	None	N/A

9.4.3 *Exit*

One of the most important things to plan when forming an entity JV is how it will end, and what happens to the JV's assets and liabilities when it ends. Unlike a simple contract, which can generally be terminated by either party for various causes or without cause (see Chapter 12), an entity JV has separate legal existence, and its termination and dissolution are often more complex. Events triggering a termination of a JV include mutual agreement of the JV members, the withdrawal of a JV member or the sale of the JV, either to a third party or to one of the members. Upon the dissolution of an entity JV, the ownership of the JV's assets, including IP, must be disentangled, with attention to the rights that each member will acquire and responsibility for the JV's liabilities.

The following case illustrates the issues that can arise when the agreements constituting a JV inadequately address issues of IP ownership and the effects of the JV's termination.

Pav-Saver Corporation v. Vasso Corporation

493 N.E.2d 423 (Ill. App., 3d Dist., 1986)

BARRY, JUSTICE

This matter before us arises out of the dissolution of the parties' partnership, the Pav-Saver Manufacturing Company.

Plaintiff, Pav-Saver Corporation (PSC), is the owner of the Pav-Saver trademark and certain patents for the design and marketing of concrete paving machines. Harry Dale is the inventor of the Pav-Saver "slip-form" paver and the majority shareholder of PSC, located in Moline. H. Moss Meersman is an attorney who is also the owner and sole shareholder of Vasso Corporation. In 1974 Dale, individually, together with PSC and Meersman, formed Pav-Saver Manufacturing Company for the manufacture and sale of Pav-Saver machines. Dale agreed to contribute his services, PSC contributed the patents and trademark necessary to the proposed operation, and Meersman agreed to obtain financing for it. The partnership agreement was drafted by Meersman and approved by attorney Charles Peart, president of PSC. The agreement contained two paragraphs which lie at the heart of the appeal and cross-appeal before us:

3. The duties, obligations and functions of the respective partners shall be:

   A. Meersman shall provide whatever financing is necessary for the joint venture, as required.
   B. (1) PAV-SAVER shall grant to the partnership without charge the exclusive right to use on all machines manufactured and sold, its trademark "PAV-SAVER" during the term of this Agreement. In order to preserve and maintain the good will and other values of the trademark PAV-SAVER, it is agreed between the parties that PAV-SAVER Corporation shall have the right to inspect from time to time the quality of machines upon which the licensed trademark PAV-SAVER is used or applied on machines for laying concrete pavement where such machines are manufactured and/or sold. Any significant changes in structure, materials or components shall be disclosed in writing or by drawings to PAV-SAVER Corporation.
   (2) PAV-SAVER grants to the partnership exclusive license without charge for its patent rights in and to its Patent No. 3,377,933 for the term of this agreement and exclusive

license to use its specifications and drawings for the Slip-form paving machine known as Model MX 6 – 33, plus any specifications and drawings for any extensions, additions and attachments for said machine for said term. It being understood and agreed that same shall remain the property of PAV-SAVER and all copies shall be returned to PAV-SAVER at the expiration of this partnership. Further, PAV-SAVER, so long as this agreement is honored and is in force, grants a license under any patents of PAV-SAVER granted in the United States and/or other countries applicable to the Slip-Form paving machine.

...

11. It is contemplated that this joint venture partnership shall be permanent, and same shall not be terminated or dissolved by either party except upon mutual approval of both parties. If, however, either party shall terminate or dissolve said relationship, the terminating party shall pay to the other party, as liquidated damages, a sum equal to four (4) times the gross royalties received by PAV-SAVER Corporation in the fiscal year ending July 31, 1973, as shown by their corporate financial statement. Said liquidated damages to be paid over a ten (10) year period next immediately following the termination, payable in equal installments.

In 1976, upon mutual consent, the PSC/Dale/Meersman partnership was dissolved and replaced with an identical one between PSC and Vasso, so as to eliminate the individual partners.

It appears that the Pav-Saver Manufacturing Company operated and thrived according to the parties' expectations until around 1981, when the economy slumped, sales of the heavy machines dropped off significantly, and the principals could not agree on the

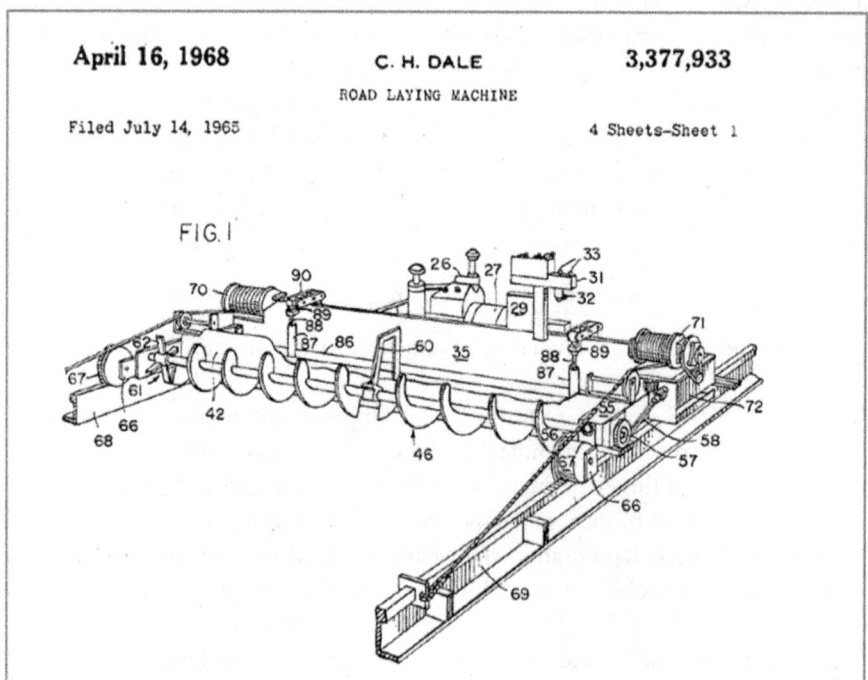

FIGURE 9.3 U.S. Patent No. 3,377,933 was assigned to Pav-Saver Corp. and licensed exclusively to the PSMC joint venture.

direction that the partnership should take to survive. On March 17, 1983, attorney Charles Peart, on behalf of PSC, wrote a letter to Meersman terminating the partnership and invoking the provisions of paragraph 11 of the parties' agreement.

In response, Meersman moved into an office on the business premises of the Pav-Saver Manufacturing Company, physically ousted Dale, and assumed a position as the day-to-day manager of the business. PSC then sued in the circuit court of Rock Island County for a court-ordered dissolution of the partnership, return of its patents and trademark, and an accounting. Vasso counter-claimed for declaratory judgment that PSC had wrongfully terminated the partnership and that Vasso was entitled to continue the partnership business, and other relief pursuant to the Uniform Partnership Act. Other related suits were filed, but need not be described as they are not relevant to the matters before us. After protracted litigation, the trial court ruled that PSC had wrongfully terminated the partnership; that Vasso was entitled to continue the partnership business and to possess the partnership assets, including PSC's trademark and patents; that PSC's interest in the partnership was $165,000, based on a $330,000 valuation for the business; and that Vasso was entitled to liquidated damages in the amount of $384,612, payable pursuant to paragraph 11 of the partnership agreement. Judgment was entered accordingly.

Both parties appealed. PSC takes issue with the trial court's failure to order the return of its patents and trademark or, in the alternative, to assign a value to them in determining the value of the partnership assets. Further, neither party agrees with the trial court's enforcement of their agreement for liquidated damages. In its cross-appeal, PSC argues that the amount determined by the formula in paragraph 11 is a penalty. Vasso, on the other hand, contends in its appeal that the amount is unobjectionable, but the installment method of payout should not be enforced.

In addition to the aforecited paragraphs of the parties' partnership agreement, the resolution of this case is controlled by the dissolution provision of the Uniform Partnership Act (Ill. Rev. Stat. 1983, ch. 106 1/2, pars. 29 through 43). The Act provides:

(2). When dissolution is caused in contravention of the partnership agreement the rights of the partners shall be as follows:

    (a) Each partner who has not caused dissolution wrongfully shall have,

       ...

      II. The right, as against each partner who has caused the dissolution wrongfully, to damages for breach of the agreement.

    (b) The partners who have not caused the dissolution wrongfully, if they all desire to continue the business in the same name, either by themselves or jointly with others, may do so, during the agreed term for the partnership and for that purpose may possess the partnership property, provided they secure the payment by bond approved by the court, or pay to any partner who has caused the dissolution wrongfully, the value of his interest in the partnership at the dissolution, less any damages recoverable under clause (2a II) of this section, and in like manner indemnify him against all present or future partnership liabilities.

    (c) A partner who has caused the dissolution wrongfully shall have:

       ...

      II. If the business is continued under paragraph (2b) of this section the right as against his co-partners and all claiming through them in respect of their interests in the

> partnership, to have the value of his interest in the partnership, less any damages caused to his co-partners by the dissolution, ascertained and paid to him in cash, or the payment secured by bond approved by the court and to be released from all existing liabilities of the partnership; but in ascertaining the value of the partner's interest the value of the good will of the business shall not be considered.

Initially we must reject PSC's argument that the trial court erred in refusing to return Pav-Saver's patents and trademark pursuant to paragraph 3 of the partnership agreement, or in the alternative that the court erred in refusing to assign a value to PSC's property in valuing the partnership assets. The partnership agreement on its face contemplated a "permanent" partnership, terminable only upon mutual approval of the parties (paragraph 11). It is undisputed that PSC's unilateral termination was in contravention of the agreement. The wrongful termination necessarily invokes the provisions of the Uniform Partnership Act so far as they concern the rights of the partners. Upon PSC's notice terminating the partnership, Vasso elected to continue the business pursuant to section 38(2)(b) of the Uniform Partnership Act. As correctly noted by Vasso, the statute was enacted "to cover comprehensively the problem of dissolution ... [and] to stabilize business." Ergo, despite the parties contractual direction that PSC's patents would be returned to it upon the mutually approved expiration of the partnership (paragraph 3), the right to possess the partnership property and continue in business upon a wrongful termination must be derived from and is controlled by the statute. Evidence at trial clearly established that the Pav-Saver machines being manufactured by the partnership could not be produced or marketed without PSC's patents and trademark. Thus, to continue in business pursuant to the statutorily granted right of the party not causing the wrongful dissolution, it is essential that paragraph 3 of the parties' agreement – the return to PSC of its patents – not be honored.

Similarly, we find no merit in PSC's argument that the trial court erred in not assigning a value to the patents and trademark. The only evidence adduced at trial to show value of this property was testimony relating to good will. It was unrefuted that the name Pav-Saver enjoys a good reputation for a good product and reliable service. However, inasmuch as the Uniform Partnership Act specifically states that "the value of the good will of the business shall not be considered", we find that the trial court properly rejected PSC's good-will evidence of the value of its patents and trademark in valuing its interest in the partnership business.

Next, we find no support for PSC's argument that the amount of liquidated damages awarded to Vasso pursuant to the formula contained in paragraph 11 of the parties' agreement is a "penalty." [T]he test for determining whether a liquidated damages clause is valid as such or void as a penalty is stated in section 356 of the *Restatement (Second) of Contracts*:

> Damages for breach by either party may be liquidated in the agreement but only at an amount that is reasonable in the light of the anticipated or actual loss caused by the breach and the difficulties of proof of loss. A term fixing unreasonably large liquidated damages is unenforceable on grounds of public policy as a penalty.

The burden of proving that a liquidated damages clause is void as a penalty rests with the party resisting its enforcement.

PSC has not and does not argue that the amount of liquidated damages was unreasonable. (Significantly, neither party purported to establish that actual damages suffered by Vasso were either more or less than $384,612.) PSC now urges, however, that "[t]he ascertainment of the value of the Pav Saver partnership for purposes of an accounting are [*sic*] easily ascertained. The accountants maintain detailed records of accounts payable and receivable and all equipment." In advancing this argument, PSC misconstrues the two-part test of a penalty: (1) whether the amount fixed is reasonable in light of the anticipated or actual loss caused by the breach; and (2) the difficulty of proving a loss has occurred, or establishing its amount with reasonable certainty. The difficulty or ease of proof of loss is a matter to be determined at the time of contracting – not, as PSC suggests, at the time of the breach.

It appears clear from the record that Meersman, with some insecurity about his partner's long-term loyalty to the newly formed partnership, insisted on a liquidated damages provision to protect his financial interests. Nonetheless the record discloses that the agreement was reviewed by Peart and not signed until it was acceptable to both parties. As of December 31, 1982, the date of its last financial statement prior to trial, Pav-Saver Manufacturing Company carried liability on notes owed to various banks amounting to $269,060. As of December 31, 1981, the loans outstanding amounted to $347,487. These loans, the record shows, were obtained primarily on the basis of Meersman's financial ability to repay and over his signature individually. The amount of liquidated damages computed according to the formula in the parties agreement – $384,612 – does not appear to be greatly disproportionate to the amount of Meersman's personal financial liability. As earlier stated, the slip-form Pav-Saver machines could not be manufactured and marketed as such without the patents and trademark contributed by Pav-Saver Corporation. Likewise, the services of Dale were of considerable value to the business.

In sum, we find there is no evidence tending to prove that the amount of liquidated damages as determined by the formula was unreasonable. Nor can we say based on the evidence of record that actual damages (as distinguished from a mere accounting) were readily susceptible to proof at the time the parties entered into their agreement. Suffice it to say, the liquidated damages clause in the parties' agreement appears to have been a legitimate matter bargained for between parties on equal footing and enforceable upon a unilateral termination of the partnership. We will not disturb the trial court's award of damages to Vasso pursuant to the liquidated damages formula.

We turn next to Vasso's arguments urging reversal of the trial court's decision to enforce paragraph 11 of the parties' agreement with respect to the manner of paying out the amount of damages determined by the formula. The paragraph provides for the liquidated sum to be paid out in equal installments over a 10-year period. The trial court held that the $384,612 owed by PSC should be paid in 120 monthly installments of $3205.10 each commencing with March 17, 1983. In support of its argument that it was entitled to a setoff of the full amount of liquidated damages, including the unaccrued balance, Vasso argues that the doctrine of equitable setoff should apply on these facts and further urges that such setoff is required by statute.

In considering whether the liquidated damages formula contained in paragraph 11 of the partnership agreement was enforceable, we necessarily scrutinized the totality of the agreement – not merely the dollar figure so determined. Certainly at first blush the formula appears to yield a suspiciously high amount that is not directly related to any anticipated damages that either party might incur upon a wrongful termination of the agreement by the other. The manner of payout however – equal installments over a 10-year period – appears to temper the effect that the amount of liquidated damages so determined would have on the party who breached the agreement. In our opinion, the validity of the clause is greatly influenced by the payout provision. What might have been a penalty appears to be a fairly bargained-for, judicially enforceable, liquidated damages provision. While, in hindsight, Vasso may sense the same insecurity in enforcement of the paragraph in toto that Meersman had hoped to avoid by insisting on the provision in 1974 and 1976, Vasso's concerns of PSC's potential insolvency are neither concrete nor sufficiently persuasive to entitle it to a right of setoff.

The primary authority cited in support of Vasso's equitable setoff argument is inapposite. There, the debtor was insolvent. In this case, PSC has been shown to have relatively little in operating finances, but has not been proved incapable of paying its creditors. Were PSC obliged to pay out the full amount of liquidated damages at this point, PSC's insolvency would be a certainty. However, PSC's assets and financial condition were known to Vasso at the time the parties agreed to become partners. Vasso cannot contend that its partner's potential insolvency in the event of a wrongful termination by it was unforeseeable at the time of contracting. We do not find that the equities so clearly favor Vasso as to require application of the doctrine of equitable setoff in disregard of the parties' agreement for installment payments.

Further, our reading of section 38(2) of the Uniform Partnership Act fails to persuade us that the statute requires a setoff of the liquidated damages. That section permits the partner causing the dissolution (PSC) to have the value of its interest in the partnership, less "any damages recoverable [by Vasso]" (subparagraph (b)) or "any damages caused [by PSC]" (subparagraph (c)), paid in cash. It does not require a cash setoff, however, in the unusual event (this case) wherein damages exceed the value of the terminating partner's interest.

Where, as here, a valid liquidated damages clause is enforceable, that clause may be implied into the statute to the extent that it does not violate the legislative intent of the Act. We do not believe that the legislative purpose of stabilizing business is frustrated by limiting Vasso's statutory setoff to past accrued damages and enforcing the payout terms of the parties' agreement. Under the circumstances, we perceive of no compelling grounds, legal or equitable, for ignoring or rewriting paragraph 11 of the parties' agreement. Therefore, all statutory references to "damages" recoverable by Vasso are supplanted by the parties' agreement for liquidated damages. As the trial court properly ruled, enforcement of the agreement results in a judgment for PSC in the amount of its share of the value of the partnership assets ($165,000) set off by past due installments of liquidated damages accrued from the date of the partnership's termination (March 17, 1983), and an ongoing obligation to pay out the balance monthly during the 10-year period which would end in March of 1993.

For the foregoing reasons, we affirm the judgment of the circuit court of Rock Island County.

Affirmed.

JUSTICE STOUDER, concurring in part and dissenting in part:

I generally agree with the result of the majority. I cannot, however, accept the majority's conclusion the defendant is entitled to retention of the patents.

The Uniform Partnership Act (UPA) is the result of an attempt to codify and make uniform the common law. Partners must act pursuant to the provisions of the Act which apply when partners have not agreed how they will organize and govern their ventures. These UPA provisions are best viewed as "default" standards because they apply in the absence of contrary agreements. The scope of the Act is to be determined by its provisions and is not to be construed to extend beyond its own proper boundaries. When the partnership contract contains provisions, imposing on one or more of the partners obligations differing from those which the law ordinarily infers from the partnership relation, the courts should strive to construe these provisions so as to give effect to the honest intentions of the partners as shown by the language of the contract and their conduct under it.

The plaintiff (PSC) brought this action at law seeking dissolution of the partnership before expiration of the agreed term of its existence. Under the Uniform Partnership Act where dissolution is caused by an act in violation of the partnership agreement, the other partners are accorded certain rights. The partnership agreement is a contract, and even though a partner may have the power to dissolve, he does not necessarily have the right to do so. Therefore, if the dissolution he causes is a violation of the agreement, he is liable for any damages sustained by the innocent partners as a result thereof. The innocent partners also have the option to continue the business in the firm name provided they pay the partner causing the dissolution the value of his interest in the partnership.

The duties and obligations of partners arising from a partnership relation are regulated by the express contract as far as they are covered thereby. A written agreement is not necessary but where it does exist it constitutes the measure of the partners' rights and obligations. While the rights and duties of the partners in relation to the partnership are governed by the Uniform Partnership Act, the Uniform Act also provides that such rules are subject to any agreement between the parties. It is where the express contract does not cover the situation or question which arises that they are determined under the applicable law, the Uniform Partnership Act.

The partnership agreement entered into by PSC and Vasso, in pertinent part, provides: 3.B.(2) [PSC] grants to the partnership exclusive license without charge for its patent rights … for the term of this agreement … [I]t being understood and agreed that same shall remain the property of [PSC] … and shall be returned to [PSC] at the expiration of this partnership …The majority holds this provision in the contract is unenforceable. The only apparent reason for such holding is that its enforcement would affect defendant's option to continue the business. No authority is cited to support such a rule.

The partnership agreement further provides:

11. … If either party shall terminate or dissolve said [partnership], the terminating party shall pay to the other party as liquidated damages [$ 384,612].

This provision becomes operative at the same time as the provision relating to the return of the patents.

Partnership agreements are governed by the same general rules of construction as are other written agreements. If their provisions are explicit and unambiguous and do not violate the duty of good faith which each partner owed his copartners, the courts should carry out the intention of the parties. The Uniform Partnership Act should not be construed to invalidate an otherwise enforceable partnership agreement entered into for a legitimate purpose.

Here, express terms of the partnership agreement deal with the status of the patents and measure of damages, the question is settled thereby. I think it clear the parties agreed the partnership only be allowed the use of the patents during the term of the agreement. The agreement having been terminated, the right to use the patents is terminated. The provisions in the contract do not conflict with the statutory option to continue the business and even if there were a conflict the provisions of the contract should prevail. The option to continue the business does not carry with it any guarantee or assurance of success and it may often well be that liquidation rather than continuation would be the better option for a partner not at fault.

As additional support for my conclusion, it appears the liquidated damages clause was insisted upon by the defendant because of earlier conduct of the plaintiff withdrawing from a former partnership. Thus, the existence of the liquidated damages clause recognizes the right of plaintiff to withdraw the use of his patents in accordance with the specific terms of the partnership agreement. Since liquidated damages depends on return of the patents, I would vacate that part of the judgment providing defendant is entitled to continue use of the patents and provide that use shall remain with plaintiff.

FIGURE 9.4 A Pav-Saver road-paving machine.

Notes and Questions

1. *JV allocations.* Table 9.2, illustrating a typical allocation of IP in an entity JV, differs substantially from Table 9.1, illustrating IP allocations in a typical two-party joint development arrangement or contractual JV. How do you explain the significant differences between these two frameworks for allocating IP?

2. *JV-developed IP.* If a JV develops IP outside of the joint field, it will often license that IP to its members in their respective reserved fields on an exclusive basis. Sometimes, the JV will charge the members royalties for these licenses. What justifies the granting of these exclusive licenses and the charging of royalties for them? Why is the situation different when the JV develops IP that is a derivative of the background IP licensed to it by a member?

3. *The Pav-Saver contributions.* In 1974, the Pav-Saver Manufacturing Co. (PSMC) was a classic three-party JV in which Dale contributed services, Meersman contributed capital and PSC contributed IP. Why do you think the JV was formed? Do these initial contributions seem reasonable to accomplish the JV's goals? Why do you think the JV was restructured in 1976 to combine the interests of Dale and PSC?

4. *A conflict of terms.* The PSMC JV agreement clearly contained drafting flaws, including the facially contradictory statements that the JV was intended to be "permanent" and could not be dissolved or terminated without the approval of both parties, and the statement that if either party terminated or dissolved the JV it would pay liquidated damages to the other. Is there any way to reconcile these statements? What do you think the parties intended when they drafted this language?

5. *The Pav-Saver result.* Following the dissolution of the PSMC JV, Vasso, as the party continuing to run the PSMC business, was entitled to retain the exclusive patent and trademark license originally contributed by PSC in exchange for a payment to PSC of $165,000 (the value of 50 percent of the business). PSC, on the other hand, was required to pay Vasso liquidated damages of $384,000 with no entitlement to the patent or trademark license. PSC thus emerged from the JV with a net cash loss of $219,000 as well as the inability to use its own patent and trademark in the business that it created. Is this result sensible? How could PSC have avoided this seemingly inequitable result?

6. *Another way?* In his dissent, Justice Souder argued that Vasso should not get the benefit of the exclusive patent license. Why not? How would Vasso operate the PSMC business without the benefit of the patent license?

7. *Trademarks and JVs.* Much of the discussion surrounding JV IP often centers on patents, but trademarks can be as, or more, important than patent rights in many JVs. In *Pav-Saver*, PSC granted the PSMC JV an exclusive license not only to its patents, but to the PAV-SAVER mark. Why did it do this?

   Unlike PSC, in many cases the members of a JV are not willing to allow the JV to use their proprietary marks to market or produce a new product. Why not? If this is the case, a new name is often devised for the JV and its product lines. The trademark rights in these names are often held by the JV itself. But what happens to those rights when the JV dissolves? As demonstrated by *Pav-Saver*, the parties should be careful to specify the fate of all JV-related IP upon a termination or dissolution of the JV.

Problem 9.4

Refer to the case *Pav-Saver v. Vasso*. You have been assigned to represent Pav-Saver Corp. (PSC) at the outset of the transactions described in the case. Draft a set of IP ownership/licensing (foreground and background) and termination provisions for the JV agreement that avoids the problems that arose in the case.

9.5 IP MAINTENANCE AND PROSECUTION

Patents and trademarks must be "prosecuted" through an examination process at the Patent and Trademark Office before they are issued as registered IP rights. After issuance, registrants must pay periodic maintenance fees and file required documentation in order to maintain these rights.[7] But, as discussed in Section 7.2.3, patent and trademark owners have significant latitude to protect, maintain and renew their registrations at their own discretion, and absent contractual requirements to the contrary courts have been reluctant to recognize any duty that they do so. Likewise, joint owners of IP generally have no duty to one another to maintain their jointly owned IP.

---

[7] See Section 8.7.

As a result, there are many circumstances under which it is necessary for the parties to an IP licensing agreement to specify which party will bear the responsibility for prosecuting and maintaining licensed IP rights, and how the parties will interact with respect to such matters.[8] Rights prosecution and maintenance are usually not a concern for nonexclusive licensees, but can be of significant importance to exclusive licensees as well as parties to joint development agreements and joint venture members.

9.5.1 *Responsibility for Prosecution and Maintenance*

Below are three different examples of clauses allocating responsibility for patent prosecution and maintenance. As you review these, consider how they differ and under what circumstances each would be most appropriate.

EXAMPLE 1: PATENT PROSECUTION (LICENSOR'S SOLE CONTROL)

Licensor shall have the sole right, in its reasonable discretion, to prosecute and maintain the patent applications and patents included in the Licensed Patents [, including defense of the patents against invalidity and opposition proceedings [1]], subject to Licensee's obligation to reimburse Licensor set forth in Section __ above [2].

EXAMPLE 2: PATENT PROSECUTION (LICENSOR'S FIRST RIGHT WITH LICENSEE STEP-IN)

Licensor shall have the sole right to prosecute and maintain the patent applications and patents included in the Licensed Patents, provided that for so long as Licensee retains exclusive rights under this Agreement, Licensor shall:

(a) notify Licensee of the status of the prosecution of all of the applications included in the Licensed Patents;
(b) consult with, and reasonably consider all suggestions made by Licensee in prosecuting the applications, and maintaining all issued patents, included in the Licensed Patents, including the countries in which to file and maintain applications and issued patents [3];
(c) notify Licensee of any intent, with respect to any country [3], to abandon or allow the lapse of any patent application or patent included within the Licensed Patents or not to oppose any action or opposition seeking to invalidate any patent [1]. Upon receipt of such notice, Licensee shall have the right, in its own name, to assume maintenance and prosecution of such patent application or patent in such country; and, in such event, Licensor shall execute such documents and provide such other documentation, data or assistance as shall be reasonably requested by Licensee to maintain or prosecute such rights, provided that upon the termination of the license(s) with respect to such Licensed IP, Licensee shall, at Licensor's request and expense, promptly assign to Licensor all of its rights in such foreign registrations and file all documentation necessary to transfer authority for such prosecution to Licensor or its designated agent [4].

---

8   Reimbursement for the costs of prosecution and maintenance is covered in Section 8.7. Responsibility for asserting licensed rights against infringers is covered in Section 11.2.

EXAMPLE 3: PATENT PROSECUTION (LICENSEE'S RIGHT)

Following the Effective Date, Licensee shall assume control, in its own name, over the prosecution and maintenance of the patent applications and patents included in the Licensed Patents at its sole expense, using counsel of its selection which are reasonably acceptable to Licensor. Licensee shall promptly provide to Licensor copies of all correspondence, applications, amendments, office actions, decisions and other materials relating to the prosecution and maintenance of the Licensed Patents. Licensor shall make its technical personnel reasonably available to Licensee, at Licensee's expense, to provide any technical or scientific information required in connection with the prosecution and maintenance of the Licensed Patents.

Upon the termination of the license(s) with respect to such Licensed IP, Licensee shall, at Licensor's request and expense, promptly assign to Licensor all of its rights in such foreign registrations and file all documentation necessary to transfer authority for such prosecution to Licensor or its designated agent [4].

DRAFTING NOTES

[1] *Invalidity proceedings* – in the United States, Europe and other countries, proceedings of various types (*inter partes review*, oppositions, etc.) can be initiated at patent offices to invalidate issued patents and trademarks. Because these proceedings are semi-administrative in nature, and are not part of court-based litigation, they are sometimes treated as part of the prosecution process.

[2] *Cost reimbursement* – as noted above, some licensors, particularly academic institutions, require that their exclusive licensees reimburse them for the costs of patent prosecution and maintenance. See Section 8.7 for a discussion of these provisions.

[3] *Countries* – some licensors will be accustomed to filing for protection only in the United States or a handful of major jurisdictions. A licensee that has global aspirations, however, may wish to secure protection in additional jurisdictions. Foreign filings can quickly become costly, however, so some licensors may not be willing to file in all countries desired by their licensees. Provisions such as these enable a licensee to assume control over foreign filings that the licensor is not willing to pursue.

[4] *Transfer back* – if the licensee is given the authority to prosecute patents in its own name in foreign jurisdictions, such rights must be transferred back to the licensor upon termination of the license. Otherwise, the licensor may be unable to grant worldwide rights to future licensees or exploit the rights in those jurisdictions itself. However, if the licensed IP is close to expiration, or of little value in a particular country, the licensor may not wish to assume such expenses. For this reason, a transfer back of prosecution authority should occur only if requested by the licensor.

9.5.2 *IP Management*

In some cases, such as joint development programs, joint ventures and large technology collaborations, the parties wish to make decisions regarding IP management collaboratively, rather than ceding this right to a single party, whether the licensor or the licensee. To do this, the agreement often calls for the formation of an IP management committee with a range of duties and responsibilities relating to IP management, prosecution and oversight. There are countless ways to organize such a committee, with one example set forth below.

EXAMPLE: IP MANAGEMENT COMMITTEE

Promptly following the Effective Date, the Parties shall form an IP Management Committee consisting of each Party's Project Manager, a representative of each Party's intellectual property office, and one other representative appointed by each Party. The Project Managers shall act as co-chairs of the Committee.

The Committee shall meet at least quarterly in person or via video conference. At least two representatives of each Party must be present in order for the Committee to conduct business. Decisions will be taken on the basis of majority vote.

The Committee shall have responsibility for the following functions connected with the IP generated by the Project:

a. evaluation of invention disclosures and decisions regarding which to advance to patent application drafting,
b. decisions regarding patent prosecution strategy, including jurisdictions in which to pursue protection,
c. selection of counsel and patent agents in various jurisdictions where protection is sought,
d. decisions regarding defense of oppositions and other challenges to patents,
e. decisions regarding licensing of project IP to third parties,
f. assessment of infringement threats and making recommendations to the Parties' management regarding enforcement of project IP against alleged infringers, it being understood that no litigation shall be commenced without the mutual written agreement of each Party [1],
g. development of an annual IP budget to be presented for review and approval by the Finance Department of each Party [2].

DRAFTING NOTES

[1] *Authority to litigate* – in general, an organization's upper management will need to be involved in any decision to initiate litigation. Thus, while an IP management committee can make recommendations, the final decision will usually rest with a party's management.

[2] *Budget* – this provision assumes that the parties will generally split the cost of IP management and prosecution. If one party will bear these costs alone, then a committee may have less authority over budgetary (and most other) matters.

Notes and Questions

1. *Nonexclusive licensees.* Why do you think that nonexclusive licensees are rarely given any authority over IP prosecution and maintenance? Are there arguments that a nonexclusive licensee could make to exercise greater control over the prosecution and maintenance of licensed rights?

2. *The impact of fields.* Examples 2 and 3 above assume that the licensee has an exclusive license in all fields of use. How should these clauses change, if at all, if the licensor has, instead, granted multiple licensees exclusive rights in different fields? Should each field-exclusive licensee have the right to dictate how the licensed rights are prosecuted and maintained?

3. *Countries.* Why might a licensee wish to protect licensed IP in more countries than the licensor? How might this strategy differ with respect to patents and trademarks?

4. *IP management.* Why do many joint projects have an IP management committee rather than a simple requirement that the parties mutually agree on decisions regarding IP management?

10

Representations, Warranties and Indemnification

In the preceding chapters we discussed a number of affirmative obligations and restrictions imposed on the parties under an intellectual property (IP) agreement. In this chapter we shift to consideration of representations and warranties – statements made by one party as of the time the agreement is executed that are intended to depict the state of the world (or at least the relevant IP) at such time. In many cases, representations and warranties are intended to induce the other party to enter into the agreement, and as such may be relied upon.[1] We next address a series of typical disclaimers of warranty and limitations on liability that are intended to allocate liability among the parties to an agreement. Further allocation of liability, usually for IP infringement, is addressed by the indemnification clauses of agreements, viewed by nonspecialists as particularly dense and impenetrable legal text that is best glossed over quickly – often to their later chagrin. This chapter concludes with a discussion of insurance requirements in license agreements, which further refine the liability exposure of the parties.

10.1 REPRESENTATIONS AND WARRANTIES

Consider the following case as you think about the types of warranties that a licensee of IP may wish to obtain from its licensor.

---

[1]   But see Roger Milgrim, Milgrim on Licensing § 23.01 (differentiating between representations and warranties as follows: "A representation is a statement as to the existence or nonexistence of a fact of state of affairs, or state of mind which acts as an inducement to contract … A warranty is a guaranty, an assurance of the existence or future existence of a fact upon which the other party may rely").

10.1.1 *Warranty of Title*

Loew's Inc. v. Wolff

101 F. Supp. 981 (S.D. Cal. 1951)

CARTER, DISTRICT JUDGE

This case raises novel questions concerning literary property and warranties, express and implied, in the sale thereof. On March 21, 1949, defendants, Victoria Wolf and Erich Wolff, sold to the plaintiff, Loew's Inc., a story in manuscript form entitled, "Case History." On that date, a regular form contract used by plaintiff was executed by the defendants. The present action is based upon alleged violations of certain provisions of this contract.

Erich Wolff, a doctor, specializing in cardiology, had met his former wife, Cathy, during chemistry lectures where she was a laboratory assistant at the institute at which he studied. Following their marriage, she later became subject to spells of extreme melancholia and attempted suicide. He investigated shock treatment and radium treatment for ovarian glands. Following her second suicide attempt, she submitted to radium treatment. A third suicide attempt followed and she died on May 22, 1942. A year and a half later, Doctor Wolff read articles in medical journals describing a pre-frontal lobotomy operation for melancholia and the marked change it produced in a patient's personality. [All of these events], as testified to by Dr. Wolff, were factual matters and in the public domain.

Victoria Wolf, a short story writer and novelist met Erich Wolff in 1943. Late that year, he first discussed with her the operation on the brain, known as a prefrontal lobotomy, as the basis of a story. She knew, and Erich Wolff told her of the tragic experiences of Wolff and his former wife. Wolff told her of the lobotomy operation; its cure of melancholia, and its transformation of the character of the patient. Due to other commitments, [however,] Victoria Wolf was unable to write the story for Erich Wolff at that time.

After his discussion with Victoria Wolf, he then contacted Elsie Foulstone, also a writer, and discussed the possibility of her aiding him in preparing a draft of the story for motion picture purposes. He told her of the facts above and she wrote a synopsis of a story entitled, "Swear Not by the Moon," based on those facts, plus additional fictional matter. The end product did not please Erich Wolff and he relieved her of any further duties.

Nothing further was done about the story until some time in 1945, when Erich Wolff again contacted Victoria Wolf and prevailed upon her to work on the story. In that year Victoria Wolf wrote a synopsis of a story entitled, "Through Narrow Streets," which was based upon the doctor's former wife's experiences, the doctor's description of a lobotomy operation and her own research concerning it, and additional fictional matter. Dissatisfied, she next wrote a revision entitled, "Brain Storm" and late in 1948 or early 1949, wrote a second revision entitled, "Case History," the story in suit. It was a combination of fact and fiction. As stated above, this story was sold to the plaintiff in March 1949 for $15,000.

The document executed by the parties was entitled "Assignment of All Rights." By its language, (Sec. 1) defendants Erich Wolff and Victoria Wolf transferred and sold to plaintiff all rights of every kind in and to the story and "the complete, unconditional and unencumbered title" thereto. Section 4 of the assignment provided that defendants represented and warranted that each was the "sole author and owner of said work, together with the title thereof"; and "the sole owner of all rights of any and all kinds whatsoever in and to said work, throughout the world"; that each had "the sole and exclusive right to dispose of each and every right herein granted"; that "neither said work nor any part thereof is in the public domain"; that "said work is original with me in all respects"; that "no incident therein contained and no part thereof is taken from or based upon any other literary or dramatic work or any photoplay, or in any way infringes upon the copyright or any other right of any individual, firm, person or corporation." ...

By Section 6, the defendants guarantee and warrant that they will "indemnify, make good, and hold harmless the purchaser of, from and against any and all loss, damage, costs, charges, legal fees, recoveries, judgments, penalties, and expenses which may be obtained against, imposed upon or suffered by the purchaser by reason of any infringement or violation or alleged violation of any copyright or any other right of any person, firm or corporation, or by reason of or from any use which may be made of said work by the purchaser, or by reason of any term, covenant, representation, or warranty herein contained, or by reason of anything whatsoever which might prejudice the securing to the purchaser of the full benefit of the rights herein granted and/or purported to be granted."

Section 7 provides that the sellers "agree duly to execute, acknowledge and deliver, and/ or to procure the due execution, acknowledgment and delivery to the purchaser of any and all further assignments and/or other instruments which in the sole judgment and discretion of the purchaser may be deemed necessary or expedient to carry out or effectuate the purposes or intent of these present instruments."

About three months after the execution of this instrument and the sale, Elsie Foulstone discovered that Erich Wolff had sold his story, and on July 1, 1949, plaintiff was notified that she claimed a portion of the proceeds of the sale because of the work she had done in 1944. On July 30, 1949, plaintiff made a demand on defendants that they obtain a quitclaim and release from Foulstone within a reasonable time or they would be compelled to rescind their agreement of March 21st. On September 21, 1949, Elsie Foulstone filed action in the Superior Court of the State of California, County of Los Angeles, naming Erich Wolff, Victoria Wolf and Metro-Goldwyn-Mayer Pictures as defendants.

[On] February 28, 1950, the Superior Court rendered a judgment in favor of defendants finding that Elsie Foulstone had no valid claim or interest in or to the story, "Case History" which was sold to the plaintiff. The present action was filed on November 2, 1949, prior to the above mentioned judgment.

At the conclusion of the trial, the court found:

1. That "Case History" was a different story from "Swear Not By the Moon," and that the only points of similarity were factual matters from the public domain.
2. That Erich Wolff collaborated with Elsie Foulstone on the story, "Swear Not By the Moon."
3. That there had been proved no fraud or fraudulent representations on the part of the defendants, Erich Wolff and Victoria Wolf.

The second cause of action, in addition to setting forth express warranties which we have found were not breached rests on plaintiff's claim to a "marketable and perfect" title, free from reasonable doubt. This raises the question of the existence and validity of what will hereafter be referred to as "implied warranties."

The plaintiff argues that an express warranty of "marketable and perfect" title, free from reasonable doubt, arose by the use of the words, "complete, unconditional and unencumbered title"; "sole author and owner of said work"; "sole owner of all rights of any and all kinds whatsoever in and to said work, throughout the world"; and "I have the sole and exclusive right to dispose of each and every right herein granted." Nowhere in this most comprehensive instrument can be found the words "marketable, perfect or free from reasonable doubt." Thus, in order to find such an express warranty it must be found that the words actually used in the "Assignment of Rights" were or are synonymous with "marketable and perfect" title.

No case has been cited by counsel nor can any be found by this court which holds that the phrase "complete, unconditional and unencumbered title" is synonymous with "marketable and perfect" title. The common meaning of the word "complete" is "Filled up, with no part, item, or element lacking." It means that the "whole" title has been given and that no part or portion of it has been kept by the seller or sold to any other person. In two cases involving the sale of real estate, the words "complete title" were found to mean the instruments which constitute the evidence of title, and not to mean the estate or interest conveyed.

The warranty of "marketability of title" is a warranty found almost exclusively in connection with the sale of real property. Such words as "merchantable title," "clear title," "good title" and "perfect title" have been held in cases involving the sale of land to mean the same as "marketable title." None of these words can be found in the present instrument. As used in this assignment the word "complete" was not meant to be synonymous with the word "marketable or perfect." It was used to mean just what the word indicated, i.e. "whole title," that is, that no other person owned any interest in the property nor was any kept by the sellers. In this respect, the plaintiffs got what they bargained for. It seems evident that the remaining words used in the assignment are not synonymous with "marketable or perfect" title.

Plaintiff argues that the law implies the warranty of marketable title in the sale of literary property. There are more than mere historical reasons for concluding that the doctrine of "marketable title" should be limited to cases involving the sale of real property. This doctrine has a basis in the traditional concepts of judicial fair play. Briefly, the doctrine developed because the courts at common law believed, and rightly so, that since the law required there be a recorded title in the sale of real estate, then that record title should be clear and free from reasonable doubt. A buyer, desiring to purchase the seller's land, would request that the seller deliver to him a "marketable" record of title to the property. If by searching the record, the title was free from reasonable doubt, it was proclaimed that the buyer had a "marketable" title and could not avoid the enforcement of the contract. If on the other hand, a defect appeared in the record title, then the common law courts felt that justice demanded that the seller either clear the record title or they would allow the buyer to avoid the contract. But the doctrine was not applied to the sale of personal property. At common law and with few exceptions the law as it exists today, there was no requirement that the sale of personal property be recorded. The doctrine of caveat emptor therefore prevailed. Without the application of this latter doctrine, it is highly doubtful that any sale of personal property would ever become final. There are no records to search. There is no way to ascertain that a cloud exists on the title. It is not a requirement that a record title be produced before a purchaser will buy the article in question. Thus, because of these differences between the sale of real and personal property, the courts neither then nor now could imply by law into a contract of sale of personal property the doctrine of "marketable" title. If they did so, then there would be no case in which the seller could rest in ease, for if any third person asserted a claim to the property the courts would be compelled to avoid the contract between the parties. To do this would be to place upon the seller an unsurmountable burden, and would leave the door open to allow a discontented purchaser to avoid any contract involving the sale of personal property.

For these reasons, in adopting the Uniform Sales Act the warranty of "marketable" title was conspicuously excluded. [It] is obvious that sales involving literary property are different in some respects from the sale of ordinary goods. The sale of literary property is more analogous to the sale of patents and patent rights. Both literary properties and patents are products of the mind, plus skill. Both utilize matters in the public domain. A review of patent cases confirms the position taken by this court.

The rule has been well put in the case of *Computing Scales Co. v. Long*, 66 S.C. 379. There the court said: "If, however, the vendor at the time of the sale knew of a valid outstanding title or encumbrance, and failed to give notice to the vendee, the element of fraud is introduced, and the vendee may rescind without waiting for actual loss to come to him. But mere dispute about the title, or the contingency of future loss, does not warrant a rescission, and, where the buyer returns the goods, and refuses to pay the purchase money, it is incumbent on him to show that there is a valid adverse claim, from which loss to him would inevitably occur. The application of the rule may sometimes result in hardship, but to adopt any other would make it possible for a purchaser to escape from his contract upon any claim coming to his notice, however, baseless or absurd it might be."

The above rules should be even more strictly applied in the sale of literary property. [In] *Golding v. R.K.O. Pictures, Inc.*, 1950, 221 P.2d 95, Justice Schauer of the Supreme Court of California refers to the fact that there are approximately thirty-six basic plots in all writing. Consequently, assertions of similarity and of plagiarism are practically a concomitant of all story writing. To establish then, a rule permitting the purchaser of literary property to return the property and demand back the purchase price upon a mere assertion of similarity or plagiarism is to create a right without the support of reason or principle, the exercise of which would result in untold hardship. There can be no other conclusion but that the law will not imply a warranty of "marketable" title in the sale of literary property.

Notes and Questions

1. *Recourse when defense is successful.* Under *Wolff*, are there any circumstances in which a licensee would have a claim under the licensor's warranty even though the licensee successfully defended against a third party? What injury would the licensee suffer under these circumstances?

2. *Comparison to leases.* Article 2A of the UCC, which relates to leases of personal property, contains the following warranty: "(a) There is in a lease contract a warranty that for the lease term no person holds a claim to or interest in the goods that arose from an act or omission of the lessor other than a claim by way of infringement or the like, which will interfere with the lessee's enjoyment of its leasehold interest" (UCC § 2A-211(a)). Is this warranty consistent with the result in *Wolff*? Should such a warranty be implied in license agreements, or is it peculiar to leases?

3. *Sole ownership.* Suppose that a license contains an express warranty that the licensor is the "sole owner" of a patent. A court then finds that another individual contributed to the invention and is a co-owner of the patent. Does this revelation constitute a breach of the warranty? What harm does the licensee suffer? Does it matter whether the license is excusive or

nonexclusive? See *Prudential Insurance Co. of America v. Premit Group*, 704 N.Y.S.2d 253 (N.Y.S.Ct. A.D. 2000) (discovery of the second co-owner was "an incurable material breach of defendants' warranty of sole ownership ... and properly released plaintiff from any obligation to make further royalty payments thereunder").

4. *Likelihood of invalidity.* What if the licensor is aware of facts that would likely make a licensed right invalid if challenged, such as prior art pertaining to a patent? In *Schlaifer Nance & Company v. Estate of Andy Warhol*, 119 F.3d 91 (2d Cir. 1997), the estate of Andy Warhol granted SNC a license to reproduce and market certain Warhol artworks, as well as his name and likeness, in the fashion, home decorating, gift, toy and entertainment industries. The license contained the following representations and warranties:

   (ii) the Artist is the sole creator and the Estate is the sole owner of the copyrights ... although certain elements of the Existing Artworks may involve or incorporate concepts in the public domain;

   (iv) except as noted on the Exhibit, the Estate has and will continue to have the sole and exclusive right to transfer to [SNC] all rights to the ... Works ...;

   (v) the ... Works [do not] infringe the rights of any third parties;

   (vi) neither the Artist nor the Estate has granted and the Estate will not grant any right, license or privilege for Licensed Products with respect to the ... Works or any portion thereof to any person or entity other than [SNC].

   The exhibit contained no exceptions (see Section 10.1.2, Note 6). Shortly after the license was granted, issues emerged regarding the estate's title and control over many of the works. Accordingly, SNC claimed that the estate's license of the works to SNC was fraudulent. The court rejected SNC's claim of fraud, holding that the circumstances of the transaction, including the disclaimers in the agreement, would have convinced any reasonable person that title in the works was uncertain. Do you agree? Are the considerations different for artistic works and technologies?

5. *Quitclaim.* In real estate transactions a transferor can transfer property without any warranty at all – a quitclaim transfer. Do such quitclaims exist with respect to IP transfers or licenses? Is this the effect of a license that lacks a warranty of validity and noninfringement?

FIGURE 10.1 After the Warhol estate granted rights in many of Andy Warhol's works to SNC, other deals began to emerge, including an exclusive license of Warhol's prints to a watchmaker.

6. *Industry-specific considerations.* In *Wolff*, the court concludes that "[t]he above rule [rejecting an implied warranty of "marketable" title] should be even more strictly applied in the sale of literary property," citing *Golding v. R.K.O. Pictures, Inc.*, 221 P.2d 95 (Cal. 1950). Do you agree? Are there other industries in which such a rule should be stringently applied? Are there any industries in which this rule should *not* be applied?

10.1.2 *Corporate Warranties*

The sample representations and warranties below are typical of a large IP licensing transaction between two sophisticated parties.

EXAMPLE: REPRESENTATIONS AND WARRANTIES

Each Party hereby represents and warrants to the other that [except as expressly set forth in the Disclosure Schedule attached hereto]:

A. *Due Organization.* It is a corporation duly organized, validly existing and in good standing under the laws of its jurisdiction of incorporation.

B. *Due Authority.* It has all necessary power and authority to execute and deliver this Agreement, and to perform its obligations hereunder.

C. *No Conflict.* The execution, delivery and performance of this Agreement and its compliance with the terms and provisions hereof does not and will not conflict with or result in a breach of any of the terms and provisions of, or constitute a default under or a violation of (i) any agreement where such conflict, breach or default would impair in any material respect the ability of such Party to perform its obligations hereunder; (ii) the provisions of its charter document or bylaws; or (iii) any Applicable Law, but, with respect to this clause (iii), only where such violation could reasonably be expected to have a material adverse effect on the ability of such Party to perform its obligations hereunder.

D. *Binding Obligation.* This Agreement has been duly authorized, executed and delivered by it and constitutes its legal, valid and binding obligation enforceable against it in accordance with its terms subject, as to enforcement, to bankruptcy, insolvency, reorganization and other laws of general applicability relating to or affecting creditors' rights and to the availability of particular remedies under general equitable principles.

E. *No Actions.* There are no actions, suits or proceedings pending or, to its knowledge, threatened against it or its Affiliates, which affect its ability to carry out its obligations under this Agreement or which challenge the validity or enforceability of the Licensed Rights.

F. *Ownership.* It is the record owner or registrant of the Licensed Rights in all relevant patent and trademark offices around the world, and there is no action currently pending or threatened challenging its ownership of such Licensed Rights.

G. *No Infringement.* [To its knowledge], as of the Effective Date, the practice of the Licensed Technology as contemplated by this Agreement will not constitute infringement or an unauthorized use of any patent, copyright, trade secret, proprietary information, license or right therein belonging to or enforceable by any Third Party.

H. *No Known Infringers.* It is not aware of any third parties that are practicing or infringing any of the Licensed Rights [other than parties to those licensing agreements listed in Exhibit H].

I. *No Other Licensees.* [uscd only if license is exclusive] As of the Effective Date, Licensor has not expressly or implicitly granted any right, title or interest in or to the Licensed Rights to any third party, nor permitted any third party to practice any of the Licensed Rights, whether with or without compensation.

Notes and Questions

1. *Corporate warranties.* Clauses A–E in the above example generally relate to the corporate good standing and authorization of a party to enter into the contemplated transaction. Most of these warranties should be expected of any reputable company doing business. Why are they expressly stated in an agreement?

2. *Material adverse effect.* In Clause C there is a qualification at the end to the effect that a failure of a party's performance to comply with applicable law will constitute a violation of the warranty only if it "could reasonably be expected to have a material adverse effect on the ability of such Party to perform its obligations." Why would the parties agree to excuse some forms of legal noncompliance in this manner? What is "material"? What kind of legal noncompliance might not have a material adverse effect (often referred to as an "MAE") on a party's performance?

3. *Intellectual property.* Clauses F and G pertain to IP. Not all agreements relating to IP have an express warranty concerning IP. Rather, many of them address IP issues through the indemnification clause discussed in Section 10.3. What are pros and cons of addressing IP issues in representations and warranties versus indemnity?

4. *Knowledge.* Clause G begins with the qualifier "To its knowledge." This is a common qualifier in representations and warranties and limits the scope of the representation to things known to the party. Just as in a contract for the sale of residential real estate, the seller is required to disclose all *known* defects in the property; an IP licensor will often argue that it cannot make any representation regarding potential IP infringements of which it is not aware. However, knowledge qualifiers in representations and warranties in IP licenses are generally more contentious and complex than they are in real estate purchase agreements. For example, whose knowledge is being assessed? That of the members of a party's engineering department? Its legal department? The executive who signed the agreement? Is knowledge "actual" or "constructive" (i.e., is there some duty of due inquiry or investigation)? What argument might a licensee make to eliminate the knowledge qualifier from the representation in Clause G? When would such an argument be successful?

5. *No other licensees.* The representation in Clause I is appropriate when an exclusive license has been granted. It assures the licensee that no other licenses, express or implicit, have previously been granted by the licensor. In considering why such a representation is not applicable to a nonexclusive license, see *Western Electric Co. v. Pacent Reproducer Corporation*, 42 F.2d 116, 116 (2d Cir. 1930), *cert. denied*, 282 U.S. 873 (1930), in which the court commented: "the patent owner may freely license others, or may tolerate infringers, and in either case no right of the [nonexclusive] patent licensee is violated. Practice of the invention by others may indeed cause him pecuniary losses, but it does him no legal injury … Infringement of the patent can no more be a legal injury to a bare licensee than a trespass upon Blackacre could be an injury to one having a nonexclusive right of way across Blackacre." Do you see any value in a nonexclusive licensee's learning about prior licensees of the licensed rights?

6. *The disclosure schedule.* In some cases a licensor cannot honestly make the statement that is set forth in a representation or warranty. The licensed IP may, in fact, be infringed by others,

an allegation of infringement may have been made against the licensor, or a third party may have a previously granted right thereto. If this is the case, and the licensor cannot give a "clean" representation or warranty, the agreement often permits the licensor to disclose these facts in a separate disclosure schedule that is delivered prior to executing the agreement and which becomes integrated into the agreement. If the licensor discloses a "breach" of a representation or warranty in the disclosure schedule, then the licensor is not liable for that breach on the theory that the licensee entered into the agreement with full knowledge. If the licensee does not wish to relieve the licensor of that particular liability, or to enter into the agreement knowing of the risk disclosed in the schedule, then the licensee may decline to execute the agreement, complete the transaction without penalizing the licensor for the disclosed matter, negotiate a reduction in the consideration, or include a specific indemnification by the licensor pertaining to the disclosed matter.

10.1.3 *Performance Warranties*

When the licensor provides the license with software, equipment, chemical reagents or other materials in addition to intangible IP rights, then the licensor will sometimes provide warranties regarding the operation or performance of those materials.

10.1.3.1 Compliance with Specifications

The most common formulation for such performance warranties is that these materials will operate "[substantially] in accordance with their Specifications and Documentation." "Specifications" are written technical documents that are agreed by the parties and appended to the agreement as an exhibit or appendix. They generally detail the technical features, dimensions and capabilities of the licensed product or materials. Documentation, on the other hand, generally refers to the standard descriptive documentation produced by the licensor and describing the licensed product or materials. It is typically less detailed than specifications. The licensee should try to ensure that such documents are as detailed and complete as possible, and that they describe every element of the licensed materials that are important to it. If a licensed product received regulatory approval, then reference may also be made to the licensor's disclosures to the relevant regulatory agency.

Licensees should also take careful note of "wiggle words" like "substantially" in performance warranties. What does it mean to operate "substantially" in accordance with specifications? Are insubstantial malfunctions acceptable? And how bad does an error need to be before it is substantial? Unfortunately, there are no clear legal rules that answer these questions, which are matters of fact unique to each specific case. If the licensee is concerned about such debates, then it should seek to eliminate from the performance warranty qualifiers such as "substantially," "materially" and the like.

10.1.3.2 Reliable Performance

In addition to compliance with specifications and documentation, a licensee may wish to ensure that a product will operate in a reliable and uninterrupted manner. Most specifications that describe the operation of a product do not include general reliability parameters, so these must often be added by attorneys to the warranties.[2] Licensors will argue against the inclusion of such general and open-ended warranties, which suggests that licensees should ensure that specifications contain as much detail as possible regarding the expected performance of licensed products.

10.1.3.3 Malicious Code

Recent reports of computer viruses and ransomware abound. Thus, when computer software will be delivered or provided, the licensee should consider requesting a warranty from the licensor that the code does not contain any computer viruses or other harmful code. This warranty is necessary in addition to typical warranties regarding software performance because harmful code need not impair the performance of the licensed software itself, but may instead give malicious parties access to the licensee's data or systems, or disrupt the operation of other software or systems.

EXAMPLE: MALICIOUS CODE

[To the knowledge of Licensor,][1] the Licensed Software, at the time of delivery [2], does not contain any disabling device, virus, worm, back door, Trojan horse, time bomb, ransomware, malware or other disruptive or malicious code that may or is intended to impair, disrupt or block their intended performance or otherwise permit unauthorized access to, hamper, delete, hijack or damage any computer system, software, network or data.

DRAFTING NOTES

[1] *Knowledge* – the licensor will usually request a "knowledge qualifier" in the warranty regarding malicious code, arguing that it should not be held liable for harmful code introduced without its knowledge by third parties (e.g., over the Internet). The licensee will respond that, as between the two parties, the licensor is in a better position to scan for and detect harmful code in its software, and to impose strict security controls on its employees who have access to it. The licensor may counter that it is nearly impossible to determine when, precisely, a virus has infected a software program, and the licensee should implement adequate scanning and security measures in all of its systems as a matter of routine. An even more licensor-protective version of the knowledge qualifier is a statement to the effect that licensor has not intentionally included any such malicious code in the licensed software.

[2] *Timing* – the licensor will likely insist that this warranty be limited to the time at which software was delivered to the licensee, as infection is more likely to occur once software is in general use than at licensor's production facility. With such a qualification, the licensee will have to prove that an infection occurred prior to installation of the software on licensee's system, which could be a difficult task.

---

²   One exception occurs in the area of computer and telecommunications networks, in which reliability is a key parameter. An important reliability metric in this area is availability or "uptime" – the amount of time that a product or service is available for use without interruption or unscheduled outage. This metric is often measured in "9s." Thus, if a service is required to have 99.9 percent availability, this is referred to as "three 9s" – the system can be "down" only 1.44 minutes during any twenty-four-hour period. By the same token, "five 9s" (99.999%) reliability permits only 0.864 seconds of downtime during any twenty-four-hour period, a very high standard indeed.

FIGURE 10.2 The 1993 film *Jurassic Park* introduced many viewers to the dangers of malicious computer code. In this classic scene, rogue computer programmer Dennis Nedry sabotages the theme park's computer system to draw attention away from his theft of dinosaur DNA.

10.1.3.4 Exclusions

As with many consumer products, a licensee's alteration of, tampering with or damage to a licensed product may void the relevant warranties. If the product is chemical or biological in nature, the licensor should also ensure that warranties are void if the product is not stored or handled in accordance with its written instructions. Examples of typical warranty exclusions are illustrated below.

EXAMPLE: WARRANTY EXCLUSIONS

Licensor shall have no obligation to correct or provide services in connection with any Errors that arise in connection with (i) any modification to the Software not made by Licensor, (ii) use of the Software in a manner, or in conjunction with software or equipment, not described in the Materials, or in any way not permitted under this Agreement, (iii) use of a superseded or obsolete version of the Software, (iv) the negligence or intentional misconduct of any user of the Software, (v) errors or defects in Third Party Software, Accessory Software, Hardware, communications equipment, peripherals or other equipment or software not provided by Licensor, or the failure by Customer to provide for regular maintenance of such Hardware and/or Software or (vi) input errors or errors associated with Customer's data. Licensor, at its option, may offer to perform troubleshooting, error correction, diagnostic or other programming services relating to the matters listed in Sections (i) to (vi) above for Customer at the Professional Services Rate.

10.1.3.5 Service Warranties

If a party provides services under an agreement, it will often warrant that those services will be provided "in a professional and workmanlike manner, in accordance with prevailing industry standards." While this recitation is fairly common, it is also notoriously imprecise. As one commentator noted nearly thirty years ago,

> Despite virtual universal adoption of the warranty of workmanlike performance by English and American jurisprudence, it remains an amorphous concept avoiding precise conceptualization. The absence of a precise formulation has created uncertainty as to the warranty's doctrinal dimensions. This in turn has produced unpredictable and uneven judicial application of the doctrine.[3]

The warranty of "professional" conduct suffers from the same lack of clarity, and "prevailing industry standards" are little better. Yet, taken together these three terms do offer the recipient of services some comfort, and a hope that truly substandard performance will convince a jury that a breach has occurred.

10.1.3.6 Duration

Many consumer products come with a warranty of thirty days, and the best will last for one year. Time periods of this duration may not be appropriate for sophisticated software systems or industrial equipment. In these cases, warranty terms may last for many years.

10.1.3.7 Remedies

Closely tied to the duration of performance warranties is the licensee's remedy if they are breached. Specifically, what happens if the licensee's multi-million-dollar inventory management system suddenly stops working, bringing its entire production line to a screeching halt? Even if the licensee has a potential monetary remedy for breach of contract and possibly a right to terminate the agreement (after a thirty-day cure period), these remedies are hardly what the licensee most wants, which is the prompt repair or replacement of the defective system. Thus, unlike "legal" warranty clauses, performance warranty clauses generally describe the specific actions that the licensor must take if the licensed products fail to comply with their warranty. These actions often include intake of the issue, problem diagnosis, initial response (sometimes a workaround) and permanent solution. As shown in the following example, many agreements classify problems as "low," "medium" or "high" priority, then assign different time requirements for each stage of response based on the severity level of the problem.

EXAMPLE: RESPONSE AND REPAIR

For purposes of Licensor's obligations under this Section, Errors in the Licensed Products shall be classified as follows:

Severity 1 – Critical problem. Application or significant module unavailable or the results produced by application are erroneous as result of error in the application. No acceptable workaround available.

---

[3] Timothy Davis, *The Illusive Warranty of Workmanlike Performance: Constructing a Conceptual Framework*, 72 Neb. L. Rev. 981 (1993).

Severity 2 – High Impact. Function limited or workaround difficult to implement.
Severity 3 – Low Impact. Cosmetic change such as screen wording or a typographical error.

		Severity	
Response	1	2	3
Problem logged	Immediate	Immediate	Immediate
Initial response from Licensor Customer Support	10 min.	60 min.	24 hours
Progress updates	Every hour	Every 6 hours	None
Temporary fix, patch or workaround	12 hours	48 hours	Next minor release
Permanent solution	3 business days	7 business days	Next major release

In addition to specifying specific remedial actions that the licensor must take upon the occurrence of an error in the licensed software, many software licensing agreements also limit the licensor's liability to the performance of such remedial actions or, if the software is not, or cannot be, repaired, to replacement of the software or, barring that, a refund of the purchase price. Such limitations, which have generally been upheld by courts, prevent the licensee from recovering damages for the harm caused by the malfunctioning software, and even from declaring a contractual breach.

EXAMPLE: ERROR REMEDIATION PROCESS AND REMEDY

In the event that Licensee identifies an Error in the Licensed Software, Licensee shall report such Error to Licensor's Level 1 Support Desk in accordance with the reporting procedures set forth in Appendix __.

Following receipt of an Error report, Licensor shall classify the Error as Severity 1, 2 or 3 in accordance with the guidelines set forth in Appendix __ and shall [use its reasonable or best efforts to] respond to such Error within the timeframes set forth in Appendix __ commensurate with the Severity of the Error.

In the event that Licensor is unable to remedy the Error within such time frames, then at Licensee's option, Licensor shall have the option either to (a) replace the Licensed Software with a new product that does not contain the Error, or (b) terminate this Agreement and Licensee's right to use the Licensed Software and refund to Licensee the license fee paid therefor [depreciated on a 5-year straight-line basis.]

This Section sets forth Licensor's sole and exclusive liability, and Licensee's sole and exclusive remedy, for any Error in the Licensed Software.

10.1.3.8 Maintenance in Lieu of Warranty

In some cases, a licensor will refuse to offer any performance warranty on products or services that it provides. Instead, it will offer a paid maintenance program under which it agrees to provide correction and repair services, as well as regular product updates and upgrades. Maintenance programs for software are discussed in more detail in Section 18.2.4.

Notes and Questions

1. *Performance warranties.* Performance warranties are typically given in software and similar licensing agreements, but not patent licenses. Why? Would you recommend that performance warranties be given more or less frequently? What purpose do they serve?

2. *Remedy.* The software remediation process described in Section 10.1.3.7 is often specified as the licensee's "sole and exclusive" remedy for failures of licensed software, with an ultimate remedy being refund of the purchase price (often on a pro-rated or depreciated basis). Is this fair? What if faulty software causes the licensee significant injury, as it did in *Mortenson v. Timberline* (reproduced in Section 17.1).

3. *Who's drafting?* Performance warranties include many components that really must be drafted (or at least outlined) by the parties' business and technical personnel. The specifications for a software program are critical to allocating the risk and responsibility for malfunctions (and *no* software works perfectly all the time), and severity levels and response times can mean the difference between a licensor's prioritizing one licensee's issues over another's. As an attorney, how would you seek to persuade business and technical personnel to engage with these contractual provisions? How much would you feel comfortable drafting and negotiating yourself?

Problem 10.1

Your client, Microware, plans to obtain an exclusive license to a software system created by DevelopIT. Microware asks you to draft a reasonable set of warranties (including remedies) to be included in the software licensing agreement, assuming the following scenarios:

a. Microware intends to distribute the software via the Apple App Store for consumer download and use.

b. Microware intends to use the software to run its own inventory-planning operation and expects to achieve significant competitive benefits using the software.

10.2 DISCLAIMERS, EXCLUSIONS AND LIMITATIONS OF LIABILITY

The court in *Loew's v. Wolff* considered whether an assignment agreement created an implied warranty of marketable title. To avoid questions like these, most IP agreements today expressly seek to disclaim and exclude all implied warranties of every kind.

DISCLAIMER

EXCEPT AS EXPRESSLY STATED ABOVE, THE LICENSED RIGHTS ARE PROVIDED "AS IS" WITH NO WARRANTY WHATSOEVER, WHETHER EXPRESS OR IMPLIED, WRITTEN OR ORAL (INCLUDING ANY WARRANTY OF MERCHANTABILITY, FITNESS FOR A PARTICULAR PURPOSE, TITLE OR NON-INFRINGEMENT, OR ARISING FROM A COURSE OF DEALING).

You may recognize many of these implied warranties as deriving from Article 2 of the Uniform Commercial Code (UCC), which pertains to sales of goods. But while the UCC does not apply to licensing transactions (see Section 2.1), attorneys drafting IP agreements have become accustomed to excluding any warranties that might arise by analogy to sales of goods.

10.2.1 *Implied Warranty of Merchantability*

An implied warranty of merchantability is created under UCC § 2-314(1). To be "merchantable," goods must (a) pass without objection in the trade under the contract description; (b) in the case of fungible goods, be of fair average quality within the description; (c) be fit for the ordinary purposes for which such goods are used; (d) run, within the variations permitted by the agreement, of even kind, quality and quantity within each unit and among all units involved; (e) be adequately contained, packaged and labeled as the agreement may require; and (f) conform to the promise or affirmations of fact made on the container or label if any.

10.2.2 *Implied Warranty of Fitness for a Particular Purpose*

An implied warranty of fitness for a particular purpose is created under UCC § 2-315. It provides that "Where the seller at the time of contracting has reason to know any particular purpose for which the goods are required and that the buyer is relying on the seller's skill or judgment to select or furnish suitable goods, there is unless excluded or modified under the next section an implied warranty that the goods shall be fit for such purpose."

10.2.3 *Implied Warranty of Title and Noninfringement*

An implied warranty of title and noninfringement is created under UCC § 2-312. The implied warranty of title provides that the title conveyed in purchased goods shall be good, and its transfer rightful; and that the goods shall be delivered free from any security interest or other lien or encumbrance of which the buyer at the time of contracting has no knowledge. The implied warranty of noninfringement provides that "goods shall be delivered free of the rightful claim of any third person by way of infringement or the like but a buyer who furnishes specifications to the seller must hold the seller harmless against any such claim which arises out of compliance with the specifications" (UCC § 2-312(3)).

10.2.4 *Course of Dealing*

Under UCC § 2-314(3), "other implied warranties may arise from course of dealing or usage of trade." Accordingly, many disclaimer clauses seek to exclude these implied warranties.

10.2.5 *Disclaiming Implied Warranties under the UCC*

Under UCC § 2-316 there are three general methods by which implied warranties may be disclaimed: (a) specific disclaimers; (b) use of general exclusionary language such as "AS IS," "with all faults" or other language which in common understanding calls the buyer's attention to the exclusion of warranties and makes plain that there is no implied warranty; and (c) a course of dealing or course of performance or usage of trade.

ALL CAPS?

Non-lawyers (and many lawyers) sometimes wonder why so many "boilerplate" contractual provisions are written in ALL CAPS. Part of the reason stems from the UCC. Section 2-316(2) states that in order to exclude or modify the implied warranty of merchantability, the text must be **conspicuous**. Likewise, to exclude or modify the implied warranty of fitness, the exclusion must be in writing and **conspicuous**.

Helpfully, the UCC also defines conspicuous for these purposes (§ 1-201(10)):

> **"Conspicuous,"** with reference to a term, means so written, displayed, or presented that a reasonable person against which it is to operate ought to have noticed it. Whether a term is "conspicuous" or not is a decision for the court. Conspicuous terms include the following: (A) a heading in capitals equal to or greater in size than the surrounding text, or in contrasting type, font, or color to the surrounding text of the same or lesser size; and (B) language in the body of a record or display in larger type than the surrounding text, or in contrasting type, font, or color to the surrounding text of the same size, or set off from surrounding text of the same size by symbols or other marks that call attention to the language.

From these humble origins, we get contracts that are laden with ALL CAPS or, better still, **BOLD ALL CAPS**.

In a recent law review article, Professor Yonathan Arbel and Andrew Toler conducted an empirical study of consumer comprehension of material written in ALL CAPS. They found that "[c]onsumers could identify their obligations no better under all-caps than under normal print—and older readers did much worse. In light of this, it is not surprising to find a consumer dislike of all-caps. Our evaluation of subjective sense of difficulty, shows that individuals rank reading as much harder when presented with text in all-caps." Accordingly, Arbel and Toler argue that "Courts should abandon their reliance on all-caps as a proxy for quality consumer consent and consider other, perhaps more contextual factors."[4]

Do you agree?

In addition to disclaimers of implied warranties, many IP agreements contain limitations on the types of monetary damages that may be available following a breach of the agreement (also frequently in ALL CAPS).

EXCLUSION OF CERTAIN DAMAGES

EXCEPT WITH RESPECT TO (i) PERSONAL INJURY, DEATH OR PROPERTY DAMAGE, (ii) A PARTY'S THIRD PARTY INDEMNIFICATION OBLIGATIONS UNDER SECTION __, OR (iii) A PARTY'S BREACH OF ITS CONFIDENTIALITY OBLIGATIONS, IN NO EVENT SHALL EITHER PARTY BE LIABLE TO THE

---

[4] Yonathan A. Arbel & Andrew Toler, *ALL-CAPS*, 17 J. Empirical L. Stud. 862 (2020).

OTHER FOR SPECIAL, INCIDENTAL, CONSEQUENTIAL, EXEMPLARY,
PUNITIVE, MULTIPLE OR OTHER INDIRECT DAMAGES, OR FOR LOSS OF
PROFITS, LOSS OF DATA OR LOSS OF USE DAMAGES, ARISING OUT OF ANY
ACTION OR OMISSION HEREUNDER, WHETHER BASED UPON WARRANTY,
CONTRACT, TORT, STATUTE, STRICT LIABILITY OR OTHERWISE, EVEN IF
REASONABLY FORESEEABLE OR IF SUCH PARTY HAS BEEN ADVISED OF
THE POSSIBILITY OF SUCH DAMAGES OR LOSSES.

10.2.6 *Special Damages*

The types of damages that are typically excluded in clauses like this fall into the general category
of "special" damages – those beyond the nonbreaching party's direct damages under the agreement (e.g., the price paid for goods or services). "Incidental" damages, defined in UCC §§ 2-710
and 2-715, include additional costs incurred by the nonbreaching party as a result of a breach,
such as storage, inspection and transport charges arising in connection with effecting cover and
otherwise incident to the breach. "Consequential" damages, in contrast, are losses and injuries
suffered by the nonbreaching party of which the breaching party had reason to know (UCC §
2-715(2)). Despite these seemingly clear distinctions under the UCC, the common law is not so
clear regarding the distinction between incidental and consequential damages. As noted by the
Restatement (Second) of Contracts, "The damages recoverable for loss that results other than
in the ordinary course of events are sometimes called 'special' or 'consequential' damages" (§
351, comment b). In fact, as recently reported by Professor Victor Goldberg, numerous judicial
decisions treat these terms as synonymous.[5]

Whatever they are, incidental and consequential damages can typically be excluded both
under the UCC and common law unless the exclusion is deemed unconscionable. Under
UCC § 2-719(3), the "limitation of consequential damages for injury to the person in the case of
consumer goods is prima facie unconscionable."

As shown in the example above, some parties also seek to limit exemplary, punitive and
multiple damages. These types of damages are typically imposed by a court at its discretion.
Examples include treble damages for "willful" patent infringement under 35 U.S.C. § 284 and
certain antitrust claims under 15 U.S.C. § 15(a). It is less clear that contractual waivers of these
types of damages will be enforceable.[6]

10.2.7 *Exceptions to Exclusions*

It may seem odd to begin a section that seeks to exclude certain types of monetary damages with
exceptions to that exclusion. Nevertheless, well-drafted damages exclusions typically include
at least some exceptions. In the example above, exception (i) relates to damages arising from

---

[5]   Victor P. Goldberg, *Consequential Damages and Exclusion Clauses*, Columbia L. & Econ. Working Paper No. 582
      at 1–2, n. 7 (2018).
[6]   See, e.g., *Kristian, et al. v. Comcast Corporation*, 446 F.3d 25 (1st Cir. 2006) (the award of treble damages under
      federal antitrust statutes cannot be waived by contract, though such a waiver may be effective with respect to treble
      damages under state antitrust statutes that are more discretionary than the federal statute), Calif. Civil Code §1668:
      "All contracts which have for their object, directly or indirectly, to exempt anyone from responsibility for his own
      fraud or willful injury to the person or property of another or violation of law, whether willful or negligent are against
      the policy of the law."

personal injury, death or physical property damage. In many cases, waivers of such damages, at least with respect to individual persons, will be deemed unconscionable or otherwise contrary to law, so this exclusion is not particularly aggressive.

Exception (ii) clarifies that a party's indemnification obligation (see Section 10.3) extends to indirect damages that may be claimed against the other party by a third-party plaintiff. In general, this exception is fair, as the indemnified party has no control over the types of damages that an aggrieved third party will seek against it, and the indemnifiability of a claim should not depend on the pleading strategy of the third-party plaintiff. This being said, are there reasons that a party might have for seeking to exclude this exception from the exclusion of indirect damages?

Exception (iii) relates to breaches of the confidentiality provisions of an agreement. The common rationale for the exclusion is that injuries arising from the disclosure of confidential information are, by their nature, speculative and in the nature of consequential and similar damages. Without the exception, the injured party would have no practical way to be compensated for its injuries.

CAP ON DAMAGES

Except with respect to (i) personal injury, death or property damage, or (ii) a party's indemnification obligations under Section __, in no event shall either Party's aggregate liability under this Agreement or for any matter or cause of action arising in connection herewith exceed [$_____] or [__ times the highest/lowest amount paid or payable by one Party to the other during [any [12-month] period during] the term hereof].

In addition to limiting the types of damages to which a party may be subject under an agreement, parties may also wish to limit their absolute financial exposure under the agreement.

10.2.8 *How Much is Enough?*

The amount of a contractual damages cap is subject to negotiation of the parties, and is sometimes one of the most contentious issues in a transaction. The cap can be an absolute dollar amount or based on the amounts due or payable under the contract, either in the aggregate or over a specified period. For large, complex transactions, different caps can be applied to different categories of potential liability under the agreement.

10.2.9 *Exceptions to the Cap*

As with the exclusions from liability, this section begins with some exceptions to the cap on liability. For reasons similar to those discussed above, the limitation of damages for personal injury and death is likely to be unenforceable (though less so for physical property damage). The exception for indemnification liability is sometimes more controversial. In most cases, a licensor that agrees to indemnify its licensee will also agree that its obligation to cover damages payable to a third party should not be subject to the contractual liability cap. In rare cases, however, a licensor may insist that its indemnity obligation be subject to a damages cap (which could be lower than the overall contractual damages cap). See Section 10.3 for a discussion.

Notes and Questions

1. *UCITA redux?* As discussed in Section 2.1 (Note 1), Article 2 of the UCC (Sales of Goods) does not apply to IP licenses. Yet, as demonstrated by the many references to the UCC above, it seems that a general set of rules relating to license agreements would be useful. This, of course, was behind the effort to create UCC Article 2B, which eventually failed and resulted in the Uniform Computer Information Transactions Act (UCITA). Yet, as noted in Chapter 2, UCITA was adopted in only two states. Does the material in this chapter make you more or less inclined to support a national code relating to IP licensing? With this in mind, would you recommend that your state adopt (or repeal) UCITA?

2. *Enforcement.* As Professor Nimmer has observed, the disclaimers, exclusions and limitations described in this chapter "are routinely enforced."[7] Should they be? Are there reasons to rethink allowing parties to limit their liability via contractual mechanisms like these? Are IP agreements different than other types of agreements in this respect?

3. *Classifying damages.* Exclusions of damages are generally viewed as contractual boilerplate, seldom warranting serious consideration or negotiation. As the Delaware Chancery Court has wryly noted with respect to one such clause, "the laundry list of precluded damages might have been put in the … Agreement by lawyers who themselves were unclear on what those terms actually mean."[8] Nevertheless, the fine distinctions among direct, indirect, consequential, special and other forms of monetary damages can become important once a contract is breached. Consider this hypothetical posed by Professor Goldberg:

    Suppose … that a licensee were to breach a patent license. If the license called for annual payments, the damages would be direct—the present value of the future stream of payments offset by any mitigation. No one questions that. What if the payments were a royalty based on sales? If the licensee were to breach, the future stream of payments would be the royalty on the future sales—losses on collateral business. Would the change in the form of compensation convert the damages from direct to consequential?[9]

4. *Lost profits.* Why do parties often try to exclude lost profits as allowable damages under their agreements?[10] Consider the characterization of lost profits by the court in *Imaging Systems Intern., Inc. v. Magnetic Resonance Plus, Inc.*, 227 Ga.App. 641, 642 (1997):

    there are two types of lost profits: (1) lost profits which are direct damages and represent the benefit of the bargain (such as a general contractor suing for the remainder of the contract price less his saved expenses), and (2) lost profits which are indirect or consequential damages such as what the user of the MRI would lose if the machine were not working and he was unable to perform diagnostic services for several patients.

    Given this analysis, would a contractual exclusion of lost profits damages exclude lost profits even if they were "direct" damages? The court addressed this question in *Elorac, Inc. v. Sanofi-Aventis Can., Inc.*, 343 F. Supp. 3d 789 (N.D. Ill. 2018). The agreement in that case included the following exclusion:

---

7   Raymond T. Nimmer & Jeff C. Dodd, *Modern Licensing Law*, Vol. 2, § 11.56 (Thomson Reuters, 2016–17).

8   *Pharmaceutical Product Development, Inc. v. TVM Life Science Ventures VI L.P.*, WL 549163 at 7 (Del. Ch. 2011) (quoted in Goldberg, supra note 5, at 1).

9   Goldberg, supra note 5, at 4.

10 For a comprehensive discussion of lost profits damages in patent cases around the world, see Christopher B. Seaman et al., *Lost Profits and Disgorgement* in Patent Remedies and Complex Products: Toward a Global Consensus 50 (C. Bradford Biddle et al., eds., Cambridge Univ. Press, 2019).

IN NO EVENT SHALL EITHER PARTY BE LIABLE TO THE OTHER PARTY FOR LOSS OF PROFITS, SPECIAL, INDIRECT, INCIDENTAL, PUNITIVE OR CONSEQUENTIAL DAMAGES ARISING OUT OF ANY BREACH OF THIS AGREEMENT

The licensor, Elorac, accused the licensee, Sanofi, of failing to use the required commercially reasonable efforts to commercialize the licensed product. Sanofi responded that even if it had breached this obligation, Elorac's only damages would be lost profits, which were expressly barred by the exclusion clause. The court disagreed. It reasoned that "loss of profits" in the exclusion clause must refer to consequential-type damages rather than "the value of the promised performance." To hold otherwise, it reasoned, would give the damages exclusion clause "unintended breadth." Rather, the court held, "a contract must be read as a whole, with effect and meaning given to every term and a reasonable effort made to harmonize the terms, so as to give effect to—not nullify—its general or primary purpose" (Id. at 805). Accordingly, Elorac's claim for monetary damages arising from Sanofi's alleged failure to commercialize survived Sanofi's motion for summary judgment. Do you concur with the court's reasoning? Are there any circumstances under which a party would rationally agree, as Sanofi argued, to exclude all damages, even for direct breach by the other party?

10.3 INTELLECTUAL PROPERTY INDEMNIFICATION

As discussed in Section 10.1, IP licensees cannot assume that the rights that they license will permit them to practice a particular technology, or that they will not later become subject to infringement claims by third parties. To address this issue, most sophisticated IP transactions include provisions by which the parties seek to allocate the risk of third-party infringement among themselves.

As Jay Dratler explains:

Once a licensing agreement has been consummated, the licensee would like to have the absolute right to use the licensed intellectual property in accordance with the terms of the agreement. Yet reality may intervene ... [A] third party may claim rights in the licensed intellectual property superior to those of licensor or licensee. Based on that claim, the third party may sue the licensee for infringement solely for exercising [its] purported rights under the licensing agreement. [Licensees] try to protect themselves against the risk of claims of this sort by asking licensors for warranties of noninfringement. They may also ask the licensor to agree, at its

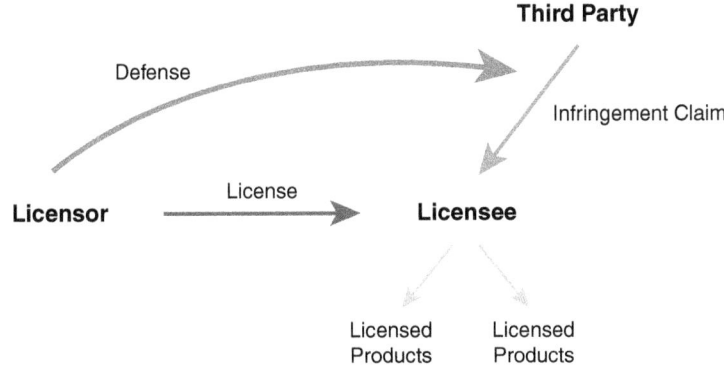

FIGURE 10.3 Illustration of the basic structure for IP indemnification.

expense, to indemnify or defend the licensee against those claims. This sort of ... covenant to indemnify or defend is generally enforceable, subject to certain rules of interpretation.[11]

Professor Michael Meurer describes a common scenario in which IP indemnity is typically required – an agreement between parties in a vertical supply chain:

> [M]uch economic activity is conducted collaboratively by a supply chain of vertically disintegrated firms, in which multiple firms are sometimes implicated in infringing activities, by making, selling, or using patented technology, or by contributing to or inducing another firm's infringement. Often patent owners have the option of suing some or all of the members of a supply chain who contribute to the design, creation, and marketing of a new technology.
>
> To illustrate, a firm named NorthPeak launched a patent enforcement campaign against supply chains active in the market for office building security technology. In 2008, the patent owner "alleged infringement by computers, routers and adapters made by 3Com Corp., Dell Inc. and 25 other manufacturers. Intel intervened in 2009 on behalf of the nine defendants that used its chips." Intel challenged the validity of claims in two patents asserted by NorthPeak in reexamination proceedings at the USPTO. The agency invalidated the relevant claims in one patent but not the other. Following a five year stay of the district court proceedings, litigation resumed and the trial judge used NorthPeak testimony in the reexaminations to construe the remaining claims narrowly, which led NorthPeak to stipulate non-infringement. NorthPeak appealed to the Federal Circuit, which affirmed the claim construction, presumably ending the lawsuit in late 2016.
>
> Because of patent assertions like this, businesses increasingly contemplate the risk of patent infringement when they negotiate contractual relations to form a supply chain. Upstream and downstream firms recognize they may be jointly liable for patent infringement because of their relationship to each other and their connection to the new product. An interesting and difficult question is: how should they manage infringement risk to maximize their joint profit? Which firm should control litigation? Or should they plan for joint control? Should they share responsibility for damages and litigation expenses? If yes, what determines each party's share?
>
> The traditional and simple answer to these questions is that the upstream firm should bear the risk of infringement because it is best able to avoid infringement. Imposing the risk of infringement on the vendor appropriately penalizes a vendor guilty of piracy. More importantly, imposing the risk on the vendor induces non-piratical vendors to make careful design and manufacturing choices, and obtain patent licenses when the risk of infringement is substantial.[12]

Notes and Questions

1. *Litigation risk.* What point does Meurer's example of the NorthPeak proceedings illustrate? Why does Meurer say that the upstream firm typically bears the risk of infringement? Are there reasons that a downstream firm (licensee/customer) should instead bear this risk?
2. *Intervention.* Why do you think that Intel intervened in the various lawsuits brought by North-Peak against computer and router manufacturers? Was this a wise business strategy for Intel?
3. *Common law indemnity.* Meurer discusses the allocation of liability among sophisticated parties through contractual instruments. But indemnity also exists under the common law, even if no contractual provisions require it. Consider the following explanation by Cynthia Cannady:

---

[11] Jay Dratler, Licensing of Intellectual Property § 10.02.
[12] Michael J. Meurer, *Allocating Patent Infringement Risk Across the Supply Chain*, 25 Tex. Intell. Prop. L.J. 251 (2018) (citations omitted).

Indemnity has three forms, common law implied contractual indemnity, equitable indemnity among concurrent tortfeasors, and contractual indemnity. The first occurs if there is a contract between the two parties, but the indemnity is not explicit. The second indemnity arises if there is no contract but there is a relationship between the two parties and a duty to a third party that makes it equitable to share the indemnity obligation. The third type of indemnity is based on the terms set forth in the contract. Whatever the type of indemnity, state contract and tort law (not IP law) govern indemnity, and federal courts will apply state law.

If no indemnity terms are set forth in the licensing or development agreement, one of the common law indemnities will apply. The common law of joint and several liability in the context of equitable indemnity is "fairly expansive." Implied contractual indemnity is unpredictable in result. For the reasons, from the licensor's point of view, it is essential to include a contractual indemnity that explicitly defines and hopefully limits the indemnity. From the licensee's perspective, a good contractual indemnity may make it easier to litigate if necessary because of attorney's fees provisions and statutes of limitations.[13]

* * *

Contractual indemnification provisions are among the most complex provisions in IP agreements. They appear in all forms of IP transactions, whether involving patents, copyrights, trademarks, trade secrets or some combination of the above. Though often allocating significant financial responsibilities among the parties, business negotiators' eyes often glaze over when it comes time to discuss the indemnification clauses. They are viewed as "lawyers" language, but don't let the complexity and seeming uniformity of these clauses fool you. Indemnification provisions are sometimes the most heavily negotiated provisions of an IP agreement, and woe be unto the junior associate who fails to address some clause that could open his or her client up to significant liability.

Read the following example of an IP indemnification clause and then consider the questions that follow.

INDEMNIFICATION BY LICENSOR

(a) *Indemnity Obligation.* Licensor shall indemnify, defend and hold harmless [1] Licensee and its Affiliates and their respective officers, directors, employees, and agents (the "Indemnified Parties") from and against any and all third party [2] claims, demands, costs, damages, settlements and liabilities (including all reasonable attorneys' fees and court costs) of any kind whatsoever, directly and to the extent arising out of claims that Licensee's manufacture, use or sale of the Licensed Product in accordance with this Agreement infringes the U.S. patent, copyright, or trademark rights of a third party or constitutes a misappropriation of the trade secrets of a third party; provided, however, that this indemnification is conditioned [3] upon: (i) Licensee providing Licensor with prompt written notice of any such claim; (ii) Licensor having sole control and authority with respect to the defense and settlement of any such claim; and (iii) Licensee cooperating fully with Licensor, at Licensor's sole cost and expense, in the defense of any such claim. Licensor shall not, without the prior written consent of Licensee, agree to any settlement of any such claim that does not include a complete release of Licensee

13 Cynthia Cannady, Technology Licensing and Development Agreements 169 (Oxford Univ. Press, 2013).

from all liability with respect thereto or that imposes any liability, obligation or restriction on Licensee. Licensee may participate in the defense of any claim through its own counsel, at its own expense.

(b) *Abatement of Infringement.* In the event that any Licensed Product is held in a suit or proceeding to infringe any patent, copyright, or trademark rights of a third party (or constitute the misappropriation of a trade secret of a third party) and the use of such Product is enjoined, or Licensor reasonably believes that it is likely to be found to infringe or constitute a misappropriation, or is likely to be enjoined, then Licensor shall, at its sole cost and expense, and at its option, either (i) procure for Licensee the right to continue manufacturing, using and selling such Licensed Product, (ii) modify such Licensed Product so that it becomes non-infringing or no longer constitutes a misappropriation, without affecting the basic functionality of such Licensed Product; provided, however, that if (i) and (ii) are not reasonably practicable, Licensor shall have the right, in its sole discretion, to terminate this Agreement with respect to such Licensed Product by giving Licensee 30 days prior written notice, upon which termination Licensor shall refund to Licensee the License Fee paid by Licensee in accordance with Section x above, depreciated on a straight-line basis over the 5-year period commencing on the Effective Date.

(c) *Exclusions.* Licensor shall have no obligation for any claim of infringement arising from: (i) any combination of the Licensed Product with products not supplied by Licensor, where such infringement would not have occurred but for such combination; (ii) the adaptation or modification of the Licensed Product, where such infringement would not have occurred but for such adaptation or modification; (iii) the use of the Licensed Product in an application for which it was not designed or intended, where such infringement would not have occurred but for such use; (iv) Licensee's continued use of a version of the Product other than the most recently released version, where such infringement would not have occurred if such most recently released version had been used; or (v) a claim based on intellectual property rights owned by Licensee or any of its Affiliates. In the event that Licensor is not required to indemnify Licensee for a claim pursuant to subsections (i), (ii), (iii) or (iv) above, Licensee agrees to indemnify, defend and hold harmless Licensor and its officers, directors, employees, and agents from and against claims, demands, costs and liabilities (including all reasonable attorneys' fees and court costs) of any kind whatsoever, arising directly or indirectly out of such claims.

(d) *Apportionment.* In the event a claim is based partially on an indemnified claim described in Section (a) above and partially on a non-indemnified claim, any payments and reasonable attorney fees incurred in connection with such claims are to be apportioned between the parties in accordance with the degree of cause attributable to each party.

(e) *Sole Remedy.* This Section X states Licensee's sole remedy and Licensor's exclusive liability in the event that the Licensed Product infringes on or misappropriates the intellectual property rights of any third party.

(f) *Cap on Liability.* Notwithstanding anything to the contrary in the foregoing, Licensor's maximum total liability under this Section X shall be [the total amount paid by Licensee under this Agreement during the immediately preceding three contract years].

DRAFTING NOTES

[1] *Hold harmless* – the term "hold harmless" is often used in conjunction with the obligation to indemnify. But what does it mean? As one court has noted,

> The terms "indemnify" and "hold harmless" have a long history of joint use throughout the lexicon of Anglo-American legal practice. The phrase "indemnify and hold harmless" appears in countless types of contracts in varying contexts. The plain fact is that lawyers have become so accustomed to using the phrase "indemnify and hold harmless" that it is often almost second nature for the drafter of a contract to include both phrases in referring to a single indemnification right … As a result of its traditional usage, the phrase "indemnify and hold harmless" just naturally rolls off the tongue (and out of the word processors) of American commercial lawyers. The two terms almost always go together. Indeed, modern authorities confirm that "hold harmless" has little, if any, different meaning than the word "indemnify."[14]

As a result, one may probably omit this term without significantly affecting the parties' rights and obligations.

[2] *Third-party claims* – see Note 3, below.

[3] *Condition versus covenant* – see Note 5, below.

Notes and Questions

1. *Indemnity versus warranty.* In the discussion of representations and warranties in Section 10.1 we mentioned that some parties forego IP representations and warranties in lieu of indemnification. Now that you have studied an IP indemnity clause, why do you think parties might prefer indemnification over warranties in this area? Think about the results that flow from a third-party infringement in either case. What happens when an unqualified warranty is breached? Does the triggering of an indemnification represent a breach of contract?

2. *Indemnification by licensor.* The above example describes the indemnification obligations of an IP licensor. IP licensees also often have indemnification obligations of their own. Considering the licensor's indemnification obligations in clause (a), against what sort of risks might the licensee be required to indemnify the licensor? Why might the licensee resist indemnifying the licensor for IP-related liabilities?

3. *Third-party claims.* Most IP indemnity clauses offer the licensee protection against third-party claims – that is, claims that the licensee, when using the licensed IP in the manner intended, infringes a third party's IP. In some indemnity clauses, however (particularly in the biopharma industry), the licensee may also seek indemnification from the licensor against its *own* internal losses and costs, in addition to damages that may be due to a third party. Why is this form of indemnification desirable for the licensee? On what grounds might the licensor object?

4. *Scope of IP covered.* In clause (a) the licensor only indemnifies against infringement of US IP rights. Is this reasonable? What if a worldwide license has been granted? Parties will often debate heavily the scope of coverage of an indemnity, sometimes listing specific countries (e.g., the United States, Canada, EU countries, Japan, Korea and China), or identifying countries where the licensed products are anticipated to be manufactured, sold or used. A

---

[14] *Majkowski v. American Imaging Management, LLC*, 913 A.2d 572, 588–89 (Del. Ch. 2006).

licensee would, of course, prefer a worldwide indemnity with no qualifications whatsoever. What reasonable objections could a licensor make to such a request?

5. *Conditions versus covenants.* Most indemnity clauses contain a set of actions that the indemnitee must take once it is notified of a claim for which it intends to seek indemnity. Thus, just as the holder of an automobile insurance policy must notify the insurer within a certain number of days if an accident occurs, the indemnitee must notify the licensor and turn over control of the claim. In clause (a) the language states that "indemnification is conditioned upon" the indemnitee taking these actions. Why are these conditions to the indemnification, rather than simple obligations of the indemnitee? What could be the different result if these actions were simply stated as obligations of the indemnitee?

6. *Control of litigation.* One of the key elements of indemnification is the licensor's (indemnitor's) ability to control the defense of any third-party claim for which indemnification is sought. In return, the indemnitor pays all costs of this defense. Why is it important for the indemnitor to control the defense? Are there situations in which an indemnitee might wish to control, or participate in, the defense of such a claim? Why does the last sentence of clause (a) give it the right to do so, but only at its expense?

7. *Abatement of infringement.* Clause (b) is what is often referred to as an "abatement" clause. Contrary to the first impression that many readers have, the abatement clause is intended to protect the *licensor*, not the licensee. It allows the licensor, if an injunction preventing the licensee's use of the licensed product is issued or likely, to terminate the applicable license. This termination avoids the licensor's potential breach of the license agreement by failing to enable the licensee to use the licensed IP and by curtailing any potential claim of inducement to infringe that may be brought against the licensor by the third-party claimant. Usually, however, the licensor is not permitted to terminate the license without compensating the licensee in some manner. The compensation structure set forth in clause (b) contemplates that the licensed product is a system that the licensee would likely have used for a five-year period. Thus, in order to terminate the license and abate the infringement, the licensor is obligated to refund to the licensee a portion of the initial license fee, pro-rated over a five-year term. Needless to say, the details of this compensatory scheme will vary dramatically based on the kind of IP being licensed and the payment structure for the original license. What complications can you see arising if (a) the injunction affects only one of several licensed technologies, and (b) the license authorized the licensee to manufacture and sell products in exchange for a running royalty?

8. *Exclusions.* Clause (c) enumerates situations in which actions of the licensee may relieve the licensor of its obligation to indemnify. This clause lists the typical exclusions that one encounters: the licensee has combined the licensed product with other, unlicensed, products; the licensee has altered or modified the licensed products or used them in a manner not intended.[15] Why is it appropriate to relieve the licensor of its indemnification obligation in these cases? Note the last part of clause (c), which requires the licensee to indemnify the licensor if an infringement arises from any of these situations. Is this always appropriate?

9. *Sole remedy.* Clause (e) provides that the indemnification provisions set out above are the licensor's sole liability, and the licensee's sole remedy, in the event that the licensed products infringe a third party's IP. What other kinds of liability is the licensor seeking to avoid here?

[15] In some industries, additional exclusions from indemnification are encountered. For example, firms that sell chips implementing popular wireless telecommunications and networking standards (e.g., UMTS, LTE, Wi-Fi) will typically exclude any indemnification for their customer's infringement of other patents covering those standards. For insight into why this might be the case, see Chapter 20.

10. *Apportionment.* Clause (d) provides an apportionment rule similar to that which exists for joint tortfeasors. How easy do you think it is to determine which portions of a claim are, and are not, subject to an indemnification obligation? Read the following case, which tackles this issue in greater detail.

11. *Limitations on indemnification liability.* Refer to the discussion of liability caps in Note 6 of Section 10.2. As noted there, a licensor that agrees to indemnify its licensee will often agree that its obligation to cover damages payable to a third party should not be subject to the contractual liability cap. In rare cases, however, a licensor may insist that its indemnity obligation be subject to a cap (which could be lower than the overall contractual damages cap). Why? Consider a chip designer that licenses IP relating to a particular circuit to the manufacturer of a much larger product, such as a television. In this transaction, the chip designer may receive a small amount, say $0.50, per $500 television sold. Yet if that television, by virtue of including the circuit, infringes a patent held by a competing television manufacturer, the court in awarding "reasonable royalty" damages[16] may base those damages on the price of the $500 television. Even at a relatively modest royalty rate of 0.5 percent, the damages would be $2.50 per infringing television, five times more than the chip designer received per television. In this circumstance, the chip designer may wish to limit its indemnification exposure to the $0.50 that it received, with the balance to be covered by the licensee. But what arguments would the television vendor make in response to the licensor to avoid imposing such a cap on its liability?

PRODUCT LIABILITY AND GENERAL LIABILITY INDEMNIFICATION

This book focuses on IP transactions, and this section covers IP indemnification clauses. This being said, there are many other types of liability for which parties seek indemnification, and many contracts include indemnification for liability involving taxes, environmental contamination, underfunded pension plans and the like, not to mention general acts of negligence and willful misconduct by employees and agents working on the other party's premises.

But beyond these general liabilities, one type of liability, and indemnification, that is very common in biopharma licensing agreements relates to product liability. Specifically, a licensee that has the right to develop and market a drug, vaccine or medical device covered by a licensor's patents will often be required to indemnify the licensor against any third-party claims arising from death or injury caused by the licensed product. The theory is that, while the licensor may have discovered the biochemical agent comprising the active ingredient of a drug, the licensee is responsible for the development, manufacture, testing and regulatory approval of the drug – all of which are usually beyond the control of the licensor. Thus, if a drug causes adverse reactions in patients or a manufacturing lot is contaminated, the licensor will wish to avoid any associated liability and be indemnified by its licensee.

By the same token, trademark licensors typically wish to limit their liability, and receive indemnification from licensees, for injury caused by products bearing licensed marks, whether they are action figures, backpacks, athletic shoes or candy bars.

---

[16] 35 U.S.C. § 284.

Southern California Gas Co. v. Syntellect, Inc.

Case No. 08-CV-941-BEN (MDD) (S.D. Cal. 2014)

BENITEZ, DISTRICT JUDGE

This case arises out of [...] SoCal Gas's purchase of an automated interactive system for handling incoming telephone calls made by Syntellect, Inc. (Syntellect). The Syntellect System is one component in SoCal Gas's system for handling customer phone calls. Among other functions, the System allowed SoCal Gas to tie an incoming call to customer information from SoCal Gas's computers. For instance, the System could obtain account records from a computer database based on the incoming phone number. Syntellect's custom application programs provided decision trees for handling calls based on the caller's inputs, enabling call flows that would allow the customer to either complete their task in the automated system, or speak to a live operator.

The purchase agreement for the Syntellect System contained a broad indemnity provision:

> [Syntellect] shall indemnify, defend and hold [SoCal Gas] ... harmless from and against any and all claims, actions, suits, proceedings, losses, liabilities, penalties, damages, costs or expenses (including attorney's fees and disbursements) of any kind whatsoever arising from (1) actual or alleged infringement or misappropriation by Syntellect or any subcontractor of any patent, copyright, trade secret, trademark, service mark, trade name or other intellectual property right in connection with the System, including without limitation, any deliverable (2) [Syntellect's] violation of any third party license to use intellectual property in connection with the System, including, without limitation, any deliverable.

The "System" includes the Vista Interactive Voice Response System, custom application programs developed by Syntellect specifically to SoCal Gas's application specifications, and all specifications and requirements included in the Request for Proposal.

SoCal Gas was sued by a third party, Ronald A. Katz Technology Licensing, L.P. (Katz), which alleged that SoCal Gas's system violated patents held by Katz. SoCal Gas asked Syntellect to defend the suit, but Syntellect refused to defend or indemnify SoCal Gas. SoCal Gas reached a settlement with Katz by entering a licensing agreement granting SoCal Gas a license to use the patents, and releasing them from liability for past use. SoCal Gas agreed to pay a licensing fee to Katz based upon past calls that had used the automated system. There were two categories of calls for which Katz demanded payment and which had actually occurred in the SoCal Gas system: 1) calls which were resolved entirely in the automated system, and 2) calls that were in the automated system, then transferred to a live customer service representative. For each minute of the entire duration of both categories of calls, SoCal Gas agreed to pay $0.011.

On March 28, 2011, this Court granted SoCal Gas's motion for partial summary adjudication on the question of whether Syntellect breached the indemnity provision by failing to defend and indemnify SoCal Gas in the Katz infringement case. Syntellect appealed to the Ninth Circuit. In a memorandum disposition, the Ninth Circuit affirmed this Court's grant of summary adjudication on the question of liability. The Ninth Circuit noted the broad language of the indemnity provision, and that California law interpreted language such as "arising from" to mean that liability will attach if the indemnitor's performance under the contract is "causally related in some manner to the injury for which indemnity

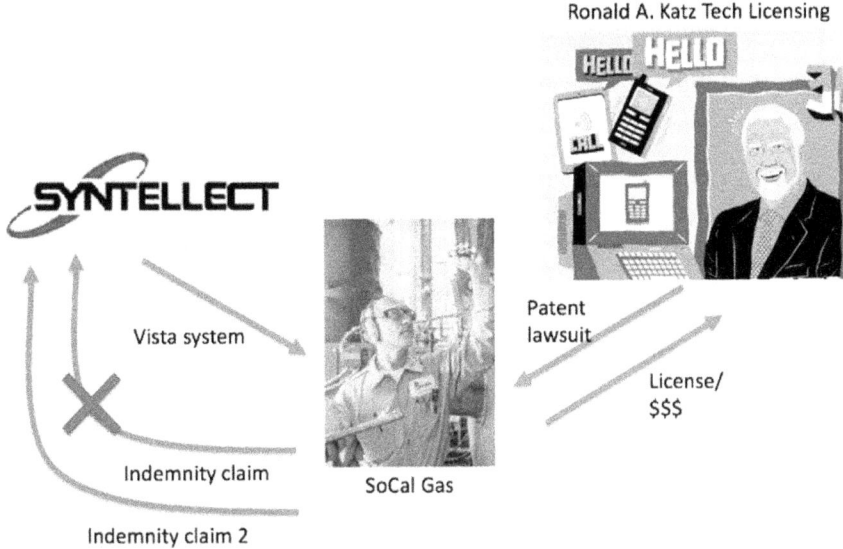

FIGURE 10.4 The parties and dispute in *SoCal Gas v. Syntellect.*

is claimed." The Court found that each of the "accused services" in the Katz complaint was "enabled by Syntellect's performance of its contractual duties." It concluded that the allegations of patent infringement were causally related to Syntellect's provision of the System, and that Syntellect was therefore liable for "damages stemming from utilization of the System."

The Ninth Circuit also found that SoCal Gas's own liability was reflected in the "presumptively reasonable amount of the settlement." However, the Ninth Circuit found that SoCal Gas must still demonstrate that the entire liability should be allocated to Syntellect. When there is a dispute over allocation, the plaintiff is required to prove the reasonableness of the proposed allocation by ordinary means, and a district court may not exclude all evidence relevant to the allocation of damages. As this Court excluded such evidence, the case was remanded for this Court to undertake this inquiry "in the first instance."

The Ninth Circuit clearly stated that it was not holding that apportionment was required, or that Syntellect could not be held responsible for the entire amount. Rather, this Court must consider evidence to determine if apportionment is necessary. To determine if apportionment is required, this Court is directed to consider the "nature of the Katz claims as they apply to the indemnity provision and to other potentially liable parties." The Ninth Circuit stated that when an indemnity obligation is "limited under the contract, an allocation of liability between culpable parties is appropriate." Apportionment is appropriate where "some portion of the liability for the alleged infringement is not embraced by Syntellect's indemnity obligation."

Discussion

As directed by the Ninth Circuit, apportionment is appropriate when the indemnity obligation is limited and "some portion of the liability for the alleged infringement is not embraced by Syntellect's indemnity obligation." The critical question is thus whether the scope of the liability provision, as determined by this Court and the Ninth Circuit, covers the entire amount of the settlement, or whether some portion of the settlement amount is not covered by the indemnity obligation and allocation is required. The parties agree that Syntellect is liable for "damages stemming from utilization of the system." SoCal Gas contends that the undisputed facts and legal conclusions demonstrate that no apportionment of liability is required. It argues that the entire amount stems from the utilization of the System, and is covered by the indemnity obligation as interpreted by the Court. Syntellect contends that part of the settlement amount exceeds the scope of the indemnity obligation. Specifically, it claims that 1) the indemnity obligation does not cover damages paid for portions of calls not conducted within the System, and 2) the indemnity obligation does not cover damages to the extent that other components of the automated call system are necessary to provide the allegedly infringing services. It argues that these categories of damages do not "[stem] from the utilization of the System."

The arguments between the parties are essentially based on the interpretation of the Ninth Circuit's language stating Syntellect is liable for damages "stemming from the utilization of the Syntellect system." It is therefore necessary for this Court to examine the indemnity provision to determine what kind of relationship the damages must have to the utilization of the System, and how the obligation is affected by the presence of other parties.

A. The Necessary Relationship Exists Between the Use of the Syntellect System and Damages Paid for Minutes Spent Waiting for an Operator or Speaking to an Operator

Syntellect argues that it should not be required to pay the portion of the licensing fee attributable to the 63% of minutes where a caller was either waiting for a live operator, or speaking to a live operator. It argues that apportionment is appropriate because such damages do not stem from the utilization of Syntellect's System. SoCal Gas contends that such minutes do stem from the utilization of the System. The factual relationship between the use of the System and the minutes spent waiting for an operator or talking to an operator is sufficient for damages for those minutes to fall within the indemnity obligation.

Syntellect essentially admitted that each of the accused services from the Katz complaint was enabled by its performance of its contractual duties. Examination of the Katz complaint confirms that all claims against SoCal Gas were based on services enabled by Syntellect's system, including the partially automated calls. It stated that Katz's inventions were "directed to the integration of telephonic systems with computer databases and live operator call centers to provide interactive call processing services." SoCal Gas was accused of using infringing call processing systems to offer automated customer services, "in some instances in connection with operators." Katz listed accused services, some of which required live operators. Katz clearly alleged that SoCal Gas violated its patents not only when a caller exclusively operated in the automated system, but when SoCal Gas provided services using the System and live operators.

It is also undisputed that the payment of the licensing fee was for the "sole purpose" of settling the patent infringement lawsuit. As SoCal Gas paid the licensing fee to settle the claims, and all claims were based on services enabled by Syntellect's System, then the entire amount of damages was paid to settle claims enabled by the System.

The contract requires Syntellect to indemnify SoCal Gas against "any and all" damages "of any kind whatsoever" arising from actual or alleged infringement of intellectual property rights, including patents, "in connection with the System." Significantly, this language is not requiring Syntellect to pay for damages "arising from" the use of the System, it requires the payment of damages "arising from" allegations of infringement in connection with the System. It is apparent that Katz's claim that the partially automated calls infringed the patent is an allegation of infringement of property rights in connection with the System. The licensing fee arose from that infringement claim. The clear terms of the contract therefore require Syntellect to pay for "any and all" damages arising from that allegation. Nothing in the contract requires a particular unit of damages to itself be traceable to the System.

Even if one were to read the Ninth Circuit's opinion to impose an additional requirement that a particular unit of damages must stem from the utilization of the system, the minutes in question meet this requirement. The licensing agreement required SoCal Gas to pay for every minute spent waiting for an operator or speaking to a live operator, if the call spent time in the automated system. If the call did not pass through the system, then no damages would be paid for those minutes. SoCal Gas argues that the damages thus stem from use of the System. SoCal Gas also asserts that it benefits from the use of the Syntellect System even after the customer is no longer actively engaging with the System. For instance, the call is tagged with relevant information, and the System could be used to help properly route a call or give information to a live operator about the call to use during the live portion of the call.

Each minute for which a licensing fee was paid was part of an allegedly infringing service enabled by the System. Syntellect's effort to isolate the minutes spent outside the system is artificial. The damages for minutes spent talking to a live operator or waiting for a live operator during a partly automated call were paid only because the minutes in question were part of an infringing service. The Syntellect System was not merely an incidental presence during those minutes. Its role was not limited to something that the callers passed through, and it was not simply present in the call system while entirely independent acts of alleged infringement took place. The System played an important role in the alleged infringement of patents by providing automation during the call and by allowing SoCal Gas to benefit from the System's ability to tag calls and help access information, even after the customer had left the system. Syntellect cannot avoid liability because the customer was not actively engaging with the System for part of the service. Apportionment of the waiting time and live operator minutes is appropriate if they are "not embraced by Syntellect's indemnity provision." As these minutes clearly are embraced by the provision, no apportionment is required on that basis.

B. Syntellect Cannot Allocate Liability to Other Components

Syntellect argues that liability must be apportioned between it and other components of the call system. It argues that because other components were required, not all of the damages stem from the use of the System. The Ninth Circuit expressly directed this Court to apportion damages if liability was not embraced by the indemnity provision. The text of the provision requires Syntellect to pay "any and all claims, actions, suits, proceedings, losses, liabilities, penalties, damages, costs or expenses of any kind whatsoever" arising from patent infringement allegations in connection with the System. This language is expansive. It makes no provision for allocation and does not purport to limit Syntellect to damages for which Syntellect is at fault. Instead, it clearly envisions that damages paid for patent allegations in connection with the Syntellect system will "all" be paid by Syntellect. Neither the text, nor the Ninth Circuit's opinion requires that the damages stem solely or primarily from the utilization of the system. Syntellect is essentially arguing that the multiple components are causally related to the damages, but the contract provides no basis for Syntellect to avoid paying the entire amount. The entire settlement amount was used to settle infringement claims in connection with the System, and Syntellect bound itself to pay "any and all" such damages.

California precedent makes clear that where a party promises to pay the damages "arising from" an activity and the party does not impose other limitations on that liability, the indemnitor must pay the full amount, even if another party's actions are casually related, or even primarily to blame for the injury.

Syntellect argues that the Ninth Circuit directed this court to consider the nature of the Katz claims as they apply to the indemnity provision "and to other potentially liable parties." However, examination of the indemnity provision in the first instance demonstrates that the existence of other potentially liable parties is immaterial in determining Syntellect's obligations. The Ninth Circuit held that "[w]here a party's indemnity obligation is limited under the contract, an allocation of liability between culpable parties is appropriate." Allocation would be necessary if Syntellect's indemnity obligation was limited in such a way that the entire award was not clearly covered. However, this Court has determined that there is no such limitation here. The only relevant limitation found in the contract is that the "claims, actions, suits, proceedings, losses, liabilities, penalties, damages, costs or expenses" arise from actual or alleged infringement or misappropriation "in connection with the System." The entire Katz settlement licensing fee fits within that requirement.

The indemnity obligation at hand makes no effort to allocate damages. Instead Syntellect agreed to indemnify SoCal Gas for "any and all" damages "of any kind whatsoever" arising from infringement claims in connection with the System. As all of the damages paid arose from infringement claims for services enabled by the use of the System, Syntellect must pay them in their entirety. It is therefore irrelevant whether other components or actions by SoCal Gas were necessary for infringement or contributed to infringement. To the extent facts related to the contributions of other parties are in dispute, they are not material, and they will not defeat summary judgment.

Conclusion

Based on the scope of the indemnity provision and the nature of the Katz claims, this Court determines that the entire Katz settlement licensing fee is within the scope of the indemnity provision, and that allocation is not appropriate.

SoCal Gas's Motion for Partial Summary Judgement is GRANTED.

Notes and Questions

1. *Patent troll defense?* The third party that sued SoCal Gas was Ronald A. Katz Technology Licensing, L.P., a well-known patent assertion entity (PAE), sometimes known as a "patent troll." Like the firm NorthPeak, mentioned in the excerpt by Meurer above, Katz's organization has sued hundreds of companies for patent infringement. As one commentator described it several years before the *Syntellect* litigation:

    Ronald A. Katz once predicted that he would someday become the wealthiest patent holder ever. By most estimates, he has achieved that goal – or will soon.

A search of federal district court filings shows that just since 2004, his company, Ronald A. Katz Technology Licensing (RAKTL), has filed more than 100 lawsuits against defendants as diverse as New York Life, General Motors and United Airlines. One report said that RAKTL had initiated more than 3,000 claims for patent violations over the last 15 years.

So who is Ronald Katz and how has he come to be such a potent force in the world of patenting?

Now in his early 70's, Katz was a cofounder in 1961 of Telecredit Inc., said to be the first company that enabled merchants to verify consumer checks by phone without the assistance of a live operator. He was awarded a patent as co-inventor of that technology.

In the 1980's, he was awarded a number of patents related to his work involving interactive telephone services. His inventions relate to toll-free numbers, automated attendants, automated call distribution, voice-response units, computer telephone integration and speech recognition …

In the late 1990's, Katz set up RAKTL to license his portfolio to companies using automated call centers. Unlike many patent holders who shy away from litigation due to its high costs and uncertainty, RAKTL has been aggressive in filing lawsuits against companies that refuse to take a license.

With several of his patents already expired and most due to end in 2009, Katz is keeping up the pace. A 2005 Forbes magazine article estimated that he had already earned $750 million in licensing fees at that time and would bring in $2 billion in fees by 2009. That would put him above the man long known as the country's most aggressive patent enforcer, Jerome Lemelson, who earned more than $1 billion in fees before his death in 1997.[17]

Given the notoriety of Katz in the telephone services sector, do you think that Syntellect and/or SoCal Gas should have known that a suit by Katz was likely? Do you think that their indemnification agreement reflected this likelihood?

2. *Refusal to defend.* Syntellect initially refused to defend or indemnify SoCal Gas after it was sued by Katz. Why might Syntellect have done so? What risks does a licensor like Syntellect run if it declines to defend a suit against one of its customers, and the customer defends and settles the suit itself?

3. *Contractual versus legal apportionment.* In *Syntellect*, the indemnification section of the purchase agreement does not contain an express apportionment clause. Rather, Syntellect argues that damages should be apportioned as a matter of law between its system and other components of SoCal Gas's call center operation (phone units, switches, etc.). The court disagrees, noting that the contractual indemnity provision "makes no effort to allocate damages," and instead requires Syntellect to pay "any and all damages of any kind whatsoever" arising from infringement by the system. Should Syntellect have included apportionment language, such as that included in sample clause (d) above, into the purchase agreement? What should such language have said? How easy or difficult would it be to allocate damages to an indemnitor when a settlement is structured in the manner that Katz offered?

10.4 INSURANCE

In order to ensure that one party (the obligor) will be able to fulfill its financial obligations under an agreement, particularly those relating to liability and indemnification, the other party (the obligee) will sometimes insist that the obligor, at its expense, procure and maintain insurance

[17] Robert Ambrogi, *For Ronald Katz, Patent Litigation Pays Billions*, BullsEye Expert Legal News, December 11, 2007, www.ims-expertservices.com/bullseye/december-2007/for-ronald-katz-patent-litigation-pays-billions.

specifically covering those obligations. In many cases, the obligee will request that it be listed as a "named insured" under the obligor's relevant insurance policy, which will enable the insurance carrier to disburse funds directly to the obligee.

Depending on the nature of the products and services covered by the agreement, as well as the size of any potential financial liability, insurance clauses can range from simple (see the example below) to very complex. In general, an obligee will be more likely to insist upon insurance coverage if the obligor is a small entity or if the potential financial exposure is very large. Thus, when a university licenses patents to a start-up company, the university will often require the start-up company to indemnify it against any and all injury and liability that may arise from the start-up's products, services and operations (particularly if it is in the biomedical field), and that this obligation be secured by a reputable third-party insurance carrier.

EXAMPLE: INSURANCE

Notwithstanding anything to the contrary contained herein, and without limiting or relieving Licensor from its indemnification obligations pursuant to Section __ above, Licensee shall obtain and maintain in full force and effect for the duration of this Agreement general liability insurance underwritten by a national insurance carrier that is reasonably acceptable to Licensor in the minimum amount of $5,000,000 per occurrence, naming Licensor as an intended beneficiary, in order to protect Licensor against any and all damages, losses, obligations and liabilities against which Licensor is indemnified pursuant to Section __ above.

Upon reasonable request by Licensor, Licensee will promptly furnish evidence of the maintenance of such insurance policy, including but not limited to originals of policies and proof of premium payments and other evidence that the policy is current and in force. In case Licensee receives notice of cancellation of the policy, it shall immediately furnish such notice to Licensor along with a written explanation of what measures it will take to reinstate the policy or obtain a replacement policy so that there is no period of lapse in insurance coverage. No insurance hereunder shall be cancelable upon less than 10 days prior written notice to Licensor.

11

Litigation-Related Clauses: Enforcement, Settlement and Dispute Resolution

It is a truism of legal practice that license agreements are negotiated in the shadow of litigation. If a prospective licensee does not enter into a license agreement for an item of intellectual property (IP), then it is liable to suit for infringement. Every prospective licensor and licensee knows this from the moment that a negotiation begins, and the (sometimes not very) tacit threat of litigation underlies every license negotiation.

In many licensing agreements, matters relating to litigation are addressed explicitly. One frequent issue is which party is permitted, or required, to bring suit to enforce licensed IP against a third-party infringer. Section 11.1 discusses the legal rules that govern an exclusive licensee's ability to bring suit against an infringer, and Section 11.2 covers contractual provisions that allocate the responsibility for enforcing licensed IP rights against infringing third parties. Sections 11.3–11.5 then turn to contractual mechanisms for resolving disputes between the parties themselves, including choice of law, forum and alternative dispute resolution mechanisms. Section 11.7 concludes by discussing contractual clauses that are unique to the settlement of IP litigation between the parties.

11.1 LICENSEE STANDING AND JOINDER

When a licensee receives an exclusive license to exploit an item of IP in a particular field, the responsibility for maximizing the economic return from that right is placed on the licensee's shoulders. Under most of the compensation mechanisms discussed in Chapter 8, the greater the revenue from exploitation of the licensed rights, the greater the licensee's profit. The licensor, who also benefits from the licensee's exploitation of the licensed rights, usually participates in these gains to a lesser degree (e.g., through a running royalty or milestone payments).

Given the financial stake that the licensee has in the licensed rights in an exclusive field, it is in the licensee's interest to ensure that no third parties are infringing the licensed rights and thereby diverting revenue from the licensee's own efforts. But what can an exclusive licensee do if a third-party infringer emerges? Does a licensee have the right to sue an infringer under licensed IP?

As you may recall from civil procedure, this question is one of standing or *locus standi* – a doctrine established under the "case or controversy" clause of Article III of the US Constitution. Standing signifies a party's ability to participate in a legal action because it bears some relation to the action. Most importantly, standing depends on whether a prospective litigant can show that it has suffered a legally redressable injury in fact arising from the matter being litigated. The Federal Circuit has recognized that those who possess "exclusionary rights" in a patent suffer an injury when their rights are infringed, giving them standing to sue (*WiAV Sols. LLC v. Motorola, Inc.*, 631 F.3d 1257, 1264–65 (Fed. Cir. 2010)).

What, specifically, must a licensee demonstrate in order to establish standing to sue a third-party infringer? This question, it turns out, is complicated and varies depending on the type of IP involved.

11.1.1 *Copyright Licensee Standing*

Let's begin with copyrights. Below are relevant portions of the Copyright Act.

17 U.S.C. 501: Infringement of Copyright

(b) The legal or beneficial owner of an exclusive right under a copyright is entitled ... to institute an action for any infringement ... while he or she is the owner of it ... The court may require the joinder, and shall permit the intervention, of any person having or claiming an interest in the copyright.

17 U.S.C. 101: Definitions

A "transfer of copyright ownership" is an assignment, mortgage, exclusive license, or any other conveyance, alienation, or hypothecation of a copyright or of any of the exclusive rights comprised in a copyright, whether or not it is limited in time or place of effect, but not including a nonexclusive license.

A common theme in standing cases (under copyright, as well as patent and trademark law) is whether a legal instrument purporting to "transfer" ownership of a right for standing purposes is actually a transfer. The Ninth Circuit focuses the issue in the following colorful anecdote:

> Abraham Lincoln told a story about a lawyer who tried to establish that a calf had five legs by calling its tail a leg. But the calf had only four legs, Lincoln observed, because calling a tail a leg does not make it so. Before us is a case about a lawyer who tried to establish that a company owned a copyright by drafting a contract calling the company the copyright owner, even though the company lacked the rights associated with copyright ownership. Heeding Lincoln's wisdom, and the requirements of the Copyright Act, we conclude that merely calling someone a copyright owner does not make it so.
>
> *Righthaven LLC v. Hoehn*, 716 F.3d 1166, 1167–68 (9th Cir. 2013)

The following case builds on the Ninth Circuit's reasoning in examining whether the *original* copyright holder has retained sufficient rights to be considered the owner for purposes of standing.

Fathers & Daughters Nevada, LLC v. Zhang

284 F. Supp. 3d 1160 (D. Or. 2018)

MICHAEL H. SIMON, DISTRICT JUDGE

Plaintiff Fathers & Daughters Nevada, LLC ("F&D") brings this action against Defendant Lingfu Zhang. F&D alleges that Defendant copied and distributed F&D's motion picture *Fathers & Daughters* through a public BitTorrent network in violation of F&D's exclusive rights under the Copyright Act. Before the Court is Defendant's motion for summary judgment. Defendant argues that F&D is not the legal or beneficial owner of the relevant exclusive rights under the Copyright Act and thus does not have standing to bring this lawsuit. For the following reasons, the Court grants Defendant's motion.

Background

A. Sales Agency Agreement

F&D is the author and registered the copyright for the screenplay and motion picture *Fathers & Daughters*. On December 20, 2013, with an effective date of April 1, 2013, F&D entered into a sales agency agreement with Goldenrod Holdings ("Goldenrod") and its sub-sales agent Voltage Pictures, LLC ("Voltage"). Under this agreement, F&D authorized Goldenrod and Voltage as "Sales Agent" to license most of the exclusive rights of

FIGURE 11.1 The 2016 film *Fathers and Daughters* starring Russell Crowe and Amanda Seyfried was the subject of the copyright dispute in *Fathers & Daughters Nevada, LLC v. Zhang*.

Fathers & Daughters, including rights to license, rent, and display the motion picture in theaters, on television, in airplanes, on ships, in hotels and motels, through all forms of home video and on demand services, through cable and satellite services, and via wireless, the internet, or streaming. F&D reserved all other rights, including merchandising, novelization, print publishing, music publishing, soundtrack album, live performance, and video game rights.

F&D further authorized Goldenrod and Voltage to execute agreements in their own name with third parties for the "exploitation" of the exclusive rights of *Fathers & Daughters* and agreed that Goldenrod and Voltage had "the sole and exclusive right of all benefits and privileges of [F&D] in the Territory, including the exclusive right to collect (in Sales Agent's own name or in the name of [F&D] …), receive, and retain as Gross Receipts any and all royalties, benefits, and other proceeds derived from the ownership and/or the use, reuse, and exploitation of the Picture …" The "Territory" is defined as the "universe."

B. Distribution Agreement with Vertical

On October 2, 2015, Goldenrod entered into a distribution agreement with Vertical Entertainment, LLC ("Vertical"). Under this agreement, Goldenrod granted to Vertical a license in the motion picture *Fathers & Daughters* in the United States and its territories for the:

> sole and exclusive right, license, and privilege … under copyright, including all extensions and renewal terms of copyright, in any and all media, and in all versions, to exploit the Rights and the Picture, including, without limitation, to manufacture, reproduce, sell, rent, exhibit, broadcast, transmit, stream, download, license, sub-license, distribute, sub-distribute, advertise, market, promote, publicize and exploit the Rights and the Picture and all elements thereof and excerpts therefrom, by any and every means, methods, forms and processes or devices, now known or hereafter devised, in the following Rights only, under copyright and otherwise.

The "rights" enumerated include … digital rights, meaning the exclusive right "in connection with any and all means of dissemination to members of the public via the internet, 'World Wide Web' or any other form of digital, wireless and/or Electronic Transmission … including, without limitation, streaming, downloadable and/or other non-tangible delivery to fixed and mobile devices," which includes "transmissions or downloads via IP protocol, computerized or computer-assisted media" and "all other technologies" … The rights granted also include the right to assign, license, or sublicense any of these rights.

The distribution agreement also purports to retain to Goldenrod the right to pursue for damages, royalties, and costs actions against those unlawfully downloading and distributing *Fathers & Daughters* via the internet, including using peer-to-peer or BitTorrent software. This clause purports to retain "the right to pursue copyright infringers in relation to works created or derived from the rights licensed pursuant to this Agreement." Shortly thereafter, however, Goldenrod and Vertical confirm and agree that "Internet and ClosedNet Rights (and all related types of transmissions) (e.g., Wireless/Mobile Rights) shall be included in the Rights licensed herein)" as long as Vertical uses commercially reasonable efforts to ensure security. Vertical was required to use commercially reasonable efforts to ensure that Vertical's internet distribution and streaming could only be received within its contract territory, was made available over a closed network where the movie could be accessed by only authorized persons, and could only be accessed in a manner that prohibited circumvention of digital security or digital rights management security features. F&D does not assert that Vertical breached this provision of the agreement or did not use commercially reasonable efforts to ensure digital security or its territorial limitations.

Discussion

F&D asserts that it is both the legal owner and the beneficial owner of the copyright to *Fathers & Daughters*, which would give F&D standing to bring this infringement suit against Defendant. F&D misstates the law of legal ownership of copyright exclusive rights and thus its argument that it is the legal owner of the exclusive rights at issue in this lawsuit is rejected. F&D also fails to present evidence that create a genuine dispute of material fact that F&D is the beneficial owner of the relevant exclusive right. Thus, that argument is similarly rejected. F&D also argues that based on a reservation of rights in the distribution agreement with Vertical and in a separate addendum to the agreements, F&D has standing. This argument also is without merit.

Standing as the Legal Owner

The legal owner of a copyright has standing. F&D argues that it is the legal owner because it registered the copyright and the copyright remains registered in its name. This simplistic view of ownership of a copyright misunderstands that copyright "ownership" can be transferred through an exclusive license (or otherwise), and can be transferred in pieces.

In the sales agency agreement, F&D authorized Goldenrod to license F&D's exclusive rights in *Fathers & Daughters*. In the distribution agreement, Goldenrod granted to Vertical a license in many of the exclusive rights of *Fathers & Daughters* as enumerated under copyright law. The first question is whether F&D, through Goldenrod, granted Vertical an exclusive license, which is a transfer of ownership, or a nonexclusive license, which is not a transfer of ownership.

The agreement is clear that Vertical was granted an exclusive license for the rights that were transferred. It is true that not all rights were transferred to Vertical, but under the Copyright Act of 1976, a copyright owner need not transfer all rights. The copyright owner may also "subdivide his or her interest" in an exclusive right by transferring his or her share "in whole or in part" to someone else.

The critical inquiry is to consider whether the substance of the rights or portions of rights that were licensed were exclusive or nonexclusive. Vertical plainly received exclusive rights. Vertical received the exclusive right to "manufacture, reproduce, sell, rent, exhibit, broadcast, transmit, stream, download, license, sub-license, distribute, sub-distribute, advertise, market, promote, publicize and exploit the Rights and the Picture and all elements thereof and excerpts therefrom" in the United States and its territories for almost all distribution outlets, except airlines and ships. This constitutes an exclusive license.

An exclusive license serves to transfer "ownership" of a copyright during the term of the license. Thus, for the exclusive rights licensed to Vertical, Vertical is the "legal owner" for standing under the Copyright Act, and not F&D. F&D argues that because it did not license to Vertical all of its rights in *Fathers & Daughters*, including rights to display the movie on airlines and ships, rights to the movie clips, and rights to stock footage, F&D remains the legal owner of the copyright with standing to bring this infringement claim. F&D misunderstands Section 501(b) of the Copyright Act.

As Section 501(b) states, and the Ninth Circuit has made clear, after a copyright owner has fully transferred an exclusive right, it is the transferee who has standing to sue for that particular exclusive right. The copyright owner need not transfer all of his or her exclusive rights, and will still have standing to sue as the legal owner of the rights that were not transferred. But the copyright owner no longer has standing to sue for the rights that have been transferred.

F&D also argues that because Paragraph 7(d) of the distribution agreement requires Vertical to use commercially reasonable efforts to ensure that its internet distribution and streaming were limited to the contract territory (the United States and its territories), were on a closed network, and were only accessible to networks prohibiting circumvention of digital rights management security and other digital security, this means that the contract reserved BitTorrent rights to Goldenrod. That is not, however, what Paragraph 7(d) provides. Paragraph 7(a) of the distribution agreement grants Vertical extremely broad rights, including comprehensive digital rights. Paragraph 7(b) grants Vertical the right to authorize others to the rights of *Fathers and Daughters*. Paragraph 7(c) reserves certain rights to Goldenrod, not relevant here. Finally, Paragraph 7(d) merely reaffirms that certain digital rights belong to Vertical and then applies commercially reasonable requirements to Vertical's exercise of those rights, primarily security terms. Paragraph 7(d) does not reserve any exclusive copyright digital rights to Goldenrod.

Under the Copyright Act, F&D is not the "legal owner" with standing to sue for infringement relating to the rights that were transferred to Vertical through its exclusive license granted in the distribution agreement. These rights include displaying or distributing copies of *Fathers & Daughters* in the United States and its territories. They further include displaying or distributing via the internet, using IP protocol, using computers, and using "all other technologies, both now or hereafter known or devised," which includes using BitTorrent protocol. In the distribution agreement Goldenrod (and therefore F&D) did not retain any fraction or portion of these digital rights. Because the infringement in this case relates to rights transferred to Vertical and there is no alleged infringement relating to display on airlines, display on ships, movie clips, stock footage, or any other rights that F&D retained, F&D does not have standing as the legal owner to bring the claims alleged.

Standing as the Beneficial Owner

A beneficial owner of a copyright may also have standing. F&D argues that it has standing as the beneficial owner of the copyright because it receives royalties for the licensing of the movie to Vertical. In support, F&D summarily asserts that the distribution agreement with Vertical states that F&D is entitled to "Licensor Net Receipts" from Vertical. The problem with this argument is that the "Licensor" in the distribution agreement is Goldenrod, not F&D. So it is Goldenrod who is entitled to those net receipts from the distribution agreement. F&D offers no argument or evidence of how the money Goldenrod receives from Vertical qualifies as royalties payable to F&D.

[T]he Court has reviewed the sales agency agreement to see if it elucidates how Goldenrod's receipts from Vertical might be payable as royalties to F&D. The sales agency agreement provides that Goldenrod may enter into license agreements and collect monies in its own name. Thus, Goldenrod may collect the monies from Vertical in Goldenrod's name. The sales agency agreement also provides, however, that monies obtained from licensing the movie shall be deemed "Gross Receipts." As described in the factual background section, the first eight steps in distributing Gross Receipts could not be considered royalties to F&D.

It is conceivable that in the final step, after the monies become "adjusted gross receipts," there may be some type of distribution that might be considered royalties to F&D. That entire section, however, is redacted in the copy provided to the Court. Thus, there is no way for the Court to know whether the adjusted gross receipts are divided in such a manner that could be considered royalties to F&D. F&D did not provide the Court with an unredacted copy or any evidence showing how F&D can be deemed to be receiving royalties. The Court would have to engage in pure speculation as to how adjusted gross receipts are divided, and the Court will not do so. Accordingly, there is no evidence before the Court that F&D receives anything from the sales agency agreement that looks like royalties, let alone that F&D receives royalties from the distribution agreement with Vertical. F&D therefore fails to show a genuine dispute that it is the beneficial owner with respect to the exclusive rights licensed to Vertical.

Contractual Reservation of Right to Sue Clause

F&D also argues that because the distribution agreement between Goldenrod and Vertical contained a reservation of the right to sue for infringement via BitTorrent and other illegal downloading via the internet, F&D has standing to sue. This argument fails for two reasons. First, the reservation of rights was to Goldenrod and not to F&D. Thus, even if the clause could convey standing, it does not convey standing to F&D.

Second, the Ninth Circuit has repeatedly held that agreements and assignments cannot convey simply a right to sue, because a right to sue is not an exclusive right under the Copyright Act. If a party cannot transfer a simple right to sue, the Court finds that a party similarly cannot retain a simple right to sue. Just as Goldenrod (or F&D) could not assign or license to Vertical or anyone else no more than the right to sue for infringement, it cannot transfer the substantive Section 501(b) rights for display and distribution in the United States and its territories, including digital rights, but retain only the right to sue for one type of infringement of those transferred rights (illegal display and distribution over the internet).

Anti-Piracy Addendum

F&D also relies on an undated "Anti-Piracy and Rights Enforcement Reservation of Rights Addendum." This document provides that "all peer-to-peer digital rights (BitTorrent, etc.) in the Picture, including international rights, are reserved to [F&D]," that F&D shall be authorized to issue Digital Millennium Copyright Act take down notices against any infringer, that F&D shall be authorized to "enforce copyrights against Internet infringers including those that use peer-to-peer technologies in violation of U.S. Copyright law," and that there shall be no cost to Vertical with regards to these enforcement actions. This document does not provide F&D with standing for two reasons.

First, the Ninth Circuit instructs courts in considering copyright assignments and agreements to consider substance over form. From the context of this document, it is clear that the peer-to-peer and BitTorrent rights being reserved to F&D are infringing rights. The substance of this Addendum is to confer no more than the right to issue take down notices and sue for copyright infringement for infringing peer-to-peer use through illegal downloading via the internet. The rights to digital display and distribution, which are exclusive rights under the Copyright Act, remain with Vertical. Accordingly, these "reserved" rights are not exclusive rights under the Copyright Act and thus do not confer standing.

Second, F&D provides no evidence in the record that this document was executed before this lawsuit was filed. As discussed above, F&D did not have any digital rights in *Fathers & Daughters* in the United States and its territories and thus did not have standing. Even if this document could provide F&D with rights that would confer standing upon F&D, standing is considered at the time a lawsuit is filed. Although there are a few exceptions to this rule, as the Ninth Circuit noted in *Righthaven LLC v. Hoehn*, 716 F.3d 1166, 1171 (9th

Cir. 2013), "permitting standing based on a property interest acquired after filing is not one of them." In *Righthaven*, the Ninth Circuit declined to decide whether a late contractual addendum to "clarify" copyright assignments "call[ed] for a new exception to the general rule." Instead, the court found that the plaintiff lacked standing either way. Under existing Ninth Circuit precedent, there is no such additional exception to the general rule.

In his motion, Defendant expressly noted that the anti-piracy addendum was undated, produced near the end of discovery, and "upon information and belief" was created after this lawsuit was filed. Notably, no other agreement in the record is undated. Additionally, in April 2015, several months before the distribution agreement was executed in October 2015, an anti-piracy agreement that was signed and dated authorized Voltage to investigate and pursue infringers, not F&D.

In its response, F&D did not dispute that the undated anti-piracy addendum was created after this lawsuit was filed, or otherwise respond to Defendant's standing argument relating to the untimeliness of this document. Nor did F&D provide any evidence as to the date this document was created. Therefore, the only reasonable inference is that this document was created after this lawsuit was filed. Accordingly, because the only reasonable inference supported by the evidence is that this document was created after the filing of this lawsuit, it is not appropriate to consider for purposes of standing.

Conclusion

Defendant's Motion for Summary Judgment is GRANTED. Plaintiff's claims are dismissed for lack of standing.

Notes and Questions

1. *The five-legged cow.* What lesson should be taken from the Ninth Circuit's discussion of Abraham Lincoln's five-legged cow in *Righthaven v. Hoehn*? How does it apply to *Fathers & Daughters Nevada*?
2. *Who should sue?* The facts of *Fathers & Daughters Nevada* reflect a fairly typical film deal: In exchange for ongoing payments, the producer of the film (F&D) exclusively licenses the distribution and commercialization rights to the film, including electronic distribution rights, to an agent (Vertical/Goldenrod). The facts recited by the court further suggest that Zhang is an internet pirate who illegally downloaded and distributed the film via the BitTorrent file-sharing system. Is there any debate regarding Zhang's infringement? Why didn't Vertical or Goldenrod sue Zhang?
3. *Legal versus beneficial ownership.* The court in *Fathers & Daughters Nevada* analyzes F&D's standing to sue in terms of both legal ownership and beneficial ownership. What is the difference between these two concepts? Why should beneficial ownership, which does not include title, convey standing to a party?
4. *Retaining the right to sue.* In *Fathers & Daughters Nevada*, F&D produced an undated addendum that allegedly demonstrated that F&D retained the right to sue online infringers. Why do you think the parties executed this addendum? The court ruled that there was insufficient evidence to show that the addendum had been executed before suit was filed, thereby eliminating its evidentiary value. But what if the addendum had clearly been executed prior to F&D filing the suit? Would that have changed the court's view? What other problem did the court find with the addendum?

5. *Copyright trolls. Righthaven LLC v. Hoehn,* 716 F.3d 1166, 1171 (9th Cir. 2013), raised the issue of standing to sue in the context of a "copyright assertion entity" (sometimes referred to as a copyright "troll"). The Ninth Circuit described Righthaven's business model as follows:

> Righthaven LLC was founded, according to its charter, to identify copyright infringements on behalf of third parties, receive "limited, revocable assignment[s]" of those copyrights, and then sue the infringers. Righthaven filed separate suits against defendants Hoehn and DiBiase for displaying copyrighted *Las Vegas Review–Journal* articles without authorization on different websites. Hoehn, who frequently commented in discussion boards at MadJackSports.com, had pasted an opinion piece about public pensions into one of his comments on the site. DiBiase, a former Assistant United States Attorney who maintained a blog about murder cases in which the victim's body was never found, reproduced an article about one of these "no body" cases on his blog.
>
> Righthaven was not the original owner of the copyrights in these articles. Stephens Media LLC, the company that owns the *Las Vegas Review–Journal,* held them at the time defendants posted the articles. After the alleged infringements occurred, but before Righthaven filed these suits, Stephens Media and Righthaven executed a copyright assignment agreement for each article. Each copyright assignment provided that, "subject to [Stephens Media's] rights of reversion," Stephens Media granted to Righthaven "all copyrights requisite to have Righthaven recognized as the copyright owner of the Work for purposes of Righthaven being able to claim ownership as well as the right to seek redress for past, present, and future infringements of the copyright … in and to the Work."

The court held that Righthaven lacked standing to sue, observing that,

> Stephens Media retained "the unfettered and exclusive ability" to exploit the copyrights. Righthaven, on the other hand, had "no right or license" to exploit the work or participate in any royalties associated with the exploitation of the work. The contracts left Righthaven without any ability to reproduce the works, distribute them, or exploit any other exclusive right under the Copyright Act. Without any of those rights, Righthaven was left only with the bare right to sue, which is insufficient for standing under the Copyright Act.

Following this holding, how do you think that copyright trolls have adjusted the language of their agreements with copyright owners in order to overcome standing issues?

11.1.2 *Patent Licensee Standing*

Under Section 281 of the Patent Act, the right to bring an action for infringement is reserved to the patentee. The patentee includes both the original assignee of a patented invention from the inventor(s), as well as its successors in interest. It also includes each joint owner of a patent, as discussed in Section 2.6.1.

Courts have interpreted the definition of "patentee" for purposes of standing as designating whichever entity holds "all substantial rights" to the patent. As the Federal Circuit explained in *Alfred E. Mann Found. for Sci. Research v. Cochlear Corp.,* 604 F.3d 1354, 1359–60 (Fed. Cir. 2010),

> [A] patent may not have multiple separate owners for purposes of determining standing to sue. Either the licensor did not transfer "all substantial rights" to the exclusive licensee, in which case the licensor remains the owner of the patent and retains the right to sue for infringement, or the licensor did transfer "all substantial rights" to the exclusive licensee, in which case the licensee becomes the owner of the patent for standing purposes and gains the right to sue on its own. In either case, the question is whether the license agreement transferred sufficient rights

to the exclusive licensee to make the licensee the owner of the patents in question. If so, the licensee may sue but the licensor may not. If not, the licensor may sue, but the licensee alone may not. When there is an exclusive license agreement, as opposed to a nonexclusive license agreement, but the exclusive license does not transfer enough rights to make the licensee the patent owner, either the licensee or the licensor may sue, but both of them generally must be joined as parties to the litigation.

We will discuss joinder in Section 11.1.5. For now, we will focus on the requirement that in order for a licensee to have standing to sue, it must have an exclusive license, and that exclusive license must convey "all substantial rights" to the licensee.

Lone Star Silicon Innovations LLC v. Nanya Tech. Corp.
925 F.3d 1225 (Fed. Cir. 2019)

O'MALLEY, CIRCUIT JUDGE

Lone Star Silicon Innovations LLC ("Lone Star") sued Appellees for infringing various patents. The district court concluded that Lone Star does not own these patents and therefore lacks the ability to assert them. We agree with the district court that Lone Star cannot assert these patents on its own.

I. Background

The asserted patents were originally assigned to AMD, which later executed an agreement purporting to transfer "all right, title and interest" in the patents to Lone Star. The transfer agreement, however, imposes several limits on Lone Star. For example, Lone Star agreed to only assert the covered patents against "Unlicensed Third Party Entit[ies]" specifically listed in the agreement. New entities can only be added if Lone Star and AMD both agree to add them. If Lone Star sues an unlisted entity, AMD has the right—without Lone Star's approval—to sublicense the covered patents to the unlisted target. AMD can also prevent Lone Star from assigning the patents or allowing them to enter the public domain. AMD and its customers can also continue to practice the patents, and AMD shares in any revenue Lone Star generates from the patents through "monetization efforts."

Lone Star sued Appellees, who are all listed as Unlicensed Third Party Entities in the transfer agreement, in successive infringement actions filed between October 2016 and December 2016. In each case, Lone Star alleged, among other things, that AMD transferred "all right, title, and interest" in the asserted patents to Lone Star.

The district court granted Appellees' motions. As the district court correctly explained, we have recognized three categories of plaintiffs in patent infringement cases. First, a patentee, i.e., one with "all rights or all substantial rights" in a patent, can sue in its own name. Second, a licensee with "exclusionary rights" can sue along with the patentee. And, finally, a licensee who lacks exclusionary rights has no authority to assert a patent (even along with the patentee). The district court concluded that it only needed to address this first category "since Lone Star claims to be an 'assignee' and 'sole owner' of the patents-in-suit."

In determining whether the agreement between AMD and Lone Star transferred "all substantial rights" to the asserted patents, the district court examined the rights transferred to Lone Star and those retained by AMD. The district court focused on three aspects of the transfer agreement in particular: (1) AMD's ability to control how Lone Star asserts or transfers the patents, (2) Lone Star's inability to practice the patents, and (3) AMD's right to share in "monetization efforts." The district court then compared the balance of rights here to previous cases where we have said agreements did or did not transfer all substantial rights. Ultimately, the district court concluded that AMD did not transfer all substantial rights in the patents to Lone Star.

After it concluded that Lone Star could not sue in its own name, the district court dismissed the case. Lone Star timely appealed.

II. Discussion

Lone Star argues that it possesses all substantial rights in the asserted patents and therefore can assert them in its own name. Appellees argue that Lone Star does not possess all substantial rights and therefore lacks standing to bring suit … We address these arguments below.

All Substantial Rights

Title 35 allows a "patentee" to bring a civil action for patent infringement. 35 U.S.C. § 281. The term patentee includes the original patentee (whether the inventor or original assignee) and "successors in title." 35 U.S.C. § 100(d). But it does not include mere licensees.

If the party asserting infringement is not the patent's original patentee, "the critical determination regarding a party's ability to sue in its own name is whether an agreement transferring patent rights to that party is, in effect, an assignment or a mere license." In distinguishing between "an assignment" and a "mere license," we "examine whether the agreement transferred all substantial rights to the patents." This inquiry depends on the substance of what was granted rather than formalities or magic words. For example, in previous cases we have reviewed how an agreement affected who could use, assert, license, or transfer the covered patents. We have also considered whether the transferor retained reversionary rights in or ongoing control over the patents. But our ultimate task is not to tally the number of rights retained against those transferred. Instead, we examine the "totality" of the agreement to determine whether a party other than the original patentee has established that it obtained all substantial rights in the patent.

Against this backdrop, Lone Star asserts two reasons why it believes it may sue in its own name. First, it argues that the transfer agreement was a complete assignment because a single provision in the agreement conveyed "all right, title and interest" in the patents to Lone Star. Second, Lone Star argues that, even if we look beyond this provision, the transfer agreement gave it all substantial rights in the patents, at least with respect to these alleged infringers. The district court rejected both arguments. We agree with the district court that, while Lone Star was given a number of rights in the transfer agreement, it was not given all substantial rights in the asserted patents.

1. "All Right, Title and Interest"

Lone Star argues that our analysis begins and ends with the transfer agreement's broad conveyance of "all right, title and interest" in the covered patents. But, as the district court correctly recognized, the rest of the agreement "substantially curtail[s] Lone Star's rights." To say that this amounts to an assignment because of the initial, broad grant ignores the total effect of the agreement.

Indeed, the Supreme Court cautioned … in *Waterman* that "[w]hether a transfer of a particular right or interest under a patent is an assignment or a license does not depend upon the name by which it calls itself, but upon the legal effect of its provisions." That is consistent with our analysis here.

2. The Totality of the Transfer Agreement

We turn next to whether the "totality" of the transfer agreement reflects a transfer of all substantial rights in the asserted patents to Lone Star. We conclude that it does not.

In considering this question, we have often focused on two salient rights: enforcement and alienation. For example, in *Intellectual Property Development, Inc. v. TCI Cablevision of California, Inc.*, 248 F.3d 1333 (Fed. Cir. 2001), we noted that the transferee could only bring suit, at least in some cases, with consent from the transferor. But, as we explained, "a transferee that receives all substantial patent rights from a transferor would never need consent from the transferor to file suit." The transferor also retained the right to prevent the transferee from assigning the patents at issue without prior consent. Again, we explained, this sort of restriction on alienation "weigh[ed] in favor of finding a transfer of fewer than all substantial rights." Taken together, these facts indicated that the transferor retained substantial rights in the patents. The extent of Lone Star's ability to enforce and alienate the asserted patents is also instructive.

As to enforcement, Lone Star needs AMD's consent to file suit against unlisted entities. For example, if Lone Star asserts the patents against a target that is not listed in the transfer agreement, then AMD can grant a sublicense and negate the lawsuit. AMD can also negate any effort to add new targets to the agreement. Lone Star's enforcement rights are, thus, illusory, at least in part. Lone Star therefore does not possess the right to sue for "all infringement." See *Sicom Sys., Ltd. v. Agilent Techs., Inc.*, 427 F.3d 971, 979 (Fed. Cir. 2005) (concluding that the right to sue for commercial infringement, but not non-commercial infringement, signified that the transferee lacked "the exclusive right to sue for all infringement"). This suggests that Lone Star therefore lacks all substantial rights in the asserted patents. See *Diamond Coating*, 823 F.3d at 621 (agreeing with a district court's conclusion that a transferee's exclusionary rights were not "unfettered" because the transferor enumerated who it wanted the transferee to sue).

Lone Star emphasizes that it possesses the right to initiate lawsuits and the right to indulge infringement (by not initiating a lawsuit) at least as to unlicensed entities, which includes Appellees. It is true that we have treated the exclusive right to sue as significant. But, as explained above, it is AMD who decides whether Lone Star can challenge or indulge infringement with respect to unlisted targets. For example, if an unlisted entity begins practicing the patents, AMD—without Lone Star's consent—can indulge that infringement by refusing to add that party to the list of approved targets. AMD could even withhold its consent conditional on payments from the unlisted target.

Lone Star insists that restrictions on suing unlisted targets are irrelevant here because Appellees are all Unlicensed Third Party Entities. But we rejected this same argument in *Sicom*:

> We find unpersuasive Sicom's response that it is not suing Appellees' customers, nor suing for non-commercial infringement, and that this court should not consider risks that are outside the scope of the facts in this case. Sicom's focus on the parties in suit is misplaced where this court has established that the intention of the parties to the Agreement and the

substance of what was granted are relevant factors in determining whether all substantial rights in a patent were conveyed.

Sicom, 427 F.3d at 979. The fact that the transfer agreement allows Lone Star to assert the patents against Appellees is important, but it is the effect of the agreement on the respective rights of the patentee and the transferee that controls. And the effect of this agreement is that AMD did not fully transfer the right to enforce its patents. The fact that AMD may have transferred some rights, with respect to certain unlisted entities, does not mean it transferred all substantial rights in the full scope of the patent.

As to alienation, the agreement restricts Lone Star's ability to transfer the asserted patents. In particular, Lone Star cannot transfer the patents to a buyer unless that buyer agrees to be bound by the same restrictions as Lone Star. Otherwise, AMD can withhold its required consent and halt the sale. While Lone Star argues that this restriction is insignificant because AMD cannot "unreasonably" withhold its consent, Lone Star concedes that it would be reasonable, indeed expected, for AMD to withhold consent if the prospective transferee refuses to be bound by the transfer agreement. Not only does this substantially restrict Lone Star's ability to transfer the patents, it ensures that AMD will always control how the patents are asserted. This is fundamentally inconsistent with a transfer of all substantial rights. Requiring Lone Star to assign the patents back to AMD, or an agent of its choice, before abandoning the patents has a similar effect.

In addition to these restrictions on enforcement and alienation, several other aspects of the agreement further support our conclusion. For example, the agreement secures a share of Lone Star's "monetization efforts" for AMD. And the agreement allows AMD and its affiliates to make, use, and sell products practicing the patents. While these facts may not be dispositive alone, together they suggest that AMD did not transfer all substantial rights in its patents to Lone Star.

Lone Star argues that the policy underpinning our "all substantial rights" test, the danger of multiple litigations against the same defendant by multiple plaintiffs, is not present here because AMD cannot sue Appellees. But we have also recognized a danger in allowing patentees to award a "hunting license" to third-parties. This additional policy concern lends support to our conclusion here.

In sum, we agree with the district court that AMD did not transfer all substantial rights in the asserted patents. Lone Star is therefore not the relevant patentee and cannot assert these patents in its own name under § 281.

Accordingly, we agree with the district court that Lone Star cannot bring suit in its own name because it does not possess all substantial rights in the asserted patents.

Notes and Questions

1. *Nonexclusive licensees.* The question of licensee standing only arises in the context of exclusive licensees. Why don't nonexclusive licensees ever get standing to sue third-party infringers? Aren't nonexclusive licensees also injured by infringing conduct in their respective fields?

2. *The question of exclusivity.* A licensee only has standing to sue an infringer if its license is exclusive. But what does "exclusive" mean in this context? *Rite-Hite Corp. v. Kelly Co. Inc.*, 56 F.3d 1538 (Fed. Cir. 1995) is best known for authorizing the recovery of certain "lost profits" damages under patent law. But *Rite-Hite* also addresses the issue of exclusivity for the

purposes of establishing standing for patent licensees. In that case, Rite-Hite, the manufac-turer of a patented device for securing a trailer to a loading dock, distributed its products both through its own direct sales organization and through a group of independent sales organiza-tions (ISOs), each granted an exclusive sales territory. The Rite-Hite direct sales organization accounted for approximately 30 percent of product sales, with the ISOs accounting for the remaining 70 percent. When Rite-Hite sued Kelley for patent infringement, the ISOs sought to join the lawsuit as co-plaintiffs. The Federal Circuit rejected the ISOs' claims, holding that their sales contracts were not exclusive patent licenses. It reasoned as follows:

> [The contracts] did not mention the word "patent" until the eve of this lawsuit. The ISO contracts permitted the ISOs only to solicit and make sales of products made by Rite-Hite in a particular "exclusive" sales territory. While the agreements conveyed the right to sell [prod-ucts] covered by the patent, any "exclusivity" related only to sales territories, not to patent rights. Even this sales exclusivity was conditional on Rite-Hite's judgment that the ISOs were doing an "adequate job."
>
> Most particularly, the ISOs had no right under the agreements to exclude anyone from mak-ing, using, or selling the claimed invention. The ISOs could not exclude from their respective territories other ISOs, third parties, or even Rite-Hite itself. Any remedy an ISO might have had for violation of its rights would lie in a breach of contract action against Rite-Hite, if the agreement was breached, not in a patent infringement action against infringers. Rite-Hite had no obligation to file infringement suits at the request of an ISO and the ISOs had no right to share in any recovery from litigation. Moreover, appellees have not contended that such obli-gations and rights are to be implied. Nor do appellees even argue that the ISOs had the right under their contracts to bring suit for infringement against another ISO or a third party, mak-ing Rite-Hite an involuntary plaintiff. To the contrary, under their agreement, if an ISO sold in another's territory, the profits were shared according to Rite-Hite's "split commission" rules.
>
> These agreements were simply sales contracts between Rite-Hite and its independent dis-tributors. They did not transfer any proprietary interest in the '847 patent and they did not give the ISOs the right to sue. If the ISOs lack a remedy in this case, it is because their agree-ments with Rite-Hite failed to make provisions for the contingency that the granted sales exclusivity would not be maintained. The ISOs could have required Rite-Hite to sue infrin-gers and arrangements could have been agreed upon concerning splitting any damage award. Apparently, this was not done.

How does the court's analysis in *Rite-Hite* compare to the more recent "all substantial rights" analysis under *Lone Star*? Which analytical framework is more likely to result in a finding of standing?

3. *The missing damages.* Judge Pauline Newman dissented from the court's decision in *Rite-Hite*. Among other things, she argued that by failing to recognize the ISOs' standing to sue, the majority allowed Kelley, the infringer, to avoid paying 70 percent of the damages it otherwise would have had to pay. That is, it should have paid damages attributable to the 70 percent of sales made by the ISOs either to the ISOs themselves or to Rite-Hite. Do you agree? Does the failure to grant standing to the ISOs represent a windfall to the infringer?

4. *Negotiating for fewer than all substantial rights.* In *Lone Star*, the court found that Lone Star lacked "all substantial rights" to the patent in question, even though the agreement purported to assign the patent to Lone Star. In particular, the court focused on a number of limitations on Lone Star's ability to exploit the patent rights to their fullest degree:

> Lone Star agreed to only assert the covered patents against "Unlicensed Third Party Entit[ies]" specifically listed in the agreement. New entities can only be added if Lone Star and AMD both agree to add them. If Lone Star sues an unlisted entity, AMD has the right—without

Lone Star's approval—to sublicense the covered patents to the unlisted target. AMD can also prevent Lone Star from assigning the patents or allowing them to enter the public domain. AMD and its customers can also continue to practice the patents, and AMD shares in any revenue Lone Star generates from the patents through "monetization efforts."

Why do you think that the parties structured their agreement in this manner? What advantages would AMD obtain from appearing to assign a patent but retaining rights such as these?

5. *All of the substantial rights.* In *Alfred E. Mann Found. for Sci. Research v. Cochlear Corp.*, 604 F.3d 1354, 1360–61 (Fed. Cir. 2010), the Federal Circuit listed a number of factors that it would consider when determining whether all substantial rights had been transferred to an exclusive licensee for standing purposes. These included:

- transfer of the exclusive right to make, use, and sell products or services under the patent
- the scope of the licensee's right to sublicense,
- the nature of license provisions regarding the reversion of rights to the licensor following breaches of the license agreement,
- the right of the licensor to receive a portion of the recovery in infringement suits brought by the licensee,
- the duration of the license rights granted to the licensee,
- the ability of the licensor to supervise and control the licensee's activities,
- the obligation of the licensor to continue paying patent maintenance fees,
- the nature of any limits on the licensee's right to assign its interests in the patent, and
- the nature and scope of the exclusive licensee's purported right to bring suit, together with the nature and scope of any right to sue purportedly retained by the licensor.

Of these, however, the court states that the licensor's right to sue accused infringers is the most important factor in determining whether an exclusive license transfers sufficient rights to render the licensee the owner of the patent. Why is this right so much more important than all the others? If none of the other factors listed above weighed in favor of a transfer of all substantial rights, but the licensor retained the right to sue infringers, what should a court conclude about the licensee's standing to sue?

6. *More substantial rights.* Does the court in *Lone Star* add any new factors to the list started by the court in *Alfred E. Mann*? Create an updated, comprehensive list of factors that a court should consider when analyzing whether a patent licensee should have standing to enforce a licensed patent against an infringer.

7. *Standing and exclusive fields.* Should a patent licensee have standing to sue an infringer if it has an exclusive license that is limited to a specific field of use? See *Intellectual Prop. Dev., Inc. v. TCI Cablevision of Cal., Inc.*, 248 F.3d 1333, 1342 (9th Cir. 2001) (holding that a licensee that is exclusive in a field does have standing to sue an infringer in that field).

8. *A troll with horns.* Lone Star Silicon Innovations, the plaintiff in *Lone Star*, is a patent assertion entity (PAE) controlled by Texas-based Longhorn IP. It "acquired" a portfolio of patents from AMD in 2016 and promptly filed several lawsuits against semiconductor manufacturers including Nanya and United Microelectronics. In fact, the rise of PAE litigation has sparked a resurgence of interest in licensee standing doctrines, and several recent cases analyze whether PAEs that acquire some, but not all, rights to patent portfolios have standing to sue.

The facts that the Federal Circuit recites, as well as those in the opinion that follows, shed light on PAE licensing practices. For example, when AMD divested its patents to Lone Star, it specifically designated competitors that Lone Star was authorized to sue, while retaining the right to veto suits against other companies. What kinds of companies might AMD have wished to prevent Lone Star from suing?

11.1.3 *Trademark Licensee Standing*

If the rules that have been developed for patent licensee standing seem confusing, then those involving trademark law are even more so, as they vary even within different sections of the Lanham Act. The below case illustrates this problem.

Gruen Marketing Corp. v. Benrus Watch Company, Inc.

955 F. Supp. 979 (N.D. Ill. 1997)

HART, DISTRICT JUDGE

Gruen Marketing Corporation ("Gruen") brings this action against defendants Benrus Watch Company, Inc. ("Benrus"), Hampden Watch Co., Inc. ("Hampden"), Irving Wein, Joseph Wein and Jim Herbert. [Defendants] move to dismiss Gruen's complaint.

I. Alleged Factual Background

Gruen, a Delaware corporation, is in the business of merchandising various products, such as watches, to major retailers and others. Benrus, a Delaware corporation, also sells watches and is the registrant for the trademark BENRUS. Hampden, a U.S. Virgin Islands corporation, assembles and sells watches for Benrus. Irving Wein controls Hampden and his son, Joseph Wein is a shareholder and officer of Benrus. Jim Herbert is a former Benrus employee.

Until June 1995, Benrus had sold its watches both with and without the BENRUS trademark. The watches not bearing the BENRUS trademark were sold as either personalized watches or private label watches. Personalized watches are sold by retailers with custom changes to the watch dial. Private label watches bear trademarks or logos of third parties, such as retailers.

In June 1995, Gruen and Benrus entered into three agreements, a License Agreement, Purchase Agreement and a Letter Agreement, each relating to Benrus' BENRUS line of watches. Pursuant to these agreements, Gruen acquired Benrus' business in BENRUS watches, including a master customer list, inventory, components and raw materials, intellectual property and a sales force to carry on the business. The License Agreement granted an exclusive license to Gruen for all uses of the BENRUS mark worldwide, except in Japan. Under the License Agreement, Benrus was not permitted to use the BENRUS mark without the prior written consent of Gruen. In addition, defendants Joseph Wein and Jim Herbert became Gruen sales agents. Gruen has paid $722,727.30 to Benrus under the License Agreement. Pursuant to the Purchase Agreement, Gruen paid $4,360,000 for all of Benrus' inventory, components and raw materials.

Despite its contractual obligations, Benrus did not discontinue using the BENRUS mark. Benrus and Irving Wein continued to use the BENRUS mark on Benrus letterhead and in other written materials. Benrus has sold watches bearing the BENRUS mark after the effective date of the License Agreement.

At a watch industry trade show in Hong Kong in September 1996, Joseph Wein stated to vendors and actual and potential customers of Gruen that Gruen was insolvent and unable to fulfill orders for BENRUS watches. Irving Wein has also made these representations, as well as stated that, in the future, Benrus will continue to sell BENRUS watches. In fact, Gruen is not insolvent and has substantial financial backing. Gruen's representatives have spent considerable time and effort to correct Irving and Joseph Wein's representations. In October 1996, Benrus diverted a shipment of watch cases from Gruen to itself. Benrus was able accomplish the diversion by using information learned as a result of its position as licensor of the BENRUS mark.

Irving Wein and Jim Herbert are former Benrus employees who became Gruen sales agents after the execution of the agreements between Benrus and Gruen. Benrus owed one of its customers a credit for returned BENRUS watches sold prior to the execution of the agreements. Joseph Wein directed the customer to apply the credit against invoices for watches purchased from Gruen. Jim Herbert persuaded certain Gruen customers to purchase Benrus' private label watches, although Herbert was working for Gruen at the time.

On November 12, 1996, Gruen filed its seven-count complaint …

II. Discussion

A. Count I: Trademark Infringement

In Count I, Gruen alleges that defendants are liable for trademark infringement because they used the BENRUS mark after the effective date of the License Agreement. Defendants argue that Gruen, as a licensee of Benrus, lacks standing to assert a claim under the Lanham Act. Gruen responds that it has standing because the License Agreement assigned, rather than merely licensed, the BENRUS trademark to Gruen.

Section 32 of the Lanham Act, 15 U.S.C. § 1114(1), grants standing to assert a claim for trademark infringement only to the "registrant" of the trademark. The term "registrant" includes the registrant and its "legal representatives, predecessors, successors and assigns." Several courts have held that a licensee has no right to sue a licensor under the Lanham Act, even where the licensee has been granted an exclusive right to use the trademark. Gruen, therefore, has standing to assert a trademark infringement claim only if the rights

FIGURE 11.2 A 1995 stainless steel Benrus "Men's Modern" watch issued to commemorate the fiftieth anniversary of D-Day.

granted to Gruen by the License Agreement amount to an assignment, as contemplated by the statute. An "assignment" of a mark is "an outright sale of all rights in that mark," whereas a license is "a limited permit to another to use the mark."

Benrus argues that the terms of the License Agreement demonstrate that Gruen is a licensee and not an assignee of the BENRUS mark. Benrus asserts that the License Agreement unequivocally reserved numerous rights in the BENRUS mark indicating that the BENRUS mark was not assigned to Gruen. For example, the License Agreement excludes Gruen from using the BENRUS mark in Japan and requires Gruen to obtain Benrus' approval for certain uses of the mark, such as advertising. In addition, Benrus reserved the right to sell BENRUS-marked goods to Jan Bell Marketing, Inc. and to use the mark on certain products sold through catalogs and direct mailings. Gruen was required to obtain Benrus' approval before assigning Gruen's rights under the License Agreement. Finally, the License Agreement contained the following provision:

> [Gruen] acknowledges that, as between [Gruen] and [Benrus], [Benrus] is the owner of all right, title and interest in and to the Licensed Mark in any form or embodiment thereof.

For its part, Gruen argues that it was assigned the BENRUS mark because "[n]otwithstanding the use of the term 'license' in an agreement, if a contract gives a party an exclusive license to use a trademark and otherwise discloses a purpose to transfer the rights in the trademark, the transfer is an assignment for purposes of the federal trademark laws." Gruen asserts that this is the case since it received the exclusive right to exploit the BENRUS mark, the right to sue for infringement, and the executory right to secure permanent transfer of the mark to Gruen. Gruen argues that its agreements with Benrus were akin to a mortgage or installment sale where Gruen's rights did not become final until future payment of funds.

Gruen's argument, however, does not overcome the express language of the License Agreement that Benrus retained ownership of the BENRUS mark. A licensee lacks standing where the agreement indicates that the licensor retains exclusive ownership of the mark. Other provisions of the agreement also support the conclusion that Gruen received only a license to use the BENRUS mark. For example, the License Agreement provides that Benrus "grants an exclusive license" to Gruen. Gruen was obligated to make royalty payments to Benrus and failure to do so terminated the license. Benrus retained the power to assure that Gruen maintained the quality of the BENRUS mark, a requirement consistent with a trademark license but not an assignment. That the License Agreement contemplated that Gruen one day would have the right to acquire title in the BENRUS mark does not mean Gruen was assigned the mark from the outset of the parties' relationship. Thus, title in the BENRUS mark did not pass to Gruen and Gruen does not have standing under 15 U.S.C. § 1114.

B. Count II: Section 43(a) of the Lanham Act[1]

Benrus moves to dismiss Count II, Gruen's Section 43(a) claim, on the same standing grounds as Gruen's trademark infringement claim. Under Section 43(a), however, a

---

[1] Section 43(a) of the Lanham Act (15 U.S.C. § 1125(a)), the "false designation of origin" provision, prohibits the making of a false statement that "(A) is likely to cause confusion, or to cause mistake, or to deceive as to the affiliation, connection, or association of such person with another person, or as to the origin, sponsorship, or approval of his or her goods, services, or commercial activities by another person, or (B) in commercial advertising or promotion, misrepresents the nature, characteristics, qualities, or geographic origin of his or her or another person's goods, services, or commercial activities" (Ed.)

plaintiff need not be the owner of a registered trademark in order to have standing to sue. Although a few cases have treated standing under Section 43(a) as interchangeable with standing under 15 U.S.C. § 1114, the better rule is that a licensee may assert a Section 43(a) claim against its licensor and third parties. Section 43(a) states that a person who violates its prohibitions shall be liable in a civil action "by any person who believes that he or she is likely to be damaged" by a prohibited act. 15 U.S.C. § 1125(a). This language is broader than the language of 15 U.S.C. § 1114(1), which states that trademark infringers "shall be liable in a civil action by the registrant." Consistent with the language of the statute, a plaintiff will be required to show "the proof of ownership of a proprietary right" or that it has "a reasonable interest to protect, which some courts have characterized as a commercial interest." Because Gruen possesses a license to use the BENRUS mark, Gruen has standing under Section 43(a) to bring an action against Benrus and the other defendants.

Benrus contends, however, that even if Gruen has standing to raise a Section 43(a) claim, Gruen has failed to state a claim beyond a breach by Benrus of the License Agreement. Because this argument is not a jurisdictional challenge, the allegations of the complaint will be taken as true and all disputed facts will be resolved in favor of the plaintiff. In Count II, Gruen alleges that Benrus' use of the BENRUS trademark constitutes false designation of origin and constitutes "passing off" of its watches as Gruen's BENRUS watches. In order to prove a claim pursuant to Section 43(a), a plaintiff must show "(1) that its trademark may be protected and (2) that the relevant group of buyers is likely to confuse the alleged infringer's products or services with those of plaintiff."

Gruen's right to relief hinges on its ability to enforce the exclusivity provision of the License Agreement. Gruen has not alleged anything beyond Benrus' alleged breach of the License Agreement. As one court has noted in considering an exclusive licensee's claim against its licensor …

> [T]his case is essentially a contract dispute between an exclusive licensee and a licensor over the right to use the trademark MEAT LOAF. Silverstar's dispute should be determined by the principles of contract law, as it is the contract that defines the parties' relationship and provides mechanisms to redress alleged breaches thereto. The Lanham Act, in contrast, establishes marketplace rules governing the conduct of parties not otherwise limited. This is not a case of either the licensee or licensor attempting to protect a trademark from unscrupulous use in the marketplace by third parties. Rather, this case involves the alleged breach of a license agreement.

[*Silverstar Enterprises, Inc. v. Aday*, 537 F. Supp. 236, 242 (S.D.N.Y. 1982)]. *Silverstar's* reasoning applies in this case. Moreover, the principle that a contractual dispute concerning a license will not give rise to a federal cause of action has been recognized in this circuit. Contract law, not the Lanham Act, governs the parties' dispute. Count II will be dismissed.

Notes and Questions

1. *Vive la différence.* Section 32 of the Lanham Act permits only the "registrant" of a trademark to bring a suit for infringement, while Section 43(a) allows "any person" who has been injured to bring a suit for false designation of goods. Is this difference justified? What would be the effect of expanding the scope of standing for trademark infringement, or narrowing the scope of standing for false designation claims?

2. *What about licensees?* Under both copyright and patent law, an exclusive licensee has standing to bring suit against an infringer. But the term "registrant" under Section 32 of the Lanham Act has not been interpreted to include licensees. Why not? Would you extend standing to exclusive trademark licensees?

3. *Breach of contract.* The court finds that Gruen does have standing to bring a false designation claim under Section 43(a) of the Lanham Act. Yet the court still dismisses Gruen's Section 43(a) claim against Benrus. Why? How might you amend Gruen's complaint to avoid this problem?

11.1.4 *Trade Secret Licensee Standing*

Because many trade secret cases are brought under state law, standing rules vary among the states. Nevertheless, it is generally understood that trade secret licensees, even nonexclusive licensees, have standing to bring claims for trade secret misappropriation.[2] This principle is embodied in the Uniform Trade Secrets Act (USTA), which has been adopted in most states, as well as the federal Defend Trade Secrets Act.[3] In fact, courts have even held that the mere lawful *possession* of a trade secret entitles the possessor to maintain a claim of trade secret misappropriation.[4]

The rationale for this departure from the standing rules for other forms of IP is not well articulated. One pair of practitioners suggests that "the harm suffered by a victim of trade secret misappropriation does not emanate solely from a violation of property rights, but also from a violation of confidence and fair and ethical business practices. Thus, anyone who possesses a trade secret, whether an exclusive licensee or not, can theoretically suffer harm via a violation of confidence."[5]

11.1.5 *Joinder*

Further complicating the question of licensee standing is the procedural issue of joinder. As discussed above, a party must have *standing* in order to participate in a lawsuit. But for a suit to be maintained and heard by a court, all necessary parties must participate in that suit. Otherwise, the resolution reached by the court may not actually dispose of the matter and, if fewer than all required plaintiffs are not joined in the suit, the defendant may be subjected to multiple liability for the same wrong. For example, suppose that a copyright is jointly owned by three co-authors. One of them sues an infringer and the court renders a judgment against the infringer, who pays damages to the asserting co-author. Can the other two co-authors now bring suit separately against the infringer? If they are successful, the infringer could end up paying the same damages three times. But if they cannot bring suit, they are deprived of an important legal right. More importantly, what if the first co-author handled the suit poorly and failed to prove infringement? Does that finding have res judicata effect on the other co-authors?

To avoid these and many other difficult questions, the Federal Rules of Civil Procedure (FRCP) require that all necessary parties to a suit be joined in the suit. FRCP 20 addresses voluntary joinder (who *may* join a suit), while FRCP 19 address mandatory joinder (who *must* join in order for the suit to move forward).

---

[2]   See Esha Bandyopadhyay & Alana Mannige, *What to Know about Licensee Standing in Trade Secret Cases*, Law360, June 16, 2020.

[3]   18 U.S.C.S. § 1836; 18 U.S.C.S. § 1839

[4]   *Advanced Fluid Sys. v. Huber*, 958 F.3d 168 (3rd Cir. 2020), *DTM Research, L.L.C. v. AT & T Corp.*, 245 F.3d 327 (4th Cir. 2001).

[5]   Bandyopadhyay & Mannige, supra note 2.

JOINDER UNDER THE FEDERAL RULES OF CIVIL PROCEDURE

Rule 19: Required Joinder of Parties

(a) Persons Required to be Joined if Feasible.

(1) *Required Party*. A person who is subject to service of process and whose joinder will not deprive the court of subject-matter jurisdiction must be joined as a party if:

  (A) in that person's absence, the court cannot accord complete relief among existing parties; or

  (B) that person claims an interest relating to the subject of the action and is so situated that disposing of the action in the person's absence may:

   (i) as a practical matter impair or impede the person's ability to protect the interest; or

   (ii) leave an existing party subject to a substantial risk of incurring double, multiple, or otherwise inconsistent obligations because of the interest.

(2) *Joinder by Court Order*. If a person has not been joined as required, the court must order that the person be made a party. A person who refuses to join as a plaintiff may be made either a defendant or, in a proper case, an involuntary plaintiff.

(b) When Joinder Is Not Feasible.
If a person who is required to be joined if feasible cannot be joined, the court must determine whether, in equity and good conscience, the action should proceed among the existing parties or should be dismissed. The factors for the court to consider include:

(1) the extent to which a judgment rendered in the person's absence might prejudice that person or the existing parties;

(2) the extent to which any prejudice could be lessened or avoided by:

  (A) protective provisions in the judgment;

  (B) shaping the relief; or

  (C) other measures;

(3) whether a judgment rendered in the person's absence would be adequate; and

(4) whether the plaintiff would have an adequate remedy if the action were dismissed for nonjoinder.

In patent cases, courts have generally held that all co-owners of a patent must join in a suit for the suit to proceed.[6] But what if a co-owner, for any of a number of reasons, is not willing to join a suit to enforce a co-owned patent? Can it be compelled to join pursuant to FRCP 19? In *STC. UNM v. Intel Corp.*, 767 F.3d 1351 (Fed. Cir. 2014), the Federal Circuit said no, holding that

the right of a patent co-owner to impede an infringement suit brought by another co-owner is a substantive right that trumps the procedural rule for involuntary joinder under Rule 19(a).

In *STC.UNM*, the fact that Sandia National Laboratory, the co-owner of the asserted patent, refused to join an infringement suit brought against Intel by STC.UNM (the licensing arm of

---

[6] See *Ethicon, Inc. v. United States Surgical Corp.*, 135 F.3d 1456, 1468 (Fed. Cir. 1998) ("An action for infringement must join as plaintiffs all co-owners").

the University of New Mexico) led the district court to dismiss the suit for failure to join all necessary parties. In affirming the district court's decision, the Federal Circuit recognized the hardship caused to STC.UNM, the co-owner who asserted the patent:

> This court is, of course, conscious of the equities at play in this case. Unless STC can secure Sandia's voluntary joinder … STC cannot enforce the '998 patent in court. STC is certainly still free to enjoy all the rights a co-owner enjoys, such as commercializing or exploiting the '998 patent through licensing without consent of the other co-owners. Admittedly, a license demand may have less bite if STC cannot sue potential licensees if they refuse (and if Sandia would not voluntarily join the suit). However, this limit on a co-owner's right to enforce a patent is one effect of the reality that each co-owner is "at the mercy" of its other co-owners.
>
> Importantly, this limit protects, *inter alia*, a co-owner's right to not be thrust into costly litigation where its patent is subject to potential invalidation. Furthermore, the rule requiring in general the participation of all co-owners safeguards against the possibility that each co-owner would subject an accused infringer to a different infringement suit on the same patent. Both concerns underpin this court's joinder requirement for patent owners.

Despite this unfortunate result for STC.UNM, the Federal Circuit did recognize two exceptions to the rule against using FRCP 19 to compel a patent co-owner to join a suit to enforce the patent:

> First, when any patent owner has granted an exclusive license, he stands in a relationship of trust to his licensee and can be involuntarily joined as a plaintiff in the licensee's infringement suit; second, if, by agreement, a co-owner waives his right to refuse to join suit, his co-owners may subsequently force him to join in a suit against infringers. [citations omitted]

Thus, unlike a co-owner of a patent, an exclusive licensee can require its licensor to join a suit as a necessary party under Rule 19. This "exception" to the rule against compelling joinder of co-owners of patents arose before the adoption of the FRCP. In *Independent Wireless Telegraph Co v. Radio Corp of America*, 269 US 459 (1926), the Supreme Court recognized that licensees cannot generally bring suit in their own name, but also concluded that an exclusive licensee should be able to join the patent owner, involuntarily if need be, to maintain suit. Otherwise, the licensee possesses a right without a remedy. Joinder "secur[es] justice to the exclusive licensee." It also honors "the obligation the [patent] owner is under to allow the use of his name and title to protect all lawful exclusive licensees and sublicensees against infringers." The joinder rule outlined in *Independent Wireless* was eventually incorporated into FRCP 19, and is generally viewed as applying both to exclusive licensees of patents and copyrights.

If a party whose joinder is required by FRCP 19(a) cannot be feasibly joined, part (b) allows a court to consider whether the case should proceed anyway or be dismissed because that party is indispensable. In *A123 Sys., Inc. v. Hydro-Quebec*, 626 F.3d 1213, 1222 (Fed. Cir. 2010), the Federal Circuit held that dismissal was appropriate because the absent patent owner, who could not be joined because it had not waived sovereign immunity, "was not only a necessary party but also an indispensable party."

Notes and Questions

1. *Rationales for refusal.* A patent holder stands to collect damages and eliminate a potential competitor by enforcing its patent in court. What reasons might the co-owner of a patent have for declining to join a suit to enforce its co-owned patent?

2. *Licensees are special.* As discussed by the Federal Circuit in *STC.UNM*, while a co-owner of a patent cannot utilize Rule 19 to require the joinder of another co-owner in an infringement suit, an exclusive licensee can. Why does a licensee have the ability to drag its licensor into litigation against its will when the co-owner of a patent does not?

3. *Joinder of whom?* Suppose a patent is jointly owned by two parties. One of the co-owners grants an exclusive license to a licensee. The licensee wishes to sue a third party for infringement. Under the rule articulated in *STC.UNM*, the licensee may involuntarily join the licensor under FRCP 19. But what about the other co-owner? The exception stated by the court in *STC.UNM* only relates to the licensor. But without the joinder of both co-owners, the suit may not be able to proceed. Should an exclusive licensee be able to involuntarily join its licensor's co-owners?

4. *Joinder as a remedy for lack of standing.* In *Lone Star* (discussed in Section 11.1.2), the district court found, and the Federal Circuit affirmed, that because Lone Star lacked "all substantial rights" in the asserted patent, it lacked standing to bring suit. However, the Federal Circuit also held that "the district court should not have dismissed this case without considering whether Advanced Micro Devices, Inc. ('AMD'), the relevant patentee, should have been joined." The Federal Circuit further explained,

> If AMD is the patentee, as the district court correctly concluded, then AMD's joinder would ordinarily be "required." And since Lone Star agreed that AMD should be joined, assuming it retained substantial rights in the asserted patents, Lone Star essentially conceded that AMD is a necessary party. The district court therefore should have considered whether AMD's joinder was feasible. If so, then AMD must be joined—involuntarily if need be. If not, then the district court should consider whether AMD is indispensable. Rather than engaging in this analysis, however, the district court declined to join AMD … But the application of Rule 19 is mandatory, not discretionary.

What could be the result if AMD did not wish to be joined in the suit? Given the context discussed in Note 8 of Section 11.1.2, how likely do you think it is that AMD would join Lone Star's suit?

5. *Joinder and copyright.* Section 501(b) of the Copyright Act provides that when a joint owner of a copyright brings an action to enforce its copyright against an infringer,

> the court may require such owner to serve written notice of the action with a copy of the complaint upon any person shown, by the records of the Copyright Office or otherwise, to have or claim an interest in the copyright, and shall require that such notice be served upon any person whose interest is likely to be affected by a decision in the case. The court may require the joinder, and shall permit the intervention, of any person having or claiming an interest in the copyright.

Unfortunately, the Act is not clear about when a court that "may" require notice to or joinder of co-owners should do so. Is the standard for joinder the same as it is under FRCP 19? Should it be? Should the Patent Act be amended to be more consistent with the Copyright Act in this regard? When might a court be justified in *not* exercising its discretion to order such co-owner notice or joinder in a copyright infringement suit?

6. *International complications.* As you have doubtless concluded by now, the rules regarding licensee standing to sue are convoluted, inconsistent and difficult to reconcile. Yet imagine the added complexity when the laws of multiple countries are involved. As described by Professor Jacques de Werra,

A review of case law shows that local courts take very different factors into account when they assess whether a license is exclusive and whether an exclusive licensee has the right to sue. Under certain legal systems, courts can admit exclusivity despite the fact that the IP owner retains certain rights. Similarly, certain courts have deemed a patent license to be exclusive even though other licenses had previously been granted to third parties, i.e. before the license agreement at issue was executed. Other courts, however, have rejected such a conclusion. For certain courts, a short contractual term of an exclusive license constitutes a reason to refuse the licensee a right to sue, while other courts consider this factor to be irrelevant. This could mean that, based on the same license agreement, which would provide for a relatively short term, the licensee could be permitted to sue in one country but be refused standing to sue in another country. The question whether a licensee can grant sublicenses can also be relevant for the courts' determinations as to whether or not a licensee has the right to sue third-party infringers.[7]

Given all this, how would you advise a client seeking to exploit its IP rights around the world, yet wishing to retain the right to enforce its IP?

11.2 AGREEMENTS TO ENFORCE

In Section 11.1 we considered when an exclusive licensee of an IP right has legal standing to bring suit to enforce that IP right, and when the IP owner must be joined in that suit in order for it to proceed. In this section we shift to a related question: How is the responsibility for pursuing infringers of a licensed IP right contractually allocated among a licensor and its exclusive licensee?

As discussed in Section 7.2.3, a licensor has no implied obligation to pursue infringers in an exclusive licensee's field. Thus, if a licensee wishes to require the licensor to pursue infringers, or to pursue infringers itself (with the consent and joinder of the licensor), these obligations must be specified in the agreement. As noted by the Federal Circuit in *Ethicon v. United States Surgical Corp.*, 135 F.3d 1456, 1465 (Fed. Cir. 1998), "A patent license agreement that binds the inventor to participate in subsequent litigation is very common."

EXAMPLE: ENFORCEMENT AGAINST THIRD-PARTY INFRINGERS

1. **Notification of Third Party Infringement.** When information comes to the attention of Licensor or Licensee to the effect that any of the Licensed Rights in the Field have been or are threatened to be infringed by a third party ("Third Party Infringement"), such party shall notify the other party in writing of such Third Party Infringement.
2. **Enforcement by Licensor.** Licensor shall have the initial right, but not the obligation, to take any action to stop such Third Party Infringement [1] and Licensee shall, at Licensor's expense, cooperate with Licensor in any such action.
3. **Enforcement by Licensee.** In the event that Licensor takes no action to stop such infringement within ninety (90) days of receipt of notice from Licensee, Licensee shall have the right to commence an action against the alleged infringer, at its own expense and in its own name [2].

---

7 Jacques de Werra, *Can Exclusive Licensees Sue for Infringement of Licensed IP Rights? A Case Study Confirming the Need to Create Global IP Licensing Rules*, 30 Harv. J. L. & Tech. 189, 195–96 (2017).

3. **Control of Litigation**. The party that initiates suit hereunder with respect to a Third Party Infringement (the "Litigating Party") shall have sole control of that proceeding and the exclusive right to employ counsel of its own selection and to direct and control the litigation. The Non-Litigating Party shall have, at its own expense, the right to participate in such action through counsel of its own selection.

4. **Settlement**. The Litigating Party shall have the sole right to settle any litigation brought hereunder, provided that if such Litigating Party is the Licensor and it desires to settle such litigation by granting a third party a license in the exclusive field of the Licensee, the Licensor shall first give the Licensee written notice of the terms of the proposed settlement, and the Licensee shall have the right to approve or reject such proposed settlement in its reasonable discretion. The failure of the Licensee to respond to such notice of settlement within ten (10) business days shall automatically constitute an approval of the terms of the proposed settlement by the Licensee.

5. **Allocation of Recoveries**. Any recovery, whether by way of settlement or judgment, from a Third Party pursuant to a legal proceeding initiated in accordance with this Section shall first be used to reimburse the Litigating Party for its actual fees, costs and expenses incurred in connection with such proceeding. The balance of such recovery shall be divided in the ratio of [__% to Licensor/Litigating Party and __% to Licensee/Non-Litigating Party] [3].

6. **Cooperation; Joinder**. The Non-Litigating Party shall cooperate fully with and supply all assistance reasonably requested by the Litigating Party in connection with any action brough hereunder, including without limitation, joining the proceeding as a party if requested [4].

DRAFTING NOTES

[1] *First right to sue* – this clause gives the licensor the first right to sue a third-party infringer, but does not require the licensor to sue. Clauses with a strict requirement to sue are rare.

[2] *Licensee's right to sue* – the above example gives the exclusive licensee the second right to sue a third-party infringer if the licensor declines to exercise its right to sue. Not all licensing agreements give the licensee the right to sue if the licensor declines to do so. Not giving this right to the licensee effectively places full control over the right to sue in the hands of the licensor, which might be appropriate if the licensee's exclusivity is only in one narrow field or if the licensor has extensive business arrangements that it does not wish a licensee to disrupt through litigation.

[3] *Split of recoveries* – if the licensor/licensee are successful in pursuing a claim of infringement against a third party and thereby receive a monetary award, they must decide how to split that award after the litigating party is reimbursed for its costs of litigation. There are many theories regarding the appropriate split of these proceeds. At one extreme, the party that litigated the claim may wish to retain all of the proceeds, given the risk it incurred in bringing the litigation. The parties may also determine a fixed formula for splitting proceeds, such as 50 percent to each party, or 75 percent to the litigating party and 25 percent to the other. Or the parties may treat such litigation proceeds as "net

sales" subject to whatever royalty obligation otherwise exists under the agreement (e.g., if the licensee pays a 10 percent royalty to the licensor, then the licensor would receive 10 percent of the litigation recovery and the licensee would retain the remaining 90 percent). Of course, in the case of an infringement, the licensee has incurred no costs of manufacturing or distributing the products triggering the payment, so permitting it to retain all but the original royalty percentage may overcompensate the licensee. Some agreements are drafted more vaguely, providing that the proceeds be divided "in proportion to the loss incurred by each party," which introduces its own evidentiary burdens. In reality, such a clause will likely require the parties to agree on a split of proceeds as part of their discussion of which of them will initiate litigation against the third-party infringer.

[4] *Agreement to join* – as discussed in Section 11.1.4, the IP owner or exclusive licensee may be required to join an infringement suit in order for the suit to proceed. Yet there are circumstances under which a party may be reluctant to join such a suit voluntarily, and the court may lack the jurisdiction to compel such party to join under FRCP 19. This provision contractually obligates a party to join a suit initiated by the other party when necessary to maintain the suit. The parties should consider carefully whether there are any exceptions to this mandatory joinder requirement that they wish to reflect in the agreement (e.g., a university may not wish to be required to sue one of its major donors).

Ryan Data Exch., Ltd. v. Graco, Inc.

913 F.3d 726 (8th Cir. 2019)

BEAM, CIRCUIT JUDGE

On September 13, 2005, [Ryan Data Exchange (Rydex)] and Graco entered into a Settlement and License Agreement (Agreement) in which Rydex granted Graco a patent license. In the instant action, the parties litigated three provisions of the Agreement at trial: (1) the provision wherein Rydex granted Graco an exclusive license to make, have made, use, and sell articles covered by the patent (§ 3.0); (2) the Agreement's provision that if a third party were to infringe the patent, Rydex would have the initial choice and obligation to prosecute the infringement (§ 11);[8] and (3) a provision stating that Graco would pay Rydex royalties of 5% of the net selling price of its product using the patent (§ 4.1).

Relevant to the instant litigation, in 2011, years after the parties entered into the Agreement, Rydex initiated a lawsuit alleging patent infringement against Badger Meter, Inc., Balcrank Corp., and Lincoln Industrial Corp. (collectively, Badger). The district court found, and the trial evidence revealed, a unique set of circumstances regarding Badger's

---

[8] Section 11 of the Agreement reads: "Should there be patent infringement relating to the licensed field of use by a third party and Licensee notifies Licensors of such infringement, Licensors shall have the initial choice and obligation to prosecute the infringement. If Licensors do not prosecute the infringement within ninety [*5] (90) days of learning of the infringement, then Licensee is free to prosecute the infringement. If Licensee prosecutes the patent infringement … the benefit of the damages or settlement achieved from the infringement shall be divided equally between Licensors on one hand and Licensee on the other after enforcement expenses incurred by Licensee have been paid" (2016 U.S. Dist. LEXIS 189569, at *4–5 (S.D. Ia. 2016)). "The Agreement also states that if in a separate action with a third party a court finds that a product equivalent to the Matrix system does not infringe the '180 Patent, 'all obligations under this Agreement will terminate'" (Id. at *5–6).

infringement, in that at the time Rydex and Graco entered into the 2005 Agreement, both parties were aware that Badger was allegedly already infringing the patent, and yet the Agreement purported to give Graco an exclusive right to the patent. In 2012 Rydex and Badger filed a stipulation of dismissal and agreed that Rydex's claims and Badger's counterclaims in the matter would be dismissed with prejudice.[9] This dismissal between Rydex and Badger is the source of Graco's claim against Rydex for failure to prosecute infringement under the Agreement.

Graco stopped paying royalties to Rydex as of December 31, 2013, as Graco believed that Rydex had breached the Agreement's exclusivity provision and the patent infringement prosecution provision (§§ 3 and 11) by allowing Badger to continue its infringement and by failing to fully prosecute the infringement claim against Badger. In May 2014, Rydex filed the instant complaint alleging breach of contract and patent infringement by Graco. Graco countersued, also alleging breach of contract and seeking declaratory judgments that the patent was invalid and that Rydex had lost its right to receive royalty payments under the Agreement due to its alleged breaches.

A jury trial was held in November 2016 on all of the contract claims then pending. During trial Graco moved pursuant to Rule 50(a) for judgment as a matter of law at the close of Rydex's case-in-chief, claiming in part that it had established through cross-examination that Rydex had breached its duty under the Agreement to prosecute the Badger litigation, and that Rydex had breached the exclusivity provision of the Agreement. In ruling on Graco's motions from the bench, the district court held as a matter of law that Rydex had breached its duty to prosecute infringement as of the date of the dismissal of the Badger litigation in 2012, and that Rydex was in breach of the exclusivity provision of the Agreement from the date of the dismissal of the Badger litigation until the expiration of the patent on March 10, 2015. Accordingly, the court granted Graco's Rule 50 motion to that extent. There was no ruling by the court as to whether Rydex breached the Agreement by failing to provide Graco an exclusive license from the date the parties entered into the Agreement in 2005 until the dismissal of the Badger litigation in 2012.

The parties discussed throughout, and after trial, how to "package" this case for the jury in light of the court's Rule 50 rulings. Accordingly, the case was presented to the jury for very particular determinations with a verdict form consisting of five narrow questions for the jury. Instruction 7, titled "Elements of Breach of Contract," stated the elements required to prove a breach of contract under Iowa law, and also instructed the jury regarding the district court's prior grant of judgment as a matter of law in favor of Graco:

> Regarding the Rydex Parties' breach of contract claim, it is for you to decide whether Graco breached the License Agreement by failing to pay royalties to the Rydex Parties for the period ending December 31, 2013, through the date of the expiration of the '180 patent on March 10, 2015.

---

[9]   The district court opinion in the case below offers additional insight as to why Rydex dismissed its infringement suit against Badger: "The Badger Defendants asserted defenses of invalidity and non-infringement concerning the '180 Patent and filed a counterclaim for declaratory judgment of invalidity and non-infringement. Rydex knew there was a risk that the Badger Litigation would end with a finding of non-infringement or that the '180 Patent was invalid, and that either would relieve Graco from royalty payments. Thereafter, Rydex did virtually nothing to prosecute the Badger Litigation: among other things, it did not serve any document requests, requests for admission, or interrogatories; it did not depose any defendant or third parties; it did not bring a motion for an injunction; and it did not attend a preliminary scheduling conference set by the court. Instead, Rydex and the defendants requested that the district court adjourn the scheduling conference so the parties could discuss settlement" (2016 U.S. Dist. LEXIS 189569 at *6–7 (S.D. Ia. 2016)).

Regarding Graco's breach of contract claim, the Court has found as a matter of law that the Rydex Parties were not required to commence an infringement action prior to the filing of the Badger Litigation. The Court has also found as a matter of law that the Rydex Parties were in breach of the duty to prosecute infringement as of the date of the dismissal of the Badger Litigation on August 15, 2012. The Court has further found as a matter of law that the Rydex Parties were in breach of the exclusivity provision of the License Agreement from the date of the dismissal of the Badger Litigation on August 15, 2012, until the expiration of the '180 patent on March 10, 2015. You must accept these facts as having been proved. It is for you to decide whether the Rydex Parties were in breach of the exclusivity provision of the License Agreement from the date the parties entered into that license agreement on September 13, 2005, through the dismissal of the Badger Litigation on August 15, 2012.

Upon deliberation, the jury found, first, that Rydex proved at trial that Graco breached the Agreement by failing to pay royalties to Rydex from December 31, 2013, through the date of the expiration of the patent on March 10, 2015; and awarded Rydex $313,000 in damages. Next, in response to the query regarding the amount of damages due Graco as a result of Rydex's breaches already determined by the court as a matter of law and laid out for the jury in Instruction 7 (i.e., its breach of duty to prosecute infringement and the breach of the exclusivity provision of the Agreement at the time of the Badger litigation dismissal), the jury answered "$0.00." As to the question to the jury as to whether Graco proved that Rydex breached the Agreement by failing to provide Graco an exclusive license from the date the parties entered into the Agreement on September 13, 2005, until the dismissal of the Badger litigation on August 15, 2012, the jury answered "no."

Notes and Questions

1. *Declining the first right to sue.* Under what circumstances might a licensor legitimately not wish to bring suit against an alleged infringer? In these circumstances, should the licensor retain the right to veto any suit by the licensee?
2. *Contract versus standing.* Suppose that a licensing agreement gives the licensor the right to sue infringers, but is silent as to the licensee's right. Should the licensee be permitted to sue if it otherwise has standing? What if the licensing agreement expressly prohibits the licensee from bringing suit? Should this contractual prohibition be disregarded if the licensee otherwise has standing?
3. *Consent to settlement.* In clause 4 of the example, the licensee is given the right to consent to a settlement proposed by the licensor, but the reverse is not true (i.e., the licensee may settle litigation without the licensor's consent). Why?
4. *Remedies.* What is the appropriate remedy when a party breaches its contractual obligation to join a lawsuit brought by the other party? A court cannot generally compel a party over which it lacks jurisdiction to join a lawsuit; can a party be compelled by contract to join a suit? What amount of monetary damages? Why do you think the jury in *Ryan Data* awarded Graco $0.00 with respect to Rydex's failure to enforce the licensed patent after 2012?
5. *Timing of enforcement.* Why do you think the jury in *Ryan Data* found that Rydex had not breached its contractual obligation to enforce the patent against Badger from 2005 through 2011? Would the result have been different if Graco had asserted this breach in 2010 instead of 2014? Why did the court hold, as a matter of law, that Rydex breached this obligation from 2012 through 2015?

Problem 11.1

Draft an enforcement clause that reflects the perspective and likely requirements of each of the following clients:

a. A small US liberal arts college that has exclusively licensed a set of educational videos to a large online learning company for distribution via the Internet.
b. A United States-based manufacturer of decorative license plates that has exclusively licensed a well-known brand from an Italian luxury goods maker in the US market.
c. A large US aircraft manufacturer that has exclusively licensed a system for onboard entertainment from a German software company.

11.3 CONTRACTUAL CHOICE OF LAW

It is not unlikely that disagreements over the terms of licensing agreements and disputes over compliance with those terms will arise, and parties are well-advised to plan in advance how they would like to resolve those disagreements. There are several types of contractual clauses that are used in this regard – those that specify which jurisdiction's substantive laws will govern an agreement (Choice of Law), those that specify which court(s) are designated to resolve disputes (Choice of Forum or Venue, discussed in Section 11.4), and those that establish alternative dispute resolution procedures (discussed in Section 11.5).

The interpretation and enforcement of every contract is conducted through the medium of a particular jurisdiction's laws. The meanings of terms such as "best efforts," "prompt response" and "reasonable notice" may differ substantially from one state to another, not to mention from one country to another. Some jurisdictions may impose implicit duties of good faith and fair dealing that color the parties' actions, and others may permit parties to rely entirely on the four corners of their contract. Some jurisdictions have more stringent data protection, personal privacy and risk disclosure rules than others, all of which could affect a party's liability for inadequate performance. And, as discussed in Section 3.3.3, Virginia and Maryland are the only two states that have enacted the Uniform Computer Information Transactions Act (UCITA), which could have a material effect on some licensing transactions. Thus, the particular body of legal rules governing the performance and interpretation of an agreement may have a substantive impact on the parties' duties and liability.

In addition to these substantive concerns, parties may wish to select a particular jurisdiction's laws in order to ensure consistency of interpretation across disputes concerning the same contract. For example, a multiparty international license agreement could be enforced in any of the countries in which a party is based or where the agreement is performed, and could be interpreted quite differently depending on the law governing the agreement. For the sake of consistency and stability, it is advisable to have all disputes arising under a single agreement or set of agreements governed by the same set of laws.

Along the same lines, it is useful to operate under the laws of a jurisdiction in which the courts have considered the issues that are likely to arise under the agreement in question. For example, the courts of Southern California have probably considered far more agreements relating to film production that the courts of, say, North Dakota. The body of case law in a particular area makes it more likely that binding precedent will exist to guide the parties' planning and behavior. This observation applies even in areas that are principally governed by federal law, such as patents, copyrights and trademarks, as the relevant federal district courts hearing such cases will necessarily draw upon local contract law in order to guide their resolution of nonfederal issues.

Finally, and perhaps most importantly, attorneys drafting, negotiating and interpreting agreements generally derive a degree of comfort from knowing that an agreement will be governed by a set of laws with which they are familiar. In some cases, this desire for familiarity is more than just a matter of comfort. The bar overseers of certain US states, particularly California, have taken a strict view of out-of-state attorneys providing advice regarding contracts governed by California law, an activity that could constitute the unauthorized practice of law.[10]

For all of these reasons, it behooves parties to select the body of substantive law[11] that will govern the interpretation of their agreement and any disputes arising out of it. And, in fact, most parties to substantial agreements today attempt to do so.[12]

EXAMPLE: GOVERNING LAW

This Agreement and its interpretation, and all disputes between the parties arising in any manner hereunder, shall be governed by and construed in accordance with the internal laws of [STATE/COUNTRY] [1] [without giving effect to any choice or conflict of law provision or rule (whether of [STATE/COUNTRY] or any other jurisdiction) that would cause the application of laws of any jurisdictions other than those of [STATE/COUNTRY]] [2].

The Parties hereby unconditionally waive their respective rights to a jury trial of any claim or cause of action arising directly or indirectly out of, related to, or in any way connected with the performance or breach of this Agreement, and/or the relationship that is being established among them [3].

DRAFTING NOTES

[1] *Which state(s)?* – the typical governing law clause specifies the laws of a single state or other jurisdiction, but it is also possible to choose the laws of multiple jurisdictions to govern different aspects of a complex transaction.[13]

[2] *Excluding conflicts principles* – suppose that a contract specifies that it will be governed by the laws of State X, but because the parties have no contacts with State X, and the performance of the contract does not affect State X, the conflicts of laws rules of State X may hold that the laws of State X should not apply to the contract. This clause seeks to avoid that outcome by overriding the conflicts rules of State X and providing that the

---

[10] See *In Re Garcia*, 335 B.R. 717 (9th Cir. BAP 2005) ("Preparation of legal documents ... are regarded as legal services. It is well settled in California that "practicing law" means more than just appearing in court ... Under California law, the practice of law includes the preparation of legal instruments and contracts by which legal rights are secured, whether the matter is pending in court or not" (citations omitted)).

[11] In contrast to substantive law, it is more difficult to select a set of procedural rules to govern a particular contract. Procedure is typically applied by the courts of a jurisdiction in a mandatory fashion that is difficult to alter by contract.

[12] John F. Coyle, *A Short History of the Choice-of-Law Clause*, 91 U. Colo. L. Rev. 1147, 1181 (2020) (citing studies finding that 70–75 percent of agreements filed with the US Securities and Exchange Commission contained choice of law clauses).

[13] See Henry E. Smith, *Modularity in Contracts: Boilerplate and Information Flow*, 104 Mich. L. Rev. 1175, 1192–93 (2006) (discussing selection of multiple state/national laws in governing law clauses).

laws of State X will apply, even if the laws of State X themselves would not apply State X's laws to the agreement. As you can imagine, the courts of many jurisdictions will not enforce such an override clause.[14] Nevertheless, attorneys often include it in their agreements.

[3] *Waiver of jury trial* – in the United States (alone among nations), jury trials are still guaranteed under the Seventh Amendment of the Constitution in all civil cases. This clause, which sometimes appears in a standalone section of an agreement, is a voluntary waiver of the parties' right to a trial by jury. It is generally considered to be enforceable. Waiving this right may or may not be advisable. Juries often sympathize with injured parties (including IP holders), and sometimes award astronomical damages in IP cases. Thus, an IP holder may be better off with a jury trial than a bench trial, in which factual matters, including monetary damages, are decided by a judge.

11.3.1 *Jurisdictional Requirements for Domestic (US) Choice of Law*

For the reasons set forth above, the parties to an agreement may find it advantageous to choose the set of laws under which their agreement will be governed. But parties do not have unlimited discretion in this regard. Within the United States, the law governing an agreement must bear some relationship to the parties or the subject matter of the agreement. As explained by § 187(2) of the *Restatement (Second) of Conflict of Laws* (1971),

> The law of the state chosen by the parties to govern their contractual rights and duties will be applied, even if the particular issue is one which the parties could not have resolved by an explicit provision in their agreement directed to that issue, unless either
> (a) the chosen state has no substantial relationship to the parties or the transaction and there is no other reasonable basis for the parties' choice, or
> (b) application of the law of the chosen state would be contrary to a fundamental policy of a state which has a materially greater interest than the chosen state in the determination of the particular issue and which … would be the state of the applicable law in the absence of an effective choice of law by the parties.

Thus, it is unlikely that a contractual choice of Utah law would be enforced with respect to an agreement between a Massachusetts-based licensor and a Texas-based manufacturer for the distribution of products in Kansas.

Notwithstanding this general rule, beginning in the 1980s a number of states enacted statutory provisions expressly permitting contracting parties to select their laws, notwithstanding the lack of any connection to the state. As Professor John Coyle explains,

> In 1984, for example, New York enacted [N.Y. Gen. Oblig. L. § 5-1401(1)] directing its courts to enforce choice-of-law clauses selecting New York law in commercial contracts for more than $250,000 even when the parties and the transaction lacked a "reasonable relation" to New York. The legislature was transparent about its motivation in passing this law—it hoped to divert legal business to New York and away from other jurisdictions, thereby generating more business for New York lawyers. The practical effect of this statute was to encourage companies with no other connection to New York to select that state's law to govern their agreements, without any concern that the choice-of-law clause would be in-validated for the lack of any "substantial relationship" to New York.

---

[14] See Michael Gruson, *Governing Law Clauses Excluding Principles of Conflict of Laws*, 37 Int'l Lawyer 1023 (2003).

In the years that followed, a number of other states followed New York in requiring their courts to enforce choice-of-law clauses selecting their law even where the transaction lacked a substantial relationship to the state ...

A statute enacted by North Carolina in 2017 goes even further. This statute stipulates that a choice-of-law clause selecting North Carolina law in a business contract is enforceable even when the parties and the transaction lack a "reasonable relation" to the state. The statute then goes on to provide that the same result should be obtained even when the contract contained a provision that was "contrary to the fundamental policy of the jurisdiction whose law would apply in the absence of the parties' choice of North Carolina law." The end result is a legal regime in which the North Carolina courts will apply that state's law to any business contract selecting the law of North Carolina, even when the transaction lacks a reasonable relation to the state and even when its law is contrary to a fundamental policy of a jurisdiction with a closer connection to the dispute.[15]

Despite the efforts of other states, New York law is by far the most popular choice of law in domestic commercial contracts due to the perceived sophistication of its courts, the enormous body of New York precedent in many areas of commercial law and the familiarity of many commercial practitioners with New York law.[16] Delaware runs a respectable but distant second.

11.3.2 *International Choice of Law*

Choice of law clauses are even more popular in international agreements than domestic agreements, with one recent study finding that 99 percent of international supply agreements filed with the US Securities and Exchange Commission contained choice of law clauses.[17] At the international level one influential convention expresses the fundamental principal governing international choice of law as "freedom of choice," a concept that is borrowed from the European Union.[18]

COALITION *for* GLOBAL
COMPETITIVENESS

FIGURE 11.3 According to its website, the North Carolina Coalition for Global Competitiveness "wants people all around the world to recognize and know North Carolina as a great place to invest, work, study, visit, partner, and live."

---

[15] Coyle, *supra* note 12, at 1179–80 (footnotes and citations omitted). Delaware has also recently enacted a choice of law statute, permitting the contractual choice of Delaware law in contracts involving more than $100,000 (6 DE Code § 2708 (2016)).

[16] See Geoffrey P. Miller & Theodore Eisenberg, *The Market for Contracts*, 30 Cardozo L. Rev. 2073 (2009).

[17] John F. Coyle & Christopher R. Drahozal, *An Empirical Study of Dispute Resolution Clauses in International Supply Contracts*, 52 Vand. J. Transnat'l L. 323 (2019).

[18] See Regulation (EC) No 593/2008 of the European Parliament and of the Council of 17 June 2008 on the law applicable to contractual obligations (Rome I), Ch. II, Art. 3 (Freedom of Choice).

Hague Conference on Private International Law

Principles on Choice of Law in International Commercial Contracts (2015)

Article 2

Freedom of Choice

1. A contract is governed by the law chosen by the parties.
2. The parties may choose –
    (a) the law applicable to the whole contract or to only part of it; and
    (b) different laws for different parts of the contract.
3. The choice may be made or modified at any time. A choice or modification made after the contract has been concluded shall not prejudice its formal validity or the rights of third parties.
4. No connection is required between the law chosen and the parties or their transaction.

Given this freedom, which laws should parties choose to govern their international contracts? One recent study of more than 4,400 international contracts finds that the most popular choices of governing law are English[19] and Swiss law, followed by US (generally New York[20]), French and German law.[21]

In Asia, Western firms often gravitate to the laws of Singapore, given its British common law heritage and the prevalence of English. Hong Kong was once the preferred choice of law in Asia, especially in the financial sector, but its gradual absorption by the People's Republic of China, along with recent political unrest, has caused it to decline in popularity. Due to their proximity to the Asia Pacific region, their English language usage and their common law heritage, Australia and New Zealand have become increasingly attractive legal systems for the resolution of disputes between North American and Asian parties.

WHEN MEETING IN THE MIDDLE SPELLS TROUBLE

Negotiation experts often encourage attorneys to "meet in the middle" when confronted by seemingly intractable issues. Choice of law is often one of those issues: Each party wants its own law to govern. As a result, parties negotiating choice of law clauses sometimes try to compromise in a way that, to the naïve observer, seems fair and equitable, but in reality is an invitation to disaster.

---

[19] It is a common mistake to refer to these laws as the laws of the "United Kingdom" because the United Kingdom also includes Scotland, which has its own parliament, statutes and common law corpus of cases. Thus, it is preferable to avoid "UK" law and choose instead the laws of "England and Wales," which are the most familiar to international practitioners.

[20] In addition to the reasons noted above, New York is a popular choice for international contracts due to the ability of foreign attorneys to be admitted to practice in New York.

[21] Gilles Cuniberti, *The International Market for Contracts: The Most Attractive Contract Laws*, 34 Nw. J. Int'l L. & Bus. 455 (2014).

Consider a licensing agreement between a Canadian university and a Japanese manufacturer. The university would strongly prefer that the agreement be governed by Canadian law, while the manufacturer would strongly prefer Japanese law. Rather than flipping a coin, the parties could try to be clever: If one party initiates litigation over the agreement, choose the law of the other party. Thus, if the university initiates a lawsuit, Japanese law will apply, and if the manufacturer initiates a lawsuit, Canadian law will apply. Voila! Not only is the result fair, but it also deters litigation, as the aggressor must deal with the law of the non-aggressor party. This Solomonic solution is actually embodied in many international agreements, but when a dispute arises it often leads to trouble.

What is wrong with this compromise? A lot! First, it provides no baseline governing law before litigation is initiated. If a party wants to assess the scope of its obligations and remedies under the agreement, it must consider both sets of laws, and a party will not know whether to plan its actions based on one set of laws or the other. Second, it is often unclear what happens if each party initiates litigation in a different jurisdiction, as often happens. Will a different set of laws govern the agreement in each proceeding? That makes little sense. Third, once a court hands down an interpretation of the agreement under one set of laws, will that interpretation be valid if the agreement is later interpreted under the other set of laws? Thus, while choosing the non-aggressor's law seems like a fair and reasonable compromise, it generally results in more conflict and uncertainty than it solves.

So, what are parties to do when they cannot agree that one or other's laws should govern their agreement? They can always choose the laws of a neutral third jurisdiction, subject to the constraints mentioned in the text. Or, if that fails, they can flip a coin.

Note: While adopting a non-aggressor choice of law provision can be inadvisable, this approach is not unreasonable when it comes to selecting a forum for litigation (see Section 11.4).

11.3.3 *International Contractual Conventions*

Responding to concerns about jurisdictional differences in the treatment of commercial issues, the United Nations Commission on International Trade Law drafted an international treaty known as the United Nations Convention on Contracts for the International Sale of Goods (UNCISG), which was first adopted in 1980. Today, there are ninety-four signatories to the Convention, including the United States and most other industrialized nations other than Iran, South Africa, Great Britain and Ireland.[22] Unless the parties expressly exclude application of the UNCISG, it will apply automatically to eligible transactions involving parties with a presence in, or doing business in, such countries. In addition, parties can voluntarily elect to apply the UNCISG to a transaction even if they do not have places of business in a ratifying country.

The UNCISG applies to contracts for the sale of goods between parties whose places of business are in ratifying countries.[23] But unlike the Uniform Commercial Code, the interpretation of "goods" for the purposes of the UNCISG can vary by country, and could, in some countries, include software and other intangibles. The most recent digest of judicial interpretations of the UNCISG explains:

---

[22] A current list of signatories can be found at https://uncitral.un.org/en/texts/salegoods/conventions/sale_of_goods/cisg/status.

[23] If a party has more than one "place of business," the place of business for determining whether the UNCISG applies is that which has the closest relationship to the contract and its performance.

28. According to case law, "goods" in the sense of the Convention are items that are, at the moment of delivery, "moveable and tangible", regardless of their shape and whether they are solid, used or new, inanimate or alive. It does not matter that the contract obliges the seller to install such goods on land unless the supply of labour or services is the preponderant part (article 3 (2)). Intangibles, such as intellectual property rights, goodwill, an interest in a limited liability company, or an assigned debt, have been considered not to fall within the Convention's concept of "goods". The same is true for a market research study. According to one court, however, the concept of "goods" is to be interpreted "extensively," perhaps suggesting that the Convention might apply to goods that are not tangible.

29. Whereas the sale of computer hardware clearly falls within the sphere of application of the Convention, the issue is not so clear when it comes to software. Some courts consider only standard software to be "goods" under the Convention; another court concluded that any kind of software, including custom-made software, should be considered "goods."[24]

As of 2016, over 4,500 cases had been decided under the UNCISG, building a growing body of decisions.[25] It should be remembered, however, that there is no single tribunal charged with adjudicating cases brought under the UNCISG. It is therefore interpreted by national courts whose interpretation of its various clauses may vary or even conflict, and which have no binding precedential effect on courts in other jurisdictions.

Many international practitioners routinely exclude application of the UNCISG due to a lack of familiarity with its provisions and because it imposes a number of unfamiliar (and possibly unwelcome) obligations on the parties. For example, Article 42(1) of the UNCISG provides that a seller "must deliver goods which are free from any right or claim of a third party based on industrial property or other intellectual property, of which at the time of the conclusion of the contract the seller knew or could not have been unaware." This type of warranty against IP infringement is often disclaimed by parties in licensing agreements (see Section 10.1.2).

In addition to the UNCISG, thirty countries, including the United States, have ratified the UN's 1974 Convention on the Limitation Period in the International Sale of Goods. This Convention establishes an automatic four-year statute of limitations on disputes arising from the sale of goods. It applies in virtually the same situations as the UNCISG. Depending on the expectations and requirements of the parties, it may also be advisable to disclaim application of this Convention.

EXAMPLE: EXCLUSION OF INTERNATIONAL CONVENTIONS

The choice of law described above shall exclude any application of the United Nations Convention on Contracts for the International Sale of Goods.

11.3.4 *Choice of Language*

It is fortunate for the American-trained attorney that the English language had, by the late twentieth century, become the global *lingua franca* for international business transactions. Examples abound of agreements between parties from countries in which English is not an official language that are drafted, negotiated and enforced entirely in English.

---

[24] United Nations Commission on International Trade Law, UNCITRAL Digest of Case Law on the United Nations Convention on Contracts for the International Sale of Goods – 2016 Edition, at 7 (citations omitted) [hereinafter UNCISG 2016 Digest].

[25] See UNCISG 2016 Digest, supra note 24, at xi.

Nevertheless, agreements among international parties are often translated into other languages, both for the convenience of non-English-speaking personnel and for filing with governmental agencies, lenders and other third parties. Some agreements are prepared in parallel versions, with translations being made with each revision. Thus, it is sometimes important to specify the "official" language of an agreement.

EXAMPLE: OFFICIAL LANGUAGE

The parties hereto have required that this Agreement and all documents relating thereto be drawn in the English language, and that the English language version shall control over all translations thereof.

Even with such a clause, some jurisdictions require more. For example, the laws of the province of Quebec, Canada, require a specific notification *in French* if the English version of an agreement will control. Thus, if an agreement will be governed by the laws of Quebec, or involves parties or performance in Quebec, the following text should be appended to the end of the official language clause: "*Les parties conviennent que cette entente ainsi que tout document accessoire soient rediges en anglais.*"

Notes and Questions

1. *The long history of choice of law.* Professor John Coyle traces the first express choice of law clause in the United States to a loan agreement executed in 1869, and finds a motion picture licensing agreement in existence as early as 1917.[26] Yet the 1934 *Restatement (First) of Conflict of Laws* does not recognize them, and, according to Professor Coyle, it was not until the early 1960s that choice of law clauses became part of mainstream contract drafting practice.[27] In your opinion, are such clauses beneficial, and should they be encouraged or discouraged in IP licensing agreements?

2. *Nonwaivable provisions of law.* If parties are operating in a country, then there are likely to be legal restrictions and requirements of local law that simply cannot be waived or overridden by selecting the law of a different jurisdiction to govern the arrangement. Obvious examples of nonwaivable legal provisions include employee protections, privacy regulations, tax laws, currency controls, anti-bribery and export control laws, and the underlying rules of IP protection and infringement.[28] Other, less common, legal provisions can act as traps for the unwary. For example, the 1986 EU Agency Directive (Council Directive 86/653/EEC) requires that a licensor or manufacturer that terminates a sales agent in the EU must pay the terminated agent an indemnity or compensation in the range of one year's full compensation. This requirement cannot be waived by contract, and has caught many non-EU principals unawares.

Problem 11.2

Assume that you are negotiating an IP licensing agreement with a large Chinese industrial firm on behalf of a California-based licensor. What would you propose as an appropriate choice of

[26] Coyle, *supra* note 12, at 1156, 1164 table 1.
[27] Id. at 1173–74.
[28] With respect to the application of foreign IP laws, see deWerra, *supra* note 7, at 195–96.

law for the agreement? What arguments would you make to persuade the other party to accept your proposal? Would it matter if the IP in question were a motion picture, a new drug or a sportswear brand?

11.4 FORUM SELECTION CLAUSES

Whereas choice of law clauses specify which body of substantive law the parties wish to govern their agreement, forum selection clauses specify the jurisdiction or physical location where they wish disputes arising under an agreement to be adjudicated.[29] Forum selection clauses often go hand in hand with dispute resolution clauses. Though there is no strict requirement that the law chosen to govern an agreement be the law of the jurisdiction in which a dispute will be resolved, it is worth remembering that judges, and the attorneys arguing before them, are most comfortable and most adept at applying the laws of their own jurisdictions.[30]

EXAMPLE: FORUM SELECTION CLAUSE

The parties irrevocably submit to the [exclusive/nonexclusive [1]] jurisdiction of the [federal and state] [2] courts sitting in [CITY/STATE/COUNTRY] for the resolution of any action or proceeding arising out of or relating to this Agreement [; *provided, however,* that each party shall have the right to institute judicial proceedings against the other party or anyone acting by, through or under such other party, in order to enforce the instituting party's rights hereunder through injunctive or similar equitable relief or to enforce the terms of a judgment or order issued by the court designated above [3]].

Each Party agrees that all claims in respect of such action or proceeding may be heard and determined in any such court, irrevocably waives any claim of inconvenient forum or other challenge to venue in such court, and agrees not to bring any action or proceeding arising out of or relating to this Agreement in any other court or tribunal.

DRAFTING NOTES

[1] *Exclusivity* – the selected forum need not be the exclusive venue for adjudicating disputes. Rather, it can be established as a forum where a party may bring suit, but would not preclude a party from bringing suit elsewhere. Choosing a nonexclusive forum effectively gives the parties a safe haven for suit, but does not mandate where their dispute must be heard. This being said, the large majority of forum selection clauses are exclusive.

[29] Forum selection clauses typically relate to judicial adjudication of disputes. For arbitration and other alternative dispute resolution mechanisms, see Section 11.5.

[30] To wit, see *Apple v. Motorola*, 2012 U.S. Dist. LEXIS 181854 at *43 (W.D. Wis., Oct. 29, 2012) ("At summary judgment, I applied Wisconsin law to Motorola's contracts with IEEE and French law to the ETSI contracts. In their motions *in limine*, both parties cite Wisconsin contract law and do not argue that French law is any different. I will apply general principles of Wisconsin contract law to interpret Motorola's commitments to both IEEE and ETSI"). One suspects that French attorneys might question the notion that the contract law of Wisconsin and France are equivalent.

[2] *Federal and state* – in the United States, parties must remember that the federal and state courts have different jurisdictional rules. Certain matters, such as patent and copyright cases, can only be heard in federal court. Some matters, such as contractual disputes between parties that do business in the same state, must be heard in state court. Thus, forum selection clauses designating a US forum usually specify that the forum for litigation will be the federal and/or state courts sitting in a particular location (e.g., New York City).

[3] *Injunctive relief* – even if the parties agree to litigate their disputes in a particular forum, it may be necessary to bring a legal action in another jurisdiction in order to enjoin infringement in that other jurisdiction (something that the selected court might not be authorized to do) or to enforce the judgment of the selected court.

Many of the same issues arising in the context of choice of law also arise in the context of choice of forum, but even more so, as the selection of a forum necessarily utilizes the limited judicial resources of the forum jurisdiction. Thus, courts generally do not hear cases over which they cannot establish both personal and subject matter jurisdiction. For example, the parties could not validly select the state courts of South Carolina to hear a patent or copyright infringement dispute, as the federal courts have exclusive subject matter jurisdiction over patent and copyright matters. Likewise, a state court in Alabama is probably unlikely to adjudicate a dispute between a Japanese and a German party over a European licensing agreement unless either party has some connection with the state of Alabama.

As with choice of law, however, some US states have deliberately opened their courts to litigation involving foreign parties. As a companion to the choice of law statute discussed above, New York General Laws § 5-1402 allows contracting parties to choose to resolve their disputes in the courts of New York, so long as their agreement is governed by New York law, the parties have contractually submitted to the jurisdiction of the New York courts and, most importantly, the dispute involves "a contract, agreement or undertaking, contingent or otherwise, in consideration of, or relating to any obligation arising out of a transaction covering in the aggregate, not less than one million dollars."

Internationally, many of the factors motivating choice of law also affect choice of forum. London, Geneva and Zurich are popular venues for international commercial litigation. Within the European Union, Ireland is a popular choice (given that English is an official language of the country), as is the Netherlands, which permits a growing number of international commercial and IP matters to be conducted in English. Similar considerations apply in Asia with respect to Singapore and Hong Kong, as well as Australia and New Zealand. For geographical (and sometimes aesthetic) reasons, Hawaii is often selected as a forum for adjudication of disputes between North American and Asian parties.

Notes and Questions

1. *Forum selection and the PTAB.* What if the parties to a patent licensing agreement select the federal and state courts of New York as the exclusive venue for the resolution of disputes relating to the agreement, and the licensee then challenges one of the licensor's patents at the Patent Trial and Appeals Board (PTAB)? Does the forum selection clause bar its PTAB action? See *Kannuu Pty Ltd., v. Samsung Electronics Co., Ltd.* (Fed. Cir. 2021).

11.5 ALTERNATIVE DISPUTE RESOLUTION

While the courts are available to resolve disputes arising in IP licensing transactions, litigation is not always an efficient or desirable mechanism for dispute resolution. Parties often wish to implement less adversarial and costly procedures for dealing with disagreements. These procedures can involve pre-litigation dispute resolution steps, such as escalation and mediation, as well as arbitration as an alternative to litigation. In this section we will discuss each of these mechanisms and the contractual terms that enable them.

11.5.1 *Escalation*

Many dispute resolution clauses establish a tiered or stepped process for resolving disputes between the parties. The first step in this process is often internal to the parties, and involves escalating a dispute from the project team, committee or managers directly involved in the project to upper-level managers or executives. This process can include one or more steps, and generally requires that the individuals to whom a dispute is escalated spend some minimum amount of time and good-faith effort toward resolution of the dispute. This route is also preferable for resolving disputes about pure business or technical decisions that professional arbitrators are ill-suited to decide.

EXAMPLE: DISPUTE ESCALATION

X. In the event of any dispute, controversy or claim of any kind or nature arising under or in connection with this Agreement (a "Dispute"), then upon the written request of either Party, each of the Parties will appoint a designated senior business executive whose task it will be to meet for the purpose of endeavoring to resolve the Dispute. The designated executives will meet as often as the Parties reasonably deem necessary in order to gather and furnish to the other all information with respect to the matter in issue which the Parties believe to be appropriate and germane in connection with its resolution. Such executives will discuss the Dispute and will negotiate in good faith to resolve the Dispute without the necessity of any formal proceeding relating thereto. The specific format for such discussions will be left to the discretion of the designated executives but may include the preparation of agreed upon statements of fact or written statements of position furnished to the other Party. No formal proceedings for the resolution of the Dispute under Sections Y or Z may be commenced until the earlier to occur of (a) a good faith conclusion by the designated executives that amicable resolution through continued negotiation of the matter in issue does not appear likely or (b) the 30th day after the initial request to negotiate the Dispute.

11.5.2 *Mediation*

Mediation involves further attempts to resolve a dispute among the parties guided by an impartial third party known as a mediator. The mediator typically has no authority to resolve a dispute or order the parties to take any action, but plays the role of a facilitator who can structure discussions and help the parties to find a pathway to resolution. In order to be effective, mediators should have the respect and trust of both parties, and are thus often selected from pools of retired judges, government officials and academics. If a mediation does not successfully resolve the parties' dispute, then a more formal adjudicatory mechanism – arbitration or litigation – is usually authorized.

EXAMPLE: MEDIATION

Y. Any Dispute that the Parties are unable to resolve through informal discussions or negotiations pursuant to Section X will be submitted to nonbinding mediation. The parties
will mutually determine who the mediator will be from a list of mediators obtained from
the American Arbitration Association office located in [CITY] (the "AAA"). If the Parties
are unable to agree on the mediator, the mediator will be selected by the AAA, and will
be an individual who has had both training and experience as a mediator of international
commercial and intellectual property matters. Within thirty days after the selection of the
mediator, the parties and their respective attorneys will meet with the mediator for one
mediation session of at least four hours.

If the Dispute cannot be settled during such mediation session or during any mutually
agreed continuation of such session, any party to this Agreement may give to the mediator
and the other party to this Agreement written notice declaring the mediation process at
an end, and such dispute will be resolved by arbitration pursuant to Section Z hereof. All
discussions pursuant to this section will be confidential and will be treated as compromise and settlement discussions. Nothing said or disclosed, and no document produced, in
the course of such discussions which is not independently discoverable may be offered or
received as evidence or used for impeachment or for any other purpose in any arbitration
or litigation. The costs of any mediation pursuant to this section will be shared equally by
the parties to this Agreement.

The use of mediation will not be construed under the doctrines of laches, waiver or
estoppel to affect adversely the rights of either party, and in particular either party may seek
a preliminary injunction or other interim judicial relief at any time if in its judgment such
action is necessary to avoid irreparable harm.

11.5.3 *Arbitration*

Arbitration is a form of private dispute resolution that serves as an alternative to judicial resolution. Arbitration is typically voluntary, so all parties to a dispute must consent to resolve the
dispute by arbitration. If arbitration is selected to resolve disputes, the parties may also specify
that arbitration will be the exclusive mechanism for dispute resolution, and thus eliminate their
ability to bring suit in court.

Many volumes have been written about arbitral dispute resolution, and the relative advantages and disadvantages of arbitration versus judicial dispute resolution.[31] Below are a few of the
factors that parties often consider when deciding whether to resolve disputes arising under an
agreement by arbitration.

11.5.3.1 Speed

It is generally believed that arbitration proceedings are completed more quickly than judicial
proceedings. The arbitrator(s) are engaged for a particular case and do not have to juggle competing case schedules as judges do. Likewise, many of the procedural steps that exist in litigation – lengthy discovery, motions, witness testimony – are eliminated or significantly curtailed

---

[31] See, e.g., Gary Born, International Commercial Arbitration (3rd ed., Wolters Kluwer, 2020).

in arbitration. Of course, while the elimination of these procedures may accelerate the dispute resolution process, it also results in a less comprehensive record.

11.5.3.2 Institutional versus Ad Hoc Arbitration

Various institutions around the world have created arbitration rules and procedures tailored to the adjudication of commercial and IP disputes. These include the American Arbitration Association (AAA) and its International Center for Dispute Resolution (ICDR), the United Nations Commission on International Trade Law (UNCITRAL), the International Court of Arbitration of the International Chamber of Commerce (ICC), the London Court of International Arbitration and the Singapore International Arbitration Centre. The World Intellectual Property Organization (WIPO), a UN agency that oversees international IP treaties, established an Arbitration and Mediation Center in 1995, and has developed arbitral rules specifically for IP disputes. The choice of an arbitral institution and rules can have a significant impact on arbitration procedure, the composition of the arbitral tribunal and the cost of the proceeding. The most important decision in this regard, however, is whether the parties wish to appoint an arbitral institution to organize and manage their arbitration ("institutional arbitration") or to manage the arbitration themselves using an existing set of arbitral rules ("ad hoc arbitration"). While ad hoc arbitration can be less costly than institutional arbitration, it places significantly greater administrative burdens on the parties and can require more frequent recourse to the courts.

11.5.3.3 Cost

Just as arbitration is typically viewed as faster than litigation, it also has the reputation of being less costly (mostly due to the streamlining of procedures noted above). This being said, the costs of the judicial system and its employees are largely borne by taxpayers, while arbitration tribunals charge the parties for their services. In some cases, arbitration fees are based on the arbitrators' hourly rates plus a surcharge for the institution that manages the arbitration, but some institutions such as the WIPO Arbitration and Mediation Center and the ICC generally charge the parties a percentage of the amount in dispute.

11.5.3.4 Case or Controversy

Courts are generally unwilling or unable to hear cases unless a genuine case or controversy between the parties exists (see Section 22.3). As such, courts seldom render advisory opinions that resolve questions about agreement interpretation or a party's duties unless one party has sued the other for breach. Arbitrators, however, will hear any matter brought before them by the parties.

11.5.3.5 Confidentiality

As a general rule, arbitration proceedings are conducted privately and all parties, including the arbitrators, are required, whether by law, ethical canon or contract, to maintain the confidentiality of the evidence presented, the parties' arguments and the arbitral award. As Sir George Jessel, Master of the Rolls, observed of arbitration agreements in 1880, "persons enter into these contracts with the express view of keeping their quarrels from the public eyes, and of avoiding that discussion in public, which must be a painful one."[32] In fact, it is this very confidentiality that often makes arbitration more attractive than litigation, in which most of the proceedings become matters of public record.

11.5.3.6 Enforceability

Because arbitration tribunals are privately convened bodies, they have no authority to enforce their awards under pain of contempt. However, in most countries arbitral awards can be enforced by the courts. In the United States, for example, the Federal Arbitration Act, 9 U.S.C. §§ 1–14 ("FAA"), enacted in 1925, ensures that all agreements to arbitrate matters involving interstate commerce are "valid, irrevocable and enforceable" in both state and federal courts. And in 1982 the US Patent Act was amended to recognize voluntary arbitration as a valid means for adjudicating disputes relating to the validity and infringement of patents (35 U.S.C. § 294).

But unlike judicial awards, which are generally enforceable only in the jurisdiction in which they were issued,[33] arbitral awards are enforceable internationally. Under the United Nations Convention on the Recognition and Enforcement of Foreign Arbitral Awards (New York, 1958), most arbitral awards rendered in accordance with a customary set of due process procedures are recognized and enforceable in all countries that are members of the Convention (166 countries as of this writing).

EXAMPLE: ARBITRATION

(a) Should the parties fail to reach agreement with respect to a Dispute [1], through the aforesaid mediation or otherwise, then the Dispute will be resolved by final and binding arbitration conducted in the English language in accordance with the [ARBITRAL RULES] of the [ARBITRAL INSTITUTE] [3] by a tribunal comprised of three independent and impartial arbitrators [4], one of which will be appointed by each of the parties, and the third of which shall have at least twenty years' experience in the field of [intellectual property licensing]. If the parties to this Agreement cannot agree on the third arbitrator, then the third arbitrator will be selected by the [ARBITRAL INSTITUTE] in accordance with the criteria set forth in the preceding sentence; provided that no person who served as a mediator pursuant to Section Y hereof with respect to such dispute may be selected as an arbitrator pursuant to this section. The seat of the arbitration shall be deemed to be [CITY] and all hearings and physical proceedings shall be held in [CITY] [2].

(b) Disputes about arbitration procedure shall be resolved by the arbitrators or, failing agreement, by the [ARBITRAL INSTITUTE]. The arbitrators may proceed to an award notwithstanding the failure of a party to participate in the proceedings.

(c) The tribunal will allow such discovery as is appropriate, consistent with the purposes of arbitration in accomplishing fair, speedy and cost effective resolution of disputes. Such

---

[32] *Russel v. Russel*, L.R. 14 Ch. D. 471 at 474.

[33] There are some exceptions to this rule that have been established by treaty. For example, the 2005 Uniform Foreign-Country Money Judgments Recognition Act had been adopted by 26 states as of 2020. It provides that certain final money judgments rendered in foreign courts pursuant to recognized standards of due process may be enforced in the courts of the adopting states.

discovery shall be limited to mutual exchange of documents relevant to the Dispute and depositions shall not be permitted unless agreed to by both parties. The tribunal will reference the rules of evidence of the Federal Rules of Civil Procedure then in effect in setting the scope of discovery.

(d) The tribunal may decide any issue as to whether, or as to the extent to which, any Dispute is subject to the arbitration and other dispute resolution provisions in this Agreement. The tribunal must base its award on the provisions of this Agreement and must render its award in writing, which must include a reasoned explanation of the basis for such award [5].

(e) Any arbitration pursuant to this section will be governed by the substantive laws specified in Section __ of this Agreement, and by the arbitration law of the Federal Arbitration Act.

(f) The award of the arbitrator[s] shall be the sole and exclusive remedy of the parties and shall be enforceable in any court of competent jurisdiction, subject only to revocation on grounds of fraud or clear bias on the part of the arbitrator.

(g) All fees, costs and expenses of the arbitrators, and all other costs and expenses of the arbitration, will be shared equally by the parties to this Agreement unless such parties agree otherwise or unless the tribunal assesses such costs and expenses against one of such parties or allocates such costs and expenses other than equally between such parties.

(h) Notwithstanding the foregoing, either party may seek a temporary restraining order and/or a preliminary injunction from a court of competent jurisdiction, to be effective pending the institution of the arbitration process and the deliberation and award of the arbitration tribunal.

(i) The limitations on liability set out in Section __ of this Agreement shall apply to an award of the arbitrators. Specifically, but without limitation, under no circumstances shall the arbitrators be authorized to award punitive or multiple damages. Any purported award of punitive or multiple damages or of other damages not permitted under Section __ hereof shall be beyond the arbitrator's authority, void, and unenforceable.

DRAFTING NOTES

[1] *Which disputes?* – Not all disputes arising under an agreement must be resolved using the same dispute resolution mechanism. Some agreements specify particular tribunals – whether arbitral or judicial – for the resolution of certain types of disputes.[34] For example, royalty calculation disputes may be referred to a neutral accounting firm, while other disputes may be referred to a more general arbitral institution. In some cases, the parties may wish to exclude an entire category of disputes (e.g., patent validity or other IP issues[35]) from arbitration, preferring instead that these be resolved through litigation.

[34] See Cathy Hwang & Matthew Jennejohn, *Deal Structure*, 113 Nw. L. Rev. 279, 328–30 (2018).
[35] See *Oracle America Inc. v Myriad Group*, 724 F.3d 1069 (9th Cir. 2013) (concerning software licensing agreement containing the following arbitration clause: "[a]ny dispute arising out of or relating to this License shall be finally settled by arbitration as set out herein, except that either party may bring any action, in a court of competent jurisdiction (which jurisdiction shall be exclusive), with respect to any dispute relating to such party's Intellectual Property Rights or with respect to Your compliance with the TCK license … ").

[2] *Location and "seat" of arbitration* – the parties must specify the physical location of the arbitration, which can be almost anywhere in the world (bearing in mind that the parties must pay the travel expenses of the arbitrators). A neutral location is often preferred, generally in a large commercial center. Note, however, that in addition to the physical location of the hearings, every arbitral proceeding must have a "seat" – the location that defines the "nationality" of the arbitration and of the award and defines the local law that will apply to the arbitration proceedings, which may or may not match the actual location of the hearings.

[3] *Arbitral institute and rules* – the parties must specify which, if any, arbitral institution will manage the arbitration or whether the parties choose ad hoc arbitration under a specified set of rules, such as the UNCITRAL Arbitration Rules.

[4] *Number of arbitrators* – most arbitral rules permit tribunals of varying sizes, the most common being a single arbitrator or a panel of three. A single arbitrator is both easier to schedule and less costly than a three-person panel. Some attorneys favor a three-person panel to avoid the risk of a single, erratic individual making all decisions. Others find that three-arbitrator tribunals add little value over a single arbitrator: The two arbitrators appointed by the parties often advocate on behalf of the parties who appointed them, leaving the deciding vote to the neutral third arbitrator – the same effect as a single arbitrator but at three times the cost.

[5] *Reasoned decision* – in an arbitration proceeding, the parties may specify whether or not the arbitrators must issue a written opinion supporting their decision and informing the parties of the grounds on which the ruling was based (a "reasoned decision"). While many institutional arbitration rules provide that the arbitrators will render a reasoned decision, this requirement may be waived by the parties, who may specify that the arbitrators simply issue an award without explanation. This approach may be desirable when parties are concerned with protecting confidential information or having the weaknesses of a patent discussed in an opinion that could be leaked to third parties or produced in discovery in another proceeding. Parties should be aware, however, that an unreasoned arbitral award is more vulnerable to subsequent judicial challenge on grounds of public policy.

Notes and Questions

1. *Dispute escalation.* Escalation of disputes is often a multi-tier process, but not all such processes include mediation or arbitration. Why might parties elect to forego either mediation or arbitration when determining how disputes will be resolved?
2. *Arbitration location.* What practical issues can arise in selecting a location for arbitration? Do you think that Zoom and other online video services will soon supplant physical hearings for international commercial arbitration?
3. *Confidentiality.* As noted in Section 11.5.3.5, the confidentiality of arbitral proceedings makes them more attractive to some parties than judicial proceedings that are conducted in the public eye. Others, however, have criticized the use of confidential arbitration proceedings because they cannot be used as precedent or to guide the conduct of other participants in the market.[36] Which view do you find more persuasive and why?

---

[36] See, e.g., Jorge L. Contreras & David L. Newman, *Developing a Framework for Arbitrating Standards: Essential Patent Disputes*, 2014 J. Dispute Resol. 23, 39–41 (2014).

4. *IP carve-outs.* As noted in Drafting Note [1], some parties choose to exclude certain types of disputes, including IP-related disputes, from arbitration. What considerations might motivate parties to exclude IP disputes, in particular, from an arbitration clause? Would you recommend this approach to your clients?

Problem 11.3

Draft a reasonable set of dispute clauses for a licensing agreement (governing law, forum selection and dispute resolution) that takes into account the likely perspectives and preferences of the following clients:

a. A Missouri-based author of a popular series of children's books who is entering into an agreement to adapt her books for a Polish television series.
b. A California-based private university that is licensing a patented vaccine technology to a New Jersey-based multinational pharmaceutical company.
c. A multinational fast-food conglomerate incorporated in Bermuda that is licensing its brand to a Taiwanese manufacturer of plush dolls for sale worldwide.

11.6 FEE SHIFTING

In many countries the losing party in litigation is required to pay the legal fees of the winner. That is not the rule in the United States, however, and awards of legal fees in IP licensing disputes litigated in the United States are rare. As a result, some licensing agreements contain express fee shifting clauses along the lines of the following example.

EXAMPLE: LEGAL FEES

For purposes of this Agreement, "Prevailing Party" [1] means the party to this Agreement that, in a final and unappealable decision in a litigation or arbitration initiated under this Agreement (an "Action"), (a) is awarded monetary damages in excess of the monetary damages awarded to the other Party, or (b) if no monetary damages are awarded in such Action, prevails in its claim for substantial nonmonetary relief such as a permanent injunction, specific performance or declaration in its favor to the exclusion of the other party, provided that if each party prevails on one or more substantial nonmonetary claims in such Action, then neither party shall be considered the "Prevailing Party" [2].

The Prevailing Party in any such Action, if any, shall be entitled to recover from the other party (the "Non-Prevailing Party") all [out-of-pocket] [3] costs and expenses incurred by the Prevailing Party in such Action, including court costs, experts and attorneys' fees, and reasonable travel and other expenses, upon delivery to the Non-Prevailing Party a statement enumerating each of these costs and expenses in reasonable detail no later than ninety (90) days following the conclusion of such Action.

DRAFTING NOTES

[1] *Prevailing Party* – the crux of a fee shifting clause is the award of legal expenses to the prevailing party in a dispute. It is thus essential to define "prevailing party" with specificity and to avoid ambiguity when, for example, each party prevails on some of its claims

or counterclaims. The above example defines prevailing in terms of the relative size of the parties' monetary damages awards, with the important caveat that if no monetary damages are awarded, the party that prevails on its claim for nonmonetary relief will be considered prevailing.

[2] *No prevailing party* – it is sometimes the case that each party "wins" some aspect of an action. If this happens, then neither party should be considered the prevailing party for the purposes of fee shifting.

[3] *Expenses* – when discussing legal costs and expenses, it is important to clarify whether the cost of a party's in-house legal team (e.g., a pro-rated share of salary and benefit costs) should be included, or whether only out-of-pocket costs paid to external counsel and experts should be covered.

11.7 SETTLEMENT LICENSE AGREEMENTS

In many cases, licensing agreements are entered in connection with the settlement of IP infringement litigation. In this scenario, the defendant infringer usually enters into a nonexclusive license agreement with the plaintiff IP owner under which ongoing use of the asserted IP is authorized. The defendant/licensee typically agrees to pay both a lump sum in consideration of past infringement, as well as an ongoing royalty for future use of the licensed IP. These payment provisions are comparable to those discussed in Chapter 8.

However, because a settlement agreement is not a normal commercial arrangement, it often lacks many of the features typically found in commercial licensing agreements such as milestones, warranties, technical assistance, support and ongoing technical cooperation.

By the same token, settlement agreements contain provisions not found in ordinary licensing agreements. Some of these are discussed below.

11.7.1 *Dismissals*

The main point of a settlement agreement is to resolve litigation between the parties. Thus, the settlement agreement usually contains a provision stipulating that this litigation will be dismissed, usually with prejudice (meaning that it cannot be brought again).

EXAMPLE: DISMISSAL OF LITIGATION

No later than one (1) business day following the Effective Date, Defendant shall complete, execute and deliver to Plaintiff stipulated worldwide dismissals and withdrawals, as applicable, of the Litigation in the forms attached hereto as Exhibits ___. Plaintiff shall thereafter promptly file with the applicable courts and other governmental authorities the fully executed stipulated dismissals and withdrawals. Any dismissals of court proceedings shall be with prejudice.

11.7.2 *Release and Covenant*

In addition to granting licenses relating to future use of IP, a settlement agreement usually includes a release of claims for past unauthorized use of that IP (infringement). Such a release exonerates the infringer (now the licensee) from its past infringing activity. Generally, a release from liability is preferred to a retroactive license, which is generally discouraged for tax, accounting and other reasons.

In addition to a release from liability, the party asserting its IP often covenants that it will not sue the alleged infringer or others (e.g., the infringer's customers and suppliers) for use of infringing products prior to the date of the settlement. Such a covenant is desirable from the defendant's standpoint, as it is often not possible to release unspecified and unnamed parties from liability, and a release does not itself exhaust the infringed patents vis-à-vis customers and other third parties. The covenant, however, can be enforced with respect to any user of an infringing product, whether specified or not.

EXAMPLE: RELEASE AND COVENANT NOT TO SUE

1. Upon receipt of the Settlement Payment, Plaintiff, on behalf of itself and its Affiliates, hereby unconditionally and irrevocably releases, remises, acquits and forever discharges Defendant and its present or former employees, directors, officers, shareholders, agents, successors, assigns, heirs, executors and administrators, in their capacities as such, from any and all debts, demands, actions, causes of action, suits, dues, sum and sums of money, accounts, reckonings, bonds, specialties, covenants, contracts, controversies, agreements, promises, doings, omissions, variances, damages, extents, executions, and liabilities of every kind and nature, at law, in equity or otherwise, liquidated or indefinite, known or unknown, suspected or unsuspected, fixed or contingent, and whether direct or indirect, hidden or concealed, arising out of or related in any way (directly, indirectly, factually, logically or legally) to the IP Rights from the beginning of time until the Effective Date.
2. Plaintiff, on behalf of itself and its Affiliates, agrees not to bring any claim of infringement (whether direct, contributory or inducement to infringe) of the IP Rights against Defendant or any of its customers, distributors, resellers or users based upon the use, sale or import of, or the practice of any method or process using or in connection with, any product manufactured, sold or imported by Defendant prior to the Effective Date.

In addition to the standard release language, if a settlement agreement implicates parties or rights in California, the parties must include a statutorily required warning pertaining to the release of unknown claims:

Unknown Claims. Plaintiff, on behalf of itself and its Affiliates, hereby irrevocably and forever expressly waives all rights that Plaintiff and/or its Affiliates may have arising under California Civil Code Section 1542 and all similar rights under the Laws of any other applicable jurisdictions with respect to the release granted by Plaintiff under Section __, above. Each Party understands that California Civil Code Section 1542 provides that:

A general release does not extend to claims which the creditor does not know or suspect to exist in his favor at the time of executing the release, which if known by him must have materially affected his settlement with the debtor.

Each Party acknowledges that it has been fully informed by its counsel concerning the effect and import of this Agreement under California Civil Code Section 1542 and similar Laws of any other applicable jurisdictions.

Given the size and market influence of California, many settlement agreements include this language even when there is no clear-cut relation to the state.

11.7.3 *Licensed Rights*

Typically, a settlement agreement following an IP dispute contains a license of the disputed IP and *only* the licensed IP. Unlike a commercial arrangement in which the licensor wishes to grant the licensee sufficient rights to develop or manufacture a particular product or carry on a particular business, a settlement license is intended to do no more than settle a dispute over IP that has been asserted. The restricted nature of the licensed IP in settlement agreements can, however, lead to problems, as illustrated in *TransCore, LP v. Elec. Transaction Consultants Corp.*, 563 F.3d 1271 (Fed. Cir. 2009) and *Endo Pharms., Inc. v. Actavis, Inc.*, 746 F.3d 1371 (Fed. Cir. 2014). In these cases (discussed in Section 4.4, Notes 3–4), settlement licenses were granted covering patents that were asserted, but the patent holder later obtained additional patents that covered the same products. In *TransCore*, the court held that the new patent, which was a continuation of one of the licensed patents, was subject to an implied license, but in *Endo*, in which the new patent was not a continuation of a licensed patent, no implied license was found. These cases illustrate the need for parties to consider carefully the scope of settlement licenses and to consider including at least other members of the same patent family in the licensed rights.

11.7.4 *No Admissions*

Even though an alleged infringer may agree to settle litigation by taking a license to the asserted IP and paying royalties for past and future use of the asserted IP, it is generally loathe to admit any wrongdoing or even that it was infringing (among other things, to avoid prejudicing itself with respect to other claims by other IP owners). Accordingly, most settlement agreements contain a "no admissions" clause along the following lines.

EXAMPLE: NO ADMISSIONS

This Agreement is entered into in order to compromise and settle disputed claims and proceedings, without any concession or admission of validity or invalidity or enforceability or non-enforceability of any IP Rights by any Party, and without any acquiescence on the part of either Party as to the merit of any claim, defense, affirmative defense, counterclaim, liabilities or damages related to any IP Rights or the Litigation. Neither this Agreement nor any part hereof shall be, or be used as, an admission of infringement, liability, validity or enforceability by either Party or its Affiliates, at any time for any purpose.

11.7.5 *Warranty*

A settlement agreement typically contains no warranties regarding the quality, validity or coverage of the asserted IP rights. However, it is important to the defendant that the plaintiff represent and warrant that entering into the settlement will actually dispose of all potential claims under the relevant IP. Accordingly, the plaintiff is often required to warrant both that it is the sole owner of the asserted IP and that it has not assigned any of its litigation claims to others who are not parties to the settlement agreement.

EXAMPLE: PLAINTIFF'S WARRANTIES

Plaintiff represents and warrants to Defendant that, as of the Effective Date,

(a) Plaintiff is the exclusive owner of all right, title and interest in, to and under the IP Rights,

(b) Plaintiff has the right to grant the licenses granted hereunder,

(c) to Plaintiff's knowledge, no third party has any enforceable right of ownership with respect to the IP Rights that may be asserted following the Effective Date, and

(d) Plaintiff has not assigned, sold, or otherwise transferred any legal claim that it has or may have against Defendant or its Affiliates to any third party (including any Affiliate) or otherwise structured its affairs in a manner so as to avoid the release of all such claims pursuant to Section __ above.

11.7.6 *No Challenge*

If a settlement agreement resolves patent or other IP litigation between the parties, then it is not uncommon for the agreement to contain a clause prohibiting the alleged infringer from later challenging the validity of the asserted IP rights. The enforceability of such no-challenge clauses is discussed in Section 22.4.

Notes and Questions

1. *Settlement licenses.* As noted above, a settlement license agreement often lacks many of the features typically found in commercial licensing agreements such as milestones, warranties, technical assistance, support and ongoing technical cooperation. Why are these features absent from settlement licenses?

2. *Release and covenant.* What would be the consequence of granting a release of claims for past infringement without a corresponding covenant not to sue? Explain using a concrete example.

3. *Plaintiff's warranties.* Why are each of the suggested warranties made by the plaintiff in a settlement agreement important? How would you advise your client, the defendant, if the plaintiff claims that it is unable to make one or more of these warranties?

4. *Later-issued patents.* Consider the *TransCore* and *Endo* cases. Why did the licensee not negotiate to include later-issued patents in its settlement license? Why would the licensor object to including such later-issued patents?

12

Term, Termination and Breach

SUMMARY CONTENTS

12.1 TERM OF AGREEMENT

Every agreement has a term – the period of time during which the agreement is in effect. This section discusses some of the basic features that define an agreement's term, following which Section 12.2 addresses issues relating to the duration of IP licenses that are granted under an agreement. The remainder of this chapter then discusses the ways that agreements and licenses can be terminated, and what effect that termination has.

EXAMPLE: TERM

Unless earlier terminated as provided in Section __ below, the Term of this Agreement shall run from the Effective Date until the third (3rd) anniversary thereof [, provided, however, that the Term shall automatically renew for additional one-year periods unless either party gives the other party written notice that it does not wish the Agreement to so renew at least sixty (60) days prior to the scheduled end of the then-current Term].

12.1.1 *Beginning of the Term*

The term of an agreement often begins when the agreement is signed by all parties or "fully executed." If an agreement does not specify another date, this is when the agreement would generally be considered effective. However, many agreements do specify a particular date after signing for effectiveness (the "Effective Date"). Sometimes a condition precedent other than execution must be met before an agreement becomes effective, such as obtaining a governmental permit or approval.

In some cases, parties wish to make their agreements effective retroactively (i.e., the agreement is effective as of January 1, even though it is not fully executed until February 20). Sometimes retroactivity of this nature is not problematic, particularly if it is just a matter of days. But if parties attempt to make an agreement retroactive over a longer period of time, unintended consequences can arise. For example, obligations triggered by the effective date of the agreement, such as up-front payments, may be overdue as soon as the agreement is signed. Likewise, obligations relating to confidentiality, noncompetition and the like could be deemed to be violated if an agreement is suddenly effective retroactively to a time before the parties were aware of the obligations that would be imposed on them. Parties should be especially wary of retroactivity that can affect tax or financial reporting obligations – it can be illegal to "shift" revenue from one quarter to another through retroactive contract dating.

12.1.2 *End of the Term: Expiration*

Most agreements have a natural ending point. The end of the term of an agreement can be specified in terms of a certain date ("the Term of this Agreement shall continue until December 31, 2025") or a defined period of time ("the Term of this Agreement shall continue until the fifth (5th) anniversary of the Effective Date").

An agreement term can also end upon the occurrence of some defined event – the sale of a company, the completion of a project or the resignation or death of an individual, for example. There are few legal constraints on the types of events that can trigger the end of an agreement term (though see Section 21.5 regarding the illegality of "*ipso facto*" bankruptcy termination clauses).

When the term of an agreement expires, the rights and obligations of the parties, including all licenses granted, typically end, subject to certain terms that may survive (see Section 12.5).

12.1.3 *Renewals and Extensions*

The term of an agreement can always be extended by mutual consent of the parties, and many agreements are extended via a series of written extensions and amendments. These are generally enforceable without additional consideration, so long as both parties agree and validly document their agreement.

Nevertheless, some parties wish to avoid the repeated need for contract extensions and instead provide for automatic renewal of their agreements at the end of their term. The above example illustrates a common formulation: The agreement will automatically renew for renewal terms of one year each unless one of the parties notifies the other, with sufficient lead time, that it does not wish the agreement to renew. Automatic renewals are useful because they eliminate the risk that the parties, years into a fruitful relationship, will forget that their agreement is about to expire. There are many examples of parties continuing to cooperate, sell products and pay royalties years after their original agreement has expired. This informal type of extension is often fine, until a dispute arises over the agreement. Then the parties must contend with the formal lack of any agreement at all or try to persuade a court of the terms on which they tacitly "renewed" their relationship.

Sometimes there is an absolute limit on automatic agreement renewals (e.g., "further provided that there shall be no more than seven (7) automatic renewals under this Agreement"). However, such limitations are uncommon in IP licensing agreements.

A key term in automatic renewals is how much notice one party must give the other of its intention not to renew the agreement. Especially if performance under an agreement requires a party to retain staff, make capital investments and conduct business with third parties, it would be unreasonable to pull the rug out from under that party with no notice at the end of the then-current term. Thus, nonrenewal notice periods are often lengthy (six months would not be unusual), depending on the level of inconvenience that the other party will suffer when the agreement ends. But no matter how generous the nonrenewal notice period may be, once it is embodied in the agreement, a party must comply with it in order to prevent the automatic renewal of the agreement from occurring. See, e.g., *Otis Elevator Co. v. George Washington Hotel Corp.*, 27 F.3d 903, 909 (3d Cir. 1994) (under Pennsylvania law, failure to comply with a ninety-day deadline for providing notice of nonrenewal prior to automatic renewal of an agreement renders termination ineffective even without a showing of prejudice by the nonterminating party).

Another issue that arises in the context of agreement renewals is the degree to which a licensor can increase its fees when the agreement is renewed. Some agreements include a cap on such increases, though it is unclear how enforceable such caps are, as the licensor may simply elect not to renew the agreement under those terms, leaving the licensee with no choice but to renegotiate at a higher rate. See *SEI Global Svcs. v. SS&C Advent*, No. 20-1148 (E.D. Pa., Oct. 23, 2020) (a software license agreement with annual renewals imposed a cap of 3 percent on fee increases, but the licensor allegedly refused to renew unless the licensee accepted a 40 percent fee increase).

Notes and Questions

1. *Numerus clausus need not apply.* As students of real property law will recall, the ancient *numerus clausus* principle provides for legal recognition of a finite set of defined forms of the estates in land: fee simple absolute, fee simple determinable, life estate, etc. The leasehold is another form of estate – one that has a defined term. With respect to leaseholds, it is not permissible to define the term except through one of the recognized forms. Thus, a leasehold may have a term of years (a fixed number of hours, days, weeks, months, years or other measurable period), or may be periodic – existing period to period until terminated. But a lease may not be for a duration that is measured by external events, such as "for the duration of the war" or "until my spouse remarries." The *numerus clausus* principle does not, however, apply to licensing agreements, which may be structured in any manner desired by the parties (within the bounds of antitrust and other legal rules). Thus, a license agreement could be terminated upon a cessation of military hostilities, a marriage or any other event that the parties desire. Is this degree of flexibility a good thing, or should licensing agreements be treated more akin to leaseholds, with fixed and invariable forms?

2. *Extension versus longer term.* If you were negotiating an agreement, would you prefer a longer term (say, ten years) or a shorter term with automatic renewals (say, five years with up to five one-year renewals)? What advantages and disadvantages are inherent in each approach?

12.2 DURATION OF LICENSES

Recall our discussion in Chapter 2 of the difference between a licensing *agreement* and an IP license. A license is a set of rights that is conveyed by one party to another, usually through the vehicle of a licensing agreement. Yet licensing agreements often contain many additional rights and obligations beyond the bare license grant. These include payment and milestone obligations, services, confidentiality, indemnification, warranties and a host of others. Accordingly, it is useful to think about the duration of particular licenses that are granted under a licensing agreement separately from the term of the licensing agreement itself.

12.2.1 *Duration Coincident with Agreement Term*

In many cases, the duration of a license will be identical to the term of the agreement under which it is granted. This duration is often explicit in the grant clause of the agreement ("Licensor hereby grants Licensee a nonexclusive license … during the Term of this Agreement"). However, if the grant clause is silent as to the duration of a license, it will typically be interpreted to run concurrently with the term of the agreement.

12.2.2 *Duration When an Agreement States No Term*

In some cases, an agreement will state no defined term, nor will the license grant clause include any temporal limitation. In these cases (which should be avoided by careful contract drafters), courts have held that the duration of the license in question is the remaining term of protection of the licensed IP rights.[1] Thus, if a license is granted in 2020 under a patent that expires in 2031, the license will last so long as the patent remains valid and enforceable – which may occur at the expiration of the patent, an earlier date if required maintenance fees are not paid or a different earlier date if the patent is invalidated or rendered unenforceable in a legal action.

12.2.3 *"Perpetual" and IP-Duration Licenses*

A number of license grant clauses provide that the license will be "perpetual." As the court in *Warner-Lambert* (reproduced below) aptly points out, "The word 'perpetuity' is often applied very loosely to contractual obligations. Indiscriminate application of the term serves only to confuse."

Technically, a perpetual license is one that remains in effect for so long as the licensed IP right remains in force, because an IP holder is generally not permitted to control or charge for the use of an IP right after its expiration (see Chapter 24 discussing IP misuse). Thus, a "perpetual" license of patents or copyrights will last only so long as the underlying IP rights remain in effect, and must thereafter end. This occurrence is called "failure" of the licensed IP, and is most often seen in the case of patent licensing. Whether a license is perpetual, lasts for the duration of the IP right or has a defined term of years, the license ends with the failure of the underlying IP right.

This being said, if a portfolio of such rights is licensed, then the license (and royalty obligation) may continue until the last-to-expire of such rights (see Section 24.4, discussing package licensing).

EXAMPLE: LICENSE GRANT WITH PERPETUAL DURATION

Licensor hereby grants to Licensee a *perpetual* royalty-bearing right and license under the Licensed Patents to make, use, sell, offer for sale and import Licensed Products in the Territory in the Field of Use.

---

[1] See Raymond T. Nimmer & Jeff C. Dodd, *Modern Licensing Law* §§ 9.4–9.5 (Thomson-Reuters, 2016–17).

EXAMPLE: LICENSE GRANT WITH DURATION TIED TO IP DURATION

Licensor hereby grants to Licensee a royalty-bearing right and license under the Licensed Patents and Licensed Know-How to make, use, sell, offer for sale and import Licensed Products in the Territory in the Field of Use until the later of (a) the expiration of the last-to-expire Licensed Patent, or (b) the Licensed Know-How is no longer used in any Licensed Product.

A perpetual license (and an accompanying perpetual obligation to pay royalties) is perhaps the most potent when trademarks, trade secrets or know-how are licensed. Unlike patents and copyrights, these IP rights have no scheduled expiration, and their licenses may continue for so long as the rights are maintained (e.g., for so long as a trademark is renewed by the owner, and for so long as a trade secret retains its trade secret status).

An important caveat, however, is that the duration of the license itself need not coincide with the duration of the licensee's obligation to pay royalties. That is, even after a trade secret becomes known to the public, thereby destroying its status as a trade secret, a royalty obligation may continue, as illustrated by the following case involving the famous Listerine formulation.[2]

Warner-Lambert Pharm. Co. v. John J. Reynolds, Inc.

178 F. Supp. 655 (S.D.N.Y. 1959)

BRYAN, DISTRICT JUDGE

Plaintiff sues under the Federal Declaratory Judgment Act, 28 U.S.C. §§ 2201 and 2202, for a judgment declaring that it is no longer obligated to make periodic payments to defendants based on its manufacture or sale of the well known product "Listerine", under agreements made between Dr. J. J. Lawrence and J. W. Lambert in 1881, and between Dr. Lawrence and Lambert Pharmacal Company in 1885.

Plaintiff is a Delaware corporation which manufactures and sells Listerine, among other pharmaceutical products. It is the successor in interest to Lambert and Lambert Pharmacal Company which acquired the formula for Listerine from Dr. Lawrence under the agreements in question. Defendants are the successors in interest to Dr. Lawrence.

For some seventy-five years plaintiff and its predecessors have been making the periodic payments based on the quantity of Listerine manufactured or sold which are called for by the agreements in suit. The payments have totaled more than twenty-two million dollars and are presently in excess of one million five hundred thousand dollars yearly.

In the early 1880's Dr. Lawrence, a physician and editor of a medical journal in St. Louis, Missouri, devised a formula for an antiseptic liquid compound which was given the name "Listerine". The agreement between Lawrence and J. W. Lambert made in 1881, and that between Lawrence and Lambert Pharmacal Company made in 1885, providing

---

[2] The interplay of perpetual royalty obligations and IP misuse is a complex and not entirely settled one. As discussed in Chapter 24, charging royalties for a patented device after the patent has expired constitutes patent misuse (see *Brulotte v. Thys*, 379 U.S. 29 (1964)), yet charging perpetual royalties for an unpatented design (see *Aronson v. Quick Point Pencil*, 440 U.S. 257 (1979)) may be permitted.

for the sale of the Lawrence formula, were entered into in that city. Lambert, and thereafter his corporation, originally engaged in the manufacture and sale of Listerine and other pharmaceutical preparations on a modest scale there. Through the years the business prospered and grew fantastically and Listerine became a widely sold and nationally known product. The Lambert Pharmacal Company, with various changes in corporate structure and name which are not material here, continued the manufacture and sale of Listerine and other preparations until March 31, 1955, when it was merged into Warner-Hudnut, Inc., a Delaware corporation, and the name of the merged corporation was changed to Warner-Lambert Pharmaceutical Company, Inc. The plaintiff in this action is the merged corporation which continues the manufacture and sale of Listerine.

Plaintiff's second amended complaint in substance alleges the following:

Prior to April 20, 1881 Dr. Lawrence furnished Lambert with an unnamed secret formula for the antiseptic compound which came to be known as "Listerine", and on or about that date Lambert executed the first of the documents with which we are concerned here. This document, in its entirety, reads as follows:

> Know all men by these presents, that for and in consideration of the fact, that Dr. J. J. Lawrence of the city of St Louis Mo has furnished me with the formula of a medicine called Listerine to be manufactured by me, that I, Jordan W Lambert, also of the city of St Louis Mo, hereby agree for myself, my heirs, executors and assigns to pay monthly to the said Dr. J. J. Lawrence his heirs, executors or assigns, the sum of twenty dollars for each and every gross of said Listerine hereafter sold by myself, my heirs, executors or assigns.

On or about May 2, 1881 Lambert began the manufacture of the formula and adopted the trademark "Listerine." The agreed payments under the 1881 agreement were reduced on October 21, 1881 by the following letter addressed to Lambert by Lawrence:

> I hereby reduce my royalty on Listerine from twenty dollars pr gross to twelve dollars pr gross on the condition that a statement of your sales made each preceding month be rendered to me promptly on or before the 10th of each month, and payment of the amount due me on said royalty be made to me or my heirs at the same time. I also hereby waive any demands of royalty on you preceding the 1st of October 1881.

They were again reduced on March 23, 1883 by a similar letter reading as follows:

> I hereby reduce my royalty on Listerine from ten pr cent on gross amount of sales to six dollars pr gross, the same reduction is hereby made on my royalty on Renalia. Wishing you great prosperity.

Thereafter Lambert assigned his rights to Listerine and other Lawrence compounds to the Lambert Pharmacal Company and this company on January 2, 1885 executed an instrument assuming Lambert's obligations under these agreements with Lawrence and other obligations on account of other formulas which Lawrence had furnished, in the following language:

> J. J. Lawrence of St Louis Mo, having originated & heretofore sold to J W Lambert, the formulae & processes for the manufacture of … Listerine … with all the rights & benefits accruing therefrom and has received therefor a monthly royalty from J. W. Lambert, and J. W. Lambert having sold said formulae of Listerine … to the Lambert Pharmacal Company …, therefore know all men by these presents that for & in consideration of these facts, the said Lambert Pharmacal Co. hereby agrees and contracts for itself & assigns to

pay to the said J. J. Lawrence, his heirs, executors & assigns, six dollars on each & every gross of Listerine ... manufactured or sold by the said Lambert Pharmacal Co. or its assigns ...

The agreements between the parties contemplated, it is alleged, "the periodic payment of royalties to Lawrence for the use of a trade secret, to wit, the secret formula for" Listerine. After some modifications made with Lawrence's knowledge and approval, the formula was introduced on the market. The composition of the compound has remained the same since then and it is still being manufactured and sold by the plaintiff.

It is then alleged that the "trade secret" (the formula for Listerine) has gradually become a matter of public knowledge through the years following 1881 and prior to 1949, and has been published in the United States Pharmacopoia, the National Formulary and the Journal of the American Medical Association, and also as a result of proceedings brought against plaintiff's predecessor by the Federal Trade Commission. Such publications were not the fault of plaintiff or its predecessors. The complaint recites the chains of interest running respectively from Lambert to the present plaintiff and from Lawrence to the defendants, and concludes with a prayer for a declaration that plaintiff is "no longer liable to the defendants" for any further "royalties".

Despite the mass of material before me the basic issue between the parties is narrow. The plaintiff claims that its obligation to make payments to the defendants under the Lawrence–Lambert agreements was terminated by the public disclosure of the Listerine formula in various medical publications. The defendants assert that the obligation continued and has not been terminated.

The plaintiff seems to feel that the 1881 and 1885 agreements are indefinite and unclear, at least as to the length of time during which they would continue in effect. I do not find them to be so. These agreements seem to me to be plain and unambiguous.

The payments to Lawrence and his successors are conditioned upon the sale (in the 1881 agreement) and the manufacture or sale (in the 1885 agreement) of the medical preparation known as Listerine which Lawrence conveyed to Lambert. The obligation to pay on each and every gross of Listerine continues as long as this preparation is manufactured or sold by Lambert and his successors. It comes to an end when they cease to manufacture or sell the preparation. There is nothing which compels the plaintiff to continue such manufacture and sale. No doubt Lambert and his successors have been and still are free at any time, in good faith and in the exercise of sound business discretion, to stop manufacturing and selling Listerine. The plain meaning of the language used in these agreements is simply that Lambert's obligation to pay is co-extensive with manufacture or sale of Listerine by him and his successors.

The plaintiff, however, claims that despite the plain language of the agreement it may continue to manufacture and sell without making the payments required by the agreements because the formula which its predecessors acquired is no longer secret. To sustain this position plaintiff invokes the shade, if not the substance, of the traditional common law distaste for contractual rights and duties unbounded by definite limitations of time and argues that absent a construction that the obligation to pay is co-extensive only with the secrecy of the formula, it must be a forbidden "perpetuity" which the law will not enforce. I find no support for the plaintiff's theory either in the cases which it cites or elsewhere.

The word "perpetuity" is often applied very loosely to contractual obligations. Indiscriminate application of the term serves only to confuse. The mere fact that an obligation under a contract may continue for a very long time is no reason in itself for declaring the contract to exist in perpetuity or for giving it a construction which would do violence to the expressed intent of the parties.

There are contracts in which the promisor's obligation has been expressly fixed to last forever. Such cases mainly arise in the field of real property and are governed by various considerations of public policy which have no pertinence here.

Contracts which omit any point of time or any condition which would terminate the promisor's liability are somewhat different. Where it appears that the parties did in fact intend that the obligation terminate at an ascertainable time, the courts, in effect, will supply the missing clause and construe the contract accordingly.

On the other hand, if it appears that no termination date was within the contemplation of the parties, or that their intention with respect thereto cannot be ascertained, the contract will be held to be terminable within a reasonable time or revocable at will, dependent upon the circumstances.

In such cases the courts are loathe to find that the absence of a terminal point indicates an intention to contract for the indefinite future, and a perpetual obligation will not usually be inferred from the absence of a terminating date or condition. While there is no hard and fast rule, the terminal date or condition of termination will be that to be ascertained from the actual though unexpressed intention of the parties or as a remedy for their neglect. If the parties intend that the obligation be perpetual they must expressly say so.

Contracts which provide no fixed date for the termination of the promisor's obligation but condition the obligation upon an event which would necessarily terminate the contract are in quite a different category and it is in this category that the 1881 and 1885 Lambert Lawrence agreements fall. On the face of the agreements the obligation of Lambert and its successors to pay is conditioned upon the continued manufacture or sale of Listerine. When they cease manufacturing or selling Listerine the condition for continued payment comes to an end and the obligation to pay terminates. This is the plain meaning of the language which the parties used.

Moreover, this is not a case in which the promisor's obligation will cease only on the occurrence of some fortuitous event unrelated to the subject matter of the contract. The obligation here is conditioned upon an event arising out of the very arrangement between the parties which is the subject matter of the contract.

In *Cammack v. J. B. Slattery & Bros.*, 241 N.Y. 39, plaintiff had furnished defendant with a secret process. Defendant's liability to make payments therefor depended upon use. There was held to be no uncertainty as to the term of the contract nor any perpetuity of obligation, but that the obligation to pay continued as long as the defendant used the secret process which it had acquired. The court expressly rejected the defendant's contention that the contract was terminable at will because it provided no fixed termination date.

Nor is there any need to resort to extrinsic evidence in order to ascertain what the intention of the parties was, or what the termination date of the obligation to pay would be, for the agreements themselves indicate the condition upon which the obligation terminates.

There is nothing unreasonable or irrational about imposing such an obligation. It is entirely rational and sensible that the obligation to make payments should be based upon the business which flows from the formula conveyed. Whether or not the obligation continues is in the control of the plaintiff itself. For the plaintiff has the right to terminate its obligation to pay whenever in good faith it desires to cease the manufacture or sale of Listerine. This would seem to end the matter.

However, plaintiff urges with vigor that the agreement must be differently construed because it involved the conveyance of a secret formula. The main thrust of its argument is that despite the language which the parties used, the court must imply a limitation upon Lambert's obligation to pay measured by the length of time that the Listerine formula remained secret.

To sustain this theory plaintiff relies upon a number of cases involving the obligations of licensees of copyrights or patents to make continuing payments to the owner or licensor, and argues that these cases are controlling here. [But all that these cases hold] is that when parties agree upon a license under a patent or copyright the court will assume, in the absence of express language to the contrary, that their actual intention as to the term is measured by the definite term of the underlying grant fixed by statute. It is quite plain that were it not for the patent and copyright features of such license agreements the term would be measured by use.

Paralleling the concept that the licensing of a patent or copyright contracts only for the statutory monopoly granted in such cases is the concept not so frequently expressed that public policy may require a termination of the obligation to pay when the patent or copyright term is ended.

I see nothing in any of the cases which the plaintiff cites dealing with patents and copyrights which supports the theory which plaintiff advances here. Plaintiff has not cited a single case in which the rules of these cases have been applied to a contract involving the conveyance of a secret formula or a trade secret.

In the patent and copyright cases the parties are dealing with a fixed statutory term and the monopoly granted by that term. This monopoly, created by Congress, is designed to preserve exclusivity in the grantee during the statutory term and to release the patented or copyrighted material to the general public for general use thereafter. This is the public policy of the statutes in reference to which such contracts are made and it is against this background that the parties to patent and copyright license agreements contract.

Here, however, there is no such public policy. The parties are free to contract with respect to a secret formula or trade secret in any manner which they determine for their own best interests. A secret formula or trade secret may remain secret indefinitely. It may be discovered by someone else almost immediately after the agreement is entered into. Whoever discovers it for himself by legitimate means is entitled to its use.

But that does not mean that one who acquires a secret formula or a trade secret through a valid and binding contract is then enabled to escape from an obligation to which he bound himself simply because the secret is discovered by a third party or by the general public. I see no reason why the court should imply such a term or condition in a contract providing on its face that payment shall be co-extensive with use. To do so here would be to rewrite the contract for the parties without any indication that they intended such a result.

It may be noted that here the parties themselves made no reference to secrecy in either the 1881 or the 1885 agreements. The word "secret" is not used anywhere in either of them. It is true that I have assumed during this discussion that the plaintiff is correct in its contention that what Lambert bargained for was a "secret" formula. But that in no way justifies the further assumption that he also bargained for continuing secrecy or that there would be failure of consideration if secrecy did not continue.

One who acquires a trade secret or secret formula takes it subject to the risk that there be a disclosure. The inventor makes no representation that the secret is non-discoverable. All the inventor does is to convey the knowledge of the formula or process which is unknown to the purchaser and which in so far as both parties then know is unknown to any one else. The terms upon which they contract with reference to this subject matter are purely up to them and are governed by what the contract they enter into provides.

If they desire the payments or royalties should continue only until the secret is disclosed to the public it is easy enough for them to say so. But there is no justification for implying such a provision if the parties do not include it in their contract, particularly where the language which they use by fair intendment provides otherwise.

The case at bar illustrates what may occur in such cases. As the undisputed facts show, the acquisition of the Lawrence formula was the base on which plaintiff's predecessors built up a very large and successful business in the antiseptic or germicide field. Even now, twenty-five or more years after it is claimed that the trade secret was disclosed to the public, plaintiff retains more than 50% of the national market in these products.

At the very least plaintiff's predecessors, through the acquisition of the Lawrence formula under this contract, obtained a head start in the field of liquid antiseptics which has proved of incalculable value through the years. There is nothing novel about business being transacted only in a small way at the outset of a contract relationship and thereafter growing far beyond what was anticipated when the contract was made. Because the business has prospered far beyond anticipations affords no basis for changing the terms of the contract the parties agreed upon when the volume was small.

There is nothing in this contract to indicate that plaintiff's predecessors bargained for more than the disclosure of the Lawrence formula which was then unknown to it. Plaintiff has pointed to no principle of law or equity which would require or permit the court gratuitously to rewrite the contract which its predecessors made for these considerations.

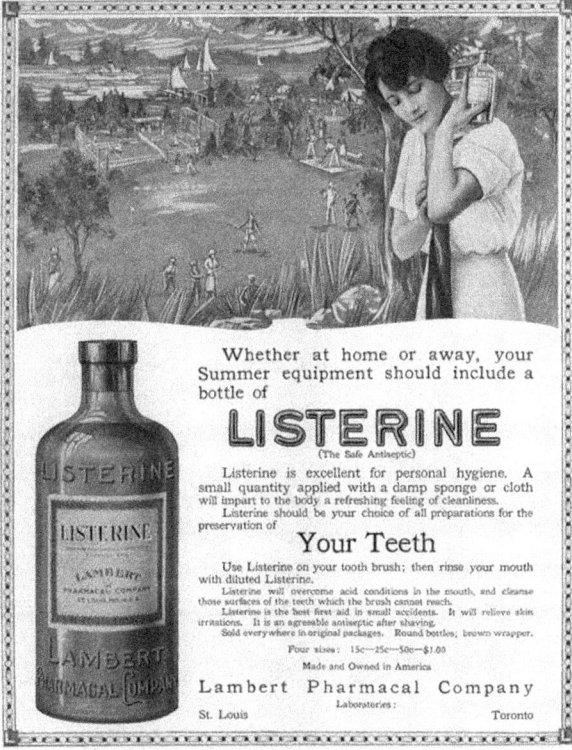

FIGURE 12.1 A 1915 advertisement for Listerine.

If plaintiff wishes to avoid its obligations under the contract it is free to do so, and, indeed, the contract itself indicates how this may be done. The fact that neither the plaintiff nor its predecessors have done so, and that the plaintiff continues to manufacture and sell Listerine under the Lawrence formula with great success, indicates how valuable the rights under the contract are and how unjust it would be to permit it to have its cake and eat it too.

Thus, I hold that under the agreements in suit plaintiff is obligated to make the periodic payments called for by them as long as it continues to manufacture and sell the preparation described in them as Listerine.

Notes and Questions

1. *No termination date.* The court in *Warner-Lambert* reasons "if it appears that no termination date was within the contemplation of the parties, or that their intention with respect thereto cannot be ascertained, the contract will be held to be terminable within a reasonable time or revocable at will, dependent upon the circumstances." Why wasn't Warner-Lambert permitted to terminate its royalty payments on Listerine?

2. *Perpetual profit.* In *Warner-Lambert*, the court distinguishes the original license of the secret Listerine formula from licenses of patents and copyrights. Yet the Listerine formula became public years before the case was brought. How does the court justify the ongoing royalty obligation when there is no apparent IP right remaining in effect? How does the court distinguish Warner-Lambert's license from a typical patent or copyright license? Keep this case in mind when you read *Aronson v. Quick Point Pencil* in Chapter 24.

3. *The rest of the Listerine story.* The court's 1956 decision in *Warner-Lambert* created a perpetual income stream for those entitled to a share of Dr. Lawrence's original Listerine royalties. John J. Reynolds, the defendant and holder of the royalty interest at suit, was a New York real estate broker who purchased the royalty interest from Dr. Lawrence's heirs for $4 million. As reported in a recent news story:

   > Reynolds in turn split up the shares and sold them to entities including the Roman Catholic Archdiocese of New York, the Salvation Army, the American Bible Society and Wellesley College. Among those who eventually acquired a stake was former New Jersey Gov. Chris Christie, whose unusual disclosure of nearly $24,000 in annual Listerine royalty income was a minor news item during his presidential campaign four years ago.[3]

   One of the slices of Reynolds' original royalty interest currently earns $32,000 per year. That slice was sold at auction in July 2020 to an anonymous bidder for $560,000. While it will take almost eighteen years for the royalty interest to pay for itself, the prospect of a perpetual payment stream, and the enduring human malady for which Listerine is one of the key antidotes, apparently made the purchase attractive.

4. *Patterns of conduct.* The court in *Warner-Lambert* notes that "where there is doubt or ambiguity as to the meaning of a contract ... the courts will follow the interpretation placed upon the contract by the parties themselves as shown by their acts and conduct." In this case, Warner-Lambert and its predecessors paid royalties for the use of Listerine for at least twenty-five years before suit was brought, substantially weakening Warner-Lambert's

---

[3] Ryan Davis, *Rare Listerine Royalty Auction Tied To 1881 Contract Flub*, Law360, July 21, 2020.

argument that royalties should not be due. But how seriously should courts take the parties' own actions if they are mistaken or contrary to the terms of a written agreement, especially if the time periods involved are substantially less than twenty-five years? In other words, how long should a party continue to profit from the other party's mistakes after it becomes aware of them?

5. *The Listerine name.* Dr. Joseph Lawrence, the inventor of Listerine, named his formulation in honor of Dr. Joseph Lister, the English physician who pioneered the use of antiseptics in surgical procedures.[4] Interestingly, the name Listerine was not registered as a trademark until 1912. The original registrant was not Dr. Lawrence, but his licensee, Lambert Pharamcal Corp., the predecessor to Warner-Lambert. Thus, the license at issue in *Warner-Lambert* was not a trademark license, as the Listerine trademark was, and still is, owned by the licensee of the formula.

6. *Rights reversions.* In 1958, Truman Capote granted Paramount Pictures the exclusive right to produce a film based on his novella *Breakfast at Tiffany's.* The 1961 film starring Audrey Hepburn and featuring the iconic song "Moon River" became a classic. In 1991, Paramount was forced to negotiate a new license with Capote's estate due to its earlier failure to obtain rights during the renewal term of the novella's copyright. The new agreement provided that if Paramount did not produce a new version of *Breakfast at Tiffany's* by 2003, then all rights in the work (other than Paramount's right to continue to distribute its original 1961 film) would revert to the estate. In 2020, when the estate sought to license the work for a television series, Paramount intervened, claiming that it possessed the television rights to *Breakfast at Tiffany's.* The estate sued, seeking a declaration that Paramount forfeited its rights under the reversion clause of the 1991 contract. *Schwartz v. Paramount Pictures Corp.* (filed Nov. 4, 2020, Cal. Sup. Ct. for Los Angeles Co.).

Such reversions are not uncommon in copyright agreements in the entertainment industry. Below is typical wording for such a clause.

EXAMPLE: REVERSION OF RIGHTS

If principal photography of the Production (which commencement of principal photography Producer does not undertake, and shall not be obligated, to do) does not commence by the date ("Reversion Date") which is [seven (7)] years after the date of Producer's exercise of the Option, then all of the Rights granted to Producer hereunder shall revert to Grantor, provided, however, that Grantor shall have no right, title or interest in or to any screenplays, treatments, outlines or other material created or developed by or for Producer based on the Rights.

Why do you think that licensees and assignees of copyright interests agree to such reversionary clauses? In some cases, the licensor to whom rights revert must repay any purchase price that the licensee has made in order to obtain the reversion. Do you think that this repayment obligation is fair? How might it be adjusted to accommodate the interests of the licensor?

---

[4] It is unclear whether Dr. Lister ever gave Lawrence permission to use his name in this manner. See Leonard F. Vernon, *From Surgical Suite to Fresh Breath: The History of Listerine®*, 4(3) Int'l J. Dentistry & Oral Health 1, 4 (2018).

7. *Perpetual conflicts.* All too often, the language of license grants is unclear or contradictory, especially when perpetual rights are purported to be granted. Consider, for example, the enterprise software license in *SEI Global Svcs. v. SS&C Advent*, No. 20-1148 (E.D. Pa., Oct. 23, 2020). On one hand, the license granted purported to be "perpetual." On the other hand, the agreement required annual renewals with fees established every year. When the licensor increased its renewal fee by 40 percent one year and the licensee refused to pay, what result?

8. *Irrevocable licenses.* In some cases the license grant clause specifies that a license is both perpetual and "irrevocable." Irrevocability is a powerful concept and indicates not only that a license has no natural end date, but also that it cannot be terminated for any cause, even breach by the licensee (see Section 12.3). For this reason, irrevocable license grants are relatively rare, but can be appropriate, for example, when a license is fully paid-up (i.e., there is no ongoing royalty obligation). When a license is fully paid, the licensee may argue that it should not be at risk of losing the license, for example, due to a breach of a confidentiality or service commitment under the agreement. Those breaches, it could argue, are addressable through monetary remedies, but loss of the license after it has been paid for is too harsh a remedy.

   Consider, however, the (not uncommon) situation in which a license is designated as irrevocable, but other provisions of the agreement suggest that it is not. For example, the court in *Fraunhofer-Gesellschaft v. Sirius XM*, 940 F.3d 1372, 1381 (Fed. Cir. 2019), describes the following contractual terms:

   Section 3.1 provides that the Master Agreement license is "irrevocable," stating that "[Fraunhofer] grants to [WorldSpace] and its Affiliates a worldwide, exclusive, irrevocable license, with the right to sublicense, under the MCM Intellectual Property Rights to make, have made, use, have used, sell, or have sold MCM Technology (and products and services incorporating or utilizing the MCM Technology) in connection with WorldSpace Business."

   On the other hand, section 7.4 states that "[n]o termination or expiration of this Agreement shall effect [sic] the rights and licenses granted to [WorldSpace] under [section 3], provided that [WorldSpace] has paid (or has agreed in writing to pay) all of the amounts specified in [section 4] as of the date of termination or expiration." Fraunhofer argues that WorldSpace has not made the required payments …

   Assuming that Fraunhofer's representation about WorldSpace's failure to pay is accurate, how would you rule regarding the survival of WorldSpace's license after the Master Agreement is terminated?

12.3 BREACH AND TERMINATION FOR CAUSE

Most licensing agreements provide for early termination before the natural expiration of the agreement. The most common cause for termination is breach of the agreement by the other party (a party cannot generally terminate for its own breach).

A breach of contract is broadly defined under Section 235(2) of the *Restatement (Second) of Contracts* as "The failure to perform at the time stated in the contract." The apparent simplicity of this definition does a disservice to the many complex obligations and requirements of IP licensing agreements, and breaches of such agreements can include not only failures to perform affirmative obligations (e.g., providing services, delivering products or paying royalties) but also violations of covenants such as the obligation to maintain information in confidence or the making of a representation or warranty that proves to be false.

Under common law, a party's breach of an agreement can give the nonbreaching party various rights and remedies including excuse of its own performance, monetary damages, injunctive relief, the right to cover and the right to terminate the agreement. These remedies are covered extensively in most first-year Contracts courses, and we will not dwell on them here, as most licensing agreements expressly call out the remedies available for breach of contract. The most common of these is termination.

EXAMPLE: TERMINATION FOR BREACH

This Agreement may be terminated prior to the expiration of its Term by either party in the event of the material breach by the other party of any provision of this Agreement, provided that the terminating party shall have notified the other party of the alleged breach and such other party shall have failed to cure such breach within thirty (30) days of the giving of such notice.

12.3.1 *Materiality*

Most clauses permitting termination of an agreement for breach require that the triggering breach be "material." In some cases, breaches of particularly important obligations (e.g., major payments or delivery of a critical deliverable such as a prototype or a manuscript) may be called out as material. However, most agreements do not specify the types of breaches that will be considered material.

If a dispute over the materiality of a breach arises, guidance can be found in a variety of sources. Nimmer and Dodd suggest that a "material" breach be defined as any breach other than an "immaterial" one, such that "materiality could simply be used to preclude a party from canceling a contract for small problems of performance."[5] Corbin, on the other hand, offers a contextual analysis:

Whether or not a breach is … material and important is a question of degree; and it must be answered by weighing the consequences in the light of the actual custom of parties in the performance of contracts similar to the one that is involved in the specific case.[6]

Below is a more detailed analytical framework provided by the *Restatement*.

RESTATEMENT (SECOND) OF CONTRACTS § 241

In determining whether a failure to render or to offer performance is material, the following circumstances are significant:

(a) the extent to which the injured party will be deprived of the benefit which he reasonably expected;
(b) the extent to which the injured party can be adequately compensated for the part of that benefit of which he will be deprived;

---

[5] Nimmer & Dodd, *supra* note 1, at § 11.18.
[6] 10 Corbin on Contracts § 53.4.

(c) the extent to which the party failing to perform or to offer to perform will suffer forfeiture;

(d) the likelihood that the party failing to perform or to offer to perform will cure his failure, taking account of all the circumstances including any reasonable assurances;

(e) the extent to which the behavior of the party failing to perform or to offer to perform comports with standards of good faith and fair dealing.

Not surprisingly, courts applying these various legal standards reach inconsistent results when assessing the materiality of contractual breaches in the IP licensing context. Even nonpayment of royalties can be deemed to be material or immaterial, depending on the circumstances.[7] Accordingly, if there are key obligations under a licensing agreement, the parties should specify that, without limiting the generality of the material breach clause, a party's failure to perform those particular obligations will be deemed to constitute a material breach.

As an illustration of the difficulty that parties and courts often have with the question of materiality, consider the following passage from a recent decision:

> it is ultimately the materiality of the breaches that was determinative of the issue and, indeed, is necessarily the reason the matters were presented to the jury despite the district court's previous rulings. Although the jury was not presented with an instruction on materiality, given the parties' discussions throughout the trial, the district court's rulings on the various motions throughout these proceedings, the evidence presented, the arguments made to the jury, and the jury instructions read in their entirety, the verdict can be characterized as one determining materiality. The materiality concept was front and center in Rydex's closing arguments; and in fact, the parties discussed issues obviously addressing materiality throughout trial and submitted the district court's holdings regarding Rydex's breaches to the jury, indicating in fact that those holdings did not carry the day in the contract dispute. The jury's conclusion that Graco be awarded $0.00 in damages as a result of Rydex's breaches, viewed under our favorable standard of review lens, indicates the jury did not find a material failing on the part of Rydex.[8]

12.3.2 *Notice*

Most termination for breach clauses require that the terminating party give written notice of the breach to the party that is allegedly in breach. This notice allows the breaching party to contest the characterization of its performance as a breach. More importantly, notice usually triggers a breaching party's right to cure the breach (see Section 12.3.3).

As noted in *Corbin on Contracts*, "Notice within the designed time period is the condition precedent to the effective exercise of the power reserved. If a party who has a power of termination by notice fails to give the notice in the form and at the time required by the Agreement, it is ineffective as a termination."[9] Accordingly, a party that fails to give a notice of breach/

---

[7]   Compare *Metabolite Labs. v. Lab. Corp. Am.*, 370 F.3d 1354 (Fed. Cir. 2004) (refusal "to pay royalties is a material breach of the license") with *USAR Sys. v. Brain Works, Inc.*, 897 F. Supp. 163 (S.D.N.Y. 1995) (failure to pay license fee was not a material breach after vendor failed to deliver contracted software).

[8]   *Ryan Data Exch., Ltd. v. Graco, Inc.*, 913 F.3d 726, 734 (8th Cir. 2019).

[9]   13 Corbin on Contracts § 68.9.

termination following the occurrence of such a breach waives its right to terminate for the breach, though it may retain other remedies, such as a claim for damages, with respect to the breach.[10]

Notice of termination must be clear and unambiguous. "[W]here the conduct of one having the right to terminate is ambiguous, he will be deemed not to have terminated the contract" (*Maloney v. Madrid Motor Corp.*, 122 A.2d 694, 696 (Pa. 1956)). The need for clarity is often defeated by a party's misplaced desire not to appear too confrontational or aggressive. For example, in *Mextel, Inc. v. Air-Shields, Inc.*, 2005 U.S. Dist. LEXIS 1281 at *65–66, Mextel allegedly failed to comply with its contractual design and development obligations relating to an electronic controller. The customer sent Mextel a letter purporting to terminate the agreement. According to the court,

> The letter listed various problems with Mextel's design and development of the controllers, including a failure to maintain good design controls and quality work standards, and then threatened that if Mextel "continues to conduct business in this manner, we will have to take appropriate action, which could include termination of Mextel as a developer/supplier as provided under the contract."

The court held that this letter did not provide adequate notice of termination, as "[a] threat of possible termination in the future does not constitute clear and unambiguous notice." Accordingly, attorneys should resist the desire of their clients to be overly polite or indirect in their communications when those communications are intended to have legal effect.

One question that is often left unanswered in the termination for breach clause is how soon after the terminating party becomes aware of the breach it must notify the breaching party. In other words, can the terminating party wait for months or years after a breach occurs before notifying the breaching party that it wishes to terminate the agreement? In effect, this would allow the nonbreaching party to hold the threat of termination over the breaching party like a trump card which it could play at any moment.

Another issue that arises is how much, if any, notice the nonbreaching party must give to the breaching party of *termination*. Suppose that the nonbreaching party notifies the breaching party of a breach and the breaching party fails to cure the breach within the allowed thirty- or sixty-day cure period. Is the agreement automatically terminated, or must the nonbreaching party then notify the breaching party of the termination of the agreement?

The answer depends on the wording of the termination for breach clause. It may provide for automatic termination if the breaching party does not cure within the designated cure period. If this is the case, then the nonbreaching party's initial notice of breach should also be drafted as a notice of termination.

But if, as in the example provided above, the clause gives the nonbreaching party the right to terminate if the breach is not cured, then we must ask how long the nonbreaching party has to issue notice of termination? If the agreement does not specify a time period (and most do not), then the common law must be consulted. As observed by the Federal Circuit in *Fraunhofer-Gesellschaft v. Sirius XM Radio*, 940 F.3d 1372, 1379 (Fed. Cir. 2018), "it is a general rule of contract law that a party exercising the right to terminate [a] contract must give notice within a reasonable time." This result is sensible, otherwise the nonbreaching party would hold a sword of Damocles over the head of the breaching party for the duration of the contract term.

---

[10] See *Carleno Coal Sales v. Ramsay Coal Co.*, 129 Colo. 393, 270 P.2d 755 (1954).

12.3.3 *Cure*

Most licensing agreements allow a breaching party to cure the breach before the other party is permitted to terminate. The cure period is often thirty days, though thoughtful drafters may establish different cure periods for different types of breaches. For example, payment errors may be quicker to cure than failures to achieve technical results.

Some types of licensing agreements, usually online and consumer licenses (see Chapter 17), do not give the licensee an opportunity to cure its breach. Rather, these agreements purport to be terminated automatically upon the licensee's breach. Though draconian, courts seem to view these automatic termination clauses as enforceable.

In addition, some agreements classify some types of breaches as "uncurable." For example, the public disclosure of a trade secret or the exposure of customer data to a hacker might not be capable of cure. As a result, some agreements qualify the cure language in their termination for breach clauses as follows:

> The breaching party shall have a period of thirty (30) days to cure any such breach that is susceptible of cure; breaches that are not susceptible of cure shall give rise to an immediate right to terminate this Agreement.

Another question that arises in the context of breach is *when* a breach is considered to be cured, and who decides whether the cure is adequate. Must the nonbreaching party be satisfied with the cure in order for it to eliminate the right to terminate? If so, the following language is often used:

> The breaching party shall have a period of thirty (30) days to cure any such breach to the reasonable satisfaction of the nonbreaching party.

Of course, this qualification gives the nonbreaching party a degree of discretion whether or not to accept a cure. For example, suppose that a biotech firm breaches its obligation to deliver a vaccine to a public health authority because the oral form of the vaccine proves to be ineffective in humans. Can the firm cure the breach by delivering an intravenous form of the vaccine instead? Can the public health authority reject this cure on the basis that its pediatric patient population is terrified of needles?

But if the nonbreaching party does not get to decide whether or not the cure is adequate, then who does? In the end, this question may have to be answered pursuant to the dispute resolution procedures of the agreement or, absent those, by a court.

12.3.4 *Excuse of Performance: Dependencies*

In addition to giving the nonbreaching party the right to terminate an agreement, a party's breach also provides grounds to excuse the nonbreaching party's performance under the agreement. For example, if one party fails to deliver a technical design or specification to the other, then the other party's obligation to pay for it or to implement that design in a product may be postponed or excused.

This principle has longstanding roots in the common law,[11] but parties that are particularly concerned about so-called "dependencies" sometimes adopt express contractual language to reflect the effect on the nonbreaching party.

---

[11]   See *Restatement (Second) of Contracts*, § 237 ("it is a condition of each party's remaining duties to render performances to be exchanged under an exchange of promises that there be no uncured material failure by the other party to render any such performance due at an earlier time").

Licensor's obligation to deliver the Deliverables specified in Schedule X shall be dependent upon Licensee's provision of the materials and authorizations specified in Schedule Y, and any delay or failure by Licensee to provide such materials and authorizations at the times specified in Schedule Y shall postpone or excuse, as the case may be, Licensee's corresponding obligation to deliver the associated Deliverables.

Notwithstanding the foregoing, any delay by Licensee in providing the required materials and authorizations of more than 30 days beyond the date specified in Schedule Y shall constitute a material breach of this Agreement by Licensee.

Notes and Questions

1. *Milestone failures as breach and termination events.* As discussed in Section 8.5, many exclusive licensing agreements include milestones that the licensee is expected to achieve on its path toward commercialization of an invention. Often, the failure to meet a milestone results in the licensee's ineligibility for a payment tied to the achievement of that milestone. But under some agreements, milestone requirements are not only payment triggers, but affirmative obligations. In these cases, failure to meet a milestone could constitute a breach of the agreement and supply grounds for termination. Under what circumstances might this approach to milestones be appropriate? An alternative approach treats the failure to meet an important milestone as grounds for termination of the agreement, but does not classify such failure as a breach. What are the relative advantages and drawbacks of this approach?

2. *Materiality.* Most licensing agreements do not specify what types of breaches rise to the level of materiality necessary to trigger a termination right. Why not? List five types of contractual breaches in an IP licensing agreement that would almost always be material, and five that would almost always be immaterial.

3. *Breach of a material term versus material breach of a term.* The example above gives a party the right to terminate the agreement upon the other party's uncured material breach of the agreement, which is the most common formulation of the termination for cause clause. But some licensing agreements formulate this clause in terms of a "breach of a material obligation under the agreement." What is the practical difference between these two formulations? Which one would be preferable in your view? See *IGEN Intl. v. Roche Diagnostics*, 335 F.3d 303 (4th Cir. 2003) (upholding the jury verdict finding that Roche's underpayment of royalties and violation of field of use restrictions were breaches of material obligations). But see *Septembertide Publishing v. Stein & Day*, 884 F.2d 675 (2nd Cir. 1989) (publisher's failure to pay one-third of required amounts did not amount to a material breach giving rise to a termination right).

4. *Incurable breaches.* As noted above, the public release of a trade secret is often considered an incurable breach. What other types of breaches of an IP licensing agreement might be considered incurable?

5. *Cure and dependencies.* Suppose that the licensor in the above example fails to deliver materials required by the licensee for its performance within thirty days of the due date. Under the language in the example, this failure constitutes a breach by the licensor. But under the termination for breach clause, each party is given thirty days to cure breaches. Does the licensor thus get an additional thirty days to deliver the required materials? What is the reason that this additional cure period may be allowed?

6. *The limits of dependencies.* Dependencies are generally effective to postpone a party's delivery obligations if the other party has delayed necessary precursor tasks. But parties should not try to expand the scope of dependencies to cover obligations that are not genuinely requirements for the other party to perform. For example, in *iXL, Inc. v. AdOutlet.Com, Inc.,* 2001 U.S. Dist. LEXIS 3784 (N.D. Ill. 2001) (discussed in Section 9.2), the court chastises a developer for attempting to broaden its customer's dependencies beyond their reasonable meaning:

> iXL points to paragraph 2.2 of the terms and conditions of the Statements of Work, which state that AdOutlet "shall perform the tasks set forth in the Statement as a condition to iXL's obligations to perform hereunder." iXL claims that this language establishes that full payment by AdOutlet is a condition precedent to AdOutlet being deemed the author and copyright holder of the source code. iXL certainly could have made full payment by AdOutlet a condition precedent. But it is hard to read paragraph 2.2 as doing so. The word "tasks" is not defined in the Agreement or in the Statements of Work. The Court finds it plausible that paragraph 2.2 is to be read in conjunction with paragraph 2.4, which provides that iXL's obligation to meet contractual deadlines is contingent upon AdOutlet complying "in a timely manner, with all reasonable requests of iXL."

   How does the example dependencies clause above avoid the problem introduced by paragraph 2.2 in the agreement between iXL and AdOutlet?

7. *Escrow of disputed sums.* If the parties disagree over the amounts due under a licensing agreement, it is sometimes advisable for the licensee to pay the disputed amounts into an escrow account administered by a neutral party (e.g., an attorney or accountant). The escrow agent is then instructed to disburse to the licensor the amount that a court or arbitrator determines to be owed. This approach demonstrates the licensee's good faith and its willingness and ability to pay the disputed amount. In *Fantasy, Inc. v. Fogerty,* 984 F.2d 1524 (9th Cir. 1993), the Ninth Circuit held that a licensee who followed this approach did not materially breach a publishing agreement. When would you recommend that a licensee establish such an escrow account? Are there any circumstances when this approach would not be desirable?

8. *Other termination events.* In addition to breach, licensing agreements often contain other events that trigger one or both parties' right to terminate. These include events of force majeure (see Section 13.6), bankruptcy or insolvency of a party (see Chapter 21), the merger or change in control of a party (see Section 13.3), the failure of a party to achieve a milestone payment (see Note 1 above) and the licensee's challenge to the validity of the licensed IP rights (see Chapter 22). The value of listing these events of termination separately is that they can trigger termination without the need to prove breach of contract. In these cases, a party may terminate without the ability to recover damages for breach. What other nonbreach events of termination might you recommend including in an IP licensing agreement?

9. *Contractual and common law termination.* With or without a contractual termination clause, a party may still have a right to terminate a contract under the common law following the other party's breach. Thus, if the parties wish to eliminate entirely one party's ability to terminate the agreement, they must do more than simply omit that party from a termination for cause clause or omit the clause entirely. Rather, the party must expressly waive its right to terminate, a legal act that may or may not be recognized by a court.

10. *Breaches by sublicensees.* What happens when a sublicensee breaches its sublicense agreement? Clearly, the sublicensor has remedies against the breaching sublicensee, including termination. But does the primary licensor have a remedy against the breaching sublicensee? Should the primary licensor have the ability to terminate a sublicense for breach without

the sublicensor's consent? And should the sublicensee's breach constitute a breach by the licensee of the primary license (i.e., the sublicensor)? Why or why not?

The law is not entirely clear or consistent on these points so, not surprisingly, parties sometimes attempt to address them contractually. How would you respond, as the licensee, to this proposed language in an IP licensing agreement:

> Licensee shall have the right to grant sublicenses to one or more sublicensees who have been approved in writing by Licensor in advance, provided, however, that any breach of the terms of any such sublicense by a sublicensee shall be deemed to constitute a material breach of this Agreement by Licensee, as to which Licensor shall have all of its available remedies, including the right of termination.

11. *Licensor's self-help remedies.* In addition to monetary damages, specific performance and termination, licensors of software and other technology products often have recourse to technical measures to address breaches of their licensing agreements. This is the technological equivalent of shutting off a customer's water or electricity for nonpayment of bills. Licensors can embed kill switches, throttles or other electronic disabling devices into their products for activation upon a licensee's breach.

Not surprisingly, licensees have objected to the use of such mechanisms, particularly when the licensor's self-help actions block access to, damage or destroy the licensee's data. Claims have been brought against licensors exercising self-help remedies under a variety of legal theories, including trespass, private nuisance and violations of the Computer Fraud and Abuse Act, 18 U.S.C. § 1030, the Electronic Communications Privacy Act, 18 U.S.C. §§ 2701-10 and other state and federal statutes. In general, courts have upheld a licensor's ability to resort to self-help measures, particularly when the licensee has consented to the use of such measures in its licensing agreement. See *Am. Computer Trust Leasing v. Jack Farrell Implement Co.*, 763 F. Supp. 1473 (D. Minn. 1991) (permitting remote deactivation of software system following licensee's failure to pay required licensing fees).[12]

If you were representing the licensee of a critical enterprise software system, what protections might you include in your licensing agreement with the software vendor to prevent a potentially catastrophic loss of data or interruption of your business?

12.4 TERMINATION WITHOUT CAUSE

In Section 12.3 we considered the conditions under which a party may terminate an agreement "for cause," namely following the other party's uncured material breach. In this section we address contractual provisions that permit parties to terminate their agreements without cause, also referred to as "at will" termination and termination "for convenience" clauses.

EXAMPLE: TERMINATION WITHOUT CAUSE

[Either party] [1] shall have the right to terminate this Agreement without cause upon 30 days prior written notice to the other party.

---

[12] For a more comprehensive discussion, see Nimmer & Dodd, *supra* note 1, § 11.34 (Electronic self-help remedies).

DRAFTING NOTES

[1] *Parties* – it is not always the case that both parties are given the right to terminate an agreement without cause. This right is often heavily negotiated.

In general, termination without cause provisions allow one or both parties to terminate an agreement on a no-fault basis. Some agreements require that a party exercising its right to terminate without cause pay a termination or "break-up" fee to the other party. The amount of this fee is entirely subject to negotiation, but is often based on the nonterminating party's loss of anticipated profits due to the termination of the relationship.

In some cases a party subjected to termination by the other party without cause has challenged the validity of the termination without cause provision of the agreement. In *Intergraph v. Intel*, 1995 F.3d 1346 (Fed. Cir. 1999), Intergraph was a member of Intel's "strategic customer" program, under which Intel provided Intergraph with various special benefits, including advance design information and samples of new versions of Intel's chips. Intergraph then sued Intel and other Intel customers for patent infringement. In response, Intel exercised its contractual right under the strategic customer program to terminate Intergraph's participation in the strategic customer program without cause. Intergraph challenged Intel's termination, alleging, among other things, that the clause was unconscionable and thus unenforceable. In rejecting Intergraph's claim, the Federal Circuit reasoned as follows:

> The district court also ruled that the at-will termination clause was "unconscionable" ... The district court rejected the argument that unconscionability as a ground of contract illegality was intended for consumer protection, and held that "the principle applies with equal force in the commercial field." We observe, however, that the Alabama courts, like others, have emphasized that "[r]ecission of a contract for unconscionability is an extraordinary remedy usually reserved for the protection of the unsophisticated and the uneducated." Although Intergraph is a much smaller company than Intel, it is one of the Fortune 1000, and does not plead inadequate legal advice in its commercial dealings. The Alabama Code comments that "The principle is one of the prevention of oppression and unfair surprise and not of disturbance of allocation of risks because of superior bargaining power." Applying this state law, the Alabama courts have recognized that "it is not the province of the court to make or remake a contract for the parties."
>
> Trade secrets and other proprietary information and products including pre-release samples of chips are commercial property, and the terms of their disclosure and use are traditional matters of commercial contract. Intergraph does not state that it objected to the mutual at-will termination provision when the contract was entered. Indeed, the district court found that when Intergraph switched [to Intel's technology, Intel] did not commit ... to provide [Intergraph] a perpetual supply of chips, pre-released chips, or confidential information [and] did not commit ... to any continued or "perpetual business relationship" with Intergraph.
>
> In an agreement relating to confidential information, negotiated between commercial entities, it is not the judicial role to rewrite the contract and impose terms that these parties did not make. Such intrusion into the integrity of contracts requires more than changed relationships. No fraud or deception is here alleged.

Notes and Questions

1. *Who can terminate for convenience?* As noted above, there are situations in which one, but not both, parties to an agreement are given the right to terminate for convenience. What circumstances might justify giving this powerful right to one party but not the other?

2. *Better than breach?* Some licensing agreements may give a party the right to terminate if certain milestones are not met. Yet terminating on that basis and admitting that a milestone was not met could have negative implications for one or both parties. In this case, it might be preferable for a party to have the right to terminate without cause, so that it does not have to publicly disclose a milestone failure. For example, in 2015 Lexicon and Sanofi-Aventis entered into a licensing agreement for worldwide development and commercialization of Lexicon's diabetes drug candidate sotagliflozin. The agreement gave Sanofi-Aventis the right to terminate if "positive results" were not achieved at certain stages of drug development and approval. When Sanofi-Aventis, citing the drug's failure in a clinical trial, exercised its right to terminate in 2019, Lexicon's stock value dropped by 70 percent.[13] Would Lexicon have been better off by giving Sanofi-Aventis the right to terminate without cause? What limitations might it have wished to put on this right?

3. *Termination payments.* Should all agreements that allow termination without cause include termination payments? Should termination payments be different depending on whether termination is triggered by the licensor or the licensee?

4. *Termination of franchisees.* Section 1-208 of the Uniform Commercial Code provides that "at will" termination of a contract may be permitted only if a party "in good faith believes that the prospect of payment or performance is impaired." The parties' freedom to contract into such a termination at will scenario is thus limited. Likewise, both federal and state laws prohibit franchisors from terminating many franchise agreements (see Section 15.5) except with "good cause." See, e.g., New Jersey Franchise Practices Act, N.J. Stat. § 56:10-5 (franchise may not be terminated, canceled or nonrenewed "without good cause").[14] Are such protections justified? Why? For more insight into the bargaining dynamics and leverage in the franchise industry, see Section 15.5. Should this type of statutory protection be advisable for other types of IP licensing agreements? Under what circumstances?

5. *Statutory termination.* As discussed in Section 2.2, Note 5, Sections 203 and 304 of the Copyright Act permit an assignor or licensor of a copyright to terminate most copyright assignments and licenses between thirty-five and forty years after they were made. Since its enactment, this statutory termination right has been exercised many times, often by musicians, authors and artists whose works are still popular decades after rights were initially signed away.

12.5 EFFECTS OF TERMINATION AND SURVIVAL

Under the common law, when an agreement is terminated, all executory rights and obligations of the parties end, while the parties' rights and obligations incurred prior to termination may, depending on the circumstances, continue (e.g., the obligation to pay for goods and services delivered prior to the termination).[15] Rather than rely upon the application of such rules, however, most parties to IP licensing agreements prefer to specify the precise effects of a termination. A number of these effects of termination are discussed below.

---

[13] Jacob Plieth, *Lexicon and Sanofi Fall Out Over Semantics*, Evaluate Vantage, July 29, 2019.

[14] There are, however, exceptions, particularly when a franchise agreement contains an express clause allowing termination without cause. See *Witmer v. Exxon*, 394 A.2d 1276, 1285 (Pa. Sup. 1978) ("Where there is no explicit termination clause …, a franchisee indeed has a reasonable expectation that the relationship will not be terminated arbitrarily without cause. However, when the actions of the franchisor are within plain and explicit enabling clauses of the lease, we find it impossible to say that the reasonable expectations of the franchisee have been violated").

[15] See, e.g., *Mextel, Inc. v. Air-Shields, Inc.*, 2005 U.S. Dist. LEXIS 1281 at *54 ("effect of both 'termination' and 'cancellation' of sale of goods means that all executory obligations on both sides are discharged, but any right based on prior breach or performance survives").

12.5.1 *Payments*

Generally, a party will be required to pay for services performed and goods delivered in compliance with an agreement prior to its termination.

EXAMPLE: SURVIVAL OF PAYMENT OBLIGATIONS

Licensor's right to receive all payments accrued and unpaid on the effective date of such termination shall survive the termination or expiration of this Agreement.

12.5.2 *Return of Materials*

There is no inherent obligation on parties to return confidential or proprietary materials after the termination of an agreement. Thus, this requirement must be included expressly if the parties are concerned about post-termination possession and use of such materials.

EXAMPLE: RETURN OF MATERIALS

Upon any expiration or termination of this Agreement, Licensee shall immediately (A) return to Licensor (or, at Licensor's option, destroy and certify in writing to Licensor that it has destroyed) the original and all copies of the Licensor Products, including compilations, translations, partial copies, archival copies, upgrades, updates, release notes and training materials relating to the Licensor Products, in Licensee's control or possession, (B) remove all Licensor Products from Licensee Offerings, (C) erase or destroy all such materials that are contained in computer memory or data storage apparatus of Licensee or under the control of Licensee or its agents, (D) return to Licensor any advertising and other materials furnished to it by Licensor, (E) remove and not thereafter use any signs containing the name or trademarks of Licensor, and (F) destroy all of its advertising matter and other preprinted matter remaining in its possession or under its control containing Licensor trade names or trademarks.

12.5.3 *Transitional Licenses*

Upon termination of a licensing agreement, unless otherwise specified, all licenses under the agreement automatically terminate. Sometimes, however, there are reasons that licenses should survive for a limited period following termination. One such reason is to give the licensee the right to sell off inventory of licensed products that were manufactured prior to the termination.[16] Sometimes, in order to sell such inventory, it is also necessary to allow the licensee to continue to use any licensed marks and brands in connection with its sales and promotion activities. Finally, particularly in the context of software licensing, it may be advisable to permit the licensee to continue to use the licensed products in order to provide support and maintenance to end user customers. All of these temporary licenses, however, should end within a reasonable period following termination.

---

[16] Recall that even absent a contractual right to sell off inventory, some courts have recognized an implied license allowing the licensee to do the same. See *McCoy v. Mitsuboshi Cutlery*, 67 F.3d 917 (Fed. Cir. 1995) (discussed in Section 4.4).

EXAMPLE: TRANSITIONAL LICENSES

Upon any expiration or termination of this Agreement, Licensee shall immediately cease all manufacture, use, sale, import, distribution and promotion of the Licensed Products, except that

a. Licensee may sell, offer to sell, advertise and promote its existing inventory of Licensed Products ("Post-Termination Sales") on a nonexclusive basis for a period not to exceed sixty (60) days following the effective date of termination (the "Post-Termination Period"); provided, however, that Royalties shall be due and payable on all Post-Termination Sales within thirty (30) days following the end of the Post-Termination Period and shall be accompanied by the report required in Section __.
b. Licensee may continue to use labeling and promotional literature bearing the Licensed Marks during the Post-Termination Period only in conjunction with the Post-Termination Sales set forth in subsection (b) above. Upon the expiration of the Post-Termination Period, all use of the Licensed Marks shall cease; all sales and offers to sell, advertising and promotion of the Licensed Products shall immediately cease; and all remaining labeling and promotional literature bearing the Licensed Marks shall be destroyed and its destruction certified by an officer of Licensee.
c. Licensee shall have the right to retain one copy of and to continue to use the Licensor Products in Object Code Form internally for a period of one year in order to support End User customers who have valid Software License Agreements in effect on the effective date of the termination or expiration of the Agreement.

12.5.4 *Transition Assistance*

In addition to the continuation of licenses, some licensees, particularly users of large enterprise software systems, may require the licensor's assistance in transitioning to a replacement system if their license terminates prior to the end of its scheduled term. A "transition assistance" clause provides this support.

EXAMPLE: TRANSITION ASSISTANCE

If the term of this Agreement or any Order Schedule is not renewed or is terminated by Licensor other than for Licensee's breach, Licensor shall, upon Licensee's written request, continue to make the Software under such a nonrenewed or terminated Order Schedule available to Licensee and shall provide transitional assistance ("Transition Services") to Licensee to the extent reasonably requested by Licensee to facilitate Licensee's smooth migration from the Software to that of a replacement supplier. Such Transition Services shall include the delivery to Licensee of all Licensee data in Licensor's custody or control, provision of historical records of Licensee's use of the Software, and other services as Licensee shall reasonably request and Licensor shall reasonably agree to provide. Licensee shall pay Licensor an hourly rate of $__ for the provision of Transition Services hereunder. In no event shall Licensor be required to provide more than __ person-hours of Transition Services.

12.5.5 *Statutory Indemnities*

Under the laws of some countries, the termination of an agreement may trigger a payment or other obligation imposed by law. An example arises under the 1986 EU Agency Directive (Council Directive 86/653/EEC), which requires that a licensor or manufacturer that terminates a sales agent in the EU must pay the terminated agent an indemnity or compensation in the range of one year's full compensation. This requirement cannot be waived by contract, and has caught many non-EU principals unawares.

12.5.6 *Effect on Sublicenses*

As discussed in Section 6.5, a sublicense conveys to the sublicensee a set of rights that a licensee has received from a prime licensor. Unless otherwise agreed by the licensee (sublicensor) and its prime licensor, a sublicense only exists while the underlying prime license remains in force. Thus, absent a special arrangement, when the prime license is terminated, all of its dependent sublicenses also terminate automatically.[17]

The automatic termination of sublicenses can be particularly harsh for sublicensees who have no control over, or visibility into, the relationship between the sublicensor and its prime licensor. Thus, when sublicenses under a prime license are anticipated, the licensee sometimes negotiates to protect its prospective sublicensees from a sudden and unexpected termination.

The most common scenario in which this occurs involves software. Consider a firm that provides a large enterprise software package that includes subsystems created by several different vendors. Each of these vendors licenses the software provider to incorporate a subsystem into the software package and to sublicense the subsystem to end users as part of the overall software package. If the license agreement between the subsystem vendor (licensor) and the software provider (licensee) terminates, it would be particularly harsh to terminate each end user's (sublicensee's) license to the entire software package, or even to the subsystem that is embedded inside of it. Thus, software licenses often permit end user sublicenses to continue following a termination of the prime license, provided that the sublicensor assigns those sublicenses to the prime licensor.

EXAMPLE: SURVIVAL OF SUBLICENSES

Following any termination or expiration of this Agreement, each sublicense granted by the Licensee to an End User with respect to the Licensed Software shall survive in accordance with its terms, provided that End User is not in breach of its End User License Agreement and such End User agrees to owe all further obligations thereunder directly to Licensor.

[17] Prior to the Federal Circuit's 2018 decision in *Fraunhofer-Gesellschaft v. Sirius XM Radio*, 940 F.3d 1372, 1380 (Fed. Cir. 2018), which definitively held that "our law does not provide for automatic survival of a sublicense" upon termination of the primary license, several commentators argued that sublicenses *should* survive such a termination. See, e.g., Ridsdale Ellis, Patent Licenses § 62 (3d ed. 1958) ("A sub-license is an independent contract and, therefor, it is not terminated by the termination of the main license, unless specifically so provided") and id. at § 63 ("Where a sub-licensee has lived up to the terms of the license it is inequitable that his license should be revoked because the main licensee has failed to do the same, especially where the sub-licensee has made extensive investments on the strengths of his license"); Brian G. Brunsvold & Dennis P. O'Reilley, Drafting Patent License Agreements 37 (BNA, 4th ed., 1998) ("An authorized sublicense is in effect an agreement with the [original] licensor. Unless the agreement with the licensee provides otherwise, the sublicense will continue despite the early termination of the license agreement"). See Section 6.5, Note 3, discussing this set of arguments.

In the above scenario, complications arise if the terminated licensee owes obligations such as support and maintenance to its sublicensees. Then, it may be necessary for the prime licensor to permit the terminated licensee to continue to use the licensed software for purposes of continuing to provide such support and maintenance to sublicensees, as contemplated by clause (c) of the above example.

Things also become more complex when sublicensees are more than passive software end users. For example, in biotechnology commercialization arrangements, a biotech company often sublicenses significant rights that it has received from a university to a large pharmaceutical company. Such sublicense agreements often contain numerous obligations of each party, significant milestone and royalty payments and complex allocations of IP. As such, the prime licensor may not wish to assume these arrangements, but instead may prefer to allow a new licensee to forge its own commercial arrangements with sublicensees. Thus, the licensor in such situations often retains the right to decide whether or not to assume particular sublicenses following the termination of the prime license.

EXAMPLE: ASSIGNMENT OF SUBLICENSES

No later than ten days following the termination or expiration of this Agreement, each sublicense that was granted by the Licensee under this Agreement and that is so designated by Licensor shall be assigned by Licensee to Licensor, and Licensor shall assume each of Licensee's rights, duties and obligations thereunder, provided that Licensor's obligations under such sublicense shall be consistent with and not exceed Licensor's obligations to Licensee under this Agreement and provided that such Sublicensee agrees in writing to owe all obligations thereunder directly to Licensor. All sublicenses that are not thus assumed by Licensor shall be terminated automatically.

On the other hand, the pharmaceutical sublicensee may not be willing to enter into a proposed sublicensing agreement unless its sublicensor obtains a commitment from the upstream IP owner to grant it a direct license in the event that the prime license is terminated (Figure 12.2). Such an agreement is called a "nondisturbance agreement" (a mechanism borrowed from the world of commercial real estate).

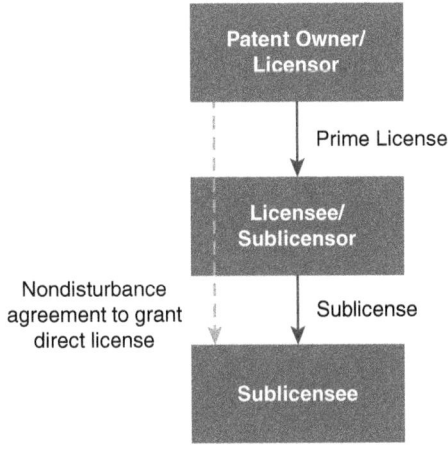

FIGURE 12.2 Operation of a nondisturbance agreement.

12.5.7 *Termination of Less than the Full Agreement*

In addition to termination of the entire agreement, some agreements provide for the termination of specific portions of an agreement. These portions generally represent large or significant sets of related rights and obligations, such as a project described in a particular statement of work, or a set of licenses relating to a particular field of use. The conditions triggering termination of a portion of an agreement are often similar to the conditions triggering termination of the entire agreement.

Agreements that permit the termination of portions of the agreement must be drafted carefully to indicate what happens to the rest of the agreement once the portion is terminated. In some cases this may be straightforward. For example, a license agreement may grant the licensee exclusive rights in three discrete fields of use. If the portion of the agreement associated with one of those fields is terminated, then the others may continue independently, unaffected by the partial termination. But in many cases there are linkages among portions of an agreement that can become incoherent if attention is not paid to the effect of such partial terminations.

12.5.8 *Sole Remedy*

Some agreements will specify that termination of the agreement is the "sole and exclusive remedy" for certain events. This type of limitation is particularly risky if it encompasses breaches of the agreement, as it is difficult to predict what damages may arise from any given breach, and termination of the agreement may not make the injured party whole following such a breach. Such sole remedy clauses are more appropriate with respect to termination without cause clauses or terminations based on failure to meet milestones, where there is less likelihood that other damages may flow from the event giving rise to termination.

12.5.9 *Survival*

In addition to the foregoing, there are a number of standard contractual terms that are routinely designated as surviving the termination of an agreement. These are typically listed in a "survival" section without much elaboration.

EXAMPLE: SURVIVAL

In addition to the foregoing, the following provisions of this Agreement shall survive any termination or expiration hereof in accordance with their terms: Section __ (Confidentiality), __ (Indemnification), __ (Warranties), __ (Limitations of Liability), __ (Compliance with Laws), __ (Dispute Resolution) and __ (Choice of Law).

Notes and Questions

1. *Survival.* Why do you think each of the provisions listed in the survival clause above would survive the termination of the agreement? What does it mean for each of these provisions to survive?
2. *The termination prenup.* Given multiple methods of terminating an agreement and the many ramifications of different types of termination, it is often useful when drafting and

negotiating an agreement to map the different obligations and rights of the parties under different termination scenarios in a large matrix. While this exercise may seem overly negative at the outset, and business representatives often shy away from discussing how their new business relationship may end, as with a good prenuptial agreement, many parties have saved significant headaches by planning the end of their relationship before it begins.

13

Other Licensing Terms: The "Boilerplate"

SUMMARY CONTENTS

In the late nineteenth century, publishing syndicates like the Western Newspaper Union began to distribute news stories, editorials and advertisements to local newspapers on prefabricated steel plates – a convenience that eliminated the papers' need to typeset this text manually. The plates were nicknamed "boilerplate" because they resembled the pressed steel plates that adorned boilers and pressure vessels. Gradually, the term boilerplate came to represent any text that is intended to be used without change. Today, it is used to refer to contractual terms, often appearing at the end of an agreement, that are viewed as standardized and routine.[1] Very few non-lawyers bother to read the boilerplate in an agreement, and its drafting and review are often delegated to junior lawyers or to nobody at all.[2]

---

[1] As explained by Professor Henry Smith, "By definition boilerplate is meant to be used in more than one contract, and boilerplate is more self-contained and less specific to a particular contract than might be expected from contract theory. Boilerplate is highly standardized, and when courts interpret boilerplate they treat it as intentionally standardized and not harboring unusual meanings. In other words, some portability of boilerplate is achieved at the price of tailoring such provisions to particular contexts." Henry E. Smith, *Modularity in Contracts: Boilerplate and Information Flow*, 104 Mich. L. Rev. 1175, 1176 (2006).

[2] See Cathy Hwang, *Unbundled Bargains: Multi-Agreement Dealmaking in Complex Mergers and Acquisitions*, 164 U. Penn. L. Rev. 1403, 1405 (2016) ("Because deal lawyers often consider confidentiality agreements straightforward and boilerplate, junior attorneys or in-house counsel usually draft them").

Yet the "boilerplate" clauses in an agreement can become critical, and sometimes make the difference between breach and compliance with the more "interesting" provisions of the agreement. In this chapter we will explore some of the boilerplate clauses in a typical intellectual property (IP) licensing agreement and their variants and implications.

13.1 FRONT MATTER

Every agreement begins with a formulaic recitation of some key information. Below, we briefly review these seemingly routine but important features of agreements.

13.1.1 *Title*

Every agreement needs a title so that it can be referenced and understood in context. Agreement titles may be long or short, but it is best to choose one that is descriptive of the agreement's content and purpose. That is, avoid calling every agreement "Agreement."

13.1.2 *Parties*

Every party to the agreement should be named and identified by its full corporate name and jurisdiction of organization. A physical headquarters address is often included as well, but this can present issues if/when the parties relocate. Notification of location changes are typically dealt with in the notices clause (see Section 13.12).

Sometimes a party is tempted to try to include all of its corporate affiliates and subsidiaries as parties to an agreement (e.g., by referring to "Party X and all of its Affiliates" as "Party X"), but this is an unwise practice when it comes to enforcement and breach of the agreement, and even understanding who the other party should look to for performance. If it is desirable to extend rights throughout a corporate family, it is preferable to name only one party to the agreement (usually the parent company), and then permit it to grant sublicenses and subcontract some of its obligations to its affiliates. Of course, if multiple members of a corporate family will have discrete, defined roles in a transaction (e.g., a manufacturing affiliate and an IP-holding affiliate), then they can and should be named separately as parties (and referred to collectively as the "X Company Parties").

EXAMPLE: INTRODUCTION

This Software Licensing Agreement ("Agreement") is made this Fifth day of May, 2020 (the "Effective Date"), by and between [1] A-Team Corporation, a Delaware corporation having its principal place of business at 123 Evergreen Terrace, Springfield, Illinois, USA 65432 ("Licensor") and B-List, LLC, a Massachusetts limited liability company having its principal place of business at 60 State Street, Boston, Massachusetts, USA 02158 ("Licensee"), each individually a "Party" and collectively the "Parties."

DRAFTING NOTES

[1] *Between and among* – the drafting convention is to say that an agreement is *between* two parties, and *among* three or more parties.

13.1.3 *Effective Date*

Every agreement comes into effect on a particular date (the "Effective Date"), whether it is the date that the agreement is fully executed, or some other date selected by the parties. Considerations regarding the choice of effective date are discussed in greater detail in Section 12.1.1. For drafting purposes, the main consideration is to specify the effective date clearly (e.g., December 1, 2020 (the "Effective Date")), and not to rely on vague descriptors such as "the date on which the last party executes this Agreement," especially if dates are not provided below signature lines at the end of the agreement.

13.1.4 *Recitals*

After the introductory paragraph listing the parties, their addresses and the effective date of the agreement, many agreements contain one or more paragraphs beginning with "Whereas, … " These "whereas clauses" are known as the recitals of an agreement. Recitals are nonoperative text – they do not (or should not) create contractual obligations. Rather, they set the stage for the agreement that is to come. As Cynthia Cannady explains, recitals "serve the purpose of helping a reader get oriented before plunging into the material terms of the agreement" and "provide background information that makes it easier to read and understand the material terms of the agreement."[3]

Because recitals are not intended to create binding contractual obligations, drafters should be careful to avoid the explicit or implicit inclusion of obligations, representations or warranties in the recitals. For example, statements like this should be avoided:

> WHEREAS, Licensor owns all right, title and interest in and to the cartoon character Dizzy Duck; and
> WHEREAS, Licensee wishes to obtain an exclusive license to reproduce and display Dizzy Duck on school supplies;

The above recital could cause problems for both the licensor and the licensee. Why? Because it could be interpreted as a *representation* by the licensor that it actually does own these rights (without the knowledge-based and other limitations contained in the actual representations and warranties later in the agreement), and because it could be interpreted as an *acknowledgment* by the licensee that the licensor actually does own these rights – a fact that the licensee may wish to challenge later. Below is a preferable set of recitals that frames the proposed transaction between the parties:

> WHEREAS, Licensor conducts an active licensing program for rights in the cartoon character Dizzy Duck; and
> WHEREAS, Licensee wishes to obtain an exclusive license to reproduce and display Dizzy Duck on school supplies; …

Or consider the equipment leasing agreement litigated in *Thomson Electric Welding Co. v. Peerless Wire Fence Co.*, 190 Mich. 496 (1916). The agreement related to the lease of electric welding machines for a term lasting "until the expiration of all the letters patent of the United States now or hereafter owned by the lessor, the inventions of which are or shall be embodied in said apparatus, or at any time involved in the use thereof." The recitals listed 111 of the

3 Cynthia Cannady, Technology Licensing and Development Agreements 112 (Oxford Univ. Press, 2013).

FIGURE 13.1 Elihu Thomson, founder of the Thomson Electric Welding Co., was one of the late nineteenth century's greatest inventors, with nearly 700 patents to his name. In addition to arc welding, he developed important advances in the fields of arc lighting. Another company founded by Thomson eventually merged with Edison Electric to become the General Electric Company.

lessor's patents covering the leased equipment. When the lessee returned the equipment after the expiration of the last of these 111 patents, the lessor claimed that it held additional patents covering the leased equipment, and that the lease was not yet expired. Accordingly, the lessor sued for remaining lease payments through the expiration of the last of these other, unlisted patents. The Michigan Supreme Court, reviewing the recital in question, considered the doctrine of "estoppel by recital" and held that "general and unlimited terms are restrained and limited by particular recitals when used in connection with them, and recitals, as well as operative clauses, should be considered as a part of the whole." As a result, the licensor was estopped from claiming that the lease ran beyond the expiration of the 111 patents listed in the recital.

13.1.5 *Acknowledgment of Consideration*

Traditionally, after the recitals there is a transitional paragraph that leads into the main body of the agreement. The putative purpose of this paragraph is to explicitly state that the agreement is made for valid consideration, fulfilling the formal contractual requirement that consideration be exchanged in order for a promise to be binding. This paragraph typically reads as follows.

EXAMPLE: ACKNOWLEDGMENT OF CONSIDERATION

NOW THEREFORE, for good and valuable consideration, the receipt of which is hereby acknowledged, the Parties hereby agree and covenant as follows:

13.2 DEFINITIONS

Every agreement contains a number of defined terms, capitalized words that, when used throughout the agreement, have the meanings ascribed specifically to them, rather than definitions that might arise from common usage or dictionaries. The definitions are among the most important elements of any agreement. As we have seen in the preceding chapters, terms such as "Licensed Rights," "Net Sales" and "Field of Use" define the very nature of the legal and financial arrangement between the parties.

Definitions may be scattered throughout the text and defined "inline" or "in context," as they are in the example of the introductory clause above. Or they may be listed – usually alphabetically – in a separate section of the agreement that appears at the beginning or end of the operative text of the agreement.[4] The placement and style of the definitions is a matter of drafting preference, but wherever they are located, definitions should be as clear and unambiguous as possible.

DRAFTING TIPS FOR DEFINITIONS

- Use Initial Caps and never hard-to-read and distracting FULL CAPS.
- Place most definitions in one section in the beginning or end of the agreement.
- List definitions in alphabetical order.
- If there are multiple related agreements, define each term once and cross-reference it in the other agreements; be sure to avoid inconsistent definitions within the same set of agreements.
- If the term is better defined in context (e.g., defined by reference to adjacent text) or is used only in one section, then define it inline, set off in parentheses and quotation marks, and preferably boldface and/or italics ("***Definition***").
- If you define terms inline, then include an index table at the end of the other definitions referencing where these definitions can be found.
- Avoid "nested" definitions (i.e., definitions that contain other defined terms that, in turn, are defined by reference to other defined terms that … ").
- There is no need to define everything: some terms are commonly understood in the relevant industry (e.g., FDA or SEC); don't waste time and paper defining other commonly used terms (e.g., Calendar Year) unless an unconventional meaning is intended (e.g., some companies adapt a fiscal year in which quarters end on Fridays).
- Never include affirmative obligations, covenants, representations, warranties or disclaimers in definitions.

Adapted with permission from material provided by Jim Farrington.

13.3 ASSIGNMENT

At the end of each agreement is often a section labeled "General Terms" or "Miscellaneous." These are the true "boilerplate" terms that cause eyes to glaze over. Or are they? Some provisions in this Miscellaneous section often get significant attention. One of the most prominent of these is the assignment clause.

---

[4] Professor Henry Smith makes an interesting argument for collecting definitions in a single section of an agreement:

[I]f definitions are not segregated and done once and for all, contracts are open to an interpretive strategy where a use of the term in one part of the contract can more easily be used in interpreting the term in another part of the contract. This type of interpretation involves far more potential interaction – and hence more complexity – than in the case of a contract with a section on definitions. (Smith, supra note 1, at 1190)

13.3.1 *The Right to Assign, Generally*

Parties generally have the right to assign their rights and duties under an agreement, as described in the *Restatement (Second) of Contracts*:

> ## RESTATEMENT (SECOND) OF CONTRACTS
>
> **§ 317(2)** A contractual right can be assigned unless
>
> (a) the substitution of a right of the assignee for the right of the assignor would materially change the duty of the obligor, or materially increase the burden or risk imposed on him by his contract, or materially impair his chance of obtaining return performance, or materially reduce its value to him, or (b) the assignment is forbidden by statute or is otherwise inoperative on grounds of public policy, or (c) assignment is validly precluded by contract.
>
> **§ 318(1)** An obligor can properly delegate the performance of his duty to another unless the delegation is contrary to public policy or the terms of his promise.

Thus, parties that wish to prevent their counterparties from assigning rights and duties under the agreement must expressly restrict this right in their agreement.

13.3.2 *The Right to Assign IP Licenses*

Notwithstanding the general rules of contract assignment noted in Section 13.3.1, IP licenses have long been treated as special cases under federal common law. As early as 1852, the Supreme Court recognized the rule that patent licensing agreements are personal and not assignable unless expressly made so (*Troy Iron & Nail Factory v. Corning*, 55 U.S. (14 How.) 193, 14 L. Ed. 383 (1852)).

Over the years this rule has evolved to differentiate between exclusive and nonexclusive IP licenses. In general, "It is well settled that a non-exclusive licensee of a patent has only a personal and not a property interest in the patent and that this personal right cannot be assigned unless the patent owner authorizes the assignment or the license itself permits assignment" (*Gilson v. Republic of Ireland*, 787 F.2d 655, 658 (D.C.Cir.1986)).

The Ninth Circuit in *Everex Systems, Inc. v. Cadtrak Corp.*, 89 F.3d 673 (9th Cir. 1996) explains the policy rationale for this rule as follows:

> Allowing free assignability ... of nonexclusive patent licenses would undermine the reward that encourages invention because a party seeking to use the patented invention could either seek a license from the patent holder or seek an assignment of an existing patent license from a licensee. In essence, every licensee would become a potential competitor with the licensor-patent holder in the market for licenses under the patents. And while the patent holder could presumably control the absolute number of licenses in existence under a free-assignability regime, it would lose the very important ability to control the identity of its licensees. Thus, any license a patent holder granted – even to the smallest firm in the product market most remote from its own – would be fraught with the danger that the licensee would assign it to the patent holder's most serious competitor, a party whom the patent holder itself might be absolutely unwilling to license. As a practical matter, free assignability of patent licenses might spell the end to paid-up licenses ... Few

FIGURE 13.2 The Supreme Court's 1852 decision in *Troy Iron & Nail* first established that patent licensing agreements are not assignable.

patent holders would be willing to grant a license in return for a one-time lump-sum payment, rather than for per-use royalties, if the license could be assigned to a completely different company which might make far greater use of the patented invention than could the original licensee.

For similar reasons, the rule against assignment of nonexclusive patent licenses has also been applied to nonexclusive copyright licenses[5] and trademark licenses.[6]

But exclusive licenses, at least in some cases, have been treated differently, as they have been construed as conveyances of IP ownership – a right that is generally amenable to free alienability by its holder.[7]

13.3.3 *Assignment of Licenses in M&A Transactions*

One of the most contentious issues relating to the assignment of IP licensing agreements arises in the context of corporate acquisitions. Specifically, what is the effect of an acquisition of a company (often called the "target" company) on licensing agreements to which it is a party?

---

[5] *Harris v. Emus Records Corp.*, 734 F.2d 1329 (9th Cir. 1984).

[6] *Tap Publications, Inc. v. Chinese Yellowpages (New York), Inc.*, 925 F. Supp. 212 (S.D.N.Y. 1996) ("the general rule is that unless the license states otherwise, the licensee's right to use the licensed mark is personal and cannot be assigned to another" (citing 2 McCarthy on Trademarks and Unfair Competition § 18.14[2]; 25.07[3] (3d ed. 1996)).

[7] See *In re Golden Books Family Entertainment, Inc.*, 269 B.R. 311 (Bankr. D. Del. 2001) (exclusive license could be assigned without licensor's consent).

Does a corporate acquisition constitute an assignment of the target company's IP licenses? And, if so, is such an assignment prohibited under applicable law?

The answer depends, in large part, on the structure through which an acquisition is effected. There are three basic forms of corporate acquisition: asset acquisitions, stock acquisitions and mergers. Parties choose the form of an acquisition for a range of tax, accounting, liability and other reasons. Treatment of IP licensing agreements is rarely an overriding consideration in choosing the form of such a transaction. Nevertheless, the choice of acquisition structure can have a significant effect on IP licensing agreements, which must often (unfortunately) be sorted out after the acquisition takes place.

In *asset acquisitions*, the acquiring company purchases some or all of the target company's assets and properties, including agreements and other IP rights, directly from the target company. In this case, the target company expressly assigns these licensing agreements to the acquirer along with its other assets. To the extent that applicable law prohibits such assignments, and they are not expressly permitted under the terms of the agreements themselves, then the target company must obtain the permission of the licensor in order to make such assignments.

Stock acquisitions involve an acquirer's purchase of a target company's stock from its prior owners. In this model, the corporate identity of the target company is unaffected by the acquisition; it remains a party to whatever agreements were in place prior to the acquisition. Thus, no assignment is generally recognized, and no consent is required from the licensor.

Mergers are statutory devices that enable an acquiror to absorb a target company into itself or into a subsidiary. After the merger, the target company no longer exists in its prior form, which is where things get complicated in terms of agreement assignment. There are three general types of merger transactions: direct mergers, forward triangular mergers and reverse triangular mergers. In a direct merger, the acquiror merges the target company directly into itself. In a forward triangular merger, the acquiror forms a wholly owned subsidiary into which it merges the target company. In a reverse triangular merger, the acquiror forms a wholly owned subsidiary that merges into the target company. After a direct merger and a forward triangular merger, the target company no longer exists. All of its assets and liabilities are absorbed, respectively, into the acquiror or its wholly owned subsidiary. In a reverse triangular merger, the target survives the merger as a wholly owned subsidiary of the acquirer. These three transaction types are illustrated in Figure 13.3.

Given these different structural outcomes, there is some debate, and inconsistency in the case law, regarding whether an IP licensing agreement can be assumed by the "surviving" company following the merger without the consent of the licensor.[8] In both a direct and a forward triangular merger the target company (licensee) is no longer in existence, so there is considerable doubt whether its licenses can be assigned to the surviving company without the licensor's consent. The best structure for allowing the assumption is the reverse triangular merger, in which the target company (the licensee) remains intact, though with a new owner. At least in Delaware, where many important mergers and acquisitions (M&A) decisions are reached, the courts have found that a reverse triangular merger does not result in an assignment of the target company's IP licenses.[9]

---

[8] See, generally, Elaine D. Ziff, *The Effect of Corporate Acquisitions on the Target Company's License Rights*, 57 Business Lawyer 767 (2002).
[9] See *Meso Scale Diagnostics, LLC v. Roche Diagnostics GmbH*, 62 A.3d 62 (Del. Ch. 2013).

DIRECT MERGER

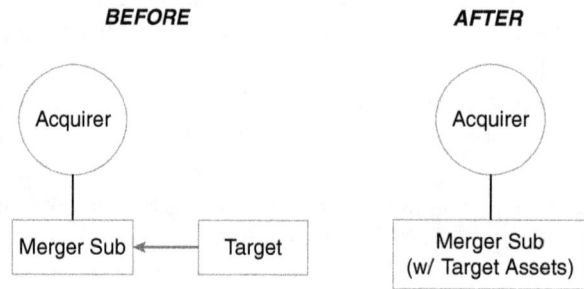

FORWARD TRIANGULAR MERGER

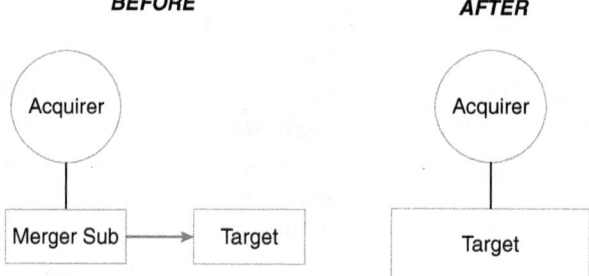

REVERSE TRIANGULAR MERGER

FIGURE 13.3　Asset acquisitions, stock acquisitions and mergers.

13.3.4 *Anti-Assignment Clauses*

Given the uncertain treatment of IP licensing agreement following the various types of transactions discussed above, parties often seek to define contractually the precise terms on which such agreements may be assigned.

EXAMPLE: ASSIGNMENT

a.　This Agreement shall be binding upon and inure to the benefit of the Parties and their respective successors and permitted assigns. Neither party may assign or transfer this Agreement in whole or in part, nor any of its rights or delegate any of its duties or obligations hereunder, without the prior written consent of the other party [which shall not be unreasonably withheld, conditioned or delayed] [except that either party may assign this Agreement in full to a successor to its business in connection with a merger or sale of all or substantially all its assets [1] [relating to the subject matter hereof] [2]].

b. For purposes of this Section, a change in the persons or entities who control 50% or more of the equity securities or voting interest of a Party in a single transaction or set of related transactions shall be considered a prohibited assignment of such Party's rights [3].

c. Any assignment made in violation of this Section shall be void, the assignee shall acquire no rights whatsoever, and the non-assigning party shall not recognize, nor shall it be required to recognize, the assignment. This provision limits both the right and the power to assign this Agreement, and the rights hereunder [3].

d. Any assignment permitted hereunder shall be evidenced by a writing executed by the assigning party and the assignee, under which the assignee expressly assumes all obligations [and liability] [4] of the assigning party. Such executed assignment document shall be provided to the non-assigning party contemporaneously with the assignment.

DRAFTING NOTES

[1] *Acquisitions* – in order to avoid the variability that often accompanies M&A transactions, parties often wish to specify that IP licensing agreements may be assigned in connection with a merger or sale of assets. This being said, not all licensors may be comfortable with a licensee's assignment of a license agreement to an acquirer that is a competitor of the licensor, or to an acquirer that is substantially larger than the original licensee (especially if an up-front fee or royalties were calculated based on estimates of the original licensee's market). In these cases, substantial negotiation often occurs around limitations on the use of the assigned license agreement by the acquirer.

[2] *Partial divestiture* – in some cases, a party may divest the division or business unit that is most related to a licensing agreement. If this is the case, the other party may wish to permit assignment of the agreement to the acquirer of that division or unit. Be aware, however, that this language can become problematic if a party simply wishes to "sell" the agreement as a freestanding asset.

[3] *Change in control* – as noted in Section 13.3.3, some types of M&A transactions (e.g., a sale of stock or a forward triangular merger) do not involve an assignment of rights to a new entity, but merely a change in ownership of an existing licensee. Nevertheless, for the reasons set forth in Item [1], a licensor may not wish to permit a license to continue if the licensee undergoes a significant "change in control." Clause (b) characterizes such changes as prohibited assignments requiring the licensor's consent. Of course, if the optional language permitting assignment in a merger is selected in clause (a), then clause (b) is unnecessary. Alternately, a change in control may be prohibited only if it involves a competitor of the other party.

[4] *The right and the power to assign* – even creating an express prohibition against assignment may not actually prevent an assignment from occurring. Restatement § 322(2) (b) provides that a "contract term prohibiting assignment of rights under the contract

… gives the obligor a right to damages for breach of the terms forbidding assignment but does not render the assignment ineffective."[10] In order to prevent assignment, the agreement must eliminate both a party's *power* to assign, as well as its *right* to assign.[11]

13.3.5 *Transfers of Rights*

Most of the above considerations relating to assignments concern the licensee and whether it may pass on to an acquiring entity the rights that it has received from the licensor. But a related topic concerns the licensor. Specifically, if a licensor assigns or transfers IP rights that it has previously licensed, what is the effect on existing licensees? As discussed in Section 3.5, an IP license generally runs with the underlying IP.

But what about the multitude of other contractual obligations contained in a licensing agreement? Licensor obligations relating to service, maintenance, technical assistance, indemnification and confidentiality are not likely to constitute part of the core license property interest, so what happens to them when the licensor transfers the underlying IP to a new owner?

One theory is that the original licensor remains obligated to perform its contractual obligations so long as they have not been assigned to someone else. Thus, if the original licensor does not assign a licensing agreement to the acquirer of the underlying IP, the original licensor is still required to perform these obligations. But this requirement may be cold comfort to the licensee, as the original licensor may have few remaining assets with which to perform those obligations. The licensee might prefer that the new owner of the underlying IP be obligated to perform the original licensor's commitments. To that end, a clause is sometimes included in the assignment section relating to transfer.

EXAMPLE: TRANSFER OF RIGHTS

Each party shall ensure that any purchaser, assignee, transferee or exclusive licensee of any of the intellectual property rights underlying the licenses and covenants granted herein ("Transferee") shall be bound by all terms and conditions contained in this Agreement, and shall require that such Transferee confirm in writing prior to any such sale, assignment, transfer or exclusive license ("Transfer"), as a condition thereof, that the licenses and other rights granted hereunder shall not be affected or diminished in any manner by such Transfer nor subject to any increased or payment or other obligation.

The following case brings together many of the issues and themes discussed above with regard to the assignment of IP licensing agreements and anti-assignment clauses.

[10] See *Rumbin v. Utica Mutual Ins. Co.*, 757 A.2d 526, 531 (Conn. 2000) (it is the "general rule that contractual provisions limiting or prohibiting assignments operate only to limit [the] parties right to assign the contract, but not their power to do so").

[11] See, e.g., *Pravin Banker Associates, Ltd. v. Banco Popular Del Peru*, 109 F.3d 850, 856 (2nd Cir. 1997) (to "preclude the power to assign, or cause an assignment … to be wholly void, [a contractual] clause must contain express provisions that any assignment shall be void or invalid if not made in a certain specified way"); *Cedar Point Apartments, Ltd. v. Cedar Point Investment Corp.*, 693 F.2d 748, 754 (8th Cir. 1982) (refusing to invalidate an assignment where "[m]erely the 'right to assign,' not the power to assign, [was] limited by the express language of the [anti-assignment] clause").

PPG Industries, Inc. v. Guardian Industries Corp.

597 F.2d 1090 (6th Cir. 1979)

LIVELY, CIRCUIT JUDGE

The question in this case is whether the surviving or resultant corporation in a statutory merger acquires patent license rights of the constituent corporations.

Prior to 1964 both PPG and Permaglass, Inc., were engaged in fabrication of glass products which required that sheets of glass be shaped for particular uses. Independently of each other the two fabricators developed similar processes which involved "floating glass on a bed of gas, while it was being heated and bent." This process is known in the industry as "gas hearth technology" and "air float technology"; the two terms are interchangeable. After a period of negotiations PPG and Permaglass entered into an agreement on January 1, 1964 whereby each granted rights to the other under "gas hearth system" patents already issued and in the process of prosecution. The purpose of the agreement was set forth in the preamble as follows:

> WHEREAS, PPG is desirous of acquiring from PERMAGLASS a world-wide exclusive license with right to sublicense others under PERMAGLASS Technical Data and PERMAGLASS Patent Rights, subject only to reservation by PERMAGLASS of non-exclusive rights thereunder; and
>
> WHEREAS, PERMAGLASS is desirous of obtaining a nonexclusive license to use Gas Hearth Systems under PPG Patent Rights, excepting in the Dominion of Canada.

This purpose was accomplished in the two sections of the agreement quoted below:

Section 3. Grant from Permaglass to PPG

3.1 Subject to the reservation set forth in Subsection 3.3 below, PERMAGLASS hereby grants to PPG an exclusive license, with right of sublicense, to use PERMAGLASS Technical Data in Gas Hearth Systems throughout the United States of America, its territories and possessions, and all countries of the world foreign thereto.

3.2 Subject to the reservation set forth in Subsection 3.3 below, PERMAGLASS hereby grants to PPG an unlimited exclusive license, with right of sublicense, under PERMAGLASS Patent Rights.

3.3 The licenses granted to PPG under Subsections 3.1 and 3.2 above shall be subject to the reservation of a non-exclusive, non-transferable, royalty-free, world-wide right and license for the benefit and use of PERMAGLASS.

Section 4. Grant from PPG to Permaglass

4.1 PPG hereby grants to PERMAGLASS a non-exclusive, non-transferable, royalty-free right and license to heat, bend, thermally temper and/or anneal glass using Gas Hearth Systems under PPG Patent Rights, excepting in the Dominion of Canada, and to use or sell glass articles produced thereby, but no license, express or implied, is hereby granted to PERMAGLASS under any claim of any PPG patent expressly covering any coating method, coating composition, or coated article.

Assignability of the agreement and of the license granted to Permaglass and termination of the license granted to Permaglass were covered in the following language:

Section 9. Assignability

9.1 This Agreement shall be assignable by PPG to any successor of the entire flat glass business of PPG but shall otherwise be non-assignable except with the consent of PERMAGLASS first obtained in writing.

9.2 This Agreement and the license granted by PPG to PERMAGLASS hereunder shall be personal to PERMAGLASS and non-assignable except with the consent of PPG first obtained in writing.

Section 11. Termination

11.2 In the event that a majority of the voting stock of PERMAGLASS shall at any time become owned or controlled directly or indirectly by a manufacturer of automobiles or a manufacturer or fabricator of glass other than the present owners, the license granted to PERMAGLASS under Subsection 4.1 shall terminate forthwith.

Eleven patents are involved in this suit. In Section 9.1 and 9.2 assignability was treated somewhat differently as between the parties, and the Section 11.2 provisions with regard to termination apply only to the license granted to Permaglass.

As of December 1969 Permaglass was merged into Guardian ... Guardian was engaged primarily in the business of fabricating and distributing windshields for automobiles and trucks. It had decided to construct a facility to manufacture raw glass and the capacity of that facility would be greater than its own requirements. Permaglass had no glass manufacturing capability and it was contemplated that its operations would utilize a large part of the excess output of the proposed Guardian facility.

FIGURE 13.4 Guardian Glass got its start as a manufacturer of automotive windshields.

Shortly after the merger was consummated PPG filed the present action, claiming infringement by Guardian in the use of apparatus and processes described and claimed in eleven patents which were identified by number and origin. The eleven patents were covered by the terms of the 1964 agreement. PPG asserted that it became the exclusive licensee of the nine patents which originated with Permaglass under the 1964 agreement and that the rights reserved by Permaglass were personal to it and non-transferable and non-assignable. PPG also claimed that Guardian had no rights with respect to the two patents which had originated with PPG because the license under these patents was personal to Permaglass and non-transferable and non-assignable except with the permission of PPG. In addition it claimed that the license with respect to these two patents had terminated under the provisions of Section 11.2 by reason of the merger.

One of the defenses pled by Guardian … was that it was a licensee of the patents in suit. It described the merger with Permaglass and claimed it "had succeeded to all rights, powers, ownerships, etc., of Permaglass, and as Permaglass' successor, defendant is legally entitled to operate in place of Permaglass under the January 1, 1964 agreement between Permaglass and plaintiff, free of any claim of infringement of the patents …"

After holding an evidentiary hearing the district court concluded that the parties to the 1964 agreement did not intend that the rights reserved by Permaglass in its nine patents or the rights assigned to Permaglass in the two PPG patents would not pass to a successor corporation by way of merger. The court held that there had been no assignment or transfer of the rights by Permaglass, but rather that Guardian acquired these rights by operation of law under the merger statutes of Ohio and Delaware. The provisions of the 1964 agreement making the license rights of Permaglass non-assignable and non-transferable were held not to apply because of the "continuity of interest inherent in a statutory merger that distinguishes it from the ordinary assignment or transfer case."

Questions with respect to the assignability of a patent license are controlled by federal law. It has long been held by federal courts that agreements granting patent licenses are personal and not assignable unless expressly made so. This has been the rule at least since 1852 when the Supreme Court decided *Troy Iron & Nail v. Corning*, 14 L. Ed. 383 (1852). The district court recognized this rule in the present case, but concluded that where patent licenses are claimed to pass by operation of law to the resultant or surviving corporation in a statutory merger there has been no assignment or transfer.

There appear to be no reported cases where the precise issue in this case has been decided. At least two treatises contain the statement that rights under a patent license owned by a constituent corporation pass to the consolidated corporation in the case of a consolidation, W. Fletcher, Cyclopedia of the Law of Corporations § 7089 (revised ed. 1973); and to the new or resultant corporation in the case of a merger, A. Deller, Walker on Patents § 409 (2d ed. 1965). However, the cases cited in support of these statements by the commentators do not actually provide such support because their facts take them outside the general rule of non-assignability. Both texts rely on the decision in *Hartford-Empire Co. v. Demuth Glass Works, Inc.*, 19 F. Supp. 626 (E.D.N.Y.1937). The agreement involved in that case specified that the patent license was assignable and its assignability was not an issue. Clearly the statement in the *Hartford-Empire* opinion that the merger conveyed to the new corporation the patent licenses owned by the old corporation results from the fact that the licenses in question were expressly made assignable, not from any general principle that such licenses pass to the resultant corporation where there is a merger. It is also noteworthy that the surviving corporation following the merger in *Hartford-Empire* was the original licensee, whereas in the present case the original licensee was merged into Guardian, which was the survivor.

Guardian relies on two classes of cases where rights of a constituent corporation have been held to pass by merger to the resultant corporation even though such rights are not otherwise assignable or transferable. It points out that the courts have consistently held that "shop rights" do pass in a statutory merger. A shop right is an implied license which accrues to an employer in cases where an employee has perfected a patentable device while working for the employer. Though the employee is the owner of the patent he is estopped from claiming infringement by the employer. This estoppel arises from the fact that the patent work has been done on the employer's time and that the employer has furnished materials for the experiments and financial backing to the employee.

The rule that prevents an employee-inventor from claiming infringement against a successor to the entire business and good will of his employer is but one feature of the broad doctrine of estoppel which underlies the shop right cases. No element of estoppel exists in the present case. The license rights of Permaglass did not arise by implication. They were bargained for at arms length and the agreement which defines the rights of the parties provides that Permaglass received non-transferable, non-assignable personal licenses. We do not believe that the express prohibition against assignment and transfer in a written instrument may be held ineffective by analogy to a rule based on estoppel in situations where there is no written contract and the rights of the parties have arisen by implication because of their past relationship.

The other group of cases which the district court and Guardian found to be analogous hold that the resultant corporation in a merger succeeds to the rights of the constituent corporations under real estate leases. The most obvious difficulty in drawing an analogy between the lease cases and those concerning patent licenses is that a lease is an interest in real property. As such, it is subject to the deep-rooted policy against restraints on alienation. [There] is no similar policy which is offended by the decision of a patent owner to make a license under his patent personal to the licensee, and non-assignable and non-transferable. In fact the law treats a license as if it contained these restrictions in the absence of express provisions to the contrary.

We conclude that the district court misconceived the intent of the parties to the 1964 agreement. We believe the district court put the burden on the wrong party in stating:

> Because the parties failed to provide that Permaglass' rights under the 1964 license agreement would not pass to the corporation surviving a merger, the Court finds that Guardian succeeded to Permaglass' license

The agreement provides with respect to the license which Permaglass granted to PPG that Permaglass reserved "a non-exclusive, non-transferable, royalty-free, world-wide right and license for the benefit and use of Permaglass." Similarly, with respect to its own two patents, PPG granted to Permaglass "a non-exclusive, non-transferable, royalty-free right and license …" Further, the agreement provides that both it and the license granted to Permaglass "shall be personal to PERMAGLASS and non-assignable except with the consent of PPG first obtained in writing."

The quoted language from Sections 3, 4 and 9 of the 1964 agreement evinces an intent that only Permaglass was to enjoy the privileges of licensee. If the parties had intended an exception in the event of a merger, it would have been a simple matter to have so provided in the agreement. Guardian contends such an exception is not necessary since it is universally recognized that patent licenses pass from a licensee to the resultant corporation in case of a merger. This does not appear to be the case. We conclude that if the parties had intended an exception in case of a merger to the provisions against assignment and transfer they would have included it in the agreement.

Thus, Sections 3, 4 and 9 of the 1964 agreement between PPG and Permaglass show an intent that the licenses held by Permaglass in the eleven patents in suit not be transferable. While this conclusion disposes of the license defense as to all eleven patents, it should be noted that Guardian's claim to licenses under the two patents which originated with PPG is also defeated by Section 11.2 of the 1964 agreement. This section addresses a different concern from that addressed in Sections 3, 4 and 9. The restrictions on transferability and assignability in those sections prevent the patent licenses from becoming the property of third parties. The termination clause, however, provides that Permaglass' license with respect to the two PPG patents will terminate if the ownership of a majority of the voting stock of Permaglass passes from the 1964 stockholders to designated classes of persons, even though the licenses themselves might never have changed hands.

Apparently PPG was willing for Permaglass to continue as licensee under the nine patents even though ownership of its stock might change. These patents originated with Permaglass and so long as Permaglass continued to use the licenses for its own benefit a mere change in ownership of Permaglass stock would not nullify the licenses. Only a transfer or assignment would cause a termination. However, the agreement provides for termination with respect to the two original PPG patents in the event of an indirect takeover of Permaglass by a change in the ownership of a majority of its stock. The fact that PPG sought and obtained a stricter provision with respect to the two patents which it originally owned in no way indicates an intention to permit transfer of licenses under the other nine in case of a merger. None of the eleven licenses was transferable; but two of them, those involving PPG's own development in the field of gas hearth technology, were not to continue even for the benefit of the licensee if it came under the control of a manufacturer of automobiles or a competitor of PPG in the glass industry "other than the present owners" of Permaglass. A consistency among the provisions of the agreement is discernible when the different origins of the various patents are considered.

Notes and Questions

1. *The federal common law of IP licenses.* As noted above, courts have long held that questions of assignability of copyright and patent licenses are matters of federal law rather than state contract law. Is there a federal law of contract? Why don't federal courts defer to the state contract laws that otherwise govern copyright and patent licensing agreements?

   Contrast this approach with trademark licenses, which have generally been treated as governed by state contract law, notwithstanding the presence of federally registered trademarks. *Tap Publications, Inc. v. Chinese Yellowpages (New York), Inc.*, 925 F. Supp. 212 (S.D.N.Y. 1996) ("The mere fact that a trademark was the subject of the contract does not convert a state-law breach of contract issue into a federal Lanham Act claim"). What might account for this difference in treatment?

2. *Exclusive vs. nonexclusive.* As discussed in *Everex* (Section 13.3.1), the general rule permits exclusive licensees to assign their rights under an IP license, but prohibits nonexclusive licensees from doing so. Do you agree with the rationale for making this distinction?

Why isn't a nonexclusive licensee treated like the holder of the copyright in a book? The owner of a copy of the book may freely sell it in competition with the copyright holder's ability to sell a new copy. Why should a nonexclusive licensee's ability to compete with the granting of new licensees by the rights holder prevent its assignment of a nonexclusive license?

3. *Remedies.* In *PPG*, did Permaglass's violation of the anti-assignment clause mean that the transfer to Guardian was ineffective, or simply that Permaglass breached the contract, giving PPG a right to seek damages and/or terminate for breach?

   As noted in Drafting Note 3 of Section 13.3.4, § 322(2)(b) of the *Restatement (Second) of Contracts* provides that a "contract term prohibiting assignment of rights under the contract … gives the obligor a right to damages for breach of the terms forbidding assignment but does not render the assignment ineffective." Is this rule sensible? What are the implications of prohibiting assignments outright? Consider the potential impact on M&A transactions.

   If the *Restatement* rule had applied in *PPG*, how would PPG's infringement claim have been affected?

4. *Change of control.* PPG also illustrates the operation of a change of control clause. How is such a clause different than an anti-assignment clause? In *PPG*, Permaglass underwent a forward merger after which it was subsumed into Guardian. Would the result have been different if Guardian acquired Permaglass through a reverse triangular merger? Why? Isn't this merely form over substance?

   An alternative approach was proposed in Section 503(2)(3) of UCITA. It provided that the prohibited assignment would be ineffective. This addresses some of the concerns with the *Restatement* approach, but introduces issues of its own. For example, if the assignment of a license is ineffective, who is left with the license after the transaction? One might assume it is the original licensee, but what if that entity is merged out of existence or exists only as a shell?

   In *First Nationwide Bank v. Florida Software Services*, 770 F. Supp. 1537 (M.D. Fla. 1991), a software licensing agreement contained a clause that deemed the transfer of more than 60 percent of the stock of the licensee to constitute an attempted transfer of the agreement, giving FSS, the licensor, a right to terminate the license. During the Savings and Loan Crisis of 1988, two licensee banks were put into receivership and then acquired by First Nationwide under a federal bailout program. In response, FSS threatened to terminate the licensing agreements unless First Nationwide paid it new license fees amounting to nearly $2 million. Though the change in control clause was clear, the court declined to enforce it, reasoning that doing so would be against public policy, and going so far as to call FSS's approach "extortion." Is this a fair characterization? Should courts have the discretion to disregard such provisions? If so, under what circumstances?

5. *Shop rights.* The court in PPG distinguishes cases holding that shop rights transfer upon a merger. How are shop rights different than license rights, and why does this distinction make a difference in the context of mergers?

13.4 PATENT MARKING

Section 237(a) of the U.S. Patent Act provides that if a patent owner wishes to recover damages for infringing activity before it formally notifies the infringer, it must mark each patented article with the relevant patent number:

Patentees, and persons making, offering for sale, or selling within the United States any patented article for or under them, or importing any patented article into the United States, may give notice to the public that the same is patented, either by fixing thereon the word "patent" or the abbreviation "pat.", together with the number of the patent … In the event of failure so to mark, no damages shall be recovered by the patentee in any action for infringement, except on proof that the infringer was notified of the infringement and continued to infringe thereafter …

Today, Section 237(a) has been amended to provide for "marking" via product packaging, documentation or internet site. But for some products, physical stamping of patent numbers on metal or plastic is still done. Accordingly, patent licensing agreements that involve the sale of products often require the licensee to mark all licensed products with the licensed patent numbers. Below is an example of such a clause.

EXAMPLE: PATENT MARKING

Licensee shall, and shall require its Affiliates and Sublicensees to, mark all Licensed Products sold or otherwise disposed of by it in the United States in a manner consistent with the marking provisions of 35 U.S.C. § 287(a). All Licensed Products shipped or sold in other countries shall be marked in such a manner as to conform with the patent laws and practice of the country to which such products are shipped or in which such products are sold.

Trademark licenses often contain similar provisions, along with detailed requirements for the size, placement and color of a licensed mark. These requirements are discussed in Section 15.4. Affixing a copyright notice to a copyrighted work is not legally required, but also often required in licensing agreements (see, e.g., Sections 19.1 and Sections 19.2 regarding required contractual notices for online content and software).

Notes and Questions

1. *Marking logic.* What kind of products do you think originally gave rise to the marking requirement? Why might such a requirement have been imposed? Does it serve any useful purpose today?

FIGURE 13.5 Historically, patented articles were marked with applicable patent numbers.

PATENT MARKING AND SOLO CUPS

Before the enactment of the America Invents Act in 2011, 35 U.S.C. § 292(a) allowed any person (a *"qui tam"* plaintiff) to bring a suit for "false marking" of a patented article. False marking included marking a product with a patent that does not cover the product or with an expired patent. The penalty for false marking was a fine up to $500 for each such product, of which a *qui tam* plaintiff was entitled to keep half.

In 2007 an enterprising patent attorney named Matthew Pequignot noticed that the iconic Solo plastic cups used at dormitory parties and backyard barbeques around the country were marked with one or more expired patent numbers. He initiated a *qui tam* suit against Solo Cup Co., seeking $500 for each of the approximately 21 billion cups that it sold after its patents expired. For good measure, Pequignot also sued Gillette and Proctor & Gamble for falsely marking billions of razors, razor blade cartridges, antiperspirants and deodorants.

It was an inspired plan, but the courts did not play along. The district courts found, and the Federal Circuit affirmed, that there was no evidence that the product manufacturers intended to deceive the public, and hence no violation of law. *Pequignot v. Solo Cup Co.*, 608 F.3d 1356 (Fed. Cir. 2010). A year later, Congress amended § 292(a) to provide that only persons who have suffered a competitive injury as a result of the false marking may bring a *qui tam* suit, and eliminating from false marking claims products that are marked with expired patent numbers, so long as the patents once covered the products.

13.5 COMPLIANCE WITH LAWS

Different attorneys take different positions about the compliance with laws clause that appears in almost every agreement. In its most basic form, the provision can be stated in a single sentence.

EXAMPLE: COMPLIANCE WITH LAWS

Each party agrees that it shall comply with all applicable federal, state and local statutes, rules, regulations, judicial orders and decrees, administrative rulings, executive orders and other legal and regulatory instruments ("Laws") with respect to its conduct, the products that it provides and the performance of its obligations under this Agreement. [Each party shall indemnify and defend the other party with respect to its failure to comply with any applicable Laws in accordance with the requirements of Section __.]

While a contractual commitment such as the one above does not make compliance with applicable laws any more or less mandatory, it does establish that a party that fails to comply with applicable laws can be found to be in breach of contract, in addition to any liability that the noncomplying party may have to regulatory or enforcement authorities. Without such an obligation, it is not at all clear that a party's violation of local health or safety regulations, tax withholding requirements, import duties, data privacy requirements or any of a thousand other legal and regulatory requirements would constitute a breach, or that the other party would have any contractual recourse for such a violation. In fact, the other party might even be implicated in the violation. Thus, the compliance with laws clause is both a useful statement of the parties' mutual intention to abide by the law, and their expectation that the other party will do so as well.

Some contract drafters, however, feel the need to explicitly enumerate a long string of laws, rules and regulations with which the parties will comply. Typical areas recited in this manner include anti-bribery regulations, export restrictions, currency controls, anti-money-laundering rules, antidiscrimination laws, and data security and privacy rules. Strictly speaking, it is not necessary to enumerate any particular area of legal compliance unless one party wishes to receive notifications or otherwise to be involved in the other party's compliance efforts (as is sometimes the case with regulatory approvals sought for food and drug products), or if one party requires the assistance of the other party to achieve compliance (which is sometimes the case with respect to international payments).

In addition to legal requirements, the parties may wish to require compliance with extralegal best practices, licensure requirements, accounting and other professional standards, conflicts of interest rules, sustainability certifications, diversity goals, codes of conduct and codes of ethics. For example, firms such as Walmart have adopted strict standards for their supply chain partners that prohibit a range of practices, whether or not illegal in the partner's country, including prohibitions on forced and child labor, unsafe working conditions and excessive working hours and assurances of fair compensation, environmentally sustainable practices and the availability of collective bargaining.[12]

Because one party may be implicated in the violation of law by the other party, it is prudent to ensure that the violating party indemnifies the other for such violations. Assuming that an agreement contains a general indemnification provision (see Section 10.3), the compliance with law provision may simply reference the general indemnification provision of the agreement.

13.6 FORCE MAJEURE

The concept of *force majeure* – literally "superior force" – has its origins in Roman law. It refers to an event beyond the control of a party that prevents that party from performing its contractual obligations. The doctrine is recognized under both the civil law and the common law, and is related to other doctrines that excuse contractual performance including impossibility, impracticability and frustration of purpose. Nevertheless, *force majeure* today is largely a contractual construct that is defined by the language of the agreement.

Force majeure is typically defined as an event that is beyond reasonable control of the affected party, was not reasonably foreseeable, has an impact that cannot be avoided through the exercise of reasonable efforts, and materially impedes a party's ability to perform its contractual obligations. Performance must typically be impossible or impractical in light of the event, not simply more burdensome. For example, an increase in the price of supplies or labor, by itself, would generally not qualify as an event of *force majeure*, as parties are expected to take price fluctuations into account when negotiating contractual commitments.

In addition to establishing the characteristics of a *force majeure* event, many *force majeure* clauses provide a list of *force majeure* events (see the example below). Depending on the language of the clause, the list may be exhaustive or nonexhaustive. Some clauses also include a generic "catch-all" phrase such as "any other events or circumstances beyond the reasonable control of the parties." Other clauses may include a list of excluded events that do not constitute *force majeure*, such as financial hardship.

---

[12]   See Walmart Stores, Inc., Standards for Suppliers Manual, April 2014, https://cdn.corporate.walmart.com/7c/c3/3d-339cb74ec9a2fad98fd43d3589/standards-for-suppliers-manual-english.pdf.

In some jurisdictions, including New York, courts will excuse performance on the basis of *force majeure* only if the *force majeure* clause specifically names the type of event that prevented a party from performing, even if the clause otherwise contains an expansive catch-all phrase.[13] Courts may also refuse to excuse a party's performance on the basis of *force majeure* if an event was foreseeable or known at the time that the agreement was executed, especially if the event is not specifically listed in the *force majeure* clause.

If a *force majeure* event has occurred within the meaning of the contractual definition, and a party cannot perform its obligations, a typical *force majeure* clause excuses that party's performance for the duration of the *force majeure* event. Some clauses set forth additional requirements on the party whose performance is excused, such as a duty to mitigate damages or to resume performance as soon as possible.

EXAMPLE: *FORCE MAJEURE*

[Except for the obligation to make payments as required under this Agreement] [1], neither Party will be liable for any failure or delay in its performance under this Agreement due to any cause beyond its reasonable control and which was not foreseeable [2], including, without limitation, acts of war, acts of God [2], earthquakes, floods, fires, embargos, riots, terrorism, sabotage [, strikes and other labor disputes] [3], [extraordinary governmental acts] [4], pandemic, quarantine or other public health emergency, [5] or failure of third party power, telecommunications or computer networks (each, a "Force Majeure Event"), provided that the affected Party: (a) gives the other Party [6] prompt notice of such Force Majeure Event and its likely impact on such Party's performance, and (b) uses its reasonable efforts to resume performance as required hereunder.

Notwithstanding the foregoing, if such Force Majeure Event causes a delay in performance of more than thirty (30) days, the unaffected Party shall have the right to terminate this Agreement without penalty upon written notice at any time prior to the affected Party's resumption of performance. [7]

DRAFTING NOTES

[1] *Exclusion of payment obligations* – some *force majeure* clauses do not allow the excuse or delay of payment obligations on the basis of *force majeure*, on the theory that it is always possible to make a payment through some mechanism.

[2] *Catch-all language* – as noted above, catch-all language is often not recognized by courts interpreting *force majeure* clauses, so an effort to list as many specific *force majeure* events as possible is recommended.

[3] *Labor issues* – some *force majeure* clauses seek to excuse performance if a party suffers a labor strike, lockout or other labor dispute. Yet this type of event is often viewed as within the control of the affected party (e.g., if it had paid its employees a reasonable wage, they would not have gone on strike).

---

[13] See *Phibro Energy, Inc. v. Empresa de Polimeros de Sines Sarl*, 720 F. Supp. 312, 318 (S.D.N.Y. 1989) (question of fact whether an "electrical mishap" that shut down production for eleven days constituted an "accident" under a contractual *force majeure* clause).

[4] *Governmental acts* – some *force majeure* clauses seek to excuse performance on the basis of "governmental acts," a broad description that could be interpreted to include ordinary health and safety regulations, taxes, tariffs and other regulatory measures that generally should not excuse performance under a contract. The intent of the "governmental acts" exclusion is to excuse performance based on unforeseen and extraordinary governmental actions such as nationalization of an industry, expropriation of private property, trade embargoes, etc.

[5] *Public health emergencies* – the COVID-19 pandemic has resulted in renewed interest in *force majeure* clauses, and will generate significant amounts of contractual litigation.

[6] *Other party* – some *force majeure* clauses refer to the other party as the "unaffected party." This terminology should be avoided, as both parties could be affected by an event of *force majeure*, though only one seeks to excuse its performance under the agreement.

[7] *Outside date* – most *force majeure* clauses require that performance be resumed within some reasonable period, often thirty days. If not, then the other party may have the right to terminate the agreement or the affected party's nonperformance may be considered a breach. While such a cutoff date may seem harsh to the affected party, it recognizes that the other party may require the flexibility to seek an alternate supplier or partner if the affected party's nonperformance will be long term.

13.7 MERGER AND ENTIRE AGREEMENT

As discussed in Section 7.3, the court in *Permanence Corp. v. Kennametal, Inc.*, 725 F. Supp. 907 (E.D. Mich. 1989) partially based its refusal to imply an obligation of best efforts on the licensee on the fact that the licensing agreement in question contained a "merger" or "integration" clause, which stated that the written agreement "contains the entire agreement of the parties." Such clauses are practically *de rigueur* in agreements today, but that does not reduce their value.

EXAMPLE: MERGER [1] OR ENTIRE AGREEMENT

This Agreement (including the documents referred to herein) constitutes the entire agreement between the Parties and supersedes any prior understandings, agreements, or representations by or between the Parties, written or oral, with respect to the subject matter hereof, including, without limitation, the [letter of intent/memorandum of understanding dated _____] [2].

DRAFTING NOTES

[1] *Merger* – the term "merger" in this context derives from the idea that the written agreement *merges* all prior understandings into itself. It has nothing to do with "mergers and acquisitions" (see Section 13.3.3).

[2] *Exclusion of pre-contract documents* – the terms of such preliminary documents such as letters of intent or memoranda of understanding (see Section 5.3) often differ from the terms of the final, negotiated agreements (the so-called "definitive agreements"). Thus, it is advisable that any such preliminary documents be expressly called out and superseded, so as to avoid interpretive conflicts.

13.8 NO WAIVER

The equitable doctrine of waiver is an affirmative defense whereby a party accused of a wrong may claim that it should not be held liable for that wrong because the accusing party has previously failed to seek redress for the same wrong, effectively waiving its right to do so. The waiver defense arises in connection with IP licensing agreements when one party has neglected to declare a breach of the agreement after repeated failures of performance by the other party. For example, if a licensee repeatedly pays its quarterly royalties more than sixty days after the date due, and the licensor fails to assert a breach, then the licensor may inadvertently waive its right to assert a breach for late payment.

To avoid this result, parties have taken to including "no waiver" clauses in their agreements along the following lines.

EXAMPLE: NO WAIVER

No waiver by either Party of any right or remedy hereunder shall be valid unless the same shall be in writing and signed by the Party giving such waiver. No waiver by either Party with respect to any default, misrepresentation, or breach of warranty or covenant hereunder shall be deemed to extend to any prior or subsequent default, misrepresentation, or breach of warranty or covenant hereunder or affect in any way any rights arising by virtue of any prior or subsequent such occurrence.

Notwithstanding the inclusion of such a clause, a court might still recognize a breaching party's waiver defense based on applicable precedent. The issue was addressed by the Eighth Circuit in *Klipsch Inc. v. WWR Technology Inc.*, 127 F.3d 729 (8th Cir. 1997):

The District Court … granted summary judgment to WWR based on the affirmative defense of waiver… The court found that Klipsch waived its right to enforce the automatic termination provision of the License Agreement by its prior acceptances of defective performance.

Klipsch advances various arguments as to why the District Court erred in granting summary judgment to WWR based on the affirmative defense of waiver. First, Klipsch contends that the agreements' non-waiver clauses prevented it from waiving the right to enforce the termination provision.

Non-waiver provisions exist in or are incorporated into each of the relevant agreements. As re executed.More importantly, parties writing online or clickwrap agreements m an example, the non-waiver provision in the License Agreement provides:

"The waiver by either party of any breach of this Agreement by the other party in a particular instance shall not operate as a waiver of subsequent breaches of the same or different kind. The failure of either party to exercise any rights under this Agreement in a particular instance shall not operate as a waiver of such party's right to exercise the same or different rights in subsequent instances."

The District Court found that under Indiana law the existence of the non-waiver provisions does not prohibit WWR from asserting the defense of waiver...

Klipsch relies upon the Indiana Supreme Court's decision in *Van Bibber v. Norris*, 419 N.E.2d 115 (Ind. 1981), to support its argument that the non-waiver provision in the License Agreement prevents WWR from asserting the defense of waiver. In *Van Bibber*, the parties entered into an installment sale security agreement, which provided for debtor's purchase of a mobile home from seller. During the course of the agreement, seller's bank accepted numerous late payments from debtor, without declaring a default. In the sixth year of the security agreement, however, after an untimely payment, the bank declared a default and repossessed the mobile home. The trial court found that the bank, through its pattern of accepting late payments, had waived its right to enforce strict compliance with the terms of the security agreement. The Indiana Supreme Court reversed, holding that the trial court improperly had ignored the security agreement's non-waiver clause, which prevented the acceptance of late payments from acting as a waiver of the bank's right to strictly enforce the terms of the agreement.

We hold that *Van Bibber* does prevent WWR from successfully asserting its waiver defense. The District Court noted that "[a] broad interpretation of *Van Bibber* would bar WWR's waiver argument," but found "that such a broad interpretation would be improper." The District Court reasoned that language in *Van Bibber* strongly indicated that the Indiana Commercial Code compelled that court's holding, and that Indiana cases decided since *Van Bibber* extend its holding only to cases involving non-waiver clauses in the mortgage context. We believe that the language in *Van Bibber* is sufficiently expansive to apply to this case. The specific purpose of the non-waiver clause as stated in *Van Bibber*, "avoiding the risk of waiver by notifying the debtor in a contract term that the secured party's acceptance of late payments cannot be relied on as treating the time provisions as modified or waived," seems equally germane to the present case. If the parties' License Agreement "is to be truly effective according to its terms, we must conclude that [Klipsch] did not waive its rights to demand strict compliance and to pursue its contract and statutory remedies."

13.9 SEVERABILITY

Despite, or sometimes because of, the best efforts of contract attorneys, courts may sometimes find certain provisions of an agreement to be invalid. The invalidity of agreement terms can, as we will see, arise from bankruptcy law, antitrust law, the laws surrounding IP misuse and various other theories.

If an agreement provision is found by a court to be invalid, a question arises regarding the effect of that invalid clause on the rest of the agreement. Does one bad apple spoil the barrel? Or should the invalid clause be surgically excised from the agreement, so that its remaining, inoffensive provisions continue in effect? Courts have wrestled with this question over the years, and in many cases have come up with answers (e.g., patent or copyright misuse generally invalidates the entire agreement – see Chapter 24).

But in an effort to avoid the uncertainty of judicial determinations, attorneys have developed contractual mechanisms to save the rest of their agreements after one provision is found to be invalid. This is known as the severability clause.

EXAMPLE: SEVERABILITY

a. Any term or provision of this Agreement that is invalid or unenforceable in any situation in any jurisdiction shall not affect the validity or enforceability of the remaining terms and provisions hereof or the validity or enforceability of the offending term or provision in any other situation or in any other jurisdiction.

b. If the final judgment of a court of competent jurisdiction declares that any term or provision hereof is invalid or unenforceable, the Parties agree that the court making the determination of invalidity or unenforceability shall have the power to limit the term or provision, to delete specific words or phrases, or to replace any invalid or unenforceable term or provision with a term or provision that is valid and enforceable and that comes closest to expressing the intention of the invalid or unenforceable term or provision, and this Agreement shall be enforceable as so modified.

In the above example, clause (a) seeks to save other terms of the Agreement when one term is found invalid. Clause (b) seeks to reform the offending clause itself to make it as enforceable as possible. For example, a court might find that the parties' ten-year noncompetition covenant is unreasonably lengthy. Instead of deleting the noncompetition covenant entirely, the parties here invite the court to substitute the original ten-year term with a shorter, more reasonable, one.

One relatively uncommon twist on the severability clause is the so-called *essentiality* clause. If a particular clause of an agreement is considered to be essential to the parties' bargain, then the invalidation of that clause could disrupt the commercial value of the agreement to one or both parties. Thus, the agreement may specify that if the essential clause is found to be invalid or unenforceable, then the entire agreement will terminate at the option of one or both of the parties.

Such clauses are rare,[14] probably for a number of reasons. For one, they draw attention to a potentially invalid or illegal clause. Second, they provide an incentive for a party wishing to terminate the agreement to challenge the legality of the essential clause.

13.10 ORDER OF PRECEDENCE AND AMENDMENT

In some cases parties will execute a variety of documents in connection with a single large transaction or series of related transactions. In addition to one or more IP licensing agreements, parties may execute service, consulting, supply, manufacturing, sponsored research, distribution, resale, agency, marketing, advertising, employment, investment and a range of other agreements, as well as multiple statements of work, service orders, purchase orders, affidavits and the like. Not surprisingly, this barrage of documents sometimes includes conflicting and contradictory terms. For example, an IP licensing agreement may call for indemnification for patent claims up to certain limits, while a related statement of work may include an uncapped indemnity and a purchase order may disclaim any responsibility for IP infringement at all. This situation resembles the classic contractual "battle of the forms," with the added twist that many of the contradictory documents are signed and negotiated agreements, rather than preprinted stock forms.

---

[14] See Smith, supra note 1, at 1194–96.

To address this problem, parties often include a clause relating to the order of precedence of the many different agreements included in their transaction. That is, in the event of a conflict, they specify which document takes precedence over the others.

EXAMPLE: PRECEDENCE

In the event of any conflict or inconsistency between the terms of this Agreement and any statement of work, work order, purchase order, invoice, correspondence or other writing issued by a party hereto, the terms of this Agreement shall control and supersede, followed by the terms of any mutually-signed statement of work, followed by any work order issued under that statement of work, followed by any written and signed correspondence, followed by any pre-printed form or clickwrap, browsewrap or similar electronic indication of assent [1], in each case whenever issued or signed [2].

The terms of a work order issued under one statement of work shall have no effect on the rights or obligations of the parties under any other statement of work or work order issued under any other statement of work.

Purchase orders shall be effective solely with respect to specifying the number and kind of products being ordered. Invoices shall be effective solely with respect to specifying the charges for products shipped and services rendered. All other terms and conditions printed or included on such purchase orders, invoices and other correspondence shall be of no effect or force.

EXAMPLE: AMENDMENT

The terms of this Agreement may be amended, modified and waived solely in a written instrument executed and dated by both parties which specifically references this Agreement and states that it is thereby being amended, and electronic means shall not suffice to evidence assent to any amendment, modification or waiver of the terms of this Agreement [1].

DRAFTING NOTES

[1] *Clickwraps* – as discussed in Chapter 17, clickwrap agreements can under many circumstances be treated as binding agreements of equal stature with negotiated and signed agreements. As a result, it is particularly important to supersede such electronic instruments, whenever they are executed.

More importantly, parties writing online or clickwrap agreements may wish to include language in those agreements that specifically prevents them from superseding the terms of prior written agreements. For example,

This Online Agreement does not affect any existing written agreement between Licensee and Licensor and may be superseded by a subsequent written agreement signed by both Licensee and Licensor. Except as indicated in the prior sentence, this Online Agreement constitutes the entire agreement between the parties with respect to the use and license of the Licensed Products, and hereby supersedes and terminates any prior agreements or understandings relating to such subject matter …[15]

---

[15] *I. Lan Systems, Inc. v. Netscout Service Level*, 183 F. Supp. 2d 328, 330 n.1 (D. Mass. 2002).

[2] *Subsequent writings* – because contract law generally permits a later writing to amend or supersede an earlier one, it is important to specify that the above order of precedence applies even to later-executed writings of lower precedence.

13.11 MUTUAL NEGOTIATION

There is an ancient rule of contract interpretation – *contra proferentem* – that states that ambiguities in a contract are resolved in favor of the nondrafting party. That is, if a contractual clause is ambiguous or incomplete, the fault lies with the drafter, and the drafter should not get the benefit of an ambiguity or omission that it could have avoided. As succinctly put by Henry Smith, "The drafter is presumed to be the cheapest cost avoider."[16]

But even if one party produces the first draft, most complex agreements today are reviewed and negotiated by counsel for both parties. Should the party that produced the first draft be placed at a perpetual disadvantage when a contract is interpreted? Or should careful records be kept of who drafted the final version of each provision in the agreement? To avoid these headaches, many agreements contain a short clause that places responsibility for drafting the agreement on *both* parties.

EXAMPLE: MUTUAL NEGOTIATION

The Parties agree that the terms and conditions of this Agreement (including any perceived ambiguity herein) shall not be construed in favor of or against any Party by reason of the extent to which any Party or its professional advisors participated in the preparation of the original or any further drafts of this Agreement, as each Party has been represented by counsel in the drafting and negotiation of this Agreement and it represents their mutual efforts.

13.12 NOTICES

Much of the day-to-day management of contracts occurs via telephone, email or in-person meetings. But when official notification is required under an agreement – notice of breach, termination, achievement of milestones, etc. – the only prudent practice is to require that such notices be in writing and physically delivered.

EXAMPLE: NOTICES

All notices, requests, demands, claims, and other communications hereunder ("Notices") shall be in writing and shall be deemed duly delivered three (3) business days after it is sent by registered or certified mail, return receipt requested, postage prepaid, or one business day after it is sent for next business day delivery via a reputable nationwide/international overnight courier service, in each case to the designated recipient set forth below:If to Licensor:

---

[16] Smith, supra note 1, at 1202.

NAME/POSITION OF LICENSOR REPRESENTATIVE [1]
DELIVERY ADDRESS

With a copy to:

LICENSOR COUNSEL [2]

If to Licensee:

NAME/POSITION OF LICENSEE REPRESENTATIVE [1]
DELIVERY ADDRESS

With a copy to:

LICENSEE COUNSEL [2]

[*Also consider special telephonic/email "expedited" notice instructions for specified events requiring immediate actions, such as data breaches* (see Section 18.1)]

Either Party may give any Notice using any other means (including personal delivery, messenger service, telecopy, ordinary mail, or electronic mail [3]), but no such Notice shall be deemed to have been duly given unless and until it actually is received by the party for whom it is intended [4].

Either Party may change the address to which Notices hereunder are to be delivered by giving the other Party notice in the manner herein set forth [5].

DRAFTING NOTES

[1] *Designated recipient* – bearing in mind that many IP licensing agreements continue for years, it is useful to identify the recipient of legal notice by position rather than name. For example, "Chief Financial Officer," "Project X Contract Manager," "General Counsel," rather than "Jane Smith," who may have left the company the year before notice was sent.

[2] *Counsel copy* – whether or not justified, there is a general belief that law firm partners are more likely to remain in their positions than corporate executives. As a result, external counsel are often listed as "copy to" addressees of formal legal notices. Another reason to include counsel (external or internal) on official notices is to ensure that someone who understands the meaning of the notice will receive and act on it in a timely fashion. In many cases the "copy to" notice does not constitute official Notice under an agreement.

[3] *Electronic mail* – in today's connected world it seems quaintly archaic to require that formal legal notice be given by certified mail or FedEx. Why not email, which is the main means of business communication today? There are many reasons. First, email is linked to an individual. If that individual leaves the employ of the relevant company, odds are good that the notice will never be delivered. Second, email is not always reliable. It can be filtered and redirected to spam folders. It can also be deleted inadvertently far more easily than a FedEx package. Third, a physical, signed document carries more weight and draws more attention than yet another email, which can get lost in the

inbox of a busy executive. Finally, email can easily be misaddressed. Thus, the requirement to send a physical letter serves to protect the sender as well as the recipient.

[4] *Effective upon receipt* – if electronic or other means are accepted as suitable for delivering official notice, then notice should be effective at the time that the message was
received (i.e., there is little need for a delay, as there is for a mailed copy).

[5] *Changing notice addresses* – every agreement should contain some provision for changing or updating the individuals and addresses to be used for notice, but regrettably few
parties avail themselves of the opportunity to make such updates.

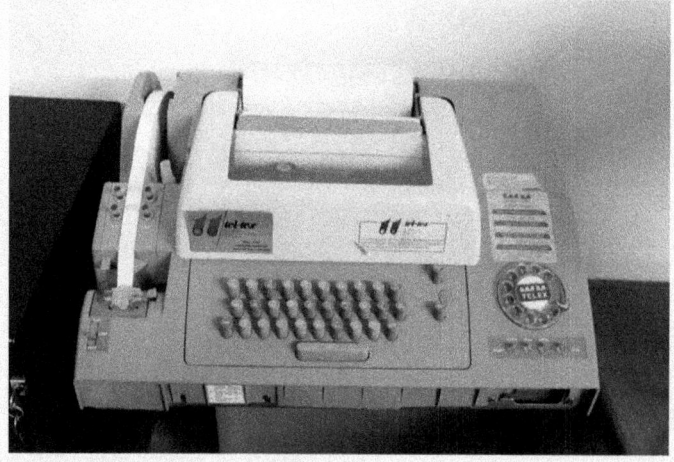

FIGURE 13.6 Many older agreements still provide for official notice by Telex or teletype
machine. This technology was a fixture in business offices from the 1950s to the 1970s and
preceded the facsimile or fax machine.

Finally, for transactions involving multiple documents (e.g., license agreements, maintenance
agreements, services agreements), it is useful to ensure that all notice provisions are consistent. This is particularly important when drafting has been split up among different counsel.
Consider stating the notice provision in the main transaction agreement and incorporating it
by reference elsewhere.

13.13 INTERPRETATION

Some agreements set forth a set of rules by which the contractual language will be interpreted,
should the need for interpretation arise. While these rules may seem obvious or trivial, each is
the result of actual disputes between parties over the years.

EXAMPLE: INTERPRETATION

(a) the use of any gender will be applicable to all genders;
(b) the word "or" is used in the inclusive sense to mean one or more of the listed words or
    phrases;

(c) the term "including" means including, without limiting the generality of any description preceding such term;

(d) any definition of or reference to any agreement or other document refers to such agreement or other document as from time to time amended or otherwise modified;

(e) any reference to any laws refer to such laws as are from time to time enacted, repealed or amended;

(f) the words "herein," "hereof" and "hereunder", and words of similar import, refer to this Agreement in its entirety and not to any particular provision hereof; and

(g) all references herein to Sections and Schedules, refer to the Sections of and Schedules to this Agreement.

(Courtesy of Jim Farrington)

Notes and Questions

1. *Giving the boilerplate its due.* As noted in this chapter, there is a lot embodied in the boilerplate clauses at the end of an agreement. Why do so few people, even attorneys, read the boilerplate, let alone negotiate it? Is this inattention to the boilerplate efficient (see the quote from Henry Smith in footnote 1)? How can you give your clients an advantage by being more attentive to these seemingly standardized clauses?

2. *Making the cut.* Attorneys are sometimes put into the awkward position of limiting the number of pages or words that their clients will tolerate in an agreement. Once the operative agreement terms are finalized, there is seldom much space for the boilerplate. How would you prioritize the different provisions discussed in this chapter? Which would you insist on including, and which would you cut?

3. *Predicting the unpredictable.* The COVID-19 pandemic of 2020 drew renewed attention to the *force majeure* clauses of agreements of all kinds. COVID-19 was unexpected, not only by public health officials, but by contract drafters. It did not manifest as an acute event, such as a hurricane or Ebola outbreak, but as a long, slow process that fundamentally altered business and economic norms over a lengthy period. Was (is) COVID-19 an event of *force majeure*? How would such a pandemic potentially affect an IP licensing agreement? Under what circumstances do you think a pandemic would excuse performance under such an agreement? How can *force majeure* clauses be drafted to take unexpected events into account while remaining enforceable?

4. *Protecting parties from themselves.* Many of the boilerplate clauses discussed in this chapter are intended to protect the parties to a contract from the unanticipated or adverse effects of their own errors, omissions and misjudgments. Which clauses are most directed to this purpose and how?

Problem 13.1

Draft the "general provisions" section of an IP licensing agreement including versions of the clauses discussed in Sections 13.3–13.13, assuming that you represent:

a. BioWhiz, a San Jose, California, biotech start-up that is in discussions with Stanford University to obtain an exclusive patent license to a groundbreaking new cancer therapy target discovered by the university.

b. Consolidated Edibles, a Minnesota-based agricultural products conglomerate that wishes to obtain exclusive rights to distribute and sell coffee grown on the Café Dulce plantation in Costa Rica.

c. SoftAsia, a medium-sized Korean video game developer that acquires the rights to video game ideas, characters and artwork from individuals located around the world.

To what degree should the boilerplate clauses be adjusted to address the likely needs of these different clients, and to what degree should they remain the same across all of the agreements?

PART III

Industry- and Context-Specific Licensing Topics

14

Academic Technology Transfer

There are approximately 200 research universities operating in the United States today. These universities, with aggregate annual research budgets in excess of $70 billion,[1] are responsible for many of the most important scientific and technological discoveries of the last century. As recounted by Jonathan Cole, "[t]he laser, magnetic-resonance imaging, FM radio, the algorithm for Google searches, global-positioning systems, DNA fingerprinting, fetal monitoring, bar codes, transistors, improved weather forecasting, mainframe computers, scientific cattle breeding, advanced methods of surveying public opinion, even Viagra had their origins in America's research universities."[2]

Universities actively seek patents and other intellectual property (IP) protection for their innovations. From 1996 to 2015, American universities obtained more than 80,000 US patents, and more than 7,600 in 2018 alone.[3] Many of these patents are licensed to start-up and mature companies. The Association for University Technology Managers (AUTM) reports that in 2018 US universities entered into 9,350 new technology license and option agreements.[4] Accordingly, any discussion of technology licensing and transactions would be incomplete without a brief stop in the world of university technology transfer.[5]

---

[1] Natl. Sci. Fnd., Rankings by Total R&D Expenditures, https://ncsesdata.nsf.gov/profiles/site?method=rankingBy-Source&ds=herd (data through 2017).

[2] Jonathan Cole, *Can American Research Universities Remain the Best in the World?* Chron. Higher Ed., January 3, 2010.

[3] *See* Assn. Univ. Tech. Managers, US Licensing Activity Survey: 2018, https://autm.net/surveys-and-tools/surveys/licensing-survey/2018-licensing-activity-survey (hereinafter AUTM 2018 Survey), and Assn. Univ. Tech. Managers, Driving the Innovation Economy Academic Technology Transfer in Numbers, https://autm.net/AUTM/media/Surveys-Tools/Documents/AUTM_2017_Infographic.pdf.

[4] AUTM 2018 Survey, *supra* note 3.

[5] Academic technology transfer is a large subject, and this chapter covers only a portion of it. Given the nature of this book, we will focus largely on agreements relating to IP licensing. For a discussion of topics including government research grants, sponsored research funding and university spinout companies, see, e.g., Jennifer Carter-Johnson, University Technology Transfer Structure and Intellectual Property Policies in Research Handbook on Intellectual Property and Technology Transfer 4 (Jacob H. Rooksby, ed., Edward Elgar, 2020).

14.1 ACADEMIC RESEARCH AND THE BAYH–DOLE ACT

Before World War II, US academic research was confined largely to the laboratory and scientific conferences.[6] But with the advent of war against technologically formidable adversaries, President Franklin D. Roosevelt placed Vannevar Bush, the Dean of MIT's School of Engineering and the founder of Raytheon, in charge of the government's new Office of Scientific Research and Development. Bush drew on his longstanding ties to MIT as he oversaw key wartime initiatives like the Manhattan Project and the development of radar. During America's post-war boom, Bush continued to shape US research policy, convinced that American academic institutions could serve the national interest through research and development. As a result, the federal government began to pour money into academic labs. In 1953, federal nondefense R&D funding was $2.2 billion. By 1980 it had reached $41.5 billion.

But although an increasing share of each year's Nobel prizes went to US scientists, relatively little academic research was finding its way into the commercial sector. Unlike Japan, where the government directly funded industrial research programs in fields like semiconductors and consumer electronics, US research had a hard time finding its way into commercial applications. It has been estimated that of the 30,000 federally owned patents in existence prior to 1980, only 5 percent were ever licensed to industry, and even fewer made their way into commercial products or services.[7] The problem, many felt, had to do with the way that patents were awarded for federally funded research.

Under prevailing federal regulations prior to 1980, IP rights in federally funded discoveries were murky. Some agencies claimed ownership over inventions that they funded, others gave rights to their grantees, others didn't specify one way or the other. A result of this lack of clarity was that few federally funded inventions were being used by the private sector. A solution to this problem was proposed by Senators Birch Bayh, a Democrat from Indiana, and Bob Dole, a Republican from Kansas. The resulting Bayh–Dole Act of 1980 made a number of tweaks to the patent system focused on federally funded research.[8]

BAYH–DOLE ACT OF 1980

35 U.S.C. § 200: Policy and Objective

It is the policy and objective of the Congress to use the patent system to promote the utilization of inventions arising from federally supported research or development; to encourage maximum participation of small business firms in federally supported research and development efforts; to promote collaboration between commercial concerns and non-profit organizations, including universities; to ensure that inventions made by nonprofit organizations and small business firms are used in a manner to promote free competition

---

[6] For a more detailed history of university technology transfer in the USA, see Carter-Johnson, *supra* note 5, at 6–12; Natl. Res. Council, Research Universities and the Future of America 37–39 (Natl. Acad. Press, 2012).

[7] Committee on Management of University Intellectual Property, Managing University Intellectual Property in the Public Interest 24 (Stephen A. Merrill & Anne-Marie Mazza eds., Natl. Res. Council, 2010); Daniel S. Greenberg, Science for Sale: The Perils, Rewards, and Delusions of Campus Capitalism 52 (Univ. Chicago Press, 2007).

[8] The Bayh–Dole Act applies to a range of nonprofit institutions and small businesses that receive federal research funding. For purposes of this chapter, however, I focus on academic institutions.

and enterprise without unduly encumbering future research and discovery; to promote the commercialization and public availability of inventions made in the United States by United States industry and labor; to ensure that the Government obtains sufficient rights in federally supported inventions to meet the needs of the Government and protect the public against nonuse or unreasonable use of inventions; and to minimize the costs of administering policies in this area.

14.1.1 *Ownership of Federally Funded Intellectual Property*

The principal feature of the Bayh–Dole Act was to allow research institutions receiving federal funding to retain ownership of the discoveries and inventions that they made using this funding.[9] The Act requires these institutions to disclose each such federally funded invention to the government, and to elect whether or not it wishes to retain rights to that invention. If the institution fails to make this disclosure within a reasonable time or to make this election within two years after the disclosure, then the government may take title to the invention (35 U.S.C. § 201(c)(1)-(2)). Then, if the institution elects to take title to the invention, it must file patent applications in the United States and any other countries where it wishes to retain rights (35 U.S.C. § 201(c)(3)). Again, if the institution fails to file such patent applications in a country, the government may take title to the invention in that country.

Despite these provisions, universities typically do not file patent applications covering every invention that is disclosed by their researchers. In many cases the potential commercial value of an invention may be small compared to the cost of filing and prosecuting a patent application, and the university's educational and research missions may better be served by permitting the researcher to publish the relevant findings and/or to release the invention, for example, on an "open source" basis. If a university wishes to discontinue prosecuting a patent application or maintaining a patent that was developed using federal funding, it must so notify the federal agency (37 C.F.R. § 401.14(f)(3)). While such a notification technically gives the agency the right to claim ownership of the invention, governmental agencies seldom exercise this right.

FIGURE 14.1 Senators Birch Bayh and Bob Dole.

---

[9] Almost all US universities require their faculty and other personnel to assign patent rights in inventions made using university resources and facilities to the university. See Section 2.3.

A related issue concerns a university's ownership of an invention when a researcher assigns the rights in that invention to a commercial research sponsor. This issue was considered in the following case.

Board of Trustees of the Leland Stanford Junior University v. Roche Molecular Systems, Inc.

563 U.S. 776 (2011)

ROBERTS, CHIEF JUSTICE

Since 1790, the patent law has operated on the premise that rights in an invention belong to the inventor. The question here is whether the Bayh–Dole Act displaces that norm and automatically vests title to federally funded inventions in federal contractors. We hold that it does not.

I

In 1985, a small California research company called Cetus began to develop methods for quantifying blood-borne levels of human immunodeficiency virus (HIV), the virus that causes AIDS. A Nobel Prize winning technique developed at Cetus—polymerase chain reaction, or PCR—was an integral part of these efforts. PCR allows billions of copies of DNA sequences to be made from a small initial blood sample.

In 1988, Cetus began to collaborate with scientists at Stanford University's Department of Infectious Diseases to test the efficacy of new AIDS drugs. Dr. Mark Holodniy joined Stanford as a research fellow in the department around that time. When he did so, he signed a Copyright and Patent Agreement (CPA) stating that he "agree[d] to assign" to Stanford his "right, title and interest in" inventions resulting from his employment at the University.

At Stanford Holodniy undertook to develop an improved method for quantifying HIV levels in patient blood samples, using PCR. Because Holodniy was largely unfamiliar with PCR, his supervisor arranged for him to conduct research at Cetus. As a condition of gaining access to Cetus, Holodniy signed a Visitor's Confidentiality Agreement (VCA). That agreement stated that Holodniy "will assign and do[es] hereby assign" to Cetus his "right, title and interest in each of the ideas, inventions and improvements" made "as a consequence of [his] access" to Cetus.

For the next nine months, Holodniy conducted research at Cetus. Working with Cetus employees, Holodniy devised a PCR-based procedure for calculating the amount of HIV in a patient's blood. That technique allowed doctors to determine whether a patient was benefiting from HIV therapy.

Holodniy then returned to Stanford where he and other University employees tested the HIV measurement technique. Over the next few years, Stanford obtained written assignments of rights from the Stanford employees involved in refinement of the technique, including Holodniy, and filed several patent applications related to the procedure. Stanford secured three patents to the HIV measurement process.

In 1991, Roche Molecular Systems, a company that specializes in diagnostic blood screening, acquired Cetus's PCR-related assets, including all rights Cetus had obtained through agreements like the VCA signed by Holodniy. After conducting clinical trials on the HIV quantification method developed at Cetus, Roche commercialized the proced-ure. Today, Roche's HIV test "kits are used in hospitals and AIDS clinics worldwide."

Some of Stanford's research related to the HIV measurement technique was funded by the National Institutes of Health (NIH), thereby subjecting the invention to the Bayh–Dole Act. Accordingly, Stanford disclosed the invention, conferred on the Government a nonexclusive, nontransferable, paid-up license to use the patented procedure, and for-mally notified NIH that it elected to retain title to the invention.

In 2005, the Board of Trustees of Stanford University filed suit against Roche, con-tending that Roche's HIV test kits infringed Stanford's patents. As relevant here, Roche responded by asserting that it was a co-owner of the HIV quantification procedure, based on Holodniy's assignment of his rights in the Visitor's Confidentiality Agreement. As a result, Roche argued, Stanford lacked standing to sue it for patent infringement. Stanford claimed that Holodniy had no rights to assign because the University's HIV research was federally funded, giving the school superior rights in the invention under the Bayh–Dole Act.

II

Although much in intellectual property law has changed in the 220 years since the first Patent Act, the basic idea that inventors have the right to patent their inventions has not. Under the law in its current form, "[w]hoever invents or discovers any new and useful pro-cess, machine, manufacture, or composition of matter … may obtain a patent therefor." 35 U.S.C. § 101.

Our precedents confirm the general rule that rights in an invention belong to the inventor. It is equally well established that an inventor can assign his rights in an invention to a third party. Thus, although others may acquire an interest in an invention, any such interest—as a general rule—must trace back to the inventor.

In accordance with these principles, we have recognized that unless there is an agree-ment to the contrary, an employer does not have rights in an invention "which is the ori-ginal conception of the employee alone." Such an invention "remains the property of him who conceived it." Ibid. In most circumstances, an inventor must expressly grant his rights in an invention to his employer if the employer is to obtain those rights.

Stanford and the United States as *amicus curiae* contend that the Bayh–Dole Act reor-ders the normal priority of rights in an invention when the invention is conceived or first reduced to practice with the support of federal funds. In their view, the Act moves inven-tors from the front of the line to the back by vesting title to federally funded inventions in the inventor's employer—the federal contractor.

[But] nowhere in the Act is title expressly vested in contractors or anyone else; nowhere in the Act are inventors expressly deprived of their interest in federally funded inventions. Instead, the Act provides that contractors may "elect to retain title to any subject inven-tion." 35 U.S.C. § 202(a). A "subject invention" is defined as "any invention of the con-tractor conceived or first actually reduced to practice in the performance of work under a funding agreement." § 201(e).

Stanford asserts that the phrase "invention of the contractor" in this provision "is natur-ally read to include all inventions made by the contractor's employees with the aid of fed-eral funding." That reading assumes that Congress subtly set aside two centuries of patent law in a statutory definition. It also renders the phrase "of the contractor" superfluous. If the phrase "of the contractor" were deleted from the definition of "subject invention," the definition would cover "any invention … conceived or first actually reduced to practice in the performance of work under a funding agreement." Reading "of the contractor" to mean "all inventions made by the contractor's employees with the aid of federal funding," as Stanford would, adds nothing that is not already in the definition, since the definition already covers inventions made under the funding agreement. That is contrary to our general "reluctan[ce] to treat statutory terms as surplusage."

Construing the phrase to refer instead to a particular category of inventions conceived or reduced to practice under a funding agreement—inventions "of the contractor," that is, those owned by or belonging to the contractor—makes the phrase meaningful in the statutory definition. And "invention owned by the contractor" or "invention belonging to the contractor" are natural readings of the phrase "invention of the contractor."

Stanford's reading of the phrase "invention of the contractor" to mean "all inventions made by the contractor's employees" is plausible enough in the abstract; it is often the case that whatever an employee produces in the course of his employment belongs to his employer. No one would claim that an autoworker who builds a car while working in a factory owns that car. But, as noted, patent law has always been different: We have rejected the idea that mere employment is sufficient to vest title to an employee's invention in the employer. Against this background, a contractor's invention—an "invention of the contractor"—does not automatically include inventions made by the contractor's employees.

The Bayh–Dole Act's provision stating that contractors may "elect to retain title" confirms that the Act does not vest title. Stanford reaches the opposite conclusion, but only because it reads "retain" to mean "acquire" and "receive." That is certainly not the common meaning of "retain." "[R]etain" means "to hold or continue to hold in possession or use." You cannot retain something unless you already have it. The Bayh–Dole Act does not confer title to federally funded inventions on contractors or authorize contractors to unilaterally take title to those inventions; it simply assures contractors that they may keep title to whatever it is they already have. Such a provision makes sense in a statute specifying the respective rights and responsibilities of federal contractors and the Government.

The Bayh–Dole Act applies to subject inventions "conceived or first actually reduced to practice in the performance of work" "funded in whole or in part by the Federal Government." Under Stanford's construction of the Act, title to one of its employee's inventions could vest in the University even if the invention was conceived before the inventor became a University employee, so long as the invention's reduction to practice was supported by federal funding. What is more, Stanford's reading suggests that the school would obtain title to one of its employee's inventions even if only one dollar of federal funding was applied toward the invention's conception or reduction to practice.

Stanford contends that reading the Bayh–Dole Act as not vesting title to federally funded inventions in federal contractors "fundamentally undermin[es]" the Act's framework and severely threatens its continued "successful application." We do not agree. Universities typically enter into agreements with their employees requiring the assignment to the university of rights in inventions. With an effective assignment, those inventions—if federally funded—become "subject inventions" under the Act, and the statute as a practical matter works pretty much the way Stanford says it should. The only significant difference is that it does so without violence to the basic principle of patent law that inventors own their inventions.

FIGURE 14.2 Stanford University failed to acquire rights in one of its researchers' inventions due to the future-looking language of its IP assignment policy. The Bayh–Dole Act did not remedy this failure.

Notes and Questions

1. *University ownership.* Why does the Bayh–Dole Act allow universities to patent federally funded inventions? Why doesn't the act award such patents to the federal funding agency? Section 105(a) of the Copyright Act provides that copyright protection is not available for any work of the US government, meaning that works of authorship made by federal personnel are largely in the public domain. Why wasn't a similar rule adopted for patents?

2. *The importance of words.* The Supreme Court, in ruling for Cetus, merely confirmed that the Bayh–Dole Act did not rescue Stanford from the results of its unfortunate drafting choices, discussed in Section 2.3, Notes 3–4. Is this fair? Should a mere contractual slip override the public policy goals of the Bayh–Dole Act?

14.1.2 *Royalty Sharing with Researchers*

Academic institutions, while excellent sources for basic research, are seldom equipped to bring their inventions to the marketplace. Accordingly, most universities seek to license their patents and other IP to the private sector (see Section 14.2). In most cases these licenses are royalty-bearing, meaning that the university will collect a royalty based on some percentage of its licensees' sales of products covered by the patents (see Section 8.2). The Bayh–Dole Act requires that universities share these royalties with individual inventors, and that the balance of the proceeds (after payment of expenses) "be utilized for the support of scientific research or education" (35 U.S.C. § 202(c)(7)(B)-(C)). Royalty-sharing arrangements vary widely among institutions. For example, Stanford University allocates the first 15 percent of net license revenue (after patenting costs) to its technology transfer office (TTO), then splits the remaining 85 percent in three equal parts among the inventors (in equal shares), their departments and the university; Washington University in St. Louis allocates 25 percent to its TTO, 35 percent to the inventors and 40 percent to the university; and Rice University allocates 37.5 percent to the inventors, 14 percent to their departments, 18.5 percent to the graduate education function, and 30 percent to the university.[10]

14.1.3 *Preference for United States Industry*

Section 204 of the Bayh–Dole Act embodies a specific preference for US manufacturing in its terms.

35 U.S.C. § 204: PREFERENCE FOR UNITED STATES INDUSTRY

Notwithstanding any other provision of this chapter, no [entity] which receives title to any subject invention … shall grant to any person the exclusive right to use or sell any subject invention in the United States unless such person agrees that any products embodying the subject invention or produced through the use of the subject invention will be manufactured substantially in the United States. However, in individual cases, the requirement for such an agreement may be waived by the Federal agency under whose funding agreement the invention was made upon a showing by the [entity] that reasonable but unsuccessful efforts have been made to grant licenses on similar terms to potential licensees that would be likely to manufacture substantially in the United States or that under the circumstances domestic manufacture is not commercially feasible.

An exclusive licensee of a federally funded invention should thus be vigilant – if a US manufacturing provision is included in the license agreement proffered by an academic institution, the licensee should evaluate whether US manufacturing will be practical under the circumstances. For example, does the licensee intend to offshore manufacturing to another country? Will its costs increase substantially if required to manufacture in the United States? Although the US manufacturing requirement is often waived by the funding agency, such waiver must be requested specifically.

Notes and Questions

1. *Bayh–Dole as an engine of global innovation?* In 2002 *The Economist* lauded the Bayh–Dole Act as "Possibly the most inspired piece of legislation to be enacted in America over the past half-century." The Act, the editors proclaimed, "unlocked all the inventions and discoveries that had been made in laboratories throughout the United States with the help of taxpayers' money [and] helped to reverse America's precipitous slide into industrial irrelevance."[11] An

---

[10] For a detailed analysis of these revenue splits, see Lisa Larrimore Ouellette & Andrew Tutt, *How Do Patent Incentives Affect University Researchers?*, 61 Intl. Rev. L. & Econ. 105883 at 9–10 (2020).

[11] Economist, "Innovation's golden goose", December 14, 2002.

industry coalition celebrating the fortieth anniversary of the Act in 2020 proudly announced that "Bayh–Dole made the United States the engine of global innovation … Thanks to Bayh–Dole, over 200 new therapies – including drugs and vaccines – have been created since 1980. The legislation has also bolstered U.S. economic output by $1.3 trillion, supported 4.2 million jobs, and led to more than 11,000 start-up companies."[12] Why would university patenting be responsible for economic growth on this scale? What is your impression of these figures?

2. *Bayh–Dole, oncomouse, and the Republic of Science.* Beginning in the 1990s, critics began to fear that the promise of licensing revenue may have caused universities to stray from their core educational and public missions. Members of the public, including a number of students, began to protest prominent academic–industry ties. One of the most heated of these incidents involved Harvard's genetically engineered "oncomouse," which the university licensed exclusively to DuPont Corporation. The arrangement led to student protests, newspaper op-eds and two rounds of Congressional hearings.[13] Eventually, in response to this flurry of negative publicity, Harvard and DuPont rescinded some of the more controversial aspects of their arrangement. In response to episodes like this, science journalist Dan Greenberg, in his influential book *Science for Sale: The Perils, Rewards, and Delusions of Campus Capitalism* (2007), asks whether "today's commercial values [have] contaminated academic research, diverting it from socially beneficial goals to mercenary service on behalf of profit-seeking corporate interests?" (p. 2).[14] What do you think of these critiques? Do they detract from the economic benefits that seem to have flowed from the Bayh–Dole Act?

3. *Royalty sharing.* As noted above, the Bayh–Dole Act requires that universities share royalties that they earn from patent licensing with individual inventors. Why? Private companies that license their patents have no such requirements. Should they? And which "inventors" should be entitled to a share of the university's royalties? In most cases, inventors for patent purposes must make a meaningful original contribution to the discovery or reduction of an invention to practice – a far higher standard than that required for authorship of a scientific paper. Should other members of the scientific team or lab that made a major breakthrough receive any compensation?[15]

4. *US manufacturing.* As noted above, the Bayh–Dole Act requires that an exclusive licensee of a federally funded invention substantially manufacture the resulting product in the United States. Why do you think this preference was included in the Act? Why does it apply only to exclusive licenses? Given the shift of manufacturing capacity overseas, how relevant do you think this preference is today? How often do you think the preference is waived by the relevant federal funding agency?

In *Ciba-Geigy Corp. v. Alza Corp.*, 804 F. Supp. 614 (1992), Ciba-Geigy obtained an exclusive license under the University of California's patents claiming a nicotine patch. Ciba-Geigy then sued Alza, claiming that Alza's Nicoderm product infringed the patent. Alza counterclaimed that Ciba-Geigy's exclusive license from the university was not valid because Ciba-Geigy had been manufacturing its own product in Germany, in violation of the US manufacturing requirement under Bayh–Dole. The court held that Alza could not

---

12   BayhDole40, https://bayhdole40.org/new-coalition-launches-to-celebrate-and-protect-the-bayh-dole-act.
13   See Daniel J. Kevles, *Of Mice and Money: The Story of the World's First Animal Patent*, 131 Daedalus 78 (2002).
14   For a more recent critique, see Rebecca S. Eisenberg and Robert Cook-Deegan, *Universities: The Fallen Angels of Bayh–Dole?* 147 Daedalus 76 (2018).
15   *See* Carter-Johnson, *supra* note 5, at 26–27 and 33–37 (discussing revenue-sharing issues).

defend against an infringement claim based on the failure of a university licensee to comply with US manufacturing requirements. Specifically, the court ruled that failing to manufacture in the United States does not automatically invalidate an exclusive license nor convert it to a nonexclusive license, so long as the government agency that funded the invention does not invoke its march-in rights (see Section 14.2). Unless and until the funding agency chose to exercise those rights (which it had shown no interest in doing), the license was unaffected. Do you agree with this result? If so, what purpose, if any, do US manufacturing rights serve today?

5. *Bayh–Dole around the world.* The apparent success of the Bayh–Dole Act in the United States has led a number of other countries to adopt legislation that seeks, in whole or in part, to replicate the benefits of the Act in their own economies. These include both developed countries such as China, Japan, France, Germany and the United Kingdom, as well as a range of mid-tier and developing countries, including Argentina, Brazil, Ethiopia, India, Indonesia, Malaysia, Nigeria, Poland, Russia and Vietnam. Do you think that local versions of the Bayh–Dole Act will be successful in each of these countries? Are there factors that would make a statutory structure such as that provided under Bayh–Dole less or more attractive in developing countries?

14.2 MARCH-IN RIGHTS UNDER THE BAYH–DOLE ACT

Because inventions subject to the Bayh–Dole Act were made using federal funding, the federal government retains some rights to these inventions even when title is held by a research institution. Under Section 202(c)(4), the funding agency has "a nonexclusive, nontransferable, irrevocable, paid-up license to practice or have practiced for or on behalf of the United States any subject invention throughout the world." This is a "government use" license, which ensures that the government is able to make use of inventions that it funds, even if they are otherwise commercialized.

A more controversial right exists under Section 203 of the Act. This section permits the funding agency to require an academic institution to license an invention to one or more third parties if necessary to "achieve practical application" of the invention or "to alleviate health or safety needs" that are "not reasonably satisfied" by the institution or its existing licensees. This right has significant implications both for the academic institution and its licensees. That is, if a university has granted an exclusive license to a private company, but that company cannot supply the licensed invention in sufficient quantities to meet health or safety needs, then the funding agency can require the university to license other manufacturers to produce the product, notwithstanding the original licensee's exclusivity.

Petition to Use Authority Under the Bayh–Dole Act to Promote Access to Fabryzyme (Agalsidase Beta), an Invention Supported By and Licensed By the National Institutes of Health under Grant No. DK-34045

August 2, 2010

Joseph M. Carik, Anita Hochendoner, and Anita Bova seek an open license under the Bayh–Dole Act that would allow supply of agalsidase beta [Fabrazyme] in the U.S. and abroad to treat Fabry patients. Specifically, this petition requests that NIH authorize responsible entities and individuals to use U.S. Patent No. 5,356,804 and U.S. Patent No. 5,580,757 in order to manufacture, import, export or sell agalsidase beta.

Background on Fabry Disease

Fabry disease is an X-linked recessive (inherited) lysosomal storage disease, which can cause [renal, heart, dermatological, ocular and other symptoms]. Fabry disease significantly shortens the life of its sufferers.

Government Role in Funding Research and Development

NIH is one of the largest funding entities for Fabry research, and is heavily invested in securing the well-being of Fabry patients. A July 22, 2010 search of the NIH Research Portfolio Online Reporting Tools (RePORT) database using the keyword "Fabry" identified 372 NIH grants. A July 23, 2010 search of clinicaltrials.gov using the key words "Fabry's Disease" identified 54 clinical trials, including 14 that were funded by the NIH, 16 identified as having received funding from Universities or other non-profit organizations, and 27 trials that received funding from industry.

Invention of Agalsidase Beta Treatment

While no cure is yet available, one of the greatest breakthroughs in scientific research on Fabry disease has been the discovery that enzyme replacement therapy with agalsidase beta (Fabrazyme) can effectively treat Fabry patients. The breakthrough was a direct result of NIH funding of grant no. DK 34045 awarded to Dr. Robert J. Desnick at the Mount

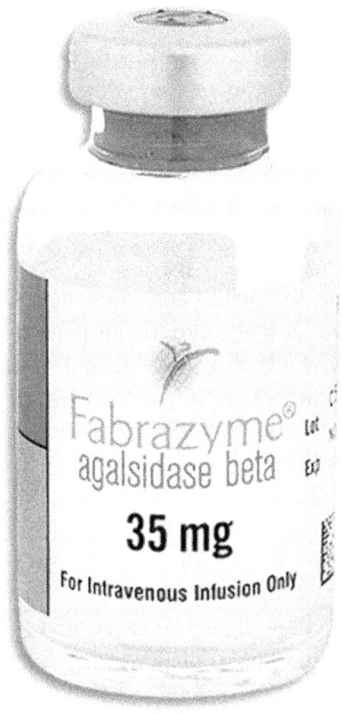

FIGURE 14.3 Genzyme's Fabrazyme.

Sinai School of Medicine of New York University. The adoption of Fabrazyme treatment has been widespread and is currently the gold standard of care for patients in the U.S. exhibiting symptoms.

Ownership and Licensing of Fabrazyme

Currently, Fabrazyme treatment is the only FDA approved enzyme replacement therapy in the United States. Genzyme, Inc. is the exclusive licensee to produce Fabrazyme.

The initial production of Fabrazyme was sufficient to meet the needs of all patients in the United States. However, in mid-2009, Genzyme decreased production as a result of a viral infection of their Allston, MA manufacturing plant. Further, in November 2009, Fabrazyme was produced which contained contaminants. The FDA initiated action against Genzyme which resulted in a consent decree including $175 million dollars in fines as profit disgorgement and oversight of the manufacture of Fabrazyme for at least 7 years.

Genzyme is only producing 30% of Fabrazyme estimated to meet the needs of patients. Current patients cannot have dosage increases, and no new patients being diagnosed are eligible to receive therapy. Although the most recent communication from Genzyme indicates that it expects to increase production by late 2011, there is no substantial guarantee that the projected date will be met.

Health Impact of Genzyme's Rationing of Fabrazyme

No cumulative data on the impact of Fabrazyme rationing is yet available; however, anecdotal data indicate that patients are struggling and at least one patient may have died due to reduced dosage (Genzyme disputes that the death was due to rationing). In addition, the petitioners have suffered immediate and significant harm due to the rationing. Specifically, Mr. Carik, Ms. Hochendoner, and Ms. Bova have had their dosage cut by 70%. They have had a return of symptoms and are now at far greater risk for cardiac disease and renal failure than before rationing began.

Genzyme Has Not Satisfied and Cannot Reasonably Satisfy the Health and Safety Needs of Fabry Patients by Rationing Drugs While Preventing Additional Sources of Manufacture

Rationing drugs does not satisfy the health and safety needs of individuals because there is no alternative treatment, and absent rationing all patients would receive their recommended treatment. The Bayh–Dole Act requires that Genzyme reasonably satisfy the health and safety needs of patients, which it has not done.

1) It is ... unreasonable, improper, and even catastrophic to limit patient access to a drug where such a limitation causes morbidity and death. The idea that drug access should be limited where there is a way to mitigate or prevent that limitation is anathema to virtually all ethical and scientific principles. Currently, 100% of Fabry patients have either limited access, or no access at all to Fabrazyme or any alternative treatment. Limiting access instead of encouraging others to make up the shortfall in manufacturing is the worst conceivable public health solution to supply shortages of publicly funded inventions.

2) It is further unreasonable and unfair to limit patient access to drug where the only impediment to its full production is a patent monopoly that was paid for in part from

the tax dollars of the patients themselves. In fact, the exception regarding health and safety concerns in Bayh–Dole Act ensures that patent laws do not trump health and safety concerns. Thus, absent an overwhelming argument that patent exclusivity is more important than drug access (e.g., critical national security concerns), there is no medically or ethically justifiable reason to limit access to Fabrazyme where a statutory remedy to the rationing exists.

3) To the extent that economic policy is to be balanced against the public need, it is further unreasonable to deny march-in rights where the petitioners or other licensees will not compete against the patentee. Specifically, granting march-in rights will not discourage industry investment in drug development, because licensees will normally not ration drug thus avoiding the instant situation altogether. Further, by granting march-in rights, Genzyme's revenues will actually increase since Genzyme sells every dose of Fabrazyme that it currently manufactures, but only meets 30% of the demand. By being granted march-in rights, the licensee will pay a reasonable 5% royalty rate to Genzyme to sell drug that Genzyme cannot otherwise produce.

4) Further it is unwise economic policy (and further unreasonable) to protect, or other-wise favor the licensee where the licensee caused the health crisis in the first place. While there is no specific remedy in the Bayh–Dole Act for licensees with "unclean hands," the drafters never anticipated that a licensee would breach the public trust by limiting access to drug that could otherwise be manufactured. Specifically, the Bayh–Dole Act has operated seamlessly and successfully for the invention of Fabrazyme until the drug was produced. The only dysfunction in the process has been Genzyme's neg-ligent manufacture of drug and the failure to obey FDA regulations. Thus, where the licensee actually caused the crisis (whether willfully or not), it is inconsistent with the objectives of Bayh–Dole to continue to reward the patentee with further patent exclusivity as it attempts to fix its own mistakes, especially while patients are suffering without a remedy.

5) It is unreasonable to deny march-in-rights where it is likely that manufacturers are motivated and encouraged to use the publicly funded patent monopoly to shift the economic costs of its errors directly to patients who, in part, funded the invention. The balance struck in the Bayh–Dole Act between public funding and private development is completely eviscerated where publicly funded pharmaceutical/biological inventions can be rationed due to negligence but, ironically, prices can be increased beyond the FDA disgorgement fees to thereby avoid the economic damages caused by that negli-gence. Thus, the grant of march-in rights assures that Genzyme will not increase prices in response to the FDA fines further vitiating an already grave health crisis to recover lost profits.

6) It is unreasonable to deny march-in rights where granting the license would harmonize with FDA actions. Specifically, the FDA has fined Genzyme $175 million dollars in disgorgement fees for its negligent manufacturing practices. If Genzyme is allowed to use its patent monopoly to shift the cost of the FDA fine to Fabry patients, then the FDA fines have no effect other than increasing the price of already limited drug. Even worse, failure to grant march-in rights after an FDA fine has the net effect of punishing the victims, not the manufacturer. While there is no provision in the Bayh–Dole Act for regulating prices directly, the remedy of march-in rights assures that the patent monopoly from a publicly funded invention cannot be misused to undermine FDA

punishments for regulatory violations. Specifically, if Genzyme attempts to profiteer from the situation, patients will turn to the march-in licensees for drug. Absent the grant of march-in rights, the FDA fines will have no deterrent effect and, worse, force the victims pay for the manufacturer's breach of regulations.

7) In addition, it is reasonable, prudent, and necessary to allow second sourcing where initial demands cannot be met and/or where market disruptions are likely to continue.

8) Finally, it unreasonable to argue that inaction is preferable to action where a remedy is available. Specifically, two possible future developments could ameliorate the crisis, the return of normal production of Fabrazyme (projected in late 2011) and/or the FDA approval of Replagal (projected date unknown) by Shire pharmaceuticals. Either development could restore access to effective enzyme replacement treatment for Fabry patients. Despite the fact that both results are hoped for by the petitioners, there is no guarantee that full access will be restored in the near future. In fact, both developments could be delayed by any number of factors. Absent an ironclad guarantee of success in the very near term for these developments, exercising march-in rights is the only immediate solution to the current problem. Because human health is at stake, it is critical for the Government act immediately to ensure that another alternative exists, even if the need for such an alternative may be hopefully mooted in longer term.

Grant of March-in Rights Is Consistent with Prior March-in Determinations

NIH has reviewed three previous petitions for march-in rights and denied exercise of the rights in each case. However, unlike previous petitions, the current petition is distinguishable for the following reasons.

Regarding interpretation of 35 U.S.C. § 203(a)(2) with regard to *In re Cellpro*, the NIH stated that reasonably satisfying a health need included "First, refraining from enforcing patent rights" and a pledge "to ensure that the product is as widely available as possible … and to ensure patient access to the fullest extent possible." Genzyme has failed to do either.

With regard to *In re Norvir* and *In re Xalatan*, the NIH refrained from acting based on pricing concerns. In both instances, the NIH determined that patients had reasonable physical access to drug, whether or not they could pay the price charged. In contrast, the instant case involves drastic drug rationing and profoundly limited physical access. There is simply not enough of the drug manufactured to treat everyone who needs it. While economic concerns are involved in the instant case and weigh heavily in favor of granting march-in rights, additional facts distinguish the instant case because physical access to the drug is the primary limiting factor preventing access.

Remedy Requested

The Bayh–Dole Act authorizes the Secretary of the Department of Health and Human Services to require that Genzyme issue licenses under terms that are reasonable under the circumstances and, if Genzyme refuses the request, to grant such licenses itself. The petitioners request that NIH use this authority to require Genzyme to issue an open license for use of the Fabrazyme patents subject to this petition. [An open license is a nonexclusive license that is available to any petitioner willing to meet standard nondiscriminatory terms.]

Right to Manufacture and Export World-Wide

The open license should include the rights to use the patents to make, sell, use, import or export Fabrazyme as either a standalone product or as a component. Additionally, the license should include access to the cell line producing Fabrazyme and any technical know-how developed in conjunction with producing the drug in order to expedite production and reduce duplication of efforts. The license should include the right to export Fabrazyme to overseas markets. These rights are necessary to restore access not only in the U.S. but also meet global treatment needs.

Royalty to the Patent Owner

The petitioners propose that the open license provide to the owners of the Fabrazyme patents a combined royalty of 5 percent of the net sales of the Fabrazyme. The five percent royalty is roughly equal to the average US pharmaceutical royalty payment, as reported by the pharmaceutical manufacturing sector to the US Internal Revenue Service. This is more than adequate given that each of the patents in question were invented through a government funding agreement, and that Genzyme has earned approximately $431 million from the sale of Fabrazyme in 2009 alone.

Conclusion

The Bayh–Dole Act provides the Federal Government with the tools it needs to address the current public health crisis caused by Genzyme's drug rationing. Petitioners request that the march-in provisions of the Bayh–Dole Act be immediately implemented in order to restore access to critical treatment for Fabry disease victims.

National Institutes of Health Office of the Director

Determination in the Case of Fabrazyme® Manufactured by Genzyme Corporation
December 1, 2010

Based upon the information currently available, NIH has determined that a march-in proceeding under 35 U.S.C. § 203(a)(2) is not warranted at the present time because any licensing plan that might result from such a proceeding would not, in our judgment, address the problem identified by the Requestors. A march-in proceeding resulting in the grant of patent use rights to a third party will not increase the supply of Fabrazyme in the short term because years of clinical studies and regulatory approval would be required before another manufacturer's product could become available to meet patients' needs in the United States. NIH has no information that a company is expecting imminent FDA approval of a competing version of an agalsidase beta product. Secondarily, the '804 patent is not an obstacle for a company to conduct clinical trials in the United States in furtherance of regulatory approval for a competing drug, because such clinical trials are exempt from infringement under the Hatch–Waxman statutory safe harbor provision (35 U.S.C. § 271(e)). Finally, Genzyme has indicated that it expects the production of Fabrazyme to be back to full supply levels in the first half of 2011. Genzyme, appears to be working diligently and in good faith to address the Fabrazyme shortage.

Notwithstanding the foregoing, NIH will continue to carefully monitor the shortage of Fabrazyme and will re-evaluate this determination immediately upon receiving any information that suggests progress toward restoring the supply of Fabrazyme to meet patient demand is not proceeding as represented.

Further, in the unlikely event that NIH receives information that a third party has a viable plan to obtain FDA approval to market agalsidase beta during the period in which Genzyme is not able to meet patient demand for Fabrazyme, and, that third party requires commercial rights to the '804 patent in order to proceed with its plan, NIH will immediately re-consider its decision to exercise its march-in authority. Toward this end, NIH has asked Mount Sinai to: (1) provide monthly reports on the status of Genzyme's progress toward addressing the supply shortage of Fabrazyme until such time as U.S. Fabry patients' needs have been met; (2) provide a copy of Genzyme's reports on the allotment of Fabrazyme to Fabry patients; and, (3) notify NIH within two business days after receiving any request from a third party for a license to the '804 patent to market agalsidase beta during the Fabrazyme shortage.

Francis S. Collins, M.D., Ph.D.
Director National Institutes of Health

Notes and Questions

1. *The Fabrazyme dispute.* Which of the petitioners' arguments for march-in rights do you feel was the strongest? Why did NIH decline to exercise its march-in rights with respect to Fabrazyme? Did NIH address all of the petitioners' concerns? Based on the petitioners' description, do you think that the Fabrazyme case was similar to or different than the previous cases in which NIH declined to exercise march-in rights?[16]

2. *March-in and royalties.* The petitioners requested that NIH require Genzyme to license other manufacturers to make and sell Fabrazyme. The requested license was royalty-bearing. That is, any other manufacturer who operated under the march-in license would be required to pay a royalty to Genzyme. Why did the petitioners request a royalty-bearing license? Wouldn't a royalty-free license have been more likely to induce other manufacturers to begin production of Fabrazyme? How did the petitioners arrive at a proposed royalty rate of 5 percent? Were they required to propose a particular royalty rate under the Bayh–Dole Act? Do you think that NIH would have been more likely to exercise its march-in rights had the petitioners proposed a 10 percent royalty rate? Would Genzyme have been less likely to object?

3. *March-in and the market.* In a 1997 petition, CellPro, the manufacturer of a stem cell separation device, asked that NIH exercise its march-in rights against patents licensed by Johns Hopkins University to the drug company Baxter, which CellPro allegedly infringed. NIH offered some insights into its reluctance to exercise those rights:

We are wary ... of forced attempts to influence the marketplace for the benefit of a single company, particularly when such actions may have far-reaching repercussions on many

---

[16] A concise summary of march-in cases brought through 2016 can be found in John R. Thomas, *March In Rights Under the Bayh Dole Act*, Congressional Research Service, August 22, 2016. Links to many of the primary documents in these cases are available at www.keionline.org/cl/march-in-royalty-free.

companies' and investors' future willingness to invest in federally funded medical technologies. The patent system, with its resultant predictability for investment and commercial development, is the means chosen by Congress for ensuring the development and dissemination of new and useful technologies. It has proven to be an effective means for the development of health care technologies. In exercising its authorities under the Bayh–Dole Act, NIH is mindful of the broader public health implications of a march-in proceeding, including the potential loss of new health care products yet to be developed from federally funded research.

To what degree should a federal agency take market factors into account when deciding whether or not to exercise march-in rights? Does it matter whether all of the statutory conditions for exercising those rights are met?

4. *March-in rights and drug pricing.* In 2016, 51 members of Congress asked the NIH to use its march-in rights under the Bayh–Dole Act to rein in the cost of prescription drugs. As explained by Rep. Lloyd Doggett (D-TX), "When drugs are developed with taxpayer funds, the government can and should act to bring relief from out-of-control drug pricing … There is a difference between earning a profit and profiteering. The Administration should use every tool it has to rein in the practice of pricing a drug at whatever the sick, suffering, or dying will pay." How could NIH's exercise of march-in rights influence drug pricing? Not surprisingly, NIH declined to act on this request. Do you agree?

5. *What's a licensee to do?* Suppose that your company is negotiating an exclusive license for an experimental new drug candidate with a major research university. Assuming that the university received at least some federal funding in support of its research, should you be concerned about march-in rights? What steps might you take in order to address those concerns?

6. *Are march-in rights illusory?* To date, no federal agency has exercised its march-in rights under the Bayh–Dole Act. Moreover, there is no practical legal or administrative mechanism available to challenge or appeal an agency determination not to exercise those rights. Should there be? What mechanism(s) might you suggest to give greater force to the prospect of march-in rights?

7. *Compulsory licensing.* If exercised by a government agency, march-in rights under the Bayh–Dole Act can require a patent licensee to grant sublicenses to third-party manufacturers, or require a patent holder to license additional manufacturers to operate under that patent. These actions are broadly classified as types of "compulsory licensing" – governmental acts that mandate the licensing of IP to others. There are many types of compulsory licenses in addition to Bayh–Dole march-in rights. In Section 16.1 we discuss various statutory compulsory licenses for musical copyrights. But perhaps the most controversial form of compulsory licensing arises when governments in the developing world have authorized local manufacturers to practice under patents held by foreign drug companies, usually to create an inexpensive version of a drug for local use. To date, the governments of Thailand, Brazil, South Africa and India, among others, have issued compulsory licenses under drug patents held by companies in the United States and Europe. Such compulsory licenses are generally not granted gratis, however, and a royalty is often paid to the foreign patent holder. How should the level of such a royalty be determined? What arguments for and against such compulsory licenses can be made?

TECHNOLOGY TRANSFER FROM US FEDERAL LABORATORIES

The US federal government operates approximately 300 different scientific laboratories across the country. These federal laboratories conduct research across a broad range of civilian and military disciplines, including nuclear physics, materials science, astronomy, meteorology, geology, oceanography and biomedicine. Like universities, federal labs patent many of their inventions and seek to license them to the commercial sector.

Federal statutes, including portions of the Bayh–Dole Act, place limitations on the ability of federal labs to license their technology on an exclusive basis. In particular, 35 U.S.C. § 209(a) requires that: (1) any such exclusive license must be a "reasonable and necessary incentive to call forth the investment capital and expenditures needed to bring the invention to practical application; or otherwise promote the invention's utilization by the public"; (2) the public must be served by granting the license, "as indicated by the applicant's intentions, plans, and ability to bring the invention to practical application or otherwise promote the invention's utilization by the public"; and (3) the scope of exclusivity is no greater than reasonably necessary to achieve these goals. The exclusive licensee must commit "to achieve practical application of the invention within a reasonable time." The agency must also ensure that "granting the license will not tend to substantially lessen competition or create or maintain a violation of the Federal antitrust laws."

FIGURE 14.4 Federal laboratories like Sandia National Laboratory in New Mexico have active technology licensing and commercialization programs.

14.3 LICENSING UNIVERSITY TECHNOLOGY

14.3.1 *The Role of the TTO*

In order to put university research to commercial use, universities must license or "transfer" technology to the private sector. To do this, most universities have established technology transfer offices (TTOs) responsible for evaluating the commercial potential of each new university invention, making decisions regarding patenting, identifying appropriate commercial partners, negotiating suitable license and option agreements, and then distributing the resulting royalties and other economic gains within the university.[17] The TTO typically employs individuals

---

[17] Some universities refer to their TTO as a technology licensing office (TLO), a technology commercialization office (TCO), an office of technology ventures and commercialization (TVC) or, in the case of the University of Utah, the "Partners for Innovation, Ventures, Outreach & Technology (PIVOT) Center."

with backgrounds in business, law and technology. While most universities, including research powerhouses such as Stanford, MIT and Harvard, operate their TTOs as internal units, sometimes falling under the jurisdiction of the university counsel or the office of the provost and sometimes operating semi-autonomously, others have elected to establish independent entities to manage IP emerging from university labs. The most notable of these is the University of Wisconsin-Madison, whose Wisconsin Alumni Research Foundation (WARF) was established in 1925 and today enters into approximately 100 commercial licensing agreements per year. It is likely that any company seeking to negotiate a license agreement with a university will deal with its TTO.[18]

14.3.2 *Nine Points for University Licensing*

In many ways, academic license agreements are no different than the ordinary business-to-business license agreements discussed elsewhere in this book. Likewise, the contractual terms of academic license agreements are largely those that are described in Part II. However, the public and educational missions of universities, the traditional role of universities as centers for open, scholarly interaction, and pressures from internal constituencies including students, researchers and alumni have led universities to observe a range of special considerations when licensing their IP.

In 2007, eleven major research universities together with the Association of American Medical Colleges (AAMC) released a document setting forth nine principles relevant to the licensing of academic technology "in the public interest and for society's benefit" (the "Nine Points Document").[19] This nonbinding set of principles relates not only to the terms of academic–industry licensing agreements, but also to issues surrounding enforcement of IP, export controls and conflicts of interest. The Nine Points document has been adopted by more than one hundred academic and research funding institutions around the world and has influenced norms and practices around university technology licensing more broadly. The Nine Points are summarized below and those that impact transactional agreements are discussed in greater detail in the following section.

IN THE PUBLIC INTEREST: NINE POINTS TO CONSIDER IN LICENSING UNIVERSITY TECHNOLOGY

MARCH 6, 2007

1. Universities should reserve the right to practice licensed inventions and to allow other nonprofit and governmental organizations to do so.
2. Exclusive licenses should be structured in a manner that encourages technology development and use.
3. Strive to minimize the licensing of "future improvements."
4. Universities should anticipate and help to manage technology transfer-related conflicts of interest.
5. Ensure broad access to research tools.

---

[18] For a discussion of the structure and role of university TTOs, see Carter-Johnson, *supra* note 5, at 12–19.
[19] The Nine Points document can be found at www.autm.net/AUTMMain/media/Advocacy/Documents/Points_to_Consider.pdf.

6. Enforcement action should be carefully considered.
7. Be mindful of export regulations.
8. Be mindful of the implications of working with patent aggregators.
9. Consider including provisions that address unmet needs, such as those of neglected patient populations or geographic areas, giving particular attention to improved therapeutics, diagnostics and agricultural technologies for the developing world.

14.3.3 *University Reserved Rights*

Point 1 of the Nine Points emphasizes one of the most important issues for universities when licensing their IP – the university must retain the right to use the licensed IP for its own internal research and educational purposes. Thus, whether the IP covers a small molecule drug target or an online safety training module, the university will retain the right for its faculty to continue to use and modify that IP in their own research and teaching activities.

This right is particularly important because, contrary to the beliefs of many academic faculty members, US law provides no inherent right to use IP for noncommercial research purposes.[20] And while limited classroom reproduction of copyrighted materials may be permitted as "fair use" under the Copyright Act (17 U.S.C. § 107(1)), there is no similar exception for patents. As a result, universities are particularly cautious to retain sufficient internal rights when granting third parties exclusive rights to their IP (this is obviously not an issue when the university only grants nonexclusive rights to third parties).

While the general principle of university retained rights is not objectionable to most exclusive licensees, the scope of the contractual exclusion can sometimes cause concern. Thus, it is one thing to permit the licensing university to retain the right to use licensed IP for its own faculty's research and educational purposes. But what about other academic institutions? The Nine Points document recommends that universities reserve noncommercial research rights not only for themselves, but for all other nonprofit and governmental organizations (p. 2).[21] Moreover, many university researchers collaborate with the private sector. Should a university's commercial collaboration partners also be permitted to conduct research using IP that has been exclusively licensed to someone else? Some university license agreements seek to retain rights that are this broad, but potential exclusive licensees may wish to seek limitations, particularly if they are concerned about competitors gaining access to university-generated technology that they have paid to develop and/or license.

14.3.4 *Publication Rights*

Another important right that universities seek to preserve in licensing agreements is the right of their researchers to publish academic papers and articles covering their discoveries. This right to disseminate knowledge is fundamental to the educational missions of universities, and generally cannot be waived.

---

[20] *See Madey v. Duke Univ.*, 307 F.3d 1351 (Fed. Cir. 2002) (holding that Duke had no right to continue to use a patented experimental laser apparatus developed by a former faculty member because the university, despite its nonprofit, educational mission, had numerous "commercial" goals such as attracting students and grant funding).

[21] Following the adoption of the Nine Points document in 2007, university licenses have notably increased their reservations of rights for all non-profit and governmental entities. See Jorge L. Contreras, *In the Public Interest: University Technology Transfer and the Nine Points Document – An Empirical Assessment*, U.C. Irvine L. Rev. (2023) (quantifying this shift).

EXAMPLE: PUBLICATION RIGHTS

Licensee acknowledges that Institution is dedicated to free scholarly exchange and to public dissemination of the results of its scholarly activities. Institution and its faculty and employees shall have the right to publish, disseminate or otherwise disclose any information relating to their research activities including, in Institution's sole discretion, information relating to the Inventions, subject to Institution's obligation to preserve the confidentiality of Licensee's Confidential Information [1].

Institution will submit the manuscript of any proposed publication to Licensee at least 30 days before publication, and Licensee shall have the right to review and comment upon such proposed publication in order to protect Licensee's Confidential Information [2]. Upon Licensee's request, publication may be delayed up to 60 additional days to enable Licensee to secure adequate intellectual property protection for the Inventions. [3].

DRAFTING NOTES

[1] *Confidential information* – in some cases, a corporate partner will provide a university with data that it considers to be confidential. This information should not be disclosed in a published paper.

[2] *Review and comment* – academics will often object to any review of their scholarly work by corporate partners, but it is increasingly common for corporate researchers to collaborate with academic scientists on research projects and to co-author any resulting papers for publication.

[3] *Delay for patent filing* – if a discovery is patentable, and if the corporate partner has the responsibility for filing patent applications, then it may seek to delay a publication that would otherwise disclose an invention in a manner that would limit patentability within the United States or elsewhere.[22] If the university has responsibility for patent prosecution, then its internal policies likely contain such a delay mechanism as well.

14.3.5 *Limiting Exclusivity*

As discussed in Section 7.1, there are valid commercial justifications for granting exclusive license rights: without exclusive rights to a particular discovery or invention, a commercial partner may not be willing to invest the substantial amounts necessary to conduct product development, complete clinical trials, and otherwise bring a product to market. Universities recognize this need, but, as the Nine Points document reminds them, "[u]niversities need to be mindful of the impact of granting overly broad exclusive rights and should strive to grant just those rights necessary to encourage development of the technology" (p. 2). The Nine Points document thus urges universities to grant exclusive licenses only when needed in order to ensure the practical application of an invention.

Moreover, the document (in Points 2, 3, 5 and 9) suggests several strategies that universities can use to soften the effect of exclusive rights:

- requiring the exclusive licensee to meet "diligence" or performance milestones toward commercial development (see Section 8.5);

- requiring the exclusive licensee to grant sublicenses to third parties to address unmet market or public health needs;
- reserving a right in the university to grant licenses to third parties to address unmet market or public health needs (akin to a "march-in" right);
- granting a company the exclusive right to *sell* a product, but not to *make* or *use* it (thus freeing others, including other research institutions, to make their own noncommercial, in-house versions of a product);
- excluding from the scope of the exclusive license grant "clinical research, professional education and training, use by public health authorities, independent validation of test results or quality verification and/or control"; and
- limiting exclusive rights to existing patents and patent applications, and not automatically licensing improvement or follow-on inventions.

The Nine Points document also echoes the advice of NIH in urging patent holders to avoid granting exclusive rights with respect to broadly applicable research tools and methods (see Section 7.1).

14.3.6 *Socially Responsible Licensing*

Since the 1980s there has been mounting public pressure to expand the availability of patented technologies, particularly so-called "essential medicines," to those who could not otherwise afford them, especially in the developing world. When the HIV antiretroviral drug Zerit, developed and patented by researchers at Yale University, became a critical part of the AIDS treatment regimen, Yale students and faculty, together with the popular press, exerted sufficient pressure on the university's exclusive licensee Bristol-Myers Squibb (BMS) to persuade the company in 2001 to make the drug available at nominal cost to patients in Africa.[23] Since the Zerit episode, an increasing number of universities have declared their support for such humanitarian or "socially responsible" licensing. Point 9 of the Nine Points document refers explicitly to a university's "social compact with society" and urges universities to structure their licensing arrangements so as to ensure that underprivileged populations have access to medical innovations. In 2009 a group of six major research universities endorsed an even stronger statement committing that their IP would not "become a barrier to essential health-related technologies needed by patients in developing countries."[24]

Potential licensing structures that reflect socially responsible licensing by universities, as suggested by the experience of essential medicines, include

- excluding developing countries from exclusive license grants;
- requiring licensees to grant sublicenses to local producers in developing countries;
- retaining university private march-in rights if products are not made suitably accessible in developing countries;

[22] In the USA an inventor may file a patent application up to one year after the first public disclosure of the invention (35 U.S.C. § 102(b)(1)). In other countries, including most European countries, there is no such grace period.

[23] See A. J. Stevens & A. E. Effort, *Using Academic License Agreements to Promote Global Social Responsibility*, 85 Les Nouvelles 86 (2008).

[24] *Statement of Principles and Strategies for the Equitable Dissemination of Medical Technologies*, https://otd.harvard.edu/upload/files/Global_Access_Statement_of_Principles.pdf (endorsed by Harvard University, Yale University, Brown University, Boston University, the University of Pennsylvania, Oregon Health & Science University and AUTM).

- prohibiting the filing of corresponding patent applications in developing countries; and
- requiring that products sold in developing countries be priced on a humanitarian basis (i.e., subsidized, at-cost or no cost).

14.3.7 *Price Controls*

The last of these approaches – controls on downstream pricing – is perhaps the most controversial. Typically, IP licensees retain flexibility to price their products as they wish, based on market and competitive factors.[25] Efforts to control the prices of prescription drugs in the United States have taken many forms, though none has yet been successful. Experiments with contractual price control mechanisms were attempted as early as the 1980s, when NIH tried to rein in drug pricing by requiring a "fair pricing" clause in all of its cooperative R&D agreements ("CRADAs") with private industry.

> This mandatory contractual language, widely reviled by the pharmaceutical industry, was adopted by NIH in response to a controversy surrounding the AIDS drug AZT. The drug, which was released in 1987 by Burroughs Wellcome, bore the then-stratospheric price tag of $8,000 per year.[26] Yet, as AIDS activists were quick to point out, Burroughs Wellcome had not been the one to discover the drug nor its effectiveness against AIDS. A failed cancer treatment, AZT's potential use against AIDS was first suspected by scientists at NIH's National Cancer Institute. To encourage Burroughs to bring AZT to market, NIH allowed the company to retain full ownership of the resulting patent. But once that happened, there was no way to constrain Burroughs' pricing of the drug, and it charged what it felt the market would bear.
>
> To prevent further instances of price gouging, in 1989 NIH inserted a new fair pricing clause into all of its CRADAs, requiring that there be a "reasonable relationship between the pricing of a licensed product, the public investment in that product, and the health and safety needs of the public." But in Varmus's view, despite its worthy aims, NIH's fair pricing clause had little impact on drug pricing. Instead, it seemed to make companies reluctant to cooperate with government labs, or at least to sign agreements with them. Which would be preferable, he must have asked, a high-minded pricing policy that resulted in little or no collaboration with the government, or more collaboration without the fair pricing policy? Ever the pragmatist, in 1995, Varmus decided to eliminate the fair pricing clause from NIH's standard research agreement, reasoning that this would better "promote research that can enhance the health of the American people."[27]

Despite the failure of contractual price control mechanisms in the United States, these mechanisms have achieved some success with respect to drug pricing in the developing world. Thus, university license agreements for biomedical discoveries may include provisions requiring that the licensee, if it sells products in less developed countries, charge prices lower than those it charges in the developed world. Some licenses, such as those promulgated by the Medicines Patent Pool (see Section 6.2.3), are focused entirely on less developed countries, and are thus entirely price constrained.

---

[25] Even in the context of technical standards, well-known FRAND (fair, reasonable and nondiscriminatory) pricing requirements apply to patent *licenses* by SDO participants, not *product* sales by their licensees.

[26] Compared to today's astronomical prices for the latest gene therapy treatments, some of which can exceed $2 million, the $8,000 price tag for AZT seems quaint. Yet, at the time, the *New York Times* called AZT "the most expensive prescription drug in history" ("AZT's Inhuman Cost," *NY Times*, August 28, 1989).

[27] Jorge L. Contreras, *Association for Molecular Pathology v. Myriad Genetics: A Critical Reassessment*, 27 Mich. Tech. L. Rev.1 (2020) (most citations omitted).

Outside of the developing world, attempts to constrain pricing of end products have been less successful, though some efforts have been made. For example, in the context of IP relevant to COVID-19, twenty-two universities and other research institutions around the world have committed to granting royalty-free licenses for technologies that may help to prevent, diagnose or treat COVID-19 under a "COVID-19 Technology Access Framework."[28] As part of the Framework, the universities expect their licensees "to distribute the resulting products as widely as possible and at a low cost that allows broad accessibility." It remains to be seen whether and to what extent licenses are granted under the Framework and with what effect.

UNIVERSITY SPINOUTS

In many cases the most promising industrial licensee of a university invention is an established enterprise that is actively pursuing the development of products in a related field. Sometimes, however, established industrial partners may not exist, particularly when technologies are in new and emerging fields. In these cases, university researchers, backed by external funders, may form start-up companies to commercialize the discoveries generated by their labs. These companies are referred to as university "spinouts." According to the AUTM, 1,080 university spinouts were formed in 2018, and were the recipients of approximately 15 percent of university technology licenses granted.[29]

In addition to licenses of university IP, spinouts often make use of university-owned facilities and equipment, as well as the services of academics, technicians and graduate students. Several universities have established incubators, shared laboratory spaces and entrepreneurship labs to encourage the formation of spinout companies by faculty, staff and students.

University spinouts have attracted significant public attention in recent years, due to both the success of a handful of these ventures and the potential conflicts of interest that plague academic investigators who actively participate in corporate research. Notable university spinouts over the years have included Bose (MIT), Digital Equipment Corporation (MIT), Google (Stanford), Myriad Genetics (U. Utah), Netscape Communications (U. Illinois), Oxford Instruments (Oxford) and RSA Data Security (MIT).

Notes and Questions

1. *Surrogate licensing.* Despite the Nine Points cautionary language concerning exclusive licensing, some universities have recently been criticized for granting exclusive licenses with extremely broad fields of use to their own spinout companies. When a university effectively grants the entire set of rights with respect to an IP portfolio to a single company, Professor Jacob Sherkow and I refer to that company as a "surrogate" because it acts as a stand-in for the university, but without its public mission and charter.

   For example, the academic institutions holding the foundational patents to the CRISPR gene editing technology (University of California Berkeley and the Broad Institute, a joint venture of Harvard and MIT) each granted to a single surrogate company broad exclusive

---

[28] See https://tlo.mit.edu/engage-tlo/covid-19/covid-19-technology-access-framework.
[29] See AUTM US Licensing Activity Survey: 2018.

licenses to use CRISPR in all fields of human therapeutics across all 20,000+ human genes. This broad exclusivity, we point out, could result in serious research bottlenecks:

> Because no single company could develop, test, and market therapeutics on the basis of even a fraction of the entire human genome … it is … unlikely that any of the surrogate companies could explore a significant fraction of the potential human health applications that CRISPR could enable, even with a range of experienced commercial partners and collaborators. If an unlicensed company has the expertise and wherewithal to develop a novel human therapy using CRISPR—even if that therapy concerns a previously unexplored gene—that company might not be able to obtain the sublicense necessary to undertake this work.[30]

    Why do universities engage in surrogate licensing? Does this practice subvert the public missions of these institutions? What can be done to limit the impact of this practice on research and discovery?

2. *Improvements*. We discussed a licensee's improvements to a licensor's technology in Section 9.1. Why does the Nine Points document suggest that universities not include improvement patents in the scope of exclusive licenses? Why might a licensee feel differently? The Nine Points document (p. 4) suggests that if improvements are included within the scope of an exclusive license, they should be limited to "inventions that are dominated by the original licensed patents, as these could not be meaningfully licensed to a third party, at least within the first licensee's exclusive field." How would this limitation address potential concerns about hold-up?

3. *Ethical licensing and field restrictions*. Some academic institutions have begun to focus on constraining the activities of their licensees based on ethical principles beyond pricing and access to medicines. For example, in the area of CRISPR gene editing, the Broad Institute has limited several of its patent licenses to industrial partners on ethical grounds. In its license of CRISPR technology to Monsanto for agricultural applications, Broad is reported to have prohibited Monsanto from: "(i) performing gene drives that spread altered genes quickly through populations, which can alter ecosystems; (ii) creating sterile 'terminator' seeds, which would impose a serious financial burden on farmers who would be forced to buy them each year; and (iii) conducting research directed to the commercialization of tobacco products, which might increase the public health burden of smoking."[31] Likewise, in its license of CRISPR technology to Editas Medicines, Broad's surrogate company, Broad excludes the right "to modify human germ cells or embryos for any purpose or to modify animal cells for the creation or commercialization of organs suitable for transplantation into humans." Restrictions like these generally take the form of exclusions from the licensee's permitted field of use (FOU), rather than contractual covenants such as fair pricing requirements. Why might a licensor wish to use FOU restrictions rather than contractual covenants under these circumstances? Would there be a benefit to using both FOU restrictions and covenants?

4. *Other terms of university licensing agreements*. While the contractual issues and terms discussed in this part of the book are among the most controversial ones raised in the area of academic technology transfer, it is worth remembering that academic licensing agreements contain many other terms as well – mostly along the lines discussed in Part II. The licensing attorney, however, should be aware of some prevalent norms in university licensing agreements. For example, technology licensed under university licenses is almost always provided

---

[30] Jorge L. Contreras & Jacob S. Sherkow, *CRISPR, Surrogate Licensing, and Scientific Discovery*, 355 Science 698, 699 (2017).

[31] Christi J. Guerrini, et al., *The Rise of the Ethical License*, 35 Nature Biotech. 22, 23 (2017).

FIGURE 14.5 Tobacco plants have been genetically modified to grow larger, faster and more efficiently. The Broad Institute prohibits licensees of its CRISPR gene editing technology from using it in connection with commercialization of the tobacco plant.

as is, without warranties of any kind (except, in some cases, as to ownership). A university will almost never indemnify a licensee. Sublicensing generally requires the consent of the university. Progress reports and milestones will usually be required. The governing law and forum of the agreement are almost always those of the university's home jurisdiction. If challenged, university attorneys will often argue that these terms are nonnegotiable, either due to strict university policy, state law, the Bayh–Dole Act or some combination of these factors. This positioning can sometimes be frustrating, but it is a reality that must be faced when dealing with academic institutions.

5. *Impact of the Nine Points.* One recent study of university licensing agreements executed before and after the Nine Points document reveals that the document had very little impact on actual university licensing practices, and that universities continued to use essentially the same licensing documents both before and after signing the Nine Points document.[32] What do you think these findings suggest about university technology transfer?

14.4 SPONSORED RESEARCH: DOLLARS AND OPTIONS

Under the traditional – some would say idealized – model of academic research, researchers select projects to pursue based on some combination of intellectual curiosity, unanswered questions in the field, and the scientific impact of their discoveries. Oftentimes, this research is funded by grants from the federal and state government, as well as private foundations. However, it is largely directed by researchers themselves.

In reality, much research that is conducted on the campuses of modern academic institutions is driven by corporate programs that use universities as outsourced R&D contractors. As Cynthia Cannady explains,

In the United States, research institutions rely increasingly on private research sponsorships, as a number of factors coincide: constraints on public funding, ambitious research agendas and university development, and physical plant expansion. Even with massive public funding of

---

[32] See Jorge L. Contreras and Jessica Maupin, *"In the Public Interest": University Technology Transfer and the Nine Points Document – An Empirical Assessment* 13 U. Cal. Irvine L. Rev. (2023).

research in the United States, there is a financial codependency between research institutions and private sponsors that increases reliance on the sponsored research model of contract.[33]

Sponsored research arrangements are effectively service contracts under which a company pays an academic institution to perform specified research activities and report the results back to the company. The services are almost always led by a particular senior investigator. If the company is a university spinout, the investigator will often have an additional consulting or founding role at the company.

University sponsored research agreements resemble many of the other technology development and service agreements discussed elsewhere in this volume. One significant difference, however, relates to IP ownership. As discussed in Section 9.2, it is typical that when one company (the client) engages a second company (the developer) to conduct R&D, the results of that R&D are owned by the client, not the developer. A university sponsored research agreement is usually different. Whether because of the Bayh–Dole Act or simply because the outcome of basic research is difficult to predict, the company sponsoring research at a university typically does not automatically obtain ownership of the resulting IP.

If the company is a university spinout that already has an exclusive license covering a particular university lab's output, then the IP generated by the sponsored research arrangement will often fall under that existing agreement. Myriad Genetics offers a good illustration of this principle.

THE MYRIAD STORY: PRELUDE TO DISCOVERY

Myriad Genetics was formed in 1991 by Dr. Mark Skolnick, a genetic epidemiologist at the University of Utah, and Peter Meldrum, a local investor. The company's goal was to locate the *BRCA1* gene that was suspected to have a high correlation with certain cases of breast cancer, and then to develop, patent and commercialize a diagnostic test for the gene.

The first thing that the new company did was enter into an exclusive license agreement with the university. Under the agreement, Myriad obtained exclusive rights to any discoveries made by Skolnick's academic lab in the area of breast cancer genetics. Whatever the lab discovered concerning *BRCA1* – or any other breast cancer gene – would be patented by the university, as required by the Bayh–Dole Act. But, practically (and legally) speaking, a university couldn't develop a commercial testing service and offer it to the public. That could only be done by a company, and, in this case, the company would be Myriad. It didn't matter that Skolnick hadn't discovered anything yet, or that his lab hadn't even begun to look for *BRCA1*. The company would simply acquire all future rights to the gene whenever it was discovered.

In exchange for this license, Myriad agreed to pay the university $250,000 to fund the lab's research, cover all of the university's patenting expenses, pay the university a 1 percent royalty on the company's future *BRCA1* testing revenue and grant the university a 2 percent ownership stake in the company.

Researchers from Myriad, the university and other collaborators isolated and patented the *BRCA1* gene in 1994. Over the lifetime of the *BRCA* patents, which were cut short by a Supreme Court ruling in 2013, Myriad paid the university approximately $40 million.[34]

---

[33] Cynthia Cannady, Technology Licensing and Development Agreements 355–56 (Oxford Univ. Press, 2013).

[34] For a detailed account of Myriad genetics and its dealings with the University of Utah, see Jorge L. Contreras, The Genome Defense: Inside the Epic Legal Battle to Determine Who Owns Your DNA (Algonquin Books, 2021).

If, however, research at a university is sponsored by an established company without an existing license to the university's technology, then the company may receive an *option* to obtain a license to the results of that research. An example option clause is given here.

EXAMPLE: SPONSORED RESEARCH AGREEMENT

Option Clause

a) In consideration of Sponsor's funding of the Research Program, Institution hereby grants to Sponsor, and Sponsor accepts, an option to obtain a license to all or any portion of the developed IPR (the "Option"). Sponsor shall have sixty (60) days from the receipt of Institution's notice that it has filed a patent application covering any developed IPR to provide Institution with written notice of its election to exercise the Option with respect to such IPR. Sponsor's failure to so notify Institution within this time period shall be deemed to be an election by Sponsor not to secure a license to such IPR, in which case Institution shall have the unrestricted right to license such IPR to third parties.

b) Should Sponsor elect to exercise its Option for any IPR, the parties agree promptly to commence negotiations, in good faith, of an exclusive License Agreement to be entered into no later than three (3) months after the date of the exercise of the Option. Such License Agreement shall take into consideration the relative contributions of both parties, including the support provided by Sponsor to the Research Program and shall include at least the following provisions:

   i. the exclusive license to Sponsor of the right to exploit the IPR in [all fields] for the duration of such IPR;

   ii an up-front license fee,

   iii. ongoing royalty payments,

   iv. reimbursement by Sponsor of past, present, and future Patent Costs,

   v. the right to grant sublicenses,

   vi. a summary of a commercial development plan for the IPR,

   vii. the right of Institution to terminate the license should Sponsor not meet specified milestones, and

   viii. indemnity and insurance provisions satisfactory to Institution's insurance carrier.

   If the parties do not execute a License Agreement by such date, Institution shall be free to offer the IPR for licensing to third parties, but for a period of one (1) year after failure to reach an agreement Institution shall not license the subject IPR to any third party on terms more favorable than those last offered to Sponsor without first offering such terms to Sponsor.

c) If Sponsor elects not to exercise its Option for any IPR pursuant to Paragraph (a), Sponsor shall have no further rights to such IPR. Notwithstanding the foregoing, Sponsor's failure to exercise the Option with respect to any particular IPR shall not limit Sponsor's rights with respect to any other IPR developed hereunder.

Notes and Questions

1. *Myriad – sponsored research, version 2.* As noted above, Myriad Genetics sponsored breast cancer genetic research conducted in Mark Skolnick's lab at the University of Utah. But Myriad was also the *recipient* of sponsored research funding, in much larger amounts, from pharmaceutical firms. Its first research sponsor was pharmaceutical giant Eli Lilly, developer of the blockbuster antidepressant Prozac. Like many large drug companies, Lilly had become interested in genetics during the 1980s. It believed that Myriad's foray into breast cancer genetics offered a promising opportunity to explore potential gene-based therapeutics. In 1992 (still two years before the *BRCA1* gene was located) Lilly entered into a sponsored research agreement with Myriad. Lilly agreed to pay Myriad $1.8 million over three years, invest another $1 million in Myriad's stock and pay Myriad a royalty of 4 percent on sales of any *BRCA1*-based drugs that Lilly developed. In exchange, Myriad granted Lilly exclusive rights to any *BRCA1*-related discoveries made by Myriad or the university, but solely in the field of breast cancer therapeutics. Myriad thus reserved for itself the sole right to exploit *BRCA1* in the diagnostics market (it sold a third company the right to make test kits – a business that never materialized).

   Why did Myriad find it advantageous to split the field into three different subfields? Why didn't the University of Utah, which owned several of the underlying patents, limit Myriad's original license to the diagnostics subfield? In other words, why did the university allow Myriad to control the therapeutic and test kit fields when Myriad had no intention of entering those markets?

2. *Sponsored research variants.* Why do sponsored research agreements look so different depending on whether the sponsor is a university spinout company versus an established company?

3. *Options and incomplete agreements.* The sample option clause shown above commits the parties to negotiate a license agreement, but only outlines a few terms of the license agreement in advance. Why aren't these terms specified in greater detail? Better still, why don't the parties attach a complete license agreement to the option, which could be exercised simply by signing the license agreement and tendering the first payment?

14.5 MATERIAL TRANSFER

Often, scientific research involves the use of unique or novel materials – cell lines, DNA, tissue samples, model organisms, plant specimens, fossilized remains, geologic core and soil samples, lunar minerals, historic artifacts, new polymers, alloys, fibers, chemical compounds and the like. In order to access such materials, researchers must either come to the place where they are stored, or request a sample for use in their own laboratory. If materials are not overly fragile or unique, many researchers are willing to send samples for others to use, but only under certain conditions. Those conditions are often set out in material transfer agreements (MTAs).

These MTAs vary in length and complexity, depending on the type of material in question. Soil samples taken from a large contaminated field might be supplied under relatively minimal terms and conditions, whereas DNA from living human subjects would usually be subject to much more stringent restrictions. The complexity of MTAs also depends on the parties involved. Generally, MTAs between academic institutions are relatively lightweight, but complications can arise when materials come from the private sector. As one National Academies report notes, "private companies often make demands that researchers—or their technology licensing offices—balk at. A company might, for instance, ask researchers to hold off in publishing their results to give it a head start in applying the results. Or it might insist on rights to an exclusive license on any invention or discovery made using its materials."[35] Do you understand why a university might find provisions like these to be objectionable?

As noted by Dr. Tania Bubela and colleagues, "Researchers commonly express frustration with institutional processes. Surveys and interview-based studies of researchers have come to the conclusion that access to research reagents is hampered by negotiations over MTAs, whose complexity rarely reflects the value to the institution of the materials to be shared."[36]

One way to simplify the MTA process is to use a standardized set of MTAs. The NIH was among the first institutions to regularize the use of MTAs in 1995. As Bubela et al. explain:

> These policies were, in part, a response to restrictions over access to two transgenic mouse technologies: OncoMouse, a mouse strain with a genetic predisposition to cancer, developed by researchers at Harvard and exclusively licensed by DuPont; and Cre-lox, a technology for generating conditional mouse mutants, developed by DuPont researchers. In both cases, the NIH stepped in to negotiate access and distribution on less restrictive terms than the original MTAs proposed by DuPont.[37]

Below are excerpts from two of NIH's standard MTAs, one for general purposes, and one geared toward biological materials. As you read these two documents, consider how they differ and why.

SIMPLE LETTER AGREEMENT (SLA) FOR THE TRANSFER OF MATERIALS

In response to Recipient's request for the Material, the Provider asks that the Recipient and the Recipient Scientist agree to the following before the Recipient receives the Material:

1. The above Material is the property of the Provider and is made available as a service to the research community.
2. This Material Is Not for Use in Human Subjects.
3. The Material will be used for teaching or not-for-profit research purposes only.
4. The Material will not be further distributed to others without the Provider's written consent. The Recipient shall refer any request for the Material to the Provider. To the extent supplies are available, the Provider or the Provider Scientist agree to make the Material available, under a separate Simple Letter Agreement to other scientists for teaching or not-for-profit research purposes only.
5. The Recipient agrees to acknowledge the source of the Material in any publications reporting use of it.
6. Any Material delivered pursuant to this Agreement is understood to be experimental in nature and may have hazardous properties. THE PROVIDER MAKES NO REPRESENTATIONS AND EXTENDS NO WARRANTIES OF ANY KIND, EITHER EXPRESSED OR IMPLIED. THERE ARE NO EXPRESS OR IMPLIED

---

[35] National Research Council, Finding the Path: Issues of Access to Research Resources 6 (Nat'l Acad. Press, 1999).

[36] Tania Bubela, Jenilee Guebert & Amrita Mishra, *Use and Misuse of Material Transfer Agreements: Lessons in Proportionality from Research, Repositories, and Litigation*, 13 PLOS Biology e1002060 at 2 (2015).

[37] Id. at 3.

WARRANTIES OF MERCHANTABILITY OR FITNESS FOR A PARTICULAR PURPOSE, OR THAT THE USE OF THE MATERIAL WILL NOT INFRINGE ANY PATENT, COPYRIGHT, TRADEMARK, OR OTHER PROPRIETARY RIGHTS. Unless prohibited by law, Recipient assumes all liability for claims for damages against it by third parties which may arise from the use, storage or disposal of the Material except that, to the extent permitted by law, the Provider shall be liable to the Recipient when the damage is caused by the gross negligence or willful misconduct of the Provider.

7. The Recipient agrees to use the Material in compliance with all applicable statutes and regulations.

8. The Material is provided at no cost, or with an optional transmittal fee solely to reimburse the Provider for its preparation and distribution costs. If a fee is requested, the amount will be indicated here: _____.

THE UNIFORM BIOLOGICAL MATERIAL TRANSFER AGREEMENT (UBMTA)
MARCH 8, 1995

1. The Provider retains ownership of the Material, including any Material contained or incorporated in Modifications.

2. The Recipient retains ownership of: (a) Modifications (except that, the Provider retains ownership rights to the Material included therein), and (b) those substances created through the use of the Material or Modifications, but which are not Progeny,[38] Unmodified Derivatives or Modifications (i.e., do not contain the original Material, Progeny, Unmodified Derivatives). If either 2(a) or 2(b) results from the collaborative efforts of the Provider and the Recipient, joint ownership may be negotiated.

3. The Recipient and the Recipient Scientist agree that the Material:

   a) is to be used solely for teaching and academic research purposes;
   b) will not be used in human subjects, in clinical trials, or for diagnostic purposes involving human subjects without the written consent of the Provider;
   c) is to be used only at the Recipient organization and only in the Recipient Scientist's laboratory under the direction of the Recipient Scientist or others working under his/her direct supervision; and
   d) will not be transferred to anyone else within the Recipient organization without the prior written consent of the Provider.

4. The Recipient and the Recipient Scientist agree to refer to the Provider any request for the Material from anyone other than those persons working under the Recipient Scientist's direct supervision. To the extent supplies are available, the Provider or the Provider Scientist agrees to make the Material available, under a separate implementing letter to this Agreement or other agreement having terms consistent with the terms of this

---

[38] "Progeny" means unmodified descendant from the Material, such as virus from virus, cell from cell, or organism from organism.

Agreement, to other scientists (at least those at Nonprofit Organization(s)) who wish to replicate the Recipient Scientist's research; provided that such other scientists reimburse the Provider for any costs relating to the preparation and distribution of the Material.

5. a) The Recipient and/or the Recipient Scientist shall have the right, without restriction, to distribute substances created by the Recipient through the use of the Original Material only if those substances are not Progeny, Unmodified Derivatives, or Modifications.

    b) Under a separate implementing letter to this Agreement (or an agreement at least as protective of the Provider's rights), the Recipient may distribute Modifications to Nonprofit Organization(s) for research and teaching purposes only.

    c) Without written consent from the Provider, the Recipient and/or the Recipient Scientist may NOT provide Modifications for Commercial Purposes.[39] It is recognized by the Recipient that such Commercial Purposes may require a commercial license from the Provider and the Provider has no obligation to grant a commercial license to its ownership interest in the Material incorporated in the Modifications. Nothing in this paragraph, however, shall prevent the Recipient from granting commercial licenses under the Recipient's intellectual property rights claiming such Modifications, or methods of their manufacture or their use.

6. The Recipient acknowledges that the Material is or may be the subject of a patent application. Except as provided in this Agreement, no express or implied licenses or other rights are provided to the Recipient under any patents, patent applications, trade secrets or other proprietary rights of the Provider, including any altered forms of the Material made by the Provider. In particular, no express or implied licenses or other rights are provided to use the Material, Modifications, or any related patents of the Provider for Commercial Purposes.

7. If the Recipient desires to use or license the Material or Modifications for Commercial Purposes, the Recipient agrees, in advance of such use, to negotiate in good faith with the Provider to establish the terms of a commercial license. It is understood by the Recipient that the Provider shall have no obligation to grant such a license to the Recipient, and may grant exclusive or non-exclusive commercial licenses to others, or sell or assign all or part of the rights in the Material to any third party(ies), subject to any pre-existing rights held by others and obligations to the Federal Government.

8. The Recipient is free to file patent application(s) claiming inventions made by the Recipient through the use of the Material but agrees to notify the Provider upon filing a patent application claiming Modifications or method(s) of manufacture or use(s) of the Material.

9. Any Material delivered pursuant to this Agreement is understood to be experimental in nature and may have hazardous properties. THE PROVIDER MAKES NO

---

[39] "Commercial Purposes" means the sale, lease, license, or other transfer of the Material or Modifications to a for-profit organization. Commercial Purposes shall also include uses of the Material or Modifications by any organization, including Recipient, to perform contract research, to screen compound libraries, to produce or manufacture products for general sale, or to conduct research activities that result in any sale, lease, license, or transfer of the Material or Modifications to a for-profit organization. However, industrially sponsored academic research shall not be considered a use of the Material or Modifications for Commercial Purposes *per se*, unless any of the above conditions of this definition are met.

REPRESENTATIONS AND EXTENDS NO WARRANTIES OF ANY KIND, EITHER EXPRESSED OR IMPLIED. THERE ARE NO EXPRESS OR IMPLIED WARRANTIES OF MERCHANTABILITY OR FITNESS FOR A PARTICULAR PURPOSE, OR THAT THE USE OF THE MATERIAL WILL NOT INFRINGE ANY PATENT, COPYRIGHT, TRADEMARK, OR OTHER PROPRIETARY RIGHTS.

10. Except to the extent prohibited by law, the Recipient assumes all liability for damages which may arise from its use, storage or disposal of the Material. The Provider will not be liable to the Recipient for any loss, claim or demand made by the Recipient, or made against the Recipient by any other party, due to or arising from the use of the Material by the Recipient, except to the extent permitted by law when caused by the gross negligence or willful misconduct of the Provider.

11. This agreement shall not be interpreted to prevent or delay publication of research findings resulting from the use of the Material or the Modifications. The Recipient Scientist agrees to provide appropriate acknowledgement of the source of the Material in all publications.

12. The Recipient agrees to use the Material in compliance with all applicable statutes and regulations, including Public Health Service and National Institutes of Health regulations and guidelines such as, for example, those relating to research involving the use of animals or recombinant DNA.

13. This Agreement will terminate on the earliest of the following dates: (a) when the Material becomes generally available from third parties, for example, through reagent catalogs or public depositories or (b) on completion of the Recipient's current research with the Material, or (c) on thirty (30) days written notice by either party to the other, or (d) on the date specified in an implementing letter, provided that:

    i. if termination should occur under 13(a), the Recipient shall be bound to the Provider by the least restrictive terms applicable to the Material obtained from the then-available sources; and

    ii. if termination should occur under 13(b) or (d) above, the Recipient will discontinue its use of the Material and will, upon direction of the Provider, return or destroy any remaining Material. The Recipient, at its discretion, will also either destroy the Modifications or remain bound by the terms of this agreement as they apply to Modifications; and

    iii. in the event the Provider terminates this Agreement under 13(c) other than for breach of this Agreement or for cause such as an imminent health risk or patent infringement, the Provider will defer the effective date of termination for a period of up to one year, upon request from the Recipient, to permit completion of research in progress. Upon the effective date of termination, or if requested, the deferred effective date of termination, Recipient will discontinue its use of the Material and will, upon direction of the Provider, return or destroy any remaining Material. The Recipient, at its discretion, will also either destroy the Modifications or remain bound by the terms of this agreement as they apply to Modifications.

14 The Material is provided at no cost, or with an optional transmittal fee solely to reimburse the Provider for its preparation and distribution costs. If a fee is requested by the Provider, the amount will be indicated in an implementing letter.

Notes and Questions

1. *Onward distribution.* Both the NIH SLA and UBMTA prohibit the onward transfer of materials by the recipient. Why? What risks may be inherent in a researcher providing such materials to a third party?

2. *Noncommercial research.* Both the NIH SLA and UBMTA require that materials be used for "teaching or not-for-profit research purposes only." What is the reason for this restriction? Some academic researchers have criticized this restriction. Why?

3. *No liability.* Both the NIH SLA and UBMTA release the provider from all liability for the materials. Why? What if the materials are more dangerous than expected (e.g., infectious, toxic, combustible or inflammable) and cause damage, injury or death at the recipient's facility?

4. *Ownership.* Both the NIH SLA and UBMTA allow the recipient to own and file for patent protection of any modifications made to the materials or results achieved using the materials. But this approach is not universally followed. Some MTAs give the provider of materials rights not only to modifications of the materials, but to anything developed using the materials (so-called "reach-through" rights [see Section 8.2.3, Note 3]). Thus, if a new drug is discovered using a reagent or cell line provided to the discoverer under such an MTA, ownership of that drug could be challenged. What is the best approach to the ownership of discoveries made using someone else's materials, that of the NIH or "reach-through" rights?

5. *Human samples.* Bubela et al. describe the additional difficulties that are presented when materials involve human samples or data:

   > Informed consent given by research participants determines the use of their samples; for example, limiting research to a specific disease. Thus, if each sample in a biobank is collected using a different consent form, the samples may be deposited on different terms. Those terms must then attach to the sample and, in turn, dictate the distribution terms. This adds a layer of complexity to the transactions managed by biobanks, requires significant informatics resources, and may impede the ability of biobanks to accept legacy materials and data from the research community. Additional constraints arise for associated data that may link to patient records or other identifiable information. In this case, MTAs must comply with national or regional privacy laws in setting conditions for storage and use of samples and associated data.[40]

   How does the UBMTA address these issues? Should it do more?

14.6 UNIVERSITIES AND COPYRIGHT

While much of the focus of university technology transfer is on patents, university personnel develop a broad range of IP beyond patented inventions. In fact, on a per capita basis, academic faculty produce far more copyrighted works – articles, books, blog posts, teaching materials, software, recordings – than inventions. Yet the Bayh–Dole Act relates only to inventions, and academic faculty generally assume that copyrighted works, even if supported by government funding, are owned by themselves rather than by their employers.

The truth is not quite so simple. As shown by Professor Shubha Ghosh, universities differ in their treatment of copyrighted material.[41] Under many university policies, computer software is treated as "technology" and subjected to the same rules as patentable inventions. University

---

[40] Bubela et al., supra note 32, at 5–6.

[41] Shubha Ghosh, Bayh–Dole Beyond Patents in Research Handbook on Intellectual Property and Technology Transfer 69, 71–80 (Jacob H. Rooksby, ed., Edward Elgar. 2020).

TTOs routinely seek to license and commercialize software developed within university labs. According to one 2011 study, software accounted for about 10 percent of both licensing activity and invention disclosures at US research universities.[42] This being said, an increasing number of university researchers are releasing software on an open source basis.[43]

The treatment of other forms of copyrighted works is less clear. Most universities appear to allow individual faculty members to retain copyright in traditional scholarly, creative and pedagogical works such as books, articles and artistic creations. An exception sometimes occurs, however, when those works are developed at the behest of the university or under a sponsored research grant. Thus, the university may claim ownership of the copyright in an online course or website that a professor develops if the university wishes to utilize it after the professor retires or departs for another university. An example of a detailed university policy governing copyrights and other forms of IP follows.

UNIVERSITY OF UTAH: POLICY 7-003: OWNERSHIP OF COPYRIGHTABLE WORKS AND RELATED WORKS

I. Purpose and Scope

A. Purpose

The Purpose of this Policy on ownership of copyrightable Works is to outline the respective rights that all members of the University community – faculty, students and staff – have in such Works created during the course of affiliation with the University. This Policy preserves the practice of allowing faculty to own the copyrights to traditional scholarly works, and at the same time seeks to protect the interests of the university in works that are created with the substantial use of university resources (see section III).

E. Types of Works Covered by this Policy

The following is a list of the types of Works that are covered by this Policy. This list is intended to be illustrative rather than definitive: literary Works, musical Works including accompanying words, dramatic Works including accompanying music, pantomimes and choreographic Works, pictorial, graphic, and sculptural Works, motion pictures and audio-visual Works, sound recordings, multi-media Works, computer programs and documentation, electronic course materials and software used in on-line courses and in the classroom, architectural Works, other Works of authorship, as defined in the U.S. Copyright Act, fixed in a tangible medium of expression, semiconductor mask Works, databases.

II. General Rules of Ownership

A. University Staff and Student-Employees

Works created by University staff and student-employees within the scope of their University employment are considered to be works made for hire, and thus are Works as to which the

---

[42] Nat'l Res. Council, Managing University Intellectual Property in the Public Interest 20 (Stephen A. Merrill and Anne-Marie Mazza, eds., Nat'l Res. Council, 2011).

[43] See Daniel Katz, *Open Source Software and University Intellectual Property Policies*, March 4, 2015, https://danielskatzblog.wordpress.com/2015/03/04/open-source-software-and-university-intellectual-property-policies-2.

University is the Owner and controls all legal rights in the Work. In contrast, Works created by University staff and student-employees outside the scope of their University employment are not covered by this Policy and are considered to be owned by the Creators, unless such Works are created through "substantial use of University resources" (as described in Section III of this Policy).

B. Faculty

The principal mission of the University is the creation and dissemination of knowledge. Therefore, the University transfers to the Creators any copyrights that it may own in a traditional scholarly Work created by University faculty members that result from teaching, research, scholarly or artistic endeavors, regardless of the medium in which the Work is expressed, unless the Work was developed with substantial use of university resources and commercial use is made of the Work. If the Creator intends to make commercial use of the Work, then disclosure must be made as required under section IV.A.

C. Students

Notwithstanding Section III ... students are the Owners of the copyright of Works for which academic credit is received, including theses, dissertations, scholarly publications, texts, pedagogical materials or other materials.

D. Independent Contractors

Any Work created by an independent contractor for the University shall be the subject of a written agreement whereby the contractor may be required to assign all rights in the Work to the University and to acknowledge that such Work constitutes work made for hire, if appropriate.

E. Assignment or Release

The University may, at its sole discretion, determine whether to assign or release to a Creator of a Work any ownership rights of the University in such Work upon such conditions as the University deems beneficial and fair to all parties. Any such release of rights must be in writing and approved by the appropriate dean or equivalent supervisor of the Creator, in consultation with the Technology Transfer Office, and by the cognizant vice president or similar administrator.

III. Substantial Use of University Resources

The following provisions provide guidance in determining whether or not the creation of a Work involved the "substantial use of University resources."

A. Categories of Substantial Use

"Substantial use of University resources" in the creation of a Work, resulting in the University being the Owner of the Work, includes, but is not limited to the following situations:

1. The University and the Creator-employee (whether faculty, staff or student) agree to create the Work, in whole or in part, as part of a specific grant, contract, appointment or assignment, with or without a reduction in other University responsibilities.

The agreement to create the work should include a clear stipulation of the copyright ownership.

2. The Work is produced through the use of University facilities not available to the general public and beyond the level of facilities and services (e.g., office space, libraries, limited secretarial and support staff, ordinary use of computers or other University facilities or equipment) that are customarily used by similarly situated colleagues of the Creator. Such facilities and services the use of which constitutes substantial use include, but are not limited to, laboratories, studios, equipment, production facilities, specialized computing resources, or special expertise of University-employed individuals.

3. The University provides significant University funding in direct support of the Work's creation. However, regular sabbatical and administrative leaves shall not count as a factor in determining substantial use.

4. The Work is significantly based upon material that is proprietary to the University, regardless of whether the Creator produced such proprietary information.

5. The Work is produced under the specific terms of a sponsored research grant or contract administered by the Office of Sponsored Projects.

IV. Commercialization and Revenue

A. Obligation to Disclose and Assign

The Creator shall promptly disclose to the Technology Transfer Office the creation of any Work in which the University has an ownership interest, as provided in Section II of this Policy. The … Creator of a Work owned by the University according to the provisions of this Policy shall promptly execute an assignment of all their rights to the University when requested to do so by the administration. The Creator shall cooperate fully with the University and the Technology Transfer Office in further protection, promotion or dissemination of the Work.

B. Revenue Sharing

1. The Creator of a Work that is owned by the University, other than a Creator of a work made for hire, shall receive a share of any royalty income or other revenue realized by the University as Owner, from the sale, licensing or other commercialization of the Work. The Creator of a Work made for hire may receive a share of royalty income or other revenue, provided that an appropriate agreement is entered into between the University and the Creator prior to the inception of the Work.

2. The Creator's share of income shall be based on a percentage of such income or revenue remaining after reimbursement of all the University's direct costs of copyright registration, licensing and other legal protection of the Work ("net revenue"). The Creator's share (which, in the case of co-Creators, shall be divided between them equally or as they shall agree in their sole discretion) shall normally be forty percent (40%) of the first twenty thousand dollars ($20,000) of net revenue, thirty-five percent (35%) of the next twenty thousand dollars ($20,000) of net revenue, and thirty percent (30%) of any additional net revenue received by the University from the Work.

C. Creators' Rights in University-Owned Works

1. The University will make reasonable efforts to consult with the Creator of a Work with respect to proposed uses to be made of the Work before it is licensed or sold to a third party. When disputes over use occur, the matter shall be referred to the cognizant vice president or similar administrator for resolution, in consultation with the Vice President for Research.

2. University-owned Works that have not been licensed or sold shall not be altered or revised without making reasonable efforts to provide the Creators an opportunity to assume the responsibility for the revision. If the Creators decline the opportunity to revise such material, the University shall assign responsibility for the revision in consultation with the appropriate department.

3. The Creator may request that University-owned Works that have not been licensed or sold be withdrawn from use when the Creator or the relevant department deems such use obsolete or inappropriate. The cognizant vice president or similar administrator shall decide disputes over the withdrawal of Works.

Notes and Questions

1. *Employment status.* In the sample policy excerpted above, why are staff, faculty, students and contractors treated differently? Do you think that different categories of employees are treated differently under the IP policies of most private companies?

2. *Categories of works.* Does it make sense under this policy to treat such a broad range of works – books, articles, art works, software, semiconductor mask layouts, databases – in the same manner? Would it be preferable to tailor the policy more specifically to each different category of work, or is there a benefit to a more uniform treatment?

3. *Adjudication.* In the policy above, most discretionary questions are left to the judgment of the university TTO. Is this appropriate? Why doesn't the policy leave such judgment questions to individual faculty members, or a committee of the faculty governing body? Are there advantages to giving this discretion to the TTO?

4. *Revenue sharing.* Why do university employees automatically receive a share of university revenue from their works that are owned by the university, but not from works made for hire? What practical reasons might exist for this distinction?

5. *Rights of authors.* Why does section IV.C give authors any rights with respect to works owned by the university? Do you think that the rights granted are too generous or not generous enough to authors?

6. *Continuing uncertainty.* Not all universities have always had detailed copyright policies. Consider the dispute between Columbia University and the estate of one of its former faculty members, Persian scholar Ehsan Yarshater, who died in 2018.[44] Yarshater founded Columbia's Center for Iranian Studies in the late 1960s. In 1973, he began to assemble the *Encyclopaedia Iranica*, a comprehensive reference work dedicated to the study of Iranian civilization. Today, the *Encyclopaedia* includes dozens of volumes with contributions from

---

[44] See Kyle Jahner, *Columbia Spat Tests Question of When Professors Own Their Work*, Bloomberg Law, November 5, 2019 (edited by the author).

more than 1,300 scholars. The Encyclopaedia Iranica Foundation created by Yarshater claims that it began to list itself as the owner of the copyright in the *Encyclopaedia* in 2003. But after Yarshater's death, Columbia claimed that it never authorized the foundation to list itself as the registered copyright owner and did not become aware of this practice until 2017. Columbia also says that it rejected the foundation's request to transfer ownership of the *Encyclopaedia* to it in 2015 under a policy allowing professors to request rights to their noncommercial work.

Could this dispute have been avoided if Columbia had a policy similar to the one excerpted above? If Columbia did have such a policy, how would the dispute over the *Encyclopaedia Iranica* have turned out?

Problem 14.1

Professor Plum, a historian, is on the faculty of Bigg University, which has adopted the copyright policy excerpted above. Over the past ten years Professor Plum has been working on a definitive biography of US president William Henry Harrison. While conducting research for the book, Plum has traveled multiple times to Harrison's birthplace in Virginia, the battlegrounds at Tippecanoe, Indiana, where he earned the nickname "Old Tippecanoe" and various sites in the former Northwest Territory where Harrison served in the government. All of these trips were funded by a grant that Plum received from Bigg University. Much of the background research for the book was performed by a series of five different undergraduate research assistants provided by the History Department at Bigg University. Recently, Professor Plum signed a publishing contract for the biography with Southern University Press, a reputable academic publisher, which paid him an advance of $10,000. Then, to Professor Plum's surprise, he received a call from a New York literary agent, who informed him that a famous Broadway producer wished to option the book for a new musical production. What obligations, if any, does Professor Plum have with respect to Bigg University?

15

Trademark and Franchise Licensing

In this chapter we will discuss some of the unique legal features and commercial practices associated with licensing agreements, including franchise agreements, that cover trademarks and associated rights such as trade dress, character copyrights and design patents.

15.1 BRAND AND CHARACTER LICENSING

According to Licensing International's 6th Annual Global Licensing Survey, sales of licensed merchandise and services reached nearly $300 billion in 2019. This impressive figure relates primarily to the licensing of trademarks and brands, though other rights such as trade dress, copyrights and design patents are also implicated in such licenses. Brands and characters are licensed for use in connection with a vast array of products and services from toys and school supplies to apparel and sports gear to restaurants, theme parks and museums. As impressive as they are, figures like this likely understate the total amount of trademark and brand licensing that occurs in the market, as they do not include the huge volume of business associated with franchise agreements in the restaurant, fast-food, hotel, retail and other industries.

Below, we discuss some of the rights that are licensed in this area beyond trademarks.

15.1.1 *Trade Dress*

In addition to registered and unregistered trademarks, brand licensing includes *trade dress*, which can also be registered or unregistered. Trade dress protection has become particularly important in the area of franchising, as it can protect the interior and exterior design of restaurants and other retail outlets.[1] In fact, one of the most important cases involving trade dress

---

[1]   See Christopher P. Bussert, *Trademark Law and Franchising: Five of the Most Significant Developments*, 40 Franchise L.J. 127, 132 (2020) ("For those franchisors who seek to create an indelible overall image of their franchised businesses in the minds of the consuming public, adopting protectable trade dress consisting of unique, yet memorable interior and exterior design elements including color schemes has gone a long way to reaching that goal").

FIGURE 15.1 In *Two Pesos v. Taco Cabana*, the Supreme Court recognized the protectable elements of Taco Cabana's interior and exterior store design – features that are regularly licensed as part of fast-food franchises.

protection centered on the décor scheme of a Tex-Mex fast-food chain in Texas, which the Supreme Court found to be distinctive and protectible:

> A festive eating atmosphere having interior dining and patio areas decorated with artifacts, bright colors, paintings and murals. The patio includes interior and exterior areas with the interior patio capable of being sealed off from the outside patio by overhead garage doors. The stepped exterior of the building is a festive and vivid color scheme using top border paint and neon stripes. Bright awnings and umbrellas continue the theme.[2]

Trade dress is not protected via a unique statute, but instead is included under the Lanham Act as a "device" used "to identify and distinguish ... goods or services ... from those manufactured or sold by others" (15 U.S.C. § 1127). As such, trade dress registrations are identical to registrations for word or symbol marks and are subject to the same limitations, duration, renewal and other requirements of registered marks. In addition, like trademarks, trade dress enjoys protection at common law.

In addition to being distinctive, in order to be entitled to protection, trade dress must not be functional. That is, a protectable feature of trade dress cannot be "essential to the use or purpose of the article or [that] affects the cost or quality of the article."[3] Thus, in the context of the Taco Cabana store design discussed above, a bright ribbon painted just below the roofline serves no functional purpose and is protectable as trade dress, while the presence of a functioning door and windows would not be protectable.

Trade dress is often difficult to define in a licensing agreement, especially if it is not registered. Even registrations for trade dress are sometimes less than illuminating. Thus, a licensing agreement (or a franchise operating manual) will often include an appendix including photographs and drawings of the licensed design/layout.

15.1.2 *Character Copyrights and Trademarks*

Fictional characters are among the most important assets for product licensing. Memorable characters from popular films, television shows, comic books, novels and children's books adorn apparel, school supplies, Happy Meals, Halloween costumes and countless other products,

---

[2] *Two Pesos, Inc. v. Taco Cabana, Inc.*, 505 U.S. 763, 765 (1992). Prior to the *Taco Cabana* case, it was generally believed that trade dress protection extended primarily to distinctive product packaging.

[3] *Inwood Laboratories, Inc. v. Ives Laboratories, Inc.*, 456 U.S. 844 (1982).

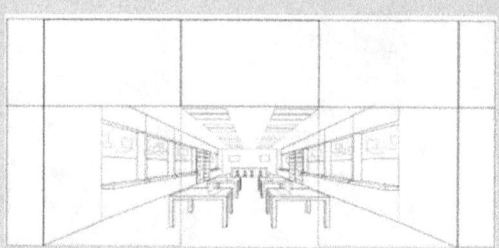

FIGURE 15.2 Apple's 2013 registration for the Apple Store layout (No. 4,277,914).

"The mark consists of the design and layout of a retail store. The store features a clear glass storefront surrounded by a paneled facade consisting of large, rectangular horizontal panels over the top of the glass front, and two narrower panels stacked on either side of the storefront. Within the store, rectangular recessed lighting units traverse the length of the store's ceiling. There are cantilevered shelves below recessed display spaces along the side walls, and rectangular tables arranged in a line in the middle of the store parallel to the walls and extending from the storefront to the back of the store. There is multi-tiered shelving along the side walls, and a [sic] oblong table with stools located at the back of the store, set below video screens flush mounted on the back wall."

form the basis for video games and animated programming and even appear in theme parks and sporting events.

Traditionally, fictional characters have been protected by copyright law, and most character licensing agreements are essentially copyright licenses. Nevertheless, there is an increasing trend to protect characters with trademarks, if they indicate a source of goods or services. The quintessential example is Mickey Mouse, whose status as a trademark has been debated for more than half a century.[4] But whatever the merits of protecting fictional characters with both copyrights and trademarks, the attentive licensing attorney should be aware that these two forms of protection exist and must be addressed in any licensing agreement.

15.1.3 *Design Patents*

Unlike the patents with which most people are familiar (so-called "utility patents," which are discussed extensively in this book), "design patents" do not cover useful inventions or discoveries. As the Patent and Trademark Office (PTO) explains, "a utility patent protects the way an article is used and works (35 U.S.C. § 101), while a design patent protects the way an article looks (35 U.S.C. § 171)."[5] Section 171 of the Patent Act defines "inventions" subject to design patent protection as "any new, original, and ornamental design for an article of manufacture."

Design patents differ from utility patents in a number of important ways. For example, the term of a design patent is fifteen years from the date of issuance, rather than twenty years from the date of filing. Moreover, design patents lack written claims – the entire protection of a design patent lies in its drawings.

Many attorneys who work in the field of character licensing are accustomed to dealing with copyrights (see Section 15.1.2), but have less familiarity with patent issues. Thus, it is important

---

4   See, e.g., Franklin Waldheim, *Mickey Mouse: Trademark or Copyright?*, 54 Trademark Rep. 865 (1964).
5   Manual of Patent Examining Procedure, § 1502.

FIGURE 15.3 In addition to the Star Wars® brand, the copyrighted Star Wars characters have been licensed for use in thousands of products from plush toys and action figures to knee socks and table lamps.

FIGURE 15.4 1932 design patent for the "Betty Boop" character.

in character licensing agreements to include both design patents and patent applications within the scope of the licensed rights, and to be aware of patent-specific issues that may not arise under pure copyright licenses (e.g., responsibility for prosecution and maintenance [Section 9.5], no-challenge clauses [Section 22.4] and adjustment of royalty rates when protection lapses [Section 8.2.2.4]).

It is also important to remember that copyrights and, to a lesser degree, trademarks cover a character in various manifestations (e.g., the copyright on Mickey Mouse covers Disney's rodent in films, and on lunchboxes, backpacks and wristwatches). Design patents, however, are drawn to the design of a specific *product* – so a design patent covering Mickey as a watch face or a plush toy would not extend to his use as a desk lamp. As a result, crafting fields of use that are of appropriate breadth for the intended business purpose and licensed rights is essential. For example, the licensor of a design patent covering a Mickey Mouse plush toy would be beyond its rights (and possibly committing patent misuse – see Chapter 24) if it sought to charge royalties on a licensee's sales of Mickey Mouse lunchboxes.

Notes and Questions

1. *IP convergence.* Commentators have bemoaned the expansion of intellectual property (IP) rights to such a degree that many simple (and complex) products are now protected under numerous IP regimes. The true extent of this trend became apparent in *Apple v. Samsung*, 137 S. Ct. 429 (2016), in which Apple's iPhone and iPad products were shown to have protection under utility patents, design patents, copyrights, trademarks, trade dress and trade secrets. Is it a problem that fictional characters like Mickey Mouse can be protected by both copyright and trademark rights?[6] What challenges does this double-coverage present for licensees? For nonlicensees? Think about this question as you read the sections in this chapter on trademark licensing.

Problem 15.1

The CEO of SportTrex, an athletic shoe and apparel manufacturer, has decided that the company will introduce a new line of sports shoes for the 8–12-year-old "tween" market. Key to marketing this new line will be the use of a famous cartoon character that will appeal to both boys and girls within the target age range. Market research suggests that the best candidate is Rarebit Rabbit, a zany cartoon character owned by Spiffy Productions. Outline (a) the rights that you would want to license from Spiffy and (b) the scope of the license grant that you would request.

15.2 NAKED TRADEMARK LICENSING AND ABANDONMENT

Until the mid-twentieth century, trademark licensing was not viewed with favor by US courts and was, in fact, treated as a species of trademark abandonment. Abandonment of a mark signifies that the owner no longer wishes to treat the mark as its own and results in a loss of ownership of the mark.

In *MacMahan Pharmacal Co. v. Denver Chemical Mfg. Co.*, 113 F. 468 (8th Cir. 1901), MacMahan, the owner of the trademark "antiphlogistine" (for an early dental anesthetic cream), brought an infringement action against Denver Chemical, the manufacturer of an "antiphlogistine" ointment used as a general topical pain reliever. In rejecting MacMahan's claim, the court held that because MacMahan had previously sold (licensed) the right to use the mark to a third party (a former Denver executive), MacMahan "evinced an intention to abandon its claim to the trade-mark." The court explained that:

---

[6] For a recent critique, see Irene Calboli, *Overlapping Trademark and Copyright Protection: A Call for Concern and Action*, 2014 U. Ill. L. Rev. Online 25 (2014); and for a more sanguine view, see Jane C. Ginsburg, *Intellectual Property as Seen by Barbie and Mickey: The Reciprocal Relationship of Copyright and Trademark Law*, 65 J. Copyright Soc'y U.S.A. 245 (2018).

A trade-mark cannot be assigned, or its use licensed, except as incidental to a transfer of the business or property in connection with which it has been used. An assignment or license without such a transfer is totally inconsistent with the theory upon which the value of a trade-mark depends and its appropriation by an individual is permitted. The essential value of a trade-mark is that it identifies to the trade the merchandise upon which it appears as of a certain origin, or as the property of a certain person … Disassociated from merchandise to which it properly appertains, it lacks the essential characteristics which alone give it value, and becomes a false and deceitful designation. It is not by itself such property as may be transferred.

For the next half-century, *MacMahan* stood for the widely accepted proposition that a "naked" trademark license, without an accompanying transfer of the underlying business, constituted an abandonment of the mark.

When the Lanham Act was enacted in 1946, codifying many years of prior common law precedent, it addressed the issue of trademark abandonment.

LANHAM ACT § 45 (15 U.S.C. § 1127)

A mark shall be deemed to be "abandoned" if either of the following occurs:

(1) When its use has been discontinued with intent not to resume such use. Intent not to resume may be inferred from circumstances. Nonuse for 3 consecutive years shall be prima facie evidence of abandonment. "Use" of a mark means the bona fide use of such mark made in the ordinary course of trade, and not made merely to reserve a right in a mark.

(2) When any course of conduct of the owner, including acts of omission as well as commission, causes the mark to become the generic name for the goods or services on or in connection with which it is used or otherwise to lose its significance as a mark. Purchaser motivation shall not be a test for determining abandonment under this paragraph.

Accordingly, if a mark owner engaged in a "course of conduct" that caused its mark to lose its significance as a mark (i.e., to indicate the origin of goods or services bearing the mark), the mark would be considered abandoned. One such "course of conduct" was naked licensing.

The Lanham Act did, however, permit licensing of trademarks, so long as the licensee was a corporate affiliate of the licensor. Such licenses did not result in abandonment of the mark because the mark's owner, in theory, retained control over the quality of the goods produced by the licensee.

In *Dawn Donut Co. v. Hart's Food Stores, Inc.*, 267 F.2d 358 (2d Cir. 1959), the Second Circuit considered the case of a trademark license in which the mark's owner did *not* own or control its licensees. Since 1922, Dawn Donut Co. used the mark DAWN on 25–100 lb bags of doughnut and cake mix, which it sold to bakeries and retail shops. It also licensed shops to operate under the DAWN name, so long as they exclusively sold Dawn Donut products. The DAWN mark received a federal trademark registration in 1927. In 1929, Hart, the operator of a grocery store chain in western New York, began to sell doughnuts and other baked goods using the slogan "Baked at midnight, delivered at Dawn" and to brand its bakery products with the mark DAWN

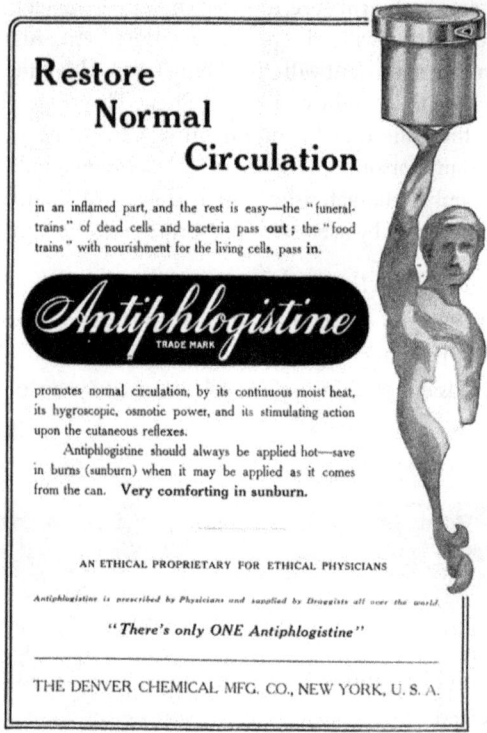

FIGURE 15.5 Denver Chemical sold its popular "Antiphlogistine" compound as a general topical analgesic.

in 1951. Dawn Donut sued Hart for infringement of the DAWN mark, and Hart responded by arguing, among other things, that Dawn Donut abandoned its mark by licensing it to unaffiliated bakeries and retailers.

Considering the case on appeal, Judge Lumbard first acknowledged the general rule that "the Lanham Act places an affirmative duty upon a licensor of a registered trademark to take reasonable measures to detect and prevent misleading uses of his mark by his licensees or suffer cancellation of his federal registration." He further explained that

> Without the requirement of control, the right of a trademark owner to license his mark separately from the business in connection with which it has been used would create the danger that products bearing the same trademark might be of diverse qualities. If the licensor is not compelled to take some reasonable steps to prevent misuses of his trademark in the hands of others the public will be deprived of its most effective protection against misleading uses of a trademark. The public is hardly in a position to uncover deceptive uses of a trademark before they occur and will be at best slow to detect them after they happen. Thus, unless the licensor exercises supervision and control over the operations of its licensees the risk that the public will be unwittingly deceived will be increased and this is precisely what the Act is in part designed to prevent. Clearly the only effective way to protect the public where a trademark is used by licensees is to place on the licensor the affirmative duty of policing in a reasonable manner the activities of his licensees.[7]

---

[7] 267 F.2d at 367.

FIGURE 15.6 Dawn Donut Co. licensed its trademark to bakeries and retailers who used its packaged mixes for doughnuts, coffee cakes, cinnamon rolls and oven goods.

The court thus established that a trademark license, even to an unaffiliated third party, might be valid, so long as the mark's owner exercised adequate "supervision and control" over the use of the mark. And determining the adequacy of such measures is a question of fact for the trial court. With this, the court eliminated the requirement that a trademark license must be accompanied by a transfer of the goodwill of the business in order to be valid, and established the "quality control" requirement that is now required of all trademark licenses.[8]

15.3 QUALITY CONTROL

15.3.1 *The Quality Control Requirement*

The "quality control" requirement for trademark licenses has, not surprisingly, generated significant discussion since it was introduced in *Dawn Donut*. The following case helps to establish the minimum threshold for adequate quality control.

Barcamerica International USA Trust v. Tyfield Importers, Inc.

289 F.3d 589 (9th Cir. 2002)

O'SCANNLAIN, CIRCUIT JUDGE

We must decide whether a company engaged in "naked licensing" of its trademark, thus resulting in abandonment of the mark and ultimately its cancellation.

Barcamerica International USA Trust ("Barcamerica") traces its rights in the Leonardo Da Vinci mark to a February 14, 1984 registration granted by the United States Patent and

---

[8] Note that while the assignment of business goodwill is no longer required for a trademark license to be valid, vestiges of this doctrine remain in the requirement that a trademark cannot be assigned without an assignment of its underlying goodwill. See Section 2.4.

Trademark Office ("PTO"), on an application filed in 1982. Barcamerica asserts that it has used the mark continuously since the early 1980s. In the district court, it produced invoices evidencing two sales per year for the years 1980 through 1993: one to a former employee and the other to a barter exchange company. Barcamerica further produced invoices evidencing between three and seven sales per year for the years 1994 through 1998. These include sales to the same former employee, two barter exchange companies, and various sales for "cash." The sales volume reflected in the invoices for the years 1980 through 1988 range from 160 to 410 cases of wine per year. Barcamerica also produced sales summaries for the years 1980 through 1996 which reflect significantly higher sales volumes; these summaries do not indicate, however, to whom the wine was sold.

In 1988, Barcamerica entered into a licensing agreement with Renaissance Vineyards ("Renaissance"). Under the agreement, Barcamerica granted Renaissance the nonexclusive right to use the "Da Vinci" mark for five years or 4,000 cases, "whichever comes first," in exchange for $2,500. The agreement contained no quality control provision. In 1989, Barcamerica and Renaissance entered into a second agreement in place of the 1988 agreement. The 1989 agreement granted Renaissance an exclusive license to use the "Da Vinci" mark in the United States for wine products or alcoholic beverages. The 1989 agreement was drafted by Barcamerica's counsel and, like the 1988 agreement, it did not contain a quality control provision. In fact, the only evidence in the record of any efforts by Barcamerica to exercise "quality control" over Renaissance's wines comprised (1) Barcamerica principal George Gino Barca's testimony that he occasionally, informally tasted of the wine, and (2) Barca's testimony that he relied on the reputation of a "world-famous winemaker" employed by Renaissance at the time the agreements were signed. (That winemaker is now deceased, although the record does not indicate when he died.) Nonetheless, Barcamerica contends that Renaissance's use of the mark inures to Barcamerica's benefit.

Cantine Leonardo Da Vinci Soc. Coop. a.r.l. ("Cantine"), an entity of Italy, is a wine producer located in Vinci, Italy. Cantine has sold wine products bearing the "Leonardo Da Vinci" tradename since 1972; it selected this name and mark based on the name of its home city, Vinci. Cantine began selling its "Leonardo Da Vinci" wine to importers in the United States in 1979. Since 1996, however, Tyfield Importers, Inc. ("Tyfield") has been the exclusive United States importer and distributor of Cantine wine products bearing the "Leonardo Da Vinci" mark. During the first eighteen months after Tyfield became Cantine's exclusive importer, Cantine sold approximately 55,000 cases of wine products bearing the "Leonardo Da Vinci" mark to Tyfield. During this same period, Tyfield spent between $250,000 and $300,000 advertising and promoting Cantine's products, advertising in *USA Today*, and such specialty magazines as *The Wine Spectator*, *Wine and Spirits*, and *Southern Beverage Journal*.

Cantine learned of Barcamerica's registration of the "Leonardo Da Vinci" mark in or about 1996, in the course of prosecuting its first trademark application in the United States. Cantine investigated Barcamerica's use of the mark and concluded that Barcamerica was no longer selling any wine products bearing the "Leonardo Da Vinci" mark and had long since abandoned the mark. As a result, in May 1997, Cantine commenced a proceeding in the PTO seeking cancellation of Barcamerica's registration for the mark based on abandonment. Barcamerica responded by filing the instant action on January 30, 1998, and thereafter moved to suspend the proceeding in the PTO. The PTO granted Barcamerica's motion and suspended the cancellation proceeding.

Although Barcamerica has been aware of Cantine's use of the "Leonardo Da Vinci" mark since approximately 1993, Barcamerica initiated the instant action only after Tyfield and Cantine commenced the proceeding in the PTO. A month after Barcamerica filed the instant action, it moved for a preliminary injunction enjoining Tyfield and Cantine from any further use of the mark. The district court denied the motion, finding, among other things, that "there is a serious question as to whether [Barcamerica] will be able to demonstrate a bona fide use of the Leonardo Da Vinci mark in the ordinary course of trade and overcome [the] claim of abandonment."

Thereafter, Tyfield and Cantine moved for summary judgment on various grounds. The district court granted the motion, concluding that Barcamerica abandoned the mark through naked licensing. The court further found that, in any event, the suit was barred by laches because Barcamerica knew several years before filing suit that Tyfield and Cantine were using the mark in connection with the sale of wine. This timely appeal followed.

[Barcamerica] first challenges the district court's conclusion that Barcamerica abandoned its trademark by engaging in naked licensing. It is well-established that "[a] trademark owner may grant a license and remain protected provided quality control of the goods and services sold under the trademark by the licensee is maintained." But "[u]ncontrolled or 'naked' licensing may result in the trademark ceasing to function as a symbol of quality and controlled source." McCarthy on Trademarks and Unfair Competition § 18:48, at 18–79 (4th ed., 2001). Consequently, where the licensor fails to exercise adequate quality control over the licensee, "a court may find that the trademark owner has abandoned the trademark, in which case the owner would be estopped from asserting rights to the trademark." Such abandonment "is purely an 'involuntary' forfeiture of trademark rights," for it need not be shown that the trademark owner had any subjective intent to abandon the mark. Accordingly, the proponent of a naked license theory "faces a stringent standard" of proof.

FIGURE 15.7 Label from a bottle of DaVinci Chianti.

Judge Damrell's analysis of this issue in his memorandum opinion and order is correct and well-stated, and we adopt it as our own. As that court explained,

> In 1988, [Barcamerica] entered into an agreement with Renaissance in which [Barcamerica] granted Renaissance the non-exclusive right to use the "Da Vinci" mark for five years or 4,000 cases, "whichever comes first." There is no quality control provision in that agreement. In 1989, [Barcamerica] and Renaissance entered into a second agreement in place of the 1998 agreement. The 1989 agreement grants Renaissance an exclusive license to use the "Da Vinci" mark in the United States for wine products or alcoholic beverages. The 1989 agreement was to "continue in effect in perpetuity," unless terminated in accordance with the provisions thereof. The 1989 agreement does not contain any controls or restrictions with respect to the quality of goods bearing the "Da Vinci" mark. Rather, the agreement provides that Renaissance is "solely responsible for any and all claims or causes of action for negligence, breach of contract, breach of warranty, or products liability arising from the sale or distribution of Products using the Licensed Mark" and that Renaissance shall defend and indemnify plaintiff against such claims.
>
> The lack of an express contract right to inspect and supervise a licensee's operations is not conclusive evidence of lack of control. "[T]here need not be formal quality control where 'the particular circumstances of the licensing arrangement [indicate] that the public will not be deceived.'" Indeed, "[c]ourts have upheld licensing agreements where the licensor is familiar with and relies upon the licensee's own efforts to control quality."
>
> Here, there is no evidence that [Barcamerica] is familiar with or relied upon Renaissance's efforts to control quality. Mr. Barca represents that Renaissance's use of the mark is "controlled by" plaintiff "with respect to the nature and quality of the wine sold under the license," and that "[t]he nature and quality of Renaissance wine sold under the trademark is good." [Barcamerica]'s sole evidence of any such control is Mr. Barca's own apparently random tastings and his reliance on Renaissance's reputation. According to Mr. Barca, the quality of Renaissance's wine is "good" and at the time plaintiff began licensing the mark to Renaissance, Renaissance's winemaker was Karl Werner, a "world famous" winemaker.
>
> Mr. Barca's conclusory statements as to the existence of quality controls is insufficient to create a triable issue of fact on the issue of naked licensing. While Mr. Barca's tastings perhaps demonstrate a minimal effort to monitor quality, Mr. Barca fails to state when, how often, and under what circumstances he tastes the wine. Mr. Barca's reliance on the reputation of the winemaker is no longer justified as he is deceased. Mr. Barca has not provided any information concerning the successor winemaker(s). While Renaissance's attorney, Mr. Goldman, testified that Renaissance "strive[s] extremely hard to have the highest possible standards," he has no knowledge of the quality control procedures utilized by Renaissance with regard to testing wine. Moreover, according to Renaissance, Mr. Barca never "had any involvement whatsoever regarding the quality of the wine and maintaining it at any level." [Barcamerica] has failed to demonstrate any knowledge of or reliance on the actual quality controls used by Renaissance, nor has it demonstrated any ongoing effort to monitor quality.
>
> [Barcamerica] and Renaissance did not and do not have the type of close working relationship required to establish adequate quality control in the absence of a formal agreement. See, e.g., *Taco Cabana Int'l, Inc.*, 932 F.2d [1113] at 1121 [(5th Cir. 1991)] (licensor and licensee enjoyed close working relationship for eight years); *Transgo, [Inc. v. Ajac Transmission Parts Corp.,]* 768 F.2d [1001] at 1017–18 (9th Cir. 1985) (licensor manufactured 90% of components sold by licensee, licensor informed licensee that if he chose to use his own parts "[licensee] wanted to know about it," licensor had ten year association with licensee and was familiar with his ability and expertise); *Taffy Original Designs,*

Inc. v. Taffy's Inc., 161 U.S.P.Q. 707, 713 (N.D.Ill.1966) (licensor and licensee were sisters in business together for seventeen years, licensee's business was a continuation of the licensor's and licensee's prior business, licensor visited licensee's store from time to time and was satisfied with the quality of the merchandise offered); *Arner v. Sharper Image Corp.*, 39 U.S.P.Q.2d 1282 (C.D.Cal.1995) (licensor engaged in a close working relationship with licensee's employees and license agreement provided that license would terminate if certain employees ceased to be affiliated with licensee). No such familiarity or close working relationship ever existed between [Barcamerica] and Renaissance. Both the terms of the licensing agreements and the manner in which they were carried out show that [Barcamerica] engaged in naked licensing of the "Leonardo Da Vinci" mark. Accordingly, [Barcamerica] is estopped from asserting any rights in the mark.

On appeal, Barcamerica does not seriously contest any of the foregoing. Instead, it argues essentially that because Renaissance makes good wine, the public is not deceived by Renaissance's use of the "Da Vinci" mark, and thus, that the license was legally acceptable. This novel rationale, however, is faulty. Whether Renaissance's wine was objectively "good" or "bad" is simply irrelevant. What matters is that Barcamerica played no meaningful role in holding the wine to a standard of quality – good, bad, or otherwise. As McCarthy explains,

> It is important to keep in mind that "quality control" does not necessarily mean that the licensed goods or services must be of "high" quality, but merely of equal quality, whether that quality is high, low or middle. The point is that customers are entitled to assume that the nature and quality of goods and services sold under the mark at all licensed outlets will be consistent and predictable.

McCarthy § 18:55, at 18–94. And "it is well established that where a trademark owner engages in naked licensing, without any control over the quality of goods produced by the licensee, such a practice is inherently deceptive and constitutes abandonment of any rights to the trademark by the licensor."

Certainly, "[I]t is difficult, if not impossible to define in the abstract exactly how much control and inspection is needed to satisfy the requirement of quality control over trademark licensees." And we recognize that "[t]he standard of quality control and the degree of necessary inspection and policing by the licensor will vary with the wide range of licensing situations in use in the modern marketplace." But in this case we deal with a relatively simple product: wine. Wine, of course, is bottled by season. Thus, at the very least, one might have expected Barca to sample (or to have some designated wine connoisseur sample) on an annual basis, in some organized way, some adequate number of bottles of the Renaissance wines which were to bear Barcamerica's mark to ensure that they were of sufficient quality to be called "Da Vinci." But Barca did not make even this minimal effort.

We therefore agree with Judge Damrell, and hold that Barcamerica engaged in naked licensing of its "Leonardo Da Vinci" mark – and that by so doing, Barcamerica forfeited its rights in the mark.

Notes and Questions

1. *Measuring quality.* Once a trademark licensor overcomes the relatively low hurdle established in *Barcamerica* (there must be *some* quality control), is there any standard governing how much quality control it must exercise over its licensees? How should the quality of a product be measured, especially when intangible factors such as the taste, body and color of a wine are relevant to consumer choice?

2. *Consistency versus quality.* The court in *Barcamerica*, adopting Professor McCarthy's reasoning, observes that "'quality control' does not necessarily mean that the licensed goods or services must be of 'high' quality, but merely of equal quality, whether that quality is high, low or middle. The point is that customers are entitled to assume that the nature and quality of goods and services sold under the mark at all licensed outlets will be consistent and predictable." Do you agree? Is there any implication that a mark like WALMART is less valuable than SAKS FIFTH AVENUE simply because the goods bearing that mark are arguably of lower quality? Is consistency with the mark owner's own product quality more important than the objective quality of the marked goods? Why?

3. *Level of policing.* How stringently must a trademark licensor police its licensees' conduct? The licensor in *Barcamerica* essentially exercised no efforts at all, but is there some marginally higher level of quality control that is required of licensors? What if the licensor itself did not closely monitor the quality of its own products or services?

4. *Process similarities.* Can a licensor rely on the fact that its licensees' quality control procedures are similar to its own? In *Barcamerica*, the court cites a number of cases establishing that a "close working relationship" between the licensor and licensee may suffice as quality control by the licensor. For example, the court cites *Taco Cabana Int'l, Inc. v. Two Pesos, Inc.*, 932 F.2d 1113 (5th Cir. 1991), *aff'd on other gnds*, 505 U.S. 763 (1992), in which the Fifth Circuit reasons that:

> Where the license parties have engaged in a close working relationship, and may justifiably rely on each parties' intimacy with standards and procedures to ensure consistent quality, and no actual decline in quality standards is demonstrated, we would depart from the purpose of the law to find an abandonment simply for want of all the inspection and control formalities … The history of the [parties'] relationship warrants this relaxation of formalities. Prior to the licensing agreement at issue, the [parties] operated Taco Cabana together for approximately eight years. Taco Cabana and TaCasita do not use significantly different procedures or products, and the brothers may be expected to draw on their mutual experience to maintain the requisite quality consistency. They cannot protect their trade dress if they operate their separate restaurants in ignorance of each other's operations, but they need not maintain the careful policing appropriate to more formal license arrangements.

Do you think that this standard of care meets the requirements for quality control established in *Dawn Donuts*?

Note the importance that the court placed on quality control procedures in *Societe Des Produits Nestle, S.A. v. Casa Helvetia, Inc.*, 982 F.2d 633 (1st Cir. 1992) (reproduced in Section 23.6.3) (discussing gray market imports, not naked licensing):

> Although Nestle and Casa Helvetia each oversees the quality of the product it sells, the record reflects, and Casa Helvetia concedes, that their procedures differ radically. The Italian PERUGINA leaves Italy in refrigerated containers which arrive at Nestle's facility in Puerto Rico. Nestle verifies the temperature of the coolers, opens them, and immediately transports the chocolates to refrigerated rooms. The company records the product's date of manufacture, conducts laboratory tests, and destroys those candies that have expired. It then transports the salable chocolates to retailers in refrigerated trucks. Loading and unloading is performed only in the cool morning hours.
>
> On the other hand, the Venezuelan product arrives in Puerto Rico via commercial air freight. During the afternoon hours, airline personnel remove the chocolates from the containers in which they were imported and place them in a central air cargo cooler. The next morning, employees of Casa Helvetia open random boxes at the airport to see if the chocolates

have melted. The company then transports the candy in a refrigerated van to a warehouse. Casa Helvetia performs periodic inspections before delivering the goods to its customers in a refrigerated van. The record contains no evidence that Casa Helvetia knows or records the date the chocolates were manufactured.

In *Casa Helvetia*, these process differences were among the factors that persuaded the court that chocolates manufactured in Italy and Venezuela were sufficiently dissimilar to warrant a ban on importing the unauthorized versions into the United States. But is this type of analysis also useful to determine whether a licensor and licensee have sufficiently similar quality control procedures to avoid a finding of naked licensing?

5. *Different classes of goods.* Trademark owners need not license their marks for use on the same types of products that they produce themselves. For example, the Walt Disney Company licenses many of its marks for use on school supplies, lunchboxes, video games and other products manufactured by others. How should a trademark owner establish quality standards for products that it does not produce itself?

6. *Higher quality.* What happens if a trademark licensee sells products that are of substantially higher quality than those of its licensor? Must the licensor enforce a uniformly *low* standard of quality among its licensees?

7. *Just say "no."* Does a licensor need to explain why it has rejected a licensee's use of a licensed mark, or tell the licensee what it must do in order to attain an acceptable quality level? In *Authentic Apparel Grp., LLC v. United States*, 989 F.3d 1008 (Fed. Cir. 2021), a trademark licensing agreement required the licensee to obtain the licensor's advance written approval of all "products, packaging, labeling, point of sale materials, trade show displays, sales materials and advertising" bearing the licensor's marks. The agreement gave the licensor "sole and absolute discretion" to approve such uses, and relieved the licensor of any damages or other liability for the "failure or refusal to grant any [such] approval." When, between 2011 and 2014, the licensor refused 41 of more than 500 such requests, the licensee sued, claiming that the licensor breached the licensing agreement and failed to act in good faith. The Federal Circuit held, and the licensee conceded, "that the approval provisions in the license agreement allowed the [licensor] to fulfill its duty to ensure quality control and thus avoid a 'naked license' of the trademarks." Do you agree? Should a trademark licensor be required to explain why it has refused a requested use of its marks? Would it matter if the licensee were obligated to pay minimum annual royalties to the licensor (as it was in *Authentic Apparel*)?

15.3.2 *Contractual Quality Control Requirements*

Must a trademark licensor include specific "quality control" language in its licensing agreement in order to satisfy the quality control requirement? The court in *Dawn Donut* answered this question in the negative, holding instead that a court must assess the mark owner's quality control efforts holistically:

> The absence … of an express contract right to inspect and supervise a licensee's operations does not mean that the plaintiff's method of licensing failed to comply with the requirements of the Lanham Act. Plaintiff may in fact have exercised control in spite of the absence of any express grant by licensees of the right to inspect and supervise. The question, then, with respect to both plaintiff's contract and non-contract licensees, is whether the plaintiff in fact exercised sufficient control.[9]

---

[9] 267 F.2d at 368.

This question was again raised in *Exxon Corp. v. Oxxford Clothes Inc.*, 109 F.3d 1070 (5th Cir. 1997), in which oil giant Exxon sued bespoke clothier Oxxford for using the letters "XX" in a manner that allegedly infringed and diluted Exxon's registered interlocking XX trademark.

As noted by the court,

> For more than two decades Exxon has aggressively protected its mark from infringement and/or dilution by seeking out and negotiating with other companies using marks similar to its own.[10] In lieu of conclusive litigation, many of these companies opted to enter "phase out" agreements with Exxon in which the other company agreed that after existing stores of stationary, advertising materials, and products bearing the offending mark were exhausted, use of that mark would be discontinued. These phase out periods afforded the potentially infringing or diluting companies time to develop and implement a new mark. The phase out agreements did not contain any quality control mechanisms ensuring the quality of goods or services offered under the offending mark during the phase out period.

In its defense, Oxxford argued that these phase-out agreements constituted "naked licenses" demonstrating Exxon's abandonment of its XX mark. "The gist of Oxxford's argument was that

FIGURE 15.8 Competing "XX" marks used by Exxon Corp. and Oxxford Clothes.

Exxon's XX trademark   Other XX marks challenged
registration   by Exxon and subject to phase-out agreements

FIGURE 15.9 Exxon's XX trademark registration and other XX marks challenged by Exxon and subject to phrase-out agreements.

---

[10] For a fascinating discussion of Exxon's trademark enforcement campaigns against other users of the letters XX, see Glynn S. Lunney, Jr., *Two-Tiered Trademarks*, 56 Hous. L. Rev. 295 (2018) – Ed.

these agreements, insofar as they authorized third parties to continue to use infringing or diluting marks with Exxon's knowledge and approval, were 'licenses'; and, because these 'licenses' contained no quality control provision, they were 'naked licenses' which, under prevailing law, could lead to forfeiture of Exxon's rights in its licensed marks."

In considering Oxxford's defense, the court reasoned as follows:

A naked license is a trademark licensor's grant of permission to use its mark without attendant provisions to protect the quality of the goods or services provided under the licensed mark. A trademark owner's failure to exercise appropriate control and supervision over its licensees may result in an abandonment of trademark protection for the licensed mark. Because naked licensing is generally ultimately relevant only to establish an unintentional trademark abandonment which results in a loss of trademark rights against the world, the burden of proof faced by third parties attempting to show abandonment through naked licensing is stringent.

The language of [15 U.S.C. § 1127] reflects that to prove "abandonment" the alleged infringer must show that, due to acts or omissions of the trademark owner, the incontestable mark has lost "its significance as a mark." This statutory directive reflects the policy considerations which underlie the naked licensing defense: "[if] a trademark owner allows licensees to depart from his quality standards, the public will be misled, and the trademark will cease to have utility as an informational device ... [a] trademark owner who allows this to occur loses his right to use the mark." Conversely, if a trademark has not ceased to function as an indicator of origin there is no reason to believe that the public will be misled; under these circumstances, neither the express declaration of Congress's intent in subsection 1127(2) nor the corollary policy considerations which underlie the doctrine of naked licensing warrant a finding that the trademark owner has forfeited his rights in the mark.

Oxxford, pointing to recent precedent in this Circuit indicating that naked licensing results in an "involuntary trademark abandonment," posits that when a defendant proves that the trademark owner has licensed its mark without any quality control provisions the courts should presume a loss of significance. We disagree. Abandonment due to naked licensing is "involuntary" because, unlike abandonment through non-use, referred to in subsection 1127(1), an intent to abandon the mark is expressly not required to prove abandonment under subsection 1127(2). In addition, a trademark owner's failure to pursue potential infringers does not in and of itself establish that the mark has lost its significance as an indicator of origin. Instead, such a dereliction on the part of the trademark owner is largely relevant only in regard to the "strength" of the mark; absent an ultimate showing of loss of trade significance, subsection 1127(2) (and the incorporated doctrine of naked licensing) is not available as a defense against an infringement suit brought by that trademark owner. We, like the district court, would find it wholly anomalous to presume a loss of trademark significance merely because Exxon, in the course of diligently protecting its mark, entered into agreements designed to preserve the distinctiveness and strength of that mark. We decline Oxxford's invitation to judicially manufacture a presumption of loss of trademark significance under the facts of this case given that had Exxon simply ignored the prior threats to its marks no such presumption would obtain.

Though courts in cases from *Dawn Donuts* to *Exxon* have held that a trademark licensor need not include quality control language in its licensing agreements to avoid a finding of trademark abandonment, most trademark licensing agreements today do include such language.

EXAMPLE: QUALITY CONTROL

Weak Version

The quality of the Licensed Product sold during the Term of this License Agreement, as well as the manner and style in which the Trademark is used by Licensee, shall be at least as high as the quality standards maintained by Licensor prior to the Effective Date.

Strong Version

Licensee may not use, offer for sale, sell, advertise, ship, or distribute any Licensed Product bearing the Trademark until Licensee has provided Licensor with a sample of the use of the Trademark on Licensed Product and has received written approval from Licensor for such use and sale during the Term. In the event that Licensor determines, following such approval, that Licensed Products do not meet its quality standards, Licensor shall so notify Licensee and [the Parties shall use their best efforts to agree upon a mutually satisfactory solution OR Licensee shall make such reasonable quality improvements to the Licensed Products as requested by Licensor [1]].

DRAFTING NOTES

[1] *Remedy* – in the strong version of a quality control clause, one must always ask what action the licensee must take if its products do not live up to the quality requirements of the licensor. Two customary choices are presented here: the parties must agree on a mutually satisfactory resolution, or the licensee must make whatever (reasonable) adjustments the licensor requests.

As shown in the above example, quality control clauses come in two general flavors: weak and strong. The weak version is a straightforward requirement that the licensee maintain quality standards commensurate with those of the licensor. There are no built-in mechanisms to ensure that such quality standards are actually being observed, or even to define what they are. In the strong version, the licensee is required to provide samples to the licensor for approval, and to adjust its products if they do not meet with the licensor's approval. As such, quality control procedures are built into the relationship of the parties.

Notes and Questions

1. *Permitting phase-out.* The court in *Exxon* concludes that "We ... would find it wholly anomalous to presume a loss of trademark significance merely because Exxon, in the course of diligently protecting its mark, entered into agreements designed to preserve the distinctiveness and strength of that mark." How did Exxon's phase-out agreements preserve the distinctiveness and strength of its XX mark? Other than expressing an admiration of Exxon's business practices and trademark enforcement diligence, what rationale does the court offer to overcome Oxxford's argument that Exxon's phase-out agreements were, in fact, naked licenses?

2. *Requiring contractual quality control.* The courts in *Dawn Donut* and *Exxon* establish that a licensor need not include quality control language in its licensing agreement in order to avoid a finding of naked licensing. Why isn't such language required? And if not, why do attorneys today routinely include quality control language in virtually all trademark licensing agreements?

3. *Weak vs. strong clauses.* Some might view the "weak" version of the quality control clause provided in the example as merely paying lip service to the notion of quality control. Yet, in some ways, this clause is *stronger* than the "strong" version of the clause. How? Which clause would you prefer if you were a licensor?

4. *Remedies.* What remedy, if any, does a licensor have against its licensee if the licensee fails to meet the licensor's quality standards but the license agreement lacks a quality control clause?

Problem 15.2

Luke, a popular Topeka DJ, operates under the trademark LUKKEN TUNES. After working local nightclubs and parties for seven years, Luke relocates to New York and licenses the mark to his former assistant, Perry, for use in Topeka. The license gives Luke the right to approve all publicity and uses of the mark by Perry. Luke, however, absorbed by the club scene in New York, fails to contact Perry for five years, and Perry fails to send Luke any promotional materials or proposals for use of the mark. Now, a new DJ has begun to operate in New York under the name LUKE-IN-TOONZ. Luke believes that there is substantial consumer confusion and wishes to bring an action for infringement against the new DJ. Can the infringer challenge Luke's mark as abandoned?

15.4 TRADEMARK USAGE GUIDELINES

TRADEMARKS, CERTIFICATION MARKS AND TECHNICAL STANDARDS

JORGE L. CONTRERAS, *CAMBRIDGE HANDBOOK OF TECHNICAL STANDARDIZATION LAW: FURTHER INTERSECTIONS OF PUBLIC AND PRIVATE LAW* 205, 213–14 (CAMBRIDGE UNIV. PRESS, 2019)

It is important to distinguish between quality control requirements and stylistic guidelines for the use of trademarks. Independently of, and in addition to, quality control requirements, many trademark owners impose restrictions on how their marks are to be presented and used (as opposed to requirements pertaining to the quality of the goods and services to which the marks are applied). While the precise requirements vary, below is a nonexhaustive list of stylistic restrictions imposed by trademark owners ... on the use of licensed marks :

- Marks must be reproduced according to specified color, size, font and placement guidelines (often including the mandatory use of a downloadable graphics file to reproduce a logo)
- Prohibition on use of a mark as a verb (e.g., "I am going to Xerox these papers")
- Prohibition on use of a mark as a noun (e.g., "DECT" is necessary in this configuration)
- Prohibition on altering the mark or combining it with other marks

- Prohibition on using the mark in a demeaning, derogatory or misleading manner
- Prohibition on registering or using the mark as, or as part of, a trade name, domain name, metatag or similar device (e.g., Bluetooth Consultants, Bluetooth-users.org)
- Prohibition on using the mark in, or as, a pun[11]
- The mark must be accompanied by the ® or ™ symbol and acknowledged as the property of the mark owner

Notes and Questions

1. *Usage guidelines.* How do trademark usage guidelines differ from quality requirements? Why are both needed?

2. *Avoiding genericide.* Some trademark owners go to great lengths to restrict how their marks are used. One recurrent concern of mark owners is *genericide* – a trademark that comes to be associated with a generic class of goods or services loses its character as an indication of origin and thus becomes unprotectable. There is a long list of marks that have been canceled over the years because they have become generic: aspirin, brassiere, escalator, linoleum, thermos, trampoline and zipper are just a few. To avoid genericide through the actions of their licensees, mark owners often draft licensing terms that prohibit uses that tend to frame their marks as generic terms (e.g., prohibiting uses of the mark as a noun [please hand me a *Kleenex*] rather than as an adjective [please hand me a *Kleenex* facial tissue]).[12] How effective do you think these measures are? What is a licensor's remedy if its licensee violates such a requirement, contributing to the cancelation of a mark on the basis of genericide?

15.5 FRANCHISING

Some of the best-known trademarks in the world are associated with franchises, which are prevalent in markets from fast-food to car dealerships to motels to tax preparation services. Legally speaking, franchises are little more than souped-up trademark licenses, often with know-how and some copyrighted materials thrown in. As such, many of the license, payment, reporting and other provisions discussed in Part II of this book are also found in franchise agreements. Yet the franchise has evolved over the years into a highly specialized, and extremely popular, form of commercial arrangement. According to the Department of Agriculture, between 2009 and 2014, the United States added nearly 18,000 mostly franchised fast-food restaurants, expanding at more than twice the rate of population growth. In this section we will explore a few of the current controversies and contractual details characterizing these unique business arrangements.

15.5.1 *The Business of Franchising*

The excerpt below discusses some of the commercial issues that face both franchisees and franchisors in today's marketplace.

---

[11] This unusual requirement was adopted by the European Telecommunications Standards Institute (ETSI), perhaps due to the inherently satiric nature of standards engineers and/or the sensitive nature of European managers ("Our trademarks represent our standards, the symbols of ETSI goodwill worldwide. They should be treated with respect as valuable assets. Accordingly, they should not be used as the object of puns").

[12] See Jorge L. Contreras, *Sui-Genericide*, 106 Iowa L. Rev. (2020) (discussing these and other genericide "countermeasures").

DISENFRANCHISED: IN THE TIGHT-FISTED WORLD OF FAST FOOD, IT'S NOT JUST THE WORKERS WHO GET A LOUSY DEAL

TIMOTHY NOAH

PACIFIC STANDARD, MARCH/APRIL 2014

BHUPINDER "BOB" BABER bought two Quiznos franchises in Long Beach, California, in 1998 and 1999. His investment totaled $500,000, and Baber's wife, Ratty, quit her job to work at the restaurants for no pay. The Babers did this because, as Bob would later recall, he "trusted in Quiznos." But, as he soon found out, being a franchisee can be a very swift and painful way to lose a lot of money.

Franchising as we know it is an American invention, and it dates back to the mid-19th century. The McCormick Harvesting Machine Company, which made reapers, and the I.M.Singer Company, which made sewing machines, found that wholesalers didn't want to carry or distribute these expensive and novel machines, nor did they want to offer parts and repair. So McCormick and Singer came up with an innovative solution: They built a network of independent agents. In return for carrying the product, the agents received a sizable cut of revenues from sales and repair, and exclusive rights to sell the machines in a certain area. In a vast country, franchising solved a lot of problems related to distribution, distance, and repairs. In subsequent decades, franchising also became the model for selling automobiles.

In the 20th century, businesses began to see the value of franchising in the service sector. Howard Johnson used franchising in the 1930s, and Ray Kroc built an empire on McDonald's franchises in the 1950s, '60s and '70s. Today, fast food is sold almost entirely through franchises. Worldwide, franchises represent about 80 percent of McDonald's

FIGURE 15.10 Beginning in 1925, Howard Johnson used franchising to expand from a single soda fountain outside of Boston into a nationwide chain of more than 1,000 orange-roofed family restaurants.[13]

---

[13] For a short history of the HoJo chain, see Adam Chandler, *The Very Last Howard Johnson's*, The Atlantic, September 9, 2016. And for a comprehensive history of America's franchised restaurant industry, see Philip Langdon, Orange Roofs, Golden Arches (Knopf, 1986) – Ed.

restaurants, 95 percent of Burger King restaurants, and 100 percent of Subway restaurants. (The rest are usually company-owned flagship restaurants in high-profile locations or restaurants relinquished by one franchisee and not yet assigned to another.)

It's not just the workers who get a lousy deal. Over the years, Bob Baber, the Quiznos franchisee, became increasingly frustrated by the terms of his contract. One of the issues that galled him the most was that Quiznos was allowed to (and did) place additional sub shops in his franchise area, creating what he felt was direct competition that cut into his profits. Baber formed the Quiznos Subs Franchise Association, a sort of franchisees' union, through which he hoped to leverage better terms. A month later, the Denver-based company terminated Baber's franchise, claiming his restaurants were not being maintained properly, and other contractual defaults. When a franchise agreement is terminated, all investment by the franchisee – including acquisition cost, equipment, and fees – is effectively flushed away. Baber and Quiznos became enmeshed in a protracted legal struggle, with Baber refinancing his house and spending nearly $100,000.

Despite such stories, people still buy into the franchise dream. For many Americans, owning a franchise seems like a starter kit for being your own boss as a small-business owner. You have the benefit of riding on a well-established national brand, and all you have to do is manage the shop. But a 1997 study by Timothy Bates, an economist at Wayne State University, concluded that "entering self-employment by purchasing an ongoing franchise operation is riskier than alternative routes." If everything goes right for a fast-food franchisee, he might enjoy a profit margin of about 10 to 12 percent, but a profit margin in the single digits is far more common. By contrast, at the corporate level, McDonald's enjoys a profit margin around 20 percent.

Well-known fast-food companies have so much clout that franchisors get to set the terms, and franchisees can take them or leave them. A 2013 McDonald's franchise agreement stipulates not only how the restaurant shall be designed and the food prepared, but also how many days a week it shall be open (seven) and during what hours (7 a.m. to 11 p.m. or "such other hours as may from time to time be prescribed by McDonald's"). In order to ensure clean finances among those with whom it partners, McDonald's requires the franchisee to submit two financial reports monthly, plus a profit and loss statement and balance sheet once a year, and McDonald's is free to examine at any time all franchisee financial records.

The more successful the brand, the tighter the leash. "Thirty years ago," says Rick Swisher, who opened Los Angeles County's first Domino's in 1981, "we ran our own business with guidelines from the franchisors as to how the product was to look." But by the time he closed his 11 Domino's franchises in 2012, he says, franchise reps were so concerned with corporate imaging that they were telling employees, "You're not answering the phone correctly."

Franchise agreements usually require the franchisee to purchase food and other items only from authorized vendors. This helps to maintain consistency in quality. More than one observer has likened contemporary franchising to sharecropping.

If a franchisee folds, moreover, the corporation may not suffer much. So long as willing buyers keep lining up, a restaurant can churn through successive franchisees.

At some point, however, squeezing franchisees becomes bad business. If too many restaurants go belly up, so could the franchisor.

Franchisees enjoy few regulatory protections at the federal level, and even at the state level, statutes intended to prevent exploitative franchising arrangements can be vague.

New Jersey's Franchise Practices Act, for instance, outlaws the imposition of "unreasonable standards of performance upon a franchisee" but doesn't define what these are.

The approach favored by Purvin, who is chairman of the American Association of Franchisees and Dealers, is to strengthen franchisees' ability to create franchisee associations to engage in something like collective bargaining. (Some franchisors actually require franchisees contractually not to join franchisee groups.) Granted, enshrining such rights of association wouldn't necessarily prevent companies from finding ways to retaliate (just as detailed labor laws don't prevent companies from finding ways to fire union supporters), and enabling franchise owners to earn larger profits wouldn't guarantee that they'd treat workers better (that's why fast food workers must themselves unionize). But it would at least make better treatment more possible.

Notes and Questions

1. *The price of franchising.* As the article by Timothy Noah illustrates, franchise relationships are often stacked in favor of the franchisor. Consider product pricing, which is often controlled by the franchisor. According to one Subway sandwich franchisee, the cost of producing a "footlong" Subway sandwich, including ingredients, labor, rent, utilities, credit card fees and royalties payable to the franchisor, is "well over $4" for a sandwich priced at about $6.[14] So when Subway announced in January 2018 that it was bringing back its "$5 Footlong" promotion, hundreds of Subway's 10,000 US franchisees protested that the promotion would cause them significant financial hardship and force some stores to close. But according to Subway, such promotions result in increased traffic and make up for losses with high profit margins on sides and drinks. How should franchisors and franchisees deal with questions of product pricing?

2. *Franchise disclosures.* In the United States, the Federal Trade Commission (FTC) oversees the promotion and sale of franchises.[15] The FTC's Franchise Rule (16 CFR Parts 436–37),

FIGURE 15.11 Subway's national $4.99 Footlong promotion reportedly hurt franchisees.

---

[14] Caitlin Dewey, *The Dark Side of Your $5 Footlong: Business Owners Say It Could Bite Them*, Wash. Post, December 28, 2017.

[15] California, Hawaii, Illinois, Indiana, Maryland, Michigan, Minnesota, New York, North Dakota, Rhode Island, South Dakota, Washington, Virginia and Wisconsin also have franchise regulations at the state level.

last updated in 2007, relates primarily to disclosures that franchisors must make when offering franchises to the public. The core of the rule (which itself runs to 133 pages, including commentary) sets out the requirements for a detailed "Franchise Disclosure Document," or FDD, that must be delivered to any prospective franchisee. Every FDD must include twenty-three sections detailing all fees, requirements, restrictions, obligations and risks associated with the franchise. In some cases, these disclosures relate directly to business risks that the franchisee will face from the franchisor itself, such as the warning:

You will not receive an exclusive territory. You may face competition from other franchisees, from outlets that we own, or from other channels of distribution or competitive brands that we control.

Given the extensive disclosures and warnings required by law, why do so many franchisees continue to experience financial disappointment, if not ruin, in franchised markets? Should the FTC or other regulatory agencies do more to protect franchisees? If so, what should they do?

FRANCHISE DISCLOSURE DOCUMENT
DUNKIN' DONUTS FRANCHISING LLC
a Delaware limited liability company
130 Royall Street
Canton, Massachusetts 02021
(781) 737-3000
www.DunkinFranchising.com

The Franchisor is DUNKIN' DONUTS FRANCHISING LLC ("Dunkin' Donuts" "we" or "DD"). We develop, operate and franchise retail stores utilizing the Dunkin' Donuts system in single-brand stores. Our franchised stores sell Dunkin' Donuts coffee, donuts, bagels, muffins, compatible bakery products, sandwiches, and other beverages.

The total investment necessary to begin operation of a DD franchise ranges from $240,250 to $1,699,850. This includes a range of $55,360 to $97,860 that must be paid to the franchisor or affiliate. This disclosure document summarizes certain provisions of your franchise agreement and other information in plain English. Read this disclosure document and all accompanying agreements carefully. You must receive this disclosure document at least 14 calendar days before you sign a binding agreement with, or make any payment to the franchisor or an affiliate in connection with the proposed franchise sale. **Note, however, that no government agency has verified the information contained in this document.**

You may wish to receive your disclosure document in another format that is more convenient for you. To discuss the availability of disclosures in different formats, contact Dunkin' Donuts Franchise Information, 3 East A, 130 Royall Street, Canton, MA 02021, 1-800-777-9983.

The terms of your contract will govern your franchise relationship. Don't rely on the disclosure document alone to understand your contract. Read all of your contract carefully. Show your contract and this disclosure document to an advisor, like a lawyer or accountant.

Buying a franchise is a complex investment. The information in this disclosure document can help you make up your mind. More information of franchising, such as "A Consumer's Guide to Buying a Franchise," which can help you understand how to use this disclosure document is available from the Federal Trade Commission. You can contact the FTC at 1-877-FTC-HELP or by writing to the FTC at 600 Pennsylvania Avenue, NW, Washington, DC 20580. You can also visit your public library for other sources of information on franchising.

There may also be laws on franchising in your state. Ask you state agencies about them.

Issuance Date: March 28, 2008

RISK FACTORS

1. THE FRANCHISE AGREEMENT AND SDA PERMIT EITHER YOU OR US TO SUBMIT DISPUTES TO A COURT OR TO ARBITRATION. THE DECISION TO ARBITRATE OR TO SUBMIT THE DISPUTE TO THE COURT SYSTEM IS BINDING, EXCEPT THAT WE HAVE THE OPTION TO SUBMIT ANY OF THE FOLLOWING ACTIONS TO A COURT: COLLECTION OF FEES; INJUNCTIVE RELIEF; PROTECTION OF OUR INTELLECTUAL PROPERTY, INCLUDING PROPRIETARY MARKS; AND TERMINATION OF FRANCHISE AGREEMENT AND SDA FOR DEFAULT. ANY ARBITRATION WILL TAKE PLACE IN THE STATE IN WHICH THE STORE IS LOCATED. SOME STATES MAY HAVE LAWS REGARDING ARBITRATION/LITIGATION. SEE ADDENDA TO CONTRACTS AND/OR FDD REQUIRED BY VARIOUS STATES (APPENDIX II).

2. THE FRANCHISE AGREEMENT STATES THAT MASSACHUSETTS LAW GOVERNS THAT AGREEMENT, AND THE SDA STATES THAT MASSACHUSETTS LAW GOVERNS THAT AGREEMENT.

FIGURE 15.12 The cover of Dunkin' Donuts 2008 Franchise Disclosure Document (508 pages in total), which discloses that a total investment of $240,250–1,699,850 is required to acquire and begin operations of a Dunkin' Donuts franchise

3. *Franchise advertising.* In addition to federal and state disclosure rules, California, Maryland, Minnesota, New York, North Dakota, Rhode Island and Washington all regulate a franchisor's advertising seeking to attract new franchisees.[16] Many of these regulations require the filing of franchise advertisements with a state agency, and some even require agency approval. Given that franchises represent significant financial investments by (presumably) sophisticated businesspersons, why do states feel that such regulation is necessary?

4. A *café without franchising*? Though most chain restaurants and cafés are franchised, there are some exceptions, most notably Starbucks. In his 1997 book *Pour Your Heart Into It*, Starbucks CEO Howard Schultz wrote:

> To me, franchisees are middlemen who would stand between us and our customer ... If we had franchised [as some executives wanted to in the 1980s], Starbucks would have lost the common culture that made us strong. We teach baristas not only how to handle the coffee properly but also how to impart to customers our passion for our products. They understand the vision and value system of the company, which is seldom the case when someone else's employees are serving Starbucks coffee.

Do you agree with Schultz's assessment? Are Starbucks employees more dedicated to quality than, say, employees of McDonald's, Subway or Quiznos? Can you think of other reasons that a corporation would choose not to franchise?

5. *Product distribution vs. business format franchises.* Franchises come in two general flavors. *Product distribution* franchises permit the franchisee to sell the franchisor's products – soft drinks, automobiles, gasoline – and to display the franchisor's logos and trademarks in connection with the sale and promotion of those products. These relationships are slightly more detailed and burdensome than ordinary product distribution agreements, but do not seek to control every aspect of the franchisee's business. Automobile dealerships are good examples of product distribution franchises. The physical showroom, layout and amenities vary from one Toyota dealership to another, but share common features such as signage, staff uniforms, promotional literature and exclusivity (i.e., a dealer cannot sell Toyotas and Chevrolets out of the same showroom). *Business format* franchises, on the other hand, exert an entirely different level of control, seeking to specify virtually every aspect of the franchised business. Most restaurant franchises, such as the Quiznos and Subway franchises discussed above, are of the business format variety. Why might a franchisor choose one type of franchise model over the other? What are the relative advantages and disadvantages of product distribution and business format franchises?

15.5.2 *The Franchise Agreement*

Franchise agreements are long and complex and are filled with requirements on the conduct of franchisees' businesses. The following case illustrates what can go wrong when a franchisee fails to live up to the expectations in its franchise agreement.

---

[16] Mark J. Burzych, *Franchise Advertising in the Digital Age: Regulators Need to Contemporaneously Address Advancing Advertising Technologies or Step Aside*, 40 Franchise L. J. 221 (2020).

IHOP Restaurants LLC v. Moeini Corp.

2018 U.S. Dist. LEXIS 19707 (S.D. Ala. 2018)

DUBOSE, CHIEF UNITED STATES DISTRICT JUDGE

This action is before the Court on the Complaint, Motion for Preliminary Injunction, and Brief in support filed by Plaintiffs IHOP Restaurants, LLC and IHOP Franchisor, LLC (IHOP), the response filed by Defendant Moeini Corporation, and IHOP's reply. Upon consideration of the motion, response and reply and the evidence presented at the hearing, and for the reasons set forth herein, the Motion for Preliminary Injunction is GRANTED.

I. Factual and Procedural Background

Defendant IHOP Franchisor is a franchisor of nationally and internationally recognized restaurants with a system of approximately 400 franchisees operating over 1,600 restaurants. Defendant IHOP Restaurants has adopted and used in interstate commerce and licensed to IHOP Franchisor and indirectly to authorized franchisees certain trademarks (the Marks), which have been registered with the United States Patent and Trademark Office, in connection with the operation of IHOP restaurants.

Mehdi Moeini began working with IHOP corporation in 1996. After working his way up to a management position, Moeni purchased his first IHOP restaurant franchise in 2004. Moeini Corporation was formed in 2006 and now owns or operates five IHOP restaurants. Two restaurants are located in Florida and three are located in Alabama. [Each Franchise Agreement has a term of 20 years.]

IHOP, through the Franchise Agreements licensed Moeini Corporation to use the IHOP Marks to identify the goods and services in the three franchised IHOP restaurants. The Marks distinguish IHOP and its franchisees from others who are not authorized or licensed to use the Marks. To insure uniformity of operation and protection of the Marks, the Franchise Agreements also require Moeini Corporation to strictly comply with IHOP's standard operating procedures, policies and rules, etc., set forth in the Franchise Agreements or in operations manual or operations bulletins. The operations bulletins are defined to "mean the Franchisor's Operations Manual, and all bulletins, notices, and supplements thereto, and all ancillary manuals, specifications and materials, as the same may be amended and revised from time to time." Franchise Agreements § 1.02. These documents are made available to IHOP franchisees through the IHOP password protected website and apply to all aspects of operating an IHOP restaurant.

Section 10.05 sets forth, in relevant part, as follows:

> Franchisee shall operate the Franchised Restaurant in strict compliance with all Applicable Laws and with the standard procedures, policies, rules and regulations established by Franchisor and incorporated herein, or in Franchisor's Operations Bulletins. Such standard procedures, policies, rules and regulations established by Franchisor may be revised from time to time as circumstances warrant, and Franchisee shall strictly comply with all such procedures as they may exist from time to time as though they were specifically set forth in this Agreement and when incorporated in Franchisor's Operations Bulletins the same shall be deemed incorporated herein by reference. By way of illustration and

without limitation, such standard procedures, policies, rules and regulations may or will specify accounting records and information, payment procedures, specifications for required supplies and purchases, including Trademarked Products, hours of operation, advertising and promotion, cooperative programs, specifications regarding required insurance, minimum standards and qualifications for employees, design and color of uniforms, menu items, methods of production and food presentation, including the size and serving thereof, standards of sanitation, maintenance and repair requirements, specifications of furniture, fixtures and equipment, flue cleaning, and fire prevention service, appearance and cleanliness of the premises, accounting and inventory methods and controls, forms and reports, and in general will govern all matters that, in Franchisor's judgment, require standardization and uniformity in all IHOP Restaurants. Franchisor or its Affiliate will furnish Franchisee with Franchisor's current Operations Bulletins upon the execution of this Agreement.

To ascertain whether an IHOP franchised restaurant is in compliance with the standards set out in the operations bulletins or policy manuals, IHOP's franchise business consultants perform periodic unannounced operations evaluation (OEs) (except in certain training and instruction circumstances) whereby its franchise business consultants will evaluate the franchisee's restaurant. The franchise business consultants rate all aspects of restaurant operation and during the relevant time period, 80% compliance on the OE is a passing score. IHOP also retains third party contractors, in this instance Ecosure, that periodically inspect food safety and cleanliness and provide an operations assessment report (OAR). As with the OEs, the inspections are unannounced and 80% compliance would pass the inspection.

At the end of 2016, Moeini Corporation lost 19 employees from the Alabama restaurants. Included were the district manager and two IHOP certified managers who left within a month. The managers then recruited other managers and employees from the restaurants. Moeini Corporation attempted to find new qualified employees to manage and work at the restaurants, but the attempt was not met with great success.

Immediately, the three restaurants began to experience deficiencies in operation. All three restaurants failed the OEs conducted in December 2016. All three restaurants passed the announced OEs for February 2017, but then failed the OEs for June and August 2017.

Additionally, during 2017, IHOP received 305 customer complaints regarding these three restaurants, which greatly exceeded the national norm for IHOP restaurants. The complaints covered many aspects of the restaurants' operations, but of primary concern to IHOP were the complaints related to food preparation, food service, food storage, food safety, cleanliness and sanitation. IHOP's Division Vice President testified that the restaurants licensed to Moeini Corporation had the highest number of complaints in the IHOP system.

If a franchisee commits a material breach of the franchise agreement, IHOP must provide written notice of the default and a period of time to cure the material breach. If the franchisee fails to cure within the time period, then the franchise agreement terminates at IHOP's election without further notice or opportunity to cure. At this point, the franchisee must, pursuant to the franchise agreements, discontinue use of the IHOP Marks and not operate the restaurants in any manner that would give the public the impression that the restaurant was authorized or licensed by IHOP.

On June 22, 2017, IHOP wrote Moeni Corporation that the three Alabama restaurants were rated as "F" on IHOP's operation rating system. IHOP pointed out two primary factors that contributed to the rating: The failure to obtain Certified General Managers at the Spanish Fort and Mobile restaurants within the time frame provided and failure of the Corporate owner or its District Manager to visit the restaurants. IHOP stated that it would send consultants to work with Moeini Corporation to improve the restaurants.

On August 4, 2017, IHOP wrote Moeini Corporation that the "results of your Operations are alarming and the Guest Complaints are the highest in the IHOP system. Additionally, your OAR results ... are below IHOP standards[.]" Again, IHOP offered assistance to improve the three restaurants. The letter also indicated that IHOP understood that Moeini Corporation was pursuing the sale of its IHOP locations, but to date no sale was indicated.

On August 23, 2017, IHOP sent Moeini Corporation a notice of default letter. IHOP notified Moeini Corporation that it had breached its "obligations under Section 10.05 of the respective Franchise Agreements" because it had failed to "operate the Restaurants in compliance with the standard procedures, policies, rules and regulations established by IHOP" as shown by the failing scores.

IHOP stated as follows:

> Pursuant to Section 12.01, you are hereby notified of your default of the Franchise Agreements, and of IHOP's intent to terminate all 3 of your Franchise Agreements if you fail to cure within 30 days of receipt of this Notice. IHOP hereby demands that you fully comply with all terms and conditions of the Franchise Agreements and pass the next OEs for each restaurant to cure.

All three restaurants failed the OEs conducted in September 2017. As of late September 2017, after the expiration of the 30-day period to cure, Moeini Corporation had not presented IHOP with any evidence that it had cured the material breach at any of the restaurants.

On September 27, 2017, IHOP sent Moeini Corporation a written notice of termination of the three Franchise Agreements.

IHOP also demanded that Moeini Corporation "de-brand and de-identify" all three restaurants "within 60 days of receipt of [the] letter, in accordance with your obligations under the Franchise Agreements ..."

IHOP continued to inspect the restaurants, for food safety and cleanliness, after the September 27, 2017 notice of termination because the IHOP Marks were still being used at the restaurants. The Mobile IHOP failed the OARS on September 29, 2017. The Spanish Fort IHOP passed the OARs on October 6, 2017. The Foley IHOP passed the OARS assessments on October 18, 2017.

During October 2017, Moeini Corporation presented one potential buyer to IHOP. Upon interview, IHOP determined that the buyer was not qualified. Another potential buyer revoked the letter of intent.

On October 26, 2017, the day before the Franchise Agreements would effectively terminate, Moeini Corporation filed a Chapter 11 bankruptcy action. On December 6, 2017, the Bankruptcy Court granted IHOP's motion for relief from the automatic stay.[17]

---

[17] For a discussion of the automatic stay in bankruptcy actions, see Section 21.1 – Ed.

In December 2017, the Division Vice President instructed two franchise business consultants to perform OEs at the three restaurants. However, Moeini Corporation denied access.

IHOP filed this action on December 29, 2017. IHOP alleges breach of the Franchise Agreements because Moeini Corporation failed to comply with IHOP's policies and procedures and operations bulletins and failed to perform contractual obligations after notice of termination of the Franchise Agreements. IHOP alleges trademark infringement pursuant to 15 U.S.C. § 1114 of the Lanham Act for continuing use of IHOP's marks for the three restaurants, without IHOP's permission, after the Franchise Agreements had been terminated. IHOP also filed a motion for preliminary injunction which is now before the Court.

II. Discussion

According to the terms of the Franchise Agreements, when a material breach occurs, IHOP has the right to terminate the Franchise Agreements if, after notice and an opportunity to cure, Moeini Corporation fails to timely cure the material breach. In relevant part, as defined and applied in the Franchise Agreements, "material breach" includes the "failure of Franchisee to comply with any other material obligation of Franchisee under the agreements, including failure to comply with Franchisor's Operations Bulletins as described in paragraph 10.05." Section 10.05 states that the franchisee Moeini Corporation "shall operate the Franchised Restaurants in strict compliance with all Applicable Laws and with the standard procedures, policies, rules and regulations established by Franchisor and incorporated herein, or in Franchisor's Operations Bulletins." The IHOP policy manuals and operations bulletins include the policies and procedures for operating an IHOP restaurant including the policies and procedures for maintaining IHOP's standards of food safety, food preparation, sanitation and cleanliness at the restaurants.

FIGURE 15.13 The (now-closed) IHOP in Spanish Fort, Alabama. Online customer reviews included comments such as "The wait for our food was about an hour, the place was not the cleanest."

The OEs, OARs, and the customer complaints significantly support IHOP's position that Moeini Corporation failed to strictly comply with IHOP's operations bulletins, as defined in § 1.02, and thus committed a material breach of the Franchise Agreements. Moreover, and importantly, repeated violations of food safety standards constitute a material breach of a restaurant franchise agreement. The corporate representative Mehdi Moeini's testimony that he disagreed with certain findings on the OEs does not change the fact there were many food safety standards that were not strictly observed as required.

The Franchise Agreements set out a seven-day or ten-day period to cure the material breach. However, consistent with the provision that IHOP may allow additional time to cure as it "may specify in the notice of default," IHOP gave Moeini Corporation thirty days to cure after receipt of the August 23, 2017 notice of default letter, or until late September 2017. The only evidence as to the condition of the restaurants during the cure period came from the three failed OEs of September 19 and 20, 2017.

Now, Moeini Corporation argues that the Franchise Agreements were not properly terminated because IHOP's franchise business consultant conducted the OEs before the 30-day period expired, and therefore, Moeini Corporation was not allowed the full 30 days to cure before IHOP declared a material breach. Although Moeini testified at the hearing that the plan was to cure and at the same time, try to sell the restaurants, there was no evidence of cure of the material breach during the 30-day time period or before the October 27, 2017 Franchise Agreement termination date. And, Moeini testified that at the end of October, he requested another 30 days to cure.

Moeini testified at the hearing that many of the low scores were the result of unreasonable inspections or assessments. He stated that during the September 2017 evaluations at the Spanish Fort and Mobile IHOP's, he objected to many of the franchise business consultant's decisions regarding the cleanliness, food safety, and other aspects of the restaurants.

In addition to the OEs and OARs showing underperformance, IHOP presented evidence and testimony regarding significant customer complaints including complaints related to sanitation, food preparation, cleanliness of the restrooms, insects, and food safety, and negative reviews on social media or internet-based restaurant review websites. IHOP's Division Vice President testified that IHOP utilized a normalized guest complaint score which is the number of complaints per 10,000 guest checks without regard to the volume of sales for the restaurants or the length of time necessary for a restaurant to generate 10,000 guest tickets. The average number of complaints was 2.9 normalized guest complaints per restaurant per month. For the year of 2017, the three restaurants at issue received 305 guest complaints and averaged between 30 and 50 normalized guest complaints per 10,000 guest tickets. The Division Vice President testified that this was the highest number of complaints in the IHOP system.

IHOP has expended substantial sums for developing, advertising and promoting its Marks. As a result, IHOP has a valuable reputation and goodwill among the public. The Marks are now associated with IHOP. They are distinctive, recognizable, and engender the goodwill upon which the IHOP franchisees depend. The complaints demonstrate that these three IHOP franchised restaurants are harming the reputation and goodwill that IHOP has developed. Importantly, as the Division Vice President testified at the hearing, the food safety concerns put the IHOP brand at great risk and if there is a food-safety related issue and guests are infected, the impact to the IHOP brand could be catastrophic, as well as the possible harm to the public.

Moreover, Moeini Corporation denied access to the restaurants for assessments and evaluations in December 2017. Therefore, IHOP has no method to monitor the restaurants and protect its brand. As stated in *IHOP Restaurants, LLC v. Len-W Foods, Inc.,* "IHOP suffers harm because the consuming public continues to believe that" these three restaurants are "authorized by IHOP. Thus, IHOP loses goodwill in the eyes of the public for each day" these restaurants continue their "poor performance."

IHOP's Motion for Preliminary Injunction is GRANTED. Accordingly, as to the three IHOP restaurants at issue in this action, Defendant Moeini Corporation is enjoined from:

(1) using the IHOP Marks or any trademark, service mark, logo, or trade name that is confusingly similar to the IHOP Marks;
(2) otherwise infringing the IHOP Marks or using any similar designation, alone or in combination with any other component;
(3) passing off any of its goods or services as those of IHOP or IHOP's authorized franchisees;
(4) causing likelihood of confusion or misunderstanding as to the source or sponsorship of its business, goods, or services;
(5) causing likelihood of confusion or misunderstanding as to its affiliation, connection, or association with IHOP and IHOP's franchisees or any of IHOP's goods or services …

Notes and Questions

1. *Franchise termination laws.* Given the extreme disproportionality between the bargaining leverage of most franchisors and franchisees, statutes have been enacted at both the federal and state levels to protect franchisees from unjustified termination. For example, the New Jersey Franchise Practices Act, N.J. Stat. § 56:10-5, provides that a franchise may not be terminated, canceled or non-renewed by the franchisor "without good cause." And the federal Petroleum Marketing Practices Act, 15 U.S.C. § 2801, *et seq.,* prohibits termination or nonrenewal of any gasoline station franchise agreement except on the basis of specifically enumerated grounds and compliance with certain notification requirements. Would such legislation have helped Moeini in the *IHOP* case? Was IHOP justified in terminating his franchises?

2. *Cure of nonperformance.* The judge in IHOP seems quite sympathetic to IHOP. Do you agree that IHOP was the "good guy" in this situation? What were Moeini's actual breaches? What more should Moeni have done to avoid a termination of the franchises?

3. *The operations manual.* In most franchise relationships, the terms of the franchisor's operations manual (which is incorporated by reference into the franchise agreement) are far more important than the terms of the franchise agreement itself. This document, often running to hundreds of pages, describes virtually every aspect of running the franchised business. As the New York Attorney General warns prospective franchisees:

   You will be told exactly how to run your business, right down to how to organize your books or where to keep the napkins. Even if you believe that the franchisor's decision is not the best one for your particular store or regional location, you will be required to follow the rules. If you are a natural entrepreneur with a creative mind, who wants to operate your business your own way, franchising is probably not for you.[18]

Why is such a detailed operational guide viewed as necessary by most franchisors?

4. *Unilateral modifications.* Like many consumer software licenses and online terms of use (see Chapter 17), the terms of a franchisor's operations manual may generally be amended by the franchisor unilaterally. But unlike a software app or website, for which the user pays a minimal amount, many franchises cost tens of thousands of dollars. Is it fair to allow the franchisor to amend contractually binding terms without the consent of the franchisee? What practical difficulties might emerge if franchisees were given a greater voice in such decisions?

Problem 15.3

You represent Rachel Ranger, an entrepreneur who has a fabulous idea for a new casual dining experience that she calls RACOON REPAST. The idea is that customers would self-serve their own meals from metal trash cans arranged throughout the dining room while blindfolded. Wait staff dressed like park rangers would help guide customers to relevant "feeding stations" (e.g., salads, meats, canned foods). Rachel wishes to franchise a chain of RACOON REPAST restaurants throughout the United States. You have been engaged to help her draft a suitable franchise agreement. List ten specific requirements that you would impose on franchisees who wished to open RACOON REPAST locations.

---

[18] N.Y. State Off. Atty. Gen., Investor Protection Bur., What to Consider Before Buying A Franchise 2 (n.d.), https://ag.ny.gov/sites/default/files/franchise_booklet.pdf.

16

Music Licensing

The licensing of musical and audiovisual content under US law is complex and somewhat arcane,[1] but it arises in an increasingly broad spectrum of transactions. Industries in which music licensing crops up include software and video games, consumer electronics, television and film, advertising and of course traditional music publishing, distribution and performance. To understand how multimedia transactions are structured today, it is first useful to gain a basic understanding of the dual nature of copyright in music, and the complex statutory framework surrounding music licensing.

16.1 THE LEGAL STRUCTURE OF MUSIC COPYRIGHT IN THE UNITED STATES

COPYRIGHT AND THE MUSIC MARKETPLACE U.S. REGISTER OF COPYRIGHTS
16–18 (2015)

1. Brief History of Copyright Protection for Music

Congress passed the first federal copyright act in 1790. That act did not provide express protection for musical compositions (or "musical works" in the parlance of the current Copyright Act), though such works could be registered as "books." Then, in 1831, Congress amended the law to provide expressly that musical works were subject to federal copyright protection. The 1831 amendment, however, provided owners of musical works with only the exclusive right to reproduce and distribute their compositions, i.e., to print and sell sheet music, because, "[a]t the time, performances were considered the vehicle by which to spur

---

[1] The goal of this chapter is not to provide an exhaustive treatment of licensing practices in the music industry, which are notoriously complex and worthy of an entire book in themselves. Rather, I hope to provide the reader with an overview of the issues to watch for when music-related transactions present themselves in a variety of contexts.

the sale of sheet music."[2] In 1897, Congress expanded the rights of music owners to include the exclusive right to publicly perform their works. With the 1909 Copyright Act, federal copyright protection for musical works was further extended by adding an exclusive right to make "mechanical" reproductions of songs in "phonorecords"—in those days, piano rolls, but in the modern era, vinyl records and CDs.[3] At the same time, Congress limited the new phonorecord right by enacting a compulsory license for this use, a topic that is addressed in greater depth below. And in 1995, Congress confirmed that an owner's exclusive right to reproduce and distribute phonorecords of musical works extends to digital phonorecord deliveries ("DPDs")—that is, the transmission of digital files embodying musical works.

Over time, new technologies changed the way people consumed music, from buying and playing sheet music, to enjoying player pianos, to listening to sound recordings on a phonograph or stereo system. But it was not until 1971, several decades after the widespread introduction of phonorecords, that Congress recognized artists' sound recordings as a distinct class of copyrighted works that were themselves deserving of federal copyright protection. This federal protection, however, was limited to sound recordings fixed on or after February 15, 1972, and, until more recently, protected only the exclusive rights of reproduction, distribution, and preparation of derivative works.

No exclusive right of public performance was granted. Then, in 1995, Congress granted sound recording owners a limited public performance right for digital audio transmissions—though, as discussed below, that right was made subject to compulsory licensing under sections 112 and 114 of the Copyright Act.

2. Musical Works versus Sound Recordings

As the above history indicates, a musical recording encompasses two distinct works of authorship: the musical work, which is the underlying composition created by the songwriter or composer along with any accompanying lyrics, and the sound recording, which is the particular performance of the musical work that has been fixed in a recording medium such as a CD or digital file. Because of this overlap, musical works and sound recordings are frequently confused. It is important to keep in mind, however, that these are separately copyrightable works.

A musical work can be in the form of sheet music, i.e., notes and lyrics written on a page, or embodied in a phonorecord, i.e., in a recording of the song. A sound recording comprises the fixed sounds that make up the recording. The musical work and sound recording are separately protected, and can be separately owned, under copyright law.

Notes and Questions

1. *Influence of the dead hand?* As the above excerpt indicates, much of our current law relating to music copyright is based on technologies that developed over a century ago. How sensible is it for our laws relating to digital downloads and streaming to harken back to the days when

---

[2] Maria A. Pallante, *ASCAP at 100*, 61 J. Copyright Soc'y 545, 545–46 (2014).
[3] Today, of course, electronic copies, either stored on a computer or a smartphone, are probably more prevalent than either of these older storage media – Ed.

FIGURE 16.1 Prior to 1972, US copyright law did not protect sound recordings, leaving performances of public domain works (such as much of the classical repertoire) entirely without protection.

vinyl records and AM/FM broadcast, let alone player piano rolls, were the primary means for distributing music?

2. *Nondramatic works*. Several important provisions of the Copyright Act, including the compulsory license under Section 115, apply only to "nondramatic" musical works. These provisions thus do not apply to musical works that are part of a dramatic production, such as an opera, ballet or musical. Why do you think this distinction exists? Does it make sense today? In practice, the distinction between dramatic and nondramatic musical works does not play a large role today. If a song from a popular musical such as *Hamilton* or *The Phantom of the Opera* is released separately from the show (e.g., on CD, streaming or download), then it is understood to be subject to Section 115. In general, it is only the performance/recording of the song in a dramatic setting itself (e.g., an unauthorized performance of *Hamilton*) that triggers this distinction. But the question still remains: Why should this distinction exist at all? Why should we treat audio works such as "The Collected Speeches of Martin Luther King, Jr." or an audio recording of *The Sound and the Fury* differently than an Andrew Lloyd Webber show tune or Lady Gaga's "Poker Face"?

16.2 LICENSING MUSICAL WORKS AND COMPOSITIONS

The divide under US copyright law between musical compositions and sound recordings has led to a bifurcated licensing system with both voluntary and statutory components. In this section we will discuss the licensing of musical compositions (works). Section 16.3 will discuss the licensing of sound recordings. With respect to each type of right licensed (composition/work and sound recording) there are two general categories of rights granted: the "mechanical" reproduction right and the performance right.

16.2.1 *The "Mechanical" Reproduction Right*

The "mechanical" right to reproduce a musical work was first recognized over a century ago:

> Until the early twentieth century, owners of musical works were compensated primarily through the reproduction and distribution of sheet music … And prices for sheet music were, as they are today, set in the free market. By the early 1900s, however, technological advances made music available for the first time via "mechanical" renderings of songs captured in player piano rolls and phonograph records. Although music publishers insisted that physical embodiments of their works were copies, the Supreme Court held otherwise in the 1908 case *White-Smith Music Publishing v. Apollo*, 209 U.S. 1, 8–9, 17–18 (1908), reasoning that such reproductions were not in a form that human beings could "see and read." With the enactment of the 1909 Copyright Act, however, Congress overrode the Court's decision and recognized copyright owners' exclusive right to make and distribute, and authorize the making and distribution, of phonorecords—i.e., mechanical reproductions—of musical works.[4]

Today, the "mechanical" reproduction right covers the reproduction of a musical work in all physical forms, including not only sheet music and player piano rolls, but vinyl records, magnetic tape, CDs, DVDs, ringtones and electronic downloads and copies of all kinds. Even some works that are electronically streamed require mechanical reproduction rights (see Note 5, below). For anachronistic reasons, all of these types of recordings are still called "phonorecords."

16.2.2 *The Compulsory License for Mechanical Reproductions under Section 115*

When the mechanical reproduction right was first incorporated into the 1909 Copyright Act, Congress was concerned that the Aeolian Company, the dominant US manufacturer of player pianos, could acquire enough exclusive rights from music publishers that it would develop a

FIGURE 16.2 Paper rolls used in player pianos were the first "mechanical" reproductions of music.

---

[4] Registrar of Copyrights, Copyright and the Music Marketplace 26 (2015).

monopoly in player piano rolls. To avoid that result, Congress simultaneously enacted the first compulsory license under US copyright law. This compulsory license is currently codified at Section 115 of the Copyright Act.

---

17 U.S. CODE § 115: SCOPE OF EXCLUSIVE RIGHTS IN NONDRAMATIC MUSICAL WORKS: COMPULSORY LICENSE FOR MAKING AND DISTRIBUTING PHONORECORDS

In the case of nondramatic musical works, the exclusive rights provided by clauses (1) and (3) of section 106, to make and to distribute phonorecords of such works, are subject to compulsory licensing under the conditions specified by this section.

(a) Availability and Scope of Compulsory License

(1) When phonorecords of a nondramatic musical work have been distributed to the public in the United States under the authority of the copyright owner, any other person … may, by complying with the provisions of this section, obtain a compulsory license to make and distribute phonorecords of the work. A person may obtain a compulsory license only if his or her primary purpose in making phonorecords is to distribute them to the public for private use, including by means of a digital phonorecord delivery.

(2) A compulsory license includes the privilege of making a musical arrangement of the work to the extent necessary to conform it to the style or manner of interpretation of the performance involved, but the arrangement shall not change the basic melody or fundamental character of the work, and shall not be subject to protection as a derivative work under this title, except with the express consent of the copyright owner.

The compulsory license under Section 115 is sometimes referred to as the "cover" license because it allows anyone to release a "cover" recording of a musical work after an initial recording of the work has been released with the authorization of the copyright owner. Recall that this license applies only to a musical composition (i.e., a song), and not to a *recording* of a song. For example, in 1984 Leonard Cohen released the song "Hallelujah," which he wrote, on his album *Various Positions*. Following its initial release, more than 300 other artists, including k.d. lang, Rufus Wainwright, John Cale and Jeff Buckley, have released their own versions of "Hallelujah."[5] So long as the cover version does not alter "the basic melody or fundamental character" of the original work, it may be released under Section 115 without the permission of the copyright owner.

Though a compulsory license permits a performer to release a version of a musical work without the permission of the copyright owner, it does not grant this right for free. Under the 1909 Copyright Act, Congress established a statutory royalty rate of two cents per copy. That rate has since been increased and is today established by the Copyright Royalty Board ("CRB"), which is composed of three administrative judges appointed by the Librarian of Congress. The following excerpt from a recent case explains the CRB's process for determining royalties for particular mechanical rights, in this case ringtones.

---

5 The song "Hallelujah" was also used to great effect in the motion picture *Shrek* (2001), but, as discussed in Section 16.4, the use of music in film requires a special set of "synchronization" licenses and is not authorized under Section 115.

Recording Industry Assn. of Am. v. Librarian of Congress
608 F.3d 861 (DC Cir. 2010)

KAVANAUGH, CIRCUIT JUDGE

By law, the Copyright Royalty Board sets the terms and rates for copyright royalties when copyright owners and licensees fail to negotiate terms and rates themselves. As part of its statutory mandate, the Board sets royalty terms and rates for what is known as the § 115 statutory license. That license allows individuals to make their own recordings of copyrighted musical works for distribution to the public without the consent of the copyright owner.

In carrying out its statutory responsibilities under 17 U.S.C. § 115, the Board instituted a … penny-rate royalty structure for cell phone ringtones, under which copyright owners receive 24 cents for every ringtone sold using their copyrighted work.

The Recording Industry Association of America challenges … the Board's decision, arguing that [it was] arbitrary and capricious for purposes of the Administrative Procedure Act.[6] We conclude that the Board's decision was reasonable and reasonably explained. We therefore affirm the Board's determination.

I A

Most songs played on the radio, sold on CDs in music stores, or digitally available on the Internet through services like iTunes embody two distinct copyrights—a copyright in the "musical work" and a copyright in the "sound recording." See 17 U.S.C. § 102. The musical work is the musical composition—the notes and lyrics of the song as they appear on sheet music. The sound recording is the recorded musical work performed by a specific artist.

Although almost always intermingled in a single song, those two copyrights are legally distinct and may be owned and licensed separately. One party might own the copyright in the words and musical arrangement of a song, and another party might own the copyright in a particular artist's recording of those words and musical notes.

This case involves licenses in a limited category of copyrighted musical works—as opposed to sound recordings. Section 115 of the Copyright Act allows an individual to make and distribute phonorecords (that is, sound recordings) of a copyrighted musical work without reaching any kind of agreement with the copyright owner. That right does not include authorization to make exact copies of an existing sound recording and distribute it; if a musical work has been recorded and copyrighted by another artist, a licensee "may exercise his rights under the [§ 115] license only by assembling his own musicians, singers, recording engineers and equipment, etc. for the purpose of recording anew the musical work that is the subject of the [§ 115] license." 2 Melville B. Nimmer & David Nimmer, Nimmer On Copyright § 8.04[A], at 8–58.5 (2009). For example, a § 115 licensee could pull together a group of musicians to record and sell a cover version of Bruce Springsteen's 1975 hit "Born to Run", but that licensee could not make copies of Springsteen's recording of that song and sell them.

The § 115 licensing regime operates in a fairly straightforward manner. When a copyright owner distributes work "to the public," § 115's provisions are triggered. Once that

---

[6] The RIAA also contested the Board's determination of a 1.5 percent monthly late fee for interest on unpaid royalties.

occurs, anyone may "obtain a compulsory license to make and distribute phonorecords of the work" under § 115 so long as the "primary purpose in making [the] phonorecords is to distribute them to the public for private use." Id. Assuming the copyright has been registered with the Copyright Office, the licensee owes the copyright owner a royalty for every phonorecord "made and distributed in accordance with the [§ 115] license." Id.

Because the § 115 license issues without any agreement between the copyright owner and the licensee, the system needs a mechanism to figure out how much the licensee owes the copyright owner and what the terms for paying that rate should be. Although that mechanism has changed over time, the Copyright Royalty Board currently serves as the rulemaking body for this system. The Board is a three-person panel appointed by the Librarian of Congress and removable only for cause by the Librarian. The Board sets the terms and rates for copyright royalties when copyright owners and licensees fail to negotiate terms and rates themselves.

As relevant here, the Copyright Act requires the Board to set "reasonable terms and rates" for royalty payments made under the § 115 license when the parties to the license fail to do so. When establishing terms and rates under that license, the Copyright Act requires the Board to balance four general and sometimes conflicting policy objectives: (1) maximizing the availability of creative works to the public; (2) providing copyright owners a fair return for their creative works and copyright users a fair income; (3) recognizing the relative roles of the copyright owners and users; and (4) minimizing any disruptive impact on the industries involved. Id. § 801(b)(1)(A)–(D).

At specified intervals, the Board holds ratemaking proceedings for licenses issued under the Copyright Act. Section 115 rate-making proceedings can occur every five years "or at such other times as the parties have agreed." Id. § 804(b)(4).

B

In 1996, the parties with an interest in the § 115 license (such as the Recording Industry Association of America, the Songwriter's Guild of America, and the National Music Publishers' Association) agreed on various terms and rates for the compulsory license. They also agreed that the settlement with respect to those terms and rates would expire 10 years later. In 2006, after the parties found they could not reach a new compromise, the Board instituted proceedings to set certain terms and rates governing the operation of the § 115 license. The process was long and complicated, involving 28 days of live testimony, more than 140 exhibits, and more than 340 pleadings, motions, and orders.

When the Board published its final determination from those proceedings in 2009, it ... established a royalty rate for cellular phone ringtones—a sound cell phones can make when they ring that often samples a popular song. It set the rate at 24 cents per ringtone sold.

The Recording Industry Association of America, known as RIAA, is a trade association representing companies that create, manufacture, and distribute sound recordings. It participated as a party in the § 115 licensing proceedings. After the Board issued its determination, RIAA filed a motion for rehearing. The Board denied the motion. RIAA now appeals ... the imposition of a penny-rate royalty structure for ringtones at 24 cents per ringtone sold.

The Board's rulings are subject to review in this Court under the arbitrary and capricious standard of the Administrative Procedure Act. 17 U.S.C. § 803(d)(3). As a general matter,

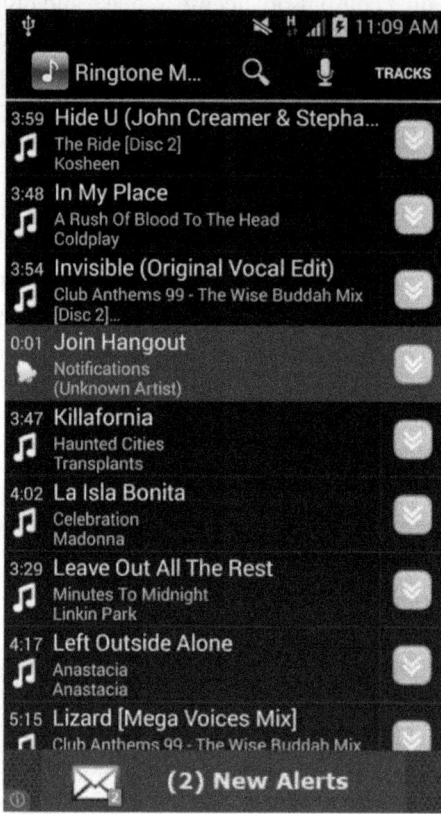

FIGURE 16.3 In 2010, the Copyright Royalty Board determined compulsory licensing rates for ringtones.

our review under that standard is deferential. And we give "substantial deference" to the ratemaking decisions of the Board because Congress expressly tasked it with balancing the conflicting statutory objectives enumerated in the Copyright Act. "To the extent that the statutory objectives determine a range of reasonable royalty rates that would serve all [the] objectives adequately but to differing degrees, the [Board] is free to choose among those rates, and courts are without authority to set aside the particular rate chosen by the [Board] if it lies within a zone of reasonableness."[7]

III

As part of the § 115 licensing proceedings, the Board established what is known as a penny-rate royalty structure for ring-tones. Under that rate, copyright owners receive 24 cents for every ringtone sold using their copyrighted work.

In the proceeding before the Board, RIAA argued for a percentage-of-revenue royalty structure under which copyright owners would receive 15 percent of the wholesale revenue derived from the sale of a ringtone. As a less preferred alternative, RIAA sought a penny-rate royalty structure in which copyright owners would receive 18 cents per ringtone sold.

7   *Recording Indus. Ass'n of America v. Copyright Royalty Tribunal,* 662 F.2d 1, 9 (D.C.Cir.1981).

Applying the § 801(b)(1) criteria, the Board settled on a penny-rate royalty structure of 24 cents per ringtone sold. With respect to the first statutory criterion it had to consider—maximizing the availability of creative work—the Board concluded that a "nominal rate[] for ring-tones" supports that objective. As to the second criterion—affording the copyright owner a fair return—the Board found that the new rates did not deprive copyright owners of a fair return on their creative works. The Board also found that the penny rate met the third statutory criterion—respecting the relative roles of the copyright owner and user. And under the fourth criterion—minimizing disruptive impact on the industry—the Board found that the rate structure it chose was reasonable and already in place in many parts of the market, minimizing any disruptive impact.

On two separate grounds, RIAA now challenges the structure of the ringtone royalty rate imposed by the Board—specifically, the fact that it is a penny rate rather than a percentage-of-revenue rate. First … RIAA alleges that the penny-rate royalty structure inappropriately departs from market analogies for voluntary licenses. Second, RIAA contends that a penny rate is unreasonable in light of falling ringtone prices.

A

As previously discussed, although existing market rates for voluntary licenses do not bind the Board when making its determinations, the Board considered those rates when selecting the penny-rate royalty structure.

The Board expressly recognized that marketplace ringtone contracts typically provide for royalty payments at the greater of (1) a penny rate ranging from 10 to 25 cents; (2) a percentage of retail revenue ranging from 10 to 15 percent; and (3) a percentage of gross revenue ranging from 9 to 20 percent.

After weighing the costs and benefits of the parties' proposals and taking into account relevant market practices, the Board concluded that a penny rate was superior to a percentage-of-revenue rate for several reasons.

First, the Board determined that a penny rate was more in line with reimbursing copyright owners for the use of their works. Under the Board's determination, every copyright owner will receive 24 cents every time a ringtone using their work is sold. By contrast, under a percentage-of-revenue system, the royalty paid to copyright owners would vary based on factors in addition to the number of ringtones sold, such as the price charged to the end consumer. This Court has validated the Board's preference for a royalty system based on the number of copyrighted works sold—like the penny rate—as being more directly tied to the nature of the right being licensed than a percentage-of-revenue rate.

Second, when looking to market analogies, the Board determined that many of the concerns driving the adoption of a percentage-of-revenue royalty structure in other instances were absent here. For example, the Board had previously concluded that a percentage-of-revenue royalty structure made sense in the satellite digital radio context because it would be difficult to measure how much a given work was actually used. In the case of ring-tones, "measuring the quantity of reproductions presents no such problems." 74 Fed. Reg. at 4516. In a market based on the sale of individual copyrighted works (like the ringtone market) as opposed to a market where copyrighted works are bundled and sold as a service to consumers (like satellite radio) figuring out how many times a copyrighted work is used (i.e., sold) is much easier.

Third, the Board found that the simplicity of using a penny-rate royalty structure supported its adoption: "No proxies need be formulated to establish the number of such reproductions," which are "readily calculable as the number of units in transactions between the parties." 74 Fed.Reg. at 4516. That simplicity contrasts sharply with the "salient difficulties" presented by RIAA's proposed percentage-of-revenue royalty structure. As the Board recognized, not least among these difficulties were definitional problems such as disagreements about what constituted "revenues."

Tying all of those strands together, the Board ultimately concluded "that a single penny-rate structure is best applied to ringtones as well as physical phonorecords and digital permanent downloads" because of "the efficiency of administration gained from a single structure when spread over the much larger number of musical works reproduced" under the § 115 licensing regime. 74 Fed.Reg. at 4517 n. 21. In the Board's view, the penny rate provided "the most efficient mechanism for capturing the value of the reproduction and distribution rights at issue." 74 Fed.Reg. at 4515.

We find nothing unreasonable about the Board's preference for a penny-rate royalty structure.

B

RIAA also argues that plummeting ring-tone prices render the penny rate inherently unreasonable. The Board considered and rejected this argument, stating: "RIAA's shrill contention that a penny-rate structure 'would be disruptive as consumer prices continue to decline' and should, therefore, be replaced by a percentage rate system in order to satisfy 801(b) policy considerations is not supported by the record of evidence in this proceeding. RIAA [does not] offer any persuasive evidence that would in any way quantify any claimed adverse impact on projected future revenues stemming from the continued application of a penny-rate structure" 74 Fed.Reg. at 4516.

Although the Board concluded that falling ringtone prices were not relevant to the choice of a penny-rate royalty as opposed to a percentage-of-revenue royalty, it did find information about declining prices useful in structuring the terms of the penny rate it chose. For example, the Board referenced concerns about reduced revenues when rejecting the copyright owners' request that selected rates be adjusted annually for inflation.

The Board examined the relevant data and determined that there was no meaningful link between the selection of a penny-rate royalty structure for ringtones and future ringtone revenues. RIAA has failed to present any basis for us to overturn that conclusion.

We affirm the Copyright Royalty Board's determination.

So ordered.

Notes and Questions

1. *Whose interests?* As discussed in *RIAA v. Librarian of Congress*, in 2009 the CRB established a compulsory license rate of 24 cents per ringtone. RIAA had initially requested a rate of 15 percent of revenue or 18 cents per ringtone. Whose interests was RIAA seeking to advance?

2. *The ringtone premium.* While the court confirmed the reasonableness of this rate, it is curious that the mechanical compulsory licensing rate for full phonorecord recordings is only 9.1 cents per copy. Why the discrepancy? The Registrar of Copyrights explains:

   It may seem counterintuitive that ringtones—which typically use only short excerpts of musical works—have a significantly higher royalty rate than full-length reproductions. Because ringtones abbreviate the full-length work, it was not immediately clear whether ringtones were eligible for the section 115 license. As a result, many ringtone sellers entered into privately negotiated licensing arrangements with publishers at rates well above the statutory rate for the full use of the song. In 2006, the Copyright Office resolved the section 115 issue, opining that ringtones were subject to compulsory licensing. But in the ensuing rate-setting proceeding before the CRB, music publishers were able to introduce the previously negotiated agreements as marketplace benchmarks, and as a result secured a much higher rate for ringtones than the rate for full songs.[8]

3. *Harry Fox and voluntary mechanical licenses.* Not all mechanical reproductions of cover versions are made under the Section 115 compulsory license. As the Registrar of Copyrights explains, many such reproductions are made pursuant to negotiated licenses:

> [I]n practice, because of the administrative burdens imposed by the [Section 115 compulsory] license—including service of a notice on the copyright owner and monthly reporting of royalties on a song-by-song basis—mechanical licensing is often handled via third-party administrators. The oldest and largest such organization is the Harry Fox Agency, Inc. ("HFA"), which was established … in 1927 and today represents over 48,000 publishers in licensing and collection activities. Mechanical licenses issued by HFA incorporate the terms of section 115, but with certain variations from the statutory provisions. Another entity that assists with mechanical licensing is Music Reports, Inc. ("MRI"), which prepares and serves statutory notices on behalf of its clients and administers monthly royalty payments in keeping with the requirements of section 115. Mechanical licenses are also issued and administered directly by music publishers in many instances.
>
> …
>
> Although the use of the section 115 statutory license has increased in recent years with the advent of digital providers seeking to clear large quantities of licenses, mechanical licensing is still largely accomplished through voluntary licenses that are issued through a mechanical licensing agency such as HFA or by the publisher directly. While HFA and other licensors typically incorporate the key elements of section 115 into their direct licenses, they may also vary those terms to some degree, such as by permitting quarterly accountings rather than the monthly statements required under the statute. That said, as observed above, the terms of the statutory license act as a ghost in the attic, effectively establishing the maximum amount a copyright owner can seek under a negotiated mechanical license.[9]

4. *The decline of mechanical reproduction.* The rise of online music consumption has caused a drastic shift in the rights being exploited by music copyright holders. As shown in Figure 16.4, between 2004 and 2013 the music industry transitioned from deriving almost all of its revenue from the sale of physical CDs to revenue that is dominated by digital downloads (also mechanical reproductions), with streaming playing an increasingly important role. Why should this shift matter to the music industry? To composers? To performing artists?

5. *Mechanical copies and digital streaming.* The streaming of music is considered a performance or broadcast, and as such is addressed by the performance licenses discussed in Section 16.3. Nevertheless, streaming services are required, as a technical matter, to make reproductions of musical works in order to operate. As a result, the Copyright Office determined in 2008 that streaming services could utilize the Section 115 compulsory licensing process to cover the reproductions made to facilitate streaming. In 2009, the CRB established the first rates under Section 115 for interactive streaming services. As a result of these developments,

---

[8] Registrar of Copyrights, supra note 4, at 30.
[9] Id. at 21.

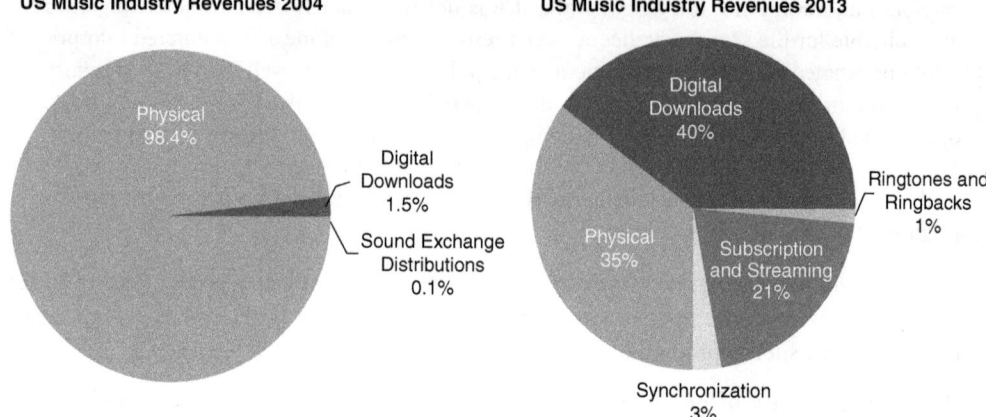

FIGURE 16.4 US music industry revenues, 2004 and 2013.

on-demand streaming services seek both mechanical and performance licenses for the musical works they use. The Music Modernization Act of 2018 created a new collecting society, the Mechanical Licensing Collective (MMA), to collect compulsory mechanical royalties from *interactive* streaming services and then distribute them to the relevant copyright holder, such as SoundExchange does for sound recordings (see Section 16.3).

6. *The rate standard.* In *RIAA v. Librarian of Congress*, Judge Kavanaugh notes that under the Copyright Act, the Board must "balance four general and sometimes conflicting policy objectives: (1) maximizing the availability of creative works to the public; (2) providing copyright owners a fair return for their creative works and copyright users a fair income; (3) recognizing the relative roles of the copyright owners and users; and (4) minimizing any disruptive impact on the industries involved." This "four-factor" rate standard was eliminated by the Music Modernization Act of 2018 and replaced by a "willing buyer, willing seller" standard, in which the Board must estimate what rate the parties would have agreed if they were bargaining in a competitive market (17 U.S.C. §§ 114(f)(1)(B), 114(f)(2)(B)). Which of these standards do you think generally results in higher royalties? Which do you suspect is easier for the Board to implement in its decision-making? Why do you think Congress amended this standard in 2018?

16.2.3 *Public Performance Rights and Performing Rights Organizations (PROs)*

Unlike the mechanical right, the public performance of musical works and compositions is not subject to compulsory licensing under the Copyright Act. Thus, anyone wishing to perform a musical work in public, either by performing it live or by playing a recording of it, must obtain a license from the copyright owner. Public performance is defined broadly and includes any performance of a work "at a place open to the public or at any place where a substantial number of persons outside of a normal circle of a family and its social acquaintances is gathered" (17 U.S.C. 101). This has been interpreted to include terrestrial (i.e., AM/FM) radio,[10] satellite and internet radio, broadcast and cable television, online services, bars, restaurants, nightclubs, sporting events, live performance venues, and commercial establishments (offices, stores, salons, elevators) that play background music.

---

[10] Terrestrial radio is a term used to describe traditional AM/FM broadcasting, derived from the fact that broadcasting and transmission facilities (i.e., towers) are located on the ground as opposed to on satellites.

COPYRIGHT AND THE MUSIC MARKETPLACE, U.S. REGISTER OF COPYRIGHTS 20, 32–34 (2015)

[A]lthough musical compositions were expressly made subject to copyright protection starting in 1831, Congress did not grant music creators the exclusive right to publicly perform their compositions until 1897. Though this right represented a new way for copyright owners to derive profit from their musical works, the sheer number and fleeting nature of public performances made it impossible for copyright owners to individually negotiate with each user for every use, or detect every case of infringement.

Songwriters and publishers almost always associate themselves with a performing rights organization ("PRO"), which is responsible for licensing their public performance rights. The two largest PROs—the American Society of Composers, Authors and Publishers ("ASCAP") and Broadcast Music, Inc. ("BMI")—together represent more than 90% of the songs available for licensing in the United States. ASCAP and BMI operate on a not-for-profit basis and, as discussed below, are subject to antitrust consent decrees that impose constraints on their membership and licensing practices. In ASCAP's case, this includes an express prohibition on licensing any rights other than public performance rights.

In addition to these larger PROs, there are two considerably smaller, for-profit PROs that license performance rights outside of direct government oversight. Nashville-based SESAC, Inc. was founded in the 1930s. SESAC's market share of the performance rights market is unclear, but appears to be at least 5% and possibly higher. Global Music Rights ("GMR"), a newcomer to the scene established in 2013, handles performance rights licensing for a select group of songwriters. While ASCAP and BMI's consent decrees prohibit them from excluding potential members who are able to meet fairly minimal criteria, SESAC and GMR have no such restriction and add new members by invitation only.

Today, the PROs provide various different types of licenses depending upon the nature of the use. Anyone who publicly performs a musical work may obtain a license from a PRO, including terrestrial, satellite and internet radio stations, broadcast and cable television stations, online services, bars, restaurants, live performance venues, and commercial establishments that play background music.

Most commonly, licensees obtain a blanket license, which allows the licensee to publicly perform any of the musical works in a PRO's repertoire for a flat fee or a percentage of total revenues. Some users opt for a blanket license due to its broad coverage of musical

FIGURE 16.5 SoundExchange, BMI, ASCAP and SESAC logos.

works and relative simplicity as compared to other types of licenses. Large commercial establishments such as bars, restaurants, concert venues, stores, and hotels often enter into blanket licenses to cover their uses, paying either a percentage of gross revenues or an annual flat fee, depending on the establishment and the type and amount of use. Terrestrial radio stations obtain blanket licenses from PROs as well, usually by means of the [Radio Music License Committee (RMLC)]. Many television stations, through the [Television Music License Committee (TMLC)], also obtain blanket licenses.

Less commonly used licenses include the per-program or per-segment license, which allows the licensee to publicly perform any of the musical works in the PRO's repertoire for specified programs or parts of their programming, in exchange for a flat fee or a percentage of that program's advertising revenue. Unlike a blanket license, the per-program or per-segment license requires more detailed reporting information, including program titles, the specific music selections used, and usage dates, making the license more burdensome for the licensee to administer.

Users can also license music directly from music publishers through a direct license or a source license. A direct license is simply a license agreement directly negotiated between the copyright owner and the user who intends to publicly perform the musical work. Source licenses are commonly used in the motion picture industry, because the PROs are prohibited from licensing public performance rights directly to movie theater owners. Instead, film producers license public performance rights for the music used in films at the same time as the synchronization rights, and pass the performance rights along to the theaters that will be showing their films. In the context of motion pictures, source licenses do not typically encompass non-theatrical performances, such as on television. Thus, television stations, cable companies, and online services such as Netflix and Hulu must obtain public performance licenses from the PROs to cover the public performance of musical works in the shows and movies they transmit to end users.

Notes and Questions

1. *Public and noncommercial broadcasting.* Section 118 of the Copyright Act creates a statutory license permitting public and noncommercial educational broadcasters to make terrestrial radio (i.e., nondigital) broadcasts of musical works at rates that are either agreed or set by the CRB. Why do you think Congress established this special licensing structure for noncommercial broadcasters? Why not subject them to the same rates charged by ASCAP and BMI to commercial broadcasters?

2. *The ASCAP/BMI antitrust decrees.* In 1934 and 1941, the Department of Justice filed actions against ASCAP and BMI under the Sherman Antitrust Act of 1890, alleging that ASCAP and BMI fixed prices for songs and committed other anticompetitive acts (see Chapter 25 for discussion of the Sherman Act). These cases were settled in 1941 with the entry of consent decrees overseen by the DOJ and enforced by federal district courts in New York:

   Although the ASCAP and BMI consent decrees are not identical, they share many of the same features. As most relevant here, the PROs may only acquire nonexclusive rights to license members' public performance rights; must grant a license to any user that applies, on terms that do not discriminate against similarly situated licensees; and must accept any songwriter or music publisher that applies to be a member, as long as the writer or publisher meets certain minimum standards.

ASCAP and BMI are also required to offer alternative licenses to the blanket license. One option is the adjustable fee blanket license, a blanket license with a carve-out that reduces the flat fee to account for music directly licensed from PRO members. Under the consent decrees, ASCAP and BMI must also provide, when requested, "through-to-the-audience" licenses to broadcast networks that cover performances not only by the networks themselves, but also by affiliated stations that further transmit those performances downstream. ASCAP and BMI are also required to provide per-program and per-segment licenses, as are described above.

ASCAP is expressly barred from licensing any rights other than its members' public performance rights (i.e., ASCAP may not license mechanical or synchronization rights). Although BMI's consent decree lacks a similar prohibition, in practice BMI does not license any rights other than public performance rights.

Finally, and perhaps most significantly, prospective licensees that are unable to agree to a royalty rate with ASCAP or BMI may seek a determination of a reasonable license fee from one of two federal district court judges in the Southern District of New York.[11]

The ASCAP consent decree was modified in 1950 and 2001. The BMI consent decree was superseded by a new decree in 1966, which was last amended in 1994. The Department of Justice has periodically reviewed the ASCAP and BMI consent decrees, and has recently indicated that the decrees may have outlived their usefulness. What do you think? Should ASCAP and BMI continue to enjoy the antitrust immunities granted to them in the mid-twentieth century?

3. *Pandora v. ASCAP.* Beginning in 2010, online streaming service Pandora developed a dispute with ASCAP regarding the rates at which ASCAP licensed works to Pandora for online streaming. Pandora initiated a rate-setting action in New York, and the court fixed the rate payable by Pandora at 1.85 percent for a five-year period. ASCAP appealed, but the Second Circuit upheld the district court's rate, holding that the district court did not commit error by establishing the 1.85 percent rate. More interestingly, in view of the "below market" rates that ASCAP was charging Pandora, three large music publishers (Universal, Sony and EMI) sought to withdraw from ASCAP the right to license their works to "new media" outlets such as Pandora. The Second Circuit, in rejecting the publishers' right to exclude new media outlets from their ASCAP licenses, held that "as ASCAP is required [under the consent decree] to license its entire repertory to all eligible users, publishers may not license works to ASCAP for licensing to some eligible users but not others."[12]

4. *How have artists fared?* Even though digital streaming services are required to pay the owners of musical works, many songwriters complain that their compensation has fallen with the rise of digital streaming. Bette Midler, a major recording star, tweeted in 2014: "@Spotify and @Pandora have made it impossible for songwriters to earn a living: three months streaming on Pandora, 4,175,149 plays = $114.11."[13]

The Registrar of Copyrights offers the following response to complaints such as Ms. Midler's:

For their part, the digital music services deny that they are the cause of the decline in songwriter income. These services note that they pay royalties for the public performance of sound recordings, while terrestrial radio does not, and so the total royalties they pay to both

---

[11] Registrar of Copyrights, supra note 4, at 36–37.
[12] *Pandora Media, Inc. v. Am. Soc'y of Composers, Authors and Publishers*, 785 F.3d 73 (2d Cir. 2015).
[13] Quoted in Registrar of Copyrights, supra note 4, at 75.

sound recording and musical work owners must be considered. Accordingly, Pandora challenged the numbers cited by Midler ... by publicizing the total amounts paid for all rights to perform the songs, including sound recording rights—stating that they paid $6,400 in royalties in Midler's case ...[14]

Who do you believe? Should the system be changed to become more favorable to composers and songwriters? How?

16.3 LICENSING SOUND RECORDINGS

In Section 16.2 we discussed the industry and statutory framework for licensing musical works or compositions. In this section we will discuss the other major set of rights that must be considered in music licensing: sound recordings. Under the Copyright Act, "sound recordings" are "works that result from the fixation of a series of musical, spoken, or other sounds, but not including the sounds accompanying a motion picture or other audiovisual work, regardless of the nature of the material objects, such as disks, tapes, or other phonorecords, in which they are embodied" (17 U.S.C. § 101). In other words, a sound recording is a particular recorded performance of a work by a particular artist. A separate copyright exists in every sound recording independent of the copyright in the underlying musical work. The protection of sound recordings in the United States was not introduced until the Copyright Act of 1976, which extends protection to all sound recordings made on or after February 15, 1972. Traditionally, we speak of the owner of a sound recording as a "record label," though that nomenclature is understandably outdated today.

16.3.1 *Reproduction and Distribution Rights*

With a few exceptions discussed below, a sound recording may not be reproduced or distributed without the authorization of the owner of the sound recording copyright. For the most part, the necessary licenses for such rights are obtained through direct negotiation between the distributor and the record label that controls the sound recording. Thus, if an online merchant wished to distribute downloaded copies of Imagine Dragons' 2013 hit "Radioactive," it would require a license from both the band's record label, KIDinaCORNER, which owns the sound recording, as well as Universal Music Publishing Group, which holds the copyright in the composition. As discussed in Section 16.2, the compulsory license under Section 115 may be available with respect to the mechanical rights to the musical work, though a license from Harry Fox Agency may also be available.

16.3.2 *Public Performance Rights: Nondigital*

When the sound recording copyright was first recognized in the United States in 1971, the exclusive right to publicly perform a sound recording was not granted. That is, the owner of a sound recording does *not* have the exclusive right to perform that sound recording and, by extension, cannot prevent others from making such a public performance. Thus, in 2004 the singer Beyoncé performed a memorable rendition of the "Star Spangled Banner" at the opening of SuperBowl XXXVIII. Anyone who bought an authorized audio recording of that performance

---

[14] Id. at 76.

has the right to play it at sporting events, high school dances, restaurants and bars and, most importantly, to broadcast it via terrestrial radio and HD radio,[15] without permission of Beyoncé or her record label, and without paying anything to do so.[16]

This result is surprising to many. The lack of an exclusive right for the public performance of a sound recording can be traced back to arguments that the public performance of phonorecords (generally via terrestrial radio) served primarily to advertise the sale of records. And since, as discussed in Section 16.3.1, the owner of a sound recording is entitled to charge a royalty for sales of phonorecords, there was no need to burden radio broadcasters with the payment of a royalty to record labels. So, to this day, terrestrial radio broadcasters, not to mention sports arenas, dance halls and restaurants, are not required to compensate the performers whose recordings they play.

Notes and Questions

1. *Political rally tunes.* Politicians wishing to rouse their supporters often adopt musical theme songs that they blast over loudspeakers at public rallies, speeches and events. In many cases, the public performance of these musical works has not been authorized by the relevant copyright holders, much to the consternation of bands and composers who do not support the player's political message. For example, in 2020 Neil Young brought suit against the Trump campaign for unauthorized use of the songs "Rockin' in the Free World" and "Devil's Sidewalk" at a number of campaign rallies. The complaint states that "in good conscience [Young] cannot allow his music to be used as a 'theme song' for a divisive, un-American campaign of ignorance and hate."[17]

   Young alleges that the Trump campaign did not have a license to publicly perform his songs. But in an increasing number of cases, campaign managers *do* acquire the necessary licenses to perform the musical compositions from ASCAP or BMI (no license being required for a live performance of the sound recording). What recourse, if any, does a musician or composer have to prevent a candidate from playing a work at a rally, even if properly licensed?[18] Does a candidate's public performance of a recorded work imply that the artist supports the candidate's political message?

   In its license agreements, BMI allows artists to opt out of having their music played at political events. The Rolling Stones, which took this option, threatened to sue the Trump campaign for playing their song "You Can't Always Get What You Want" at a political rally in Tulsa, Oklahoma.[19] What would be the basis for the Rolling Stones' claim?

---

[15] Though HD radio technology is technically "digital," HD radio is treated comparably to AM/FM analog radio for the purposes of the Act.

[16] Because the "Star Spangled Banner" is in the public domain, there is no musical work copyright to contend with in this scenario.

[17] *Young v. Donald J. Trump For President, Inc.*, Case No. 1:20-cv-06063 (S.D.N.Y., filed June 8, 2020).

[18] Donald Trump, in particular, has attracted the ire of recording artists. In addition to Neil Young, performers/groups Adele, Steven Tyler from Aerosmith, Rihanna, Pharrell Williams, R.E.M., Elton John, Dee Snider from Twisted Sister, Queen, the Rolling Stones, Nickelback, Prince, Tom Petty, Brendon Urie from Panic! At the Disco, and Guns n' Roses have all objected to Trump's public performance of their works. See Antonia Noori Farzan, *Rihanna Doesn't Want Trump Playing Her Music at His "Tragic Rallies," But She May Not Have a Choice*, Wash. Post, November 5, 2018; Andrew Solender, *All the Artists Who Have Told Trump to Stop Using Their Songs at His Rallies*, Forbes, June 28, 2020.

[19] Assoc. Press, *Rolling Stones Threatening to Sue Trump over Using Band's Songs*, June 28, 2020.

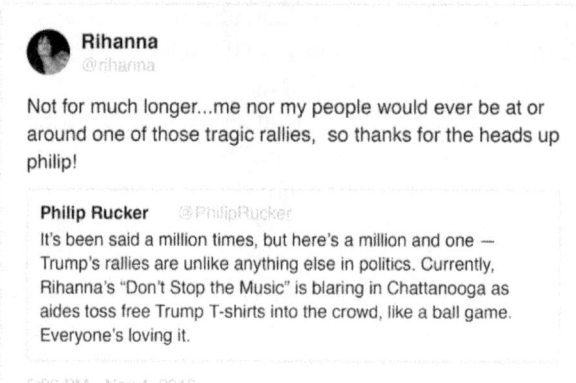

FIGURE 16.6 Recording artist Rihanna objected via Twitter to the Trump campaign's performance of her song "Don't Stop the Music."

16.3.3 *Public Performance Rights: Digital*

By 1995 Congress had become convinced that the owners of sound recordings deserved to receive some revenue from digital transmissions made via satellite radio and the Internet. But rather than create a general performance right for sound recordings, Congress elected to leave in place the existing no-royalty structure for terrestrial radio, reasoning that, unlike digital services, traditional radio broadcasters posed no threat to the recording industry. The resulting Digital Performance Right in Sound Recordings Act of 1995 (DPRSRA) created a specific set of rules for digital performances of sound recordings in Sections 112 and 114 of the Copyright Act.

16.3.3.1 Interactive and Noninteractive Services

The digital performance rights created under Sections 112 and 114 depend on whether a digital broadcast service is classified as "interactive" or "noninteractive." Noninteractive services are those that resemble traditional radio broadcasts and which the user has little opportunity to customize. These include satellite radio and webcasting. An interactive service, on the other hand, is one that enables a listener to receive either "a transmission of a program specially created for the recipient," or "on request, a transmission of a particular sound recording, whether or not as part of a program, which is selected by or on behalf of the recipient." Spotify is a typical example of an interactive digital service, in which the songs streamed to the listener are determined by the listener's choices. Nevertheless, there are a number of gray areas between interactive and noninteractive services which are discussed in the *Launch Media* case excerpted below.

16.3.3.2 The Statutory License for Noninteractive Services

Under Sections 112 and 114, noninteractive digital services may avail themselves of a compulsory license to publicly perform sound recordings at rates established by the CRB. All such royalties are paid to an independent nonprofit entity called SoundExchange. After deducting an administrative fee, SoundExchange distributes royalties paid under Section 114 to the owner of the sound recording copyright (50 percent), the featured recording artist(s) (45 percent), an agent representing nonfeatured musicians who perform on the recording (2.5 percent), and an agent representing nonfeatured vocalists who perform on the recording (2.5 percent). It distributes royalties paid under Section 112 directly to the sound recording owner. Through 2015, SoundExchange had distributed more than $2 billion to artists and record labels.

16.3.3.3 Privately Negotiated Licenses for Interactive Services

Interactive digital broadcasters cannot take advantage of the compulsory licenses under Sections 112 and 114. Instead, they must negotiate licenses directly with record labels to broadcast their sound recordings. As explained by the Registrar of Copyrights,

> It is common for a music service seeking a sound recording license from a label to pay a substantial advance against future royalties, and sometimes an administrative fee. Other types of consideration may also be involved. For example, the major labels acquired a reported combined 18% equity stake in the on-demand streaming service Spotify allegedly based, at least in part, on their willingness to grant Spotify rights to use their sound recordings on its service.[20]

Because significant sums of money can depend on whether a digital music service is treated as noninteractive or interactive, disputes over this distinction have arisen as the music streaming industry has matured. The *Launch Media* case exemplifies the interpretations that have had to be made in this area.

Arista Records, LLC v. Launch Media, Inc.
578 F.3D 148 (2D CIR. 2009)

WESLEY, CIRCUIT JUDGE

We are the first federal appellate court called upon to determine whether a webcasting service that provides users with individualized internet radio stations—the content of which can be affected by users' ratings of songs, artists, and albums—is an interactive service within the meaning of 17 U.S.C. § 114(j)(7). If it is an interactive service, the webcasting service would be required to pay individual licensing fees to those copyright holders of the sound recordings of songs the webcasting service plays for its users. If it is not an interactive service, the webcasting service must only pay a statutory licensing fee set by the Copyright Royalty Board. A jury determined that the defendant does not provide an interactive service and therefore is not liable for paying the copyright holders, a group of recording companies, a licensing fee for each individual song. The recording companies appeal claiming that as a matter of law the webcasting service is an interactive service.

Background

Launch operates an internet radio website, or "webcasting" service, called LAUNCHcast, which enables a user to create "stations" that play songs that are within a particular genre or similar to a particular artist or song the user selects. BMG holds the copyrights in the sound recordings of some of the songs LAUNCHcast plays for users.

BMG, as a sound recording copyright holder, has no copyright in the general performance of a sound recording, but BMG does have the exclusive right "to perform the copyrighted [sound recording] publicly by means of a digital audio transmission". Launch does

---

[20] Registrar of Copyrights, supra note 4, at 52.

not dispute that LAUNCHcast provides a digital audio transmission within the definition of § 106(6). BMG has a right to demand that those who perform—i.e., play or broadcast—its copyrighted sound recording pay an individual licensing fee to BMG if the performance of the sound recording occurs through an "interactive service."

An interactive service is defined as a service "that enables a member of the public to receive a transmission of a program specially created for the recipient, or on request, a transmission of a particular sound recording …, which is selected by or on behalf of the recipient." If a digital audio transmission is not an interactive service and its "primary purpose … is to provide to the public such audio or other entertainment programming," the transmitter need only pay a compulsory or statutory licensing fee set by the Copyright Royalty Board.

At trial, BMG claimed that between November 1999 and May 2001 Launch—through LAUNCHcast—provided an interactive service and therefore was required to obtain individual licenses from BMG to play BMG's sound recordings. The jury returned a verdict in favor of Launch.

BMG appeals … arguing that LAUNCHcast is an interactive service as a matter of law because LAUNCHcast is "designed and operated to enable members of the public to receive transmissions of programs specially created for them." BMG claims that under the DMCA there is no tipping point for the level of influence a user must assert before the program becomes an interactive service—all that matters is that the alleged copyright infringer is "transmi[tting] … a program specially created for" the user.

Discussion

The parties do not materially disagree on how LAUNCHcast works; their point of conflict centers on whether the program is "interactive" as defined by the statute. An "interactive service" according to the statute "is one that enables a member of the public to receive a transmission of a program specially created for the recipient, or on request, a transmission of a particular sound recording, whether or not as part of a program, which is selected by or on behalf of the recipient." The statute provides little guidance as to the meaning of its operative term "specially created."

BMG sees the issue as a simple one. BMG argues that any service that reflects user input is specially created for and by the user and therefore qualifies as an interactive service. But we should not read the statute so broadly. The meaning of the phrase in question must significantly depend on the context in which Congress chose to employ it.

Congress extended the first copyright protection for sound recordings in 1971 by creating a right "[t]o reproduce and distribute" "tangible" copies of sound recordings. Sound Recording Act of 1971 (the "SRA"). Congress drafted the SRA to address its concern about preventing "phonorecord piracy due to advances in duplicating technology." Notably, unlike the copyright of musical works, the sound recording copyright created by the SRA did not include a right of performance. Therefore, holders of sound recording copyrights—principally recording companies such as BMG—had no right to extract licensing fees from radio stations and other broadcasters of recorded music. The reason for this lack of copyright protection in sound recordings, as the Third Circuit has put it, was that the "recording industry and [radio] broadcasters existed in a sort of symbiotic relationship wherein the recording industry recognized that radio airplay was free advertising that lured consumers to retail stores where they would purchase recordings." *Bonneville Int'l Corp.*,

347 F.3d at 487. As the *Bonneville* court also noted, however, the relationship has been, and continues to be, "more nuanced" and occasionally antagonistic.

With the inception and public use of the internet in the early 1990s, the recording industry became concerned that existing copyright law was insufficient to protect the industry from music piracy. At the time, the United States Register of Copyrights referred to the internet as "the world's biggest copying machine." What made copying music transmitted over the internet more dangerous to recording companies than traditional analog copying with a tape recorder was the fact that there is far less degradation of sound quality in a digital recording than an analog recording. Although data transmission over the internet was slow—in 1994 it took on average twenty minutes to download one song—the recording industry foresaw the internet as a threat to the industry's business model. If an internet user could listen to music broadcast over, or downloaded from, the internet for free, the recording industry worried that the user would stop purchasing music. Jason Berman, president of the Recording Industry Association of America (the "RIAA"), the lobbying arm of the recording industry, stated in 1994 that without a copyright in a right of performance via internet technology, the industry would be "unable to compete in this emerging digital era." Berman warned that "digital delivery would siphon off and eventually eliminate the major source of revenue for investing in future recordings" and that "[o]ver time, this [would] lead to a vast reduction in the production of recorded music."

In light of these concerns, and recognizing that "digital transmission of sound recordings [were] likely to become a very important outlet for the performance of recorded music," Congress enacted the Digital Performance Right in Sound Recordings Act of 1995 (the "DPSR"), giving sound recording copyright holders an exclusive but "narrow" right to perform—play or broadcast—sound recordings via a digital audio transmission. The right was limited to exclusive performance of digital audio transmissions through paid subscriptions services and "interactive services." While non-interactive subscription services qualified for statutory licensing, interactive services were required to obtain individual licenses for each sound recording those interactive services played via a digital transmission. Under the DPSR, interactive service was defined as one that enables a member of the public to receive, on request, a transmission of a particular sound recording chosen by or on behalf of the recipient. The ability of individuals to request that particular sound recordings be performed for reception by the public at large does not make a service interactive. If an entity offers both interactive and non-interactive services (either concurrently or at different times), the non-interactive component shall not be treated as part of an interactive service.

Fairly soon after Congress enacted the DPSR, critics began to call for further legislation, charging that the DPSR was too narrowly drawn and did not sufficiently protect sound recording copyright holders from further internet piracy. For instance, webcasting services, which provide free—i.e., nonsubscription—services that do not provide particular sound recording on request and are therefore not interactive within the meaning of term under the DPSR, at that time fell outside the sound recording copyright holder's right of control. Recording companies became concerned that these webcasting services were allowing users to copy music transmitted to their computer via webcast for free, or to listen to these webcasting services in lieu of purchasing music. Record companies were concerned that these webcasting services were causing a diminution in record sales, which the companies feared would cut into profits and stunt development of the recording industry. According to Cary Sherman, Senior Executive Vice President and General Counsel of the RIAA, by 1997, the record industry was losing $1 million a day due to music piracy.

In light of these concerns, Congress enacted the current version of § 114 under the DMCA in 1998. The term "interactive service" was expanded to include "those that are specially created for a particular individual." As enacted, the definition of "interactive service" was now a service "that enables a member of the public to receive a transmission of a program specially created for the recipient, or on request, a transmission of a particular sound recording, whether or not as part of a program, which is selected by or on behalf of the recipient."

According to the House conference report,

> The conferees intend that the phrase "program specially created for the recipient" be interpreted reasonably in light of the remainder of the definition of "interactive service." For example, a service would be interactive if it allowed a small number of individuals to request that sound recordings be performed in a program specially created for that group and not available to any individuals outside of that group. In contrast, a service would not be interactive if it merely transmitted to a large number of recipients of the service's transmissions a program consisting of sound recordings requested by a small number of those listeners.

The House report continued that a transmission is considered interactive "if a transmission recipient is permitted to select particular sound recordings in a prerecorded or predetermined program." Id. at 88. "For example, if a transmission recipient has the ability to move forward and backward between songs in a program, the transmission is interactive. It is not necessary that the transmission recipient be able to select the actual songs that comprise the program."

In sum, from the SRA to the DMCA, Congress enacted copyright legislation directed at preventing the diminution in record sales through outright piracy of music or new digital media that offered listeners the ability to select music in such a way that they would forego purchasing records.

[*The court next describes the complex methodology by which LAUNCHcast dynamically creates a "personalized radio station" for each user based on the user's ratings of songs, albums and artists, similar ratings by DJs followed by the user, songs deleted or skipped by the user and songs played for the user within the past three hours.*]

Given LAUNCHcast's format, we turn to the question of whether LAUNCHcast is an interactive service as a matter of law. As we have already noted, a webcasting service such as LAUNCHcast is interactive under the statute if a user can either (1) request—and have played—a particular sound recording, or (2) receive a transmission of a program "specially created" for the user. A LAUNCHcast user cannot request and expect to hear a particular song on demand; therefore, LAUNCHcast does not meet the first definition of interactive. But LAUNCHcast may still be liable if it enables the user to receive a transmission of a program "specially created" for the user. It comes as no surprise to us that the district court, the parties, and others have struggled with what Congress meant by this term.

The language and development of the DPSR and DMCA make clear that Congress enacted both statutes to create a narrow copyright in the performance of digital audio transmissions to protect sound recording copyright holders—principally recording companies—from the diminution in record sales. Congress created this narrow right to ensure that "the creation of new sound recordings and musical works [would not] be discouraged," and to prevent the "threat to the livelihoods of those whose income depends upon revenues derived from traditional record sales."

Contrary to BMG's contentions, Congress was clear that the statute sought to prevent further decreases in revenues for sound recording copyright holders due to significant reductions in record sales, perceived in turn to be a result of the proliferation of interactive listening services.[21] If the user has sufficient control over the interactive service such that she can predict the songs she will hear, much as she would if she owned the music herself and could play each song at will, she would have no need to purchase the music she wishes to hear. Therefore, part and parcel of the concern about a diminution in record sales is the concern that an interactive service provides a degree of predictability—based on choices made by the user—that approximates the predictability the music listener seeks when purchasing music.

The current version § 114(j)(7) was enacted because Congress determined that the DPSR was not up to the task of protecting sound recording copyright holders from diminution in record sales, presumably because programs not covered by the DPSR's definition of interactive service provided a degree of control—predictability—to internet music listeners that dampened the music listeners' need to purchase music recordings. By giving sound recording copyright holders the right to require individual licenses for transmissions of programs specially created for users, Congress hoped to plug the loophole the DPSR had left open for webcasting services.

Launch does not deny that each playlist generated when a LAUNCHcast user selects a radio station is unique to that user at that particular time. However, this does not necessarily make the LAUNCHcast playlist specially created for the user. Based on a review of how LAUNCHcast functions, it is clear that LAUNCHcast does not provide a specially created program within the meaning of § 114(j)(7) because the webcasting service does not provide sufficient control to users such that playlists are so predictable that users will choose to listen to the webcast in lieu of purchasing music, thereby—in the aggregate—diminishing record sales.

First, the rules governing what songs are pooled … ensure that the user has almost no ability to choose, let alone predict, which specific songs will be pooled in anticipation for selection to the playlist. Second, the selection of songs … to be included in the playlist is governed by rules preventing the user's explicitly rated songs from being anywhere near a majority of the songs on the playlist.

Even the ways in which songs are rated include variables beyond the user's control. For instance, the ratings by all of the user's subscribed-to DJs are included in the playlist selection process. When the user rates a particular song, LAUNCHcast then implicitly rates all other songs by that artist, subjecting the user to many songs the user may have never heard or does not even like. There are restrictions placed on the number of times songs by a particular artist or from a particular album can be played, and there are restrictions on consecutive play of the same artist or album. Finally, because each playlist is unique to

---

[21] While file-sharing services like Napster initially caused a decline in record sales, recently webcasting services have been credited with "becom[ing] a massive driver in digital [music] sales" by exposing users to new music and providing an easy link to sites where users can purchase this music. The difference between the two types of services likely explains the different effect on record sales. File-sharing services allow users to copy music files to their computer, thereby enabling the user to listen to the music at any time. Webcasting services, however, do not allow the user to download the files of the music being webcast, and therefore do not enable music piracy.

each user each time the user logs in, a user cannot listen to the playlist of another user and anticipate the songs to be played from that playlist, even if the user has selected the same preferences and rated all songs, artists, and albums identically as the other user. Relatedly, a user who hears a song she likes and wants to hear again cannot do so by logging off and back on to reset her station to disable the restriction against playing the same song twice on a playlist. Even if a user logs off LAUNCHcast then logs back on and selects the same station, the user will still hear the remainder of the playlist to which she had previously been listening with its restrictions still in operation, provided there were at least eight songs left to be played on the playlist—or, in other words, until the user listens to at least forty-two of the playlist's songs.

Finally, after navigating these criteria to … generate a playlist, LAUNCHcast randomly orders the playlist. This randomization is limited by restrictions on the consecutive play of artists or albums,[22] which further restricts the user's ability to choose the artists or albums they wish to hear. LAUNCHcast also does not enable the user to view the unplayed songs in the playlist, ensuring that a user cannot sift through a playlist to choose the songs the user wishes to hear.

It appears the only thing a user can predict with certainty—the only thing the user can control—is that by rating a song at zero the user will not hear that song on that station again. But the ability not to listen to a particular song is certainly not a violation of a copyright holder's right to be compensated when the sound recording is played.

In short, to the degree that LAUNCHcast's playlists are uniquely created for each user, that feature does not ensure predictability. Indeed, the unique nature of the playlist helps Launch ensure that it does not provide a service so specially created for the user that the user ceases to purchase music. LAUNCHcast listeners do not even enjoy the limited predictability that once graced the AM airwaves on weekends in America when "special requests" represented love-struck adolescents' attempts to communicate their feelings to "that special friend." Therefore, we cannot say LAUNCHcast falls within the scope of the DMCA's definition of an interactive service created for individual users.

When Congress created the sound recording copyright, it explicitly characterized it as "narrow." There is no general right of performance in the sound recording copyright. There is only a limited right to performance of digital audio transmission with several exceptions to the copyright, including the one at issue in this case. We find that LAUNCHcast is not an interactive service within the meaning of 17 U.S.C. § 114(j)(7).

The district court's judgment of May 16, 2007 in favor of Appellee is hereby AFFIRMED with costs.

Notes and Questions

1. *Legislative intent.* What do you make of the Congressional rationale for giving record labels the exclusive right to perform sound recordings digitally? Should this right have been extended to terrestrial radio and other nondigital broadcast channels?

2. *Interactive versus noninteractive digital services.* Following the *Launch Media* decision, personalized music streaming services such as Pandora and Rdio took pains to ensure that they

---

[22] Under the "sound recording performance complement," webcasters are limited to playing no more than three selections from a given record in a three-hour period (17 U.S.C. § 114(d)(2)(C)(i), (j)(13)) – Ed.

continue to be recognized as noninteractive services. Why should so much ride on whether a digital music service is interactive or noninteractive? Does this distinction make sense today?

3. *SoundExchange*. As noted above, after deducting an administrative fee, SoundExchange distributes royalties paid under Section 114 to the owner of the sound recording copyright (50 percent), the featured recording artist(s) (45 percent), an agent representing nonfeatured musicians who perform on the recording (2.5 percent) and an agent representing nonfeatured vocalists who perform on the recording (2.5 percent). Is this split sensible?

4. *Pre-1972 sound recordings*. When Congress granted federal copyright protection to sound recordings in 1971, it extended protection only to recordings created on or after February 15, 1972. Sound recordings fixed before that date are protected not by federal law, but by a patchwork of inconsistent and often vague state laws. The disparate treatment of pre-1972 sound recordings under federal and state law has given rise to a number of significant policy issues. For example, some digital broadcasters, including YouTube and Spotify, have negotiated deals with record labels that expressly cover pre-1972 sound recordings, and others, such as Music Choice, pay statutory rates for pre-1972 recordings to SoundExchange. Sirius XM and Spotify, however, have taken the position that state law does not grant the owners of sound recordings any exclusive right to perform those sound recordings; accordingly, they do not pay royalties either to owners directly or to SoundExchange for performances of pre-1972 sound recordings. This position has led to significant litigation. As summarized by the Registrar of Copyrights:

> Recently, three courts—two in California and one in New York—have held that the unauthorized public performance of pre-1972 sound recordings violates applicable state law. In the initial case, a California federal district court ruled that Sirius XM infringed rights guaranteed to plaintiffs by state statute. A state court in California subsequently adopted the federal court's reading of the California statute in a second action against Sirius XM. Following these decisions, in a third case against Sirius XM, a federal district court in New York has indicated that the public performance of pre-1972 sound recordings constitutes common law copyright infringement and unfair competition under New York law. Notably, the reasoning employed in these decisions is not expressly limited to digital performances (i.e., internet streaming and satellite radio); they thus could have potentially broad implications for terrestrial radio (currently exempt under federal law for the public performance of sound recordings) as well. In the meantime, similar lawsuits have been filed against other digital providers, including Pandora, Google, Apple's Beats service, and Rdio, alleging the unauthorized use of pre-1972 recordings.[23]

The Music Modernization Act of 2018 seeks to bring some clarity to this area by requiring that noninteractive digital services such as Sirius XM and Pandora pay performance royalties to SoundExchange for pre-1972 sound recordings at rates established by the CRB, while interactive services such as Spotify and Apple Music would continue to negotiate private licenses with record labels. What the MMA does not do, however, is establish a general performance right for pre-1972 (or post-1972) sound recordings, leaving terrestrial radio stations, sports arenas, bars, restaurants, office buildings and supermarkets free to perform these sound recordings without charge.

5. *International rights*. The United States is something of an outlier with respect to sound recording rights. As observed by the Registrar of Copyrights in 2015, "[v]irtually all industrialized

---

[23] Registrar of Copyrights, supra note 4, at 54-55.

nations recognize a more complete public performance right for sound recordings than does the United States ... Only a handful of countries – including Iran and North Korea – lack [the exclusive right to publicly perform a sound recording]."[24] Why do you think the United States diverges from international norms to this degree? Do you think the US position helps or hurts recording artists as compared to other countries?

16.4 SYNCHRONIZATION RIGHTS

All of the rights and licenses discussed so far in this chapter relate to the distribution and performance of music on a standalone basis. To incorporate music into an audiovisual work – a film, television program, advertisement, music video or video game – a separate license is required from both the owner of the copyright in the musical work and the sound recording. This right is generally called a "synchronization (or 'synch') license" with respect to the musical work, and a "master recording license" with respect to the sound recording. Although the Copyright Act does not refer explicitly to a synchronization or master recording right, these are generally understood to be aspects of a copyright owner's reproduction and derivative work rights.

There is no statutory scheme for licensing music for audiovisual works, and all such arrangements must be negotiated separately. In practice, similar amounts are typically paid to acquire synch rights for a musical work and its sound recording. A number of specialized intermediaries exist to facilitate licensing of musical works in multimedia productions. These include companies such as Greenlight, Dashbox, Cue Songs and Rumblefish, which provide online services that offer different songs for synchronization purposes.

In the early 2000s, major record labels and publishers entered into "New Digital Media Agreements" ("NDMAs") to allow labels efficiently to obtain licenses from their major publisher counterparts so they could pursue new digital products and exploit music videos in online markets. These licensing arrangements, in turn, became a model for a more recent 2012 agreement between UMG and NMPA that allowed UMG to seek similar rights from smaller independent publishers on an "opt-in" basis. The licensing arrangement includes rights for the use of musical works in "MTV-style" videos, live concert footage, and similar exploitations.

Like the major record labels, larger music publishers have entered into direct licensing relationships with the on-demand video provider YouTube that allow them some amount of control over the use of user-uploaded videos incorporating their music and provide for payment of royalties. Following the settlement of infringement litigation by a class of independent music publishers against YouTube in 2011, NMPA and its licensing subsidiary HFA announced an agreement with YouTube under which smaller publishers could choose to license their musical works to YouTube by opting in to prescribed licensing terms. Those who choose to participate in the arrangement grant YouTube the right to "reproduce, distribute and to prepare derivative works (including synchronization rights)" for videos posted by YouTube's users. The license does not, however, cover the public performance right. Music publishers who opt into the YouTube deal receive royalties from YouTube and have some ability to manage the use of their music through HFA, which administers the relationship and can access YouTube's content identification tools on behalf of individual publishers. Over 3,000 music publishers have entered into this licensing arrangement with YouTube.

---

[24] Id. at 45.

Another developing area is the market for so-called "micro-licenses" for music that is used in videos of modest economic value, such as wedding videos and corporate presentations. In the past, income received by rightsholders from licensing such uses might not overcome administrative or other costs. But the market is moving to take advantage of technological developments — especially online applications — that make micro-licensing more viable. This includes the aforementioned services like Rumblefish, but also efforts by NMPA, HFA, and RIAA to license more synchronization rights through programs that allow individual copyright owners to effectuate small licensing transactions.[25]

Notes and Questions

1. *Synch rates.* Rates for synchronization rights vary dramatically based on the intended use of a song and the popularity of the song. The use of a song in a single US television episode broadcast for a five-year term would run approximately $1,000. That rate increases to $7,000–10,000 if rights are worldwide with no expiration. Fees for motion picture synchronization can be significantly higher, running into the low six figures for recent hits that are used in the opening or closing credits.

2. *Clearing rights in advance.* The producer of a work that requires music licenses is well-advised to obtain those rights as early in the production process as possible. Once principal photography for a motion picture has been completed, altering a scene to remove a work that has not been authorized can be prohibitively expensive. Take, for example, the case of performer Sam Cooke, owner of the hit song "Wonderful World." After Cooke's death in 1964 his manager, the notorious music industry figure Allen Klein, who also managed the Beatles and the Rolling Stones, gained control of the copyright in Cooke's songs.

   When Klein saw a rough cut of the Harrison Ford movie *Witness* in 1984 and realised the barn dance sequence would have to be reshot if the producers couldn't get "Wonderful World", he demanded and got $200,000 for the use of that one song, thereby triggering the sync-rights gold rush that rages to this day. He was, as Goodman puts it, "the first hardball player in a slow-pitch league".[26]

3. *Works made for hire.* Not all music synchronized with video content is subject to the licensing considerations discussed above. Much of the music that accompanies video – TV theme songs, advertising jingles, video game soundtracks – is commissioned specifically for the programming that it accompanies. As such, the copyright owner is considered to be the commissioner of the work (usually the production company). Though composition credits may be given under industry collective bargaining agreements, the individual composers and performers of such works generally do not collect ongoing royalties.

4. As you have seen in this chapter, music licensing can be complex, with numerous moving parts and parties in every transaction. Table 16.1 can help to organize the different rights and parties involved in a given transaction.

---

[25] Id. at 58.
[26] David Hepworth, *The Biggest Bastard in Pop: How Allen Klein Changed the Game for Music Revenue*, NewStatesman America, February 9, 2016.

FIGURE 16.7 John Williams, who composed the music for *Star Wars*, won the 1978 Oscar for Best Original Score. But as a work made for hire, the copyright in the score was owned by a subsidiary of Twentieth Century Fox, which distributed the film.

TABLE 16.1 *Summary of music licensing provisions*

	Musical composition	Sound recording
Print (musical score, lyrics)	Negotiated between composer and publisher	N/A
Performance right (live performance, broadcast, streaming)	Licensed by PROs (ASCAP, BMI, SESAC)	***Live performance, analog or* HD *broadcast*:** No license needed ***Digital broadcast*** (section 114) – *noninteractive* (streaming, webcast, satellite radio – Pandora): compulsory license collected by SoundExchange – *interactive* (Spotify): license negotiated with performer/record label
Mechanical right (reproduction and distribution of copies: CD, DVD, MP3, ringtones, iTunes downloads, interactive streaming)	***First release***: negotiated by publisher and composer ***Subsequent (cover) recordings***: – Section 115 compulsory license, OR – negotiated license with Harry Fox Agency or publisher ***Interactive streaming***: Section 115 compulsory blanket license administered by Mechanical Licensing Collective	Negotiated license with performer/record label
Synchronization with video (film, TV, advertising, music video, video games)	Synchronization license negotiated with publisher	Master recording license negotiated with performer/record label

16.5 MUSIC SAMPLING

It is increasingly common in certain musical genres – hip hop, rap, dance club – to incorporate or "sample" short portions of existing sound recordings into new, combined works. Some artists, operating primarily online (e.g., Girl Talk), create works of significant length and complexity doing nothing more than combining portions of dozens or hundreds of existing works over a new beat or rhythm track. As such, sampling usually implicates both the copyright in a musical composition and a sound recording.[27]

Absent the existence of a legal exception such as "fair use,"[28] copying or imitating even a very small segment of a copyrighted musical work generally requires permission of the copyright holder.[29] Failure to obtain that permission constitutes copyright infringement.

Professors Kembrew McLeod and Peter DiCola have extensively analyzed the practice of sampling in the music industry.

As shown in the Table 16.2,[30] the use of a "small" sample of a work of "medium" popularity would cost $2,500 (up-front) or $0.01 per copy for the sound recording rights, and $4,000 (up-front) or 10 percent of revenues for the musical composition rights, while a "small" sample of a "superstar" recording (e.g., the Beatles or Led Zeppelin) would cost $100,000 or $0.15 per copy for the sound recording, and 100 percent of revenue or assignment of the copyright in the new work for the musical composition (a prohibitive proposition).

Against this backdrop, MacLeod and DiCola analyzed two popular albums by the artists Public Enemy and the Beastie Boys. They identified a total of 81 and 125 identifiable samples on

TABLE 16.2 *Sampling costs*

Profile of the sampled work	Use in the sampling work		
	Small	Moderate	Extensive
Low	SR: $0 to $500 MC: Not infringement	SR: $2,500 or $0.01/copy MC: $4,000 or 10%	SR: $5,000 or $0.025/copy MC: 25%
Medium	SR: $2,500 or $0.01/copy MC: $4,000 or 10%	SR: $5,000 or $0.025/copy MC: 25%	SR: $15,000 or $0.05/ copy MC: 40%
High	SR: $5,000 or $0.025/copy MC: 25%	SR: $15,000 or $0.05/copy MC: 40%	SR: $25,000 or $0.10/copy MC: 50% or co-ownership
Famous	SR: $50,000 or $0.12/copy MC: 100% (assignment)		
Superstar	SR: $100,000 or $0.15/copy MC: 100% (assignment)		

SR denotes the sound recording copyright in the sampled song; MC denotes the musical composition copyright in the sampled song.

[27] Sampling should not be confused with unauthorized use of a musical composition. For example, in the famous fair use case *Campbell v. Acuff-Rose Music, Inc.*, 510 U.S. 569 (1994), the band 2LiveCrew appropriated the principal melody and several lyrics from Roy Orbison's popular ballad "Pretty Woman." 2LiveCrew did not incorporate Orbison's actual sound recording into their work; they merely used the musical composition owned by his publisher without authorization.

[28] Under Section 107 of the Copyright Act, certain uses of copyrighted material that otherwise would be infringing are permitted "for purposes such as criticism, comment, news reporting, teaching ..., scholarship, or research."

[29] As the court famously held in *Bright Tunes Music v. Harrisongs Music*, 420 F. Supp. 177 (S.D.N.Y. 1976), as little as three consecutive notes can constitute infringement of a song if they are confusingly similar to the original.

[30] Kembrew MacLeod and Peter DiCola, Creative License: The Law and Culture of Digital Sampling (Duke University Press, 2011) table 2, p. 55 (the authors credit Whitney Broussard for contributions to the table).

each album and estimated the cost that would have been required to clear and license each of these samples.[31] The end result of this analysis: If the two artists had cleared the rights necessary to sample each of the works on their albums, Public Enemy would have lost $4.47 per copy sold, and the Beastie Boys would have lost $7.87 per copy sold.[32]

As the above passage illustrates, many bands do not clear all necessary rights with respect to sampled tracks, often with few or no consequences. Yet artists who are sampled without permission have become increasingly litigious, and the rise of sampling infringement suits is clearly having an impact on the industry.

Notes and Questions

1. *"Bittersweet Symphony."* One of the most notorious sampling cases on record pitted Allen Klein (again), this time in his capacity as the manager of the Rolling Stones, against Brit-pop group The Verve. The controversy concerned The Verve's 1997 hit single "Bittersweet Symphony," which gained fame both on the pop charts as well as the soundtrack to the 1999 teen romance film *Cruel Intentions.* Though the lyrics were original, the instrumental backing was partially sampled from a slowed-down symphonic version of the Rolling Stones' song "The Last Time." The Verve licensed a five-note segment of the recording from the Stones in exchange for 50 percent of the song's royalties, but Klein claimed that they exceeded this licensed use. He sued on behalf of Stones members Mick Jagger and Keith Richards, and won. As a result, The Verve forfeited all songwriting royalties and publishing rights to "Bittersweet Symphony," and Jagger and Richards were credited as its writers. To make matters worse, Andrew Oldham, another former Rolling Stones manager who owned the sound recording that was sampled, sued The Verve for $1.7 million in mechanical royalties. In the end, the Verve lost all control of their biggest hit. It was used in a Nike commercial without their permission, earning them nothing. Then, when "Bittersweet Symphony" was nominated for a "Best Song" Grammy, Jagger and Richards, and not the Verve, were named on the ballot.[33] Were The Verve treated unfairly by Klein and his clients? As the attorney for The Verve, how would you have advised them to avoid some of their legal woes?

   In an unexpected turn of events, in 2019 Mick Jagger and Keith Richards of the Rolling Stones voluntarily assigned their rights in "Bittersweet Symphony" back to Richard Ashcroft of The Verve. Ashcroft, who announced the resolution of the decades-long dispute at a British music awards event, called it, "a kind and magnanimous gesture from Mick and Keith."[34]

2. *Amending the law to accommodate sampling?* What, if anything, should be done about the law and music sampling? MacLeod and DiCola offer several possibilities, including the enactment of a compulsory licensing scheme for sampling (along the lines of the existing licenses under Sections 114 and 115 of the Copyright Act), the establishment of a "de minimis" threshold for music copyright infringement and the expansion of "fair use" to cover sampling more explicitly. What problem are MacLeod and DiCola trying to solve? Which, if any, of these proposals do you think would be effective?

[31] Id. at 57–58.
[32] Id. at 60.
[33] Jordan Runtagh, *Songs on Trial: 12 Landmark Music Copyright Cases*, Rolling Stone, June 8, 2016.
[34] Jem Aswad, *Rolling Stones Give "Bittersweet Symphony" Songwriter Royalties to the Verve's Richard Ashcroft*, Variety, May 23, 2019.

17

Consumer and Online Licensing

SUMMARY CONTENTS

> Has this happened to you? You plunk down a pretty penny for the latest and greatest software, speed back to your computer, tear open the box, shove the CDROM into the computer, click on "install" and, after scrolling past a license agreement which would take at least fifteen minutes to read, find yourself staring at the following dialog box: "I agree." Do you click on the box? You probably do not agree in your heart of hearts, but you click anyway, not about to let some pesky legalese delay the moment for which you've been waiting. Is that "clickwrap" license agreement enforceable?
>
> *I.Lan Systems, Inc. v. Netscout Service Level*, 183 F. Supp. 2d 328 (D. Mass. 2002)

Standardized end user and consumer license agreements have a bad reputation. Professor Margaret Jane Radin associates them with "democratic degradation."[1] Chief Justice John Roberts has admitted that he does not read them (see Section 17.3, Note 2). But, for better or worse, these maligned instruments have become a part of US law that is not likely to disappear entirely in the foreseeable future. As a result, it is worth spending some time to understand the contours and ramifications of these ubiquitous contractual documents.

This chapter reviews the development of consumer license agreements through their three principal phases of development: the paper "shrinkwrap" agreements that accompanied packaged software, the electronic "clickwrap" or "click-through" agreements that emerged with the popularization of the Internet, and the even more amorphous "browsewrap" agreements that seemingly bind users to website terms and other contractual commitments without any affirmative indication of assent. The principal issue in the discussion and cases that follow is contract *formation* – is a valid and enforceable contract formed under the various circumstances that are described? Once a contract is found to exist, then routine principles of contract interpretation that are described elsewhere in this book apply.

---

[1]   Margaret Jane Radin, Boilerplate: The Fine Print, Vanishing Rights, and the Rule of Law 168–69 (Princeton University Press, 2012).

17.1 SHRINKWRAP LICENSES

Beginning in the 1980s, the computer software industry had to contend with a question that had not previously been asked: how to license valuable intellectual property (IP) to thousands, if not millions, of consumer software users in an efficient and effective manner. Clearly, it would not be possible to execute a signed license agreement with every consumer who purchased a diskette containing a computer game or utility. Nor did the industry want to rely solely on copyright law to protect their products, as the book and magazine publishing industries had done for centuries. Though a consumer who purchased a copy of a software program on magnetic tape, a diskette or a hard drive might "own" that copy, it should obtain no rights, by implication or otherwise, to exercise rights in the manufacturer's copyright. While the copyright laws prevented purchasers of books from illegally photocopying and distributing them, photocopying a book took a lot of effort – more than the average consumer would be willing to expend for a relatively modest payoff. Computer software, on the other hand, could be copied and redistributed with the click of a button. In the view of the industry, more robust protection than the law provided was needed (more on this below).

The answer that the industry arrived at was the "shrinkwrap" license agreement, a paper license agreement affixed to the package in which a software program was sold, visible through the clear plastic shrinkwrap surrounding the package. The consumer's assent to the terms of the license was evidenced by her tearing open the package and using the software within. One of the first legal tests of this licensing structure came in the now-seminal *ProCD* case.

ProCD, Inc. v. Zeidenberg
86 F.3d 1447 (7th Cir. 1996)

EASTERBROOK, CIRCUIT JUDGE

Must buyers of computer software obey the terms of shrinkwrap licenses? The district court held not, for two reasons: first, they are not contracts because the licenses are inside the box rather than printed on the outside; second, federal law forbids enforcement even if the licenses are contracts. The parties and numerous amici curiae have briefed many other issues, but these are the only two that matter – and we disagree with the district judge's conclusion on each. Shrinkwrap licenses are enforceable unless their terms are objectionable on grounds applicable to contracts in general (for example, if they violate a rule of positive law, or if they are unconscionable).

I

ProCD, the plaintiff, has compiled information from more than 3,000 telephone directories into a computer database. We may assume that this database cannot be copyrighted, although it is more complex, contains more information (nine-digit zip codes and census industrial codes), is organized differently, and therefore is more original than the single alphabetical directory at issue in *Feist Publications, Inc. v. Rural Telephone Service Co.*, 499 U.S. 340 (1991). ProCD sells a version of the database, called SelectPhone, on CD-ROM discs. (CD-ROM means "compact disc – read only memory." The "shrinkwrap license" gets its name from the fact that retail software packages are covered in plastic or cellophane "shrinkwrap," and some vendors, though not ProCD, have written licenses that

FIGURE 17.1 ProCD's SelectPhone product (*c*.1996).

become effective as soon as the customer tears the wrapping from the package. Vendors prefer "end user license," but we use the more common term.) A proprietary method of compressing the data serves as effective encryption too. Customers decrypt and use the data with the aid of an application program that ProCD has written. This program, which is copyrighted, searches the database in response to users' criteria (such as "find all people named Tatum in Tennessee, plus all firms with 'Door Systems' in the corporate name"). The resulting lists (or, as ProCD prefers, "listings") can be read and manipulated by other software, such as word processing programs.

The database in SelectPhone cost more than $10 million to compile and is expensive to keep current. It is much more valuable to some users than to others. The combination of names, addresses, and SIC codes enables manufacturers to compile lists of potential customers. Manufacturers and retailers pay high prices to specialized information inter-mediaries for such mailing lists; ProCD offers a potentially cheaper alternative. People with nothing to sell could use the database as a substitute for calling long distance infor-mation, or as a way to look up old friends who have moved to unknown towns, or just as an electronic substitute for the local phone book. ProCD decided to engage in price discrimination, selling its database to the general public for personal use at a low price (approximately $150 for the set of five discs) while selling information to the trade for a higher price. It has adopted some intermediate strategies too: access to the SelectPhone (trademark) database is available via the America Online service for the price America Online charges to its clients (approximately $3 per hour), but this service has been tailored to be useful only to the general public.

If ProCD had to recover all of its costs and make a profit by charging a single price – that is, if it could not charge more to commercial users than to the general public – it would have to raise the price substantially over $150. The ensuing reduction in sales would harm consumers who value the information at, say, $200. They get consumer surplus of $50 under the current arrangement but would cease to buy if the price rose substantially. If because of high elasticity of demand in the consumer segment of the market the only way to make a profit turned out to be a price attractive to commercial users alone, then all consumers would lose out – and so would the commercial clients, who would have to pay more for the listings because ProCD could not obtain any contribution toward costs from the consumer market.

To make price discrimination work, however, the seller must be able to control arbitrage. An air carrier sells tickets for less to vacationers than to business travelers, using advance purchase and Saturday-night-stay requirements to distinguish the categories. A producer of movies segments the market by time, releasing first to theaters, then to pay-per-view services, next to the videotape and laserdisc market, and finally to cable and commercial tv. Vendors of computer software have a harder task. Anyone can walk into a retail store and buy a box. Customers do not wear tags saying "commercial user" or "consumer user." Anyway, even a commercial-user-detector at the door would not work, because a consumer could buy the software and resell to a commercial user. That arbitrage would break down the price discrimination and drive up the minimum price at which ProCD would sell to anyone.

Instead of tinkering with the product and letting users sort themselves – for example, furnishing current data at a high price that would be attractive only to commercial customers, and two-year-old data at a low price – ProCD turned to the institution of contract. Every box containing its consumer product declares that the software comes with restrictions stated in an enclosed license. This license, which is encoded on the CD-ROM disks as well as printed in the manual, and which appears on a user's screen every time the software runs, limits use of the application program and listings to non-commercial purposes.

Matthew Zeidenberg bought a consumer package of SelectPhone in 1994 from a retail outlet in Madison, Wisconsin, but decided to ignore the license. He formed Silken Mountain Web Services, Inc., to resell the information in the SelectPhone database. The corporation makes the database available on the Internet to anyone willing to pay its price – which, needless to say, is less than ProCD charges its commercial customers. Zeidenberg has purchased two additional SelectPhone packages, each with an updated version of the database, and made the latest information available over the World Wide Web, for a price, through his corporation. ProCD filed this suit seeking an injunction against further dissemination that exceeds the rights specified in the licenses (identical in each of the three packages Zeidenberg purchased). The district court held the licenses ineffectual because their terms do not appear on the outside of the packages. The court added that the second and third licenses stand no different from the first, even though they are identical, because they might have been different, and a purchaser does not agree to – and cannot be bound by – terms that were secret at the time of purchase.

II

Following the district court, we treat the licenses as ordinary contracts accompanying the sale of products, and therefore as governed by the common law of contracts and the Uniform Commercial Code. Whether there are legal differences between "contracts" and "licenses" (which may matter under the copyright doctrine of first sale) is a subject for another day. Zeidenberg does argue, and the district court held, that placing the package of software on the shelf is an "offer," which the customer "accepts" by paying the asking price and leaving the store with the goods. In Wisconsin, as elsewhere, a contract includes only the terms on which the parties have agreed. One cannot agree to hidden terms, the judge concluded. So far, so good – but one of the terms to which Zeidenberg agreed by purchasing the software is that the transaction was subject to a license. Zeidenberg's position therefore must be that the printed terms on the outside of a box are the parties' contract – except for printed terms that refer to or incorporate other terms. But why would Wisconsin fetter the parties' choice in this way? Vendors can put the entire terms of a contract on the outside of a box only by using microscopic type, removing other information that buyers might find more useful (such as what the software does, and on which computers it works), or both. The "Read Me" file included with most software, describing system requirements and potential incompatibilities, may be equivalent to ten pages of type; warranties and license restrictions take still more space. Notice on the outside, terms on the inside, and a right to return the software for a refund if the terms are unacceptable (a right that the license expressly extends), may be a means of doing business valuable to buyers and sellers alike. Doubtless a state could forbid the use of standard contracts in the software business, but we do not think that Wisconsin has done so.

Transactions in which the exchange of money precedes the communication of detailed terms are common. Consider the purchase of insurance. The buyer goes to an agent, who explains the essentials (amount of coverage, number of years) and remits the premium to the home office, which sends back a policy. On the district judge's understanding, the terms of the policy are irrelevant because the insured paid before receiving them. Yet the device of payment, often with a "binder" (so that the insurance takes effect immediately even though the home office reserves the right to withdraw coverage later), in advance of the policy, serves buyers' interests by accelerating effectiveness and reducing transactions costs. Or consider the purchase of an airline ticket. The traveler calls the carrier or an agent, is quoted a price, reserves a seat, pays, and gets a ticket, in that order. The ticket contains elaborate terms, which the traveler can reject by canceling the reservation. To use the ticket is to accept the terms, even terms that in retrospect are disadvantageous. Just so with a ticket to a concert. The back of the ticket states that the patron promises not to record the concert; to attend is to agree. A theater that detects a violation will confiscate the tape and escort the violator to the exit. One could arrange things so that every concertgoer signs this promise before forking over the money, but that cumbersome way of doing things not only would lengthen queues and raise prices but also would scotch the sale of tickets by phone or electronic data service.

Consumer goods work the same way. Someone who wants to buy a radio set visits a store, pays, and walks out with a box. Inside the box is a leaflet containing some terms, the most important of which usually is the warranty, read for the first time in the comfort of home. By Zeidenberg's lights, the warranty in the box is irrelevant; every consumer gets the standard warranty implied by the UCC in the event the contract is silent; yet so far as we are aware no state disregards warranties furnished with consumer products. Drugs come with a list of ingredients on the outside and an elaborate package insert on the inside. The package insert describes drug interactions, contraindications, and other vital information – but, if Zeidenberg is right, the purchaser need not read the package insert, because it is not part of the contract.

Next consider the software industry itself. Only a minority of sales take place over the counter, where there are boxes to peruse. A customer may place an order by phone in response to a line item in a catalog or a review in a magazine. Much software is ordered over the Internet by purchasers who have never seen a box. Increasingly software arrives by wire. There is no box; there is only a stream of electrons, a collection of information that includes data, an application program, instructions, many limitations ("MegaPixel 3.14159 cannot be used with Byte-Pusher 2.718"), and the terms of sale. The user purchases a serial number, which activates the software's features. On Zeidenberg's arguments, these unboxed sales are unfettered by terms – so the seller has made a broad warranty and must pay consequential damages for any shortfalls in performance, two "promises" that if taken seriously would drive prices through the ceiling or return transactions to the horse-and-buggy age.

According to the district court, the UCC does not countenance the sequence of money now, terms later. One of the court's reasons – that by proposing as part of the draft Article 2B a new UCC sec. 2-2203 that would explicitly validate standard-form user licenses, the American Law Institute and the National Conference of Commissioners on Uniform Laws have conceded the invalidity of shrinkwrap licenses under current law, depends on a faulty inference. To propose a change in a law's text is not necessarily to propose a change in the law's effect. New words may be designed to fortify the current rule with a more precise text that curtails uncertainty.

What then does the current version of the UCC have to say? We think that the place to start is sec. 2-204(1): "A contract for sale of goods may be made in any manner sufficient to show agreement, including conduct by both parties which recognizes the existence of such a contract." A vendor, as master of the offer, may invite acceptance by conduct, and may propose limitations on the kind of conduct that constitutes acceptance. A buyer may accept by performing the acts the vendor proposes to treat as acceptance. And that is what happened. ProCD proposed a contract that a buyer would accept by using the software after having an opportunity to read the license at leisure. This Zeidenberg did. He had no choice, because the software splashed the license on the screen and would not let him proceed without indicating acceptance. So although the district judge was right to say that a contract can be, and often is, formed simply by paying the price and walking out of the store, the UCC permits contracts to be formed in other ways. ProCD proposed such a different way, and without protest Zeidenberg agreed. Ours is not a case in which a consumer opens a package to find an insert saying "you owe us an extra $10,000" and the seller files suit to collect. Any buyer finding such a demand can prevent formation of the contract by returning the package, as can any consumer who concludes that the terms of the license make the software worth less than the purchase price. Nothing in the UCC requires a seller to maximize the buyer's net gains.

Section 2-606, which defines "acceptance of goods", reinforces this understanding. A buyer accepts goods under sec. 2-606(1)(b) when, after an opportunity to inspect, he fails to make an effective rejection under sec. 2-602(1). ProCD extended an opportunity to reject if a buyer should find the license terms unsatisfactory; Zeidenberg inspected the package, tried out the software, learned of the license, and did not reject the goods. We refer to sec. 2-606 only to show that the opportunity to return goods can be important; acceptance of an offer differs from acceptance of goods after delivery; but the UCC consistently permits the parties to structure their relations so that the buyer has a chance to make a final decision after a detailed review.

Some portions of the UCC impose additional requirements on the way parties agree on terms. A disclaimer of the implied warranty of merchantability must be "conspicuous." UCC sec. 2-316(2), incorporating UCC sec. 1-201(10). Promises to make firm offers, or to negate oral modifications, must be "separately signed." UCC secs. 2-205, 2-209(2). These special provisos reinforce the impression that, so far as the UCC is concerned, other terms may be as inconspicuous as the forum-selection clause on the back of the cruise ship ticket in *Carnival Lines*. Zeidenberg has not located any Wisconsin case – for that matter, any case in any state – holding that under the UCC the ordinary terms found in shrinkwrap licenses require any special prominence, or otherwise are to be undercut rather than enforced. In the end, the terms of the license are conceptually identical to the contents of the package. Just as no court would dream of saying that SelectPhone (trademark) must contain 3,100 phone books rather than 3,000, or must have data no more than 30 days old, or must sell for $100 rather than $150 – although any of these changes would be welcomed by the customer, if all other things were held constant – so, we believe, Wisconsin would not let the buyer pick and choose among terms. Terms of use are no less a part of "the product" than are the size of the database and the speed with which the software compiles listings. Competition among vendors, not judicial revision of a package's contents, is how consumers are protected in a market economy. ProCD has rivals, which may elect to compete by offering superior software, monthly updates, improved terms of use, lower price, or a better compromise among these elements. As we stressed above, adjusting terms in buyers' favor might help Matthew Zeidenberg today (he already has the software) but would lead to a response, such as a higher price, that might make consumers as a whole worse off.

III

The district court held that, even if Wisconsin treats shrinkwrap licenses as contracts, § 301(a) of the Copyright Act prevents their enforcement. The relevant part of § 301(a) preempts any "legal or equitable rights [under state law] that are equivalent to any of the exclusive rights within the general scope of copyright as specified by section 106 in works of authorship that are fixed in a tangible medium of expression and come within the subject matter of copyright as specified by sections 102 and 103." ProCD's software and data are "fixed in a tangible medium of expression," and the district judge held that they are "within the subject matter of copyright." The latter conclusion is plainly right for the copyrighted application program, and the judge thought that the data likewise are "within the subject matter of copyright" even if, after *Feist*, they are not sufficiently original to be copyrighted. One function of § 301(a) is to prevent states from giving special protection to works of authorship that Congress has decided should be in the public domain, which it can accomplish only if "subject matter of copyright" includes all works of a type covered by sections 102 and 103, even if federal law does not afford protection to them.

But are rights created by contract "equivalent to any of the exclusive rights within the general scope of copyright"? Three courts of appeals have answered "no." The district court disagreed with these decisions, but we think them sound. Rights "equivalent to any of the exclusive rights within the general scope of copyright" are rights established by law – rights that restrict the options of persons who are strangers to the author. Copyright law forbids duplication, public performance, and so on, unless the person wishing to copy or perform the work gets permission; silence means a ban on copying. A copyright is a right against the world. Contracts, by contrast, generally affect only their parties; strangers may do as they please, so contracts do not create "exclusive rights." Someone who found a copy of SelectPhone on the street would not be affected by the shrinkwrap license – though the federal copyright laws of their own force would limit the finder's ability to copy or transmit the application program.

Think for a moment about trade secrets. One common trade secret is a customer list. After *Feist*, a simple alphabetical list of a firm's customers, with address and telephone numbers, could not be protected by copyright. Yet *Kewanee Oil Co. v. Bicron Corp.*, 416 U.S. 470 (1974), holds that contracts about trade secrets may be enforced – precisely because they do not affect strangers' ability to discover and use the information independently. If the amendment of § 301(a) in 1976 overruled *Kewanee* and abolished consensual protection of those trade secrets that cannot be copyrighted, no one has noticed – though abolition is a logical consequence of the district court's approach. Think, too, about everyday transactions in intellectual property. A customer visits a video store and rents a copy of *Night of the Lepus*. The customer's contract with the store limits use of the tape to home viewing and requires its return in two days. May the customer keep the tape, on the ground that § 301(a) makes the promise unenforceable?

A law student uses the LEXIS database, containing public-domain documents, under a contract limiting the results to educational endeavors; may the student resell his access to this database to a law firm from which LEXIS seeks to collect a much higher hourly rate? Suppose ProCD hires a firm to scour the nation for telephone directories, promising to pay $100 for each that ProCD does not already have. The firm locates 100 new directories, which it sends to ProCD with an invoice for $10,000. ProCD incorporates the directories into its database; does it have to pay the bill? Surely yes; *Aronson v. Quick Point Pencil Co.*, 440 U.S. 257 (1979), holds that promises to pay for intellectual property may be enforced even though federal law (in *Aronson*, the patent law) offers no protection against third-party uses of that property.[2] But these illustrations are what our case is about. ProCD offers software and data for two prices: one for personal use, a higher price for commercial use. Zeidenberg wants to use the data without paying the seller's price; if the law student and Quick Point Pencil Co. could not do that, neither can Zeidenberg.

Although Congress possesses power to preempt even the enforcement of contracts about intellectual property … courts usually read preemption clauses to leave private contracts unaffected. *American Airlines, Inc. v. Wolens*, 513 U.S. 219 (1995), provides a nice illustration. A federal statute preempts any state "law, rule, regulation, standard, or other provision … relating to rates, routes, or services of any air carrier." Does such a law preempt the law of contracts – so that, for example, an air carrier need not honor a quoted price (or a contract to reduce the price by the value of frequent flyer miles)? The Court allowed that it is possible to read the statute that broadly but thought such an interpretation would make little sense. Terms and conditions offered by contract reflect private ordering, essential to the efficient functioning of markets. Although some principles that carry the name of contract law are designed to defeat rather than implement consensual transactions, the rules that respect private choice are not preempted by a clause such as § 1305(a)(1). Section 301(a) plays a role similar to § 1301(a)(1): it prevents states from substituting their own regulatory systems for those of the national government. Just as § 301(a) does not itself interfere with private transactions in intellectual property, so it does not prevent states from respecting those transactions. Like the Supreme Court in *Wolens*, we think it prudent to

---

[2]   For a further discussion of *Aronson*, see Chapter 24.

refrain from adopting a rule that anything with the label "contract" is necessarily outside the preemption clause: the variations and possibilities are too numerous to foresee.

Aronson emphasized that enforcement of the contract between Aronson and Quick Point Pencil Company would not withdraw any information from the public domain. That is equally true of the contract between ProCD and Zeidenberg. Everyone remains free to copy and disseminate all 3,000 telephone books that have been incorporated into ProCD's database. Anyone can add SIC codes and zip codes. ProCD's rivals have done so. Enforcement of the shrinkwrap license may even make information more readily available, by reducing the price ProCD charges to consumer buyers. To the extent licenses facilitate distribution of object code while concealing the source code (the point of a clause forbidding disassembly), they serve the same procompetitive functions as does the law of trade secrets. Licenses may have other benefits for consumers: many licenses permit users to make extra copies, to use the software on multiple computers, even to incorporate the software into the user's products. But whether a particular license is generous or restrictive, a simple two-party contract is not "equivalent to any of the exclusive rights within the general scope of copyright" and therefore may be enforced.

REVERSED AND REMANDED.

Notes and Questions

1. *Shrinkwrap and assent.* The original "shrinkwrap" software licenses were visible in their entirety through the clear plastic packaging of the software box or diskette. By the time of *ProCD*, however, software vendors, not wishing to detract from the visual appeal of their packaging, included only a sticker indicating that licensing terms could be found inside the box, on the theory that if a consumer opened the box, then read the terms and was dissatisfied, he or she could return the product for a refund. What practical difficulties arise from this theory? How many consumers to you think requested such refunds? What risks exist for the software vendor in this scenario?

2. *ProCD and the rise of the EULA.* The *ProCD* case stands for two important principles of law. First, as discussed above, shrinkwrap license agreements can be enforceable contracts. But the second principle established in *ProCD* is equally important: the Copyright Act does not preempt state contract law when it seeks to cover material protected (or not protected) by copyright. As the court in *ProCD* notes, it was not the first court to rule in this manner on preemption, and the Supreme Court's decision in *Aronson* laid the groundwork for *ProCD*, though in the area of patents rather than copyrights. But *ProCD* opened the door to consumer software contracts (end user license agreements or "EULAs") that grew in length and contained an increasing number of legal terms that went well beyond the restrictions imposed by the Copyright Act. Just a few of the terms included in typical EULAs are:

   - limitations on the number of users/devices;
   - restrictions on uses (noncommercial, educational, no spam);
   - prohibitions on rental, resale, reverse engineering and transfer;
   - limitations and exclusions of warranty and damages;
   - consent to use of personal data; and
   - disputes will be resolved by arbitration in a designated locale.

Are EULA terms like this reasonable? How many consumers to you think are aware of the EULA limitations on the hundreds of different software programs that they use on a daily basis? This issue is discussed in greater detail in Section 17.3.

3. *Preemption and the "extra element."* Most courts that have reviewed application of Section 301 of the Copyright Act to state law claims adopt what has been described as the "extra element" test. Under this approach, a state law claim is not preempted if it requires proof of a qualitatively extra or different element from that required to prove infringement. *ProCD*, and a number of other decisions, stand for the proposition that a contract claim involves that extra element. How would you describe the "extra element" that is involved? What types of claims might be subject to preemption? Does Judge Easterbrook suggest any of these in *ProCD*?

4. *Reverse engineering.* As in *ProCD*, in the absence of misuse or overreaching, courts have enforced standard-form contracts even if the contract terms give an IP holder rights beyond those afforded by copyright, patent or other applicable laws. For example, in *Bowers v. Baystate Technologies, Inc.*, 320 F.3d 1317 (Fed. Cir. 2003), the Federal Circuit held that a shrinkwrap license agreement prohibiting reverse engineering of software was not preempted by the copyright law, even though reverse engineering would likely have been permissible as fair use under copyright law. The *Bowers* decision was criticized by Judge Dyk, who dissented. In his view, such contractual clauses had the potential to displace the protections of federal law in a manner that would not have been permissible had they been enacted by a state legislature. Judge Dyk acknowledges that parties may in "freely negotiated" agreements give up rights like fair use that are otherwise available under the law, but doing so under a contract of adhesion, which effectively gives the user no alternative, should not be permitted.[3] Which of these positions do you find more persuasive?

M.A. Mortenson Company, Inc. v. Timberline Software Corp.
998 P.2d 305 (Wash. 2000)

JOHNSON, JUSTICE

Mortenson is a nationwide construction contractor. Respondent Timberline is a software developer located in Beaverton, Oregon. Respondent Softworks, an authorized dealer for Timberline, is located in Kirkland, Washington and provides computer-related services to contractors such as Mortenson.

Since at least 1990, Mortenson has used Timberline's Bid Analysis software to assist with its preparation of bids. Mortenson had used Medallion, an earlier version of Bid Analysis, at its Minnesota headquarters and its regional offices. In early 1993, Mortenson installed a new computer network operating system at its Bellevue office and contacted Mark Reich (Reich), president of Softworks, to reinstall Medallion. Reich discovered, however, that the Medallion software was incompatible with Mortenson's new operating system. Reich informed Mortenson that Precision, a newer version of Bid Analysis, was compatible with its new operating system.

Mortenson wanted multiple copies of the new software for its offices, including copies for its corporate headquarters in Minnesota and its northwest regional office in Bellevue.

---

[3] See a discussion of the contractual prohibition on reverse engineering in Section 18.2.5.

Reich informed Mortenson he would place an order with Timberline and would deliver eight copies of the Precision software to the Bellevue office, after which Mortenson could distribute the copies among its offices.

After Reich provided Mortenson with a price quote, Mortenson issued a purchase order dated July 12, 1993, confirming the agreed upon purchase price, set up fee, delivery charges, and sales tax for eight copies of the software. The purchase order indicated that Softworks, on behalf of Timberline, would "[f]urnish current versions of Timberline Precision Bid Analysis Program Software and Keys" and "[p]rovide assistance in installation and system configuration for Mortenson's Bellevue Office." The purchase order also contained the following notations:

> Provide software support in converting Mortenson's existing Bid Day Master Files to a format accepted by the newly purchased Bid Day software. This work shall be accomplished on a time and material basis of $85.00 per hour. Format information of conversion of existing D-Base Files to be shared to assist Mortenson Mid-West programmers in file conversion.
>
> — System software support and upgrades to be available from Timberline for newly purchased versions of Bid Day Multi-User.
>
> — At some future date should Timberline upgrade "Bid Day" to a windows version, M.A. Mortenson would be able to upgrade to this system with Timberline crediting existing software purchase toward that upgrade on a pro-rated basis to be determined later.

Below the signature line the following was stated: "ADVISE PURCHASING PROMPTLY IF UNABLE TO SHIP AS REQUIRED. EACH SHIPMENT MUST INCLUDE A PACKING LIST. SUBSTITUTIONS OF GOODS OR CHANGES IN COSTS REQUIRE OUR PRIOR APPROVAL." The purchase order did not contain an integration clause.

Reich signed the purchase order and ordered the requested software from Timberline. When Reich received the software, he opened the three large shipping boxes and checked the contents against the packing invoice. Contained inside the shipping boxes were several smaller boxes, containing program diskettes in plastic pouches, installation instructions, and user manuals. One of the larger boxes also contained the sealed protection devices for the software.

All Timberline software is distributed to its users under license. Both Medallion and Precision Bid Analysis are licensed Timberline products. In the case of the Mortenson shipment, the full text of Timberline's license agreement was set forth on the outside of each diskette pouch and the inside cover of the instruction manuals. The first screen that appears each time the program is used also references the license and states, "[t]his software is licensed for exclusive use by: Timberline Use Only." Further, a license to use the protection device was wrapped around each of the devices shipped to Mortenson. The following warning preceded the terms of the license agreement:

> CAREFULLY READ THE FOLLOWING TERMS AND CONDITIONS BEFORE USING THE PROGRAMS. USE OF THE PROGRAMS INDICATES YOUR ACKNOWLEDGEMENT THAT YOU HAVE READ THIS LICENSE, UNDERSTAND IT, AND AGREE TO BE BOUND BY ITS TERMS AND CONDITIONS. IF YOU DO NOT AGREE TO THESE TERMS AND CONDITIONS, PROMPTLY RETURN THE PROGRAMS AND USER MANUALS TO THE PLACE OF PURCHASE AND

YOUR PURCHASE PRICE WILL BE REFUNDED. YOU AGREE THAT YOUR USE OF THE PROGRAM ACKNOWLEDGES THAT YOU HAVE READ THIS LICENSE, UNDERSTAND IT, AND AGREE TO BE BOUND BY ITS TERMS AND CONDITIONS.

Under a separate subheading, the license agreement limited Mortenson's remedies and provided:

LIMITATION OF REMEDIES AND LIABILITY

NEITHER TIMBERLINE NOR ANYONE ELSE WHO HAS BEEN INVOLVED IN THE CREATION, PRODUCTION OR DELIVERY OF THE PROGRAMS OR USER MANUALS SHALL BE LIABLE TO YOU FOR ANY DAMAGES OF ANY TYPE, INCLUDING BUT NOT LIMITED TO, ANY LOST PROFITS, LOST SAVINGS, LOSS OF ANTICIPATED BENEFITS, OR OTHER INCIDENTAL, OR CONSEQUENTIAL DAMAGES ARISING OUT OF THE USE OR INABILITY TO USE SUCH PROGRAMS, WHETHER ARISING OUT OF CONTRACT, NEGLIGENCE, STRICT TORT, OR UNDER ANY WARRANTY, OR OTHERWISE, EVEN IF TIMBERLINE HAS BEEN ADVISED OF THE POSSIBILITY OF SUCH DAMAGES OR FOR ANY OTHER CLAIM BY ANY OTHER PARTY. TIMBERLINE'S LIABILITY FOR DAMAGES IN NO EVENT SHALL EXCEED THE LICENSE FEE PAID FOR THE RIGHT TO USE THE PROGRAMS.

Reich personally delivered the software to Mortenson's Bellevue office, and was asked to return at a later date for installation. The parties dispute what happened next. According to Neal Ruud (Ruud), Mortenson's chief estimator at its Bellevue office, when Reich arrived to install the software Reich personally opened the smaller product boxes contained within the large shipping boxes and also opened the diskette packaging. Reich inserted the diskettes into the computer, initiated the program, contacted Timberline to receive the activation codes, and wrote down the codes for Mortenson. Reich then started the programs and determined to the best of his knowledge they were operating properly. Ruud states that Mortenson never saw any of the licensing information described above, or any of the manuals that accompanied the software. Ruud adds that copies of the programs purchased for other Mortenson offices were forwarded to those offices.

Reich claims when he arrived at Mortenson's Bellevue office he noticed the software had been opened and had been placed on a desk, along with a manual and a protection device. Reich states he told Mortenson he would install the program at a single workstation and "then they would do the rest." Reich proceeded to install the software and a Mortenson employee attached the protection device. Reich claims he initiated and ran the program, and then observed as a Mortenson employee repeated the installation process on a second computer. An employee then told Reich that Mortenson would install the software at the remaining stations.

In December 1993, Mortenson utilized the Precision Bid Analysis software to prepare a bid for a project at Harborview Medical Center in Seattle. On the day of the bid, the software allegedly malfunctioned multiple times and gave the following message: "Abort: Cannot find alternate." Clerk's Papers at 60. Mortenson received this message 19 times that day. Nevertheless, Mortenson submitted a bid generated by the software. After Mortenson was awarded the Harborview Medical Center project, it learned its bid was approximately $1.95 million lower than intended.

FIGURE 17.2 Mortenson used Timberline's Precision Bid Analysis software to prepare a bid for a project at Harborview Medical Center in Seattle. The software malfunctioned.

Mortenson filed an action in King County Superior Court against Timberline and Softworks alleging breach of express and implied warranties. Timberline moved for summary judgment of dismissal in July 1997, arguing the limitation on consequential damages in the licensing agreement barred Mortenson's recovery. Mortenson countered that its entire contract with Timberline consisted of the purchase order and it never saw or agreed to the provisions in the licensing agreement.

Analysis

Terms of the Contract

Mortenson [argues that] even if the purchase order was not an integrated contract, Timberline's delivery of the license terms merely constituted a request to add additional or different terms, which were never agreed upon by the parties. Mortenson claims under RCW 62A.2-207 the additional terms did not become part of the contract because they were material alterations. Timberline responds that the terms of the license were not a request to add additional terms, but part of the contract between the parties. Timberline further argues that so-called "shrinkwrap" software licenses have been found enforceable by other courts, and that both trade usage and course of dealing support enforcement in the present case. For its section 2-207 analysis, Mortenson relies on *Step-Saver Data Sys., Inc. v. Wyse Tech.*, 939 F.2d 91 (3d Cir.1991). Mortenson claims *Step-Saver* is controlling, as "virtually every element of the transaction in the present case is mirrored in Step-Saver." We disagree.

First, *Step-Saver* did not involve the enforceability of a standard license agreement against an end user of the software, but instead involved its applicability to a value added retailer who simply included the software in an integrated system sold to the end user. In fact, in *Step-Saver* the party contesting applicability of the licensing agreement had been assured the license did not apply to it at all. Such is not the case here, as Mortenson was the end user of the Bid Analysis software and was never told the license agreement did not apply.

Further, in *Step-Saver* the seller of the program twice asked the buyer to sign an agreement comparable to their disputed license agreement. Both times the buyer refused, but the seller continued to make the software available. In contrast, Mortenson and Timberline had utilized a license agreement throughout Mortenson's use of the Medallion and Precision Bid Analysis software. Given these distinctions, we find *Step-Saver* to be inapplicable to the present case. We conclude this is a case about contract formation, not contract alteration. As such, RCW 62A.2-204, and not RCW 62A.2-207, provides the proper framework for our analysis.

RCW 62A.2-204 states:

(1) A contract for sale of goods may be made in any manner sufficient to show agreement, including conduct by both parties which recognizes the existence of such a contract.
(2) An agreement sufficient to constitute a contract for sale may be found even though the moment of its making is undetermined.
(3) Even though one or more terms are left open a contract for sale does not fail for indefiniteness if the parties have intended to make a contract and there is a reasonably certain basis for giving an appropriate remedy.

Although no Washington case specifically addresses the type of contract formation at issue in this case, a series of recent cases from other jurisdictions have analyzed shrinkwrap licenses under analogous statutes.

In *ProCD*, which involved a retail purchase of software, the Seventh Circuit held software shrinkwrap license agreements are a valid form of contracting under Wisconsin's version of U.C.C. section 2-204, and such agreements are enforceable unless objectionable under general contract law such as the law of unconscionability. The court stated, "[n]otice on the outside, terms on the inside, and a right to return the software for a refund if the terms are unacceptable (a right that the license expressly extends), may be a means of doing business valuable to buyers and sellers alike."

In *Hill*, the customer ordered a computer over the telephone and received the computer in the mail, accompanied by a list of terms to govern if the customer did not return the product within 30 days. Relying in part on *ProCD*, the court held the terms of the "accept-or-return" agreement were effective, stating, "[c]ompetent adults are bound by such documents, read or unread." Elaborating on its holding in *ProCD*, the court continued:

The question in *ProCD* was not whether terms were added to a contract after its formation, but how and when the contract was formed – in particular, whether a vendor may propose that a contract of sale be formed, not in the store (or over the phone) with the payment of money or a general "send me the product," but after the customer has had a chance to inspect both the item and the terms. ProCD answers "yes," for merchants and consumers alike.

Interpreting the same licensing agreement at issue in *Hill*, the New York Supreme Court, Appellate Division concluded shrinkwrap license terms delivered following a mail order purchase were not proposed additions to the contract, but part of the original agreement between the parties. The court held U.C.C. section 2-207 did not apply because the contract was not formed until after the period to return the merchandise.

We find the approach of the *ProCD*, *Hill*, and *Brower* courts persuasive and adopt it to guide our analysis under RCW 62A.2-204. We conclude because RCW 62A.2-204 allows a contract to be formed "in any manner sufficient to show agreement ... even though the moment of its making is undetermined," it allows the formation of "layered contracts" similar to those envisioned by *ProCD*, *Hill* and *Brower*. We, therefore, hold under RCW 62A.2-204 the terms of the license were part of the contract between Mortenson and Timberline, and Mortenson's use of the software constituted its assent to the agreement, including the license terms.

The terms of Timberline's license were either set forth explicitly or referenced in numerous locations. The terms were included within the shrinkwrap packaging of each copy of Precision Bid Analysis; they were present in the manuals accompanying the software; they were included with the protection devices for the software, without which the software could not be used. The fact the software was licensed was also noted on the introductory screen each time the software was used. Even accepting Mortenson's contention it never saw the terms of the license, it was not necessary for Mortenson to actually read the agreement in order to be bound by it.

Furthermore, the U.C.C. defines an "agreement" as "the bargain of the parties in fact as found in their language or by implication from other circumstances including course of dealing or usage of trade or course of performance". Mortenson and Timberline had a course of dealing; Mortenson had purchased licensed software from Timberline for years prior to its upgrade to Precision Bid Analysis. All Timberline software, including the prior version of Bid Analysis used by Mortenson since at least 1990, is distributed under license. Moreover, extensive testimony and exhibits before the trial court demonstrate an unquestioned use of such license agreements throughout the software industry. Although Mortenson questioned the relevance of this evidence, there is no evidence in the record to contradict it. While trade usage is a question of fact, undisputed evidence of trade usage may be considered on summary judgment.

As the license was part of the contract between Mortenson and Timberline, its terms are enforceable unless "objectionable on grounds applicable to contracts in general."

We affirm the Court of Appeals, upholding the trial court's order of summary judgment of dismissal and denial of the motions to vacate and amend.

Notes and Questions

1. *Offer and counteroffer.* Though cases like *ProCD* and *Mortenson* generally established that shrinkwrap agreements are enforceable contracts, some courts have declined to enforce them under certain circumstances. One such case is *Step-Saver Data Sys., Inc. v. Wyse Technology*, 939 F.2d 91, 102–03 (3d Cir. 1991), which the court in *Mortenson* distinguished. In that case, Step-Saver was a value-added reseller (VAR) that obtained computer terminals from Wyse and software operating systems from TSL. Step-Saver combined these components with IBM computers and sold them as a package to consumers. When consumers complained that the system did not work, Step-Saver brought a warranty claim against TSL. TSL argued, in response, that a box-top disclaimer accompanying its operating system software negated any warranties to Step-Saver or its customers. The court disagreed, holding that in order for the warranty disclaimer to form part of the contract between TSL and Step-Saver, it must constitute a formal counteroffer by TSL, without which TSL was unwilling to complete the transaction.

On its face, the box-top license states that TSL will refund the purchase price if the purchaser does not agree to the terms of the license. Even with such a refund term, however, [TSL] may be relying on the purchaser's investment in time and energy in reaching this point in the transaction to prevent the purchaser from returning the item. Because a purchaser has made a decision to buy a particular product and has actually obtained the product, the purchaser may use it despite the refund offer, regardless of the additional terms specified after the contract formed. But we need not decide whether such a refund offer could ever amount to a conditional acceptance; the undisputed evidence in this case demonstrates that the terms of the license were not sufficiently important that TSL would forego its sales to Step-Saver if TSL could not obtain Step-Saver's consent to those terms. [A Step-Saver employee] testified that TSL assured him that the box-top license did not apply to Step-Saver, as Step-Saver was not the end user of the Multilink Advanced program. Supporting this testimony, TSL on two occasions asked Step-Saver to sign agreements that ... contained warranty disclaimer and limitation of remedy terms similar to those contained in the box-top license. Step-Saver refused to sign the agreements; nevertheless, TSL continued to sell copies of Multilink Advanced to Step-Saver.

With this reasoning in mind, what should a licensor like TSL do in order to limit its liability to resellers like Step-Saver?

2. *Invoicing and terms beyond software.* Software vendors are not alone in their use of standardized consumer contracts. For example, in *Greenfield v. Twin Vision Graphics, Inc.*, 268 F. Supp. 2d 358 (D.N.J. 2003), a court enforced a restriction on the use of a commercial photograph that was contained in a photographer's invoice. The court distinguished *Step-Saver*, reasoning that TSL continued to provide the Multilink software even after Step-Saver refused to enter into a contract with the requested disclaimer. The photographer, in contrast, did not provide additional services after sending the invoice, nor did the customer reject the terms of the invoice. *Puget Sound Financial, LLC v. Unisearch, Inc.*, 47 P.3d 940 (Wash. 2002) also involved a term contained in an invoice – a damages limitation relating to services provided by a public records search firm. The court held that the damages limitation became part of the contract whether or not the customer expressly agreed to the invoice containing the terms because the limitation was common in the trade and routinely used in such contracts. Given these decisions, what limits exist on the ability of product and service vendors to impose contractual restrictions and terms on customers through invoices and other post-transaction documentation?

FIGURE 17.3 A 1980s-era computer terminal of the type at issue in *Step-Saver*.

3. *Seed tag licenses.* For years, Monsanto and other sellers of genetically modified seeds and other proprietary agricultural products have affixed legal terms to the bags and packaging of these products. Known as "seed tag" licenses, these terms generally prohibit the purchaser from selling new seeds that result from the planting of the original seeds (see discussion of *Bowman v. Monsanto* in Section 23.4, Note 8). Recently, however, this practice has invaded the consumer market. In 2020, a surprised Twitter user circulated a photo of a EULA on a plastic bag of Carnival brand seedless grapes. It read:

> The recipient of the produce contained in this package agrees not to propagate or reproduce any portion of this produce, including "but not limited to" seeds, stems, tissue, and fruit.

Is there any product the use of which is not susceptible to limitation by contract of adhesion?

4. *Unconscionability.* Despite general skepticism toward standard-form contracts, US law has generally accepted that they are enforceable, so long as they do not rise (or fall) to the level of unconscionability. While there is no clear definition of unconscionability, the *Restatement (Second) of Contracts* § 208 (Comment), explains, somewhat unhelpfully:

> The determination that a contract or term is or is not unconscionable is made in the light of its setting, purpose and effect. Relevant factors include weaknesses in the contracting process like those involved in more specific rules as to contractual capacity, fraud, and other invalidating causes; the policy also overlaps with rules which render particular bargains or terms unenforceable on grounds of public policy.

In *AT&T Mobility, LLC v. Concepcion*, 563 U.S. 333 (2011), the Supreme Court summarized the California law of unconscionability as requiring "a 'procedural' and a 'substantive' element, the former focusing on 'oppression' or 'surprise' due to unequal bargaining power, the latter on 'overly harsh' or 'one-sided' results." One common challenge to online agreements arises from arbitration clauses that require consumers to participate

FIGURE 17.4 Vendors have sought to control the use of products, including seedless grapes, through "shrinkwrap" agreements.

in binding arbitration, often in distant cities, in order to resolve disputes under the agreements. In *Carey v. Uber Technologies, Inc.*, Case No. 1:16-cv-1058 (N.D. Ohio Mar. 27, 2017), a district court applied the procedural unconscionability test to uphold a contractual clause that delegated the question of whether an issue was arbitrable to the arbitrator. The court found that the user's assent to the clickwrap terms and the opportunity to opt out of the arbitration provision defeated any finding of procedural unconscionability. Likewise, in *Corwin v. NYC Bike Share, LLC*, 238 F. Supp. 3d 475 (S.D.N.Y. 2017), the court held that an injury release in a clickwrap agreement was not unconscionable because the full text of the release agreement was embedded within the registration page, the user could not continue to register before manifesting assent and the terms were in plain view. Given these precedents, what kind of shrinkwrap license terms, if any, might a court find unconscionable?

The doctrine of unconscionability under US law today is distinctly anemic. Amit Elazari Bar On has recently proposed that unconscionability be reinvigorated along the lines used in Israel. There, according to Elazari, "if a term in a standard form contract meets the criteria of unconscionability presumptions, the burden of proof is borne by the drafter, who must prove that, in view of the contract as a whole and its particular circumstances, the condition in question is justified and reasonable."[4] How might Elazari's proposal change the frequency of unconscionability findings in the United States? If you were advising a software or online services provider, would you recommend that they support or oppose such a change to the law? Why?

17.2 CLICKWRAP AND BROWSEWRAP LICENSES

In the mid-1990s, firms began to distribute consumer software and services via the Internet. In doing so, they had to contend with means for imposing binding contractual terms on users. Without a physical software disc or CD, they could not rely on the tried-and-true shrinkwrap method, but they quickly adapted the principles of *ProCD* to the online realm. What emerged were contractual terms presented to the user in electronic, on-screen form only, in which the user's assent was manifested through clicking an "I ACCEPT" or similar graphic button. Initially, courts struggled with the ability of parties to form contracts electronically through the click of a button on a computer screen. However, they soon accepted the notion that such "clickwrap" or "click-through" agreements offered sufficient evidence of assent to form binding contracts if the user's notice and assent were clear.

A committee of the American Bar Association, writing early in the evolution of clickwrap agreements, proposed a series best practices for the creation of legally binding clickwrap agreements.[5] The principles articulated by the ABA Committee recommended that online terms be clearly displayed, and users be given an opportunity to review them, that users have the opportunity to manifest their acceptance or rejection of the terms, that an opportunity to correct errors be provided, and that records be maintained to prove assent. Over the years, online agreements meeting these guidelines have generally been found to be enforceable.

---

4   Amit Elazari Bar On, *Unconscionability 2.0 and the IP Boilerplate: A Revised Doctrine of Unconscionability for the Information Age*, 34 Berkeley Tech. L.J. 567, 681–82 (2019).

5   Christina L. Kunz, Maureen F. Del Duca, Heather Thayer & Jennifer Debrow, *Click-Through Agreements: Strategies for Avoiding Disputes on Validity of Assent*, 57 Business Lawyer 401 (2001). Over the years, the ABA Joint Working Group on Electronic Contracting Practices (the "ABA Committee") has played an important role in analyzing the enforceability of electronic consumer agreements.

Some software vendors, however, sought to streamline the contracting process further by eliminating the consumer's click – after all, traditional shrinkwrap agreements simply required the user to open a package and begin to use a software program in order to be bound. A new generation of agreements thus emerged that sought to bind the user simply by virtue of his or her use of the licensed software, website or service. These agreements became known as "browsewrap" agreements.[6] The following case is one of the first to deal thoroughly with the issues that they raised.

Specht v. Netscape Communications, Inc.

306 F.3d 17 (2d Cir. 2002)

SOTOMAYOR, CIRCUIT JUDGE

This is an appeal from a judgment of the Southern District of New York denying a motion by defendants-appellants Netscape Communications Corporation and its corporate parent, America Online, Inc. (collectively, "defendants" or "Netscape"), to compel arbitration and to stay court proceedings. In order to resolve the central question of arbitrability presented here, we must address issues of contract formation in cyberspace. Principally, we are asked to determine whether plaintiffs-appellees ("plaintiffs"), by acting upon defendants' invitation to download free software made available on defendants' webpage, agreed to be bound by the software's license terms (which included the arbitration clause at issue), even though plaintiffs could not have learned of the existence of those terms unless, prior to executing the download, they had scrolled down the webpage to a screen located below the download button. We agree with the district court that a reasonably prudent Internet user in circumstances such as these would not have known or learned of the existence of the license terms before responding to defendants' invitation to download the free software, and that defendants therefore did not provide reasonable notice of the license terms. In consequence, plaintiffs' bare act of downloading the software did not unambiguously manifest assent to the arbitration provision contained in the license terms.

We also agree with the district court that plaintiffs' claims relating to the software at issue – a "plug-in" program entitled SmartDownload ("SmartDownload" or "the plug-in program"), offered by Netscape to enhance the functioning of the separate browser program called Netscape Communicator ("Communicator" or "the browser program") – are not subject to an arbitration agreement contained in the license terms governing the use of Communicator ... We therefore affirm the district court's denial of defendants' motion to compel arbitration and to stay court proceedings.

Background

In three related putative class actions, plaintiffs alleged that, unknown to them, their use of SmartDownload transmitted to defendants private information about plaintiffs' downloading of files from the Internet, thereby effecting an electronic surveillance of their online

---

[6] The ABA Committee defined "browsewrap" agreements as "all electronically presented terms and conditions that [do] not require the user to expressly manifest assent, such as by clicking 'yes,' or 'I agree'." Christina L. Kunz, et al., *Browse-Wrap Agreements: Validity of Implied Assent in Electronic Form Agreements*, 59 Business Lawyer 279 (2003).

activities in violation of two federal statutes, the Electronic Communications Privacy Act, 18 U.S.C. §§ 2510 et seq., and the Computer Fraud and Abuse Act, 18 U.S.C. § 1030.

In the time period relevant to this litigation, Netscape offered on its website various software programs, including Communicator and SmartDownload, which visitors to the site were invited to obtain free of charge. It is undisputed that [plaintiffs] downloaded Communicator from the Netscape website. These plaintiffs acknowledge that when they proceeded to initiate installation of Communicator, they were automatically shown a scrollable text of that program's license agreement and were not permitted to complete the installation until they had clicked on a "Yes" button to indicate that they accepted all the license terms. If a user attempted to install Communicator without clicking "Yes," the installation would be aborted. All five named user plaintiffs expressly agreed to Communicator's license terms by clicking "Yes." The Communicator license agreement that these plaintiffs saw made no mention of SmartDownload or other plug-in programs, and stated that "[t]hese terms apply to Netscape Communicator and Netscape Navigator" and that "all disputes relating to this Agreement (excepting any dispute relating to intellectual property rights)" are subject to "binding arbitration in Santa Clara County, California."

Although Communicator could be obtained independently of SmartDownload, all the named user plaintiffs, except Fagan, downloaded and installed Communicator in connection with downloading SmartDownload. Each of these plaintiffs allegedly arrived at a Netscape webpage captioned "SmartDownload Communicator" that urged them to "Download With Confidence Using SmartDownload!" At or near the bottom of the screen facing plaintiffs was the prompt "Start Download" and a tinted button labeled "Download." By clicking on the button, plaintiffs initiated the download of SmartDownload. Once that process was complete, SmartDownload, as its first plug-in task, permitted plaintiffs to

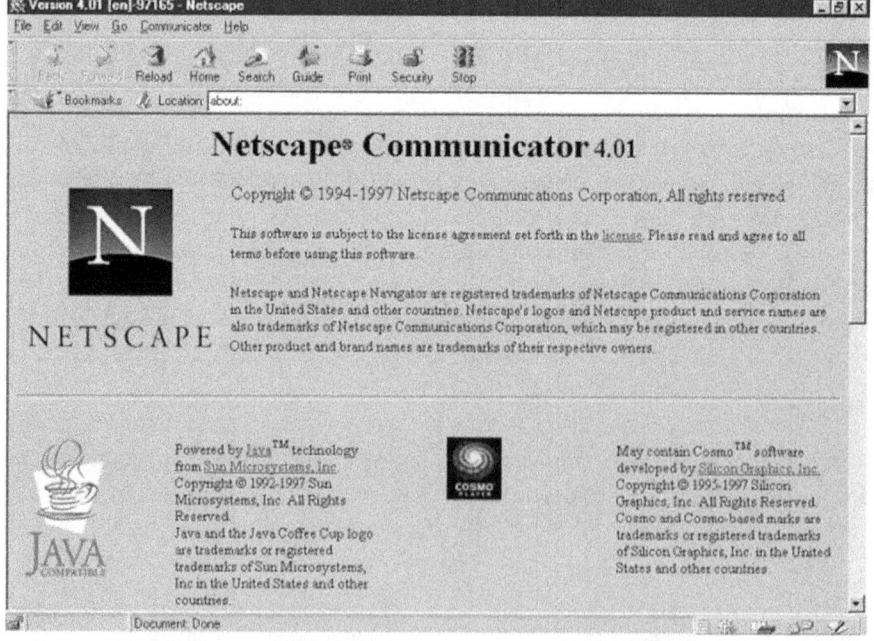

FIGURE 17.5 Netscape Navigator was the most popular early web browser.

proceed with downloading and installing Communicator, an operation that was accompanied by the clickwrap display of Communicator's license terms described above.

The signal difference between downloading Communicator and downloading SmartDownload was that no clickwrap presentation accompanied the latter operation. Instead, once plaintiffs Gibson, Gruber, Kelly, and Weindorf had clicked on the "Download" button located at or near the bottom of their screen, and the downloading of SmartDownload was complete, these plaintiffs encountered no further information about the plug-in program or the existence of license terms governing its use. The sole reference to SmartDownload's license terms on the "SmartDownload Communicator" webpage was located in text that would have become visible to plaintiffs only if they had scrolled down to the next screen.

Had plaintiffs scrolled down instead of acting on defendants' invitation to click on the "Download" button, they would have encountered the following invitation: "Please review and agree to the terms of the Netscape SmartDownload software license agreement before downloading and using the software." Plaintiffs Gibson, Gruber, Kelly, and Weindorf averred in their affidavits that they never saw this reference to the SmartDownload license agreement when they clicked on the "Download" button. They also testified during depositions that they saw no reference to license terms when they clicked to download SmartDownload, although under questioning by defendants' counsel, some plaintiffs added that they could not "remember" or be "sure" whether the screen shots of the SmartDownload page attached to their affidavits reflected precisely what they had seen on their computer screens when they downloaded SmartDownload.

In sum, plaintiffs Gibson, Gruber, Kelly, and Weindorf allege that the process of obtaining SmartDownload contrasted sharply with that of obtaining Communicator. Having selected SmartDownload, they were required neither to express unambiguous assent to that program's license agreement nor even to view the license terms or become aware of their existence before proceeding with the invited download of the free plug-in program. Moreover, once these plaintiffs had initiated the download, the existence of SmartDownload's license terms was not mentioned while the software was running or at any later point in plaintiffs' experience of the product.

Even for a user who, unlike plaintiffs, did happen to scroll down past the download button, SmartDownload's license terms would not have been immediately displayed in the manner of Communicator's clickwrapped terms. Instead, if such a user had seen the notice of SmartDownload's terms and then clicked on the underlined invitation to review and agree to the terms, a hypertext link would have taken the user to a separate webpage entitled "License & Support Agreements." The first paragraph on this page read, in pertinent part:

> The use of each Netscape software product is governed by a license agreement. You must read and agree to the license agreement terms BEFORE acquiring a product. Please click on the appropriate link below to review the current license agreement for the product of interest to you before acquisition. For products available for download, you must read and agree to the license agreement terms BEFORE you install the software. If you do not agree to the license terms, do not download, install or use the software.

Below this paragraph appeared a list of license agreements, the first of which was "License Agreement for Netscape Navigator and Netscape Communicator Product Family

(Netscape Navigator, Netscape Communicator and Netscape SmartDownload)." If the user clicked on that link, he or she would be taken to yet another webpage that contained the full text of a license agreement that was identical in every respect to the Communicator license agreement except that it stated that its "terms apply to Netscape Communicator, Netscape Navigator, and Netscape SmartDownload." The license agreement granted the user a nonexclusive license to use and reproduce the software, subject to certain terms:

> BY CLICKING THE ACCEPTANCE BUTTON OR INSTALLING OR USING NETSCAPE COMMUNICATOR, NETSCAPE NAVIGATOR, OR NETSCAPE SMARTDOWNLOAD SOFTWARE (THE "PRODUCT"), THE INDIVIDUAL OR ENTITY LICENSING THE PRODUCT ("LICENSEE") IS CONSENTING TO BE BOUND BY AND IS BECOMING A PARTY TO THIS AGREEMENT. IF LICENSEE DOES NOT AGREE TO ALL OF THE TERMS OF THIS AGREEMENT, THE BUTTON INDICATING NON-ACCEPTANCE MUST BE SELECTED, AND LICENSEE MUST NOT INSTALL OR USE THE SOFTWARE.

Among the license terms was a provision requiring virtually all disputes relating to the agreement to be submitted to arbitration:

> Unless otherwise agreed in writing, all disputes relating to this Agreement (excepting any dispute relating to intellectual property rights) shall be subject to final and binding arbitration in Santa Clara County, California, under the auspices of JAMS/EndDispute, with the losing party paying all costs of arbitration.

Unlike the four named user plaintiffs who downloaded SmartDownload from the Netscape website, the fifth named plaintiff, Michael Fagan, claims to have downloaded the plug-in program from a "shareware" website operated by ZDNet, an entity unrelated to Netscape. Shareware sites are websites, maintained by companies or individuals, that contain libraries of free, publicly available software. The pages that a user would have seen while downloading SmartDownload from ZDNet differed from those that he or she would have encountered while downloading SmartDownload from the Netscape website. Notably, instead of any kind of notice of the SmartDownload license agreement, the ZDNet pages offered only a hypertext link to "more information" about SmartDownload, which, if clicked on, took the user to a Netscape webpage that, in turn, contained a link to the license agreement. Thus, a visitor to the ZDNet website could have obtained SmartDownload, as Fagan avers he did, without ever seeing a reference to that program's license terms, even if he or she had scrolled through all of ZDNet's webpages.

Discussion

Whether governed by the common law or by Article 2 of the Uniform Commercial Code ("UCC"), a transaction, in order to be a contract, requires a manifestation of agreement between the parties. Mutual manifestation of assent, whether by written or spoken word or by conduct, is the touchstone of contract. Although an onlooker observing the disputed transactions in this case would have seen each of the user plaintiffs click on the SmartDownload "Download" button, a consumer's clicking on a download button does not communicate assent to contractual terms if the offer did not make clear to the consumer that clicking on the download button would signify assent to those terms. California's common law is clear that "an offeree, regardless of apparent manifestation of his consent, is not bound by inconspicuous contractual provisions of which he is unaware, contained in a document whose contractual nature is not obvious."

Arbitration agreements are no exception to the requirement of manifestation of assent. "This principle of knowing consent applies with particular force to provisions for arbitration." Clarity and conspicuousness of arbitration terms are important in securing informed assent. "If a party wishes to bind in writing another to an agreement to arbitrate future disputes, such purpose should be accomplished in a way that each party to the arrangement will fully and clearly comprehend that the agreement to arbitrate exists and binds the parties thereto." Thus, California contract law measures assent by an objective standard that takes into account both what the offeree said, wrote, or did and the transactional context in which the offeree verbalized or acted.

A. The Reasonably Prudent Offeree of Downloadable Software

Defendants argue that plaintiffs must be held to a standard of reasonable prudence and that, because notice of the existence of SmartDownload license terms was on the next scrollable screen, plaintiffs were on "inquiry notice" of those terms. We disagree with the proposition that a reasonably prudent offeree in plaintiffs' position would necessarily have known or learned of the existence of the SmartDownload license agreement prior to acting, so that plaintiffs may be held to have assented to that agreement with constructive notice of its terms. See Cal. Civ.Code § 1589 ("A voluntary acceptance of the benefit of a transaction is equivalent to a consent to all the obligations arising from it, so far as the facts are known, or ought to be known, to the person accepting."). It is true that "[a] party cannot avoid the terms of a contract on the ground that he or she failed to read it before signing." Marin Storage & Trucking, 89 Cal.App.4th at 1049. But courts are quick to add: "An exception to this general rule exists when the writing does not appear to be a contract and the terms are not called to the attention of the recipient. In such a case, no contract is formed with respect to the undisclosed term."

Most of the cases cited by defendants in support of their inquiry-notice argument are drawn from the world of paper contracting. As [these] cases suggest, receipt of a physical document containing contract terms or notice thereof is frequently deemed, in the world of paper transactions, a sufficient circumstance to place the offeree on inquiry notice of those terms. "Every person who has actual notice of circumstances sufficient to put a prudent man upon inquiry as to a particular fact, has constructive notice of the fact itself in all cases in which, by prosecuting such inquiry, he might have learned such fact." Cal. Civ.Code § 19. These principles apply equally to the emergent world of online product delivery, pop-up screens, hyperlinked pages, clickwrap licensing, scrollable documents, and urgent admonitions to "Download Now!" What plaintiffs saw when they were being invited by defendants to download this fast, free plug-in called SmartDownload was a screen containing praise for the product and, at the very bottom of the screen, a "Download" button. Defendants argue that under the principles set forth in the cases cited above, a "fair and prudent person using ordinary care" would have been on inquiry notice of SmartDownload's license terms.

We are not persuaded that a reasonably prudent offeree in these circumstances would have known of the existence of license terms. Plaintiffs were responding to an offer that did not carry an immediately visible notice of the existence of license terms or require unambiguous manifestation of assent to those terms. Thus, plaintiffs' "apparent manifestation of … consent" was to terms contained in a document whose contractual nature [was] not obvious. Moreover, the fact that, given the position of the scroll bar on their computer screens, plaintiffs may have been aware that an unexplored portion of the Netscape web-page remained below the download button does not mean that they reasonably should have concluded that this portion contained a notice of license terms. In their deposition testimony, plaintiffs variously stated that they used the scroll bar "[o]nly if there is some-thing that I feel I need to see that is on – that is off the page," or that the elevated position of the scroll bar suggested the presence of "mere formalities, standard lower banner links" or "that the page is bigger than what I can see." Plaintiffs testified, and defendants did not refute, that plaintiffs were in fact unaware that defendants intended to attach license terms to the use of SmartDownload.

We conclude that in circumstances such as these, where consumers are urged to download free software at the immediate click of a button, a reference to the existence of license terms on a submerged screen is not sufficient to place consumers on inquiry or constructive notice of those terms. The SmartDownload webpage screen was "printed in such a manner that it tended to conceal the fact that it was an express acceptance of [Netscape's] rules and regulations." Internet users may have, as defendants put it, "as much time as they need" to scroll through multiple screens on a webpage, but there is no reason to assume that viewers will scroll down to subsequent screens simply because screens are there. When products are "free" and users are invited to download them in the absence of reasonably conspicuous notice that they are about to bind themselves to contract terms, the transactional circumstances cannot be fully analogized to those in the paper world of arm's-length bargaining. In the next two sections, we discuss case law and other legal authorities that have addressed the circumstances of computer sales, software licensing, and online transacting. Those authorities tend strongly to support our conclusion that plaintiffs did not manifest assent to SmartDownload's license terms.

B. Shrinkwrap Licensing and Related Practices

Defendants cite certain well-known cases involving shrinkwrap licensing and related commercial practices in support of their contention that plaintiffs became bound by the SmartDownload license terms by virtue of inquiry notice. For example, in *Hill v. Gateway 2000, Inc.*, 105 F.3d 1147 (7th Cir.1997), the Seventh Circuit held that where a purchaser had ordered a computer over the telephone, received the order in a shipped box contain-ing the computer along with printed contract terms, and did not return the computer within the thirty days required by the terms, the purchaser was bound by the contract. In *ProCD, Inc. v. Zeidenberg*, the same court held that where an individual purchased software in a box containing license terms which were displayed on the computer screen every time the user executed the software program, the user had sufficient opportunity to review the terms and to return the software, and so was contractually bound after retaining the product.

These cases do not help defendants. To the extent that they hold that the purchaser of a computer or tangible software is contractually bound after failing to object to printed license terms provided with the product, *Hill* and *Brower* do not differ markedly from the cases involving traditional paper contracting discussed in the previous section. Insofar as the purchaser in ProCD was confronted with conspicuous, mandatory license terms every time he ran the software on his computer, that case actually undermines defendants' contention that downloading in the absence of conspicuous terms is an act that binds plaintiffs to those terms. In Mortenson, the full text of license terms was printed on each sealed diskette envelope inside the software box, printed again on the inside cover of the user manual, and notice of the terms appeared on the computer screen every time the purchaser executed the program. In sum, the foregoing cases are clearly distinguishable from the facts of the present action.

C. Online Transactions

Cases in which courts have found contracts arising from Internet use do not assist defendants, because in those circumstances there was much clearer notice than in the present case that a user's act would manifest assent to contract terms ...

After reviewing the California common law and other relevant legal authority, we conclude that under the circumstances here, plaintiffs' downloading of SmartDownload did not constitute acceptance of defendants' license terms. Reasonably conspicuous notice of the existence of contract terms and unambiguous manifestation of assent to those terms by consumers are essential if electronic bargaining is to have integrity and credibility. We hold that a reasonably prudent offeree in plaintiffs' position would not have known or learned, prior to acting on the invitation to download, of the reference to SmartDownload's license terms hidden below the "Download" button on the next screen. We affirm the district court's conclusion that the user plaintiffs, including Fagan, are not bound by the arbitration clause contained in those terms.

For the foregoing reasons, we affirm the district court's denial of defendants' motion to compel arbitration and to stay court proceedings.

Notes and Questions

1. *A victory for browsewrap.* Despite the holding in *Specht*, two years later the Second Circuit upheld the enforceability of a browsewrap agreement. In *Register.com v. Verio, Inc.*, 356 F.3d 393 (2d Cir. 2004), the court found that a user's downloading of factual data from a website was sufficient to indicate its assent to the site's online terms of use. The Register site enabled users to access the Internet's centralized "WHOIS" database, which contains information relating to the identity of Internet domain name registrants. A user making a WHOIS query through The Register site would receive a reply furnishing the requested WHOIS information, accompanied by a legend stating that: "By submitting a WHOIS query, you agree that you will use this data only for lawful purposes and that under no circumstances will you use this data to ... support the transmission of mass unsolicited, commercial advertising or solicitation via email" (i.e., The Register sought to prohibit the use of WHOIS data to fuel email spam). Importantly, this notice arrived *after* the user submitted its WHOIS request. The court analyzed The Register's online agreement as follows:

Verio contends that in no instance did it receive legally enforceable notice of the conditions Register intended to impose. If Verio had submitted only one query, or even if it had submitted only a few sporadic queries, that would give considerable force to its contention that it obtained the WHOIS data without being conscious that Register intended to impose conditions, and without being deemed to have accepted Register's conditions. But Verio was daily submitting numerous queries, each of which resulted in its receiving notice of the terms Register exacted. Furthermore, Verio admits that it knew perfectly well what terms Register demanded. Verio's argument fails. The situation might be compared to one in which plaintiff P maintains a roadside fruit stand displaying bins of apples. A visitor, defendant D, takes an apple and bites into it. As D turns to leave, D sees a sign, visible only as one turns to exit, which says "Apples – 50 cents apiece."

D does not pay for the apple. Thereafter, each day, several times a day, D revisits the stand, takes an apple, and eats it. D never leaves money. In our view, however, D cannot continue on a daily basis to take apples for free, knowing full well that P is offering them only in exchange for 50 cents in compensation. Verio's circumstance is effectively the same. Each day Verio repeatedly enters Register's computers and takes that day's new WHOIS data. Each day upon receiving the requested data, Verio receives Register's notice of the terms on which it makes the data available – that the data not be used for mass solicitation via direct mail, email, or telephone. Verio acknowledges that it continued drawing the data from Register's computers with full knowledge that Register offered access subject to these restrictions. Verio is no more free to take Register's data without being bound by the terms on which Register offers it, than D was free, in the example, once he became aware of the terms of P's offer. We recognize that contract offers on the Internet often require the offeree to click on an "I agree" icon. And no doubt, in many circumstances, such a statement of agreement by the offeree is essential to the formation of a contract. But not in all circumstances. [It] is standard contract doctrine that when a benefit is offered subject to stated conditions, and the offeree makes a decision to take the benefit with knowledge of the terms of the offer, the taking constitutes an acceptance of the terms, which accordingly become binding on the offeree.

Do you agree with the court's analysis? What do you think of the court's $0.50 apple analogy? Do you think that Verio had more or less knowledge of the applicable restrictions than an ordinary user of The Register site? How does this case accord with *Specht*? Could Netscape have prevailed on a similar theory?

2. *Browsewrap today.* Courts remain divided over the enforceability of browsewrap agreements. Those following *Specht* have generally found that, even without multiple or repeat transactions, "the enforceability of browsewrap agreements depends upon whether 'there is evidence that the user has actual or constructive notice of the site's terms.'" *Mohammed v. Uber Techs., Inc.*, 237 F. Supp. 3d 719, 731 n.8 (N.D. Ill. 2017). Generally, this "actual or constructive notice" should occur *before* the user begins to use the site in question.

In the end, the assessment of browsewrap agreements often boils down to a question of website design and layout. One court derived the following "general principles" from the growing body of case law on this subject:

First, "terms of use" will not be enforced where there is no evidence that the website users had notice of the agreement

Second, "terms of use" will be enforced when a user is encouraged by the design and content of the website and the agreement's webpage to examine the terms clearly available through hyperlinkage

Third, "terms of use" will not be enforced where the link to a website's terms is buried at the bottom of a webpage or tucked away in obscure corners of the website where users are unlikely to see it.[7]

Why are website design and layout so important to the enforceability of online agreements? Do lawyers now need to become familiar with graphical design principles in addition to contract law, or is graphical design now an integral *part* of contract law?

---

7   *Berkson v. Gogo LLC*, 97 F. Supp. 3d 359, 401–02 (E.D.N.Y. 2015).

3. *Feels like paper?* Some courts continue to analyze electronic contracts as though they were electronic versions of paper contracts. For example, the court in *Hubbert v. Dell Corp.*, 844 N.E.2d 965, 968 (Ill. 2006) considered the enforceability of online terms that included hyperlinks to numerous other documents. It held that hyperlinks "should be treated the same as a multipage written paper contract. The blue hyperlink simply takes a person to another page of the contract, similar to turning the page of a written paper contract." Do you agree? How often do you click through the linked documents in online terms?

   In contrast, the ABA Committee argues that electronic and paper contracts are inherently different:

   To equate digital contracts with paper contracts is to ignore the difference that tangibility makes. The recipient of a paper contract is more likely to skim the pages for capitalized and bolded terms than is a recipient of an electronic contract with terms that remain hidden until the hyperlink is clicked.[8]

   Which view do you find more persuasive? In the end, does it matter whether electronic contracts can be analogized to their paper counterparts?

4. *Automated scraping and acceptance.* The legal analysis of shrinkwrap and browsewrap agreements depends on a finding that there was sufficient assent to support contract formation. Yet what happens when both the presentation of the agreement and its "acceptance" are accomplished without human intervention? The Internet today teems with automated programs, agents, bots and spiders that crawl across billions of webpages collecting ("scraping"), compiling and analyzing information for their creators. Can these automated devices "assent" to a website's terms of use? Many websites contain prohibitions on automated access in their online terms of use, but are these prohibitions enforceable against an automated bot or spider? Some website operators have argued that, even absent contractual assent, unauthorized access to a website may be prohibited by the Computer Fraud and Abuse Act, 18 U.S.C. § 1030, or common law doctrines such as trespass.[9]

5. *Contracting authority.* One recurrent issue with online agreements is whether the person purporting to agree to the terms of the license has the legal authority to enter into the agreement. For example, a five-year-old can easily click "I ACCEPT" on a computer screen, but lacks the requisite legal capacity to make a contract. Likewise, if a low-level employee of a company purports to bind his or her company pursuant to a clickwrap agreement when downloading a piece of software, is the company legally bound? Does it matter whether the software is a $0.99 app or a $50 million enterprise resource management system? What duty does the licensor have to ensure that the person on the other side of the click actually has authority to bind the licensee?

   It may be for this reason that companies like IBM have adopted across-the-board policies prohibiting their employees from clicking to accept any agreement in connection with their work duties. Do you think this approach is effective? What drawbacks might a company implementing such a policy face?

   Courts have wrestled with the issue of apparent authority and clickwrap agreements. See *National Auto Lenders, Inc. v. SysLOCATE, Inc.*, 686 F. Supp. 2d 1318 (S.D.Fla. 2010), in

---

[8] Nancy S. Kim, Juliet M. Moringiello & John E. Ottaviani, *Notice and Assent Through Technological Change: The Enduring Relevance of the Work of the ABA Joint Working Group on Electronic Contracting Practices*, 75 Business Lawyer 1725, 1734 (2020).

[9] See Kevin Emerson Collins, *Cybertrespass and Trespass to Documents*, 54 Clev. St. L. Rev. 41 (2006).

which the licensee (NAL) informed a software vendor (SysLOCATE) that only its executives could make decisions on behalf of their company. As a result, when lower-level employees clicked to accept a software agreement proffered on the vendor's website, the court found that provisions in the software agreement requiring disputes to be resolved through arbitration were not enforceable.

6. *Supersedure*. If clickwrap, browsewrap and other electronic terms are considered to be binding contracts, then they can supersede prior written agreements, including agreements that were negotiated and signed by the parties. Why might this effect be considered risky by some parties? What might a party do in order to avoid this risk? For a hint, see Section 13.10, dealing with the precedence of agreements.

17.3 THE (D)EVOLUTION OF CONSUMER LICENSES

Firms and their attorneys do not observe developments in the law of technology licensing passively. Rather, as the below academic study demonstrates, they adapt their agreements to take new legal developments into account.

SET IN STONE? CHANGE AND INNOVATION IN CONSUMER STANDARD-FORM CONTRACTS
FLORENCIA MAROTTA-WURGLER AND ROBERT TAYLOR, 88 NYU L. REV. 240 (2013)

In this Article, we examine the innovation and evolution of a common type of mass-market consumer standard, End User License Agreements (EULAs). EULAs are an important type of online standard-form contract and have been at the forefront of various regulatory debates. Recently, the American Law Institute approved the Principles of the Law of Software Contracts (Law of Software Contracts), which focuses in large part on mass-market transactions involving EULAs. We use a sample of EULAs from 264 mass-market software firms between 2003 and 2010 to track changes to thirty-two common contractual terms. Our methodology measures the relative buyer-friendliness of each term relative to the default rules of Article 2 of the Uniform Commercial Code (U.C.C.) to examine how the pro-seller bias of EULAs changes over time. Since buyers need to become informed about terms to "shop" around effectively, we measure changes in contract length and readability. We begin exploring the firm, product, and market characteristics that are associated with contract changes. Finally, we record relevant court decisions around the sample period to evaluate whether the sample contracts are sensitive to changes in the enforceability of terms.

There are a number of interesting results. Thirty-nine percent of the sample firms made material changes to their contracts during the seven-year period, despite the fact that the product being licensed was held as constant as possible. While there is no absolute baseline against which to measure contract stickiness, our results contrast with the high degree of standardization and stickiness that has generally been observed in sovereign-bond contracting. In our study, a material change occurs when a EULA changes at least one of the thirty-two terms that we track. The list of terms is fairly comprehensive, as explained in Part II. Contracts have also gotten considerably longer on average but no easier to read;

despite being ostensibly written for the consumer, the average license agreement remains, by standard textual analysis criteria, as hard to read as an article in a scientific journal. Increased contract complexity over time is problematic in this context because it increases the cost of becoming informed, which, in the absence of intermediaries who can simplify information, might weaken a market disciplining mechanism.

We find that most of the terms that changed have become more pro-seller relative to the original contract. Most of these changes are driven by firms opting out of U.C.C. Article 2 default rules in favor of relatively more pro-seller terms. Clauses that changed the most (in that they have become relatively more pervasive) are forum-selection and arbitration clauses, restrictions on reverse engineering, and restrictions on transfer. While most terms are likely to change away from the default rules, terms that are more pro-seller relative to the default rules are almost twice as likely to change away from those defaults as terms that benefit buyers, all else being equal. That is, pro-buyer defaults are relatively less sticky than pro-seller defaults. We also document innovations, as new and largely pro-seller terms have been introduced even in the absence of strong property rights. In particular, seven terms that were virtually absent in 2003 emerged by 2010. These relate to remote disablement of software, firms' ability to collect user information, and terms related to the rights and software of third parties. Most of these new terms allow sellers to increase control over users, which is possible because of technological innovation. What parties are associated with change? We find that younger, growing, and large firms, as well as firms with legal departments, are more likely to innovate. We hypothesize that young and growing firms might be more sophisticated and ambitious, and thus more willing to experiment. We test the hypothesis that contract changes might have been shaped by increased legal certainty on the enforceability of such terms. We find that the terms that have become more enforceable during the sample period were more likely to be used in a pro-seller sense, consistent with this hypothesis.

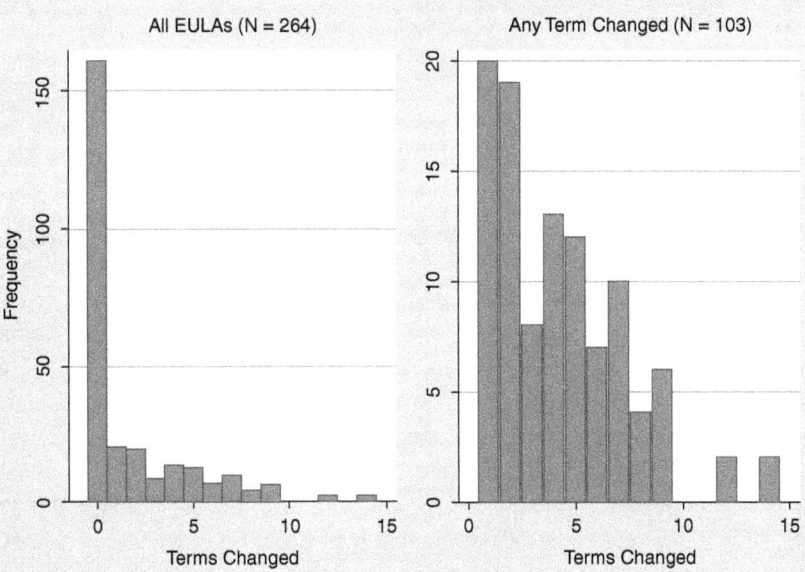

FIGURE 17.6 Number of terms changed, 2003 vs. 2010.

Next, we explore the appearance and adoption of innovative terms. We identified seven terms that were rare or absent at the beginning of the period and fell into the three categories of modification and termination, information collection, and third parties. Terms allowing the drafter to unilaterally modify the agreement are examples of changes borrowed from other areas, such as credit card agreements and online Terms of Use. Terms that define the relationship between the user and third parties are innovations in the narrower sense of the term, as these terms allow software providers to contract out some of the functionalities of their products, arguably to parties who can provide them in a better way at a lower cost. Most of these terms take advantage of technological changes (such as electronic licensing) that allow sellers to exercise more control over buyers' use of the product. As explained above, we do not mean to imply that the terms that we designate "innovative" are economically efficient or good in any welfare sense. All we can say for sure is that they are novel.

Who are the innovators and who are those who adopt the terms later on? Controlling for contract length, the results show that young and larger companies are more likely to adopt innovative terms. A possible explanation for this finding is that larger firms have more resources and are thus more likely to be aware of technological changes that present opportunities to revise EULAs, or that these firms receive more cutting-edge legal advice. Younger firms might be more sophisticated and also more attuned to technological innovations.

We [also] explore the role of in-house counsel in the evolution of fine print ... In both 2003 and 2010, the presence of lawyers is associated with more pro-seller bias. Again, lawyers are associated not with change in terms per se, but with a negative change in bias over the sample period. Of course, firm size and the presence of legal counsel are highly correlated, so it might be hard to identify the contribution of legal counsel to change in terms. We assume that firms with legal departments are likely to assign the job of revising and drafting terms to lawyers.

[L]awyers are also associated with innovation, as firms with lawyers are more likely to adopt innovative terms at the beginning of the sample period. [The data] shows no effect between the presence of lawyers and adoption of the innovative terms at the end of the period. This might be because such firms adopted them earlier. Firms without legal departments might look at the contracts of other firms and copy the innovative terms. This possibility is consistent with accounts of various firms in the sample with whom we communicated. In contrast to previous studies, we find that lawyers (at least those who work in-house) appear to be involved in revising and innovating in mass-market agreements.

Conventional wisdom suggests that standard-form contracts are essentially static given that they are rarely invoked, govern relatively low-price items that are unlikely to be the source of litigation, and are not protected by property rights. This study finds change and innovation in several aspects of common consumer standard-form contracts. Contrary to studies of innovation in law firms, it finds that in-house lawyers are associated with new terms. Almost forty percent of the contracts we examined saw at least one standard term change over the period between 2003 and 2010; some changed more than ten terms. While this number could be perceived as low, especially in an industry as dynamic as software, the results challenge conventional views that a large fraction of consumer fine print is set in stone. We find that contracts have become longer but no simpler to read. On average, EULAs accumulate more terms over time, a process consistent with the observation that the process of contract creation involves the overlaying of terms without much revision. Drafters might be thinking myopically about the effect of the particular term being added as opposed to the meaning of the contract as a whole. The implication of this trend is that, to the extent consumers read terms to comparison shop, the cost of becoming informed about terms has increased. The cost is also higher for would-be intermediaries such as ratings websites and consumer nonprofits. An important implication of this is that proposals for increased contract disclosure are less likely to be effective because what is increasingly costly for consumers is not gaining access to the contract but reading it. Any type of disclosure reform might be more effective if it included directives for plainer and more succinct language. Consumer advocates, who have been lobbying for plain-language laws in consumer agreements for some time, may have picked up this trend.

Notes and Questions

1. *Directional evolution.* Is it a surprise that EULA terms have steadily grown more pro-seller over the years? Under what circumstances might new pro-consumer terms become ingrained in EULAs?

2. *Does anybody read the fine print?* What do you think about the usefulness of EULA terms given statements like those of Chief Justice John G. Roberts of the US Supreme Court in response to a question during a 2010 speech:

   Roberts admitted he doesn't usually read the computer jargon that is a condition of accessing websites … "It is a problem," he added, "because the legal system obviously is to blame for that." Providing too much information defeats the purpose of disclosure, since no one reads it, he said. "What the answer is," he said, "I don't know."[10]

   What is "the answer" in your opinion?

3. *A thicket of restrictions?* Much information that is publicly available on the Web is now used for epidemiological and public health research. Genetic epidemiologists have made

FIGURE 17.7 Chief Justice Roberts admits that he doesn't read the fine print …

[10] Debra Cassens Weiss, *Chief Justice Roberts Admits He Doesn't Read the Computer Fine Print*, ABA J., October 20, 2010.

important discoveries using automated web crawling techniques (see Section 17.2, Note 4) to gather information from tens of millions of individual genealogy records contained online. Yet, as one recent study has found, many genealogy websites contain terms of use that place numerous restrictions on this publicly accessible data.[11] Restrictions include:

- *genealogical use only*: limits usage to personal, private or professional genealogical use;
- *no commercial use*: prohibits any commercial use of content;
- *no downloads*: prohibits downloading all or significant portions of other users' content;
- *no automated access*: prohibits automated scraping, crawling and/or harvesting of content;
- *no transfer*: prohibits unauthorized distribution, reproduction, retransmission, publication, sale, exploitation (commercial or otherwise) or any other form of transfer of any portion of the content;

Most of these restrictions, individually and in combination, appear to prohibit scientific research. Yet, it seems that most researchers are unaware of, or do not understand, such restrictions and, to date, no such restrictions appear to have been enforced against biomedical researchers. Is there an issue here? Would the answer change if more website operators began to enforce their online terms? What do you think about a system in which legally enforceable online terms exist but are widely ignored and seldom enforced?

4. *Unilateral modification.* One of the contractual terms identified by Marotta-Wurgler and Taylor is the licensor's unilateral ability to amend the terms of the contract. Think about it. Would you knowingly agree to a contract in which the other party could unilaterally amend the terms simply by notifying you? The very idea sounds absurd, but unilateral amendments to consumer contracts are now pervasive. In a recent article, Shmuel Becher and Uri Benoliel report that of 500 browsewrap agreements used with popular US websites, 81.6 percent could be modified unilaterally by the licensor.[12] They find that "[c]ommon modifications include, for example, a change in fees, a modification of a dispute resolution clause, or revision of the firm's privacy policy. In fact, unilateral modifications can address virtually every aspect of a contract." Does the realization that every aspect of an online contract is malleable give you pause? Does it make such instruments less than contracts? Should it?

   Courts appear to be divided over the enforceability of contract terms that are unilaterally amended, as well as the general principle of unilateral amendment. At least one court has held that terms of service that permitted a provider to amend the terms at any time rendered the entire contract illusory.[13] Do you agree? Why shouldn't a party be entitled to agree that terms may be amended by the other party in the future?

5. *The innovations of lawyers.* Marotta-Wurgler and Taylor observe that the "innovation" in online contracting terms has largely been driven not by changes in technology or product offerings, but by lawyers. In your view, has this degree of legal innovation helped or hindered the marketplace?

---

[11] Jorge L. Contreras, et al., *Legal Terms of use and Public Genealogy Websites*, 7 J. L. & Biosci. (2020).

[12] Shmuel I. Becher & Uri Benoliel, *Sneak in Contracts: An Empirical and Legal Analysis of Unilateral Modification Clauses in Consumer Contracts*, 55 Ga. L. Rev. (2020).

[13] *Harris v. Blockbuster, Inc.*, 622 F. Supp. 2d 396 (N.D. Tex. 2009). For a review of recent cases, see Juliet M. Moringiello & John E. Ottaviani, *Online Contracts: We May Modify These Terms at Any Time, Right?*, Business L. Today, May 20, 2016.

Problem 17.1

Find an online EULA on your computer, tablet or phone. How long is it? Read it. What terms does it contain that surprise you? Would you have agreed to these terms if you were negotiating the agreement in person, or on behalf of a client?

Now put the shoe on the other foot. If you represented the company that wrote the EULA, what additional terms might be beneficial for your client that you could include in the agreement? How close to the line of unconscionability would you advise your client to venture?

18

Software, Data and the Cloud

Software and data licensing are tied to a significant amount of global commerce. While many aspects of the licensing agreements in these industries are similar to those in other industries, there are a number of unique features that characterize licenses of software and data.

18.1 DATA AND DATABASES

Analysts estimate that the global market for data will grow from \$139 billion in 2020 to \$229 billion by 2025.[1] Data fuels financial markets, consumer sales, advertising, healthcare, political campaigning, natural resources extraction and thousands of other industries, small and large. Yet surprisingly little is known or written about the licensing of data and database products.[2] This section offers an introduction to this increasingly important field.

18.1.1 *Protecting the Unprotectable*

Despite the expansive reach of US copyright law, no copyright exists in facts, information or data. This principle was established by the Supreme Court more than a century ago in the seminal case *International News Service v. Associated Press*, 248 U.S. 215 (1918), in which the Court held that the news of the day, independent of its expression in a particular news story, is not subject to copyright. The Court reaffirmed this principle three decades ago in *Feist Publications v. Rural Telephone*, 499 U.S. 340 (1991), explaining "That there can be no valid copyright in facts is universally understood. The most fundamental axiom of copyright law is that no author may copyright his ideas or the facts he narrates." In *Feist*, the compiler of a telephone directory

---

[1] Markets and Markets, Big Data Market by Component, Deployment Mode, Organization Size, Business Function (Operations, Finance, and Marketing and Sales), Industry Vertical (BFSI, Manufacturing, and Healthcare and Life Sciences), and Region – Global Forecast to 2025, www.marketsandmarkets.com/Market-Reports/big-data-market-1068.html.

[2] The term database has several meanings. First, a database is a type of computer program that can store and provide access to large quantities of data. In another sense, a database is the collection of data elements contained in a software database program. For the purposes of this chapter, we will use the latter meaning.

argued that copyright should be recognized in its compilation of names and telephone numbers – the product of significant labor and effort. Nevertheless, the Court flatly rejected this "sweat of the brow" theory of protection. It notes that "The same is true of all facts – scientific, historical, biographical, and news of the day. They may not be copyrighted and are part of the public domain available to every person." Under the principles set forth in *Feist*, the compiler of a collection of data may obtain a "thin" copyright in any creative arrangement and selection of entries in a database, but no copyright in the data elements themselves, singly or in the aggregate.

The situation is different in Europe. In 1996, the EU adopted Directive 96/9 on the Legal Protection of Databases (the EU Database Directive), granting fifteen years of legal protection to any collection of data, information or other material that is arranged in a systematic or methodological way, provided that it is accessible by electronic or other means and its producer has made a "substantial investment" in its compilation. Around the same time, a significant debate occurred in the United States regarding the advisability of enacting similar database protection legislation. Despite the introduction of several different proposals in Congress, no such legislation was enacted, leaving databases without formal legal protection in the United States.[3] More recently, the EU enacted the General Data Protection Regulation (GDPR), a sweeping set of legislation intended to protect individual data, which is discussed in greater detail in Section 18.1.4.

This being said, there are numerous legal tools at the disposal of a US database owner to prevent the unauthorized use of data that it has compiled. For example, Section 1201 of the Digital Millennium Copyright Act of 1998 (DMCA) prohibits the circumvention of technological devices that are intended to control access to copyrighted works. In other words, hacking the protections that a database owner implements to protect its data could be a violation of the DMCA, even if the use of the protected data is not a copyright infringement.[4] Claims for unauthorized use of data are also available under theories of trade secret misappropriation, unfair competition and trespass (sometimes referred to as "cybertrespass").[5]

In addition, there are ongoing efforts to "propertize" data in the United States, thus overcoming the precedent established in *INS v. AP* and other cases, as discussed in the following article relating to individual health information.

THE FALSE PROMISE OF HEALTH DATA OWNERSHIP
JORGE L. CONTRERAS, 94 *N.Y.U. L. REV.* 624, 626–33 (2019)

Debates regarding data ownership and privacy have been brewing in academic circles since the emergence of computers and digital records in the 1960s, but it was the growth of the Internet in the late 1990s and early 2000s that sparked widespread debate among cyberlaw and intellectual property scholars. In recent years, increasing wealth inequality and the rise of digital platforms have fueled a renewed conversation about the ownership of personal information.

---

[3] J. H. Reichman & Paul F. Uhlir, *A Contractually Reconstructed Research Commons for Scientific Data in a Highly Protectionist Intellectual Property Environment*, 66 L. & Contemp. Probs. 315, 374–76, 388–95 (2003).

[4] See Raymond T. Nimmer, *Issues in Modern Licensing of Factual Information and Databases* in Research Handbook on Intellectual Property Licensing 99, 112–15 (Jacques de Werra, ed., Edward Elgar, 2013).

[5] See id. at 105–12, 115–16.

Joining this debate, some health law scholars have raised concerns regarding individual autonomy, privacy and distributive justice in arguing for the propertization of genetic and other health information. In his bestselling book *The Patient Will See You Now*, cardiologist and patient advocate Eric Topol asserts that "[t]he ownership of property is essential to emancipation. It's unquestionably appropriate, a self-evident truth, that each individual is entitled to own all of his or her medical data." Popular awareness of these issues has been fueled, among other things, by the story of Henrietta Lacks, an indigent African-American cancer patient whose excised tumor cells formed the basis of a multi-billion industry while her descendants continued to live in poverty. At least six U.S. states have enacted legislation purporting to grant individuals ownership of their genetic information (though one has since repealed that legislation). And even former President Barack Obama once opined that "if somebody does a test on me or my genes … that's mine."

But the push toward individual data ownership has gained the most momentum thanks to a new crop of technology-focused startups. In a global health data market worth an estimated $67 to $100 billion per year, these aspiring data intermediaries seek to use Blockchain and mobile apps to enable consumers to control, and get paid for, the use of their Individual Health Information (IHI), and in the process retain a healthy portion of the proceeds. These firms include Nebula Genomics (co-founded by Harvard Medical School professor and genomics pioneer George Church), Genos (a spinout from Chinese sequencing giant BGI-Shenzhen), DNASimple (a recent contestant on the ABC television show Shark Tank), Invitae (seeking to sell "genome management" services) and LunaDNA (backed by equipment manufacturer Illumina). The motivations of these firms may be summed up by the Chairman of Genos, who has publicly stated that "our business is to make money enabling researchers and individuals to connect and transact with each other."

In a less commercial vein, Unpatient.org, a short-lived not-for-profit effort by Topol and Leonard Kish, sought to empower patients through data ownership. Unpatient.org released its own "Data Ownership Manifesto" which proclaimed that "[d]ata that reflects you should belong to you," rather than to healthcare providers and pharmaceutical companies.

But perhaps the most intriguing addition to the propertization camp is Hu-manity.org, which approaches the issue of data propertization from the perspective of international human rights, arguing that a "31st human right" in personal data ownership should be recognized under the Universal Declaration of Human Rights, following from which individuals should be able to sell, and profit from, access to their data.

In each of these business models, the aspiring data intermediary acts as the consumer's authorized agent in selling or licensing her IHI to healthcare providers, pharmaceutical manufacturers, and anyone else interested in it, remitting a share of the revenue back to the consumer and, of course, retaining a portion for itself. While the idea that consumers, as a matter of equity and distributive fairness, should share in the profits earned from the use of their data is not a new one, it is only today, with the advent of technologies such as Blockchain and pervasive mobile connectivity, that markets in IHI have become feasible.

Though there are differences among these proposed offerings, an individual who signed up with one of these data intermediaries would be given the ability to opt-in to one or more research studies and contribute all or a portion of her stored data to the study. In some cases, an individual may not wish to share certain types of information, such as a family history of schizophrenia or an HIV-positive diagnosis. In that case, the intermediary could screen the studies offered to the individual or exclude IHI relating to the sensitive subject area. DNAsimple advertises that it will pay donors for saliva samples to help genetic disease research. Genos estimates that IHI payments to consumers would be in the range of $50 to $250; while LunaDNA offers participants a mere $3.50 for the use of their genetic marker data and $21 for a full genomic sequence.

The linchpin of this new business model is the recognition of an individual's ownership of IHI. Without it, companies, hospitals, insurers, and data intermediaries can (and today do) aggregate and sell individual health information without consulting, or paying, the individual. But if consumers owned their data, anyone who tried to use or sell it without permission would be stealing (or at least converting) that data. Ownership of IHI would potentially invest individuals with powerful and legally enforceable mechanisms to prevent intrusion, appropriation, and exploitation of information that they do not wish to share—authority that seems particularly desirable in today's world of untrammeled data exploitation.

Recognizing a property right in IHI, of course, would represent a significant departure from current U.S. law, which has held for more than a century that data—objective information and facts—cannot be owned as property. As Justice Louis Brandeis wrote, facts are "free as the air to common use." This longstanding rule has been applied consistently to information ranging from the news of the day, stock recommendations, and sports scores to the sequence of naturally occurring human DNA. The federal court in *Greenberg v. Miami Children's Hospital Research Institute, Inc.* expressly rejected property-based claims under which the plaintiffs sought a share of the profits made using discoveries based on their children's genetic data. Thus, under current law, facts—raw information about the world—once generally known, cannot be owned.

Numerous scholars have argued against the creation of a new form of personal property covering individual data. Their objections range from moral and dignitary concerns over commodification of the individual, to utilitarian concerns about barriers that individual ownership of health information could impose on biomedical research and its potential impact on patient safety and public health, to a sense that the propertization of IHI is unnecessary in view of existing common law and regulatory protections of individual privacy and safety.

But, as noted above, the current movement toward ownership of IHI is driven, to an increasing degree, by concerns over privacy, autonomy, and distributive justice. These core ethical considerations are difficult to balance against a "communitarian" instrumental analysis. Thus, even if granting individuals ownership over IHI is likely to impede scientific research and public health monitoring, this cost may be acceptable to those who value personal privacy and autonomy above aggregate net benefits to society.

Notes and Questions

1. *No protection for data.* Why doesn't US law recognize copyright in data? Should the United States move toward a database protection regime similar to that in the EU?

2. *Health data.* What do advocates for recognizing property interests in personal health data hope to gain? Do you think, as the author suggests, that "granting individuals ownership over IHI is likely to impede scientific research and public health monitoring"? Is this cost worth the benefit of such ownership?

18.1.2 *Licensing Data*

If a data licensing agreement will cover the EU, then the licensor may rely on the *sui generis* protection afforded by the EU Database Directive as a licensable intellectual property (IP) right. To do so, the definition of IP in the agreement should include "data and database rights" or language to the same effect. This small modification allows data to be licensed on terms similar to those used for patents and copyrights.

In the United States, database licensors have largely compensated for this lack of *per se* legal protection by relying on a combination of trade secret law, restrictive contractual terms and technological access and control mechanisms. These are discussed in greater detail below.

18.1.2.1 Trade Secrets

Trade secret protection for databases is a tricky subject. At one extreme, a database may contain information that is entirely proprietary to the database creator, such as a company's internal sales and production figures, or the results of an internal safety testing program. In these instances, assuming that the information in the database otherwise meets the statutory requirements for trade secret protection, the data within the database can be considered to be protected by trade secret law. At the other extreme, a database may contain public information that is readily accessible to others, such as stock prices or sports scores. In these cases, trade secret protection is probably not available for the data (though, as we will see below, such databases can be protected quite effectively through contractual terms of use).

In the middle lies a gray area. A database may contain information that is technically public, but the collection and combination of which is not straightforward. As explained by the Ninth Circuit in the context of the Economic Espionage Act, 18 U.S.C. § 1839(3),

> A trade secret may consist of a compilation of data, public sources or a combination of proprietary and public sources. It is well recognized that it is the secrecy of the claimed trade secret as a whole that is determinative. The fact that some or all of the components of the trade secret are well-known does not preclude protection for a secret combination, compilation, or integration of the individual elements. The theoretical possibility of reconstructing the secret from published materials containing scattered references to portions of the information or of extracting it from public materials unlikely to come to the attention of the appropriator will not preclude relief against the wrongful conduct. Expressed differently, a compilation that affords a competitive advantage and is not readily ascertainable falls within the definition of a trade secret.[6]

Thus, many data and database licensing agreements refer to trade secrets as the IP being licensed, though doing so may involve some risk that portions of the license grant may be invalidated if the data is no longer viewed as having trade secret status.[7]

18.1.2.2 Data Licensing as a Contractual Matter

When there is no trade secret or other underlying IP right to support a license of data under US law (e.g., a database of stock prices or sports scores), licensing agreements often elide the

---

[6]   *United States v. Nosal*, 844 F.3d 1024, 1042 (9th Cir. 2016).
[7]   See the famous "Listerine" case, *Warner-Lambert Pharm. Co. v. John J. Reynolds, Inc.*, discussed in Section 12.2 (holding that the loss of trade secret status did not override the parties' intent that royalties be paid in perpetuity).

question of what rights, specifically, are being "licensed." Rather, they often state that the data in question is being licensed without reference to a particular set of IP rights.

EXAMPLE: DATABASE LICENSE

a. Licensor hereby grants Licensee a worldwide, nonexclusive license during the term of this Agreement to incorporate the Database into the Licensee Product in the manner described in Appendix A, and to license the Licensee Product to users (directly or indirectly through one or more sublicensees) for the users' internal purposes only and for a period as long as the Agreement is in effect.

b. The Parties agree and acknowledge that any use of the Database not expressly authorized by the foregoing clause (a) is strictly prohibited. Without limiting the generality of the foregoing, Licensee and the users are expressly prohibited from (i) sublicensing or reselling the Database or any data elements included therein on a standalone basis separate from the Licensee Products; (ii) using or allowing third parties to use the Database for the purpose of compiling, enhancing, verifying, supplementing, adding to or deleting from any mailing list, geographic or trade directories, business directories, classified directories, classified advertising, or other compilation of information which is sold, rented, published, furnished or in any manner provided to a third party; (iii) using the Database in any service or product not specifically authorized in this Agreement or offering it through any third party other than the sublicensees; or (iv) disassembling, decompiling, reverse engineering, modifying or otherwise altering the Database, other than as required to provide the products and services permitted under this Agreement, or any part thereof without Licensor's prior written consent, which consent may be withheld in Licensor's sole discretion.

The absence of an underlying IP right results in several challenges for the data licensor. First, it means that if the licensee violates the licensing agreement, the licensor cannot bring an infringement suit. Rather, it is left with only its contractual remedies. Second, because the licensor lacks contractual privity with third parties who obtain and use the data that the licensee impermissibly disclosed or disseminated, it cannot bring contractual claims against them. And without an IP claim, the licensor has little recourse against such third parties.

The lack of an underlying IP right also makes it particularly important for the licensor to construct a contractual framework that emulates the existence of an IP right, as shown in clause (b) of the above example. This text makes it clear that the "license" granted in clause (a) is the only use that the licensee is permitted to make of the licensed data, even if there is no underlying IP right that would prevent other uses. It is also beneficial, in these cases, to specify the types of uses that are *not* permitted, as shown above.

It has been said that "data is the new oil," and data has, for decades, fueled the oil and gas industry itself. Vast quantities of geophysical data are generated in the search for new fossil fuel reservoirs, and the petroleum exploration and production (E&P) industry was one of the pioneers of the use of "big data" in its operations. The following case involves a license of E&P data that went awry.

M.D. Mark, Inc. v. Kerr-McGee Corp.

565 F.3d 753 (10th Cir. 2009)

BRISCOE, CIRCUIT JUDGE

Plaintiff M.D. Mark, Inc. (Mark) filed this action alleging that defendants Kerr-McGee Corporation (Kerr-McGee) and Oryx Energy Company breached the terms of seismic data license agreements and also misappropriated seismic data owned by Mark. Mark prevailed on its claims at trial and was awarded $25,266,381 in compensatory damages. Kerr-McGee now appeals, attacking each aspect of the jury's liability findings, as well as the amount of the damage award. [W]e affirm the district court's judgment in all respects.

I

PGI, Mark and the Seismic Data

In the 1970's and 1980's, a Texas-based company called Professional Geophysics, Inc. (PGI) developed, at substantial expense, a collection of geophysical information called seismic data. PGI in turn licensed that data, for a fee, to members of the oil and gas industry for exploration purposes. In 1991, PGI declared bankruptcy and Mark, a Texas-based company, purchased PGI's database for $1.4 million, or approximately $53 per mile for approximately 26,000 miles of data. Mark then began, and continues to this day, to license that data.

Sun/Oryx

In the early 1980's, the Sun Exploration & Production Company (Sun), a Delaware corporation headquartered in Houston, Texas, entered into a series of license agreements with PGI covering approximately 16,000 miles of seismic data. In December 1985, Sun created a subsidiary called Sun Operating Limited Partnership (SOLP) and transferred to it a group of assets, including the seismic data licensed from PGI. In doing so, however, Sun apparently did not transfer to SOLP any of the underlying license agreements. In May 1989, Sun changed its name to Oryx Energy Company (Oryx).

Kerr-McGee

Between 1984 and 1994, Kerr-McGee, an Oklahoma-based corporation, entered into a series of license agreements in its own name with PGI and Mark covering approximately 775 miles of seismic data. Kerr-McGee itself, however, did not engage in any oil or gas exploration. Instead, all such exploration was conducted by its subsidiaries, including Kerr-McGee Oil and Gas Corporation (KMOG).

Merger Between Kerr-McGee and Oryx and Subsequent Changes

On October 14, 1998, Kerr-McGee and Oryx entered into a written agreement pursuant to which Oryx would merge into Kerr-McGee. That merger was approved by the companies' shareholders on February 26, 1999.

Communications Between Oryx/Kerr-McGee and Mark re Merger

On October 16, 1998, Mark, aware of the pending merger between Kerr-McGee and Oryx, sent a letter to Oryx reminding it that Oryx had licensed "certain PGI … seismic data" and that "[t]hose licenses [we]re not transferable, as stated in the agreements." The letter went on to state:

> However, M.D. Mark will allow the data to be transferred and licensed to Kerr-McGee upon the payment of a transfer fee and the execution of a current M.D. Mark license agreement. This offer to transfer the data is valid for thirty (30) days from the date of this letter. If, however, Kerr-McGee does not wish to transfer the data, then M.D. Mark is requesting the immediate return of its data within thirty (30) days.

Oryx apparently responded to the letter by telephoning Mark and asking additional questions about the proposed transfer fee.

On November 11, 1998, Marilyn Davies, the president of Mark, sent another letter to Oryx stating, in pertinent part:

> As we discussed, M.D. Mark would authorize Kerr McGee to have access to this seismic data for about $200 per mile if all of the data was retained. The fee would go higher if Kerr McGee chose to retain only certain data sets instead of the entire volume …
>
> Since the actual consummation of the [merger] deal won't take place until 1st Quarter 1999, M.D. Mark will extend its offer to transfer the data until thirty (30) days after the merger/consolidation/control change date.

No further response was received from Oryx until February 11, 1999, when Patricia Horsfall, Oryx's manager of exploration, sent a letter … to Mark stating, in pertinent part:

> Contingent upon approval of the merger by the companies' shareholders, your records will need to be changed to reflect the name change of the Licensee, under the referenced Seismic Data License Agreement(s), from Oryx Energy Company to Kerr-McGee Oil & Gas Corporation, a subsidiary of Kerr-McGee, located in Houston.

On February 17, 1999, Davies sent a letter to Horsfall stating that "the PGI seismic [data] is not transferable, assignable, etc. and cannot be made available to Kerr-McGee without prior written approval from M.D. Mark and the payment of an authorization or transfer fee." Davies' letter further stated that, in the absence of such authorization or transfer fee, "the licenses of all PGI seismic data in Oryx's possession w[ould] be automatically terminated" upon the closing of the merger, and all "data must be returned."

On March 26, 1999, Salazar, Kerr-McGee's in-house counsel, sent a letter to Mark stating:

> Please be advised that Kerr-McGee Corporation will not pay a transfer fee for any data subject to a license from PGI to Oryx Energy Company or any of its predecessors. We are in the process of packaging all data identified on our records as being subject to any such license and will be shipping it to you as soon as packaging is complete.

On March 31, 1999, Davies acknowledged Salazar's March 26, 1999 letter and requested that all data be "returned to [Mark's] storage facilities" in Houston, Texas. Davies' letter outlined all of the types of material that needed to be returned to Mark, and stated, in conclusion, "that any and all licenses to PGI seismic data re [*sic*] now terminated."

On August 16, 2000, Davies sent a letter to Salazar stating that "[t]he option of returning the data ha[d] been withdrawn," and enclosed an invoice in the amount of $3,000,000 "reflecting the charges based on the discount given to a volume license purchase." On

August 29, 2000, Salazar sent a letter to Davies stating that it "remain[ed] [Kerr-McGee's] intention to retain the data ... and to not pay a transfer fee."

This Lawsuit

On February 16, 2001, Mark filed suit against Kerr-McGee and Oryx in Colorado state court asserting claims for misappropriation of trade secrets, breach of contract, tortious interference with contract, and unjust enrichment. On March 7, 2001, Kerr-McGee removed the action to federal district court in Colorado, premised on diversity jurisdiction.

During discovery, it was determined that Kerr-McGee was in possession of 3,175 miles of Mark's seismic data that was not covered by any of the existing license agreements between PGI or Mark and Kerr-McGee, Sun, or Oryx. This discovery gave rise to an additional claim of misappropriation by Mark against Kerr-McGee.

The case proceeded to trial on September 17, 2007. During trial, the parties and the district court focused on three categories of seismic data underlying Mark's claims 2:

Category 1 Data – this category encompassed approximately 15,745 miles of seismic data licensed by Sun/Oryx from PGI/Mark prior to Oryx's merger into Kerr-McGee;
Category 2 Data – this category encompassed the 775 miles of seismic data licensed directly by Kerr-McGee from PGI/Mark prior to the merger; and
Category 3 Data – this category encompassed approximately 3,175 miles of seismic data found during discovery to be in Kerr-McGee's possession but not covered by any preexisting license agreements (this is sometimes referred to as the "bootleg data").

At the conclusion of all the evidence, the jury found that:

Oryx breached one or more of the license agreements it entered into with PGI/Mark, covering Category 1 data, by "transferr[ing] the license agreement[s] to Kerr McGee Corp, without prior approval," and that Mark suffered $15,745,000 in damages as a result of the breach;

Kerr-McGee breached one or more of its own pre-merger license agreements with PGI/Mark, covering Category 2 data, by "transfer[ring] license[s] to Kerr McGee Oil & Gas [Corporation]" without "prior consent," by failing to return all data to Mark, and by failing to safeguard Mark's trade secrets, and that Mark suffered $968,750 in damages as result of this conduct; and

Kerr-McGee "gained access to and possessed PGI data [i.e., Category 3 data] through improper means" beginning in at least 1996, Kerr-McGee also, after the merger with Oryx, wrongfully transferred control of the Category 1 data to a Kerr-McGee subsidiary, id., and that Mark suffered $25,266,381 in damages as a result of Kerr-McGee's misconduct regarding the Category 1 and Category 3 data.

On September 28, 2007, the district court entered judgment in favor of Mark and against Kerr-McGee in the amount of $25,266,381.

[The parties appealed].

II

1. Challenges to the Jury's Liability Findings Regarding Category 1 Data

Kerr-McGee ... attacks the jury's findings that Oryx and Kerr-McGee misappropriated Category 1 seismic data. More specifically, Kerr-McGee contends that there was no evidence of any "wrongful transfer" of the Category 1 data from Oryx or Kerr-McGee to a Kerr-McGee subsidiary, as was necessary to a finding of misappropriation under the district court's instructions.

It is true that Kerr-McGee presented evidence in its defense suggesting that the Category 1 data was not transferred to KMOG, and instead "was left in the former Oryx subsidiary SOLP ... " However ... the evidence presented at trial ... suggested that the employees of Kerr-McGee and its subsidiaries generally paid little heed to corporate formalities, instead viewed Kerr-McGee and its subsidiaries as a "family," and readily shared seismic data without regard to any limitations imposed by the underlying license agreements. In light of this evidence, we cannot say that the jury's misappropriation findings were "clearly, decidedly, or overwhelmingly against the weight of the evidence."

2. Challenges to the Jury's Liability Findings Regarding Category 2 Data

The jury found, with regard to the Category 2 data, that Kerr-McGee breached one or more of its own pre-merger license agreements with PGI/Mark by "transfer[ring] license[s] [covering Category 2 data] to Kerr McGee Oil & Gas," i.e., KMOG, without "prior consent," by failing to return all data to Mark, and by failing to safeguard Mark's trade secrets.

As previously noted, Mark presented, during its case-in-chief, the testimony of Kerr-McGee's in-house attorney Carlos Salazar. Salazar testified, in pertinent part, that Kerr-McGee itself did not engage in any oil and gas exploration. Instead, Salazar testified, such exploration was handled by Kerr-McGee's subsidiaries. Further, Salazar testified that he and other Kerr-McGee employees "considered [Kerr-McGee] to be a family of companies," and "didn't ... see anything wrong with affiliates and subsidiaries exchanging [seismic data] information." ... Marilyn Young, a Kerr-McGee-employed attorney who oversaw Kerr-McGee's family of subsidiaries, testified ... that "Kerr-McGee wanted all [of] its oil and gas exploration and development and production to go through" KMOG, and that, in 2002, the subsidiaries were reorganized in a fashion such that KMOG oversaw Onshore LP.

In addition to this testimony, the jury was presented with a copy of the 1994 Agreement between Kerr-McGee and Mark. That agreement required Kerr-McGee, absent "written permission" from Mark, to "maintain the Data on its premises at all times" and prohibited Kerr-McGee from "provid[ing] copies [of the data] to third parties for removal from [Kerr-McGee]'s premises for any purpose." Notably, the agreement provided that these requirements "appl[ied] even in the event of a corporate reorganization ... or a merger," and that "no disclosure" could "be made to any parties involved in such actions, even if such parties [we]re the surviving entities after such corporate reorganization ... or merger." Lastly, the agreement provided that in the event of a breach by Kerr-McGee, Mark could terminate the agreement and require the return of "all physical evidence of the Data including any reprocessing of the Data."

In light of this evidence, we are unable to conclude that the jury's findings regarding the Category 2 data were "clearly, decidedly, or overwhelmingly against the weight of the evidence." Thus, in turn, we conclude that the district court did not abuse its discretion in denying Kerr-McGee's motion for new trial as to the Category 2 data issues.

3. Challenges to the Jury's Liability Findings Regarding Category 3 Data

The jury found that Kerr-McGee gained access to and possessed through improper means the Category 3 data.

Turning now to the evidence presented at trial, it is true, as asserted by Kerr-McGee, that Mark did not produce any direct evidence that Kerr-McGee acquired the Category 3 data by means of theft, bribery, misrepresentation, or breach or inducement of a breach of a duty to maintain secrecy or not to disclose a trade secret. Importantly, however, Mark's evidence established that:

> Mark regularly maintained records of the data sets it licensed to third parties, and those records showed no license or delivery of the Category 3 data to Kerr-McGee, Oryx/Sun or any Kerr-McGee subsidiary;
>
> [A]lthough Kerr-McGee was in possession of the Category 3 data, it could not produce a single employee, former or present, who could explain how Kerr-McGee obtained the data, when the data was obtained, or how or when it may have been utilized by Kerr-McGee or any of its subsidiaries;
>
> Kerr-McGee could produce no license agreements or other records validating its possession of the Category 3 data; and
>
> [T]he Category 3 data films possessed by Kerr-McGee were of arguably poor quality, thereby allowing the jury to reasonably infer they were not originals provided directly by Mark to Kerr-McGee.

In our view, this circumstantial evidence was more than sufficient to have allowed the jury to reasonably infer that Kerr-McGee utilized one of the improper means listed in the district court's instructions to obtain access to the Category 3 data. Thus, we conclude the district court did not abuse its discretion in denying Kerr-McGee's Rule 59 motion for new trial with respect to the jury's findings regarding the Category 3 data.

The judgment of the district court is AFFIRMED.

Notes and Questions

1. *Intercompany sharing.* M.D. *Mark* relates in large part to a licensee's sharing of licensed data among a group of affiliated companies. Both the jury and the court found that such sharing violated the terms of the relevant data licensing agreements. Why do you think that such data sharing among affiliated companies was prohibited? What harm did M.D. Mark suffer from Kerr-McGee's internal sharing of the data? Do you think that M.D. Mark was reasonable in its request for a transfer fee for the licensed data?

2. *Good lawyering.* What would you have done to avoid, or reduce, liability if you had represented Kerr-McGee before and during the events described in this case, at least with respect to the Category 1 and 2 data?

3. *Bootleg data.* How do you think Kerr-McGee came into possession of the Category 3 data? Do you think the jury's inferences were fair, given the lack of direct evidence of misappropriation?

4. *Return of data.* What does it mean to "return" data that can be copied an infinite number of times?

18.1.3 *Noncircumvention and Noncompetition in Data Licensing*

In some cases, parties licensing data may seek additional contractual protections to prevent the misuse of their licensed data. The following case describes one such contractual mechanism.

Eden Hannon & Co. v. Sumitomo Trust & Banking Co.

914 F.2d 556 (4th Cir. 1990)

RUSSELL, CIRCUIT JUDGE

Eden Hannon & Co. ("EHC") is an investment company located in Alexandria, Virginia, and Sumitomo Trust & Banking Co. is a New York subsidiary of a Japanese bank. This appeal involves the competition between EHC and Sumitomo to purchase an investment portfolio from Xerox Corporation. In the past, EHC has produced extensive economic models for the purpose of valuing Xerox lease portfolios, bidding on these portfolios, and selling the income rights to the portfolios to institutional investors. In the late summer of 1988, Sumitomo indicated interest in purchasing a portfolio through EHC. To that end, Sumitomo signed a "Nondisclosure and Noncircumvention" agreement with EHC, in order to protect the confidential information that EHC later shared with Sumitomo. In violation of that agreement, and after taking possession of EHC's confidential analyses, Sumitomo bid on the December 1988 Xerox portfolio, won the bid, and made a direct purchase of the portfolio. EHC had bid also on that portfolio, and its bid was ranked third by Xerox officials.

EHC subsequently filed this suit, stating four counts: misappropriation of trade secrets, breach of contract, breach of fiduciary duty, and breach of the duty of good faith and fair dealing. Sumitomo denied these allegations. [The district court] found that Sumitomo's actions constituted a breach of contract, and found that a misappropriation of trade secrets had not been proven. As a remedy, the district judge enjoined Sumitomo from repeating its violation of the Nondisclosure and Noncircumvention Agreement. Both parties have appealed the rulings adverse to their positions, and we affirm in part, reverse in part, and remand.

I

The "portfolio" that Xerox sells is composed of the right to receive the stream of income from a group of copiers leased by Xerox, and to receive the residual value of the copiers when the leases expire or are terminated. This is known as the Xerox Partnership Asset Strategy ("PAS") Program. Four times a year, Xerox invites a limited number of investors to bid for a portfolio, which typically contains several hundred copiers leased by Xerox to various customers for terms usually ranging from one to three years. EHC has been a regular bidder and frequent winner in the past, winning ten quarterly bids in the first three-and-a-half years of the program. The bids submitted to Xerox are not just dollar figures; instead, a bid consists of several components, and each component addresses how an element of the projected revenue stream would be divided between Xerox and the successful bidder.

EHC does not bid with its own money in these sales. Instead, it arranges in advance for a bank or insurance company to provide the monetary investment, and in return that investor receives all of the revenue generated by the leases.

Given that EHC's value is in its knowledge, it must guard that knowledge jealously. On the other hand, it must also disclose a great amount of its confidential analysis regarding a proposed bid on a portfolio in order to convince an institution to bid from $25 million to more than $60 million on a single portfolio. To that end, EHC requires any interested investor to sign a "Nondisclosure and Noncircumvention Agreement" (an "Agreement") before it can receive any of EHC's confidential information. This Agreement requires that the investor not disclose the information it receives from EHC to other parties. Most importantly, it also requires that the potential investor "not independently pursue lease transactions" with Xerox's PAS Program "for a period equal to the term of the Purchase Agreement." Since the copiers are usually leased for one to three years, we presume that this term would prevent an investor from independently pursuing a portfolio for approximately three years.

Sumitomo was a potential investor interested in the PAS portfolio. Immediately after EHC won the June 1988 portfolio bid, a Sumitomo officer, Ragheed Shanti, based in the United States, telephoned EHC to express interest. In order to evaluate the PAS program, Shanti attempted to obtain EHC's economic data on their winning June bid. EHC insisted that it could not disclose that information without an Agreement signed by a Sumitomo representative. Shanti tried to avoid signing an Agreement, and then attempted to water down the provision that would require Sumitomo not to "independently pursue" portfolio purchases ... EHC refused this substitution, and Shanti eventually signed the original Agreement on the part of Sumitomo. During these negotiations over the language of the Agreement, Sumitomo admitted to EHC that it was also considering financing a portfolio bid by a competitor of EHC, DPF Leasing Services, Inc. ("DPF"). EHC indicated that the Agreement would not prevent Sumitomo from financing a competitor's bid. However, EHC did not want to create a new competitor that would use EHC's information to bid directly against it. Thus, the understanding between EHC and Sumitomo was that Sumitomo could finance a competitor's bid, but it could not directly bid (i.e., "independently pursue") on a portfolio during the "term of the Purchase Agreement."

Once the Agreement was signed, EHC disclosed a great amount of confidential bidding information to Sumitomo. However, Sumitomo and EHC could not reach a deal on a bid for the next portfolio to be offered in December, 1988.

This did not prevent Sumitomo from participating in the bidding for the December portfolio, however. In fact, Sumitomo bid directly on the portfolio, in clear violation of the Agreement with EHC. In submitting its bid, Sumitomo worked through Gerry Sherman, who was a former employee of DPF, a competitor of EHC. Sherman had formed his own one-man company, Oasis, which would work on bids for Xerox PAS portfolios. Sherman had experience from his days at DPF in the economic modelling and bidding process for such portfolios. Sumitomo argues that Oasis won the December bid by carrying out the same functions as EHC would have carried out.

This is not true. To us, and to the district court, it is clear that Oasis was merely a stalking horse for Sumitomo, and that Sumitomo was the direct bidder for the December portfolio. Unfortunately, it is unclear whether Sherman also provided the financial advice to Sumitomo that enabled it to make its bid. Sherman did work on the Xerox PAS Program when he was employed by EHC's competitor, DPF. Sumitomo has claimed that it gained all of its knowledge on how to value and bid for a Xerox portfolio from Sherman. While Sumitomo admits that it had possession of the confidential materials it got from EHC, it claims that it did not use these materials at all. It states that after negotiations fell through with EHC on August 25, 1988, Shanti put these materials in a box and never looked at them again. In a close call, the district judge found that Sumitomo had not misappropriated EHC's trade secrets, and thus, the district judge must have found Sumitomo's story more credible on this point.

FIGURE 18.1 In the 1980s, Xerox sold investment portfolios comprising revenue streams from hundreds of leased photocopier machines.

Since our disposition of this case does not depend on knowing whether Sumitomo actually used this information, we will not dwell on the point. However, we have our doubts about the correctness of this finding.

II

The Supreme Court of Virginia has decided several cases involving agreements not to compete in the employment law arena, and those cases are substantially similar to the case at bar. In many employment contracts, there is language stating that upon termination of the employment relationship, the employee is restricted from competing with the employer within a certain amount of time and within a certain geographical area (for the purposes of this opinion, these are called "employment agreements"). The Virginia courts have held repeatedly that employment agreements are enforceable if they pass a three-part reasonableness test:

(1) Is the restraint, from the standpoint of the employer, reasonable in the sense that it is no greater than is necessary to protect the employer in some legitimate business interest?

(2) From the standpoint of the employee, is the restraint reasonable in the sense that it is not unduly harsh and oppressive in curtailing his legitimate efforts to earn a livelihood?

(3) Is the restraint reasonable from the standpoint of sound public policy?

Paramount Termite Control Co. v. Rector, 380 S.E.2d 922, 924 (Va. 1989). The agreements that pass this test may be enforced in equity.

The Noncircumvention and Nondisclosure Agreement … is nearly identical in purpose to an employment agreement. Most importantly, an employment agreement enables an employer to expose his employees to the firm's trade secrets. Similarly, a noncircumvention agreement enables potential joint venturers to share confidential information regarding a possible deal. In both instances, the idea is to share trade secrets so that business can be conducted without losing control over the secrets. Often, the value of a firm is its special knowledge, and this knowledge may not be an idea protectible by patent or copyright. If that firm cannot protect that knowledge from immediate dissemination to competitors, it may not be able to reap the benefits from the time and money invested in building that knowledge. If firms are not permitted to construct a reasonable legal mechanism to protect that knowledge, then the incentive to engage in the building of such knowledge will be greatly reduced. Free riders will capture this information at little or no cost and produce a product cheaper than the firm which created the knowledge, because it will not have to carry the costs of creating that knowledge in its pricing. Faced with this free rider problem, this information may not be created, and thus everybody loses. To counteract that problem, an employer can demand that employees sign an employment agreement as a condition of their contract, and thus protect the confidential information. This means that if an employer takes in an employee and exposes that employee to trade secrets, the employer does not have to allow the employee to go across the street and set up shop once that employee has mastered the information. Although it was not explained in this detail, Virginia has recognized this interest in protecting confidential information.

These employment agreements (or in the present case, a noncircumvention agreement) are often necessary because it can be very difficult to prove the theft of a trade secret by a former employee. Often, the purpose of an employment agreement can be to prevent the dissemination of trade secrets, yet a mere ban on using trade secrets after the termination of employment would be difficult to enforce. Judge Lord explained the problem well in *Greenberg v. Croydon Plastics Co.*, 378 F.Supp. 806, 814 (E.D.Pa.1974):

> Plaintiffs in trade secret cases, who must prove by a fair preponderance of the evidence disclosure to third parties and use of the trade secret by the third parties, are confronted with an extraordinarily difficult task. Misappropriation and misuse can rarely be proved by convincing direct evidence. In most cases plaintiffs must construct a web of perhaps ambiguous circumstantial evidence from which the trier of fact may draw inferences which convince him that it is more probable than not that what the plaintiffs allege happened did in fact take place. Against this often delicate construct of circumstantial evidence there frequently must be balanced defendants' witnesses who directly deny everything.

Actually, Judge Lord's description of the problem covers just the tip of the iceberg. There are several problems with trying to prevent former employees from illegally using the former employer's trade secrets, and these problems are caused by the status of the law regarding the misappropriation of trade secrets. First, as Judge Lord depicted so well, it is difficult to prove that the trade secret was actually used. Second, the former employee tends to get "one free bite" at the trade secret. Most courts will refuse to enjoin the disclosure or use of a trade secret until its illegal use is imminent or until it has already occurred. By that time, much of the damage may be done. Third, even if a clearly illegal use of the trade secret by a former employee can be shown, most courts will not enjoin that person from working for the competition on that basis. Instead, they will merely enjoin future disclosure of the trade secret. Yet, policing the former employee's compliance with that injunction will be difficult. Finally, even if the employee does not maliciously attempt to use his former employer's trade secrets in the new employer's workplace, avoiding this use can be difficult. It would be difficult for the employee to guard the trade secret of the former employer and be effective for the new employer.

In order to avoid these problems, many employers ask their employees to sign noncompetition agreements. These agreements prevent an employee from working with the competition within a limited geographical range of the former employer and for a limited time. As seen above, Virginia courts will only enforce these agreements if they are reasonable. Yet, when they are valid, they make the guarding of a trade secret easier since they remove the opportunity for the former employee to pass on the trade secret to the competition, either malevolently or benevolently. This does not supplant the need for law protecting trade secrets. Non-competition agreements cannot prevent disclosure anywhere in the world and until the end of time, for they would be held unreasonable. Instead, a non-competition agreement will merely prevent the illegal use of a trade secret next door in the near future, where the use might do the most damage.

EHC's position regarding potential investors was the same as an employer–employee relationship in regard to the use of trade secrets. The thing that made EHC valuable was its expertise in valuing lease portfolios. EHC would "sell" its knowledge of the value of a particular PAS portfolio to investors for a percentage of the profit. It was necessary for EHC to share its confidential economic models and projections on the particular bid in order to attract investors. Yet, if it gave this information to an investor without restriction, that investor would merely make the bid directly and cut EHC out of the deal, after EHC's investment in expertise and research made the bid possible.

EHC could have merely prohibited its potential customers from using its information if that customer became a rival bidder. Indeed, this was the essence of Shanti's counterproposal regarding the language of the agreement, which was rejected by EHC. Such an arrangement would have become an unenforceable honor system. In the present case, Sumitomo has denied that it used the materials it received from EHC, and claimed that it gained its expertise primarily from Gerry Sherman. The trial judge ultimately ruled that there had not been a misappropriation of trade secrets, but his ruling was based on Sumitomo's denials and the citing of Sherman's experience in the area. The trial court did not definitively discover whether Sumitomo actually used these materials, and there was no way that it could have found out. For that reason, EHC chose to include in its agreement with potential investors the noncircumvention clause. Armed with that agreement, EHC could protect its information by merely showing that an investor was competing contrary to the agreement, without having to prove that it was actually using EHC's confidential information.

One reason why [EHC] had a noncircumvention clause was to prevent its disclosures from creating new competitors. The competition for the PAS portfolios was already keen. Xerox invited a limited number of businesses to bid for the portfolios, and there were many other businesses who wanted a chance to bid that were seeking invitations. EHC had a legitimate fear that it would let a new bidder through the door if it educated that investor and gave it contacts to Xerox. Thus a reasonable noncircumvention clause was constructed to place a reasonable limit on competition from a temporary ally.

Thus, EHC's noncircumvention agreement is merely a twist on employment noncompetition agreements that have been recognized by the Virginia courts. That being so, we will briefly discuss the application of Virginia's three-factor test for reasonableness to the case at bar. We have reworked the terms of the test so that it will address noncircumvention agreements.

1. *Is the restraint on circumvention no broader than is necessary, from the standpoint of the trade secret holder, to protect the holder from the disclosure of its confidential information?* Yes. The limitation provided by the noncircumvention clause did not prevent Sumitomo from doing many things. Sumitomo could still invest in a bid won by a

competitor of EHC; it could use this information internally in order to put together its own bid for lease portfolios offered by companies other than Xerox; and Sumitomo could bid directly for PAS portfolios in approximately three or four years after the Agreement was signed. This was a narrowly drawn limitation.

2. *From the standpoint of the party that received the confidential information, is the restraint reasonable in the sense that it is not unduly harsh and oppressive in curtailing the legitimate efforts of that party to conduct its business?* Yes. Most importantly, Sumitomo could still invest immediately in any winning bids, including EHC's competitors. Also, Sumitomo could bid directly on any other lease program other than Xerox's, and it could directly invest in Xerox's PAS Program after several years. Furthermore, presumably Sumitomo can make (and has made) money in its other banking activities.

3. *Is the restraint reasonable from the standpoint of sound public policy?* Yes. This factor overlaps the area covered by the first two factors to a great extent. Presumably, public policy seeks to protect the development of trade secrets without ruining competition or driving the receiver of confidential information out of business. As discussed above, this noncircumvention agreement satisfies those concerns. EHC's economic modeling process receives some protection, the bidding for Xerox PAS portfolios remains highly competitive, and Sumitomo will certainly remain a profitable bank.

Notes and Questions

1. *Noncircumvention.* How does noncircumvention differ from nondisclosure (as discussed in Section 5.2)? Why do you think that EHC included both types of restrictions in its agreement? How did Sumitomo allegedly breach the noncircumvention provision of its agreement with EHC? Did Sumitomo also violate the nondisclosure provisions?

2. *Nonuse.* Sumitomo claimed that it did not use the data obtained from EHC, and the district court agreed. Why did the Fourth Circuit find this fact to be irrelevant?

3. *Suspicious behavior.* The Fourth Circuit in *Eden Hannon* seems to make much of the admittedly suspicious behavior exhibited by Sumitomo's employee Ragheed Shanti and its consultant Gerry Sherman. Why does this behavior matter in establishing the breach of contract claims made by EHC?

4. *Employee noncompetition agreements.* The court in *Eden Hannon* bases its analysis of the parties' Noncircumvention and Nondisclosure Agreement on the law of employee noncompetition agreements. How are these two types of agreement similar? Do you think that agreements between sophisticated business parties should be judged by the same standards as agreements between an employer and its employees?

5. *Free riders.* What is the "free rider" problem identified by the court as a justification for restrictive noncompetition and other agreements?

6. *State-level variation?* Note that employee noncompetition agreements are seemingly permitted in Virginia. Yet in some states, such as California, such agreements are far more difficult to enforce. Would a California court have viewed the agreement between EHC and Sumitomo differently as well?

7. *Data versus other types of licenses.* Are noncircumvention/noncompetition agreements more important in data licenses than in other types of licensing agreements like patents or copyrights? Why?

18.1.4 *Data Privacy*

As noted in Section 18.1.1, there is a plethora of recent legislation relating to the protection and privacy of individual data.[8] The most prominent recent legislative enactment in this area has been the EU's General Data Protection Regulation (GDPR), which has caused companies around the world to scramble to adjust their data-handling practices and online privacy policies.[9] Data privacy legislation also exists at the US federal level in certain industries, namely healthcare (with the Privacy Rule under the Health Insurance Portability and Accountability Act of 1996 [HIPAA][10]) and consumer financial information (with the Gramm-Leach-Bliley Act[11]).

At the state level, all fifty states, the District of Columbia, Guam, Puerto Rico and the Virgin Islands have enacted legislation requiring private and governmental entities to notify individuals of breaches of security involving personally identifiable information.[12] In addition, states such as California have also enacted broadly applicable data privacy laws that apply to all entities holding personal data in the state or affecting the state's residents.[13]

Beyond these legislative and regulatory mechanisms, governmental oversight exists to protect individual data and privacy. Since the early days of internet commerce, the US Federal Trade Commission (FTC), which is authorized to police unfair and deceptive business practices, has monitored the collection and use of consumer data by online vendors.[14] In recent years, the FTC has investigated and brought actions for deceptive data claims and practices against prominent companies including Uber, Vizio, BLU and AshleyMadison.com.[15] The FTC has also been active in policing the data security practices of healthcare providers and personal genomics testing companies. In 2014 it filed charges against two companies, Genelink, Inc. and foru International, among other things, for failing to maintain adequate and reasonable data security for their customers' personal information.[16] These claims were settled with the companies agreeing to "establish and maintain comprehensive data security programs and submit to security audits by independent auditors every other year for 20 years."[17] Two years later, the FTC found medical testing company LabMD liable for data security practices "lacking even basic precautions to protect the sensitive consumer information maintained on its computer system."[18]

---

[8] Individual data refers to data identifying an individual human subject's identity, address, financial, health or other personal information. This being said, vast quantities of data, such as the Xerox lease information and seismological data discussed in the cases in Sections 18.1.2 and 18.1.3, would not be subject to data privacy regulation.

[9] For an overview, see Meg Leta Jones & Margot E. Kaminski, *An American's Guide to the GDPR*, 98 Denver L. Rev. 1 (2020).

[10] 45 C.F.R. Parts 160 & 164 (2003) (hereinafter HIPAA Privacy Rule) (pertaining to the use and handling of protected health information by healthcare providers and related entities).

[11] Requires that financial institutions include privacy notices and limit the sharing of nonpublic personal information (NPI) – "personally identifiable financial information (i) provided by a consumer to a financial institution, (ii) resulting from a transaction or service performed for the consumer, or (iii) otherwise obtained by the financial institution" (15 U.S.C. § 6809(4)).

[12] See Natl. Conf. of State Legislators, Security Breach Notification Laws, www.ncsl.org/research/telecommunications-and-information-technology/security-breach-notification-laws.aspx.

[13] California Consumer Privacy Act of 2018, AB 375 (codified at Cal. Civ. Code Div. 3, Part 4, Title 1.81.5 [commencing with Section 1798.100]).

[14] See Fed. Trade Comm'n, Privacy Online: Fair Information Practices in the Electronic Marketplace (2000); Fed. Trade Comm'n, Privacy & Data Security Update: 2016 at 1 (2017).

[15] See Fed. Trade Comm'n, Privacy and Security Enforcement – Press Releases, www.ftc.gov/news-events/media-resources/protecting-consumer-privacy/privacy-security-enforcement.

[16] Id.

[17] Id.

[18] *In re. LabMD, Inc.*, Docket No. 9357, Opinion of the Commission 1 (F.T.C. 2016).

This panoply of regulation – state, federal and international – coupled with monitoring and enforcement by governmental agencies has sweeping consequences for transactions involving data and databases. These include:

- the structuring of internal systems and processes to secure personal data;
- the creation and updating of compliant data privacy policies and notifications;
- the development of mechanisms to obtain and record individual consent to data practices and to take necessary measures to address information by nonconsenting individuals; and
- implementing response and remediation plans to address consumer complaints and data breaches.

But while these measures will undoubtedly require substantial resources, both financial and personnel, they need not lead to an excess of additional contractual verbiage in data licensing agreements. The following example illustrates language that may be used to supplement a data licensee's obligations with respect to data privacy and security regulations.

EXAMPLE: DATA SECURITY AND PRIVACY

a. Licensee shall, at its sole expense, comply with all applicable Laws regarding the storage and handling of personally identifiable information ("PII"), obtaining consent from individuals for the collection, storage and use of PII, and the notification of individuals and relevant governmental agencies in the event of a breach of security pertaining to PII, an unauthorized release, disclosure or exposure of PII or other unauthorized data or information disclosure [1].

b. Within 24 hours after discovering or being informed of any breach of Licensee's security measures pertaining to PII, any unauthorized access to or release of PII, or of any other event requiring notification under applicable Law (a "Data Breach"), Licensee shall notify Licensor of the Data Breach using the expedited Notification procedure specified in Section __ [2], and shall keep Licensor fully apprised of Licensee's investigation and response to such Data Breach. Licensee shall implement all additional security and privacy measures reasonably requested by Licensor in response to such Data Breach.

c. Licensee shall, at its sole expense [3], prepare and disseminate all notifications required by Law to all individuals affected by a Data Breach, as soon as possible, but in no event later than required by Law. Licensee shall consult with Licensor during the preparation of such notifications and shall incorporate Licensor's reasonable suggestions with regard thereto.

d. Licensee shall indemnify and defend Licensor against any losses arising out of claims related to any Data Breach in accordance with the provisions of Section __ [4].

DRAFTING NOTES

[1] *Compliance* – strictly speaking, it is not necessary to require specifically that the licensee comply with applicable data privacy and protection laws, as compliance is typically required under the general compliance with law clause found in most agreements (see

Section 13.5). However, if the licensing of PII forms an important component of an agreement, then it may be prudent to call out compliance with data privacy and security laws simply to raise awareness of this key issue.

[2] *Expedited notification* – some agreements provide special expedited email or telephonic notice instructions for events requiring immediate action (see Section 13.12).

[3] *Data subject notification* – many state statutes require that written notice of data breaches be provide to all affected individuals, which could number in the millions. As a result, this obligation can be costly, and it is important that responsibility for this cost be allocated between the licensor and licensee.

[4] *Indemnification* – assuming that an agreement contains a general indemnification provision (see Section 10.3), the data breach provision may simply reference the general indemnification provision of the agreement. Alternately, the general indemnification clause may be adjusted to specify that data breaches are subject to its requirements.

Notes and Questions

1. *Data privacy versus value*. Most data privacy regulation seeks to protect personally identifiable information obtained from individuals. How valuable is this information? What are the consequences of its unauthorized disclosure or use? Why is this type of data protected so much more stringently than valuable commercial data such as the seismological geophysical data in *Kerr-McGee* or the Xerox portfolio data in *Eden Hannon*?

2. *Data privacy vs. trade secrecy*. Does an individual have trade secret protection over his or her personally identifiable data? What about when a corporation collects that data and includes it in a customer or patient database? Why would trade secrecy status vary depending on who holds the data?

3. *Data privacy proliferation*. How can enterprises simultaneously manage compliance with data protection, security and breach regulations in all fifty states, the federal government, the EU and elsewhere? Is the protection afforded by this legislation worth the significant burden of compliance?

18.2 PROPRIETARY SOFTWARE LICENSING

The software industry today is almost too large to size accurately. Almost every electronic product – from medical devices to automobiles to kitchen appliances – contains software, and in many cases cannot operate without it. This section provides a brief background concerning the legal protection of computer software, as well as considerations for software licensing. The subject of "open source software" (OSS) licensing, an important phenomenon, is addressed in Section 19.2.

18.2.1 *Source Code and Object Code*

The classic legal model of computer software contemplates two basic forms of code: *source code* – programming language instructions written (usually) by a human author; and *object code* – the machine-readable executable version of a source code program.[19] Under this

---

[19] Today, there are many variants on the classic model, including pseudocode and interpreted programming languages such as HTML and JavaScript, which do not require compilation to execute.

classic model, a source code program is "compiled" by another program, called a compiler, to form the object code version of the program. Object code is what most people are familiar with when they download or install a computer program – it is the file often labeled with the suffix ".exe" or similar designation.

Anyone who has taken an introductory computer class will recognize some of the programming languages in the example below.

EXAMPLE: SOURCE CODE

C[20]

```
Int main(…)
{
…Printf("Hello World");
    …
}
```

HTML[21]

```
== History =={{Main|History of copyright}}[[File:European Output of
Books 500-1800.png|thumb|upright=2|European output of books before the
advent of copyright, 500s to 1700s. Blue shows printed books. [[Log-
lin plot]]; a straight line therefore shows an exponential increase.]]
```

Perl[22]

```
#!/usr/bin/perl -w
# 531-byte qrpff-fast, Keith Winstein and Marc Horowitz <sipb-iap-
dvd@mit.edu>
# MPEG 2 PS VOB file on stdin -> descrambled output on stdout
#   arguments: title  key  bytes  in  least  to  most-significant
order$_='while(read+STDIN,$_,2048){$a=29;$b=73;$c=142;$t=255;@
t=map{$_%16or$t^=$c^=(
$m=(11,10,116,100,11,122,20,100)[$_/16%8])&110;$t^=(72,@
z=(64,72,$a^=12*($_%16
-2?0:$m&17)),$b^=$_%64?12:0,@z)[$_%8]}(16..271);if((@a=unx"C*",$_)
[20]&48){$h
=5;$_=unxb24,join"",@b=map{xB8,unxb8,chr($_^$a[-$h+84])}@ARGV;s/   …
$/1$&/;$
```

<p>[20] This simple program, known as "Hello, World" was introduced in 1972 by Brian Kernignan, one of the developers of the C programming language.</p>

<p>[21] Hypertext markup language (HTML), now maintained by the Worldwide Web Consortium (see Chapter 20), is used to design web pages. This sample is from the Wikipedia page for the topic "Copyright." The source code for every web page is available through a browser option.</p>

<p>[22] "Perl" refers to a family of computer programming languages that emerged in 1987. This example "script," known as "Qrpff," allows the user to "break" the CSS encryption of a DVD. It was considered when it was written in 2001 by some to violate the Digital Millennium Copyright Act's prohibition on anti-circumvention measures.</p>

```
d=unxV,xb25,$_;$e=256|(ord$b[4])«9|ord$b[3];$d-$d»8^($f=$L&)$d»12
^$d»4^
$d^$d/8))«17,$e=$e»8^($t&($g=($q=$e»14&7^$e)^$q*8^$q«6))«9,$_
=$t[$_]^
(($h»=8)+=$f+(~$g&$t))for@a[128..$#a]}print+x"C*",@a}';s/x/
pack+/g;eval
```

These examples of source code are very different, just as different human languages differ in grammar, character sets and vocabulary. Yet each has the power to convert human instructions into commands that can be executed by a computer. As Professor Sonia Katyal has observed, "source code is much more than just lines of commands — it comprises the lifeblood of software, embodying both the potential of the creativity that produces the code and the functionality that the code achieves."[23]

Object code, on the other hand, is comprehensible only to the true computer savant. As one such savant has written, "All computer code is human readable. Some forms are simply more convenient to read than others."[24] Object code is also referred to as "binary" or "machine" code, as it is processed and executed directly by a computer.

EXAMPLE: OBJECT CODE[25]

```
10110100
11111111
01011100
10100101
```

18.2.2 *Legal Protection of Software*

Legal rules concerning software began to emerge in the 1970s when software first left government labs and corporate data processing centers and began to enter the mainstream marketplace. Among the most heated debates that occurred during that era concerned the most sensible mode of legal protection for software: patent, copyright, trade secret or something new? Eventually, copyright protection prevailed as the primary mode of protecting software in the United States.[26]

18.2.2.1 Copyright

Given the analogy between software created using written programming languages and other written works of authorship (books, articles, etc.), it was felt that computer software was best

---

[23] Sonia K. Katyal, *The Paradox of Source Code Secrecy*, 104 Cornell L. Rev. 1183, 1194 (2020).

[24] David S. Touretzky, *Source vs. Object Code: A False Dichotomy*, July 12, 2000, www.cs.cmu.edu/~dst/DeCSS/object-code.txt.

[25] This code is a binary representation of the Hello World program written in the C programming language.

[26] See National Commission on New Technological Uses of Copyrighted Works (CONTU), *Final Report on the National Commission on New Technological Uses of Copyrighted Works*, July 31, 1978 (reproduced in 3 Computer L.J. 53 [1981]).

considered a "literary work" for the purposes of copyright protection.[27] This is the case even though lines of computer code are purely functional in nature, and copyright generally excludes the functional elements of a work.[28] By extension, the executable object code version of a computer program, even though it is incomprehensible to most people, is deemed to constitute a different representation of that same copyrightable work and, thus, is also subject to copyright, though this position was heavily contested at the outset.[29]

Beginning in the 1980s, courts began to distinguish between protectable forms of software expression and unprotectable ideas regarding software architecture and structure.[30] In *Whelan Associates, Inc. v. Jaslow Dental Laboratory, Inc.*, 797 F.2d 1222 (3d Cir. 1986), the court held that a software program's "structure, sequence, and organization" were eligible for copyright protection. And in *Google v. Oracle*, the Supreme Court confirmed that certain functional elements of computer code – particularly so-called application programmer interfaces (APIs) – can be protected by copyright.[31] As suggested by the dispute in *Google v. Oracle*, the lines separating protectable and unprotectable software content remain blurred today.

Finally, the screen displays and other images produced by computer software are protected by copyright, even though these images are not necessarily "fixed" in a tangible medium (i.e., they are intangible projections or manifestations of the illumination of different electronic elements in a computer screen).[32] Moreover, these images often change in a manner enabled by the programmer, but controlled by the user. Nevertheless, the different configurations and motions of an avatar in a video game would generally be owned by the designer of the game. However, there is a limit to this logic, and the text typed by the user of a word processing program or the music composed with a music synthesis program are owned by the user.

One consequence of treating computer software as a copyrightable work is that its reproduction is an exclusive right of the copyright owner. Yet "reproduction" in the copyright sense has two distinct connotations in the context of software: first is making copies of the software for distribution to others, but a second connotation involves the inevitable reproduction of every computer program in the memory of a computer when the program is executed. The Ninth Circuit confirmed that this "transient" copy is, indeed, a copy for the purposes of the Copyright Act in *MAI Systems Corp. v. Peak Computer Inc.*, 991 F.2d 511 (9th Cir. 1993). In *MAI*, the court held that even though a licensee was authorized to reproduce MAI's software as part of its use, a third-party maintenance provider, Peak, was not so authorized. Thus, when Peak performed maintenance services on the licensee's computers, thereby creating a transient copy of MAI's software, Peak was found to infringe.[33]

---

[27] US Copyright Office, Compendium of U.S. Copyright Office Practices § 721 (2017).

[28] 1 Nimmer on Copyright § 2A.10.

[29] US Copyright Office, supra note 27, § 721.5. See Pamela Samuelson, *CONTU Revisited: The Case against Copyright Protection for Computer Programs in Machine-Readable Form*, 33 Duke L.J. 663 (1984); Arthur R. Miller, *Copyright Protection for Computer Programs, Databases, and Computer-Generated Works: Is Anything New Since CONTU?* 106 Harv. L. Rev. 97 (1993).

[30] 4 Nimmer on Copyright § 13.03[F]; Miller, supra note 29.

[31] *Google LLC v. Oracle Am., Inc.*, 141 S.Ct. 1183 (2021).

[32] Some of the earliest software copyright cases involved the layout of pull-down menus used in business spreadsheets and similar software. See *Lotus Dev. Corp. v. Borland Int'l, Inc.*, 516 U.S. 233 (1996).

[33] Though the *MAI* decision has been roundly criticized (see Aaron Perzanowski, *Fixing RAM Copies*, 104 Nw. U. L. Rev. 1067 [2010]), it appears to remain the law, and software licensees that wish to engage third-party maintenance providers are well-advised to ensure that their licensing agreements permit usage and reproduction of licensed software by contractors working on their behalf.

18.2.2.2 Patents

The eligibility of computer software and algorithms for patent protection has fluctuated over time. It has long been the case that abstract ideas, such as mathematical formulas, are not eligible patent subject matter. In *Gottschalk v. Benson*, 403 U.S. 63 (1972), the Supreme Court rejected a patent claiming "a method for converting binary-coded-decimal … numerals into pure binary numerals" using a general-purpose digital computer. The Court reasoned that the "claim is so abstract and sweeping as to cover both known and unknown uses of the … conversion [method]." As a result, the claims were considered to be abstract ideas that were ineligible for patent protection. Six years later, in *Parker v. Flook*, 437 U.S. 584 (1978), the Supreme Court held that a patent claiming several conventional applications of a novel mathematical formula was similarly drawn to ineligible subject matter.

It was not until 1981, in *Diamond v. Diehr*, 450 U.S. 175 (1981), that the Supreme Court upheld a patent claiming computer software. The claimed method employed the well-known Arrhenius equation to calculate and control the temperature in a process for curing rubber. The Court held that, while the Arrhenius equation itself was not patentable, the claimed method for curing rubber was an industrial process of a type that has historically enjoyed patent protection. The use of the equation and a computer were incidental to the patentable inventive process.

Software patents differ substantially from copyrights covering computer software. Copyright protects the expression of a work – the lines of code written by a programmer, the executable version of that code and the screen displays and images generated by the code. Patents, on the other hand, protect software functionality at a higher level. Actual source code is seldom included in a patent application, and in many cases software patents simply describe, and claim, the functions accomplished by particular programs.[34]

AMAZON'S ONE-CLICK PURCHASING PATENT

U.S. Pat. No. 5,960,411 (September 28, 1999)

1. A method of placing an order for an item comprising:

under control of a client system, displaying information identifying the item; and

in response to only a single action being performed, sending a request to order the item along with an identifier of a purchaser of the item to a server system;

under control of a single-action ordering component of the server system, receiving the request;

retrieving additional information previously stored for the purchaser identified by the identifier in the received request; and

generating an order to purchase the requested item for the purchaser identified by the identifier in the received request using the retrieved additional information; and

fulfilling the generated order to complete purchase of the item whereby the item is ordered without using a shopping cart ordering model.

---

34 Mark A. Lemley, *Software Patents and the Return of Functional Claiming*, 2013 Wisc. L. Rev. 905 (2013).

The vagueness, potential overbreadth and poor quality of many software patents led to significant criticism of software patenting in the 2000s. Notorious examples of questionable software patents emerged, including Amazon's "one-click shopping" patent, British Telecom's patent that allegedly covered "the Internet" and Apple's patents covering basic smartphone gestures such as "tap to zoom." Compounding these issues, the 2000s also saw the rise of significant patent litigation initiated by so-called patent assertion entities (colloquially known as "patent trolls") that took advantage of broad and vague patent claim language to seek monetary settlements from firms across the electronics and computing industry. The system came under heavy fire from the popular media, scholars and even the Obama Administration.

Perhaps in response to some of these issues, the Supreme Court again turned its attention to algorithmic patents in 2010. In *Bilski v. Kappos*, 561 U.S. 593 (2010), the Court held that an algorithm for calculating a fixed price for monthly utility bills was an unpatentable abstract idea. Then, in *Alice Corp. v. CLS Bank*, 573 U.S. 208 (2014), the Court rejected patent claims drawn to a computer-implemented electronic escrow service for facilitating financial transactions, holding that the invention was merely an abstract idea. The Court also observed that claiming a generic computer implementation of such an abstract idea cannot transform it into a patent-eligible invention. *Alice* overturned much existing wisdom and practice regarding software patenting and appears to be responsible, at least initially, for a sharp increase in the number of software patent applications that have been rejected on eligibility grounds, and patents that have been invalidated, either at the Patent Trial and Appeals Board (PTAB) or in the courts.[35]

18.2.2.3 Trade Secrets

Computer software may be treated as a trade secret, even when copyright and patent protection are also available. The principal source of software trade secrecy is its source code – the human-readable instructions that are generally invisible and inaccessible to a user of an executable (object code) program (see Section 18.3.3.3).[36]

Yet trade secrecy is also sought with respect to the object code versions of programs. Take, for example, software developed by an enterprise and used internally for key strategic purposes, such as economic forecasting, oil and gas exploration or programmed securities trading. The enterprise could be seriously injured if a competitor obtained an executable version of such a program, or even its readouts and displays.

The issue becomes murkier, however, when dealing with computer software that has been publicly distributed.[37] Despite the inconsistency that seems to arise when treating something distributed to the public as a secret, a combination of contractual confidentiality requirements and the inherent difficulty of extracting intelligible source code from executable object code has resulted in a general recognition of trade secret protection for the internal mechanics of publicly distributed executable software programs.[38]

---

[35] Jasper L. Tran, *Two Years after Alice v. CLS Bank*, 98 J. Pat. & Trademark Off. Soc'y 354 (2016). Colleen Chien & Jiun Ying Wu, *Decoding Patentable Subject Matter*, 2018 Patently-O Patent L.J. 1 (2018). For an overview of software patenting issues, see Gregory J. Kirsch & Charley F. Brown, *Software Patents* in Bioinformatics, Medical Informatics and the Law 80 (Jorge L. Contreras et al., eds., 2022).

[36] Needless to say, open source code software, in which source code is made freely available to the public, is not subject to trade secret protection (see Section 19.2).

[37] Jay Dratler, Jr., *Trade Secret Law: An Impediment to Trade in Computer Software*, 1 Santa Clara Computer & High-Tech. L.J. 27, 45–47 (1985).

[38] 1 Milgrim on Trade Secrets § 1.09[5][b].

18.2.3 *Software Licensing*

As noted above, computer software can be, and often is, covered by a range of IP rights including copyright, trade secret and patent. As discussed in Section 6.1.4, software licenses are generally *product* licenses rather than *rights* licenses. That is, a blanket license is granted under all IP covering a particular software program, rather than enumerating the specific IP rights being licensed. Below are some other special provisions that are encountered in software licensing agreements.[39]

18.2.3.1 Software Use Licenses

Object Code. Most software licenses authorize the licensee to use the licensed software in executable, object code form. Whether the licensed software is an enterprise inventory management system, a consumer photo-editing app or an algorithm embedded in a pacemaker, the user only requires an executable version of the software, and the licensor is only willing to share object code with the user. Generally, these licenses do not permit the licensee to modify the software or to distribute it to third parties (other than its own affiliates).

User Limits. Such licenses sometimes include limits on the number of individual users that may access or use the software. These limits may be stated in terms of a maximum number of registered users, or in terms of the number of concurrent "seats" that may use the software at any given time. Thus, an app intended for individual use may be authorized for use on a single smartphone or other device. An enterprise software system may be limited to use by fifteen individual user IDs in the licensee's finance department. And a university mathematical simulation program may be limited to use by no more than fifty concurrent users at any given time. Often, technical measures enforce these limitations, and avoidance or circumvention of such measures can constitute both a breach of the licensing agreement as well as a violation of the Digital Millennium Copyright Act. And, as the Federal Circuit held in *Bitmanagement Software GmbH v. United States*, 989 F.3d 938 (Fed. Cir. 2021), failing to track and exceeding seat limitations for a licensed software system may constitute a breach of a license condition giving rise to a claim for copyright infringement in addition to breach of contract.

Internal Use Only. Many software use licenses are limited to the licensee's "internal business purposes." This limitation ensures that the licensee cannot use the software for "service bureau" purposes – permitting others to access and use the software remotely. When software contains "internal use" restrictions, the licensee should ensure that its external consultants, contractors, collaborators and business partners are also entitled to access and use the software to the extent necessary to support the licensee's business or to perform services for the licensee.

18.2.3.2 Software Distribution Agreements

One common form of software licensing agreement authorizes the licensee to distribute the licensed software to others, rather than use the licensed software for its own internal purposes. These agreements have various labels, including "original equipment manufacturer" (OEM), "value-added reseller" (VAR) and distribution agreements.

---

[39] In addition to the materials covered in this chapter, see also Section 10.1.3 covering "performance" warranties for software products.

OEMs. OEM agreements typically authorize the licensee to incorporate the licensed software into another software program or a hardware device. For example, the vendor of an electronic French grammar checker might license this program to Microsoft for incorporation into Microsoft Word, or the developer of road-mapping software might license it to Toyota for incorporation into its vehicles. Often, the licensee (OEM) sells the combined product under its own name, and the licensor is recognized only briefly (e.g., on a "splash" screen when its software is launched, or in the product user manual).

VARs. VAR and distribution agreements, on the other hand, typically limit the licensee to distributing or reselling the software as a standalone product or combined with other software in a manner that does not require substantial integration (e.g., reselling a video game as part of a video game "ten pack"). Some of these licensees may provide value-added services, such as software installation, support and training, along with the licensed software. In these cases, the licensor's software is usually identified by name (requiring a trademark license if the licensee will advertise or promote it).

APIs. Incorporation of one program into another sometimes requires the licensee to access and modify the source code of the licensed software (see below). However, this is usually not required, as software often includes object code "application programmer interfaces" or APIs that enable the integration of software programs without the need to access or modify source code. It is important to recall, however, that APIs themselves may constitute copyrightable code, which was the subject of the dispute in *Oracle v. Google* (Oracle alleged that Google infringed the copyright in Oracle's APIs for the Java programming language by incorporating them into the Android operating system without Oracle's permission).

18.2.3.3 Proprietary Source Code Licenses

Unlike the developers of OSS (see Section 19.2), the licensors of proprietary software seldom make the source code of their programs available to licensees. As discussed above, most typical uses of software – whether for internal use or incorporation into other products – require only object code. In some cases, however, a licensee may require access to the source code of licensed software. Some situations in which this might occur include the following:

- The licensed software will be incorporated into a proprietary program or device in a manner that requires detailed knowledge of licensee's larger systems, which knowledge the licensor lacks.
- The licensee requires modifications or customizations to the licensed software to reflect its own proprietary algorithms, formulas or processes.
- The licensee wishes the flexibility to modify the licensed software as it desires, without relying on the licensor.
- The licensee plans to use the software in a mission-critical application and wishes to verify independently that it contains no bugs, defects or vulnerabilities, and that it operates in a manner that will not compromise other licensee systems.
- The licensor is a small company with a limited track record, and the licensee does not have confidence that the licensor will be available indefinitely to make required modifications, updates and upgrades to the software.

In these and other cases, the licensor may grant the licensee access to the source code of a proprietary software program, together with rights to reproduce, modify and create derivative works of the source code and then to use or distribute modified versions of the object code program that is derived from that source code. Unless the software is OSS, it is highly unlikely that the licensee will be granted the right to distribute or disclose the source code itself, or modifications of that source code.

EXAMPLE: SOURCE CODE LICENSE GRANTS

Licensor hereby grants to Licensee, and Licensee accepts, a nonexclusive, nontransferable right and license:

a. to modify, reproduce and prepare Derivative Works of the Source Code, and to incorporate those Derivative Works into Licensee Programs to produce Modified Licensee Programs;
b. to reproduce and distribute Modified Licensee Programs in Object Code form to Licensee's end user customers in the Territory pursuant to End User Sublicense Agreements meeting the requirements of Section __ below.

Licenses of proprietary source code require the parties consider several issues that do not arise in the context of typical software licenses or OSS licenses.

Confidentiality. A software proprietor's source code is often a valuable trade secret. Thus, source code releases are often governed by strict confidentiality restrictions – sometimes more strict than even the ordinary confidentiality terms applied to information exchanged under an agreement. For example, the number and identity of individuals to whom source code may be released is often specified, there are requirements regarding heightened security measures that must be applied to the storage and transmission of source code (e.g., encryption, password-protected directories). Likewise, the duration of confidentiality provisions relating to source code are often indefinite, rather than limited to a period of years, and almost always survive the termination of the license agreement. Often, the licensee must produce evidence that it has destroyed or permanently deleted all copies of source code and modifications thereto once its license has terminated.

Ownership. If the licensee is granted the right to modify the licensor's source code, then the parties must agree who will own those modifications. If the modifications are to be owned by the licensee, then the parties must also agree whether the licensor will receive a grantback license of any kind. These issues are discussed at length in Section 9.1.2.

Disclaimer of Warranties. If a licensee has the right to modify the licensor's source code, then the licensor will usually seek to disclaim any warranty or liability for errors or disruptions in the operation of the software, whether or not they are directly traceable to the licensee's modifications. While this may seem harsh for the licensee, it is often impossible to determine with precision what, precisely, has caused a software fault, particularly in large and complex systems (see Section 10.1.3.3, discussing warranty exclusions).

Escrow. Often, source code is "licensed," but placed in a third-party escrow account and released to the licensee only if the licensor fails to meet its warranty or maintenance obligations, or if the licensor suffers a bankruptcy or similar event that makes it likely that it will be unable to perform in the future (see Section 21.6).

18.2.4 *Maintenance, Support, Updates and Upgrades*

As noted in Section 10.1.3.8, many enterprise and OEM software licensing agreements include paid maintenance, support and other services by the licensor. The charge for these services is often based on a percentage (15–25 percent) of the annual licensing fee for the software. While the types of services included in these relationships can vary, below is a rough summary of what each generally entails.

Maintenance. Software "maintenance" generally means the correction of software errors and issues, often in accordance with a timescale that depends on the severity of the issue (see Sections 10.1.3.7 and 10.1.3.8).[40] Most maintenance plans include the provision of regular updates of the software (see below). Upgrades, on the other hand, may be included, but may also be offered by the licensor as new products subject to additional charges.

Support. Support generally refers to training and helpdesk support for the licensee's personnel who are using the licensed software. If the licensee has its internal "Level 1" helpdesk (which interacts directly with users), then the licensor may provide only "Level 2" and "Level 3" support. Level 2 support personnel generally interact with Level 1 personnel and do not take queries directly from users. Level 2 personnel are generally understood to be senior or specialist personnel with a higher degree of skill and familiarity with the software. Note that neither Level 1 or Level 2 support personnel are responsible for correcting errors in the software itself, only for responding to the large number of user inquiries and problems that can be resolved through the normal operation of the software. Level 3 support is often referred to as "engineering" support, and becomes involved only if an error in the software is detected or there is a compatibility issue with other software or hardware. Level 3 support personnel typically deal only with Level 2 support, and not with the Level 1 helpdesk or users. Level 3 support may be available only if the licensor also provides maintenance services to the licensee.

Patch or Correction. A software "patch" or "correction" is usually modified code that can be installed to address a problem or error in a software program.

Workaround. A workaround is a temporary way to avoid the consequences of a software error without actually correcting the error. For example, if a system uses the wireless Bluetooth protocol to connect to an office printer but the Bluetooth module malfunctions, a workaround might be to connect the system to the printer using a physical USB cable. This is not a correction of the software error in the Bluetooth module, but can often be implemented quickly to ensure that users can continue to use the system while a more permanent correction is developed or installed.

Updates. Software updates are new releases of a software program that correct errors, close security holes, ensure compatibility with new versions of hardware or operating systems, add support for new devices and make cosmetic changes. Updates are often designated by incremental increases of the software version number to the right of the decimal point (e.g., version 3.2 to 3.3 or 5.4.4 to 5.4.5, also called "point updates").

Upgrades. Software upgrades, often designated by increments to the left of the decimal point (e.g., version 3.2 to 4.0), are major modifications to a program that introduce substantial new features, performance or functionality.

---

[40] Computer hardware also comes with "maintenance" plans, which include configuration, repair and tuning of equipment, as well as installation of available software updates and upgrades. Hardware maintenance is often offered by third parties. Licensees engaging third-party software providers for hardware and software maintenance should ensure that their licensing agreements permit such third parties to access and reproduce licensed software. See note 33, supra, and accompanying text.

18.2.5 *Reverse Engineering Restrictions*

The term "reverse engineering" has its roots in the hardware world. It refers to the process of taking apart and inspecting a device to determine how it works, usually with the goal of building one's own device or creating another device that interacts with it.[41] From a hardware standpoint there is little that can be done to prevent reverse engineering. While patents may prevent one from making or using a new and infringing device, they are not effective at preventing the disassembly of a validly acquired device (particularly given recent judicial interpretations invalidating "conditional sales" of patented articles – see Section 23.5).

In the software industry, however, prohibitions on reverse engineering are viewed as more enforceable, both under trade secret and copyright law. These prohibitions are intended to prevent the user of a software program from reverse engineering an executable object code version of the software to derive its source code (or at least a source code approximation of what it does). In addition to reverse engineering, this process is also called disassembly or decompilation. While each of these activities is, from a technical standpoint, slightly different, the goal of each is to take the long string of zeros and ones comprising an object code program and convert it into human-readable source code. This, in turn, reveals how a proprietary software program works and, in theory, allows the reverse engineer to replicate it or to create products that interface directly with it (i.e., if the vendor does not provide an API to enable interoperability).

Reverse engineering of software code has long been a subject of dispute. In *NEC Corp. v. Intel Corp.*, 1989 U.S. Dist. LEXIS 1409 (N.D. Cal. 1989), the court held that NEC's reverse engineering of copyrighted microcode contained in Intel chips did not constitute an infringement of Intel's copyright.[42] A series of other cases found that the disassembly of video game console software in order to create game cartridges compatible with those consoles was a fair use under copyright law.[43] A few years later, § 1201(f) of the Digital Millennium Copyright Act expressly permitted reverse engineering for the sole purpose of achieving interoperability.

These legal developments led to the proliferation of contractual prohibitions on reverse engineering. Such prohibitions have, in turn, been challenged as preempting copyright law (which seemingly permits reverse engineering), but the prohibitions have largely been upheld (*Bowers v. Baystate Technologies, Inc.*, 320 F.3d 1317 (Fed. Cir. 2003, discussed in Section 17.1, Note 4)). Thus, prohibitions on reverse engineering are now standard features of the software licensing landscape.

EXAMPLE: PROHIBITION ON REVERSE ENGINEERING

Licensee agrees that it shall not, through manual or automated means, reverse engineer, reverse compile, reverse assemble, decompile, disassemble or otherwise seek to derive a Source Code version of the Licensed Software or otherwise to discern its internal architecture, structure or design.

---

[41] For example, one might reverse engineer a competitor's laser printer and printer cartridges in order to produce third-party cartridge replacements.

[42] See Jorge L. Contreras, Laura Handley & Terrance Yang, NEC v. Intel: *Breaking New Ground in the Law of Copyright*, 3 Harv. J.L. & Tech. 209 (1990).

[43] See *Atari Games v. Nintendo*, 975 F.2d 832, (Fed. Cir. 1992), *Sega v. Accolade*, 977 F.2d 1510 (9th Cir. 1992).

Notes and Questions

1. *Is software special?* Think of five ways that software licenses differ from licenses for other copyrighted works such as literary works and musical compositions. Now think of five ways that software licenses differ from patent licenses. How important are these differences? What would happen if a software program were licensed under an agreement used to license a motion picture for theatrical display, or a patent covering a new method of sequencing DNA?

2. *Source code.* Why is software source code treated so carefully? Think about the special measures taken to protect software source code when you read Section 19.2 about OSS licensing.

3. *Reverse engineering.* Why is reverse engineering routinely prohibited by software licensing agreements? Why do courts uphold these prohibitions, given the ample precedent establishing that reverse engineering does not constitute copyright infringement?

4. *Noncircumvention.* Noncircumvention clauses such as that discussed in the *Eden Hannon* case are not common in the software industry. Why not? Could a software vendor achieve advantages from such clauses that it might not otherwise be able to achieve using the provisions discussed in this section?

5. *Maintenance.* At 15–25 percent of the licensing fee per year, software maintenance programs are not cheap. Why does a licensee need to obtain maintenance services from the licensor? If you represented a licensee, are there any services typically included in a maintenance program that you would recommend your client forego (in an effort to reduce the annual charge for the program)? Other than revenue generation, why do you think that software licensors often insist that licensees purchase maintenance programs from them?

Problem 18.1

Your client AirBrain has designed a robotic carrier pigeon. In order to keep on track while flying it requires geospatial navigation software. As there is no existing pigeon-based navigation software, your development team believes that the fastest way to market is to adapt the navigation software developed by Boeing for commercial aircraft. Draft the licensing terms that you would propose to Boeing, including fallback positions if Boeing rejects your initial offers.

18.3 LICENSING IN THE CLOUD

The Role of Patent Pledges in the Cloud

Liza Vertinsky, *Patent Pledges: Global Perspectives on Patent Law's Private Ordering Frontier* 260–62 (Jorge L. Contreras & Meredith Jacob, eds., Edward Elgar, 2017)

The U.S. National Institute of Standards and Technology (NIST) defines cloud computing as "a model for enabling convenient, on-demand network access to a shared pool of configurable computing resources (e.g., networks, servers, storage, applications, and services) that can be rapidly provisioned and released with minimal management effort or service provider interaction." Put more simply, cloud computing is a form of computing that utilizes shared computer resources accessed over the internet or through mobile devices to deliver on-demand computing services. The cloud is a metaphor for the large data centers that perform the computing tasks desired by the end users.

This idea of concentrating computing resources at the center of a network rather than in user terminals is not new, but rather marks a return to the mainframe models of the 1950s, 1960s and 1970s. The use of the term "cloud computing" to refer to a distinct model of computing is new, however, and the rapid growth in cloud computing applications and services has produced what is now considered to be a distinct cloud computing industry.

While there are many firms offering different kinds of cloud computing applications and services, the industry is dominated by a small number of large firms. Amazon, Google, Microsoft and IBM are among the leaders in terms of market share and market influence, with Amazon by far in the lead in terms of market share. Other companies important in the cloud computing space include Salesforce.com, which pioneered software as a service, VMware and its competitor Citrix, which offer software for clouds, and Rackspace, which is leading a large coalition for free cloud software and provides its own public cloud and related services. On top of cloud computing platforms sit an increasing number of successful cloud computing companies such as LinkedIn (offers cloud based recruiting software), NetSuite (offers cloud-based business software), WorkDay (offers cloud based HR and finance software) and AthenaHealth (offers cloud based services for electronic health records), to name a few, all of which offer software as a service in targeted areas.

While the market leaders operate in all major segments of cloud computing and provide platforms for both developers and consumers, their business models and the ways in which these companies compete and expect to make money vary. In its current form the cloud computing market has been roughly stratified into three different segments: infrastructure as a service (IaaS), platform as a service (PaaS), and software as a service (SaaS). IaaS involves raw computing resources, analogous to virtualized hardware, providing customers with computing infrastructure for data storage, management and manipulation. It allows companies to outsource computing equipment and resources while giving them flexibility in how to deploy the infrastructure for their own purposes. Amazon has by far the lion's share of this market with its Amazon Web Services (AWS) platform. PaaS provides a platform and environment for building applications and services over the internet, operating essentially as a cloud based operating system. Microsoft and Google are among the market leaders in this segment, although Amazon's AWS is increasingly encompassing services that resemble those offered by a PaaS platform. PaaS examples include Google AppEngine, Microsoft Azure, and AWS Elastic Beanstalk. SaaS involves preconfigured software applications offered as a web based service to end users, like Google Docs and Gmail. These market categories increasingly overlap, however, as firms compete with alternative cloud platforms and accommodate new and disruptive technologies.

The cloud computing market is also differentiated into private, public and hybrid clouds. Private clouds are computing platforms that are under the control of a single customer, operated within the customer's firewall and under its own control. Public clouds can be used by anyone anywhere, based on a model of pooled, shared computing resources accessed over the internet. Hybrid clouds involve a combination of public and private cloud computing, allowing companies to keep certain computing functions or databases in house and have others externally provided via a public cloud. Amazon and Google focus primarily on public clouds, IBM began with a focus on private clouds but has subsequently found the need to embrace hybrid and public cloud strategies as well, and Microsoft has taken the lead in offering hybrid clouds.

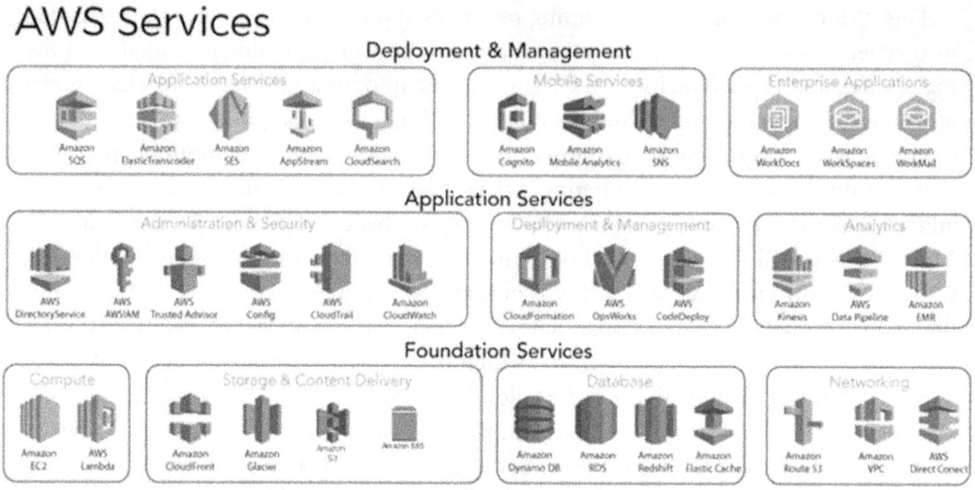

AWS Services

FIGURE 18.2 Amazon makes a range of applications available on a service-basis through Amazon Web Services (AWS).

Microsoft's cloud computing platform is called Azure. Below is an excerpt from a Microsoft document explaining the advantages of Azure to companies that are considering offering their own software and services to customers through the Azure platform.

Intellectual Property Protection: Azure Helps Protect your IP

Debra Shinder, Microsoft Corp. (n.d.), https://aka.ms/Azure-Trusted-IP

Business method and software patents provide a lucrative opportunity for non-practicing entities (NPEs), who stockpile large numbers of patents with no intention of developing products, but for the purpose of suing companies and individuals for infringement. This type of cloud-based patent litigation is increasing, and lawsuits and countersuits can cost your organization money and time and damage your reputation. The aggressive tactics of NPEs discourage innovation.

Trust in the cloud encompasses not only the assurance of security, privacy, compliance, and resiliency, but also clarity and confidence that your innovations will be protected against frivolous infringement claims, including when you co-develop innovative solutions working together with a cloud provider. Microsoft Azure IP Advantage and the Shared Innovation Initiative can help offer that assurance.

IP in the Cloud

As computing shifts to the cloud, new risks to innovation emerge. These include risks to developers, to Azure customer organizations working in the cloud, and to customers who co-create intellectual property with Microsoft as part of their digital transformation.

Microsoft trust and IP initiatives build on one another to provide protections to all three of these categories.

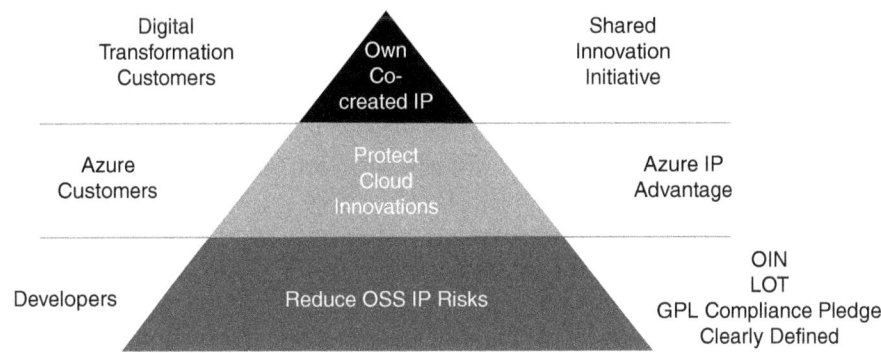

Azure IP Advantage

Intellectual property is increasingly being created, stored, and shared in digital form. Digital transformation has brought a paradigm shift to the business environment as companies embrace new approaches to creating, communicating, and interacting with customers, partners, and the public.

NPEs see this as an opportunity; they collect and hoard patents and then assert patent infringement against innovators. This is a growing concern for cloud services customers, and the fear of a patent suit discourages innovation in the cloud. Cloud providers can help their customers reduce the risk to be able to innovate with confidence, and Microsoft Azure offers best-in-industry protection against IP risks. Azure IP Advantage includes:

- **Uncapped indemnification**. This covers claims for IP infringement and extends to open source software (OSS) incorporated by Microsoft in Azure services (for example, Apache Hadoop used for Azure HDInsight). It is provided by default for all Microsoft cloud customers.
- **Patent Pick**. Microsoft provides a portfolio of 10,000 patents that customers can pick from and use to deter and defend against patent lawsuits. It is available to consuming Azure customers with an Azure usage of $1 k/m over the last three months who have not filed a patent infringement lawsuit against another Azure customer for their Azure workloads in the last two years. This helps to discourage excessive litigation.
- **Springing license**. This provides peace of mind with future patent protection; if Microsoft sells any of its patents to an NPE in the future, its customers will receive a license, so the NPE won't have an infringement suit against the customer. This is available to all consuming Azure customers with an Azure usage of $1 k/m over the last three months. Unlike other cloud providers, Microsoft does not require a reciprocal commitment from the customer for its patents. In addition, Microsoft is a member of the LOT Network, a non-profit community of companies that was formed to preserve the traditional uses of patents while providing immunization against the patent troll problem.

These protections help free companies to concentrate more on building their businesses, leveraging open source software, and serving their customers, and less on dealing with patent litigation.

Shared Innovation Initiative

Every company today is becoming in part a software company. Companies are increasingly collaborating with their cloud providers to co-create intellectual property to transform their business operations. There is growing concern that without an approach that ensures customers own key patents to these new solutions, tech companies will use the knowledge to enter their customers' market and compete against them—perhaps even using the IP that customers helped create.

Microsoft developed its Shared Innovation Initiative in response to these concerns when customers collaborate with Microsoft to develop new products and services that run on the Azure platform. We've created contract terms that lay out these principles for engagements where the parties are co-creating new IP. Shared Innovation builds on our approach outlined in the AIPA, and is based on seven guiding principles:

1. **Respect for ownership of existing technology.** We each own the existing technology and IP that we bring to the table when we partner together. As we work with customers, we'll ensure that we similarly will each own the improvements made to our respective technologies that result from our collaboration.
2. **Assuring customer ownership of new patents and design rights**. As we work together to create new technology, our customers, rather than Microsoft, will own any patents that result from our shared innovation work.
3. **Support for open source**. If our shared innovation results in the creation of source code and our customers so choose, Microsoft will work with them to contribute to an open source project any code the customer is licensed to use.
4. **Licensing back to Microsoft**. Microsoft will receive a license back to any patents and design rights in the new technology that results from the shared innovation, but the license will be limited to improving our platform technologies.
5. **Portability**. We won't impose contractual restrictions that prevent customers from porting to other platforms the new, shared innovations they own.
6. **Transparency and clarity**. We will work with customers to ensure transparency and clarity on all IP issues as the shared innovation project moves forward.
7. **Learning and improvement**. We'll continue to learn from this work and use this learning to improve further our shared innovation work.

Notes and Questions

1. *The cloud.* What is the "cloud"? How many of your daily activities involve use of a service provided via the cloud? (There may be more than you think.) As Liza Vertinsky points out, cloud computing is not new – it goes back to the roots of the computing industry in the 1950s. Why do you think that, after a long dormancy from the 1990s through the 2010s, cloud computing has recently made a comeback?
2. *Service not software.* From a contracting standpoint, the principal difference between obtaining software through physical media (disc or download) and through a SaaS model via the cloud is that cloud-based software delivery services typically don't provide the user with a copy of the executable program itself. Rather, the software is accessed through a browser or "thin" app front-end, but the bulk of the program – its guts – are stored and executed

remotely. Thus, a SaaS license is really a service contract. While some small software elements may be downloaded to the user's computer, the crux of the contractual relationship that is established is not one of licensor–licensee, but of service provider–customer. What advantages and disadvantages can you see to obtaining access to a program remotely through SaaS rather than obtaining a physical copy of the software to run on your own computer? SaaS applications are priced in various ways, but one common method is a monthly service fee – just like a cable or phone service contract – rather than a one-time "purchase price" for a software program. What advantages and disadvantages exist with these different "purchase" models?

3. *Public, private, hybrid.* What relative advantages and disadvantages do you think a software vendor would derive from offering its software through a public, private or hybrid cloud platform? What are the differences among these three cloud structures?

4. *IP risks in the cloud.* Microsoft offers its customers (companies that host their software on the Azure cloud platform) several novel IP-related incentives. What threat is Microsoft responding to? Why is this threat of concern to customers of cloud-based services? How does each of Microsoft's Azure IP initiatives (uncapped indemnity, patent pick and springing license) respond to this threat? Which of these initiatives do you think offers customers the greatest protection from IP threats?

5. *Shared Innovation Initiative.* Microsoft's Shared Innovation Initiative is aimed at companies that wish to develop new software offerings for the Azure platform. How do the IP allocation terms of the Shared Innovation Initiative differ from what one might expect in a collaboration between Microsoft (one of the world's largest corporations) and a developer of software for its platform (see Section 9.3, discussing allocation of IP in joint development projects)? Why do you think Microsoft took this approach? Which of the Shared Innovation Initiative program features do you think is most important to Microsoft? To its customers?

19

Public Licenses: Open Source, Creative Commons and IP Pledges

SUMMARY CONTENTS

This chapter discusses licenses that are granted to the public at large, typically without monetary compensation. Like consumer EULAs, these "public" licenses are made available to potential users online, do not require signature, delivery or formal execution, and are generally effective automatically upon the user's download or use of the licensed content. Despite their relative informality, such licenses underlie vast quantities of online content, computer software and even patent rights today. Below, we discuss the history, motivations and strategies of three distinct types of public licensing: Creative Commons online content licenses, open source software (OSS) licenses and patent pledges.

19.1 CREATIVE COMMONS AND OPEN CONTENT LICENSING

THE CREATIVE COMMONS
LAWRENCE LESSIG, 64 *Montana Law Review* 1, 10–13 (2004)

In the beginning of the Internet, the architecture of the Internet disabled any ability to control the distribution of copyrighted works. That meant that if we had this triad among all, some, and none, the effective protection of the original Internet was none. The architecture meant that copyright was not respected because anybody could copy and perfectly distribute any copyrighted work without control.

That extreme begot another: the terror of the copyright industry, which in 1995, in response to the Internet launched a campaign to change the technical and legal infrastructure that defined the Internet, to change the Internet from an architecture of no control into an architecture of total control. So again, instead of a triad, we have increasingly an architecture of total control over everything. We have thus moved from one extreme to the other: from the extreme of total freedom to total control, and this is the shift the law is encouraging.

We're setting up a regime that thinks as if the world is either one or the other when it is in fact neither. Some want total control, some want no control, but most want this balance in the middle. Not "all rights reserved," not "no rights reserved," but increasingly the idea of "some rights reserved." My content is out there, I want you to respect it in some ways, but I want you to use it in lots of ways that traditional "all rights reserved" models would not permit.

Enter an organization that I have helped start called the Creative Commons. Think of it as pushing, as another founder, James Boyle, describes it, as a kind of environmentalism for culture. The idea here is that we need to build a layer of reasonable copyright law, by showing the world a layer of reasonable copyright law resting on top of the extremes. Take this world that is increasingly a world by default regulating all and change it into a world where once again we can see the mix between all, none, and some, using the technology of the Creative Commons.

This change is done through the voluntary action of individuals – creators, content owners. They take voluntary action by marking their content with a tag that expresses a kind of freedom. They use these tags then to build a kind of balance into the system to restore this reasonableness into the system by giving people a way to say, "I don't believe in this extremism."

For example, if you go to the Creative Commons Web site (http://creativecommons .org), you are given a very simple choice by which you can select the freedoms you want to grant. You can say, "I want people to give me attribution or not," or you can say, "I want people to use this for commercial use or not," or you can say, "I want to allow people to modify this or not," or you can use what we call a "share alike" license that says, whatever freedoms you got from me, you have to pass on to someone else.

Once you make these selections, the technology then produces a license that is comprised of three separate layers. One layer is a human-readable version of that license. Another is the lawyer-readable version of the license – the license. And a third layer is a machine-readable version of the license, which enables computers to understand what freedoms you are granting.

These three layers live together in a "Creative Commons" tag. And in four months, more than 400,000 pages have appeared on the Internet linking back to these licenses. Four hundred thousand have said, we believe in a kind of freedom associated with our content that is not the extreme.

Now we want this 400,000 to turn into 10,000,000. Because if there are 10,000,000 people out there who say we don't believe in the extremes, then this debate is no longer a debate between copyright owners and anarchists. Instead, it is increasingly a debate between extremists and those who believe in a tradition that expresses a freedom more fundamental. Beyond the permissions of fair use, these licenses give people ways to say go ahead, sample me, share me, copy me, liberate me, and together they restore something of balance in this debate. And this balance, we believe, will enable a different kind of creativity: creativity built upon a tradition of building upon the works of others, freely. A free culture, not the permission culture that our law has produced.

There is an extraordinary potential enabled by a technology that is increasingly threatened and destroyed. The potential for a different, critical, democratic creativity, is increasingly being forced into last century's model for doing business.

> It is a world where the dinosaurs have been given the power to control evolution. A system where last century's powerful has the ability to veto next century's innovators. In such a world, creativity and innovation die. The free culture that defined our tradition has been eroded, not by idealists, but by lobbyists. The free culture that we have lived under now is under threat. And we have an obligation, all of us, to engage in this practice to enable this freedom again.

Lessig's vision of ten million Creative Commons (CC) tags has been more than fulfilled. The CC website today claims that more than 500 million online images are available under CC licenses. As Lessig and others intended, the appeal of the CC licensing system is its simplicity and its intuitiveness. Users can choose to apply one of six different combinations of four different licensing options to their works. Each option is described in simple, plain language and identified by an intuitive icon.

Thus, if I wish to post a photo to a social media site and make it available for anyone else to use for any purpose so long as they give me credit (attribution), I can tag the photo with the "CC BY" symbol, and the CC Attribution license will apply. If I also wish to stipulate that my photo cannot be modified in any way, then I can tag it with the "CC BY ND" (Attribution, No Derivatives) license.[1] If I want to be sure that my photo remains free for all to use, even if someone incorporates it into a proprietary database or website, then I can add the "SA" (Share Alike) tag. And if I wish to prohibit commercial uses (e.g., using my photo in a corporate ad), then I can use "NC" (Non-Commercial). As shown in Figure 19.1, there are only six permitted combinations of these four licensing tags (out of fifteen possible combinations), reflecting the designers' views of the most frequent and logical types of uses that should be permitted.

The CC suite of licenses appears simple, but a sophisticated legal structure underlies its streamlined user-facing tags. That is, the tag "CC BY ND" does not itself convey a license to the user. Rather, when a tag is attached to an online image or other content, it includes a hyperlink to a more comprehensive licensing agreement that is hosted on CC's website. For example, the full text of the CC BY NC ND 4.0 license can be found at https://creativecommons.org/licenses/by-nc-nd/4.0/legalcode.

By many measures, the CC licensing framework has been phenomenally successful. Professor Jane Ginsburg points to four important design features that have contributed to the success of the CC model: its overall simplicity, its extension of credit to authors (included in each of the six permitted licenses), its ability to authorize use of the licensed content instantly and forever, and its potential to expand distribution of a work through search engines.[2] These features have made CC licensing a standard feature of online platforms and social media sites.

Notes and Comments

1. *Which rights reserved?* In Lessig's view, why is a third option necessary for copyrighted material in addition to "all rights reserved" and "no rights reserved"?
2. *Public licenses.* The CC licenses are "public" licenses. That is, they are not specifically negotiated between copyright owners and users, but are publicly posted and can be "accepted" by

---

[1] The CC licenses also include a version number reflecting updates that have been made over the years. The current version is 4.0, so a full CC tag would read: "This work is licensed under a *CC BY 4.0 license.*"

[2] Jane C. Ginsburg, Authors' Transfer and License Contracts under US Copyright Law in Research Handbook on Intellectual Property Licensing 3, 23 (Jacques de Werra, ed., Edward Elgar, 2013).

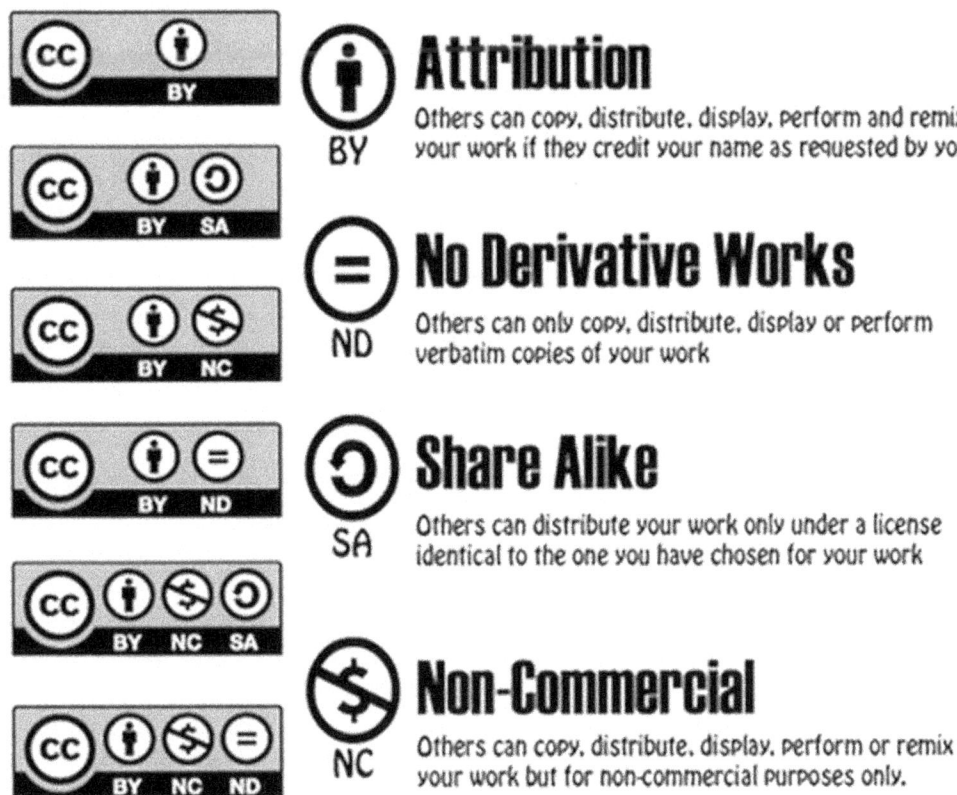

FIGURE 19.1 The Creative Commons suite of licenses.

anyone who wishes to use the licensed content. Thus, the introduction to the CC BY NC ND 4.0 license reads as follows:

> By exercising the Licensed Rights (defined below), You accept and agree to be bound by the terms and conditions of this Creative Commons Attribution-NonCommercial-NoDerivatives 4.0 International Public License ("Public License"). To the extent this Public License may be interpreted as a contract, You are granted the Licensed Rights in consideration of Your acceptance of these terms and conditions, and the Licensor grants You such rights in consideration of benefits the Licensor receives from making the Licensed Material available under these terms and conditions.

How consistent is the CC approach to that recognized by courts in the context of consumer EULAs and terms of use discussed in Chapter 17? Why aren't more IP licenses structured as public licenses?

3. *Permitted combinations.* Why did the designers of the CC licenses only permit six out of fifteen possible combinations of the four licensing tags? Can you think of any useful combinations beyond the six permitted ones?

4. *The importance of attribution.* In one early survey of CC licenses, 98 percent of users selected the BY attribution requirement – far more than any of the other licensing options. For this reason, when it revamped its licensing options, CC included the "BY" requirement in all options (i.e., there is no CC licensing option that omits "BY"). Why do you think attribution is so important to content creators?

CC is fairly flexible when it comes to specifying how attribution must be made. The license states:

> You may satisfy the conditions in Section 3(a)(1) in any reasonable manner based on the medium, means, and context in which You Share the Licensed Material. For example, it may be reasonable to satisfy the conditions by providing a URI or hyperlink to a resource that includes the required information.

Is this flexible approach ideal? How might it be abused?

5. *Sharealike and Copyleft.* The Share Alike or "SA" feature of CC licenses resembles the controversial "copyleft" approach to some OSS software promoted by the Free Software Foundation and others (see Section 19.2). As such, CC SA is probably the least commonly used variant of the CC licensing suite. What is the rationale for imposing an SA licensing requirement? Why do you think it is not widely used? Keep these issues in mind as you review Section 19.2 and 19.3.

6. *Applications.* The core application for CC licenses is digital content, particularly images such as photographs, drawings and artworks. But the CC licenses are general copyright licenses that are not strictly limited to visual images. It is not difficult to imagine how CC licensing could be used for text – blog posts, academic articles, short stories, poems. But what about music? In the mid-2000s, CC created three music sampling licenses,[3] but those have since been discontinued in favor of the general suite of six licenses. Likewise, CC has experimented with licenses for scientific data, though that project has also been discontinued. And despite the growth of OSS licensing (see Section 19.2), CC licenses are seldom used for software. Why does CC licensing appear to be limited to visual images? Are there other logical expansions for the use of CC licensing?

7. *Database rights.* As discussed in Section 18.1, databases, *per se*, are not protected under US intellectual property law, though they are protected in the EU and other jurisdictions. Thus, the CC licenses, which are intended to apply internationally, include a provision stating that "Where the Licensed Rights include Sui Generis Database Rights that apply to Your use of the Licensed Material," the licenses granted with respect to copyrights are also granted with respect to those database rights. Under what circumstances do you think that this provision could become important?

8. *CC 0.* In addition to its suite of licenses, CC also permits users to select a CC o or "No Rights Reserved" tag for their content. As CC explains,

> CC o enables scientists, educators, artists and other creators and owners of copyright- or database-protected content to waive those interests in their works and thereby place them as completely as possible in the public domain, so that others may freely build upon, enhance and reuse the works for any purposes without restriction under copyright or database law.

Why was the CC o option necessary? Does this option conflict with Lessig's original plan to create a system that offered options other than "all rights reserved" and "no rights reserved"?

9. *Choice of law?* The CC licenses do not include an express choice of law provision (see Section 11.3). Why do you think this term was omitted?

10. *The business of CC.* Creative Commons is not a governmental body or an international organization, but a nonprofit corporation based in the United States, with local chapters

---

[3]　See Michael W. Carroll, *Creative Commons and the New Intermediaries*, 2006 Mich. St. L. Rev. 45, 47–48 (2006).

around the world. Is it advisable to entrust the licensing structure for so much online content to a single private organization? What would happen to CC licenses if the Creative Commons corporation were to be liquidated or simply disappear? Is there any viable competitor to CC today? Is there a need for one, now that the CC licenses are published and available online? Why is a legal entity needed at all for a self-executing licensing framework?

19.2 THE OPEN SOURCE PHENOMENON

As discussed in Section 18.2.1, a computer program's "source code" is a version of the program written in a human-readable programming language such as C++, Perl, BASIC or Fortran. Most proprietary software is licensed and distributed in object code or executable form. But beginning in the 1970s, a group of software developers in Cambridge, Massachusetts, began to make their source code publicly available too. This trend began the "free software" or "open source software" (OSS) movement, which today is at the heart of a multi-billion-dollar industry.

19.2.1 *Origins: The Free Software Movement*

The excerpt below is by Richard Stallman, who is generally credited as the father of the free software movement.

> **THE GNU OPERATING SYSTEM AND THE FREE SOFTWARE MOVEMENT**
> **RICHARD STALLMAN,** *Open Sources: Voices from the Open Source Revolution* (1999)

> When I started working at the MIT Artificial Intelligence Lab in 1971, I became part of a software-sharing community that had existed for many years. Sharing of software was not limited to our particular community; it is as old as computers, just as sharing of recipes is as old as cooking. But we did it more than most.
>
> We did not call our software "free software," because that term did not yet exist, but that is what it was. Whenever people from another university or a company wanted to port and use a program, we gladly let them. If you saw someone using an unfamiliar and interesting program, you could always ask to see the source code, so that you could read it, change it, or cannibalize parts of it to make a new program.
>
> The situation changed drastically in the early 1980s when Digital discontinued the PDP-10 series. The modern computers of the era, such as the VAX or the 68020, had their own operating systems, but none of them were free software: you had to sign a nondisclosure agreement even to get an executable copy.
>
> This meant that the first step in using a computer was to promise not to help your neighbor. A cooperating community was forbidden. The rule made by the owners of proprietary software was, "If you share with your neighbor, you are a pirate. If you want any changes, beg us to make them."
>
> One assumption is that software companies have an unquestionable natural right to own software and thus have power over all its users … Interestingly, the U.S. Constitution and legal tradition reject this view; copyright is not a natural right, but an artificial government-imposed monopoly that limits the users' natural right to copy.

Another unstated assumption is that the only important thing about software is what jobs it allows you to do—that we computer users should not care what kind of society we are allowed to have.

A third assumption is that we would have no usable software (or would never have a program to do this or that particular job) if we did not offer a company power over the users of the program. This assumption may have seemed plausible, before the free software movement demonstrated that we can make plenty of useful software without putting chains on it.

If we decline to accept these assumptions, and judge these issues based on ordinary common-sense morality while placing the users first, we arrive at very different conclusions. Computer users should be free to modify programs to fit their needs, and free to share software, because helping other people is the basis of society.

So I looked for a way that a programmer could do something for the good. I asked myself, was there a program or programs that I could write, so as to make a community possible once again?

The answer was clear: what was needed first was an operating system. That is the crucial software for starting to use a computer. With an operating system, you can do many things; without one, you cannot run the computer at all. With a free operating system, we could again have a community of cooperating hackers—and invite anyone to join. And anyone would be able to use a computer without starting out by conspiring to deprive his or her friends.

I chose to make the system compatible with Unix so that it would be portable, and so that Unix users could easily switch to it. The name GNU was chosen following a hacker tradition, as a recursive acronym for "GNU's Not Unix."

The term "free software" is sometimes misunderstood—it has nothing to do with price. It is about freedom. Here, therefore, is the definition of free software. A program is free software, for you, a particular user, if:

You have the freedom to run the program, for any purpose.

You have the freedom to modify the program to suit your needs. (To make this freedom effective in practice, you must have access to the source code, since making changes in a program without having the source code is exceedingly difficult.)

You have the freedom to redistribute copies, either gratis or for a fee.

You have the freedom to distribute modified versions of the program, so that the community can benefit from your improvements.

In January 1984 I quit my job at MIT and began writing GNU software. Leaving MIT was necessary so that MIT would not be able to interfere with distributing GNU as free software. If I had remained on the staff, MIT could have claimed to own the work, and could have imposed their own distribution terms, or even turned the work into a proprietary software package.

I began work on GNU Emacs [a text editing program] in September 1984, and in early 1985 it was beginning to be usable … At this point, people began wanting to use GNU Emacs, which raised the question of how to distribute it. So I announced that I would mail a tape to whoever wanted one, for a fee of $150. In this way, I started a free software distribution business, the precursor of the companies that today distribute entire Linux-based GNU systems.

If a program is free software when it leaves the hands of its author, this does not necessarily mean it will be free software for everyone who has a copy of it. For example, public domain software (software that is not copyrighted) is free software; but anyone can make a proprietary modified version of it. Likewise, many free programs are copyrighted but distributed under simple permissive licenses that allow proprietary modified versions.

The goal of GNU was to give users freedom, not just to be popular. So we needed to use distribution terms that would prevent GNU software from being turned into proprietary software. The method we use is called "copyleft."

Copyleft uses copyright law, but flips it over to serve the opposite of its usual purpose: instead of a means of privatizing software, it becomes a means of keeping software free.

The central idea of copyleft is that we give everyone permission to run the program, copy the program, modify the program, and distribute modified versions—but not permission to add restrictions of their own. Thus, the crucial freedoms that define "free software" are guaranteed to everyone who has a copy; they become inalienable rights.

For an effective copyleft, modified versions must also be free. This ensures that work based on ours becomes available to our community if it is published. When programmers who have jobs as programmers volunteer to improve GNU software, it is copyleft that prevents their employers from saying, "You can't share those changes, because we are going to use them to make our proprietary version of the program."

The requirement that changes must be free is essential if we want to ensure freedom for every user of the program. The companies that privatized the X Window System usually made some changes to port it to their systems and hardware. These changes were small compared with the great extent of X, but they were not trivial. If making changes was an excuse to deny the users freedom, it would be easy for anyone to take advantage of the excuse.

A related issue concerns combining a free program with non-free code. Such a combination would inevitably be non-free; whichever freedoms are lacking for the non-free part would be lacking for the whole as well. To permit such combinations would open a hole big enough to sink a ship. Therefore, a crucial requirement for copyleft is to plug this hole: anything added to or combined with a copylefted program must be such that the larger combined version is also free and copylefted.

The specific implementation of copyleft that we use for most GNU software is the GNU General Public License, or GNU GPL for short.

As interest in using Emacs was growing, other people became involved in the GNU project, and we decided that it was time to seek funding once again. So in 1985 we created the Free Software Foundation, a tax-exempt charity for free software development. The FSF also took over the Emacs tape distribution business; later it extended this by adding other free software (both GNU and non-GNU) to the tape, and by selling free manuals as well.

The free software philosophy rejects a specific widespread business practice, but it is not against business. When businesses respect the users' freedom, we wish them success.

Selling copies of Emacs demonstrates one kind of free software business. When the FSF took over that business, I needed another way to make a living. I found it in selling services relating to the free software I had developed. This included teaching, for subjects such as how to program GNU Emacs and how to customize GCC, and software development, mostly porting GCC to new platforms.

FIGURE 19.2 Richard Stallman, founder of the free software movement, speaking in Oslo as Saint IGNUcius in 2009.

Today each of these kinds of free software business is practiced by a number of corporations. Some distribute free software collections on CD-ROM; others sell support at levels ranging from answering user questions to fixing bugs to adding major new features. We are even beginning to see free software companies based on launching new free software products.

Watch out, though—a number of companies that associate themselves with the term "Open Source" actually base their business on non-free software that works with free software. These are not free software companies, they are proprietary software companies whose products tempt users away from freedom. They call these "value added," which reflects the values they would like us to adopt: convenience above freedom.

Teaching new users about freedom became more difficult in 1998, when a part of the community decided to stop using the term "free software" and say "open source software" instead.

Some who favored this term aimed to avoid the confusion of "free" with "gratis"—a valid goal. Others, however, aimed to set aside the spirit of principle that had motivated the free software movement and the GNU project, and to appeal instead to executives and business users, many of whom hold an ideology that places profit above freedom, above community, above principle. Thus, the rhetoric of "Open Source" focuses on the potential to make high quality, powerful software, but shuns the ideas of freedom, community, and principle.

We can't take the future of freedom for granted. Don't take it for granted! If you want to keep your freedom, you must be prepared to defend it.

Notes and Questions

1. *Software and morality.* Stallman's rhetoric is steeped in notions of morality and justice. Is this moralistic attitude surprising when discussing a field such as software development? Do developers of automotive engines, chemical solvents or even chemotherapy agents speak in the same terms about their work? Why is software different? Would the software world today

look different if Richard Stallman had simply moved on to a different project at MIT instead of beginning to develop free software? Would OSS have emerged as a market phenomenon in any event?

2. *Nondisclosure.* Stallman takes great offense at the nondisclosure agreement that he was required to sign. Why?

3. *Assumptions of the software industry.* What three pre-existing assumptions does Stallman posit about the software industry? Do you think that Stallman's depiction of the realities of the software industry of the 1970s were accurate? Was his response a sensible reaction to these realities?

4. A *question of terminology.* Why does Stallman object to the use of the term "open source software"? Why do you think that many preferred this term to "free software"? Consider these questions when you read Section 19.2.2.

5. *Copyleft.* What is "copyleft"? Why does Stallman view it as fundamentally important to free software? Why does Stallman believe that it is necessary that the GPL be applied not only to redistribution of GPL programs, but to *modifications* of those programs? What does he seek to avoid? Consider these issues as you read the next section and the details of the GPL's copyleft provisions.

6. *Free software versus the public domain.* Somewhat surprisingly, Stallman did not argue that software should be contributed to the public domain. He explains that "public domain software (software that is not copyrighted) is free software; but anyone can make a proprietary modified version of it." What did he mean? Why did he prefer copyleft to the public domain?

7. *Value-added.* What does Stallman describe as "value-added" software and why does he object to it? How does this differ from the paid services that Stallman himself provided with respect to software?

19.2.2 *Defining Open Source Software*

The year 1998 was a watershed in the OSS world. The Linux operating system, created in 1991 by a twenty-one-year-old Finnish undergraduate named Linus Torvalds, was quickly becoming the operating system of choice for corporate enterprises. In that year, database vendors Oracle, Sybase and Informix all announced Linux-compatible products, and Torvalds appeared on the cover of *Forbes* magazine.[4] IBM announced that it would distribute and support the OSS Apache web server. Red Hat, a company devoted to OSS software distribution and support, was formed with backing from Intel and Netscape. And Netscape itself announced that it would release the source code for its popular Navigator web browser.

That year also saw the formation of the Open Source Initiative (OSI), an educational, advocacy and stewardship organization dedicated to open software development. The organization grew out of a February 1998 meeting in Palo Alto, California, shortly after the Netscape announcement. Among the organizers of the meeting was Eric Raymond, the author of a 1997 manifesto on open software development titled *The Cathedral and the Bazaar*. As explained on the OSI website:

> The conferees believed the pragmatic, business-case grounds that had motivated Netscape to release their code illustrated a valuable way to engage with potential software users and

---

[4] Josh McHugh, *For the Love of Hacking*, Forbes, August 10, 1998.

developers, and convince them to create and improve source code by participating in an engaged community. The conferees also believed that it would be useful to have a single label that identified this approach and distinguished it from the philosophically- and politically-focused label "free software." Brainstorming for this new label eventually converged on the term "open source"…[5]

With this new label in hand, OSI presented itself to the world as the arbiter of what constitutes an open source license, and what does not. To this end, it created a list of characteristics that it felt all open source licenses should possess and in 1999 identified fourteen such licenses that met its criteria, including the GPL, the BSD license, the Artistic License (featured in *Jacobsen v. Katzer*, discussed in Section 19.2.4) and the Mozilla Public License. These were the first OSI "certified" licenses. Since then, OSI has slightly expanded its list of characteristics to ten, and has certified over 100 different OSS licenses.[6] OSI's current list of OSS characteristics is reproduced here.

THE OPEN SOURCE DEFINITION[7]

Introduction

Open source doesn't just mean access to the source code. The distribution terms of open source software must comply with the following criteria:

1. Free Redistribution

The license shall not restrict any party from selling or giving away the software as a component of an aggregate software distribution containing programs from several different sources. The license shall not require a royalty or other fee for such sale.

2. Source Code

The program must include source code, and must allow distribution in source code as well as compiled form. Where some form of a product is not distributed with source code,

---

5   Open Source Initiative, History of the OSI, https://opensource.org/history. Immediately after the February meeting, Raymond updated *The Cathedral and the Bazaar* to replace the term "free software" with "open source." www.catb .org/esr/writings/homesteading/cathedral-bazaar/

6   See https://opensource.org/licenses/alphabetical (as of December 2, 2020, there were 105 different licenses on OSI's certification list).

7   https://opensource.org/osd.html.

there must be a well-publicized means of obtaining the source code for no more than a reasonable reproduction cost, preferably downloading via the Internet without charge. The source code must be the preferred form in which a programmer would modify the program. Deliberately obfuscated source code is not allowed. Intermediate forms such as the output of a preprocessor or translator are not allowed.

3. Derived Works

The license must allow modifications and derived works, and must allow them to be distributed under the same terms as the license of the original software.

4. Integrity of the Author's Source Code

The license may restrict source-code from being distributed in modified form only if the license allows the distribution of "patch files" with the source code for the purpose of modifying the program at build time. The license must explicitly permit distribution of software built from modified source code. The license may require derived works to carry a different name or version number from the original software.

5. No Discrimination Against Persons or Groups

The license must not discriminate against any person or group of persons.

6. No Discrimination Against Fields of Endeavor

The license must not restrict anyone from making use of the program in a specific field of endeavor. For example, it may not restrict the program from being used in a business, or from being used for genetic research.

7. Distribution of License

The rights attached to the program must apply to all to whom the program is redistributed without the need for execution of an additional license by those parties.

8. License Must Not Be Specific to a Product

The rights attached to the program must not depend on the program's being part of a particular software distribution. If the program is extracted from that distribution and used or distributed within the terms of the program's license, all parties to whom the program is redistributed should have the same rights as those that are granted in conjunction with the original software distribution.

9. License Must Not Restrict Other Software

The license must not place restrictions on other software that is distributed along with the licensed software. For example, the license must not insist that all other programs distributed on the same medium must be open source software.

10. License Must Be Technology-Neutral

No provision of the license may be predicated on any individual technology or style of interface.

Notes and Questions

1. *The OSI definition.* OSI's definition of OSS is clearly inspired by Richard Stallman's ideas, but is phrased in more neutral language. Are there any ways that the OSI definition falls short of Stallman's goals? Does the OSI definition go beyond Stallman's original ideas? Which of the ten OSI attributes of OSS do you think are the most important? The least important?

2. *Free redistribution.* There is considerable confusion in the industry over the ability to charge for OSS. OSI's Definition 1 states that an OSS license "shall not require a royalty or other fee" for the sale or reproduction of OSS software. Yet Richard Stallman himself makes it clear that a software developer may charge for OSS software and emphasizes that the term "free software" "has nothing to do with price." So what does OSI mean in Definition 1?

3. *No copyleft?* OSI's definition is notably silent on the issue of copyleft. Why is this feature of OSS, which was so important to Stallman, omitted from the OSI definition?

4. *Export controls.* OSI Definition 5 requires that OSS not discriminate against any person or group, which sounds like an admirable goal. But OSI explains that Definition 5 is intended to prevent software licensors from prohibiting the export of software to users in countries that are subject to national (i.e., US) export restrictions, such as Cuba, North Korea, Iran and the like. Why would OSI wish to ban prohibitions on such software exports, particularly if they are mandated by law?

5. *Commercial use.* Definition 6 prohibits discrimination against different business models. In particular, it prohibits OSS licenses from containing restrictions on commercial use along the lines of the Creative Commons Non-Commercial (NC) licensing model. OSI goes so far as saying that "We want commercial users to join our community, not feel excluded from it." Why doesn't OSI recognize an "NC" OSS license? Isn't this something that Richard Stallman would approve of?

6. *The anti-NDA clause.* The annotations to the OSI definition explain that Definition 7 is intended to "forbid closing up software by indirect means such as requiring a non-disclosure agreement." Is this how you originally read the definition? What problem is this clause trying to avoid?

7. *Technology neutrality.* OSI Definitions 8 and 10 seek to divorce OSS from any particular software or hardware dependencies. Why is this approach perceived as beneficial?

FIGURE 19.3   Eric Raymond, one of the founders of OSI, in 2004.

8. *OSS license proliferation.* Once OSI set itself up as a certifier of OSS licenses, it received a flood of licenses from groups seeking certification – companies, nonprofit organizations, attorneys, standards bodies and more. As OSI explains,

> This explosion of choice in licensing reflected both the interest in Open Source as well as the many particular ways in which people wanted to create and or manage their Open Source software. Unfortunately, while all of these licenses provide the freedom to read, modify, and share source code, many of the licenses were legally incompatible with other free and open source licenses, seriously constraining the ways in which developers could innovate by combining rather than merely extending Open Source software.[8]

As a result, in 2004, OSI began a process to "clear out the licensing deadwood so as to make more room (and potentially ensure greater license compatibility) for the more popular licenses." It formed a License Proliferation Committee, which produced a report in 2006 recommending that OSI-certified licenses be classified according to popularity, and that in addition to OSI's substantive criteria for determining whether licenses comply with the OSS definition, certification also take into account three additional questions: (1) Is the license duplicative? (2) Is the license clearly written, simple and understandable? And (3) is the license reusable?[9] Today, there are over 100 OSI-certified OSS licenses, but only 8 in the category "popular and widely-used or with strong communities."[10] These are:

- Apache License 2.0 (Apache-2.0)
- 3-clause BSD license (BSD-3-Clause)
- 2-clause BSD license (BSD-2-Clause)
- GNU General Public License (GPL)
- GNU Lesser General Public License (LGPL)
- MIT license (MIT)
- Mozilla Public License 2.0 (MPL-2.0)
- Common Development and Distribution License 1.0 (CDDL-1.0)
- Eclipse Public License 2.0 (EPL-2.0)

What is the problem with license proliferation? Why did the License Proliferation Committee recommend that the most popular OSI-certified licenses be identified and grouped together? When might you recommend that a client develop its own OSS license and seek OSI certification for it?

19.2.3 *The BSD Licenses*

Researchers at AT&T Bell Laboratories developed the Unix operating system in the late 1960s and liberally shared its source code with researchers at other institutions. A copy of Unix was sent to the University of California Berkeley in 1974, and in 1978 researchers there released a version of Unix known as the Berkeley Software Distribution, or BSD. Berkeley researchers released their software under various simple licensing terms, and in 1990 standardized their use around what became known as the original BSD license.

---

[8] OSI, The Licence Proliferation Project, https://opensource.org/proliferation.
[9] OSI, Report of License Proliferation Committee and Draft FAQ (2006), https://opensource.org/proliferation-report.
[10] OSI, Open Source Licenses by Category, https://opensource.org/licenses/category.

FIGURE 19.4 A "daemon" is a type of software agent. This demon
in sneakers came to be associated with the BSD project.

The original BSD license contained four short clauses plus a disclaimer of warranties and limitation of liability. One of those clauses (#3) caused considerable consternation in the industry. It read:

3. All advertising materials mentioning features or use of this software must display the following acknowledgement: This product includes software developed by the <organization>.

The problem with the so-called "advertising clause" was its cumulative effect. That is, when a developer used a piece of BSD code distributed by Berkeley, it was not burdensome to include a one-sentence acknowledgment of Berkeley in the ad. But when that developer passed along its software to someone else, who passed it along to someone else, and so on, the number of required acknowledgments quickly outnumbered the actual text of any advertisement. Richard Stallman claims that he counted seventy-five such notices in a 1997 software program released under this license.[11] As a result, Berkeley amended the BSD license in 1999 to remove the advertising clause.

This left a version of the BSD license with three clauses, which became known as the Revised or Modified BSD License. An even simpler version containing just one clause (in addition to the disclaimers) was also released in 1999.

BSD 1-CLAUSE LICENSE (AKA SIMPLIFIED BSD LICENSE)

Copyright (c) [Year]
[Name of Organization] [All rights reserved].
Redistribution and use in source and binary forms, with or without modification, are permitted provided that the following conditions are met:

Redistributions of source code must retain the above copyright notice, this list of conditions and the following disclaimer.

---

11   Richard Stallman, The BSD License Problem, www.gnu.org/licenses/bsd.html

THIS SOFTWARE IS PROVIDED BY [Name of Organization] "AS IS" AND ANY EXPRESS OR IMPLIED WARRANTIES, INCLUDING, BUT NOT LIMITED TO, THE IMPLIED WARRANTIES OF MERCHANTABILITY AND FITNESS FOR A PARTICULAR PURPOSE ARE DISCLAIMED. IN NO EVENT SHALL [Name of Organization] BE LIABLE FOR ANY DIRECT, INDIRECT, INCIDENTAL, SPECIAL, EXEMPLARY, OR CONSEQUENTIAL DAMAGES (INCLUDING, BUT NOT LIMITED TO, PROCUREMENT OF SUBSTITUTE GOODS OR SERVICES; LOSS OF USE, DATA, OR PROFITS; OR BUSINESS INTERRUPTION) HOWEVER CAUSED AND ON ANY THEORY OF LIABILITY, WHETHER IN CONTRACT, STRICT LIABILITY, OR TORT (INCLUDING NEGLIGENCE OR OTHERWISE) ARISING IN ANY WAY OUT OF THE USE OF THIS SOFTWARE, EVEN IF ADVISED OF THE POSSIBILITY OF SUCH DAMAGE.

BSD 3-CLAUSE LICENSE (AKA REVISED OR MODIFIED BSD LICENSE)

Copyright <YEAR> <COPYRIGHT HOLDER>
Redistribution and use in source and binary forms, with or without modification, are permitted provided that the following conditions are met:

1. Redistributions of source code must retain the above copyright notice, this list of conditions and the following disclaimer.
2. Redistributions in binary form must reproduce the above copyright notice, this list of conditions and the following disclaimer in the documentation and/or other materials provided with the distribution.
3. Neither the name of the copyright holder nor the names of its contributors may be used to endorse or promote products derived from this software without specific prior written permission.

THIS SOFTWARE IS PROVIDED BY THE COPYRIGHT HOLDERS AND CONTRIBUTORS "AS IS" AND ANY EXPRESS OR IMPLIED WARRANTIES, INCLUDING, BUT NOT LIMITED TO, THE IMPLIED WARRANTIES OF MERCHANTABILITY AND FITNESS FOR A PARTICULAR PURPOSE ARE DISCLAIMED. IN NO EVENT SHALL THE COPYRIGHT HOLDER OR CONTRIBUTORS BE LIABLE FOR ANY DIRECT, INDIRECT, INCIDENTAL, SPECIAL, EXEMPLARY, OR CONSEQUENTIAL DAMAGES (INCLUDING, BUT NOT LIMITED TO, PROCUREMENT OF SUBSTITUTE GOODS OR SERVICES; LOSS OF USE, DATA, OR PROFITS; OR BUSINESS INTERRUPTION) HOWEVER CAUSED AND ON ANY THEORY OF LIABILITY, WHETHER IN CONTRACT, STRICT LIABILITY, OR TORT (INCLUDING NEGLIGENCE OR OTHERWISE) ARISING IN ANY WAY OUT OF THE USE OF THIS SOFTWARE, EVEN IF ADVISED OF THE POSSIBILITY OF SUCH DAMAGE.

The BSD licenses were among the first to be certified by OSI. Today, the BSD licenses are widely used, largely because of their simplicity and their lack of restrictions and obligations. They contain no copyleft or other burdensome restrictions or obligations. To use an analogy from the world of real property conveyances, the BSD licenses most closely resemble quitclaim deeds – they allow any use of the licensed software in source and object code forms, and release the provider from all liability. As we will see below, this simplified approach diverged significantly from that of Richard Stallman and the Free Software Foundation (FSF).

Notes and Questions

1. *BSD and OSI compliance?* OSI lists ten elements that define OSS licenses. The BSD licenses were among the first that it certified in 1999. How do the BSD licenses embody the ten OSI definitional elements?
2. *Attribution.* As discussed in Section 19.1 (Note 4), creators of copyrighted works are most interested in getting credit for their work, even if they give it away for free. The BSD and most other OSS licenses (including the GNU GPL) provide for attribution by requiring that subsequent distributors of OSS software reproduce any copyright notices that are included in the original source code. The theory is that when a user modifies a portion of that code, it should add itself to the copyright notice, thereby accumulating a list of all contributors to the code. Is this a sensible approach to attribution? Why don't OSS licenses use the simpler approach exemplified by the CC BY licensing tag?
3. *Corporate appropriation?* The BSD licenses contain no copyleft requirement, meaning that a recipient of BSD-licensed code can take that code, modify it and include it in a proprietary software program distributed under a traditional, non-OSS license. In other words, code that was once OSS can be appropriated and turned into proprietary code. Not surprisingly, the FSF and other OSS advocates objected strongly to this possibility. But it has made the BSD license extremely popular among corporate users of OSS. Do you think that the original BSD license drafters at UC Berkeley were right to omit a copyleft provision or not? How does the historical development of BSD (as opposed to the GNU project) help to explain why this approach was chosen?
4. *Disclaimers.* The BSD licenses are famously (and refreshingly) short. In fact, the majority of their text is devoted to a disclaimer of warranties and limitation of liability. Why are liability disclaimers the focus of these agreements? How do these liability provisions differ between the 1-Clause and 3-Clause BSD licenses?

19.2.4 *The GNU General Public License*

Without a doubt, the most famous and infamous OSS license is the Free Software Foundation's (FSF) GNU General Public License (GPL). Richard Stallman released version 1 of the GPL in February 1989. The agreement embodied the principles of freedom and copyleft that he espoused when creating the GNU project. The original GPL was short by the standards of IP licensing agreements, running to just over 1,600 words. Version 2, which added some corrections and clarifications, was released in 1991 and amounted to around 2,500 words. GPL v2 was adopted broadly by many significant OSS projects, most notably the Linux operating system. And even though Stallman was not part of the OSI project, and in fact vocally objected to its rejection of his "free software" terminology, the GPL heavily influenced OSI's definition of OSS and GPL v2 was the first OSS license to be certified by OSI.

But over the years, as the law and norms of the software industry evolved, GPL v2 started to become outdated. Concerns emerged over how the GPL should handle developments such as the Digital Millennium Copyright Act (DMCA) of 1998, digital rights management, software patents and compatibility with the dozens of new OSS licenses being certified by OSI. As a result, in 2005 the FSF began a public consultation process to update the GPL. Over the eighteen-month consultation period, more than 2,600 written comments were submitted. GPL v3 was released in June 2007, comprising over 5,200 words.

GPL v3 was controversial for a number of reasons, including its treatment of patents and digital rights management. As a result, many OSS projects, including Linux, declined to "upgrade" from GPL v2 to v3 (more on this below). Nevertheless, the GPL licenses, principally v2 and v3, remain important documents in the OSS ecosystem. Their language is, however, notoriously turgid and requires a significant amount of background knowledge and lore to parse. For this reason, it is not reproduced here. Instead, some of its more significant and controversial provisions are summarized and discussed below.[12]

19.2.4.1 Access to Source Code

The *sine qua non* of OSS licensing is the availability of the source code underlying a computer program. The GPL, which was created with the goal of source code availability in mind, contains detailed prescriptions on when and how source code must be provided or made available to recipients of the software. Importantly, the requirement to deliver source code can be met in a variety of ways, including by providing a physical disc or other medium, making it available for download from a network server or peer-to-peer service or, if the software is embedded in a physical device, extending a written offer valid for three years to provide such source code.

19.2.4.2 Copyleft: The "Viral" Nature of GPL

Today, the GPL is probably best known for the "viral" effect of its copyleft provisions. That is, if a piece of software is distributed under the GPL, then anyone who redistributes that software, *or any modified version of that software*, must also distribute it under the GPL. Thus, like a biological virus, the GPL propagates itself from user to user. But the real threat perceived by the GPL was not the continuing need to license GPL'd code under the GPL, but the risk that the GPL'd code could infect any proprietary code with which it was combined, making the entire combined work subject to the GPL.

To be specific, § 5(c) of the GPL provides that "You must license the entire work, as a whole, under this License to anyone who comes into possession of a copy." Section 0 defines a "covered work" as "either the unmodified Program or a work based on the Program," and provides that to

---

¹² The interested student may find the full text of GPL v3 (and prior versions of the GPL) at www.gnu.org/licenses/gpl-3.0.en.html.

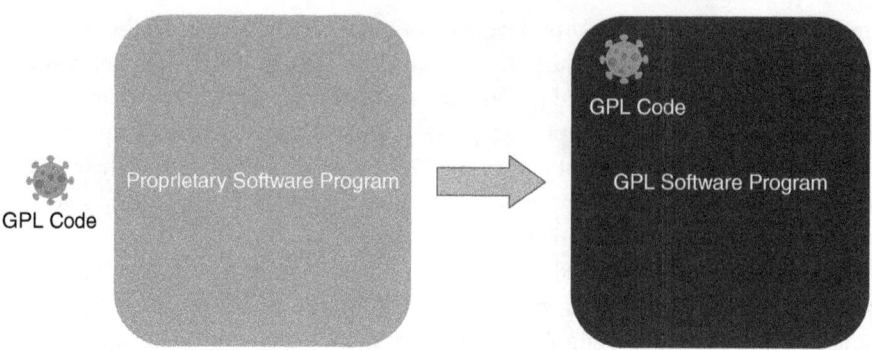

FIGURE 19.5 Graphical illustration of the perceived "viral effect" of GPL software combined with proprietary software. OSS advocates claim that representations like this overstate the risk of using GPL software.

"modify" a work means "to copy from or adapt all or part of the work in a fashion requiring copyright permission, other than the making of an exact copy. The resulting work is called a 'modified version' of the earlier work or a work 'based on' the earlier work." While these provisions, read together, are less than clear, they are generally understood to mean that a larger program that incorporates GPL'd software should itself become subject to the GPL.

This being said, the GPL does recognize an exception of "mere aggregation" of separate works on the same "storage or distribution medium." Thus, distributing a proprietary program and a GPL program on the same CD would not "infect" the proprietary program with the GPL. This exception, however, has given cold comfort to commercial users, who are generally more concerned with proprietary programs that might actually call or access the GPL'd code.

19.2.4.3 Anti-Anti-Circumvention

The enactment of the DMCA in 1998 galled many in the OSS and hacker communities, particularly the "anti-circumvention" provisions of 17 U.S.C. § 1201. These provisions made it illegal to attempt to circumvent any "technological measure that effectively controls access to a [copyrighted] work." As such, the DMCA prohibited the hacking of encryption and digital rights management protections. In response, GPL v3 expressly states that any software code covered by the GPL will *not* be deemed to be part of such a technological measure. In other words, it ensured that no one would be liable for hacking any code covered by the GPL, whether it was used in a protection system or not.

19.2.4.4 Anti-Tivoization

In 1999, TiVo released one of the first consumer digital video recorders (DVR), which allowed viewers to make digital recordings of broadcast television programs. As a significant improvement over tape-based VCR machines, the TiVo DVR became incredibly popular. It incorporated the Linux kernel, which was licensed under GPL v2. But because the Linux software controlled a complex hardware device, TiVo prevented users from uploading modified versions of the Linux software to the DVR. This restriction infuriated the FSF and Richard Stallman, who claimed that TiVo had violated the GPL in spirit, if not in fact. So when GPL v3 was proposed in 2005, it contained a provision that became known as the "Anti-Tivoization" clause. The lengthy clause, which is included in Section 6 of GPL v3, was heavily negotiated and bears

FIGURE 19.6 In 1999 TiVo introduced the first successful mass-market DVR device. It ran the Linux kernel.

the signs of a Frankenstein contractual clause negotiated by committee. In effect, it requires that consumer hardware devices intended for home use (i.e., not equipment used in hospitals, factories, etc.) allow end users to upload modified versions of GPL software, so long as this will not interfere with their operation. It also permits the manufacturer to void warranties and service commitments when modified software is installed.

There were significant objections to the Anti-Tivoization clause, including by Linus Torvalds, the creator of Linux. Torvalds believed that hardware manufacturers were entitled to prevent users from uploading modified software to their hardware products, and didn't see why doing so violated the OSS spirit. As a result, Torvalds never "upgraded" the Linux license from GPL v2 to v3 (and Linux remains under v2 today).

19.2.4.5 Patentleft

The preface to the GPL states that "every program is threatened constantly by software patents." But concerns about patents and OSS are not unique to the FSF and OSS advocates. Professor Greg Vetter points out that patent law may be "particularly threatening" to [OSS] for a variety of reasons.[13] And IBM, the holder of one of the largest patent portfolios in the world, observed in 2005 that

> Patents ... must be considered when OSS is developed. When OSS is created and licensed, it must, as a practical matter, carry with it a grant of license to any patents concerning the software that the author holds. Doing otherwise creates an untenable situation, wherein any users of that OSS may become inadvertent infringers of the patent. Some licenses ... include an explicit grant of a patent license, but most do not.[14]

To address patent issues, "the GPL assures that patents cannot be used to render [a] program non-free." How, exactly, does the GPL do this? In typical fashion, the answer is complex. It involves four parts, all contained in § 11 of the GPL:

i.   *Present and Future Patent License.* Section 11, ¶ 2 describes "essential patent claims" as all patent claims owned or controlled by a contributor to the licensed code currently or in the future. Under ¶ 3, each such contributor grants to each user of the code

[13] Greg R. Vetter, *Commercial Free and Open Source Software: Knowledge Production, Hybrid Appropriability, and Patents*, 77 Fordham L. Rev. 2087, 2093 (2009).
[14] Peter G. Capek, et al., *A History of IBM's Open-Source Involvement and Strategy*, 44 IBM Syst. J. 249 (2005).

a non-exclusive, worldwide, royalty-free patent license under the contributor's essential patent claims, to make, use, sell, offer for sale, import and otherwise run, modify and propagate the contents of its contributor version.

The GPL thus makes it clear that a patent holder who distributes software under the GPL ("Licensor") cannot later sue users of that software for patent infringement.

One concern with this provision is that it covers not only the software contribution made by the licensor, but all other software contained in the relevant GPL program. Thus, if a licensor obtains a GPL program to which seventy-five previous contributors have contributed, then modifies it and redistributes it under the GPL, the licensor's patents are licensed with respect to the entire GPL program, even the portions written by the other seventy-five contributors. This is the case even if some of those other contributors were intentionally infringing the licensor's patents.[15]

ii. *Third Party Licenses.* In addition to the patent license described above, Section 11, ¶ 5 addresses patents held by third parties. It provides that:

> If you convey a covered work, knowingly relying on a patent license, and the Corresponding Source of the work is not available for anyone to copy, free of charge and under the terms of this License, through a publicly available network server or other readily accessible means, then you must either (1) cause the Corresponding Source to be so available, or (2) arrange to deprive yourself of the benefit of the patent license for this particular work, or (3) arrange, in a manner consistent with the requirements of this License, to extend the patent license to downstream recipients.

> Thus, if a licensor of GPL code has the benefit of a license under a third-party patent, and recipients of that GPL code do not have the right to operate under that third-party patent license (i.e., the licensor does not have the right to sublicense), then the licensor must do one of three things. The first and third options are effectively the same: the licensor must extend the rights under the patent license to all users of the GPL code on a royalty-free basis (i.e., "under the terms of this License"). In most cases, this will be impossible. This leaves the licensor with option 2, under which it must disavow the benefits of the patent license with respect to itself. How it would do this is unclear, but the idea, presumably, is that the licensor will be motivated to find ways to extend patent licenses or sublicenses to users of the GPL code if it is itself stripped of the benefit of its patent licenses.

iii. *No One-Off Patent Licenses.* Section 11, ¶ 6 addresses a situation in which a licensor grants a patent license to some (but not all) parties receiving a piece of GPL code (e.g., in a litigation settlement). If that happens, then the license "is automatically extended to all recipients of the covered work and works based on it." Again, it is not clear how this automatic expansion of rights would legally occur, but it will certainly make licensors think twice before granting one-off patent licensors to recipients of GPL code.

---

[15] The GPL is not unique in requiring a broad patent license covering an entire product, as opposed to the licensor's contributions. The Mozilla Public License takes a similar approach. In contrast, the Apache 2.0 license contains a patent license that is limited to the licensor's contributions:

each Contributor hereby grants to You a perpetual, worldwide, non-exclusive, no-charge, royalty-free, irrevocable (except as stated in this section) patent license to make, have made, use, offer to sell, sell, import, and otherwise transfer the Work, where such license applies only to those patent claims licensable by such Contributor that are necessarily infringed by their Contribution(s) alone or by combination of their Contribution(s) with the Work to which such Contribution(s) was submitted.

iv. *Discriminatory Licenses.* Section 11, ¶ 7 seeks to eliminate the benefits that Licensors and selected users might receive from cross-licenses and other private arrangements. As one commentator explains:

> Section 11(7) stemmed from a 2006 cross-licensing agreement between Microsoft and Novell. As a result of this agreement, Microsoft and Novell customers were granted protection against the other party's patent claims. Section 11(7) was incorporated into the draft licence text at the time; it is a narrow clause which is tailored at such cross-licensing agreements. It covers only one of numerous possible cases which can be easily circumvented by minor modifications made by the affected entities.[16]

Notes and Questions

1. *The SaaS loophole and the Affero General Public License.* The GPL requires that anyone who "conveys" software covered by the GPL to another must provide the recipient with the source code of that software. But the GPL contains an important exception stating that "Mere interaction with a user through a computer network, with no transfer of a copy, is not conveying." That is, an entity's use of GPL-licensed software *to provide services to others* does not constitute a conveyance, so long as software code is not actually transferred to the service recipient. This "loophole" allows firms to obtain software under the GPL, modify its source code, then make that modified software remotely available to users on a "software as a service" (SaaS) basis (see Section 18.3), all while avoiding the obligation to make their own source code modifications publicly available. The appearance of this "SaaS loophole" in GPL v3 (also known as the "ASP" [application service provider] loophole) shocked many in the OSS community, and seemed to contradict the fundamental "open source" precepts of the FSF.[17] Yet, through the difficult negotiation and public commenting process that led to GPL v3, it remained. The concession to OSS purists was the concurrent release in 2007 of the GNU Affero General Public License, a version of the GPL that closes the SaaS loophole by providing that

> if you modify the Program, your modified version must prominently offer all users interacting with it remotely through a computer network (if your version supports such interaction) an opportunity to receive the Corresponding Source of your version by providing access to the Corresponding Source from a network server at no charge, through some standard or customary means of facilitating copying of software.

The degree to which the Affero GPL has been adopted is uncertain. Some commentators see evidence that it is gaining in popularity.[18] Yet major online service providers such as Google have reportedly banned its use.[19] How would you advise a client that is interested in offering a SaaS environment using OSS? Would you recommend avoiding or embracing the Affero GPL?

---

[16] Hendrick Schöttle, *Open Source Software and Patents: How the GPLv3 Affects Patent Portfolios*, Intl. L. Off., February 5, 2013, www.internationallawoffice.com/Newsletters/Tech-Data-Telecoms-Media/International/Osborne-Clarke/Open-source-software-and-patents-how-the-GPLv3-affects-patent-portfolios.

[17] Richard Stallman has written at length about the nonfree nature of SaaS services. Richard Stallman, *Who Does That Server Really Serve?*, www.gnu.org/philosophy/who-does-that-server-really-serve.en.html.

[18] Phil Odence, *The Quietly Accelerating Adoption of the AGPL*, August 14, 2017, www.synopsys.com/blogs/software-security/using-agpl-adoption.

[19] Cade Metz, *Google Open Source Guru: "Why We Ban the AGPL,"* March 31, 2011, www.theregister.com/2011/03/31/google_on_open_source_licenses.

2. *The LGPL.* When the FSF released GPL v2 in 1991, it also released a licensing agreement called the "Library GPL" or LGPL. The LGPL was intended to be used with software "libraries" – standalone software modules used to perform discrete functions, such as time zone conversions or the calculation of square roots. Libraries can be used by application programs such as databases, spreadsheets and word processors, but remain relatively independent of these larger programs.

In the early days, commercial software developers were reluctant to use libraries released under the GPL because they were concerned that "linking" a commercial program to the library would cause the entire linked body of software (application plus library) to become GPL software (i.e., through the viral effect of the GPL's copyleft provisions). To address this concern, the FSF developed the LGPL.

For most purposes, a software library released under the LGPL is treated just like software released under the ordinary GPL. The source code of the library is provided to users, and if it is modified, the modified source code is also covered by the LGPL. The major difference between the LGPL and the ordinary GPL is how they treat other programs that are "linked" to the covered software. Section 5 of the original LGPL provided that

A program that contains no derivative of any portion of the Library, but is designed to work with the Library by being compiled or linked with it, is called a "work that uses the Library". Such a work, in isolation, is not a derivative work of the Library, and therefore falls outside the scope of this License.[20]

Thus, if I create a time zone utility and release it as a library under the LGPL, and UPS wishes to use this utility in its proprietary delivery scheduling software, the LGPL library will not "contaminate" UPS's proprietary software so long as my library is kept separate from the proprietary software.

This exception to the copyleft feature of the GPL was enthusiastically welcomed by corporate software developers. Now they could use OSS libraries without the risk of contaminating their proprietary software. But it was perhaps this very enthusiasm that caused the FSF to step back from the LGPL licensing model. When it updated the LGPL in 1999, it changed its name from the "Library GPL" to the "*Lesser* GPL" and published a warning to developers titled "Why you shouldn't use the Lesser GPL for your next library."[21]

Given the importance of distinguishing between a work that "uses" an LGPL library and a work "based on" an LGPL library, a significant amount of lore and guidance has developed over the years, most of which is comprehensible only to computer programmers (and then only partially). For example, much of the debate focuses on whether a proprietary software program links with an LGPL library in a manner that is "static" (embedding the library into the code of the proprietary program) or "dynamic" (where a proprietary program accesses the library "on the fly" as it is executed). Many commentators argue that dynamic linking should not result in a combined program "based on" the library, while static linking *could* result in a combined program subject to the copyleft terms of the LGPL. But the FSF itself seems to take the position that *both* static and dynamic linking create such a combined program.[22] While the issue has never been litigated, many companies continue to view the LGPL as a relatively "safe" OSS license.

---

[20] Later versions of the LGPL have altered (and obfuscated) this text substantially.

[21] Free Software Fndn, *Why You Shouldn't Use the Lesser GPL for Your Next Library*, 1999, www.gnu.org/licenses/why-not-lgpl.html.

[22] See Michael Pavento, *A Practical Guide to Open Source Software* 3–4 (2012) (the linking debate).

Why do you think the FSF discourages use of its own LGPL? If the FSF dislikes the LGPL so much, why didn't it revoke the license entirely, instead of reissuing it with a warning? As an attorney advising a software client, how would you explain the LGPL and its potential effect when the OSS community and the FSF themselves cannot seem to agree on its precise meaning?

3. *The GPL and patents.* GPL v3 contains more patent-related language than any other OSS license and seeks rights well beyond the straightforward, though broad, patent license contained in § 11, ¶ 3. Why are the additional rights under ¶¶ 5, 6 and 7 needed? What would be the effect of eliminating these provisions from the GPL?

4. *Implied patent licenses.* Unlike the GPL, the BSD licenses contain no provisions relating to patents. Is it likely that someone distributing software under the BSD license could later sue users for patent infringement? GPL v2 likewise contains no explicit patent license, but commentators have suggested that users of GPL v2 code would have a strong implied license argument if the distributor later sued them for patent infringement.[23] And § 11, ¶ 8 of the GPL v3 itself states that nothing in the GPL "shall be construed as excluding or limiting any implied license or other defenses to infringement that may otherwise be available to you under applicable patent law." Does a user of OSS software licensed under these different licenses have an implied license under the patents of the OSS licensor? If so, what is the likely scope of this implied license? Why do you think the FSF included so much language about patents in GPL v3 if implied licenses were already understood to exist under OSS programs, including under GPL v2? (See Chapter 4 for a discussion of implied licenses.)

5. *Microsoft and the Linux patent litigation.* The FSF was somewhat vindicated in its worries about patents when, in 2009, Microsoft began to file patent infringement suits, first against electronics manufacturers using the Linux kernel, and later against mobile device makers using the Android operating system. According to one estimate, Microsoft earned $3.4 billion from patent licenses on Android, including $1 billion from Samsung alone.[24] As noted above, Linux and its variants (including Android) are licensed under GPL v2, which lacks the patent clauses of GPL v3. But Microsoft, which was not a major contributor to these OSS projects, would not likely have been subject to the patent licensing provisions of GPL v3 even if they had applied. What, if anything, could the FSF have done to prevent Microsoft's litigation campaign?[25]

6. *Defensive termination.* The Apache License 2.0, which grants a patent license more limited in scope than that under GPL v3, § 11, ¶ 3, contains a provision that is not found in the GPL. Section 3 of the Apache License provides that

> If You institute patent litigation against any entity (including a cross-claim or counterclaim in a lawsuit) alleging that the Work or a Contribution incorporated within the Work constitutes direct or contributory patent infringement, then any patent licenses granted to You under this License for that Work shall terminate as of the date such litigation is filed.

23 Pavento, *supra* note 21, at 8.
24 See Steven J. Vaughan-Nichols, *Microsoft Open-Sources Its Patent Portfolio*, ZDNet, October 10, 2018, www.zdnet .com/article/microsoft-open-sources-its-entire-patent-portfolio.
25 In 2018, Microsoft reversed course and joined the Open Innovation Platform, pledging to allow rivals to operate under 60,000 Microsoft patents relating to Linux without charge. Klint Finley, *Microsoft Calls a Truce in the Linux Patent Wars*, Wired, November 10, 2018.

This is called a "defensive termination" clause. It results in the automatic termination of the patent licenses granted by the OSS licensor if the user sues the licensor for patent infringement with respect to the licensed OSS. Why do you think such a clause is not included in the GPL? (See Section 20.1.4 for a discussion of defensive termination in the context of licenses of standards-essential patents.) Note that copyright licenses are not terminated by this provision. Why not?

19.2.5 *Enforcement of OSS Licenses*

In the discussion of OSS licenses to this point, we have assumed that such licenses are binding and enforceable legal agreements. Yet this was not always clear. There have been a handful of cases in the United States and Europe interpreting and enforcing the terms of OSS licenses.[26] The following is among the best known of these.

Jacobsen v. Katzer

535 F.3d 1373 (Fed. Cir. 2008)

HOCHBERG, DISTRICT JUDGE (by designation)

We consider here the ability of a copyright holder to dedicate certain work to free public use and yet enforce an "open source" copyright license to control the future distribution and modification of that work. Appellant Robert Jacobsen ("Jacobsen") appeals from an order denying a motion for preliminary injunction. Jacobsen holds a copyright to computer programming code. He makes that code available for public download from a website without a financial fee pursuant to the Artistic License, an "open source" or public license. Appellees Matthew Katzer and Kamind Associates, Inc. (collectively "Katzer/Kamind") develop commercial software products for the model train industry and hobbyists. Jacobsen accused Katzer/Kamind of copying certain materials from Jacobsen's website and incorporating them into one of Katzer/Kamind's software packages without following the terms of the Artistic License. Jacobsen brought an action for copyright infringement and moved for a preliminary injunction.

The District Court held that the open source Artistic License created an "intentionally broad" nonexclusive license which was unlimited in scope and thus did not create liability for copyright infringement [and] denied the motion for a preliminary injunction. We vacate and remand.

I

Jacobsen manages an open source software group called Java Model Railroad Interface ("JMRI"). Through the collective work of many participants, JMRI created a computer programming application called DecoderPro, which allows model railroad enthusiasts to use their computers to program the decoder chips that control model trains. DecoderPro files are available for download and use by the public free of charge from an open source incubator website called SourceForge; Jacobsen maintains the JMRI site on SourceForge.

---

[26] For an only slightly outdated compendium of cases, see Heather J. Meeker, *Open Source and the Age of Enforcement*, 4 Hastings Sci. & Tech. L.J. 267 (2012).

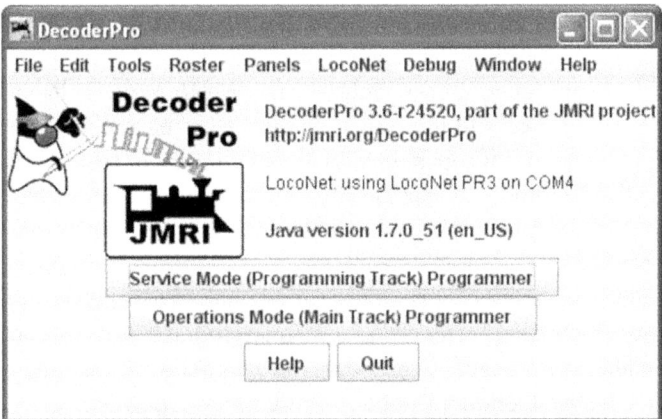

FIGURE 19.7 Screenshot from the DecoderPro model railroad control software released by Jacobsen for the JMRI project.

The downloadable files contain copyright notices and refer the user to a "COPYING" file, which clearly sets forth the terms of the Artistic License.

Katzer/Kamind offers a competing software product, Decoder Commander, which is also used to program decoder chips. During development of Decoder Commander, one of Katzer/Kamind's predecessors or employees is alleged to have downloaded the decoder definition files from DecoderPro and used portions of these files as part of the Decoder Commander software. The Decoder Commander software files that used DecoderPro definition files did not comply with the terms of the Artistic License. Specifically, the Decoder Commander software did not include (1) the authors' names, (2) JMRI copyright notices, (3) references to the COPYING file, (4) an identification of SourceForge or JMRI as the original source of the definition files, and (5) a description of how the files or computer code had been changed from the original source code. The Decoder Commander software also changed various computer file names of DecoderPro files without providing a reference to the original JMRI files or information on where to get the Standard Version.

Jacobsen moved for a preliminary injunction, arguing that the violation of the terms of the Artistic License constituted copyright infringement and that, under Ninth Circuit law, irreparable harm could be presumed in a copyright infringement case. The District Court found that Jacobsen had a cause of action only for breach of contract, rather than an action for copyright infringement based on a breach of the conditions of the Artistic License. Because a breach of contract creates no presumption of irreparable harm, the District Court denied the motion for a preliminary injunction.

Jacobsen appeals the finding that he does not have a cause of action for copyright infringement. Although an appeal concerning copyright law and not patent law is rare in our Circuit, here we indeed possess appellate jurisdiction. In the district court, Jacobsen's operative complaint against Katzer/Kamind included not only his claim for copyright infringement, but also claims seeking a declaratory judgment that a patent issued to Katzer is not infringed by Jacobsen and is invalid. Therefore the complaint arose in part under the patent laws.

II. A

Public licenses, often referred to as "open source" licenses, are used by artists, authors, educators, software developers, and scientists who wish to create collaborative projects and to dedicate certain works to the public. Several types of public licenses have been designed to provide creators of copyrighted materials a means to protect and control their copyrights. Creative Commons, one of the amici curiae, provides free copyright licenses to allow parties to dedicate their works to the public or to license certain uses of their works while keeping some rights reserved.

Open source licensing has become a widely used method of creative collaboration that serves to advance the arts and sciences in a manner and at a pace that few could have imagined just a few decades ago. For example, the Massachusetts Institute of Technology ("MIT") uses a Creative Commons public license for an OpenCourseWare project that licenses all 1800 MIT courses. Other public licenses support the GNU/Linux operating system, the Perl programming language, the Apache web server programs, the Firefox web browser, and a collaborative web-based encyclopedia called Wikipedia. Creative Commons notes that, by some estimates, there are close to 100,000,000 works licensed under various Creative Commons licenses. The Wikimedia Foundation, another of the amici curiae, estimates that the Wikipedia website has more than 75,000 active contributors working on some 9,000,000 articles in more than 250 languages.

Open Source software projects invite computer programmers from around the world to view software code and make changes and improvements to it. Through such collaboration, software programs can often be written and debugged faster and at lower cost than if the copyright holder were required to do all of the work independently. In exchange and in consideration for this collaborative work, the copyright holder permits users to copy, modify and distribute the software code subject to conditions that serve to protect downstream users and to keep the code accessible. By requiring that users copy and restate the license and attribution information, a copyright holder can ensure that recipients of the redistributed computer code know the identity of the owner as well as the scope of the license granted by the original owner. The Artistic License in this case also requires that changes to the computer code be tracked so that downstream users know what part of the computer code is the original code created by the copyright holder and what part has been newly added or altered by another collaborator.

Traditionally, copyright owners sold their copyrighted material in exchange for money. The lack of money changing hands in open source licensing should not be presumed to mean that there is no economic consideration, however. There are substantial benefits, including economic benefits, to the creation and distribution of copyrighted works under public licenses that range far beyond traditional license royalties. For example, program creators may generate market share for their programs by providing certain components free of charge. Similarly, a programmer or company may increase its national or international reputation by incubating open source projects. Improvement to a product can come rapidly and free of charge from an expert not even known to the copyright holder. The Eleventh Circuit has recognized the economic motives inherent in public licenses, even where profit is not immediate. See *Planetary Motion, Inc. v. Techsplosion, Inc.*, 261 F.3d 1188, 1200 (11th Cir. 2001) (Program creator "derived value from the distribution [under a public license] because he was able to improve his Software based on suggestions sent by end-users ... It is logical that as the Software improved, more end-users used his Software, thereby increasing [the programmer's] recognition in his profession and the likelihood that the Software would be improved even further.").

B

The parties do not dispute that Jacobsen is the holder of a copyright for certain materials distributed through his website. Katzer/Kamind also admits that portions of the DecoderPro software were copied, modified, and distributed as part of the Decoder Commander software. Accordingly, Jacobsen has made out a prima facie case of copyright infringement. Katzer/Kamind argues that they cannot be liable for copyright infringement because they had a license to use the material. Thus, the Court must evaluate whether the use by Katzer/Kamind was outside the scope of the license. The copyrighted materials in this case are downloadable by any user and are labeled to include a copyright notification and a COPYING file that includes the text of the Artistic License. The Artistic License grants users the right to copy, modify, and distribute the software:

> provided that [the user] insert a prominent notice in each changed file stating how and when [the user] changed that file, and provided that [the user] do at least ONE of the following:

a) place [the user's] modifications in the Public Domain or otherwise make them Freely Available, such as by posting said modifications to Usenet or an equivalent medium, or placing the modifications on a major archive site such as ftp.uu.net, or by allowing the Copyright Holder to include [the user's] modifications in the Standard Version of the Package.
b) use the modified Package only within [the user's] corporation or organization.
c) rename any non-standard executables so the names do not conflict with the standard executables, which must also be provided, and provide a separate manual page for each nonstandard executable that clearly documents how it differs from the Standard Version, or
d) make other distribution arrangements with the Copyright Holder.

The heart of the argument on appeal concerns whether the terms of the Artistic License are conditions of, or merely covenants to, the copyright license. Generally, a "copyright owner who grants a nonexclusive license to use his copyrighted material waives his right to sue the licensee for copyright infringement" and can sue only for breach of contract. If, however, a license is limited in scope and the licensee acts outside the scope, the licensor can bring an action for copyright infringement.

Thus, if the terms of the Artistic License allegedly violated are both covenants and conditions, they may serve to limit the scope of the license and are governed by copyright law. If they are merely covenants, by contrast, they are governed by contract law. The District Court did not expressly state whether the limitations in the Artistic License are independent covenants or, rather, conditions to the scope; its analysis, however, clearly treated the license limitations as contractual covenants rather than conditions of the copyright license.

Jacobsen argues that the terms of the Artistic License define the scope of the license and that any use outside of these restrictions is copyright infringement. Katzer/Kamind argues that these terms do not limit the scope of the license and are merely covenants providing contractual terms for the use of the materials, and that his violation of them is neither compensable in damages nor subject to injunctive relief. Katzer/Kamind's argument is premised upon the assumption that Jacobsen's copyright gave him no economic rights because he made his computer code available to the public at no charge. From this assumption, Katzer/Kamind argues that copyright law does not recognize a cause of action for non-economic rights. The District Court based its opinion on the breadth of the Artistic License terms, to which we now turn.

III

The Artistic License states on its face that the document creates conditions: "The intent of this document is to state the conditions under which a Package may be copied." The Artistic License also uses the traditional language of conditions by noting that the rights to copy, modify, and distribute are granted "provided that" the conditions are met. Under California contract law, "provided that" typically denotes a condition.

The conditions set forth in the Artistic License are vital to enable the copyright holder to retain the ability to benefit from the work of downstream users. By requiring that users who modify or distribute the copyrighted material retain the reference to the original source files, downstream users are directed to Jacobsen's website. Thus, downstream users know about the collaborative effort to improve and expand the SourceForge project once they learn of the "upstream" project from a "downstream" distribution, and they may join in that effort.

The District Court interpreted the Artistic License to permit a user to "modify the material in any way" and did not find that any of the "provided that" limitations in the Artistic License served to limit this grant. The District Court's interpretation of the conditions of the Artistic License does not credit the explicit restrictions in the license that govern a downloader's right to modify and distribute the copyrighted work. The copyright holder here expressly stated the terms upon which the right to modify and distribute the material depended and invited direct contact if a downloader wished to negotiate other terms. These restrictions were both clear and necessary to accomplish the objectives of the open source licensing collaboration, including economic benefit. Moreover, the District Court did not address the other restrictions of the license, such as the requirement that all modification from the original be clearly shown with a new name and a separate page for any such modification that shows how it differs from the original.

Copyright holders who engage in open source licensing have the right to control the modification and distribution of copyrighted material. As the Second Circuit explained in *Gilliam v. ABC*, 538 F.2d 14, 21 (2d Cir. 1976), the "unauthorized editing of the underlying work, if proven, would constitute an infringement of the copyright in that work similar to any other use of a work that exceeded the license granted by the proprietor of the copyright." Copyright licenses are designed to support the right to exclude; money damages alone do not support or enforce that right. The choice to exact consideration in the form of compliance with the open source requirements of disclosure and explanation of changes, rather than as a dollar-denominated fee, is entitled to no less legal recognition. Indeed, because a calculation of damages is inherently speculative, these types of license restrictions might well be rendered meaningless absent the ability to enforce through injunctive relief.

In this case, a user who downloads the JMRI copyrighted materials is authorized to make modifications and to distribute the materials "provided that" the user follows the restrictive terms of the Artistic License. A copyright holder can grant the right to make certain modifications, yet retain his right to prevent other modifications. Indeed, such a goal is exactly the purpose of adding conditions to a license grant. The Artistic License, like many other common copyright licenses, requires that any copies that are distributed contain the copyright notices and the COPYING file.

It is outside the scope of the Artistic License to modify and distribute the copyrighted materials without copyright notices and a tracking of modifications from the original computer files. If a downloader does not assent to these conditions stated in the COPYING file, he is instructed to "make other arrangements with the Copyright Holder." Katzer/Kamind did not make any such "other arrangements." The clear language of the Artistic License creates conditions to protect the economic rights at issue in the granting of a public license. These conditions govern the rights to modify and distribute the computer programs and files included in the downloadable software package. The attribution and modification transparency requirements directly serve to drive traffic to the open source incubation page and to inform downstream users of the project, which is a significant economic goal of the copyright holder that the law will enforce. Through this controlled spread of information, the copyright holder gains creative collaborators to the open source project; by requiring that changes made by downstream users be visible to the copyright holder and others, the copyright holder learns about the uses for his software and gains others' knowledge that can be used to advance future software releases.

IV

For the aforementioned reasons, we vacate and remand. While Katzer/Kamind appears to have conceded that they did not comply with the aforedescribed conditions of the Artistic License, the District Court did not make factual findings on the likelihood of success on the merits in proving that Katzer/Kamind violated the conditions of the Artistic License.

The judgment of the District Court is vacated and the case is remanded for further proceedings consistent with this opinion.

FIGURE 19.8 *Jacobsen v. Katzer* concerned OSS used to control model trains.

Notes and Questions

1. *The artistic license.* The OSS license used by Jacobsen was the Artistic License, an OSI-certified, but relatively uncommon, license (OSI places the Artistic License in the "Other/Miscellaneous" category). Given this, how useful is *Jacobsen v. Katzer* for interpreting other, more popular, OSS licenses, such as the GPL and BSD licenses? Does the court's holding extend generally to all OSS licenses, or is it specific to the Artistic License?

2. *Economic harm and free software.* Katzer argued that Jacobsen was not entitled to any economic damages "because he made his computer code available to the public at no charge." What did the court think of this argument? Assuming that Katzer breached the attribution requirement of the Artistic License, what harm did Jacobsen suffer?

3. *Covenant versus condition.* Did the court find that the attribution requirements of the Artistic License were contractual covenants or conditions to the copyright license? What is the significance of this distinction?

4. *What breach?* The district court in *Jacobsen* did not make factual findings regarding the scope of Katzer's use of the DecoderPro software. On remand, what did Katzer need to show to avoid liability?

5. *What dispute?* The district court in *Jacobsen* notes that "[Katzer and Kamind] represent that they have voluntarily ceased all potentially infringing activities utilizing any of the disputed material and … both parties conceded that the disputed material is no longer of value." If this is the case, why did the parties continue to litigate? What did Jacobsen hope to gain with the injunction that he sought?[27]

Problem 19.1

Softbot downloads a copy of the PlanEt workflow planning software from Mikro Software, Inc. (MSI) for $100. In addition, Softbot pays MSI $5,000 for a copy of the software source code and agrees to a one-year maintenance agreement with MSI. The PlanEt source code is licensed under GPL v3, and MSI is listed as its owner in the copyright notice, along with two of its employees. Softbot incorporates the PlanEt code into its Factotum factory management system and begins distributing it to large manufacturing entities around the world. The price of Factotum is $3 million. Before incorporating the PlanEt code into Factotum, Softbot makes significant modifications. When Softbot distributes Factotum, it requires the customer to sign a customary software licensing agreement that prohibits reverse engineering, accessing the source code and attempting to modify the code. What legal recourse does MSI have against Softbot?

19.3 OPEN SOURCE IN THE COMMERCIAL MARKET

Early OSS advocates like Richard Stallman and the FSF felt that OSS should never be combined with proprietary, commercial software. As Stallman famously wrote in 1999, "To permit such combinations would open a hole big enough to sink a ship." This anti-corporate sentiment, and the "viral" nature of Stallman's GPL, frightened corporate IT managers and software developers. They feared that using even a tiny piece of GPL code in a commercial program

---

[27] See Meeker, supra note 25, at 277 (on remand, the district court issued an injunction in favor of Jacobsen. The case settled soon thereafter).

FIGURE 19.9 Major OSS successes include the Linux and Android operating systems, the Apache web server, the Firefox browser and Red Hat, which provides services related to Linux.

could result in the entire program becoming OSS – a potentially catastrophic result for a company in the business of selling proprietary software.

Yet as the market for OSS grew, and OSS products like Linux, the Apache web server and the Android mobile operating system began to be adopted globally, that fear began to diminish. Nonviral OSS licenses such as BSD, MIT and Apache were viewed as "friendly" to proprietary software. And even GPL code such as Linux could be used safely within a corporate enterprise or in a commercial system, so long as modifications were not made to the software itself, and it was well-segregated from any proprietary programs with which it was distributed.

Today, OSS has come far from its underground, countercultural origins in the 1970s and has assumed a prominent place in the mainstream software industry. In 2019 IBM paid $34 billion for RedHat, a pioneer in distributing and providing services for Linux and other OSS tools, and in 2018 Microsoft paid $7.5 billion in stock to acquire GitHub, a leading platform for OSS development. Deals of this magnitude signal that major corporations view OSS "not as a fad or an adjunct but as a core part of how [they] will make software in the future."[28] In this section we explore how OSS is integrated into commercial software products, services and business models.

19.3.1 *Open Source as a Business Model*

What is the thinking behind corporate strategies involving OSS? The following two excerpts present different perspectives on corporate OSS approaches.

COMMERCIAL FREE AND OPEN SOURCE SOFTWARE: KNOWLEDGE PRODUCTION, HYBRID APPROPRIABILITY, AND PATENTS
GREG R. VETTER, 77 *Fordham Law Review* 2087, 2088–94 (2009)

Compare Robert Jacobsen [the OSS developer who served as plaintiff in *Jacobsen v. Katzer*] to MetaCarta, a company involved in both proprietary software development and related services for its users, and involved with certain niche open source communities relating to software for displaying geographic information. I choose MetaCarta as a stylized example

---

[28] Klint Finley, *Why 2018 Was a Breakout Year for Open Source Deals*, Wired, December 23, 2018.

because it is not involved in any litigation of which I am aware. But it has a noteworthy approach to its role in the greater world of free and open source software (FOSS) development. MetaCarta contributes some of its software to the FOSS community by acting as the organizing hub for three FOSS projects. This is not unheard-of. More uniquely, however, it also actively seeks a small portfolio of patents in related areas of software technology. Following a trend, MetaCarta is backed by venture capital investors while explicitly embracing the FOSS movement. Compared to a for-profit entity such as MetaCarta, Robert Jacobsen is a sympathetic figure for a court. He was a volunteer developing FOSS with public benefit spillovers. His motivations likely fit within some of the typically offered explanations for FOSS volunteerism: to scratch a technological itch; to have fun; to participate in a community; to learn; or to enhance career prospects. MetaCarta's motivations are those of a for-profit firm with investors hoping for return and market share. While software patenting has become common among information technology companies, much of the FOSS movement would see it as nonbeneficial. MetaCarta, however, represents a trend: "commercial FOSS" that hybridizes proprietary software appropriation techniques with conventional FOSS volunteerism-centric development.

Jacobsen and MetaCarta illustrate a dualism in FOSS that channels the knowledge production and distribution influences of the movement and could impact the perspective of future courts as they engage other licensing law issues likely to arise ... On one side of the dualism is the free software strand within the FOSS movement, while on the other is the open source strand. Each correlates to different licensing models and to different practices to gather satisfaction from writing and supplying software. The free software strand would typically use licenses with a mechanism known as copyleft to ensure that the original license conditions (often requiring source code availability and sometimes prohibiting ongoing royalties) remain in place for downstream versions of the software. With this, appropriating value from the software is biased toward services and other economic complements whenever the FOSS developer needs value to accrue to her in a pecuniary fashion.

Jacobsen's story is the narrative of the stylized FOSS developer who codes and shares for nonpecuniary satisfactions. Jacobsen's group did not use a copyleft license, but many similarly situated groups do so. For historical reasons developers often choose the Free Software Foundation's (FSF) General Public License (GPL), which is a strong copyleft license locking the software under its scope into a development mode characterized by source code availability and a prohibition against ongoing royalties to run the software.

MetaCarta's narrative is that of open source software development within a for-profit company. It applies an attribution-only license to the projects it stewards, meaning that others can deploy or use the software however they wish so long as such later deployment gives attribution to the software's originators. Open source developers sometimes start projects under an attribution-only license to allow for the future involvement of a company under a proprietary or hybridized model. The attribution-only license allows for the possibility to later release the software under either the GPL or as proprietary software, or perhaps as both in a dual-licensing strategy. MetaCarta has the twist of involving itself with patents. Other commercial FOSS entities, however, use kindred mechanisms, such as dual licensing, to rig an appropriability mix that allows some benefits of FOSS development to contribute to the prospects of the entity. Hopefully, as a result, the entity is therefore also a better (more financially viable) steward for the FOSS projects.

FOSS's influences on knowledge production and distribution ... must be considered in light of the free software/open source dualism, but also in light of appropriability. The weight of the literature to date treats FOSS as a nonmarket, peer-production method of developing and distributing new knowledge. FOSS has generated new knowledge in the sense of new collaboration models for software development and market deployment; inspired other movements, such as Creative Commons or free culture generally; and it provides or supports numerous technology platforms, including important elements of the Internet's past and future development.

This impressive scorecard of knowledge production is bronzed by FOSS benefits in knowledge distribution. Simply put, FOSS created a sea change in the availability of source code to study and learn coding and software technology at every level of complexity and in an incredibly diverse array of languages and information technology environments. In other ways, however, the benefits of FOSS are less clear. Superior code quality, in terms of lower defects and greater resistance to problems, is often argued to be a FOSS benefit for structural reasons. Empirical evidence on the point, however, is mixed, although many high-profile FOSS projects are clearly of very high quality. A reframed question is more to the point: is the quality of software developed with the methods of the FOSS movement of higher quality compared to traditional proprietary software development? If so, this is a part of FOSS's contribution to knowledge creation for the information technology ecosystem.

Software is of greater benefit not only if its quality is high, but also if it provides superior functionality. Often superior functionality means new functionality; that is, technology innovation from some programmatic processing, presentation, or interfacing that is novel and heretofore not in existence within information technology. The creation of new nonplatform software functionality may not yet be a primary strength of FOSS development. Assuming this is true, it raises a knowledge production question for FOSS: can the movement gain momentum in generating new nonplatform functionality as opposed to primarily moving functionality from one platform to another, or commoditizing existing software products?

Is the mechanism to gain this momentum in the nonpecuniary satisfaction of volunteer developers coupled with the leveraging of economic complements under the free software approach? Or, is the path in open source appropriability with commercial FOSS experiments such as MetaCarta?

These questions are not in a vacuum because other new appropriability mechanisms for software have mainstreamed in the last decade. Thus, the traditional models, such as the proprietary software product vendor model and the custom software developer model, now compete with advertising-supported software and web-delivered software as a service.

A History of IBM's Open-Source Involvement and Strategy

Peter G. Capek, et al., 44 *IBM Systems Journal* 249 (2005)[29]

The origins and principles of free software and of open-source software (OSS) may lead the casual observer to conclude that they are a world apart from—if not opposed to—more traditional software development, use, and evolution. An alternative view sees OSS

---

[29] Reprint Courtesy of International Business Machines Corporation, © 2005 International Business Machines Corporation.

as essentially an alternative business model which provides types of flexibility, opportunity, and benefits different than those provided by the conventional model. IBM was among the earliest of the major computer companies to embrace opensource software and was probably the first to realize that doing so could be consistent with our business goals. Indeed, a problem with which IBM has long contended is that of how to provide to our customers internally developed software that was not planned to be a product, without the inevitable support and product issues.

In December of 1998, an effort was first made to understand the broad strategic implications for IBM of open-source software. At that point, it was clear that the OSS phenomenon was taking hold in a substantial way. Most visibly, Linux was starting to appear widely in the media, but more importantly, parts of our customer organizations were starting to pay attention, with Linux reportedly being used in some cases without the involvement or blessing of corporate IT organizations. Quickly, we realized that whether this evolved into an important force or whether it remained a minor fad, the potential was such that it was important to understand its implications for our customers and for us and be able to respond appropriately. Before 1999, our involvement was on a case-by-case basis.

...

An important issue was the quality of software that was produced by open-source communities and their collaboration. Much of IBM's product software development was historically quite structured, with substantial initial planning and design, followed by implementation, unit and system testing phases, and of course ongoing support and maintenance. Many at IBM had the impression—partly from what appeared in the business and technical press—that open-source software efforts were closer to the other end of the spectrum in terms of structure and management discipline, and they were accordingly skeptical that the quality of the open-source software produced could be sufficient to be relevant to us and our customers.

These early fears turned out to be unfounded. Even at that time (ca. 1999), the quality of the software from the open-source projects investigated was impressive. It was clear that this development style attracted very skilled developers, and that the overlap between developers and users of a particular OSS project made possible excellent and open communication, rapid development cycles, and intensive real-environment testing, ultimately producing software that was often very good and sometimes excellent by our standards. At the same time, it was immediately clear that there were important areas where IBM's large and excellent technical community could make significant contributions, having substantial experience, and in doing so, our customers could be helped to reap the benefits of our expertise in an open context. In more recent years, the possibility of inverting the model has been investigated, whereby our proprietary development activities can benefit from what has been learned from the open community.

...

From the outset, it was clear that a host of legal and business considerations needed to be understood if IBM was going to participate in any OSS activities in a meaningful way. Much of the participation and development of OSS at that time was done by individuals acting on their own. There were some early efforts that were more organized and which involved small companies, but these were, for the most part, companies organized around their opensource participation. A few notable examples included companies that were using open source in their own operations and contributing enhancements and development to it for the broader good.

IBM, of course, had a large software business, which could not be put at risk; therefore, it was important that any risks associated with OSS be identified, and the legal, strategic, and business issues surrounding open source and its licensing be understood. Where needed, procedures would have to be established to ensure that our participation was principled and appropriate.

...

More generally, a strategy was planned that allowed us to add value for our customers in the areas where our ability to do so was greatest. This was clearly in the broad area of what is called middleware, and not in operating systems, because our enterprise customers benefit more directly from middleware functions than from operating-system functions; analogous statements can be made in other areas. Consequently, our strategy for open-source participation was one which effectively minimized the distinctions at the operating-system level and allowed us to retain the ability to differentiate where we could have the greatest impact.

...

Complexity sets in with software because most substantial open-source software has many authors and is developed in a collaborative and informal manner by people with no particular legal relationship. For these projects, it is often difficult years later to know reliably whether the person granting a license had the right to do so. For instance, was a particular contributor the author of the code, and did he have the right to grant a license, or did his employer acquire that right when he wrote it? Although some projects, including those under the Free Software Foundation, have long required assignment of copyright by each contributor including written signatures, this has not been a universal practice. Recently, more software community leaders have recognized the importance of creating clarity of code "pedigree" and rights, and IBM has worked to assist some open-source projects to increase the rigor of their processes in this area. Examples of these efforts are the Linux kernel and its Developer's Certificate of Origin and the Apache Software Foundation and its Contributor License Agreement.

Another legal consideration was the proliferation of licenses used for open-source projects. None of these licenses had been interpreted by any court, and they varied greatly in terms of their legal robustness and completeness. Many of them were unclear with respect to the granting of intellectual property rights. As a commercial organization, we felt it was important to encourage a model in which commercial products could be based on open-source efforts, and we needed to identify a license that would permit such a model. Thus, IBM created, used, and encouraged the use of, what is now known as the CPL, or Common Public License. This license has been well received by the community, and its use seems to be increasing. It has been certified as an open-source license by the Open Source Initiative. Our goals in creating this license were to provide a means for commercial organizations to base products on open-source efforts, to encourage a common OSS practice of making modifications and enhancements available as source code, and to provide a model which could help to shape other open-source licenses. In our opinion, this license provides a good balance between open-source and commercial efforts and encourages enhancements to open-source projects.

Notes and Questions

1. *OSS dualism*. Explain the "dualism" that Vetter observes in the OSS world.
2. *Commercial hurdles*. What strategic and business assumptions did IBM have to overcome before it was convinced that adoption of OSS was a sensible commercial move?
3. *Small vs. large*. Compare the OSS strategies of Robert Jacobsen, MetaCarta and IBM. How do they differ? What are their similarities?
4. *Software pedigree*. Why does IBM raise the issue of a software program's "pedigree" as a concern? The authors mention that the FSF once required that contributors assign copyright in their software contributions to the FSF. Why would they do that? IBM and others elected not to require such assignments, but developed alternative methods of ensuring software pedigree. What do you think these alternative methods entailed?
5. *License proliferation*. One of the challenges that IBM notes is the proliferation of OSS licenses – a problem that OSI was considering at about the same time (see Section 19.2.2). In IBM's case, this concern resulted in IBM developing its own form of OSS license. Why did IBM take this approach? Some observers have called company-specific OSS licenses "vanity licenses." What benefits can you see in allowing every company to create its own form of OSS license versus using a small set of widely adopted OSS licenses?

19.3.2 *Integrating OSS with Commercial Products*

How, precisely, should OSS be integrated with commercial products? This section addresses some of the practical legal and contracting issues that arise when integrating OSS and commercial software, both for internal use within an enterprise and in a software product or service for distribution to others.

19.3.2.1 Considerations for Using OSS in a Corporate Enterprise

Corporate IT managers who are considering the use of OSS products within the enterprise must consider a host of technical issues including the following:

1. Do the enterprise's internal IT staff have the expertise to install and operate the OSS software without external assistance, or must external consultants be hired?
2. How will the OSS be integrated with existing systems?
3. Does the OSS meet all data security and privacy requirements imposed by internal corporate policies as well as external regulatory and licensing agencies (e.g., HIPAA for medical records)?
4. Is it necessary to customize the OSS for internal usage, or will it satisfy internal needs in its current form?
5. Is a commercial substitute available at a reasonable cost?
6. How important is the availability of technical support, help, maintenance and updates? Can these be provided by internal IT staff?
7. What experiences have other similarly situated enterprises had with this OSS product?
8. What licensing restrictions surround the use of the OSS?
9. Is there any chance that the OSS, or a system that includes the OSS, will be shared with third-party partners, collaborators or affiliates in a manner that will constitute "distribution" of the code triggering OSS licensing requirements such as source code availability?
10. How closely is the OSS code integrated into proprietary code? Can it introduce security vulnerabilities?

19.3.2.2 Considerations for Incorporating OSS into a Distributed Product

A host of OSS modules, libraries and applications that perform a wide range of functions are available for minimal or no cost. It is tempting to use these OSS programs in commercial products, as they reduce costs and accelerate development schedules. What's more, many software engineers are familiar with OSS code that they used (or wrote) in graduate school or at prior jobs. Product developers and managers, however, should consider a variety of factors before permitting OSS to be incorporated into a commercial hardware or software product.

1. What type of license is the OSS covered by? A "viral" license such as GPL, or a license that requires broad patent grants, such as GPL or Mozilla, may be disqualifying. Permissive licenses such as BSD, MIT and Apache may be more acceptable. Careful study of the projected integration of the OSS code into proprietary software should be made before accepting OSS licensed under the LGPL.
2. Is the larger product intended to be released on an OSS basis? If so, then a "viral" license such as GPL may not be as problematic as it might be if the larger product were intended to be released on a proprietary basis.
3. How important is the support of an OSS community of developers to the acceptance, adoption and dissemination of the product?
4. How will the product be supported and updated? Does the internal staff have the ability to support the OSS code?
5. Bearing in mind that most OSS comes with no warranty or liability, what risks are involved in the operation of the product, and what harm might arise if the OSS malfunctions? Is the product a pacemaker, a nuclear reactor controller or a new Solitaire app?
6. Can the OSS be validated in terms of security, privacy and regulatory compliance?
7. Is there a reasonably priced commercial alternative to the OSS code?
8. How closely is the OSS code integrated into proprietary code? Can it introduce security vulnerabilities?

19.3.2.3 Required Notices and Licensing Terms

Even companies like Apple that have traditionally favored the use of proprietary code have integrated OSS with some of their commercial software products. When doing so, a company must be careful to disclose any applicable OSS licensing terms in its relevant product licensing agreements, just as it must for any other third-party software integrated into its products (see Section 9.2.1.2). Below is an example of the text that Apple includes in one of its recent software license agreements to address OSS requirements.

APPLE BIG SUR MACOS LICENSE (2020)[30]

Open Source. Certain components of the Apple Software, and third party open source programs included with the Apple Software, have been or may be made available by Apple on its Open Source web site (https://www.opensource.apple.com/) (collectively

---

[30] www.apple.com/legal/sla/docs/macOSBigSur.pdf.

the "Open-Sourced Components"). You may modify or replace only these Open-Sourced Components; provided that: (i) the resultant modified Apple Software is used, in place of the unmodified Apple Software, on Apple-branded computers you own or control, as long as each such Apple computer has a properly licensed copy of the Apple Software on it; and (ii) you otherwise comply with the terms of this License and any applicable licensing terms governing use of the Open-Sourced Components. Apple is not obligated to provide any updates, maintenance, warranty, technical or other support, or services for the resultant modified Apple Software. You expressly acknowledge that if failure or damage to Apple hardware results from modification of the Open-Sourced Components of the Apple Software, such failure or damage is excluded from the terms of the Apple hardware warranty.

Certain software libraries and other third party software included with the Apple Software are free software and licensed under the terms of the GNU General Public License (GPL) or the GNU Library/Lesser General Public License (LGPL), as the case may be. You may obtain a complete machine-readable copy of the source code for such free software under the terms of the GPL or LGPL, as the case may be, without charge except for the cost of media, shipping, and handling, upon written request to Apple at opensource@apple.com. The GPL/LGPL software is distributed in the hope that it will be useful, but WITHOUT ANY WARRANTY, without even the implied warranty of MERCHANTABILITY or FITNESS FOR A PARTICULAR PURPOSE. A copy of the GPL and LGPL is included with the Apple Software.

Notes and Questions

1. *Enterprise versus product.* How do the considerations for IT managers considering using an OSS program within an enterprise differ from the considerations for software product developers considering using an OSS program in a product for distribution? What should be the greatest concerns for each?

2. *Dual licensing.* It is important to remember that neither the GPL nor any other OSS license requires the owner of a copyright in a software program to assign or give up that copyright. Accordingly, the owner of a software program that releases it under an OSS license retains copyright in that program. And, as such, the owner may decide to release the program under both an OSS license *and* a proprietary license. Why would a copyright owner do this? Companies like MySQL have developed "dual-licensing" programs. They make their software available for free on an OSS basis (sometimes under the GPL), but also offer a commercial licensing option that comes with user support, maintenance and a warranty. This option is often attractive to corporate IT managers. While they would save some money by using the free OSS version, they also value the ability to get support from the software vendor. What drawbacks might a software vendor face with a dual-licensing approach?

Problem 19.2

You are the general counsel of FishFry Corp. (NYSE: FFC), a publicly traded Seattle-based manufacturer of deep-frying equipment for the fast-food restaurant market. FFC's flagship product is the FF-1000 (so-named because it heats the cooking oil to a temperature of 1000°F). The

FF-1000 uses a sophisticated proprietary sensor-plus-software system to monitor and adjust cooking temperature during use. Unfortunately, due to the "health food craze" that is sweeping the nation, the deep-fried food market is suffering and FFC's customers are not inclined to upgrade their equipment. Worse, FFC's biggest competitor, HeißFrei GmbH, a German manufacturer, has just released the SuperHeiß-1001, which cooks at one degree hotter *and* is priced $100 less than the FF-1000. But there may be hope! FFC's chief engineer, Haddock Sturgeon, just came by your office and mentioned that a well-known thermodynamics engineer at the University of East Nevada recently released a new, highly efficient, open source code temperature control algorithm on his website. The software was developed as part of a research project on geothermal energy, but Haddock is pretty sure that his team can make any necessary modifications and integrate it into the FF-1000 control system. Best of all, it's free, and it will make the FF-1000 15 percent more energy efficient, a big selling point for customers. What questions and concerns do you have regarding Haddock's plan?

19.3.3 OSS *Due Diligence*

The issue of open source "contamination" of proprietary code often arises in the context of acquisition transactions. That is, when an acquirer is considering the purchase of a target company or a division of another company, it may wish to understand the licensing regimes governing the target's products. This is particularly important if the target is a small company or university spinoff, in which software developers and engineers are accustomed to working with OSS code.

The bulk of an acquirer's "due diligence" in considering such an acquisition should be technical and include code reviews and walkthroughs with the target's technical personnel. But legal due diligence is also advisable. This includes reviewing the licensing agreements that apply to the target company's products.

EXAMPLE: OPEN SOURCE REPRESENTATION AND WARRANTY

"Open Source Materials" means all software or other material that is distributed as "free software," "open source software" or under a similar licensing or distribution model, including, but not limited to, the GNU General Public License (GPL), GNU Lesser General Public License (LGPL), Mozilla Public License (MPL), BSD Licenses, and the Apache License.

Open Source Code. Section __ of the Disclosure Schedule lists all Open Source Materials that Company has utilized in any way in the Exploitation of Company Offerings or Internal Systems and describes the manner in which such Open Source Materials have been utilized, including, without limitation, whether and how the Open Source Materials have been modified and/or distributed by Company. Except as specifically disclosed in Section __ of the Disclosure Schedule, Company has not (i) incorporated Open Source Materials into, or combined Open Source Materials with, the Customer Offerings; (ii) distributed Open Source Materials in conjunction with any other software developed or distributed by Company; or (iii) used Open Source Materials that create, or purport to create, obligations for Company with respect to the Customer Offerings or grant, or purport to grant, to any third party, any rights or immunities under Intellectual Property rights (including, but not limited to, using any Open Source Materials that require, as a condition of Exploitation of such Open Source Materials, that other Software incorporated into, derived from or distributed with such Open Source Materials be (a) disclosed or distributed in source code form, (b) licensed for the purpose of making derivative works, or (c) redistributable at no charge or minimal charge).

Notes and Questions

1. *The importance of OSS review.* Why is it important for an acquirer to understand the degree to which a target company employs OSS in its products?
2. *Black Duck.* In many cases, the recollections and records of a target company's personnel are inadequate to identify the OSS code within a large product code base. Since the early 2000s, products have been available to scan a code base to detect OSS code included within it, and to identify the applicable licensing terms. One early entrant into this market was Black Duck Software, a firm formed in 2002 by former Microsoft employees and acquired by Synopsis in 2017. Black Duck deploys algorithms to scan a code base for incidences of more than 2,700 known OSS programs.

    OSS proponents have charged that firms like Black Duck exist only to spread fear, uncertainty and doubt (FUD) about OSS. What do you think? Is OSS scanning/auditing a useful service, or merely a ploy by proprietary software giants to discredit OSS?

19.4 PATENT PLEDGES

The previous sections of this chapter have focused largely on public licenses of copyrighted material – online content and software. While several OSS licenses include explicit or implicit terms relating to patents, these are not their primary focus. Yet the rise of commercial OSS in the 1990s, particularly the Linux operating system, motivated several large companies to eliminate the potential barriers to large-scale adoption of OSS software presented by their patent portfolios. The solution that they arrived at were public-facing patent "pledges."

PATENT PLEDGES: BETWEEN THE PUBLIC DOMAIN AND MARKET EXCLUSIVITY
Jorge L. Contreras, 2015 *Michigan State Law Review* 787

Patent pledges are "[public] commitments voluntarily made by patent holders to limit the enforcement or other exploitation of their patents." These pledges encompass a wide range of technologies and firms: from promises by multinational corporations like IBM and Google not to assert patents against open source software users; to commitments by developers of industry standards to grant licenses on terms that are fair, reasonable, and non-discriminatory (FRAND); to the recent announcement by Tesla Motors that it will not enforce its substantial patent portfolio against any company making electric vehicles in "good faith."

Despite this diversity in content and form, patent pledges share a number of unifying features. The public nature of patent pledges distinguishes them from the broad array of formal licenses that patent holders routinely grant in commercial transactions. First, patent pledges are not made to direct contractual counterparties or business partners, *but to the public at large,* or at least to large segments of certain markets. Second are the motivations that lead patent holders to make patent pledges. In general, these motivations fall into two broad categories: (1) inducing other market participants to adopt, and make investments in, a standardized technology or other common technology platform; and (2) "soft" factors including communitarianism, altruism, and the desire for improved public relations. Broadly speaking, this Article addresses the first category of pledges, those that are made with an intention to induce movement in the relevant technology market, and which I have termed "actionable" pledges.

To understand the reasons that patent holders make patent pledges, it is first important to consider the beneficial market-wide effects that patent pledges can have. For example, technical interoperability standards enable devices manufactured by different vendors to interoperate automatically and without significant user intervention. The Wi-Fi wireless networking suite of standards is a good example. Any computer, tablet, smart phone, or other device that implements the relevant Wi-Fi standard can communicate with any other device that implements the same standard. The manufacturers of those devices need not interact at all during the development and manufacturing of their respective products. So long as two devices comply with the relevant standard, they can communicate with each other.

The benefits that can be achieved through widespread product interoperability are known as "network effects" and generally increase as the number of compatible devices grows. The interoperability of different vendors' products opens markets for new products and services, fostering innovation, competition, consumer choice, and economic growth. As observed by the principal U.S. antitrust agencies, standards enabling product interoperability "are widely acknowledged to be one of the engines of the modern economy." The same holds true for some software platforms, particularly those that are characterized by open application program interfaces (APIs) or are distributed in open-source form. The broad availability of such software platforms can give rise to market-wide cost savings and efficiencies, and can promote consumer choice and competition, as exemplified by the Linux and Android operating systems.

Patent pledges create an environment in which multiple firms are more likely to adopt particular standards or open-technology platforms, resulting in greater product interoperability and increased network effects. Why? This is because the holder of patents, which might otherwise be used to block a competitor from developing and selling a compatible product, commits to limit the use of those patents. This commitment might come close to contributing the patent to the public domain, for example, by pledging not to enforce a software patent against any company with fewer than twenty-five employees. At the other end of the spectrum, the pledge might simply be to grant royalty-bearing patent licenses on terms that are "fair, reasonable and non-discriminatory." In both cases, patent owners limit their statutory right to enforce their patents. By doing so, they seek to induce market participants to adopt *their preferred* standards or technology platforms. In other words, such pledges create a "safe space" in which product development and innovation can flourish with a reduced threat of patent enforcement. Such commitments thus benefit the market broadly, but also guide the market toward the patent holder's own products and technologies, which benefits the patent holder. Patent pledges thus have the potential to produce a number of beneficial market effects, which alone should be sufficient reason to respect and enforce them.

However, there is another reason that patent pledges, as a general rule, should be treated as legally enforceable obligations. This justification is based on the reliance of other market actors on these pledges. Manufacturers who rely on a patent holder's promise not to block the sale of a product will often make costly investments on that basis. These investments could include product design and development, marketing, materials, capital equipment, information technology, employee training, and supply chain management. Once such investments have been made, the manufacturer is said to be "locked-in" and cannot switch to an alternative technology without significant, and potentially prohibitive, cost. Thus, it is important to enforce the patent holder's pledge to protect other market actors who have relied on those pledges in making investments that, in the end, are likely to have a socially beneficial effect.

Various theories have been advanced regarding the most appropriate legal framework for enforcing patent pledges. These include common law contract, antitrust law, patent misuse, and other theories based in equity and property law. Each of these approaches has theoretical or practical drawbacks that I have previously discussed at length. As an alternative, I have proposed a new theory termed "market reliance," which begins with the equitable doctrine of promissory estoppel and adds to it a rebuttable presumption of reliance adapted from the "fraud-on-the-market" theory under Federal securities law. The market-reliance approach, which focuses on a patent holder's behavior-inducing promise to the market, may enable patent pledges to be recognized and enforced without the need to prove the elements of contract formation, antitrust injury or specific reliance.

But as I have also explained elsewhere, any reliance-based approach requires that the relevant promise have some degree of visibility to the market, even if individual market actors are not aware of specific pledges made with respect to specific patents. Thus, pledges that are posted on a web site and taken down the next day, or are substantially changed after they are made, raise questions regarding their later enforcement. If an initial announcement attracted sufficient public attention, such pledges might influence markets significantly. Yet if their appearance and disappearance went unnoticed, then it is likely they would have no impact on the market. And, of course, most situations will fall somewhere between these two extremes.

Patent pledges have already shaped critical technology markets and enabled the interoperability of a vast range of products and services. However, as patent litigation in these markets has increased, the premises and assumptions underlying these pledges have begun to show stress. I have proposed both a theoretical framework (market reliance) and a practical resource (the pledge registry) that, it is hoped, will solidify the legal foundation for this critical middle ground between the public domain and market exclusivity.

ALL OUR PATENT ARE BELONG TO YOU!
Elon Musk, CEO [Tesla Motors], June 12, 2014

Yesterday, there was a wall of Tesla patents in the lobby of our Palo Alto headquarters. That is no longer the case. They have been removed, in the spirit of the open source movement, for the advancement of electric vehicle technology.

Tesla Motors was created to accelerate the advent of sustainable transport. If we clear a path to the creation of compelling electric vehicles, but then lay intellectual property landmines behind us to inhibit others, we are acting in a manner contrary to that goal. **Tesla will not initiate patent lawsuits against anyone who, in good faith, wants to use our technology**.

When I started out with my first company, Zip2, I thought patents were a good thing and worked hard to obtain them. And maybe they were good long ago, but too often these days they serve merely to stifle progress, entrench the positions of giant corporations and enrich those in the legal profession, rather than the actual inventors. After Zip2, when I realized that receiving a patent really just meant that you bought a lottery ticket to a lawsuit, I avoided them whenever possible.

At Tesla, however, we felt compelled to create patents out of concern that the big car companies would copy our technology and then use their massive manufacturing, sales and marketing power to overwhelm Tesla. We couldn't have been more wrong. The unfortunate reality is the opposite: electric car programs (or programs for any vehicle that doesn't burn hydrocarbons) at the major manufacturers are small to non-existent, constituting an average of far less than 1% of their total vehicle sales.

At best, the large automakers are producing electric cars with limited range in limited volume. Some produce no zero emission cars at all.

FIGURE 19.10 Elon Musk, the flamboyant CEO of Tesla Motors, pledged all of the company's patents in a 2014 blog post.

Given that annual new vehicle production is approaching 100 million per year and the global fleet is approximately 2 billion cars, it is impossible for Tesla to build electric cars fast enough to address the carbon crisis. By the same token, it means the market is enormous. Our true competition is not the small trickle of non-Tesla electric cars being produced, but rather the enormous flood of gasoline cars pouring out of the world's factories every day.

We believe that Tesla, other companies making electric cars, and the world would all benefit from a common, rapidly-evolving technology platform.

Technology leadership is not defined by patents, which history has repeatedly shown to be small protection indeed against a determined competitor, but rather by the ability of a company to attract and motivate the world's most talented engineers. We believe that applying the open source philosophy to our patents will strengthen rather than diminish Tesla's position in this regard.

Notes and Questions

1. *Pledge plus public license.* Like the Creative Commons licensing tags, some patent pledges include both a short public pledge statement as well as a public license containing more detailed terms. This approach was used, for example, by the Open COVID Pledge (www .opencovidpledge.org),[31] under which a number of IP holders pledged patents and copyrights to fight the COVID-19 pandemic. What are the advantages of this two-tiered pledge approach? Can you think of any disadvantages?

2. *Tesla's pledge.* Do you think that the pledge made by Elon Musk in a blog post legally binds his company, Tesla Motors? Why do you think that Musk approached this important grant of rights in this relatively informal manner? As it turns out, Tesla's legal department also had concerns with Musk's pledge, and a year later reissued it on Tesla's corporate website in more robust legal terms. Was this revision necessary?

3. *Motivations for pledges.* What do you think motivated Tesla to make its pledge? Why did it sacrifice potential royalty income, or market exclusivity, for no apparent financial gain? Likewise, why did several large IP holders like IBM, Microsoft, Amazon and Facebook make the Open COVID Pledge? Do you think their motivations differed from Tesla's motivation to pledge its electric vehicle patents?[32]

---

[31] See also Jorge L. Contreras, *The Open COVID Pledge: Design, Implementation and Preliminary Assessment of an Intellectual Property Commons,* 2021 Utah L. Rev. 833 (2021).

[32] Jorge L. Contreras, *Patent Pledges,* 47 Ariz. St. L.J. 543, 573–92 (2015).

20

Technical Standards: Fair, Reasonable and Nondiscriminatory (FRAND) Licensing[1]

20.1 STANDARDS, STANDARDIZATION AND PATENTS

Technical interoperability standards like Wi-Fi, 3G/4G/5G, Bluetooth and USB enable devices made by different manufacturers – whether laptops, smartphones, automobiles or heart monitors – to communicate with very little effort by the end user. Today, these standards impact virtually all aspects of the modern networked economy. The existence of these standards, and the widespread product interoperability that they enable, give rise to significant market efficiencies known as "network effects." Such standards can increase innovation, efficiency and consumer choice; reduce barriers to market entry; foster public health and safety; and enable efficient and reliable international trade. As the Ninth Circuit has observed, "[w]hen we connect to WiFi in a coffee shop, plug a hairdryer into an outlet, or place a phone call, we owe thanks to standard-setting organizations."[2]

THE GREAT BALTIMORE FIRE AND STANDARDS

The critical importance of interoperability standards is illustrated by the tragic story of the 1904 Baltimore fire. At the outbreak of the fire, which portended to be large, fire crews were called in from as far away as Washington, DC. But when they arrived, the crews discovered that their fire hoses could not be coupled to the fire hydrants in Baltimore due to differences in shape, diameter and thread count. As a result, the fire fighters stood by helplessly as more than seventy city blocks were destroyed.

---

[1] This chapter deals with the contractual, pseudo-contractual and governance issues raised by technical standard setting. Antitrust issues associated with standards development are discussed in Chapters 25 and 26.

[2] *Microsoft Corp. v. Motorola, Inc.*, 795 F.3d 1024 (9th Cir. 2015).

FIGURE 20.1 A lack of standardized fire hydrant couplings resulted in a tragic loss of life and property in the 1904 Baltimore fire.

20.1.1 *The SDO Ecosystem*

Most of the technical standards currently deployed throughout the world were developed collaboratively by market participants in voluntary standards-development organizations (SDOs, also referred to as "standard-setting organizations" or SSOs). SDOs range from large, governmentally recognized bodies that address a diverse range of standardization projects (e.g., the International Organization for Standardization [ISO]), to established private sector groups that address the standardization needs of major industry segments (e.g., the European Telecommunications Standards Institute [ETSI], Internet Engineering Task Force [IETF], and Institute for Electrical and Electronics Engineers [IEEE]) to smaller groups often referred to as "consortia" that focus on one or a handful of related standards (e.g., the HDMI Forum, Bluetooth Special Interest Group, USB Forum). Because of the significant market benefits that are made possible by technical standards, a high degree of cooperation among competitors has long been tolerated by antitrust and competition law authorities, which might otherwise discourage such large-scale coordination efforts among competitors.[3]

20.1.2 *Patents and Standards*

Many of the technological features specified by standards can be patented. Such patents are typically obtained by those participants in a standardization activity that make technical

---

[3] See Section 25.8, for a discussion of antitrust issues and due process requirements for SDOs.

FIGURE 20.2 A 2017 meeting of the Internet Engineering Task Force (IETF).

contributions to the standard (SDOs themselves almost never obtain patent protection over their standards). However, to the extent that patents cover technologies that are "essential" to the implementation of a standard ("standards-essential patents" or "SEPs"), concerns can arise.

Ordinarily, if the manufacturer of a product that allegedly infringes a patent is unable, or does not wish, to obtain a license on the terms offered by the patent holder, the manufacturer has three options: stop selling the infringing product, design around the patent or do neither and risk liability as an infringer. With standardized products, however, the manufacturer's choices are more limited, as designing around the patent may be impossible or may make the product noncompliant with a commercially necessary standard (e.g., who would sell a smartphone today without Wi-Fi capability?). Moreover, once a standard is approved and released by an SDO, manufacturers may make significant internal investments on the basis of the standard. In such cases, the cost of switching from the standardized technology to an alternative technology may be prohibitive (a situation often referred to as "lock-in"). Once manufacturers are locked into a particular standardized technology, the holders of SEPs covering that technology may be able to extract fees that exceed the value of their patented technology, simply because the manufacturer is unable to switch to an alternative technology without incurring substantial costs. As explained by the Ninth Circuit, "The tactic of withholding a license unless and until a manufacturer agrees to pay an unduly high royalty rate for an SEP is referred to as 'hold-up.'"[4]

The risk of hold-up is likely to increase as the number of parties holding SEPs covering a single standard rises. Complex technological products may implement dozens, if not hundreds of standards, each of which may be covered by hundreds or thousands of patents held by a wide range of parties. As such, the aggregation of royalty demands by multiple patent holders could

---

[4] *Microsoft v. Motorola*, 795 F.3d at 1031 (citing *Ericsson, Inc. v. D-Link Sys., Inc.*, 773 F.3d 1201, 1209 (Fed. Cir. 2014)).

lead to high costs on implementing standards-compliant products. This situation is sometimes referred to as "royalty stacking." Royalty stacking can arise "when a standard implicates numerous patents, perhaps hundreds, if not thousands," each of which bears a royalty that must be paid by product manufacturers and which "may become excessive in the aggregate."[5] When royalty stacking occurs, "(1) the cumulative royalties paid for patents incorporated into a standard exceed the value of the feature implementing the standard, and (2) the aggregate royalties obtained for the various features of a product exceed the value of the product itself."[6]

20.1.3 *SDO IP Policies*

In order to mitigate the threats of patent hold-up and royalty stacking, many SDOs have adopted internal policies that are binding on their participants. These policies fall into two general categories: disclosure policies and licensing policies. Disclosure policies require SDO participants to disclose SEPs that they hold, generally prior to the approval of a relevant standard. These disclosures are often made available to the public via the Internet. Early disclosure of SEPs enables standards developers to decide whether or not to approve a design that is covered by these SEPs, to choose an alternative, noninfringing technology, to modify a draft standard before it is approved to eliminate the infringing feature, or to seek licenses to the patented technology.

Licensing policies, on the other hand, require SEP holders to grant manufacturers of standardized products licenses to use their SEPs on terms that are either royalty-free (RF) or "fair, reasonable and nondiscriminatory" (FRAND). These commitments are intended to assure product manufacturers that they will be able to obtain all SEP licenses necessary to manufacture a standardized product. FRAND or RF licensing commitments are required of all SDOs accredited by the American National Standards Institute (ANSI) and are also utilized widely among other SDOs around the world.

ESSENTIAL REQUIREMENTS, SECTION 3.1.1.B

A holder of standards-essential patents must offer all implementers of the standard "reasonable terms and conditions that are demonstrably free of any unfair discrimination."

Before diving into the issues surrounding FRAND royalty rates, it is important to make two ancillary points. First, a FRAND commitment, such as the one illustrated above, is not itself a license. It is a promise to enter into a license. As such, it is a binding obligation, but it is not itself a conveyance of rights to the licensee.[7] Second, most SDO licensing commitments require that

---

5   *Ericsson v. D-Link*, 773 F.3d at 1209.
6   *Microsoft v. Motorola*, 795 F.3d at 1031.
7   This point is discussed in Jorge L. Contreras, *A Market Reliance Theory for FRAND Commitments and Other Patent Pledges*, 2015 Utah L. Rev. 479, 497–98 (2015).

all terms of a SEP license be fair and reasonable, not only the royalty provisions. For obvious reasons, royalty rates have gotten most of the attention in recent FRAND litigation (see below), but there are other significant terms in every FRAND license agreement that should not be ignored. In most cases, these terms (scope, duration, disclaimers, indemnity, etc.) are similar or identical to comparable terms in other patent license agreements, which are discussed elsewhere in this volume. In many respects, FRAND patent licenses share similarities with open source code software licenses (Section 19.2), inasmuch as they are nonexclusive and carry few or no warranties or indemnities. Some have also required the licensee to grant a license in improvements, or its own patents, back to the licensor, sometimes at no charge.

20.1.4 *The Challenge of Defining FRAND Royalty Rates*

Despite the appeal of FRAND licensing commitments, a consistent, practical and readily enforceable definition of the level of a FRAND royalty for a given patent/standard, or a methodology for calculating FRAND royalties more generally, has proven difficult to achieve. Virtually no SDO defines precisely what this phrase means, and many SDOs affirmatively disclaim any role in establishing, interpreting or adjudicating the reasonableness of FRAND royalties. As explained in the common patent policy adopted by ISO, ITU and IEC, "The detailed arrangements arising from patents (licensing, royalties, etc.) are left to the parties concerned, as these arrangements might differ from case to case." Some SDOs even go so far as to *prohibit* discussions of royalties and other licensing terms at SDO meetings, making the development of a consensus view on the precise meaning of FRAND difficult. This lack of clarity has contributed to litigation over FRAND commitments.

These disputes have arisen when a SEP holder and a product manufacturer cannot agree on the terms of a license and there is disagreement whether the patent holder's proposed royalty is "reasonable." However, FRAND disputes can also involve the reasonableness of nonroyalty terms, such as requirements that the vendor license-back its own patents to the patent holder ("reciprocity") or that the license be "suspended" if the manufacturer threatens the patent holder with litigation ("defensive suspension").[8] When parties cannot agree on license terms, no license is granted and any product that conforms to a standard may infringe the patent holder's SEPs. The parties are thus left in a difficult and ambiguous situation, which has led to a vigorous debate within industry, government and academia regarding the scope and contour of FRAND obligations. Some of the specific issues arising in these disputes are discussed in the following sections.

Notes and Questions

1. *Essentiality*. The SDO disclosure and licensing policies described above relate primarily to patents that are "essential" to the SDO's standards. This qualifier is important, as SDOs would likely be overstepping their bounds if they sought to require patent holders to disclose or license patents that did not directly impact a manufacturer's ability to implement the SDO's standards. But what, exactly, does "essential" mean? This question has been heavily debated, and SDOs generally take one of three approaches. Some speak in terms of patents that are "technically" essential to a standard, some speak in terms of those that are "commercially"

---

[8] Defensive suspension or termination clauses also appear in open source software (OSS) licenses. See Section 19.2, Note 5.

essential, and some do not specify which of these approaches they prefer. The following excerpt highlights some of the issues that can arise with respect to this critical definition:

One major divide among SDO patent policies is whether they define an "essential" patent claim as covering a technology that must, as a technical or engineering matter, be included in a product implementing a standard (technical essentiality) or whether that patented technology, though not strictly required as a technical matter, is the only commercially feasible way that the standard can be implemented (i.e., considering factors such as manufacturing cost, efficiency, reliability, manufacturability, etc.) (commercial essentiality).

For example, suppose that a municipal electrical standard specifies a range of tolerances (pressure, temperature, corrosion resistance, puncture resistance, etc.) for wiring conduits. Such conduits are typically made from aluminum, though other materials could also be used to make such conduits. Thus, a patent covering the use of aluminum conduits for wiring would not be technically essential to the standard, as one could use various other materials. But suppose that the only alternative material that met the other tolerance requirements of the specification were gold. Aluminum conduit costs an average of $0.15 per meter, while gold conduit, if such a thing were ever made, would cost $2,000.00 per meter. Under this scenario, a patent covering aluminum conduit might no longer be considered technically essential to the standard, as gold, technically speaking, could also be used to make compliant conduits. Nevertheless, given these two alternatives, there is no commercially feasible alternative to aluminum. Thus, when the only technical substitute for aluminum conduit is significantly more costly, a patent covering the use of aluminum conduit would likely be commercially essential to the standard.

But what if, in addition to aluminum and gold, polyvinyl chloride (PVC) is also a suitable material for conduit which meets all the requirements of the specification. PVC costs $0.45 per meter: three times more than aluminum, but far less than gold. Is PVC, at three times the cost of aluminum, a commercially feasible substitute for aluminum? If so, is an aluminum conduit patent still commercially essential to the implementation of the conduit standard? What if the cost of PVC conduit dropped to $0.25 per meter? Or to $0.16? Just how different must the qualities and pricing of a substitute technology (PVC) be before another technology (aluminum) is no longer considered commercially essential to the standard?

This question of degree must be factored into the analysis by SDOs deciding how to define essentiality. While technical essentiality may seem rather unforgiving and unfairly exclude some patents from the reach of the SDO's policy (e.g., a patent on aluminum conduit, when gold exists as a technically, though not commercially, feasible alternative), the virtually limitless gradations of pricing, quality and availability that factor into commercial manufacturing decisions could make determinations as to commercial essentiality hopelessly fraught.[9]

What advantages and drawbacks do each of the approaches outlined above have for SDO participants, the SDO itself, and the standards that are developed? Given these considerations, how would you define "essentiality" in a new SDO's patent policy?

2. *De facto standards.* The standards discussed in this chapter are generally known as "voluntary consensus standards" and are developed by groups of competitors within SDOs. However, not all standards are created in this way. Several important standards that are widely deployed in the market were developed by a single firm and became so broadly used that they have come to be considered standards (generally known as "de facto" standards). An example is Adobe's Portable Document Format (PDF). Though Adobe originally

---

[9] Jorge L. Contreras, Essentiality and Standards Essential Patents in Cambridge Handbook of Technical Standardization Law: Competition, Antitrust, and Patents, 209, 217–18 (Jorge L. Contreras, ed., Cambridge Univ. Press, 2017).

developed PDF as a proprietary document format, PDF has become so widespread that Adobe has made available the tools necessary to read and convert PDF documents to the industry generally. Yet because Adobe developed PDF on its own and without the involvement of an SDO, the standard carries no FRAND or other licensing commitments to third parties. Should firms like Adobe be required to license patents covering de facto standards to others, including their competitors? Some commentators have argued that they should, while others worry that doing so could be problematic.[10] What do you think?

3. *Patent pools.* As we will discuss in greater detail in Chapter 26, patent pools are created when the holders of patents wish to license their patents collectively, at uniform rates via a single point of contact. Over the years, patent pools have formed to facilitate the licensing of patents covering several important standards including Advanced Audio Coding (AAC), Digital Video Broadcast (DVB) and Digital Video Disc (DVD). The Department of Justice has reviewed several of these pooling arrangements and has generally concluded that they are likely to have significant procompetitive effects.[11]

Yet most SDO-developed standards are not associated with patent pools, and the licensing of SEPs is conducted on a bilateral basis between individual SEP holders and product manufacturers. One recent study found that of more than 250 standards implemented in a new laptop computer, only 3 percent of them were subject to SEP licensing under a patent pool, while 75 percent were covered by FRAND licensing policies and 22 percent were subject to royalty-free licensing.[12]

One of the principal reasons patent pools are used infrequently in the context of voluntary consensus standards relates to "essentiality," discussed in Note 1 above:

[P]atent pools must ensure, with a high degree of certainty, that all patents placed in the pool are essential. This requirement flows from the risk that a patent pool may stifle competition if it contains patents covering substitute technologies. Under this theory, including substitute technologies in the pool could effectively fix prices on competing technologies. For this reason, the parties forming patent pools typically engage in a lengthy and expensive process (usually through external counsel engaged for the purpose) of vetting each patent that is proposed to be included in the pool and ensuring its essentiality.

Such a vetting process would typically be cost-prohibitive in the context of SDO-based standards. Some SDOs produce hundreds or thousands of standards in a wide range of product areas. Many SDO standards are never widely adopted or have limited application, so much of an up-front investment of resources to determine essentiality would be wasted. In contrast, relatively little up-front investment is required to identify SEPs in SDOs: patents are voluntarily declared essential by patent holders and essentiality is not tested unless and until litigation ensues. While this structure relies on litigation to resolve questions regarding patent essentiality, its significant up-front cost savings makes it far more desirable in the SDO context.[13]

Given these differences, do you see any way to increase the efficiency of SEP licensing for SDOs?

---

[10] Compare Robert P. Merges & Jeffrey M. Kuhn, *An Estoppel Doctrine for Patented Standards*, 97 Calif. L. Rev. 1, 4 (2009) (arguing that Adobe and other holders of de facto standards should be required to make their patents broadly available under the doctrine of equitable estoppel) with Contreras, *Market Reliance*, supra note 7, at 522–23 (significant mischief could ensue from requiring involuntary licensing of proprietary technologies).

[11] US Dep't Justice & Fed. Trade Comm'n, Antitrust Enforcement and Intellectual Property Rights: Promoting Innovation and Competition 71 (2007).

[12] Brad Biddle, Andrew White & Sean Woods, How Many Standards in a Laptop? (And Other Empirical Questions), in Int'l Telecomm. Union Sec. Telecomm. Standardization Kaleidoscope Acad. Conf. Proc. 123 (2010).

[13] Jorge L. Contreras, *Fixing FRAND: A Pseudo-Pool Approach to Standards-Based Patent Licensing*, 79 Antitrust L.J. 47, 76–77 (2013).

As discussed above, many SDOs require that their participants disclose patents that are likely to be "essential" to standards under development by the SDO. However, the specific conditions under which such disclosures must be made are sometimes hazy. The cases in this section address what happens when an SDO participant allegedly fails to comply with its obligation to disclose SEPs to an SDO.

Qualcomm Inc. v. Broadcom Corp.

548 F.3d 1004 (Fed. Cir. 2008)

PROST, CIRCUIT JUDGE

I. Background

This case presents the question of whether Qualcomm waived its right to assert its patents by failing to disclose them to the JVT SSO. The asserted patents relate to video compression technology. The '104 Patent issued in 1995 and is entitled, "Adaptive Block Size Image Compression Method and System." The '767 Patent issued in 1996 and is entitled, "Interframe Video Encoding and Decoding System." Qualcomm is the assignee of the '104 and '767 Patents.

In late 2001, the JVT was established as a joint project by two parent SSOs: (1) the Video Coding Experts Group ("VCEG") of the International Telecommunication Union Telecommunication Standardization Sector ("ITU-T"); and (2) the Moving Picture Experts Group ("MPEG") of the International Organization for Standardization ("ISO") and the International Electrotechnical Commission ("IEC"). The JVT was created to develop a single "technically aligned, fully interoperable" industry standard for video compression technology. The standard developed by the JVT was later named the H.264 standard. In May 2003, the ITU-T and ISO/IEC adopted and published the official H.264 standard.

Plaintiff Qualcomm is a member of the American National Standards Institute ("ANSI"), which is the United States representative member body in the ISO/IEC, and was an active dues-paying member for many years prior to 2001. It is also a member of the ITU-T and a participant in the JVT. Qualcomm did not disclose the '104 and '767 Patents to the JVT prior to release of the H.264 standard in May 2003.

On October 14, 2005, Qualcomm filed the present lawsuit against Broadcom in the United States District Court for the Southern District of California, claiming that Broadcom infringed the '104 and '767 Patents by making products compliant with the H.264 video compression standard. A jury trial was held from January 9, 2007, to January 26, 2007. The jury returned a unanimous verdict as to non-infringement and validity, finding that (1) Broadcom does not infringe the '104 and '767 Patents; and (2) the '104 and '767 Patents were not shown to be invalid. The jury also returned a unanimous advisory verdict as to the equitable issues, finding by clear and convincing evidence that (1) the '104 Patent is unenforceable due to inequitable conduct; and (2) the '104 and '767 Patents are unenforceable due to waiver.

On March 21, 2007, the district court entered an order (1) finding in favor of Qualcomm and against Broadcom on Broadcom's counterclaim of inequitable conduct as to the '104

Patent; (2) finding in favor of Broadcom and against Qualcomm on Broadcom's affirmative defense of waiver as to the '104 and '767 Patents; and (3) setting a hearing on an Order to Show Cause as to the appropriate remedy for Qualcomm's waiver. The district court's conclusion that Qualcomm waived its rights to assert the '104 and '767 Patents was based on Qualcomm's conduct before the JVT.

Throughout discovery, motions practice, trial, and even post-trial, Qualcomm adamantly maintained that it did not participate in the JVT during development of the H.264 standard. Despite numerous requests for production and interrogatories requesting documents relating to Qualcomm's JVT participation prior to adoption of the H.264 standard, Qualcomm repeatedly represented to the court that it had no such documents or emails. On January 24, 2007, however, one of the last days of trial, a Qualcomm witness testified that she had emails that Qualcomm previously claimed did not exist. Later that day, Qualcomm produced twenty-one emails belonging to that witness. As the district court later discovered, these emails were just the "tip of the iceberg," as over two hundred thousand more pages of emails and electronic documents were produced post-trial. The district court later determined that these documents and emails "indisputably demonstrate that Qualcomm participated in the JVT from as early as January 2002, that Qualcomm witnesses ... and other engineers were all aware of and a part of this participation, and that Qualcomm knowingly attempted in trial to continue the concealment of evidence."

On August 6, 2007, after a hearing on the Order to Show Cause, the district court entered an Order on Remedy for Finding of Waiver, ordering the '104 and '767 Patents (and their continuations, continuations-in-part, divisions, reissues, and any other derivatives thereof) unenforceable against the world.

This appeal followed.

II. Discussion

By failing to disclose relevant intellectual property rights ("IPR") to an SSO prior to the adoption of a standard, a "patent holder is in a position to 'hold up' industry participants from implementing the standard. Industry participants who have invested significant resources developing products and technologies that conform to the standard will find it prohibitively expensive to abandon their investment and switch to another standard." In order to avoid "patent hold-up," many SSOs require participants to disclose and/or give up IPR covering a standard.

In *Rambus Inc. v. Infineon Technologies* AG, this court considered the question of whether the plaintiff, Rambus, had a duty to disclose information about patents or patent applications to the Joint Electron Device Engineering Council ("JEDEC"), which is an SSO associated with the Electronic Industries Alliance ("EIA"). 318 F.3d 1081, 1096 (Fed. Cir. 2003). It stated that, "[b]efore determining whether Rambus withheld information about patents or applications in the face of a duty to disclose, this court first must ascertain what duty Rambus owed JEDEC." In determining what duty, if any, Rambus owed JEDEC, our court considered both the language of the written EIA/JEDEC IPR policy and the members' treatment of said language. It determined that the written policy did not impose a direct duty on members expressly requiring disclosure of IPR information. "Nevertheless, because JEDEC members treated the language of [the policy] as imposing a disclosure duty, this court likewise treat[ed] this language as imposing a disclosure duty."

After considering evidence regarding the JEDEC members' understanding of the JEDEC policy, this court determined that "Rambus's duty to disclose extended only to claims in patents or applications that reasonably might be necessary to practice the standard." Applying that rationale to the claims at issue and the evidence in the case, it stated that "[t]he record shows that Rambus's claimed technology did not fall within the JEDEC disclosure duty." Accordingly, this court concluded that "substantial evidence does not support the jury's verdict that Rambus breached its duties under the EIA/JEDEC policy."

A. Existence of Disclosure Duty

Determining whether Qualcomm had a duty to disclose the '104 and '767 Patents to the JVT involves two questions. First, we must determine whether the written JVT IPR policies impose any disclosure obligations on participants (apart from the submission of technical proposals). Second, to the extent the written JVT IPR policies are ambiguous, we must determine whether the JVT participants understood the policies as imposing such obligations.

The district court first considered the written JVT IPR policies. Specifically, the district court considered the JVT ToR, which encompass patent and copyright IPR. As the district court noted, the IPR disclosure provisions of the JVT IPR policies apply to Qualcomm, as a member of the ITU-T and participant in the JVT.

Section 3 of the JVT ToR is entitled "IPR Policy & Guidelines." Subsection 3.2, entitled "Collection of IPR information during the standardization process," reads:

> According to the ITU-T and ISO/IEC IPR policy, members/experts are encouraged to disclose as soon as possible IPR information (of their own or anyone else's) associated with any standardization proposal (of their own or anyone else's). Such information should be provided on a best effort basis …

As the district court observed, it is clear from a review of the JVT IPR policies that identification of IPR by JVT participants is critical to the development of an effective industry standard.

On appeal, the threshold dispute between the parties is whether the written JVT IPR policies impose any disclosure duty on participants apart from the submission of technical proposals. Qualcomm argues that the written JVT IPR policies require disclosure only when a technical proposal is made, and that disclosure is merely encouraged from participants not submitting technical proposals. Broadcom, however, argues that the written policies of both the JVT and its parent organizations impose disclosure obligations on participants (apart from the submission of technical proposals). Additionally, Broadcom submits that, to the extent there is any ambiguity in the written policies, the understanding of the JVT participants controls.

Pointing to subsection 3.2, Qualcomm argues that the express language of the written JVT policies only requires disclosure when a technical proposal is made, and that disclosure is merely "encouraged" from participants not making technical proposals. Thus, Qualcomm argues that the district court erred in holding that Qualcomm waived patent rights by breaching an "unwritten" JVT disclosure duty. In addition to the language of subsection 3.2, Qualcomm points to the JVT patent disclosure form, which states: "JVT requires that all technical contributions be accompanied with this form. Anyone with knowledge of any patent affecting the use of JVT work, of their own or any other entity ('third parties'), is strongly encouraged to submit this form as well."

As Broadcom notes, however, subsection 3.2 expressly incorporates a "best effort[s]" standard. When asked at oral argument whether there is any evidence in the record that Qualcomm made any efforts, let alone best efforts, to disclose IPR information associated with any standardization proposal, Qualcomm responded, "No, we didn't because we did not view that as imposing a duty on us." On rebuttal, Qualcomm clarified this response by arguing that the use of best efforts is merely "encouraged," not required.

We disagree with Qualcomm's reading of subsection 3.2. While Qualcomm places much emphasis on the use of the word "encouraged" in subsection 3.2, we agree with Broadcom that, when considered in light of the relevant context, this language applies to the timing of the disclosure (i.e., encouraged to disclose as soon as possible), not the disclosure duty itself. Thus, while the language of the JVT IPR policies may not expressly require disclosure by all participants in all circumstances (e.g., if relevant IPR is not disclosed despite the use of best efforts), it at least incorporates a best efforts standard (even apart from the submission of technical proposals). By Qualcomm's own admission, it did not present evidence of any efforts, much less best efforts, to disclose patents associated with the standardization proposal (of their own or anyone else's) to the JVT prior to the release of the H.264 standard.

In sum, we conclude that Qualcomm, as a participant in the JVT prior to the release of the H.264 standard, did have IPR disclosure obligations, as discussed above, under the written policies of both the JVT and its parent organizations.

JVT Participants' Understanding of the JVT IPR Policies

Even if we were to read the written IPR policies as not unambiguously requiring by themselves the aforementioned disclosure obligations, our conclusion as to the disclosure obligations of JVT participants would nonetheless be the same. That is because the language of the JVT IPR policies coupled with the district court's unassailable findings and conclusions as to the JVT participants' understanding of the policies further establishes that the policies imposed disclosure duties on participants (apart from the submission of technical proposals). As previously discussed, even though the *Rambus* court determined that there was not an express disclosure duty in the JEDEC patent policy in that case, it treated the policy as imposing a disclosure duty because the members treated it as imposing a disclosure duty.

In the present case, while the district court concluded that there was no express disclosure requirement in the written policies apart from the submission of technical proposals, it found "clear and convincing evidence that JVT participants treated the JVT IPR Policies as imposing a duty to disclose," and "that Qualcomm was aware of this treatment as early as August 2002," prior to the release of the H.264 standard in May 2003. Specifically, the district court noted that, "like *Rambus*, in addition to the written guidelines, JVT participants also learned of the patent disclosure policy from attendance of JVT meetings."

The district court considered witness testimony, including testimony from Qualcomm employees, indicating that it was the practice of the chairman of the JVT, Gary Sullivan, to discuss the JVT IPR policies at every meeting. The district court also considered testimony indicating that JVT participants sometimes submitted disclosures without an accompanying technical proposal.

Qualcomm attempts to distinguish *Rambus* by arguing that the JEDEC patent policy in *Rambus* was silent as to whether members had a disclosure duty, while the written JVT IPR policies are "unambiguous," and "expressly specify disclosure duties only in conjunction with a submission". Thus, Qualcomm argues that the district court erred by inferring a disclosure duty that is "directly contrary to the written JVT policy." As previously discussed, however, we disagree with Qualcomm's interpretation of the written JVT IPR policies in the present case. Moreover, even if we were to read the written IPR policies as not unambiguously requiring by themselves the aforementioned disclosure obligations, the disclosure duty found by the district court based on the understanding of the JVT participants is certainly not "directly contrary to the written JVT policy."

B. Scope of Disclosure Duty

Having concluded that Qualcomm, as a participant in the JVT prior to release of the H.264 standard, had a duty to disclose patents, we turn to the question of the scope of the disclosure duty. In Rambus, although the JEDEC IPR policy did not use the language "related to," the parties consistently agreed that the policy required disclosure of patents "related to" the standardization work of the committee. The parties disagreed, however, in their interpretation of "related to". The court considered evidence regarding the JEDEC members' understanding of the JEDEC policy, and concluded that "Rambus's duty to disclose extended only to claims in patents or applications that reasonably might be necessary to practice the standard". The court reasoned that, "[t]o hold otherwise would contradict the record evidence and render the JEDEC disclosure duty unbounded. Under such an amorphous duty, any patent or application having a vague relationship to the standard would have to be disclosed". The court noted, "[j]ust as lack of compliance with a well-defined patent policy would chill participation in open standard-setting bodies, after-the-fact morphing of a vague, loosely defined policy to capture actions not within the actual scope of that policy likewise would chill participation in open standard-setting bodies."

In the present case, the district court noted that the JVT IPR policies refer to IPR information "associated with" any standardization proposal or "affecting the use" of JVT work. Applying the reasoning of *Rambus*, the district court concluded that this language requires only that JVT participants disclose patents that "reasonably might be necessary" to practice the H.264 standard. To hold otherwise, the district court explained, "would render the JVT disclosure duty inappropriately 'unbounded,' 'amorphous,' and 'vague.'"

On appeal, Qualcomm argues that we should reject the district court's formulation of the "reasonably might be necessary" standard. Qualcomm characterizes the "reasonably might be necessary" formulation from *Rambus* as follows: "it must be reasonably clear at the time that the patent or application would actually be necessary to practice the standard." Thus, according to Qualcomm, when the *Rambus* court explained the standard in terms of whether the patent or application "reasonably might be necessary" to practice the standard, the court really meant that the patent or application must "actually be necessary" to practice the standard. Qualcomm submits that "[i]t is nonsensical to conceive that an SSO would require disclosure to design a standard around a patent when the standard does not read on the patent in the first place."

We disagree with Qualcomm's characterization of the standard applied in *Rambus*. The plain language used by the *Rambus* court ("reasonably might be necessary") contradicts Qualcomm's claim that the *Rambus* formulation requires that a patent must "actually be necessary" in order to trigger a disclosure duty. The *Rambus* court explained the "reasonably might be necessary" standard by stating that "the disclosure duty operates when a reasonable competitor would not expect to practice the standard without a license under the undisclosed claims."

It further clarified that the "reasonably might be necessary" standard is an objective standard, which "does not depend on a member's subjective belief that its patents do or do not read on the proposed standard." Likewise, in the present case, we agree with the district court that the language requires JVT participants to disclose patents that "reasonably might be necessary" to practice the H.264 standard. This is an objective standard, which applies when a reasonable competitor would not expect to practice the H.264 standard without a license under the undisclosed claims. This formulation does not require that the patents ultimately must "actually be necessary" to practice the H.264 standard.

C. Breach of Disclosure Duty

Having concluded that the proper scope of the disclosure duty requires JVT participants to disclose patents that "reasonably might be necessary" to practice the H.264 standard, we next address the question of whether Qualcomm breached this disclosure duty. It is undisputed that Qualcomm did not disclose the '104 and '767 Patents to the JVT prior to the release of the H.264 standard. Thus, Qualcomm breached its disclosure duty if, as the district court found by clear and convincing evidence, the '104 and '767 Patents "reasonably might be necessary" to practice the H.264 standard.

As previously mentioned, the district court found clear and convincing evidence that the '104 and '767 Patents "reasonably might be necessary" to practice the H.264 standard. In reaching this conclusion, the district court relied on the testimony from several Qualcomm witnesses. For example, the district court relied on testimony from Qualcomm's H.264 expert, who testified at trial that "the claims of the ['104] patent map onto the H.264 standard, so that devices or systems that practice H.264 actually practice claims of the '104 patent." Additionally, inter alia, the district court relied on an email from a Qualcomm employee discussing the coverage of the '767 Patent, and describing it as a "core patent relevant to H.264."

Qualcomm argues that the finding of non-infringement here refutes any finding that it breached a disclosure duty. Broadcom responds, however, that it is inconsistent for Qualcomm to now argue that the asserted patents do not meet the "reasonably might be necessary" standard, when Qualcomm accused Broadcom's products of infringement in this case solely because they practiced the H.264 standard. Broadcom also points to testimony of Qualcomm's own JVT participants in support of its claim that JVT participants considered that the asserted patents "reasonably might be necessary" to practice the H.264 standard.

On appeal, Qualcomm does not present any arguments comparing the asserted claims to the H.264 standard in an attempt to show that they do not meet the "reasonably might be necessary" formulation. Indeed, Broadcom argues that if Qualcomm truly believes that the asserted patents do not meet the "reasonably might be necessary" standard, then it necessarily lacked a Rule 11 basis to bring this litigation in the first place.

We are not persuaded by Qualcomm's arguments on this point, and are unable to reconcile its ex post argument that the asserted patents do not meet the "reasonably might be necessary" standard with its ex ante arguments regarding infringement. Based on the foregoing, we conclude that the district court did not err in finding clear and convincing evidence that the '104 and '767 Patents fell within the "reasonably might be necessary" standard. Thus, the district court properly determined that Qualcomm breached its disclosure duty by failing to disclose the '104 and '767 Patents to the JVT prior to the release of the H.264 standard in May 2003.

Accordingly, we turn to the question of whether it was within the district court's equitable authority to enter an unenforceability remedy in this case.

D. Equitable Remedies

The district court analyzed the consequence of Qualcomm's failure to disclose the '104 and '767 Patents under the framework of waiver as a consequence of silence in the face of a duty to speak. The parties disagree on whether waiver was the appropriate equitable framework, and whether the scope of the unenforceability remedy was within the district court's equitable authority.

Waiver

First, we address the question of whether waiver was the appropriate equitable doctrine to apply in this case. Qualcomm argues that the district court's findings do not constitute waiver as a matter of law. It argues that "true waiver" requires a voluntary or intentional relinquishment of a known right.

Specifically, Qualcomm claims that the district court's findings in this case run directly contrary to any claim that Qualcomm intended to voluntarily waive its patent rights. On this point, we agree with Qualcomm. The following finding by the district court certainly suggests that Qualcomm did not intend to waive its patent rights:

> The Court finds by clear and convincing evidence that Qualcomm intentionally organized a plan of action to shield the '104 and '767 patents from consideration by the JVT with the anticipation that (1) the resulting H.264 standard would infringe those patents and (2) Qualcomm would then have an opportunity to be an indispensable licensor to anyone in the world seeking to produce an H.264-compliant product.

Therefore, rather than establishing that Qualcomm intentionally relinquished its rights, the district court's findings demonstrate that Qualcomm intentionally organized a plan to shield its patents from consideration by the JVT, intending to later obtain royalties from H.264-compliant products. Thus, in these circumstances, it appears that "true waiver" is not the appropriate framework.

As Broadcom notes, however, the district court's formulation of the law of waiver was not limited to "true waiver," but also addressed "implied waiver." The district court's advisory jury instruction stated:

> In order to prove waiver, Broadcom must show by clear and convincing evidence either that Qualcomm, with full knowledge of the material facts, intentionally relinquished its rights to enforce the 104 and 767 patents or that its conduct was so inconsistent with an intent to enforce its rights as to induce a reasonable belief that such right has been relinquished.

Broadcom submits that "[t]he second element of that instruction correctly states the long-established doctrine of implied waiver."

Qualcomm responds that "[e]ven if a duty to disclose had been breached, this breach is best explained as negligence, oversight, or thoughtlessness, which does not create a waiver." In the present case, however, the district court found clear and convincing evidence that Qualcomm knew that the asserted patents "reasonably might be necessary" to practice that H.264 standard, and that it intentionally did not disclose them to the JVT. These findings demonstrate much more than "negligence, oversight, or thoughtlessness."

Qualcomm also argues that any "nondisclosure did not cause any harm to Broadcom or any other entity." Qualcomm submits that there is no harm because (1) the jury's non-infringement verdict conclusively establishes that the asserted patents are not needed to produce H.264-compliant products, and (2) even if the asserted patents were needed to practice the H.264 standard, Qualcomm would be willing to license them. We disagree. Even if Qualcomm agreed not to pursue an injunction in this case, injunctions are not the only type of harm. Forcing a party to accept a license and pay whatever fee the licensor demands, or to undergo the uncertainty and cost of litigation (which in this case was substantial), are significant burdens.

Qualcomm further argues that "[t]he district court never found detrimental reliance by Broadcom because of its misconception that such reliance is not an element of a defense premised on conduct that allegedly is objectively misleading to a reasonable person." In essence, it appears that Qualcomm wants to benefit from its intentional nondisclosure of the asserted patents by arguing that Broadcom cannot succeed on an implied waiver defense without specific findings as to detrimental reliance by Broadcom.

We disagree with Qualcomm's contention that the district court's findings in this case were insufficient to support the application of an implied waiver defense. The district court found that JVT participants understood the JVT IPR policies as imposing a disclosure duty, that Qualcomm participated in the JVT prior to release of the H.264 standard, and that Qualcomm was silent in the face of its disclosure duty. Indeed, the district court stated that "participants in the JVT project shared the aims and policies of the JVT and considered themselves obligated to identify IPR owned or known by them, whether or not they made technical proposals for study." As the district court noted, "Broadcom, ignorant of the existence of the '104 and '767 patents, designed and is in the process of manufacturing numerous H.264-compliant products." In light of the record in this case in its entirety, it would be improper to allow Qualcomm to rely on the effect of its misconduct to shield it from the application of the equitable defense of implied waiver.

In sum, we agree with the district court that, "[a] duty to speak can arise from a group relationship in which the working policy of disclosure of related intellectual property rights ('IPR') is treated by the group as a whole as imposing an obligation to disclose information in order to support and advance the purposes of the group." Not only did the district court find that Qualcomm was silent in the face of a disclosure duty in the SSO context, it also found clear and convincing evidence that Qualcomm had knowledge, prior to the adoption of the H.264 standard in May 2003, that the JVT participants understood the policies as imposing a disclosure duty, that the asserted patents "reasonably might be necessary" to practice the H.264 standard, and that Qualcomm intentionally organized a plan to shield said patents from consideration by the JVT, planning to demand license fees from those seeking to produce H.264-compliant products. Then, after participating in the JVT and shielding the asserted patents from consideration during development of the H.264 standard, Qualcomm filed a patent infringement lawsuit against Broadcom, alleging infringement primarily, if not solely, based on Broadcom's H.264 compliance. In these circumstances, we conclude that it was within the district court's authority, sitting as a court of equity, to determine that Qualcomm's misconduct falls within the doctrine of waiver.

Unenforceability Remedy

On August 6, 2007, after a hearing on the Order to Show Cause, the district court entered an Order on Remedy for Finding of Waiver, ordering the '104 and '767 Patents (and their continuations, continuations-in-part, divisions, reissues, and any other derivatives thereof) unenforceable against the world. In reaching this conclusion, the district court rejected Qualcomm's argument that Broadcom may not have any remedies beyond itself, because it raised waiver as an affirmative defense rather than as a counterclaim or cross-claim. The district court noted that this court has upheld the unenforceability of a patent to the world due to inequitable conduct even when pled as an affirmative defense.

Qualcomm argues that the remedy of unenforceability entered on Broadcom's defense of waiver is contrary to law. It submits that once the jury returned a non-infringement verdict the district court lacked any legal basis to consider the affirmative defense of waiver. It appears to base this argument largely on the fact that Broadcom pled waiver only as an affirmative defense, as opposed to a counterclaim. Thus, Qualcomm argues that, because waiver was pled as an affirmative defense, it cannot result in a judgment of unenforceability. We disagree. It was entirely appropriate for the district court to address the defense of waiver after the jury returned a non-infringement verdict. As the district court noted, this court has upheld judgments of unenforceability based on inequitable conduct even where pled as an affirmative defense. We see no reason why an affirmative defense of waiver cannot similarly result in a judgment of unenforceability.

Broadcom also submits that "[t]he district court, sitting in equity, had the authority to grant relief as a result of Qualcomm's conduct." By analogy, it claims that successful assertion of the defenses of inequitable conduct, equitable estoppel, and patent misuse has resulted in unenforceability judgments. In response to Broadcom's analogy to inequitable conduct, Qualcomm argues "the rationale for a remedy of unenforceability for inequitable conduct before the PTO—that such conduct taints the property right ab initio—is simply not present for waiver based on post-PTO conduct before a private SSO." In response to the patent misuse analogy, Qualcomm states that "[w]hen patent misuse is proven, a court may temporarily suspend the owner's ability to enforce the patent while the improper practice and its effects remain ongoing."

In addition to the analogy to inequitable conduct, we find the remedy of unenforceability based on post-issuance patent misuse instructive in this case. As Qualcomm notes, the successful assertion of patent misuse may render a patent unenforceable until the misconduct can be purged; it does not render the patent unenforceable for all time. In *B. Braun Medical, Inc. v. Abbott Laboratories*, this court stated:

> [T]he patent misuse doctrine is an extension of the equitable doctrine of unclean hands, whereby a court of equity will not lend its support to enforcement of a patent that has been misused. Patent misuse arose, as an equitable defense available to the accused infringer, from the desire to restrain practices that did not in themselves violate any law, but that drew anticompetitive strength from the patent right, and thus were deemed to be contrary to public policy. When used successfully, this defense results in rendering the patent unenforceable until the misuse is purged.

124 F.3d 1419, 1427 (Fed. Cir. 1997). In light of the foregoing, we agree with Qualcomm that patent misuse does not render a patent unenforceable for all time. Contrary to Qualcomm's arguments, however, the limited scope of unenforceability in the patent misuse context does not necessarily lead to the conclusion that an unenforceability remedy is unavailable in the waiver context in the present case. Instead, we conclude that a district court may in appropriate circumstances order patents unenforceable as a result of silence in the face of

an SSO disclosure duty, as long as the scope of the district court's unenforceability remedy is properly limited in relation to the underlying breach.

While the scope of an unenforceability remedy in the patent misuse context is limited to rendering the patent unenforceable until the misuse is purged, the scope of the district court's unenforceability remedy in the present case was not limited in relation to Qualcomm's misconduct in the SSO context. The basis for Broadcom's waiver defense was Qualcomm's conduct before the JVT during development of the H.264 standard, including intentional nondisclosure of patents that it knew "reasonably might be necessary" to practice the standard. The district court correctly recognized that the remedy for waiver in the SSO context should not be automatic, but should be fashioned to give a fair, just, and equitable response reflective of the offending conduct. In determining the appropriate equitable remedy in this case, the district court properly considered the extent of the materiality of the withheld information and the circumstances of the nondisclosure relating to the JVT proceedings. While we agree with the district court that there is an "obvious connection between the '104 and '767 patents and H.264 compliant products," we do not discern such a connection between the asserted patents and products that are not H.264-compliant, and neither party points us to any such connection.

Accordingly, based on the district court's findings, the broadest permissible unenforceability remedy in the circumstances of the present case would be to render the '104 and '767 Patents (and their continuations, continuations-in-part, divisions, reissues, and any other derivatives thereof) unenforceable against all H.264-compliant products (including the accused products in this case, as well as any other current or future H.264-compliant products). Accordingly, we vacate the unenforceability remedy and remand with instructions to enter an unenforceability remedy limited in scope to any H.264-compliant products.

Notes and Questions

1. *Rambus v. Infineon.* Perhaps the best-known case of a failure to disclose patents to an SDO involves Rambus, Inc., a developer of semiconductor memory technology. Much has been written about the decade-long legal battles in which Rambus sought to assert its patents against implementers of dynamic random access memory (DRAM) technology standardized by JEDEC, a voluntary SDO in which Rambus participated in the early 1990s. In the cases (which involved US and EU enforcement agencies, as well as multiple semiconductor companies), Rambus escaped liability largely because some (but not all) of the triers of fact determined that the JEDEC patent policy was too vague to prohibit the conduct that Rambus allegedly committed. Or, as concluded by the Federal Circuit in *Rambus v. Infineon* (Fed. Cir. 2003), the JEDEC policy suffered from "a staggering lack of defining details" that left SDO participants with "vaguely defined expectations as to what they believe the policy requires." In hindsight, it is easy to criticize JEDEC and its counsel for poor drafting, but can you think of any factors that might have led to the deliberate creation of such an imprecise policy?

2. *Policy language.* The outcome of *Broadcom* hangs on whether or not Qualcomm had a duty to disclose two of its patents to JVT. The court concedes that the language of JVT's patent policy does not expressly create this obligation, yet imposes this obligation on Qualcomm based on the general understanding of JVT participants. Is it valid to impose a legal obligation based on non-lawyers' (mis)understanding of legal policies? How does the court

reconcile its holding with that of *Rambus v. Infineon*, in which no duty to disclose was found under a similarly unclear policy?[14]

3. *Noninfringement.* At the district court, the jury found that Qualcomm's patents were not infringed by Broadcom. What does this finding imply regarding the essentiality of Qualcomm's patents to the H.264 standard? Why did the Federal Circuit give little weight to the jury's noninfringement finding or Qualcomm's argument that, as a result, Broadcom suffered no harm from Qualcomm's failure to disclose the patents at issue?

4. *Unenforceability.* In *Broadcom*, the district court held that Qualcomm's undisclosed patents were unenforceable as against the entire world. The Federal Circuit vacated this holding and remanded to narrow the scope of the unenforceability remedy. Was this a victory for Qualcomm? What practical difference is there between an unenforceability order as to the entire world and as to a standard with respect to which the patent is essential? Even with the Federal Circuit's narrowing of the district court's unenforceability order, patent unenforceability is a remarkably strong remedy. Was this remedy justified in this case? Why?

5. *Nondisclosure as an antitrust violation?* After the Federal Circuit's 2003 ruling in *Rambus v. Infineon*, the Federal Trade Commission initiated a separate action against Rambus, arguing that its failure to disclose relevant patents to JEDEC violated US antitrust law. In 2006, the FTC ruled against Rambus, finding that it had violated both the Sherman Act and the FTC Act through its deceptive conduct toward JEDEC. The FTC's ruling was overturned on technical antitrust grounds in 2008 by the Court of Appeals for the DC Circuit.[15] Nevertheless, it is still generally understood that an SDO participant's intentional failure to disclose relevant patents to the SDO in violation of its policies could result in serious penalties. Why is violation of SDO disclosure policies viewed as harmful to competition?

6. *Disclosure of licensing terms.* The disclosure policies at issue in the *Rambus* and *Broadcom* cases discussed above concern the disclosure of patents that are (or may be) essential to the implementation of technical standards. In addition, at least one SDO[16] has adopted a policy requiring the disclosure of not only patents essential to its standards, but also the most restrictive licensing terms (i.e., the highest royalty rates) on which the patent holder will license those patents to others. Surprisingly, such "ex ante" licensing disclosure policies have proven controversial and have been vehemently opposed by patent holders at other SDOs. Why do you think that a patent holder would object to disclosing its licensing terms for standards-essential patents?[17] What benefits might such disclosures offer to SDOs and the market?

20.3 FRAND ROYALTY RATES

One of the most complex issues arising with respect to FRAND licensing is the royalty level that complies with a SEP holder's commitment to grant a license on terms that are "fair and reasonable." As noted above, most SDOs offer little guidance regarding the actual FRAND royalty level. Thus, the determination of FRAND royalty rates is typically left to bilateral negotiations among SEP holders and manufacturers of standardized products. Not surprisingly, there

---

[14] For a discussion of implied duties under SDO policies, see Jorge L. Contreras, *Private Law, Conflicts of Law, and a Lex Mercatoria of Standards Development Organizations*, 2019 Eur. Rev. Private L. 245 (2019).

[15] *Rambus Incorporated v. FTC*, 522 F.3d 456 (D.C. Cir. 2008).

[16] VITA, the VMEBus International Trade Association, a small SDO that develops electronics standards for avionics and defense applications.

[17] For a discussion of the controversy surrounding this issue, see Jorge L. Contreras, *Technical Standards and Ex Ante Disclosure: Results and Analysis of an Empirical Study*, 53 Jurimetrics 163 (2013).

is sometimes disagreement whether a royalty rate is compliant with the SEP holder's FRAND commitment. In some cases, a SEP holder and a manufacturer may disagree whether the royalty rate demanded by the SEP holder for such a license is FRAND, and the manufacturer may sue the SEP holder for breaching its FRAND commitment. In other cases, a SEP holder may sue a manufacturer for infringing its SEPs, and the manufacturer may raise as an affirmative defense the SEP holder's obligation to grant the manufacturer a license on FRAND terms. In both of these scenarios, one of the central questions is whether the royalty rate that the SEP holder sought to charge the manufacturer was FRAND.

20.3.1 *FRAND Royalties in the United States and the Georgia-Pacific Framework*

Under the U.S. Patent Act, the principal measure of damages for patent infringement is a "reasonable royalty." As a result, several courts that have calculated FRAND royalty rates have looked to traditional methodologies for determining reasonable royalty damages. The calculation of reasonable royalty damages in the United States has generally followed the fifteen-factor framework established in 1970 by *Georgia-Pacific Corp. v. U.S. Plywood Corp.*, 318 F. Supp. 1116 (S.D.N.Y. 1970). However, because this framework assumes that the patent holder and the infringer have no pre-existing relationship, and that the patent holder is not otherwise constrained in its ability to determine its royalty rate, many of the assumptions underlying the *Georgia-Pacific* analysis do not apply in cases involving FRAND-encumbered SEPs.

In *Microsoft v. Motorola*, the federal District Court for the Western District of Washington sought to determine both a reasonable royalty and a range of reasonable royalties for Motorola's patents covering two industry standards. In doing so, the court looked first to the reasonable royalty damages analysis in *Georgia-Pacific*, including its hypothetical negotiation framework. It reasoned that the parties to a hypothetical negotiation would set [F]RAND[18] royalty rates by "looking at the importance of the SEPs to the standard and the importance of the standard and the SEPs to the products at issue." However, he also noted that "[f]rom an economic perspective, a RAND commitment should be interpreted to limit a patent holder to a reasonable royalty on the economic value of its patented technology itself, apart from the value associated with incorporation of the patented technology into the standard."

Ultimately, the court adopted a modified version of the *Georgia-Pacific* framework in which it altered twelve of the fifteen factors to take Motorola's RAND commitment into account. After establishing this analytical framework, the court looked to several "comparable" sets of license agreements, including some patent pools, to evaluate the basis for Motorola's RAND royalty rates.

The RAND royalty rates determined by the court in *Microsoft* were significantly lower than the rates originally demanded by Motorola. For example, with respect to SEPs covering the H.264 audio-video encoding standard, Motorola initially demanded a royalty of 2.25 percent of the end price of Microsoft products embodying the standard. Thus, for a low-end $500 computer, the per-unit royalty would have been $11.25. The court, in assessing the value of Motorola's patents to the H.264 standard and the value of the standard to the overall products in which it was embodied, determined a FRAND royalty rate of $0.00555 per unit. Based on these results, Motorola's initial royalty demand to Microsoft was more than 2,000 times higher than the "reasonable" royalty rate determined by the court.

---

[18] Most courts and commentators who have considered the issue use the terms FRAND and RAND interchangeably.

In *Innovatio IP Ventures*, 956 F. Supp. 2d 925 (N.D. Ill. 2013), Innovatio, a patent assertion entity (PAE) holding twenty-three SEPs covering the 802.11 Wi-Fi standards, sent demand letters to hundreds of coffee shops, motels, supermarkets and other retail establishments that offered public Wi-Fi access (thereby allegedly infringing the SEPs), in each case seeking a modest monetary settlement. The case was consolidated and the court considered Innovatio's proposed royalty of 6 percent of the end price of products such as wireless access points, laptops, tablets and barcode scanners, resulting in potential royalties ranging from $3.39 to $36.90 per unit. In assessing the appropriate RAND royalty rate, the District Court for the Northern District of Illinois largely followed the framework described in *Microsoft* for the determination of RAND royalties. In particular, it applied a modified *Georgia-Pacific* analysis that simulates a hypothetical bilateral negotiation in the context of RAND obligations. After assessing the value of Innovatio's SEPs, the court held that the appropriate FRAND royalty was only $0.0956 per unit, making Innovatio's initial royalty proposals between 35 and 386 times higher than the adjudicated FRAND royalty rate.

In *Ericsson v. D-Link*, 773 F.3d 1201, 1226 (Fed. Cir. 2014), the FRAND royalty rate was determined by a jury. Thus, the Federal Circuit, on appeal, was limited to reviewing the trial court's instructions to the jury. In the appeal, the Federal Circuit reversed and remanded the jury verdict based, in part, on the district court's instruction to apply the fifteen *Georgia-Pacific* factors without modification. The Federal Circuit affirmed that, "[i]n a case involving RAND-encumbered patents, many of the *Georgia-Pacific* factors simply are not relevant; many are even contrary to RAND principles." The Federal Circuit noted several respects in which the *Georgia-Pacific* factors were both irrelevant and contrary to the RAND commitment under consideration. Thus, like the court in *Microsoft*, the Federal Circuit criticized the use of several specific *Georgia-Pacific* factors when considering royalties subject to RAND commitments.

The Federal Circuit in *Ericsson v. D-Link* made several other important rulings. In particular, it held that an accused infringer seeking to raise the issue of hold-up to a jury must introduce actual evidence of the SEP holder's hold-up behavior. Because this evidence was not introduced by the alleged infringer, the court was justified in not instructing the jury on the question of hold-up. The court used similar reasoning with respect to the question of royalty stacking and held that actual evidence of stacking must be introduced in order for the question to be considered by the jury.

20.3.2 *Bottom-Up versus Top-Down Royalty Determinations*

In most of the cases discussed in Section 20.1, the courts determined FRAND royalties in a "bottom-up" manner. That is, they calculated the royalty due to the patent holder based primarily on the alleged value of the patents in suit, without regard to the overall number or value of patents covering the standard in question or the results reached by other courts addressing the same standards. In fact, as the Federal Circuit emphasized in *Ericsson v. D-Link*, a court may not even instruct the jury regarding royalty stacking without actual evidence of stacking. When such bottom-up approaches are used, royalties due to individual patent holders are determined in an uncoordinated manner independently of one another, and the total royalty burden associated with a standard emerges only as the sum of its individual components. The problem with such bottom-up approaches is that courts may use different royalty criteria and factors case by case, even when patents covering the same features of the same standard are involved, thus yielding inconsistent and potentially excessive results. For example, as shown

TABLE 20.1 *US-litigated FRAND royalty determinations for 802.11 (Wi-Fi) standard-essential patents*[19]

Case	Court (year)	Royalty
Microsoft v. Motorola	W.D. Wash. (2013)	$0.035 per unit
In re Innovatio	N.D. Ill. (2013)	$0.0956 per unit
Ericsson v. D-Link	E.D. Tex. (2013)	$0.15 per unit
Realtek v. LSI	N.D. Cal. (2014)	0.12% of net sales
CSIRO v. Cisco	E.D. Tex. (2014)	Up to $1.90 per unit

in Table 20.1, in 2013 and 2014 five different US district courts calculated royalties for a total of thirty-five SEPs covering IEEE's Wi-Fi standards using different methodologies, with widely divergent results.

The aggregate royalty for these thirty-five SEPs amounted to approximately 4.5 percent of the total sale price of a typical $50 Wi-Fi router. Yet it has been estimated that there are approximately 3,000 patents covering the Wi-Fi standard. If the royalty for each of these patents were calculated in a similarly uncoordinated, bottom-up manner, the aggregate patent royalty on a Wi-Fi router could easily surpass the product's total selling price by at least an order of magnitude. And even if, as suggested by some commentators, this effect might be reduced because many of these SEPs are held by the same large firms, the total number of firms holding SEPs covering Wi-Fi is still significantly larger than the number of adjudicated cases to date.

Given the growing recognition of these issues, commentators, courts and policy makers have become increasingly attracted to mechanisms that take into account the aggregate royalty burden associated with a standard when considering the royalties owed to any particular patent holder. Thus, as noted by the European Commission in a recent communication regarding SEPs, "an individual SEP cannot be considered in isolation. Parties need to take into account a reasonable aggregate rate for the standard, assessing the overall added value of the technology." Royalty calculation methodologies that seek to address these issues can broadly be termed "top-down" approaches because they look first to the overall level of royalties associated with a standard and then allocate a portion of this total to individual patent holders. Top-down approaches implicitly recognize that when multiple patents cover a single standard, the rate charged by one SEP holder will necessarily affect the rates that the other SEP holders are able to obtain from a given manufacturer. Of course, the biggest challenge of a top-down approach is determining the overall royalty rate for the patents covering a particular standard.

Notes and Questions

1. *Top-down vs. bottom-up.* What are the relative advantages and drawbacks of top-down and bottom-up approaches to calculating FRAND royalties? Do these advantages and drawbacks apply to patents other than SEPs?
2. *Vive la différence?* Are there advantages or disadvantages to the multiple methods of calculating FRAND royalties recognized by the courts? How might different judicial approaches to FRAND royalty calculation influence licensing negotiations among SEP holders and manufacturers of standardized products?

[19] Jason R. Bartlett and Jorge L. Contreras, *Rationalizing FRAND Royalties: Can Interpleader Save the Internet of Things*, 36 Rev. Litigation 285, 288 (2017) (citations omitted).

3. *Third-party beneficiaries.* In general, a FRAND commitment is made by a SEP holder as part of its agreement to participate in an SDO, whether through a written membership agreement, the SDO's corporate bylaws, or a formal policy adopted by the SDO's board or membership. In all of these cases, the SEP holder's formal commitment runs to the SDO rather than to third-party manufacturers of standardized products. Yet it is precisely those manufacturers who will benefit most directly from the SEP holder's commitment: They are the ones to which the SEP holder must grant licenses on FRAND terms. More importantly, it is they, rather than the SDOs themselves, who are far more likely to seek to enforce a SEP holder's FRAND commitment in court. Do you understand why this is the case?

   As a result of this mismatch, manufacturers seeking to enforce FRAND commitments against SEP holders have often sought to do so as intended third-party beneficiaries of the SEP holders' FRAND commitments. As described in Section 301 of the *Restatement (Second) of Contracts*,

   > Unless otherwise agreed between promisor and promisee, a beneficiary of a promise is an intended beneficiary if recognition of a right to performance in the beneficiary is appropriate to effectuate the intention of the parties and … the circumstances indicate that the promisee intends to give the beneficiary the benefit of the promised performance.

   What challenges might a product manufacturer face in seeking to enforce a SEP holder's FRAND commitment as a third-party beneficiary?[20] What if some countries do not recognize a third-party beneficiary doctrine in their contract law?[21]

4. *Royalty-free standards.* Not all SEPs are licensed on FRAND terms. In fact, SEPs covering broadly adopted standards such as USB, Bluetooth, HTML, HTTP, the World Wide Web

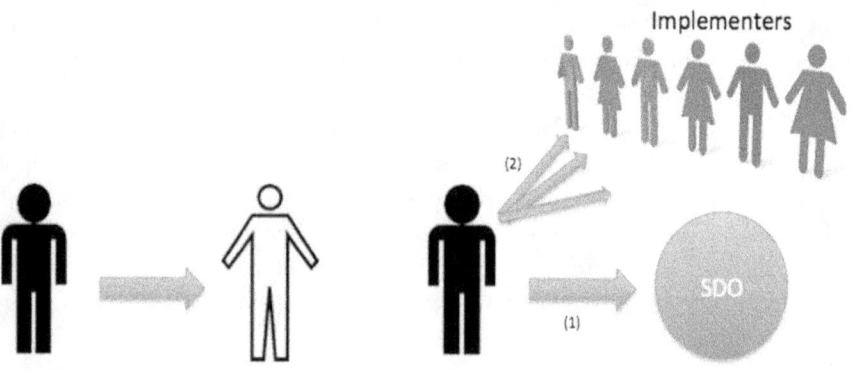

(A) Contract Paradigm - Black to White: "I will grant you a license"   *(B) Standards Paradigm – Black to SDO "I will grant Implementers a license"*

FIGURE 20.3   (a) Contract paradigm – black to white: "I will grant you a license." (b) Standards Paradigm – black to SDO: "I will grant implementers a license."

---

[20]   See Contreras, *Market Reliance*, supra note 7, at 508-14.

[21]   According to Professor Thomas Cotter, courts outside the United States have not found contract theory to be a particularly strong theory of enforcing FRAND commitments (especially with regard to third-party beneficiary status). See Thomas F. Cotter, *Comparative Law and Economics of Standard-Essential Patents and FRAND Royalties*, 22 Tex. Intell. Prop. L.J. 311 (2014) (discussing cases from Germany, the Netherlands and the Republic of Korea).

and the Internet Protocol are all made available on a royalty-free basis. Why would the SDOs behind these standards, and their members, choose this approach? Is this corporate philanthropy, or are there commercial reasons to release a standard on a royalty-free basis? And if it works for them, why aren't all SEPs licensed on a royalty-free basis?[22]

5. *Disclosure versus licensing commitments.* Not all SDOs require their participants to license SEPs, whether on FRAND or any other terms. The principal example of such an SDO is IETF, which requires its participants to disclose any of their patents or patent applications that may cover an IETF standard that they have helped to develop, but does not require them to license those patents to anyone. Is this a major oversight, or can you think of a reason that IETF may have adopted this approach?[23] Despite IETF's lack of a patent licensing commitment, most IETF participants voluntarily commit to license their patents to implementers of IETF standards on a royalty-free basis. What might motivate companies to do this?

20.4 NONDISCRIMINATION AND FRAND COMMITMENTS

The terms offered under a FRAND license must be not only fair and reasonable, but "nondiscriminatory." Like "fair" and "reasonable," there is significant debate concerning the meaning and contours of the obligation to grant licenses on terms that are "nondiscriminatory."

There is a general consensus that in order to comply with the nondiscrimination prong of the FRAND commitment, a SEP holder must treat "similarly situated" licensees in a similar manner. Several commentators have understood this constraint to allow a SEP holder to charge different royalty rates to implementers based on their size or market share (often with the understanding that larger players are likely to sell more licensed products and thus pay higher levels of royalties). In *Unwired Planet v. Huawei*, the UK High Court for Patents reasoned that a FRAND royalty rate should be set based on the value of the licensed patents, not on the size of other characteristics of the licensee. Thus, "all licensees who need the same kind of licence will be charged the same kind of rate" and "[s]mall new entrants are entitled to pay a royalty based on the same benchmark as established large entities."

Likewise, in *TCL v. Ericsson*, the federal District Court for the Central District of California concluded that similarly situated firms are "all firms reasonably well-established in the world market [for telecommunications products]." 2017 U.S. Dist. LEXIS 214003 (C.D. Cal. 2017). The court expressly excluded from this group "local kings" – firms that sell most of their products in a single country (e.g., India's Karbonn and China's Coolpad). The firms that the court found to be similarly situated to TCL were Apple, Samsung, Huawei, LG, HTC and ZTE. The SEP holder, Ericsson, argued that Apple and Samsung are not similar to TCL given their greater market shares and brand recognition, but the court rejected this argument, reasoning that "the prohibition on discrimination would mean very little if the largest, most profitable firms could always be a category unto themselves simply because they were the largest and most profitable firms."[24]

---

[22] For a discussion of this issue and its manifestation in two related but very different industries – wireless telecommunications and the Internet – see Jorge L. Contreras, *A Tale of Two Layers: Patents, Standards and the Internet*, 93 Denver L. Rev. 855 (2016).

[23] See id.

[24] The district court decision in this case was reversed and remanded by the Federal Circuit on other grounds.

20.4.1 *Hard-Edged Nondiscrimination*

In *Unwired Planet*, the UK court asks what happens if, after a FRAND rate is agreed between a SEP holder and an implementer, the implementer discovers that the SEP holder has, previously or subsequently, granted more favorable terms (i.e., a lower royalty rate) to another "similarly situated" implementer? Has the SEP holder violated its nondiscrimination commitment? Interestingly, the court rules that a SEP licensee cannot challenge a license granted to it on FRAND terms if it later discovers that a similarly situated licensee is paying a lower rate for the same patents unless the difference would "distort competition" between the two licensees. In reaching this conclusion, the court rejects the notion that the ND prong of FRAND implies a "hard-edged" obligation that places an absolute ceiling on the rate that a SEP holder may charge to other licensees. That is, some level of "discrimination" might be permitted, so long as the discrepancy between rates does not distort competition.

20.4.2 *Level Discrimination*

One of the most hotly debated issues concerning the ND prong of FRAND is whether a FRAND commitment requires a SEP holder to grant a license to all applicants, or whether the SEP holder may refuse to license certain categories of potential licensees (usually "upstream" component vendors) so that they may instead license other categories of licensees (usually "downstream" product vendors that purchase components from upstream vendors). This approach is largely motivated by the doctrine of patent exhaustion (see Chapter 23.4), under which a patent holder may collect a royalty only once per patented article. Thus, if a standardized technology is implemented in a chip, the SEP holder may collect a royalty either from the manufacturer of the chip, the assembler of the circuit board on which the chip resides, the producer of the smartphone in which the board is installed or the user of the smartphone that utilizes the chip. But it cannot collect royalties from more than one of these parties in the supply chain. The SEP is "exhausted" once a product is sold by an authorized licensee, and the SEP holder cannot collect royalties from further downstream users of the patented technology.

There is thus a significant debate regarding the ability of SEP holders, under their FRAND commitments, to refuse to grant licenses to upstream component manufacturers who seek SEP licenses. Courts and commentators are divided on this issue. The US Court of Appeals for the Ninth Circuit held in *Microsoft v. Motorola* that a SEP holder, in its declarations to the ITU, promised to "grant a license to an unrestricted number of applicants on a worldwide, nondiscriminatory basis." Likewise, the district court in *FTC v. Qualcomm*, 2018 U.S. Dist. LEXIS 190051, *11–12 (N.D. Cal. 2018) found that the policies of two SDOs, the Telecommunications Industry Association (TIA) and the Alliance for Telecommunications Industry Solutions (ATIS), required Qualcomm to grant licenses to "all applicants."[25]

Nevertheless, some have argued that the "nondiscrimination" prong of FRAND does not require SEP holders to offer licenses to every applicant, but only to avoid discrimination within the class of applicants that the SEP holder chooses to license. SEP holders who refuse to license component vendors have argued that by instead licensing such component vendors' downstream customers, they have, in effect, "indirectly licensed" the component vendors, and that refusing to license component vendors does not discriminate against competitors. In other

---

[25] This ruling was later vacated by the Ninth Circuit as moot. *FTC v. Qualcomm*, slip op. at *20 (9th Cir., Aug. 11, 2020).

words, so long as no component vendors receive licenses, no one component maker is placed at a competitive disadvantage compared to the others. This reasoning was accepted by the district court in *Ericsson v. D-Link*, which held that Ericsson did not violate its nondiscrimination commitment to ETSI by offering licenses only to vendors of "fully compliant" products and refusing to grant licenses to chip and component vendors.

Notes and Questions

1. *Interpretive differences.* As the cases in this section indicate, different courts have interpreted SDO licensing commitments differently. To some degree, these differences may arise from language variations in the SDO policies under consideration. But not always. To what degree should one US district court's interpretation of an SDO policy bind other courts that are interpreting the same SDO policy? What about different SDO policies?

2. *International variation.* As with so many things (chips vs. fries, hood vs. bonnet, football vs. soccer), the British and American approaches to nondiscrimination in FRAND licenses seem to be at odds with one another. Does this transatlantic divergence matter? Why? In recent years, courts in China have also taken an active role in interpreting SDO FRAND commitments, often with strikingly different results than those in the United States. What implications might arise from these and other international differences in interpretation?[26]

3. *Making policies clear.* The reader should by now have realized that if SDO policies were more explicit about their requirements, disagreements like the ones described in this section would be less likely to occur. As the National Academies of Science observed:

   Ideally, SSO policies should clarify the nature of rights and obligations transferred with an SEP in a manner that promotes widespread implementation of standards without creating additional transaction costs that could impede the otherwise efficient transfer of patent rights. To achieve that balance, SSOs need to consider both the legal implications of their IPR policies and their practical effects on different stakeholders.[27]

   Some SDOs have sought to clarify their IP policies. For example, in 2015 the IEEE amended its IP policy to describe various expectations associated with its FRAND commitment, including an express obligation to grant SEP licenses to all applicants. Why don't more SDOs clarify their policies to avoid disagreement over their meaning and intent? What vested interests do you think might work against clarity of SDO policies? The IEEE's 2015 policy amendments were met with fierce opposition. Who do you think opposed them and why?

4. *The origin of patent access requirements.* Commitments to license patents on FRAND terms have their origin in a series of antitrust remedial orders extending back to the early 1940s. These orders were put in place to remedy a range of anticompetitive arrangements that patent holders had created using their patents. More than 100 such orders were entered by the 1970s.[28] Today's FRAND obligations are different, as they are voluntary commitments made by participants in SDOs. If the commitment is the same, does it matter that one is imposed

---

[26] For a discussion of the implications of divergent national approaches to global FRAND licenses, see Jorge L. Contreras, *The New Extraterritoriality: FRAND Royalties, Anti-Suit Injunctions and the Global Race to the Bottom in Disputes over Standards-Essential Patents*, 25(2) B.U. J. Sci. & Tech. L. 251 (2019).

[27] Natl. Research Council, Intellectual Property Challenges for Standard-Setting in the Global Economy 83 (Keith Maskus & Stephen A. Merrill, ed., Natl. Acad. Press, 2013).

[28] See Jorge L. Contreras, *A Brief History of FRAND: Analyzing Current Debates in Standard-Setting and Antitrust through a Historical Lens*, 80 Antitrust L.J. 39 (2015).

by a court but the other is made voluntarily? Should these commitments be interpreted in a similar manner, or does the voluntary nature of today's FRAND commitments make them so unlike their mandatory predecessors that comparison is unwarranted?

20.5 EFFECT OF A FRAND COMMITMENT ON INJUNCTIVE RELIEF

One of the remedies available to a patent holder when its patent is infringed is an injunction – a court order that prohibits the infringer from continuing to infringe the patent. Often, the entry of an injunction means that the infringer may no longer manufacture or sell the infringing product, or that it must design around the patent so that the product no longer infringes. But what happens when a product implements a widely adopted industry standard and infringes a SEP that the SEP holder has committed to license on FRAND terms? May the patent holder seek or obtain an injunction blocking the manufacturer from making and selling the standardized product?

The analysis of injunctive relief in US patent cases takes its current form from the landmark US Supreme Court decision in *eBay Inc. v. MercExchange, L.L.C.*, 547 U.S. 388 (2006). In *eBay*, the Court held that the decision to grant or deny an injunction is an act of judicial discretion that must be exercised in accordance with "well-established principles of equity." The Court articulated a four-factor equitable test to be applied by courts considering the grant of injunctive relief. This test requires the plaintiff seeking an injunction to demonstrate:

1. that it has suffered an irreparable injury;
2. that remedies available at law (i.e., monetary damages) are inadequate to compensate it for that injury;
3. that considering the balance of hardships between the plaintiff and defendant, a remedy in equity is warranted; and
4. that the public interest would not be disserved by the award of an injunction.

In view of these factors, some have argued that a SEP holder, by making a FRAND commitment, implicitly concedes that remedies available at law (i.e., monetary damages) must be adequate to compensate it for the infringement. They reason that, by committing to grant everyone a license on FRAND terms, the SEP holder has agreed not to exclude others from the market, but only to collect a "reasonable" royalty to compensate it for the infringement of its SEPs. As a result, they argue that the second *eBay* factor can never be satisfied by a patent holder that has made a FRAND commitment, and therefore such a SEP holder should generally be precluded from seeking injunctive relief to prevent others from operating under its SEPs. The interplay of FRAND commitments with the US law of patent injunctions has given rise to several judicial decisions as well as guidance from regulatory and enforcement agencies in the United States.

In *Microsoft Corp. v. Motorola, Inc.*, Motorola sought an injunction to prevent Microsoft's continued infringement of Motorola's patents covering two industry standards (IEEE's 802.11 and ITU's H.264) as to which Motorola made FRAND commitments. The court evaluated Motorola's request for an injunction in view of the four *eBay* factors and determined that Motorola did not suffer an irreparable injury or show that monetary damages would be inadequate to compensate it for the infringement. Accordingly, the court denied Motorola's request for an injunction.

In *Realtek Semiconductor Corp. v. LSI Corp.*, the US District Court for the Northern District of California held that a SEP holder breached its FRAND commitment by seeking injunctive relief against an implementer of a standard before the patent holder offered a license to the implementer. Again, the injunction was denied.

These district court decisions laid the groundwork for the Court of Appeals for the Federal Circuit to consider the issue of injunctive relief in *Apple, Inc. v. Motorola, Inc.*, in which the district judge (Richard Posner, sitting by designation from the Seventh Circuit) denied Motorola's request for an injunction against Apple's sale of products that allegedly infringed a SEP covering part of the UMTS 3G wireless telecommunications standard published by the European Telecommunications Standards Association (ETSI). The fractured, three-way opinion of the Federal Circuit is excerpted below.

Apple, Inc. v. Motorola, Inc.

757 F.3d 1286 (Fed. Cir. 2014)

REYNA, CIRCUIT JUDGE

Apple moved for summary judgment that Motorola was not entitled to an injunction for infringement of the '898 patent. The '898 patent is a SEP and, thus, Motorola has agreed to license it on fair, reasonable, and non-discriminatory licensing ("FRAND") terms. The district court granted Apple's motion, stating:

> I don't see how, given FRAND, I would be justified in enjoining Apple from infringing the '898 unless Apple refuses to pay a royalty that meets the FRAND requirement. By committing to license its patents on FRAND terms, Motorola committed to license the '898 to anyone willing to pay a FRAND royalty and thus implicitly acknowledged that a royalty is adequate compensation for a license to use that patent. How could it do otherwise? How could it be permitted to enjoin Apple from using an invention that it contends Apple must use if it wants to make a cell phone with UMTS telecommunications capability—without which it would not be a cell phone.

To the extent that the district court applied a per se rule that injunctions are unavailable for SEPs, it erred.

While Motorola's FRAND commitments are certainly criteria relevant to its entitlement to an injunction, we see no reason to create, as some amici urge, a separate rule or analytical framework for addressing injunctions for FRAND-committed patents. The framework laid out by the Supreme Court in *eBay*, as interpreted by subsequent decisions of this court, provides ample strength and flexibility for addressing the unique aspects of FRAND committed patents and industry standards in general. A patentee subject to FRAND commitments may have difficulty establishing irreparable harm. On the other hand, an injunction may be justified where an infringer unilaterally refuses a FRAND royalty or unreasonably delays negotiations to the same effect. To be clear, this does not mean that an alleged infringer's refusal to accept any license offer necessarily justifies issuing an injunction. For example, the license offered may not be on FRAND terms. In addition, the public has an interest in encouraging participation in standard-setting organizations but also in ensuring that SEPs are not overvalued. While these are important concerns, the district courts are more than capable of considering these factual issues when deciding whether to issue an injunction under the principles in *eBay*.

Applying those principles here, we agree with the district court that Motorola is not entitled to an injunction for infringement of the '898 patent. Motorola's FRAND commitments, which have yielded many license agreements encompassing the '898 patent, strongly suggest that money damages are adequate to fully compensate Motorola for any infringement. Similarly, Motorola has not demonstrated that Apple's infringement has caused it irreparable harm. Considering the large number of industry participants that are already using the system claimed in the '898 patent, including competitors, Motorola has not provided any evidence that adding one more user would create such harm. Again, Motorola has agreed to add as many market participants as are willing to pay a FRAND royalty. Motorola argues that Apple has refused to accept its initial licensing offer and stalled negotiations. However, the record reflects that negotiations have been ongoing, and there is no evidence that Apple has been, for example, unilaterally refusing to agree to a deal. Consequently, we affirm the district court's grant of summary judgment that Motorola is not entitled to an injunction for infringement of the '898 patent.

Rader, Chief Judge, Dissenting-in-Part

I join the court's opinion in its entirety, except for the affirmance of the district court's denial of Motorola's request for an injunction. To my eyes, the record contains sufficient evidence to create a genuine dispute of material fact on Apple's posture as an unwilling licensee whose continued infringement of the '898 patent caused irreparable harm. Because of the unique and intensely factual circumstances surrounding patents adopted as industry standards, I believe the district court improperly granted summary judgment. Therefore, on this narrow point, I respectfully dissent in part.

At the outset, a patent adopted as a standard undoubtedly gains value by virtue of that adoption. This enhancement complicates the evaluation of the technology independent of the standardization. By the same token, the standardization decision may also simply reflect and validate the inherent value of the technology advance accomplished by the patent. Untangling these value components (at the heart of deciding whether a putative licensee was "unwilling" to license, and thus irreparable harm and other injunction factors) requires intense economic analysis of complex facts. In sum, right from the theoretical outset, this question is not likely to be susceptible to summary adjudication.

In reciting the legal principles for an injunction, this court accurately states the inquiries. Those principles supply no per se rule either favoring or proscribing injunctions for patents in any setting, let alone the heightened complexity of standardized technology. This court notes that a patent owner in a standard context "may have difficulty establishing irreparable harm … [but] an injunction may be justified where an infringer unilaterally refuses a FRAND royalty or unreasonably delays negotiations to the same effect."

Market analysts will no doubt observe that a "hold out" (i.e., an unwilling licensee of an SEP seeking to avoid a license based on the value that the technological advance contributed to the prior art) is equally as likely and disruptive as a "hold up" (i.e., an SEP owner demanding unjustified royalties based solely on value contributed by the standardization). These same complex factual questions regarding "hold up" and "hold out" are highly relevant to an injunction request. In sum, differentiating "hold up" from "hold out" requires some factual analysis of the sources of value—the inventive advance or the standardization.

The record in this case shows evidence that Apple may have been a hold out. This evidence alone would create a dispute of material fact.

More important, the district court made no effort to differentiate the value due to inventive contribution from the value due to standardization. Without some attention to that perhaps dispositive question, the trial court was adrift without a map, let alone a compass or GPS system. In fact, without that critical inquiry, the district court could not have properly applied the *eBay* test as it should have.

Instead of a proper injunction analysis, the district court effectively considered Motorola's FRAND commitment as dispositive by itself: "Motorola committed to license the '898 to anyone willing to pay a FRAND royalty and thus implicitly acknowledged that a royalty is adequate compensation for a license to use that patent. How could it do otherwise?" To the contrary, Motorola committed to offer a FRAND license, which begs the question: What is a "fair" and "reasonable" royalty? If Motorola was offering a fair and reasonable royalty, then Apple was likely "refus[ing] a FRAND royalty or unreasonably delay[ing] negotiations." In sum, the district court could not duck the question that it did not address; was Motorola's FRAND offer actually FRAND?

Furthermore, the district court acknowledged the conflicting evidence about Apple's willingness to license the '898 patent: "Apple's refusal to negotiate for a license (if it did refuse—the parties offer competing accounts, unnecessary for me to resolve, of why negotiations broke down) was not a defense to a claim by Motorola for a FRAND royalty." Yet this scenario, adequately presented by this record, is precisely one that the court today acknowledges may justify an injunction.

In my opinion, the court should have allowed Motorola to prove that Apple was an unwilling licensee, which would strongly support its injunction request. The court states that "the record reflects that negotiations have been ongoing," but, as the district court even acknowledged, Motorola asserts otherwise—that Apple for years refused to negotiate while nevertheless infringing the '898 patent. Motorola should have had the opportunity to prove its case that Apple's alleged unwillingness to license or even negotiate supports a showing that money damages are inadequate and that it suffered irreparable harm. The district court refused to develop the facts necessary to apply *eBay* as it should have. Consequently, the case should be remanded to develop that record. For these reasons, I respectfully dissent in part.

Prost, Circuit Judge, Concurring in Part and Dissenting in Part

I concur in the majority's judgment that Motorola is not entitled to an injunction for infringement of the '898 patent. However, I write separately to note my disagreement with the majority's suggestion that an alleged infringer's refusal to negotiate a license justifies the issuance of an injunction after a finding of infringement.

As an initial matter, I agree with the majority that there is no need to create a categorical rule that a patentee can never obtain an injunction on a FRAND-committed patent. Rather, FRAND commitment should simply be factored into the consideration of the *eBay* framework. Moreover, I agree that a straightforward application of the *eBay* factors does not necessarily mean that injunctive relief would never be available for a FRAND-committed patent. However, I disagree as to the circumstances under which an injunction might be appropriate.

Motorola argues—and the majority agrees—that an injunction might be appropriate where an alleged infringer "unilaterally refuses a FRAND royalty or unreasonably delays negotiations to the same effect." Motorola insists that in the absence of the threat of an injunction, an infringer would have no incentive to negotiate a license because the worst-case scenario from a patent infringement lawsuit is that it would have to pay the same amount it would have paid earlier for a license.

I disagree that an alleged infringer's refusal to enter into a licensing agreement justifies entering an injunction against its conduct, for several reasons. First, as Apple points out, an alleged infringer is fully entitled to challenge the validity of a FRAND-committed patent before agreeing to pay a license on that patent, and so should not necessarily be punished for less than eager negotiations. Second, there are many reasons an alleged infringer might prefer to pay a FRAND license rather than undergoing extensive litigation, including litigation expenses, the possibility of paying treble damages or attorney's fees if they are found liable for willful infringement, and the risk that the fact-finder may award damages in an amount higher than the FRAND rates. Indeed, as Motorola itself pointed out, we have previously acknowledged that a trial court may award an amount of damages greater than a reasonable royalty if necessary "to compensate for the infringement." *Stickle v. Heublein, Inc.*, 716 F.2d 1550, 1563 (Fed. Cir. 1983). Thus, if a trial court believes that an infringer previously engaged in bad faith negotiations, it is entitled to increase the damages to account for any harm to the patentee as a result of that behavior.

But regardless, none of these considerations alters the fact that monetary damages are likely adequate to compensate for a FRAND patentee's injuries. I see no reason, therefore, why a party's pre-litigation conduct in license negotiations should affect the availability of injunctive relief.

Instead, an injunction might be appropriate where, although monetary damages could compensate for the patentee's injuries, the patentee is unable to collect the damages to which it is entitled. For example, if an alleged infringer were judgment-proof, a damages award would likely be an inadequate remedy. Or, if a defendant refused to pay a court-ordered damages award after being found to infringe a valid FRAND patent, a court might be justified in including an injunction as part of an award of sanctions.

But regardless, these circumstances are not present in this case, and I agree with the district court that under the facts here, Motorola cannot show either irreparable harm or inadequacy of damages. I would therefore affirm the district court's denial of Motorola's claim for injunctive relief for the '898 patent.

Notes and Questions

1. *Three judges, three opinions.* What is the crux of the disagreement among the three Federal Circuit judges in *Apple v. Motorola*? Which of the judges do you most agree with?

2. *Holdout.* In the plurality opinion in *Apple v. Motorola*, Judge Reyna comments that "an injunction may be justified where an infringer unilaterally refuses a FRAND royalty or unreasonably delays negotiations to the same effect." This type of behavior by potential licensees is often referred to as "holdout" or "reverse hold-up." Chief Judge Rader argues that holdout "is equally as likely and disruptive as a 'hold up.'" Do you agree? Are hold-up and holdout just two sides of the same coin, or different types of wrongs? How should each be treated by the courts?

3. *Enhanced damages for FRAND violations?* In her concurring opinion in *Apple v. Motorola*, Judge Prost makes that point that a SEP holder that is denied injunctive relief may not be entirely out of luck, as courts have the discretion to increase a damages awarded if the

infringer engaged in "willful" infringement. Is the likelihood of an enhanced damages award higher with respect to SEPs than other patents? Why?[29]

4. *The FTC and injunctive relief.* The Federal Trade Commission has also determined that a SEP holder subject to a FRAND commitment should be limited in its ability to seek injunctive relief from a potential SEP licensee. In late 2012 and 2013, the FTC brought actions under Section 5 of the FTC Act against Robert Bosch GmbH and Motorola Mobility (since acquired by Google) to address these companies' threats of injunctive relief against potential SEP licensees. The FTC's claims were settled by consent decrees in which the SEP holders agreed not to seek injunctive relief against an infringer of FRAND-committed patents unless the infringer was beyond the jurisdiction of the US courts, stated in writing that it would not accept a license of the patent, refused to enter into a license agreement determined by a court or arbitrator to comply with the FRAND requirement, or failed to provide written confirmation of an offer of a FRAND license. How do these exceptions square with the opinions in *Apple v. Motorola*?

5. *The European approach: Huawei v. ZTE.* Under the national laws of some European countries, Germany in particular, injunctions are issued almost automatically once a patent holder establishes that its patent has been infringed, and prior to any adjudication of the validity of the asserted patent. This strong presumption in favor of injunctions is somewhat offset by the effect of Article 102 of the Treaty on the Functioning of the European Union (TFEU), which prohibits the "abuse of a dominant position." In some cases, dominance may be conferred by patent rights, and SEPs in particular. Thus, it is possible that a SEP holder's attempt to obtain an injunction against the manufacturer of a standardized product could constitute a violation of Article 102.

The analytical framework for assessing abuse of dominance with SEPs subject to FRAND commitments was established by the European Court of Justice (ECJ) in 2015 in *Huawei v. ZTE*. In *Huawei*, the ECJ held that if a SEP holder possesses market dominance, then in order to avoid violating Article 102, the SEP holder must comply with a series of procedural steps. Likewise, in order to preserve its ability to challenge the SEP holder's conduct under Article 102, the infringer must comply with a similar series of procedural steps. The combination of these behavioral requirements has been referred to as the *Huawei* "choreography," which includes the following steps:

1. the patentee must notify the defendant of the alleged infringement;
2. the defendant must show its willingness to license on FRAND terms;
3. the patentee must make a specific, written offer for a license on FRAND terms;
4. the defendant must diligently respond to that offer without delaying tactics;
5. if the defendant rejects the patentee's offer, it must make a counteroffer on FRAND terms; and
6. if the patentee rejects the counteroffer, the defendant must provide appropriate security (including for past use) and be able to render an account of its acts of use.

In the years since the *Huawei* decision, a number of cases in Germany and other jurisdictions have helped to clarify these requirements, though they seem to raise as many questions as they answer.[30] Should courts in the United States look to the *Huawei* framework when

[29] For a discussion of this issue, see Jorge L. Contreras, et al., The Effect of FRAND Commitments on Patent Remedies, in Patent Remedies and Complex Products: Toward a Global Consensus, Ch. 5 (C. Bradford Biddle et al., ed., Cambridge Univ. Press, 2019).
[30] For a summary of *Huawei* and subsequent cases, see Robin Jacob & Alexander Milner, Lessons from *Huawei v. ZTE*, 4iP Council research report, October 2016, www.4ipcouncil.com/news/latest-research-4ip-council-lessons-huawei-v-zte.

assessing parties' compliance with FRAND obligations? Does it matter that *Huawei* is a case about European competition law, and not contractual interpretation?

6. *Waiver.* Given the legal uncertainty surrounding the availability of injunctive relief, particularly on an international basis, some SDOs have sought to address the issue in their IP policies. While an SDO's internal policies do not affect underlying legal rules, they can impose contractual restraints on SDO members' behavior and establish presumptions that can be considered by courts when assessing a request for injunctive relief. Below is an example of a contractual waiver of injunctive relief included in IEEE's patent policy (note that in IEEE, SEP holders make licensing commitments under written Letters of Assurance, or LOAs):

IEEE STANDARDS ASSOCIATION
IEEE-SA Standards Board Bylaws (December 2017)

"Prohibitive Order" shall mean an interim or permanent injunction, exclusion order, or similar adjudicative directive that limits or prevents making, having made, using, selling, offering to sell, or importing a Compliant Implementation.

An Accepted LOA … signifies that reasonable terms and conditions, including without compensation or under Reasonable Rates, are sufficient compensation for a license to use those Essential Patent Claims and precludes seeking, or seeking to enforce, a Prohibitive Order except as provided in this policy.

The Submitter of an Accepted LOA who has committed to make available a license for one or more Essential Patent Claims agrees that it shall neither seek nor seek to enforce a Prohibitive Order based on such Essential Patent Claim(s) in a jurisdiction unless the implementer fails to participate in, or to comply with the outcome of, an adjudication, including an affirming first-level appellate review, if sought by any party within applicable deadlines, in that jurisdiction by one or more courts that have the authority to: determine Reasonable Rates and other reasonable terms and conditions; adjudicate patent validity, enforceability, essentiality, and infringement; award monetary damages; and resolve any defenses and counterclaims. In jurisdictions where the failure to request a Prohibitive Order in a pleading waives the right to seek a Prohibitive Order at a later time, a Submitter may conditionally plead the right to seek a Prohibitive Order to preserve its right to do so later, if and when this policy's conditions for seeking, or seeking to enforce, a Prohibitive Order are met.

What is prohibited by the above policy clause? Under what circumstances is a SEP holder permitted to seek a prohibitive order against the implementer of an IEEE standard? What is the purpose of the final sentence of this policy language?

As noted above, the IEEE policy has been controversial. Who might have opposed the adoption of the clause shown above? On what basis? Do you think that the clause will have a positive or negative effect on standards development at IEEE? Why?

20.6 THE TRANSFER OF FRAND COMMITMENTS

In Chapter 2 we considered issues arising from the assignment and transfer of IP rights. In Section 13.3 we addressed the assignment and transfer of IP licenses. FRAND commitments raise a new set of issues: when a patent as to which a FRAND commitment has been made is transferred, what happens to that commitment?[31] Does the commitment only bind the firm that made the commitment, or does the commitment travel with the patent to bind its new owner? Absent specific language in the relevant SDO policy, the answer is less than clear.

This issue first received broad attention in connection with a patent covering part of IEEE's 802.3 Fast Ethernet standard. In 1994, the patent's original owner, National Semiconductor, committed to IEEE that it would license the patent for a flat fee of $1,000 to any party implementing the standard. National Semiconductor later sold the patent, which was eventually acquired by Negotiated Data Solutions (N-Data), a PAE run by a former National Semiconductor attorney. N-Data announced that while it would license the patent on FRAND terms, it did not intend to honor National Semiconductor's original $1,000 licensing offer. The FTC brought an action claiming that N-Data's disavowal of National Semiconductor's commitment constituted an unfair method of competition, as well as an unfair act or practice, in violation of Section 5 of the FTC Act (see Chapter 25). The case was settled with a consent decree pursuant to which N-Data agreed to honor National Semiconductor's original $1,000 licensing commitment.[32]

The issue of transfers arose again in 2011, when bankrupt Nortel Networks, a contributor to several SDOs, proposed the sale of its assets, including approximately 4,000 patents, in a bankruptcy sale on a "free and clear" basis.[33] Several product vendors, together with IEEE, argued that Nortel's "free and clear" sale could erase the patent licensing commitments that Nortel had previously made to SDOs, including IEEE. Ultimately, the purchaser of the patents, a consortium including several large product vendors, voluntarily agreed to abide by Nortel's prior FRAND commitments and the issue was not adjudicated.[34]

Because the law remains unsettled in this regard, an increasing number of SDOs require participants that transfer SEPs as to which FRAND commitments have been made to ensure that those commitments are binding on subsequent owners of those SEPs. The policy approach adopted by IETF is shown below.

RFC 8179/BCP 79: INTELLECTUAL PROPERTY RIGHTS IN IETF TECHNOLOGY (MAY 2017)

Internet Engineering Task Force

5.5.c. It is likely that IETF will rely on licensing declarations and other information that may be contained in an IPR disclosure and that implementers will make technical, legal, and commercial decisions on the basis of such commitments and information. Thus, when licensing declarations and other information, comments, notes, or URLs for further information are contained in an IPR disclosure, the persons making such disclosure agree and

---

[31] This question is separate from the fate of licenses that have been executed in response to a FRAND commitment. Those licenses, as discussed in Chapter 11, likely continue following the transfer of the underlying patents. FRAND commitments, however, are commitments to enter into licenses, rather than licenses themselves.

[32] *Negotiated Data Solutions LLC*, No. C-4234, 2008 WL 4407246 (F.T.C. Sept. 22, 2008).

[33] Under Section 363(f) of the US Bankruptcy Code, a bankruptcy trustee or debtor in possession may sell the bankruptcy estate's assets "free and clear of any interest in such property." See Chapter 21 for a further discussion of bankruptcy issues in IP licensing transactions.

[34] *In re Nortel Networks, Inc.*, 469 B.R. 478, 488 (Bankr. D. Del. 2012). ("On July 11, 2011, the Court entered an order approving the sale of Nortel's Residual Patent Assets, representing some 6,000 patents for telecommunications, internet, wireless, and other technology, to Rockstar Bidco, LP.")

acknowledge that the commitments and information contained in such disclosure shall be irrevocable and will attach, to the extent permissible by law, to the associated IPR, and all implementers of Implementing Technologies will be justified and entitled to rely on such materials in relating to such IPR, whether or not such IPR is subsequently transferred to a third party by the IPR holder making the commitment or providing the information. IPR holders making IPR disclosures that contain licensing declarations or providing such information, comments, notes, or URLs for further information must ensure that such commitments are binding on any transferee of the relevant IPR, and that such transferee will use reasonable efforts to ensure that such commitments are binding on a subsequent transferee of the relevant IPR, and so on.

Notes and Questions

1. *A noncontested policy.* Unlike SDO policy amendments seeking to clarify the method of calculating FRAND royalties or limiting the ability of SDO members to seek injunctive relief, policy language requiring SEP licensing commitments to travel with transferred patents has not been particularly controversial.[35] Why not? Are there parties that might not wish FRAND licensing commitments to continue after a SEP is transferred to a new owner?

2. *The view from the government.* As noted above, the FTC brought an action against N-Data when it disavowed National Semiconductor's original SEP licensing commitment to IEEE. It raised similar concerns in its 2012 and 2013 actions against Motorola Mobility and Robert Bosch (see Section 20.4, Note 4). Officials from the DOJ and the European Commission have also encouraged SDOs to clarify that SEP licensing commitments travel with the underlying patents when they are transferred. Why are government enforcement agencies so interested in this topic? Why is this issue primarily addressed by antitrust and competition enforcement agencies rather than the legislature or other administrative agencies? What arguments might exist that such FRAND commitments do not travel with the underlying patents?

3. *FRAND as servitude?* One academic theory that has been proposed in the literature is that FRAND commitments relating to SEPs can be analogized to real property servitudes (easements, covenants) that "run with the land." When a piece of real estate is sold, easements across that property continue to bind the new owner. Likewise, FRAND commitments made with respect a patent should continue to bind each successive owner of the patent. What do you think of this theory? Property-based analogies have not been embraced by courts assessing FRAND commitments. Why not?[36] Compare this reluctance with courts' willingness to treat other aspects of patent and copyright licenses as "running with the right" (see Section 3.5).

---

[35] For a discussion of contested versus noncontested SDO policy amendments, see Justus Baron, et al., *Making the Rules: The Governance of Standard Development Organizations and their Policies on Intellectual Property Rights*, JRC Science for Policy Report EUR 29655 at 157–58 (March 2019).

[36] For a discussion and critique of these theories, see Contreras, Market Reliance, supra note 7, at 536–38.

PART IV

Advanced Licensing Topics

Bankruptcy and Insolvency Issues

US bankruptcy law can be invoked voluntarily or involuntarily when a company (a debtor) is unable to meet its obligations to its creditors. The law is designed to protect both debtors and creditors by modifying the relationship between a debtor's assets and its obligations. Two general types of bankruptcy proceeding are available under the US Bankruptcy Code: liquidation under Chapter 7 and reorganization under Chapter 11.[1]

In a Chapter 7 liquidation the debtor ceases all operations and its assets are collected and sold by a court-appointed trustee. The order in which the proceeds from this sale are distributed to the creditors depends on the type of debt owed. The filing of a bankruptcy proceeding initiates this process by creating a bankruptcy "estate" to which the debtor's property is transferred and assigning a trustee to manage the property. These actions are taken to protect the interests of the creditors during the pendency of the proceeding.

In contrast, under Chapter 11 the debtor continues to operate its business as a "debtor in possession" (DIP) with a fiduciary duty to maintain its assets for the benefit of its creditors. In the proceeding, the debtor's liabilities and obligations are reorganized in a manner that is designed to optimize the debtor company's ongoing value. As part of the proceeding, the debtor's plan of reorganization must be approved by both the creditors and the court. Once the proceeding is concluded, the debtor's business, obligations and debts are restructured and it may continue operations as an independent company.

21.1 AUTOMATIC STAY OF PROCEEDINGS

The filing of a bankruptcy petition in the United States triggers an automatic stay of most efforts to collect from, enforce rights against or take or use property of the bankruptcy estate.

[1] This chapter focuses exclusively on corporate bankruptcy and insolvency proceedings. Different rules apply to individual debtors in certain cases. Insolvency, which unlike "bankruptcy" is generally a matter of state law, means that the sum of the debtor's assets is less than the sum of its existing obligations (debts), or that the debtor is unable to pay its obligations as they become due.

11 U.S.C. § 362(a): AUTOMATIC STAY

(a) Except as provided in subsection (b) of this section, a petition filed under [this title] operates as a stay, applicable to all entities, of –

    (1) the commencement or continuation, including the issuance or employment of process, of a judicial, administrative, or other action or proceeding against the debtor that was or could have been commenced before the commencement of the case under this title, or to recover a claim against the debtor that arose before the commencement of the case under this title;

    (2) the enforcement, against the debtor or against property of the estate, of a judgment obtained before the commencement of the case under this title;

    (3) any act to obtain possession of property of the estate or of property from the estate or to exercise control over property of the estate;

    (4) any act to create, perfect, or enforce any lien against property of the estate;

    (6) any act to collect, assess, or recover a claim against the debtor that arose before the commencement of the case under this title;

The automatic stay under the Bankruptcy Code is a powerful tool. It demonstrates the priority that bankruptcy proceedings have over other actions, precluding otherwise lawful actions unless the actor obtains permission from the Bankruptcy Court. As explained by the Ninth Circuit, its purpose is "to give the debtor a breathing spell from creditors, to stop all collection efforts, and to permit the debtor to attempt repayment or reorganization."[2] Thus, any other legal actions that may impact a bankruptcy proceeding by removing property from the bankruptcy estate are frozen as of the date the proceeding commences.

Keep these principles in mind as you read the following case involving the automatic stay.

United States v. Inslaw, Inc.

932 F.2d 1467 (D.C. Cir. 1991)

WILLIAM, CIRCUIT JUDGE

    Inslaw, Inc., after filing for reorganization under Chapter 11 of the Bankruptcy Code, invoked § 362(a) to secure bankruptcy court adjudication of … its prolonged dispute with the Department of Justice over the Department's right to use a case-tracking software system that Inslaw had provided under contract. Inslaw claimed that the Department had violated the stay provision by continuing, and expanding, its use of the software [PROMIS] in its U.S. Attorneys' offices [after the bankruptcy filing]. The bankruptcy court found a willful violation and the district court affirmed on appeal. [We reverse.]

    [Inslaw's] major allegation concerns the Department's use of enhanced PROMIS after the filing of the bankruptcy petition. The bankruptcy court concluded first that the privately-funded enhancements to PROMIS were proprietary trade secrets owned by

---

[2] *Computer Comm. Inc. v. Codex*, 824 F.2d 725 (9th Cir. 1987).

Inslaw, and then that the Department's continued use of these enhancements, and in particular its post-petition installation of enhanced PROMIS in 23 U.S. Attorneys' offices (in addition to the 22 where Inslaw had made installations), were a "willful exercise of control over the property of the estate."

The automatic stay protects "property of the estate." This estate is created by the filing of a petition and comprises property of the debtor "wherever located and by whomever held," including (among other things) "all legal or equitable interests of the debtor in property as of the commencement of the case." 11 U.S.C. § 541(a)(1) (1988). It is undisputed that this encompasses causes of action that belong to the debtor, as well as the debtor's intellectual property, such as interests in patents, trademarks and copyrights. The estate also includes property recoverable under the Code's "turnover" provisions, which allow the trustee to recover property that "was merely out of the possession of the debtor, yet remained 'property of the debtor.'"

In its brief, Inslaw refers rather vaguely to its interest in the enhanced PROMIS software as the "property of the estate" over which the Department supposedly exercised control. But for meaningful analysis, Inslaw's interests must be examined separately. One set of interests consists of (1) the computer tapes containing copies of the source and object codes that Inslaw sent to the Department on April 20, 1983 and (2) the copies of enhanced PROMIS that Inslaw installed on Department hardware between August 1983 and January 1984. As to these, Inslaw held no possessory interest when it filed for bankruptcy on February 7, 1985. Nor can it claim a possessory interest over them through the Code's turnover provisions, [because] as Inslaw freely admits, the Department held possession of the copies under a claim of ownership (its view of the contract …) and claimed the right to use enhanced PROMIS without further payment. [A] debtor cannot use the turnover provisions to liquidate contract disputes or otherwise demand assets whose title is in dispute. Indeed, Inslaw never sought possession of the copies under the turnover provisions.

The bankruptcy court instead identified the relevant property as Inslaw's intangible trade secret rights in the PROMIS enhancements. It then found that the Department's continuing use of these intangible enhancements was an "exercise of control" over property of the estate.

If the bankruptcy court's idea of the scope of "exercise of control" were correct, the sweep of § 362(a) would be extraordinary – with a concomitant expansion of the jurisdiction of the bankruptcy court. Whenever a party against whom the bankrupt holds a cause of action (or other intangible property right) acted in accord with his view of the dispute rather than that of the debtor-in-possession or bankruptcy trustee, he would risk a determination by a bankruptcy court that he had "exercised control" over intangible rights (property) of the estate.

[Such] assertions of bankruptcy court jurisdiction raise severe constitutional problems. Even apart from constitutional concerns, Inslaw's view of § 362(a) would take it well beyond Congress's purpose. The object of the automatic stay provision is essentially to solve a collective action problem – to make sure that creditors do not destroy the bankrupt estate in their scramble for relief. Fulfillment of that purpose cannot require that every party who acts in resistance to the debtor's view of its rights violates § 362(a) if found in error by the bankruptcy court. Thus, someone defending a suit brought by the debtor does not risk violation of § 362(a)(3) by filing a motion to dismiss the suit, though his resistance may burden rights asserted by the bankrupt. Nor does the filing of a *lis pendens* violate the stay (at least where it does not create a lien), even though it alerts prospective buyers to a hazard and may thereby diminish the value of estate property. And the commencement and continuation of a cause of action against the debtor that arises post-petition, and so is not stayed by § 362(a)(1), does not violate § 362(a)(3). Since willful violations of the stay expose the offending party to liability for compensatory damages, costs, attorney's fees, and, in some circumstances, punitive damages, see 11 U.S.C. § 362(h) (1988), it is difficult to believe that Congress intended a violation whenever someone already in possession of property mistakenly refuses to capitulate to a bankrupt's assertion of rights in that property.

[Our] understanding of § 362(a) does not expose bankrupts to any troubling hazard. Here, for example, Inslaw retains whatever intangible property rights it had in enhanced PROMIS at the time of filing. If the Department has violated the [contract,] Inslaw as debtor-in-possession has all the access to court enjoyed by any victim of a contract breach by the United States government. If [the alleged modification of the contract] was induced by fraud, [then] Inslaw has its contract remedies or perhaps a suit for conversion. Assuming that its privately-funded enhancements to PROMIS qualify as proprietary trade secrets, [it] may be able to sue the government under the Trade Secrets Act or even under the Administrative Procedure Act for improper disclosures of its trade secrets by government officials.

[Because] the Department has taken no actions since the filing of the bankruptcy petition that violate the automatic stay, the bankruptcy court must, as both a statutory and constitutional matter, defer to adjudication of these matters by other forums. So ordered.

Notes and Questions

1. *The* Inslaw *saga.* The *Inslaw* decision excerpted above is just one small piece in a sprawling legal dispute that improbably combines software licensing with international espionage, illicit arms deals and government cover-ups. According to Inslaw, the Department of Justice played a significant role in forcing the company into bankruptcy, which led to the above litigation regarding the DOJ's rights following Inslaw's filing. According to news reports, television programs and fragments of the case record, Inslaw licensed its PROMIS software to the US Department of Justice (DOJ) to help prosecutors monitor case records. But the DOJ, possibly with the help of the National Security Agency (NSA), modified the software without Inslaw's permission to enable it to spy on its users. The DOJ, possibly in coordination with high-ranking officials of the Reagan Administration, then allegedly distributed copies of the software to US allies, including the UK, Israel and Australia, using it to collect information surreptitiously from these countries.[3]

2. *Exercise of control.* The Bankruptcy Court in *Inslaw* found that the DOJ's continued use of the proprietary PROMIS software after Inslaw's bankruptcy filing constituted an "exercise of control" over Inslaw's trade secrets, which was subject to the automatic stay. The DC Circuit reversed, holding that the DOJ's use of property was *not* the exercise of control over that property. Given this holding, what kind of activity *would* constitute the attempted exercise of control of a software program licensed by the debtor to a third party?

3. *Post-petition actions not stayed.* In *Inslaw*, the court notes that the automatic stay does not prohibit a defendant from defending against a suit brought by the debtor-in-possession, nor

---

[3] Ryan Gallagher, *Dirtier than Watergate*, New Statesman, April 20, 2011.

does it prohibit "the commencement and continuation of a cause of action against the debtor that arises post-petition." By the same token, the court suggests that Inslaw could bring a post-petition action for damages or intellectual property infringement against the DOJ for its unauthorized use of the PROMIS software. Even so, the DOJ's use of the software, even if unauthorized, does not fall within the scope of the automatic stay in bankruptcy.

4. *Actions barred.* In *Computer Communications, Inc. v. Codex Corp.*, 824 F.2d 725 (9th Cir. 1987), CCI and Codex were parties to a contract whereby Codex would purchase computer equipment from CCI. Shortly after CCI filed for bankruptcy, Codex sought to terminate the agreement in accordance with its terms. Among other things (see Section 21.5 for a discussion of the rule against *ipso facto* bankruptcy clauses), CCI argued that Codex was barred by the automatic stay from terminating the contract without permission of the bankruptcy court. The Ninth Circuit agreed with CCI, holding that the termination of a contract constituted an attempt to exert control over an intangible asset of the debtor (the contract). It explained:

> The legislative history emphasizes that the stay is intended to be broad in scope. Congress designed it to protect debtors and creditors from piecemeal dismemberment of the debtor's estate. The automatic stay statute itself provides a summary procedure for obtaining relief from the stay. All parties benefit from the fair and orderly process contemplated by the automatic stay and judicial relief procedure. Judicial toleration of an alternative procedure of self-help and post hoc justification would defeat the purpose of the automatic stay. Accordingly, we affirm the bankruptcy and district courts on the ground that Codex violated the automatic stay by unilaterally terminating the contract ...

5. *Congressional intent?* The court in *Inslaw* notes that "it is difficult to believe that Congress intended a violation [of the automatic stay] whenever someone already in possession of property mistakenly refuses to capitulate to a bankrupt's assertion of rights in that property." What situation was the court referring to?

Problem 21.1

Which of the following actions would most likely be permitted in view of the automatic stay created by the debtor's filing for bankruptcy?

a. A licensor delivers the debtor a notice terminating a copyright license one day prior to filing for bankruptcy.
b. A licensor files an action in state court, one week after the debtor's filing for bankruptcy, seeking an injunction against the debtor who has licensed the licensor's trademarks and trade name.
c. A licensor files a lawsuit for patent infringement against the debtor one week prior to the debtor's filing for bankruptcy.

21.2 THE BANKRUPTCY ESTATE

As noted above, filing a bankruptcy petition causes an immediate and automatic transfer of all the debtor's "property" into the bankruptcy estate. This transfer has an immediate impact on entities dealing with the debtor and can substantially change the terms on which their relationship was built. Since the goal of a bankruptcy proceeding is to maximize value for creditors, the description of "property" included in the bankruptcy estate is broad.

Section 541(a) of the Bankruptcy Code provides that the bankruptcy estate "is comprised of … all legal or equitable interests of the debtor in property as of the commencement of the case [and various designated types of property acquired after commencement of the case]." The key point in time for this purpose is thus the commencement of the bankruptcy case.

"Property of the estate" generally includes intellectual property (IP) rights, license rights, lawsuits and all other tangible and intangible assets of potential value at the time of a bankruptcy filing, as well as all "proceeds, product, offspring, rents, and profits of or from property of the estate." The definition of proceeds is quite important in determining what assets the creditors have access to.

Thus, in *Keen, Inc. v. Gecker*, 264 F. Supp. 659 (N.D. Ill. 2003), the court held that a patent application pending at the time of a bankruptcy filing was the property of the bankruptcy estate, as were any royalties earned after the patent issued (i.e., as "proceeds" arising from that property). In contrast, if the debtor begins a new line of research *after* the bankruptcy filing, and that research leads to an important new discovery that the debtor patents, that patent and its proceeds would *not* form part of the bankruptcy estate, as they arose after the filing.

The question of what assets are included in the bankruptcy estate is important for several reasons, including the degree to which the creditors of the bankrupt debtor are entitled to receive the proceeds of those assets.

Problem 21.2

Spendthrift Corp. is a producer of industrial chemicals. Suppose that in January 2013, Spendthrift discovers and files a patent application for a new nontoxic solvent. In December 2014, Spendthrift then files for reorganization under Chapter 11 of the Bankruptcy Code. The patent issues in March 2015, and in April the DIP licenses the patent to Ajax Corp. for an up-front royalty of $1 million. In June 2015, the DIP sells the patent to Bromide Corp. for $2 million. In August 2015, the DIP hires Rita Reagent, a world-renowned chemist. Rita immediately invents a heat-resistant lubricant compound and the DIP files a patent application on the invention. The lubricant patent issues in record time in July 2016. The DIP then sells this patent to Lubrizol, Inc. for $3 million. In October 2016, the DIP enters into a consulting agreement with Bromide relating to the manufacture of solvents made using the technology claimed in the 2015 patent. Which assets are included in Spendthrift's bankruptcy estate, and which are not?

21.3 EXECUTORY CONTRACTS AND SECTION 365(n)

Among the debtor's assets and property that are transferred to the bankruptcy estate are contract rights that existed at the time of filing for bankruptcy. However, in the case of contracts that have not been fully performed at the time of filing (so-called "executory" contracts), Section 365 of the Bankruptcy Code gives the trustee in bankruptcy or the debtor in possession the right to choose whether or not to assume such contracts.

The purpose of this powerful right is to allow the trustee to maximize the value of the estate's assets. As such, it may assume those contracts that would be beneficial to the debtor, while rejecting those that would be burdensome or uneconomical to perform.

If a contract is assumed, the responsibilities of the contract may be retained or assigned by the trustee, subject to court approval. If a contract is rejected, the debtor ceases its performance. Such nonperformance may constitute a breach of the contract, leaving the other contracting party with a claim for monetary damages against the estate that is adjudicated along with the claims of other creditors.

Originally, the Bankruptcy Code did not give much guidance regarding the treatment of IP licenses under Section 365. On one hand, the most significant legal event to occur under a licensing agreement – the grant of the license – occurs upon execution of the agreement. On the other hand, most licensing agreements include a range of ongoing commitments by the parties, including the payment of running royalties, confidentiality, indemnification and so forth. Given these factors, should an IP licensing agreement that was in place before a filing for bankruptcy generally be considered an executory contract or not? And if it is an executory contract, may a trustee in bankruptcy reject it long after the license has been granted?

The Fourth Circuit considered this question in the well-known case *Lubrizol Enterprises, Inc. v. Richmond Metal Finishers, Inc.*, 756 F.2d 1043 (4th Cir. 1985). In that case, Richmond Metal Finishers (RMF) granted Lubrizol a nonexclusive license to utilize a metal coating process technology. The agreement required Lubrizol to pay periodic royalties to RMF. A year after the license was granted, RMF filed for bankruptcy under Chapter 11. As part of its plan to emerge from bankruptcy, RMF sought, pursuant to § 365(a), to characterize the agreement as executory and to reject it in order to facilitate a sale or licensing of the technology at a more favorable price. Lubrizol, not wishing to lose its rights under the agreement, argued that the agreement was largely performed and thus not executory.

The Fourth Circuit disagreed. First, it noted that under prevailing precedent, "a contract is executory if the obligations of both the bankrupt and the other party to the contract are so far unperformed that the failure of either to complete the performance would constitute a material breach excusing the performance of the other." Next, it outlined the as-yet unperformed duties of each of the parties:

> RMF owed the following duties to Lubrizol under the agreement: (1) to notify Lubrizol of any patent infringement suit and to defend in such suit; (2) to notify Lubrizol of any other use or licensing of the process, and to reduce royalty payments if a lower royalty rate agreement was reached with another licensee; and (3) to indemnify Lubrizol for losses arising out of any misrepresentation or breach of warranty by RMF. Lubrizol owed RMF reciprocal duties of accounting for and paying royalties for use of the process and of cancelling certain existing indebtedness.

Given these continuing obligations of both parties, the court held that the agreement was executory and permitted RMF to cancel it, leaving Lubrizol without the license that it had already paid a significant amount to secure.

The *Lubrizol* case led to a significant outcry in the technology sector, as firms quickly realized that the rights that they had under license were vulnerable to cancelation if their licensor entered bankruptcy proceedings. As a result, Congress convened hearings and three years later enacted the Intellectual Property Bankruptcy Act of 1988, which was codified as Section 365(n) of the Bankruptcy Code. As explained by one commentator:

> In enacting section 365(n), Congress recognized that technological development and innovation are advanced by encouraging solvent licensees to invest in start-up companies. Indeed, the economic reality is that intellectual property is often developed by undercapitalized companies relying on the financial support of solvent licensees to provide "venture capital" for development. To encourage investment in intellectual property and to protect the rights of licensees who contribute financing, research, development, manufacturing, or marketing skills, Congress limited the power of debtor-licensors to "reject" licenses as executory contracts.

As the judiciary committees observed, it would be inequitable if a licensee who funded the development of the intellectual property, or who invested substantial monies in anticipation of using or marketing the technology, were denied the benefit of its bargain. It would also be unjust if the debtor or creditors' committee could unilaterally disclose jointly developed trade secrets, patents, or copyrightable information. Such disclosures would have a devastating effect on the licensee's business, possibly even causing its bankruptcy. The judiciary committees compared the licensee's predicament to that of a lessee of real property because in both instances the consequences of the debtor's breach is not compensable in monetary damages.[4]

Section 365(n), which is reproduced below, effectively eliminates the effect of a bankrupt licensor's rejection of an executory IP license by allowing the licensee to continue to enjoy the benefits of that license, so long as it continues to make all required payments (the subject of the *Prize Frize* case excerpted below).

BANKRUPTCY CODE SECTION 365(n)

(1) If the trustee rejects an executory contract under which the debtor is a licensor of a right to intellectual property, the licensee under such contract may elect –

    (A) to treat such contract as terminated by such rejection if such rejection by the trustee amounts to such a breach as would entitle the licensee to treat such contract as terminated by virtue of its own terms, applicable nonbankruptcy law, or an agreement made by the licensee with another entity; or

    (B) to retain its rights (including a right to enforce any exclusivity provision of such contract, but excluding any other right under applicable nonbankruptcy law to specific performance of such contract) under such contract ... to such intellectual property ... as such rights existed immediately before the case commenced, for (i) the duration of such contract ...

(2) If the licensee elects to retain its rights, as described in paragraph (1)(B) of this subsection, under such contract –

    (A) the trustee shall allow the licensee to exercise such rights;

    (B) the licensee shall make all royalty payments due under such contract for the duration of such contract ...

(3) If the licensee elects to retain its rights, as described in paragraph (1)(B) of this subsection, then on the written request of the licensee the trustee shall –

    (A) to the extent provided in such contract ... provide to the licensee any intellectual property ... held by the trustee; and

    (B) not interfere with the rights of the licensee as provided in such contract ... to such intellectual property ... including any right to obtain such intellectual property ... from another entity.

---

[4] Marjorie F. Chertok, *Structuring License Agreements with Companies in Financial Difficulty: Section 365(n) – Divining Rod or Obstacle Course?* 65 St. John's L. Rev. 1045 (1991).

In Re Prize Frize, Inc.

32 F.3d 426 (9th Cir. 1994)

NOONAN, CIRCUIT JUDGE

This case, of first impression in any circuit, turns on whether license fees, paid by a licensee for the use of technology, patents, and proprietary rights, are "royalties" within the meaning of 11 U.S.C. § 365(n)(2)(B) and, as such, must continue to be paid after the licensor in bankruptcy has exercised its statutory right to reject the contract.

Facts

The debtor, Prize Frize, Inc., is the owner and licensor of all technology, patents, proprietary rights and related rights used in the manufacture and sale of a French fry vending machine. On March 6, 1991, the debtor entered into a License Agreement granting an exclusive license to utilize the proprietary rights and to manufacture, use and sell the vending machine. In consideration for the license to use the proprietary information and related rights, the licensee agreed to pay the debtor a $1,250,000 license fee – $300,000 to be paid within ten days of execution of the agreement with the balance due in $50,000 monthly payments. The licensee also agreed to pay royalty payments based on a percentage of franchise fees, of net marketing revenues and of any sales of the machines or certain related products. The license agreement also provided that if there was a failure of design and/or components of the machines to the extent that they were not fit for their intended use and were withdrawn from service, then the licensee's obligations would be suspended for a period of 180 days, during which time the debtor was entitled to cure any defect. Encino Business Management, Inc. (EBM) is the successor licensee under this license.

The debtor filed its Chapter 11 petition on March 12, 1991. In September of 1991, EBM, which had become the licensee, stopped making the $50,000 per month license fee payments and has made no payments since. EBM contends that there is a design defect in the machines which caused the machines to be withdrawn from service and which allowed the suspension of its obligation to pay the debtor.

The debtor subsequently filed a motion to reject the license agreement with EBM and to compel EBM to elect whether it wished to retain its rights under section 365(n)(1). EBM did not file a written response to the motion. At the hearing, EBM's counsel indicated that he did not oppose rejection. He disputed, however, that EBM should be required to immediately pay $350,000 in past due license fee payments, contending that the obligation to make such payments was suspended because of the purported design defect.

The bankruptcy court entered an order indicating that the debtor might reject the agreement, that EBM might elect whether to retain its rights under the agreement pursuant to section 365(n)(1) and that if EBM elected to retain its rights under the agreement it must do the following: (1) make all license fee payments presently due in the amount of $350,000 within seven days of its election; (2) pay the $400,000 balance of the license fee in monthly installments of $50,000; and (3) waive any and all rights of setoff with respect to the contract and applicable non-bankruptcy law and any claim under section 503(b) arising from performance under the agreement. The court's order also stated that assuming, arguendo, that EBM's payment obligations were properly suspended, the 180-day suspension period had ended and the September to March monthly payments were now due.

EBM appealed.

Analysis

Section 365 of the Bankruptcy Code is an intricate statutory scheme governing the treatment by the trustee in bankruptcy or the debtor-in-possession of the executory contracts of the debtor. There is no dispute that the license agreement between EBM and the debtor was executory, i.e. there were obligations on both sides which to some extent were unperformed. Consequently, the debtor had the right to reject the contract. However, section 365(n)(1) qualifies this right when the debtor is "a licensor of a right to intellectual property." There is no dispute that the debtor is such a licensor. Consequently, EBM as "the licensee under such contract" could make an election. § 365(n)(1). EBM could either treat the contract as terminated as provided by (n)(1)(A), or EBM could retain its rights to the intellectual property for the duration of the contract and any period for which the contract might be extended by the licensee as of right under applicable nonbankruptcy law.

EBM elected to retain its rights. It was then obligated to "make all royalty payments due under such contract." By the terms of the statute EBM was also "deemed to waive any right of setoff it may have with respect to such contract under this title or applicable nonbankruptcy law."

Section 365(n) has struck a fair balance between the interests of the bankrupt and the interests of a licensee of the bankrupt's intellectual property. The bankrupt cannot terminate and strip the licensee of rights the licensee had bargained for. The licensee cannot retain the use of those rights without paying for them. It is essential to the balance struck that the payments due for the use of the intellectual property should be analyzed as "royalties," required by the statute itself to be met by the licensee who is enjoying the benefit of the bankrupt's patents, proprietary property, and technology. [The] legislative history buttresses this commonsense interpretation of "royalties" in the statute.

EBM's principal argument is that the licensing agreement itself makes a distinction between what the agreement calls "license fees" and what the agreement calls "royalty payments." The "royalty payments" in the agreement are percentages payable on the retail sales price of each machine sold by EBM; the "license fees" in the agreement are the sums here in dispute which were to be paid for the license to manufacture and sell the vending machine. EBM's argument is not frivolous. Nonetheless the parties by their choice of names cannot alter the underlying reality nor change the balance that the Bankruptcy Code has struck. Despite the nomenclature used in the agreement, the license fees to be paid by EBM are royalties in the sense of section 365(n). Section 365(n) speaks repeatedly of "licensor" and "licensee" with the clear implication that payments by licensee to licensor for the use of intellectual property are, indifferently, "licensing fees" or "royalties," and, as royalties, must be paid by the licensee who elects to keep its license after the licensor's bankruptcy. The same indifference to nomenclature in referring to a licensee's lump sum or percentage-of-sales payments as royalties is apparent in patent cases.

EBM's fallback position on appeal is that the debtor has been freed by its rejection of the contract from the obligations assumed by the debtor under Article V ("Representations, Warranties and Covenants by PFI") of the agreement. These obligations included the debtor's agreement to hold EBM harmless from any claim arising out of events preceding the agreement, to defend any infringement suit relating to technology or design included in the machine, and to prosecute at its own expense any infringers of the rights granted by the agreement. The debtor also represented that the design of the Stand-Alone Machine was free from material defects. These obligations raise the question whether it is proper to consider all of the license fees as royalties or whether some portion of the fees should be allocated to payment for the obligations assumed by the debtor. Neither the bankruptcy court nor the BAP addressed this possibility. They did not because EBM did not present this question to them. It is consequently too late to raise it here. EBM still has its unsecured claim for breach of the entire license agreement that § 365(g) accords it. As its appeal was non-frivolous, no attorney's fees are awarded.

As what the licensing agreement denominates "license fees" must be regarded as "royalty payments" for purposes of § 365(n)(1)(B), the judgment [is] AFFIRMED.

Notes and Questions

1. *Executory contracts: copyright.* The issues discussed above are not unique to patent licenses. In *Otto Preminger Films, Ltd. v. Quintex Entertainment, Ltd.*, 950 F.2d 1492 (9th Cir. 1991), the Ninth Circuit held that a contract relating to the colorization of several motion pictures was executory. Among other things, the contract required the licensor to: (1) refrain from selling the rights to subdistribute the movies to third parties; (2) indemnify and defend the licensee; and (3) exercise creative control over the colorization and marketing of the pictures. In addition, the licensee remained contractually obligated to give accountings and pay royalties for future sales of the pictures.

   Likewise, in *In re Select-A-Seat Corp.*, 625 F.2d 290 (9th Cir. 1980), the court held that an exclusive software license was executory because the licensee remained obligated to pay the licensor a portion of the licensee's annual net return from use of the software, while the licensor remained obligated not to sell its software packages to other parties.

   All things considered, do these agreements sound executory to you? If so, what obligations would need to be eliminated to make these agreements non-executory? Realistically, are there any IP licensing agreements that are not executory by these standards?

2. *The* Lubrizol *effect.* As noted above, Congress enacted Section 365(n) as a direct response to the *Lubrizol* decision. What was so wrong with *Lubrizol*? And if Section 365(a) allows the rejection of other executory contracts, why should IP licenses be treated differently?[5]

3. *The effect of 365(n).* Do you agree with the court in *Prize Frize* that "Section 365(n) has struck a fair balance between the interests of the bankrupt and the interests of a licensee of the bankrupt's intellectual property"?

4. *Trademark licenses.* Section 101(35A) of the Bankruptcy Code defines "intellectual property" as including trade secrets, patented inventions, plant varieties, copyrighted works and semiconductor mask works. Notably absent from this list are trademarks. One reason for this omission, it has been argued, is that a trademark licensor is required to exercise quality control over the goods and services sold under its mark (see Section 15.3). If a trademark licensor is in bankruptcy, and is required to allow its licensees to retain their right to use its marks, then the licensor will necessarily be required to exert effort to police the use of those marks – an effort that may not serve to maximize the value of the bankruptcy estate.

   Courts were divided over the ability of a trademark licensor to reject trademark licenses in bankruptcy. The confusion was finally resolved by the Supreme Court in *Mission Product*

---

[5] Note that there is a similar exclusion in the Bankruptcy Code for real estate leases. 11 U.S.C. 365(h)(1) prohibits a debtor landlord from evicting a tenant who does not wish to vacate the premises.

Holdings v. Tempnology, LLC, 139 S. Ct. 1652, 1662 (2019). There, the Court looked not to Section 365(n), which admittedly does not include trademarks within its ambit, but to the effect of breach on licenses outside of the bankruptcy context. That is, Section 365(g) of the Bankruptcy Code provides that if a trustee in bankruptcy rejects a debtor's obligations under an executory contract, that rejection constitutes a breach of the agreement. But outside the bankruptcy context, a breach of contract by a licensor of IP does not automatically terminate the licensee's rights. The licensee's rights cease only if the licensee elects to terminate the contract for the licensor's breach. Upon a licensor's breach, the licensee gains a remedy in damages against the licensor, and may also continue to enjoy its rights under the agreement. Why, then, the Court asks, should a debtor licensor's breach in bankruptcy change this situation? "A debtor's property does not shrink by happenstance of bankruptcy, but it does not expand, either." Accordingly, a bankrupt trademark licensor may reject and stop performing its obligations under an executory license, but it cannot "rescind the license already conveyed." So, the Court concludes, "the licensee can continue to do whatever the license authorizes." Do you agree with the Court's reasoning in *Mission Product*? Why would the Court protect trademark licensees contrary to the Congressional intent made evident by leaving trademarks out of the IP exclusion under Section 365(n)? Should Congress again correct the courts, as it did after the decision in *Lubrizol*?

5. *Contractual bankruptcy clauses.* Never wishing to forego an opportunity to include new clauses in license agreements, transactional attorneys have developed contractual language directed to Section 365(n) which often takes the following form:

> *Rights in Bankruptcy.* Licensor acknowledges and agrees that the licenses and rights granted in this Section by Licensor to Licensee with respect to the Licensed Rights are licenses and rights to "intellectual property" within the definition of Section 101(35A) of the Code. The parties hereto further agree that, in the event of the commencement of a bankruptcy proceeding by or against Licensor under the Code, Licensee shall be entitled, at its option, to retain all its rights under this Agreement, including without limitation [list], pursuant to Code Section 365(n). Rejection pursuant to Section 365 of the Code constitutes a material breach of the contract and entitles the aggrieved party to terminate upon written notice.

Is this language necessary? What advantages may lie in including it in an agreement?

21.4 ASSIGNMENT BY BANKRUPT LICENSEE

In a bankruptcy proceeding, the "debtor in possession" (DIP) is technically considered a separate legal entity from the debtor company itself. Accordingly, when the DIP takes possession of the assets of the debtor (the bankruptcy estate), those assets are assigned from the debtor to the DIP. This transfer is described in Section 541(c) of the Bankruptcy Code, which provides that a contract of the debtor becomes property of the bankruptcy estate "notwithstanding any provision in an agreement, transfer instrument, or applicable nonbankruptcy law … that restricts or conditions transfer of such interest by the debtor."

However, there is an exception for executory contracts. Section 365 of the Code provides:

(c) The trustee may not assume or assign any executory contract or unexpired lease of the debtor, whether or not such contract or lease prohibits or restricts assignment of rights or delegation of duties, if –

(1)   (A) applicable law excuses a party, other than the debtor, to such contract or lease from accepting performance from or rendering performance to an entity other than the debtor

or the debtor in possession, whether or not such contract or lease prohibits or restricts assignment of rights or delegation of duties; and

(B) such party does not consent to such assumption or assignment

Thus, under Section 365(c)(1)(A), if applicable law does not permit the assignment of an executory contract, it may not be assigned by the trustee.

How does this rule apply to IP licenses? As discussed in Section 13.3, a licensee's interest in a nonexclusive copyright or patent license may not be transferred without the consent of the licensor. In *Everex Systems, Inc. v. Cadtrax Corp.*, 89 F.3d 673 (9th Cir. 1996), the Ninth Circuit confirmed that the rule of nonassignability applies in the bankruptcy context. In *Everex*, the court held that a nonexclusive patent license could not be assumed or assigned even though it was found to be an executory contract for bankruptcy purposes because, under federal law, a nonexclusive license is only assignable with the consent of the licensor.

But in *Institut Pasteur v. Cambridge Biotech Corp.*, 104 F.3d 489 (1st Cir. 1997), the First Circuit refused to follow the Ninth Circuit's lead. It held that when a debtor sought to assign a nonexclusive patent license to the DIP, the assignment did not run afoul of the rule against assignability, as the only difference between the pre-petition debtor and the post-petition DIP was pro forma:

> Where the particular transaction envisions that the debtor-in-possession would assume and continue to perform under an executory contract, the bankruptcy court cannot simply presume as a matter of law that the debtor-in-possession is a legal entity materially distinct from the pre-petition debtor with whom the nondebtor party ... contracted. Rather, sensitive to the rights of the nondebtor party ... the bankruptcy court must focus on the performance actually to be rendered by the debtor-in-possession with a view to ensuring that the nondebtor party ... will receive the full benefit of [its] bargain.

Notes and Questions

1. *Assignment to one's self.* Considering the decisions in *Everex* and *Institut Pasteur*, what do you think of applying the prohibition on assignment to an assignment of an agreement from a pre-petition debtor to a post-petition DIP? Which court's reasoning seems more practical?

2. *Overriding prohibitions on assignment.* Section 365(f)(1) of the Bankruptcy Code allows a trustee in bankruptcy (or a debtor in possession) to assign many of the debtor's executory contracts even if the contracts themselves forbid assignment. What is the rationale for this rule? Why should a trustee be permitted to override the parties' agreed prohibition on assignment of an agreement?

21.5 *IPSO FACTO* CLAUSES

Section 365(e)(1) of the Bankruptcy Code provides that:

> Notwithstanding a provision in an executory contract ... or in applicable law, an executory contract ... of the debtor may not be terminated or modified, and any right or obligation under such contract ... may not be terminated or modified, at any time after the commencement of the case solely because of a provision in such contract or lease *that is conditioned on* -

(A) the insolvency or financial condition of the debtor at any time before the closing of the case;

(B) the commencement of a case under this title; or

(C) the appointment of or taking possession by a trustee in a case under this title or a custodian before such commencement.

In effect, this provision prohibits the parties to an executory contract, such as an IP license, from agreeing that the contract will terminate upon the initiation of a bankruptcy proceeding or other event under the Code (there are some exceptions to this rule, for example, for personal service contracts). Thus, under US law, *ipso facto* (by the very fact or act) bankruptcy termination clauses are facially invalid. This result was confirmed in *Computer Communications, Inc. v. Codex Corp.*, 824 F.2d 725 (9th Cir. 1987), in which the parties entered into a technology development and purchase agreement that stipulated that certain events, including bankruptcy, would constitute default under the agreement. Two days after the parties executed the agreement, Computer Communications, Inc. (CCI) filed a petition for reorganization under Chapter 11. Shortly thereafter, Codex notified CCI that it was terminating the agreement under the bankruptcy clause. The district court held, however, that § 365(e)(1) prevented Codex from unilaterally terminating the contract. The Ninth Circuit affirmed, though on slightly different grounds.

Despite the relatively clear rule under § 365(e)(1), it is common to see *ipso facto* clauses in the termination sections of agreements, particularly IP licensing agreements. An example of such a clause follows.

EXAMPLE: TERMINATION FOR INSOLVENCY CLAUSE

Without prejudice to either party's other rights and remedies, either party shall have the right to terminate this Agreement upon written notice to the other upon:

(a) the entry of an order for relief against the other party under Title 7 or 11 of the United States Bankruptcy Code ("Code");

(b) the commencement of an involuntary proceeding under the Code against the other party, if not dismissed within 30 days after such commencement;

(c) the making by the other party of a general assignment for the benefit of creditors;

(d) the appointment of or taking possession by a receiver, liquidator, assignee, custodian, trustee, or other similar official of some or all of the business or property of the other party;

(e) the institution by or against the other party of any bankruptcy, reorganization, arrangement, insolvency or similar proceedings under the laws of any jurisdiction;

(f) the other party becoming insolvent or generally failing to pay its debts as they become due; or

(g) any action or omission on the part of or against the other party that would lead to the dissolution or winding up of substantially all of its business.

In order to enable the parties to exercise their rights under this Section __, each party hereby agrees to provide the other party with written notice promptly upon the occurrence of any of the events listed in Subsections (a) to (g) above.

Notes and Questions

1. *Illegal or customary?* Given that *ipso facto* bankruptcy termination clauses are invalid under US law, why are they so common in IP licensing agreements? Bankruptcy experts offer several explanations for this seeming discrepancy:

   - These clauses were permissible prior to the enactment of the 1979 Bankruptcy Act, and attorneys may simply include them in agreements due to force of habit.
   - Such clauses may be valid outside of the United States and thus remain useful in international agreements.
   - The US law prohibiting *ipso facto* clauses could change to recognize the validity of such clauses, so it is safest to retain the clauses against such a day.
   - The Code only prohibits termination that is triggered upon the filing or existence of a "case" under the Bankruptcy Code. Less formal indicia of a debtor's insolvency may not run afoul of the *ipso facto* rule.

   Which of these rationales is most convincing to you? Would you include an ipso facto bankruptcy termination clause in a contract you were drafting? Why or why not?

Problem 21.3

Your client, Acme Sports, licenses its trademarks, trade secrets and copyrights to third parties around the world in connection with the marketing and manufacturing of athletic wear. Acme Sports has entered into hundreds of these licensing agreements, all of which must be renewed every five years. Acme Sports would like to have the option to terminate a licensing agreement if the licensee files for bankruptcy. As the next round of renewals approaches, what would you, as Acme Sports' lawyer, recommend? Would you recommend a provision in the contract specifying that Acme Sports may terminate the contract if the licensee becomes insolvent? What about a provision that terminates the contract if a party files for bankruptcy?

21.6 BANKRUPTCY AND ESCROW

A licensee of technology – particularly software – will often depend on the licensor to maintain, update and correct errors in the licensed technology throughout the licensee's period of use. But what happens if the licensor becomes unable to perform those maintenance, updating and error correction services, either through insolvency, bankruptcy or otherwise? If the technology is complex and its inner workings are described in designs, documentation or computer "source code" (see Section 18.1) that are not provided to the licensee as part of its license, then the licensee has little chance of assuming these critical functions once the licensor is out of the picture. As a result, a very expensive technology system may become useless to the licensee that has paid for it.

To guard against this scenario, some licensees require the licensor to place software source code and other design information in "escrow" against the day when the licensor is no longer able to provide critical support and maintenance services.

Technology Licensing: A Practitioner's Guide
Heather J. Meeker, 4th ed., 2018 at 90–93

An independent trustee—usually a firm in the business of doing technology escrows—is appointed as the escrow agent for licensor and licensee. The parties enter into a three-way agreement that is essentially a trust arrangement. The licensor delivers a copy of the source code to the escrow agent, and is usually required to deliver a source code update whenever it delivers a corresponding object code update to the licensee under the agreement. Upon occurrence of a triggering event, the escrow agent delivers the escrowed source code to the licensee. The escrow agreement, or the original license agreement, should include a license grant that is effective upon delivery by the escrow agent.

Most of the provisions of escrow agreements are not heavily negotiated. Sometimes the parties negotiate who will pay the fees. Typically the licensee pays these fees, if only because a licensor nearing bankruptcy may not place escrow fees at the top of its financial priorities, and the escrow agent may not be willing to release an escrow deposit with fees due in arrears. Parties also negotiate the dispute resolution mechanism if there is a disagreement over whether a triggering event has occurred. Licensees usually want fast arbitration, because obtaining the source code a year after a bug has appeared and maintenance has ended does not do much to address the licensee's quiet enjoyment issue.

The heavily negotiated provisions are the trigger events. Some of them relate to bankruptcy, and some do not:

- Filing of Chapter 7 (also cessation of business in the ordinary course, liquidation without filing of a bankruptcy provision). This trigger is ubiquitous and seldom controversial.
- Filing of Chapter 11. The licensor may argue that, for the reasons discussed above, Chapter 11 will not be likely to interrupt maintenance services.
- Breach of the Licensor's Maintenance Obligations. Licensors are wary of agreeing to this, particularly if the maintenance obligations in the agreement are vague or stringent.
- Change of Control of Licensor. This is a "poison pill" for an acquisition of the licensor, and the licensor usually tries to negotiate against it.

When drafting and negotiating licenses that involve escrows, the parties may attach an executed escrow agreement as an exhibit to the document. However, the parties often do not have time to set up the escrow or have the escrow agent sign the document before executing the underlying license. In those cases, you might use the following provision, which is drafted to favor the licensor:

Escrow. No later than 30 days after the Effective Date, the parties shall enter into a source code escrow agreement with [an escrow agent reasonably acceptable to both parties] [name of escrow agent], pursuant to which Licensor shall make Licensee the beneficiary of source code and source materials embodying the Software that are deposited by Licensor with such agent. Licensor hereby grants to Licensee the right to use, reproduce, and prepare derivative works of the source code and source materials for the Software and derivative works thereof; provided that Licensee may exercise such rights only in the event of a release of such materials pursuant to such source code escrow agreement, and only for the purpose of maintaining and correcting errors in the Software. The parties agree that such release will take place only if and when Licensor ceases business in the ordinary course. Licensee shall pay all fees associated with such escrow account.

Note the present language of grant in the license: "Licensor hereby grants to Licensee ... provided that Licensee may exercise such rights only in the event of a release of such materials pursuant to such source code escrow agreement." This is the proper way to draft this provision, as opposed to: "Licensor shall grant to Licensee ... upon a release of such materials pursuant to such source code escrow agreement." This is an issue for the licensee's counsel to spot. The obligation to grant a license may be more difficult to enforce, because it could require a court to mandate the granting of a license, and courts are reluctant to grant mandatory injunctions.

The Flow-Down Problem

There is a lurking issue in software escrows that is rarely considered by licensees. Few software developers today develop their entire product from scratch. Suppose a licensor (DevCo) provides an escrow for a licensee (DistyCo) that intends to redistribute the software. DistyCo's customers also want an escrow of source code in the event DistyCo goes out of business. But part of the software provided by DistyCo to its customers belongs to licensors like DevCo. DistyCo's escrow for its customers will not work, because DistyCo probably cannot grant its customers any rights in Devco's source code. If it did, then in the type of escrow provision described above, a failure of the business of DistyCo would trigger release of the source code of DevCo. DevCo is likely to take a dim view of this.

If this problem arises, one way to solve it is as follows:

> If Licensee is in material breach of its support obligations for the Software to any customer of Licensee to whom Licensee has licensed the Software under this Agreement, Licensor shall, at its sole option and discretion, either (a) assume Licensee's rights and obligations for support of the Software with respect to such customer, including without limitation making such customer the beneficiary of and granting such customer the rights in Software source code and source materials of this Section ___, or (b) instruct the escrow agent to release the source code and source materials to such customer, and grant to such customer the right to use, reproduce, prepare derivative works of, perform, display and transmit the source code and source materials for the Software and derivative works thereof.

This will address the customer's need for continuing access to technology, but not force DevCo to lose control of its source code.

Escrows in the 21st Century

Escrows have always had their issues. They are often not properly updated by the Licensor, so the binaries the Licensee is using does not correspond with the software in escrow. Source code is often poorly documented, and the Licensee often does not have the human resources to fix problems, even if it has access to source code. Software runs in a larger computing environment, and it is very difficult to capture that environment in an escrow.

Software escrows used to be ubiquitous in software licensing deals, but today, they are much rarer. One reason is that computing has tended to become vertically dis-integrated, so it may be easier to find substitutes for software whose vendor is no longer available. Another is that many technologists are skeptical about the value of escrows, for the reasons given above. Another reason is the rise of cloud computing or SaaS—it is nearly impossible to properly capture a SaaS product in an escrow. So, today, many licensees dispense with the escrow terms of license agreements.

The good news is that open source software has changed how escrows are done. It might be counterintuitive, but open source is great to put in escrow—mainly so that a licensee can capture the exact computing environment for the application it is licensing, with no worries about the right to include these third party components. Open source software has also changed the expectations of licensees; engineers now expect to get source code and not just binaries from vendors, so the function of escrows has changed.

Twenty years ago, asking for an escrow was an expected part of a software license. Today, if you demand an escrow on behalf of a licensee, the licensor may challenge you about why it is necessary, so be prepared to discuss the practicalities of software escrows.

FIGURE 21.1 Some technology escrow providers.

Notes and Questions

1. *Escrowed materials.* The excerpt from Meeker above focuses on software source code. Do you think that the same considerations would apply to an escrow of other technical information, such as manufacturing diagrams for a mechanical part, bills of materials, ingredients lists and the like?

2. *Escrow in practice.* Escrow agents are risk-averse, and escrow agreements typically go out of their way to protect the escrow agent from any potential liability. Thus, if a triggering event occurs and the licensee makes a request to obtain source code or other materials from escrow, any objection on the part of the licensor will usually be sufficient to prevent the release until a court has ordered the escrow agent to comply. Why do escrow agents include these provisions in their agreements? Does waiting for a court order frustrate the entire purpose of the escrow?

3. *Two-party versus three-party escrow.* Technology escrow agreements often come in two flavors: two-party and three-party. Three-party agreements are among the licensor, licensee and escrow agent and specify the conditions under which the agent will release the escrowed materials to the licensee. Two-party agreements only involve the licensor and the agent. These agreements provide for the escrow of materials and payment of the agent's fees. In addition, the licensor provides the agent with a list – updated periodically – of licensees who are permitted to make claims against the escrow account. Which of these contractual approaches would you prefer if you were the licensee? The licensor?

4. *Escrow and OSS.* Meeker writes that open source software is "great" to escrow. Why is this? If source code for this software is already available, why would the parties need to spend money on an escrow?

22

Estoppel and No-Challenge Clauses

What happens when an intellectual property (IP) license is granted, but the underlying IP is later found to be invalid? Is the license still in effect? More importantly, is the licensee still required to pay for it? The answer to these questions is generally "no." Invalid IP is a legal nullity that cannot be licensed. Moreover, as we will see in Section 24.3, an IP holder commits misuse if it tries to charge royalties after a patent or copyright expires.

But when IP is licensed, who has the greatest incentive to challenge the validity of that IP? Validity challenges are often brought by infringers who are threatened or sued by the IP owner. But what if the infringers have all taken licenses? In many cases, the most logical, if not the only, party with an incentive and standing to challenge an IP right is one of its existing licensees, especially if that licensee is obligated to pay ongoing royalties for the continued use of that IP right.

It thus becomes important to understand when the licensee of an IP right can challenge the validity of licensed IP. And, if such challenges are *legally* permitted, can the licensee be *contractually* prohibited from making such a challenge? These seemingly straightforward questions have been the subject of extensive litigation and implicate the very foundations of IP law itself. In this chapter we will review the doctrines of assignor and licensee estoppel, then review the requirements for challenging licensed IP under the Declaratory Judgment Act. We conclude with a discussion of contractual clauses that limit IP challenges by licensees in agreements licensing patents, copyrights and trademarks.

22.1 ASSIGNOR ESTOPPEL

To understand the restraints on a licensee's ability to challenge IP that it has licensed, it is instructive to consider a related doctrine – assignor estoppel. This doctrine, which originated in England in the late eighteenth century, provides that one who sells a patent for valuable consideration may not thereafter challenge the validity of the patent that it has sold.[1] The idea harkens back to the

---

[1] For a review of these historical cases, see William C. Rooklidge, *Licensee Validity Challenges and the Obligation to Pay Accrued Royalties: Lear v. Adkins Revisited* – Part 1, 68 J. Pat. & Trademark Off. Soc'y 506, 508–12 (1986).

real property doctrine of "estoppel by deed," which holds that a seller of property by deed cannot later assert defects in the deed to claim back any right in the property. In effect, it prevents a seller from profiting by its own dishonesty. The Supreme Court recently revisited this ancient doctrine.

Minerva Surgical, Inc. v. Hologic, Inc.
210 L. Ed. 2d 689 (U.S. 2021)

KAGAN, JUSTICE[2]

In *Westinghouse Elec. & Mfg. Co. v. Formica Insulation Co.*, 266 U. S. 342 (1924), this Court approved the "well settled" patent-law doctrine of "assignor estoppel." That doctrine, rooted in an idea of fair dealing, limits an inventor's ability to assign a patent to another for value and later contend in litigation that the patent is invalid. The question presented here is whether to discard this century-old form of estoppel. Continuing to see value in the doctrine, we decline to do so. But in upholding assignor estoppel, we clarify that it reaches only so far as the equitable principle long understood to lie at its core. The doctrine applies when, but only when, the assignor's claim of invalidity contradicts explicit or implicit representations he made in assigning the patent.

I

The invention sparking this lawsuit is a device to treat abnormal uterine bleeding, a medical condition affecting many millions of women. Csaba Truckai, a founder of the company Novacept, Inc., invented the device—called the NovaSure System—in the late 1990s. He soon afterward filed a patent application, and assigned his interest in the application—as well as in any future "continuation applications"—to Novacept. The NovaSure System, as described in Truckai's patent application, uses an applicator head to destroy targeted cells in the uterine lining. To avoid unintended burning or ablation (tissue removal), the head is "moisture permeable," meaning that it conducts fluid out of the uterine cavity during treatment. The PTO issued a patent, and in 2001 the Food and Drug Administration (FDA) approved the device for commercial distribution. But neither Truckai nor Novacept currently benefits from the NovaSure System patent. In 2004, Novacept sold its assets, including its portfolio of patents and patent applications, to another company (netting Truckai individually about $8 million). And in another sale, in 2007, respondent Hologic, Inc. acquired all patent rights in the NovaSure System. Today, Hologic sells that device throughout the United States.

Not through with inventing, Truckai founded in 2008 petitioner Minerva Surgical, Inc. There, he developed a supposedly improved device to treat abnormal uterine bleeding. Called the Minerva Endometrial Ablation System, the device (like the NovaSure System) uses an applicator head to remove cells in the uterine lining. But the new device, relying on a different way to avoid unwanted ablation, is "moisture impermeable": It does not remove any fluid during treatment. The PTO issued a patent for the device, and in 2015 the FDA approved it for commercial sale.

Meanwhile, in 2013, Hologic filed a continuation application requesting to add claims to its patent for the NovaSure System. Aware of Truckai's activities, Hologic drafted one of

---

[2] Justices Barrett, Gorsuch and Thomas dissented from the majority's opinion, largely on historical statutory interpretation grounds. Justice Alito dissented separately on different grounds.

those claims to encompass applicator heads generally, without regard to whether they are moisture permeable. The PTO in 2015 issued the altered patent as requested.

A few months later, Hologic sued Minerva for patent infringement. Minerva rejoined that its device does not infringe. But more relevant here, it also asserted that Hologic's amended patent is invalid. The essential problem, according to Minerva, is that the new, broad claim about applicator heads does not match the invention's description, which addresses their water-permeability. In response, Hologic invoked the doctrine of assignor estoppel. Because Truckai assigned the original patent application, Hologic argued, he and Minerva (essentially, his alter-ego) could not impeach the patent's validity. The District Court agreed that assignor estoppel barred Minerva's invalidity defense, and also ruled that Minerva had infringed Hologic's patent. At a trial on damages, a jury awarded Hologic about $5 million.

The Court of Appeals for the Federal Circuit mainly upheld the judgment, focusing on assignor estoppel. The court first "decline[d] Minerva's invitation to 'abandon [that] doctrine.'" Citing both this Court's precedents and equitable principles, the court affirmed the doctrine's "continued vitality." An assignor, the court stated, "should not be permitted to sell something and later to assert that what was sold is worthless, all to the detriment of the assignee." The assignor makes an "implicit representation" that the rights "he is assigning (presumably for value) are not worthless." It would "work an injustice," the court reasoned, to "allow the assignor to make that representation at the time of assignment (to his advantage) and later to repudiate it (again to his advantage)." The court then applied assignor estoppel to bar Truckai and Minerva from raising an invalidity defense. Here, the court rejected Minerva's argument that because "Hologic broadened the claims" after "Truckai's assignment," it would "be unfair to block Truckai (or Minerva) from challenging the breadth of those claims." Relying on circuit precedent, the court deemed it "irrelevant that, at the time of the assignment, the inventor's patent application[] w[as] still pending" and that the assignee "may have later amended the claims" without the inventor's input.

We granted certiorari to consider the important issues raised in the Federal Circuit's judgment. Assignor estoppel, we now hold, is well grounded in centuries-old fairness principles, and the Federal Circuit was right to uphold it. But the court failed to recognize the doctrine's proper limits. The equitable basis of assignor estoppel defines its scope: The doctrine applies only when an inventor says one thing (explicitly or implicitly) in assigning a patent and the opposite in litigating against the patent's owner.

II

Courts have long applied the doctrine of assignor estoppel to deal with inconsistent representations about a patent's validity. The classic case (different in certain respects from the one here) begins with an inventor who both applies for and obtains a patent, then assigns it to a company for value. Later, the inventor/assignor joins a competitor business, where he develops a similar—and possibly infringing—product. When the assignee company sues for infringement, the assignor tries to argue—contrary to the (explicit or implicit) assurance given in assigning the patent—that the invention was never patentable, so the patent was never valid. That kind of about-face is what assignor estoppel operates to prevent—or, in legalese, estop. As one of the early American courts to use the doctrine held: The assignor is not "at liberty to urge [invalidity] in a suit upon his own patent against a party who derives title to that patent through him." Woodward v. Boston Lasting Mach. Co., 60 F. 283, 284 (CA1 1894). Or as the Federal Circuit held in modern times:

The assignor's explicit or "implicit representation" that the patent he is assigning is "not worthless … deprive[s] him of the ability to challenge later the [patent's] validity."

Assignor estoppel got its start in late 18th-century England and crossed the Atlantic about a hundred years later. In the first recorded case, Lord Kenyon found that a patent assignor "was by his own oath and deed estopped" in an infringement suit from "attempt[ing] to deny his having had any title to convey." That rule took inspiration from an earlier doctrine—estoppel by deed—applied in real property law to prevent a conveyor of land from later asserting that he had lacked good title at the time of sale. Lord Kenyon's new patent formulation of the doctrine grew in favor throughout the 1800s as an aspect of fair dealing: When "the Defendant sold and assigned th[e] patent to the Plaintiffs as a valid one," it "does not lie in his mouth to say that the patent is not good." Within a decade or two, the doctrine was "so well established and generally accepted that citation of authority is useless."

This Court first considered—and unanimously approved—assignor estoppel in 1924, in *Westinghouse v. Formica*. Speaking through Chief Justice Taft, the Court initially invoked the doctrine's uniform acceptance in the lower courts. The first decision applying assignor estoppel, the Court recounted, was soon "followed by a myriad." "[L]ater cases in nearly all the Circuit Courts of Appeal" were "to the same point" as the first, adding up to a full "forty-five years of judicial consideration and conclusion." Such a "well settled" rule, in the Court's view, should "not [be] lightly disturb[ed]." And so it was not disturbed, lightly or otherwise. Rather, the Court added its own voice to that pre-existing "myriad." We announced that an assignor "is estopped to attack" the "validity of a patented invention which he has assigned." "As to the rest of the world," the Court explained, "the patent may have no efficacy"; but "the assignor can not be heard to question" the assignee's rights in what was conveyed.

Westinghouse, like its precursor decisions, grounded assignor estoppel in a principle of fairness. "If one lawfully conveys to another a patented right," the Court reasoned, "fair dealing should prevent him from derogating from the title he has assigned." After all, the "grantor purports to convey the right to exclude others"; how can he later say, given that representation, that the grantee in fact possesses no such right? The Court supported that view of equity by referring to estoppel by deed. Under that doctrine, the Court explained, "a grantor of a deed of land" cannot "impeach[] the effect of his solemn act" by later claiming that the grantee's title is no good. *Westinghouse*, 266 U. S., at 350. "The analogy" was "clear": There was "no reason why the principles of estoppel by deed should not apply to [the] assignment of a patent right." In the latter context too, the Court held, the assignor could not fairly "attack" the validity of a right he had formerly sold.

After thus endorsing assignor estoppel, the Court made clear that the doctrine has limits. Although the assignor cannot assert in an infringement suit that the patent is invalid, the Court held that he can argue about how to construe the patent's claims. Here, the Court addressed the role in patent suits of prior art—the set of earlier inventions (and other information) used to decide whether the specified invention is novel and non-obvious enough to merit a patent. "Of course," the Court said, the assignor cannot use prior art in an infringement suit "to destroy the patent," because he "is estopped to do this." But he can use prior art to support a narrow claim construction—to "construe and narrow the claims of the patent, conceding their validity." "Otherwise," the Court explained, a judge "would be denied" the "most satisfactory means" of "reaching a just conclusion" about the patent's scope—a conclusion needed to resolve the infringement charge. "The distinction" thus established, the Court thought, "may be a nice one, but seems to be workable." And, indeed, the Court applied it to decide the case at hand for the assignor, finding that he had not infringed the properly narrowed claim.

Finally, the Court left for another day several other questions about the contours of assignor estoppel. One concerned privity: When was an assignor so closely affiliated with another party that the latter would also be estopped? Another related to consideration: What if an assignor had received only a nominal amount of money for transferring the patent? But the question that most interested the Court was whether estoppel should operate differently if the assignment was not of a granted patent but of a patent application—as in fact was true in that case. The Court saw a possible distinction between the two. In a patent application, the Court began, the inventor "swor[e] to" a particular "specification." But the exact rights at issue were at that point "inchoate"—not "certainly defined." And afterward, the Court (presciently) observed, the claims might be "enlarge[d]" at "the instance of the assignee" beyond what the inventor had put forward. That might weaken the case for estoppel. But the Court decided not to decide the issue, given its holding that the assignor had not infringed the (narrowed) patent claim anyway.

III

Minerva's main argument here, as in the Federal Circuit, is that "assignor estoppel should be eliminated"—and indeed has been already. We reject that view. The doctrine has lasted for many years, and we continue to accept the fairness principle at its core. Minerva's back-up contention is that assignor estoppel "should be constrained." On that score, we find that the Federal Circuit has applied the doctrine too expansively. Today, we clarify the scope of assignor estoppel, including in the way *Westinghouse* suggested.

A

In its quest to abolish assignor estoppel, Minerva lodges three main arguments. The first two offer different reasons for why the doctrine is already defunct: because Congress repudiated it in the Patent Act of 1952 and because, even if not, this Court's post-*Westinghouse* cases leave no room for the doctrine to continue. The third, by contrast, is a present-day policy claim: that assignor estoppel "imposes" too high a "barrier to invalidity challenges" and so keeps bad patents alive.

[*Discussion of statutory interpretation of 1952 Patent Act omitted*]

We likewise do not accept Minerva's view that two of our post-*Westinghouse* decisions have already interred assignor estoppel. According to Minerva, *Scott Paper Co. v. Marcalus Mfg. Co.* "eliminated any justification for assignor estoppel and 'repudiated' the doctrine." And if that were not enough, Minerva continues, our decision in *Lear, Inc. v. Adkins*, 395 U. S. 653 (1969),[3] also "eviscerated any basis for assignor estoppel." But we think the words "eliminated," "repudiated," and "eviscerated" are far off. *Scott Paper* and *Lear* in fact retained assignor estoppel; all they did was police the doctrine's boundaries (just as *Westinghouse* did and we do today).

Whatever a worked-up dissent charged, *Scott Paper* did nothing more than decline to apply assignor estoppel in a novel and extreme circumstance. The petitioner in *Scott Paper* made the same ask Minerva does here: to abolish the *Westinghouse* rule. The Court expressly declined that request. And it restated the "basic principle" animating assignor

---

[3] *Lear* is reproduced and discussed in Section 22.2.

estoppel, describing it as "one of good faith, that one who has sold his invention may not, to the detriment of the purchaser, deny the existence of that which he has sold." The Court, to be sure, declined to apply the doctrine in the case before it. There, estoppel would have prevented the assignor from making a device on which the patent had expired—a device, in other words, that had already entered the public domain. The Court could not find any precedent for applying estoppel in that situation. And the Court thought that doing so would carry the doctrine too far, reasoning that the public's interest in using an already-public invention outweighs the "interest in private good faith." But the Court did not question—again, it reaffirmed—the principle of fairness on which assignor estoppel rests in more common cases, where the assignee is not claiming to control a device unequivocally part of the public domain. In those cases, the doctrine remained intact.

Lear gives Minerva still less to work with. In that case, the Court considered and toppled a different patent estoppel doctrine. Called licensee estoppel, it barred (as its name suggests) a patent licensee from contesting the validity of the patent on a device he was paying to use. Minerva's basic claim is that as goes one patent estoppel rule, so goes another. But *Lear* did not purport to decide the fate of the separate assignor estoppel doctrine. To the contrary, the Court stated that the patent holder's "equities" in the assignment context "were far more compelling than those presented in the typical licensing arrangement." 395 U. S., at 664. And so they are.

In sum, *Scott Paper* and *Lear* left *Westinghouse* right about where they found it—as a bounded doctrine designed to prevent an inventor from first selling a patent and then contending that the thing sold is worthless. *Westinghouse* saw that about-face as unfair; *Scott Paper* and *Lear* never questioned that view. At the same time, *Westinghouse* realized that assignor estoppel has limits: Even in approving the doctrine, the Court made clear that not every assignor defense in every case would fall within its scope. *Scott Paper* and *Lear* adopted a similar stance. They maintained assignor estoppel, but suggested (if in different ways) that the doctrine needed to stay attached to its equitable moorings. The three decisions together thus show not the doctrinal "eviscerat[ion]" Minerva claims, but only the kind of doctrinal evolution typical of common-law rules.

Finally, we do not think, as Minerva claims, that contemporary patent policy—specifically, the need to weed out bad patents—supports overthrowing assignor estoppel. And we continue to think the core of assignor estoppel justified on the fairness grounds that courts applying the doctrine have always given. Assignor estoppel, like many estoppel rules, reflects a demand for consistency in dealing with others. When a person sells his patent rights, he makes an (at least) implicit representation to the buyer that the patent at issue is valid—that it will actually give the buyer his sought-for monopoly. In later raising an invalidity defense, the assignor disavows that implied warranty. And he does so in service of regaining access to the invention he has just sold. By saying one thing and then saying another, the assignor wants to profit doubly—by gaining both the price of assigning the patent and the continued right to use the invention it covers. That course of conduct by the assignor strikes us, as it has struck courts for many a year, as unfair dealing—enough to outweigh any loss to the public from leaving an invalidity defense to someone other than the assignor.

B

Still, our endorsement of assignor estoppel comes with limits—true to the doctrine's reason for being. Just as we guarded the doctrine's boundaries in the past, so too we do so today.

Assignor estoppel should apply only when its underlying principle of fair dealing comes into play. That principle, as explained above, demands consistency in representations about a patent's validity: What creates the unfairness is contradiction. When an assignor warrants that a patent is valid, his later denial of validity breaches norms of equitable dealing. And the original warranty need not be express; as we have explained, the assignment of specific patent claims carries with it an implied assurance. But when the assignor has made neither explicit nor implicit representations in conflict with an invalidity defense, then there is no unfairness in its assertion. And so there is no ground for applying assignor estoppel.

One example of non-contradiction is when the assignment occurs before an inventor can possibly make a warranty of validity as to specific patent claims. Consider a common employment arrangement. An employee assigns to his employer patent rights in any future inventions he develops during his employment; the employer then decides which, if any, of those inventions to patent. In that scenario, the assignment contains no representation that a patent is valid. How could it? The invention itself has not come into being. And so the employee's transfer of rights cannot estop him from alleging a patent's invalidity in later litigation.

A second example is when a later legal development renders irrelevant the warranty given at the time of assignment. Suppose an inventor conveys a patent for value, with the warranty of validity that act implies. But the governing law then changes, so that previously valid patents become invalid. The inventor may claim that the patent is invalid in light of that change in law without contradicting his earlier representation. What was valid before is invalid today, and no principle of consistency prevents the assignor from saying so.

Most relevant here, another post-assignment development—a change in patent claims— can remove the rationale for applying assignor estoppel. *Westinghouse* itself anticipated this point, which arises most often when an inventor assigns a patent application, rather than an issued patent. As *Westinghouse* noted, "the scope of the right conveyed in such an assignment" is "inchoate"—"less certainly defined than that of a granted patent." 266 U. S., at 352–353. That is because the assignee, once he is the owner of the application, may return to the PTO to "enlarge[]" the patent's claims. And the new claims resulting from that process may go beyond what "the assignor intended" to claim as patentable. *Westinghouse* did not need to resolve the effects of such a change, but its liberally dropped hints—and the equitable basis for assignor estoppel—point all in one direction. Assuming that the new claims are materially broader than the old claims, the assignor did not warrant to the new claims' validity. And if he made no such representation, then he can challenge the new claims in litigation: Because there is no inconsistency in his positions, there is no estoppel. The limits of the assignor's estoppel go only so far as, and not beyond, what he represented in assigning the patent application.

The Federal Circuit, in both its opinion below and prior decisions, has failed to recognize those boundaries. Minerva (recall, Truckai's alter-ego) argued to the court that estoppel should not apply because it was challenging a claim that was materially broader than the ones Truckai had assigned. But the court declined to consider that alleged disparity. Citing circuit precedent, the court held it "irrelevant" whether Hologic had expanded the assigned claims: Even if so, Minerva could not contest the new claim's validity. For the reasons given above, that conclusion is wrong. If Hologic's new claim is materially broader than the ones Truckai assigned, then Truckai could not have warranted its validity in making the assignment. And without such a prior inconsistent representation, there is no basis for estoppel.

We remand this case to the Federal Circuit to now address what it thought irrelevant: whether Hologic's new claim is materially broader than the ones Truckai assigned. The parties vigorously disagree about that issue. In Truckai's view, the new claim expanded on the old by covering non-moisture-permeable applicator heads. In Hologic's view, the claim matched a prior one that Truckai had assigned. Resolution of that issue in light of all relevant evidence will determine whether Truckai's representations in making the assignment conflict with his later invalidity defense—and so will determine whether assignor estoppel applies.

IV

This Court recognized assignor estoppel a century ago, and we reaffirm that judgment today. But as the Court recognized from the beginning, the doctrine is not limitless. Its boundaries reflect its equitable basis: to prevent an assignor from warranting one thing and later alleging another. Assignor estoppel applies when an invalidity defense in an infringement suit conflicts with an explicit or implicit representation made in assigning patent rights. But absent that kind of inconsistency, an invalidity defense raises no concern of fair dealing—so assignor estoppel has no place.

For these reasons, we vacate the judgment of the Federal Circuit and remand the case for further proceedings consistent with this opinion.

It is so ordered.

Notes and Questions

1. *Contracting for estoppel.* In *Hologic*, Minerva (the assignor) argued that the doctrine of assignor estoppel should be abolished entirely. Among other things, it noted that "[a]n assignee who seeks protection against future competition from an assignor need simply negotiate a covenant not to compete in their agreement." How is a covenant not to compete different than assignor estoppel? Given these differences, how would you respond to Minerva's argument?

2. *Assignor estoppel in the modern workplace.* Prior to *Hologic*, Professor Mark Lemley argued that the assignor estoppel doctrine is largely unnecessary in today's economy.

   The nineteenth-century vision of assignor estoppel was directed at people who themselves sold a patent for profit. But modern assignor estoppel no longer is. Not only does it reach companies that never made such a promise, it extends to patents that did not exist at the time of the deal. More important, assignor estoppel is regularly applied to bind employee-inventors on the basis of their assignment of the patent to their employers. But nothing about the modern employee-inventor suggests that they are selling their inventions to their employers for profit. Employees are regularly required to assign all their inventions as a condition of employment. Those assignment agreements are standard-form contracts, usually presented to the employee on their first day of work, after they have quit their prior job and perhaps relocated. So they apply by definition to inventions that have not yet been made. Companies and universities impose them on all their employees, not just designated inventors; as a research assistant in law school, for instance, I was forced to assign all the inventions I might make during law school. And the employees are not normally paid extra in exchange for assigning their rights. Indeed, employees are sometimes compelled to disclose their inventions against their will so the employer can turn it into a patent. Even if they aren't, the signing of the inventor's declaration is a relatively perfunctory act, done long after the employer himself has decided to pursue a patent. Employees may sign an inventorship form even if they doubt the validity of the invention because they fear to lose their job if they don't. And if the employee can't or won't sign the agreement, the law … allows the company to apply for a patent in their name without the employee's signature, simply by attesting that they were obligated to assign the invention.[4] Employees who assign their inventions have no ownership or financial interest in any patents that result. The employer holds legal title to the invention even if it was assigned before it was made.[5]

How does the Court in *Minerva* address Professor Lemley's arguments? Are you satisfied with its response?

22.2 LICENSEE ESTOPPEL

Just as the doctrine of assignor estoppel prevents the assignor of a patent from later challenging the validity of that patent, the related doctrine of licensee estoppel prohibits a patent licensee from challenging the validity of a licensed patent. Licensee estoppel has been described as "one of the oldest doctrines in the field of patent law."[6] The theory behind the doctrine is that a licensee should not be permitted to enjoy the benefits of a licensing agreement (i.e., protection from suit by the patentee) while simultaneously seeking to void the patent that forms the basis of the agreement. The Supreme Court upheld the doctrine in *Automatic Radio Manufacturing Co. v. Hazeltine Research, Inc.*, 339 U.S. 827, 836 (1950),[7] but reversed its position and effectively abolished the doctrine in *Lear v. Adkins*, one of the most famous cases in patent law.

Lear, Inc. v. Adkins
395 U.S. 653 (1969)

HARLAN, JUSTICE

In January of 1953, John Adkins, an inventor and mechanical engineer, was hired by Lear Incorporated for the purpose of solving a vexing problem the company had encountered in its efforts to develop a gyroscope which would meet the increasingly demanding requirements of the aviation industry. The gyroscope is an essential component of the navigational system in all aircraft, enabling the pilot to learn the direction and altitude of his airplane. With the development of the faster airplanes of the 1950's, more accurate gyroscopes were needed, and the gyro industry consequently was casting about for new techniques which would satisfy this need in an economical fashion. Shortly after Adkins was hired, he developed a method of construction at the company's California facilities which improved gyroscope accuracy at a low cost. Lear almost immediately incorporated Adkins' improvements into its production process to its substantial advantage.

I

At the very beginning of the parties' relationship, Lear and Adkins entered into a rudimentary one-page agreement which provided that although "[a]ll new ideas, discoveries,

---

4   35 U.S.C. § 116 (2012).
5   Mark A. Lemley, *Rethinking Assignor Estoppel*, 54 Houston L. Rev. 513, 516 (2016).
6   *Lear, Inc. v. Adkins*, 67 Cal. 2d 882, 891, 435 P. 2d 321, 325–326 (1967).
7   Discussed in the context of package licensing and patent misuse in Section 24.4.

inventions etc. related [to] vertical gyros become the property of Mr. John S. Adkins," the inventor promised to grant Lear a license as to all ideas he might develop "on a mutually satisfactory royalty basis." As soon as Adkins' labors yielded tangible results it quickly became apparent to the inventor that further steps should be taken to place his rights to his ideas on a firmer basis. On February 4, 1954, Adkins filed an application with the Patent Office in an effort to gain federal protection for his improvements. At about the same time, he entered into a lengthy period of negotiations with Lear in an effort to conclude a licensing agreement which would clearly establish the amount of royalties that would be paid.

These negotiations finally bore fruit on September 15, 1955, when the parties approved a complex 17-page contract which carefully delineated the conditions upon which Lear promised to pay royalties for Adkins' improvements. The parties agreed that "if the United States Patent Office refuses to issue a patent on the substantial claims [contained in Adkins' original patent application] or if such a patent so issued is subsequently held invalid then in any of such events Lear at its option shall have the right forthwith to terminate the specific license so affected or to terminate this entire Agreement ..."

As the contractual language indicates, Adkins had not obtained a final Patent Office decision as to the patentability of his invention at the time the licensing agreement was concluded. Indeed, he was not to receive a patent until January 5, 1960.

The progress of Adkins' effort to obtain a patent followed the typical pattern. In his initial application, the inventor made the ambitious claim that his entire method of constructing gyroscopes was sufficiently novel to merit protection. The Patent Office, however, rejected this initial claim, as well as two subsequent amendments, which progressively narrowed the scope of the invention sought to be protected. Finally, Adkins narrowed his claim drastically to assert only that the design of the apparatus used to achieve gyroscope accuracy was novel. In response, the Office issued its 1960 patent, granting a 17-year monopoly on this more modest claim.

During the long period in which Adkins was attempting to convince the Patent Office of the novelty of his ideas, however, Lear had become convinced that Adkins would never receive a patent on his invention and that it should not continue to pay substantial royalties on ideas which had not contributed substantially to the development of the art of gyroscopy. In 1957, after Adkins' patent application had been rejected twice, Lear announced that it had searched the Patent Office's files and had found a patent which it believed had fully anticipated Adkins' discovery. As a result, the company stated that it would no longer pay royalties on the large number of gyroscopes it was producing at its plant in Grand Rapids, Michigan (the Michigan gyros). Payments were continued on the smaller number of gyros produced at the company's California plant for two more years until they too were terminated on April 8, 1959 (the California gyros).

As soon as Adkins obtained his patent in 1960, he brought this lawsuit in the California Superior Court. He argued to a jury that both the Michigan and the California gyros incorporated his patented apparatus and that Lear's failure to pay royalties on these gyros was a breach both of the 1955 contract and of Lear's quasi-contractual obligations. Although Lear sought to raise patent invalidity as a defense, the trial judge directed a verdict of $16,351.93 for Adkins on the California gyros, holding that Lear was estopped by its licensing agreement from questioning the inventor's patent. The trial judge took a different approach when it came to considering the Michigan gyros. Noting that the Company claimed that it had developed its Michigan designs independently of Adkins' ideas, the court instructed the jury to award the inventor recovery only if it was satisfied that Adkins' invention was novel, within the meaning of the federal patent laws. When the jury returned a verdict for Adkins of $888,122.56 on the Michigan gyros, the trial judge granted Lear's motion for judgment notwithstanding the verdict, finding that Adkins' invention had been completely anticipated by the prior art.

Once again both sides appealed, this time to the California Supreme Court, which took yet another approach to the problem presented. The court rejected the Court of Appeals' conclusion that the 1955 license gave Lear the right to terminate its royalty obligations in 1959. Since the 1955 agreement was still in effect, the court concluded, relying on the language we have already quoted, that the doctrine of estoppel barred Lear from questioning the propriety of the Patent Office's grant. The court's adherence to estoppel, however, was not without qualification. After noting Lear's claim that it had developed its Michigan gyros independently, the court tested this contention by considering "whether what is being built by Lear [in Michigan] springs entirely" (emphasis supplied) from the prior art. Applying this test, it found that Lear had in fact "utilized the apparatus patented by Adkins throughout the period in question," reinstating the jury's $888,000 verdict on this branch of the case.

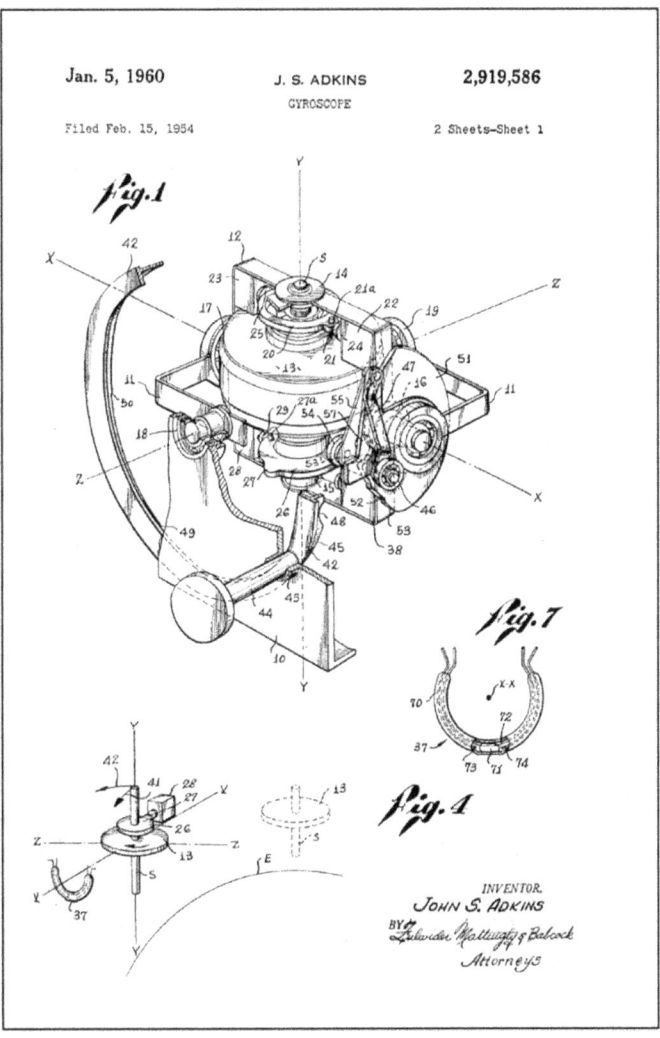

FIGURE 22.1 The gyroscope invention in *Lear v. Adkins*.

II

Since the California Supreme Court's construction of the 1955 licensing agreement is solely a matter of state law, the only issue open to us is raised by the court's reliance upon the doctrine of estoppel to bar Lear from proving that Adkins' ideas were dedicated to the common welfare by federal law. In considering the propriety of the State Court's decision, we are well aware that we are not writing upon a clean slate. The doctrine of estoppel has been considered by this Court in a line of cases reaching back into the middle of the 19th century. Before deciding what the role of estoppel should be in the present case and in the future, it is, then, desirable to consider the role it has played in the past.

A

While the roots of the doctrine have often been celebrated in tradition, we have found only one 19th century case in this Court that invoked estoppel in a considered manner. And that case was decided before the Sherman Act made it clear that the grant of monopoly power to a patent owner constituted a limited exception to the general federal policy favoring free competition. *Kinsman v. Parkhurst*, 18 How. 289 (1855).

In [1892], this Court found the doctrine of patent estoppel so inequitable that it refused to grant an injunction to enforce a licensee's promise never to contest the validity of the underlying patent. "It is as important to the public that competition should not be repressed by worthless patents, as that the patentee of a really valuable invention should be protected in his monopoly …" *Pope Manufacturing Co. v. Gormully*, 144 U.S. 224, 234 (1892).

Although this Court invoked an estoppel in 1905 without citing or considering *Pope's* powerful argument, the doctrine was not to be applied again in this Court until it was revived in *Automatic Radio Manufacturing Co. v. Hazeltine Research, Inc.*, which declared, without prolonged analysis, that licensee estoppel was "the general rule." In so holding, the majority ignored the teachings of a series of decisions this Court had rendered during the 45 years since [*United States v. Harvey Steel Co.*, 196 U.S. 310 (1905)] had been decided. During this period, each time a patentee sought to rely upon his estoppel privilege before this Court, the majority created a new exception to permit judicial scrutiny into the validity of the Patent Office's grant. Long before *Hazeltine* was decided, the estoppel doctrine had been so eroded that it could no longer be considered the "general rule," but was only to be invoked in an ever-narrowing set of circumstances.

B

The estoppel rule was first stringently limited in a situation in which the patentee's equities were far more compelling than those presented in the typical licensing arrangement. *Westinghouse Electric & Manufacturing Co. v. Formica Insulation Co.*, 266 U.S. 342 (1924), framed a rule to govern the recurring problem which arises when the original patent owner, after assigning his patent to another for a substantial sum, claims that the patent is worthless because it contains no new ideas. The courts of appeals had traditionally refused to permit such a defense to an infringement action on the ground that it was improper both "to sell and keep the same thing." Nevertheless, *Formica* imposed a limitation upon estoppel which was radically inconsistent with the premises upon which the "general rule" is based. The Court held that while an assignor may not directly attack the validity of a patent by reference to the prior state of the art, he could introduce such evidence to narrow the claims made in the patent. "The distinction seems a nice one but seems to be workable."

Workable or not, the result proved to be an anomaly: if a patent had some novelty *Formica* permitted the old owner to defend an infringement action by showing that the invention's novel aspects did not extend to include the old owner's products; on the other hand, if a patent had no novelty at all, the old owner could not defend successfully since he would be obliged to launch the direct attack on the patent that Formica seemed to forbid. The incongruity of this position compelled at least one court of appeals to carry the logic of the Formica exception to its logical conclusion. In 1940 the Seventh Circuit held that a licensee could introduce evidence of the prior art to show that the licensor's claims were not novel at all and thus successfully defend an action for royalties.

In *Scott Paper Co. v. Marcalus Manufacturing Co.*, 326 U.S. 249 (1945), this Court adopted a position similar to the Seventh Circuit's, undermining the basis of patent estoppel even more than [*Westinghouse*] had done. In *Scott*, the original patent owner had attempted to defend an infringement suit brought by his assignee by proving that his product was a copy of an expired patent. The Court refused to permit the assignee to invoke an estoppel, finding that the policy of the patent laws would be frustrated if a manufacturer was required to pay for the use of information which, under the patent statutes, was the property of all. Chief Justice Stone, for the Court, did not go beyond the precise question presented by a manufacturer who asserted that he was simply copying an expired patent. Nevertheless it was impossible to limit the *Scott* doctrine to such a narrow compass. If patent policy forbids estoppel when the old owner attempts to show that he did no more than copy an expired patent, why should not the old owner be also permitted to show that the invention lacked novelty because it could be found in a technical journal or because it was obvious to one knowledgeable in the art? The *Scott* exception had undermined the very basis of the "general rule."

III

> *"federal law requires that all ideas in general circulation be dedicated to the common good unless they are protected by a valid patent"*

The uncertain status of licensee estoppel in the case law is a product of judicial efforts to accommodate the competing demands of the common law of contracts and the federal law of patents. On the one hand, the law of contracts forbids a purchaser to repudiate his promises simply because he later becomes dissatisfied with the bargain he has made. On the other hand, federal law requires that all ideas in general circulation be dedicated to the common good unless they are protected by a valid patent. When faced with this basic conflict in policy, both this Court and courts throughout the land have naturally sought to develop an intermediate position which somehow would remain responsive to the radically different concerns of the two different worlds of contract and patent. The result has been a failure. Rather than creative compromise, there has been a chaos of conflicting case law, proceeding on inconsistent premises. Before renewing the search for an elusive middle ground, we must reconsider on their own merits the arguments which may properly be advanced on both sides of the estoppel question.

A

It will simplify matters greatly if we first consider the most typical situation in which patent licenses are negotiated. In contrast to the present case, most manufacturers obtain a license after a patent has issued. Since the Patent Office makes an inventor's ideas public when it issues its grant of a limited monopoly, a potential licensee has access to the inventor's ideas even if he does not enter into an agreement with the patent owner. Consequently, a manufacturer gains only two benefits if he chooses to enter a licensing agreement after the patent has issued. First, by accepting a license and paying royalties for a time, the licensee may have avoided the necessity of defending an expensive infringement action during the period when he may be least able to afford one. Second, the existence of an unchallenged patent may deter others from attempting to compete with the licensee.

Under ordinary contract principles the mere fact that some benefit is received is enough to require the enforcement of the contract, regardless of the validity of the underlying patent. Nevertheless, if one tests this result by the standard of good-faith commercial dealing, it seems far from satisfactory. For the simple contract approach entirely ignores the position of the licensor who is seeking to invoke the court's assistance on his behalf. Consider, for example, the equities of the licensor who has obtained his patent through a fraud on the Patent Office. It is difficult to perceive why good faith requires that courts should permit him to recover royalties despite his licensee's attempts to show that the patent is invalid.

Even in the more typical cases, not involving conscious wrongdoing, the licensor's equities are far from compelling. A patent, in the last analysis, simply represents a legal conclusion reached by the Patent Office. Moreover, the legal conclusion is predicated on factors as to which reasonable men can differ widely. Yet the Patent Office is often obliged to reach its decision in an ex parte proceeding, without the aid of the arguments which could be advanced by parties interested in proving patent invalidity. Consequently, it does not seem to us to be unfair to require a patentee to defend the Patent Office's judgment when his licensee places the question in issue, especially since the licensor's case is buttressed by the presumption of validity which attaches to his patent. Thus, although licensee estoppel may be consistent with the letter of contractual doctrine, we cannot say that it is compelled by the spirit of contract law, which seeks to balance the claims of promisor and promisee in accord with the requirements of good faith.

Surely the equities of the licensor do not weigh very heavily when they are balanced against the important public interest in permitting full and free competition in the use of ideas which are in reality a part of the public domain. Licensees may often be the only individuals with enough economic incentive to challenge the patentability of an inventor's discovery. If they are muzzled, the public may continually be required to pay tribute to would-be monopolists without need or justification. We think it plain that the technical requirements of contract doctrine must give way before the demands of the public interest in the typical situation involving the negotiation of a license after a patent has issued.

We are satisfied that *Automatic Radio Co. v. Hazeltine Research, Inc.*, itself the product of a clouded history, should no longer be regarded as sound law in respect of its "estoppel" holding, and that holding is now overruled.

> *"Licensees may often be the only individuals with enough economic incentive to challenge the patentability of an inventor's discovery. If they are muzzled, the public may continually be required to pay tribute to would-be monopolists without need or justification."*

B

The terms of the 1955 agreement provide that royalties are to be paid until such time as "the patent is held invalid," and the fact remains that the question of patent validity has not been finally determined in this case. Thus, it may be suggested that although Lear must be allowed to raise the question of patent validity in the present lawsuit, it must also be required to comply with its contract and continue to pay royalties until its claim is finally vindicated in the courts.

The parties' contract, however, is no more controlling on this issue than is the State's doctrine of estoppel, which is also rooted in contract principles. The decisive question is whether overriding federal policies would be significantly frustrated if licensees could be required to continue to pay royalties during the time they are challenging patent validity in the courts.

It seems to us that such a requirement would be inconsistent with the aims of federal patent policy. Enforcing this contractual provision would give the licensor an additional economic incentive to devise every conceivable dilatory tactic in an effort to postpone the day of final judicial reckoning. We can perceive no reason to encourage dilatory court tactics in this way. Moreover, the cost of prosecuting slow-moving trial proceedings and defending an inevitable appeal might well deter many licensees from attempting to prove patent invalidity in the courts. The deterrence effect would be particularly severe in the many scientific fields in which invention is proceeding at a rapid rate. In these areas, a patent may well become obsolete long before its 17-year term has expired. If a licensee has reason to believe that he will replace a patented idea with a new one in the near future, he will have little incentive to initiate lengthy court proceedings, unless he is freed from liability at least from the time he refuses to pay the contractual royalties. Lastly, enforcing this contractual provision would undermine the strong federal policy favoring the full and free use of ideas in the public domain. For all these reasons, we hold that Lear must be permitted to avoid the payment of all royalties accruing after Adkins' 1960 patent issued if Lear can prove patent invalidity.

The judgment of the Supreme Court of California is vacated and the case is remanded to that court for further proceedings not inconsistent with this opinion.

Notes and Questions

1. *State versus federal.* Why was *Lear* appealed to the US Supreme Court from the California Supreme Court, rather than from a federal appellate court? Why do you think that Adkins brought his suit in state rather than federal court?

2. *Patent policy.* Justice Harlan bases the holding in *Lear* in large part on the existence of a federal policy that favors the invalidation of improperly issued patents. What is the justification for such a policy, and from what legal source does it derive?

3. *Balance of the equities.* In weighing the value of the licensee estoppel doctrine, the *Lear* Court says that "the licensor's equities are far from compelling," even in the face of the presumption of validity of patents issued by the PTO. Why?

4. *Economic incentives.* Why is it likely that "Licensees may often be the only individuals with enough economic incentive to challenge the patentability of an inventor's discovery"? Should this matter? What about the licensor's economic position?

5. *Why not assignor estoppel?* Why does the Court in *Lear* distinguish between licensee and assignor estoppel? Why does it permit assignor estoppel to survive when it abolishes licensee estoppel?

6. *Contract doctrine.* What does Justice Harlan mean in *Lear* when he writes, "although licensee estoppel may be consistent with the letter of contractual doctrine, we cannot say that it is compelled by the spirit of contract law"? What "spirit" of contract law is he referring to, and why does it militate against the licensee estoppel doctrine?

7. *Termination.* The agreement in *Lear* states: "if the [PTO] refuses to issue a patent on the substantial claims ... Or if such patent so issued is subsequently held invalid then ... Lear at its option shall have the right forthwith to *terminate* the specific license so affected or to *terminate* this entire Agreement ..." (emphasis added). Why would Lear wish to terminate its license? Did it actually exercise its right of termination? Why or why not?

8. *Pre-issuance royalties.* The Court in *Lear* avoids the question of whether Lear must pay Adkins royalties for the period from when the licensing agreement was signed in 1955 until the patent issued in 1960. This, the Court concedes, is a question of state contract law, as no patent right yet exists: "it squarely raises the question whether, and to what extent, the States may protect the owners of unpatented inventions who are willing to disclose their ideas to manufacturers only upon payment of royalties." How would you answer this question? As it turns out, the Court did answer this question ten years later in *Aronson v. Quick Point Pencil Co.*, 440 U.S. 257 (1979) (discussed and reproduced in Section 24.3.2).

9. *Benefit of the bargain?* In Part III.B of *Lear*, Justice Harlan acknowledges that under the licensing agreement royalties are to be paid until such time as "the patent is held invalid." He also notes that, at the time of writing, the patent had not yet been held invalid. Given that the patent issued in 1960 and the Court's decision was rendered in 1969, it would likely be 1970 or later before Adkins' patent was finally determined to be invalid (cutting approximately seven years from its full duration). According to the express language of the licensing agreement, if the patent were found to be invalid, Lear was required to pay royalties for the period through the invalidity finding (i.e., 1960 through 1970 [assuming that is when invalidity was found]). But the Court says that if the patent is eventually found invalid, Lear should be relieved of the payment of any future royalties from *the date of the patent's issuance* (1960). The difference is ten full years of royalties – a significant amount. Why doesn't the Court hold Lear to its contractual bargain?

10. *Is Lear still needed?* Some commentators have observed that when *Lear* was decided in 1969, a patent licensee was the party most likely to challenge the validity of a patent. However, in the intervening years, it has become much easier and much less expensive to challenge the validity of patents before they are licensed, including at the Patent Trial and Appeals Board (PTAB). Given the increased ease with which patent validity may be challenged today, is there less justification for eliminating the licensee estoppel doctrine? See Rob Merges, Patents, *Validity Challenges, and Private Ordering: A New Dispensation for the Easy-Challenge Era* (working paper, Dec. 2021)

11. *License eviction.* Prior to *Lear*, the doctrine of licensee estoppel held that a licensee was not permitted to dispute the validity of a licensed patent in order to avoid paying royalties. Yet an exception was recognized when the patent was invalidated in a separate proceeding not brought by the licensee. If that occurred, the licensee was said to be "evicted" from the license. As the court explained in *Drackett Chem. Co. v. Chamberlain Co.*, 63 F.2d 853, 854 (6th Cir. 1933):

> The subject-matter of such a contract is essentially the monopoly which the grant confers: the right of property which it creates, and, when this monopoly has been destroyed, and the

exclusive rights of manufacture, sale, and use, purported to have been created by the patent, are judicially decreed to be no longer exclusive, but are thrown open to the public at large, there has been a complete failure of consideration – an eviction – which should justify a termination of the contract. Prior to such eviction, the mere invalidity of the patent is properly held not to be a sufficient defense, because the licensee may still continue to enjoy all the benefits of a valid patent. It may be respected, and the licensee would then have just what he bargained for ... It is only when, by judicial decree or otherwise, it is published to the world that the monopoly is destroyed, that the licensee can claim a corresponding release from his obligation to pay royalties.

Did the doctrine of eviction ameliorate the policy effects of the licensee estoppel doctrine? What perverse results might this doctrine have created?

FIGURE 22.2 The Drackett Chemical Company of Cincinnati, Ohio, created many household cleaning products that are still in use, including Windex, Dawn and Drāno.

12. *Restitution of paid royalties.* The Court in *Lear* holds that "Lear must be permitted to avoid the payment of all royalties accruing after Adkins' 1960 patent issued if Lear can prove patent invalidity." But Lear stopped paying royalties in 1957, when it believed that it found prior art that would invalidate Adkins' patent. So if the patent were found invalid in 1970 (using our hypothetical from Note 9), Lear would have no obligation to pay royalties to Adkins for the period from 1960 to 1970. But what if Lear, like a good licensee, *had* paid royalties to Adkins for part of that period (say from 1960 to 1965) before realizing that the patent was likely invalid and ceasing its royalty payments? When the patent was finally invalidated in 1970, would Lear receive a refund of the royalties it paid during the five-year period that it thought the patent was valid? Under the doctrine of "license eviction," the answer is generally no.

In *Drackett*, 63 F.2d at 855, the licensee had paid royalties under a licensing agreement for some years before the licensed patent was invalidated in a different proceeding. Once the licensee was thus "evicted" from its license (see Note 10), it had no further obligation to pay royalties under the licensing agreement. However, the court also held that "there was no such mistake of fact (the validity of the patents) as would warrant a recovery of royalties already paid" – implying that only the contractual doctrines of mistake of fact or, perhaps, fraud in the inducement might give rise to a claim for recovery of paid royalties.

The Sixth Circuit revisited the eviction doctrine in *Troxel Mfg. Co. v. Schwinn Bicycle Co.*, 465 F.2d 1253 (6th Cir. 1972) to determine whether *Drackett* had been overturned by *Lear*. That is, whether *Lear* implies that an invalid patent is invalidated *ab initio* – from the moment it was issued – thus giving the licensee a claim for restitution of all royalties previously paid. In an opinion that continues to be cited today, the Sixth Circuit held not:

> A rule that licensees can recover all royalties paid on a patent which later is held to be invalid would do far more than "unmuzzle" licensees. It would give the licensee the advantage of a "heads-I-win, tails-you-lose" option. *Lear* states that it is in the public interest to encourage an early adjudication of invalidity of patents. Application of the holding of the District Court could defeat early adjudication of invalidity and encourage tardy and marginal litigation. If the licensee could recover royalties paid (subject to any statute of limitations) on the basis of an adjudication of invalidity accomplished by another litigant, without incurring

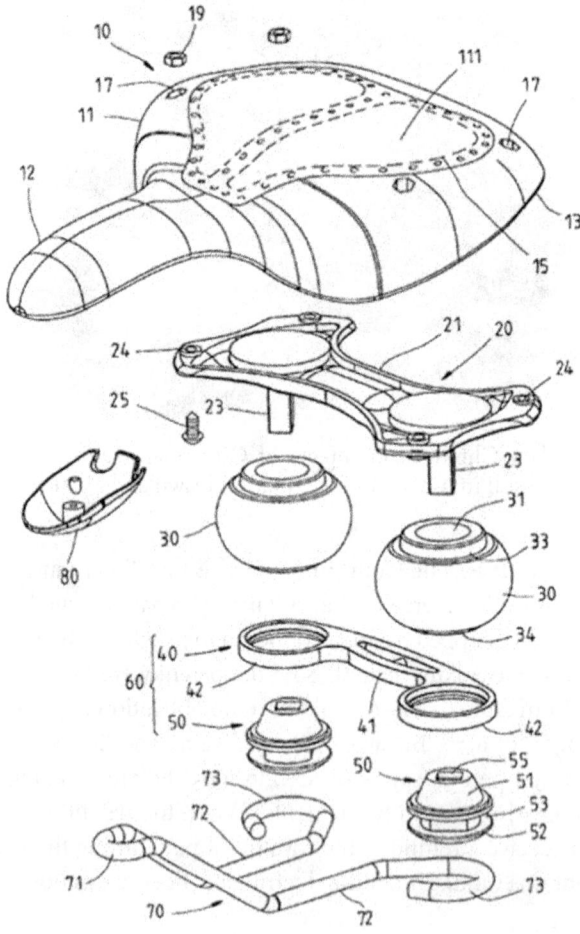

FIGURE 22.3 In *Troxel v. Schwinn*, Schwinn held a design patent for a bicycle seat issued in 1966. After Schwinn accused Troxel of infringement, Troxel took a license in 1967. Later that year, Troxel notified Schwinn that Goodyear was also selling infringing bicycle seats. Schwinn sued Goodyear, and the patent was found to be invalid in 1969. Troxel then sued to recover royalties previously paid to Schwinn under its licensing agreement.

the expense or trouble of litigation, there would be less inducement for him to challenge the patent and thus remove an invalid patent from the competitive scene. He would be more likely to wait for somebody else to battle the issue because he would have nothing to lose by the delay.

Rather than stimulating early litigation to test patent validity, such an interpretation of *Lear* would make it advantageous for a licensee to postpone litigation, enjoy the fruits of his licensing agreement, and sue for repayment of royalties near the end of the term of the patent. When a licensed patent is about to expire and the threat of injunction no longer exists, a licensee would have little to lose in bringing an action to recover all the money he has paid in royalties on the ground of the invalidity of the patent. The licensee would have a chance to regain all the royalties paid while never having been subjected to the risk of an injunction. Such an interpretation of *Lear* would defeat one of the expressed purposes of the court in announcing that decision.

Do you agree with the court's reasoning? Does the result in *Troxel* diminish the force of *Lear*? What arguments might be made that a licensee *should* be entitled to recoup paid royalties after a licensed patent is found to be invalid?

22.3 VALIDITY CHALLENGES UNDER THE DECLARATORY JUDGMENT ACT

In the assignee estoppel cases discussed in Section 22.1, the assignee of a patent was sued for infringement, then raised the invalidity of the asserted patent as a defense. The patentee, in turn, argued that the assignee was estopped from raising the invalidity defense. After *Lear*, a licensee that believed that a licensed patent was invalid could stop paying royalties and then assert invalidity when the patentee sued it for breach of contract and, after the licensor terminated the licensing agreement for breach, patent infringement.

Though the Supreme Court in *Lear* sought to "unmuzzle" licensees and enable them to challenge potentially invalid patents, the pathway cleared by *Lear* was, in reality, a difficult one for licensees. That is, if the licensee wishes to stop paying royalties on a questionable patent, it must intentionally breach the licensing agreement and wait to be sued for nonpayment and infringement before asserting its claim of invalidity. And, of course, there is always a chance (sometimes a large one) that the invalidity defense will fail and the patent will be upheld, in which case the licensee will be no more than a willful infringer. Thus, in order to take advantage of the freedom to challenge afforded by *Lear*, the licensee must take a substantial risk.

There is, of course, another option. As discussed in Section 5.1, the Declaratory Judgment Act, 28 U.S.C. § 2201, provides that "In a case of actual controversy … any court of the United States … may declare the rights and other legal relations of any interested party seeking such a declaration." And, as cases such as *SanDisk v. STMicroelectronics* demonstrate (see Section 5.1), such declaratory judgment actions may be brought to establish the validity of a patent before it is asserted in litigation. Thus, there is a route for parties to challenge the validity of patents in court before they are sued by the patent holder.

There is, however, a catch. The Declaratory Judgment Act requires that in order for a court to hear a declaratory judgment action, there must be "a case of actual controversy." In Section 5.1 we discussed situations in which a patent holder approaches an alleged infringer, and what degree of "threat" is necessary to give rise to an "actual controversy." Though the standard has varied over the years, an unlicensed party that may be infringing a patent can often make out a case for declaratory judgment after being "approached" by a patent holder with a licensing offer.

But when one is actually *licensed* under the patent, where is the threat? Unlike an alleged infringer, a licensee in good standing is not threatened by the patent holder. Does this fact prevent licensees from challenging licensed patents under the Declaratory Judgment Act? In *Gen-Probe Inc. v. Vysis, Inc.*, 359 F.3d 1376 (Fed. Cir. 2004), the Federal Circuit held that under the Declaratory Judgment Act, no case or controversy exists while a license remains in force. To challenge a licensed patent, the licensee must stop paying royalties and breach the licensing agreement. This breach creates a case or controversy, which gives the licensee jurisdiction under the Act. However, it also places the licensee in a difficult spot: It is in breach of the contract, it could be subject to contractual damages, it risks treble damages for willful infringement as well as the loss of its right to operate its business if the patent is ultimately found to be valid, and it also loses any other benefits that it enjoyed under the terminated licensing agreement (e.g., licenses under *other* patents or IP rights not being challenged). Nevertheless, Judge Rader, writing for the court, explained that:

> [P]ermitting Gen-Probe to pursue a lawsuit without materially breaching its license agreement yields undesirable results. Vysis voluntarily relinquished its statutory right to exclude by granting Gen-Probe a nonexclusive license. In so doing, Vysis chose to avoid litigation as an avenue of enforcing its rights. Allowing this action to proceed would effectively defeat those contractual covenants and discourage patentees from granting licenses. In other words, in this situation, the licensor would bear all the risk, while licensee would benefit from the license's effective cap on damages or royalties in the event its challenge to the patent's scope or validity fails.
>
> Under these circumstances, there is not a reasonable apprehension of suit. Therefore, this court holds that no actual controversy supports jurisdiction under the Declaratory Judgment Act for Gen-Probe's suit against Vysis over the … patent.

This result, harsh as it was for licensees, remained in force for only three years. In 2007, the Supreme Court overturned *Gen-Probe* in *MedImmune, Inc. v. Genentech, Inc.*, 549 U.S. 118 (2007). In 1997, MedImmune entered into a licensing agreement with Genentech for multiple patents and patent applications. In 2001, one of the patent applications matured into an issued patent and Genentech notified MedImmune that royalties were due with respect to MedImmune's respiratory drug Synagis. MedImmune believed that the patent, as issued, was invalid. In response, it did two things. First, to avoid breaching the agreement, it paid the royalties demanded by Genentech (albeit under protest). Second, it brought an action in district court seeking a declaration of the patent's invalidity. Citing *Gen-Probe*, the district court dismissed MedImmune's claim, and the Federal Circuit affirmed. In an opinion written by Justice Scalia, the Supreme Court reversed.

First, the Court recognized that MedImmune considered Genentech's royalty demand letter "to be a clear threat to enforce the … patent, terminate the 1997 license agreement, and sue for patent infringement if [MedImmune] did not make royalty payments as demanded." In considering whether MedImmune was required to cease making royalty payments in order to avail itself of the Declaratory Judgment Act, Justice Scalia analogized the situation to one in which a petitioner is permitted to challenge the Constitutionality of a law without actually violating the law, or to ask a court to opine on the legality of demolishing a building before "drop[ping] the wrecking ball." In these examples, it is reasonable for a court to recognize the existence of a "controversy" without the need for the plaintiff to inflict substantial self-injury upon itself. Likewise, the Court held that MedImmune "was not required, insofar as Article III is concerned, to break or terminate its 1997 license agreement before seeking a declaratory judgment in federal court that the underlying patent is invalid, unenforceable, or not infringed."

In ruling for MedImmune, the Court quoted the standard for declaratory judgment relief articulated in *Maryland Casualty Co. v. Pacific Coal & Oil Co.*, 312 U.S. 270, 273 (1941):

> Whether the facts alleged, under all circumstances, show that there is a substantial controversy between parties having adverse legal interests of sufficient immediacy and reality to warrant the issuance of a declaratory judgment.

In doing so, it eliminated any requirement that a licensee breach its licensing agreement in order to challenge the validity of licensed patents.

Notes and Questions

1. *MedImmune and Lear.* At the Federal Circuit, MedImmune argued that "under *Lear v. Adkins*, it has the absolute right to challenge the validity or enforceability of the patent, whether or not it breaches the license and whether or not it can be sued by the patentee." The Federal Circuit, relying on *Gen-Probe*, rejected this argument. But the Supreme Court hardly mentioned *Lear* in its opinion. Why not? Does the ruling in *MedImmune* support or contradict the policy considerations raised in *Lear*?

2. *Incentives.* The Court's decision in *MedImmune* makes it easier for a licensee to challenge the validity of a licensed patent. What types of conduct might this decision encourage?

3. *What is a threat?* In *MedImmune*, as in many biopharma licensing disputes, a single Genentech patent was at issue. MedImmune successfully argued that its failure to pay royalties with respect to that patent would expose it to an infringement suit by Genentech – a threat sufficient to confer standing on MedImmune to challenge the patent in a declaratory judgment action. In contrast, in *Apple Inc. v. Qualcomm Inc.*, 992 F.3d 1378 (Fed. Cir. 2021), Apple and Qualcomm settled global patent litigation with an agreement under which Qualcomm granted Apple a six-year royalty-bearing license to tens of thousands of patents. After this, Apple continued to prosecute invalidity challenges against two Qualcomm patents at the Patent Trial and Appeals Board (PTAB); these challenges were appealed to the Federal Circuit. The Federal Circuit held that Apple lacked standing to maintain its suit.[8] First, it reasoned that the invalidity of the two patents, even if proven, would not affect Apple's royalty obligation under the global licensing agreement.[9] Second, Apple provided no evidence that it would manufacture a product that infringed the patents after the expiration of the licensing agreement. Finally, Apple's contention that Qualcomm had exhibited a pattern of suing licensees, including Apple, after licensing agreements expired was too speculative to confer standing on Apple. Do you agree? Under what circumstances, if any, should Apple be permitted to challenge patents within the large portfolio licensed by Qualcomm? Is there a public interest arising under *Lear* in allowing such challenges?

4. *Declaratory Judgment Jurisdiction.* In *Red Wing Shoe Co. v. Hockerson-Halberstadt, Inc.*, 148 F.3d 1355 (Fed. Cir. 1998), HHI, a Louisiana-based patent assertion entity (PAE), sent Red Wing a demand letter and invitation to license. HHI then entered into correspondence

---

[8]   The Federal Circuit's holding did not limit Apple's ability to challenge Qualcomm's patents at the PTAB. It observed that "nearly any person" may initiate such an administrative challenge, with no requirement of constitutional standing.

[9]   As discussed in Section 24.4, parties are permitted to bundle together multiple patents at a single royalty rate, without adjusting the rate each time an individual patent expires, so long as the arrangement is for the mutual convenience of the parties.

with Red Wing, in which HHI granted Red Wing an extension of time and then rebutted Red Wing's contentions of noninfringement. At that point, Red Wing brought a declaratory judgment action against HHI in its home jurisdiction of Minnesota. HHI moved to dismiss based on a lack of personal jurisdiction. Red Wing argued that the three letters sent by HHI to Red Wing at its Minnesota location "not only sought to inform Red Wing of potential infringement but also solicited business with Red Wing in Minnesota." The district court determined that it lacked personal jurisdiction over HHI and the Federal Circuit affirmed. In *Trimble Inc. v. Perdiemco LLC*, 997 F.3d 1147 (Fed. Cir. 2021), the plaintiff PAE exchanged a total of twenty-two communications with the defendant over a period of three months. This, the court ruled, "easily satisfied" the personal jurisdiction requirement in a declaratory judgment action brought by the defendant in its home jurisdiction. The court specifically held that *Red Wing* did not compel a finding in the plaintiff's favor on the facts of this case. Given these two data points (three versus twenty-two communications), just how much correspondence must a patent holder have with a potential licensee before being subject to the jurisdiction of the defendant's home court? To what extent do these cases encourage patent holders to adopt a "sue first, talk later" strategy?

22.4 NO-CHALLENGE CLAUSES

22.4.1 *Agreements Not to Challenge*

Lear eliminated the estoppel doctrine that prevented licensees from challenging the validity of licensed patents, and *MedImmune* opened the way for licensees to challenge validity through declaratory judgment actions without having to breach their licensing agreements. With these new avenues open for challenges to the validity of licensed patents, it is not surprising that transactional practices quickly adapted to prohibit such challenges through so-called "no-challenge" or "no-contest" clauses. Below is an example of such a clause.

EXAMPLE: NO-CHALLENGE

a. Licensee agrees that it shall not, at any time in the future, directly or indirectly aid, assist or participate in any action contesting or seeking to limit the validity, scope or enforceability of any Licensed Patent in any court, review board or tribunal or before any patent office or administration anywhere in the world, or knowingly disclose to any third party or to the public any document, record, prior art or other information that could have the effect of assisting in any current or future action contesting the validity, scope or enforceability of any Licensed Patent, except as may be required by law or order of any court of competent jurisdiction.

b. Licensee expressly waives any and all invalidity and unenforceability defenses that it may have in any future litigation, arbitration or proceeding relating to the Licensed Patents.

As you can see, the above example prohibits the licensee both from affirmatively challenging the validity of any licensed patent (both in court and at the PTO) and from asserting any invalidity defense in any future proceeding with licensor.

Not surprisingly, the rise of no-challenge clauses soon led to litigation over their enforceability in a range of contexts. *Lear* remains strong precedent, and its general encouragement of validity challenges has prevented the widespread adoption of no-challenge clauses. Yet these clauses appear in a widening group of licensing agreements, as discussed in *Flex-Foot*.

Flex-Foot, Inc. v. CRP, Inc.
238 F.3d 1362 (Fed. Cir. 2001)

LINN, CIRCUIT JUDGE

Background

This is the third litigation between [CRP, Inc. d/b/a Springlite ("Springlite")] and [Flex-Foot, Inc. and Van L. Phillips (collectively "Flex-Foot")] regarding U.S. Patent No. 4,822,363 (the " '363 patent"). In 1989, Flex-Foot brought the first lawsuit against Springlite for infringement of the '363 patent. That action was promptly settled and dismissed by way of a settlement agreement and a corresponding license agreement in which Springlite agreed to pay a royalty on the accused Springlite device.

Springlite contends that its primary motivation in settling with Flex-Foot at that time was economic. Springlite did not have the financial resources to defend against Flex-Foot's infringement claims. Neither the settlement agreement nor the license agreement acknowledged that Springlite's device infringed the '363 patent. In addition, neither agreement barred Springlite from later challenging the validity of the '363 patent. In fact, the license expressly provided that it would expire upon judicial determination that the '363 patent was invalid.

Springlite brought a second action in 1993 (the "DJ action"), seeking a declaration that the '363 patent was invalid. The parties thereafter conducted discovery and fully briefed a motion for summary judgment regarding Springlite's invalidity allegations. While that motion was pending, however, the parties settled the case in March 1994 via another settlement agreement (the "March 1994 Settlement Agreement") and corresponding license agreement (the "March 1994 License Agreement").

The March 1994 Settlement Agreement contains language making it clear that Springlite waived its right to challenge the validity and enforceability of the '363 patent. Specifically, paragraph 7.1 states:

> 7.1 The CRP Group agrees not to challenge or cause to be challenged, directly or indirectly, the validity or enforceability of the '913 patent and/or the '363 patent in any court or other tribunal, including the United States Patent and Trademark Office. As to the '363 and '913 patents only, the CRP Group waives any and all invalidity and unenforceability defenses in any future litigation, arbitration, or other proceeding.

In addition, paragraph 6 of the March 1994 License Agreement states:

> CRP agrees not to challenge or cause to be challenged, directly or indirectly, the validity or unenforceability, or scope of the '913 patent and/or the '363 patent in any court or tribunal, or before the United States Patent and Trademark Office or in any arbitration proceeding. This waiver is expressly limited to challenges to the '363 and '913 patents, but applies without exception to any and all products which CRP may make, use or sell in the

future. CRP also waives any argument that the licensed products are not covered by one or more claims of the '913 or '363 patent.

The March 1994 Settlement Agreement also required arbitration of any infringement claims. Pursuant to the March 1994 Settlement Agreement and the March 1994 License Agreement, the parties entered into a stipulation for dismissal of the DJ action with prejudice.

In 1997, Flex-Foot filed a complaint alleging that Springlite's "G-Foot" prosthetic foot device infringed the '363 patent (the "1997 Complaint"). In accordance with the March 1994 Settlement Agreement, the 1997 Complaint was sent to arbitration. In January 1999, Flex-Foot successfully obtained an arbitration award from the American Arbitration Association ("AAA"). That decision, rendered by a panel of three patent attorneys mutually selected by the parties, found that the accused Springlite device literally infringed asserted claims 16 and 17 of the '363 patent. The arbitration panel awarded Flex-Foot the costs of the arbitration. Soon thereafter, Springlite requested that the arbitrators clarify or modify their award, as well as set forth clear statements about the scope of the contested claim elements. The arbitrators declined both requests.

As a defense to the charge of infringement in the 1997 Complaint, Springlite alleged invalidity of the '363 patent, and subsequent to the arbitrators' award, filed a motion with the district court to vacate the award and consider the invalidity defense. In response, Flex-Foot filed a motion to affirm the arbitration award. The district court granted Flex-Foot's motion to confirm the arbitration award and entered a permanent injunction against Springlite, concluding that Springlite was "collaterally estopped" from challenging the validity and enforceability of Flex-Foot's '363 patent.

Springlite appeals the arbitration panel's award and the district court's judgment to this court. We have jurisdiction over Springlite's appeal from the district court's judgment.

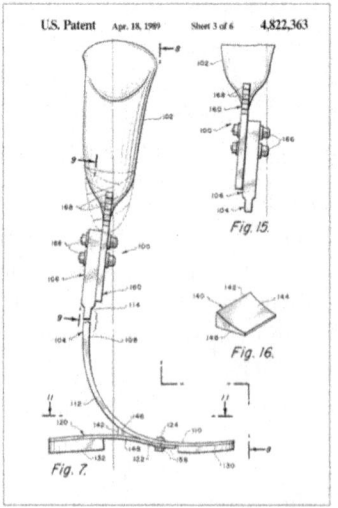

FIGURE 22.4 Flex-Foot's patented "bladerunner" prosthesis design gained worldwide attention when used by South Africa's Oscar Pistorius to run the 400 m sprint at the 2012 London Olympics.

Discussion

The arbitration award did not address Springlite's challenge to the validity of the '363 patent. Upon … reviewing the award, the district court held that the validity of Flex-Foot's patents could not be litigated. It so held because it determined that Springlite was collaterally estopped from challenging the validity of the '363 patent, based on paragraph 7.1 of the March 1994 Settlement Agreement and paragraph 6 of the March 1994 Licensing Agreement.

Springlite argues that the district court's holding – that it is collaterally estopped from challenging the validity of the '363 patent – is in error. Springlite contends that it did not agree to enter into any type of judgment adjudicating the issues of infringement and validity. Despite Springlite's protestations, we note that Springlite did agree to a dismissal with prejudice following a settlement agreement that included a promise that Springlite would not challenge the validity of the '363 patent. We hold that … such a dismissal with prejudice and accompanying settlement agreement certainly gives rise to contractual estoppel of Springlite's challenge to the '363 patent's validity. The question is whether such contractually created estoppel is void as against public policy pursuant to *Lear v. Adkins*.

Springlite does not contend that its intent in entering into the March 1994 Settlement Agreement and March 1994 Licensing Agreement was anything other than a waiver of future challenges to the '363 patent's validity. Instead, Springlite argues that it should be entitled, under the public policy rationale set forth in Lear, to renege on its prior written agreement with Flex-Foot.

In *Lear*, notably, the license did not contain, and was not accompanied by, any promise by the licensee not to challenge the validity of the patent. This distinguishing fact is meaningful because it implicates the important policy of enforcing settlement agreements and res judicata. Indeed, the important policy of enforcing settlement agreements and res judicata must themselves be weighed against the federal patent laws' prescription of full and free competition in the use of ideas that are in reality a part of the public domain.

In addition to the present case being meaningfully distinguishable from *Lear*, we note that this court has in the past distinguished a number of other cases from *Lear*.

[*Hemstreet v. Spiegel, Inc.*, 851 F.2d 348 (Fed. Cir. 1988)] concerns settlement of an infringement trial that had progressed for a single week. The settlement, which included a stipulation requiring the licensee to make payments without regard to any subsequent determination of invalidity or unenforceability, was memorialized in a settlement order signed by the parties' representatives and the district court. The court's settlement order dismissed the action and stated that "the issues of validity, unenforceability and infringement of" the patents were finally concluded and disposed of. In a subsequent lawsuit, the parties disputed whether the settlement order created res judicata. We held that a dismissal based upon a settlement order in which "'the issues of validity, enforceability and infringement of' the patents in suit were finally concluded and disposed of," barred a subsequent challenge to the validity and enforceability of those patents by the same party, whether or not the settlement order and dismissal actually adjudicated patent validity to create res judicata. We also stated, "there is a compelling public interest and policy in upholding and enforcing settlement agreements voluntarily entered into" because enforcement of settlement agreements encourages parties to enter into them – thus fostering judicial economy.

Thus, the holding in *Hemstreet* was premised on the policy that while the federal patent laws favor full and free competition in the use of ideas in the public domain over the technical requirements of contract doctrine, settlement of litigation is more strongly favored by the law. Clearly, the importance of res judicata and its hierarchical position in the realm of public policy was not a relevant consideration in Lear and therefore the Supreme Court never evaluated the importance of res judicata and whether it trumps the patent laws' prescription of full and free competition in the use of ideas that are in reality a part of the public domain. See id.

This court had the occasion to revisit *Lear's* holding in [*Foster v. Hallco Mfg. Co.*, 947 F.2d 469 (Fed. Cir. 1991)]. *Foster* concerns termination of an infringement suit via a consent decree, i.e., a decision by the court to which the parties have agreed. In the consent decree, Foster acknowledged the validity and infringement of the patents at issue. About four years after entry of the consent decree, Foster began making a new device, and informed the patentee Hallco that the device did not infringe the patents at issue in the prior litigation. Hallco disagreed. When Foster subsequently filed a declaratory judgment action that the patents were invalid and unenforceable, Hallco asserted an affirmative defense of res judicata, based on the consent decree declaring that the patents are valid and enforceable. Foster alleged that, because the consent decree was essentially an agreement not to challenge the patent, it therefore was unenforceable under *Lear*.

We held that *Lear's* abrogation of licensee estoppel did not change the fact that a consent decree gives rise to res judicata. The *Foster* court could not conclude that the public policy expressed in *Lear* is so overriding that challenges to validity must be allowed when, under normal principles of res judicata applicable to a consent judgment, such judgment would be precluded. *Foster* echoes *Hemstreet's* teaching that there is a strong public interest in settlement of patent litigation and that upholding the terms of a settlement encourages patent owners to agree to settlements – thus fostering judicial economy. These interests are relevant to the instant case, even though this case deals with a settlement agreement and resulting dismissal with prejudice, rather than a consent decree.

> *"while the federal patent laws favor full and free competition in the use of ideas in the public domain over the technical requirements of contract doctrine, settlement of litigation is more strongly favored by the law"*

We note that this is the third litigation between Flex-Foot and Springlite. Springlite has already challenged the validity of the '363 patent twice, voluntarily ending that challenge via settlement and licensing agreements on both occasions. In the latest settlement agreement, Springlite promised not to challenge the validity and enforceability of the '363 patent. There has been no allegation that the latest settlement was anything other than a voluntary waiver of future challenges to the '363 patent's validity. Moreover, in this challenge, the parties conducted discovery and fully briefed opposing summary judgment motions on the issue of invalidity. The latest settlement occurred on the eve of the summary judgment briefing. Indeed, Springlite's behavior is exactly the type of behavior that both *Hemstreet* and *Foster* were concerned with when they noted the strong public interest in enforcing settlements. Settlement agreements must be enforced if they are to remain effective as a means for resolving legal disagreements. Upholding the terms of settlement agreements encourages patent owners to agree to settlements and promotes judicial economy.

Once an accused infringer has challenged patent validity, has had an opportunity to conduct discovery on validity issues, and has elected to voluntarily dismiss the litigation with prejudice under a settlement agreement containing a clear and unambiguous undertaking not to challenge validity and/or enforceability of the patent in suit, the accused infringer is contractually estopped from raising any such challenge in any subsequent proceeding.

Based on the clear and unambiguous waiver of future challenges to the validity of the '363 patent in the settlement agreement voluntarily entered into by the parties in this case, we hold that Springlite is contractually estopped from challenging the validity of the '363 patent and affirm the district court's judgment in favor of Flex-Foot.

Notes and Questions

1. *Competing policy goals.* In *Flex-Foot*, the Federal Circuit relies on two earlier decisions, *Hemstreet* and *Foster*, which expressed different policy goals than *Lear*. In fact, the policy goals expressed in these cases appear to have been strong enough to overcome *Lear's* aversion restrictions on the ability to challenge patents on invalidity grounds. What policy goals were set forth in *Hemstreet* and *Foster*, and why are they more influential than those set forth in *Lear*?

2. *Beyond settlements? Flex-Foot* establishes that no-challenge clauses are enforceable in settlement agreements, given overriding policy considerations favoring the settlement of litigation. What other types of agreements might categorically be held to permit no-challenge clauses?

3. *What is a challenge? Lear* and most other cases interpreting a licensee's ability to "challenge" the validity of a licensed patent involve a licensee's assertion of the affirmative defenses of patent invalidity and unenforceability. But what about other actions that could narrow the scope of the licensed patent claims? Are these prohibited "challenges"?

   In *Transocean Offshore Deepwater Drilling, Inc. v. Noble Corp. PLC*, 451 F. Supp. 3d 690 (S.D. Tex. 2020), the parties had entered into a settlement agreement containing the following no-challenge clause:

   Licensee covenants that it will not participate as a party or financially support a third party in any administrative or court proceeding or effort in the world to invalidate, oppose, nullify, reexamine, reissue or otherwise challenge the validity, enforceability, or scope of any claim of the Licensed Patents.

   In a subsequent infringement suit between the parties, the licensee argued that the licensor had disavowed claim scope by distinguishing prior art and proposed a construction of previously construed claim language that narrows the scope of the claim. The licensor argued that these actions amounted to "challenges" to the "scope of any claims of the Licensed Patents," in violation of the contractual no-challenge clause.

   The court, however, threw up its hands, holding that "the meaning of the language 'challenge the ... scope of any claim' is uncertain and doubtful, and the language is reasonably susceptible to more than one meaning." Do you agree that the language of the no-challenge clause is irredeemably vague? If so, how would you amend this language so that it is sufficiently clear to prohibit (or allow) the licensee's actions? Does the language in the example clause above address the court's concern?

22.4.2 *No-Challenge Clauses in Copyright and Trademark Licenses*

Lear was a patent case, and the public interest goals that it expressed were largely related to patents. But there are reasons that owners of other IP rights might like to include no-challenge clauses in their licensing agreements. Does *Lear* prohibit this? Or is the old doctrine of licensee estoppel still alive and well outside of patent law, making such contractual prohibitions unnecessary?

The Seventh Circuit considered these questions as they pertain to copyright in *Saturday Evening Post v. Rumbleseat Press, Inc.*, 816 F.2d 1191 (7th Cir. 1987). In 1979 the Saturday Evening Post Company granted Rumbleseat Press an exclusive license to manufacture porcelain dolls derived from certain Norman Rockwell illustrations that appeared in the *Saturday Evening Post*. Paragraph 9 of the license agreement provided that Rumbleseat "shall not, during the Original Term [of the agreement] or any time thereafter dispute or contest, directly or indirectly, [the] validity of any of the copyrights … which [the Post] may have obtained."

The Seventh Circuit found Saturday Evening Post's no-challenge clause to be valid and enforceable. Judge Richard Posner, writing for the court, first considered the salutary effects of such a clause:

FIGURE 22.5 Porcelain figurine based on a Norman Rockwell illustration.

Without it the licensee always has a club over the licensor's head: the threat that if there is a dispute the licensee will challenge the copyright's validity. The threat would discourage copyright licensing and might therefore retard rather than promote the diffusion of copyrighted works. Also, a no-contest clause might actually accelerate rather than retard challenges to invalid copyrights, by making the would-be licensee think hard about validity before rather than after he signed the licensing agreement. Rumbleseat had, in fact, used its expressed doubts of the validity of the Post's copyrights to obtain a lower royalty rate in the negotiations for the license.

He then discusses whether policy considerations, particularly those set forth in *Lear*, weighed against such clauses in copyright agreements. He finds that they do not, noting first that "the logic of *Lear* does not extend to copyright licenses." He explains:

A patent empowers its owner to prevent anyone else from making or using his invention; a copyright just empowers its owner to prevent others from copying the particular verbal or pictorial or aural pattern in which he chooses to express himself. The economic power conferred is much smaller. There is no need for a rule that would automatically invalidate every no-contest clause. If a particular clause is used to confer monopoly power beyond the small amount that the copyright laws authorize, the clause can be attacked under section 1 of the Sherman Act as a contract in restraint of trade. Rumbleseat does not argue that the clause here restrained trade in that sense. The fact that we can find no antitrust case – or for that matter any other reported case – that deals with a no-contest clause in a copyright license is evidence that these clauses are not such a source of significant restraints on freedom to compete as might warrant a per se rule of illegality.

Thus, the court held that there were no countervailing policy considerations that weighed strongly against Saturday Evening Post's no-challenge clause, and upheld the clause.

A different result obtains, however, in the area of certification marks, as discussed in the following case.

Idaho Potato Comm. v. M&M Produce Farm & Sales
335 F.3d 130 (2d Cir. 2003)

FEINBERG, CIRCUIT JUDGE

Plaintiff Idaho Potato Commission ("IPC") appeals from a May 2002 Memorandum and Order ("May 2002 Order") of the United States District Court for the Southern District of New York (Brieant, J.), vacating a $ 41,962 jury award for the IPC in its certification mark infringement suit under the Lanham Act against M&M Produce Farm and Sales, M&M Packaging, Inc., and Matthew and Mark Rogowski individually (collectively "M&M").

Defendant M&M cross-appeals from the court's August 1998 Memorandum and Order ("August 1998 Order") … holding that M&M was barred from seeking cancellation of the IPC marks by a no-challenge provision in its licensing agreement with the IPC. M&M argues on appeal that the no-challenge provision should not be enforced because it violates the public policy embodied in the Lanham Act.

Background

The IPC is an agency created by Idaho statute to promote the sale of Idaho russet potatoes and to prevent the substitution of potatoes grown in other regions as Idaho potatoes. To further these goals, the IPC has registered a number of certification marks with the United States Patent and Trademark Office, two of which are relevant to this appeal: (1) the word "IDAHO" in a distinctive font; and (2) the phrase "GROWN IN IDAHO" written inside an outline of the boundaries of the state of Idaho (collectively "the IPC marks"). Each mark certifies that "goods so marked are grown in the State of Idaho."

The IPC controls its marks through an elaborate licensing system that seeks to ensure the quality and geographic authenticity of potatoes packed in containers bearing the IPC marks. This system requires everyone in the chain of distribution, from in-state growers to out-of-state repackers and resellers, to be licensed in order to use the IPC certification marks on their packaging. Licensed vendors are also prevented from selling Idaho potatoes to non-licensed customers for repacking or reselling.

The standard licensing agreements provide licensees with the right to use the IPC marks, an important benefit because certified Idaho potatoes sell for more than non-Idaho potatoes. In return, licensees agree, among other things, to use the IPC marks only on potatoes that are certified as grown in Idaho and that meet the IPC's other quality standards. Licensees also agree to maintain purchase and sale records so that the IPC can check periodically for compliance and prevent "counterfeiting" (putting non-Idaho potatoes in bags bearing the IPC marks.)

M&M is a small business in New York owned and operated by two brothers, Matthew and Mark Rogowski. M&M's main business is growing onions on a small farm, but because onions are a seasonal crop, the brothers also repack potatoes to stay in business throughout the year. In 1990, M&M entered into a licensing agreement with the IPC and was given the right to use the IPC's certification marks, subject to the terms in the agreement. While M&M was a licensee, it would purchase potatoes in bulk from licensed Idaho potato vendors and would repackage those potatoes into small five-pound bags bearing the certification marks.

In 1994, M&M received a notice of audit from the IPC requesting M&M's records with regard to all Idaho potatoes bought and sold. Because M&M did not produce sufficient records, the IPC considered M&M in breach of the licensing agreement and requested that M&M return its license. In February 1995, M&M voluntarily gave up the license and consequently no longer had the right to use the IPC marks.

After returning the license, however, M&M continued repacking Idaho potatoes in bags with the IPC marks.

FIGURE 22.6 One of the Idaho Potato Commission's certification marks for Idaho-grown potatoes.

In November 1997, the IPC filed the current lawsuit against M&M alleging: (1) trademark infringement, (2) false designation of origin and dilution, and (3) unlawful and unfair competition in violation of various New York and Idaho statutes and common law.

In response, M&M filed counterclaims for, among other things, cancellation of the IPC marks under federal and state law. M&M argued that the IPC marks should be cancelled for numerous reasons, including that the IPC abused its marks by: discriminately refusing to certify potatoes that were grown in Idaho, imposing standards for certification beyond the geographic origin the marks are registered to certify, and using its certification marks for purposes other than to certify, all in violation of the Lanham Act. M&M also alleged that the IPC lacks the independence necessary for certification mark owners under the Lanham Act.

[The district] court held [in the August 1998 Order] that M&M was estopped from challenging the IPC marks by a provision in its licensing agreement in which M&M (1) acknowledged that the marks "are valid, registered marks;" and (2) agreed that it would "not during the term of the agreement, or at any time thereafter, attack the title or any rights" of the IPC in the relevant marks.

M&M cross-appeals from the August 1998 Order holding M&M estopped from attacking the validity of the IPC marks.

Discussion

Because the jury's verdict against M&M was predicated on the IPC's ownership of valid certification marks, we first discuss M&M's cross-appeal challenging the district court's August 1998 ruling that M&M was … estopped by the licensing agreement from attacking those marks.

The facts relevant to the issue are not in dispute. M&M signed a licensing agreement with the IPC in which M&M recognized the validity of the IPC marks and promised not to attack the rights of the IPC in those marks during the term of the agreement or at any time thereafter. The basic question on the facts before us, therefore, is whether such a provision in a certification mark licensing agreement is enforceable against a licensee when the licensee no longer holds a license. This question has apparently not yet been squarely decided by any federal circuit court.

M&M contends that the no-challenge provision in its licensing agreement should not be enforced because it violates the public policy embodied in the Lanham Act. It argues that by requiring licensees to forever waive their statutory right to challenge the IPC's marks, the IPC effectively avoids enforcement of the Lanham Act. M&M relies principally on the Supreme Court's opinion in *Lear, Inc. v. Adkins*, which held that the contract doctrine of licensee estoppel was trumped by the federal policy embodied in the patent laws. M&M argues that *Lear* should apply to certification mark licenses as it does to patent licenses because the public interest in both is similar.

We begin our analysis with the Supreme Court's opinion in *Lear*. The general rule of licensee estoppel provides that when a licensee enters into an agreement to use the intellectual property of a licensor, the licensee effectively recognizes the validity of that property and is estopped from contesting its validity in future disputes. As noted above, the Supreme Court in *Lear* held that the doctrine does not necessarily control in disputes over the validity of patents. The Court identified in the patent laws the "strong federal policy favoring the full and free use of ideas in the public domain."

Courts applying the principles articulated in *Lear* to patent disputes have enforced no-challenge contract provisions only when the interests in doing so outweigh the public interest in discovering invalid patents. Thus, in *Flex-Foot*, the United States Court of Appeals for the Federal Circuit recently enforced an estoppel provision in a settlement agreement only after determining that the public policy in favor of settlements outweighed the public interest in patents.

Other courts, including this one, have weighed these interests to reach differing results, but each has recognized the applicability of the balancing test first articulated in *Lear*.

The *Lear* balancing test has also been frequently applied to trademark licensing contracts. As the district court here correctly noted, courts in this context have generally precluded licensees from challenging the validity of a mark they have obtained the right to use. However, courts have done so only after considering the public interest in trademarks. For example, in *Beer Nuts, Inc. v. King Nut Co.*, the Sixth Circuit explicitly used the *Lear* balancing test in upholding a written agreement not to challenge the validity of a trademark. The court distinguished the public policy of trademarks—guarding the public from being deceived into purchasing an unwanted product—from that of patents and held, "When the balancing test is employed in the instant situation, we conclude that the public interest in [trademarks] ... is not so great that it should take precedence over the rule of the law of contracts that a person should be held to his undertakings."

The IPC maintains that the *Lear* balancing test is inapplicable because unlike the contract in *Lear*, which was silent concerning the rights of the licensee to challenge the patent, the contract signed by M&M specifically precluded M&M from challenging the IPC's marks. However, this distinction does not negate the applicability of the *Lear* balancing test to the contract in this case. *Lear* itself recognized that federal policy embodied in the law of intellectual property can trump even explicit contractual provisions. The licensor in *Lear* argued that based on the licensee's explicit contractual agreement to pay royalties until invalidity of the patent had been determined by a court, the licensee was required to pay royalties for the duration of the litigation even if the patent in question was eventually declared invalid. The *Lear* Court disagreed and refused to enforce the contract on the same basis that it refused to apply licensee estoppel: "The parties' contract, however, is no more controlling on this issue than is the State's doctrine of estoppel, which is also rooted in contract principles." *Lear* makes clear that courts should weigh the federal policy embodied in the law of intellectual property against even explicit contractual provisions and render unenforceable those provisions that would undermine the public interest. Thus, the explicit contractual provision in the licensing agreement between the IPC and M&M is no barrier to application of the *Lear* balancing test.

We turn now to application of this balancing test to the current dispute. In doing so, we must identify the public interest in certification marks and the public injury that might result from enforcement of the estoppel provision in the contract between M&M and the IPC. The IPC argues, and the district court agreed, that the trademark cases enforcing no-challenge provisions noted above are controlling with regard to certification marks because "certification marks are generally treated the same as trademarks." Although we recognize that trademarks and certification marks are "generally treated the same," we conclude that the difference between the public interests in certification marks and trademarks compels a different result in this context.

In the trademark context ... "[a] dealer's good will is protected ... in order that the purchasing public may not be enticed into buying A's product when it wants B's product."

Thus, agreements that allow the continued use of confusingly similar trademarks injure the public, and the important issue in litigation over trademark contracts is the public confusion that might result from enforcing the contract.

Significantly, trademark owners are granted a monopoly over their marks and can choose to license the marks to others on whatever conditions they deem appropriate, so long as confusion does not result. The same is not true of certification marks. Certification mark licensing programs are "a form of limited compulsory licensing," 3 McCarthy on Trademarks and Unfair Competition § 19.96, and the certifier has a "duty ... to certify the goods or services of any person who meets the standards and conditions which the mark certifies."

That the owner of a certification mark "cannot refuse to license the mark to anyone on any ground other than the standards it has set," 3 McCarthy at § 19.96, is an important distinction between the policies embodied in trademarks and certification marks. It is true that certification marks are designed to facilitate consumer expectations of a standardized product, much like trademarks are designed to ensure that a consumer is not confused by the marks on a product. But the certification mark regime protects a further public interest in free and open competition among producers and distributors of the certified product. It protects the market players from the influence of the certification mark owner, and aims to ensure the broadest competition, and therefore the best price and quality, within the market for certified products. From our review of the cases, it appears to us that this interest is akin to the public interest in the "full and free use of ideas in the public domain" embodied in the patent laws. *Lear*, 395 U.S. at 674.

We believe that the estoppel provision in the contract between M&M and the IPC injures this public interest in a number of ways. First, the provision places a non-quality-control related restriction on the sellers of the certified product and other licensees that benefits the mark owner in contravention of the mark owner's obligation not to interfere with a free market for products meeting the certification criteria. Second, as in *Lear*, parties that have entered into a licensee relationship with the IPC may often be the only individuals with enough economic incentive to challenge the IPC's licensing scheme, and thus the only individuals with enough incentive to force the IPC to conform to the law.

Finally, to decide the issue of public injury we must look to the public interest implicated by the merits of the licensee's challenges. M&M alleges, among other things, that: (1) the IPC is a corporate entity dominated by producers of the certified products and that such domination violates the provisions in 15 U.S.C. § 1064(5)(B); (2) the IPC uses the goodwill derived from the certification marks as a trademark in violation of § 1064(5)(C); (3) the IPC imposes certification standards other than those that the certification mark is registered to certify in violation of § 1064(5)(D); and (4) the IPC discriminately refuses to certify potatoes that meet the standards for certification, also in violation of § 1064(5)(D). All of these challenges implicate the public interest in maintaining a free market for the certified product unaffected by the possible competing economic interests of the certification mark owner.

We believe these public interests are more substantial and more likely to be harmed if M&M is not allowed to press its claims than the public interests and de minimis harm alleged in the trademark-related cases that upheld contractual no-challenge provisions. See, e.g., *Beer Nuts*, 477 F.2d at 329 (holding that public interest in guarding against depletion of general vocabulary insufficient to override contract law). Also, this case lacks a strong countervailing public interest other than the general interest in enforcing written contracts (like the interest in settlements) that persuaded courts to enforce contractual no-challenge provisions in other agreements. See, e.g., *Flex-Foot*, 238 F.3d at 1368. We therefore conclude that the district court erred in finding M&M contractually estopped as a matter of law from challenging the IPC marks.

[W]e therefore vacate the district court's August 1998 Order holding M&M estopped as a matter of law from bringing its counterclaims for cancellation of the IPC marks and remand for consideration of those claims on the merits.

Notes and Questions

1. Lear *beyond patents*. Why does Judge Posner conclude that the reasoning of *Lear* should not be extended to copyrights? Are the policies expressed in Lear limited solely to patents? Do you agree with limiting *Lear* in this manner? In *Idaho Potato*, Judge Feinberg does not seem to display the same reluctance to apply *Lear* in the context of trademarks. What might account for this difference in approaches?

2. *Economic power*. Do you agree with Judge Posner's statement in *Saturday Evening Post* that the "economic power" conferred by copyrights is "much smaller" than that conferred by patents? Surely some copyrights are more valuable than others, just as some patents are more valuable than others and, by extension, some copyrights are more valuable than some patents. Is Judge Posner's reasoning, then, based on a law of averages?

3. *The rarity of copyright invalidity*. In *Saturday Evening Post*, "the Post had copyrighted each of the magazines in which the [Norman Rockwell] illustrations appeared but had not copyrighted the illustrations separately." This omission caused Rumbleseat to question the validity of the Post's copyright in the illustrations. Such an omission, however, is relatively rare, and today, with the elimination of the copyright registration requirement, a nonissue. Is this why Judge Posner observed that "we can find no ... other reported case that deals with a no-contest clause in a copyright license"? Compare this situation with that of patents, every one of which can be (and usually is) subject to a validity challenge when asserted. Does the relative infrequency of copyright validity challenges make the decision in *Saturday Evening Post* easier? Note that Judge Posner is careful to distinguish between the validity of the Post's copyrights in the Rockwell illustrations and "the copyrightability of the Rockwell dolls." Why bother to make this distinction? Would the result change if the no-challenge clause related to the copyrightability of a porcelain doll, or possibly a software program?

4. *The* Lear *balancing test*. In *Idaho Potato*, Judge Feinberg views *Lear* as requiring a court to "balance" the "strong federal policy favoring the full and free use of ideas in the public domain" against whatever policy factors favor the enforcement of a particular no-challenge clause. He refers numerous times to the *Lear* "balancing test." Yet neither the Supreme Court in *Lear* nor the Federal Circuit in its major opinions applying *Lear* refer to such a "balancing test." Is Judge Feinberg's characterization of *Lear* accurate? If so, why do so few courts assessing no-challenge clauses in patent cases use this terminology?

5. *Public policy and certification marks*. Judge Feinberg identifies separate public policies concerning a party's ability to challenge the validity of trademarks and certification marks. What are these different public policy interests and why are they so different?

In reviewing earlier trademark cases such as *Beer Nuts*, he seems to acknowledge that "the public interest in [trademarks] ... is not so great that it should take precedence over the rule of the law of contracts that a person should be held to his undertakings." Yet in striking down the Idaho Potato Commission's no-challenge clause, he favorably compares the strong public policy interests favoring challenges to potentially invalid certification marks, as well as other behaviors of certification mark owners. But unlike the enforceability of settlement agreements, which, under *Flex-Foot*, is supported by a strong public interest, the interest of certification mark owners in no-challenge clauses is a mere "general interest in enforcing written contracts." As a result, the factors supporting challenges to certification marks outweigh those supporting no-challenge clauses, and the Commission's no-challenge clause was rejected. Do you agree with the results of Judge Feinberg's various balancing exercises? Why isn't the goal of trademarks – avoiding consumer confusion – as or more important than the goal of certification marks?

Review the below summary of the state of the law regarding no-challenge clauses in licensing agreements for different types of IP. Do these rules make sense to you? What, if anything, would you change?

> ## SUMMARY: LEGAL STATUS OF NO-CHALLENGE CLAUSES IN LICENSING AGREEMENTS
>
> **Patents** – generally barred (*Lear*), but permitted in settlement agreements (*Flex-Foot*)
> **Copyrights** – generally permitted (*Saturday Evening Post*)
> **Trademarks** – generally permitted (*Beer Nuts*)
> **Certification Marks** – generally barred (*Idaho Potato*)

22.4.3 *Other Penalties for Validity Challenges*

As discussed in the preceding sections, no-challenge clauses are not likely to be enforced in nonsettlement patent licensing agreements. As a result, licensors have developed a set of alternative contractual provisions that seek to discourage licensees from challenging the validity of licensed IP, and to penalize those that do.

Licensee Patent Validity Challenges Following *MedImmune*: Implications for Patent Licensing

Alfred C. Server & Peter Singleton, 3 *Hastings Sci. & Tech. L.J.* 243, 417–38 (2010)

Considering the various problems and uncertainties associated with the "no-challenge" clause, it is reasonable to conclude that its use in a typical license agreement should be avoided. As we will see in the sections that follow, other pro-licensor contract provisions can be used, whether alone or in combination, that have a far greater likelihood of being enforceable and are associated with significantly less risk of giving rise to unintended consequences.

"Termination-for-Challenge" Clause

A "termination-for-challenge" clause, also referred to as a "no-challenge termination" clause, confers upon a patent licensor the right to terminate the license agreement in the event that the licensee challenges the validity of the licensed patent. If enforceable, the provision provides a contractual means of counteracting the effect of the Supreme Court's *MedImmune* decision, which relieved a licensee of the jurisdictional requirement of having to repudiate its patent license agreement before challenging the licensed patent. By permitting a licensor to terminate the license agreement upon the licensee's patent challenge, the "termination-for-challenge" clause places the licensee in the same position it would have been in prior to the *MedImmune* Court's rejection of the Federal Circuit's *Gen-Probe* holding, i.e., in order to bring a patent challenge, a licensee is required to risk losing the benefits of its patent license. Not surprisingly, the "termination-for-challenge" clause is encountered with increasing frequency in the aftermath of [*MedImmune*]. However, the question of whether the clause is enforceable is not a simple one.

Unlike the "no-challenge" clause, a "termination-for-challenge" clause does not eliminate one of the protections of the *Lear* doctrine. In the words of one commentator, "[t]his type of contractual provision does not bar a licensee from challenging the patent's validity. It merely gives the licensor the right to terminate the license in such a case, enabling the licensor to sue the licensee for infringement."[10] The "termination-for-challenge" clause differs from the "no-challenge" clause in another important respect. While the latter has been the subject of judicial review on a number of occasions (as discussed in the preceding section), the "termination-for-challenge" clause has only rarely been evaluated by a court.

One such evaluation was provided ... in *Bayer AG v. Housey Pharmaceuticals, Inc.*, 228 F. Supp. 2d 467 (D. Del. 2002). Bayer, the plaintiff in the case, sought a declaratory judgment that the Housey patents were unenforceable as a result of Housey's misuse of the patents.[11] Among the alleged acts of misuse was the inclusion in patent license agreements with third parties of the following provision:

> [LICENSOR] acknowledges the LICENSEE is not estopped from contesting the validity or enforceability of the Licensed Patent Rights. However, LICENSEE acknowledges that such an attack on validity or enforceability of the Licensed Patent Rights is inconsistent with the purposes of this License Agreement. Accordingly, LICENSEE hereby agrees that if it decides to assert its right to contest the Licensed Patent Rights, in whole or in part, that ... [LICENSOR] shall have the right, at ... [LICENSOR's] option, to terminate this License Agreement by giving written notice thereof to LICENSEE. Further, unless terminated by ... [LICENSOR], LICENSEE agrees to make all payments due under this License Agreement notwithstanding any challenge ... by LICENSEE ... to the Licensed Patent Rights, so long as the applicable patent(s) or patent application(s) remain in effect.

Bayer contended that the provision was an attempt "to muzzle licensees in violation of *Lear*" and its presence in the Housey license agreements constituted patent misuse. The district court in *Bayer* began its analysis by restating the dual protections afforded a patent licensee under the *Lear* doctrine, namely, that a licensee cannot be barred from challenging the validity of a licensed patent nor required to pay royalties to the licensor during the pendency of its patent challenge. Concluding that neither of these protections can be eliminated by the agreement of contracting parties, the court held that the portion of the

[10] Christian Chadd Taylor, No-*Challenge Termination Clauses: Incorporating Innovation Policy and Risk Allocation into Patent Licensing Law*, 69 Ind. L.J. 231 (1993).
[11] The doctrine of patent misuse is discussed in Chapter 24.

Housey provision under consideration that obligated the licensee to continue to pay royalties while challenging the licensed patent was unenforceable. The court went on to note, however, that the inclusion of this unenforceable portion of the provision in the Housey license agreements did not constitute patent misuse. What is significant for the purpose of this section is that the *Bayer* court found no fault with the "termination-for-challenge" portion of the Housey provision. The fact that the district court selectively rejected the royalty payment portion of the provision suggests that the basis for the rejection was that that portion of the provision, in contrast to the "termination-for-challenge" portion, directly eliminated one of the protections of the *Lear* doctrine.

The *Bayer* decision, however, is only a tacit endorsement of the "termination-for-challenge" clause, and questions as to the provision's enforceability remain to be answered …

In the end, a decision by a patent licensor to use a "termination-for-challenge" clause in its license agreement involves a degree of uncertainty that is not likely to be lessened in the near future, but such a decision is probably justified on the basis of the available information. Unlike in the case of a typical "no-challenge" clause, which eliminates one of the protections of the *Lear* doctrine and is almost certainly unenforceable, there is credible support for the enforceability of a "termination-for-challenge" clause.

Royalty Payment Provisions

Another type of pro-licensor contract provision that is receiving increasing attention is one that links a licensee's patent validity challenge with its obligation to pay royalties under the license agreement. This type of provision can vary on the basis of the event that triggers a consequence (e.g., the patent challenge itself as opposed to the failure of the challenge) and the nature of the consequence (e.g., a continuing obligation to pay the agreed-to royalties as opposed to an increase in the royalty amount to be paid by the licensee). At least one variation of this type of provision has been ruled unenforceable in that it eliminated one of the protections of the *Lear* doctrine. Other variations, however, are likely to be enforceable, especially one that requires an increase in the royalty payment obligation of a licensee whose patent challenge fails, reflecting the added value of a patent that has been adjudicated as valid.

The relationship between a patent licensee's right to challenge the validity of the licensed patent and its obligation to pay royalties was originally explored in *Lear*. Recall that the Supreme Court in *Lear* ruled that an express contractual obligation of a licensee to pay royalties "until such time as the 'patent *** is held invalid,'" effectively requiring the licensee to pay during the pendency of any patent challenge, is unenforceable (the second prong of the *Lear* doctrine). According to the *Lear* Court, such an obligation would encourage a licensor to postpone a final determination regarding the licensed patent's validity and could deter the licensee from bringing the patent challenge in the first place, thereby frustrating the public's interest in eliminating worthless patents. Considering the holding in *Lear*, it is not surprising that a district court in *Bayer* rejected a royalty payment provision that stated that

> LICENSEE agrees to make all payments due under this License Agreement notwithstanding any challenge … by LICENSEE … to the Licensed Patent Rights, so long as the applicable patent(s) or patent application(s) remain in effect.

As was already discussed in the preceding section, the Bayer court concluded that the provision was unenforceable in that it impermissibly eliminated one of the protections of the *Lear* doctrine, but its inclusion in the license agreement was not patent misuse.

The *Bayer* court did not consider the question of whether a licensee that exercises its *Lear*-protected right to withhold agreed-to royalties during the pendency of its patent challenge and, thereby, breaches an unenforceable royalty payment provision such as the one under consideration in the case could have its license agreement terminated by the licensor on the basis of the breach. [P]ost-*Lear* district court decisions ... support the view that the nonpayment of agreed-to royalties associated with a patent challenge is an insufficient basis for the termination of a license agreement, in light of the public's interest in the early adjudication of patent invalidity. In contrast, the Federal Circuit's "challenge-but-face-the-consequence" [e.g., *Gen-Probe* – Ed.] decisions take the position that a breach by a licensee of a contractual provision in the course of bringing a patent challenge can subject the licensee to an unwanted consequence, including the loss of rights under the license agreement, despite the public policy articulated in *Lear*.

While a royalty payment provision that eliminates one of the protections of the *Lear* doctrine (such as the one rejected in *Bayer*) is almost certainly unenforceable, assessing the enforceability of other pro-licensor royalty payment provisions presents a greater challenge. For example, one of the provisions that has been suggested in response to [*MedImmune*] would require a licensee that brings a patent validity challenge to pay increased royalties. The U.S. Government, in its *MedImmune* Brief, noted that such a provision could "anticipate and ameliorate the effects of the filing of a declaratory judgment action by a licensee [challenging the validity of the licensed patent]." However, as stated in the Government's Brief, the enforceability of such a provision "is an open question in light of the strong public policy favoring patent challenges as reflected in *Pope* and *Lear*." A provision that burdens a patent licensee with an unwanted consequence for the mere act of challenging the validity of the licensed patent could be viewed as too much of a disincentive to challenge to be compatible with the "spirit of *Lear*."

One way to lessen the impact of a pro-licensor contract provision that calls for an increase in a licensee's royalty payment obligation following a patent challenge is to have the increase triggered only by an unsuccessful challenge by the licensee, i.e., one in which the challenged patent is ultimately adjudicated as valid. There is a reasonable basis for such a royalty increase that is not punitive in nature, namely, that a patent that has been adjudicated as valid is of greater value than one that is merely presumed to be valid as a result of its issuance.

A number of other royalty payment provisions have been proposed to account for the increased likelihood of a licensee patent validity challenge following [*MedImmune*], although to the authors' knowledge none has undergone judicial review where compatibility with *Lear* was at issue. Some of these provisions are intended to maximize a licensor's return on a licensed patent prior to any patent challenge by the licensee (e.g., requiring the licensee to pay a higher royalty from the outset than would otherwise have been sought in the absence of the increased threat of a challenge). Other provisions are designed to guarantee the continuation of a licensee's royalty payment despite a patent challenge (e.g., making the royalty payment obligation independent of the validity of the licensed patent). Putting aside the question of whether a licensee would agree to any of these royalty payment provisions, each such provision must be assessed for its enforceability and effect ... What can be said with respect to all of these provisions is the following: (1) the more punitive the provision, burdening a licensee for merely exercising its *Lear*-protected right to challenge the validity of the licensed patent, the greater the risk of unenforceability, and (2) the possibility that the inclusion of the provision in a patent license agreement constitutes patent misuse must be given careful consideration.

Other Pro-Licensor Contract Provisions

In the aftermath of [*MedImmune*], patent licensors have been particularly active in crafting pro-licensor contract provisions to account for an increased likelihood of a licensee patent validity challenge.

A contract provision that is increasingly popular among patent licensors requires that a licensee that intends to challenge the validity of the licensed patent provide advanced notice to the licensor and disclose the basis for the challenge. The following is an example of such a provision:

> In the event LICENSEE intends to assert in any forum that any LICENSED PATENT is invalid …, LICENSEE will, not less than ninety (90) days prior to making any such assertion, provide to LICENSOR a complete written disclosure of each and every basis then known to LICENSEE for such assertion and, with such disclosure, will provide LICENSOR with a copy of any document or publication upon which LICENSEE intends to rely in support of such assertion. LICENSEE's failure to comply with this provision will constitute a material breach of this Agreement.[12]

A provision of this type will allow for a dialogue between licensor and licensee that may avert a patent challenge and will, if necessary, aid the licensor in its preparation of a defense of its patent.

Other pro-licensor contract provisions are intended to limit the information available to a licensee in its challenge of the licensed patent. For example, a patent license agreement may contain a provision that expressly prohibits the licensee from using any confidential information of the licensor, provided to the licensee under the agreement, in challenging the licensed patent. An even more restrictive provision has been suggested that "requir[es] … that the licensee disclose the prior art it knows about before entering the license, and provid[es] … that the licensee will have the right to challenge validity in defense to an action for royalties, or as [a] declaratory judgment claim based only on other and closer prior art that the licensee learns of after entering the license."[13]

One of the more frequently encountered pro-licensor provisions obligates a licensee that challenges the validity of the licensed patent to pay the patent holder's litigation costs, including attorney's fees, that result from the challenge. Such a provision varies on the basis of whether the licensee's payment obligation attaches irrespective of the success of its challenge or only in the event that the patent challenge fails.

The list of pro-licensor contract provisions, to be used alone or in combination, will grow as creative transactional attorneys continue to grapple with the increased likelihood of a licensee patent validity challenge following *MedImmune*. In the absence of case law confirming the enforceability of such a provision, its inclusion in a patent license agreement will entail a degree of uncertainty … In the end, however, a number of pro-licensor contract provisions will fall within a gray zone where a finding of patent misuse is unlikely, but the question of enforceability will remain open until resolved by a court. The licensor

---

[12] Brian G. Brunsvold & Dennis P. O'Reilley, Drafting Patent License Agreements, 169–70 (5th ed., BNA Books, 2004).
[13] John W. Schlicher, *Patent Licensing, What to Do After* MedImmune v. Genentech, 89 J. Pat. & Trademark Off. Soc'y 364, 392 (2007).

inclined to incorporate such a provision will need to be advised as to the risk of unenforceability, which risk increases to the extent that the provision appears to penalize a licensee
for a patent validity challenge in a manner and to a degree that is likely to prevent the
challenge in the first place, thereby frustrating the important public interest, articulated in
Lear, in eliminating worthless patents.

SUMMARY: OTHER CONTRACTUAL PENALTIES FOR VALIDITY CHALLENGES

- Termination-on-challenge
- Loss of exclusivity
- Payment of royalties required during challenge
- Royalty increases upon challenge
- Royalty increases upon unsuccessful challenge
- Licensee advance notice of challenges
- No use of licensor's confidential information in making any challenge
- Licensee disclosure of known prior art and limitation of challenges to that art
- Licensee bears licensor's legal costs, win or lose
- Mandatory arbitration of validity disputes

Notes and Questions

1. *Untested clauses*. Server and Singleton describe a range of contractual provisions that have
   been used in lieu of no-challenge clauses to deter licensees from challenging the validity
   of licensed patents. None of these provisions have been tested in the courts. As such, how
   would you advise a licensor client that wished to include such clauses in a licensing agreement? How would you describe the risks and benefits of such clauses?
2. *Value of adjudicated patents*. Server and Singleton reason that "a patent that has been adjudicated as valid is of greater value than one that is merely presumed to be valid as a result of
   its issuance." Why would this be the case? What impact does such an observation have on
   the enforceability of clauses triggered by patent validity challenges?
3. *Arbitration of validity challenges*. Why might some licensors prefer that licensee challenges
   to the validity of licensed patents be resolved through binding arbitration rather than litigation? Consider the effect of arbitral decisions on other current or future licensees.

Problem 22.1

Your client, Monop O. Liszt, is a famed pianist who has developed a suite of ingenious music
synthesis software applications. He has applied for patents on these inventions and has registered the copyrights in the software source code. Liszt now wishes to license his software on a
nonexclusive basis to computer, electronic keyboard, film production and music distribution
companies around the world. Because he is an individual without a large litigation budget, however, he would like to limit the ability of his licensees to challenge his IP rights. Prepare a draft
set of provisions that you would recommend inserting into his standard form of software licensing agreement to achieve this goal, explaining the relative risks and benefits of each provision.

23

First Sale and Exhaustion

When you buy a physical book from your local bookshop or online retailer, you exchange a sum of money for legal title to the physical copy of that book (we'll cover electronic books shortly). Of course, buying a book does not give you any ownership interest in the author's copyright. Thus, by spending $30 to acquire a physical book, you do not gain the right to make additional copies of that book, to adapt it for television or to translate it into another language. You simply own the physical copy that you bought. By the same token, once you purchase the book from a retailer, neither the author nor the publisher has any further right to limit or charge you for the right to read the book, to lend it to your sister or to sell it on eBay. The publisher has authorized the retailer to sell you the book, and once they have granted that right they have no ability to further control its destiny.

This result, which should correspond with your intuitive understanding of how markets in copyrighted goods work, arises from what is known as the "first sale" doctrine. A similar doctrine known as "exhaustion" applies with respect to goods marked with trademarks and to patented articles. Despite their intuitive and straightforward origins, the modern application of the first sale and exhaustion doctrines to multi-component technologies distributed through multi-tier, international supply chains is fraught with complications that have made these doctrines among the most complex in the intellectual property (IP) transactional landscape. In this chapter we will review the basic doctrines of first sale and exhaustion, and then explore how they have evolved in the modern marketplace.

23.1 COPYRIGHT FIRST SALE

Today, the copyright first sale doctrine is embodied in Section 109(a) of the Copyright Act. It provides that "the owner of a particular copy … lawfully made under this title, or any person authorized by such owner, is entitled, without the authority of the copyright owner, to sell or otherwise dispose of the possession of that copy." That is, someone who owns a valid copy of a copyrighted work may further sell, transfer, donate or otherwise dispose of that copy without permission of the copyright owner, notwithstanding the copyright owner's exclusive right to distribute copies of the work under Section 106(3) of the Act.

Prior to the enactment of the 1976 version of the Act, the extent of the first sale doctrine was not so clear. The following case is one of the first to wrestle with the extent and scope of the first sale doctrine.

Bobbs-Merrill Co. v. Straus

210 U.S. 339 (1908)

DAY, JUSTICE

The complainant in the circuit court, appellant here, the Bobbs-Merrill Company, brought suit against the respondents, appellees here, Isidor Straus and Nathan Straus, partners as R. H. Macy & Company, in the Circuit Court of the United States for the Southern District of New York to restrain the sale of a copyrighted novel, entitled "The Castaway," at retail at less than $1 for each copy. The circuit court dismissed the bill on final hearing. The decree of the circuit court was affirmed on appeal by the circuit court of appeals.

The appellant is the owner of the copyright upon "The Castaway," obtained on the eighteenth day of May, 1904, in conformity to the copyright statutes of the United States. Printed immediately below the copyright notice, on the page in the book following the title page, is inserted the following notice:

> The price of this book at retail is one dollar net. No dealer is licensed to sell it at a less price, and a sale at a less price will be treated as an infringement of the copyright.

Macy & Company, before the commencement of the action, purchased copies of the book for the purpose of selling the same at retail. Ninety percent of such copies were purchased by them at wholesale at a price below the retail price by about forty percent, and

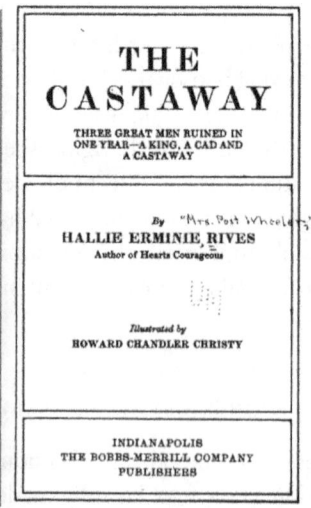
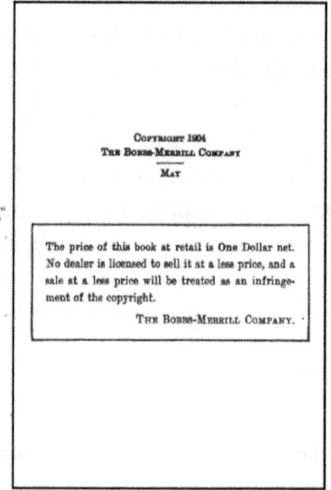

FIGURE 23.1 *The Castaway: Three Great Men Ruined in One Year – A King, A Cad and a Castaway,* by Hallie Ermine Rives (1904).

ten percent of the books purchased by them were purchased at retail, and the full price paid therefor.

It is stipulated in the record:

Defendants at the time of their purchase of copies of the book, knew that it was a copyrighted book, and were familiar with the terms of the notice printed in each copy thereof, as above set forth, and knew that this notice was printed in every copy of the book purchased by them.

The wholesale dealers from whom defendants purchased copies of the book obtained the same either directly from the complainant or from other wholesale dealers at a discount from the net retail price, and at the time of their purchase knew that the book was a copyrighted book, and were familiar with the terms of the notice printed in each copy thereof, as described above, and such knowledge was in all wholesale dealers through whom the books passed from the complainants to defendants. But the wholesale dealers were under no agreement or obligation to enforce the observance of the terms of the notice by retail dealers, or to restrict their sales to retail dealers who would agree to observe the terms stated in the notice.

The defendants have sold copies of the book at retail at the uniform price of eighty-nine cents a copy, and are still selling, exposing for sale, and offering copies of the book at retail at the price of eighty-nine cents per copy, without the consent of the complainant.

The present case involves rights under the copyright act. The facts disclose a sale of a book at wholesale by the owners of the copyright at a satisfactory price, and this without agreement between the parties to such sale obligating the purchaser to control future sales, and where the alleged right springs from the protection of the copyright law alone. It is contended that this power to control further sales is given by statute to the owner of such a copyright in conferring the sole right to "vend" a copyrighted book.

Recent cases in this Court have affirmed the proposition that copyright property under the federal law is wholly statutory, and depends upon the right created under the acts of Congress passed in pursuance of the authority conferred under Article I, § 8, of the federal Constitution:

To promote the progress of science and useful arts, by securing, for limited times, to authors and inventors, the exclusive right to their respective writings and discoveries.

The learned counsel for the appellant in this case, in the argument at bar, disclaims relief because of any contract, and relies solely upon the copyright statutes, and rights therein conferred. The copyright statutes ought to be reasonably construed with a view to effecting the purposes intended by Congress. They ought not to be unduly extended by judicial construction to include privileges not intended to be conferred, nor so narrowly construed as to deprive those entitled to their benefit of the rights Congress intended to grant.

At common law, an author had a property in his manuscript, and might have redress against anyone who undertook to realize a profit from its publication without authority of the author.

While the nature of the property and the protection intended to be given the inventor or author as the reward of genius or intellect in the production of his book or work of art is to be considered in construing the act of Congress, it is evident that to secure the author the right to multiply copies of his work may be said to have been the main purpose of the copyright statutes.

This fact is emphasized when we note the title to the act of Congress, passed at its first session: "An Act for the Encouragement of Learning, by Securing the Copies of Maps, Charts, and Books, to the Authors and Proprietors of Such Copies, during the Times Therein Mentioned." 1 Stat. at Large, by Peters, c. 15, p. 124.

In order to secure this right, it was provided in that statute, as it has been in subsequent ones, that the authors of books, their executors, administrators, or assigns, shall have the "sole right and liberty of printing, reprinting, publishing, and vending" such book for a term of years, upon complying with the statutory conditions set forth in the act as essential to the acquiring of a valid copyright. Each and all of these statutory rights should be given such protection as the act of Congress requires, in order to secure the rights conferred upon authors and others entitled to the benefit of the act. Let us see more specifically what are the statutory rights, in this behalf, secured to one who has complied with the provisions of the law and become the owner of a copyright. They may be found in §§ 4952 ... of the Revised Statutes of the United States, and are as follows:

> Any citizen of the United States or resident therein, who shall be the author, inventor, designer, or proprietor of any book, map, chart, dramatic or musical composition, engraving, cut, print, or photograph or negative thereof, or of a painting, drawing, chromo, statute, statuary, and of models or designs intended to be perfected as works of the fine arts, and the executors, administrators, or assigns of any such person, shall, upon complying with the provisions of this chapter, have the sole liberty of printing, reprinting, publishing, completing, copying, executing, finishing, and vending the same.

It is the contention of the appellant that the circuit court erred in failing to give effect to the provision of § 4952, protecting the owners of the copyright in the sole right of vending the copyrighted book or other article, and the argument is that the statute vested the whole field of the right of exclusive sale in the copyright owner; that he can part with it to another to the extent that he sees fit, and may withhold to himself, by proper reservations, so much of the right as he pleases.

What does the statute mean in granting "the sole right of vending the same?" Was it intended to create a right which would permit the holder of the copyright to fasten, by notice in a book or upon one of the articles mentioned within the statute, a restriction upon the subsequent alienation of the subject matter of copyright after the owner had parted with the title to one who had acquired full dominion over it and had given a satisfactory price for it? It is not denied that one who has sold a copyrighted article, without restriction, has parted with all right to control the sale of it. The purchaser of a book, once sold by authority of the owner of the copyright, may sell it again, although he could not publish a new edition of it.

In this case, the stipulated facts show that the books sold by the appellant were sold at wholesale, and purchased by those who made no agreement as to the control of future sales of the book, and took upon themselves no obligation to enforce the notice printed in the book, undertaking to restrict retail sales to a price of one dollar per copy.

The precise question therefore in this case is, does the sole right to vend (named in § 4952) secure to the owner of the copyright the right, after a sale of the book to a purchaser, to restrict future sales of the book at retail, to the right to sell it at a certain price per copy, because of a notice in the book that a sale at a different price will be treated as an infringement, which notice has been brought home to one undertaking to sell for less than the named sum? We do not think the statute can be given such a construction, and it is to be remembered that this is purely a question of statutory construction. There is no claim in this case of contract limitation, nor license agreement controlling the subsequent sales of the book.

In our view, the copyright statutes, while protecting the owner of the copyright in his right to multiply and sell his production, do not create the right to impose, by notice, such as is disclosed in this case, a limitation at which the book shall be sold at retail by future purchasers, with whom there is no privity of contract. This conclusion is reached in view of the language of the statute, read in the light of its main purpose to secure the right of multiplying copies of the work – a right which is the special creation of the statute. True, the statute also secures, to make this right of multiplication effectual, the sole right to vend copies of the book, the production of the author's thought and conception. The owner of the copyright in this case did sell copies of the book in quantities and at a price satisfactory to it. It has exercised the right to vend. What the complainant contends for embraces not only the right to sell the copies, but to qualify the title of a future purchaser by the reservation of the right to have the remedies of the statute against an infringer because of the printed notice of its purpose so to do unless the purchaser sells at a price fixed in the notice. To add to the right of exclusive sale the authority to control all future retail sales by a notice that such sales must be made at a fixed sum would give a right not included in the terms of the statute, and, in our view, extend its operation, by construction, beyond its meaning, when interpreted with a view to ascertaining the legislative intent in its enactment.

The decree of the circuit court of appeals is Affirmed.

Notes and Questions

1. *Resale price maintenance.* In *Bobbs-Merrill*, the court analyzes, as a matter of statutory interpretation, whether the copyright owner's exclusive right to "vend" includes a right to dictate the prices at which future owners may resell a book. The practice of setting minimum resale prices is referred to as "resale price maintenance," and it warrants special scrutiny under the antitrust laws (see Section 25.4). Antitrust issues aside, why do you think that Bobbs-Merrill wished to set a minimum resale price for books that it had already sold to retailers? How would Bobbs-Merrill profit from Macy's sale of the book at $1.00 rather than $0.89?

2. *Contract.* Bobbs-Merrill incorporated its price maintenance clause in the book itself. From a contract law standpoint, how binding to you think this restriction was on retailers like Macy's?

3. *The right to vend.* The Court in *Bobbs-Merrill* held that a copyright owner's statutory exclusive right to vend a book did not extend to the control of the terms of downstream sales of the book. Why not? What language in the Copyright Act persuaded the Court that this was the correct outcome?

4. *Limits of first sale.* As set forth in Section 109(a) of the Copyright Act today, the owner of a particular copy of a work has the right to "sell or otherwise dispose of the possession of that copy." In other words, the first sale exhausts the copyright owner's exclusive right to transfer a copy of a work, which was granted under Section 106(3) of the Copyright Act. But the first sale doctrine does not exhaust the other exclusive rights granted to a copyright holder under Section 106, namely, the right to reproduce the work (§ 106(1)), the right to make derivative works (§ 106(2)) and the right to publicly perform the work (§§ 106(4)–(6)). Why is the first sale doctrine limited to transfers of copies of copyrighted works?

23.2 SOFTWARE SALE VERSUS LICENSE

The *Bobbs-Merrill* case established the first sale principle in copyright law, a principle that was later codified in Section 109(a) of the Copyright Act. But the first sale doctrine depends on there being an authorized *sale* of a copyrighted work. What if a work is licensed rather than sold? Does the first sale doctrine apply?

These questions are extremely important in the case of computer software. Even though software vendors convey copies of their software to users, either on tangible media (discs or memory devices) or electronically, the common practice in the software industry is to refer to software as licensed rather than sold. So, what rights does a consumer obtain when she downloads an app to her smartphone? Does she "own" a copy of the software, which she can then resell or exploit as she would a book, or is she merely a licensee who does not own the copy in her possession? Numerous cases considered this issue from the 1990s through the 2000s, most questioning the software vendor's ability to impose restrictions on further transfer of the software on the user. The following case, decided in the circuit that is home to the majority of the US software industry, effectively put the issue to rest.

Vernor v. Autodesk, Inc.

621 F.3d 1102 (9th Cir. 2010)

CALLAHAN, CIRCUIT JUDGE

Timothy Vernor purchased several used copies of Autodesk, Inc.'s AutoCAD Release 14 software ("Release 14") from one of Autodesk's direct customers, and he resold the Release 14 copies on eBay. Vernor brought this declaratory judgment action against Autodesk to establish that these resales did not infringe Autodesk's copyright. The district court issued the requested declaratory judgment, holding that Vernor's sales were lawful because of two of the Copyright Act's affirmative defenses that apply to owners of copies of copyrighted works, the first sale doctrine and the essential step defense.

Autodesk distributes Release 14 pursuant to a limited license agreement in which it reserves title to the software copies and imposes significant use and transfer restrictions on its customers. We determine that Autodesk's direct customers are licensees of their copies of the software rather than owners, which has two ramifications. Because Vernor did not purchase the Release 14 copies from an owner, he may not invoke the first sale doctrine, and he also may not assert an essential step defense on behalf of his customers. For these reasons, we vacate the district court's grant of summary judgment to Vernor and remand for further proceedings.

I.

A. Autodesk's Release 14 Software and Licensing Practices

The material facts are not in dispute. Autodesk makes computer-aided design software used by architects, engineers, and manufacturers. It has more than nine million customers. It first released its AutoCAD software in 1982. It holds registered copyrights in all versions of the software including the discontinued Release 14 version, which is at issue in this case. It provided Release 14 to customers on CD-ROMs.

Since at least 1986, Autodesk has offered AutoCAD to customers pursuant to an accompanying software license agreement ("SLA"), which customers must accept before installing the software. A customer who does not accept the SLA can return the software for a full refund. Autodesk offers SLAs with different terms for commercial, educational institution, and student users. The commercial license, which is the most expensive, imposes the fewest restrictions on users and allows them software upgrades at discounted prices.

The SLA for Release 14 first recites that Autodesk retains title to all copies. Second, it states that the customer has a nonexclusive and nontransferable license to use Release 14. Third, it imposes transfer restrictions, prohibiting customers from renting, leasing, or transferring the software without Autodesk's prior consent and from electronically or physically transferring the software out of the Western Hemisphere. Fourth, it imposes significant use restrictions:

YOU MAY NOT: (1) modify, translate, reverse engineer, decompile, or disassemble the Software ... (3) remove any proprietary notices, labels, or marks from the Software or Documentation; (4) use ... the Software outside of the Western Hemisphere; (5) utilize any computer software or hardware designed to defeat any hardware copy-protection device, should the software you have licensed be equipped with such protection; or (6) use the Software for commercial or other revenue-generating purposes if the Software has been licensed or labeled for educational use only.

Fifth, the SLA provides for license termination if the user copies the software without authorization or does not comply with the SLA's restrictions. Finally, the SLA provides that if the software is an upgrade of a previous version:

[Y]ou must destroy the software previously licensed to you, including any copies resident on your hard disk drive ... within sixty (60) days of the purchase of the license to use the upgrade or update .... Autodesk reserves the right to require you to show satisfactory proof that previous copies of the software have been destroyed.

Autodesk takes measures to enforce these license requirements. It assigns a serial number to each copy of AutoCAD and tracks registered licensees. It requires customers to input "activation codes" within one month after installation to continue using the software. The customer obtains the code by providing the product's serial number to Autodesk. Autodesk issues the activation code after confirming that the serial number is authentic, the copy is not registered to a different customer, and the product has not been upgraded. Once a customer has an activation code, he or she may use it to activate the software on additional computers without notifying Autodesk.

B. Autodesk's Provision of Release 14 Software to CTA

In March 1999, Autodesk reached a settlement agreement with its customer Cardwell/Thomas & Associates, Inc. ("CTA"), which Autodesk had accused of unauthorized use of its software. As part of the settlement, Autodesk licensed ten copies of Release 14 to CTA. CTA agreed to the SLA, which appeared (1) on each Release 14 package that Autodesk provided to CTA; (2) in the settlement agreement; and (3) on- screen, while the software is being installed.

CTA later upgraded to the newer, fifteenth version of the AutoCAD program, AutoCAD 2000. It paid $495 per upgrade license, compared to $3,750 for each new license. The SLA for AutoCAD 2000, like the SLA for Release 14, required destruction of copies of previous versions of the software, with proof to be furnished to Autodesk on request. However, rather than destroying its Release 14 copies, CTA sold them to Vernor at an office sale with the handwritten activation codes necessary to use the software.

C. Vernor's eBay Business and Sales of Release 14

Vernor has sold more than 10,000 items on eBay. In May 2005, he purchased an authentic used copy of Release 14 at a garage sale from an unspecified seller. He never agreed to the SLA's terms, opened a sealed software packet, or installed the Release 14 software. Though he was aware of the SLA's existence, he believed that he was not bound by its terms. He posted the software copy for sale on eBay.

Autodesk filed a Digital Millennium Copyright Act ("DMCA") take-down notice with eBay claiming that Vernor's sale infringed its copyright, and eBay terminated Vernor's auction.[1] Autodesk advised Vernor that it conveyed its software copies pursuant to non-transferable licenses, and resale of its software was copyright infringement. Vernor filed a DMCA counter-notice with eBay contesting the validity of Autodesk's copyright claim. Autodesk did not respond to the counter-notice. eBay reinstated the auction, and Vernor sold the software to another eBay user.

In April 2007, Vernor purchased four authentic used copies of Release 14 at CTA's office sale. The authorization codes were handwritten on the outside of the box. He listed the four copies on eBay sequentially, representing, "This software is not currently installed on any computer." On each of the first three occasions, the same DMCA process ensued. Autodesk filed a DMCA take-down notice with eBay, and eBay removed Vernor's auction. Vernor submitted a counter-notice to which Autodesk did not respond, and eBay reinstated the auction.

When Vernor listed his fourth, final copy of Release 14, Autodesk again filed a DMCA take-down notice with eBay. This time, eBay suspended Vernor's account because of Autodesk's repeated charges of infringement. Vernor also wrote to Autodesk, claiming that he was entitled to sell his Release 14 copies pursuant to the first sale doctrine, because he never installed the software or agreed to the SLA. In response, Autodesk's counsel directed Vernor to stop selling the software. Vernor filed a final counter-notice with eBay. When Autodesk again did not respond to Vernor's counter-notice, eBay reinstated Vernor's account. At that point, Vernor's eBay account had been suspended for one month, during which he was unable to earn income on eBay.

Vernor currently has two additional copies of Release 14 that he wishes to sell on eBay. Although the record is not clear, it appears that Vernor sold two of the software packages that he purchased from CTA, for roughly $600 each, but did not sell the final two to avoid risking further suspension of his eBay account.

III.

The Copyright Act confers several exclusive rights on copyright owners, including the exclusive rights to reproduce their works and to distribute their works by sale or rental. Id. § 106(1), (3). The exclusive distribution right is limited by the first sale doctrine, an

---

[1] Under the Digital Millennium Copyright Act, 17 U.S.C. § 512(c)(3), a copyright holder may notify an online service provider such as eBay that a user of the service has posted infringing material on the service. In order to benefit from the liability exclusions under the Act, the service provider must act promptly to take down the infringing content – Ed.

FIGURE 23.2　Autodesk's AutoCAD 14 software.

affirmative defense to copyright infringement that allows owners of copies of copyrighted works to resell those copies. The exclusive reproduction right is limited within the software context by the essential step defense, another affirmative defense to copyright infringement that is discussed further infra. Both of these affirmative defenses are unavailable to those who are only licensed to use their copies of copyrighted works.

This case requires us to decide whether Autodesk sold Release 14 copies to its customers or licensed the copies to its customers. If CTA owned its copies of Release 14, then both its sales to Vernor and Vernor's subsequent sales were non-infringing under the first sale doctrine. However, if Autodesk only licensed CTA to use copies of Release 14, then CTA's and Vernor's sales of those copies are not protected by the first sale doctrine and would therefore infringe Autodesk's exclusive distribution right.

We turn to our precedents governing whether a transferee of a copy of a copyrighted work is an owner or licensee of that copy. We then apply those precedents to CTA's and Vernor's possession of Release 14 copies.

1. *United States v. Wise,* 550 F.2d 1180 (9th Cir. 1977)

In *Wise,* a criminal copyright infringement case, we considered whether copyright owners who transferred copies of their motion pictures pursuant to written distribution agreements had executed first sales. The defendant was found guilty of copyright infringement based on his for-profit sales of motion picture prints. The copyright owners distributed their films to third parties pursuant to written agreements that restricted their use and transfer. On appeal, the defendant argued that the government failed to prove the absence of a first sale for each film. If the copyright owners' initial transfers of the films were first sales, then the defendant's resales were protected by the first sale doctrine and thus were not copyright infringement.

To determine whether a first sale occurred, we considered multiple factors pertaining to each film distribution agreement. Specifically, we considered whether the agreement

(a) was labeled a license, (b) provided that the copyright owner retained title to the prints, (c) required the return or destruction of the prints, (d) forbade duplication of prints, or (e) required the transferee to maintain possession of the prints for the agreement's duration. Our use of these several considerations, none dispositive, may be seen in our treatment of each film print.

For example, we reversed the defendant's conviction with respect to *Camelot*. It was unclear whether the *Camelot* print sold by the defendant had been subject to a first sale. Copyright owner Warner Brothers distributed *Camelot* prints pursuant to multiple agreements, and the government did not prove the absence of a first sale with respect to each agreement. We noted that, in one agreement, Warner Brothers had retained title to the prints, required possessor National Broadcasting Company ("NBC") to return the prints if the parties could select a mutual agreeable price, and if not, required NBC's certification that the prints were destroyed. We held that these factors created a license rather than a first sale.

We further noted, however, that Warner Brothers had also furnished another *Camelot* print to actress Vanessa Redgrave. The print was provided to Redgrave at cost, and her use of the print was subject to several restrictions. She had to retain possession of the print and was not allowed to sell, license, reproduce, or publicly exhibit the print. She had no obligation to return the print to Warner Brothers. We concluded, "While the provision for payment for the cost of the film, standing alone, does not establish a sale, when taken with the rest of the language of the agreement, it reveals a transaction strongly resembling a sale with restrictions on the use of the print." There was no evidence of the print's whereabouts, and we held that "[i]n the absence of such proof," the government failed to prove the absence of a first sale with respect to this Redgrave print. Since it was unclear which copy the defendant had obtained and resold, his conviction for sale of *Camelot* had to be reversed.

Thus, under *Wise*, where a transferee receives a particular copy of a copyrighted work pursuant to a written agreement, we consider all of the provisions of the agreement to determine whether the transferee became an owner of the copy or received a license. We may consider (1) whether the agreement was labeled a license and (2) whether the copyright owner retained title to the copy, required its return or destruction, forbade its duplication, or required the transferee to maintain possession of the copy for the agreement's duration. We did not find any one factor dispositive in *Wise*: we did not hold that the copyright owner's retention of title itself established the absence of a first sale or that a transferee's right to indefinite possession itself established a first sale.

2. The "MAI Trio" of Cases

Over fifteen years after *Wise*, we again considered the distinction between owners and licensees of copies of copyrighted works in three software copyright cases, the "*MAI* trio". See *MAI Sys. Corp. v. Peak Computer, Inc.*, 991 F.2d 511 (9th Cir. 1993); *Triad Sys. Corp. v. Se. Express Co.*, 64 F.3d 1330 (9th Cir. 1995); *Wall Data, Inc. v. Los Angeles County Sheriff's Dep't*, 447 F.3d 769 (9th Cir. 2006). In the *MAI* trio, we considered which software purchasers were owners of copies of copyrighted works for purposes of a second affirmative defense to infringement, the essential step defense.

The enforcement of copyright owners' exclusive right to reproduce their work under the Copyright Act, 17 U.S.C. § 106(1), has posed special challenges in the software context. In order to use a software program, a user's computer will automatically copy the software into the computer's random access memory ("RAM"), which is a form of computer data storage. Congress enacted the essential step defense to codify that a software user who is the "owner of a copy" of a copyrighted software program does not infringe by making a copy of the computer program, if the new copy is "created as an essential step in the utilization of the computer program in conjunction with a machine and … is used in no other manner." 17 U.S.C. § 117(a)(1).

The Copyright Act provides that an "owner of a copy" of copyrighted software may claim the essential step defense, and the "owner of a particular copy" of copyrighted software may claim the first sale doctrine. 17 U.S.C. §§ 109(a), 117(a)(1). The *MAI* trio construed the phrase "owner of a copy" for essential step defense purposes. Neither Vernor nor Autodesk contends that the first sale doctrine's inclusion of the word "particular" alters the phrase's meaning, and we "presume that words used more than once in the same statute have the same meaning throughout." Accordingly, we consider the *MAI* trio's construction of "owner of a copy" controlling in our analysis of whether CTA and Vernor became "owner[s] of a particular copy" of Release 14 software.

In *MAI* and *Triad*, the defendants maintained computers that ran the plaintiffs' operating system software. When the defendants ran the computers, the computers automatically loaded plaintiffs' software into RAM. The plaintiffs in both cases sold their software pursuant to restrictive license agreements, and we held that their customers were licensees who were therefore not entitled to claim the essential step defense. We found that the defendants infringed plaintiffs' software copyrights by their unauthorized loading of copyrighted software into RAM. In *Triad*, the plaintiff had earlier sold software outright to some customers. We noted that these customers were owners who were entitled to the essential step defense, and the defendant did not infringe by making RAM copies in servicing their computers.

In *Wall Data*, plaintiff sold 3,663 software licenses to the defendant. The licenses (1) were non-exclusive; (2) permitted use of the software on a single computer; and (3) permitted transfer of the software once per month, if the software was removed from the original computer. The defendant installed the software onto 6,007 computers via hard drive imaging, which saved it from installing the software manually on each computer. It made an unverified claim that only 3,663 users could simultaneously access the software.

The plaintiff sued for copyright infringement, contending that the defendant violated the license by "over-installing" the software. The defendant raised an essential step defense, contending that its hard drive imaging was a necessary step of installation. On appeal, we held that the district court did not abuse its discretion in denying the defendant's request for a jury instruction on the essential step defense. Citing *MAI*, we held that the essential step defense does not apply where the copyright owner grants the user a license and significantly restricts the user's ability to transfer the software. Since the plaintiff's license imposed "significant restrictions" on the defendant's software rights, the defendant was a licensee and was not entitled to the essential step defense.

In *Wall Data*, we acknowledged that *MAI* had been criticized in a Federal Circuit decision, but declined to revisit its holding, noting that the facts of *Wall Data* led to the conclusion that any error in the district court's failure to instruct was harmless. Even if the defendant owned its copies of the software, its installation of the software on a number of computers in excess of its license was not an essential step in the software's use.

We read *Wise* and the *MAI* trio to prescribe three considerations that we may use to determine whether a software user is a licensee, rather than an owner of a copy. First, we consider whether the copyright owner specifies that a user is granted a license. Second, we consider whether the copyright owner significantly restricts the user's ability to transfer the software. Finally, we consider whether the copyright owner imposes notable use restrictions. Our holding reconciles the *MAI* trio and *Wise*, even though the *MAI* trio did not cite *Wise*.

In response to *MAI*, Congress amended § 117 to permit a computer owner to copy software for maintenance or repair purposes. See 17 U.S.C. § 117(c). However, Congress did not disturb *MAI's* holding that licensees are not entitled to the essential step defense.

IV.

We hold today that a software user is a licensee rather than an owner of a copy where the copyright owner (1) specifies that the user is granted a license; (2) significantly restricts the user's ability to transfer the software; and (3) imposes notable use restrictions. Applying our holding to Autodesk's SLA, we conclude that CTA was a licensee rather than an owner of copies of Release 14 and thus was not entitled to invoke the first sale doctrine or the essential step defense.

> *"a software user is a licensee rather than an owner of a copy [of a software program] where the copyright owner (1) specifies that the user is granted a license; (2) significantly restricts the user's ability to transfer the software; and (3) imposes notable use restrictions."*

Autodesk retained title to the software and imposed significant transfer restrictions: it stated that the license is nontransferable, the software could not be transferred or leased without Autodesk's written consent, and the software could not be transferred outside the Western Hemisphere. The SLA also imposed use restrictions against the use of the software outside the Western Hemisphere and against modifying, translating, or reverse-engineering the software, removing any proprietary marks from the software or documentation, or defeating any copy protection device. Furthermore, the SLA provided for termination of the license upon the licensee's unauthorized copying or failure to comply with other license restrictions. Thus, because Autodesk reserved title to Release 14 copies and imposed significant transfer and use restrictions, we conclude that its customers are licensees of their copies of Release 14 rather than owners.

CTA was a licensee rather than an "owner of a particular copy" of Release 14, and it was not entitled to resell its Release 14 copies to Vernor under the first sale doctrine. 17 U.S.C. § 109(a). Therefore, Vernor did not receive title to the copies from CTA and accordingly could not pass ownership on to others. Both CTA's and Vernor's sales infringed Autodesk's exclusive right to distribute copies of its work.

Because Vernor was not an owner, his customers are also not owners of Release 14 copies. Therefore, when they install Release 14 on their computers, the copies of the software that they make during installation infringe Autodesk's exclusive reproduction right because they too are not entitled to the benefit of the essential step defense.

V.

Although our holding today is controlled by our precedent, we recognize the significant policy considerations raised by the parties and amici on both sides of this appeal.

Autodesk, the Software & Information Industry Association ("SIIA"), and the Motion Picture Association of America ("MPAA") have presented policy arguments that favor our result. For instance, Autodesk argues in favor of judicial enforcement of software license agreements that restrict transfers of copies of the work. Autodesk contends that this (1) allows for tiered pricing for different software markets, such as reduced pricing for students or educational institutions; (2) increases software companies' sales; (3) lowers prices for all consumers by spreading costs among a large number of purchasers; and (4) reduces the incidence of piracy by allowing copyright owners to bring infringement actions against unauthorized resellers. SIIA argues that a license can exist even where a customer (1) receives his copy of the work after making a single payment and (2) can indefinitely possess a software copy, because it is the software code and associated rights that are valuable rather than the inexpensive discs on which the code may be stored. Also, the MPAA argues that a customer's ability to possess a copyrighted work indefinitely should not compel a finding of a first sale, because there is often no practically feasible way for a consumer to return a copy to the copyright owner.

Vernor, eBay, and the American Library Association ("ALA") have presented policy arguments against our decision. Vernor contends that our decision (1) does not vindicate the law's aversion to restraints on alienation of personal property; (2) may force everyone purchasing copyrighted property to trace the chain of title to ensure that a first sale occurred; and (3) ignores the economic realities of the relevant transactions, in which the copyright owner permanently released software copies into the stream of commerce without expectation of return in exchange for upfront payment of the full software price. eBay contends that a broad view of the first sale doctrine is necessary to facilitate the creation of secondary markets for copyrighted works, which contributes to the public good by (1) giving consumers additional opportunities to purchase and sell copyrighted works, often at below-retail prices; (2) allowing consumers to obtain copies of works after a copyright owner has ceased distribution; and (3) allowing the proliferation of businesses.

The ALA contends that the first sale doctrine facilitates the availability of copyrighted works after their commercial lifespan, by inter alia enabling the existence of libraries, used bookstores, and hand-to-hand exchanges of copyrighted materials. The ALA further contends that judicial enforcement of software license agreements, which are often contracts of adhesion, could eliminate the software resale market, require used computer sellers to delete legitimate software prior to sale, and increase prices for consumers by reducing price competition for software vendors. It contends that Autodesk's position (1) undermines 17 U.S.C. § 109(b)(2), which permits non-profit libraries to lend software for non-commercial purposes, and (2) would hamper efforts by non-profits to collect and preserve out-of-print software. The ALA fears that the software industry's licensing practices could be adopted by other copyright owners, including book publishers, record labels, and movie studios.

These are serious contentions on both sides, but they do not alter our conclusion that our precedent from *Wise* through the *MAI* trio requires the result we reach. Congress is free, of course, to modify the first sale doctrine and the essential step defense if it deems these or other policy considerations to require a different approach.

Notes and Questions

1. *Policy factors.* In Part V of its opinion, the court in *Vernor* discusses a number of public policy rationales both supporting and refuting the treatment of software as licensed rather than sold. It acknowledges that while there are "serious contentions on both sides," these do not alter the court's conclusion, which it purports to base on its own binding precedent. Which side of the debate do you feel has the stronger policy arguments in its favor?

2. *The essential step defense.* As noted by the court in *Vernor*, § 117(a)(1) of the Copyright Act provides that the "owner of a copy" of a copyrighted software program does not infringe by making a copy of the computer program if the new copy is "created as an essential step in the utilization of the computer program in conjunction with a machine and … is used in no other manner." In effect, this provision was intended to insulate the vast majority of software users whose computers "copy" every software program into their memory as part of the execution of that program. But what happens to this essential step defense if software users do not "own" copies of the software programs? Is anything still covered by the essential step defense? How does the court deal with this issue? Should Congress step in to amend § 117(a)(1) further? If so, what amendment would you propose?

3. *Doubling down on MAI.* In *Vernor*, the Ninth Circuit acknowledges that its 1993 decision in *MAI* was criticized by the Federal Circuit. In *DSC Commc'ns Corp. v. Pulse Commc'ns, Inc.*, 170 F.3d 1354, 1360 (Fed. Cir. 1999), the Federal Circuit states:

   In the leading case on section 117 ownership, the Ninth Circuit considered an agreement in which MAI, the owner of a software copyright, transferred copies of the copyrighted software to Peak under an agreement that imposed severe restrictions on Peak's rights with respect to those copies. The court held that Peak was not an "owner" of the copies of the software for purposes of section 117 and thus did not enjoy the right to copy conferred on owners by that statute. The Ninth Circuit stated that it reached the conclusion that Peak was not an owner because Peak had licensed the software from MAI. That explanation of the court's decision has been criticized for failing to recognize the distinction between ownership of a copyright, which can be licensed, and ownership of copies of the copyrighted software. Plainly, a party who purchases copies of software from the copyright owner can hold a license under a copyright while still being an "owner" of a copy of the copyrighted software for purposes of section 117. We therefore do not adopt the Ninth Circuit's characterization of all licensees as non-owners.

   Despite this criticism, the Federal Circuit later concedes that the Ninth Circuit was correct to consider Peak to be a licensee, and not an owner, of the software in question. What's more, the Federal Circuit found that the software user in its own case should be treated as a licensee and not an owner. Given these results, is it surprising that the Ninth Circuit effectively doubled-down on *MAI* in *Vernor*?

4. *MAI and software maintenance.* The Ninth Circuit's *MAI* case is perhaps most infamous for its holding that a computer maintenance provider was liable for infringement when it ran a client's software for maintenance purposes. As noted by the Ninth Circuit in *Vernor*, "In response to *MAI*, Congress amended § 117 to permit a computer owner to copy software for maintenance or repair purposes." Section 117(c) of the Copyright Act reads as follows:

   (c) Machine Maintenance or Repair.—Notwithstanding the provisions of section 106, it is not an infringement for the owner or lessee of a machine to make or authorize the making of a copy of a computer program if such copy is made solely by virtue of the activation of a machine that lawfully contains an authorized copy of the computer program, for purposes only of maintenance or repair of that machine, if—

(1) such new copy is used in no other manner and is destroyed immediately after the maintenance or repair is completed; and

(2) with respect to any computer program or part thereof that is not necessary for that machine to be activated, such program or part thereof is not accessed or used other than to make such new copy by virtue of the activation of the machine.

Thus, the exception to infringement under Section 117(c) is based on a user's ownership of a "machine," rather than its ownership of a copy of a software program, as is the exclusion under § 117(a)(1). Did Congress get it right in § 117(c) but not § 117(a)(1)? Should Congress seek to reconcile these statutory provisions?

5. *Back to books.* Suppose that the *Bobbs-Merrill* case had been heard the year after *Vernor* was decided. Do you think that the court would have reached a different conclusion? What if Bobbs-Merrill, instead of printing its $1.00 resale price limitation on the copyright page of each book, packaged the book in a cellophane wrapper through which the resale limitation was clearly visible. Would this change the outcome? What if Bobbs-Merrill distributed books under a "shrinkwrap" license agreement (see Section 17.1) that included the resale price limitation? Finally, what if Bobbs-Merrill had entered into a "Book Supply and Resale Agreement" with Macy's which contained a contractual clause imposing the resale price limitation? At what point would the first sale doctrine yield to a contractual arrangement between the parties?

6. *Software and things.* Even if software programs themselves are licensed to consumers, software increasingly inhabits tangible products from kitchen appliances to automobiles. These products are still bought and sold. What does it mean, then, to purchase a programmable toaster? Does the consumer own the aluminum body and circuitry, but not the software inside the device? What does that mean when the consumer wishes to sell the toaster, or donate it to charity, or throw it away? Licensees are not usually permitted to exercise these rights with respect to licensed software. Does the software producer thus begin to exert control over the consumer's right to dispose of his or her tangible property? If not, do we need to rethink the answer to the sale versus license question?

7. *A step back?* A year after *Vernor*, the Ninth Circuit decided *UMG Recordings v. Augusto*, 628 F.3d 1175 (9th Cir. 2011). The case related to promotional music CDs that UMG distributed to music critics and radio disc jockeys. The CDs were labeled with printed notices such as:

This CD is the property of the record company and is licensed to the intended recipient for personal use only. Acceptance of this CD shall constitute an agreement to comply with the terms of the license. Resale or transfer of possession is not allowed and may be punishable under federal and state laws.

Augusto acquired some of these CDs through unknown channels and sold them on eBay. UMG sued Augusto for copyright infringement, alleging that he violated UMG's exclusive right to distribute the CDs. The Ninth Circuit ruled in favor of Augusto, holding that, unlike copies of computer software,

under all the circumstances of the CDs' distribution, the recipients were entitled to use or dispose of them in any manner they saw fit, and UMG did not enter a license agreement for the CDs with the recipients. Accordingly, UMG transferred title to the particular copies of its promotional CDs and cannot maintain an infringement action against Augusto for his subsequent sale of those copies.

What do you make of this holding, especially in view of the express language on the CD labels that "This CD is the property of the record company and is licensed to the intended recipient"? Is this case consistent with *Vernor*? How does the holding of *UMG* gibe with shrinkwrap license cases such as *ProCD v. Zeidenberg* (see Chapter 17)?

8. *First sale in the digital world?* Some argue that the debate over whether the "purchase" of software on physical media is moot today, as almost all consumer software is distributed via online download, either to a computer or a phone. In addition to software, most music and a growing percentage of books are also delivered electronically, with no physical copy conveyed. As such, most of this electronic content is explicitly licensed to consumers, with no pretense of sale. What does this mean for the first sale doctrine under *Bobbs-Merrill*? Do consumers own any of their books, music or software today? What are the implications of not owning one's content?

9. *Digital exhaustion?* Professor Ariel Katz resists the rumor that "the first-sale doctrine is dying." He reasons:

> Once we ... recall that the legal significance of property rights, including intellectual property rights, lies not in the object to which the property rights relate, but in the legal relations between people with respect to that object, we can realize what exhaustion simply means: the right to transfer a lawfully obtained bundle of rights with respect to a work from one person to another, without seeking the ... owner's permission. The bundle of rights may relate to a tangible object embodying a work (such as a book), or it may comprise a set of permissions obtained under a license in relation to a work in digital format (such as a license to download an e-book and install it on one or more devices). In principle, exhaustion could apply to the latter bundle just as it applies to the former.[2]

As such, Professor Katz argues that the "sale" of a software program, a song file or an electronic book should exhaust the copyright owner's rights to the same degree as the sale of a computer disc, a music CD or a printed book. Do you agree?

23.3 TRADEMARK EXHAUSTION AND FIRST SALE

The gravamen of a trademark infringement claim is consumer confusion as to the source of a marked product. For this reason, the law generally recognizes the right of the owner of a marked product, whether a handbag or a luxury car, to resell it without permission of the manufacturer. The source is still the same manufacturer, even if the particular product has been used. As explained by the Ninth Circuit in *Sebastian Int'l, Inc. v. Longs Drug Stores Corp.*, 53 F.3d 1073, 1077 (9th Cir. 1995):

> The right of a producer to control distribution of its trademarked product does not extend beyond the first sale of the product. Resale by the first purchaser of the original article under the producer's trademark is neither trademark infringement nor unfair competition.

Yet complications arise when a marked product is altered or repackaged in some way before being resold. The following case summarizes the law surrounding first sale and exhaustion of trademark rights.

---

[2] Ariel Katz, *Digital Exhaustion: North American Observations* in Research Handbook on Electronic Commerce Law 137, 139 (John A. Rothchild, ed., Edward Elgar, 2016).

Au-Tomotive Gold Inc. v. Volkswagen of America, Inc.

603 F.3d 1133 (9th Cir. 2010)

WILLIAM A. FLETCHER, CIRCUIT JUDGE

We are asked to decide whether the sale by Au-Tomotive Gold ("Auto Gold") of marquee license plates bearing Volkswagen badges purchased from Volkswagen constitutes trademark infringement, or whether the sale of the plates is protected by the "first sale" doctrine. In *Au-Tomotive Gold, Inc. v. Volkswagen of America, Inc.* ("*Auto Gold I*"), 457 F.3d 1062 (9th Cir. 2006), we concluded that Auto Gold's production and sale of automobile accessories bearing Volkswagen's trademarks created a sufficient likelihood of confusion to constitute trademark infringement. We remanded to the district court to address Auto Gold's "first sale" and other defenses. On remand, the district court granted summary judgment and a permanent injunction to Volkswagen.

We affirm. We hold that the "first sale" doctrine does not provide a defense because Auto Gold's marquee license plates create a likelihood of confusion as to their origin.

I. Facts and Proceedings Below

Auto Gold produces and sells automobile accessories for specific makes of cars. Volkswagen and its subsidiary Audi are car manufacturers with well-known trademarks. The trademark at issue in this appeal is the familiar Volkswagen logo consisting of the letters "VW" inside a circle.

Beginning in the 1990s, Auto Gold produced and sold products bearing Volkswagen and Audi trademarks without permission from Volkswagen or Audi. It sold four products: license plates, license plate frames, key chains, and marquee license plates. The first three products used replicas of the companies' trademarks. However, the marquee license plates used actual VW badges purchased on the open market from a Volkswagen dealer. Auto Gold asserts its "first sale" defense only as to the marquee plates.

The marquee license plates are plain silver or black plates on which Auto Gold has mounted the VW badges. These badges are sold by Volkswagen and are ordinarily used as replacements for the badges found on the hoods or trunks of Volkswagen vehicles. Auto Gold purchased the badges, altered them by removing prongs and (in some cases) gold-plating them, and mounted them on the marquee plates. The plates were packaged with labels that explained that the plates were not produced or sponsored by Volkswagen.

Both parties accept for purposes of this appeal that Volkswagen had knowledge of Auto Gold's products as early as January 1999. In September 1999, a Volkswagen representative sent a letter to Auto Gold requesting that it cease using the trademarks. When Auto Gold refused to do so, a Volkswagen representative sent a second letter in October 1999. A Volkswagen representative sent a third letter in February 2001.

On April 19, 2001, Auto Gold filed suit seeking a declaratory judgment that its activities did not constitute an infringement or dilution of Volkswagen or Audi trademarks. Volkswagen and Audi counterclaimed, alleging federal trademark counterfeiting and infringement under § 32 of the Lanham Act, false designation, trademark dilution, and related state-law claims. Both parties moved for summary judgment.

The district court granted summary judgment to Auto Gold on all claims, holding that under the doctrine of "aesthetic functionality" the trademarks were "functional" and therefore not protected by trademark law. We reversed. We held that "the use of Volkswagen and Audi's marks is neither aesthetic nor independent of source identification." Rather, we held, consumers buy Auto Gold products because of the products' identification with the companies' brands. We then remanded to the district court for consideration of Auto Gold's "first sale" and other related defenses.

The district court rejected Auto Gold's "first sale" [defense] and granted Volkswagen summary judgment and a permanent injunction. Auto Gold timely appealed.

III. Discussion

Auto Gold argues that because it purchased actual VW badges from a Volkswagen dealer for use on the marquee license plates, the "first sale" doctrine protects the sale of the plates. We hold that the "first sale" doctrine does not provide a defense because the plates create a likelihood of confusion as to their origin. We do not base our holding on a likelihood of confusion among purchasers of the plates. Rather, we base it on the likelihood of post-purchase confusion among observers who see the plates on purchasers' cars.

1. Background

The "first sale" doctrine was first introduced in an opinion by Justice Holmes in *Prestonettes, Inc. v. Coty*, 264 U.S. 359 (1924). Prestonettes purchased toilet powder and perfumes produced and trademarked by Coty. Prestonettes incorporated the Coty products into its own products by combining the powder with a binder to create a cream and by rebottling the perfumes into smaller bottles. The Supreme Court held that Prestonettes did not violate trademark law. "The defendant of course by virtue of its ownership had a right to compound or change what it bought, to divide either the original or the modified product, and to sell it so divided."

The Court further held that Prestonettes could identify the components of its products as being Coty trademarked products so long as its labels were not misleading. For example, Prestonettes could place a label on the perfume bottles stating, "Prestonettes, Inc., not connected with Coty, states that the contents are Coty's ... independently rebottled in New York." It rejected Coty's argument that Prestonettes should not be allowed to use the Coty trademark in its description of the product because Prestonettes's products might be inferior. It wrote, "If the compound was worse than the constituent, it might be a misfortune to [Coty], but [Coty] would have no cause of action, as [Prestonettes] was exercising the rights of ownership and only telling the truth. The existence of a trademark would have no bearing on the question." The Court relied on the fact that consumers would not be confused about the manufacturer of the product. "A trade-mark only gives the right to prohibit the use of it so far as to protect the owner's good will against the sale of another's product as his."

Application of the "first sale" doctrine has generally focused on the likelihood of confusion among consumers. In *Sebastian Int'l, Inc. v. Longs Drug Stores Corp.*, 53 F.3d 1073, 1077 (9th Cir. 1995), we held that the "first sale" doctrine protected Longs when it purchased Sebastian hair products from a distributor and sold them in its own store despite Sebastian's efforts to allow only "Sebastian Collective Members" to sell the products. We recognized the principle that "the right of a producer to control distribution of its trademarked product does not extend beyond the first sale of the product." We emphasized that this rule "preserves an area of competition by limiting the producer's power to control the resale of its product," while ensuring that "the consumer gets exactly what the consumer bargains for, the genuine product of the particular producer."

FIGURE 23.3 In *Enesco v. Price/Costco*, Costco repackaged porcelain angels manufactured by Enesco in allegedly inferior packaging.

We also applied the "first sale" doctrine in *Enesco Corp. v. Price/Costco Inc.*, 146 F.3d 1083, 1084–85 (9th Cir. 1998), in which Costco purchased porcelain figurines manufactured by Enesco, repackaged them in allegedly inferior packaging, and sold them in its own stores. We held that Costco could repackage and sell the Enesco figurines, but that it was required to place labels on the packages that disclosed to the public that Costco had repackaged Enesco's original product. We rejected Enesco's argument that it would be harmed, even with this disclosure, because of the poor quality of the packaging. "The critical issue is whether the public is likely to be confused as a result of the lack of quality control."

A separate line of cases further illustrates the central role of the likelihood of confusion, including post-purchase confusion, in trademark infringement claims. In this line of cases, we have held that producers committed trademark infringement by selling refurbished or altered goods under their original trademark. None of these cases directly addressed the "first sale" doctrine, but they establish that activities creating a likelihood of post-purchase confusion, even among non-purchasers, are not protected.

In *Karl Storz Endoscopy-America, Inc. v. Surgical Tech., Inc.* ("*Surgi-Tech*"), 285 F.3d 848, 852–53 (9th Cir. 2002), SurgiTech repaired Storz endoscopes at the request of hospitals that owned them. Surgi-Tech sometimes rebuilt the endoscopes, replacing every part and retaining only the block element bearing Storz's trademarks. At an earlier time, Surgi-Tech had etched its own mark into rebuilt endoscopes to make clear what it had done, but Surgi-Tech had stopped that practice. Storz submitted evidence of confusion on the part of surgeons who were not the purchasers of the endoscopes but who used them and mistakenly blamed Storz when they malfunctioned. We held that there was a triable issue of fact on Storz's trademark infringement claim, even though there was no claim of purchaser confusion. We relied entirely on the possibility of confusion among non-purchasers, noting that such confusion "may be no less injurious to the trademark owner's reputation than confusion on the part of the purchaser at the time of sale."

We also relied on the likelihood of non-purchaser confusion in *Rolex Watch, U.S.A., Inc. v. Michel Co.*, 179 F.3d 704 (9th Cir. 1999). The defendant sold used Rolex watches that had been "reconditioned" or "customized" with non-Rolex parts. We agreed with the district court that "retention of the original Rolex marks on altered 'Rolex' watches ... was deceptive and misleading as to the origin of the non-Rolex parts, and likely to cause confusion to subsequent or downstream purchasers, as well as to persons observing the product."

In both *Surgi-Tech* and *Rolex*, we made clear that the defendants did not deceive the direct purchasers of the products. Rather, in both cases, we found trademark infringement based on a likelihood of confusion on the part of non-purchasers.

2. Application to the Marquee Plates

We held in *Auto Gold I* that the marquee license plates create a likelihood of post-purchase confusion on the part of observers of the plates. "Shorn of their disclaimer-covered packaging, Auto Gold's products display no indication visible to the general public that the items are not associated with Audi or Volkswagen. The disclaimers do nothing to dispel post-purchase confusion." It is likely that a person on the street who sees an Auto Gold marquee license plate with a VW badge will associate the plate with Volkswagen. Indeed, customers buy marquee license plates principally to demonstrate to the general public an association with Volkswagen. "The demand for Auto Gold's products is inextricably tied to the trademarks themselves."

Auto Gold, however, maintains that the likelihood of post-purchase confusion does not matter. Auto Gold argues, first, that confusion among non-purchasers is irrelevant in "first sale" cases. However, Auto Gold cannot point to any case in which a court has held that the "first sale" doctrine applies when there is a likelihood of post-purchase confusion. In *Prestonettes*, there was no suggestion that a third-party could be confused about, or even be aware of, the origin of the facial cream or perfume used by a purchaser. Likewise, there was no possibility of post-purchase confusion as to the origin of the hair products in Sebastian or the porcelain figurines in *Enesco*.

In each case in which a court has applied the "first sale" doctrine, the court either had good reason not to be concerned with post-purchase confusion or took steps to avoid addressing the issue. In *Alexander Binzel Corp.*, the court noted that Binzel sold its parts to be incorporated into welding guns produced by other manufacturers. The defendant's "use of Binzel nozzles is fully consistent with Binzel's profit motive as well as the manner Binzel has chosen to control its product's reputation." In *Dad's Kid Corp.*, the court noted that baseball trading cards are regularly repackaged, displayed, or mounted, and that there was therefore "no likelihood that anyone will be confused as to origin by reason of Dad's Kid's treatment of genuine cards." In *Scarves by Vera, Inc.*, the court noted that the plaintiff's trademark could be seen on some of the defendant's bags. It therefore insisted that a disclaimer label be sewn into the bag near the clasp, and plainly visible to anyone opening the handbag.

Post-purchase confusion creates a free-rider problem. Auto Gold contends that in "first sale" cases "the element of 'free-riding' present in other post-purchase confusion cases disappears because the producer has paid the price asked by the trademark owner for the 'ride.'" This contention misses the point. When a producer purchases a trademarked product, that producer is not purchasing the trademark. Rather, the producer is purchasing a product that has been trademarked. If a producer profits from a trademark because of post-purchase confusion about the product's origin, the producer is, to that degree, a free-rider.

For example, a producer may purchase non-functioning Rolex watches and refurbish them with non-Rolex parts, leaving only the original casing. Even if the producer adequately explains the nature of the refurbished watches to purchasers, the producer nonetheless infringes on Rolex's trademarks by profiting from the Rolex name. In such a case, the purchasers buy the watches in order to make others think that they have bought a true Rolex watch. The same holds true for new but relatively cheap products that prominently display a well-known trademark. If the producer purchases such a trademarked product and uses that product to create post-purchase confusion as to the source of a new product, the producer is free-riding even though it has paid for the trademarked product.

Next, Auto Gold argues that there is no trademark infringement because its marquee plates are of high quality. But likelihood of confusion, not quality control, is "the 'keystone' of trademark law." *Westinghouse Elec. Corp. v. Gen. Circuit Breakers & Elec. Supply Inc.*, 106 F.3d 894, 900 (9th Cir. 1997). Courts have consistently held for plaintiffs where there is a possibility of confusion, even where defendants are not selling lower quality goods. See, e.g., *Levi Strauss & Co. v. Blue Bell, Inc.*, 632 F.2d 817, 821–22 (9th Cir. 1980) (pocket tabs on Wrangler jeans infringed upon Levi's trademark by creating a likelihood of post-purchase confusion despite no contention that Wrangler jeans were of lower quality). Similarly, courts have consistently held for defendants where there was no possibility of confusion, despite the fact that the defendants may have lowered the quality of goods. See, e.g., *Prestonettes*, 264 U.S. at 367; *Enesco Corp.*, 146 F.3d at 1087.

Finally, Auto Gold argues that the public interest is served by the competition that results from the availability of its products. It may be true that Auto Gold's activities serve to reduce the price paid by consumers for marquee plates. But trademark law protects trademark holders from the competition that results from trademark infringement, irrespective of its effect on prices.

We therefore conclude that the district court correctly granted summary judgment to Volkswagen on its trademark infringement claim.

AFFIRMED.

Notes and Questions

1. *Point of confusion.* Much of the court's reasoning in *Auto Gold* hangs on the distinction between confusion at the point of sale versus post-purchase confusion. What is the significance of this distinction in the first sale analysis? Do you agree with the court's determination that post-purchase confusion should be the deciding factor in such cases?

2. *Who is confused?* Closely related to the point at which confusion is measured is the question of whose confusion is relevant. If confusion is at the point of sale, then the customer making the purchase is the one likely to be confused, and the one that the law seeks to protect. But who is the victim of post-purchase confusion? If the purpose of trademark law is to prevent consumer confusion as to the source of goods, why should the law protect individuals who are not making the decision to purchase the particular good in question? Who is really being protected here?

3. *The public interest.* As noted by the court, "Auto Gold argues that the public interest is served by the competition that results from the availability of its products." Do you agree with Auto Gold? Why did the court summarily dismiss this argument? Are there public interest factors that should be considered in trademark exhaustion cases?

4. *Used, refurbished and like new.* As noted in the introduction to this section, the owner of a trademarked product is free to resell it without the authorization of the trademark owner on the theory that the product was genuinely produced by the trademark owner. This right is limited, however, if the reseller claims that the product is "new" or if the reseller has altered, reconditioned or repackaged the product. In *Surgi-Tech* and *Rolex*, discussed by the court in *Auto Gold*, substantial reconditioning of branded products altered them sufficiently that resale under their original brand was deemed to be likely to cause consumer confusion. But in cases such as *Prestonettes* and *Enesco*, repackaging of a branded product was permitted so long as the reseller adequately informed the consumer. Given that Auto Gold did not make any changes to the VW sticker that it used on its marquee license plates, how would you square the holding in *Auto Gold* with these precedentys?

23.4 PATENT EXHAUSTION

Just as with copyrighted materials and goods bearing trademarks, patented articles are subject to an exhaustion doctrine. The Supreme Court offers the rationale for this doctrine in *United States v. Univis Lens Co.*, 316 U.S. 241, 251 (1942):

> the purpose of the patent law is fulfilled with respect to any particular article when the patentee has received his reward for the use of his invention by the sale of the article, and that, once that purpose is realized, the patent law affords no basis for restraining the use and enjoyment of the thing sold.

Yet the patent exhaustion doctrine originated long before the Court's decision in *Univis*. The following early case helped to establish the modern contours of the exhaustion doctrine.[3]

Adams v. Burke
84 U.S. 453 (1873)

On the 26th day of May, 1863, letters-patent were granted to Merrill & Horner, for a certain improvement in coffin lids, giving to them the exclusive right of making, using, and vending to others to be used, the said improvement.

On the 13th day of March, 1865, Merrill & Horner, the patentees, by an assignment duly executed and recorded, assigned Lockhart & Seelye, of Cambridge, in Middlesex County, Massachusetts, all the right, title, and interest which the said patentees had in the invention described in the said letters-patent, for, to, and in a circle whose radius is ten miles, having the city of Boston as a centre. They subsequently assigned the patent, or what right they retained in it, to one Adams.

Adams now filed a bill in the court below, against a certain Burke, an undertaker, who used in the town of Natick (a town about seventeen miles from Boston, and therefore outside of the circle above mentioned) coffins with lids of the kind patented, alleging him to be an infringer of their patent, and praying for an injunction, discovery, profits, and other relief suitable against an infringer.

---

3 For a more complete early history of the doctrine, see Alfred C. Server & William J. Casey, *Contract-Based Post-Sale Restrictions on Patented Products Following* Quanta, 64 Hastings L.J. 561, 564–75 (2013).

The Defendant Pleaded in Bar:

"That he carries on the business of an undertaker, having his place of business in Natick, in said district; that, in the exercise of his said business, he is employed to bury the dead; that when so employed it is his custom to procure hearses, coffins, and whatever else may be necessary or proper for burials, and to superintend the preparation of graves, and that his bills for his services in each case, and the coffin, hearse, and other articles procured by him, are paid by the personal representatives of the deceased; that, since the date of the alleged assignment to the plaintiff of an interest in the invention secured by the said letters-patent, he has sold no coffins, unless the use of coffins by him in his said business, as above described, shall be deemed a sale; has used no coffins, except in his said business as aforesaid; and has manufactured no coffins containing the said invention; and that since the said he has used in his business as aforesaid, in Natick, no coffin containing the invention secured by said letters-patent, except such coffins containing said invention as have been manufactured by said Lockhart & Seelye, within a circle, whose radius is ten miles, having the city of Boston as its centre, and sold within said circle by said Lockhart & Seelye, without condition or restriction."

Mr. Justice MILLER delivered the opinion of the court.

The question presented by the plea in this case is a very interesting one in patent law, and the precise point in it has never been decided by this court, though cases involving some of the consideration which apply to it have been decided, and others of analogous character are frequently recurring. The vast pecuniary results involved in such cases, as well as the public interest, admonish us to proceed with care, and to decide in each case no more than what is directly in issue.

We have repeatedly held that where a person had purchased a patented machine of the patentee or his assignee, this purchase carried with it the right to the use of that machine so long as it was capable of use, and that the expiration and renewal of the patent, whether in favor of the original patentee or of his assignee, did not affect this right. The true ground on which these decisions rest is that the sale by a person who has the full right to make, sell, and use such a machine carries with it the right to the use of that machine to the full extent to which it can be used in point of time.

The right to manufacture, the right to sell, and the right to use are each substantive rights, and may be granted or conferred separately by the patentee. But, in the essential nature of things, when the patentee, or the person having his rights, sells a machine or instrument whose sole value is in its use, he receives the consideration for its use and he parts with the right to restrict that use. The article, in the language of the court, passes without the limit of the monopoly. That is to say, the patentee or his assignee having in the act of sale received all the royalty or consideration which he claims for the use of his invention in that particular machine or instrument, it is open to the use of the purchaser without further restriction on account of the monopoly of the patentees.

If this principle be sound as to a machine or instrument whose use may be continued for a number of years, and may extend beyond the existence of the patent, as limited at the time of the sale, and into the period of a renewal or extension, it must be much more applicable to an instrument or product of patented manufacture which perishes in the first use of it, or which, by that first use, becomes incapable of further use, and of no further value. Such is the case with the coffin-lids of appellant's patent.

It seems to us that, although the right of Lockhart & Seelye to manufacture, to sell, and to use these coffin-lids was limited to the circle of ten miles around Boston, that a purchaser from them of a single coffin acquired the right to use that coffin for the purpose for which all coffins are used. That so far as the use of it was concerned, the patentee had received his consideration, and it was no longer within the monopoly of the patent. It would be to engraft a limitation upon the right of use not contemplated by the statute nor within the reason of the contract to say that it could only be used within the ten-miles circle. Whatever, therefore, may be the rule when patentees subdivide territorially their patents, as to the exclusive right to make or to sell within a limited territory, we hold that in the class of machines or implements we have described, when they are once lawfully made and sold, there is no restriction on their use to be implied for benefit of the patentee or his assignees or licensees.

A careful examination of the plea satisfies us that the defendant, who, as an undertaker, purchased each of these coffins and used it in burying the body which he was employed to bury, acquired the right to this use of it freed from any claim of the patentee, though purchased within the ten-mile circle and used without it.

The decree of the Circuit Court dismissing the plaintiff's bill is, therefore,
AFFIRMED.

Notes and Questions

1. *The power of exhaustion.* Lockhart & Seelye had the right to manufacture and sell patented coffin lids within a ten-mile radius of Boston. Burke, who purchased a coffin from them, used it in Natick, beyond the ten-mile radius. Yet the Court denied the claim of Adams, who

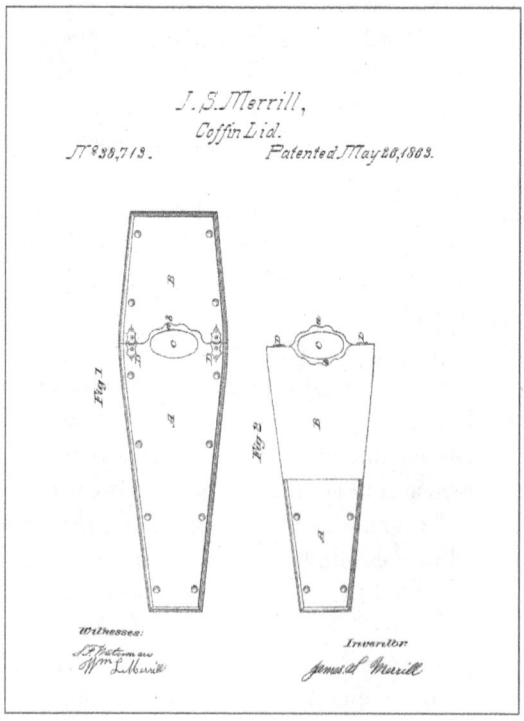

FIGURE 23.4 Figures from U.S. Patent No. 38,713 (May 26, 1863) "Improvement in Coffin Lids."

was the owner of the patent rights beyond the ten-mile radius. Why? Because when Lockhart & Scclye made an authorized sale to Burke, the patent rights in that coffin were exhausted and Adams could no longer assert them against those particular coffins. This is a potent concept. What if Lockhart & Seelye set up a coffin factory and began to ship their coffins around the world? Should Adams feel aggrieved? At what point might Adams have a claim against a user of a Lockhart & Seelye coffin beyond the ten-mile radius?

2. *A limitation on use?* What if the original patentee had assigned to Lockhart & Seelye only the right to manufacture coffins *for use* within a ten-mile radius of Boston? Could Adams then have argued that the right to use the patented coffins outside of the ten-mile radius was never granted to Lockhart & Seelye, and thus could not be exhausted by their sale to Burke? How would such a limitation on the scope of the right conveyed differ from a contractual clause that simply prohibited Lockhart & Seelye from permitting any coffin they sold to be used outside of their permitted ten-mile radius? For more on this issue, see Section 23.5.

Quanta Computer, Inc. v. LG Electronics
553 U.S. 617 (2008)

THOMAS, JUSTICE

For over 150 years this Court has applied the doctrine of patent exhaustion to limit the patent rights that survive the initial authorized sale of a patented item. In this case, we decide whether patent exhaustion applies to the sale of components of a patented system that must be combined with additional components in order to practice the patented methods. The Court of Appeals for the Federal Circuit held that the doctrine does not apply to method patents at all and, in the alternative, that it does not apply here because the sales were not authorized by the license agreement. We disagree on both scores. Because the exhaustion doctrine applies to method patents, and because the license authorizes the sale of components that substantially embody the patents in suit, the sale exhausted the patents.

I

Respondent LG Electronics, Inc. (LGE), purchased a portfolio of computer technology patents in 1999, including the three patents at issue here: U.S. Patent Nos. 4,939,641 ('641); 5,379,379 ('379); and 5,077,733 ('733) (collectively LGE Patents). The main functions of a computer system are carried out on a microprocessor, or central processing unit, which interprets program instructions, processes data, and controls other devices in the system. A set of wires, or bus, connects the microprocessor to a chipset, which transfers data between the microprocessor and other devices, including the keyboard, mouse, monitor, hard drive, memory, and disk drives.

The data processed by the computer are stored principally in random access memory, also called main memory. Frequently accessed data are generally stored in cache memory, which permits faster access than main memory and is often located on the microprocessor itself. Id., at 84. When copies of data are stored in both the cache and main memory, problems may arise when one copy is changed but the other still contains the original "stale" version of the data. The '641 patent addresses this problem. It discloses a system for ensuring that the most current data are retrieved from main memory by monitoring data requests and updating main memory from the cache when stale data are requested. The '379 patent relates to the coordination of requests to read from, and write to, main memory. The '733 patent addresses the problem of managing the data traffic on a bus connecting two computer components, so that no one device monopolizes the bus.

LGE licensed a patent portfolio, including the LGE Patents, to Intel Corporation (Intel). The cross-licensing agreement (License Agreement) permits Intel to manufacture and sell microprocessors and chipsets that use the LGE Patents (the Intel Products). The License Agreement authorizes Intel to "make, use, sell (directly or indirectly), offer to sell, import or otherwise dispose of" its own products practicing the LGE Patents. Notwithstanding this broad language, the License Agreement contains some limitations.

Relevant here, it stipulates that no license

is granted by either party hereto ... to any third party for the combination by a third party of Licensed Products of either party with items, components, or the like acquired ... from sources other than a party hereto, or for the use, import, offer for sale or sale of such combination.

The License Agreement purports not to alter the usual rules of patent exhaustion, however, providing that, "[n]otwithstanding anything to the contrary contained in this Agreement, the parties agree that nothing herein shall in any way limit or alter the effect of patent exhaustion that would otherwise apply when a party hereto sells any of its Licensed Products."

In a separate agreement (Master Agreement), Intel agreed to give written notice to its own customers informing them that, while it had obtained a broad license "ensur[ing] that any Intel product that you purchase is licensed by LGE and thus does not infringe any patent held by LGE," the license "does not extend, expressly or by implication, to any product that you make by combining an Intel product with any non-Intel product."

The Master Agreement also provides that "a breach of this Agreement shall have no effect on and shall not be grounds for termination of the Patent License."

Petitioners, including Quanta Computer (collectively Quanta), are a group of computer manufacturers. Quanta purchased microprocessors and chipsets from Intel and received the notice required by the Master Agreement. Nonetheless, Quanta manufactured computers using Intel parts in combination with non-Intel memory and buses in ways that practice the LGE Patents. Quanta does not modify the Intel components and follows Intel's specifications to incorporate the parts into its own systems.

LGE filed a complaint against Quanta, asserting that the combination of the Intel Products with non-Intel memory and buses infringed the LGE Patents. The District Court granted summary judgment to Quanta, holding that, for purposes of the patent exhaustion doctrine, the license LGE granted to Intel resulted in forfeiture of any potential infringement actions against legitimate purchasers of the Intel Products. In a subsequent order limiting its summary judgment ruling, the court held that patent exhaustion applies only to apparatus or composition-of-matter claims that describe a physical object, and does not apply to process, or method, claims that describe operations to make or use a product.

The Court of Appeals for the Federal Circuit affirmed in part and reversed in part. It agreed that the doctrine of patent exhaustion does not apply to method claims. In the alternative, it concluded that exhaustion did not apply because LGE did not license Intel to sell the Intel Products to Quanta for use in combination with non-Intel products.

We granted certiorari.

FIGURE 23.5 The parties in *Quanta v. LGE*: LGE, which held three patents covering aspects of a chip's design; Intel, which manufactured chips under license from LG; and Quanta, which purchased Intel chips for use in its computers.

II

The longstanding doctrine of patent exhaustion provides that the initial authorized sale of a patented item terminates all patent rights to that item.

[*The early history of patent exhaustion is omitted*]

This Court most recently discussed patent exhaustion in *United States v. Univis Lens Co.*, 316 U.S. 241 (1942), on which the District Court relied. Univis Lens Company, the holder of patents on eyeglass lenses, licensed a purchaser to manufacture lens blanks[4] by fusing together different lens segments to create bi- and tri-focal lenses and to sell them to other Univis licensees at agreed-upon rates. Wholesalers were licensed to grind the blanks into the patented finished lenses, which they would then sell to Univis-licensed prescription retailers for resale at a fixed rate. Finishing retailers, after grinding the blanks into patented lenses, would sell the finished lenses to consumers at the same fixed rate. The United States sued Univis under the Sherman Act, alleging unlawful restraints on trade.[5] Univis asserted its patent monopoly rights as a defense to the antitrust suit. The Court granted certiorari to determine whether Univis' patent monopoly survived the sale of the lens blanks by the licensed manufacturer and therefore shielded Univis' pricing scheme from the Sherman Act.

The Court assumed that the Univis patents containing claims for finished lenses were practiced in part by the wholesalers and finishing retailers who ground the blanks into lenses, and held that the sale of the lens blanks exhausted the patents on the finished lenses. The Court explained that the lens blanks "embodi[ed] essential features of the patented device and [were] without utility until … ground and polished as the finished lens of the patent." The Court noted that:

> where one has sold an uncompleted article which, because it embodies essential features
> of his patented invention, is within the protection of his patent, and has destined the

---

4 Lens blanks are "rough opaque pieces of glass of suitable size, design and composition for use, when ground and polished, as multifocal lenses in eyeglasses."

5 For a discussion of the Sherman Antitrust Act of 1890, see Chapter 25 – Ed.

article to be finished by the purchaser in conformity to the patent, he has sold his invention so far as it is or may be embodied in that particular article.

In sum, the Court concluded that the traditional bar on patent restrictions following the
sale of an item applies when the item sufficiently embodies the patent—even if it does not
completely practice the patent—such that its only and intended use is to be finished under
the terms of the patent.

With this history of the patent exhaustion doctrine in mind, we turn to the parties'
arguments.

III. A

LGE argues that the exhaustion doctrine is inapplicable here because it does not apply
to method claims, which are contained in each of the LGE Patents. LGE reasons that,
because method patents are linked not to a tangible article but to a process, they can
never be exhausted through a sale. Rather, practicing the patent—which occurs upon each
use of an article embodying a method patent—is permissible only to the extent rights are
transferred in an assignment contract. Quanta, in turn, argues that there is no reason to
preclude exhaustion of method claims, and points out that both this Court and the Federal
Circuit have applied exhaustion to method claims. It argues that any other rule would
allow patent holders to avoid exhaustion entirely by inserting method claims in their patent
specifications.

Quanta has the better of this argument. Nothing in this Court's approach to patent
exhaustion supports LGE's argument that method patents cannot be exhausted. It is true
that a patented method may not be sold in the same way as an article or device, but methods nonetheless may be "embodied" in a product, the sale of which exhausts patent rights.
Our precedents do not differentiate transactions involving embodiments of patented methods or processes from those involving patented apparatuses or materials. To the contrary,
this Court has repeatedly held that method patents were exhausted by the sale of an item
that embodied the method. These cases rest on solid footing. Eliminating exhaustion for
method patents would seriously undermine the exhaustion doctrine. Patentees seeking to
avoid patent exhaustion could simply draft their patent claims to describe a method rather
than an apparatus. Apparatus and method claims "may approach each other so nearly that
it will be difficult to distinguish the process from the function of the apparatus." By characterizing their claims as method instead of apparatus claims, or including a method claim
for the machine's patented method of performing its task, a patent drafter could shield
practically any patented item from exhaustion.

This case illustrates the danger of allowing such an end-run around exhaustion. On
LGE's theory, although Intel is authorized to sell a completed computer system that practices the LGE Patents, any downstream purchasers of the system could nonetheless be
liable for patent infringement. Such a result would violate the longstanding principle that,
when a patented item is "once lawfully made and sold, there is no restriction on [its] use
to be implied for the benefit of the patentee." We therefore reject LGE's argument that
method claims, as a category, are never exhaustible.

B

We next consider the extent to which a product must embody a patent in order to trigger
exhaustion. Quanta argues that, although sales of an incomplete article do not necessarily

exhaust the patent in that article, the sale of the microprocessors and chipsets exhausted LGE's patents in the same way the sale of the lens blanks exhausted the patents in *Univis.* Just as the lens blanks in *Univis* did not fully practice the patents at issue because they had not been ground into finished lenses, Quanta observes, the Intel Products cannot practice the LGE Patents—or indeed, function at all—until they are combined with memory and buses in a computer system ... We agree with Quanta that *Univis* governs this case. As the Court there explained, exhaustion was triggered by the sale of the lens blanks because their only reasonable and intended use was to practice the patent and because they "embodie[d] essential features of [the] patented invention." Each of those attributes is shared by the microprocessors and chipsets Intel sold to Quanta under the License Agreement.

First, *Univis* held that "the authorized sale of an article which is capable of use only in practicing the patent is a relinquishment of the patent monopoly with respect to the article sold." Here, LGE has suggested no reasonable use for the Intel Products other than incorporating them into computer systems that practice the LGE Patents. Nor can we discern one: A microprocessor or chipset cannot function until it is connected to buses and memory. And here, as in *Univis*, the only apparent object of Intel's sales to Quanta was to permit Quanta to incorporate the Intel Products into computers that would practice the patents.

Second, the lens blanks in *Univis* "embodie[d] essential features of [the] patented invention." Like the Univis lens blanks, the Intel Products constitute a material part of the patented invention and all but completely practice the patent. Here, as in *Univis*, the incomplete article substantially embodies the patent because the only step necessary to practice the patent is the application of common processes or the addition of standard parts. Everything inventive about each patent is embodied in the Intel Products.

C

Having concluded that the Intel Products embodied the patents, we next consider whether their sale to Quanta exhausted LGE's patent rights. Exhaustion is triggered only by a sale authorized by the patent holder.

FIGURE 23.6 An Intel chip integrated into a computer board.

LGE argues that there was no authorized sale here because the License Agreement does not permit Intel to sell its products for use in combination with non-Intel products to practice the LGE Patents. It cites *General Talking Pictures Corp. v. Western Elec. Co.*, 304 U.S. 175 and 305 U.S. 124 (1938), in which the manufacturer sold patented amplifiers for commercial use, thereby breaching a license that limited the buyer to selling the amplifiers for private and home use. The Court held that exhaustion did not apply because the manufacturer had no authority to sell the amplifiers for commercial use, and the manufacturer "could not convey to petitioner what both knew it was not authorized to sell." LGE argues that the same principle applies here: Intel could not convey to Quanta what both knew it was not authorized to sell, i.e., the right to practice the patents with non-Intel parts.

LGE overlooks important aspects of the structure of the Intel–LGE transaction. Nothing in the License Agreement restricts Intel's right to sell its microprocessors and chipsets to purchasers who intend to combine them with non-Intel parts. It broadly permits Intel to "make, use, [or] sell" products free of LGE's patent claims. To be sure, LGE did require Intel to give notice to its customers, including Quanta, that LGE had not licensed those customers to practice its patents. But neither party contends that Intel breached the agreement in that respect. In any event, the provision requiring notice to Quanta appeared only in the Master Agreement, and LGE does not suggest that a breach of that agreement would constitute a breach of the License Agreement. Hence, Intel's authority to sell its products embodying the LGE Patents was not conditioned on the notice or on Quanta's decision to abide by LGE's directions in that notice.

LGE points out that the License Agreement specifically disclaimed any license to third parties to practice the patents by combining licensed products with other components. But the question whether third parties received implied licenses is irrelevant because Quanta asserts its right to practice the patents based not on implied license but on exhaustion. And exhaustion turns only on Intel's own license to sell products practicing the LGE Patents.

Alternatively, LGE invokes the principle that patent exhaustion does not apply to post-sale restrictions on "making" an article. But this is simply a rephrasing of its argument that combining the Intel Products with other components adds more than standard finishing to complete a patented article. As explained above, making a product that substantially embodies a patent is, for exhaustion purposes, no different from making the patented article itself. In other words, no further "making" results from the addition of standard parts—here, the buses and memory—to a product that already substantially embodies the patent.

The License Agreement authorized Intel to sell products that practiced the LGE Patents. No conditions limited Intel's authority to sell products substantially embodying the patents. Because Intel was authorized to sell its products to Quanta, the doctrine of patent exhaustion prevents LGE from further asserting its patent rights with respect to the patents substantially embodied by those products.[6]

---

[6] [n. 7] We note that the authorized nature of the sale to Quanta does not necessarily limit LGE's other contract rights. LGE's complaint does not include a breach-of-contract claim, and we express no opinion on whether contract damages might be available even though exhaustion operates to eliminate patent damages. See *Keeler v. Standard Folding Bed Co.*, 157 U.S. 659, 666 (1895) ("Whether a patentee may protect himself and his assignees by special contracts brought home to the purchasers is not a question before us, and upon which we express no opinion. It is, however, obvious that such a question would arise as a question of contract, and not as one under the inherent meaning and effect of the patent laws").

IV

The authorized sale of an article that substantially embodies a patent exhausts the patent holder's rights and prevents the patent holder from invoking patent law to control post-sale use of the article. Here, LGE licensed Intel to practice any of its patents and to sell products practicing those patents. Intel's microprocessors and chipsets substantially embodied the LGE Patents because they had no reasonable noninfringing use and included all the inventive aspects of the patented methods. Nothing in the License Agreement limited Intel's ability to sell its products practicing the LGE Patents. Intel's authorized sale to Quanta thus took its products outside the scope of the patent monopoly, and as a result, LGE can no longer assert its patent rights against Quanta. Accordingly, the judgment of the Court of Appeals is reversed.

Notes and Questions

1. *Exhaustion of method claims.* According to some observers, the Court thought that the principal holding of *Quanta* established that patent exhaustion applied to method claims. As Justice Thomas writes, failing to recognize patent exhaustion of method claims would be "an end-run around exhaustion." What did he mean?

2. *Embodiment of a patent.* The Court in *Quanta* relies heavily on its earlier reasoning in *Univis*, in which patents covering finished optical lenses were found to be exhausted upon the patentee's sale of unfinished lens blanks. How can an unpolished piece of glass embody the "essential features" of an optical lens? By the same token, how can Intel's chips, which lacked the buses and memory claimed in LGE's patents, exhaust those patents?

3. *Exhaustion policy?* As noted by Fred Server and William Casey, the *Quanta* decision has been criticized for

   perpetuating a draconian per se rule against post-sale vertical restraints that runs counter to the trend in competition law to evaluate such restraints with greater subtlety and to view them more favorably ... exacerbated by the Court's recurring failure to articulate a clear and compelling policy rationale in support of the doctrine.[7]

   Do you agree with this critique? What do you think the Court viewed as the overriding policy concern of patent exhaustion? Do you think that a more nuanced test for patent exhaustion, perhaps modeled on "rule of reason" analysis under antitrust law (see Section 25.1), is warranted?

4. *A license exclusion?* The license agreement between LGE and Intel stated that "no license is granted ... to any third party for the combination by a third party of Licensed Products ... with items, components, or the like acquired ... from sources other than a party hereto, or for the use, import, offer for sale or sale of such combination." What was the purpose of this clause? Why do you think it was written in terms of no license rights being granted to a third party? Why do you think that Intel, knowing that it planned to sell chips to computer manufacturers like Quanta, agreed to this exclusionary language?[8]

---

[7] Server & Casey, supra note 3, at 580.

[8] For a discussion of the parties' possible business motives in this transaction, see Amelia Smith Rinehart, *Contracting Patents: A Modern Patent Exhaustion Doctrine*, 23 Harv. J. L. Tech. 483, 521 (2010).

What do you make of the additional clause in the License Agreement, "nothing herein shall in any way limit or alter the effect of patent exhaustion that would otherwise apply when a party hereto sells any of its Licensed Products." Why would the parties include such a clause in the License Agreement? Which of them do you think insisted on this clause?

Of course, the Court, in analyzing the license agreement, concluded that the exclusionary language was largely irrelevant. Quanta was not arguing that it had obtained a license from LGE, it was arguing that LGE's patent rights were exhausted upon Intel's sale of chips. Why was this such an important difference?

If LGE really wanted to limit the rights that Intel's customers obtained, couldn't LGE have limited the rights that it granted to Intel in the first place? That is, could LGE's license to Intel have been limited to manufacturing and selling chips on a standalone basis, but not combining the chips with other computer components? Would such a limitation have defeated patent exhaustion? What might have Intel's reaction been to such language?

5. *Customer notification and limitations.* Under a separate master agreement between LGE and Intel, Intel agreed to notify its customers that Intel's broad license from LGE "does not extend, expressly or by implication, to any product that you make by combining an Intel product with any non-Intel product." What was the purpose of this notification requirement? Why would Intel agree to this requirement? Did such a notice have any legal effect on Intel's customers?

6. *Other contractual limitations?* Footnote 7 of the *Quanta* opinion (reproduced in the case above) has occasioned significant speculation. The Court seemingly leaves open the door to a breach of contract claim even if patent rights have been exhausted. Thus, if Intel had failed to notify Quanta of LGE's position that computer manufacturers were not licensed under LGE's patents, LGE might have a breach of contract claim against Intel. What damages might be available to LGE if such a claim were successful, given the exhaustion of LGE's patents?

7. *What is an exhaustive license?* What constitutes a "license" for the purposes of patent exhaustion? The license that LGE granted to Intel clearly exhausted LGE's patents. But what if the agreement were less clear? For example, in *De Forest Radio Telephone Co. v. United States*, 273 U.S. 236, 241 (1927), the Supreme Court held that "No formal granting of a license is necessary in order to give it effect. Any language used by the owner of the patent, or any conduct on his part exhibited to another from which that other may properly infer that the owner consents to his use of the patent in making or using it, or selling it, upon which the other acts, constitutes a license." And in *Ortho Pharmaceutical Corp. v. Genetics Institute, Inc.*, 52 F.3d 1026, 1031 (Fed. Cir. 1995), the Federal Circuit wrote that "A license may amount to no more than a covenant by the patentee not to sue the licensee for making, using or selling the patented invention." Given this precedent, could a patent holder's conduct short of granting a formal license agreement exhaust its patents?

Consider, for example, the "CDMA ASIC Agreements" that patent owner Qualcomm entered into with makers of wireless telecommunication chips, as described in *FTC v. Qualcomm* (9th Cir., Aug. 11, 2020). As described by the court, these agreements "allow Qualcomm's competitors to practice Qualcomm's [patents] royalty-free," though they are not called licenses. Could such agreements exhaust Qualcomm's patents?[9]

8. *Exhaustion and self-propagating inventions – patented plants.* In *Bowman v. Monsanto*, 569 U.S. 278 (2013), Monsanto patented a genetic modification that makes soybean plants

---

9 For a more in-depth consideration of this question, see Jorge L. Contreras, *"No License, No Problem" – Is Qualcomm's Ninth Circuit Antitrust Victory a Patent Exhaustion Defeat?*, Patently-O blog, August 31, 2020.

resistant to glyphosate, a potent herbicide marketed by Monsanto as Roundup.[10] Monsanto and its licensees sell these seeds to growers who are contractually permitted to use or sell the resulting soybeans for consumption (human or animal). However, they must also agree not to save any of the harvested soybeans for replanting. One farmer, Vernon Bowman, however, thought he found a way to circumvent Monsanto's replanting restrictions. As the Court explains, he

went to a grain elevator; purchased "commodity soybeans" intended for human or animal consumption; and planted them in his fields. Those soybeans came from prior harvests of other local farmers. And because most of those farmers also used Roundup Ready seed, Bowman could anticipate that many of the purchased soybeans would contain Monsanto's patented technology. When he applied a glyphosate-based herbicide to his fields, he confirmed that this was so; a significant proportion of the new plants survived the treatment, and produced in their turn a new crop of soybeans with the Roundup Ready trait. Bowman saved seed from that crop to use in his late-season planting the next year—and then the next, and the next, until he had harvested eight crops in that way. Each year, that is, he planted saved seed from the year before (sometimes adding more soybeans bought from the grain elevator), sprayed his fields with glyphosate to kill weeds (and any non-resistant plants), and produced a new crop of glyphosate-resistant—i.e., Roundup Ready—soybeans.

After discovering this practice, Monsanto sued Bowman for infringing its patents on Roundup Ready seed. Bowman raised patent exhaustion as a defense, arguing that Monsanto could not control his use of the soybeans because they were the subject of a prior authorized sale (from local farmers to the grain elevator).

The Supreme Court, in a unanimous decision, ruled against Bowman, reasoning as follows:

Under the patent exhaustion doctrine, Bowman could resell the patented soybeans he purchased from the grain elevator; so too he could consume the beans himself or feed them to his animals ... But the exhaustion doctrine does not enable Bowman to make additional patented soybeans without Monsanto's permission (either express or implied). And that is precisely what Bowman did. He took the soybeans he purchased home; planted them in his fields at the time he thought best; applied glyphosate to kill weeds (as well as any soy plants lacking the Roundup Ready trait); and finally harvested more (many more) beans than he started with. That is how "to 'make' a new product," to use Bowman's words, when the original product is a seed. Because Bowman thus reproduced Monsanto's patented invention, the exhaustion doctrine does not protect him.

What do you think of the Court's reasoning with respect to patent exhaustion? Should all of Monsanto's patent rights have been exhausted with respect to each seed once it was sold the first time? Does it make a difference that a seed, by its very nature, will grow into a soybean plant without substantial alteration by its owner?

The Court, in supporting its result, also relies on several policy and instrumentalist arguments, attempting to demonstrate that any other result would be irrational:

Were the matter otherwise, Monsanto's patent would provide scant benefit. After inventing the Roundup Ready trait, Monsanto would, to be sure, "receiv[e] [its] reward" for the first seeds it sells. But in short order, other seed companies could reproduce the product and market it to growers, thus depriving Monsanto of its monopoly. And farmers themselves need only buy the seed once, whether from Monsanto, a competitor, or (as here) a grain elevator.

---

[10] The plaintiffs in several class actions also allege that glyphosate is a carcinogen that has caused them significant personal injury and death.

The grower could multiply his initial purchase, and then multiply that new creation, ad infinitum—each time profiting from the patented seed without compensating its inventor. Bowman's late-season plantings offer a prime illustration.

What alternative policy arguments would you raise if you represented Bowman?

9. *Exhaustion across IP types.* Now that you have seen how the first sale and exhaustion doctrines work across copyright, trademark and patent law, what common features can you identify among these three bodies of law? What important differences do you find?

23.5 CONDITIONAL SALES AND POST-SALE RESTRICTIONS

Ever since *Adams v. Burke*, patent licensors have experimented with contractual mechanisms to limit the rights that their licensees can impart to purchasers of licensed products. They sought to limit contractually the rights granted to licensees in such a way that the licensees' sale of products would not, under the right circumstances, exhaust the patent. For example, what if the patent holders in *Adams v. Burke* had expressly limited Lockhart & Seelye's rights to the sale of coffins for use within a ten-mile radius of Boston? Would Burke's use outside of that radius have constituted patent infringement?

The question of the effect of "conditional sales" of patented articles was addressed by the Federal Circuit in *Mallinckrodt, Inc. v. Medipart, Inc.*, 976 F.2d 700 (Fed. Cir. 1992). In that case, Mallinckrodt produced a patented device known as "UltraVent" which delivered a radioactive aerosol mist to the lungs of a patient for the diagnosis and treatment of pulmonary disease. Each UltraVent device was marked "Single Use Only." The package insert provided with each unit stated that the entire contaminated device should be disposed of as biohazardous waste material. Contrary to these instructions, several hospitals that purchased UltraVent devices did not dispose of them after the first use, but instead shipped them to Medipart, which sterilized and returned them to the hospitals as "reconditioned" devices. The hospitals then used these reconditioned devices in apparent violation of their "single use only" labeling. Mallinckrodt, upon learning of this practice, sued Medipart for patent infringement and inducement to infringe. It argued, among other things, that:

- the restriction on reuse could be construed as a label license for a specified field of use, wherein the field is single (i.e., disposable) use;
- the restriction is valid and enforceable under the patent law because the use is within the scope of the patent grant, and the restriction does not enlarge the patent grant;
- a license to less than all uses of a patented article is well recognized and a valid practice under patent law;
- the restriction is reasonable because it is based on health, safety, efficacy, and liability considerations and violates no public policy; and
- use in violation of the restriction is patent infringement.

The federal circuit agreed with Mallinckrodt, reasoning that:

If the sale of the UltraVent was validly conditioned under the applicable law such as the law governing sales and licenses, and if the restriction on reuse was within the scope of the patent grant or otherwise justified, then violation of the restriction may be remedied by action for patent infringement.

UltraVent™
Radioaerosol Delivery System
For Single Patient Use

Caution:

Rx Federal (U.S.A.) Law restricts this
ONLY device to sale by or on the order of a
physician.

**Ventilation Kit and Shield Instructions
For Use**

Warning:

This ventilation kit is FOR SINGLE
PATIENT USE ONLY. Reuse can cause
Single use cross-infection. After using this
ventilation kit once, it should be disposed
of using appropriate techniques for the
disposal of biohazardous materials.

(PHT) This product contains DEHP. The
intended use limits exposure to
DEHP transient contact, minimizing the risk
of DEHP release from the device. In order
to avoid undue risk of DEHP exposure in
children and nursing or pregnant women,
product should only be used as directed.

Assembly Instructions:

1. Remove the UltraVent Ventilation
   Kit from its packaging. Components
   include:

FIGURE 23.7 A portion of the product information brochure for Mallinckrodt's UltraVent device.

Impression Products, Inc. v. Lexmark International, Inc.

137 S. Ct. 1523 (2017)

ROBERTS, CHIEF JUSTICE

I

The underlying dispute in this case is about laser printers—or, more specifically, the cartridges that contain the powdery substance, known as toner, that laser printers use to make an image appear on paper. Respondent Lexmark International, Inc. designs, manufactures, and sells toner cartridges to consumers in the United States and around the globe. It owns a number of patents that cover components of those cartridges and the manner in which they are used. When toner cartridges run out of toner they can be refilled and used again. This creates an opportunity for other companies—known as remanufacturers—to acquire empty Lexmark cartridges from purchasers in the United States and abroad, refill them with toner, and then resell them at a lower price than the new ones Lexmark puts on the shelves. Not blind to this business problem, Lexmark structures its sales in a way that encourages customers to return spent cartridges. It gives purchasers two options: One is to buy a toner cartridge at full price, with no strings attached. The other is to buy a cartridge at roughly 20 percent off through Lexmark's "Return Program." A customer who buys through the Return Program still owns the cartridge but, in exchange for the lower price, signs a contract agreeing to use it only once and to refrain from transferring the empty cartridge to anyone but Lexmark. To enforce this single-use/no-resale restriction, Lexmark installs a microchip on each Return Program cartridge that prevents reuse once the toner in the cartridge runs out.

Lexmark's strategy just spurred remanufacturers to get more creative. Many kept acquiring empty Return Program cartridges and developed methods to counteract the effect of the microchips. With that technological obstacle out of the way, there was little to prevent the re-manufacturers from using the Return Program cartridges in their resale business. After all, Lexmark's contractual single-use/no-resale agreements were with the initial customers, not with downstream purchasers like the remanufacturers.

Lexmark, however, was not so ready to concede that its plan had been foiled. In 2010, it sued a number of remanufacturers, including petitioner Impression Products, Inc., for patent infringement with respect to two groups of cartridges. One group consists of Return Program cartridges that Lexmark sold within the United States. Lexmark argued that, because it expressly prohibited reuse and resale of these cartridges, the remanufacturers infringed the Lexmark patents when they refurbished and resold them. The other group consists of all toner cartridges that Lexmark sold abroad and that remanufacturers imported into the country. Lexmark claimed that it never gave anyone authority to import these cartridges, so the remanufacturers ran afoul of its patent rights by doing just that.

Eventually, the lawsuit was whittled down to one defendant, Impression Products, and one defense: that Lexmark's sales, both in the United States and abroad, exhausted its patent rights in the cartridges, so Impression Products was free to refurbish and resell them, and to import them if acquired abroad. Impression Products filed separate motions to dismiss with respect to both groups of cartridges. The District Court granted the motion as to the domestic Return Program cartridges, but denied the motion as to the cartridges Lexmark sold abroad. Both parties appealed.

The Federal Circuit considered the appeals *en banc* and ruled for Lexmark with respect to both groups of cartridges. The court began with the Return Program cartridges that Lexmark sold in the United States. Relying on its decision in *Mallinckrodt, Inc. v. Medipart, Inc.*, 976 F. 2d 700 (1992), the Federal Circuit held that a patentee may sell an item and retain the right to enforce, through patent infringement lawsuits, "clearly communicated … lawful restriction[s] as to post-sale use or resale." The exhaustion doctrine, the court reasoned, derives from the prohibition on making, using, selling, or importing items "without authority." When you purchase an item you presumptively also acquire the authority to use or resell the item freely, but that is just a presumption; the same authority does not run with the item when the seller restricts post-sale use or resale. Because the parties agreed that Impression Products knew about Lexmark's restrictions and that those restrictions did not violate any laws, the Federal Circuit concluded that Lexmark's sales had not exhausted all of its patent rights, and that the company could sue for infringement when Impression Products refurbished and resold Return Program cartridges.

Judge Dyk, joined by Judge Hughes, dissented. In their view, selling the Return Program cartridges in the United States exhausted Lexmark's patent rights in those items because any "authorized sale of a patented article … free[s] the article from any restrictions on use or sale based on the patent laws."

[*The Court's discussion of international exhaustion is contained in* Section 23.6]

We granted certiorari to consider the Federal Circuit's decisions … and now reverse.

II. A

First up are the Return Program cartridges that Lexmark sold in the United States. We conclude that Lexmark exhausted its patent rights in these cartridges the moment it sold them. The single-use/no-resale restrictions in Lexmark's contracts with customers may have been clear and enforceable under contract law, but they do not entitle Lexmark to retain patent rights in an item that it has elected to sell.

The Patent Act grants patentees the "right to exclude others from making, using, offering for sale, or selling [their] invention[s]." 35 U. S. C. §154(a). For over 160 years, the doctrine of patent exhaustion has imposed a limit on that right to exclude. The limit functions automatically: When a patentee chooses to sell an item, that product "is no longer within the limits of the monopoly" and instead becomes the "private, individual property" of the purchaser, with the rights and benefits that come along with ownership. A patentee is free to set the price and negotiate contracts with purchasers, but may not, "by virtue of his patent, control the use or disposition" of the product after ownership passes to the purchaser. *United States v. Univis Lens Co.*, 316 U. S. 241, 250 (1942). The sale "terminates all patent rights to that item." *Quanta Computer, Inc. v. LG Electronics, Inc.*, 553 U. S. 617, 625 (2008).

This well-established exhaustion rule marks the point where patent rights yield to the common law principle against restraints on alienation. The Patent Act "promote[s] the progress of science and the useful arts by granting to [inventors] a limited monopoly" that allows them to "secure the financial rewards" for their inventions. But once a patentee sells an item, it has "enjoyed all the rights secured" by that limited monopoly. *Keeler v. Standard Folding Bed Co.*, 157 U. S. 659, 661 (1895). Because "the purpose of the patent law is fulfilled … when the patentee has received his reward for the use of his invention," that law furnishes "no basis for restraining the use and enjoyment of the thing sold." *Univis*, 316 U. S., at 251.

This venerable principle is not, as the Federal Circuit dismissively viewed it, merely "one common-law jurisdiction's general judicial policy at one time toward anti-alienation restrictions." Congress enacted and has repeatedly revised the Patent Act against the backdrop of the hostility toward restraints on alienation. That enmity is reflected in the exhaustion doctrine. The patent laws do not include the right to "restrain[] … further alienation" after an initial sale; such conditions have been "hateful to the law from Lord Coke's day to ours" and are "obnoxious to the public interest." *Straus v. Victor Talking Machine Co.*, 243 U. S. 490, 501 (1917). "The inconvenience and annoyance to the public that an opposite conclusion would occasion are too obvious to require illustration." *Keeler*, 157 U. S., at 667.

But an illustration never hurts. Take a shop that restores and sells used cars. The business works because the shop can rest assured that, so long as those bringing in the cars own them, the shop is free to repair and resell those vehicles. That smooth flow of commerce would sputter if companies that make the thousands of parts that go into a vehicle could keep their patent rights after the first sale. Those companies might, for instance, restrict resale rights and sue the shop owner for patent infringement. And even if they refrained from imposing such restrictions, the very threat of patent liability would force the shop to invest in efforts to protect itself from hidden lawsuits. Either way, extending the patent rights beyond the first sale would clog the channels of commerce, with little benefit from the extra control that the patentees retain. And advances in technology, along with increasingly complex supply chains, magnify the problem.

This Court accordingly has long held that, even when a patentee sells an item under an express restriction, the patentee does not retain patent rights in that product. In *Boston Store of Chicago v. American Graphophone Co.*, for example, a manufacturer sold graphophones—one of the earliest devices for recording and reproducing sounds—to retailers under contracts requiring those stores to resell at a specific price. When the manufacturer brought a patent infringement suit against a retailer who sold for less, we concluded that there was "no room for controversy" about the result: By selling the item, the manufacturer placed it "beyond the confines of the patent law, [and] could not, by qualifying restrictions as to use, keep [it] under the patent monopoly."

Two decades later, we confronted a similar arrangement in *Univis*. There, a company that made eyeglass lenses authorized an agent to sell its products to wholesalers and retailers only if they promised to market the lenses at fixed prices. The Government filed an antitrust lawsuit, and the company defended its arrangement on the ground that it was exercising authority under the Patent Act. We held that the initial sales "relinquish[ed] ... the patent monopoly with respect to the article[s] sold," so the "stipulation ... fixing resale prices derive[d] no support from the patent and must stand on the same footing" as restrictions on unpatented goods.

It is true that *Boston Store* and *Univis* involved resale price restrictions that, at the time of those decisions, violated the antitrust laws. But in both cases it was the sale of the items, rather than the illegality of the restrictions, that prevented the patentees from enforcing those resale price agreements through patent infringement suits. And if there were any lingering doubt that patent exhaustion applies even when a sale is subject to an express, otherwise lawful restriction, our recent decision in *Quanta* settled the matter. In that case, a technology company—with authorization from the patentee—sold microprocessors under contracts requiring purchasers to use those processors with other parts that the company manufactured. One buyer disregarded the restriction, and the patentee sued for infringement. Without so much as mentioning the lawfulness of the contract, we held that the patentee could not bring an infringement suit because the "authorized sale ... took its products outside the scope of the patent monopoly."

Turning to the case at hand, we conclude that this well-settled line of precedent allows for only one answer: Lexmark cannot bring a patent infringement suit against Impression Products to enforce the single-use/no-resale provision accompanying its Return Program cartridges. Once sold, the Return Program cartridges passed outside of the patent monopoly, and whatever rights Lexmark retained are a matter of the contracts with its purchasers, not the patent law.

B

The Federal Circuit reached a different result largely because it got off on the wrong foot. The "exhaustion doctrine," the court believed, "must be understood as an interpretation of" the infringement statute, which prohibits anyone from using or selling a patented article "without authority" from the patentee. Exhaustion reflects a default rule that a patentee's decision to sell an item "presumptively grant[s] 'authority' to the purchaser to use it and resell it." But, the Federal Circuit explained, the patentee does not have to hand over the full "bundle of rights" every time. If the patentee expressly withholds a stick from the bundle—perhaps by restricting the purchaser's resale rights—the buyer never acquires that withheld authority, and the patentee may continue to enforce its right to exclude that practice under the patent laws.

The misstep in this logic is that the exhaustion doctrine is not a presumption about the authority that comes along with a sale; it is instead a limit on "the scope of the patentee's rights." *United States v. General Elec. Co.*, 272 U. S. 476, 489 (1926). The right to use, sell, or import an item exists independently of the Patent Act. What a patent adds—and grants exclusively to the patentee—is a limited right to prevent others from engaging in those practices. Exhaustion extinguishes that exclusionary power. As a result, the sale transfers the right to use, sell, or import because those are the rights that come along with ownership, and the buyer is free and clear of an infringement lawsuit because there is no exclusionary right left to enforce.

The Federal Circuit also expressed concern that preventing patentees from reserving patent rights when they sell goods would create an artificial distinction between such sales and sales by licensees. Patentees, the court explained, often license others to make and sell their products, and may place restrictions on those licenses. A computer developer could, for instance, license a manufacturer to make its patented devices and sell them only for non-commercial use by individuals. If a licensee breaches the license by selling a computer for commercial use, the patentee can sue the licensee for infringement. And, in the Federal Circuit's view, our decision in *General Talking Pictures Corp. v. Western Elec. Co.*, 304 U. S. 175 (1938), established that—when a patentee grants a license "under clearly stated restrictions on post-sale activities" of those who purchase products from the licensee—the patentee can also sue for infringement those purchasers who knowingly violate the restrictions. If patentees can employ licenses to impose post-sale restrictions on purchasers that are enforceable through infringement suits, the court concluded, it would make little sense to prevent patentees from doing so when they sell directly to consumers.

The Federal Circuit's concern is misplaced. A patentee can impose restrictions on licensees because a license does not implicate the same concerns about restraints on alienation as a sale. Patent exhaustion reflects the principle that, when an item passes into commerce, it should not be shaded by a legal cloud on title as it moves through the marketplace. But a license is not about passing title to a product, it is about changing the contours of the patentee's monopoly: The patentee agrees not to exclude a licensee from making or selling the patented invention, expanding the club of authorized producers and sellers. Because the patentee is exchanging rights, not goods, it is free to relinquish only a portion of its bundle of patent protections.

A patentee's authority to limit licensees does not, as the Federal Circuit thought, mean that patentees can use licenses to impose post-sale restrictions on purchasers that are enforceable through the patent laws. So long as a licensee complies with the license when selling an item, the patentee has, in effect, authorized the sale. That licensee's sale is treated, for purposes of patent exhaustion, as if the patentee made the sale itself. The result: The sale exhausts the patentee's rights in that item. A license may require the licensee to impose a restriction on purchasers, like the license limiting the computer manufacturer to selling for non-commercial use by individuals. But if the licensee does so—by, perhaps, having each customer sign a contract promising not to use the computers in business—the sale nonetheless exhausts all patent rights in the item sold. The purchasers might not comply with the restriction, but the only recourse for the licensee is through contract law, just as if the patentee itself sold the item with a restriction.

    General Talking Pictures involved a fundamentally different situation: There, a licensee "knowingly ma[de] ... sales ... outside the scope of its license." We treated the sale "as if no license whatsoever had been granted" by the patentee, which meant that the patentee could sue both the licensee and the purchaser—who knew about the breach—for infringement. This does not mean that patentees can use licenses to impose post-sale restraints on purchasers. Quite the contrary: The licensee infringed the patentee's rights because it did not comply with the terms of its license, and the patentee could bring a patent suit against the purchaser only because the purchaser participated in the licensee's infringement. *General Talking Pictures*, then, stands for the modest principle that, if a patentee has not given authority for a licensee to make a sale, that sale cannot exhaust the patentee's rights.

> *"if a patentee has not given authority for a licensee to make a sale, that sale cannot exhaust the patentee's rights"*

    In sum, patent exhaustion is uniform and automatic. Once a patentee decides to sell—whether on its own or through a licensee—that sale exhausts its patent rights, regardless of any post-sale restrictions the patentee purports to impose, either directly or through a license.

Notes and Questions

1. *Post-sale restrictions.* Cases like *Mallinckrodt* and *Impression Products* revolve around the desire of a patent holder to impose restrictions on users of patented articles after their first sale. As a general matter, why do patent holders wish to impose such restrictions after they have been compensated for the sale of a patented article? Do you think this approach is more common in certain types of industries?

2. *Infringement versus breach of contract.* In many cases, patent holders who impose post-sale restrictions on purchasers of patented products seek to enforce these restrictions as a matter of patent law (i.e., the user who fails to comply is infringing the patent) rather than as a breach of contract. Why? What role does privity of contract play in this calculation?

3. *Choice of defendant.* In *Mallinckrodt*, the patent holder chose to sue the party who sterilized and reconditioned used UltraVent devices rather than the hospitals who used the devices in violation of the single-use restriction. Why? Would there be any advantages to suing the hospitals themselves?

4. *The smooth flow of commerce.* The Supreme Court in *Impression Products* reasons that the "smooth flow of commerce would sputter if companies that make the thousands of parts that go into a vehicle could keep their patent rights after the first sale." What does this mean? Is this conclusion true with respect to all types of products and services, or is it specific to reusable items like printer ink cartridges?

5. *The end of post-sale restrictions?* Many commentators have questioned whether *Quanta*, and then *Impression Products*, effectively overrule *Mallinckrodt*, thus eliminating a patent holder's ability to impose post-sale restrictions on patented products as a matter of patent law (i.e., disregarding the purely contractual restrictions discussed in footnote 7 of *Quanta*). What

do you think? Are there any post-sale restrictions that survive *Quanta*, and then *Impression Products*? Did *Impression Products* close any loopholes potentially left open by *Quanta*?

6. *Copyright versus patent.* How does the Supreme Court's reasoning in patent exhaustion cases like *Quanta* and *Impression Products* contrast with the lower courts' treatment of copyrighted works under cases such as *Bobbs-Merrill* and *Vernor*? Is the difference more about copyright versus patent law, or about the unusual evolution of the software distribution market?

23.6 INTERNATIONAL FIRST SALE, EXHAUSTION AND GRAY MARKETS

In the cases discussed so far, we have largely focused on patents and sales of patented products in the United States. As they usually do, things become more complicated once we introduce the international distribution of products into the mix. Yet, given the global nature of many product markets – from tennis shoes and designer handbags to films and recorded music to smartphones and microchips, a consideration of international issues is unavoidable in any conscientious treatment of exhaustion issues. International issues can arise with respect to all types of IP. In this chapter we will consider cases (one of which you have seen before) that have defined the law in this area.

23.6.1 *International First Sale and Copyrights*

Kirtsaeng v. John Wiley & Sons, Inc.

568 U.S. 519 (2013)

BREYER, JUSTICE

Section 106 of the Copyright Act grants "the owner of copyright under this title" certain "exclusive rights," including the right "to distribute copies … of the copyrighted work to the public by sale or other transfer of ownership." 17 U. S. C. §106(3). These rights are qualified, however, by the application of various limitations [including] the "first sale" doctrine (§109).

Section 109(a) sets forth the "first sale" doctrine as follows:

> Notwithstanding the provisions of section 106(3) [the section that grants the owner exclusive distribution rights], the owner of a particular copy or phonorecord *lawfully made under this title* … is entitled, without the authority of the copyright owner, to sell or otherwise dispose of the possession of that copy or phonorecord. (Emphasis added.)

Thus, even though §106(3) forbids distribution of a copy of, say, the copyrighted novel *Herzog* without the copyright owner's permission, §109(a) adds that, once a copy of *Herzog* has been lawfully sold (or its ownership otherwise lawfully transferred), the buyer of *that copy* and subsequent owners are free to dispose of it as they wish. In copyright jargon, the "first sale" has "exhausted" the copyright owner's §106(3) exclusive distribution right.

What, however, if the copy of *Herzog* was printed abroad and then initially sold with the copyright owner's permission? Does the "first sale" doctrine still apply? Is the buyer, like the buyer of a domestically manufactured copy, free to bring the copy into the United States and dispose of it as he or she wishes?

To put the matter technically, an "importation" provision, §602(a)(1), says that

> "[i]mportation into the United States, without the authority of the owner of copyright under this title, of copies … of a work that have been acquired outside the United States is an infringement of the exclusive right to distribute copies … *under section 106* … ." 17 U. S. C. §602(a)(1) (emphasis added).

Thus §602(a)(1) makes clear that importing a copy without permission violates the owner's exclusive distribution right. But in doing so, §602(a)(1) refers explicitly to the §106(3) exclusive distribution right. As we have just said, §106 is by its terms "[s]ubject to" … §109(a)'s "first sale" limitation. Do those same modifications apply—in particular, does the "first sale" modification apply—when considering whether §602(a)(1) prohibits importing a copy?

In *Quality King Distributors, Inc. v. L'anza Research Int'l, Inc.*, 523 U. S. 135, 145 (1998), we held that §602(a)(1)'s reference to §106(3)'s exclusive distribution right incorporates the later subsections' limitations, including, in particular, the "first sale" doctrine of §109. Thus, it might seem that, §602(a)(1) notwithstanding, one who buys a copy abroad can freely import that copy into the United States and dispose of it, just as he could had he bought the copy in the United States.

But *Quality King* considered an instance in which the copy, though purchased abroad, was initially manufactured in the United States (and then sent abroad and sold). This case is like *Quality King* but for one important fact. The copies at issue here were manufactured abroad. That fact is important because §109(a) says that the "first sale" doctrine applies to "a particular copy or phonorecord lawfully made under this title." And we must decide here whether the five words, "lawfully made under this title," make a critical legal difference.

Putting section numbers to the side, we ask whether the "first sale" doctrine applies to protect a buyer or other lawful owner of a copy (of a copyrighted work) lawfully manufactured abroad. Can that buyer bring that copy into the United States (and sell it or give it away) without obtaining permission to do so from the copyright owner? Can, for example, someone who purchases, say at a used bookstore, a book printed abroad subsequently resell it without the copyright owner's permission?

In our view, the answers to these questions are, yes. We hold that the "first sale" doctrine applies to copies of a copyrighted work lawfully made abroad.

I. A

Respondent, John Wiley & Sons, Inc., publishes academic textbooks. Wiley obtains from its authors various foreign and domestic copyright assignments, licenses and permissions—to the point that we can, for present purposes, refer to Wiley as the relevant American copyright owner. Wiley often assigns to its wholly owned foreign subsidiary, John Wiley & Sons (Asia) Pte Ltd., rights to publish, print, and sell Wiley's English language textbooks abroad. Each copy of a Wiley Asia foreign edition will likely contain language making clear that the copy is to be sold only in a particular country or geographical region outside the United States.

For example, a copy of Wiley's American edition says, "Copyright © 2008 John Wiley & Sons, Inc. All rights reserved … Printed in the United States of America." A copy of Wiley Asia's Asian edition of that book says:

Copyright © 2008 John Wiley & Sons (Asia) Pte Ltd[.] All rights reserved. This book is authorized for sale in Europe, Asia, Africa, and the Middle East only and may be not exported out of these territories. Exportation from or importation of this book to another region without the Publisher's authorization is illegal and is a violation of the Publisher's rights. The Publisher may take legal action to enforce its rights ... Printed in Asia.

Both the foreign and the American copies say:

No part of this publication may be reproduced, stored in a retrieval system, or transmitted in any form or by any means ... except as permitted under Sections 107 or 108 of the 1976 United States Copyright Act.

The upshot is that there are two essentially equivalent versions of a Wiley textbook, each version manufactured and sold with Wiley's permission: (1) an American version printed and sold in the United States, and (2) a foreign version manufactured and sold abroad. And Wiley makes certain that copies of the second version state that they are not to be taken (without permission) into the United States.

Petitioner, Supap Kirtsaeng, a citizen of Thailand, moved to the United States in 1997 to study mathematics at Cornell University. He paid for his education with the help of a Thai Government scholarship which required him to teach in Thailand for 10 years on his return. Kirtsaeng successfully completed his undergraduate courses at Cornell, successfully completed a Ph.D program in mathematics at the University of Southern California, and then, as promised, returned to Thailand to teach. While he was studying in the United States, Kirtsaeng asked his friends and family in Thailand to buy copies of foreign edition English-language textbooks at Thai book shops, where they sold at low prices, and mail them to him in the United States. Kirtsaeng would then sell them, reimburse his family and friends, and keep the profit.

FIGURE 23.8 J. Walker, *Fundamentals of Physics* (Wiley, 8th ed. (US), 2008) – one of the textbooks at issue in *Kirtsaeng v. Wiley*.

B

In 2008 Wiley brought this federal lawsuit against Kirtsaeng for copyright infringement. Wiley claimed that Kirtsaeng's unauthorized importation of its books and his later resale of those books amounted to an infringement of Wiley's §106(3) exclusive right to distribute as well as §602's related import prohibition. Kirtsaeng replied that the books he had acquired were "'lawfully made'" and that he had acquired them legitimately. Thus, in his view, §109(a)'s "first sale" doctrine permitted him to resell or otherwise dispose of the books without the copyright owner's further permission.

The District Court held that Kirtsaeng could not assert the "first sale" defense because, in its view, that doctrine does not apply to "foreign-manufactured goods" (even if made abroad with the copyright owner's permission). The jury then found that Kirtsaeng had willfully infringed Wiley's American copyrights by selling and importing without authorization copies of eight of Wiley's copyrighted titles. And it assessed statutory damages of $600,000 ($75,000 per work).

On appeal, a split panel of the Second Circuit agreed with the District Court. It pointed out that §109(a)'s "first sale" doctrine applies only to "the owner of a particular copy ... *lawfully made under this title*." (emphasis added). And, in the majority's view, this language means that the "first sale" doctrine does not apply to copies of American copyrighted works manufactured abroad.

We granted Kirtsaeng's petition for certiorari to consider this question in light of different views among the Circuits.

II

We must decide whether the words "lawfully made under this title" restrict the scope of §109(a)'s "first sale" doctrine geographically. The Second Circuit, the Ninth Circuit, Wiley, and the Solicitor General (as amicus) all read those words as imposing a form of geographical limitation. The Second Circuit held that they limit the "first sale" doctrine to particular copies "made in territories in which the Copyright Act is law," which (the Circuit says) are copies "manufactured domestically," not "outside of the United States." Wiley agrees that those five words limit the "first sale" doctrine "to copies made in conformance with the [United States] Copyright Act where the Copyright Act is applicable," which (Wiley says) means it does not apply to copies made "outside the United States" and at least not to "foreign production of a copy for distribution exclusively abroad." Similarly, the Solicitor General says that those five words limit the "first sale" doctrine's applicability to copies "'made subject to and in compliance with [the Copyright Act],'" which (the Solicitor General says) are copies "made in the United States." And the Ninth Circuit has held that those words limit the "first sale" doctrine's applicability (1) to copies lawfully made in the United States, and (2) to copies lawfully made outside the United States but initially sold in the United States with the copyright owner's permission.

Under any of these geographical interpretations, §109(a)'s "first sale" doctrine would not apply to the Wiley Asia books at issue here. And, despite an American copyright owner's permission to make copies abroad, one who buys a copy of any such book or other copyrighted work—whether at a retail store, over the Internet, or at a library sale—could not resell (or otherwise dispose of) that particular copy without further permission.

Kirtsaeng, however, reads the words "lawfully made under this title" as imposing a non-geographical limitation. He says that they mean made "in accordance with" or "in compliance with" the Copyright Act. In that case, §109(a)'s "first sale" doctrine would apply to copyrighted works as long as their manufacture met the requirements of American copyright law. In particular, the doctrine would apply where, as here, copies are manufactured abroad with the permission of the copyright owner.

In our view, §109(a)'s language, its context, and the common-law history of the "first sale" doctrine, taken together, favor a non-geographical interpretation. We also doubt that Congress would have intended to create the practical copyright-related harms with which a geographical interpretation would threaten ordinary scholarly, artistic, commercial, and consumer activities. See Part II–D, infra. We consequently conclude that Kirtsaeng's nongeographical reading is the better reading of the Act.

B

[W]e normally presume that the words "lawfully made under this title" carry the same meaning when they appear in different but related sections. But doing so here produces surprising consequences. Consider:

(1) Section 109(c) says that, despite the copyright owner's exclusive right "to display" a copyrighted work (provided in §106(5)), the owner of a particular copy "lawfully made under this title" may publicly display it without further authorization. To interpret these words geographically would mean that one who buys a copyrighted work of art, a poster, or even a bumper sticker, in Canada, in Europe, in Asia, could not display it in America without the copyright owner's further authorization.

(2) Section 109(e) specifically provides that the owner of a particular copy of a copyrighted video arcade game "lawfully made under this title" may "publicly perform or display that game in coin-operated equipment" without the authorization of the copyright owner. To interpret these words geographically means that an arcade owner could not ("without the authority of the copyright owner") perform or display arcade games (whether new or used) originally made in Japan.

(3) Section 110(1) says that a teacher, without the copyright owner's authorization, is allowed to perform or display a copyrighted work (say, an audiovisual work) "in the course of face-to-face teaching activities"—unless the teacher knowingly used "a copy that was not lawfully made under this title." To interpret these words geographically would mean that the teacher could not (without further authorization) use a copy of a film during class if the copy was lawfully made in Canada, Mexico, Europe, Africa, or Asia.

C

A relevant canon of statutory interpretation favors a nongeographical reading. "[W]hen a statute covers an issue previously governed by the common law," we must presume that "Congress intended to retain the substance of the common law."

The "first sale" doctrine is a common-law doctrine with an impeccable historic pedigree. In the early 17th century Lord Coke explained the common law's refusal to permit restraints on the alienation of chattels: A law that permits a copyright holder to control the resale or other disposition of a chattel once sold is ... "against Trade and Traffi[c], and bargaining and contracting."

With these last few words, Coke emphasizes the importance of leaving buyers of goods free to compete with each other when reselling or otherwise disposing of those goods. American law too has generally thought that competition, including freedom to resell, can work to the advantage of the consumer.

The "first sale" doctrine also frees courts from the administrative burden of trying to enforce restrictions upon difficult-to-trace, readily movable goods. And it avoids the selective enforcement inherent in any such effort. Thus, it is not surprising that for at least a century the "first sale" doctrine has played an important role in American copyright law. See *Bobbs-Merrill Co. v. Straus*, 210 U. S. 339 (1908).

The common-law doctrine makes no geographical distinctions; nor can we find any in *Bobbs-Merrill* (where this Court first applied the "first sale" doctrine) or in §109(a)'s predecessor provision, which Congress enacted a year later. Rather, as the Solicitor General acknowledges, a straightforward application of *Bobbs-Merrill* would not preclude the "first sale" defense from applying to authorized copies made overseas. And we can find no language, context, purpose, or history that would rebut a "straightforward application" of that doctrine here.

D

Associations of libraries, used-book dealers, technology companies, consumer-goods retailers, and museums point to various ways in which a geographical interpretation would fail to further basic constitutional copyright objectives, in particular "promot[ing] the Progress of Science and useful Arts." U. S. Const., Art. I, §8, cl. 8.

The American Library Association tells us that library collections contain at least 200 million books published abroad; that many others were first published in the United States but printed abroad because of lower costs; and that a geographical interpretation will likely require the libraries to obtain permission (or at least create significant uncertainty) before circulating or otherwise distributing these books.

How, the American Library Association asks, are the libraries to obtain permission to distribute these millions of books? How can they find, say, the copyright owner of a foreign book, perhaps written decades ago? They may not know the copyright holder's present address. And, even where addresses can be found, the costs of finding them, contacting owners, and negotiating may be high indeed. Are the libraries to stop circulating or distributing or displaying the millions of books in their collections that were printed abroad?

Used-book dealers tell us that, from the time when Benjamin Franklin and Thomas Jefferson built commercial and personal libraries of foreign books, American readers have bought used books published and printed abroad. The dealers say that they have "operat[ed] ... for centuries" under the assumption that the "first sale" doctrine applies. But under a geographical interpretation a contemporary tourist who buys, say, at Shakespeare and Co. (in Paris), a dozen copies of a foreign book for American friends might find that she had violated the copyright law. The used-book dealers cannot easily predict what the foreign copyright holder may think about a reader's effort to sell a used copy of a novel. And they believe that a geographical interpretation will injure a large portion of the used-book business.

Technology companies tell us that "automobiles, microwaves, calculators, mobile phones, tablets, and personal computers" contain copyrightable software programs or packaging. Many of these items are made abroad with the American copyright holder's permission and then sold and imported (with that permission) to the United States. A geographical interpretation would prevent the resale of, say, a car, without the permission of the holder of each copyright on each piece of copyrighted automobile software. Yet there is no reason to believe that foreign auto manufacturers regularly obtain this kind of permission from their software component suppliers, and Wiley did not indicate to the contrary when asked. Without that permission a foreign car owner could not sell his or her used car.

Retailers tell us that over $2.3 trillion worth of foreign goods were imported in 2011. American retailers buy many of these goods after a first sale abroad. And, many of these items bear, carry, or contain copyrighted "packaging, logos, labels, and product inserts and instructions for [the use of] everyday packaged goods from floor cleaners and health and beauty products to breakfast cereals." The retailers add that American sales of more traditional copyrighted works, "such as books, recorded music, motion pictures, and magazines" likely amount to over $220 billion. A geographical interpretation would subject many, if not all, of them to the disruptive impact of the threat of infringement suits.

Art museum directors ask us to consider their efforts to display foreign-produced works by, say, Cy Twombly, René Magritte, Henri Matisse, Pablo Picasso, and others. A geographical interpretation, they say, would require the museums to obtain permission from the copyright owners before they could display the work—even if the copyright owner has already sold or donated the work to a foreign museum. What are the museums to do, they ask, if the artist retained the copyright, if the artist cannot be found, or if a group of heirs is arguing about who owns which copyright?

Neither Wiley nor any of its many amici deny that a geographical interpretation could bring about these "horribles"—at least in principle. Rather, Wiley essentially says that the list is artificially invented. It points out that a federal court first adopted a geographical interpretation more than 30 years ago. Yet, it adds, these problems have not occurred. Why not? Because, says Wiley, the problems and threats are purely theoretical; they are unlikely to reflect reality.

[T]he fact that harm has proved limited so far may simply reflect the reluctance of copyright holders so far to assert geographically based resale rights. They may decide differently if the law is clarified in their favor. Regardless, a copyright law that can work in practice only if unenforced is not a sound copyright law. It is a law that would create uncertainty, would bring about selective enforcement, and, if widely unenforced, would breed disrespect for copyright law itself.

Thus, we believe that the practical problems that petitioner and his amici have described are too serious, too extensive, and too likely to come about for us to dismiss them as insignificant—particularly in light of the ever-growing importance of foreign trade to America. The upshot is that copyright-related consequences along with language, context, and interpretive canons argue strongly against a geographical interpretation of §109(a).

IV

For these reasons we conclude that the considerations supporting Kirtsaeng's nongeographical interpretation of the words "lawfully made under this title" are the more persuasive. The judgment of the Court of Appeals is reversed, and the case is remanded for further proceedings consistent with this opinion.

Notes and Questions

1. *Statutory interpretation.* Justice Breyer's analysis in *Kirtsaeng* focuses in excruciating detail on the language of Section 109(a) of the Copyright Act – the statutory codification of the first sale doctrine. Yet Chief Justice Roberts hardly considers statutory language at all in *Impression Products*. Why is there such a difference in approach as between copyright and patent law with respect to international exhaustion?

23.6.2 *International Patent Exhaustion*

Impression Products, Inc. v. Lexmark International, Inc.
137 S. Ct. 1523 (2017)

ROBERTS, CHIEF JUSTICE

[*The case background and a discussion of exhaustion, generally, are contained in* Section 23.5.]

Our conclusion that Lexmark exhausted its patent rights when it sold the domestic Return Program cartridges goes only halfway to resolving this case. Lexmark also sold toner cartridges abroad and sued Impression Products for patent infringement for "importing [Lexmark's]invention into the United States." 35 U. S. C. §154(a). Lexmark contends that it may sue for infringement with respect to all of the imported cartridges—not just those in the Return Program—because a foreign sale does not trigger patent exhaustion unless the patentee "expressly or implicitly transfer[s] or license[s]" its rights. The Federal Circuit agreed, but we do not. An authorized sale outside the United States, just as one within the United States, exhausts all rights under the Patent Act. This question about international exhaustion of intellectual property rights has also arisen in the context of copyright law. Under the "first sale doctrine," which is codified at 17 U. S. C. §109(a), when a copyright owner sells a lawfully made copy of its work, it loses the power to restrict the purchaser's freedom "to sell or otherwise dispose of … that copy." In *Kirtsaeng v. John Wiley & Sons, Inc.*, we held that this "'first sale' [rule] applies to copies of a copyrighted work lawfully made [and sold] abroad." We began with the text of §109(a), but it was not decisive: The language neither "restrict[s] the scope of [the] 'first sale' doctrine geographically," nor clearly embraces international exhaustion. What helped tip the scales for global exhaustion was the fact that the first sale doctrine originated in the common law's refusal to permit restraints on the alienation of chattels. That common-law doctrine makes no geographical distinctions. The lack of any textual basis for distinguishing between domestic and international sales meant that "a straightforward application" of the first sale doctrine required the conclusion that it applies overseas.

Applying patent exhaustion to foreign sales is just as straightforward. Patent exhaustion, too, has its roots in the antipathy toward restraints on alienation, and nothing in the text or history of the Patent Act shows that Congress intended to confine that borderless common law principle to domestic sales. In fact, Congress has not altered patent exhaustion at all; it remains an unwritten limit on the scope of the patentee's monopoly. And differentiating the patent exhaustion and copyright first sale doctrines would make little theoretical or practical sense: The two share a "strong similarity … and identity of purpose," and many everyday products—"automobiles, microwaves, calculators, mobile phones, tablets, and personal computers"—are subject to both patent and copyright protections, see *Kirtsaeng*, 568 U.S., at 545. There is a "historic kinship between patent law and copyright law," and the bond between the two leaves no room for a rift on the question of international exhaustion.

Lexmark sees the matter differently. The Patent Act, it points out, limits the patentee's "right to exclude others" from making, using, selling, or importing its products to acts that occur in the United States. 35 U. S. C. §154(a). A domestic sale, it argues, triggers exhaustion because the sale compensates the patentee for "surrendering [those] U. S. rights." A foreign sale is different: The Patent Act does not give patentees exclusionary powers abroad. Without those powers, a patentee selling in a foreign market may not be able to sell its product for the same price that it could in the United States, and therefore is not sure to receive "the reward guaranteed by U. S. patent law." Absent that reward, says Lexmark, there should be no exhaustion. In short, there is no patent exhaustion from sales abroad because there are no patent rights abroad to exhaust.

The territorial limit on patent rights is, however, no basis for distinguishing copyright protections; those protections "do not have any extraterritorial operation" either. Nor does the territorial limit support the premise of Lexmark's argument. Exhaustion is a separate limit on the patent grant, and does not depend on the patentee receiving some undefined premium for selling the right to access the American market. A purchaser buys an item, not patent rights. And exhaustion is triggered by the patentee's decision to give that item up and receive whatever fee it decides is appropriate "for the article and the invention which it embodies." *Univis*, 316 U. S., at 251. The patentee may not be able to command the same amount for its products abroad as it does in the United States. But the Patent Act does not guarantee a particular price, much less the price from selling to American consumers. Instead, the right to exclude just ensures that the patentee receives one reward—of whatever amount the patentee deems to be "satisfactory compensation," *Keeler*, 157 U. S., at 661—for every item that passes outside the scope of the patent monopoly.

This Court has addressed international patent exhaustion in only one case, *Boesch v. Gräff*, decided over 125 years ago. All that case illustrates is that a sale abroad does not exhaust a patentee's rights when the patentee had nothing to do with the transaction. *Boesch*—from the days before the widespread adoption of electrical lighting—involved a retailer who purchased lamp burners from a manufacturer in Germany, with plans to sell them in the United States. The manufacturer had authority to make the burners under German law, but there was a hitch: Two individuals with no ties to the German manufacturer held the American patent to that invention. These patentees sued the retailer for infringement when the retailer imported the lamp burners into the United States, and we rejected the argument that the German manufacturer's sale had exhausted the American patentees' rights. The German manufacturer had no permission to sell in the United States from the American patentees, and the American patentees had not exhausted their patent rights in the products because they had not sold them to anyone, so "purchasers from [the German manufacturer] could not be thereby authorized to sell the articles in the United States." 133 U. S. 697, 703 (1890).

Our decision did not, as Lexmark contends, exempt all foreign sales from patent exhaustion. Rather, it reaffirmed the basic premise that only the patentee can decide whether to make a sale that exhausts its patent rights in an item. The American patentees did not do so with respect to the German products, so the German sales did not exhaust their rights.

Finally, the United States, as an amicus, advocates what it views as a middle-ground position: that "a foreign sale authorized by the U. S. patentee exhausts U. S. patent rights unless those rights are expressly reserved." Its position is largely based on policy rather than principle. The Government thinks that an overseas "buyer's legitimate expectation" is that a "sale conveys all of the seller's interest in the patented article," so the presumption should be that a foreign sale triggers exhaustion. But, at the same time, lower courts long ago coalesced around the rule that "a patentee's express reservation of U.S. patent rights at the time of a foreign sale will be given effect," so that option should remain open to the patentee.

The theory behind the Government's express-reservation rule also wrongly focuses on the likely expectations of the patentee and purchaser during a sale. Exhaustion does not arise because of the parties' expectations about how sales transfer patent rights. More is at stake when it comes to patents than simply the dealings between the parties, which can be addressed through contract law. Instead, exhaustion occurs because, in a sale, the patentee elects to give up title to an item in exchange for payment. Allowing patent rights to stick remora-like to that item as it flows through the market would violate the principle against restraints on alienation. Exhaustion does not depend on whether the patentee receives a premium for selling in the United States, or the type of rights that buyers expect to receive. As a result, restrictions and location are irrelevant; what matters is the patentee's decision to make a sale.

The judgment of the United States Court of Appeals for the Federal Circuit is reversed, and the case is remanded for further proceedings consistent with this opinion.

It is so ordered.

JUSTICE GINSBURG, concurring in part and dissenting in part.

I concur in the Court's holding regarding domestic exhaustion—a patentee who sells a product with an express restriction on reuse or resale may not enforce that restriction through an infringement lawsuit, because the U.S. sale exhausts the U.S. patent rights in the product sold. I dissent, however, from the Court's holding on international exhaustion. A foreign sale, I would hold, does not exhaust a U.S. inventor's U.S. patent rights. Patent law is territorial. When an inventor receives a U.S. patent, that patent provides no protection abroad. A U.S. patentee must apply to each country in which she seeks the exclusive right to sell her invention.

Because a sale abroad operates independently of the U.S. patent system, it makes little sense to say that such a sale exhausts an inventor's U.S. patent rights. U.S. patent protection accompanies none of a U.S. patentee's sales abroad—a competitor could sell the same patented product abroad with no U.S.-patent-law consequence. Accordingly, the foreign sale should not diminish the protections of U.S. law in the United States.

The majority disagrees, in part because this Court decided, in *Kirtsaeng v. John Wiley & Sons, Inc.*, 568 U. S. 519, 525 (2013), that a foreign sale exhausts U. S. copyright protections. Copyright and patent exhaustion, the majority states, "share a strong similarity." I dissented from our decision in *Kirtsaeng* and adhere to the view that a foreign sale should not exhaust U.S. copyright protections.

But even if I subscribed to *Kirtsaeng's* reasoning with respect to copyright, that decision should bear little weight in the patent context. Although there may be a "historical kinship" between patent law and copyright law, the two "are not identical twins". The Patent Act contains no analogue to 17 U.S.C. §109(a), the Copyright Act first-sale provision analyzed in *Kirtsaeng*. More importantly, copyright protections, unlike patent protections,

> are harmonized across countries. Under the Berne Convention, which 174 countries have joined, members "agree to treat authors from other member countries as well as they treat their own." The copyright protections one receives abroad are thus likely to be similar to those received at home, even if provided under each country's separate copyright regime.
>
> For these reasons, I would affirm the Federal Circuit's judgment with respect to foreign exhaustion.

FIGURE 23.9 Justice Ruth Bader Ginsburg dissented in both *Kirtsaeng* and *Impression Products*.

Notes and Questions

1. *Copyright versus patent.* Despite the difference in approach discussed in Note 1, Chief Justice Roberts relies in his reasoning in *Impression Products* on the "historical kinship" between patent law and copyright law. Justice Ginsburg, dissenting, argues that the two "are not identical twins." What is the crux of this disagreement between the justices? Which view of the relationship between patent and copyright law do you consider to be stronger?

23.6.3 *International Trademark Exhaustion and the Gray Market*

As discussed in Section 23.3, "genuine" trademarked goods may be resold without the authorization of the trademark owner. This is also the case internationally. An overseas purchaser of an authorized marked product may import it into the United States so long as the foreign product is "genuine," or manufactured under authority of the mark owner. Take the example of Nike athletic shoes. Nike may authorize a manufacturer in Thailand to manufacture a particular type of branded shoe. Under its contract with Nike, the Thai manufacturer may then sell those shoes for $20 per pair to Nike's authorized wholesalers, who distribute them to retailers in the United States who sell them to consumers for $150 per pair. But suppose that the Thai manufacturer makes a few extra shoes and sells them at $30 per pair to discount Nike retailers in the United States, who then sell them to consumers for $50 per pair? It is possible that the Thai manufacturer is violating its contract with Nike, but can Nike prevent the sale of the shoes by the discount retailers in the United States under trademark law if they are the exact same shoes that authorized resellers are selling for $150? This scenario illustrates what is called the "gray market" for trademarked goods.

Made in Thailand under license from Nike (TL)

Imported to U.S.

Sold in U.S. w/o permission of Nike (US)

FIGURE 23.10 Flow of goods in the "gray market."

You will note the similarities in this scenario to those described in *Kirtsaeng* and *Impression Products*. Yet trademark law was the first place in which international exhaustion was recognized – long before the Supreme Court intervened in the copyright and patent areas.

The key question in international trademark exhaustion cases[11] is whether the imported goods are, in fact, "genuine," as trademark law does not extend to the sale of genuine goods. But as the Third Circuit explained in *Iberia Foods Corp. v. Romeo*, 150 F.3d 298, 303 (3d Cir. 1998), where imported goods are marketed under identical marks but are materially different, the alleged infringer's goods are considered "non-genuine" and the sale of the goods constitutes infringement. This leads, naturally, to the question of what constitutes a "material difference" for purposes of international trademark exhaustion. The question has attracted significant attention and is addressed in detail in the following case.

Societe Des Produits Nestle, S.A. v. Casa Helvetia, Inc.
982 F.2d 633 (1st Cir. 1992)

SELYA, CIRCUIT JUDGE

This bittersweet appeal requires us to address the protection that trademark law affords a registrant against the importation and sale of so-called "gray goods," that is, trademarked goods manufactured abroad under a valid license but brought into this country in derogation of arrangements lawfully made by the trademark holder to ensure territorial exclusivity. As we explain below, the scope of protection turns on the degree of difference between the product authorized for the domestic market and the allegedly infringing product. In the case before us, the difference is sufficiently marked that the domestic product warrants protection.

I. Background

PERUGINA chocolates originated in Italy and continue to be manufactured there. They are sold throughout the world and cater to a sophisticated consumer, a refined palate, and an indulgent budget. Societe Des Produits Nestle, S.A. (Nestle S.P.N.) owns the PERUGINA trademark.

---

[11] This section focuses on the treatment of international trademark exhaustion under US law. Of course, every country can approach the issue slightly differently. For a summary and comparison of approaches in other jurisdictions see Irene Calboli, *The Relationship between Trademark Exhaustion and Free Movement of Goods: A Review of Selected Jurisdictions and Regional Organizations* in The Cambridge Handbook of International and Comparative Trademark Law 589 (Irene Calboli & Jane C. Ginsburg, eds., Cambridge, Univ. Press, 2020).

FIGURE 23.11 Nestlé sought to prevent its former distributor from importing Venezuelan Perugina-branded chocolates into Puerto Rico.

For many years, defendant-appellee Casa Helvetia, Inc. was the authorized distributor of PERUGINA chocolates in Puerto Rico. On November 28, 1988, however, Nestle S.P.N. forsook Casa Helvetia and licensed its affiliate, Nestle Puerto Rico, Inc. (Nestle P.R.), as the exclusive Puerto Rican distributor.

At this point, the plot thickened. Nestle S.P.N. had previously licensed an independent company, Distribuidora Nacional de Alimentos La Universal S.A. (Alimentos), to manufacture and sell chocolates bearing the PERUGINA mark in Venezuela. The Venezuelan sweets differ from the Italian sweets in presentation, variety, composition, and price. In March 1990, without obtaining Nestle S.P.N.'s consent, Casa Helvetia began to purchase the Venezuelan-made chocolates through a middleman, import them into Puerto Rico, and distribute them under the PERUGINA mark.

This maneuver drew a swift response. Charging that Casa Helvetia's marketing of the Venezuelan candies infringed both Nestle S.P.N.'s registered trademark and Nestle P.R.'s right of exclusive distributorship, Nestle S.P.N. and Nestle P.R. (hereinafter collectively "Nestle") sued under the Lanham Act. They claimed that Casa Helvetia's use of the PERUGINA label was "likely to confuse consumers into the mistaken belief that the Venezuelan chocolates are the same as the Italian chocolates and are authorized by Nestle for sale in Puerto Rico." And, they asserted that, because the PERUGINA name in Puerto Rico is associated with Italian-made chocolates, the importation of materially different Venezuelan chocolates threatened to erode "the integrity of the PERUGINA trademarks as symbols of consistent quality and goodwill in Puerto Rico."

The district court consolidated the hearing on preliminary injunction with the hearing on the merits, and, after taking testimony, ruled in the defendants' favor. It held that the differences between the Italian-made and Venezuelan-made candies did not warrant injunctive relief in the absence of demonstrated consumer dissatisfaction, harm to plaintiffs' good will, or drop-off in product quality. This appeal followed.

II. The Lanham Act Claims

Two amaranthine principles fuel the Lanham Act. One aims at protecting consumers. The other focuses on protecting registrants and their assignees. These interlocking principles, in turn, are linked to a concept of territorial exclusivity.

1. *Animating Principles*. Every product is composed of a bundle of special characteristics. The consumer who purchases what he believes is the same product expects to receive those special characteristics on every occasion. Congress enacted the Lanham Act to realize this expectation with regard to goods bearing a particular trademark. The Act's prophylaxis operates not only in the more obvious cases, involving the sale of inferior goods in derogation of the registrant's mark, but also in the less obvious cases, involving the sale of goods different from, although not necessarily inferior to, the goods that the customer expected to receive. By guaranteeing consistency, a trademark wards off both consumer confusion and possible deceit.

The system also serves another, equally important, purpose by protecting the trademark owner's goodwill. Once again, this protection comprises more than merely stopping the sale of inferior goods. Even if an infringer creates a product that rivals or exceeds the quality of the registrant's product, the wrongful sale of the unauthorized product may still deprive the registrant of his ability to shape the contours of his reputation.

2. *Territoriality*. In general, trademark rights are congruent with the boundaries of the sovereign that registers (or recognizes) the mark. Such territoriality reinforces the basic goals of trademark law. Because products are often tailored to specific national conditions, see *Lever Bros. Co. v. United States*, 877 F.2d 101, 108 (D.C. Cir. 1989), a trademark's reputation (and, hence, its goodwill) often differs from nation to nation. Because that is so, the importation of goods properly trademarked abroad but not intended for sale locally may confuse consumers and may well threaten the local mark owner's goodwill. It is not surprising, then, that the United States Supreme Court long ago recognized the territoriality of trademark rights.

Of course, territoriality only goes so far. By and large, courts do not read [prior cases] to disallow the lawful importation of identical foreign goods carrying a valid foreign trademark. See, e.g., *NEC Elecs., Inc. v. Cal Circuit Abco*, 810 F.2d 1506 (9th Cir.), *cert. denied*, 484 U.S. 851 (1987). Be that as it may, territorial protection kicks in under the Lanham Act where two merchants sell physically different products in the same market and under the same name, for it is this prototype that impinges on a trademark holder's goodwill and threatens to deceive consumers. Indeed, without such territorial trademark protection, competitors purveying country-specific products could exploit consumer confusion and free ride on the goodwill of domestic trademarks with impunity. Such a scenario would frustrate the underlying goals of the Lanham Act, the "plain language and general sweep" of which "undeniably bespeak an intention to protect domestic trademark holders." *Lever Bros.*, 877 F.2d at 105. Thus, where material differences exist between similarly marked goods, the Lanham Act honors the important linkage between trademark law and geography.

In this case … liability necessarily turns on the existence *vel non* of material differences between the products of a sort likely to create consumer confusion. Because the presence or absence of a material difference – a difference likely to cause consumer confusion – is the pivotal determinant of Lanham Act infringement in a gray goods case, the lower court's insistence on several other evidentiary showings was inappropriate.

III. The Materiality Threshold

When a trial court misperceives and misapplies the law, remand may or may not be essential. Here, a final judgment under the correct rule of law requires only the determination of whether reported differences between the Venezuelan and Italian products are material.

It follows, then, that we must examine the legal standard for materiality before deciding whether to remand.

Under the Lanham Act, only those appropriations of a mark that are likely to cause confusion are prohibited. Ergo, when a product identical to a domestic product is imported into the United States under the same mark, no violation of the Lanham Act occurs. In such a situation, consumers get exactly the bundle of characteristics that they associate with the mark and the domestic distributor can be said to enjoy in large measure his investment in goodwill. By the same token, using the same mark on two blatantly different products normally does not offend the Lanham Act, for such use is unlikely to cause confusion and is, therefore, unlikely to imperil the goodwill of either product.

The probability of confusion is great, however, when the same mark is displayed on goods that are not identical but that nonetheless bear strong similarities in appearance or function. Gray goods often fall within this category. Thus, when dealing with the importation of gray goods, a reviewing court must necessarily be concerned with subtle differences, for it is by subtle differences that consumers are most easily confused. For that reason, the threshold of materiality must be kept low enough to take account of potentially confusing differences – differences that are not blatant enough to make it obvious to the average consumer that the origin of the product differs from his or her expectations.

There is no mechanical way to determine the point at which a difference becomes "material." Separating wheat from chaff must be done on a case-by-case basis. Bearing in mind the policies and provisions of the Lanham Act as they apply to gray goods, we can confidently say that the threshold of materiality is always quite low in such cases. See *Lever Bros.*, 877 F.2d at 103, 108 (finding minor differences in ingredients and packaging between versions of deodorant soap to be material); *Ferrero*, 753 F. Supp. at 1241–49, 1247 (finding a one-half calorie difference in chemical composition of breath mints, coupled with slight differences in packaging and labeling, to be material); *PepsiCo Inc. v. Nostalgia*, 18 U.S.P.Q.2D (BNA) at 1405 (finding "differences in labeling, packaging and marketing methods" to be material); *PepsiCo v. Giraud*, 7 U.S.P.Q.2D (BNA) at 1373 (finding differences not readily apparent to the consumer – container volume, packaging, quality control, and advertising participation – to be material); *Dial Corp.*, 643 F. Supp. at 952 (finding differences in formulation and packaging of soap products to be material).

We conclude that the existence of any difference between the registrant's product and the allegedly infringing gray good that consumers would likely consider to be relevant when purchasing a product creates a presumption of consumer confusion sufficient to support a Lanham Act claim. Any higher threshold would endanger a manufacturer's investment in product goodwill and unduly subject consumers to potential confusion by severing the tie between a manufacturer's protected mark and its associated bundle of traits.

The alleged infringer, of course, may attempt to rebut this presumption, but in order to do so he must be able to prove by preponderant evidence that the differences are not of the kind that consumers, on average, would likely consider in purchasing the product.

"the existence of any difference between the registrant's product and the allegedly infringing gray good that consumers would likely consider to be relevant when purchasing a product creates a presumption of consumer confusion sufficient to support a Lanham Act claim."

The alleged infringer, of course, may attempt to rebut this presumption, but in order to do so he must be able to prove by preponderant evidence that the differences are not of the kind that consumers, on average, would likely consider in purchasing the product.

IV. Materiality in This Case

Having fashioned the standard of materiality and examined the record in light of that standard, we are drawn to the conclusion that remand is not required. The district court determined that the products are different but that the differences are not material. Although this determination is tainted by a misunderstanding of the applicable legal principles, the court's subsidiary findings are, nonetheless, reasonably explicit and subject to reuse. Hence, we proceed to take the lower court's supportable findings of fact, couple them with other, uncontradicted facts, and, using the rule of law articulated above, determine for ourselves whether the admitted differences between the Venezuelan-made chocolates and the Italian-made chocolates are sufficiently material to warrant injunctive relief.

A Catalog of Differences.

The district court identified numerous differences between the competing products. Because the record supports these findings and the parties do not contest their validity, we accept them. We add, however, other potentially significant distinctions made manifest by the record.

1. Quality Control. Although Nestle and Casa Helvetia each oversees the quality of the product it sells, the record reflects, and Casa Helvetia concedes, that their procedures differ radically. The Italian PERUGINA leaves Italy in refrigerated containers which arrive at Nestle's facility in Puerto Rico. Nestle verifies the temperature of the coolers, opens them, and immediately transports the chocolates to refrigerated rooms. The company records the product's date of manufacture, conducts laboratory tests, and destroys those candies that have expired. It then transports the salable chocolates to retailers in refrigerated trucks. Loading and unloading is performed only in the cool morning hours.

   On the other hand, the Venezuelan product arrives in Puerto Rico via commercial air freight. During the afternoon hours, airline personnel remove the chocolates from the containers in which they were imported and place them in a central air cargo cooler. The next morning, employees of Casa Helvetia open random boxes at the airport to see if the chocolates have melted. The company then transports the candy in a refrigerated van to a warehouse. Casa Helvetia performs periodic inspections before delivering the goods to its customers in a refrigerated van. The record contains no evidence that Casa Helvetia knows or records the date the chocolates were manufactured.

2. Composition. The district court enumerated a number of differences in ingredients. The Italian BACI candies have five percent more milk fat than their Venezuelan counterparts, thus prolonging shelf life. Furthermore, the Italian BACI chocolates contain Ecuadorian and African cocoa beans, fresh hazelnuts, and cooked sugar syrup, whereas the corresponding Venezuelan candies are made with domestic beans, imported hazelnuts, and ordinary crystal sugar.

3. Configuration. The district court specifically noted that the Italian chocolates in the Maitre Confiseur and Assortment collections come in a greater variety of shapes than the Venezuelan pieces.

4. Packaging. The district court observed differences in the "boxes, wrappers and trays" between the Italian and Venezuelan versions of the various chocolate assortments. For example, the packages from Italy possess a glossy finish and are either silver, brown, or gold in color. The Venezuelan boxes lack the shiny finish. They are either blue, red,

or yellow in color. While the Italian sweets sit in gold or silver trays, their Venezuelan counterparts rest on white or transparent trays. The Italian boxes depict the chocolates inside and describe the product in English, French, and Italian. The Venezuelan packages describe the contents only in Spanish and English. Moreover, only the BACI box illustrates what is inside.

5. Price. The district court pointed out that while the Venezuelan and Italian BACI collections contain the same quantity of chocolate (8 oz.), the Italian BACI sells for $12.99 and the Venezuelan BACI costs $7.50. The record also reflects that the Italian version of the Assortment collection (14.25 oz. for $26.99) weighs less and is more expensive than the Venezuelan version (15.6 oz. for $22.99).

Applying the Standard

Applying the legal standard discussed in Part III, supra, to the record at bar, it is readily apparent that material differences exist between the Italian and Venezuelan PERUGINA. These differences – which implicate quality, composition, packaging, and price – if not overwhelming, are certainly relevant. We run the gamut.

Differences in quality control methods, although not always obvious to the naked eye, are nonetheless important to the consumer. The precautions a company takes to preserve a food product's freshness are a prime example. Here, the parties' quality control procedures differ significantly. Even if Casa Helvetia's quality control measures are as effective as Nestle's – a dubious proposition on this record – the fact that Nestle is unable to oversee the quality of the goods for the entire period until they reach the consumer is significant in ascertaining whether a Lanham Act violation exists. Regardless of the offending goods' actual quality, courts have issued Lanham Act injunctions solely because of the trademark owner's inability to control the quality of the goods bearing its name. Thus, the substantial variance in quality control here creates a presumption of customer confusion as a matter of law.

The differences in presentation of the candies are also material. Although the district court dismissed the differences in packaging as "subtle," subtle differences are, as we have said, precisely the type that heighten the presumption of customer confusion. Consumers are more likely to be confused as to the origin of different goods bearing the same name when both goods are substantially identical in appearance. Furthermore, the differences in presentation and chocolate shape strike us as more than subtle. Glossy veneers, gold and silver wraps, and delicate sculpting add to the consumer's perception of quality. In the market for premium chocolates, often purchased as gifts, an elegant-looking package is an important consideration. The cosmetic differences between the Italian-made and the Venezuelan-made PERUGINA, therefore, might well perplex consumers and harm Nestle's goodwill.

We are also hesitant to dismiss as trivial the differences in ingredients. While the district court may be correct in suggesting that "the ultimate consumer is [not] concerned about the country of origin of cocoa beans and hazelnuts," the measure of milk fat in the chocolates is potentially significant. Certainly, consumers care about the expected shelf life of food products.

Price, without doubt, is also a variable with which purchasers are concerned. To the consumer (perhaps a gift buyer) who relishes a higher price for its connotation of quality and status, as well as to the chocolate aficionado who values his wallet more than his image, a difference of nearly five and a half dollars (or, put another way, 73 percent) on a half-pound box of chocolate is a relevant datum. Furthermore, the fact that consumers are willing to pay over five dollars more for the Italian-made chocolate than for its Venezuelan counterpart may suggest that consumers do care about the other differences between the two products. Afforded perfect information, consumers indifferent between the two would presumably not be willing to pay more for one than for the other.

We need go no further. Given the low threshold of materiality that applies in gray goods cases, we find the above dissimilarities material in the aggregate. The use of the same PERUGINA label on chocolates manifesting such differences is presumptively likely to cause confusion. Casa Helvetia could, of course, have offered evidence to rebut this presumption – but it has not done so. There is no proof that retailers explain to consumers the differences between the Italian and Venezuelan products. The record is likewise devoid of any evidence that consumers are indifferent about quality control procedures, packaging, ingredients, or price. Because the differences between the Italian and Venezuelan PERUGINA chocolates are material, the district court erred in denying plaintiffs' trademark infringement and unfair competition claims.

Reversed and remanded for the entry of appropriate injunctive relief and for further proceedings not inconsistent herewith.

Notes and Questions

1. *A low threshold.* As the court notes in *Nestle*, there is a low threshold of materiality that applies in gray goods cases. Why is the threshold so low? Is there any limiting principle that could be applied to the types of details that could constitute a material difference between imported and domestic products?

2. *Price?* One of the most surprising holdings of *Nestle* was that differences in price alone could support a finding that an imported product was materially different than a domestic product, even if the products were otherwise identical. If this is the case, would the discount retailers of Thai-manufactured Nike athletic shoes discussed in the introduction to this section be liable for trademark infringement? Is this outcome consistent with the purpose of the trademark exhaustion doctrine?

3. *Consumer preferences.* The court in *Nestle* observes that "The record is … devoid of any evidence that consumers are indifferent about quality control procedures, packaging, ingredients, or price." What if the defendant had conducted consumer taste tests and surveys demonstrating that most consumers could not tell the difference between the Italian and Venezuelan chocolates, and didn't really care about the other factors? Would the result have changed?

4. *An international difference.* As shown in the *Kirtsaeng* and *Impression Products* cases, the tests for exhaustion of copyrighted and patented products do not change depending on whether the product originates domestically or abroad (those cases largely considering whether international exhaustion should exist at all). In trademark cases, however, the tests for exhaustion are somewhat different for domestic and international products. Consider that the Venezuelan PERUGINA chocolates found to be infringing in *Nestle* were unaltered when distributed in Puerto Rico. They were the exact products manufactured by Nestle's authorized Venezuelan producer, Alimentos. Unlike the refurbished surgical instrument in *Surgi-Tech* or the watches in *Rolex*, Casa Helvetia made no changes at all to the candies produced

and packaged by Alimentos. So why was Casa Helvetia liable for trademark infringement when reselling these authorized goods in Puerto Rico?

5. *Cure by labeling*? Professor Irene Calboli notes that "several countries allow importers and/ or national distributors to cure these differences [in imported products] by affixing disclaimers to the goods clearly notifying that these goods have been imported by third parties and may be of a different quality."[12] Would such a label notification have addressed any potential consumer confusion in *Nestle*? Should the United States allow parallel imports of slightly different products so long as consumers are warned?

[12] Calboli, supra note 11, at 605.

24

Intellectual Property Misuse

Intellectual property rights, particularly patents and copyrights, are powerful legal instruments that give their owners exclusive rights over potentially broad fields of technical and creative output. Not surprisingly, actors holding rights of such potency often seek to use them to their greatest commercial advantage. And, at times, these uses have overstepped the line of legitimate business competition and entered a realm that the law has deemed worthy of sanction.

The antitrust laws, discussed in Chapter 25, were created to curb abuses in the competitive landscape by limiting both collusive agreements among competitors and abusive practices by monopolists. Yet merely holding a patent or a copyright does not necessarily give its owner power to distort competition in a particular market.[1] After all, many modern technology devices are covered by thousands of patents held by hundreds of different firms, and it is unlikely that any one patent or group of patents confers the type of market power necessary to trigger the antitrust laws.[2] Yet the owners of intellectual property (IP) rights may still overstep the bounds of legitimate competition in ways that public policy seeks to contain. Redress for this conduct must therefore come from the IP laws themselves, rather than the antitrust laws. The IP-based doctrines that have arisen to address the anticompetitive or abusive use of IP rights are loosely classified as intellectual property "misuse."

In this chapter we will explore the origins of misuse doctrine and its evolution into several distinct doctrines that remain important today. Understanding these doctrines is of critical importance to the transactional licensing attorney because, as we will see, IP misuse almost always arises in the context of a licensing agreement that – with or without ill intent – oversteps the line.

---

[1]   Though this principle was long believed to be true, the Supreme Court definitively confirmed it in *Illinois Tool Works Inc. v. Independent Ink, Inc.*, 547 U.S. 28 (2006) (discussed in Section 25.6).

[2]   An exception may exist with respect to patents that are essential to practice industry-wide standards. See Section 25.6, Note 4.

24.1 THE ORIGINS OF THE MISUSE DOCTRINE

Though the doctrine has existed since at least 1917,[3] most discussions of IP misuse begin with the Supreme Court's famous decision in *Morton Salt v. Suppiger*, which gave a name to a species of abusive use of patents that was distinct from previously recognized offenses under the antitrust laws.

Morton Salt Co. v. G.S. Suppiger Co.
314 U.S. 488 (1942)

STONE, CHIEF JUSTICE

Respondent brought this suit in the district court for an injunction and an accounting for infringement of its Patent No. 2,060,645, of November 10, 1936, on a machine for depositing salt tablets, a device said to be useful in the canning industry for adding predetermined amounts of salt in tablet form to the contents of the cans.

Upon petitioner's motion ... the trial court, without passing on the issues of validity and infringement, granted summary judgment dismissing the complaint. It took the ground that respondent was making use of the patent to restrain the sale of salt tablets in competition with its own sale of unpatented tablets, by requiring licensees to use with the patented machines only tablets sold by respondent. The Court of Appeals for the Seventh Circuit reversed because it thought that respondent's use of the patent was not shown to violate § 3 of the Clayton Act, as it did not appear that the use of its patent substantially lessened competition or tended to create a monopoly in salt tablets.[4] We granted certiorari because of the public importance of the question presented and of an alleged conflict of the decision below with [prior cases].

The Clayton Act authorizes those injured by violations tending to monopoly to maintain suit for treble damages and for an injunction in appropriate cases. But the present suit is for infringement of a patent. The question we must decide is not necessarily whether respondent has violated the Clayton Act, but whether a court of equity will lend its aid to protect the patent monopoly when respondent is using it as the effective means of restraining competition with its sale of an unpatented article.

Both respondent's wholly owned subsidiary and the petitioner manufacture and sell salt tablets used and useful in the canning trade. The tablets have a particular configuration rendering them capable of convenient use in respondent's patented machines. Petitioner makes and leases to canners unpatented salt deposition machines, charged to infringe respondent's patent. For reasons we indicate later, nothing turns on the fact that petitioner also competes with respondent in the sale of the tablets, and we may assume for purposes of this case that petitioner is doing no more than making and leasing the

---

[3] *Motion Picture Patents Co. v. Universal Film Manufacturing Corp.*, 243 U.S. 502 (1917).

[4] Chief Justice Stone's summary of the Seventh Circuit's decision, 117 F.2d 968 (7th Cir. 1941), is not entirely accurate. The Circuit did not find that "the use of [Suppiger's] patent" did not "substantially lessen[] competition or tend[] to create a monopoly in salt tablets." Rather, the Circuit reversed the district court's summary judgment in favor of Morton on the ground that the lower court entered judgment "without an inquiry into the facts." The Circuit reasoned that, given the lack of factual inquiry in the case below, it was "not able to determine the monopolistic extent of plaintiff's contract." Id. at 972.

alleged infringing machines. The principal business of respondent's subsidiary, from which its profits are derived, is the sale of salt tablets. In connection with this business, and as an adjunct to it, respondent leases its patented machines to commercial canners, some two hundred in all, under licenses to use the machines upon condition and with the agreement of the licensees that only the subsidiary's salt tablets be used with the leased machines.

It thus appears that respondent is making use of its patent monopoly to restrain competition in the marketing of unpatented articles, salt tablets, for use with the patented machines, and is aiding in the creation of a limited monopoly in the tablets not within that granted by the patent. A patent operates to create and grant to the patentee an exclusive right to make, use and vend the particular device described and claimed in the patent. But a patent affords no immunity for a monopoly not within the grant and the use of it to suppress competition in the sale of an unpatented article may deprive the patentee of the aid of a court of equity to restrain an alleged infringement by one who is a competitor. It is the established rule that a patentee who has granted a license on condition that the patented invention be used by the licensee only with unpatented materials furnished by the licensor, may not restrain as a contributory infringer one who sells to the licensee like materials for like use.

The grant to the inventor of the special privilege of a patent monopoly carries out a public policy adopted by the Constitution and laws of the United States, "to promote the Progress of Science and useful Arts, by securing for limited Times to … Inventors the exclusive Right" to their "new and useful" inventions. But the public policy which includes inventions within the granted monopoly excludes from it all that is not embraced in the invention. It equally forbids the use of the patent to secure an exclusive right or limited monopoly not granted by the Patent Office and which it is contrary to public policy to grant.

It is a principle of general application that courts, and especially courts of equity, may appropriately withhold their aid where the plaintiff is using the right asserted contrary to the public interest. Respondent argues that this doctrine is limited in its application to those cases where the patentee seeks to restrain contributory infringement by the sale to licensees of competing unpatented articles, while here respondent seeks to restrain petitioner from a direct infringement, the manufacture and sale of the salt tablet depositor. It is said that the equitable maxim that a party seeking the aid of a court of equity must come into court with clean hands applies only to the plaintiff's wrongful conduct in the particular act or transaction which raises the equity, enforcement of which is sought; that where, as here, the patentee seeks to restrain the manufacture or use of the patented device, his conduct in using the patent to restrict competition in the sale of salt tablets does not foreclose him from seeking relief limited to an injunction against the manufacture and sale of the infringing machine alone.

Undoubtedly equity does not demand that its suitors shall have led blameless lives; but additional considerations must be taken into account where maintenance of the suit concerns the public interest as well as the private interests of suitors. Where the patent is used as a means of restraining competition with the patentee's sale of an unpatented product, the successful prosecution of an infringement suit even against one who is not a competitor in such sale is a powerful aid to the maintenance of the attempted monopoly of the unpatented article, and is thus a contributing factor in thwarting the public policy underlying the grant of the patent. Maintenance and enlargement of the attempted monopoly of the unpatented article are dependent to some extent upon persuading the public of the validity of the patent, which the infringement suit is intended to establish. Equity may rightly withhold its assistance from such a use of the patent by declining to entertain a suit for infringement, and should do so at least until it is made to appear that the improper practice has been abandoned and that the consequences of the misuse of the patent have been dissipated.

The reasons for barring the prosecution of such a suit against one who is not a competitor with the patentee in the sale of the unpatented product are fundamentally the same as those which preclude an infringement suit against a licensee who has violated a condition of the license by using with the licensed machine a competing unpatented article, or against a vendee of a patented or copyrighted article for violation of a condition for the maintenance of resale prices. It is the adverse effect upon the public interest of a successful infringement suit in conjunction with the patentee's course of conduct which disqualifies him to maintain the suit, regardless of whether the particular defendant has suffered from the misuse of the patent. Similarly equity will deny relief for infringement of a trademark where the plaintiff is misrepresenting to the public the nature of his product either by the trademark itself or by his label. The patentee, like these other holders of an exclusive privilege granted in the furtherance of a public policy, may not claim protection of his grant by the courts where it is being used to subvert that policy.

It is unnecessary to decide whether respondent has violated the Clayton Act, for we conclude that in any event the maintenance of the present suit to restrain petitioner's manufacture or sale of the alleged infringing machines is contrary to public policy and that the district court rightly dismissed the complaint for want of equity.

REVERSED.

FIGURE 24.1 G.S. Suppiger Co. leased its patented salt-depositing machines to canneries with a contractual requirement that they purchase unpatented salt tablets exclusively from Suppiger. When Suppiger sued Morton Salt for selling an allegedly infringing salt-depositing machine, Morton accused Suppiger of misusing its machine patents to corner the market for salt tablets.

Notes and Questions

1. *Public policy.* The Court in *Morton Salt* bases its decision largely on public policy grounds. Chief Justice Stone famously writes, "equity does not demand that its suitors shall have led blameless lives; but additional considerations must be taken into account where maintenance of the suit concerns the public interest as well as the private interests of suitors." What public policy is at stake in the case, and how is it advanced by the recognition of patent misuse as a defense to infringement?

2. *Antitrust or not?* The Court in *Morton Salt* states that Suppiger's contractual restriction "restrain[s] competition in the marketing of unpatented articles, salt tablets, for use with the patented machines, and is aiding in the creation of a limited monopoly in the tablets not within that granted by the patent." This sounds a lot like an antitrust claim, yet the Court later states that it is "unnecessary to decide whether respondent has violated the Clayton Act" (and the Seventh Circuit below found insufficient facts to prove such a violation). Why did the Supreme Court brush aside the antitrust laws to create the new doctrine of patent misuse in this case?[5]

3. *The crux of misuse.* The Court seems to identify the crux of Suppiger's misuse as "aiding in the creation of a limited monopoly in the tablets not within that granted by the patent." That is, Suppiger's offense was seeking to expand its patent monopoly (in the machines) beyond its granted scope (i.e., to the tablets). The expansion of a patent (or copyright) monopoly beyond what was granted by the government is thus the gravamen of misuse claims. What is so bad about such an expansion, so long as it is accomplished via mutual agreement of the affected parties?

4. *Injury?* Recall that the *Morton Salt* case was brought as an infringement action by Suppiger against Morton. Morton did not allege any particular harm from Suppiger's alleged misuse of the asserted patent. Morton presented no evidence that it lost potential sales of salt tablets to users of Suppiger's machines or even that Suppiger overcharged customers for its salt tablets. So, who was injured by Suppiger's misuse? And why should a provision in a licensing agreement between Suppiger and its customers have anything to do with whether or not Morton is liable for selling infringing machines?

5. *A drastic remedy.* The Court's remedy for Suppiger's patent misuse was drastic: Suppiger lost the ability to enforce its patent against Morton, even if Morton had been infringing. How can such a drastic remedy be justified?

6. *No cause of action.* In *Morton Salt*, Suppiger sued Morton for selling salt-depositing machines that allegedly infringed Suppiger's patent. Morton raised Suppiger's alleged misuse of its machine patents as an affirmative defense. Interestingly, unlike an antitrust claim, patent misuse is *only* an affirmative defense and gives rise to no independent cause of action. Should it be?

7. *Blameless lives?* In *Morton Salt*, Chief Justice Stone cryptically observes that "equity does not demand that its suitors shall have led blameless lives." He is perhaps referring to the fact, noted in the Seventh Circuit opinion below, that Morton "also leases its machine to the trade and provides in its lease that *the lessee shall use only salt tablets made by it.*" 117 F.2d

---

5 Judge Richard Posner considers these issues in *USM Corp. v. SPS Techs., Inc.,* 694 F.2d 505, 511 (7th Cir. 1982) ("Since the antitrust laws as currently interpreted reach every practice that could impair competition substantially, it is not easy to define a separate role for a doctrine also designed to prevent an anticompetitive practice – the abuse of a patent monopoly. One possibility is that the doctrine of patent misuse, unlike antitrust law, condemns any patent licensing practice that is even trivially anticompetitive, at least if it has no socially beneficial effects").

at 970 (emphasis added). Thus, Morton employed precisely the same exclusive purchasing provision as Suppiger. What do you make of this coincidence? Why did the Supreme Court pay it so little heed? Does it matter than Suppiger's salt-depositing machine was patented, but Morton's was not? How would you answer one commentator's question "[s]hould not Morton be estopped by its own conduct from asserting the misuse defense?"[6]

24.2 MISUSE BY SCOPE EXPANSION: TYING AND STATUTORY REFORM

As we will see in Section 25.5, the improper use of leverage in one market to support sales in another market is known as "tying," a practice that is condemned by the antitrust laws. In a sense, Suppiger's requirement that users of its patented machines buy its unpatented salt tablets can also be viewed as a type of illegal "tie." Liability for this form of tying misuse, however, is different than that under the antitrust laws. With tying misuse, there is no requirement that the tying party (Suppiger) have market power in the market for the tying product (salt-depositing machines) or that the claimant establish any injury from the alleged tie. It is simply enough that the misuse occur to trigger the drastic remedy of patent unenforceability.

Following *Morton Salt*, the courts considered a number of cases in which a patent holder sought to use its patents to exert control over unpatented articles. In *Mercoid Corp. v. Minneapolis-Honeywell Regulator Co.*, 320 U.S. 680 (1944), the Supreme Court considered a patent held by Minneapolis-Honeywell covering a furnace thermostat control system. Each such system includes three thermostats that control the switching of the furnace stoker and the fan. While the combination of these components was covered by the patent, the individual thermostatic switches used in the system were not patented.

Minneapolis-Honeywell granted five manufacturers a royalty-bearing license under the patent to make thermostatic switches designed for use in the patented furnace system. The licensing agreement required each such manufacturer to include a notice with each switch, informing the customer that its purchase of the switch included a license for one installation of the patented furnace system. The only way for a customer to obtain a license to install and use the patented system, apparently, was to purchase a thermostatic switch from one of the licensed manufacturers.

Mercoid, a switch manufacturer, refused to take a license. When Mercoid then sold thermostatic switches that were compatible with the patented furnace system, Minneapolis-Honeywell sued Mercoid for contributory infringement – supplying a necessary part of the patented system, even if it did not itself infringe the full patent.[7] Mercoid raised the defense of patent misuse, arguing that Minneapolis-Honeywell, in its five licensing agreements with other switch manufacturers, was collecting royalties on the sale of unpatented switches. The Supreme Court, citing *Morton Salt*, ruled in favor of Mercoid, holding that

> The legality of any attempt to bring unpatented goods within the protection of the patent is measured by the anti-trust laws[8] not by the patent law ... [T]he effort here made to control competition in this unpatented device plainly violates the anti-trust laws ... It follows that [Mercoid] is entitled to be relieved against the consequences of those acts. It likewise

---

[6]   L. Peter Farkas. *Can a Patent Still be Misused?* 59 Antitrust L.J. 677, 681 (1990).

[7]   At this time, contributory patent infringement was recognized under the common law, but was not yet embodied in the Patent Act.

[8]   Though the court references the "anti-trust laws," it does not refer to the Sherman Act, Clayton Act or other specific antitrust law. It can be assumed that the Court was referring to patent misuse, per its recent decision in *Morton Salt*.

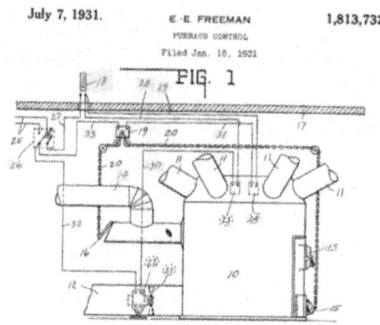
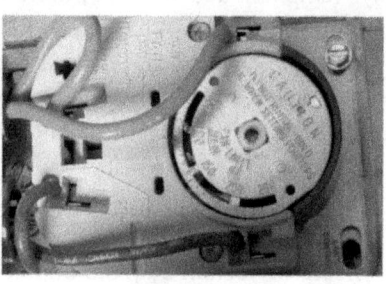

FIGURE 24.2 The 1931 Minneapolis-Honeywell furnace control system patent and a Honeywell furnace switch (unpatented).

follows that [Minneapolis-Honeywell] may not obtain from a court of equity any decree which directly or indirectly helps it to subvert the public policy which underlies the grant of its patent.

The court did not seem to care that Mercoid's thermostatic switch was a critical element of the patented Minneapolis-Honeywell system. It explained that "However worthy it may be, however essential to the patent, an unpatented part of a combination patent is no more entitled to monopolistic protection than any other unpatented device." Thus, like Suppiger's attempt to control the supply of unpatented salt pellets, Minneapolis-Honeywell was barred by the misuse doctrine from using its patent to control the sale of unpatented thermostatic switches.

The *Mercoid* decision set off alarm bells throughout the industry. Effectively, it meant that a patent holder could not stop a supplier from selling a critical but unpatented component designed for use in a patented system, even if the *only use* for that component was in the patented system. In other words, a patent on a complex mechanical system was virtually worthless unless an infringer sold the entire system as a whole. The sale of components that were not separately patented could not be prevented.

The result of this public outcry was the inclusion of a new statutory prohibition on contributory infringement in the 1952 version of the Patent Act. This section, now codified as 35 U.S.C. § 271(c), provides that

> Whoever [sells] a component of a patented machine, manufacture, combination or composition, or a material or apparatus for use in practicing a patented process, constituting a material part of the invention, knowing the same to be especially made or especially adapted for use in an infringement of such patent, and not a staple article or commodity of commerce suitable for substantial noninfringing use, shall be liable as a contributory infringer.

Section 271(c) clarifies the law of contributory patent infringement, establishing that the seller of a component of a patented system can be held liable for contributory infringement, so long as the component is not a "staple article" (e.g., sale of a screw, nail or wire should not result in contributory infringement by the seller even if the component is used in a patented system).

But the 1952 Act went further. In addition to establishing the framework for contributory patent infringement, it clarified the law of patent *misuse*, now codified in Section 271(d):

(d) No patent owner otherwise entitled to relief for infringement or contributory infringement of a patent shall be denied relief or deemed guilty of misuse or illegal extension of the patent right by reason of his having done one or more of the following:

(1) derived revenue from acts which if performed by another without his consent would constitute contributory infringement of the patent;
(2) licensed or authorized another to perform acts which if performed without his consent would constitute contributory infringement of the patent;
(3) sought to enforce his patent rights against infringement or contributory infringement

This new provision exonerates patent holders from three actions for which Minneapolis-Honeywell was condemned in *Mercoid*: charging a royalty to someone who is not directly infringing a patent; licensing someone to sell a noninfringing product if it would contribute to someone else's infringement; and enforcing a patent against a contributory infringer.

Even with these modifications, the patent misuse doctrine had its detractors, some of them highly placed. For example, Senator Orrin Hatch (R-Ut), a long-time champion of strong IP rights, remarked:

> The patent misuse doctrine has come to provide a defense even to a person who knowingly infringes a valid patent and is not affected by the conduct held to be misuse. If there ever existed a reason for this harsh result, it is long gone.

Hatch's comments were not idle posturing. In 1988, the Senate passed a sweeping bill that all but eliminated the doctrine. Eventually, a less extreme version of the bill was enacted as the Patent Misuse Reform Act of 1988.[9] It adds two additional exclusions from patent misuse already present under § 271(d), providing that it shall not be misuse if a patent owner has:

(4) refused to license or use any rights to the patent; or
(5) conditioned the license of any rights to the patent or the sale of the patented product on the acquisition of a license to rights in another patent or purchase of a separate product, unless, in view of the circumstances, the patent owner has *market power* in the relevant market for the patent or patented product on which the license or sale is conditioned.

Clause 4 of the 1988 amendment codifies a venerable doctrine under patent law: A patent owner may choose whether and with whom to conduct business; it need not grant a license to any particular party, and is free to refuse to grant such a license.[10]

Clause 5, however, effects a more significant change. It effectively reconnects the misuse doctrine to antitrust law – a connection that was severed by the Supreme Court in *Morton Salt*. That is, it provides that tying-based patent misuse will not be found unless the patent holder has "market power in the relevant market for the patent or patented product" (i.e., the tying product). As such, tying misuse now requires a similar level of market leverage as the offense of tying under the antitrust laws (see Section 25.5).

---

9   For a summary of this history, see Farkas, supra, note 6, at 681–84.
10   See Kenneth J. Burchfiel, *Patent Misuse and Antitrust Reform: "Blessed be the Tie?"* 4 Harv. J.L. & Tech. 1, 6 (1991) ("It is clear that prior to the amendment there was no duty to license another to make, use or sell a patented invention, which are the basic exclusive rights granted by a United States patent. The right of the patentee to prevent others from practicing the invention has long been regarded as absolute, and Section 271(d)(4) was intended only to codify this established principle"). This clause may have been a reaction to statements by the US Department of Justice in its 1987 business review letter to the MPEG-2 pool, which promoted "nondiscriminatory" licensing to all competitors as a procompetitive feature of the pool (see discussion in Section 26.3, Note 3).

Notes and Questions

1. *Contributory and direct infringers.* In *Mercoid*, Minneapolis-Honeywell sued Mercoid for contributory patent infringement under the old common law regime. Even before the 1952 Act this was a risky move, as Mercoid was only selling an unpatented component of Minneapolis-Honeywell's patented furnace control system. In order to establish a claim for contributory infringement, the alleged contributory infringer must be contributing to a direct infringement by somebody else. In this case, the direct infringer would be anyone who installed a furnace control system covered by the patent. Why didn't Minneapolis-Honeywell simply sue these direct infringers? What was attractive about suing Mercoid?

2. *Legislative override.* It is not uncommon in IP law for Congress to enact laws specifically designed to overrule unpopular judicial decisions.[11] What commercial interests were most opposed to the patent misuse doctrine? How do you explain a concerted industrial lobbying effort in this regard, given that cases in which patent misuses arises often involve two large corporations (e.g., Morton Salt and Suppiger)?

3. *Codifying contributory infringement.* Why did Congress feel the need to codify the law of contributory patent infringement in 1952? Other than overriding the decision in *Mercoid*, what else did this statutory enactment have?

4. *Antitrust and misuse.* Prior to 1988, many commentators felt that patent misuse should be treated as a species of antitrust violation, and no more. Section 271(d)(5) achieved this goal, in part, for tying-type misuse. But patent misuse is still a separate legal doctrine, distinct from antitrust law. How does misuse differ from antitrust law, even after the 1988 amendments?

5. *Other forms of scope expansion.* In *Bayer AG v. Housey Pharmaceuticals, Inc.*, 169 F. Supp. 2d 328 (2001), Housey licensed four patents relating to screening methods for therapeutic compounds to more than thirty different companies. Housey offered two different payment options for this license: a lump-sum payment based on the licensee's R&D budget, or a running royalty based on the licensee's sale of therapeutic compounds discovered using the patented method. Bayer attempted to negotiate a license with Housey, but the parties could not come to terms and Bayer sought a declaratory judgment that Housey had committed patent misuse by charging royalties based on compounds not covered by its patent claims. The court, echoing the reasoning of the "package licensing" cases *Automatic Radio* and *Zenith* (discussed in Section 24.4), held that Housey had not committed misuse, as it did not condition the grant of its license on the payment of royalties on unpatented products, but rather offered this as an option.[12]

24.3 MISUSE BY TERM EXPANSION: POST-EXPIRATION ROYALTIES

24.3.1 *The Long Shadow of* Brulotte

As the Supreme Court established in *Morton Salt*, patent misuse constitutes the expansion of the patent monopoly beyond the scope granted by the Patent and Trademark Office (PTO). The tying-type misuse claims discussed above each involved the purported expansion of a patent's

---

[11] For another example in the context of IP licensing, see Section 21.3, discussing the enactment of § 265(n) of the Bankruptcy Code in response to the Court's decision in *Lubrizol Enterprises, Inc. v. Richmond Metal Finishers, Inc.*

[12] For an analysis of this case and the application of the patent misuse doctrine to "reach-through" royalty arrangements (discussed in more detail in Section 8.2.3.2, Note 3), see Alfred C. Server, Nader Mousavi & Jane M. Love, *Reach-Through Rights and the Patentability, Enforcement, and Licensing of Patents on Drug Discovery Tools*, 1 Hastings Sci. Tech. L.J. 21, 90–92 (2009).

reach to unpatented articles sold by the patent holder or its licensees (e.g., salt tablets, sensors). But a patent monopoly can be expanded in other ways.

In *Brulotte v. Thys Co.*, 379 U.S. 29 (1964),[13] Thys Co. held twelve patents covering the process of mechanized hop-picking and hop-picking machines. Walter Brulotte and Raymond Charvet were hop farmers in Yakima County, Washington. They each purchased portable Thys hop-picking machines that they acquired second-hand. When Thys approached the farmers with its patents, each agreed to take a license under which he would pay Thys minimum annual royalties of $500 for seventeen years from the date of the original purchase.[14] They also agreed during this period not to remove the machines from Yakima County. Brulotte's royalty obligation was scheduled to expire in 1958, Charvet's in 1960. Both farmers ceased to pay Thys royalties in 1952, and the last of the patents expired in 1957. When Thys sued to recover unpaid royalties, the farmers argued that Thys committed patent misuse by charging royalties and seeking to control the location of the machines after expiration of the patents.

Justice Douglas, writing for the Supreme Court, reasoned that

> a patentee's use of a royalty agreement that projects beyond the expiration date of the patent is unlawful *per se*. If that device were available to patentees, the free market visualized for the post-expiration period would be subject to monopoly influences that have no proper place there … The exaction of royalties for use of a machine after the patent has expired is an assertion of monopoly power in the post-expiration period when, as we have seen, the patent has entered the public domain.

THYS PORTABLE

HOP PICKERS

AVAILABLE FOR

*IMMEDIATE
DELIVERY*

Cancellation of some 1947 export orders has made available to domestic growers several of these proven mechanical pickers. Though designed as portable pickers, these machines make very satisfactory stationary units, enabling growers of low wire yards to profit by their great capacity and efficiency.

Write or Wire

Thys Co. **John Deere-Lindeman Co.**
RFD 2, Box 630 1011 South First Street
Sacramento, Cal. Yakima, Washington

FIGURE 24.3 Prior to the introduction of mechanical hop-picking equipment, the harvesting of hops was a labor-intensive manual process, as illustrated by this photograph (left) of hop pickers in Yakima County, Washington.

---

[13] Many of the most relevant (and interesting) facts in this case can be found in the decision below of the Washington Supreme Court, 382 P.2d 271 (Wash. 1963).

[14] At this time, the duration of a patent was seventeen years from the date of issuance.

Justice Harlan dissented from the Court's decision, arguing that the payment of royalties following expiration of the patents should be treated as an extension of payment terms, rather than an expansion of the patent monopoly:

> The essence of the majority opinion may lie in some notion that "patent leverage" being used by Thys to exact use payments extending beyond the patent term somehow allows Thys to extract more onerous payments from the farmers than would otherwise be obtainable. If this be the case, the Court must in some way distinguish long-term use payments from long-term installment payments of a flat-sum purchase price. For the danger which it seems to fear would appear to inhere equally in both, and as I read the Court's opinion, the latter type of arrangement is lawful despite the fact that failure to pay an installment under a conditional sales contract would permit the seller to recapture the machine, thus terminating – not merely restricting – the farmer's use of it.

Criticisms of this nature continued in the years following *Brulotte*. In *Scheiber v. Dolby Laboratories, Inc.*, 293 F.3d 1014 (7th Cir. 2002), Judge Richard Posner reasoned that "charging royalties beyond the term of the patent does not lengthen the patentee's monopoly; it merely alters the timing of royalty payments." Nevertheless, he followed *Brulotte*, but only because he was compelled to, complaining that "we have no authority to overrule a Supreme Court decision no matter how dubious its reasoning strikes us, or even how out of touch with the Supreme Court's current thinking the decision seems."

Despite nearly continual criticism by commentators and lower courts, *Brulotte* has remained good law, and was most recently affirmed in no uncertain terms by the Supreme Court in the following case.

Kimble v. Marvel Entertainment, LLC
576 U.S. 446 (2015)

KAGAN, JUSTICE

In *Brulotte v. Thys Co.*, 379 U.S. 29 (1964), this Court held that a patent holder cannot charge royalties for the use of his invention after its patent term has expired. The sole question presented here is whether we should overrule *Brulotte*. Adhering to principles of stare decisis, we decline to do so. Critics of the *Brulotte* rule must seek relief not from this Court but from Congress.

I

In 1990, petitioner Stephen Kimble obtained a patent on a toy that allows children (and young-at-heart adults) to role-play as "a spider person" by shooting webs—really, pressurized foam string—"from the palm of [the] hand." … Respondent Marvel Entertainment, LLC (Marvel) makes and markets products featuring Spider–Man, among other comic-book characters. Seeking to sell or license his patent, Kimble met with the president of Marvel's corporate predecessor to discuss his idea for web-slinging fun. Soon afterward, but without remunerating Kimble, that company began marketing the "Web Blaster"—a toy that, like Kimble's patented invention, enables would-be action heroes to mimic Spider–Man through the use of a polyester glove and a canister of foam.

Kimble sued Marvel in 1997 alleging, among other things, patent infringement. The parties ultimately settled that litigation. Their agreement provided that Marvel would

FIGURE 24.4 *Kimble v. Marvel* involved a licensing agreement entered into to settle patent litigation over the popular "Web Blaster" toy.

purchase Kimble's patent in exchange for a lump sum (of about a half-million dollars) and a 3% royalty on Marvel's future sales of the Web Blaster and similar products. The parties set no end date for royalties, apparently contemplating that they would continue for as long as kids want to imitate Spider–Man (by doing whatever a spider can).

And then Marvel stumbled across *Brulotte*, the case at the heart of this dispute. In negotiating the settlement, neither side was aware of *Brulotte*. But Marvel must have been pleased to learn of it. *Brulotte* had read the patent laws to prevent a patentee from receiving royalties for sales made after his patent's expiration. So the decision's effect was to sunset the settlement's royalty clause. On making that discovery, Marvel sought a declaratory judgment in federal district court confirming that the company could cease paying royalties come 2010—the end of Kimble's patent term. The court approved that relief, holding that *Brulotte* made "the royalty provision ... unenforceable after the expiration of the Kimble patent." The Court of Appeals for the Ninth Circuit affirmed, though making clear that it was none too happy about doing so. "[T]he *Brulotte* rule," the court complained, "is counterintuitive and its rationale is arguably unconvincing."

We granted certiorari, to decide whether, as some courts and commentators have suggested, we should overrule *Brulotte*. For reasons of stare decisis, we demur.

II

Patents endow their holders with certain superpowers, but only for a limited time. In crafting the patent laws, Congress struck a balance between fostering innovation and ensuring public access to discoveries. While a patent lasts, the patentee possesses exclusive rights to the patented article—rights he may sell or license for royalty payments if he so chooses. But a patent typically expires 20 years from the day the application for it was filed. And when the patent expires, the patentee's prerogatives expire too, and the right to make or use the article, free from all restriction, passes to the public.

In a related line of decisions, we have deemed unenforceable private contract provisions limiting free use of such inventions. In *Scott Paper Co. v. Marcalus Mfg. Co.*, 326 U.S.

249 (1945), for example, we determined that a manufacturer could not agree to refrain from challenging a patent's validity. Allowing even a single company to restrict its use of an expired or invalid patent, we explained, "would deprive … the consuming public of the advantage to be derived" from free exploitation of the discovery. And to permit such a result, whether or not authorized "by express contract," would impermissibly undermine the patent laws.

Brulotte was brewed in the same barrel. There, an inventor licensed his patented hop-picking machine to farmers in exchange for royalties from hop crops harvested both before and after his patents' expiration dates. The Court (by an 8–1 vote) held the agreement unenforceable—"unlawful per se"—to the extent it provided for the payment of royalties "accru[ing] after the last of the patents incorporated into the machines had expired."

The *Brulotte* rule, like others making contract provisions unenforceable, prevents some parties from entering into deals they desire. As compared to lump-sum fees, royalty plans both draw out payments over time and tie those payments, in each month or year covered, to a product's commercial success. And sometimes, for some parties, the longer the arrangement lasts, the better—not just up to but beyond a patent term's end. A more extended payment period, coupled (as it presumably would be) with a lower rate, may bring the price the patent holder seeks within the range of a cash-strapped licensee. (Anyone who has bought a product on installment can relate.). Or such an extended term may better allocate the risks and rewards associated with commercializing inventions—most notably, when years of development work stand between licensing a patent and bringing a product to market. As to either goal, *Brulotte* may pose an obstacle.

Yet parties can often find ways around *Brulotte*, enabling them to achieve those same ends. To start, Brulotte allows a licensee to defer payments for pre-expiration use of a patent into the post-expiration period; all the decision bars are royalties for using an invention after it has moved into the public domain. A licensee could agree, for example, to pay the licensor a sum equal to 10% of sales during the 20-year patent term, but to amortize that amount over 40 years. That arrangement would at least bring down early outlays, even if it would not do everything the parties might want to allocate risk over a long timeframe. And parties have still more options when a licensing agreement covers either multiple patents or additional non-patent rights. Under *Brulotte*, royalties may run until the latest-running patent covered in the parties' agreement expires. Too, post-expiration royalties are allowable so long as tied to a non-patent right—even when closely related to a patent. That means, for example, that a license involving both a patent and a trade secret can set a 5% royalty during the patent period (as compensation for the two combined) and a 4% royalty afterward (as payment for the trade secret alone). Finally and most broadly, Brulotte poses no bar to business arrangements other than royalties—all kinds of joint ventures, for example—that enable parties to share the risks and rewards of commercializing an invention.

Contending that such alternatives are not enough, Kimble asks us to abandon *Brulotte* in favor of "flexible, case-by-case analysis" of post-expiration royalty clauses "under the rule of reason." Used in antitrust law, the rule of reason requires courts to evaluate a practice's effect on competition by "taking into account a variety of factors, including specific information about the relevant business, its condition before and after the [practice] was imposed, and the [practice's] history, nature, and effect." Of primary importance in this context, Kimble posits, is whether a patent holder has power in the relevant market and so might be able to curtail competition. Resolving that issue, Kimble notes, entails "a full-fledged economic inquiry into the definition of the market, barriers to entry, and the like."

III

Overruling precedent is never a small matter. Stare decisis—in English, the idea that today's Court should stand by yesterday's decisions—is "a foundation stone of the rule of law." Application of that doctrine, although "not an inexorable command," is the "preferred course because it promotes the evenhanded, predictable, and consistent development of legal principles, fosters reliance on judicial decisions, and contributes to the actual and perceived integrity of the judicial process." It also reduces incentives for challenging settled precedents, saving parties and courts the expense of endless relitigation.

Respecting stare decisis means sticking to some wrong decisions. The doctrine rests on the idea, as Justice Brandeis famously wrote, that it is usually "more important that the applicable rule of law be settled than that it be settled right." *Burnet v. Coronado Oil & Gas Co.*, 285 U.S. 393, 406 (1932) (dissenting opinion). To reverse course, we require as well what we have termed a "special justification"—over and above the belief "that the precedent was wrongly decided."

And Congress has spurned multiple opportunities to reverse *Brulotte*—openings as frequent and clear as this Court ever sees. *Brulotte* has governed licensing agreements for more than half a century. During that time, Congress has repeatedly amended the patent laws, including the specific provision on which Brulotte rested. *Brulotte* survived every such change. Indeed, Congress has rebuffed bills that would have replaced *Brulotte's* per se rule with the same antitrust-style analysis Kimble now urges. Congress's continual reworking of the patent laws—but never of the *Brulotte* rule—further supports leaving the decision in place.

Nor yet are we done, for the subject matter of *Brulotte* adds to the case for adhering to precedent. *Brulotte* lies at the intersection of two areas of law: property (patents) and contracts (licensing agreements). And we have often recognized that in just those contexts—"cases involving property and contract rights"—considerations favoring stare decisis are "at their acme." That is because parties are especially likely to rely on such precedents when ordering their affairs. To be sure, Marvel and Kimble disagree about whether *Brulotte* has actually generated reliance. Marvel says yes: Some parties, it claims, do not specify an end date for royalties in their licensing agreements, instead relying on *Brulotte* as a default rule ... Overturning *Brulotte* would thus upset expectations, most so when long-dormant licenses for long-expired patents spring back to life. Not true, says Kimble: Unfair surprise is unlikely, because no "meaningful number of [such] license agreements ... actually exist." To be honest, we do not know (nor, we suspect, do Marvel and Kimble). But even uncertainty on this score cuts in Marvel's direction. So long as we see a reasonable possibility that parties have structured their business transactions in light of *Brulotte*, we have one more reason to let it stand.

As against this superpowered form of stare decisis, we would need a superspecial justification to warrant reversing *Brulotte*. But the kinds of reasons we have most often held sufficient in the past do not help Kimble here. If anything, they reinforce our unwillingness to do what he asks.

IV. B

Kimble also seeks support from the wellspring of all patent policy: the goal of promoting innovation. *Brulotte*, he contends, "discourages technological innovation and does significant damage to the American economy." Recall that would-be licensors and licensees may benefit from post-patent royalty arrangements because they allow for a longer payment period and a more precise allocation of risk. If the parties' ideal licensing agreement is barred, Kimble reasons, they may reach no agreement at all. And that possibility may discourage invention in the first instance. The bottom line, Kimble concludes, is that some "breakthrough technologies will never see the light of day."

Maybe. Or, then again, maybe not. While we recognize that post-patent royalties are sometimes not anticompetitive, we just cannot say whether barring them imposes any meaningful drag on innovation. As we have explained, *Brulotte* leaves open various ways—involving both licensing and other business arrangements—to accomplish payment deferral and risk-spreading alike. Those alternatives may not offer the parties the precise set of benefits and obligations they would prefer. But they might still suffice to bring patent holders and product developers together and ensure that inventions get to the public. Neither Kimble nor his amici have offered any empirical evidence connecting *Brulotte* to decreased innovation; they essentially ask us to take their word for the problem. And the United States, which acts as both a licensor and a licensee of patented inventions while also implementing patent policy, vigorously disputes that *Brulotte* has caused any "significant real-world economic harm." Truth be told, if forced to decide that issue, we would not know where or how to start.

V

What we can decide, we can undecide. But stare decisis teaches that we should exercise that authority sparingly. Finding many reasons for staying the stare decisis course and no "special justification" for departing from it, we decline Kimble's invitation to overrule *Brulotte*.

For the reasons stated, the judgment of the Court of Appeals is affirmed.

Notes and Questions

1. *Deferred payments. Brulotte* has been criticized – from Justice Harlan's original dissent to the dissenting justices in *Kimble* – for seeming to disregard the parties' reasonable desire to spread payments over time. But Justice Douglas understood the concept of installment payments, and rejected the argument that Thys was simply allowing the licensee farmers to make payments over time. "The royalty payments due for the post-expiration period are by their terms for use during that period, and are not deferred payments for use during the pre-expiration period." 379 U.S. at 31. "The sale or lease of unpatented machines on long-term payments based on a deferred purchase price or on use would present wholly different considerations." 379 U.S. at 32. What distinction does Justice Douglas draw regarding the nature of the post-expiration payments, and why is it so important?

2. *Nonroyalty obligations.* In *Brulotte*, Justice Douglas is careful to note that the obligations imposed on the farmers after expiration of the Thys patents included not only the payment of royalties, but also an agreement not to move the machines out of Yakima County. Yet this point is seldom raised in the critiques of *Brulotte*. What is its significance, and how does it support the Court's holding?

3. *Per se vs. rule of reason.* In *Kimble*, Kimble asks the Court to replace the *per se* rule of *Brulotte* with the more flexible "rule of reason" approach adopted in most antitrust cases

today. We will discuss the differences between *per se* and rule of reason approaches in greater detail in Chapter 25. But for now, consider why Justice Kagan declined this invitation.

4. *A market power requirement?* In *Scheiber v. Dolby Laboratories, Inc.*, 293 F.3d 1014 (7th Cir. 2002), a licensor seeking to charge post-expiration royalties argued that under 35 U.S.C. § 271(d)(5) he could be found to have engaged in patent misuse only if he possessed "market power in the market for the conditioning product." Judge Posner responded, correctly, that § 271(d)(5) only applies by its terms to tying-type patent misuse. But should the statute be so limited? Should the market power requirement of § 271(d)(5) be extended to other forms of patent misuse, such as the type of term-extension misuse alleged in *Brulotte* and *Kimble*?

5. *Effects on innovation.* Kimble argued that retaining the *Brulotte* rule would discourage technological innovation. Why? Justice Kagan seems skeptical of his theory. How convincing do you find it?

6. *Patent vs. contract.* Justice Alito, who wrote a dissenting opinion in *Kimble*, returns to the well-worn debate over the nature of IP licenses: whether they are interests in property or contracts (see Chapter 3). As Justice Alito writes, "A licensing agreement that provides for the payment of royalties after a patent's term expires does not enlarge the patentee's monopoly or extend the term of the patent. It simply gives the licensor a contractual right." Why is this distinction important?

7. *Drafting around* Brulotte. Marvel argues that contracting parties depend on the rule in *Brulotte* when drafting their licensing agreements. "Some parties, it claims, do not specify an end date for royalties in their licensing agreements, instead relying on *Brulotte* as a default rule … Overturning *Brulotte* would thus upset expectations, most so when long-dormant licenses for long-expired patents spring back to life." How much credence do you give to this argument? Would it be a good practice to draft a licensing agreement with no end date in reliance on a case that prohibits the payment of royalties after the expiration of the licensed patents?

8. *The* Brulotte *windfall.* In *Kimble*, Justice Kagan writes that Marvel "stumbled" across *Brulotte*, implying that neither party was aware of the case when they drafted the settlement agreement including the perpetual royalty clause. Does this matter? What if Marvel, a large corporation represented by high-priced lawyers, did know about *Brulotte*, but simply allowed Kimble, a garage inventor, to enter into an invalid agreement. Would this change the outcome? Recall Chief Justice Stone's comment in *Morton Salt* that "equity does not demand that its suitors shall have led blameless lives." Does that sentiment apply here as well?

9. *Hybrid licensing.* In *Kimble*, Justice Kagan explains how parties can easily avoid the problems imposed by *Brulotte* through contractual drafting. We discussed one of these techniques in Section 8.2.2.4 – hybrid rates, in which the license covers both patents and unpatented know-how, and the combined royalty rate is lower in jurisdictions, and at times, that no patents are in force. What other drafting techniques does Justice Kagan imply might avoid the *Brulotte* rule?

24.3.2 *The Limits of* Brulotte: Aronson v. Quick Point *and Unpatented Articles*

Not long after the Supreme Court's decision in *Brulotte*, the Court considered another case – *Aronson v. Quick Point Pencil Co.*, 440 U.S. 257 (1979) – that quietly established the outer limits of the *Brulotte* misuse doctrine. In 1955, Jane Aronson filed a patent application for a novel form of keyholder into which a photo or corporate logo could be inserted. While the patent application was pending, she negotiated a contract for the manufacture and sale of the keyholder with a St. Louis-based office supply manufacturer, Quick Point Pencil Co. The relevant facts are set forth by the district court:

> On June 26, 1956, [Aronson] entered into an agreement with [Quick Point] which gives [Quick Point] the exclusive license and right to make and sell key holders of the type shown in [Aronson's] patent application … which was filed with the United States Patent Office on October 25, 1955 … The agreement was amended on June 27, 1956. The agreement provides that [Quick Point] would pay [Aronson] royalties at the rate of 5 percent and if no patent was issued within five years of June 27, 1956 the royalties would be reduced to 2½ percent "as long as [Quick Point] continue[s] to sell the same."
>
> [Quick Point] commenced manufacturing key holders in July of 1956 and paid a five percent royalty on gross sales until June 26, 1961, when the royalty was reduced to two and one-half percent. On that date [Aronson] had not been granted a patent …
>
> On January 27, 1959, the parties executed a supplementary agreement, which provided for royalties on key holders sold in combination with rulers, watches and other items. This agreement did not otherwise alter any terms of the original agreements.
>
> [Quick Point] paid royalties … in excess of $200,000.00 from July 9, 1957 to September, 1975.[15]
>
> [O]n September 27, 1961, the Board of Patent Appeals held this was an unpatentable invention.[16]

In 1975, Quick Point sought a declaratory judgment that the royalty agreement was unenforceable. The Eighth Circuit agreed. Citing *Brulotte*, it reasoned that "if Aronson actually had obtained a patent, Quick Point would have escaped its royalty obligations either if the patent were held to be invalid or upon its expiration after 17 years. Accordingly, it concluded that a licensee should be relieved of royalty obligations when the licensor's efforts to obtain a contemplated patent prove unsuccessful."

The Supreme Court reversed. Chief Justice Burger explained:

> No decision of this Court relating to patents justifies relieving Quick Point of its contract obligations. We have held that a state may not forbid the copying of an idea in the public domain which does not meet the requirements for federal patent protection. Enforcement of Quick Point's agreement, however, does not prevent anyone from copying the keyholder. It merely requires Quick Point to pay the consideration which it promised in return for the use of a novel device which enabled it to preempt the market.

The Court's move here is an interesting one. Rather than characterizing the royalty payable to Aronson as an impermissible expansion of the nonexistent patent right that she never obtained, the Court treats the agreement as dealing entirely with nonpatent matters. As a result, the federal patent law doctrine of misuse is wholly inapplicable to her arrangement with Quick Point. As Chief Justice Burger further explains:

> On this record it is clear that the parties contracted with full awareness of both the pendency of a patent application and the possibility that a patent might not issue. The clause de-escalating the royalty by half in the event no patent issued within five years makes that crystal clear. Quick Point apparently placed a significant value on exploiting the basic novelty of the device, even if no patent issued; its success demonstrates that this judgment was well founded. Assuming, arguendo, that the initial letter and the commitment to pay a 5% royalty was subject to federal

---

[15] As detailed by the Supreme Court, Quick Point paid Aronson total royalties of $203,963.84 on sales of over $7 million.

[16] 425 F. Supp. 600 (E.D. Mo. 1976).

patent law, the provision relating to the 2 1/2% royalty was explicitly independent of federal law. The cases and principles relied on by the Court of Appeals and Quick Point [e.g., *Brulotte* – Ed.] do not bear on a contract that does not rely on a patent, particularly where, as here, the contracting parties agreed expressly as to alternative obligations if no patent should issue.

Commercial agreements traditionally are the domain of state law. State law is not displaced merely because the contract relates to intellectual property which may or may not be patentable; the states are free to regulate the use of such intellectual property in any manner not inconsistent with federal law. In this as in other fields, the question of whether federal law preempts state law "involves a consideration of whether that law stands as an obstacle to the accomplishment and execution of the full purposes and objectives of Congress." *Kewanee Oil Co. v. Bicron Corp.*, 416 U. S. 470, 479 (1974). If it does not, state law governs.

In *Kewanee Oil Co.*, we reviewed the purposes of the federal patent system. First, patent law seeks to foster and reward invention; second, it promotes disclosure of inventions to stimulate further innovation and to permit the public to practice the invention once the patent expires; third, the stringent requirements for patent protection seek to assure that ideas in the public domain remain there for the free use of the public.

Enforcement of Quick Point's agreement with Aronson is not inconsistent with any of these aims. Permitting inventors to make enforceable agreements licensing the use of their inventions in return for royalties provides an additional incentive to invention. Similarly, encouraging Aronson to make arrangements for the manufacture of her keyholder furthers the federal policy of disclosure of inventions; these simple devices display the novel idea which they embody wherever they are seen.

Notes and Questions

1. *Royalties without patents.* In *Brulotte*, Thys Co. was found liable for patent misuse by charging royalties after its patents had expired – when the patented inventions were in the public domain. But in *Aronson*, the Court held that Aronson was entitled to charge Quick Point a royalty on her invention, even though it was never patented. How does the Supreme Court's decision in *Aronson* square with *Brulotte*?

2. *Fixing* Brulotte. Given the decision in *Aronson*, how might you advise Thys Co. today regarding contractual wording that would accomplish its business goals without constituting patent misuse?

3. *When patents come and go.* In *Aronson*, the Court holds that the contract between Aronson and Quick Point was governed by principles of state contract law, as no patent had ever issued. But what if a patent had issued? Presumably, federal law would govern the contract while the patent was in force. But what if the patent were found invalid by a court five years after its issuance? Would state contract law then become applicable, or is the rule "once federal, always federal"? Under this hypothetical, would Aronson be entitled to charge Quick Point a royalty at the reduced rate after the patent was invalidated? If so, why didn't that approach work for Thys in *Brulotte*?

4. *No-challenge clauses as patent misuse?* In a 2010 article, the authors speculate whether a licensor's use of a "no-challenge" clause in a patent licensing agreement (discussed in Section 22.4) should be interpreted as an act of patent misuse.[17] As noted in Section 22.4, no-challenge clauses in ordinary patent licensing agreements are generally unenforceable

---

[17] Alfred C. Server & Peter Singleton, *Licensee Patent Validity Challenges Following MedImmune: Implications for Patent Licensing*, 3 Hastings Sci. & Tech. L.J. 243, 412–16 (2010). See also id. at 419, discussing a claim of misuse in connection with a "termination-for-challenge" clause.

under the Supreme Court's precedent in *Lear v. Adkins*. But as discussed in this chapter, a finding of misuse has far greater ramifications for the patent holder, including the broad unenforceability of the patent against others. How might a no-challenge clause potentially fit within the rubric of patent misuse? Do you think that the existence of such a clause in a licensing agreement, whether or not enforced, should constitute misuse? What about other types of clauses discouraging licensees from challenging patents (see Section 22.4.3)?

24.4 MISUSE BY BUNDLING: PACKAGE LICENSING

A third form of potential patent misuse arose when the early patent aggregator and licensing entity Hazeltine Research began to license a large portfolio of patents to manufacturers in the electronics and broadcast industries beginning in the 1940s. Below are two leading cases involving Hazeltine's "package" licenses of large portfolios of patents.

Automatic Radio Mfg. Co. v. Hazeltine Research, Inc.
339 U.S. 827 (1950)

MINTON, JUSTICE

This is a suit by respondent Hazeltine Research, Inc., as assignee of the licensor's interest in a nonexclusive patent license agreement covering a group of 570 patents and 200 applications, against petitioner Automatic Radio Manufacturing Company, Inc., the licensee, to recover royalties. The patents and applications are related to the manufacture of radio broadcasting apparatus. Respondent and its corporate affiliate and predecessor have for some twenty years been engaged in research, development, engineering design and testing and consulting services in the radio field. Respondent derives income from the licensing of its patents, its policy being to license any and all responsible manufacturers of radio apparatus at a royalty rate which for many years has been approximately one percent. Petitioner manufactures radio apparatus, particularly radio broadcasting receivers.

The license agreement in issue, which appears to be a standard Hazeltine license, was entered into by the parties in September 1942, for a term of ten years. By its terms petitioner acquired permission to use, in the manufacture of its "home" products, any or all of the patents which respondent held or to which it might acquire rights. Petitioner was not, however, obligated to use respondent's patents in the manufacture of its products. For this license, petitioner agreed to pay respondent's assignor royalties based upon a small percentage of petitioner's selling price of complete radio broadcasting receivers, and in any event a minimum of $ 10,000 per year.

This suit was brought to recover the minimum royalty due for the year ending August 31, 1946, for an accounting of other sums due, and for other relief. The District Court ... sustained the motion of respondent for judgment. The validity of the license agreement was upheld against various charges of misuse of the patents, and judgment was entered for the recovery of royalties and an accounting, and for a permanent injunction restraining petitioner from failing to pay royalties, to keep records, and to render reports during the life of the agreement. The Court of Appeals affirmed, and we granted certiorari in order to consider important questions concerning patent misuse and estoppel to challenge the validity of licensed patents.

The questions for determination are whether a misuse of patents has been shown, and whether petitioner may contest the validity of the licensed patents, in order to avoid its obligation to pay royalties under the agreement.

It is insisted that the license agreement cannot be enforced because it is a misuse of patents to require the licensee to pay royalties based on its sales, even though none of the patents are used. Petitioner directs our attention to the "Tie-in" cases. These cases have condemned schemes requiring the purchase of unpatented goods for use with patented apparatus or processes, prohibiting production or sale of competing goods, and conditioning the granting of a license under one patent upon the acceptance of another and different license. Petitioner apparently concedes that these cases do not, on their facts, control the instant situation. It is obvious that they do not. There is present here no requirement for the purchase of any goods. Hazeltine does not even manufacture or sell goods; it is engaged solely in research activities. Nor is there any prohibition as to the licensee's manufacture or sale of any type of apparatus. The fact that the license agreement covers only "home" apparatus does not mean that the licensee is prohibited from manufacturing or selling other apparatus. And finally, there is no conditioning of the license grant upon the acceptance of another and different license.

But petitioner urges that this case "is identical in principle" with the "Tie-in" cases. It is contended that the licensing provision requiring royalty payments of a percentage of the sales of the licensee's products constitutes a misuse of patents because it ties in a payment on unpatented goods. That which is condemned as against public policy by the "Tie-in" cases is the extension of the monopoly of the patent to create another monopoly or restraint of competition – a restraint not countenanced by the patent grant. See, e. g., *Mercoid Corp. v. Mid-Continent Investment Co.*, 320 U.S. 661, *Morton Salt Co. v. Suppiger Co.*, 314 U.S. 488. The principle of those cases cannot be contorted to circumscribe the instant situation. This royalty provision does not create another monopoly; it creates no restraint of competition beyond the legitimate grant of the patent. The right to a patent includes the right to market the use of the patent at a reasonable return.

The licensing agreement in issue was characterized by the District Court as essentially a grant by Hazeltine to petitioner of a privilege to use any patent or future development of Hazeltine in consideration of the payment of royalties. Payment for the privilege is required regardless of use of the patents. The royalty provision of the licensing agreement was sustained by the District Court and the Court of Appeals on the theory that it was a convenient mode of operation designed by the parties to avoid the necessity of determining whether each type of petitioner's product embodies any of the numerous Hazeltine patents. The Court of Appeals reasoned that since it would not be unlawful to agree to pay a fixed sum for the privilege to use patents, it was not unlawful to provide a variable consideration measured by a percentage of the licensee's sales for the same privilege.

The mere accumulation of patents, no matter how many, is not in and of itself illegal. And this record simply does not support incendiary, yet vague, charges that respondent uses its accumulation of patents "for the exaction of tribute" and collects royalties "by means of the overpowering threat of disastrous litigation." We cannot say that payment of royalties according to an agreed percentage of the licensee's sales is unreasonable. Sound business judgment could indicate that such payment represents the most convenient method of fixing the business value of the privileges granted by the licensing agreement. We are not unmindful that convenience cannot justify an extension of the monopoly of the patent.

But as we have already indicated, there is in this royalty provision no inherent extension of the monopoly of the patent. Petitioner cannot complain because it must pay royalties whether it uses Hazeltine patents or not. What it acquired by the agreement into which it entered was the privilege to use any or all of the patents and developments as it desired to use them. If it chooses to use none of them, it has nevertheless contracted to pay for the privilege of using existing patents plus any developments resulting from respondent's continuous research. We hold that in licensing the use of patents to one engaged in a related enterprise, it is not *per se* a misuse of patents to measure the consideration by a percentage of the licensee's sales.

The judgment of the Court of Appeals is Affirmed.

MR. JUSTICE DOUGLAS, with whom MR. JUSTICE BLACK concurs, dissenting.

We are, I think, inclined to forget that the power of Congress to grant patents is circumscribed by the Constitution. The patent power, of all legislative powers, is indeed the only one whose purpose is defined. Article I, § 8 describes the power as one "To promote the Progress of Science and useful Arts, by securing for limited Times to Authors and Inventors the exclusive Right to their respective Writings and Discoveries." This statement of policy limits the power itself.

The Court in its long history has at times been more alive to that policy than at other times. During the last three decades it has been as devoted to it (if not more so) than at any time in its history. I think that was due in large measure to the influence of Mr. Justice Brandeis and Chief Justice Stone. They were alert to the danger that business – growing bigger and bigger each decade – would fasten its hold more tightly on the economy through the cheap spawning of patents and would use one monopoly to beget another through the leverage of key patents. They followed in the early tradition of those who read the Constitution to mean that the public interest in patents comes first, reward to the inventor second.

Mr. Justice Brandeis and Chief Justice Stone did not fashion but they made more secure one important rule designed to curb the use of patents. It is as follows: One who holds a patent on article A may not license the use of the patent on condition that B, an unpatented article, be bought. Such a contract or agreement would be an extension of the grant of the patent contrary to a long line of decisions. For it would sweep under the patent an article that is unpatented or unpatentable. Each patent owner would become his own patent office and, by reason of the leverage of the patent, obtain a larger monopoly of the market than the Constitution or statutes permit.

That is what is done here. Hazeltine licensed Automatic Radio to use 570 patents and 200 patent applications. Of these Automatic used at most 10. Automatic Radio was obligated, however, to pay as royalty a percentage of its total sales in certain lines without regard to whether or not the products sold were patented or unpatented. The inevitable result is that the patentee received royalties on unpatented products as part of the price for the use of the patents.

The patent owner has therefore used the patents to bludgeon his way into a partnership with this licensee, collecting royalties on unpatented as well as patented articles.

A plainer extension of a patent by unlawful means would be hard to imagine.

Zenith Radio Corp. v. Hazeltine Research, Inc.

395 U.S. 100 (1969)

WHITE, JUSTICE

Petitioner Zenith Radio Corporation (Zenith) is a Delaware Corporation which for many years has been successfully engaged in the business of manufacturing radio and television sets for sale in the United States and foreign countries. A necessary incident of Zenith's operations has been the acquisition of licenses to use patented devices in the radios and televisions it manufactures, and its transactions have included licensing agreements with respondent Hazeltine Research, Inc. (HRI), an Illinois corporation which owns and licenses domestic patents, principally in the radio and television fields.

Until 1959, Zenith had obtained the right to use all HRI domestic patents under HRI's so-called standard package license. In that year, however, with the expiration of Zenith's license imminent, Zenith declined to accept HRI's offer to renew, asserting that it no longer required a license from HRI. Negotiations proceeded to a stalemate, and in November 1959, HRI brought suit in the Northern District of Illinois, claiming that Zenith television sets infringed HRI's patents on a particular automatic control system. Zenith's answer alleged invalidity of the patent asserted and noninfringement, and further alleged that HRI's claim was unenforceable because of patent misuse as well as unclean hands through conspiracy with foreign patent pools. On May 22, 1963, more than three years after its answer had been filed, Zenith filed a counterclaim against HRI for treble damages and injunctive relief, alleging violations of the Sherman Act by misuse of HRI patents, including the one in suit ...

The District Court, sitting without a jury, ruled for Zenith in the infringement action ... On the counterclaim, the District Court ruled, first that HRI had misused its domestic patents by attempting to coerce Zenith's acceptance of a five-year package license, and by insisting on extracting royalties from unpatented products.

With respect to Zenith's patent misuse claim, the Court of Appeals affirmed the treble-damage award against HRI, but modified in certain respects the District Court's injunction against further misuse.

We granted certiorari.

[The] only misuse issue we need consider at length is whether the Court of Appeals was correct in striking the last clause from Paragraph A of the injunction, which enjoined HRI from

> Conditioning directly or indirectly the grant of a license to defendant-counterclaimant, Zenith Radio Corporation, or any of its subsidiaries, under any domestic patent upon the taking of a license under any other patent or upon the paying of royalties on the manufacture, use or sale of apparatus not covered by such patent.

This paragraph of the injunction was directed at HRI's policy of insisting upon acceptance of its standard five-year package license agreement, covering the 500-odd patents within its domestic licensing portfolio and reserving royalties of the licensee's total radio and television sales, irrespective of whether the licensed patents were actually used in the products manufactured.

In striking the last clause of Paragraph A the Court of Appeals, in effect, made two determinations. First, under its view of *Automatic Radio Mfg. Co. v. Hazeltine Research, Inc.*, 339 U.S. 827 (1950), conditioning the grant of a patent license upon payment of royalties on unpatented products was not misuse of the patent. [W]e reverse the Court of Appeals. We hold that conditioning the grant of a patent license upon payment of royalties on products which do not use the teaching of the patent does amount to patent misuse.

The trial court's injunction does not purport to prevent the parties from serving their mutual convenience by basing royalties on the sale of all radios and television sets, irrespective of the use of HRI's inventions. The injunction reaches only situations where the patentee directly or indirectly "conditions" his license upon the payment of royalties on unpatented products – that is, where the patentee refuses to license on any other basis and leaves the licensee with the choice between a license so providing and no license at all. Also, the injunction takes effect only if the license is conditioned upon the payment of royalties "on" merchandise not covered by the patent – where the express provisions of the license or their necessary effect is to employ the patent monopoly to collect royalties, not for the use of the licensed invention, but for using, making, or selling an article not within the reach of the patent.

A patentee has the exclusive right to manufacture, use, and sell his invention. The heart of his legal monopoly is the right to invoke the State's power to prevent others from utilizing his discovery without his consent. The law also recognizes that he may assign to another his patent, in whole or in part, and may license others to practice his invention. But there are established limits which the patentee must not exceed in employing the leverage of his patent to control or limit the operations of the licensee. Among other restrictions upon him, he may not condition the right to use his patent on the licensee's agreement to purchase, use, or sell, or not to purchase, use, or sell, another article of commerce not within the scope of his patent monopoly. His right to set the price for a license does not extend so far, whatever privilege he has "to exact royalties as high as he can negotiate." And just as the patent's leverage may not be used to extract from the licensee a commitment to purchase, use, or sell other products according to the desires of the patentee, neither can that leverage be used to garner as royalties a percentage share of the licensee's receipts from sales of other products; in either case, the patentee seeks to extend the monopoly of his patent to derive a benefit not attributable to use of the patent's teachings.

In *Brulotte v. Thys Co.*, the patentee licensed the use of a patented machine, the license providing for the payment of a royalty for using the invention after, as well as before, the expiration date of the patent. Recognizing that the patentee could lawfully charge a royalty for practicing a patented invention prior to its expiration date and that the payment of this royalty could be postponed beyond that time, we noted that the post-expiration royalties were not for prior use but for current use, and were nothing less than an effort by the patentee to extend the term of his monopoly beyond that granted by law. *Brulotte* thus articulated in a particularized context the principle that a patentee may not use the power of his patent to levy a charge for making, using, or selling products not within the reach of the monopoly granted by the Government.

Automatic Radio is not to the contrary; it is not authority for the proposition that patentees have carte blanche authority to condition the grant of patent licenses upon payment of royalties on unpatented articles.

The Court's opinion in *Automatic Radio* did not deal with the license negotiations which spawned the royalty formula at issue and did not indicate that HRI used its patent leverage to coerce a promise to pay royalties on radios not practicing the learning of the patent. No such inference follows from a mere license provision measuring royalties by the licensee's total sales even if, as things work out, only some or none of the merchandise employs the patented idea or process, or even if it was foreseeable that some undetermined portion would not contain the invention. It could easily be, as the Court indicated in *Automatic Radio*, that the licensee as well as the patentee would find it more convenient and efficient from several standpoints to base royalties on total sales than to face the burden of figuring royalties based on actual use. If convenience of the parties rather than patent power dictates the total-sales royalty provision, there is no misuse of the patents and no forbidden conditions attached to the license.

The Court also said in *Automatic Radio* that if the licensee bargains for the privilege of using the patent in all of his products and agrees to a lump sum or a percentage-of-total-sales royalty, he cannot escape payment on this basis by demonstrating that he is no longer using the invention disclosed by the patent. We neither disagree nor think such transactions are barred by the trial court's injunction. If the licensee negotiates for "the privilege to use any or all of the patents and developments as [he] desire[s] to use them," he cannot complain that he must pay royalties if he chooses to use none of them. He could not then charge that the patentee had refused to license except on the basis of a total-sales royalty.

But we do not read *Automatic Radio* to authorize the patentee to use the power of his patent to insist on a total-sales royalty and to override protestations of the licensee that some of his products are unsuited to the patent or that for some lines of his merchandise he has no need or desire to purchase the privileges of the patent. In such event, not only would royalties be collected on unpatented merchandise, but the obligation to pay for nonuse would clearly have its source in the leverage of the patent.

We also think patent misuse inheres in a patentee's insistence on a percentage-of-sales royalty, regardless of use, and his rejection of licensee proposals to pay only for actual use. Unquestionably, a licensee must pay if he uses the patent. Equally, however, he may insist upon paying only for use, and not on the basis of total sales, including products in which he may use a competing patent or in which no patented ideas are used at all. There is nothing in the right granted the patentee to keep others from using, selling, or manufacturing his invention which empowers him to insist on payment not only for use but also for producing products which do not employ his discoveries at all.

Of course, a licensee cannot expect to obtain a license, giving him the privilege of use and insurance against infringement suits, without at least footing the patentee's expenses in dealing with him. He cannot insist upon paying on use alone and perhaps, as things turn out, pay absolutely nothing because he finds he can produce without using the patent. If the risks of infringement are real and he would avoid them, he must anticipate some minimum charge for the license – enough to insure the patentee against loss in negotiating and administering his monopoly, even if in fact the patent is not used at all. But we discern no basis in the statutory monopoly granted the patentee for his using that monopoly to coerce an agreement to pay a percentage royalty on merchandise not employing the discovery which the claims of the patent define.

Judgment of Court of Appeals affirmed in part and reversed in part, and case remanded.

MR. JUSTICE HARLAN, dissenting in part.

I do not join Part III [of the Court's opinion], in which the Court holds that a patent license provision which measures royalties by a percentage of the licensee's total sales is lawful if included for the "convenience" of both parties but unlawful if "insisted upon" by the patentee.

My first difficulty with this part of the opinion is that its test for validity of such royalty provisions is likely to prove exceedingly difficult to apply and consequently is apt to engender uncertainty in this area of business dealing, where certainty in the law is particularly desirable. In practice, it often will be very hard to tell whether a license provision was included at the instance of both parties or only at the will of the licensor. District courts will have the unenviable task of deciding whether the course of negotiations establishes "insistence" upon the suspect provision. Because of the uncertainty inherent in such determinations, parties to existing and future licenses will have little assurance that their agreements will be enforced. And it may be predicted that after today's decision the licensor will be careful to embellish the negotiations with an alternative proposal, making the court's unraveling of the situation that much more difficult.

Such considerations lead me to the view that any rule which causes the validity of percentage-of-sales royalty provisions to depend upon subsequent judicial examination of the parties' negotiations will disserve rather than further the interests of all concerned. Hence, I think that the Court has fallen short in failing to address itself to the question whether employment of such royalty provisions should invariably amount to patent misuse.

[A] possible justification for the Court's result might be that a royalty based directly upon use of the patent will tend to spur the licensee to "invent around" the patent or otherwise acquire a substitute which costs less, while a percentage-of-sales royalty can have no such effect because of the licensee's knowledge that he must pay the royalty regardless of actual patent use. No hint of such a rationale appears in the Court's opinion. Moreover, under this theory a percentage-of-sales royalty would be objectionable largely because of resulting damage to the rest of the economy, through less efficient allocation of resources, rather than because of possible harm to the licensee. Hence, the theory might not admit of the Court's exception for provisions included for the "convenience" of both parties.

Because of its failure to explain the reasons for the result reached ... the Court's opinion is of little assistance in answering the question which I consider to be the crux of this part of the case: whether percentage-of-sales royalty provisions should be held without exception to constitute patent misuse. A recent economic analysis argues that such provisions may have two undesirable consequences. First, as has already been noted, employment of such provisions may tend to reduce the licensee's incentive to substitute other, cheaper "inputs" for the patented item in producing an unpatented end-product. Failure of the licensee to substitute will, it is said, cause the price of the end-product to be higher and its output lower than would be the case if substitution had occurred. Second, it is suggested that under certain conditions a percentage-of-sales royalty arrangement may enable the patentee to garner for himself elements of profit, above the norm for the industry or economy, which are properly attributable not to the licensee's use of the patent but to other factors which cause the licensee's situation to differ from one of "perfect competition," and that this cannot occur when royalties are based upon use.

If accepted, this economic analysis would indicate that percentage-of-sales royalties should be entirely outlawed. However, so far as I have been able to find, there has as yet been little discussion of these matters either by lawyers or by economists. And I find scant illumination on this score in the briefs and arguments of the parties in this case. The Court has pointed out both today and in *Automatic Radio* that percentage-of-sales royalties may be administratively advantageous for both patentee and licensee. In these circumstances, confronted, as I believe we are, with the choice of holding such royalty provisions either valid or invalid across the board, I would, as an individual member of the Court, adhere for the present to the rule of *Automatic Radio.*

FIGURE 24.5 Decided nearly two decades apart, *Automatic Radio* and *Zenith* both involved licenses by Hazeltine, an early electronics patent aggregator and licensing entity.

Notes and Questions

1. *Total sales royalties.* How is the royalty payable to Hazeltine calculated in each of *Automatic Radio* and *Zenith,* and why does the licensee in each case contend that it constitutes patent misuse?

2. *Convenience versus compulsion.* The Court in *Zenith* distinguishes its earlier decision in *Automatic Radio* by drawing a fine line between "total sales" royalties that are established for the "convenience of the parties" (not misuse) versus those on which the licensor "insists" (misuse). In his dissent, Justice Harlan observes that "District courts will have the unenviable task of deciding whether the course of negotiations establishes 'insistence' upon the suspect provision," and that "[b]ecause of the uncertainty inherent in such determinations, parties to existing and future licenses will have little assurance that their agreements will be enforced." As a result, Justice Harlan argued that package licensing should be "either valid or invalid across the board." Do you agree with Justice Harlan's assessment, or are you comfortable with the majority's confidence in courts' ability to differentiate between these two modes of conduct? If you were representing a licensor of a large portfolio of patents, how would you advise it to approach the negotiation of its royalties with prospective licensees?

3. *A preferred payment?* Justices Douglas and Black dissented from the Court's opinion in *Automatic Radio.* Among other things, they expressed concern that Hazeltine licensed, and required Automatic Radio to pay for, 570 patents and 200 patent applications, of which Automatic Radio used "at most 10." But on what basis would they have preferred Automatic

Radio to pay for the use of Hazeltine's patents? Should patent aggregators like Hazeltine be required to price patents on an *à la carte* basis? Is that reasonable when hundreds or, today, thousands of patents are involved in a single license?

4. *Inverse dissents? Automatic Radio* and *Zenith* are viewed, in many respects, like inverse images of one another. In addition to many other similarities, each decision drew a pointed dissent. But did the Court in *Zenith* adopt the reasoning of the dissent in *Automatic Radio*, or vice versa? Why not?

5. *Package licensing and market power*. As noted above, in 1988 Congress enacted the Patent Misuse Reform Act, which added "market power" to the elements required to find patent misuse of the tying variety (codified at 35 U.S.C. § 271(d)(5)). This market power requirement also applies to package licensing misuse (i.e., conditioning the license of any rights to a patent on the acquisition of a license to rights in another patent). Yet the enactment of § 271(d)(5) does not seem to have substantially altered the convenience vs. compulsion test established under *Automatic Radio* and *Zenith*.[18] How would § 271(d)(5) have affected the analysis in each of these cases had it been enacted at the time of the licenses in question?

6. *Package licensing and incentives*. In his dissent in *Zenith*, Justice Harlan offers up an alternative rationale supporting the majority's decision: that allowing package licenses will decrease a licensee's incentive to "invent around" the licensed patents or to employ substitute and cheaper technologies in its products, resulting in decreased innovation and higher consumer prices.[19] Why does Justice Harlan believe that this result is possible? Why didn't the majority rely on this line of reasoning in its own opinion?

7. *Patent misuse and irrationality*. Professor Mark Lemley has written:

> [T]he patent misuse doctrine is indefensible from an economic standpoint for several reasons. First, the sanction imposed bears no relation to the injury caused. Second, the sanction duplicates antitrust remedies in many cases, leading to an excessive level of deterrence. Third, the doctrine often pays the sanction as a windfall to an unrelated third party, thereby encouraging infringement while failing to compensate those actually injured. These economic problems lead one seriously to question the continued vitality of the patent misuse doctrine as a whole.

What are examples of each of Professor Lemley's three specific critiques of the patent misuse doctrine? Do you agree that the patent misuse doctrine should be abolished?

8. *Packaged patents and standards*. The Federal Circuit considered patent misuse in a series of cases involving the alleged infringement by compact disc manufacturer Princo of a group of pooled patents covering the CD-R and CD-RW standards. In one such case, *U.S. Philips Corp. v. ITC*, 424 F.3d 1179 (Fed. Cir. 2005), Princo asserted that Philips (the administrator of the relevant patent pools) committed patent misuse by offering to license all of the pooled patents as a single package, without the option to license individual patents separately. In other words, by tying undesired patents to desired patents. The International Trade Commission (ITC) found misuse by tying, but the Federal Circuit reversed, reasoning that package licensing does not constitute patent misuse *per se* because it potentially reduces transaction costs and creates other efficiencies, and thus does not lack any

---

[18] See Burchfiel, supra note 10, at 8–9.

[19] Similar arguments have been made with respect to patent pools. See Section 26.4, discussing complementarity and substitutability of patents included in pools.

redeeming value (the general standard for *per se* illegality). Likewise, the Federal Circuit reversed the ITC's finding of patent misuse under the "rule of reason" because the ITC "failed to consider the efficiencies that package licensing may produce." The court further noted that when "a patentholder has a package of patents, all of which are necessary to enable a licensee to practice particular technology, it is well established that the patentee may lawfully insist on licensing the patents as a package and may refuse to license them individually, since the group of patents could not reasonably be viewed as distinct products." That is, if all packaged patents are essential to the particular standard, then, in theory, all of the packaged patents should be considered part of the same tying product, hence offering them together cannot constitute misuse. However, if some patents not essential to the standard are included in the package, misuse may again be possible. This is among the reasons that antitrust authorities have generally recommended that patent pools include only patents that are complements (essential to a particular standard or technology), and not substitutes. See Sections 26.3 and 26.4.

9. *Packaging non-essential patents.* In *Philips*, Princo also alleged that some of the pooled patents were not actually essential to the relevant CD standards. The Federal Circuit, acknowledging this possibility, reasoned that "in a fast-developing field such as the one at issue in this case, it seems quite likely that questions will arise over time, such as what constitutes an 'essential' patent," and that *per se* liability for patent misuse should not arise due to technological changes that were not foreseeable at the time of licensing. And with respect to the analysis under the rule of reason, "evidence did not show that including those patents in the patent packages had a negative effect on commercially available technology" – in effect, Princo did not meet its burden of establishing a sufficient anticompetitive harm. As a result, the alleged nonessentiality of some of the pooled patents did not give rise to liability for patent misuse in this case, though the Federal Circuit did not rule out the prospect of such liability upon a sufficient showing of evidence. What evidence might this be?

SUMMARY: PATENT MISUSE DOCTRINE TODAY

Enforcement against non-patented components: not misuse (§ 271(d)(1)–(3) [1952])
Refusal to license: not misuse (§ 271(d)(4) [1988])
Tying: rule of reason, requires market power (§ 271(d)(5) [1988])
Package licensing: permitted for mutual convenience, so long as there is no compulsion (*Automatic Radio*, *Zenith*), requires market power (§ 271(d)(5) [1988])
Unpatented articles: no misuse (*Aronson*)
Post-term royalties: *per se* illegal (*Brulotte*, *Kimble*)

24.5 NONCOMPETITION AND COPYRIGHT MISUSE

Misuse of IP is not entirely limited to the patent world. Though far fewer in number, there have been cases involving the misuse of copyrights as well.

Lasercomb v. Reynolds

911 F.2d 970 (4th Cir. 1990)

SPROUSE, CIRCUIT JUDGE

Appellants and defendants below are Larry Holliday, president and sole shareholder of Holiday Steel Rule Die Corporation (Holiday Steel), and Job Reynolds, a computer programmer for that company. Appellee is Lasercomb America, Inc. (Lasercomb), the plaintiff below. Holiday Steel and Lasercomb were competitors in the manufacture of steel rule dies that are used to cut and score paper and cardboard for folding into boxes and cartons. Lasercomb developed a software program, Interact, which is the object of the dispute between the parties. Using this program, a designer creates a template of a cardboard cutout on a computer screen and the software directs the mechanized creation of the conforming steel rule die.

In 1983, before Lasercomb was ready to market its Interact program generally, it licensed four prerelease copies to Holiday Steel which paid $35,000 for the first copy, $17,500 each for the next two copies, and $2,000 for the fourth copy. Lasercomb informed Holiday Steel that it would charge $2,000 for each additional copy Holiday Steel cared to purchase. Apparently ambitious to create for itself an even better deal, Holiday Steel circumvented the protective devices Lasercomb had provided with the software and made three unauthorized copies of Interact which it used on its computer systems. Perhaps buoyed by its success in copying, Holiday Steel then created a software program called "PDS-1000," which was almost entirely a direct copy of Interact, and marketed it as its own CAD/CAM die-making software. These infringing activities were accomplished by Job Reynolds at the direction of Larry Holliday.

There is no question that defendants engaged in unauthorized copying, and the purposefulness of their unlawful action is manifest from their deceptive practices ... When Lasercomb discovered Holiday Steel's activities, it registered its copyright in Interact and filed this action against Holiday Steel, Holliday, and Reynolds on March 7, 1986. Lasercomb claimed copyright infringement, breach of contract, misappropriation of trade secret, false designation of origin, unfair competition, and fraud. Defendants filed a number of counterclaims. On March 24, 1986, the district court entered a preliminary injunction, enjoining defendants from marketing the PDS-1000 software.

Holliday and Reynolds [do] not dispute that they copied Interact, but they contend that Lasercomb is barred from recovery for infringement by its concomitant culpability. They assert that, assuming Lasercomb had a perfected copyright, it impermissibly abused it. This assertion of the "misuse of copyright" defense is based on language in Lasercomb's standard licensing agreement, restricting licensees from creating any of their own CAD/CAM die-making software.

The offending paragraphs read:

D. Licensee agrees during the term of this Agreement that it will not permit or suffer its directors, officers and employees, directly or indirectly, to write, develop, produce or sell computer assisted die making software.

E. Licensee agrees during the term of this Agreement and for one (1) year after the termination of this Agreement, that it will not write, develop, produce or sell or assist others in the writing, developing, producing or selling computer assisted die making software, directly or indirectly without Lasercomb's prior written consent. Any such activity undertaken without Lasercomb's written consent shall nullify any warranties or agreements of Lasercomb set forth herein.

The "term of this Agreement" referred to in these clauses is ninety-nine years.

Defendants were not themselves bound by the standard licensing agreement. Lasercomb had sent the agreement to Holiday Steel with a request that it be signed and returned. Larry Holliday, however, decided not to sign the document, and Lasercomb apparently overlooked the fact that the document had not been returned. Although defendants were not party to the restrictions of which they complain, they proved at trial that at least one Interact licensee had entered into the standard agreement, including the anticompetitive language.

The district court rejected the copyright misuse defense for three reasons. First, it noted that defendants had not explicitly agreed to the contract clauses alleged to constitute copyright misuse. Second, it found "such a clause is reasonable in light of the delicate and sensitive area of computer software." And, third, it questioned whether such a defense exists. We consider the district court's reasoning in reverse order.

The philosophy behind copyright ... is that the public benefits from the efforts of authors to introduce new ideas and knowledge into the public domain. To encourage such efforts, society grants authors exclusive rights in their works for a limited time.

Although the patent misuse defense has been generally recognized since *Morton Salt*, it has been much less certain whether an analogous copyright misuse defense exists. This uncertainty persists because no United States Supreme Court decision has firmly established a copyright misuse defense in a manner analogous to the establishment of the patent misuse defense by Morton Salt. The few courts considering the issue have split on whether the defense should be recognized, and we have discovered only one case which has actually applied copyright misuse to bar an action for infringement.

We are of the view, however, that since copyright and patent law serve parallel public interests, a "misuse" defense should apply to infringement actions brought to vindicate either right.

[And] while it is true that the attempted use of a copyright to violate antitrust law probably would give rise to a misuse of copyright defense, the converse is not necessarily true – a misuse need not be a violation of antitrust law in order to comprise an equitable defense to an infringement action. The question is not whether the copyright is being used in a manner violative of antitrust law (such as whether the licensing agreement is "reasonable"), but whether the copyright is being used in a manner violative of the public policy embodied in the grant of a copyright.

Lasercomb undoubtedly has the right to protect against copying of the Interact code. Its standard licensing agreement, however, goes much further and essentially attempts to suppress any attempt by the licensee to independently implement the idea which Interact expresses. The agreement forbids the licensee to develop or assist in developing any kind of computer-assisted die-making software. If the licensee is a business, it is to prevent all its directors, officers and employees from assisting in any manner to develop computer-assisted die-making software. Although one or another licensee might succeed in negotiating out the noncompete provisions, this does not negate the fact that Lasercomb is attempting to use its copyright in a manner adverse to the public policy embodied in copyright law, and that it has succeeded in doing so with at least one licensee.

The language employed in the Lasercomb agreement is extremely broad. Each time Lasercomb sells its Interact program to a company and obtains that company's agreement to the noncompete language, the company is required to forego utilization of the creative abilities of all its officers, directors and employees in the area of CAD/CAM die-making software. Of yet greater concern, these creative abilities are withdrawn from the public. The period for which this anticompetitive restraint exists is ninety-nine years, which could be longer than the life of the copyright itself.

FIGURE 24.6 Lasercomb's software related to the computer-aided design of steel rule dies for cutting cardboard.

We previously have considered the effect of anticompetitive language in a licensing agreement in the context of patent misuse. *Compton v. Metal Products, Inc.*, 453 F.2d 38 (4th Cir.1971), cert. denied, 406 U.S. 968 (1972). Compton had invented and patented coal auguring equipment. He granted an exclusive license in the patents to Joy Manufacturing, and the license agreement included a provision that Compton would not "engage in any business or activity relating to the manufacture or sale of equipment of the type licensed hereunder" for as long as he was due royalties under the patents. Suit for infringement of the Compton patents was brought against Metal Products, and the district court granted injunctive relief and damages. On appeal we held that relief for the infringement was barred by the misuse defense, stating:

> The need of Joy to protect its investment does not outweigh the public's right under our system to expect competition and the benefits which flow therefrom, and the total withdrawal of Compton from the mining machine business ... everywhere in the world for a period of 20 years unreasonably lessens the competition which the public has a right to expect, and constitutes misuse of the patents.

We think the anticompetitive language in Lasercomb's licensing agreement is at least as egregious as that which led us to bar the infringement action in *Compton*, and therefore amounts to misuse of its copyright. Again, the analysis necessary to a finding of misuse is similar to but separate from the analysis necessary to a finding of antitrust violation. The misuse arises from Lasercomb's attempt to use its copyright in a particular expression, the Interact software, to control competition in an area outside the copyright, i.e., the idea of computer-assisted die manufacture, regardless of whether such conduct amounts to an antitrust violation.

In its rejection of the copyright misuse defense, the district court emphasized that Holiday Steel was not explicitly party to a licensing agreement containing the offending language. However, again analogizing to patent misuse, the defense of copyright misuse is available even if the defendants themselves have not been injured by the misuse. In *Morton Salt*, the defendant was not a party to the license requirement that only Morton-produced salt tablets be used with Morton's salt-depositing machine. Nevertheless, suit against defendant for infringement of Morton's patent was barred on public policy grounds. Similarly, in *Compton*, even though the defendant Metal Products was not a party to the license agreement that restrained competition by Compton, suit against Metal Products was barred because of the public interest in free competition.

Therefore, the fact that appellants here were not parties to one of Lasercomb's standard license agreements is inapposite to their copyright misuse defense. The question is whether Lasercomb is using its copyright in a manner contrary to public policy, which question we have answered in the affirmative.

Notes and Questions

1. *Patent versus copyright.* Why do you think that there have been comparatively few cases involving copyright misuse in comparison to the number of cases involving patent misuse? Is this difference due to a fundamental difference between copyright and patent law, or the licensing practices of copyright versus patent owners, or something else?

2. *What is copyright misuse?* In *Lasercomb*, the court finds that "the anticompetitive language in Lasercomb's licensing agreement is at least as egregious as that which led us to bar the infringement action in *Compton*, and therefore amounts to misuse of its copyright." What kind of standard of review is this? *Compton* was a patent misuse case. As discussed in Supreme Court cases since *Morton Salt*, the standard for assessing patent misuse is whether or not the licensor impermissibly attempted to expand the scope of the patent grant. Is this the standard for copyright misuse according to the Fourth Circuit? Or should copyright misuse, as suggested by the Fourth Circuit, be determined based on whether or not the offending licensing language is more or less egregious than the language in one or more patent misuse cases? How should one measure egregiousness? How would you describe a better test for copyright misuse?

3. *A need for statutory reform?* Why did the 1988 Patent Misuse Reform Act cover only patents? Is a statutory reform effort needed to address copyright misuse?

4. *Copyright misuse through suppression of speech.* In *Video Pipeline, Inc. v. Buena Vista Home Entertainment, Inc.*, 342 F.3d 191 (3d Cir. 2003), Video Pipeline created and displayed "clip previews" (short, two-minute segments) of approximately sixty-two Disney films on its website without Disney's permission. Disney accused Video Pipeline of copyright infringement and Video Pipeline responded that Disney had misused its copyright and, as a result, should not receive the protection of copyright law. Specifically, Video Pipeline pointed to the licensing agreements that Disney entered into with other websites authorizing them to display trailers of Disney films. Those agreements contained the following clause:

   The Website in which the Trailers are used may not be derogatory to or critical of the entertainment industry or of [Disney] (and its officers, directors, agents, employees, affiliates, divisions and subsidiaries) or of any motion picture produced or distributed by [Disney] ... [or]

of the materials from which the Trailers were taken or of any person involved with the production of the Underlying Works. Any breach of this paragraph will render this license null and void and Licensee will be liable to all parties concerned for defamation and copyright infringement, as well as breach of contract.

According to Video Pipeline, this prohibition leveraged Disney's copyright in its trailers to suppress free speech and criticism of Disney, and is thus copyright misuse. In assessing Video Pipeline's claim, the Third Circuit recognized the defense of copyright misuse, but held that Video Pipeline had not established misuse in this case. The court explained:

Misuse often exists where the patent or copyright holder has engaged in some form of anti-competitive behavior. More on point, however, is the underlying policy rationale for the misuse doctrine set out in the Constitution's Copyright and Patent Clause: "to promote the Progress of Science and useful Arts." The "ultimate aim" of copyright law is "to stimulate artistic creativity for the general public good." Put simply, our Constitution emphasizes the purpose and value of copyrights and patents. Harm caused by their misuse undermines their usefulness.

Anti-competitive licensing agreements may conflict with the purpose behind a copyright's protection by depriving the public of the would-be competitor's creativity. The fair use doctrine and the refusal to copyright facts and ideas also address applications of copyright protection that would otherwise conflict with a copyright's constitutional goal. But it is possible that a copyright holder could leverage its copyright to restrain the creative expression of another without engaging in anti-competitive behavior or implicating the fair use and idea/expression doctrines.

The licensing agreements in this case do seek to restrict expression by licensing the Disney trailers for use on the internet only so long as the web sites on which the trailers will appear do not derogate Disney, the entertainment industry, etc. But we nonetheless cannot conclude on this record that the agreements are likely to interfere with creative expression to such a degree that they affect in any significant way the policy interest in increasing the public store of creative activity. The licensing agreements do not, for instance, interfere with the licensee's opportunity to express such criticism on other web sites or elsewhere. There is no evidence that the public will find it any more difficult to obtain criticism of Disney and its interests, or even that the public is considerably less likely to come across this criticism, if it is not displayed on the same site as the trailers. Moreover, if a critic wishes to comment on Disney's works, the fair use doctrine may be implicated regardless of the existence of the licensing agreements. Finally, copyright law, and the misuse doctrine in particular, should not be interpreted to require Disney, if it licenses its trailers for display on any web sites but its own, to do so willy-nilly regardless of the content displayed with its copyrighted works.

 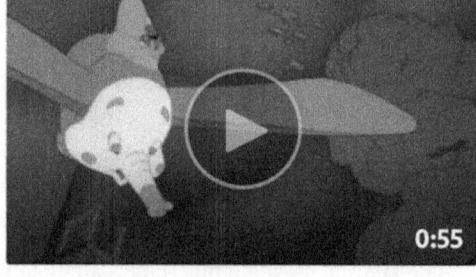

FIGURE 24.7 Video Pipeline allegedly displayed short clips of more than sixty Disney films on its website without authorization.

Indeed such an application of the misuse doctrine would likely decrease the public's access to Disney's works because it might as a result refuse to license at all online display of its works.

Thus, while we extend the patent misuse doctrine to copyright, and recognize that it might operate beyond its traditional anti-competition context, we hold it inapplicable here. On this record Disney's licensing agreements do not interfere significantly with copyright policy (while holding to the contrary might, in fact, do so).

How convincing is Video Pipeline's case for copyright misuse? Is the Third Circuit's test for copyright misuse in *Video Pipeline* any clearer than the Fourth Circuit's test in *Lasercomb*? Under what fact patterns might a claim for copyright misuse be established based on suppression of speech?

Antitrust and Competition Issues

This chapter offers a broad overview of the impact of US antitrust laws on intellectual property (IP) licensing and transactions. It is by no means comprehensive, and there are numerous texts that deal with these issues in far greater depth.[1] A basic understanding of antitrust law is, however, critical to the analysis of IP licensing arrangements. As I observed over many years of legal practice, to the uninitiated, anticompetitive arrangements often seem like great business ideas – activities like price fixing, market allocation, even concerted refusals to deal can be profitable and beneficial for those who engage in them. Unfortunately, they are illegal. As a result, this chapter offers a summary of the antitrust doctrines that arise frequently in IP- and technology-focused transactions. Antitrust issues also play a role in the analysis of joint ventures, which are discussed in Section 9.4, and IP pools, which are discussed in Chapter 26 (a preview of this topic is presented in Section 25.5).

Antitrust law can be a particularly challenging subject, as the law, and even the basic premises underlying it, have evolved over time. As you read this chapter, consider how antitrust attitudes toward IP have shifted over the last fifty years, from the suspicion evidenced by the "Nine No-Nos" to the relatively permissive posture adopted in recent cases.

---

[1] See, e.g., Christopher R. Leslie, Antitrust Law and Intellectual Property Rights (Oxford Univ. Press, 2011); Mark R. Patterson, Antitrust Law in the Online Economy: Selected Cases and Materials (Amazon, 2020).

SHERMAN ANTITRUST ACT OF 1890

Section 1

Every contract, combination in the form of trust or otherwise, or conspiracy, in restraint of trade or commerce among the several States, or with foreign nations, is declared to be illegal …

Section 2

Every person who shall monopolize, or attempt to monopolize, or combine or conspire with any other person or persons, to monopolize any part of the trade or commerce among the several States, or with foreign nations, shall be deemed guilty of a felony …

At their most fundamental level, the antitrust laws are intended to protect free market competition from private restraint. In the United States, the principal antitrust statute is the Sherman Antitrust Act of 1890 (15 U.S.C. §§ 1–38). The Sherman Act has two main goals, described in its first two sections. Section 1 of the Sherman Act is described as prohibiting unlawful combinations – concerted action by competitors – and Section 2 is described as prohibiting monopolization – unilateral action. Though these two statutory sections are brief (often referred to as Constitutional in scope), they have spawned volumes of commentary and case law over more than a century. In addition to the Sherman Act, other US statutes address antitrust issues, including the Clayton Act of 1914 (15 U.S.C. §§ 12–27, 29 U.S.C. §§ 52–53), which deals primarily with mergers and acquisitions, and the Robinson–Patman Act (15 U.S.C. § 13), which deals with price discrimination. In addition, most states have their own competition laws, which overlap with federal laws to differing degrees.

On the other hand, IP rights, by their very nature, afford their owners exclusive rights over certain works and inventions. They are sometimes referred to as legally sanctioned monopolies. Intellectual property licenses are arrangements among multiple parties. It should thus be obvious that IP licensing intersects with, and can run afoul of, the antitrust laws in a variety of ways.

FIGURE 25.1 The Sherman Act was enacted to combat the worst abuses of sprawling business "trusts."

ANTITRUST ENFORCEMENT IN THE UNITED STATES

Unlike most countries, the United States has not one, but two federal agencies with jurisdiction to enforce the antitrust laws: the Department of Justice (DOJ) acting through its Antitrust Division, and the Federal Trade Commission (FTC), an independent federal agency formed in 1914. These two agencies have overlapping but not entirely coextensive jurisdiction over antitrust matters.

The DOJ has sole authority to prosecute criminal violations of the antitrust laws. The DOJ also issues Business Review Letters (BRL) in response to inquiries from private parties. In BRLs the DOJ indicates whether it would likely prosecute a proposed transaction.

The FTC is chartered under the Federal Trade Commission Act (15 U.S.C. § 41 *et seq.*). Section 5 of the FTC Act bans "unfair methods of competition" and "unfair or deceptive acts or practices." The Supreme Court has held that violations of the Sherman Act necessarily violate the FTC Act. Thus, while the FTC does not technically enforce the Sherman Act, it can prosecute the same types of conduct under the FTC Act. There is also some debate over the extent to which § 5 of the FTC Act, particularly its ban on "unfair methods of competition," prohibits conduct beyond the bounds of the Sherman Act.

The DOJ and FTC have historically coordinated their antitrust enforcement activities, and have produced numerous joint statements regarding their views of the law. Nevertheless, the agencies do not always see eye to eye. During the Trump Administration, in particular, the DOJ and FTC have taken opposing views on antitrust issues, particularly when they involve IP. The most stark example of this divergence occurred during the FTC's enforcement action against Qualcomm, in which the DOJ intervened several times in support of the defendant.

In addition to the FTC and DOJ, private parties can also bring suits to enforce the Sherman Act, though their remedies are limited to monetary and injunctive relief – criminal penalties being available only to the DOJ. Only the FTC may enforce the FTC Act.

In considering statements and opinions issued by the US antitrust enforcement agencies, it is important to remember that these agencies *enforce* the antitrust laws, they do not *make* the antitrust laws. As in other areas of federal law, Congress enacts the laws, which are then interpreted by the courts. Just as the FBI, another unit of the DOJ, investigates violations of and enforces federal criminal laws, the DOJ's Antitrust Division investigates potential antitrust violations and, if it feels that a violation has occurred, it may bring an action in court. But the DOJ's determination that a violation of antitrust law has occurred does not make it so, any more than the FBI's seizure of an alleged felon's assets automatically passes muster under the Fourth Amendment.

FIGURE 25.2 Unlike most countries, the United States has two antitrust enforcement agencies with overlapping jurisdiction and sometimes conflicting policies.

25.1 *PER SE* ILLEGALITY VERSUS THE RULE OF REASON

From the early twentieth century through the 1970s, US antitrust authorities and courts had a relatively dim view of IP. As one DOJ official explained, "The prevailing view in the 1970s was that antitrust law and IP law shared no common purpose. One created monopolies and the other sought to prevent them, so the two regimes were seen as not only in tension, but in conflict."[2] As a result, during the first three-quarters of the twentieth century, many arrangements involving IP were found to violate the antitrust laws.[3] Various licensing practices that were condemned were summed up in 1970 by a DOJ official in a list that came to be known as the "Nine No-Nos."[4] The Nine No-Nos are summarized as follows:

1. royalties not reasonably related to sales of the patented products;
2. restraints on licensees' commerce outside the scope of the patent (tie-outs);
3. requiring the licensee to purchase unpatented materials from the licensor (tie-ins);
4. mandatory package licensing;
5. requiring the licensee to assign to the patentee patents that may be issued to the licensee after the licensing arrangement is executed (exclusive grantbacks):
6. licensee veto power over grants of further licenses;
7. restraints on sales of unpatented products made with a patented process;
8. post-sale restraints on resale; and
9. setting minimum prices on resale of the patent products.

Committing any of the Nine No-Nos was viewed as a *per se* violation of the antitrust laws. That is, if a party was found to engage in one of these practices, antitrust liability was effectively automatic. Views of the role and scope of US antitrust law began to change in the late 1970s,

---

[2] Makan Delrahim, "*The times they are a'changin'*": *The Nine No-No's in 2019*, Remarks as Prepared for the Licensing Executives Society (LES) 2019 Annual Meeting, October 21, 2019 at 2.

[3] For a summary of several of these early cases, see Jorge L. Contreras, *A Brief History of FRAND: Analyzing Current Debates in Standard-Setting and Antitrust through a Historical Lens*, 80 Antitrust L.J. 39 (2015).

[4] See Richard Gilbert & Carl Shapiro, *Antitrust Issues in the Licensing of Intellectual Property: The Nine No-No's Meet the Nineties*, Brookings Papers on Economic Activity: Microeconomics 283, 285 (1997).

influenced by the rise of the "Chicago School" of law and economics and by the publication of Robert Bork's deeply flawed but highly influential book *The Antitrust Paradox* (1978). Thus, by the early 1980s the DOJ began to reconsider the validity of the Nine No-Nos. In 1988, the DOJ issued a policy statement that shifted its analysis of most IP licensing practices from *per se* illegality to a "rule of reason" approach in which the potential anticompetitive effects of an arrangement are balanced against its procompetitive effects.[5] Under the rule of reason, an arrangement will be condemned only if the anticompetitive effects outweigh the procompetitive effects.

In 1995, the DOJ and FTC jointly released a set of Antitrust Guidelines for the Licensing of Intellectual Property. As explained by Richard Gilbert and Carl Shapiro, the DOJ–FTC Guidelines embody three core principles regarding IP licensing:

- an explicit recognition of the generally procompetitive nature of licensing arrangements;
- a clear rejection of any presumption that IP necessarily creates market power in the antitrust context; and
- an endorsement of the validity of applying the same general antitrust approach to the analysis of conduct involving IP that the agencies apply to conduct involving other forms of tangible or intangible property.[6]

These core principles and the other elements of the 1995 DOJ–FTC Guidelines proved remarkably influential and long-lasting. They were only updated once, in 2017, and have largely retained their original intent and scope. We will see elements from the DOJ–FTC Guidelines throughout this chapter.

While the current approach to antitrust liability largely relies on the "rule of reason" analysis, there are still some areas of *per se* liability.

25.2 PRICE FIXING

Chief among the areas of *per se* liability today is price fixing and the related activity of bid rigging. Both are forms of impermissible collusion that violate Section 1 of the Sherman Act. Because liability is *per se*, "where such a collusive scheme has been established, it cannot be justified under the law by arguments or evidence that, for example, the agreed-upon prices were reasonable, the agreement was necessary to prevent or eliminate price cutting or ruinous competition, or the conspirators were merely trying to make sure that each got a fair share of the market."[7]

The DOJ defines price fixing as follows:

Price fixing is an agreement among competitors to raise, fix, or otherwise maintain the price at which their goods or services are sold. It is not necessary that the competitors agree to charge exactly the same price, or that every competitor in a given industry join the conspiracy. Price fixing can take many forms, and any agreement that restricts price competition violates the law. Other examples of price-fixing agreements include those to:

- Establish or adhere to price discounts.
- Hold prices firm.

---

[5]   See Gilbert & Shapiro, *supra* note 4, at 286.
[6]   Id. at 287.
[7]   US Dept. Justice (DOJ), Price Fixing, Bid Rigging, and Market Allocation Schemes: What They Are and What to Look For, www.justice.gov/atr/price-fixing-bid-rigging-and-market-allocation-schemes (June 25, 2015).

- Eliminate or reduce discounts.
- Adopt a standard formula for computing prices.
- Maintain certain price differentials between different types, sizes, or quantities of products.
- Adhere to a minimum fee or price schedule.
- Fix credit terms.
- Not advertise prices.

In many cases, participants in a price-fixing conspiracy also establish some type of policing mechanism to make sure that everyone adheres to the agreement.[8]

Three Executives Indicted for Their Roles in the DRAM Price-Fixing & Bid-Rigging Conspiracy

US Department of Justice, October 18, 2006

WASHINGTON – A federal grand jury in San Francisco today returned an indictment against two executives from Samsung Electronics Ltd. (Samsung) and one executive from Hynix Semiconductor America Inc. (Hynix America) for their participation in a global conspiracy to fix DRAM prices, the Department of Justice announced.

Including today's charge, four companies and 16 individuals have been charged and fines totaling more than $731 million have resulted from the Department's ongoing antitrust investigation into the DRAM industry. The $731 million in criminal fines is the second highest total obtained by the Department of Justice in a criminal antitrust investigation into a specific industry.

The indictment, filed today in the U.S. District Court in San Francisco, charged that Il Ung Kim, Young Bae Rha, and Gary Swanson participated with co-conspirators in the conspiracy from on or about April 1, 2001, until on or about June 15, 2002. At the time of the conspiracy, Kim was vice president of marketing for the memory division at Samsung. Rha was vice president of sales and marketing for the memory division at Samsung. Both Kim and Rha are citizens and residents of Korea. At the time of the conspiracy, Swanson was senior vice president of memory sales and marketing for Hynix America, the U.S.-based subsidiary of Hynix Semiconductor Inc. (Hynix), which is headquartered in Korea. Swanson is a resident and citizen of the United States.

DRAM is the most commonly used semiconductor memory product, providing high-speed storage and retrieval of electronic information for a wide variety of computer, telecommunication and consumer electronic products. DRAM is used in personal computers, laptops, workstations, servers, printers, hard disk drives, personal digital assistants (PDAs), modems, mobile phones, telecommunication hubs and routers, digital cameras, video recorders and TVs, digital set-top boxes, game consoles and digital music players. There were approximately $7.7 billion in DRAM sales in the United States alone in 2004.

---

[8] DOJ, Price Fixing, *supra* note 7.

The indictment charges that Kim, Rha, Swanson, and their co-conspirators carried out the conspiracy in a variety of ways, including:

- Attending meetings and participating in telephone conversations in the U.S. and elsewhere to discuss the prices of DRAM to be sold to certain original equipment manufacturers (OEMs);
- Agreeing during those meetings and telephone conversations to charge prices of DRAM at certain levels to be sold to certain OEMs;
- Exchanging information on sales of DRAM to certain OEM customers, for the purpose of monitoring and enforcing adherence to the agreed-upon prices;
- Agreeing during those meetings and telephone conversations to raise and maintain prices of DRAM to be sold to certain OEMs;
- Agreeing during those meetings and telephone discussions to rig the online auction, sponsored by Compaq Computer Corporation on Nov. 29, 2001, by not submitting a bid in the auction, or by submitting intentionally high prices on the bids in the auction ...

The Samsung employees agreed to serve prison terms ranging from seven to eight months and to each pay a $250,000 fine. In total, four companies have been charged with price-fixing in the DRAM investigation. Samsung pleaded guilty to the price fixing conspiracy and was sentenced to pay a $300 million criminal fine in November 2005. Hynix, the world's second largest DRAM manufacturer, pleaded guilty and was sentenced to pay a $185 million criminal fine in May 2005. Japanese manufacturer Elpida Memory pleaded guilty and was sentenced to pay an $84 million fine in March 2006. German manufacturer Infineon pleaded guilty and was sentenced to pay a $160 million criminal fine in October 2004.

Notes and Questions

1. *The continuing DRAM saga.* In July 2006, shortly before the DOJ press release excerpted above, thirty-three states, including California, Massachusetts, Florida, New York and Pennsylvania, filed a class action lawsuit against DRAM makers alleging that their price-fixing scheme injured consumers, state agencies, universities and other groups. Two of the defendants reached a settlement for $113 million in 2007, and the remainder of the class action settled in 2010 for $173 million. Then, in 2018, another class action lawsuit was filed against DRAM manufacturers, this time for price fixing activity from 2016 to 2017. Why do you think the antitrust enforcement authorities are so intent on prosecuting price fixing? Are criminal penalties, including jail time, warranted by the offense?

2. *Output restrictions.* The classic price-fixing scenario is the one described in the DRAM case: executives of competing companies secretly collude to set prices for their products. But there are other avenues for price fixing. One of these is restricting output. As explained by the FTC:

> An agreement to restrict production, sales, or output is just as illegal as direct price fixing, because reducing the supply of a product or service drives up its price. For example, the FTC challenged an agreement among competing oil importers to restrict the supply of lubricants by refusing to import or sell those products in Puerto Rico. The competitors were seeking to pressure the legislature to repeal an environmental deposit fee on lubricants, and warned of lubricant shortages and higher prices. The FTC alleged that the conspiracy was an unlawful

---

[9] Fed. Trade Comm'n (FTC), Price Fixing, www.ftc.gov/tips-advice/competition-guidance/guide-antitrust-laws/dealings-competitors/price-fixing.

horizontal agreement to restrict output that was inherently likely to harm competition and that had no countervailing efficiencies that would benefit consumers.[9]

Are output restrictions just as harmful as explicit price fixing? Should they be subject to *per se* antitrust liability?

3. *Uncoordinated price movements.* Everyone has probably noticed that in many industries – air travel, higher education, retail gasoline – competing vendors offer prices that are surprisingly similar, and such prices often rise and fall in unison. Such coordinated price changes do not always indicate that illegal price fixing has occurred. As the FTC explains:

> Not all price similarities, or price changes that occur at the same time, are the result of price fixing. On the contrary, they often result from normal market conditions. For example, prices of commodities such as wheat are often identical because the products are virtually identical, and the prices that farmers charge all rise and fall together without any agreement among them. If a drought causes the supply of wheat to decline, the price to all affected farmers will increase. An increase in consumer demand can also cause uniformly high prices for a product in limited supply.
>
> ...
>
> Q: Our company monitors competitors' ads, and we sometimes offer to match special discounts or sales incentives for consumers. Is this a problem?
>
> A: No. Matching competitors' pricing may be good business, and occurs often in highly competitive markets. Each company is free to set its own prices, and it may charge the same price as its competitors as long as the decision was not based on any agreement or coordination with a competitor.[10]

Where should the law draw the line between collusive price fixing and natural price convergence in competitive industries?

4. *Buyer-side cartels.* Just as a group of sellers who conspire to fix prices is a *per se* violation of Section 1 of the Sherman Act, so is a conspiracy among buyers to pressure suppliers to lower their prices, to refrain from selling to their competitors or to otherwise distort the market. Such buyer cartels, sometimes referred to as oligopsonies, typically arise with respect to tangible goods, but have also been alleged with respect to intangibles such as employee wages. By the same token, buyer cartels can, in theory, occur with respect to IP licenses. Consider a patent holder, for example, as the supplier of non-exclusive licenses, and potential licensees as its customers. Were the customers to collude improperly to pressure the patent holder to lower its license rates, a *per se* violation could be found.

The specter of such buyer-side arrangements has been raised in the context of industry standard-setting (see Chapter 20). For example, potential manufacturers of a standardized product could, in theory, pressure a patent holder to lower its royalty rate for a patent covering a standard (eventually approaching zero) on the threat that the manufacturers will otherwise cause the relevant standards-development organization (SDO) to "work around" the patent and exclude it from the standard.[11] Both the DOJ and the FTC, however, have indicated that coordination and information sharing among the members of an SDO can have significant procompetitive benefits, including preventing patent holders from charging excessive licensing fees. Accordingly, the agencies have indicated that a rule of reason analysis should be utilized in such cases. Which approach – *per se* liability or the rule of reason – do you find more persuasive in this context?

---

[10] FTC, Price Fixing, *supra* note 9.

[11] See J. Gregory Sidak, *Patent Holdup and Oligopsonistic Collusion in Standard-Setting Organizations*, 5 J. Comp. L. & Econ. 123 (2009).

As explained by the FTC, "Plain agreements among competitors to divide sales territories or assign customers are almost always illegal. These arrangements are essentially agreements not to compete: 'I won't sell in your market if you don't sell in mine.'"[12] For example, the FTC has prosecuted an arrangement in which two chemical companies agreed that one would not sell in North America if the other would not sell in Japan. In addition to dividing sales territories on a geographic basis, illegal market allocation may involve assigning a specific percentage of available business to each producer or assigning certain customers to each seller. The case that follows examines an allocation scheme that arose in the context of "store brand" groceries.

United States v. Topco Associates, Inc.

405 U.S. 596 (1972)

MARSHALL, JUSTICE

The United States brought this action for injunctive relief against alleged violation by Topco Associates, Inc. (Topco), of § 1 of the Sherman Act. Following a trial on the merits, the United States District Court for the Northern District of Illinois entered judgment for Topco, and we now reverse the judgment of the District Court.

I

Topco is a cooperative association of approximately 25 small and medium-sized regional supermarket chains that operate stores in some 33 States. Each of the member chains operates independently; there is no pooling of earnings, profits, capital, management, or advertising resources. No grocery business is conducted under the Topco name. Its basic function is to serve as a purchasing agent for its members.[13] In this capacity, it procures and distributes to the members more than 1,000 different food and related nonfood items, most of which are distributed under brand names owned by Topco. The association does not itself own any manufacturing, processing, or warehousing facilities, and the items that it procures for members are usually shipped directly from the packer or manufacturer to the members. Payment is made either to Topco or directly to the manufacturer at a cost that is virtually the same for the members as for Topco itself.

All of the stock in Topco is owned by the members, with the common stock, the only stock having voting rights, being equally distributed. The board of directors, which controls the operation of the association, is drawn from the members and is normally composed of high-ranking executive officers of member chains. It is the board that elects the association's officers and appoints committee members, and it is from the board that the principal executive officers of Topco must be drawn. Restrictions on the alienation of stock and the procedure for selecting all important officials of the association from within the ranks of

---

12 FTC, Market Division or Customer Allocation, www.ftc.gov/tips-advice/competition-guidance/guide-antitrust-laws/dealings-competitors/market-division-or.

13 [n.2] In addition to purchasing various items for its members, Topco performs other related functions: e.g., it insures that there is adequate quality control on the products that it purchases; it assists members in developing specifications on certain types of products (e.g., equipment and supplies); and it also aids the members in purchasing goods through other sources.

its members give the members complete and unfettered control over the operations of the association.

Topco was founded in the 1940's by a group of small, local grocery chains, independently owned and operated, that desired to cooperate to obtain high quality merchandise under private labels in order to compete more effectively with larger national and regional chains.[14] With a line of canned, dairy, and other products, the association began. It added frozen foods in 1950, fresh produce in 1958, more general merchandise equipment and supplies in 1960, and a branded bacon and carcass beef selection program in 1966. By 1964, Topco's members had combined retail sales of more than $2 billion; by 1967, their sales totaled more than $2.3 billion, a figure exceeded by only three national grocery chains.

Members of the association vary in the degree of market share that they possess in their respective areas. The range is from 1.5% to 16%, with the average being approximately 6%. While it is difficult to compare these figures with the market shares of larger regional and national chains because of the absence in the record of accurate statistics for these chains, there is much evidence in the record that Topco members are frequently in as strong a competitive position in their respective areas as any other chain. The strength of this competitive position is due, in some measure, to the success of Topco-brand products. Although only 10% of the total goods sold by Topco members bear the association's brand names, the profit on these goods is substantial and their very existence has improved the competitive potential of Topco members with respect to other large and powerful chains.

It is apparent that from meager beginnings approximately a quarter of a century ago, Topco has developed into a purchasing association wholly owned and operated by member chains, which possess much economic muscle, individually as well as cooperatively.

II

The United States charged that, beginning at least as early as 1960 and continuing up to the time that the complaint was filed, Topco had combined and conspired with its members to violate [§ 1 of the Sherman Act] in two respects. First, the Government alleged that there existed:

> a continuing agreement, understanding and concert of action among the co-conspirator member firms acting through Topco, the substantial terms of which have been and are that each co-conspirator or member firm will sell Topco-controlled brands only within the marketing territory allocated to it, and will refrain from selling Topco-controlled brands outside such marketing territory.

---

[14] [n.3] The founding members of Topco were having difficulty competing with larger chains. This difficulty was attributable in some degree to the fact that the larger chains were capable of developing their own private-label programs. Private-label products differ from other brand-name products in that they are sold at a limited number of easily ascertainable stores. A&P, for example, was a pioneer in developing a series of products that were sold under an A&P label and that were only available in A&P stores. It is obvious that by using private-label products, a chain can achieve significant cost economies in purchasing, transportation, warehousing, promotion, and advertising. These economies may afford the chain opportunities for offering private-label products at lower prices than other brand-name products. This, in turn, provides many advantages of which some of the more important are: a store can offer national-brand products at the same price as other stores, while simultaneously offering a desirable, lower priced alternative; or, if the profit margin is sufficiently high on private-brand goods, national-brand products may be sold at reduced price. Other advantages include: enabling a chain to bargain more favorably with national-brand manufacturers by creating a broader supply base of manufacturers, thereby decreasing dependence on a few, large national-brand manufacturers; enabling a chain to create a "price-mix" whereby prices on special items can be lowered to attract customers while profits are maintained on other items; and creation of general goodwill by offering lower priced, higher quality goods.

The division of marketing territories to which the complaint refers consists of a number of practices by the association. Article IX, § 2, of the Topco bylaws establishes three categories of territorial licenses that members may secure from the association:

(a) "Exclusive—An exclusive territory is one in which the member is licensed to sell all products bearing specified trademarks of the Association, to the exclusion of all other persons.

(b) "Non-exclusive—A non-exclusive territory is one in which a member is licensed to sell all products bearing specified trademarks of the Association, but not to the exclusion of others who may also be licensed to sell products bearing the same trademarks of the Association in the same territory.

(c) "Coextensive—A coextensive territory is one in which two (2) or more members are licensed to sell all products bearing specified trademarks of the Association to the exclusion of all other persons ..."

When applying for membership, a chain must designate the type of license that it desires. Membership must first be approved by the board of directors, and thereafter by an affirmative vote of 75% of the association's members. If, however, the member whose operations are closest to those of the applicant, or any member whose operations are located within 100 miles of the applicant, votes against approval, an affirmative vote of 85% of the members is required for approval. Because, as indicated by the record, members cooperate in accommodating each other's wishes, the procedure for approval provides, in essence, that members have a veto of sorts over actual or potential competition in the territorial areas in which they are concerned.

Following approval, each new member signs an agreement with Topco designating the territory in which that member may sell Topco-brand products. No member may sell these products outside the territory in which it is licensed. Most licenses are exclusive, and even those denominated "coextensive" or "non-exclusive" prove to be de facto exclusive.

FIGURE 25.3 Some of the brands developed by Topco.

Exclusive territorial areas are often allocated to members who do no actual business in those areas on the theory that they may wish to expand at some indefinite future time and that expansion would likely be in the direction of the allocated territory. When combined with each member's veto power over new members, provisions for exclusivity work effectively to insulate members from competition in Topco-brand goods. Should a member violate its license agreement and sell in areas other than those in which it is licensed, its membership can be terminated under the bylaws. Once a territory is classified as exclusive, either formally or de facto, it is extremely unlikely that the classification will ever be changed.

The Government maintains that this scheme of dividing markets violates the Sherman Act because it operates to prohibit competition in Topco-brand products among grocery chains engaged in retail operations. The Government also makes a subsidiary challenge to Topco's practices regarding licensing members to sell at wholesale. Under the bylaws, members are not permitted to sell any products supplied by the association at wholesale, whether trademarked or not, without first applying for and receiving special permission from the association to do so. Before permission is granted, other licensees (usually retailers), whose interests may potentially be affected by wholesale operations, are consulted as to their wishes in the matter. If permission is obtained, the member must agree to restrict the sale of Topco products to a specific geographic area and to sell under any conditions imposed by the association. Permission to wholesale has often been sought by members, only to be denied by the association. The Government contends that this amounts not only to a territorial restriction violative of the Sherman Act, but also to a restriction on customers that in itself is violative of the Act.

Topco's answer to the complaint is illustrative of its posture in the District Court and before this Court:

> Private label merchandising is a way of economic life in the food retailing industry, and exclusivity is the essence of a private label program; without exclusivity, a private label would not be private. Each national and large regional chain has its own exclusive private label products in addition to the nationally advertised brands which all chains sell. Each such chain relies upon the exclusivity of its own private label line to differentiate its private label products from those of its competitors and to attract and retain the repeat business and loyalty of consumers. Smaller retail grocery stores and chains are unable to compete effectively with the national and large regional chains without also offering their own exclusive private label products.
>
> The only feasible method by which Topco can procure private label products and assure the exclusivity thereof is through trademark licenses specifying the territory in which each member may sell such trademarked products.

Topco essentially maintains that it needs territorial divisions to compete with larger chains; that the association could not exist if the territorial divisions were anything but exclusive; and that by restricting competition in the sale of Topco-brand goods, the association actually increases competition by enabling its members to compete successfully with larger regional and national chains.

III

On its face, § 1 of the Sherman Act appears to bar any combination of entrepreneurs so long as it is "in restraint of trade." Theoretically, all manufacturers, distributors, merchants, sellers, and buyers could be considered as potential competitors of each other. Were § 1 to be read in the narrowest possible way, any commercial contract could be deemed to violate it. The history underlying the formulation of the antitrust laws led this Court to conclude, however, that Congress did not intend to prohibit all contracts, nor even all contracts that might in some insignificant degree or attenuated sense restrain trade or competition. In lieu of the narrowest possible reading of § 1, the Court adopted a "rule of reason" analysis for determining whether most business combinations or contracts violate the prohibitions of the Sherman Act. An analysis of the reasonableness of particular restraints includes consideration of the facts peculiar to the business in which the restraint is applied, the nature of the restraint and its effects, and the history of the restraint and the reasons for its adoption.

While the Court has utilized the "rule of reason" in evaluating the legality of most restraints alleged to be violative of the Sherman Act, it has also developed the doctrine that certain business relationships are per se violations of the Act without regard to a consideration of their reasonableness. In *Northern Pacific R. Co. v. United States*, 356 U.S. 1, 5 (1958), Mr. Justice Black explained the appropriateness of, and the need for, per se rules:

> [T]here are certain agreements or practices which because of their pernicious effect on competition and lack of any redeeming virtue are conclusively presumed to be unreasonable and therefore illegal without elaborate inquiry as to the precise harm they have caused or the business excuse for their use. This principle of per se unreasonableness not only makes the type of restraints which are proscribed by the Sherman Act more certain to the benefit of everyone concerned, but it also avoids the necessity for an incredibly complicated and prolonged economic investigation into the entire history of the industry involved, as well as related industries, in an effort to determine at large whether a particular restraint has been unreasonable — an inquiry so often wholly fruitless when undertaken.

It is only after considerable experience with certain business relationships that courts classify them as per se violations of the Sherman Act. One of the classic examples of a per se violation of § 1 is an agreement between competitors at the same level of the market structure to allocate territories in order to minimize competition. Such concerted action is usually termed a "horizontal" restraint, in contradistinction to combinations of persons at different levels of the market structure, e.g., manufacturers and distributors, which are termed "vertical" restraints. This Court has reiterated time and time again that "(h)orizontal territorial limitations ... are naked restraints of trade with no purpose except stifling of competition."

We think that it is clear that the restraint in this case is a horizontal one, and, therefore, a per se violation of § 1. The District Court failed to make any determination as to whether there were per se horizontal territorial restraints in this case and simply applied a rule of reason in reaching its conclusions that the restraints were not illegal. In so doing, the District Court erred.

United States v. Sealy, Inc., is, in fact, on all fours with this case. Sealy licensed manufacturers of mattresses and bedding to make and sell products using the Sealy trademark. Like Topco, Sealy was a corporation owned almost entirely by its licensees, who elected the Board of Directors and controlled the business. Just as in this case, Sealy agreed with the licensees not to license other manufacturers or sellers to sell Sealy-brand products in a designated territory in exchange for the promise of the licensee who sold in that territory not to expand its sales beyond the area demarcated by Sealy. The Court held that this was a horizontal territorial restraint, which was *per se* violative of the Sherman Act.

Whether or not we would decide this case the same way under the rule of reason used by the District Court is irrelevant to the issue before us. The fact is that courts are of limited utility in examining difficult economic problems. Our inability to weigh, in any meaningful sense, destruction of competition in one sector of the economy against promotion of competition in another sector is one important reason we have formulated per se rules.

In applying these rigid rules, the Court has consistently rejected the notion that naked restraints of trade are to be tolerated because they are well intended or because they are allegedly developed to increase competition.

Antitrust laws in general, and the Sherman Act in particular, are the Magna Carta of free enterprise. They are as important to the preservation of economic freedom and our free-enterprise system as the Bill of Rights is to the protection of our fundamental personal freedoms. And the freedom guaranteed each and every business, no matter how small, is the freedom to compete—to assert with vigor, imagination, devotion, and ingenuity whatever economic muscle it can muster. Implicit in such freedom is the notion that it cannot be foreclosed with respect to one sector of the economy because certain private citizens or groups believe that such foreclosure might promote greater competition in a more important sector of the economy.

The District Court determined that by limiting the freedom of its individual members to compete with each other, Topco was doing a greater good by fostering competition between members and other large supermarket chains. But, the fallacy in this is that Topco has no authority under the Sherman Act to determine the respective values of competition in various sectors of the economy. On the contrary, the Sherman Act gives to each Topco member and to each prospective member the right to ascertain for itself whether or not competition with other supermarket chains is more desirable than competition in the sale of Topco-brand products. Without territorial restrictions, Topco members may indeed "(cut) each other's throats." But we have never found this possibility sufficient to warrant condoning horizontal restraints of trade.

The Court has previously noted with respect to price fixing, another *per se* violation of the Sherman Act, that:

> The reasonable price fixed today may through economic and business changes become the unreasonable price of tomorrow. Once established, it may be maintained unchanged because of the absence of competition secured by the agreement for a price reasonable when fixed.

A similar observation can be made with regard to territorial limitations.

There have been tremendous departures from the notion of a free-enterprise system as it was originally conceived in this country. These departures have been the product of congressional action and the will of the people. If a decision is to be made to sacrifice competition in one portion of the economy for greater competition in another portion this too is a decision that must be made by Congress and not by private forces or by the courts. Private forces are too keenly aware of their own interests in making such decisions and courts are ill-equipped and ill-situated for such decisionmaking. To analyze, interpret, and evaluate the myriad of competing interests and the endless data that would surely be brought to bear on such decisions, and to make the delicate judgment on the relative values to society of competitive areas of the economy, the judgment of the elected representatives of the people is required.

> Just as the territorial restrictions on retailing Topco-brand products must fall, so must the territorial restrictions on wholesaling. The considerations are the same, and the Sherman Act requires identical results.
>
> We also strike down Topco's other restrictions on the right of its members to wholesale goods. These restrictions amount to regulation of the customers to whom members of Topco may sell Topco-brand goods. Like territorial restrictions, limitations on customers are intended to limit intra-brand competition and to promote inter-brand competition. For the reasons previously discussed, the arena in which Topco members compete must be left to their unfettered choice absent a contrary congressional determination.
>
> We reverse the judgment of the District Court and remand the case for entry of an appropriate decree.

Notes and Questions

1. *Good intentions*? The Court in *Topco* states that it "has consistently rejected the notion that naked restraints of trade are to be tolerated because they are well intended or because they are allegedly developed to increase competition." Why shouldn't intent matter when analyzing restraints such as those imposed in *Topco*?

2. *Bad intentions*. Just as a party's good or innocent intentions don't affect antitrust analysis, its intent to compete ruthlessly in the market doesn't either. As Judge Easterbrook of the Seventh Circuit wrote in A.A. *Poultry v. Rose Acre*, 881 F.2d 1396 (7th Cir. 1989):

   > Firms intend to ... crush their rivals if they can. Intent to harm without more offers too vague a standard ... Rivalry is harsh, and consumers gain the most when firms slash costs to the bone and pare price down to cost, all in pursuit of more business ... If courts use the vigorous, nasty pursuit of sales as evidence of a forbidden intent, they run the risk of penalizing the motive forces of competition.

   Do you agree with Judge Easterbrook's reasoning? Is a firm's ruthlessness irrelevant to antitrust analysis? Should it be?

3. Per se *liability*. Market allocation is one of the few remaining areas of *per se* antitrust liability. Do you think that the harm arising from arrangements such as that described in *Topco* warrants *per se* liability? How comparable is market allocation to price fixing? Are the potential injuries to competition similar?

4. *The Magna Carta of free enterprise*. Why does Justice Marshall refer to the Sherman Act as "the Magna Carta of free enterprise"? Do you agree with his characterization? Are there other laws that are equally as important to the free enterprise system? What would happen to the market economy if there were no antitrust laws?

5. *The reformed Topco program*. On remand, the district court entered the following order, which was summarily affirmed by the Supreme Court (414 U.S. 801 (1975)):

   > Defendant is ordered and directed ... to amend its bylaws, Membership and Licensing Agreements, resolutions, rules and regulations to eliminate therefrom any provision which in any way limits or restricts the territories within which or the persons to whom any member firm may sell Topco brand products.
   >
   > ...
   >
   > Notwithstanding the foregoing provisions, nothing in this Final Judgment shall prevent defendant from creating or eliminating areas or territories of prime responsibility of member firms; from designating the location of the place or places of business for which a trademark

license is issued; from determining warehouse locations to which it will ship products; from terminating the membership of any organization which does not adequately promote the sale of Topco brand products; from formulating and implementing passovers or other procedures for reasonable compensation for good will developed for defendant's trademarks in geographic areas in which another member firm begins to sell trademarked products; or from engaging in any activity rendered lawful by subsequent legislation enacted by the Congress of the United States.

How are the activities that Topco and its members are permitted to engage in under this order different than those that were challenged by the DOJ? How will Topco's new restrictions promote competition?

6. *The IP licensing "safety zone."* Recognizing the inherent procompetitive features of IP licensing arrangements, the DOJ and FTC established in § 4.3 of their 2017 *Antitrust Guidelines for the Licensing of Intellectual Property* an antitrust "safety zone" for licensing arrangements.[15] There, the agencies indicate that they "will not challenge a restraint in an intellectual property licensing arrangement" (other than a restraint that is "facially anticompetitive") if "the licensor and its licensees collectively account for no more than twenty percent of each relevant market significantly affected by the restraint," or "four or more independently controlled entities in addition to the parties to the licensing arrangement possess the required specialized assets or characteristics and the incentive to engage in research and development that is a close substitute of the research and development activities of the parties to the licensing agreement." In effect, these guidelines recognize that below a certain level of market dominance, even otherwise anticompetitive arrangements have limited potential to harm competition in the market. The exception, of course, is "facially anticompetitive" activity, which is generally understood to mean any conduct that would be *per se* illegal. Do you agree with the idea of thresholds below which antitrust enforcement will not be pursued? Why doesn't this logic apply to *per se* illegal conduct? Should it?

ANTITRUST REMEDIES

Violation of the Sherman Act is a felony punishable by a fine of up to $100 million for corporations, and a fine of up to $1 million and up to ten years imprisonment (or both) for individuals. Under some circumstances, the maximum fine may be increased to twice the gain or loss involved, and restitution to victims may be ordered. Only the Department of Justice has the authority to prosecute criminal actions under the Sherman Act, but rarely does so with respect to anticompetitive conduct involving IP.

The FTC may impose fines on parties that have violated an existing order prohibiting certain conduct. In July 2019, the FTC imposed a fine of $5 billion on Google for allegedly violating a 2012 FTC order relating to consumer privacy.

In addition to criminal sanctions and fines, private parties injured "by reason of anything forbidden in the antitrust laws" may bring suit and "shall recover threefold the damages by him sustained, and the cost of suit, including a reasonable attorney's fee" (15 U.S.C. § 15(a)).

---

[15] US DOJ & FTC, Antitrust Guidelines for the Licensing of Intellectual Property (1995). The 1995 Guidelines were updated in 2017 with only minor changes. US DOJ & FTC, Antitrust Guidelines for the Licensing of Intellectual Property (2017) [hereinafter DOJ–FTC 2017 Licensing Guidelines].

Both government enforcement agencies and private plaintiffs may seek preliminary and permanent injunctive relief to prevent the continuation of anticompetitive
conduct. Injunctive relief may consist of relatively common "cease and desist" orders
(behavioral remedies), as well as "structural" remedies that require a firm to divest
portions of its business. Structural remedies are the most common in merger cases,
but have also been imposed in large monopolization cases. The most famous of these
is the 1984 break-up of AT&T, which split the massive enterprise into a long-distance
carrier, seven regional service operators (the "Baby Bells") and an equipment supplier
(Western Electric). In the *Microsoft* case (see Section 25.6), the district court ordered
Microsoft to divest its internet browser operations, though that order was eventually
overturned on appeal.

Many remedial measures in antitrust cases are imposed not through judicial decisions,
but through orders by the enforcement agency. If the government and the defendant agree
to settle litigation brought by the agency, they may stipulate the terms of settlement in
a mutually agreed "consent decree," which is submitted to the court for entry into the
record. Though not fully adjudicated, a consent decree has the force of judicial decision,
enforceable on penalty of contempt. If, on the other hand, the defendant denies the allegations brought by the government or otherwise rejects the terms of a proposed order, the
parties may litigate and the court may fashion a remedial decree based on its assessment
of the case and the parties' respective arguments. Such a decree is termed a "contested
decree."

The compulsory licensing of patents and other IP rights is sometimes required under
antitrust remedial orders. From the 1940s through the 1970s, federal courts in antitrust
cases approved more than 100 remedial patent licensing decrees, often requiring that patents be licensed to potential users on "fair, reasonable and nondiscriminatory" terms in
order to remedy anticompetitive arrangements involving those patents.[16]

25.4 VERTICAL RESTRAINTS: RESALE PRICE MAINTENANCE

The antitrust violations discussed above have related largely to conspiracies among competitors –
so-called "horizontal" arrangements. Anticompetitive arrangements can also exist, however,
between suppliers and resellers or manufacturers and customers in what are called "vertical"
relationships. For example, a manufacturer may assign different geographical markets to different distributors of its products. Unlike the horizontal territorial restraints discussed in *Topco*,
this type of vertical territorial restraint is generally viewed as permissible under the rule of reason. See Continental T.V., Inc. v. GTE Sylvania Inc., 433 U.S. 36 (1977).

Resale price maintenance is an arrangement whereby an "upstream" supplier or licensor requires that its "downstream" distributors, resellers or licensees sell products at certain
minimum prices. That is, the supplier establishes a floor on prices of downstream products.
Traditionally, this practice looked a lot like price fixing, which is *per se* illegal under Section 1
of the Sherman Act. However, in the following case the Supreme Court establishes that such
vertical restraints should be evaluated under the "rule of reason."

---

[16] See Contreras, *FRAND History, supra* note 3 (cataloging and discussing these historical consent decrees).

Leegin Creative Leather Products, Inc. v. PSKS, Inc., dba Kay's Kloset

551 U.S. 877 (2007)

KENNEDY, JUSTICE

In *Dr. Miles Medical Co. v. John D. Park & Sons Co.*, 220 U. S. 373 (1911), the Court established the rule that it is per se illegal under §1 of the Sherman Act, 15 U. S. C. §1, for a manufacturer to agree with its distributor to set the minimum price the distributor can charge for the manufacturer's goods. The question presented by the instant case is whether the Court should overrule the per se rule and allow resale price maintenance agreements to be judged by the rule of reason, the usual standard applied to determine if there is a violation of §1. The Court has abandoned the rule of per se illegality for other vertical restraints a manufacturer imposes on its distributors. Respected economic analysts, furthermore, conclude that vertical price restraints can have procompetitive effects. We now hold that *Dr. Miles* should be overruled and that vertical price restraints are to be judged by the rule of reason.

I

Petitioner, Leegin Creative Leather Products, Inc. (Leegin), designs, manufactures, and distributes leather goods and accessories. In 1991, Leegin began to sell belts under the brand name "Brighton." The Brighton brand has now expanded into a variety of women's fashion accessories. It is sold across the United States in over 5,000 retail establishments, for the most part independent, small boutiques and specialty stores. Leegin's president, Jerry Kohl, also has an interest in about 70 stores that sell Brighton products. Leegin asserts that, at least for its products, small retailers treat customers better, provide customers more services, and make their shopping experience more satisfactory than do larger, often impersonal retailers. Kohl explained: "[W]e want the consumers to get a different experience than they get in Sam's Club or in Wal-Mart. And you can't get that kind of experience or support or customer service from a store like Wal-Mart."

Respondent, PSKS, Inc. (PSKS), operates Kay's Kloset, a women's apparel store in Lewisville, Texas. Kay's Kloset buys from about 75 different manufacturers and at one time sold the Brighton brand. It first started purchasing Brighton goods from Leegin in 1995. Once it began selling the brand, the store promoted Brighton. For example, it ran Brighton advertisements and had Brighton days in the store. Kay's Kloset became the destination

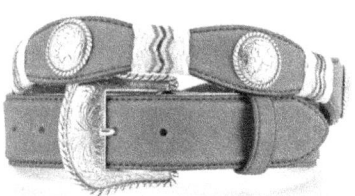

FIGURE 25.4 Brighton handbag and belt by Leegin.

retailer in the area to buy Brighton products. Brighton was the store's most important brand and once accounted for 40 to 50 percent of its profits.

In 1997, Leegin instituted the "Brighton Retail Pricing and Promotion Policy." Following the policy, Leegin refused to sell to retailers that discounted Brighton goods below suggested prices. The policy contained an exception for products not selling well that the retailer did not plan on reordering. In the letter to retailers establishing the policy, Leegin stated:

> "In this age of mega stores like Macy's, Bloomingdales, May Co. and others, consumers are perplexed by promises of product quality and support of product which we believe is lacking in these large stores. Consumers are further confused by the ever popular sale, sale, sale, etc.
>
> "We, at Leegin, choose to break away from the pack by selling [at] specialty stores; specialty stores that can offer the customer great quality merchandise, superb service, and support the Brighton product 365 days a year on a consistent basis.
>
> "We realize that half the equation is Leegin producing great Brighton product and the other half is you, our retailer, creating great looking stores selling our products in a quality manner."

Leegin adopted the policy to give its retailers sufficient margins to provide customers the service central to its distribution strategy. It also expressed concern that discounting harmed Brighton's brand image and reputation.

A year after instituting the pricing policy Leegin introduced a marketing strategy known as the "Heart Store Program." It offered retailers incentives to become Heart Stores, and, in exchange, retailers pledged, among other things, to sell at Leegin's suggested prices. Kay's Kloset became a Heart Store soon after Leegin created the program. After a Leegin employee visited the store and found it unattractive, the parties appear to have agreed that Kay's Kloset would not be a Heart Store beyond 1998. Despite losing this status, Kay's Kloset continued to increase its Brighton sales.

In December 2002, Leegin discovered Kay's Kloset had been marking down Brighton's entire line by 20 percent. Kay's Kloset contended it placed Brighton products on sale to compete with nearby retailers who also were undercutting Leegin's suggested prices. Leegin, nonetheless, requested that Kay's Kloset cease discounting. Its request refused, Leegin stopped selling to the store. The loss of the Brighton brand had a considerable negative impact on the store's revenue from sales.

PSKS sued Leegin in the United States District Court for the Eastern District of Texas. It alleged, among other claims, that Leegin had violated the antitrust laws by "enter[ing] into agreements with retailers to charge only those prices fixed by Leegin." Leegin planned to introduce expert testimony describing the procompetitive effects of its pricing policy. The District Court excluded the testimony, relying on the per se rule established by *Dr. Miles*. At trial PSKS argued that the Heart Store program, among other things, demonstrated Leegin and its retailers had agreed to fix prices. Leegin responded that it had established a unilateral pricing policy lawful under §1, which applies only to concerted action. The jury agreed with PSKS and awarded it $1.2 million. Pursuant to 15 U. S. C. §15(a), the District Court trebled the damages and reimbursed PSKS for its attorney's fees and costs. It entered judgment against Leegin in the amount of $3,975,000.80.

The Court of Appeals for the Fifth Circuit affirmed. On appeal Leegin did not dispute that it had entered into vertical price-fixing agreements with its retailers. Rather, it contended that the rule of reason should have applied to those agreements. The Court of Appeals rejected this argument. We granted certiorari to determine whether vertical minimum resale price maintenance agreements should continue to be treated as per se unlawful.

II

The rule of reason is the accepted standard for testing whether a practice restrains trade in violation of §1. In its design and function the rule distinguishes between restraints with anticompetitive effect that are harmful to the consumer and restraints stimulating competition that are in the consumer's best interest.

The rule of reason does not govern all restraints. Some types "are deemed unlawful per se." The *per se* rule, treating categories of restraints as necessarily illegal, eliminates the need to study the reasonableness of an individual restraint in light of the real market forces at work; and, it must be acknowledged, the per se rule can give clear guidance for certain conduct. Restraints that are per se unlawful include horizontal agreements among competitors to fix prices or to divide markets.

Resort to per se rules is confined to restraints, like those mentioned, "that would always or almost always tend to restrict competition and decrease output." To justify a per se prohibition a restraint must have "manifestly anticompetitive" effects and "lack of any redeeming virtue."

As a consequence, the per se rule is appropriate only after courts have had considerable experience with the type of restraint at issue, and only if courts can predict with confidence that it would be invalidated in all or almost all instances under the rule of reason. It should come as no surprise, then, that "we have expressed reluctance to adopt per se rules with regard to restraints imposed in the context of business relationships where the economic impact of certain practices is not immediately obvious." And, as we have stated, a "departure from the rule-of-reason standard must be based upon demonstrable economic effect rather than ... upon formalistic line drawing."

III

The Court has interpreted *Dr. Miles* as establishing a *per se* rule against a vertical agreement between a manufacturer and its distributor to set minimum resale prices. In *Dr. Miles* the plaintiff, a manufacturer of medicines, sold its products only to distributors who agreed to resell them at set prices. The Court found the manufacturer's control of resale prices to be unlawful. It relied on the common-law rule that "a general restraint upon alienation is ordinarily invalid." The Court then explained that the agreements would advantage the distributors, not the manufacturer, and were analogous to a combination among competing distributors, which the law treated as void.

The reasoning of the Court's more recent jurisprudence has rejected the rationales on which *Dr. Miles* was based. By relying on the common-law rule against restraints on alienation, the Court justified its decision based on "formalistic" legal doctrine rather than "demonstrable economic effect". Yet the Sherman Act's use of "restraint of trade" "invokes the common law itself, and not merely the static content that the common law had assigned to the term in 1890." The general restraint on alienation, especially in the age when then-Justice Hughes used the term, tended to evoke policy concerns extraneous to the question that controls here. Usually associated with land, not chattels, the rule arose from restrictions removing real property from the stream of commerce for generations.

The Court should be cautious about putting dispositive weight on doctrines from antiquity but of slight relevance.

Dr. Miles, furthermore, treated vertical agreements a manufacturer makes with its distributors as analogous to a horizontal combination among competing distributors. In later cases, however, the Court rejected the approach of reliance on rules governing horizontal restraints when defining rules applicable to vertical ones. Our recent cases formulate antitrust principles in accordance with the appreciated differences in economic effect between vertical and horizontal agreements, differences the *Dr. Miles* Court failed to consider.

The reasons upon which *Dr. Miles* relied do not justify a *per se* rule. As a consequence, it is necessary to examine, in the first instance, the economic effects of vertical agreements to fix minimum resale prices, and to determine whether the per se rule is nonetheless appropriate.

A

Though each side of the debate can find sources to support its position, it suffices to say here that economics literature is replete with procompetitive justifications for a manufacturer's use of resale price maintenance. The few recent studies documenting the competitive effects of resale price maintenance also cast doubt on the conclusion that the practice meets the criteria for a per se rule.

The justifications for vertical price restraints are similar to those for other vertical restraints. Minimum resale price maintenance can stimulate interbrand competition—the competition among manufacturers selling different brands of the same type of product—by reducing intrabrand competition—the competition among retailers selling the same brand. The promotion of interbrand competition is important because "the primary purpose of the antitrust laws is to protect [this type of] competition." A single manufacturer's use of vertical price restraints tends to eliminate intrabrand price competition; this in turn encourages retailers to invest in tangible or intangible services or promotional efforts that aid the manufacturer's position as against rival manufacturers. Resale price maintenance also has the potential to give consumers more options so that they can choose among low-price, low-service brands; high-price, high-service brands; and brands that fall in between.

Absent vertical price restraints, the retail services that enhance interbrand competition might be underprovided. This is because discounting retailers can free ride on retailers who furnish services and then capture some of the increased demand those services generate. Consumers might learn, for example, about the benefits of a manufacturer's product from a retailer that invests in fine showrooms, offers product demonstrations, or hires and trains knowledgeable employees. Or consumers might decide to buy the product because they see it in a retail establishment that has a reputation for selling high-quality merchandise. If the consumer can then buy the product from a retailer that discounts because it has not spent capital providing services or developing a quality reputation, the high-service retailer will lose sales to the discounter, forcing it to cut back its services to a level lower than consumers would otherwise prefer. Minimum resale price maintenance alleviates the problem because it prevents the discounter from undercutting the service provider. With price competition decreased, the manufacturer's retailers compete among themselves over services.

Resale price maintenance, in addition, can increase interbrand competition by facilitating market entry for new firms and brands. "[N]ew manufacturers and manufacturers entering new markets can use the restrictions in order to induce competent and aggressive retailers to make the kind of investment of capital and labor that is often required in the distribution of products unknown to the consumer." New products and new brands are essential to a dynamic economy, and if markets can be penetrated by using resale price maintenance there is a procompetitive effect.

Resale price maintenance can also increase interbrand competition by encouraging retailer services that would not be provided even absent free riding. It may be difficult and inefficient for a manufacturer to make and enforce a contract with a retailer specifying the different services the retailer must perform. Offering the retailer a guaranteed margin and threatening termination if it does not live up to expectations may be the most efficient way to expand the manufacturer's market share by inducing the retailer's performance and allowing it to use its own initiative and experience in providing valuable services.

B

While vertical agreements setting minimum resale prices can have procompetitive justifications, they may have anticompetitive effects in other cases; and unlawful price fixing, designed solely to obtain monopoly profits, is an ever present temptation. Resale price maintenance may, for example, facilitate a manufacturer cartel. An unlawful cartel will seek to discover if some manufacturers are undercutting the cartel's fixed prices. Resale price maintenance could assist the cartel in identifying price-cutting manufacturers who benefit from the lower prices they offer. Resale price maintenance, furthermore, could discourage a manufacturer from cutting prices to retailers with the concomitant benefit of cheaper prices to consumers.

Vertical price restraints also "might be used to organize cartels at the retailer level." A group of retailers might collude to fix prices to consumers and then compel a manufacturer to aid the unlawful arrangement with resale price maintenance. In that instance the manufacturer does not establish the practice to stimulate services or to promote its brand but to give inefficient retailers higher profits. Retailers with better distribution systems and lower cost structures would be prevented from charging lower prices by the agreement.

A horizontal cartel among competing manufacturers or competing retailers that decreases output or reduces competition in order to increase price is, and ought to be, per se unlawful. To the extent a vertical agreement setting minimum resale prices is entered upon to facilitate either type of cartel, it, too, would need to be held unlawful under the rule of reason. This type of agreement may also be useful evidence for a plaintiff attempting to prove the existence of a horizontal cartel.

Resale price maintenance, furthermore, can be abused by a powerful manufacturer or retailer. A dominant retailer, for example, might request resale price maintenance to forestall innovation in distribution that decreases costs. A manufacturer might consider it has little choice but to accommodate the retailer's demands for vertical price restraints if the manufacturer believes it needs access to the retailer's distribution network. A manufacturer with market power, by comparison, might use resale price maintenance to give retailers an incentive not to sell the products of smaller rivals or new entrants. As should be evident, the potential anticompetitive consequences of vertical price restraints must not be ignored or underestimated.

C

Notwithstanding the risks of unlawful conduct, it cannot be stated with any degree of confidence that resale price maintenance "always or almost always tend[s] to restrict competition and decrease output." Vertical agreements establishing minimum resale prices can have either procompetitive or anticompetitive effects, depending upon the circumstances in which they are formed. And although the empirical evidence on the topic is limited, it does not suggest efficient uses of the agreements are infrequent or hypothetical. As the rule would proscribe a significant amount of procompetitive conduct, these agreements appear ill suited for per se condemnation.

Respondent contends, nonetheless, that vertical price restraints should be per se unlawful because of the administrative convenience of per se rules. That argument suggests per se illegality is the rule rather than the exception. This misinterprets our antitrust law. Per se rules may decrease administrative costs, but that is only part of the equation. Those rules can be counterproductive. They can increase the total cost of the antitrust system by prohibiting procompetitive conduct the antitrust laws should encourage. They also may increase litigation costs by promoting frivolous suits against legitimate practices. The Court has thus explained that administrative "advantages are not sufficient in themselves to justify the creation of per se rules," and has relegated their use to restraints that are "manifestly anticompetitive". Were the Court now to conclude that vertical price restraints should be per se illegal based on administrative costs, we would undermine, if not overrule, the traditional "demanding standards" for adopting per se rules. Any possible reduction in administrative costs cannot alone justify the *Dr. Miles* rule.

Respondent also argues the per se rule is justified because a vertical price restraint can lead to higher prices for the manufacturer's goods. Respondent is mistaken in relying on pricing effects absent a further showing of anticompetitive conduct. For, as has been indicated already, the antitrust laws are designed primarily to protect interbrand competition, from which lower prices can later result. The Court, moreover, has evaluated other vertical restraints under the rule of reason even though prices can be increased in the course of promoting procompetitive effects. And resale price maintenance may reduce prices if manufacturers have resorted to costlier alternatives of controlling resale prices that are not per se unlawful.

Respondent's argument, furthermore, overlooks that, in general, the interests of manufacturers and consumers are aligned with respect to retailer profit margins. The difference between the price a manufacturer charges retailers and the price retailers charge consumers represents part of the manufacturer's cost of distribution, which, like any other cost, the manufacturer usually desires to minimize. A manufacturer has no incentive to overcompensate retailers with unjustified margins. The retailers, not the manufacturer, gain from higher retail prices. The manufacturer often loses; interbrand competition reduces its competitiveness and market share because consumers will "substitute a different brand of the same product." As a general matter, therefore, a single manufacturer will desire to set minimum resale prices only if the "increase in demand resulting from enhanced service … will more than offset a negative impact on demand of a higher retail price."

The implications of respondent's position are far reaching. Many decisions a manufacturer makes and carries out through concerted action can lead to higher prices. A manufacturer might, for example, contract with different suppliers to obtain better inputs that improve product quality. Or it might hire an advertising agency to promote awareness of its goods. Yet no one would think these actions violate the Sherman Act because they lead to higher prices. The antitrust laws do not require manufacturers to produce generic goods that consumers do not know about or want. The manufacturer strives to improve its product quality or to promote its brand because it believes this conduct will lead to increased demand despite higher prices. The same can hold true for resale price maintenance.

Resale price maintenance, it is true, does have economic dangers. If the rule of reason were to apply to vertical price restraints, courts would have to be diligent in eliminating their anticompetitive uses from the market. This is a realistic objective, and certain factors are relevant to the inquiry. For example, the number of manufacturers that make use of the practice in a given industry can provide important instruction. When only a few manufacturers lacking market power adopt the practice, there is little likelihood it is facilitating a manufacturer cartel, for a cartel then can be undercut by rival manufacturers. Likewise, a retailer cartel is unlikely when only a single manufacturer in a competitive market uses resale price maintenance. Interbrand competition would divert consumers to lower priced substitutes and eliminate any gains to retailers from their price-fixing agreement over a single brand. Resale price maintenance should be subject to more careful scrutiny, by contrast, if many competing manufacturers adopt the practice.

The source of the restraint may also be an important consideration. If there is evidence retailers were the impetus for a vertical price restraint, there is a greater likelihood that the restraint facilitates a retailer cartel or supports a dominant, inefficient retailer. If, by contrast, a manufacturer adopted the policy independent of retailer pressure, the restraint is less likely to promote anticompetitive conduct. A manufacturer also has an incentive to protest inefficient retailer-induced price restraints because they can harm its competitive position.

As a final matter, that a dominant manufacturer or retailer can abuse resale price maintenance for anticompetitive purposes may not be a serious concern unless the relevant entity has market power. If a retailer lacks market power, manufacturers likely can sell their goods through rival retailers. And if a manufacturer lacks market power, there is less likelihood it can use the practice to keep competitors away from distribution outlets.

The rule of reason is designed and used to eliminate anticompetitive transactions from the market. This standard principle applies to vertical price restraints. A party alleging injury from a vertical agreement setting minimum resale prices will have, as a general matter, the information and resources available to show the existence of the agreement and its scope of operation. As courts gain experience considering the effects of these restraints by applying the rule of reason over the course of decisions, they can establish the litigation structure to ensure the rule operates to eliminate anticompetitive restraints from the market and to provide more guidance to businesses. Courts can, for example, devise rules over time for offering proof, or even presumptions where justified, to make the rule of reason a fair and efficient way to prohibit anticompetitive restraints and to promote procompetitive ones.

For all of the foregoing reasons, we think that were the Court considering the issue as an original matter, the rule of reason, not a per se rule of unlawfulness, would be the appropriate standard to judge vertical price restraints.

The judgment of the Court of Appeals is reversed, and the case is remanded for proceedings consistent with this opinion.

Notes and Questions

1. *MSRP.* Many suppliers, from book publishers to automobile manufacturers, print a "manufacturer's suggested retail price" (MSRP) on the packaging or documentation of their products. How does this common practice differ from Leegin's "Heart Store Program"? Is there an anticompetitive threat from MSRPs?

2. *Injury.* PSKS was not part of the Heart Store Program when it brought suit against Leegin, and the vertical restraint that it alleged to be anticompetitive was between Leegin and other retailers. What injury did PSKS allege? Isn't a manufacturer entitled to sell its products to whomever it chooses? How could Leegin's discontinuation of sales to PSKS violate the antitrust laws?

3. *Resale price maintenance and price fixing.* How does the Court differentiate resale price maintenance (RPM) from horizontal price fixing? Couldn't the same procompetitive benefits that the Court identifies with respect to RPM be used to justify horizontal price fixing as well?

4. *Value-added services.* In finding procompetitive justifications for Leegin's RPM program, the Court notes that "Many decisions a manufacturer makes and carries out through concerted action can lead to higher prices. A manufacturer might, for example, contract with different suppliers to obtain better inputs that improve product quality. Or it might hire an advertising agency to promote awareness of its goods. Yet no one would think these actions violate the Sherman Act because they lead to higher prices." Leegin wanted retailers carrying its products to offer individualized customer attention and a high level of support. But was requiring retailers to charge minimum prices the best or most effective way to achieve this goal? What else might Leegin have done to ensure that retailers provided these enhanced services? Would these alternatives have been more or less likely than RPM to ensure that such enhanced services were provided?

5. *Legislative reversals.* Both federal and state legislative proposals have been made to reverse the effects of the *Leegin* decision. Some state efforts have even been successful.[17] Who would have an interest in reinstating the *per se* illegality rule for RPM? Would you support such an effort in your state?

6. *Discounts and distributed retail.* In an interview about the PSKS case, one customer said that she liked the 20 percent discount that Kay Stores offered on Leegin products, but when Kay Stores stopped carrying Leegin products she found them on eBay at a 50 percent discount.[18] Given the reality of massively distributed retail today, do RPM programs make business sense anymore?

7. *Maximum prices. Leegin* dealt with minimum prices that a manufacturer wished to impose on its retailers. What about maximum prices? Is any antitrust concern raised when a manufacturer requires its resellers to impose prices no higher than a set maximum? Isn't a maximum price inherently good for consumers? In *State Oil Co. v. Khan*, 522 U.S. 3 (1997), the Supreme Court held that a vertical restraint on the maximum resale price of a product should be examined under the rule of reason, rather than constitute a *per se* violation of the antitrust laws. What procompetitive justifications can you find for maximum price restraints?

25.5 UNILATERAL CONDUCT: TYING

So far, we have discussed anticompetitive agreements among parties in either horizontal or vertical relationships, all falling under the banner of concerted conduct under Section 1 of the Sherman Act. But unilateral conduct, the subject of Section 2 of the Sherman Act, can also give rise to antitrust liability.

---

[17] See *Darush v. Revision LP*, No. CV 12-10296 GAF (AGRx), 2013 WL 1749539, at *6 (C.D. Cal. Apr. 10, 2013) (vertical RPM *per se* illegal under California's Cartwright Act) and Md. Code Ann., Commercial Law, § 11-204(b) ("[A] contract, combination, or conspiracy that establishes a minimum price below which a retailer, wholesaler, or distributor may not sell a commodity or service is an unreasonable restraint of trade or commerce").

[18] See Maria Halkias, *Mr. Smith to Washington Goes*, Dallas Morning News, March 25, 2007.

One such form of unilateral conduct is the tying arrangement or "tie-in," in which one party agrees to sell, lease or license one product (the "tying product," which is usually protected by the seller's IP) only on the condition that the buyer also purchase from the seller another product (the "tied product," which is often not covered by the seller's IP).[19] The buyer who wishes to purchase, lease or license the tying product is thus left with no option but to purchase unwanted (or overpriced) tied products. And because the tying product is typically covered by the seller's IP, the buyer has no choice but to obtain it from the seller.

As noted in Section 25.1, tying arrangements were once considered *per se* illegal – one of the Nine No-Nos of IP licensing. In *Jefferson Parish Hosp. Dist. No. 2 v. Hyde*, 466 U.S. 2, 12 (1984), the Supreme Court confirmed that tying arrangements remain *per se* illegal. However, the Court has also recognized a number of factors that tend to soften the application of the *per se* test in cases of tying. Thus, to establish illegal tying, the following four elements must be proved:

1. the existence of at least two distinct products or services;
2. the sale of the tying product or service is conditioned on the purchase of the tied product or service;
3. the defendant has sufficient economic or market power over the tying product to restrain competition for another product; and
4. the amount of commerce involved is not insubstantial.[20]

In some circuits, courts have even permitted a defendant to introduce evidence that there was a legitimate business rationale for the alleged tie-in, causing many practitioners (as well as the DOJ and FTC[21]) to view tying as being subject to the "rule of reason" for all practical purposes, notwithstanding the Supreme Court's adherence to the *per se* label.

In tying cases there must be both a tying product and a tied product. The tying product can generally be covered by any form of IP – patent, copyright or trademark. The following case focuses on an alleged anticompetitive tie involving trademarks.

Siegel v. Chicken Delight, Inc.

448 F.2d 43 (9th Cir. 1971)

MERRILL, CIRCUIT JUDGE

This antitrust suit is a class action in which certain franchisees of Chicken Delight seek treble damages for injuries allegedly resulting from illegal restraints imposed by Chicken Delight's standard form franchise agreements. The restraints in question are Chicken Delight's contractual requirements that franchisees purchase certain essential cooking equipment, dry-mix food items, and trademark bearing packaging exclusively from Chicken Delight as a condition of obtaining a Chicken Delight trademark license. These requirements are asserted to constitute a tying arrangement, unlawful per se under Sec. 1 of the Sherman Act.

---

[19] As discussed in Chapter 24, tying arrangements, exemplified by *Morton Salt v. Suppiger*, may also form the basis for a claim of IP misuse.
[20] *Eastman Kodak Co. v. Image Technical Servs., Inc.*, 504 U.S. 451 (1992).
[21] See US DOJ & FTC, Antitrust Enforcement and Intellectual Property Rights: Promoting Innovation and Competition 114 (2007) ("as a matter of their prosecutorial discretion, the Agencies will apply the rule of reason when evaluating intellectual property tying and bundling agreements") [hereinafter DOJ–FTC 2007 IP Report].

After five weeks of trial to a jury in the District Court, plaintiffs moved for a directed verdict, requesting the court to rule upon four propositions of law: (1) That the contractual requirements constituted a tying arrangement as a matter of law; (2) that the alleged tying products – the Chicken Delight name, symbols, and system of operation – possessed sufficient economic power to condemn the tying arrangement as a matter of law; (3) that the tying arrangement had not, as a matter of law, been justified; and (4) that, as a matter of law, plaintiffs as a class had been injured by the arrangement.

The court ruled in favor of plaintiffs on all issues except part of the justification defense, which it submitted to the jury. On the questions submitted to it, the jury rendered special verdicts in favor of plaintiffs. Chicken Delight has taken this interlocutory appeal from the trial court rulings and verdicts.

I. Factual Background

Over its eighteen years existence, Chicken Delight has licensed several hundred franchisees to operate home delivery and pick-up food stores. It charged its franchisees no franchise fees or royalties. Instead, in exchange for the license granting the franchisees the right to assume its identity and adopt its business methods and to prepare and market certain food products under its trademark, Chicken Delight required its franchisees to purchase a specified number of cookers and fryers and to purchase certain packaging supplies and mixes exclusively from Chicken Delight. The prices fixed for these purchases were higher than, and included a percentage markup which exceeded that of, comparable products sold by competing suppliers.

II. The Existence of an Unlawful Tying Arrangement

In order to establish that there exists an unlawful tying arrangement plaintiffs must demonstrate *First*, that the scheme in question involves two distinct items and provides that one (the tying product) may not be obtained unless the other (the tied product) is also purchased. *Times-Picayune Publishing Co. v. United States*, 345 U.S. 594, 613–614 (1953). *Second*, that the tying product possesses sufficient economic power appreciably to restrain competition in the tied product market. *Northern Pacific R. Co. v. United States*, 356 U.S. 1, 6 (1958). *Third*, that a "not insubstantial" amount of commerce is affected by the arrangement. *International Salt Co. v. United States*, 332 U.S. 392 (1947). Chicken Delight concedes that the third requirement has been satisfied. It disputes the existence of the first two. Further it asserts that, even if plaintiffs should prevail with respect to the first two requirements, there is a *fourth* issue: whether there exists a special justification for the particular tying arrangement in question.

A. Two Products

The District Court ruled that the license to use the Chicken Delight name, trademark, and method of operations was "a tying item in the traditional sense," the tied items being the cookers and fryers, packaging products, and mixes.

The court's decision to regard the trademark or franchise license as a distinct tying item is not without precedent. In *Susser v. Carvel Corp.*, 332 F.2d 505 (2d Cir. 1964), all three judges regarded as a tying product the trademark license to ice cream outlet franchisees, who were required to purchase ice cream, toppings and other supplies from the franchisor. Nevertheless, Chicken Delight argues that the District Court's conclusion conflicts with the purposes behind the strict rules governing the use of tying arrangements.

The hallmark of a tie-in is that it denies competitors free access to the tied product market, not because the party imposing the arrangement has a superior product in that market, but because of the power or leverage exerted by the tying product. *Northern Pac. R. Co. v. United States, supra.* Rules governing tying arrangements are designed to strike, not at the mere coupling of physically separable objects, but rather at the use of a dominant desired product to compel the purchase of a second, distinct commodity. In effect, the forced purchase of the second, tied product is a price exacted for the purchase of the dominant, tying product. By shutting competitors out of the tied product market, tying arrangements serve hardly any purpose other than the suppression of competition.

Chicken Delight urges us to hold that its trademark and franchise licenses are not items separate and distinct from the packaging, mixes, and equipment, which it says are essential components of the franchise system. To treat the combined sale of all these items as a tie-in for antitrust purposes, Chicken Delight maintains, would be like applying the antitrust rules to the sale of a car with its tires or a left shoe with the right. Therefore, concludes Chicken Delight, the lawfulness of the arrangement should not be measured by the rules governing tie-ins. We disagree.

In determining whether an aggregation of separable items should be regarded as one or more items for tie-in purposes in the normal cases of sales of products the courts must look to the function of the aggregation. Consideration is given to such questions as whether the amalgamation of products resulted in cost savings apart from those reductions in sales expenses and the like normally attendant upon any tie-in, and whether the items are normally sold or used as a unit with fixed proportions.

Where one of the products sold as part of an aggregation is a trademark or franchise license, new questions are injected. In determining whether the license and the remaining ("tied") items in the aggregation are to be regarded as distinct items which can be traded in distinct markets consideration must be given to the function of trademarks.

The burgeoning business of franchising has made trademark licensing a widespread commercial practice and has resulted in the development of a new rationale for trademarks as representations of product quality. This is particularly true in the case of a franchise system set up not to distribute the trademarked goods of the franchisor, but, as here, to conduct a certain business under a common trademark or trade name. Under such a type of franchise, the trademark simply reflects the goodwill and quality standards of the enterprise which it identifies. As long as the system of operation of the franchisees lives up to those quality standards and remains as represented by the mark so that the public is not misled, neither the protection afforded the trademark by law nor the value of the trademark to the licensee depends upon the source of the components.

This being so, it is apparent that the goodwill of the Chicken Delight trademark does not attach to the multitude of separate articles used in the operation of the licensed system or in the production of its end product. It is not what is used, but how it is used and what results that have given the system and its end product their entitlement to trademark protection. It is to the system and the end product that the public looks with the confidence that established goodwill has created.

Thus, sale of a franchise license, with the attendant rights to operate a business in the prescribed manner and to benefit from the goodwill of the trade name, in no way requires the forced sale by the franchisor of some or all of the component articles. Just as the quality of a copyrighted creation cannot by a tie-in be appropriated by a creation to which the copyright does not relate, *United States v. Paramount Pictures, Inc.*, 334 U.S. 131, 158 (1948), so here attempts by tie-in to extend the trademark protection to common articles (which the public does not and has no reason to connect with the trademark) simply because they are said to be essential to production of that which is the subject of the trademark, cannot escape antitrust scrutiny.

Chicken Delight's assertions that only a few essential items were involved in the arrangement does not give us cause to reach a different conclusion. The relevant question is not whether the items are essential to the franchise, but whether it is essential to the franchise that the items be purchased from Chicken Delight. This raises not the issue of whether there is a tie-in but rather the issue of whether the tie-in is justifiable, a subject to be discussed below.

We conclude that the District Court was not in error in ruling as matter of law that the arrangement involved distinct tying and tied products.

B. Economic Power

Under the per se theory of illegality, plaintiffs are required to establish not only the existence of a tying arrangement but also that the tying product possesses sufficient economic power to appreciably restrain free competition in the tied product markets. *Northern Pacific R. Co. v. United States, supra.*

Chicken Delight points out that while it was an early pioneer in the fast food franchising field, the record establishes that there has recently been a dramatic expansion in this area, with the advent of numerous firms, including many chicken franchising systems, all competing vigorously with each other. Under the circumstances, it contends that the existence of the requisite market dominance remained a jury question.

The District Court ruled, however, that Chicken Delight's unique registered trademark, in combination with its demonstrated power to impose a tie-in, established as matter of law the existence of sufficient market power to bring the case within the Sherman Act.

We agree.

It can hardly be denied that the Chicken Delight trademark is distinctive; that it possesses goodwill and public acceptance unique to it and not enjoyed by other fast food chains. It is now clear that sufficient economic power is to be presumed where the tying product is patented or copyrighted.

Just as the patent or copyright forecloses competitors from offering the distinctive product on the market, so the registered trademark presents a legal barrier against competition. It is not the nature of the public interest that has caused the legal barrier to be erected that is the basis for the presumption, but the fact that such a barrier does exist. Accordingly we see no reason why the presumption that exists in the case of the patent and copyright does not equally apply to the trademark.

Thus we conclude that the District Court did not err in ruling as matter of law that the tying product – the license to use the Chicken Delight trademark – possessed sufficient market power to bring the case within the Sherman Act.

C. Justification

Chicken Delight maintains that, even if its contractual arrangements are held to constitute a tying arrangement, it was not an unreasonable restraint under the Sherman Act. Three different bases for justification are urged.

First, Chicken Delight contends that the arrangement was a reasonable device for measuring and collecting revenue. There is no authority for justifying a tying arrangement on this ground. Unquestionably, there exist feasible alternative methods of compensation for the franchise licenses, including royalties based on sales volume or fees computed per unit of time, which would neither involve tie-ins nor have undesirable anticompetitive consequences.

Second, Chicken Delight advances as justification the fact that when it first entered the fast food field in 1952 it was a new business and was then entitled to the protection afforded by *United States v. Jerrold Electronics Corp.*, *supra*, 187 F.Supp. 545. As to the period here involved – 1963 to 1970 – it contends that transition to a different arrangement would be difficult if not economically impossible.

We find no merit in this contention. Whatever claim Chicken Delight might have had to a new business defense in 1952 – a question we need not decide – the defense cannot apply to the 1963–70 period. To accept Chicken Delight's argument would convert the new business justification into a perpetual license to operate in restraint of trade.

The third justification Chicken Delight offers is the "marketing identity" purpose, the franchisor's preservation of the distinctiveness, uniformity and quality of its product. In the case of a trademark this purpose cannot be lightly dismissed. Not only protection of the franchisor's goodwill is involved. The licensor owes an affirmative duty to the public to assure that in the hands of his licensee the trademark continues to represent that which it purports to represent. For a licensor, through relaxation of quality control, to permit inferior products to be presented to the public under his licensed mark might well constitute a misuse of the mark.

However, to recognize that such a duty exists is not to say that every means of meeting it is justified. Restraint of trade can be justified only in the absence of less restrictive alternatives. In cases such as this, where the alternative of specification is available, the language used in *Standard Oil Co. v. United States*, *supra*, 337 U.S. at 306, in our view states the proper test, applicable in the case of trademarks as well as in other cases:

> the protection of the good will of the manufacturer of the tying device – fails in the usual situation because specification of the type and quality of the product to be used in connection with the tying device is protection enough. The only situation, indeed, in which the protection of good will may necessitate the use of tying clauses is where specifications for a substitute would be so detailed that they could not practicably be supplied.

The District Court found factual issues to exist as to whether effective quality control could be achieved by specification in the case of the cooking machinery and the dip and spice mixes. These questions were given to the jury under instructions; and the jury, in response to special interrogatories, found against Chicken Delight.

Notes and Questions

1. *Tying product.* In *Chicken Delight*, the "tying product" is the Chicken Delight trademark. Is a trademark a product? Does a trademark possess characteristics similar, for example, to a patented salt-depositing machine?
2. *Market power.* As noted by the court, "the tying product [must possess] sufficient economic power appreciably to restrain competition in the tied product market." Clearly the owner of a trademark controls the use of that mark with respect to the relevant classes of goods and services. But is that the relevant market? Benjamin Klein and Lester Saft argue that

"Chicken Delight, although it possesses a trademark, does not possess any economic power in the relevant market in which it operates – the fast food franchising (or perhaps, more generally, the franchising) market."[22] According to Klein and Saft, Chicken Delight, a relatively small operation compared to fast-food giants such as McDonald's and Kentucky Fried Chicken, had little market power, despite its trademark. How does this observation affect your view of the court's conclusion that a tying arrangement existed?

3. *Consideration.* How was Chicken Delight compensated in this arrangement? Is it relevant that it charged its franchisees no franchise fees or royalties?

4. *Tied products.* Eleven years after *Chicken Delight*, in *Krehl v. Baskin Robbins Ice Cream Co.*, 664 F.2d 1348 (9th Cir. 1982), the Ninth Circuit sought to distinguish *Chicken Delight* on the basis of the type of franchise arrangement that it used.

In *Chicken Delight*, we were confronted with a situation where the franchisor conditioned the grant of a franchise on the purchase of a catalogue of miscellaneous items used in the franchised business. These products were neither manufactured by the franchisor nor were they of a special design uniquely suited to the franchised business. Rather, they were commonplace paper products and packaging goods, readily available in the competitive market place. In evaluating this arrangement, we stated that, "in determining whether the (trademark) ... and the remaining ... items ... are to be regarded as distinct items ... consideration must be given to the function of trademarks." Because the function of the trademark in *Chicken Delight* was merely to identify a distinctive business format, we found the nexus between the trademark and the tied products to be sufficiently remote to warrant treating them as separate products.

A determination of whether a trademark may appropriately be regarded as a separate product requires an inquiry into the relationship between the trademark and the products allegedly tied to its sale. In evaluating this relationship, consideration must be given to the type of franchising system involved. In *Chicken Delight*, we distinguished between two kinds of franchising systems: 1) the business format system; and 2) the distribution system. A business format franchise system is usually created merely to conduct business under a common trade name. The franchise outlet itself is generally responsible for the production and preparation of the system's end product. The franchisor merely provides the trademark and, in some cases, supplies used in operating the franchised outlet and producing the system's products. Under such a system, there is generally only a remote connection between the trademark and the products the franchisees are compelled to purchase. This is true because consumers have no reason to associate with the trademark, those component goods used either in the operation of the franchised store or in the manufacture of the end product. "Under such a type of franchise, the trade-mark simply reflects the goodwill and quality standards of the enterprise it identifies. As long as ... franchisees (live) up to those quality standards ... neither the protection afforded the trade-mark by law nor the value of the trade-mark ... depends upon the source of the components."

Where, as in *Chicken Delight*, the tied products are commonplace articles, the franchisor can easily maintain its quality standards through other means less intrusive upon competition. Accordingly, the coerced purchase of these items amounts to little more than an effort to impede competition on the merits in the market for the tied products.

Where a distribution type system, such as that employed by Baskin-Robbins, is involved, significantly different considerations are presented. Under the distribution type system, the franchised outlets serve merely as conduits through which the trademarked goods of the franchisor

[22] Benjamin Klein & Lester F. Saft, *The Law and Economics of Franchise Tying Contracts*, 28 J. L. Econ. 345, 356 (1985).

flow to the ultimate consumer. These goods are generally manufactured by the franchisor or, as in the present case, by its licensees according to detailed specifications. In this context, the trademark serves a different function. Instead of identifying a business format, the trademark in a distribution franchise system serves merely as a representation of the end product marketed by the system. "It is to the system and the end product that the public looks with the confidence that the established goodwill has created." Consequently, sale of substandard products under the mark would dissipate this goodwill and reduce the value of the trademark. The desirability of the trademark is therefore utterly dependent upon the perceived quality of the product it represents. Because the prohibition of tying arrangements is designed to strike solely at the use of a dominant desired product to compel the purchase of a second undesired commodity, the tie-in doctrine can have no application where the trademark serves only to identify the alleged tied product. The desirability of the trademark and the quality of the product it represents are so inextricably interrelated in the mind of the consumer as to preclude any finding that the trademark is a separate item for tie-in purposes.

In the case at bar, the District Court found that the Baskin-Robbins trademark merely served to identify the ice cream products distributed by the franchise system. Based on our review of the record, we cannot say that this finding is clearly erroneous. Accordingly, we conclude that the District Court did not err in ruling that the Baskin-Robbins trademark lacked sufficient independent existence apart from the ice cream products allegedly tied to its sale, to justify a finding of an unlawful tying arrangement.

Affirmed.

Do you agree? Does it matter that the tied products in *Chicken Delight* included "cookers and fryers" and "dry-mix food items" in addition to "commonplace paper products and packaging goods, readily available in the competitive market place"?

5. *Block booking.* The practice of "block booking" in the motion picture industry involved the movie studio policy of licensing films to theaters and television networks only in packages that included both desirable and less desirable titles. As explained by the Supreme Court in *United States v. Loew's, Inc.*, 371 U.S. 38 (1962),

> [a studio] negotiated four contracts that were found to be block booked. Station WTOP was to pay $118,800 for the license of 99 pictures, which were divided into three groups of 33 films, based on differences in quality. To get "Treasure of the Sierra Madre," "Casablanca," "Johnny Belinda," "Sergeant York," and "The Man Who Came to Dinner," among others, WTOP also had to take such films as "Nancy Drew Troubleshooter," "Tugboat Annie Sails Again," "Kid Nightingale," "Gorilla Man," and "Tear Gas Squad."

Thus, if the station wished to broadcast *Casablanca*, it also had to pay for *The Gorilla Man* and a host of other "B" movies, whether it wanted them or not. Block booking arrangements have generally been treated by the courts as tying arrangements, and have largely been condemned on that basis. Do you think that the result would be different if these arrangements had been evaluated under a "rule of reason" approach?

6. *Platform software products and the rule of reason.* In the government's massive antitrust case against Microsoft, one of the allegations was that Microsoft illegally tied its Internet Explorer web browser (IE) to its ubiquitous Windows operating system by contractually requiring computer manufacturers to license a copy of IE with every copy of Windows and prohibiting them from removing or uninstalling IE from computers using Windows. The district court, applying the Supreme Court's *per se* rule, found an illegal tie (87 F. Supp. 2d 30 (D.D.C. 2000)). On appeal, the DC Circuit (253 F.3d 34 (D.C. Cir. 2001)) questioned the *per se* rule itself, reasoning that

FIGURE 25.5 With "block booking," in order to show classic films like *Casablanca*, television stations and movie theaters were also required to license, and pay for, "B" movies like *The Gorilla Man*.

because of the pervasively innovative character of platform software markets, tying in such markets may produce efficiencies that courts have not previously encountered and thus the Supreme Court had not factored into the per se rule as originally conceived.

Among the examples of efficiencies that could have flowed from Microsoft's tying of IE to Windows were ease of integration with third-party applications and consumer preference for an integrated product:

These arguments all point to one conclusion: we cannot comfortably say that bundling in platform software markets has so little "redeeming virtue," and that there would be so "very little loss to society" from its ban, that "an inquiry into its costs in the individual case [can be] considered [] unnecessary."

Accordingly, the Circuit remanded to the district court for reconsideration of the tying claim under the rule of reason. In view of the heightened burden imposed by the rule of reason test, the DOJ dropped its tying claim on remand.[23]

7. *No license, no chips?* In order to obtain a license to the valuable Chicken Delight trademark (tying product), franchisees were required, among other things, to purchase Chicken Delight's commodity packaging (tied products). In this context, consider *FTC v. Qualcomm* (N.D. Cal. 2018). There, Qualcomm was accused of enforcing a "no license – no chips" policy, under which smartphone manufacturers (OEMs) who desired to purchase Qualcomm's wireless communication chips were required to enter into separate royalty-bearing patent

---

[23] David S. Evans, *Introduction*, in Microsoft, Antitrust and The New Economy: Selected Essays 1, 6 (David S. Evans ed., Springer, 2002).

license agreements. In finding that Qualcomm violated Section 2 of the Sherman Act (a monopolization claim – see Section 25.6), the district court explained,

Qualcomm wields its chip monopoly power to coerce OEMs to sign patent license agreements. Specifically, Qualcomm threatens to withhold OEMs' chip supply until OEMs sign patent license agreements on Qualcomm's preferred terms. In some cases, Qualcomm has even cut off OEMs' chip supply, although the threat of cutting off chip supply has been more than sufficient to coerce OEMs into signing Qualcomm's patent license agreements and avoiding the devastating loss of chip supply.[24]

Interestingly, the court did not explicitly characterize Qualcomm's "no license – no chips" policy as an illegal tying arrangement. Rather, it considered a range of Qualcomm's licensing practices together, concluding that they "strangled competition" in the relevant chip markets and "harmed rivals, OEMs, and end consumers in the process."[25] Is the district court describing a tying agreement here? If so, why not say so explicitly? Does it matter that both the presumably tying products (the chips) and the tied product (the license) are patented?

In any event, the Ninth Circuit reversed, holding that:

If Qualcomm were to refuse to license its SEPs to OEMs unless they first agreed to purchase Qualcomm's chips ("no chips, no license"), then rival chip suppliers indeed might have an antitrust claim under both §§ 1 and 2 of the Sherman Act based on exclusionary conduct. This is because OEMs cannot sell their products without obtaining Qualcomm's SEP licenses, so a "no chips, no license" policy would essentially force OEMs to either purchase Qualcomm's chips or pay for both Qualcomm's and a competitor's chips (similar to the no-win situation faced by OEMs in the Caldera case). But unlike a hypothetical "no chips, no license" policy, "no license, no chips" is chip neutral: it makes no difference whether an OEM buys Qualcomm's chip or a rival's chips. The policy only insists that, whatever chip source an OEM chooses, the OEM pay Qualcomm for the right to practice the patented technologies embodied in the chip, as well as in other parts of the phone or other cellular device.[26]

What does the Ninth Circuit view as the crucial difference between "no license – no chips" and "no chips – no license"? Why might the latter be a potential violation of the Sherman Act, but not the former?

25.6 MONOPOLIZATION AND MARKET POWER

The possession of a monopoly in a given market is not itself a violation of the antitrust laws. Monopolies may be gained in a variety of legitimate ways including "growth or development as a consequence of a superior product, business acumen, or historic accident."[27] Rather, it is the willful acquisition or maintenance of monopoly power through anticompetitive, predatory or exclusionary conduct that violates § 2 of the Sherman Act.

In order to prove a case of monopolization, the plaintiff must first show that the defendant had "market power" in a relevant market. As explained by the DOJ and FTC, "Market power is the ability profitably to maintain prices above, or output below, competitive levels for a significant period of time."[28]

[24] *FTC v. Qualcomm Inc.*, 411 F. Supp. 3d 658, 698 (N.D. Cal. 2019), *rev'd* 969 F.3d 974 (9th Cir. 2020).
[25] Id. at 812.
[26] *FTC v. Qualcomm Inc.*, 969 F.3d 97, 1002–03 (9th Cir. 2020).
[27] *United States v. Grinnell Corp.*, 384 U.S. 563, 570–71 (1966).
[28] DOJ-FTC, 2017 Licensing Guidelines, supra note 15, at 4.

FIGURE 25.6 Häagen-Dazs successfully argued that inexpensive and expensive ice cream products compete in the same market.

Market power is always defined by reference to a particular *market*. In antitrust cases, two types of market are generally considered: product and geographic markets. Entire books have been written about the complex exercise of defining markets in antitrust cases.[29] Geographic markets are defined based on the ability of suppliers to sell beyond their immediate locations, taking into account factors such as transportation costs, buyer convenience and customer preferences. To grossly oversimplify, the principal factors that are evaluated when defining a product market include the degree to which different products can function as substitutes for one another, the degree of price elasticity among different products and the degree to which producers can easily shift from production of one product to another. Thus, in one well-known case involving an exclusive distribution arrangement among Häagen-Dazs and its distributors, potential markets could have included the market for all frozen desserts, packaged ice cream, packaged premium ice cream or packaged super-premium ice cream.[30]

In *United States v. Microsoft*, the court established that the relevant market was "Intel-compatible PC operating systems" and that Microsoft controlled more than 95 percent of that market (253 F.3d at 51). Microsoft argued, unsuccessfully, that the market should have been defined to include non-Intel-compatible operating systems such as Mac OS, operating systems for non-PC devices such as handheld devices, and middleware products such as Netscape Navigator and Java. But the court, in applying the rule that "the relevant market must include all products reasonably interchangeable by consumers for the same purposes," excluded these other products from the definition of Microsoft's market (Id. at 52–54).

One particularly thorny issue in market definition is the role that IP rights play in defining a market. Some have argued that the owner of a patent, copyright or trade secret has a "monop-oly" over the use of that right. But does that IP right give its owner real power over any particular market? The following case, in which an illegal tie was alleged, considers the issue.

---

[29] See, e.g., ABA Section of Antitrust Law, Market Definition in Theory and Case Studies (ABA, 2012).

[30] *See In re Super Premium Ice Cream Distribution Antitrust Litigation*, 691 F. Supp. 1262, 1268 (N.D. Cal. 1988) (finding that "all grades of ice creams compete with one another for customer preference and for space in the retailers' freezers" and "gradations among various qualities of ice cream are not sufficient to establish separate relevant markets for the purposes of determining market power" and finally holding that "the relevant market is ice cream generally").

Illinois Tool Works Inc. v. Independent Ink, Inc.

547 U.S. 28 (2006)

STEVENS, JUSTICE

In *Jefferson Parish Hospital Dist. No. 2 v. Hyde*, 466 U. S. 2 (1984), we repeated the well-settled proposition that "if the Government has granted the seller a patent or similar monopoly over a product, it is fair to presume that the inability to buy the product elsewhere gives the seller market power." This presumption of market power, applicable in the antitrust context when a seller conditions its sale of a patented product (the "tying" product) on the purchase of a second product (the "tied" product), has its foundation in the judicially created patent misuse doctrine. In 1988, Congress substantially undermined that foundation, amending the Patent Act to eliminate the market power presumption in patent misuse cases. 35 U. S. C. §271(d). The question presented to us today is whether the presumption of market power in a patented product should survive as a matter of antitrust law despite its demise in patent law. We conclude that the mere fact that a tying product is patented does not support such a presumption.

I

Petitioners, Trident, Inc., and its parent, Illinois Tool Works Inc., manufacture and market printing systems that include three relevant components: (1) a patented piezoelectric impulse ink jet printhead; (2) a patented ink container, consisting of a bottle and valved cap, which attaches to the printhead; and (3) specially designed, but unpatented, ink. Petitioners sell their systems to original equipment manufacturers (OEMs) who are licensed to incorporate the printheads and containers into printers that are in turn sold to companies for use in printing barcodes on cartons and packaging materials. The OEMs agree that they will purchase their ink exclusively from petitioners, and that neither they nor their customers will refill the patented containers with ink of any kind.

Respondent, Independent Ink, Inc., has developed an ink with the same chemical composition as the ink sold by petitioners. After an infringement action brought by Trident against Independent was dismissed for lack of personal jurisdiction, Independent ... alleged that petitioners are engaged in illegal tying and monopolization in violation of §§1 and 2 of the Sherman Act.

After discovery, the District Court granted petitioners' motion for summary judgment on the Sherman Act claims. It rejected respondent's submission that petitioners "necessarily have market power in the market for the tying product as a matter of law solely by virtue of the patent on their printhead system, thereby rendering [the] tying arrangements *per se* violations of the antitrust laws." Finding that respondent had submitted no affirmative evidence defining the relevant market or establishing petitioners' power within it, the court concluded that respondent could not prevail on either antitrust claim.

After a careful review of the "long history of Supreme Court consideration of the legality of tying arrangements," the Court of Appeals for the Federal Circuit reversed the District Court's decision as to respondent's §1 claim. We granted certiorari to undertake a fresh examination of the history of both the judicial and legislative appraisals of tying arrangements. Our review is informed by extensive scholarly comment and a change in position by the administrative agencies charged with enforcement of the antitrust laws.

II

American courts first encountered tying arrangements in the course of patent infringement litigation. Such a case came before this Court in *Henry v. A. B. Dick Co.*, 224 U. S. 1 (1912), in which, as in the case we decide today, unpatented ink was the product that was "tied" to the use of a patented product through the use of a licensing agreement. Without commenting on the tying arrangement, the Court held that use of a competitor's ink in violation of a condition of the agreement—that the rotary mimeograph "'may be used only with the stencil, paper, ink and other supplies made by A. B. Dick Co.'"—constituted infringement of the patent on the machine. Chief Justice White dissented, explaining his disagreement with the Court's approval of a practice that he regarded as an "attempt to increase the scope of the monopoly granted by a patent ... which tend[s] to increase monopoly and to burden the public in the exercise of their common rights." [I]n this Court's subsequent cases reviewing the legality of tying arrangements we, too, embraced Chief Justice White's disapproval of those arrangements.

In the years since *A. B. Dick*, four different rules of law have supported challenges to tying arrangements. They have been condemned as improper extensions of the patent monopoly under the patent misuse doctrine, as unfair methods of competition under §5 of the Federal Trade Commission Act, as contracts tending to create a monopoly under §3 of the Clayton Act, and as contracts in restraint of trade under §1 of the Sherman Act. In all of those instances, the justification for the challenge rested on either an assumption or a showing that the defendant's position of power in the market for the tying product was being used to restrain competition in the market for the tied product. As we explained in *Jefferson Parish*, "[o]ur cases have concluded that the essential characteristic of an invalid tying arrangement lies in the seller's exploitation of its control over the tying product to force the buyer into the purchase of a tied product that the buyer either did not want at all, or might have preferred to purchase elsewhere on different terms."

Over the years, however, this Court's strong disapproval of tying arrangements has substantially diminished. Rather than relying on assumptions, in its more recent opinions the Court has required a showing of market power in the tying product. Our early opinions consistently assumed that "[t]ying arrangements serve hardly any purpose beyond the suppression of competition." *Standard Oil Co.*, 337 U. S., at 305–306. In 1962, in *Loew's*, 371 U. S., at 47–48, the Court relied on this assumption despite evidence of significant competition in the market for the tying product. And as recently as 1969, Justice Black, writing for the majority, relied on the assumption as support for the proposition "that, at least when certain prerequisites are met, arrangements of this kind are illegal in and of themselves, and no specific showing of unreasonable competitive effect is required." *Fortner Enterprises, Inc. v. United States Steel Corp.*, 394 U. S. 495, 498–499 (*Fortner I*). Explaining the Court's decision to allow the suit to proceed to trial, he stated that "decisions rejecting the need for proof of truly dominant power over the tying product have all been based on a recognition that because tying arrangements generally serve no legitimate business purpose that cannot be achieved in some less restrictive way, the presence of any appreciable restraint on competition provides a sufficient reason for invalidating the tie."

Reflecting a changing view of tying arrangements, four Justices dissented in *Fortner I*, arguing that the challenged "tie"—the extension of a $2 million line of credit on condition that the borrower purchase prefabricated houses from the defendant—might well have served a legitimate purpose. In his opinion, Justice White noted that promotional tie-ins may provide "uniquely advantageous deals" to purchasers. And Justice Fortas concluded that the arrangement was best characterized as "a sale of a single product with the incidental provision of financing."

The dissenters' view that tying arrangements may well be procompetitive ultimately prevailed; indeed, it did so in the very same lawsuit. After the Court remanded the suit in *Fortner I*, a bench trial resulted in judgment for the plaintiff, and the case eventually made its way back to this Court. Upon return, we unanimously held that the plaintiff's failure of proof on the issue of market power was fatal to its case—the plaintiff had proved "nothing more than a willingness to provide cheap financing in order to sell expensive houses." *United States Steel Corp. v. Fortner Enterprises, Inc.*, 429 U. S. 610, 622 (1977) (*Fortner II*).

The assumption that "[t]ying arrangements serve hardly any purpose beyond the suppression of competition," rejected in *Fortner II*, has not been endorsed in any opinion since. Instead, it was again rejected just seven years later in Jefferson Parish, where, as in *Fortner II*, we unanimously reversed a Court of Appeals judgment holding that an alleged tying arrangement constituted a per se violation of §1 of the Sherman Act. Like the product at issue in the *Fortner* cases, the tying product in *Jefferson Parish*—hospital services—was unpatented, and our holding again rested on the conclusion that the plaintiff had failed to prove sufficient power in the tying product market to restrain competition in the market for the tied product—services of anesthesiologists.

In rejecting the application of a *per se* rule that all tying arrangements constitute antitrust violations, we explained:

> [W]e have condemned tying arrangements when the seller has some special ability—usually called "market power"—to force a purchaser to do something that he would not do in a competitive market …
>
> Per se condemnation—condemnation without inquiry into actual market conditions—is only appropriate if the existence of forcing is probable. Thus, application of the per se rule focuses on the probability of anticompetitive consequences …
>
> For example, if the Government has granted the seller a patent or similar monopoly over a product, it is fair to presume that the inability to buy the product elsewhere gives the seller market power. Any effort to enlarge the scope of the patent monopoly by using the market power it confers to restrain competition in the market for a second product will undermine competition on the merits in that second market. Thus, the sale or lease of a patented item on condition that the buyer make all his purchases of a separate tied product from the patentee is unlawful.

Notably, nothing in our opinion suggested a rebuttable presumption of market power applicable to tying arrangements involving a patent on the tying good. Instead, it described the rule that a contract to sell a patented product on condition that the purchaser buy unpatented goods exclusively from the patentee is a *per se* violation of §1 of the Sherman Act.

Justice O'Connor wrote separately in *Jefferson Parish*. In her opinion, she questioned not only the propriety of treating any tying arrangement as a *per se* violation of the Sherman Act, but also the validity of the presumption that a patent always gives the patentee significant market power, observing that the presumption was actually a product of our patent misuse cases rather than our antitrust jurisprudence. It is that presumption, a vestige of the Court's historical distrust of tying arrangements, that we address squarely today.

III

Justice O'Connor was, of course, correct in her assertion that the presumption that a patent confers market power arose outside the antitrust context as part of the patent misuse doctrine. That doctrine had its origins in *Motion Picture Patents Co. v. Universal Film Mfg. Co.*, 243 U. S. 502 (1917), which found no support in the patent laws for the proposition that a patentee may "prescribe by notice attached to a patented machine the conditions of its use and the supplies which must be used in the operation of it, under pain of infringement of the patent." Although *Motion Picture Patents Co.* simply narrowed the scope of possible patent infringement claims, it formed the basis for the Court's subsequent decisions creating a patent misuse defense to infringement claims when a patentee uses its patent "as the effective means of restraining competition with its sale of an unpatented article." *Morton Salt Co. v. G. S. Suppiger Co.*, 314 U.S. 488, 490 (1942).

Without any analysis of actual market conditions, these patent misuse decisions assumed that, by tying the purchase of unpatented goods to the sale of the patented good, the patentee was "restraining competition," *Morton Salt*, 314 U. S., at 490, or "secur[ing] a limited monopoly of an unpatented material," *Mercoid*, 320 U. S., at 664. In other words, these decisions presumed "[t]he requisite economic power" over the tying product such that the patentee could "extend [its] economic control to unpatented products." *Loew's*, 371 U. S., at 45–46.

The presumption that a patent confers market power migrated from patent law to antitrust law in *International Salt*. In that case, we affirmed a District Court decision holding that leases of patented machines requiring the lessees to use the defendant's unpatented salt products violated §1 of the Sherman Act and §3 of the Clayton Act as a matter of law. Although the Court's opinion does not discuss market power or the patent misuse doctrine, it assumes that "[t]he volume of business affected by these contracts cannot be said to be insignificant or insubstantial and the tendency of the arrangement to accomplishment of monopoly seems obvious."

Indeed, later in the same Term we cited *International Salt* for the proposition that the license of "a patented device on condition that unpatented materials be employed in conjunction with the patented device" is an example of a restraint that is "illegal per se." And in subsequent cases we have repeatedly grounded the presumption of market power over a patented device in *International Salt*.

IV

Although the patent misuse doctrine and our antitrust jurisprudence became intertwined in *International Salt*, subsequent events initiated their untwining. This process has ultimately led to today's reexamination of the presumption of per se illegality of a tying arrangement involving a patented product, the first case since 1947 in which we have granted review to consider the presumption's continuing validity.

Three years before we decided *International Salt*, this Court had expanded the scope of the patent misuse doctrine to include not only supplies or materials used by a patented device, but also tying arrangements involving a combination patent and "unpatented material or [a] device [that] is itself an integral part of the structure embodying the patent." *Mercoid*, 320 U. S., at 665. In reaching this conclusion, the Court explained that it could see "no difference in principle" between cases involving elements essential to the inventive character of the patent and elements peripheral to it; both, in the Court's view, were attempts to "expan[d] the patent beyond the legitimate scope of its monopoly."

[*See discussion of the Patent Misuse Reform Act of 1988 in Section 24.2.*]

While the 1988 [Patent Act] amendment does not expressly refer to the antitrust laws, it certainly invites a reappraisal of the per se rule announced in *International Salt*. A rule denying a patentee the right to enjoin an infringer is significantly less severe than a rule that makes the conduct at issue a federal crime punishable by up to 10 years in prison. It would be absurd to assume that Congress intended to provide that the use of a patent that merited punishment as a felony would not constitute "misuse." Moreover, given the fact that the patent misuse doctrine provided the basis for the market power presumption, it would be anomalous to preserve the presumption in antitrust after Congress has eliminated its foundation.

After considering the congressional judgment reflected in the 1988 amendment, we conclude that tying arrangements involving patented products should be evaluated under the standards applied in cases like *Fortner II* and *Jefferson Parish* rather than under the *per se* rule applied in *Morton Salt* and *Loew's*. While some such arrangements are still unlawful, such as those that are the product of a true monopoly or a marketwide conspiracy, that conclusion must be supported by proof of power in the relevant market rather than by a mere presumption thereof.

V

Rather than arguing that we should retain the rule of *per se* illegality, respondent contends that we should endorse a rebuttable presumption that patentees possess market power when they condition the purchase of the patented product on an agreement to buy unpatented goods exclusively from the patentee. Respondent recognizes that a large number of valid patents have little, if any, commercial significance, but submits that those that are used to impose tying arrangements on unwilling purchasers likely do exert significant market power. Hence, in respondent's view, the presumption would have no impact on patents of only slight value and would be justified, subject to being rebutted by evidence offered by the patentee, in cases in which the patent has sufficient value to enable the patentee to insist on acceptance of the tie.

As we have already noted, the vast majority of academic literature recognizes that a patent does not necessarily confer market power. Similarly, while price discrimination may provide evidence of market power, particularly if buttressed by evidence that the patentee has charged an above-market price for the tied package, it is generally recognized that it also occurs in fully competitive markets. We are not persuaded that the combination of these two factors should give rise to a presumption of market power when neither is sufficient to do so standing alone. Rather, the lesson to be learned from *International Salt* and the academic commentary is the same: Many tying arrangements, even those involving patents and requirements ties, are fully consistent with a free, competitive market. For this reason, we reject both respondent's proposed rebuttable presumption and their narrower alternative.

Congress, the antitrust enforcement agencies, and most economists have all reached the conclusion that a patent does not necessarily confer market power upon the patentee. Today, we reach the same conclusion, and therefore hold that, in all cases involving a tying arrangement, the plaintiff must prove that the defendant has market power in the tying product.

Reversed.

Notes and Questions

1. *The prevalence of market power.* The existence of power in a defined market is not only relevant to tying cases like *Illinois Tool Works*, but also to antitrust cases involving monopolization and to horizontal arrangements among competitors that are evaluated under the rule of reason. For an agreement to be condemned under the rule of reason, the parties must be shown both to have restrained competition in a defined product and geographic market, and to have played a significant role in that market. Why is market power so central to antitrust analysis? Why aren't arrangements that are otherwise intended to disadvantage competitors condemned absent market power?

2. *When does IP create market power?* The Court in *Illinois Tool Works* held that the existence of a patent covering a product does not automatically result in market power in any relevant market. But when might a patent or other IP right confer market power on its owner? Would this determination depend on the industry? For example, would it be more likely to find that a patent holder had market power in the pharmaceutical industry versus the software industry?

3. *The DOJ–FTC Guidelines.* The Court in *Illinois Tool Works* notes that in their 1995 Guidelines on Antitrust and IP, the DOJ and FTC state that they "will not presume that a patent, copyright, or trade secret necessarily confers market power upon its owner." This position appears to have influenced the Court in eliminating its own presumption that IP rights do create market power. What weight should courts, and the Supreme Court in particular, give to the prosecutorial views of the antitrust enforcement agencies? The DOJ and FTC revised their IP Guidelines in 2017, leaving their discussion of market power largely unchanged. But what if the agencies had reversed course and again established a presumption – to be used as a guide in their enforcement activities – that IP rights do create market power? Should the Court reassess its decision in *Illinois Tool Works* based on the revised DOJ–FTC position? Does it matter that the leaders of the DOJ and FTC are political appointees who change office periodically, particularly in election years?[31]

4. *Standards-essential patents and market power.* In Chapter 20 we discussed technical standards bodies and standards-essential patents (SEPs). Assume that a SEP is essential to a standard that is used in 80 percent of all smartphones in the world. Does that SEP confer market power on its owner? What if the SEP is only one of 40,000 SEPs covering that standard? Professor Herbert Hovenkamp, one of the leading authorities on US antitrust law, writes:

> Questions about the market power of individual SEP patents are … heavily derivative of questions about the power of the standard setting organization for which the patent is essential. If a patent is truly essential, then it has whatever power is enjoyed by the standard to which it is essential. Most large SSOs that employ SEPS and dominate their industries presumably have significant power. In that case, a properly identified SEP can be presumed to have market power as well. In many other settings, however, standards are less likely to have power for the simple reason that the organization is only one of many alternative standard setting organizations, or else because compliance with a standard is not all that valuable.[32]

With the above caveat in mind, Professor Hovenkamp suggests that "FRAND status create a presumption of sufficient market power, which can be defeated by a showing that firms

---

[31] For some of the implications of such changes see Jorge L. Contreras, *Taking it to the Limit: Shifting U.S. Antitrust Policy Toward Standards Development*, 103 Minn. L. Rev. Headnotes 66 (2018).

[32] Herbert Hovenkamp, *FRAND and Antitrust*, 105 Cornell L. Rev. 101, 119 (2020).

operating under the SSO can find a suitable substitute for the FRAND-encumbered patent in question, readily and at low cost." Do you agree? Under what circumstances might the ownership of a SEP not create market power?

5. *IP misuse versus antitrust*. The Court in *Illinois Tool Works* states that "[a]lthough the patent misuse doctrine and our antitrust jurisprudence became intertwined in *International Salt*, subsequent events initiated their untwining." As discussed in Chapter 24, patent misuse today is treated as a distinct category of wrong under the patent laws, and not as a form of antitrust violation. This means, of course, that an action for patent misuse can succeed without the elements that are necessary to prove an antitrust case, including, notably, the requirement of market power. Is this a good result? Are there reasons why patent misuse and antitrust law should be "retwined"?

6. *Barriers to entry*. Having a large share of a defined market alone is not sufficient to prove market power. An antitrust plaintiff must also show that the market occupied by an accused monopolist is subject to significant barriers to entry. For example, patents covering the major features of a product could make it impossible for competitors to enter the market for that product. But barriers to entry need not be imposed by formal legal exclusivities. In *United States v. Microsoft*, the court considered structural features of the software operating system market dominated by Microsoft's Windows. It concluded that

(1) most consumers prefer operating systems for which a large number of applications have already been written; and (2) most developers prefer to write for operating systems that already have a substantial consumer base. This "chicken-and-egg" situation ensures that applications

FIGURE 25.7 Microsoft's Windows operating system captured 95 percent of the relevant operating system market.

will continue to be written for the already dominant Windows, which in turn ensures that consumers will continue to prefer it over other operating systems.[33]

Accordingly, Microsoft's 95 percent share of the relevant operating system market plus the inherent difficulty that would be faced by any competing operating system combined to demonstrate that Microsoft possessed market power in the relevant market. What other forms of "structural" barriers to entry might play a role in a market power determination?

25.7 REFUSALS TO DEAL: UNILATERAL AND CONCERTED

In general, a party is free to choose its business partners.[34] This precept is especially true with respect to IP. As discussed in Section 24.2, the Patent Misuse Reform Act of 1988 makes it clear that a patent holder is not liable for patent misuse because it "refused to license or use any rights to the patent" (35 U.S.C. § 271(d)(4)). Analogous rules exist under copyright and trade secret law. Thus, absent a contractual or other voluntary commitment to license IP rights to others (e.g., the FRAND commitments as discussed in Chapter 20), an IP owner may freely choose to grant licenses to some and refuse to grant licenses to others. Even the possession of market power does not automatically "impose on [an] intellectual property owner an obligation to license the use of that property to others."[35]

One potential exception to this general rule arises via the so-called "essential facilities" doctrine, under which a monopolist may be required to make available to its competitors some resource or facility that is essential to compete in the market.[36] The origin of this principle is often traced to *United States v. Terminal R.R. Ass'n of St. Louis*, 224 U.S. 383, 391–97 (1912), in which thirty-eight companies conspired to prevent their competitors from utilizing "every feasible means of railroad access to St. Louis," including its only two rail bridges and ferry service. The Supreme Court struck down the arrangement as an unlawful restraint of trade and ordered the defendants to open membership in their association to "any existing or future railroad." Though several cases have raised the specter that an IP right may be treated as an essential facility under the right circumstances, no case has yet held this.[37]

Unlike unilateral refusals to grant licenses, which are seldom found to violate the antitrust laws, agreements to do so among competitors – colloquially known as "group boycotts" – are subject to *per se* liability under Section 1 of the Sherman Act. The following case explores this practice in the context of the distribution of copyrighted films.

The Movie 1 & 2 v. United Artists Communications

909 F.2d 1245 (9th Cir. 1990)

BREWSTER, DISTRICT JUDGE

The Movie 1 & 2 ("The Movie") appeals a district court judgment dismissing its case against numerous antitrust defendants. This case involves allegations that two motion

---

[33] 253 F.3d at 54.
[34] This freedom of association does not apply in the context of consumer transactions, as to which a variety of antidiscrimination and common carrier rules apply.
[35] DOJ–FTC, 2017 Licensing Guidelines, supra note 15, at 4.
[36] See *MCI Comm. Corp. v. AT&T*, 708 F.2d 1081, 1132–33 (7th Cir. 1983).
[37] For a discussion and summary of the case law, see Herbert Hovenkamp, Mark D. Janis & Mark A. Lemley, *Unilateral Refusals to License*, 2 J. Comp. L. & Econ. 1 (2006).

picture exhibitors in Santa Cruz, California, entered into an illegal film licensing agreement in which 19 national film distributors participated, and that the exhibitors attempted to monopolize, conspired to monopolize, and did monopolize the film exhibition market in Santa Cruz. The United States District Court for the Northern District of California ... granted the defendants' multiple motions for summary judgment as to all of the antitrust claims.

Background

Appellant The Movie is a general partnership consisting of Harold Snyder and his two sons, David and Larry Snyder. In February of 1984, the Snyders opened a motion picture theatre in Santa Cruz, California. The two-screen theatre, which has 225 seats in each auditorium, is located in downtown Santa Cruz in a converted storefront which it shares with a moped shop. The Snyders' intent was to exhibit both "commercial" and "art" films on a first-run basis.

The exhibitor defendants in this case were two of The Movie's competitors, UA, which operates five theaters in Santa Cruz with a total of twelve screens, and the Nickelodeon, which operates two theatres with a total of four screens. The distributor defendants included ten major motion picture distributors ("Group I") and nine smaller independent distribution companies ("Group II").

The relevant geographic market in this case is the greater Santa Cruz area, which includes Aptos, Scotts Valley, and Capitola. The relevant product market is first-run motion pictures. Although theatres can either show "first-run" films or subsequently run "sub-run" films, first-run films provide the greatest grossing potential. The Santa Cruz area has only ten theatres at present. UA's five theatres exhibit primarily first-run "commercial" films. The Nickelodeon's two theatres exhibit primarily first-run and vintage "art" films. The only other competitors in Santa Cruz are two non-defendant independent exhibitors who apparently show primarily sub-run films.

This circuit has recognized the existence of relevant submarkets within a product market. We are satisfied with the appellant's division of the relevant market in this case into two categories, "commercial" and "art" films.

The appellant alleges that The Movie was unable to obtain licenses to first-run commercial or art films from the defendant distributors, who concertedly refused to deal with it. Appellant alleges that the distributors cooperated in an illegal "split agreement" between UA and the Nickelodeon, whereby nearly all first-run commercial films were licensed to UA and nearly all first-run art films were licensed to the Nickelodeon. A split agreement is an exhibitor agreement which divides a normally competitive market by allocating films to particular members with the understanding that there will be no bidding among members for licensing rights to the films assigned.

Appellant alleges that the split agreement in this case was part of a boycott against The Movie, which had the purpose of eliminating it as a competitor, a restraint of trade in violation of section 1 of the Sherman Act.

Discussion

Section 1 of the Sherman Act prohibits "[e]very contract, combination ... or conspiracy, in restraint of trade." Appellant's section 1 claims allege an illegal agreement between the exhibitors and the distributors in the form of a "group boycott" aimed at excluding The Movie from the Santa Cruz theatre market.

FIGURE 25.8 The Nickelodeon Theater in Santa Cruz, Cal.

The Supreme Court has emphasized, however, that the Sherman Act does not restrict "the long recognized right of a trader ... engaged in an entirely private business, freely to exercise his own independent discretion as to the parties with whom he will deal." *United States v. Colgate Co.*, 250 U.S. 300, 307 (1919). Because of a supplier's right to choose his customers and set his own terms, antitrust plaintiffs are required to do more than merely allege conspiracy and unequal treatment in order to take a case to trial. According to the law of this circuit, once a defendant rebuts the allegations of conspiracy with "probative evidence supporting an alternative interpretation of a defendant's conduct," the plaintiff must come forward with specific factual support of its conspiracy allegations to avoid summary judgment.

The defendants in this case did offer some evidence from which a trier of fact could reasonably have found that their refusal to deal with The Movie was based on legitimate and sound business judgment. Following such a showing of a plausible and justifiable reason for a defendant's conduct, a plaintiff must provide specific factual support for its allegations of conspiracy which tends to show that the defendant was not acting independently. Accordingly, we examine appellant's evidence in support of its conspiracy allegations.

The Distributor Defendants

The distributors possessed an absolute right to refuse to license films to The Movie as long as their decisions were based upon independent business judgment. The distributors presented evidence to the trial court from which a trier of fact could find that the decision to license films to UA and the Nickelodeon rather than to The Movie was based on such factors as the perceived inferiority and consequently lower grossing potential of The Movie's theatre house and the allegedly inferior terms offered in The Movie's bids. Thus … the defendants rebutted the allegations of conspiracy, and it was incumbent upon the plaintiff to come forward with specific factual support of its conspiracy claim. We believe the plaintiff did present ample evidence to rebut defendants' evidence of independent business decisions and to support plaintiff's allegations of an illegal boycott. We, therefore, reverse the trial court's summary adjudication of the section 1 claims against all of the Group I distributor defendants.

Appellees contend that the lower court's record contained no admissible evidence or assertion of any defendant distributors' having received superior bids from The Movie and having rejected them in favor of defendant exhibitors. While it could be argued, as appellees also urge here, that none of the appellant's bids were superior, that determination is an issue of fact which should be decided by summary judgment only if the trial court can find that no reasonable jury could find on that question in favor of the non-moving party. Some of the bids were arguably superior.

There was evidence before the trial court indicating that these distributors had refused to even receive bids from The Movie until they received threatening correspondence from The Movie's attorney. The distributors have cited no legitimate business justification for a refusal to even receive an exhibitor's bid, nor can this court conceive of how such conduct could reflect sound business judgment. To the contrary, such behavior raises the inference that the distributors would not have licensed films to The Movie even if presented with consistent lucrative bids superior to those of the other exhibitors. This circuit has recognized that a distributor's repeated rejection of lucrative bids in an anticompetitive market environment raises an inference of conspiratorial antitrust conduct. The evidence that UA reaped roughly 96.9% of all revenues from first-run commercial films shown in Santa Cruz reflects an anticompetitive market situation. In such an environment, the distributors' refusal to even receive a new exhibitor's bids "tends to exclude the possibility of independent action," and at least raises an issue of fact as to their participation in the alleged boycott.

This circuit has recognized that it is not necessary for a plaintiff to show an explicit agreement among defendants in support of a Sherman Act conspiracy, and that concerted action may be inferred from circumstantial evidence of the defendant's conduct and course of dealings. We conclude, therefore, that appellant did present sufficient evidence to present a triable issue on the section 1 claim of conspiracy to restrain trade in the form of a group boycott of appellant through split agreements. Our conclusion is reached in the context of evidence before the trial court of awards of films without any bids at all, bid negotiations excluding appellant, bid-tipping, adjustments to licensing agreements made to UA regularly, but to appellant rarely, if ever, and the statistics of film licenses awarded. The appellant should, therefore, have been allowed to proceed to trial on the section 1 claims against the Group I distributors. We accordingly reverse the trial court's grant of summary judgment as to these defendants.

Evaluation of the Unreasonable Restraint of Trade Allegations Under the "Per Se" Rule or the "Rule of Reason"

To the extent that the district court held that a split agreement should be evaluated under the rule of reason because it constituted a non-price restraint of trade, the court erred. It should have applied the illegal per se rule.

Appellees contend that the district court referred to the rule of reason in mere dicta and, therefore, that the issue to which it referred cannot be the basis for a reversal. They argue that the district court never reached the question whether the rule of reason or the per se analysis should be used because both first require proof of an agreement, such as a split agreement, which the court failed to find. Since we find an issue of fact exists regarding the existence of a split agreement, we address the applicability of the "rule of reason" analysis.

This circuit has recently ruled on this issue. In *Harkins*, 850 F.2d at 486, we noted that per se treatment is appropriate "where joint efforts by firms disadvantage competitors by inducing suppliers or customers to deny relationships the competitors need in order to compete." We concluded that an alleged split agreement, if proven, would be illegal per se. Appellees dispute the appellant's reliance on *Harkins* on several grounds. First, they claim that the "per se rule" in that case was only dicta. Second, they claim that all cases finding per se treatment appropriate for a split agreement have demonstrated that the agreement was to depress film rentals to the distributors, eliminate guarantees to those distributors, or otherwise affect the terms of licensing for films, i.e., antitrust injury. Appellees contend that appellants have failed to even allege these factors. One of the cases relied on in *Harkins*, appellees point out, *Northwest Wholesale Stationers, Inc. v. Pacific Stationery Printing Co.*, 472 U.S. 284 (1985), supports the proposition that a per se analysis is not appropriate where no antitrust injury has been alleged. The United States Supreme Court in that case found that plaintiff failed to prove an antitrust violation when it demonstrated injury to itself but not to competition.

In the instant case, however, the split agreement is allegedly employed to restrict entry of other exhibitors into the Santa Cruz market for any film. If so, such conduct would cause antitrust injury in the form of a boycott, a conspiracy in restraint of trade in violation of 15 U.S.C. § 1. In fact, in *Northwest Wholesale Stationers*, the court opined that in cases of group boycotts that directly or indirectly cut off necessary access to customers or suppliers, the per se rule applies because the likelihood of antitrust injury is clear.

On remand, the trial court should instruct the jury accordingly.

Notes and Questions

1. *Unilateral versus concerted conduct.* Why are unilateral refusals to license IP generally tolerated under the antitrust laws, but concerted refusals to license are not? Why is it that the Supreme Court has labeled collusion as "the supreme evil of antitrust"? *Verizon Communications, Inc. v. Law Offices of Curtis V. Trinko, LLP*, 540 U.S. 398, 408 (2004).

2. *Market allocation or group boycott?* As explained by the court in *The Movie*, "A split agreement is an exhibitor agreement which divides a normally competitive market by allocating films to particular members with the understanding that there will be no bidding among members for licensing rights to the films assigned." On its face, this sounds like a market allocation scheme discussed in Section 25.3. Why did The Movie instead challenge the split agreement as a group boycott? How might the antitrust have differed between these two theories?

3. *Antitrust injury.* In *Northwest Wholesale Stationers*, the Supreme Court held that the plaintiff failed to prove an antitrust violation when it demonstrated injury to itself but not to competition. Why should that matter? Isn't the plaintiff's job in a lawsuit to prove that it was injured? Why would the Supreme Court deny recovery to a private plaintiff because it failed

FIGURE 25.9 The National Electrical Code is published by the National Fire Protection Association.

to prove injury to "competition" broadly writ? Should safeguarding overall market competition be the responsibility of the enforcement agencies rather than private plaintiffs?

25.8 ANTITRUST ISSUES AND DUE PROCESS IN STANDARD SETTING

As discussed in Chapter 20, the development of technical interoperability standards is often conducted by groups of competitors under the auspices of one or more standards-development organizations (SDOs). Given the coordinated work of dozens of different competitors to produce shared technical specifications, standardization has long been the subject of antitrust scrutiny.

Today, the conduct of participants within an SDO is typically governed by detailed rules imposed by SDOs in order to limit antitrust liability, both for the SDO and for its participants. But this was not always the case. The following case explores some of the ways that participants in an SDO can act in a manner that is anticompetitive.

Allied Tube v. Indian Head, Inc.

486 U.S. 492 (1988)

BRENNAN, JUSTICE

I

The National Fire Protection Association (Association) is a private, voluntary organization with more than 31,500 individual and group members representing industry, labor, academia, insurers, organized medicine, firefighters, and government. The Association, among other things, publishes product standards and codes related to fire protection through a process known as "consensus standard making." One of the codes it publishes is the National Electrical Code (Code), which establishes product and performance requirements for the design and installation of electrical wiring systems. Revised every three years, the Code is the most influential electrical code in the nation. A substantial number of state and local governments routinely adopt the Code into law with little or no change; private certification laboratories, such as Underwriters Laboratories, normally will not list and label an electrical product that does not meet Code standards; many underwriters will refuse to insure structures that are not built in conformity with the Code, and many electrical inspectors, contractors, and distributors will not use a product that falls outside the Code.

Among the electrical products covered by the Code is electrical conduit, the hollow tubing used as a raceway to carry electrical wires through the walls and floors of buildings. Throughout the relevant period, the Code permitted using electrical conduit made of steel, and almost all conduit sold was in fact steel conduit. Starting in 1980, respondent began to offer plastic conduit made of polyvinyl chloride. Respondent claims its plastic conduit offers significant competitive advantages over steel conduit, including pliability, lower installed cost, and lower susceptibility to short circuiting. In 1980, however, there was also a scientific basis for concern that, during fires in high-rise buildings, polyvinyl chloride conduit might burn and emit toxic fumes.

Respondent initiated a proposal to include polyvinyl chloride conduit as an approved type of electrical conduit in the 1981 edition of the Code. Following approval by one of the Association's professional panels, this proposal was scheduled for consideration at the 1980 annual meeting, where it could be adopted or rejected by a simple majority of the members present. Alarmed that, if approved, respondent's product might pose a competitive threat to steel conduit, petitioner, the Nation's largest producer of steel conduit, met to plan strategy with, among others, members of the steel industry, other steel conduit manufacturers, and its independent sales agents. They collectively agreed to exclude respondent's product from the 1981 Code by packing the upcoming annual meeting with new Association members whose only function would be to vote against the polyvinyl chloride proposal.

Combined, the steel interests recruited 230 persons to join the Association and to attend the annual meeting to vote against the proposal. Petitioner alone recruited 155 persons – including employees, executives, sales agents, the agents' employees, employees from two divisions that did not sell electrical products, and the wife of a national sales director. Petitioner and the other steel interests also paid over $100,000 for the membership, registration, and attendance expenses of these voters. At the annual meeting, the steel group voters were instructed where to sit and how and when to vote by group leaders who used walkie-talkies and hand signals to facilitate communication. Few of the steel group voters had any of the technical documentation necessary to follow the meeting. None of them spoke at the meeting to give their reasons for opposing the proposal to approve polyvinyl chloride conduit. Nonetheless, with their solid vote in opposition, the proposal was rejected and returned to committee by a vote of 394 to 390. Respondent appealed the membership's vote to the Association's Board of Directors, but the Board denied the appeal on the ground that, although the Association's rules had been circumvented, they had not been violated.[38]

---

[38] Respondent also sought a tentative interim amendment to the Code, but that was denied on the ground that there was not sufficient exigency to merit an interim amendment. The Association subsequently approved use of polyvinyl chloride conduit for buildings of less than three stories in the 1984 Code, and for all buildings in the 1987 Code.

In October, 1981, respondent brought this suit in Federal District Court, alleging that petitioner and others had unreasonably restrained trade in the electrical conduit market in violation of § 1 of the Sherman Act. A bifurcated jury trial began in March, 1985. Petitioner conceded that it had conspired with the other steel interests to exclude respondent's product from the Code, and that it had a pecuniary interest to do so. The jury, instructed under the rule of reason that respondent carried the burden of showing that the anticompetitive effects of petitioner's actions outweighed any procompetitive benefits of standard-setting, found petitioner liable. In answers to special interrogatories, the jury found that petitioner did not violate any rules of the Association and acted, at least in part, based on a genuine belief that plastic conduit was unsafe, but that petitioner nonetheless did "subvert" the consensus standard-making process of the Association. The jury also made special findings that petitioner's actions had an adverse impact on competition, were not the least restrictive means of expressing petitioner's opposition to the use of polyvinyl chloride conduit in the marketplace, and unreasonably restrained trade in violation of the antitrust laws. The jury then awarded respondent damages, to be trebled, of $3.8 million for lost profits resulting from the effect that excluding polyvinyl chloride conduit from the 1981 Code had of its own force in the marketplace. No damages were awarded for injuries stemming from the adoption of the 1981 Code by governmental entities.

II

[*The Court's discussion of the Noerr–Pennington doctrine, which immunizes certain conduct that can be characterized as petitioning the government, is omitted.*]

Typically, private standard-setting associations, like the Association in this case, include members having horizontal and vertical business relations. There is no doubt that the members of such associations often have economic incentives to restrain competition and that the product standards set by such associations have a serious potential for anticompetitive harm. See *American Society of Mechanical Engineers, Inc. v. Hydrolevel Corp.*, 456 U. S. 556 (1982). Agreement on a product standard is, after all, implicitly an agreement not to manufacture, distribute, or purchase certain types of products. Accordingly, private standard-setting associations have traditionally been objects of antitrust scrutiny. When, however, private associations promulgate safety standards based on the merits of objective expert judgments and through procedures that prevent the standard-setting process from being biased by members with economic interests in stifling product competition, those private standards can have significant procompetitive advantages. It is this potential for procompetitive benefits that has led most lower courts to apply rule-of-reason analysis to product standard-setting by private associations.

[T]he validity of [petitioner's efforts to influence the Code] must ... be evaluated under the standards of conduct set forth by the antitrust laws that govern the private standard-setting process. The antitrust validity of these efforts is not established, without more, by petitioner's literal compliance with the rules of the Association, for the hope of procompetitive benefits depends upon the existence of safeguards sufficient to prevent the standard-setting process from being biased by members with economic interests in restraining competition. An association cannot validate the anticompetitive activities of its members simply by adopting rules that fail to provide such safeguards ...

What petitioner may not do (without exposing itself to possible antitrust liability for direct injuries) is bias the process by, as in this case, stacking the private standard-setting body with decisionmakers sharing their economic interest in restraining competition.

Notes and Questions

1. *The antitrust issue.* The *Allied Tube* case was not decided on antitrust grounds, and the Court's discussion of the antitrust issues is largely dicta. Nevertheless, the Court clearly recognized the potential for antitrust violations in the defendants' conduct. Under what theories might antitrust liability lie in this case?

2. *Inadvertent collusion?* The Court in *Allied Tube* notes that "the jury found that petitioner did not violate any rules of the Association and acted, at least in part, based on a genuine belief that plastic conduit was unsafe, but that petitioner nonetheless did 'subvert' the consensus standard-making process of the Association." If Allied Tube did not violate any NFPA rules, and actually thought that plastic was an unsafe material for electrical conduit, could it be found liable for violating the Sherman Act? Should there be liability for inadvertent or negligent harm to competition?

3. *More bad behavior at SDOs.* The Court in *Allied Tube* cites its earlier decision involving the American Society of Mechanical Engineers (ASME). Like *Allied Tube*, *ASME v. Hydrolevel*, 456 U.S. 556 (1982), involved allegedly bad behavior at a large SDO. Specifically, the chair of an ASME subcommittee responsible for certifying the compliance of boiler pressure valves with ASME standards ruled that a competitor's valves did not meet the standards and were thus unsafe. The Supreme Court held that ASME itself could be held liable for these misrepresentations, as the weight of the SDO's reputation greatly enhanced the anticompetitive effects of its members' conduct. Why do you think SDOs offer a particularly attractive venue for anticompetitive conduct? Unlike ASME, the NFPA itself was not charged with anticompetitive conduct. To what degree do you think SDOs should be liable for the anticompetitive conduct of their members? Based on the facts of *Allied Tube*, should NFPA have shared antitrust liability with Allied Tube and its allies?

4. *Circular A-119 and SDO due process.* In the late 1970s, observers began to appreciate both the power of SDOs to shape industry practices and their potential to foster anticompetitive behavior. At the same time, there was a strong movement in the United States to shift technical activity from the government to the private sector. In 1980, the Office of Management and Budget (OMB) released a memorandum known as OMB Circular A-119 to the heads of federal agencies.[39] Circular A-119 encouraged each federal agency to adopt privately developed "voluntary standards" in lieu of governmentally developed standards when specifying the characteristics of goods and services to be procured by the agency. In order to qualify as an SDO developing "voluntary standards," the SDO had to abide by a list of "due process and other basic criteria" set out in Circular A-119. These criteria included having public meetings, broadly based representation, consensus decision-making, an appeals process and so forth. Circular A-119 has evolved over the years, and now covers both federal procurement and regulatory activities. Due in part to Circular A-119, the Supreme Court's holdings in *ASME* and *Allied Tube* and other national and international legal developments, most SDOs today have adopted rules imposing due process requirements (openness, balance, consensus, appeal) on their standardization activities.[40] Why are due process requirements important for technical standards development, which might seem like a value-neutral technical activity?

---

[39] Off. Mgt. Budget, Federal Participation in the Development and Use of Voluntary Standards; Final Issuance, 45 Fed. Reg. 4326 (1980).

[40] For a brief history of these developments, see Justus Baron, Jorge L. Contreras & Pierre Larouche, *Balance and Standardization: Implications for Competition and Antitrust Analysis*, 84 Antitrust L.J. 301 (2022).

5. *Due process and policy making.* The anticompetitive activity condemned in cases like *ASME* and *Allied Tube* related to an SDO's standardization activities – is a particular pressure valve compliant? Is PVC an appropriate material for electrical conduit? As a result, the due process requirements that SDOs implemented in the wake of these cases and Circular A-119 focused largely on the standardization process: how standards are proposed, developed, debated and approved at an SDO. But what about the SDO's own internal policies? Must the SDO members follow similar due process requirements when formulating, say, the SDO's patent policy? This question has been hotly debated in recent years as SDOs such as the IEEE have adopted policies that are opposed by some SDO members (see Chapter 20). Is adopting an SDO policy different than developing a technical standard? Is the antitrust risk the same for SDO policies as it is for technical standards? Should the same due process requirements apply in both contexts?[41]

25.9 REVERSE PAYMENT SETTLEMENTS: "PAY FOR DELAY"

Federal Trade Commission v. Actavis, Inc.

570 U.S. 136 (2013)

BREYER, JUSTICE,

Company A sues Company B for patent infringement. The two companies settle under terms that require (1) Company B, the claimed infringer, not to produce the patented product until the patent's term expires, and (2) Company A, the patentee, to pay B many millions of dollars. Because the settlement requires the patentee to pay the alleged infringer, rather than the other way around, this kind of settlement agreement is often called a "reverse payment" settlement agreement. And the basic question here is whether such an agreement can sometimes unreasonably diminish competition in violation of the antitrust laws. See, e.g., 15 U.S.C. § 1 (Sherman Act prohibition of "restraint[s] of trade or commerce").

In this case, the Eleventh Circuit dismissed a Federal Trade Commission (FTC) complaint claiming that a particular reverse payment settlement agreement violated the antitrust laws. In doing so, the Circuit stated that a reverse payment settlement agreement generally is "immune from antitrust attack so long as its anticompetitive effects fall within the scope of the exclusionary potential of the patent." And since the alleged infringer's promise not to enter the patentee's market expired before the patent's term ended, the Circuit found the agreement legal and dismissed the FTC complaint. In our view, however, reverse payment settlements such as the agreement alleged in the complaint before us can sometimes violate the antitrust laws. We consequently hold that the Eleventh Circuit should have allowed the FTC's lawsuit to proceed.

I A

Apparently most if not all reverse payment settlement agreements arise in the context of pharmaceutical drug regulation, and specifically in the context of suits brought under statutory provisions allowing a generic drug manufacturer (seeking speedy marketing

[41] For an overview and analysis of this question, see Justus Baron, et al., *Making the Rules: The Governance of Standard Development Organizations and their Policies on Intellectual Property Rights*, JRC Science for Policy Report EUR 29655 at 148–64 (March 2019).

approval) to challenge the validity of a patent owned by an already-approved brand-name drug owner. We consequently describe four key features of the relevant drug-regulatory framework established by the Drug Price Competition and Patent Term Restoration Act of 1984. That Act is commonly known as the Hatch–Waxman Act.

First, a drug manufacturer, wishing to market a new prescription drug, must submit a New Drug Application to the federal Food and Drug Administration (FDA) and undergo a long, comprehensive, and costly testing process, after which, if successful, the manufacturer will receive marketing approval from the FDA.

Second, once the FDA has approved a brand-name drug for marketing, a manufacturer of a generic drug can obtain similar marketing approval through use of abbreviated procedures. The Hatch–Waxman Act permits a generic manufacturer to file an Abbreviated New Drug Application specifying that the generic has the "same active ingredients as," and is "biologically equivalent" to, the already-approved brand-name drug. In this way the generic manufacturer can obtain approval while avoiding the "costly and time-consuming studies" needed to obtain approval "for a pioneer drug."

Third, the Hatch–Waxman Act sets forth special procedures for identifying, and resolving, related patent disputes. It requires the pioneer brand-name manufacturer to list in its New Drug Application the "number and the expiration date" of any relevant patent. And it requires the generic manufacturer in its Abbreviated New Drug Application to "assure the FDA" that the generic "will not infringe" the brand-name's patents.

The generic can provide this assurance in one of several ways. It can certify that the brand-name manufacturer has not listed any relevant patents. It can certify that any relevant patents have expired. It can request approval to market beginning when any still-in-force patents expire. Or, it can certify that any listed, relevant patent "is invalid or will not be infringed by the manufacture, use, or sale" of the drug described in the Abbreviated New Drug Application. Taking this last-mentioned route (called the "paragraph IV" route), automatically counts as patent infringement, and often "means provoking litigation." If the brand-name patentee brings an infringement suit within 45 days, the FDA then must withhold approving the generic, usually for a 30–month period, while the parties litigate patent validity (or infringement) in court.

Fourth, Hatch–Waxman provides a special incentive for a generic to be the first to file an Abbreviated New Drug Application taking the paragraph IV route. That applicant will enjoy a period of 180 days of exclusivity (from the first commercial marketing of its drug). During that period of exclusivity no other generic can compete with the brand-name drug. If the first-to-file generic manufacturer can overcome any patent obstacle and bring the generic to market, this 180–day period of exclusivity can prove valuable, possibly worth several hundred million dollars. Indeed, the Generic Pharmaceutical Association said in 2006 that the "vast majority of potential profits for a generic drug manufacturer materialize during the 180–day exclusivity period." The 180-day exclusivity period, however, can belong only to the first generic to file.

B. 1

In 1999, Solvay Pharmaceuticals, a respondent here, filed a New Drug Application for a brand-name drug called AndroGel. The FDA approved the application in 2000. In 2003, Solvay obtained a relevant patent and disclosed that fact to the FDA, as Hatch–Waxman requires.

Later the same year another respondent, Actavis, Inc. (then known as Watson Pharmaceuticals), filed an Abbreviated New Drug Application for a generic drug modeled after AndroGel. Subsequently, Paddock Laboratories, also a respondent, separately filed an Abbreviated New Drug Application for its own generic product. Both Actavis and Paddock certified under paragraph IV that Solvay's listed patent was invalid and their drugs did not infringe it. A fourth manufacturer, Par Pharmaceutical, likewise a respondent, did not file an application of its own but joined forces with Paddock, agreeing to share the patent litigation costs in return for a share of profits if Paddock obtained approval for its generic drug.

Solvay initiated paragraph IV patent litigation against Actavis and Paddock. Thirty months later the FDA approved Actavis' first-to-file generic product, but, in 2006, the patent-litigation parties all settled. Under the terms of the settlement Actavis agreed that it would not bring its generic to market until August 31, 2015, 65 months before Solvay's patent expired (unless someone else marketed a generic sooner). Actavis also agreed to promote AndroGel to urologists. The other generic manufacturers made roughly similar promises. And Solvay agreed to pay millions of dollars to each generic—$12 million in total to Paddock; $60 million in total to Par; and an estimated $19–$30 million annually, for nine years, to Actavis. The companies described these payments as compensation for other services the generics promised to perform, but the FTC contends the other services had little value. According to the FTC the true point of the payments was to compensate the generics for agreeing not to compete against AndroGel until 2015.

2

On January 29, 2009, the FTC filed this lawsuit against all the settling parties, namely, Solvay, Actavis, Paddock, and Par. The FTC's complaint (as since amended) alleged that respondents violated § 5 of the Federal Trade Commission Act by unlawfully agreeing "to share in Solvay's monopoly profits, abandon their patent challenges, and refrain from launching their low-cost generic products to compete with AndroGel for nine years." The District Court held that these allegations did not set forth an antitrust law violation. It accordingly dismissed the FTC's complaint. The FTC appealed.

The Court of Appeals for the Eleventh Circuit affirmed the District Court. It wrote that "absent sham litigation or fraud in obtaining the patent, a reverse payment settlement is immune from antitrust attack so long as its anticompetitive effects fall within the scope of the exclusionary potential of the patent."

The FTC sought certiorari. Because different courts have reached different conclusions about the application of the antitrust laws to Hatch–Waxman-related patent settlements, we granted the FTC's petition.

II A

Solvay's patent, if valid and infringed, might have permitted it to charge drug prices sufficient to recoup the reverse settlement payments it agreed to make to its potential generic competitors. And we are willing to take this fact as evidence that the agreement's "anticompetitive effects fall within the scope of the exclusionary potential of the patent." But we do not agree that that fact, or characterization, can immunize the agreement from antitrust attack.

For one thing, to refer, as the Circuit referred, simply to what the holder of a valid patent could do does not by itself answer the antitrust question. The patent here may or may not be valid, and may or may not be infringed. "[A] valid patent excludes all except its owner from the use of the protected process or product". And that exclusion may permit the patent owner to charge a higher-than-competitive price for the patented product. But an invalidated patent carries with it no such right. And even a valid patent confers no right to exclude products or processes that do not actually infringe. The paragraph IV litigation in this case put the patent's validity at issue, as well as its actual preclusive scope. The parties' settlement ended that litigation. The FTC alleges that in substance, the plaintiff agreed to pay the defendants many millions of dollars to stay out of its market, even though the defendants did not have any claim that the plaintiff was liable to them for damages. That form of settlement is unusual. And, for reasons discussed in Part II-B, infra, there is reason for concern that settlements taking this form tend to have significant adverse effects on competition.

Given these factors, it would be incongruous to determine antitrust legality by measuring the settlement's anticompetitive effects solely against patent law policy, rather than by measuring them against procompetitive antitrust policies as well. And indeed, contrary to the Circuit's view that the only pertinent question is whether "the settlement agreement ... fall[s] within" the legitimate "scope" of the patent's "exclusionary potential," this Court has indicated that patent and antitrust policies are both relevant in determining the "scope of the patent monopoly"—and consequently antitrust law immunity—that is conferred by a patent.

Thus, the Court in *Line Material* explained that "the improper use of [a patent] monopoly," is "invalid" under the antitrust laws and resolved the antitrust question in that case by seeking an accommodation "between the lawful restraint on trade of the patent monopoly and the illegal restraint prohibited broadly by the Sherman Act." To strike that balance, the Court asked questions such as whether "the patent statute specifically gives a right" to restrain competition in the manner challenged; and whether "competition is impeded to a greater degree" by the restraint at issue than other restraints previously approved as reasonable. In short, rather than measure the length or amount of a restriction solely against the length of the patent's term or its earning potential, as the Court of Appeals apparently did here, this Court answered the antitrust question by considering traditional antitrust factors such as likely anticompetitive effects, redeeming virtues, market power, and potentially offsetting legal considerations present in the circumstances, such as here those related to patents. See Part II-B, infra. Whether a particular restraint lies "beyond the limits of the patent monopoly" is a conclusion that flows from that analysis and not, as the Chief Justice suggests, its starting point.

For another thing, this Court's precedents make clear that patent-related settlement agreements can sometimes violate the antitrust laws. In *United States v. Singer Mfg. Co.*, 374 U.S. 174 (1963), for example, two sewing machine companies possessed competing patent claims; a third company sought a patent under circumstances where doing so might lead to the disclosure of information that would invalidate the other two firms' patents. All three firms settled their patent-related disagreements while assigning the broadest claims to the firm best able to enforce the patent against yet other potential competitors. The Court did not examine whether, on the assumption that all three patents were valid, patent law would have allowed the patents' holders to do the same. Rather, emphasizing that the Sherman Act "imposes strict limitations on the concerted activities in which patent owners may lawfully engage," it held that the agreements, although settling patent disputes, violated the antitrust laws. And that, in important part, was because "the public interest in granting patent monopolies" exists only to the extent that "the public is given a novel and useful invention" in "consideration for its grant."

Similarly, both within the settlement context and without, the Court has struck down overly restrictive patent licensing agreements—irrespective of whether those agreements produced supra-patent-permitted revenues. We concede that in *United States v. General Elec. Co.*, 272 U.S. 476 (1926), the Court permitted a single patentee to grant to a single licensee a license containing a minimum resale price requirement. But in *Line Material*, the Court held that the antitrust laws forbid a group of patentees, each owning one or more patents, to cross-license each other, and, in doing so, to insist that each licensee maintain retail prices set collectively by the patent holders. The Court was willing to presume that the single-patentee practice approved in General Electric was a "reasonable restraint" that "accords with the patent monopoly granted by the patent law," but declined to extend that conclusion to multiple-patentee agreements: "As the Sherman Act prohibits agreements to fix prices, any arrangement between patentees runs afoul of that prohibition and is outside the patent monopoly." In *New Wrinkle*, 342 U.S., at 378, the Court held roughly the same, this time in respect to a similar arrangement in settlement of a litigation between two patentees, each of which contended that its own patent gave it the exclusive right to control production. That one or the other company (we may presume) was right about its patent did not lead the Court to confer antitrust immunity. Far from it, the agreement was found to violate the Sherman Act.

Finally in *Standard Oil Co. (Indiana)*, the Court upheld cross-licensing agreements among patentees that settled actual and impending patent litigation, which agreements set royalty rates to be charged third parties for a license to practice all the patents at issue (and which divided resulting revenues). But, in doing so, Justice Brandeis, writing for the Court, warned that such an arrangement would have violated the Sherman Act had the patent holders thereby "dominate[d]" the industry and "curtail[ed] the manufacture and supply of an unpatented product." These cases do not simply ask whether a hypothetically valid patent's holder would be able to charge, e.g., the high prices that the challenged patent-related term allowed. Rather, they seek to accommodate patent and antitrust policies, finding challenged terms and conditions unlawful unless patent law policy offsets the antitrust law policy strongly favoring competition.

Finally, the Hatch–Waxman Act itself does not embody a statutory policy that supports the Eleventh Circuit's view. Rather, the general procompetitive thrust of the statute, its specific provisions facilitating challenges to a patent's validity, see Part I-A, supra, and its later-added provisions requiring parties to a patent dispute triggered by a paragraph IV filing to report settlement terms to the FTC and the Antitrust Division of the Department of Justice, all suggest the contrary. Those interested in legislative history may also wish to examine the statements of individual Members of Congress condemning reverse payment settlements in advance of the 2003 amendments. *See, e.g.*, 148 Cong. Rec. 14437 (2002) (remarks of Sen. Hatch) ("It was and is very clear that the [Hatch–Waxman Act] was not designed to allow deals between brand and generic companies to delay competition").

B

The Eleventh Circuit's conclusion finds some degree of support in a general legal policy favoring the settlement of disputes. The Circuit's related underlying practical concern consists of its fear that antitrust scrutiny of a reverse payment agreement would require the parties to litigate the validity of the patent in order to demonstrate what would have happened to competition in the absence of the settlement. Any such litigation will prove time consuming, complex, and expensive. The antitrust game, the Circuit may believe, would not be worth that litigation candle.

We recognize the value of settlements and the patent litigation problem. But we nonetheless conclude that this patent-related factor should not determine the result here. Rather, five sets of considerations lead us to conclude that the FTC should have been given the opportunity to prove its antitrust claim.

First, the specific restraint at issue has the "potential for genuine adverse effects on competition." The payment in effect amounts to a purchase by the patentee of the exclusive right to sell its product, a right it already claims but would lose if the patent litigation were to continue and the patent were held invalid or not infringed by the generic product. Suppose, for example, that the exclusive right to sell produces $50 million in supracompetitive profits per year for the patentee. And suppose further that the patent has 10 more years to run. Continued litigation, if it results in patent invalidation or a finding of noninfringement, could cost the patentee $500 million in lost revenues, a sum that then would flow in large part to consumers in the form of lower prices.

We concede that settlement on terms permitting the patent challenger to enter the market before the patent expires would also bring about competition, again to the consumer's benefit. But settlement on the terms said by the FTC to be at issue here—payment in return for staying out of the market—simply keeps prices at patentee-set levels, potentially producing the full patent-related $500 million monopoly return while dividing that return between the challenged patentee and the patent challenger. The patentee and the challenger gain; the consumer loses. Indeed, there are indications that patentees sometimes pay a generic challenger a sum even larger than what the generic would gain in profits if it won the paragraph IV litigation and entered the market. The rationale behind a payment of this size cannot in every case be supported by traditional settlement considerations. The payment may instead provide strong evidence that the patentee seeks to induce the generic challenger to abandon its claim with a share of its monopoly profits that would otherwise be lost in the competitive market.

But, one might ask, as a practical matter would the parties be able to enter into such an anticompetitive agreement? Would not a high reverse payment signal to other potential challengers that the patentee lacks confidence in its patent, thereby provoking additional challenges, perhaps too many for the patentee to "buy off?" Two special features of Hatch–Waxman mean that the answer to this question is "not necessarily so." First, under Hatch–Waxman only the first challenger gains the special advantage of 180 days of an exclusive right to sell a generic version of the brand-name product. See Part I-A, supra. And as noted, that right has proved valuable—indeed, it can be worth several hundred million dollars. Subsequent challengers cannot secure that exclusivity period, and thus stand to win significantly less than the first if they bring a successful paragraph IV challenge. That is, if subsequent litigation results in invalidation of the patent, or a ruling that the patent is not infringed, that litigation victory will free not just the challenger to compete, but all other potential competitors too (once they obtain FDA approval). The potential reward available to a subsequent challenger being significantly less, the patentee's payment to the initial challenger (in return for not pressing the patent challenge) will not necessarily provoke subsequent challenges. Second, a generic that files a paragraph IV after learning that the first filer has settled will (if sued by the brand-name) have to wait out a stay period of (roughly) 30 months before the FDA may approve its application, just as the first filer did.

These features together mean that a reverse payment settlement with the first filer (or, as in this case, all of the initial filers) "removes from consideration the most motivated challenger, and the one closest to introducing competition." The dissent may doubt these provisions matter, but scholars in the field tell us that "where only one party owns a patent, it is virtually unheard of outside of pharmaceuticals for that party to pay an accused infringer to settle the lawsuit." 1 H. Hovenkamp, M. Janis, M. Lemley, & C. Leslie, IP and Antitrust § 15.3, p. 15–45, n. 161 (2d ed. Supp. 2011). It may well be that Hatch–Waxman's unique regulatory framework, including the special advantage that the 180-day exclusivity period gives to first filers, does much to explain why in this context, but not others, the patentee's ordinary incentives to resist paying off challengers (i.e., the fear of provoking myriad other challengers) appear to be more frequently overcome.

Second, these anticompetitive consequences will at least sometimes prove unjustified. As the FTC admits, offsetting or redeeming virtues are sometimes present. The reverse payment, for example, may amount to no more than a rough approximation of the litigation expenses saved through the settlement. That payment may reflect compensation for other services that the generic has promised to perform—such as distributing the patented item or helping to develop a market for that item. There may be other justifications. Where a reverse payment reflects traditional settlement considerations, such as avoided litigation costs or fair value for services, there is not the same concern that a patentee is using its monopoly profits to avoid the risk of patent invalidation or a finding of noninfringement. In such cases, the parties may have provided for a reverse payment without having sought or brought about the anticompetitive consequences we mentioned above. But that possibility does not justify dismissing the FTC's complaint. An antitrust defendant may show in the antitrust proceeding that legitimate justifications are present, thereby explaining the presence of the challenged term and showing the lawfulness of that term under the rule of reason.

Third, where a reverse payment threatens to work unjustified anticompetitive harm, the patentee likely possesses the power to bring that harm about in practice. At least, the "size of the payment from a branded drug manufacturer to a prospective generic is itself a strong indicator of power"—namely, the power to charge prices higher than the competitive level. An important patent itself helps to assure such power. Neither is a firm without that power likely to pay "large sums" to induce "others to stay out of its market." In any event, the Commission has referred to studies showing that reverse payment agreements are associated with the presence of higher-than-competitive profits—a strong indication of market power.

Fourth, an antitrust action is likely to prove more feasible administratively than the Eleventh Circuit believed. The Circuit's holding does avoid the need to litigate the patent's validity (and also, any question of infringement). But to do so, it throws the baby out with the bath water, and there is no need to take that drastic step. That is because it is normally not necessary to litigate patent validity to answer the antitrust question (unless, perhaps, to determine whether the patent litigation is a sham). An unexplained large reverse payment itself would normally suggest that the patentee has serious doubts about the patent's survival. And that fact, in turn, suggests that the payment's objective is to maintain supracompetitive prices to be shared among the patentee and the challenger rather than face what might have been a competitive market—the very anticompetitive consequence that underlies the claim of antitrust unlawfulness. The owner of a particularly valuable patent might contend, of course, that even a small risk of invalidity justifies a large payment. But, be that as it may, the payment (if otherwise unexplained) likely seeks to prevent the risk of competition. And, as we have said, that consequence constitutes the relevant anticompetitive harm. In a word, the size of the unexplained reverse payment can provide a workable surrogate for a patent's weakness, all without forcing a court to conduct a detailed exploration of the validity of the patent itself.

Fifth, the fact that a large, unjustified reverse payment risks antitrust liability does not prevent litigating parties from settling their lawsuit. They may, as in other industries, settle in other ways, for example, by allowing the generic manufacturer to enter the patentee's market prior to the patent's expiration, without the patentee paying the challenger to stay out prior to that point. Although the parties may have reasons to prefer settlements that include reverse payments, the relevant antitrust question is: What are those reasons? If the basic reason is a desire to maintain and to share patent-generated monopoly profits, then, in the absence of some other justification, the antitrust laws are likely to forbid the arrangement.

In sum, a reverse payment, where large and unjustified, can bring with it the risk of significant anticompetitive effects; one who makes such a payment may be unable to explain and to justify it; such a firm or individual may well possess market power derived from the patent; a court, by examining the size of the payment, may well be able to assess its likely anticompetitive effects along with its potential justifications without litigating the validity of the patent; and parties may well find ways to settle patent disputes without the use of reverse payments. In our view, these considerations, taken together, outweigh the single strong consideration — the desirability of settlements — that led the Eleventh Circuit to provide near-automatic antitrust immunity to reverse payment settlements.

III

The FTC urges us to hold that reverse payment settlement agreements are presumptively unlawful and that courts reviewing such agreements should proceed via a "quick look" approach, rather than applying a "rule of reason." We decline to do so. In *California Dental*, we held (unanimously) that abandonment of the "rule of reason" in favor of presumptive rules (or a "quick-look" approach) is appropriate only where "an observer with even a rudimentary understanding of economics could conclude that the arrangements in question would have an anticompetitive effect on customers and markets." (Breyer, J., concurring in part and dissenting in part). We do not believe that reverse payment settlements, in the context we here discuss, meet this criterion.

That is because the likelihood of a reverse payment bringing about anticompetitive effects depends upon its size, its scale in relation to the payor's anticipated future litigation costs, its independence from other services for which it might represent payment, and the lack of any other convincing justification. The existence and degree of any anticompetitive consequence may also vary as among industries. These complexities lead us to conclude that the FTC must prove its case as in other rule-of-reason cases.

It is so ordered.

Notes and Questions

1. *Size matters*. In *Actavis*, Justice Breyer repeatedly focuses on the size of the settlement payment (up to $270 million to Actavis over nine years, and lesser amounts to two other generic manufacturers), reasoning that "a court, by examining the size of the payment, may well be able to assess its likely anticompetitive effects along with its potential justifications without litigating the validity of the patent." How can the size of a payment give clues as

to anticompetitive conduct? Does the overall size of the market matter? For instance, is Solvay's $171–270 million payment to Actavis large in comparison to its $500 million in anticipated profits from AndroGel?

2. *Market power.* In a dissenting opinion, Chief Justice Roberts suggests that the Court should have asked whether the challenged settlement agreement "gives Solvay monopoly power beyond what the patent already gave it." Why does he feel that this is the relevant legal question? How does Justice Breyer address this concern?

3. *Injury.* Justice Breyer states that under the terms of the settlement agreement, "the consumer loses," as generic entry typically drives down the price of prescription drugs. But while consumer prices may be higher than they otherwise would be, is this a harm to competition constituting a violation of the antitrust laws (see Section 25.7, Note 3)? How so? Are any competitors harmed by the settlement among Solvay and the generic manufacturers?

4. *Permissible settlements.* Notwithstanding the result in *Actavis*, branded pharmaceutical manufacturers continue to settle patents disputes with generic drug manufacturers. In fact, the number of such settlements has increased since the *Actavis* decision. According to the FTC (which collects data on pharmaceutical patent settlements),[42] in fiscal year 2012 pharmaceutical companies reported 88 final settlements of patent litigation. That figure increased to 232 settlements in 2016. The difference, of course, is that far fewer of the settlements post-*Actavis* contained reverse payments or other forms of compensation to the generic manufacturer. Thus, in 2004, none of the final settlements reported to the FTC included reverse payments. Then, when lower courts started to approve such payments in 2005, the number of reverse payments began to increase. The FTC reports that in 2006 and 2007, 40–50 percent of all final settlements filed with the FTC included reverse payments. By 2016, no reverse payment settlements were reported. What do these statistics imply about the responsiveness of private industry to changes in the antitrust laws?

5. *No-AG agreements.* In the aftermath of *Actavis*, pharmaceutical firms found creative ways to structure patent settlements to delay generic entry, while at the same time avoiding explicit pay-for-delay arrangements. One of those methods involved a branded pharmaceutical firm's ability, after patent expiration, to launch a generic version of its own drug, called an "authorized generic," or AG. An AG is not prohibited from entering the market during the first generic filer's 180-day exclusivity period under the Hatch–Waxman Act. Price competition between the AG and the first-filer's generic have the potential to erode the first-filer's profit during the 180-day exclusivity period by up to 60 percent. For lucrative drugs, that margin can translate into hundreds of millions of dollars.[43] Thus, pharmaceutical firms realized that a branded manufacturer's promise to refrain from introducing an AG during the first-filer's exclusivity period had a clear cash value. Accordingly, firms began to enter into settlement agreements in which a generic first-filer would withdraw its challenge to a pharmaceutical patent and agree not to enter the market for a number of years. Instead of paying the generic firm (as Solvay did in *Actavis*), the pharmaceutical firm would agree not to release its own generic version of the drug during the generic manufacturer's 180-day period of exclusivity. Not surprisingly, these no-AG agreements were soon found to be equivalent to the pay-for-delay settlements condemned in *Actavis*. See *King Drug Co. of Florence, Inc. v. SmithKline Beecham Corp.*, 791 F.3d 388 (3d Cir. 2015) (Lamictal Direct Purchaser Litigation).

---

[42] See FTC, *Then, Now, and Down the Road: Trends in Pharmaceutical Patent Settlements after FTC v. Actavis*, May 28, 2019, www.ftc.gov/news-events/blogs/competition-matters/2019/05/then-now-down-road-trends-pharmaceutical-patent.

[43] See FTC, *Authorized Generic Drugs: Short-Term Effects and Long-Term Impact*, August 2011.

6. *Other forms of compensation.* Even with direct pay-for-delay and no-AG settlements out of the picture, enterprising pharmaceutical firms have found ways to entice generic manufacturers to delay their entry into lucrative drug markets. These arrangements include declining royalty structures in which a generic's obligation to pay royalties to a branded pharmaceutical manufacturer is substantially reduced or eliminated if the branded manufacturer sells an AG, or the transfer of valuable products or equipment by the branded pharmaceutical manufacturer to the generic manufacturer. Is it realistic to hope that all such arrangements will eventually be addressed (and prohibited) by the courts, or is it inevitable that creative attorneys will constantly figure out ways to circumvent the latest judicial decision to achieve the ends of their clients? Would legislation in this area help? If so, what legislation might you propose?

26

Intellectual Property Pools and Aggregation

As we saw in Chapter 25, agreements among competitors that restrain trade can violate Section 1 of the Sherman Act. Such anticompetitive agreements can involve trademarks, copyrights, patents and other intellectual property (IP) rights. If they seek to fix prices, allocate markets or impose similar restraints on competition, such agreements are *per se* illegal; otherwise they are evaluated under the rule of reason, balancing their procompetitive and anticompetitive effects.

In this chapter we will consider an important category of agreements among competitors – those in which IP rights are combined or "pooled" for various purposes. The first documented patent pool in the United States was formed in 1856 by three leading manufacturers of sewing machines.[1] Since then, IP pools have evolved and grown in complexity. Though the specifics vary from pool to pool, at the most general level, IP pools involve the aggregation and centralized licensing of IP rights held by different parties. In some cases, this centralized licensing function is carried out by one of the pool members, and in others it is performed by an independent pool administrator. Some pools grant licenses only to pool members, while others make licenses available to members and nonmembers alike. The crux of an IP pooling arrangement today is typically the aggregation of the pool members' rights for licensing to users in a single trans-action, with the proceeds of that transaction allocated among the pool members according to some predetermined formula. Such pooling arrangements can have numerous procompetitive effects, but without certain precautions, they can also harm or reduce competition.

> The crux of an IP pooling arrangement is the aggregation of the pool members' rights for more convenient licensing.

---

[1] For an informative history of the Singer Combination, see Adam Mossoff, *The Rise and Fall of the First American Patent Thicket: The Sewing Machine War of the 1850s*, 53 Ariz. L. Rev. 165 (2011).

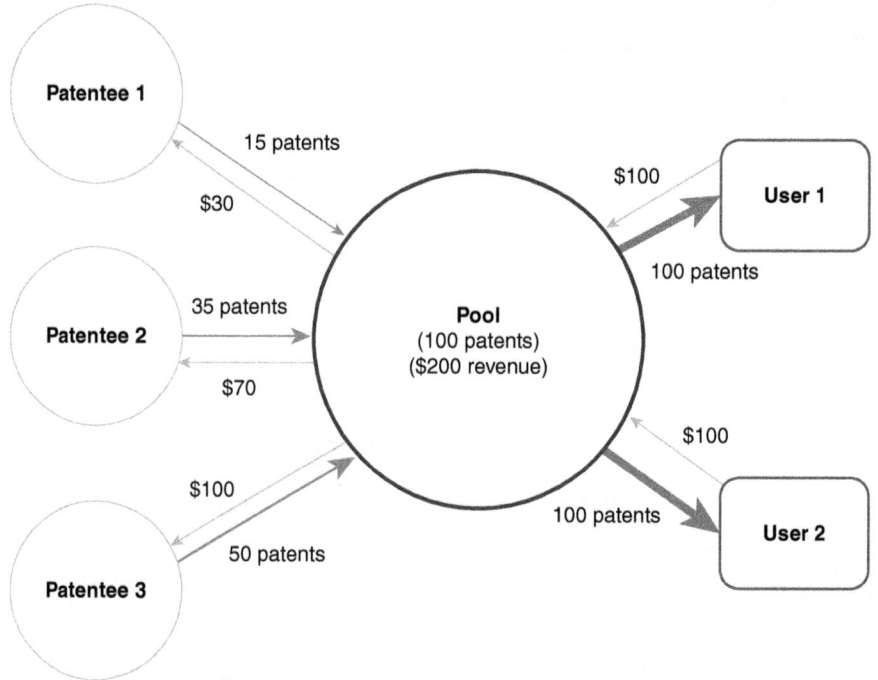

FIGURE 26.1 Basic structure of a patent pool with per-patent allocation of royalties and no pool administration charges.

As we will discuss in the remainder of this chapter, IP pools vary in a number of important respects, but they often share a number of key features, including the following:

- Rights are licensed (or assigned) by the members to a centralized pool administrator (one of the members or an independent third party).
- The administrator grants licenses of the pooled rights to third-party licensees/users.
- The pooled rights are licensed as a bundle, not separately.
- Any interested party may obtain a license.
- Royalties are charged to all licensees on a consistent basis.
- Licenses are granted using relatively simple, standardized form agreements.
- Licenses are nonexclusive.
- Income received by the pool is allocated to the pool members according to a predetermined formula, usually after the deduction of administrative fees and charges.

As you review the materials in this chapter, bear in mind that IP pools have impacted a broad range of industries over the past century, from motion pictures and recorded music to aviation and automobiles to semiconductors and telecommunications.[2] Pools have enabled transactions involving dozens, hundreds or thousands of individual IP rights that otherwise might have been impossible to effect, but some have crossed the line into anticompetitive territory. The complexity in structuring, forming and operating effective IP pools arises to a large degree from walking the tightrope between procompetitive and anticompetitive features.

---

[2] For an informative catalog of patent pools from the early twentieth century to today, see Michael Mattioli, *Power and Governance in Patent Pools*, 27 Harv. J. L. Tech. 421, 446–47, 463–65, Appendix (2014).

26.1 THEORIES OF IP POOLING: EFFICIENCY AND ENABLEMENT

There are two fundamental motivating forces behind IP pooling, which I refer to as *efficiency* and *enablement*. Efficiency is relatively easy to grasp. If a firm holds twelve patents covering different aspects of an electric motor, it is more efficient for a motor manufacturer to license all twelve in a single transaction than to license them one by one. The manufacturer can thus pay a single royalty for each motor that it sells, and does not have to determine which motors practice which patents and account for each separately. As we saw in Section 24.4, parties to a licensing transaction may find the convenience of licensing a bundle of patents to be mutually beneficial, even if the royalty remains constant as some of the patents in the bundle expire (*Automatic Radio v. Hazeltine* (U.S. 1950)). Such package licensing runs afoul of the antitrust and patent misuse laws only when it becomes coercive (*Zenith v. Hazeltine* (U.S. 1969)).

So, if efficiencies can be gained by licensing a single holder's patents in a bundle, then it stands to reason that bundling patents held by *multiple* patent holders should create even greater efficiencies. Thus, in the example above, instead of one firm holding twelve patents covering electric motors, suppose that twelve different firms each held one such patent. Then, in order to make electric motors, a manufacturer would have to negotiate successfully with twelve different parties – a substantially more costly and time-consuming proposition. But aggregating the twelve firms' patents into a single pool and licensing them together, as a single bundle, would enable the manufacturer, again, to acquire the necessary rights in a single transaction: a substantial gain in efficiency.

The efficiency justification for IP pools is even more pronounced with respect to copyrights. As discussed in Chapter 16, every composer, lyricist and musician holds a copyright interest in the songs that he or she creates, and the public broadcast and performance of music potentially involves thousands of copyright licenses. The aggregation and pooling of these rights is thus essential to distribution of music, film and other copyrighted works. Performing rights organizations such as ASCAP, BMI and SEASAC, discussed in Section 16.2, have aggregated and pooled copyrights in musical works for more than a century, thereby enabling the broad dissemination of musical works through radio broadcast, live performance and online distribution channels. As we saw in Section 25.5 (Note 5), the Hollywood studios of the mid-twentieth century sought to package their films into bundles that they licensed to movie theaters and television stations for public viewing. By and large, these "block booking" arrangements, in which popular films like *Casablanca* were bundled with B-movies like *The Gorilla Man*, and in which the distributor had no choice but to pay for them all, have been held to constitute illegal tying arrangements. Even so, it is not hard to see the transactional efficiencies that studios, as well as theaters and television networks, would enjoy by conducting business with large bundles of content, rather than individual titles. When a few licensors each control a large number of copyrighted works, pooling is a natural inclination.

But pooling is useful not only to reduce the number of individual licenses that must be negotiated. It also serves the important, and related, function of *enabling* market activity by assembling complementary rights. In an influential 1998 paper,[3] Michael Heller and Rebecca Eisenberg identify a phenomenon known as an "anticommons," a situation in which the rights necessary to accomplish a particular task (e.g., building a motor, developing a drug) are held by dispersed parties that are difficult to assemble. This phenomenon is also known as a patent

---

[3] Michael A. Heller & Rebecca S. Eisenberg, *Can Patents Deter Innovation? The Anticommons in Biomedical Research*, 280 Science 698 (1998).

or IP "thicket." Heller and Eisenberg observe that "a [scarce] resource is prone to underuse in a 'tragedy of the anticommons' when multiple owners each have a right to exclude others ... and no one has an effective privilege of use." In other words, if a set of IP rights is required to manufacture a particular product, and a potential manufacturer is unable to acquire the necessary permissions from each of the different rights holders, then it will not be legally permitted to produce the product.

Heller and Eisenberg analogize the anticommons that developed among retail operators in the Soviet Union to patents covering biomedical innovations, theorizing that a large number of patents held by different parties could stifle lifesaving innovations. One potential solution to the anticommons problem is pooling: "When the background legal rules threaten to waste resources, people often rearrange rights sensibly and create order through private arrangements." Pooling of necessary or blocking IP rights, then, enables the production of goods that would otherwise be absent from the market. Or, as economist Carl Shapiro has written, patent pooling is a "natural and effective method[] used by market participants to cut through the patent thicket."[4]

IP pooling thus accomplishes two related but distinct functions: increasing transactional *efficiency* by reducing the number of license negotiations in which any given licensee must engage, and clearing blocking IP positions to *enable* the broader creation of goods covered by IP.

Notes and Questions

1. *Nonexclusivity.* Almost all IP pools license their pooled assets on a nonexclusive basis. Why do you think this is? What would be the disadvantage of licensing pooled assets on an exclusive basis?

2. *Allocation systems.* When a pool grants a license, the licensee typically pays a royalty to the pool for all of the rights contained in the pool. It is up to the pool administrator to allocate that royalty among the individual pool members. The method by which royalties are allocated among pool members is often a closely guarded secret. In some cases, royalties may be simply split evenly among pool members, as they were in *Standard Oil (Indiana)* (see Section 26.3, footnote 8) (a *per capita* system). In other cases, royalties may be allocated to members based on the number of IP rights that each has contributed (e.g., if a member contributed 5 of 100 patents to the pool, then it would be entitled to 5 percent of the royalties received by the pool) (*patent counting*).[5] Hybrids of per capita and per patent allocation systems also exist, as illustrated by the RFID patent pool, in which "half of the royalties are allocated to participants based on the number of patents contributed by each participant, and the other half are allocated substantially equally among participants."[6] Finally, royalties may be allocated to a member based on the *value* of the IP that it has contributed (*value-based allocation*). This system is sometimes used to allocate larger shares of a pool's revenue to early or "founder" members of the pool.[7] What advantages and disadvantages do you see with respect to each of these allocation methodologies?

4   Carl Shapiro, *Navigating the Patent Thicket: Cross Licenses, Patent Pools, and Standard Setting* in Innovation Policy and the Economy, Volume 1, 119, 119 (Adam B. Jaffe, Josh Lerner & Scott Stern, ed., MIT Press, 2001).
5   See Mattioli, *supra* note 2, at 446–47 (describing the per-patent allocation system in the MPEG-2 patent pool).
6   Letter from Thomas O. Barnett, Assistant Attorney Gen., Antitrust Div. of the Dep't of Justice, to William F. Dolan and Geoffrey Oliver, Jones Day (October 21, 2008).
7   See Mattioli, *supra* note 2, at 441–42 (describing percentage-based allocation system of the early-twentieth-century raisin patent pool).

3. *When pools compete.* Most IP pooling arrangements are voluntary, meaning that rights holders may elect to participate or not. In some cases, multiple pools cover the same product, so that a would-be manufacturer must obtain a license from each pool in order to manufacture the product. An example can be found in DVD technology:

> In late 1995, it was reported that four "core" DVD developers of a ten-member DVD consortium would enter into a patent pooling agreement to administer the licensing of DVD patents. The core members, Philips, Sony, Matsushita and Toshiba, reportedly extended an open invitation to secondary patent holders claiming rights to DVD-related patents.
>
> In August, 1996, after a period of failed negotiations among the core consortium members, Sony and Philips announced that they would form their own DVD pool, with Philips to be the licensor. Philips stated that "[t]here were so many differences of opinion that we could not wait for these to be settled." Pioneer Electronics subsequently joined this three-firm pool. Six months later, Hitachi, Matsushita, Mitsubishi, Time Warner, Toshiba and JVC formed their own patent pool. Industry analysts warned that without a single, unitary pool, the price of DVD technology would increase since a piecemeal licensing system would push the cost of the technology higher.[8]

   Notwithstanding the split among the principal DVD patent holders, the two DVD patent pools (which became known as the DVD3C and DVD6C pools) operated side by side for years and reduced the number of licenses required by manufacturers of DVD players and discs from ten to two. The DVD format became one of the most broadly adopted standards in the world. Yet time has overtaken even the DVD. The DVD6C pool announced that it would stop offering new patent licenses on January 1, 2020.[9]

4. *Pooling holdouts.* Given the voluntary nature of IP pools, it is also possible that some IP holders will elect not to join any pool. Research by Anne Layne-Farrar and Josh Lerner[10] suggests that most patent pools today are incomplete. They found that nine major patent pools directed at significant technology standards (e.g., DVD, 3G, Bluetooth) had coverage rates of between 10 and 89 percent of the total patents believed to be necessary to practice the standards. Why might an IP holder "hold out" and decline to join a pool?[11] If pools enhance the overall efficiency of markets, how might IP holders be encouraged to join pools rather than licensing and asserting their rights independently?

5. *Royalty stacking and Cournot complements.* Commentators have also suggested that pooling complementary IP can reduce the overall *cost* of obtaining licenses to that IP. The theory of complementary production inputs originated with French mathematician Antoine Augustin Cournot in 1838. Carl Shapiro explains Cournot's insight and its application to modern technology markets as follows:

> Cournot considered the problem faced by a manufacturer of brass who had to purchase two key inputs, copper and zinc, each controlled by a monopolist. As Cournot demonstrated, the resulting price of brass was higher than would arise if a single firm controlled trade in both copper and zinc, and sold these inputs to a competitive brass industry (or made the brass itself). Worse yet, the combined profits of the producers were lower as well in the presence

---

[8] Robert P. Merges, *Institutions for Intellectual Property Transactions: The Case of Patent Pools* 32 (August, 1999 revision), www.law.berkeley.edu/files/pools.pdf.

[9] DVD6C Licensing Group, Information, www.dvd6cla.com/index.html.

[10] Anne Layne-Farrar & Josh Lerner, *To Join or Not to Join: Examining Patent Pool Participation and Rent Sharing Rules*, 29 Int'l J. Indus. Org. 294, 299 (2011).

[11] For thorough discussions of the business motivations for holding out in the context of patent pools, see Layne-Farrar and Lerner, *supra* note 10, at 296–97; Michael Mattioli, *Patent Pool Outsiders*, 33 Berkeley Tech. L.J. 225, 239–46 (2018).

of complementary monopolies. So, the sad result of the balkanized rights to copper and zinc was to harm both consumers and producers. The same applies today when multiple companies control blocking patents for a particular product, process, or business method.

How can the inefficiency associated with multiple blocking patents be eliminated? One natural and attractive solution is for the copper and zinc suppliers to join forces and offer their inputs for a single, package price to the brass industry. The two monopolist suppliers will find it in their joint interest to offer a package price that is less than these two components sold for when priced separately. The blocking patent version of this principle is that the rights holders will find it attractive to create a package license or patent pool.

[I]f the two patent holders see benefits from enabling many others to make products that utilize their intellectual property rights, a patent pool, under which all the blocking patents are licensed in a coordinated fashion as a package, can be an ideal outcome. [This] simple theory … suggests that coordinating such licensing can lead to *lower* royalty rates than would independent pricing (licensing) of the two companies' patents.[12]

Do you see why combining patents (or other IP rights) in a pool might lower the overall cost of licensing these rights? How do you think this concept affects the likelihood that certain patent holders will hold out and refuse to join a pool (see Note 4)?

6. *The mystery of the missing biotech patent pools.* Despite cautionary predictions by scholars like Heller and Eisenberg, few patent pools – and none of commercial significance – have emerged in the biotechnology sector. Even in 1998, Heller and Eisenberg recognized that a number of structural and institutional factors might work against the formation of pools in the biotech sector, including transaction costs associated with accumulating sufficient rights to practice biotechnology inventions, the divergent interests of biotech patent holders and cognitive biases causing researchers to overestimate the value of their own discoveries. Other factors may also be at work, including "the need for at least some market exclusivity in an environment with extremely high costs of product development, clinical trials and regulatory approval; patent holders' desire to retain control over their assets; and concerns over compromising commercial secrecy by collaborating with others."[13] What do you make of the lack of patent pools in the biotechnology sector, when pooling activity in areas such as electronics and telecommunications has only increased?

7. *New forms of fragmentation.* Heller and Eisenberg identified the potential of patents to fragment markets for innovation in biotechnology, yet that anticommons and the accompanying stifling of innovation does not seem to have occurred for a variety of reasons. Nevertheless, concerns have been raised regarding other trends toward fragmentation of rights that could cause similar or even greater hurdles to innovation. Consider the following:

A spate of recent legal disputes in the U.S. ha[s] led to increasing calls for personal ownership of genetic and other health information. [D]espite the good intentions behind many of these proposals, granting individuals an enforceable property interest in information about themselves … could pose significant impediments to data-driven research, particularly in the coming era of mega-cohort studies involving a million and more individuals.

Thus, while Heller and Eisenberg worried that fragmented interests held by a few dozen or hundred patent owners could severely impede biomedical research, the possibility that millions of individual data subjects could demand clearance, oversight or payment in order to use their data … has far more dramatic ramifications for biomedical research.[14]

---

[12]   Shapiro, *supra* note 4, at 123 (emphasis in original).
[13]   Jorge L. Contreras, *The Anticommons at Twenty: Concerns for Research Continue*, 361 Science 335, 336 (2018).
[14]   Id. at 336–37.

Is the type of rights fragmentation identified in the above excerpt similar to the fragmentation that could arise due to dispersed patent ownership? Could this type of data ownership fragmentation effectively be addressed by pooling solutions?

26.2 ANTITRUST ANALYSIS OF PATENT POOLS

The earliest patent pools emerged prior to the enactment of the Sherman Antitrust Act of 1890. But almost as soon as the Sherman Act became law, antitrust enforcers turned an eye toward the pooling arrangements that large industrial concerns created using patents. In the following case, the Supreme Court considered such an arrangement led by John D. Rockefeller's infamous Standard Oil Trust.

Standard Oil Co. (Indiana) v. United States
283 U.S. 163 (1931)

BRANDEIS, JUSTICE

This suit was brought by the United States in June, 1924, in the federal court for northern Illinois, to enjoin further violation of section 1 and section 2 of the Sherman Anti-Trust Act. The violation charged is an illegal combination to create a monopoly and to restrain interstate commerce by controlling that part of the supply of gasoline which is produced by the process of cracking. Control is alleged to be exerted by means of seventy-nine contracts concerning patents relating to the cracking art. The parties to the several contracts are named as defendants. Four of them own patents covering their respective cracking processes, and are called the primary defendants. Three of these, the Standard Oil Company of Indiana, the Texas Company, and the Standard Oil Company of New Jersey, are themselves large producers of cracked gasoline. The fourth, Gasoline Products Company, is merely a licensing concern. The remaining forty-six defendants manufacture cracked gasoline under licenses from one or more of the primary defendants. They are called secondary defendants.

The violation of the Sherman Act now complained of rests substantially on the making and effect of three contracts entered into by the primary defendants. The history of these agreements may be briefly stated. For about half a century before 1910, gasoline had been manufactured from crude oil exclusively by distillation and condensation at atmospheric pressure. When the demand for gasoline grew rapidly with the widespread use of the automobile, methods for increasing the yield of gasoline from the available crude oil were sought. It had long been known that from a given quantity of crude, additional oils of high volatility could be produced by "cracking"; that is, by applying heat and pressure to the residuum after ordinary distillation. But a commercially profitable cracking method and apparatus for manufacturing additional gasoline had not yet been developed. The first such process was perfected by the Indiana Company in 1913; and for more than seven years this was the only one practiced in America. During that period the Indiana Company not only manufactured cracked gasoline on a large scale, but also had licensed fifteen independent concerns to use its process and had collected, prior to January 1, 1921, royalties aggregating $15,057,432.46.

Meanwhile, since the phenomenon of cracking was not controlled by any fundamental patent, other concerns had been working independently to develop commercial processes of their own. Most prominent among these were the three other primary defendants, the Texas Company, the New Jersey Company, and the Gasoline Products Company. Each of these secured numerous patents covering its particular cracking process. Beginning in 1920, conflict developed among the four companies concerning the validity, scope, and ownership of issued patents. One infringement suit was begun; cross-notices of infringement, antecedent to other suits, were given; and interferences were declared on pending applications in the Patent Office. The primary defendants assert that it was these difficulties which led to their executing the three principal agreements which the United States attacks; and that their sole object was to avoid litigation and losses incident to conflicting patents.

The three agreements differ from one another only slightly in scope and terms. Each primary defendant was released thereby from liability for any past infringement of patents of the others. Each acquired the right to use these patents thereafter in its own process. Each was empowered to extend to independent concerns, licensed under its process, releases from past, and immunity from future claims of infringement of patents controlled by the other primary defendants. And each was to share in some fixed proportion the fees received under these multiple licenses. The royalties to be charged were definitely fixed in the first contract; and minimum sums per barrel, to be divided between the Texas and Indiana companies, were specified in the second and third.

[P]ooling arrangements may obviously result in restricting competition. The limited monopolies granted to patent owners do not exempt them from the prohibitions of the Sherman Act and supplementary legislation. Hence the necessary effect of patent interchange agreements, and the operations under them, must be carefully examined in order to determine whether violations of the Act result.

The Government contends that the three agreements constitute a pooling by the primary defendants of the royalties from their several patents; that thereby competition between them in the commercial exercise of their respective rights to issue licenses is eliminated; that this tends to maintain or increase the royalty charged secondary defendants and hence to increase the manufacturing cost of cracked gasoline; that thus the primary defendants exclude from interstate commerce gasoline which would, under lower competitive royalty rates, be produced; and that interstate commerce is thereby unlawfully restrained. There is no provision in any of the agreements which restricts the freedom of the primary defendants individually to issue licenses under their own patents alone or under the patents of all the others; and no contract between any of them, and no license agreement with a secondary defendant executed pursuant thereto, now imposes any restriction upon the quantity of gasoline to be produced, or upon the price, terms, or conditions of sale, or upon the territory in which sales may be made. The only restraint thus charged is that necessarily arising out of the making and effect of the provisions for cross-licensing and for division of royalties.

The Government concedes that it is not illegal for the primary defendants to cross-license each other and the respective licensees; and that adequate consideration can legally be demanded for such grants. But it contends that the insertion of certain additional provisions in these agreements renders them illegal. It urges, first, that the mere inclusion of the provisions for the division of royalties, constitutes an unlawful combination under the Sherman Act because it evidences an intent to obtain a monopoly. This contention is unsound. Such provisions for the division of royalties are not in themselves conclusive evidence of illegality. Where there are legitimately conflicting claims or threatened interferences, a settlement by agreement, rather than litigation, is not precluded by the Act. An interchange of patent rights and a division of royalties according to the value attributed by the parties to their respective patent claims is frequently necessary if technical advancement is not to be blocked by threatened litigation. If the available advantages are upon on reasonable terms to all manufacturers desiring to participate, such interchange may promote rather than restrain competition.[15]

The Government next contends that the agreements to maintain royalties violate the Sherman [Act] because the fees charged are onerous. The argument is that the competitive advantage which the three primary defendants enjoy of manufacturing cracked gasoline free of royalty, while licensees must pay to them a heavy tribute in fees, enables these primary defendants to exclude from interstate commerce cracked gasoline which would, under lower competitive royalty rates, be produced by possible rivals. This argument ignores the privileges incident to ownership of patents. Unless the industry is dominated, or interstate commerce directly restrained, the Sherman Act does not require cross-licensing patentees to license at reasonable rates others engaged in interstate commerce. The allegation that the royalties charged are onerous is, standing alone, without legal significance; and, as will be shown, neither the alleged domination, nor restraint of commerce, has been proved.

The main contention of the Government is that even if the exchange of patent rights and division of royalties are not necessarily improper and the royalties are not oppressive, the three contracts are still obnoxious to the Sherman Act because specific clauses enable the primary defendants to maintain existing royalties and thereby to restrain interstate commerce. The provisions which constitute the basis for this charge are these. The first contract specifies that the Texas Company shall get from the Indiana Company one-fourth of all royalties thereafter collected under the latter's existing license agreements; and that all royalties received under licenses thereafter issued by either company shall be equally divided. Licenses granting rights under the patents of both are to be issued at a fixed royalty – approximately that charged by the Indiana Company when its process was alone in the field. By the second contract, the Texas Company is entitled to receive one-half of the royalties thereafter collected by the Gasoline Products Company from its existing licensees, and a minimum sum per barrel for all oil cracked by its future licensees. The third contract gives to the Indiana Company one-half of all royalties thereafter paid by existing licensees of the New Jersey Company, and a similar minimum sum for each barrel treated by its future licensees, subject in the latter case to reduction if the royalties charged by the Indiana and Texas companies for their processes should be reduced.[16] The alleged effect of these provisions is to enable the primary defendants, because of their monopoly

---

[15] [n.6] Such agreements, varying in purpose, scope, and validity, are not uncommon. Conflict of patents in the automobile industry, and the early difficulties encountered with an alleged basic patent, led to an agreement in 1915, by which the members of the National Automobile Chamber of Commerce cross-licensed each other without royalty for the use of all patent improvements. Interchange of basic aviation patents was made during the [first] world war, at the suggestion of the National Advisory Committee for Aeronautics. Various patent exchanges existing in the radio industry are detailed in the Report of the Federal Trade Commission on the Radio Industry (1923).

[16] [n.8] Payments received by the Texas and Indiana companies under the second and third contracts are divided equally by these companies pursuant to the terms of the first. That contract further provides that all royalties received after January 1, 1937, even from existing licensees, are to be divided equally between the two companies.

of patented cracking processes, to maintain royalty rates at the level established originally for the Indiana process.

The rate of royalties may, of course be a decisive factor in the cost of production. If combining patent owners effectively dominate an industry, the power to fix and maintain royalties is tantamount to the power to fix prices. Where domination exists, a pooling of competing process patents, or an exchange of licenses for the purpose of curtailing the manufacture and supply of an unpatented product, is beyond the privileges conferred by the patents and constitutes a violation of the Sherman Act. The lawful individual monopolies granted by the patent statutes cannot be unitedly exercised to restrain competition. But an agreement for cross-licensing and division of royalties violates the Act only when used to effect a monopoly, or to fix prices, or to impose otherwise an unreasonable restraint upon interstate commerce. In the case at bar, the primary defendants own competing patented processes for manufacturing an unpatented product which is sold in interstate commerce; and agreements concerning such processes are likely to engender the evils to which the Sherman Act was directed. We must, therefore, examine the evidence to ascertain the operation and effect of the challenged contracts.

> "an agreement for cross-licensing and division of royalties violates the [Sherman] Act only when used to effect a monopoly, or to fix prices, or to impose otherwise an unreasonable restraint upon interstate commerce"

No monopoly, or restriction of competition, in the business of licensing patented cracking processes resulted from the execution of these agreements. Up to 1920 all cracking plants in the United States were either owned by the Indiana Company alone, or were operated under licenses from it. In 1924 and 1925, after the cross-licensing arrangements were in effect, the four primary defendants owned or licensed, in the aggregate, only 55 percent of the total cracking capacity, and the remainder was distributed among twenty-one independently owned cracking processes. This development and commercial expansion of competing processes is clear evidence that the contracts did not concentrate in the hands of the four primary defendants the licensing of patented processes for the production of cracked gasoline. Moreover, the record does not show that after the execution of the agreements there was a decrease of competition among them in licensing other refiners to use their respective processes.

No monopoly, or restriction of competition, in the production of either ordinary or cracked gasoline has been proved. The output of cracked gasoline in the years in question was about 26 percent of the total gasoline production. Ordinary or straight run gasoline is indistinguishable from cracked gasoline and the two are either mixed or sold interchangeably. Under these circumstances the primary defendants could not effectively control the supply or fix the price of cracked gasoline by virtue of their alleged monopoly of the cracking processes, unless they could control, through some means, the remainder of the total gasoline production from all sources. Proof of such control is lacking. Evidence of the total gasoline production by all methods, of each of the primary defendants and their licensees is either missing or unsatisfactory in character. The record does not accurately show even the total amount of cracked gasoline produced, or the production of each of the licensees, or competing refiners.

No monopoly, or restriction of competition, in the sale of gasoline has been proved. On the basis of testimony relating to the marketing of both cracked and ordinary gasoline, the master found that the defendants were in active competition among themselves and with other refiners; that both kinds of gasoline were refined and sold in large quantities by other companies; and that the primary defendants and their licensees neither individually or collectively controlled the market price or supply of any gasoline moving in interstate commerce. There is ample evidence to support these findings.

Thus it appears that no monopoly of any kind, or restraint of interstate commerce, has been effected either by means of the contracts or in some other way. In the absence of proof that the primary defendants had such control of the entire industry as would make effective the alleged domination of a part, it is difficult to see how they could by agreeing upon royalty rates control either the price or the supply of gasoline, or otherwise restrain competition. By virtue of their patents they had individually the right to determine who should use their respective processes or inventions and what the royalties for such use should be. To warrant an injunction which would invalidate the contracts here in question, and require either new arrangements or settlement of the conflicting claims by litigation, there must be a definite factual showing of illegality.

FIGURE 26.2 In this iconic 1904 illustration from *Puck*, the Standard Oil Company is depicted as a malignant octopus wrapping its tentacles around state and federal legislatures, the White House and representatives of the steel, copper and shipping industries.

Notes and Questions

1. *Elimination of blocking positions.* One of the major procompetitive benefits that the Supreme Court finds in the oil cracking pool is the elimination of blocking positions imposed by competitors' patents. That is, the four members of the cracking pool each held patents that could block the others from practicing the technology to its fullest potential, thus depriving the market of the most beneficial gasoline products. As the Court notes, "An interchange

of patent rights and a division of royalties according to the value attributed by the parties to their respective patent claims is frequently necessary if technical advancement is not to be blocked by threatened litigation." Then, in footnote 8, the Court notes several other instances in which patent pools have facilitated the progress of technical advancement in industries such as automobiles, aviation and radio. How does a patent pool enable competitors to avoid each other's "blocking" patents?[17]

2. *Onerous royalties and exclusion.* The government's principal objection to the cracking pool revolved around the parties' royalty arrangements, which it claimed to be onerous. Who was allegedly harmed by these royalty arrangements, and what effect did the government claim that they had on the market? How did the court respond to these allegations? Under what circumstances does the Court suggest that members of a patent pool might be required to limit the royalties that they charge?

3. *Price fixing by pooling.* Even if the pooling parties had no obligation to limit the royalties that they charged to others, the government still maintained that the parties' royalty arrangement

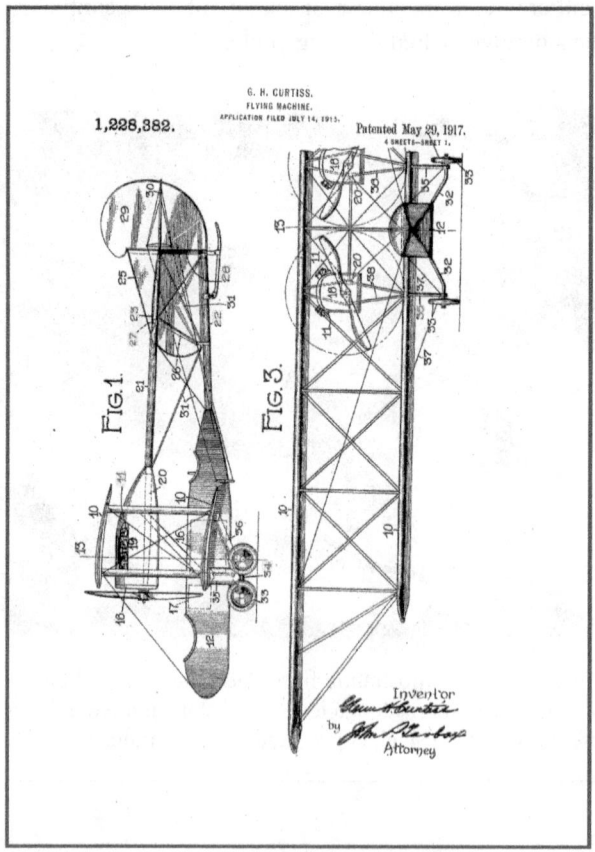

FIGURE 26.3 The US Navy pressured feuding aircraft manufacturers Curtiss and Wright to form an early aviation patent pool prior to US entry into World War I. The Manufacturers Aircraft Association (MAA) pool continued until it was disbanded by the Department of Justice in the 1970s.

---

[17] See Richard J. Gilbert, *Antitrust for Patent Pools: A Century of Policy Evolution*, 2004 Stan. Tech. L. Rev. 3, § II.C (2004) (discussing *Standard Oil (Indiana)*).

was anticompetitive because it allowed them to maintain royalty rates at their original levels without the reductions that might result from competition. How did the court respond to this argument?

4. *The courts crack down on pools.* Despite the favorable view of patent pools offered by the Supreme Court in *Standard Oil (Indiana)*, judicial attitudes toward patent pools soured soon thereafter, following a general trend toward stricter application of the antitrust laws from the 1940s through 1970s.[18] In cases from *Hartford-Empire Co. v. United States*, 323 U.S. 386 (1945) through *United States v. Mfrs. Aircraft Ass'n*, 1975 WL 405109 (S.D.N.Y. Nov. 12, 1975), arrangements among competitors involving patent pools were found to reduce competition and were ordered dissolved.[19] Nevertheless, patent pools increased in popularity again beginning in the 1980s, as antitrust law again adopted a more lenient approach to IP arrangements.

Antitrust Guidelines for the Licensing of Intellectual Property
US Department of Justice and Federal Trade Commission, 2017

5.5 Cross-Licensing and Pooling Arrangements[20]

[Pooling] arrangements may provide procompetitive benefits by integrating complementary technologies, reducing transaction costs, clearing blocking positions, and avoiding costly infringement litigation. By promoting the dissemination of technology … pooling arrangements are often procompetitive.

[P]ooling arrangements can have anticompetitive effects in certain circumstances. For example, collective price or output restraints in pooling arrangements, such as the joint marketing of pooled intellectual property rights with collective price setting or coordinated output restrictions, may be deemed unlawful if they do not contribute to an efficiency-enhancing integration of economic activity among the participants. When … pooling arrangements are mechanisms to accomplish naked price-fixing or market division, they are subject to challenge under the per se rule.

Pooling arrangements generally need not be open to all who would like to join. However, exclusion from … pooling arrangements among parties that collectively possess market power may, under some circumstances, harm competition. In general, exclusion from a pooling … arrangement among competing technologies is unlikely to have anticompetitive effects unless (1) excluded firms cannot effectively compete in the relevant market for the good incorporating the licensed technologies and (2) the pool participants collectively possess market power in the relevant market. If these circumstances exist, the Agencies will evaluate whether the arrangement's limitations on participation are reasonably related to the efficient development and exploitation of the pooled technologies and will assess the net effect of those limitations in the relevant market.

Another possible anticompetitive effect of pooling arrangements may occur if the arrangement deters or discourages participants from engaging in research and development, thus

---

[18] This trend is also discussed in Section 25.1.

[19] See Gilbert, *supra* note 17, at § II.D, and Jorge L. Contreras, *A Brief History of FRAND: Analyzing Current Debates in Standard Setting and Antitrust Through a Historical Lens*, 80 Antitrust L.J. 39, 51–72 (2015).

[20] In this section the agencies also discuss cross-licensing arrangements, which are omitted from this excerpt for the sake of clarity. The 2017 Guidelines update an earlier set of Guidelines issued in 1995, with few amendments.

retarding innovation. For example, a pooling arrangement that requires members to grant licenses to each other for current and future technology at minimal cost may reduce the incentives of its members to engage in research and development because members of the pool have to share their successful research and development and each of the members can free ride on the accomplishments of other pool members. However, such an arrangement can have procompetitive benefits, for example, by exploiting economies of scale and integrating complementary capabilities of the pool members, (including the clearing of blocking positions), and is likely to cause competitive problems only when the arrangement includes a large fraction of the potential research and development in a research and development market.

Notes and Questions

1. *Members-only pools.* The DOJ and FTC are careful to say that "[p]ooling arrangements generally need not be open to all who would like to join." That is, closed or members-only pools are permitted. But this concept has significant caveats. When might it be anticompetitive for a pool to exclude those who would like to join?
2. *Innovation effects.* The agencies are particularly concerned with pools that discourage future R&D and innovation. How might pooling IP rights discourage the members from pursuing R&D activities? How might pooling IP increase R&D activity among the members? How should an agency draw the line between pooling activity that promotes and harms innovation?

26.3 PATENT POOLS FOR STANDARDS

As discussed in Chapter 20, many industry standards are developed through the collaboration of different parties, whether through a commercial agreement, a joint venture or a standards-development organization (SDO). Parties that contribute technology to a standardization effort sometimes obtain patents covering those technical contributions. In addition to licensing requirements imposed by SDOs and private licensing arrangements among standards developers, some standards have become the subject of patent pools.

MPEG-2 Business Review Letter

US Department of Justice Antitrust Division, June 26, 1997

Gerrard R. Beeney, Esq.
Sullivan & Cromwell
125 Broad Street
New York, NY 10004–2498
Dear Mr. Beeney:

This is in response to your request on behalf of the Trustees of Columbia University, Fujitsu Limited, General Instrument Corp., Lucent Technologies Inc., Matsushita Electric Industrial Co., Ltd., Mitsubishi Electric Corp., Philips Electronics N.V.,

Scientific-Atlanta, Inc., and Sony Corp. (collectively the "Licensors"), Cable Television Laboratories, Inc. ("CableLabs"), MPEG LA, L.L.C. ("MPEG LA"), and their affiliates for the issuance of a business review letter pursuant to the Department of Justice's Business Review Procedure, 28 C.F.R. § 50.6. You have requested a statement of the Department of Justice's antitrust enforcement intentions with respect to a proposed arrangement pursuant to which MPEG LA will offer a package license under the Licensors' patents that are essential to compliance with the MPEG-2 compression technology standard, and distribute royalty income among the Licensors.

I. The Proposed Arrangement

A. The MPEG-2 Standard

The MPEG-2 standard has been approved as an international standard by the [Moving] Picture Experts Group of the International Organization for Standards (ISO) and the International Electrotechnical Commission (IEC) and by the International Telecommunication Union Telecommunication Standardization Sector (ITU-T).

The video and systems parts of the MPEG-2 standard will be applied in many different products and services in which video information is stored and/or transmitted, including cable, satellite and broadcast television, digital video disks, and telecommunications. However, compliance with the standards will infringe on numerous patents owned by many different entities. Consequently, a number of firms that participated in the development of the standard formed the MPEG-2 Intellectual Property Working Group ("IP Working Group") to address intellectual property issues raised by the proposed standard. Among other things, the IP Working Group sponsored a search for the patents that covered the technology essential to compliance with the proposed standard and explored the creation of a mechanism to convey those essential intellectual property rights to MPEG-2 users. That exploration led ultimately to an agreement among the Licensors, CableLabs and Baryn S. Futa establishing MPEG LA as a Delaware Limited Liability Company.

Each of the Licensors owns at least one patent that the IP Working Group's patent search identified as essential to compliance with the video and/or systems parts of the MPEG-2 standard (hereinafter "MPEG-2 Essential Patent" or "Essential Patent"). Among them, they account for a total of 27 Essential Patents, which are most, but not all, of the Essential Patents. Pursuant to a series of four proposed agreements, the Licensors will combine their Essential Patents into a single portfolio (the "Portfolio") in the hands of a common licensing administrator that would grant licenses under the Portfolio on a non-discriminatory basis, collect royalties, and distribute them among the Licensors pursuant to a pro-rata allocation based on each Licensor's proportionate share of the total number of Portfolio patents in the countries in which a particular royalty-bearing product is made and sold.

This arrangement is embodied in a network of four proposed agreements: (1) an Agreement Among Licensors, in which the Licensors commit to license their MPEG-2 Essential Patents jointly through a common License Administrator and agree on basic items including the Portfolio license's authorized fields of use, the amount and allocation of royalties, and procedures for adding patents to, and deleting them from, the Portfolio;

(2) a Licensing Administrator Agreement between the Licensors and MPEG LA, pursuant to which MPEG LA assumes the tasks of licensing the Portfolio to MPEG-2 users and collecting and distributing royalty income; (3) a license from each Licensor to MPEG LA for the purpose of granting the Portfolio License; and (4) the Portfolio license itself.

B. MPEG LA

Pursuant to the Licensing Administrator Agreement, MPEG LA will: (1) grant a worldwide, nonexclusive sublicense under the Portfolio to make, use and sell MPEG-2 products "to each and every potential Licensee who requests an MPEG-2 Patent Portfolio License and shall not discriminate among potential licensees"; (2) solicit Portfolio licensees; (3) enforce and terminate Portfolio license agreements; and (4) collect and distribute royalties. For this purpose, each MPEG-2 Licensor will grant MPEG LA a nonexclusive license under its Essential Patents, while retaining the right to license them independently for any purpose, including for making MPEG-2-compliant products.

The Licensing Administrator Agreement places the day-to-day conduct of MPEG LA's business, including its licensing activities, under the sole control of Futa and his staff. The other owners retain some control, however, over "major decisions," including approval of budgets and annual financial statements, extraordinary expenditures, entry into new businesses, mergers and acquisitions, and the sale or dissolution of the corporation.

C. The MPEG-2 Portfolio

As noted above, the Portfolio initially will consist of 27 patents, which constitute most, but not all, Essential Patents. These 27 patents were identified in a search carried out by an independent patent expert under the sponsorship of the IP Working Group. Once the MPEG-2 standard was largely in place, the IP Working Group issued a public call for the submission of patents that might be infringed by compliance with the MPEG-2 standard. CableLabs, whose COO Futa was an active participant in the IP Working Group, retained an independent patent expert familiar with the standard and the relevant technology to review the submissions. In all, the expert and his assistant reviewed approximately 8,000 United States patent abstracts and studied about 800 patents belonging to over 100 different patentees or assignees. No submission was refused, and no entity or person that was identified as having an essential patent was in any way excluded from the effort in forming the proposed joint licensing program.

The proposed agreement among the Licensors creates a continuing role for an independent expert as an arbiter of essentiality. It requires the retention of an independent expert to review patents submitted to any of the Licensors for inclusion in the Portfolio and to review any Portfolio patent which an MPEG-2 Licensor has concluded is not essential or as to which anyone has claimed a good-faith belief of non-essentiality. In both cases, the Licensors are bound by the expert's opinion.

The Portfolio's composition may also change for other reasons. A patent will be deleted promptly from the Portfolio upon a final adjudication of invalidity or unenforceability by a tribunal of competent jurisdiction in the country of its issuance. The expiration of a Licensor's last-to-expire Portfolio patent, or a final adjudication of invalidity or unenforceability of its last remaining Portfolio patent, terminates the Licensor's participation in the Portfolio and the Agreement Among Licensors. Each MPEG-2 Licensor may terminate its participation in the Portfolio license on 30 days' notice; however, all existing Portfolio licenses will remain intact.

D. The Portfolio License

The planned license from MPEG LA to users of the MPEG-2 standards is a worldwide, nonexclusive, nonsublicensable license under the Portfolio patents for the manufacture, sale, and in most cases, use of: (1) products and software designed to encode and/or decode video information in accordance with the MPEG-2 standard; (2) products and software designed to generate MPEG-2 program and transport bitstreams; and (3) so-called "intermediate products," such as integrated circuit chips, used in the aforementioned products and software.

The Portfolio license expires January 1, 2000, but is renewable at the licensee's option for a period of not less than five years, subject to "reasonable amendment of its terms and conditions." That "reasonable amendment" may not, however, increase royalties by more than 25%. Each Portfolio licensee may terminate its license on 30 days' written notice. The per-unit royalties are those agreed upon in the Agreement Among Licensors, but they are subject to reduction pursuant to a "most-favored-nation" clause. The royalty obligations are predicated on actual use of one or more of the licensed patents in the unit for which the royalty is assessed. The Portfolio license imposes no obligation on the licensee to use only the licensed patents and explicitly leaves the licensee free independently to develop "competitive video products or video services which do not comply with the MPEG-2 Standard."

The Portfolio license will list the Portfolio patents in an attachment. It also explicitly addresses the licensee's ability, and possible need, to obtain Essential Patent rights elsewhere. The Portfolio license states that each Portfolio patent is also available for licensing independently from the MPEG-2 Licensor that had licensed it to MPEG LA and that the license may not convey rights to all Essential Patents.

The license's grantback provision requires the licensee to grant any of the Licensors and other Portfolio licensees a nonexclusive worldwide license or sublicense, on fair and reasonable terms and conditions, on any Essential Patent that it has the right to license or sublicense. The Licensors' per-patent share of royalties is the basis for determining a fair and reasonable royalty for the grantback. Alternatively, a licensee that controls an Essential Patent may choose to become an MPEG-2 licensor and add its patent to the Portfolio. Failure to honor the grantback requirement constitutes a material breach of the license, giving MPEG LA the right to terminate the license unless the licensee has cured the breach within 60 days after MPEG LA sends it notice of the breach.

A separate provision allows for partial termination of a licensee's Portfolio license as to a particular MPEG-2 Licensor's patents. Pursuant to Section 6.3, an MPEG-2 Licensor may direct MPEG LA to withdraw its patents from the Portfolio license if the licensee has (a) brought a lawsuit or other proceeding against the MPEG-2 Licensor for infringement of an Essential Patent or an MPEG-2 Related Patent ("Related Patent") and (b) refused to grant the MPEG-2 Licensor a license under the Essential Patent or MPEG-2 Related Patent on fair and reasonable terms and conditions. As with the grantback, the per-patent share of Portfolio license royalties is the basis for determining a fair and reasonable royalty for the licensee's patent. Upon the withdrawal of the MPEG-2 Licensor's patents from the licensee's Portfolio license, the licensee may seek a license on the withdrawn patents directly

FIGURE 26.4 Patents covering many important standards today are licensed through patent pools.

from the MPEG-2 Licensor, which remains subject to its undertaking to the ISO and/or the ITU-T to license on fair and reasonable terms and conditions.

II. Analysis

A. The Patent Pool in General

An aggregation of patent rights for the purpose of joint package licensing, commonly called a patent pool, may provide competitive benefits by integrating complementary technologies, reducing transaction costs, clearing blocking positions, and avoiding costly infringement litigation. By promoting the dissemination of technology, patent pools can be procompetitive. Nevertheless, some patent pools can restrict competition, whether among intellectual property rights within the pool or downstream products incorporating the pooled patents or in innovation among parties to the pool.

A starting point for an antitrust analysis of any patent pool is an inquiry into the validity of the patents and their relationship to each other. A licensing scheme premised on invalid or expired intellectual property rights will not withstand antitrust scrutiny. And a patent pool that aggregates competitive technologies and sets a single price for them would raise serious competitive concerns. On the other hand, a combination of complementary intellectual property rights, especially ones that block the application for which they are jointly licensed, can be an efficient and procompetitive method of disseminating those rights to would-be users.

Based on your representations to us about the complementary nature of the patents to be included in the Portfolio, it appears that the Portfolio is a procompetitive aggregation of intellectual property. The Portfolio combines patents that an independent expert has determined to be essential to compliance with the MPEG-2 standard; there is no technical alternative to any of the Portfolio patents within the standard. Moreover, each Portfolio patent is useful for MPEG-2 products only in conjunction with the others. The limitation of the Portfolio to technically essential patents, as opposed to merely advantageous ones, helps ensure that the Portfolio patents are not competitive with each other and that the Portfolio license does not, by bundling in non-essential patents, foreclose the competitive implementation options that the MPEG-2 standard has expressly left open.

The continuing role of an independent expert to assess essentiality is an especially effective guarantor that the Portfolio patents are complements, not substitutes. The relevant provisions of the Agreement Among Licensors appear well designed to ensure that the expert will be called in whenever a legitimate question is raised about whether or not a particular patent belongs in the Portfolio; in particular, they seem designed to reduce the likelihood that the Licensors might act concertedly to keep invalid or non-essential patents in the Portfolio or to exclude other essential patents from admission to the Portfolio.

B. Specific Terms of the Agreements

Despite the potential procompetitive effects of the Portfolio license, we would be concerned if any specific terms of any of the contemplated agreements seemed likely to restrain competition. Such possible concerns might include the likelihood that the Licensors could use the Portfolio license as a vehicle to disadvantage competitors in downstream product markets; to collude on prices outside the scope of the Portfolio license, such as downstream MPEG-2 products; or to impair technology or innovation competition, either within the MPEG-2 standard or from rival compression technologies. It appears, however, that the proposed arrangement will not raise any significant competitive concerns.

1. EFFECT ON RIVALS

There does not appear to be any potential for use of the Portfolio license to disadvantage particular licensees. The Agreement Among Licensors commits the Licensors to nondiscriminatory Portfolio licensing, and the Licensing Administrator agreement both vests sole licensing authority in MPEG LA and explicitly requires MPEG LA to offer the Portfolio license on the same terms and conditions to all would-be licensees. Thus, maverick competitors and upstart industries will have access to the Portfolio on the same terms as all other licensees. The Portfolio license's "most-favored-nation" clause ensures further against any attempt to discriminate on royalty rates.

Although it offers the Portfolio patents only as a package, the Portfolio license does not appear to be an illegal tying agreement. The conditioning of a license for one intellectual property right on the license of a second such right could be a concern where its effect was to foreclose competition from technological alternatives to the second. In this instance, however, the essentiality of the patents – determined by the independent expert – means that there is no technological alternative to any of them and that the Portfolio license will not require licensees to accept or use any patent that is merely one way of implementing the MPEG-2 standard, to the detriment of competition. Moreover, although a licensee cannot obtain fewer than all the Portfolio patents from MPEG LA, the Portfolio license informs potential licensees that licenses on all the Portfolio patents are available individually from their owners or assignees. While the independent expert mechanism should ensure that the Portfolio will never contain any unnecessary patents, the independent availability of each Portfolio patent is a valuable failsafe. The list of Portfolio patents attached to the Portfolio license will provide licensees with information they need to assess the merits of the Portfolio license.

2. FACILITATION OF COLLUSION

From what you have told us, there does not appear to be anything in the proposed agreements that is likely to facilitate collusion among Licensors or licensees in any market. Although

MPEG LA is authorized to audit licensees, confidentiality provisions prohibit it from transmitting competitively sensitive information among the Licensors or other licensees. Further, since the contemplated royalty rates are likely to constitute a tiny fraction of MPEG-2 products' prices, at least in the near term, it appears highly unlikely that the royalty rate could be used during that period as a device to coordinate the prices of downstream products.

3.EFFECT ON INNOVATION

It further appears that nothing in the arrangement imposes any anticompetitive restraint, either explicitly or implicitly, on the development of rival products and technologies. Nothing in the Agreement Among Licensors discourages, either through outright prohibition or economic incentives, any Licensor from developing or supporting a rival standard. As noted above, the Portfolio license explicitly leaves licensees free independently to make products that do not comply with the MPEG-2 standard and premises royalty obligations on actual use of at least one Portfolio patent. Since the Portfolio includes only Essential Patents, the licensee's manufacture, use or sale of MPEG-2 products will necessarily infringe the Portfolio patents. By weeding out non-essential patents from the Portfolio, the independent-expert mechanism helps ensure that the licensees will not have to pay royalties for making MPEG-2 products that do not employ the licensed patents.

The license's initial duration, to January 1, 2000, does not present any competitive concern. While the open-ended renewal term of "no less than five years" holds open the possibility of a perpetual license, its competitive impact will depend substantially on whether any of the "reasonable amendments" made at that time increase the license's exclusionary impact. While the term "reasonable" is the Portfolio license's only limitation on the Licensors' ability to impose onerous non-royalty terms on licensees at renewal time, the 25% cap on royalty increases and the "most-favored-nation" clause appear to constrain the Licensors' ability to use royalties to exploit any locked-in installed base among its licensees.

Nor does the Portfolio license's grantback clause appear anticompetitive. Its scope, like that of the license itself, is limited to Essential Patents. It does not extend to mere implementations of the standard or even to improvements on the essential patents. Rather, the grantback simply obliges licensees that control an Essential Patent to make it available to all, on a nonexclusive basis, at a fair and reasonable royalty, just like the Portfolio patents. This will mean that any firm that wishes to take advantage of the cost savings afforded by the Portfolio license cannot hold its own essential patents back from other would-be manufacturers of MPEG-2 products. While easing, though not altogether clearing up, the holdout problem, the grantback should not create any disincentive among licensees to innovate. Since the grantback extends only to MPEG-2 Essential Patents, it is unlikely that there is any significant innovation left to be done that the grantback could discourage. The grantback provision is likely simply to bring other Essential Patents into the Portfolio, thereby limiting holdouts' ability to exact a supracompetitive toll from Portfolio licensees and further lowering licensees' costs in assembling the patent rights essential to their compliance with the MPEG-2 standard.

In different circumstances, the right of partial termination set forth in Section 6.3 of the Portfolio license could raise difficult competition issues. That section provides that, on instruction from any Licensor, MPEG LA ... shall withdraw from a particular licensee's portfolio license that Licensor's patent or patents if the licensee has sued the Licensor for infringement of an Essential Patent or a Related Patent and refused to grant a license on the allegedly infringed patent on "fair and reasonable terms."

The partial termination right may enable Licensors to obtain licenses on Related Patents at royalty levels below what they would have been in a competitive market. Consequently, the partial termination right may dampen licensees' incentives to invest in research and development of MPEG-2 implementations, undercutting somewhat the benefits of the openness of the MPEG-2 standard and the prospects for improvements on the Essential Patents.

This impact on the incentive to innovate within the MPEG-2 standard would be of particular concern were the partial termination right designed to benefit all portfolio licensees. In that event, the partial termination right would function much like a compulsory grantback into the Portfolio. Licensees that owned Related Patents would not be able to choose among and negotiate freely with potential users of their inventions. The licensees' potential return from their R&D investments could be curtailed drastically, and the corresponding impact on their incentive to innovate could be significant.

Here, however, the partial termination right, unlike the grantback, protects only the Licensors. Other portfolio licensees have no right under the pool license to practice fellow licensees' inventions. And the Licensors are likely to be restrained in exercising their partial termination rights because the development of Related Patents will enhance MPEG-2 and, thus, the value of the Portfolio. The long-term interest of the Licensors is generally to encourage innovation in Related Patents, not to stifle it.

Moreover, the partial termination right may have procompetitive effects to the extent that it functions as a nonexclusive grantback requirement on licensees' Related Patents. It could allow Licensors and licensees to share the risk and rewards of supporting and improving the MPEG-2 standard by enabling Licensors to capture some of the value they have added to licensees' Related Patents by creating and licensing the Portfolio. In effect, the partial termination right may enable Licensors to realize greater returns on the Portfolio license from the licensees that enjoy greater benefits from the license, while maintaining the Portfolio royalty at a level low enough to attract licensees that may value it less. This in turn could lead to more efficient exploitation of the Portfolio technology.

Therefore, in light of both its potentially significant procompetitive effects and the limited potential harm it poses to Portfolio licensees' incentives to innovate, the partial-termination clause appears on balance unlikely to be anticompetitive.

III. Conclusion

Like many joint licensing arrangements, the agreements you have described for the licensing of MPEG-2 Essential Patents are likely to provide significant cost savings to Licensors and licensees alike, substantially reducing the time and expense that would otherwise be required to disseminate the rights to each MPEG-2 Essential Patent to each would-be licensee. Moreover, the proposed agreements that will govern the licensing arrangement have features designed to enhance the usual procompetitive effects and mitigate potential anticompetitive dangers. The limitation of the Portfolio to technically essential patents and the use of an independent expert to be the arbiter of that limitation reduces the risk that the patent pool will be used to eliminate rivalry between potentially competing technologies. Potential licensees will be aided by the provision of a clear list of the Portfolio patents, the availability of the Portfolio patents independent of the Portfolio, and the warning that the Portfolio may not contain all Essential Patents. The conditioning of licensee royalty liability on actual use of the Portfolio patents, the clearly stated freedom of licensees to develop and use alternative technologies, and the imposition of obligations on licensees' own patent rights that do not vitiate licensees' incentives to innovate, all serve to protect competition in the development and use of both improvements on, and alternatives to, MPEG-2 technology.

For these reasons, the Department is not presently inclined to initiate antitrust enforcement action against the conduct you have described. This letter, however, expresses the Department's current enforcement intention. In accordance with our normal practices, the Department reserves the right to bring an enforcement action in the future if the actual operation of the proposed conduct proves to be anticompetitive in purpose or effect.

Sincerely,
    Joel I. Klein, Assistant Attorney General

KEY DESIGN FEATURES FOR STANDARDS PATENT POOLS

The DOJ's MPEG-2 letter formalized a list of features that has come to be viewed as an industry best practice for the design of patent pools. While, strictly speaking, these features are not legally required, they appear to have influenced the DOJ's favorable evaluation of the MPEG-2 pool and several other pools that it has evaluated since. These features include the following:

1. *Transparency* – the pool's royalty rates and terms are publicly disclosed.
2. *Nondiscrimination* – the pool offers the same rates and terms to all similarly situated licensees, and will grant a license to any applicant that accepts those terms.
3. *Independence* – pool members are permitted to license their patents independently of the pool.
4. *Voluntariness* – pool members and licensees are not required to use the standard(s) covered by the pool in their products.
5. *Essentiality* – the pool will assess each pooled patent for essentiality to the standard.
6. *Complementarity* – the pool will not cover technologies that compete with or can be viewed as substitutes for one another.

Notes and Questions

1. *MPEG grew.* When the DOJ issued its business review letter on the MPEG-2 pool, the pool contained twenty-seven patents. At its peak in the early 2010s, the MPEG-2 pool contained over 1,000 patents.[21] Do you think that the guidelines outlined by the DOJ in its business review letter apply equally to a pool of twenty-seven versus 1,000+ patents? Why or why not?
2. *Fair and reasonable royalties.* Recall the Supreme Court's conclusion in *Standard Oil (Indiana)* that "Unless the industry is dominated, or interstate commerce directly restrained, the Sherman Act does not require cross-licensing patentees to license at reasonable rates others engaged in interstate commerce." How does this holding square with the FRAND obligations that are often imposed by SDOs on participants in standards development?

---

[21]   The last of the MPEG-2 pooled patents is believed to have expired in 2018.

When a pool is formed around patents that are essential to a particular standard that is subject to a FRAND commitment, should that commitment bind the pool?

3. *Nondiscrimination.* The DOJ notes that the MPEG-2 pool will license its patents on a "nondiscriminatory" basis and "explicitly requires MPEG LA to offer the Portfolio license on the same terms and conditions to all would-be licensees." Why is this requirement important from a competition standpoint? How does the pool's "most-favored-nation" clause further prevent any attempt to discriminate on royalty rates? The most-favored and nondiscrimination provisions of the pool agreement ensure that all licensees are treated in a consistent manner, but what if everyone is treated equally unfairly?

Nondiscriminatory licensing does not mean, of course, that every licensee must pay exactly the same amount to a pool. Many patent royalties are based on a percentage of the licensee's revenue, meaning that licensees who sell more licensed products pay more. Some pools charge different rates based on the type of product that the licensee produces. For example, in 2016, for a DVD video player, the DVD6C pool charged the greater of (1) 4 percent of the net selling price (up to a maximum of $8 per player) or (2) $4 per player; while for a DVD disc, the pool charged $0.05 per disc.[22] Do you see any competitive risks in a patent pool charging different rates based on the types of products to be manufactured? What about differences based on the size or sales volume of the licensee?

DVD players and DVD discs are fundamentally different products, even if they are intended to work together. Maybe this difference justifies differential pricing of pooled patents. But can differential pricing be justified when the same product (e.g., a wireless communications chip) is sold for use in different applications (e.g., an electric meter versus a smartphone versus an automobile versus a passenger airplane)? On one hand, a chip is a chip is a chip. But on the other hand, the value that such a chip brings to different applications may differ appreciably. Is it nondiscriminatory to charge users of a patented article different prices based on the value of the larger product in which they will incorporate the article?

4. *Independent licensing.* The DOJ notes that in the MPEG-2 pool, "each Portfolio patent is also available for licensing independently from the MPEG-2 Licensor that ... licensed it to MPEG LA." The DOJ has consistently emphasized the procompetitive benefits of allowing pool members to license their patents independently of the pool. It explained in 2013,

> Having the option to license independently of a pool can mitigate the effects of potential market power. For example, independent licensing can encourage competition and create incentives for innovators to invent around some of the patents in a pool. Efficiencies from licensing outside of a pool are more likely when the transaction costs of negotiating with multiple licensors are not prohibitive.[23]

As noted by Layne-Farrar and Lerner, "most modern pool agreements allow for independent licensing by pool members outside of the pool."[24] Nevertheless, not all pools have followed this pattern. In 1998, the FTC issued a complaint against two suppliers of patented photorefractive keratectomy (PRK) (eye surgery) equipment. In 1992, the suppliers, VISX, Inc. and Summit Technology, Inc., formed a partnership called Pillar Point Partners (PPP), in

---

22 DVD6C Licensing Group, Royalty Rates under DVD6C Licensing Program, www.dvd6cla.com/royaltyrate.html.
23 Letter from William J. Baer, Assistant Attorney General to Garrard R. Beeney, Sullivan & Cromwell, LLP, dated March 26, 2013 [IPXI Letter].
24 Layne-Farrar & Lerner, *supra* note 10, at 296.

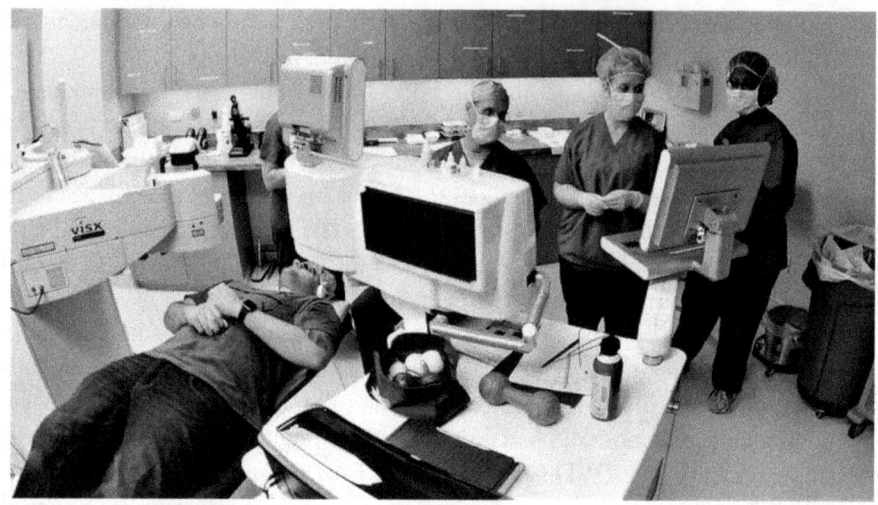

FIGURE 26.5 Two manufacturers of PRK equipment for laser eye surgery pooled their patents in an arrangement challenged by the FTC.

which they pooled their PRK patents. The agreement provided that PPP would have the exclusive right to license the parties' respective PRK patents to third parties, and that either party could veto the decision to grant such a license. Between 1992 and 1998, PPP granted no licenses to third parties. The FTC alleged that the pooling arrangement had the effect of eliminating competition between VISX and Summit in the market for PRK technology licensing. In settling the FTC's claims, the parties agreed to dissolve PPP and not to interfere with one another's licensing of their PRK technology.[25]

5. *Voluntary adoption.* In its MPEG-2 letter, the DOJ notes that the pool "explicitly leaves licensees free independently to make products that do not comply with the MPEG-2 standard." In other words, licensees are free to make products that comply with MPEG-2 standards or not, and are also free to adopt and use standards that compete with MPEG-2. Why is this freedom important?

6. *Grantback.* The MPEG-2 pool requires licensees to grant any of the pool licensors a nonexclusive worldwide license to any essential patent that it has the right to license on fair and reasonable terms. In their 2017 *Antitrust Guidelines for the Licensing of IP*, the DOJ and FTC analyze grantback clauses as follows:

> The Agencies will evaluate a grantback provision under the rule of reason, considering its likely effects in light of the overall structure of the licensing arrangement and conditions in the relevant markets. An important factor in the Agencies' analysis of a grantback will be whether the licensor has market power in a relevant technology or research and development market. If the Agencies determine that a particular grantback provision is likely to reduce significantly licensees' incentives to invest in improving the licensed technology, the Agencies will consider the extent to which the grantback provision has offsetting procompetitive effects, such as (1) promoting dissemination of licensees' improvements to the licensed technology, (2) increasing the licensors' incentives to disseminate the licensed technology,

---

[25]   *In Re Summit Tech. Inc. and VISX, Inc.*, FTC Docket No. 9286, Complaint (filed Mar. 24, 1998).

or (3) otherwise increasing competition and output in a relevant technology or research and development market. In addition, the Agencies will consider the extent to which grantback provisions in the relevant markets generally increase licensors' incentives to innovate in the first place.[26]

How would these considerations affect the agencies' evaluation of the MPEG-2 pool? Do you think that the pool had market power in 1997? What about in 2013? How important is it that the pool permits licensees to charge a reasonable royalty for their essential patents, rather than requiring grantback licenses to be free of charge? Why does the DOJ conclude that "the grantback should not create any disincentive among licensees to innovate"?

7. *Defensive termination.* Another feature of the MPEG-2 license agreement is a "partial termination" right, which enables a pool member to cause the pool to terminate a licensee's license under any of the member's patents if that licensee has sued the licensor for infringement of an essential patent and has refused to grant the pool member a license on fair and reasonable terms. In effect, the partial termination right is a backstop to the licensee's grantback obligation. If it fails to grant a FRAND license to a pool member, that member may withdraw those patents that the pool has licensed to the intransigent licensee. For this reason, clauses of this nature are often referred to as "defensive" termination clauses. Why do you think that a defensive termination clause is needed in addition to the grantback clause discussed above? Would a defensive termination clause be sufficient without the grantback?

In assessing the MPEG-2 pool, the DOJ reasons that "[i]n different circumstances, the right of partial termination … could raise difficult competition issues." In particular, the DOJ expresses concern that "[t]he partial termination right may enable Licensors to obtain licenses on Related Patents at royalty levels below what they would have been in a competitive market. Consequently, the partial termination right may dampen licensees' incentives to invest in research and development of MPEG-2 implementations." Why are these concerns alleviated under the licensing framework proposed by the MPEG-2 pool? Would the number of market participants in the pool matter to this analysis?

8. *Essentiality.* One of the key features of the MPEG-2 pool, and most patent pools today, is that "The Portfolio combines patents that an independent expert has determined to be essential to compliance with the MPEG-2 standard." In effect, only "essential" patents may be included in the pool. Why is it important that non-essential patents be excluded from the pool? Why is an independent-expert evaluation desirable?

Of course, independent patent evaluation does not come cheap. Professors Robert Merges and Michael Mattioli determined that the organizer of the MPEG Audio pool (unrelated to the MPEG-2 pool) paid attorney fees of approximately $7,500 per patent evaluated for essentiality. With around 700 patents, this resulted in a price tag of approximately $5,250,000.[27] Is this cost worth it? Is there a less expensive way to determine essentiality of patents covering complex technology standards?

Compare the approach taken by SDOs as described in Section 20.1 (Notes 1 and 3). SDOs permit their participants to self-declare which patents are essential to their standards. There

[26] US DOJ & FTC, Antitrust Guidelines for the Licensing of Intellectual Property, § 5.6, 33–34 (2017).

[27] Robert P. Merges & Michael Mattioli, *Measuring the Costs and Benefits of Patent Pools*, 78 Ohio St. L.J. 281, 306 (2017). See also Jorge L. Contreras, *Essentiality and Standards-Essential Patents* in Cambridge Handbook of Technical Standardization Law: Competition, Antitrust, and Patents 209, 215–16 (Jorge L. Contreras, ed., Cambridge Univ. Press, 2017) (discussing costs and benefits of validating essentiality).

is no cost to the SDO, but there is also no verification whether those patents are essential or not. Independent studies have estimated that so-called over-declaration is rampant at SDOs, as patent holders have little incentive *not* to declare any particular patent as essential to a standard.[28] Which approach to patent essentiality do you think is better: that of patent pools, which spend large sums independently evaluating each patent, or of SDOs, which spend nothing, but get a less accurate view of whether or not patents are essential to their standards?

9. *Complementarity.* Closely related to the issue of essentiality is that of complementarity. From an antitrust perspective, patents included in a pool should be essential to practice one *particular* standard, not a variety of different standards that could act as substitutes for one another. In other words, patents within a pool should be complementary, but not substitutes. The theory behind this important requirement is the subject of Section 26.4.

10. *Beyond standards.* While many of the recent DOJ business review letters concerning patent pools have revolved around technical standards, pools continue to be formed and planned around other technologies with fragmented IP ownership. Returning to the world of bio-technology, one of these areas is CRISPR gene-editing technology. Foundational patents relating to CRISPR are held by the University of California and the Broad Institute (a joint venture of Harvard and MIT), as well as several foreign universities. In 2017, MPEG LA, the creator of the MPEG-2 patent pool, proposed a pool relating to CRISPR patents. So far, the Broad Institute has indicated its interest in joining:

> [J]ust as MPEG LA's pioneering pool license model helped assure the success of digital video in the consumer electronics industry with convenient one-stop access to relevant intellectual property, now CRISPR can benefit from MPEG LA's patent pool approach with an impact far more profound.
>
> MPEG LA's CRISPR Cas-9 Joint Licensing Platform will give technology owners the opportunity to share in mass-market royalties from their CRISPR technology while enjoying, with other developers, broad access to other important CRISPR technologies. As a voluntary market-based business solution to the patent access problem tailored to balance, incentivize and resolve competing market and public interests, an independently managed patent pool is the best hope for unleashing CRISPR's full potential for the benefit of humanity.[29]

Some commentators have questioned the viability of a CRISPR patent pool as proposed by MPEG LA:

> We believe that the lack of commercial patent pooling and FRAND licensing in the biopharma sector is due to the high cost of product development, clinical trials, and regulatory approval required to market new drugs and treatments. In many cases, private-sector firms that incur these costs will be profitable (and viable) only if they can leverage the market exclusivity afforded by patent rights for a limited period. Indeed, this is an animating concern behind much of the lengthy and costly development of cancer therapeutics today. Because patent pools do not lend themselves to exclusive licensing, even when commercially desirable in narrow fields, we question whether patent pooling for CRISPR would ultimately be successful.[30]

Which view do you find to be more persuasive?

---

[28]   See Contreras, *Essentiality, supra* note 27, at 222–25.

[29]   MPEG LA, CRISPR, www.mpegla.com/crispr/initiative.

[30]   Jorge L. Contreras & Jacob S. Sherkow, *Patent Pools for CRISPR Technology: Response,* 355 Science 1274 (2017).

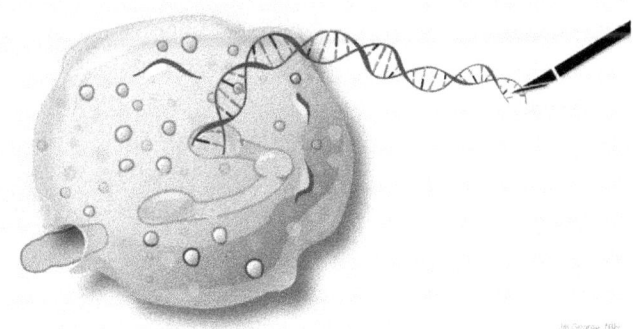

FIGURE 26.6 Can patent pools promote the broad accessibility of CRISPR gene-editing technology?

26.4 COMPLEMENTARITY AND ESSENTIALITY IN PATENT POOLS

As noted in the DOJ's MPEG-2 letter, the limitation of the MPEG-2 pool to patents essential to the MPEG-2 standard, and excluding patents that covered substitute technologies, was an important factor in finding that the pool would not result in anticompetitive effects. This rationale has been adopted in every subsequent pool that has been reviewed by the DOJ,[31] and was taken to its most extreme point in the Third Generation Patent Platform Partnership (3GPP) pooling structure, which involved five different competing standards for third-generation wireless communications.

3GPP Business Review Letter

US Department of Justice Antitrust Division, November 12, 2002

Ky P. Ewing, Esq.
 Vinson & Elkins L.L.P.
 1455 Pennsylvania Avenue, N.W.
 Washington, D.C. 20004–1008
 Dear Mr. Ewing:
 This letter responds to your request on behalf of the 3G Patent Platform Partnership ("Partnership") for the issuance of a business review letter pursuant to the Department of Justice Business Review Procedure, 28 C.F.R. § 50.6.

I. The IMT-2000 Family of 3G Standards

There are two generations of wireless communications systems in use today in the United States and other nations. The first uses analog transmission technology, while the second generation ("2G") uses various digital transmission technologies and makes possible the provision of some additional services along with voice telephony. The third generation

---

[31] European competition law authorities take an even stronger view of this principle, stating that "The creation of a technology pool ... composed solely or predominantly of substitute technologies amounts to a price fixing cartel." Guidelines on the Application of Article 101 of the Treaty on the Functioning of the European Union to Technology Transfer Agreements (2014/C 89/03) of Mar. 28, 2014, ¶ 245.

("3G") of wireless communication systems, also involving the use of digital transmission technologies, will enable not only wireless voice telephony, but also the transmission of data at rates much higher than those of the second generation systems, making additional applications possible.

As with the second generation, there will not be a single global 3G radio interface technology. Pursuant to its International Mobile Telephony-2000 ("IMT-2000") project, the International Telecommunication Union ("ITU") has approved five different radio interface technologies for use in 3G systems, which determine how a signal travels over the air from a user's handset to an operator's terrestrial network:

- IMT-Multicarrier ("IMT-MC"), also known as CDMA-2000
- IMT-Direct Spread ("IMT-DS"), also known as Wideband-CDMA ("W-CDMA")
- IMT-Time Code ("IMT-TC"), also known as TD-CDMA4
- IMT-Single Carrier ("IMT-SC"), also known as UWC-136 or TDMA-EDGE
- IMT-Frequency Time ("IMT-FT"), also known as Digital Enhanced Cordless Telecommunications ("DECT")

Each 3G radio interface technology has evolved from one or more of the 2G technologies. W-CDMA, for example, is a descendant of the Global Standard for Mobile Communications ("GSM"), the 2G technology mandated throughout Europe and used in some other areas in the world as well. CDMA-2000, in contrast, has evolved out of IS-955 Code Division Multiple Access ("CDMA"), one of the two most widely used 2G technologies in the U.S., while TDMAEDGE builds on IS-136 Time Division Multiple Access ("TDMA"), the other most widely used 2G technology in the U.S. By design, each 3G technology will afford a degree of backwards compatibility with networks employing the 2G technology from which it evolved. While an operator's choice of 2G technology is likely to be a significant factor in its choice of 3G technology, it does not appear to be determinative. Several substantial wireless operators in various countries, including the United States, have indicated that they are considering a 3G radio interface technology other than the one evolving most directly from the technology in the operator's 2G installed base. Moreover, since many nations are awarding more licenses for 3G service than they had for 2G or are making additional spectrum available that could be acquired by other operators, there will likely be new entrants into 3G service unconstrained by installed base considerations. The alternatives available to an operator for its 3G radio interface standard could constrain prices or other terms offered by the owners of 3G patents, to the extent that individual patents are not essential for all five standards.

As with most standardized technology, utilization of any of the interface standards may implicate the patent rights of numerous entities. As of June 2000, a total of 45 firms had claimed ownership of at least one patent essential to compliance with one or more of the 3G radio interface standards to at least one standards-related body. Consequently, it appears likely that any operator of a 3G wireless system and any manufacturer of 3G equipment, whether handsets or network infrastructure, regardless of the particular radio interface technology it adopts, will need to acquire licenses from multiple patent holders, and for some standards may need licenses for a large number of patents. Each such patent owner could exclude an operator or manufacturer from the use of a 3G technology by denying it a license.

II. The Proposed 3G Patent Platform Arrangement

The 3G Patent Platform serves several distinct functions, including identifying, evaluating and certifying patents essential to compliance with one or more of the five distinct 3G standards in the IMT-2000 "family," and providing a mechanism by which licensors and licensees can enter into a Standard License Agreement for each 3G patent applicable to a technology … As the Platform Specification makes clear, there will not actually be a single 3G Patent Platform entity, but rather a number of entities created with distinct personnel and responsibilities to carry out the various functions identified in the Platform Specification, and to ensure that where such functions may implicate competitive considerations among the five technologies, competitive choices are made independently for each technology rather than on a common basis.

The Platform will carry out licensing functions through five separate and independent Platform Companies ("PlatformCos"), one for each of the five 3G radio interface technologies, with a separate Licensing Administrator ("LA") and a separate board of directors for each PlatformCo. The members of each PlatformCo will be the two subscribers initially chosen by the Partnership from firms likely to hold essential patents, and all licensors that thereafter submit patents for evaluation and are certified as holding essential patents applicable to that 3G technology. Each PlatformCo is to be managed by its board of directors, consisting of one representative of each licensor member, which will be responsible for decisions on royalty rates and license terms, while decisions on any changes to PlatformCo governing documents are made by PlatformCo members. The licensing functions assigned to each PlatformCo are to be conducted by its LA, recognizing the potentially competitively sensitive nature of these functions, but the LA generally does not act as a licensor and the LA's responsibilities do not include the actual collection or distribution of royalties for licensors.

The five PlatformCos can have a limited number of shared functions, coordinated through a Management Company ("ManCo") with which the PlatformCos are initially expected to enter into a service agreement, and a Common Administrator ("CA") and an Evaluation Service Provider ("ESP") to whom specific Manco responsibilities will be assigned or outsourced. The functions of ManCo are defined as: (1) patent evaluation service outsourced to the ESP; (2) evaluation-related services most likely outsourced to the CA; (3) education of third parties about the 3G Platform concept; and (4) industry-wide market research and analysis, as opposed to research and analysis for or regarding a specific company. The CA, whose responsibilities are focused on assisting the evaluation process and providing general information about 3G, will initially be selected by the Partnership but thereafter the five PlatformCos will be responsible collectively for appointing a CA. The members of ManCo are not limited to licensors, unlike the PlatformCos, but can include licensees and other interested parties in the industry. ManCo will be managed by a board of directors chosen by the members, and will also have non-voting representatives of each of the five PlatformCos on its board committees.

Once a licensor or licensee participates in any of the evaluation or-licensing processes established for a PlatformCo, it becomes subject to that PlatformCo's licensing obligations. Licensors who submit any of their patents for evaluation are required to make all of their essential patents related to that specific 3G technology available under the relevant

PlatformCo's standard licensing terms to licensees that want to avail themselves of those terms. In turn, licensees who accept either a Standard License or an Interim License agreement from a licensor are required to submit all of their 3G-related patents for evaluation of essentiality, and to make such patents available under the platform terms if they are found to be essential. This "grant-back" obligation extends to third parties who receive sublicenses or make products using licensed technology on behalf of a licensee. However, this obligation is specific to the individual PlatformCos associated with a 3G technology, "and shall not be across PlatformCos," so that submitting patents for evaluation or accepting a Standard or Interim License with respect to one 3G technology does not oblige a patent holder to submit its essential patents for review, to become a PlatformCo member, or to accept the platform licensing terms with respect to any of the other four 3G technologies. Patent holders and licensees can avoid the grant-back obligation entirely by negotiating bilateral licenses outside the Platform without using an Interim License. Licensors may also leave their PlatformCo on one year's notice, though they remain obligated to license essential patents under the PlatformCo's licensing requirements during that year and existing licenses remain in place after the resignation takes effect.

[*Description of how the PlatformCos will evaluate essentiality of patents and license them to third parties is omitted.*]

III. Analysis

It is reasonably likely that essential patents associated with a single 3G technology, as defined in the Platform Specification, will be complements rather than substitutes. Essential patents by definition have no substitutes; one needs licenses to each of them in order to comply with the standard. The arrangements proposed in connection with the Platform, including (1) the limitation of patents to those "technically" essential to compliance, (2) the provisions for review of essentiality by competent experts without conflicts of interest and payment of the costs of evaluation through fees assessed on applicants, (3) retention of the experts by the ESP rather than directly by licensors, and (4) the financial incentives of licensors to object to the inclusion of others' non-essential patents that could lower per-patent compensation under the royalty formula, provide reasonable assurance that patents combined in a single PlatformCo for a 3G radio interface technology will not be substitutes for one another. In the future, patent holders for a specific 3G technology are free to develop new mechanisms to reduce costs of identification and licensing of essential patents which could further enhance competition, without affecting differences between technologies based on market forces.

There is however, publicly available evidence that several of the five 3G radio interface technologies have been competing with each other for adoption by wireless system operators and could continue to be the basis for competition among operators once 3G wireless services are on the market. There is a reasonable possibility that the five 3G radio interface technologies will continue to be substitutes for each other, and we would expect the owners of intellectual property rights essential to these technologies to compete, including through price, to persuade operators to adopt their technology. The actual Platform arrangements have been structured to take into account substitutability between 3G technologies by creating an independent PlatformCo to handle all licensing matters, including setting of actual royalty rates, with respect to each individual 3G technology. Though the five PlatformCos will operate under a standard Platform Specification, including a common methodology for calculating royalties due, and at least at the outset will make use of standard license terms, each PlatformCo will have the ability to modify license terms over time, and from the outset each PlatformCo will independently determine the key values used to calculate royalties.

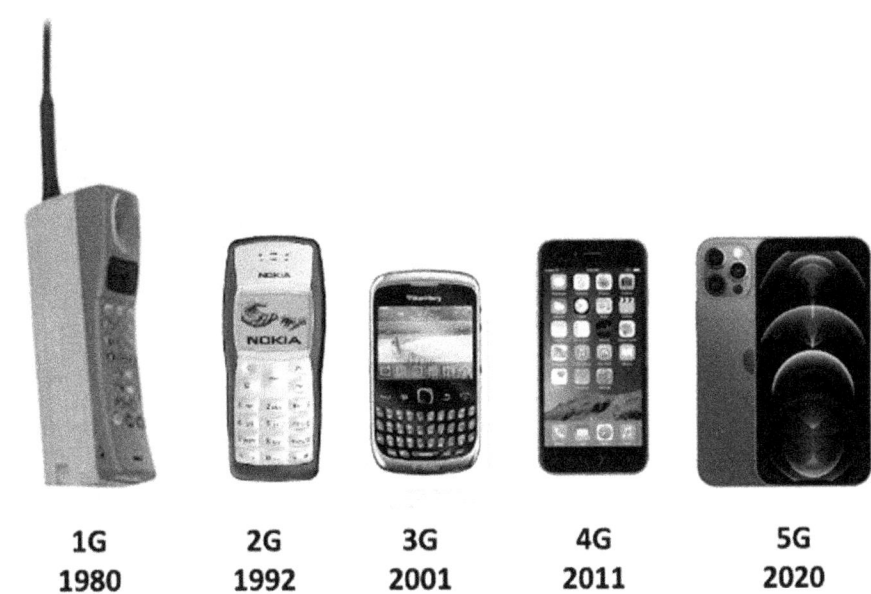

1G **2G** **3G** **4G** **5G**
1980 **1992** **2001** **2011** **2020**

FIGURE 26.7 Cellular communication protocols have evolved to enable better, faster and higher bandwidth connections and voice, data and video content transmission.

Notes and Questions

1. *And the winner is?* Though the 3GPP pool included patents for five 3G standards, it soon became apparent that only one of the five contenders would emerge as the victor. The W-CDMA standard known as UMTS (Universal Mobile Telecommunications Standard), based on the European GSM 2G standard, was quickly adopted and rolled out in Europe and Japan. In South Korea, both major telecommunications carriers adopted the Qualcomm-backed CDMA-2000 standard, as did Verizon Wireless in the United States. AT&T and T-Mobile (an offshoot of Deutsche Telekom), however, opted for the European-style UMTS. US carriers remained split through the 2000s, causing incompatibility among their networks (i.e., an AT&T phone could not connect to Verizon's network). However, with the advent of the 4G LTE standard in 2010, all major carriers around the world have moved to a single compatible standard. Are there any benefits to having a diversity of communications standards, or is the world better off with a single standard?
2. *Five standards, five pools.* As described in the DOJ's 3GPP letter, each 3G standard had its own patent pool with separate administration and licensing. This structure was necessary to ensure that only patents essential to the individual 3GPP standards would be included in each pool, and that the standards would be able to compete with one another. Was this degree of patent segregation really necessary?
3. *Nonessential patents.* Sometimes, parties to a patent pool may inadvertently include a nonessential patent in the pool, or a standard may change so that a patent originally included

in the pool becomes nonessential. Is this a problem? The Federal Circuit considered the question in *Princo Corp. v. International Trade Com'n*, 616 F.3d 1318 (Fed. Cir. 2010). There, Philips and Sony collaborated to create a standard for recordable and writable compact discs (CD-R/RW). While the standard was under development, each of Philips and Sony (as well as other companies) committed to pool their patents required to implement the standard. But by the time the final standard was agreed, it no longer contained technology covered by one of Sony's patents (referred to as the Lagadec patent). Princo, a Taiwanese disc manufacturer, entered into a license for the pooled patents, but then stopped paying royalties after it realized that the Lagadec patent was not essential to practice the CD-R/RW standard. Princo argued that including the Lagadec patent in the pool constituted anticompetitive conduct by Sony and Philips.[32] The Federal Circuit rejected Princo's arguments, reasoning that Philips' and Sony's engineers determined that the Lagadec technology was not a viable solution for recordable CDs. As a result, the Lagadec technology could not compete with or substitute for the final CD-R/RW standard. Therefore, its inclusion in the pool was not a violation of the antitrust laws. Do you agree? Why or why not?

4. *Defensive patent aggregation.* In response to perceived litigation threats from patent assertion entities, a new breed of firm called a "defensive patent aggregator" has emerged. The most prominent of these is RPX Corp. RPX claims that since its inception in 2008, it has acquired more than 60,000 patents in industries including automotive, electronics, computers, e-commerce, financial services, software, media, communications, networking and semiconductors.[33] As a result, RPX may represent the largest aggregation of patents ever assembled. Yet, as the Supreme Court made clear in *Automatic Radio Mfg. Co. v. Hazeltine Research, Inc.*, 339 U.S. 827, 834 (1950), "The mere accumulation of patents, no matter how many, is not in and of itself illegal."

RPX charges its member companies annual subscription fees based on their annual revenue, with fees ranging from tens of thousands to millions of dollars. RPX grants each of its 300+ members a license to practice all of RPX's aggregated patent rights. These licenses last while a company is a member of RPX, and become perpetual after a certain number of years. Members are not required to grant RPX or other members any of their own patent rights. As such, RPX may be the largest patent aggregation ever created, but it differs substantially from the pools discussed in this chapter in a number of important respects:

- RPX does not obtain patent rights from its members, but from third parties.
- RPX's patents cover many different technologies that, in theory, might compete or act as substitutes for one another, and are not evaluated for essentiality to any particular standard.
- The fees paid by RPX members to the pool are not disclosed, and vary from member to member.

Given these differences, how relevant to patent aggregators like RPX are the DOJ's and FTC's analyses of the procompetitive effects of patent pools? Do you see any potential antitrust issues in such patent aggregation structures? Given the close question in *Princo*, which involved just one patent that was not essential to the CD-R/RW standard, does it matter that RPX members receive licenses to thousands of patents covering technologies that could

---

[32] Princo also alleged patent misuse, discussed in Chapter 24.
[33] RPX Corp., The RPX Network, www.rpxcorp.com/platform/rpx-network; RPX Corp., 2017 Annual Report on Form 10-K.

act as substitutes for one another? What might the effect of such an arrangement be on innovation?

In 2012, RPX was sued by Cascades Computer Innovations LLC,[34] a patent assertion entity that sought to sell or license a portfolio of patents to RPX. When the deal failed to materialize, Cascades alleged that RPX represented an illegal *buyer's* cartel that depressed the price for the patents that it sought to sell. The case was dismissed on other grounds prior to a hearing on the merits of the antitrust claim. But what do you think of Cascades' theory? Is it relevant that RPX members can direct RPX to negotiate to acquire particular patent portfolios that they view as threats?[35]

---

[34] *Cascades Computer Innovation LLC v. RPX Corp.*, Case No. 12-cv-01143-YGR (N.D. Cal., filed Mar. 2012).

[35] See Matthew W. Callahan & Jason M. Schultz, Is Patent Reform via Private Ordering Anticompetitive? An Analysis of Open Patent Agreements in Patent Pledges: Global Perspectives on Patent Law's Private Ordering Frontier 151, 159–60 (Jorge L. Contreras & Meredith Jacob, ed., Edward Elgar, 2017) (antitrust analysis of open patent agreements, contrasting with defensive patent aggregators).

Index

CPSIA information can be obtained
at www.ICGtesting.com
Printed in the USA
LVHW022043170123
737295LV00005B/235